CHAMBERS

OFFICIAL

SCRABBLE®

CHAMBERS

OFFICIAL

SCRABBLE®

W₄ O₁ R₁ D₂ S₁

4th EDITION

Managing Editor
Catherine Schwarz

SCRABBLE $^{®}$ is a registered trademark of J W Spear & Sons Ltd,
Maidenhead SL6 4UB, England, a Mattel Company, and is used
under licence from Mattel Europa B.V.

CHAMBERS
An imprint of Chambers Harrap Publishers Ltd
7 Hopetoun Crescent
Edinburgh EH7 4AY

This edition first published in harback by Chambers 1999
Paperback edition 2000

Reprinted 2000, 2001, 2002 (twice), 2003

First edition published by Chambers 1988; second edition published 1990;
third edition published 1994

Copyright © Chambers Harrap Publishers Ltd 1999

ISBN 0-550 12004-1 Paperback
ISBN 0-550-14190-1 Hardback

Publishing Manager
Elaine Higgleton

Designed and typeset by Chambers Harrap Publishers Ltd
Printed and bound in Great Britain by Cox & Wyman Ltd, Reading, Berkshire

Preface to fourth edition

Official Scrabble® Words (OSW) is established as the definitive work on Scrabble, indispensable whether solving those family arguments or dealing with word challenges in Scrabble clubs and tournaments all around the world. This fourth edition is published following on from publication of a new edition of *The Chambers Dictionary* in 1998.

Despite company changes, a close relationship, dating back to Spear's decision to use *The Chambers Dictionary* at the 1980 National Scrabble Championships, still exists between Spear's Games (now part of Mattel Inc) and Chambers (now part of Chambers Harrap Publishers Ltd). I know that Scrabble players throughout the English-speaking world are most appreciative of the rich fund of useful Scrabble words contained in *The Chambers Dictionary*, which is complementary to OSW and should be consulted when you want to check the meaning of a word.

With the many changes in the 1998 edition of the Dictionary, a complete review of all the words in it was required for OSW. Once again, the Main Committee, many of whom have been involved in producing all four editions of OSW, deserve thanks, along with Catherine Schwarz and her colleagues at Chambers for their painstaking work. Special mention is also due to the Initial Adjudicating Committee, both in the UK and in Australia, for their dedication in highlighting areas of change.

I, and I'm sure many others, have derived huge satisfaction from playing Scrabble over many years now. This new edition of OSW and the many new words it contains are going to make Scrabble even more enjoyable and entertaining.

Philip Nelkon
Manager–Scrabble Clubs
Spear's Games

Main Committee

Darryl Francis, *London Scrabble League*
Ian Gucklhorn, *London Scrabble League*
Terry Kirk, *London Scrabble League*
Allan Simmons, *Onwords Scrabble Magazine*
Jim Warmington, *Australian Scrabble Players Association*

Initial adjudicating committee

UK

David Acton, *Middlesex League*
Amy Byrne, *Edinburgh Scrabble Club*
Andrew Cook, *Oxford City Scrabble Club*
Andrew Fisher, *UK-Scrabble*
Helen R Gipson, *East Berks Scrabble Club*
Helen Grayson, *Aireborough Scrabble Club*
Mary Grylls, *Melton Scrabble Club*
Barry Grossman, *London Scrabble League*
Sheila Hockey, *London Scrabble League*
Terry Hollington, *Southampton Scrabble Club*
Josef Kollar, *Hythe Scrabble Club*
Donald Macleod, *Edinburgh Scrabble Club*
Roger Phillips
Evan Simpson, *Middlesex League*
Roy Upton, *Derby Scrabble Club*
Wilma Warwick, *Leith Scrabble Club*

Australia

Roger Blom, *Camberwell Scrabble Club*
Ruth Fewings, *Bendigo Scrabble Club*
Alistair Kane, *Dandenong Scrabble Club*
Sue Kyatt, *Knox Scrabble Club*
Joan Rosenthal, *Balmain BUGS Scrabble Club*
Margaret Warmington, *Balwyn Scrabble Club*

The publishers wish to acknowledge with thanks the computing help of Peter Schwarz in the compilation and revision of this edition of *Official Scrabble® Words*, and the support of Philip Nelkon of Spear's Games.

Introduction

This fourth edition of *Official Scrabble® Words* is based on *The Chambers Dictionary* (1998), the latest in a long line of Chambers dictionaries. All words listed in that dictionary are permitted in Scrabble except:

> those only spelt with an initial capital letter;
> abbreviations and symbols;
> prefixes and suffixes;
> those requiring apostrophes and hyphens.

Official Scrabble® Words (OSW) lists, and is the official authority for, all allowable words of up to 9 letters long and their inflections (plurals etc). For longer words, *The Chambers Dictionary* is the authority. A number of words listed in *The Chambers Dictionary*, and hence in OSW, may be offensive to some people, or may not conform to 'political correctness'. These words are however part of the English language, which the Dictionary naturally reflects. We therefore have not followed the American Scrabble movement in disallowing such words for Scrabble.

Every relevant entry in *The Chambers Dictionary* has been thoroughly examined and considered for inclusion in OSW. Derivative forms have been carefully considered too, and appropriate inflections – plurals, verb forms, and comparatives and superlatives – have been included. Many new words have been added to the Dictionary, and there have been other changes: some words have changed or augmented their labels (both part-of-speech and classification), some have changed their hyphenation or capitalization status, others have moved on from being abbreviations – all resulting in hundreds of new entries in this edition of OSW. Inevitably such changes, along with other Dictionary judgements, have resulted in a small number of deletions from the previous edition of OSW.

In the compilation of this edition of OSW, a small number of errors were found in *The Chambers Dictionary*. Those confirmed by the publisher have not been perpetuated in OSW.

Allowable words

This edition of *Official Scrabble® Words* is the final authority on allowed Scrabble words where the uninflected form of the word is up to 9 letters long. It is based on the 1998 edition of *The Chambers Dictionary*. All words listed in that dictionary are permitted in Scrabble except for those in the categories mentioned above.

It should be noted that the entries that are labelled 'symbol' (for example FF, LM) are now, as well as abbreviations, barred from Scrabble use.

One particular entry in OSW worthy of special mention is PH. Since in the Dictionary the capitalized letter is not the initial letter, and since PH is not deemed to be an abbreviation or a symbol, it has been included here, along with its plural PHS.

The approaches that have been taken to various groups of words in this edition of OSW are explained below.

Accents

Accents are not shown in this edition of *Official Scrabble® Words*. As there are no accented letters in the English-language Scrabble sets, it was felt unnecessary to retain accents in OSW. Where *The Chambers Dictionary* shows a word with an accent, the accent has been ignored in OSW.

Adverbs

Adverbs have been included in *Official Scrabble® Words* if they are included in *The Chambers Dictionary*. No attempt has been made to include adverbial forms which are not explicitly shown in the Dictionary.

Comparatives and Superlatives

This edition of *Official Scrabble® Words* sees the inclusion of more comparative and superlative forms than were in the previous edition. We have considered the possible comparative and superlative forms of all adjectives in OSW, and we have based our final selection on a range of criteria. These have included commonness or familiarity of the adjective, number of syllables, meaning, and whether the adjective is dialect, obsolete or foreign. We also took into account the euphony of the -ER and -EST forms, current usage, data from language corpora, including the British National Corpus®, and listings in other dictionaries. We cannot say that we have applied a mechanical formula in deciding which comparatives and superlatives to include. We have allowed the -IER and the -IEST forms of most one- and two-syllable adjectives ending in -Y, and some of three syllables, but not all. We have not excluded the comparative and superlative forms of all adjectives of three syllables or more – some have been included. We have not excluded the comparative and superlative forms of all adjectives ending in certain specific groups of letters, such as -ATE, -ENT, and -ID. Again, some have been included.

Definitions

This edition of *Official Scrabble® Words* contains a separate appendix listing the 2- and 3-letter words, with basic definitions, intended as aids in memorizing these important Scrabble words. For fuller treatment of these words, and to know the meaning of any other word in OSW, *The Chambers Dictionary* should be consulted.

Foreign Words

Foreign words appearing in *The Chambers Dictionary* have been included in *Official Scrabble® Words*. Where a specific plural form appears in the Dictionary, we have included only that form. Where no plural is shown in the Dictionary, we have used our judgement, and the appropriate plural form has been included. In some instances, this will be a foreign plural; in others, it will be an English plural (usually the addition of an -S). Occasionally, both types of plural will be included. Do be aware that not all plural forms in OSW are explicitly shown in *The Chambers Dictionary*. For example, as no plural form is shown in the Dictionary for STERNUM, we have included both of the plural forms STERNA and STERNUMS.

Interjections

Interjections are not treated as nouns, but as parts of speech which do not permit plurals. In *Official Scrabble® Words*, an interjection has no inflected forms, unless explicitly indicated in *The Chambers Dictionary*. A plural is only allowed if an interjection is also shown to be a noun; and verb forms are only allowed if an interjection is also shown to be a verb.

Some examples:

> AW, QUOTHA and UM are interjections only, so no inflected forms are allowed;
> EH is an interjection and a verb, so the inflected verb forms EHS, EHED and EHING are allowed;

OOH is an interjection, verb and noun, so the verb forms
OOHS, OOHED and OOHING are allowed;
OOHS is also the plural form of the noun.

If *The Chambers Dictionary* quite clearly lists a plural form of an interjection (for example, as at LO and OHO), then that is allowable.

Letters and letter sounds

Names of letters and letter sounds appearing in *The Chambers Dictionary* are included in *Official Scrabble® Words*, as there is nothing in the rules of Scrabble to bar the use of such words. Accordingly, OSW lists familiar letter names (for example, AITCH, MU, NU, and XI) as well as unfamiliar ones (for example, DIGAMMA, SAMPI, VAU and WYNN). Their plural forms are also included.

Obsolete Words

Obsolete words are included in *Official Scrabble® Words*, along with many of their relevant inflected forms (such as plurals and verb inflections). We have included plurals of obsolete nouns, and we have included verb inflections of obsolete verbs. We have not included comparative and superlative forms of obsolete adjectives, or derivatives of obsolete words, unless these are explicitly shown in *The Chambers Dictionary*. (For example, BROACH and BROACHER are both allowable words, and BROCH is in the Dictionary as an obsolete spelling of BROACH – so BROACH, BROACHER and BROCH are all allowable, but we have not included BROCHER.)

Words marked in *The Chambers Dictionary* as being from the works of Shakespeare, Spenser and Milton have been treated in the same way as obsolete words.

Order of Words

All the words in *Official Scrabble® Words* are listed in strict alphabetical sequence, regardless of length. It is important to bear this in mind, particularly when checking the validity of plurals.

For example:

> the plural of FAD is not listed immediately after FAD but is shown at its correct alphabetical place between FADOS and FADY;
> to determine whether FAB has a plural or not it is necessary to check between the entries FABRICS and FABULAR. It is not listed there, so FABS is not allowed.

Plurals

With few exceptions, we have included in *Official Scrabble® Words* the plurals of all nouns. Plural forms have been shown for all nouns ending in -ISM, -ITY and -NESS; while these plurals may be little used in regular English, all are available for use if needed in the English language. We have also included the plural forms of chemicals, chemical elements, minerals, man-made materials, natural minerals, fibres, drugs, gases, rocks, oils, vitamins, enzymes, diseases, illnesses and the like.

The plurals of many foreign words are included. For many words there are now two plural forms – an English plural and a foreign plural (for example, STERNUMS and STERNA). However, some words that previously only had an -S plural now only have a foreign plural. Where the compilers have found no evidence for these -S forms, only the foreign plurals are now included. For example, the plural of ANCILE is now only ANCILIA, although previously it was only ANCILES.

Word Lengths

Official Scrabble® Words users may well want to understand what criteria have been employed in considering word lengths. In compiling OSW we began by listing all the valid but uninflected words of length up to (and including) 9 letters. We then allowed the relevant inflections of these (namely plurals, verb forms, and comparatives and superlatives), resulting in words up to 13 letters long. (It is possible for a 9-letter verb to double a final consonant before adding -ING, giving 13 letters in all!)

Here are some examples:

the 9-letter noun CACODEMON gives rise to the 10-letter plural CACODEMONS;
the 9-letter noun CACOPHONY gives rise to the 11-letter plural CACOPHONIES;
the 9-letter noun CANTHARIS gives rise to the 11-letter plural CANTHARIDES;
the 9-letter verb CALCULATE gives rise to these verb inflections: CALCULATED, CALCULATES and CALCULATING, having 10 or 11 letters;
the 8-letter verb CARBURET gives rise to these verb inflections: CARBURETS, CARBURETTED and CARBURETTING, having 9, 11 or 12 letters

If any inflected form of a 9-letter word is also a singular noun in its own right, then a plural form of that noun is also included.

For example:

> the 9-letter verb CATERWAUL gives rise to these verb inflections: CATERWAULS, CATERWAULED and CATERWAULING; but since CATERWAULING is also shown in *The Chambers Dictionary* as a noun, the plural form of CATERWAULINGS has been included here;
> the 8-letter verb CROSSCUT gives rise to these verb inflections: CROSSCUTS and CROSSCUTTING; but since CROSSCUTTING is also shown in the Dictionary as a noun, the plural form CROSSCUTTINGS has been included here.

There are a few instances of 9-letter adjectives which add an -S to become 10-letter nouns. For example, CANONICAL thus becomes CANONICALS, which is included. For convenience in adjudication, other similar cases are treated likewise: for example, the adverbs EARTHWARD and EARTHWARDS are both included.

There are instances of singular nouns having more than 9 letters, but with plurals of 9 letters or less. The singulars have not been included here, but the plurals have. For example, the singular AUDITORIUM has 10 letters, so hasn't been included, but its plural AUDITORIA has 9 letters, so is included.

Official Scrabble® Words will not answer every possible query regarding the validity of words. Remember that for words longer than 9 letters, and their inflected forms, you will have to turn to *The Chambers Dictionary*. For example, AUDITORIUM, mentioned above, is perfectly valid for use in Scrabble; it's just that it isn't included here. There are plenty of other 10–15 letter words that could be played legitimately in Scrabble, and are in *The Chambers Dictionary*.

A

AA	ABATEMENT	ABDUCTED	ABHORS	ABLEIST
AARDVARK	ABATEMENTS	ABDUCTEE	ABID	ABLER
AARDVARKS	ABATES	ABDUCTEES	ABIDANCE	ABLES
AARDWOLF	ABATING	ABDUCTING	ABIDANCES	ABLEST
AARDWOLVES	ABATIS	ABDUCTION	ABIDDEN	ABLET
AAS	ABATOR	ABDUCTIONS	ABIDE	ABLETS
AASVOGEL	ABATORS	ABDUCTOR	ABIDED	ABLING
AASVOGELS	ABATTIS	ABDUCTORS	ABIDES	ABLINS
ABA	ABATTOIR	ABDUCTS	ABIDING	ABLOOM
ABAC	ABATTOIRS	ABEAM	ABIDINGLY	ABLOW
ABACA	ABATTU	ABEAR	ABIDINGS	ABLUSH
ABACAS	ABATURE	ABEARING	ABIES	ABLUTION
ABACI	ABATURES	ABEARS	ABIGAIL	ABLUTIONS
ABACK	ABAXIAL	ABED	ABIGAILS	ABLY
ABACS	ABAYA	ABEIGH	ABILITIES	ABNEGATE
ABACTINAL	ABAYAS	ABELE	ABILITY	ABNEGATED
ABACTOR	ABB	ABELES	ABIOSES	ABNEGATES
ABACTORS	ABBA	ABELIA	ABIOSIS	ABNEGATING
ABACUS	ABBACIES	ABELIAS	ABIOTIC	ABNEGATOR
ABACUSES	ABBACY	ABERRANCE	ABJECT	ABNEGATORS
ABAFT	ABBAS	ABERRANCES	ABJECTED	ABNORMAL
ABALONE	ABBATIAL	ABERRANCIES	ABJECTING	ABNORMALS
ABALONES	ABBE	ABERRANCY	ABJECTION	ABNORMITIES
ABAMPERE	ABBES	ABERRANT	ABJECTIONS	ABNORMITY
ABAMPERES	ABBESS	ABERRATE	ABJECTLY	ABNORMOUS
ABAND	ABBESSES	ABERRATED	ABJECTS	ABOARD
ABANDED	ABBEY	ABERRATES	ABJOINT	ABODE
ABANDING	ABBEYS	ABERRATING	ABJOINTED	ABODED
ABANDON	ABBOT	ABESSIVE	ABJOINTING	ABODEMENT
ABANDONED	ABBOTS	ABESSIVES	ABJOINTS	ABODEMENTS
ABANDONEE	ABBOTSHIP	ABET	ABJURE	ABODES
ABANDONEES	ABBOTSHIPS	ABETMENT	ABJURED	ABODING
ABANDONING	ABBS	ABETMENTS	ABJURER	ABOIDEAU
ABANDONS	ABCEE	ABETS	ABJURERS	ABOIDEAUS
ABANDS	ABCEES	ABETTAL	ABJURES	ABOIL
ABAS	ABDABS	ABETTALS	ABJURING	ABOITEAU
ABASE	ABDICABLE	ABETTED	ABLATE	ABOITEAUS
ABASED	ABDICANT	ABETTER	ABLATED	ABOLISH
ABASEMENT	ABDICATE	ABETTERS	ABLATES	ABOLISHED
ABASEMENTS	ABDICATED	ABETTING	ABLATING	ABOLISHES
ABASES	ABDICATES	ABETTOR	ABLATION	ABOLISHING
ABASH	ABDICATING	ABETTORS	ABLATIONS	ABOLITION
ABASHED	ABDICATOR	ABEYANCE	ABLATIVAL	ABOLITIONS
ABASHEDLY	ABDICATORS	ABEYANCES	ABLATIVE	ABOLLA
ABASHES	ABDOMEN	ABEYANCIES	ABLATIVES	ABOLLAE
ABASHING	ABDOMENS	ABEYANCY	ABLATOR	ABOLLAS
ABASHLESS	ABDOMINA	ABEYANT	ABLATORS	ABOMASA
ABASHMENT	ABDOMINAL	ABHOR	ABLAUT	ABOMASAL
ABASHMENTS	ABDUCE	ABHORRED	ABLAUTS	ABOMASI
ABASING	ABDUCED	ABHORRENT	ABLAZE	ABOMASUM
ABASK	ABDUCENT	ABHORRER	ABLE	ABOMASUS
ABATABLE	ABDUCES	ABHORRERS	ABLED	ABOMASUSES
ABATE	ABDUCING	ABHORRING	ABLEISM	ABOMINATE
ABATED	ABDUCT	ABHORRINGS	ABLEISMS	ABOMINATED

ABOMINATES	ABREACTING	ABSEILED	ABSTRUSE	ABYSSES
ABOMINATING	ABREACTS	ABSEILING	ABSTRUSER	ACACIA
ABONDANCE	ABREAST	ABSEILINGS	ABSTRUSEST	ACACIAS
ABONDANCES	ABREGE	ABSEILS	ABSURD	ACADEME
ABORAL	ABREGES	ABSENCE	ABSURDER	ACADEMES
ABORD	ABRICOCK	ABSENCES	ABSURDEST	ACADEMIA
ABORDED	ABRICOCKS	ABSENT	ABSURDISM	ACADEMIAS
ABORDING	ABRIDGE	ABSENTED	ABSURDISMS	ACADEMIC
ABORDS	ABRIDGED	ABSENTEE	ABSURDIST	ACADEMICS
ABORE	ABRIDGER	ABSENTEES	ABSURDISTS	ACADEMIES
ABORIGEN	ABRIDGERS	ABSENTING	ABSURDITIES	ACADEMISM
ABORIGENS	ABRIDGES	ABSENTLY	ABSURDITY	ACADEMISMS
ABORIGIN	ABRIDGING	ABSENTS	ABSURDLY	ACADEMIST
ABORIGINE	ABRIM	ABSEY	ABTHANE	ACADEMISTS
ABORIGINES	ABRIN	ABSEYS	ABTHANES	ACADEMY
ABORIGINS	ABRINS	ABSINTH	ABULIA	ACAJOU
ABORNE	ABROACH	ABSINTHE	ABULIAS	ACAJOUS
ABORNING	ABROAD	ABSINTHES	ABUNA	ACALEPH
ABORT	ABROADS	ABSINTHS	ABUNAS	ACALEPHAN
ABORTED	ABROGATE	ABSIT	ABUNDANCE	ACALEPHANS
ABORTEE	ABROGATED	ABSITS	ABUNDANCES	ACALEPHE
ABORTEES	ABROGATES	ABSOLUTE	ABUNDANCIES	ACALEPHES
ABORTING	ABROGATING	ABSOLUTER	ABUNDANCY	ACALEPHS
ABORTION	ABROGATOR	ABSOLUTES	ABUNDANT	ACANTH
ABORTIONS	ABROGATORS	ABSOLUTEST	ABUNE	ACANTHA
ABORTIVE	ABROOKE	ABSOLVE	ABURST	ACANTHAS
ABORTS	ABROOKED	ABSOLVED	ABUSAGE	ACANTHIN
ABORTUARIES	ABROOKES	ABSOLVER	ABUSAGES	ACANTHINE
ABORTUARY	ABROOKING	ABSOLVERS	ABUSE	ACANTHINS
ABOUGHT	ABRUPT	ABSOLVES	ABUSED	ACANTHOID
ABOULIA	ABRUPTER	ABSOLVING	ABUSER	ACANTHOUS
ABOULIAS	ABRUPTEST	ABSONANT	ABUSERS	ACANTHS
ABOUND	ABRUPTION	ABSORB	ABUSES	ACANTHUS
ABOUNDED	ABRUPTIONS	ABSORBATE	ABUSING	ACANTHUSES
ABOUNDING	ABRUPTLY	ABSORBATES	ABUSION	ACAPNIA
ABOUNDS	ABRUPTS	ABSORBED	ABUSIONS	ACAPNIAS
ABOUT	ABSCESS	ABSORBENT	ABUSIVE	ACARI
ABOUTS	ABSCESSED	ABSORBENTS	ABUSIVELY	ACARIAN
ABOVE	ABSCESSES	ABSORBER	ABUT	ACARIASES
ABRADANT	ABSCIND	ABSORBERS	ABUTILON	ACARIASIS
ABRADANTS	ABSCINDED	ABSORBING	ABUTILONS	ACARICIDE
ABRADE	ABSCINDING	ABSORBS	ABUTMENT	ACARICIDES
ABRADED	ABSCINDS	ABSTAIN	ABUTMENTS	ACARID
ABRADES	ABSCISE	ABSTAINED	ABUTS	ACARIDAN
ABRADING	ABSCISED	ABSTAINER	ABUTTAL	ACARIDANS
ABRAID	ABSCISES	ABSTAINERS	ABUTTALS	ACARIDEAN
ABRAIDED	ABSCISIN	ABSTAINING	ABUTTED	ACARIDEANS
ABRAIDING	ABSCISING	ABSTAINS	ABUTTER	ACARIDIAN
ABRAIDS	ABSCISINS	ABSTERGE	ABUTTERS	ACARIDIANS
ABRAM	ABSCISS	ABSTERGED	ABUTTING	ACARIDS
ABRASION	ABSCISSA	ABSTERGES	ABUZZ	ACARINE
ABRASIONS	ABSCISSAE	ABSTERGING	ABVOLT	ACAROID
ABRASIVE	ABSCISSAS	ABSTINENT	ABVOLTS	ACAROLOGIES
ABRASIVES	ABSCISSE	ABSTRACT	ABY	ACAROLOGY
ABRAXAS	ABSCISSES	ABSTRACTED	ABYE	ACARPOUS
ABRAXASES	ABSCISSIN	ABSTRACTER	ABYEING	ACARUS
ABRAY	ABSCISSINS	ABSTRACTERS	ABYES	ACATER
ABRAYED	ABSCOND	ABSTRACTEST	ABYING	ACATERS
ABRAYING	ABSCONDED	ABSTRACTING	ABYSM	ACATES
ABRAYS	ABSCONDER	ABSTRACTS	ABYSMAL	ACATOUR
ABRAZO	ABSCONDERS	ABSTRICT	ABYSMALLY	ACATOURS
ABRAZOS	ABSCONDING	ABSTRICTED	ABYSMS	ACAUDAL
ABREACT	ABSCONDS	ABSTRICTING	ABYSS	ACAUDATE
ABREACTED	ABSEIL	ABSTRICTS	ABYSSAL	ACAULINE

The Chambers Dictionary is the authority for many longer words; see *OSW* Introduction, page xii

ACAULOSE	ACCLAIMING	ACCOUTRE	ACERBER	ACHIMENES
ACCABLE	ACCLAIMS	ACCOUTRED	ACERBEST	ACHING
ACCEDE	ACCLIMATE	ACCOUTRES	ACERBIC	ACHINGLY
ACCEDED	ACCLIMATED	ACCOUTRING	ACERBITIES	ACHINGS
ACCEDENCE	ACCLIMATES	ACCOY	ACERBITY	ACHKAN
ACCEDENCES	ACCLIMATING	ACCOYED	ACEROSE	ACHKANS
ACCEDER	ACCLIVITIES	ACCOYING	ACEROUS	ACHROMAT
ACCEDERS	ACCLIVITY	ACCOYLD	ACERS	ACHROMATS
ACCEDES	ACCLIVOUS	ACCOYS	ACERVATE	ACHY
ACCEDING	ACCLOY	ACCREDIT	ACES	ACICULAR
ACCEND	ACCLOYED	ACCREDITED	ACESCENCE	ACICULATE
ACCENDED	ACCLOYING	ACCREDITING	ACESCENCES	ACID
ACCENDING	ACCLOYS	ACCREDITS	ACESCENCIES	ACIDER
ACCENDS	ACCOAST	ACCRETE	ACESCENCY	ACIDEST
ACCENSION	ACCOASTED	ACCRETED	ACESCENT	ACIDFREAK
ACCENSIONS	ACCOASTING	ACCRETES	ACETABULA	ACIDFREAKS
ACCENT	ACCOASTS	ACCRETING	ACETAL	ACIDIC
ACCENTED	ACCOIED	ACCRETION	ACETALS	ACIDIER
ACCENTING	ACCOIL	ACCRETIONS	ACETAMIDE	ACIDIEST
ACCENTOR	ACCOILS	ACCRETIVE	ACETAMIDES	ACIDIFIED
ACCENTORS	ACCOLADE	ACCREW	ACETATE	ACIDIFIER
ACCENTS	ACCOLADES	ACCREWED	ACETATES	ACIDIFIERS
ACCENTUAL	ACCOMPANIED	ACCREWING	ACETIC	ACIDIFIES
ACCEPT	ACCOMPANIES	ACCREWS	ACETIFIED	ACIDIFY
ACCEPTANT	ACCOMPANY	ACCRUAL	ACETIFIES	ACIDIFYING
ACCEPTANTS	ACCOMPANYING	ACCRUALS	ACETIFY	ACIDITIES
ACCEPTED	ACCOMPT	ACCRUE	ACETIFYING	ACIDITY
ACCEPTER	ACCOMPTED	ACCRUED	ACETONE	ACIDLY
ACCEPTERS	ACCOMPTING	ACCRUES	ACETONES	ACIDNESS
ACCEPTING	ACCOMPTS	ACCRUING	ACETOSE	ACIDNESSES
ACCEPTIVE	ACCORAGE	ACCUMBENT	ACETOUS	ACIDOSES
ACCEPTOR	ACCORAGED	ACCURACIES	ACETYL	ACIDOSIS
ACCEPTORS	ACCORAGES	ACCURACY	ACETYLENE	ACIDS
ACCEPTS	ACCORAGING	ACCURATE	ACETYLENES	ACIDULATE
ACCESS	ACCORD	ACCURSE	ACETYLS	ACIDULATED
ACCESSARIES	ACCORDANT	ACCURSED	ACH	ACIDULATES
ACCESSARY	ACCORDED	ACCURSES	ACHAENIA	ACIDULATING
ACCESSED	ACCORDER	ACCURSING	ACHAENIUM	ACIDULENT
ACCESSES	ACCORDERS	ACCURST	ACHAENIUMS	ACIDULOUS
ACCESSING	ACCORDING	ACCUSABLE	ACHAGE	ACIDY
ACCESSION	ACCORDION	ACCUSAL	ACHAGES	ACIERAGE
ACCESSIONED	ACCORDIONS	ACCUSALS	ACHARNE	ACIERAGES
ACCESSIONING	ACCORDS	ACCUSE	ACHARYA	ACIERATE
ACCESSIONS	ACCOST	ACCUSED	ACHARYAS	ACIERATED
ACCESSORIES	ACCOSTED	ACCUSER	ACHATES	ACIERATES
ACCESSORY	ACCOSTING	ACCUSERS	ACHE	ACIERATING
ACCIDENCE	ACCOSTS	ACCUSES	ACHED	ACIFORM
ACCIDENCES	ACCOUNT	ACCUSING	ACHENE	ACING
ACCIDENT	ACCOUNTED	ACCUSTOM	ACHENES	ACINI
ACCIDENTS	ACCOUNTING	ACCUSTOMED	ACHENIA	ACINIFORM
ACCIDIE	ACCOUNTINGS	ACCUSTOMING	ACHENIAL	ACINOSE
ACCIDIES	ACCOUNTS	ACCUSTOMS	ACHENIUM	ACINOUS
ACCINGE	ACCOURAGE	ACE	ACHENIUMS	ACINUS
ACCINGED	ACCOURAGED	ACED	ACHES	ACKEE
ACCINGES	ACCOURAGES	ACEDIA	ACHIER	ACKEES
ACCINGING	ACCOURAGING	ACEDIAS	ACHIEST	ACKERS
ACCIPITER	ACCOURT	ACELLULAR	ACHIEVE	ACKNEW
ACCIPITERS	ACCOURTED	ACER	ACHIEVED	ACKNOW
ACCITE	ACCOURTING	ACERATE	ACHIEVER	ACKNOWING
ACCITED	ACCOURTS	ACERB	ACHIEVERS	ACKNOWN
ACCITES	ACCOUTER	ACERBATE	ACHIEVES	ACKNOWNE
ACCITING	ACCOUTERED	ACERBATED	ACHIEVING	ACKNOWS
ACCLAIM	ACCOUTERING	ACERBATES	ACHILLEA	ACLINIC
ACCLAIMED	ACCOUTERS	ACERBATING	ACHILLEAS	ACME

The Chambers Dictionary is the authority for many longer words; see *OSW* Introduction, page xii

ACMES	ACRASIAS	ACTING	ACTUARIAL	ADAWING
ACMITE	ACRATIC	ACTINGS	ACTUARIES	ADAWS
ACMITES	ACRAWL	ACTINIA	ACTUARY	ADAXIAL
ACNE	ACRE	ACTINIAE	ACTUATE	ADAYS
ACNES	ACREAGE	ACTINIAN	ACTUATED	ADD
ACOCK	ACREAGES	ACTINIANS	ACTUATES	ADDAX
ACOEMETI	ACRED	ACTINIAS	ACTUATING	ADDAXES
ACOLD	ACRES	ACTINIC	ACTUATION	ADDEBTED
ACOLUTHIC	ACRID	ACTINIDE	ACTUATIONS	ADDED
ACOLYTE	ACRIDER	ACTINIDES	ACTUATOR	ADDEEM
ACOLYTES	ACRIDEST	ACTINISM	ACTUATORS	ADDEEMED
ACOLYTH	ACRIDIN	ACTINISMS	ACTURE	ADDEEMING
ACOLYTHS	ACRIDINE	ACTINIUM	ACTURES	ADDEEMS
ACONITE	ACRIDINES	ACTINIUMS	ACUITIES	ADDEND
ACONITES	ACRIDINS	ACTINOID	ACUITY	ADDENDA
ACONITIC	ACRIDITIES	ACTINOIDS	ACULEATE	ADDENDS
ACONITINE	ACRIDITY	ACTINON	ACULEATED	ADDENDUM
ACONITINES	ACRIMONIES	ACTINONS	ACULEI	ADDER
ACONITUM	ACRIMONY	ACTINS	ACULEUS	ADDERS
ACONITUMS	ACROBAT	ACTION	ACUMEN	ADDERWORT
ACORN	ACROBATIC	ACTIONED	ACUMENS	ADDERWORTS
ACORNED	ACROBATICS	ACTIONER	ACUMINATE	ADDICT
ACORNS	ACROBATS	ACTIONERS	ACUMINATED	ADDICTED
ACOSMISM	ACROGEN	ACTIONING	ACUMINATES	ADDICTING
ACOSMISMS	ACROGENIC	ACTIONIST	ACUMINATING	ADDICTION
ACOSMIST	ACROGENS	ACTIONISTS	ACUMINOUS	ADDICTIONS
ACOSMISTS	ACROLEIN	ACTIONS	ACUPOINT	ADDICTIVE
ACOUCHI	ACROLEINS	ACTIVATE	ACUPOINTS	ADDICTS
ACOUCHIES	ACROLITH	ACTIVATED	ACUSHLA	ADDING
ACOUCHIS	ACROLITHS	ACTIVATES	ACUSHLAS	ADDIO
ACOUCHY	ACROMIA	ACTIVATING	ACUTE	ADDIOS
ACOUSTIC	ACROMIAL	ACTIVATOR	ACUTELY	ADDITION
ACOUSTICS	ACROMION	ACTIVATORS	ACUTENESS	ADDITIONS
ACQUAINT	ACRONICAL	ACTIVE	ACUTENESSES	ADDITIVE
ACQUAINTED	ACRONYCAL	ACTIVELY	ACUTER	ADDITIVES
ACQUAINTING	ACRONYM	ACTIVISM	ACUTES	ADDLE
ACQUAINTS	ACRONYMIC	ACTIVISMS	ACUTEST	ADDLED
ACQUEST	ACRONYMS	ACTIVIST	ACYCLIC	ADDLEMENT
ACQUESTS	ACROPETAL	ACTIVISTS	ACYCLOVIR	ADDLEMENTS
ACQUIESCE	ACROPHONIES	ACTIVITIES	ACYCLOVIRS	ADDLES
ACQUIESCED	ACROPHONY	ACTIVITY	ACYL	ADDLING
ACQUIESCES	ACROPOLIS	ACTON	ACYLS	ADDOOM
ACQUIESCING	ACROPOLISES	ACTONS	AD	ADDOOMED
ACQUIGHT	ACROSOME	ACTOR	ADAGE	ADDOOMING
ACQUIGHTING	ACROSOMES	ACTORS	ADAGES	ADDOOMS
ACQUIGHTS	ACROSPIRE	ACTRESS	ADAGIO	ADDORSED
ACQUIRAL	ACROSPIRES	ACTRESSES	ADAGIOS	ADDRESS
ACQUIRALS	ACROSS	ACTS	ADAMANT	ADDRESSED
ACQUIRE	ACROSTIC	ACTUAL	ADAMANTLY	ADDRESSEE
ACQUIRED	ACROSTICS	ACTUALISE	ADAMANTS	ADDRESSEES
ACQUIRES	ACROTER	ACTUALISED	ADAPT	ADDRESSER
ACQUIRING	ACROTERIA	ACTUALISES	ADAPTABLE	ADDRESSERS
ACQUIST	ACROTERS	ACTUALISING	ADAPTED	ADDRESSES
ACQUISTS	ACROTISM	ACTUALIST	ADAPTER	ADDRESSING
ACQUIT	ACROTISMS	ACTUALISTS	ADAPTERS	ADDRESSOR
ACQUITE	ACRYLIC	ACTUALITE	ADAPTING	ADDRESSORS
ACQUITES	ACRYLICS	ACTUALITES	ADAPTION	ADDREST
ACQUITING	ACT	ACTUALITIES	ADAPTIONS	ADDS
ACQUITS	ACTA	ACTUALITY	ADAPTIVE	ADDUCE
ACQUITTAL	ACTABLE	ACTUALIZE	ADAPTOR	ADDUCED
ACQUITTALS	ACTED	ACTUALIZED	ADAPTORS	ADDUCENT
ACQUITTED	ACTIN	ACTUALIZES	ADAPTS	ADDUCER
ACQUITTING	ACTINAL	ACTUALIZING	ADAW	ADDUCERS
ACRASIA	ACTINALLY	ACTUALLY	ADAWED	ADDUCES

The Chambers Dictionary is the authority for many longer words; see *OSW* Introduction, page xii

ADDUCIBLE	ADIABATIC	ADMEASURES	ADOPTION	ADULATOR
ADDUCING	ADIAPHORA	ADMEASURING	ADOPTIONS	ADULATORS
ADDUCT	ADIEU	ADMEN	ADOPTIOUS	ADULATORY
ADDUCTED	ADIEUS	ADMIN	ADOPTIVE	ADULT
ADDUCTING	ADIEUX	ADMINICLE	ADOPTS	ADULTERER
ADDUCTION	ADIOS	ADMINICLES	ADORABLE	ADULTERERS
ADDUCTIONS	ADIPOCERE	ADMINS	ADORABLY	ADULTERIES
ADDUCTIVE	ADIPOCERES	ADMIRABLE	ADORATION	ADULTERY
ADDUCTOR	ADIPOSE	ADMIRABLY	ADORATIONS	ADULTHOOD
ADDUCTORS	ADIPOSITIES	ADMIRAL	ADORE	ADULTHOODS
ADDUCTS	ADIPOSITY	ADMIRALS	ADORED	ADULTS
ADEEM	ADIT	ADMIRANCE	ADORER	ADUMBRATE
ADEEMED	ADITS	ADMIRANCES	ADORERS	ADUMBRATED
ADEEMING	ADJACENCIES	ADMIRE	ADORES	ADUMBRATES
ADEEMS	ADJACENCY	ADMIRED	ADORING	ADUMBRATING
ADEMPTION	ADJACENT	ADMIRER	ADORINGLY	ADUNC
ADEMPTIONS	ADJECTIVE	ADMIRERS	ADORN	ADUNCATE
ADENINE	ADJECTIVES	ADMIRES	ADORNED	ADUNCATED
ADENINES	ADJOIN	ADMIRING	ADORNING	ADUNCITIES
ADENITIS	ADJOINED	ADMISSION	ADORNMENT	ADUNCITY
ADENITISES	ADJOINING	ADMISSIONS	ADORNMENTS	ADUNCOUS
ADENOID	ADJOINS	ADMISSIVE	ADORNS	ADUST
ADENOIDAL	ADJOINT	ADMIT	ADOS	ADUSTED
ADENOIDS	ADJOINTS	ADMITS	ADOWN	ADUSTING
ADENOMA	ADJOURN	ADMITTED	ADPRESS	ADUSTS
ADENOMAS	ADJOURNED	ADMITTING	ADPRESSED	ADVANCE
ADENOMATA	ADJOURNING	ADMIX	ADPRESSES	ADVANCED
ADENOSINE	ADJOURNS	ADMIXED	ADPRESSING	ADVANCES
ADENOSINES	ADJUDGE	ADMIXES	ADRAD	ADVANCING
ADEPT	ADJUDGED	ADMIXING	ADREAD	ADVANTAGE
ADEPTER	ADJUDGES	ADMIXTURE	ADREADED	ADVANTAGED
ADEPTEST	ADJUDGING	ADMIXTURES	ADREADING	ADVANTAGES
ADEPTLY	ADJUNCT	ADMONISH	ADREADS	ADVANTAGING
ADEPTNESS	ADJUNCTLY	ADMONISHED	ADRED	ADVECTION
ADEPTNESSES	ADJUNCTS	ADMONISHES	ADRENAL	ADVECTIONS
ADEPTS	ADJURE	ADMONISHING	ADRENALIN	ADVENE
ADEQUACIES	ADJURED	ADMONITOR	ADRENALINS	ADVENED
ADEQUACY	ADJURES	ADMONITORS	ADRENALS	ADVENES
ADEQUATE	ADJURING	ADNASCENT	ADRIFT	ADVENING
ADERMIN	ADJUST	ADNATE	ADROIT	ADVENT
ADERMINS	ADJUSTED	ADNATION	ADROITER	ADVENTIVE
ADESPOTA	ADJUSTER	ADNATIONS	ADROITEST	ADVENTIVES
ADESSIVE	ADJUSTERS	ADNOMINAL	ADROITLY	ADVENTS
ADESSIVES	ADJUSTING	ADNOUN	ADRY	ADVENTURE
ADHARMA	ADJUSTOR	ADNOUNS	ADS	ADVENTURED
ADHARMAS	ADJUSTORS	ADO	ADSCRIPT	ADVENTURES
ADHERE	ADJUSTS	ADOBE	ADSCRIPTS	ADVENTURING
ADHERED	ADJUTAGE	ADOBES	ADSORB	ADVERB
ADHERENCE	ADJUTAGES	ADONISE	ADSORBATE	ADVERBIAL
ADHERENCES	ADJUTANCIES	ADONISED	ADSORBATES	ADVERBS
ADHERENT	ADJUTANCY	ADONISES	ADSORBED	ADVERSARIES
ADHERENTS	ADJUTANT	ADONISING	ADSORBENT	ADVERSARY
ADHERER	ADJUTANTS	ADONIZE	ADSORBENTS	ADVERSE
ADHERERS	ADJUVANCIES	ADONIZED	ADSORBING	ADVERSELY
ADHERES	ADJUVANCY	ADONIZES	ADSORBS	ADVERSER
ADHERING	ADJUVANT	ADONIZING	ADSUM	ADVERSEST
ADHESION	ADJUVANTS	ADOORS	ADULARIA	ADVERSITIES
ADHESIONS	ADLAND	ADOPT	ADULARIAS	ADVERSITY
ADHESIVE	ADLANDS	ADOPTED	ADULATE	ADVERT
ADHESIVES	ADMAN	ADOPTEE	ADULATED	ADVERTED
ADHIBIT	ADMASS	ADOPTEES	ADULATES	ADVERTENT
ADHIBITED	ADMASSES	ADOPTER	ADULATING	ADVERTING
ADHIBITING	ADMEASURE	ADOPTERS	ADULATION	ADVERTISE
ADHIBITS	ADMEASURED	ADOPTING	ADULATIONS	ADVERTISED

The Chambers Dictionary is the authority for many longer words; see *OSW* Introduction, page xii

ADVERTISES	AEFALD	AEROFOILS	AESTIVATES	AFFIRM
ADVERTISING	AEFAULD	AEROGRAM	AESTIVATING	AFFIRMANT
ADVERTISINGS	AEGIRINE	AEROGRAMS	AETHER	AFFIRMANTS
ADVERTIZE	AEGIRINES	AEROGRAPH	AETHERS	AFFIRMED
ADVERTIZED	AEGIRITE	AEROGRAPHS	AETIOLOGIES	AFFIRMER
ADVERTIZES	AEGIRITES	AEROLITE	AETIOLOGY	AFFIRMERS
ADVERTIZING	AEGIS	AEROLITES	AFALD	AFFIRMING
ADVERTS	AEGISES	AEROLITH	AFAR	AFFIRMS
ADVEW	AEGLOGUE	AEROLITHS	AFARA	AFFIX
ADVEWED	AEGLOGUES	AEROLITIC	AFARAS	AFFIXED
ADVEWING	AEGROTAT	AEROLOGIES	AFAWLD	AFFIXES
ADVEWS	AEGROTATS	AEROLOGY	AFEAR	AFFIXING
ADVICE	AEMULE	AEROMANCIES	AFEARD	AFFLATED
ADVICEFUL	AEMULED	AEROMANCY	AFEARED	AFFLATION
ADVICES	AEMULES	AEROMETER	AFEARING	AFFLATIONS
ADVISABLE	AEMULING	AEROMETERS	AFEARS	AFFLATUS
ADVISABLY	AENEOUS	AEROMETRIES	AFFABLE	AFFLATUSES
ADVISE	AEOLIAN	AEROMETRY	AFFABLY	AFFLICT
ADVISED	AEOLIPILE	AEROMOTOR	AFFAIR	AFFLICTED
ADVISEDLY	AEOLIPILES	AEROMOTORS	AFFAIRE	AFFLICTING
ADVISER	AEOLIPYLE	AERONAUT	AFFAIRES	AFFLICTINGS
ADVISERS	AEOLIPYLES	AERONAUTS	AFFAIRS	AFFLICTS
ADVISES	AEON	AERONOMIES	AFFEAR	AFFLUENCE
ADVISING	AEONIAN	AERONOMY	AFFEARD	AFFLUENCES
ADVISINGS	AEONS	AEROPHOBE	AFFEARE	AFFLUENT
ADVISOR	AERATE	AEROPHOBES	AFFEARED	AFFLUENTS
ADVISORS	AERATED	AEROPHONE	AFFEARES	AFFLUENZA
ADVISORY	AERATES	AEROPHONES	AFFEARING	AFFLUENZAS
ADVOCAAT	AERATING	AEROPHYTE	AFFEARS	AFFLUX
ADVOCAATS	AERATION	AEROPHYTES	AFFECT	AFFLUXES
ADVOCACIES	AERATIONS	AEROPLANE	AFFECTED	AFFLUXION
ADVOCACY	AERATOR	AEROPLANES	AFFECTER	AFFLUXIONS
ADVOCATE	AERATORS	AEROS	AFFECTERS	AFFOORD
ADVOCATED	AERIAL	AEROSHELL	AFFECTING	AFFOORDED
ADVOCATES	AERIALIST	AEROSHELLS	AFFECTION	AFFOORDING
ADVOCATING	AERIALISTS	AEROSOL	AFFECTIONED	AFFOORDS
ADVOCATOR	AERIALITIES	AEROSOLS	AFFECTIONING	AFFORCE
ADVOCATORS	AERIALITY	AEROSPACE	AFFECTIONS	AFFORCED
ADVOUTRER	AERIALLY	AEROSPACES	AFFECTIVE	AFFORCES
ADVOUTRERS	AERIALS	AEROSTAT	AFFECTS	AFFORCING
ADVOUTRIES	AERIE	AEROSTATS	AFFEER	AFFORD
ADVOUTRY	AERIER	AEROTAXES	AFFEERED	AFFORDED
ADVOWSON	AERIES	AEROTAXIS	AFFEERING	AFFORDING
ADVOWSONS	AERIEST	AEROTONE	AFFEERS	AFFORDS
ADWARD	AERIFORM	AEROTONES	AFFERENT	AFFOREST
ADWARDED	AERO	AEROTRAIN	AFFIANCE	AFFORESTED
ADWARDING	AEROBE	AEROTRAINS	AFFIANCED	AFFORESTING
ADWARDS	AEROBES	AERY	AFFIANCES	AFFORESTS
ADYNAMIA	AEROBIC	AESC	AFFIANCING	AFFRAP
ADYNAMIAS	AEROBICS	AESCES	AFFICHE	AFFRAPPED
ADYNAMIC	AEROBIONT	AESCULIN	AFFICHES	AFFRAPPING
ADYTA	AEROBIONTS	AESCULINS	AFFIDAVIT	AFFRAPS
ADYTUM	AEROBOMB	AESIR	AFFIDAVITS	AFFRAY
ADZ	AEROBOMBS	AESTHESES	AFFIED	AFFRAYED
ADZE	AEROBUS	AESTHESIA	AFFIES	AFFRAYING
ADZES	AEROBUSES	AESTHESIAS	AFFILIATE	AFFRAYS
AE	AEROBUSSES	AESTHESIS	AFFILIATED	AFFRENDED
AECIA	AERODART	AESTHETE	AFFILIATES	AFFRET
AECIDIA	AERODARTS	AESTHETES	AFFILIATING	AFFRETS
AECIDIUM	AERODROME	AESTHETIC	AFFINE	AFFRICATE
AECIUM	AERODROMES	AESTHETICS	AFFINED	AFFRICATES
AEDES	AERODYNE	AESTIVAL	AFFINES	AFFRIGHT
AEDILE	AERODYNES	AESTIVATE	AFFINITIES	AFFRIGHTED
AEDILES	AEROFOIL	AESTIVATED	AFFINITY	AFFRIGHTING

AFFRIGHTS	AFTERWARD	AGENTED	AGIOTAGES	AGOGIC
AFFRONT	AFTERWARDS	AGENTIAL	AGIST	AGOGICS
AFFRONTE	AFTERWORD	AGENTING	AGISTED	AGOING
AFFRONTED	AFTERWORDS	AGENTIVE	AGISTER	AGON
AFFRONTEE	AFTMOST	AGENTIVES	AGISTERS	AGONE
AFFRONTING	AGA	AGENTS	AGISTING	AGONIC
AFFRONTINGS	AGACANT	AGERATUM	AGISTMENT	AGONIES
AFFRONTS	AGACANTE	AGERATUMS	AGISTMENTS	AGONISE
AFFUSION	AGACERIE	AGES	AGISTOR	AGONISED
AFFUSIONS	AGACERIES	AGGER	AGISTORS	AGONISES
AFFY	AGAIN	AGGERS	AGISTS	AGONISING
AFFYDE	AGAINST	AGGRACE	AGITATE	AGONIST
AFFYING	AGALACTIA	AGGRACED	AGITATED	AGONISTES
AFGHAN	AGALACTIAS	AGGRACES	AGITATES	AGONISTIC
AFGHANS	AGALLOCH	AGGRACING	AGITATING	AGONISTICS
AFIELD	AGALLOCHS	AGGRADE	AGITATION	AGONISTS
AFIRE	AGAMI	AGGRADED	AGITATIONS	AGONIZE
AFLAJ	AGAMIC	AGGRADES	AGITATIVE	AGONIZED
AFLAME	AGAMID	AGGRADING	AGITATO	AGONIZES
AFLATOXIN	AGAMIDS	AGGRATE	AGITATOR	AGONIZING
AFLATOXINS	AGAMIS	AGGRATED	AGITATORS	AGONS
AFLOAT	AGAMOID	AGGRATES	AGITPROP	AGONY
AFLUTTER	AGAMOIDS	AGGRATING	AGITPROPS	AGOOD
AFOOT	AGAMOUS	AGGRAVATE	AGLEAM	AGORA
AFORE	AGAPAE	AGGRAVATED	AGLEE	AGORAS
AFOREHAND	AGAPE	AGGRAVATES	AGLET	AGOROT
AFORESAID	AGAR	AGGRAVATING	AGLETS	AGOUTA
AFORETIME	AGARIC	AGGREGATE	AGLEY	AGOUTAS
AFOUL	AGARICS	AGGREGATED	AGLIMMER	AGOUTI
AFRAID	AGARS	AGGREGATES	AGLITTER	AGOUTIES
AFREET	AGAS	AGGREGATING	AGLOW	AGOUTIS
AFREETS	AGAST	AGGRESS	AGMA	AGOUTY
AFRESH	AGATE	AGGRESSED	AGMAS	AGRAFFE
AFRIT	AGATES	AGGRESSES	AGNAIL	AGRAFFES
AFRITS	AGATEWARE	AGGRESSING	AGNAILS	AGRAPHA
AFRO	AGATEWARES	AGGRESSOR	AGNAME	AGRAPHIA
AFRONT	AGAVE	AGGRESSORS	AGNAMED	AGRAPHIAS
AFROS	AGAVES	AGGRI	AGNAMES	AGRAPHIC
AFT	AGAZE	AGGRIEVE	AGNATE	AGRAPHON
AFTER	AGAZED	AGGRIEVED	AGNATES	AGRARIAN
AFTERCARE	AGE	AGGRIEVES	AGNATIC	AGRASTE
AFTERCARES	AGED	AGGRIEVING	AGNATICAL	AGRAVIC
AFTERDECK	AGEDNESS	AGGRO	AGNATION	AGREE
AFTERDECKS	AGEDNESSES	AGGROS	AGNATIONS	AGREEABLE
AFTEREYE	AGEE	AGGRY	AGNISE	AGREEABLY
AFTEREYED	AGEING	AGHA	AGNISED	AGREED
AFTEREYEING	AGEINGS	AGHAS	AGNISES	AGREEING
AFTEREYES	AGEISM	AGHAST	AGNISING	AGREEMENT
AFTEREYING	AGEISMS	AGILA	AGNIZE	AGREEMENTS
AFTERGAME	AGEIST	AGILAS	AGNIZED	AGREES
AFTERGAMES	AGEISTS	AGILE	AGNIZES	AGREGE
AFTERGLOW	AGELAST	AGILELY	AGNIZING	AGREGES
AFTERGLOWS	AGELASTIC	AGILER	AGNOMEN	AGREMENS
AFTERHEAT	AGELASTS	AGILEST	AGNOMENS	AGREMENT
AFTERHEATS	AGELESS	AGILITIES	AGNOMINA	AGREMENTS
AFTERINGS	AGELONG	AGILITY	AGNOMINAL	AGRESTAL
AFTERMATH	AGEN	AGIN	AGNOSIA	AGRESTIAL
AFTERMATHS	AGENCIES	AGING	AGNOSIAS	AGRESTIC
AFTERMOST	AGENCY	AGINGS	AGNOSTIC	AGRIMONIES
AFTERNOON	AGENDA	AGINNER	AGNOSTICS	AGRIMONY
AFTERNOONS	AGENDAS	AGINNERS	AGO	AGRIN
AFTERS	AGENE	AGIO	AGOG	AGRIOLOGIES
AFTERTIME	AGENES	AGIOS	AGOGE	AGRIOLOGY
AFTERTIMES	AGENT	AGIOTAGE	AGOGES	AGRISE

The Chambers Dictionary is the authority for many longer words; see *OSW* Introduction, page xii

AGRISED	AIDE	AIRFLOWS	AIRSTREAMS	AKOLUTHOSES
AGRISES	AIDED	AIRFOIL	AIRSTRIP	AKVAVIT
AGRISING	AIDER	AIRFOILS	AIRSTRIPS	AKVAVITS
AGRIZE	AIDERS	AIRFRAME	AIRT	ALA
AGRIZED	AIDES	AIRFRAMES	AIRTED	ALAAP
AGRIZES	AIDFUL	AIRGAP	AIRTIGHT	ALAAPS
AGRIZING	AIDING	AIRGAPS	AIRTIME	ALABAMINE
AGROLOGIES	AIDLESS	AIRGLOW	AIRTIMES	ALABAMINES
AGROLOGY	AIDOI	AIRGLOWS	AIRTING	ALABASTER
AGRONOMIC	AIDOS	AIRGRAPH	AIRTS	ALABASTERS
AGRONOMICS	AIDS	AIRGRAPHS	AIRWARD	ALACK
AGRONOMIES	AIERIES	AIRHEAD	AIRWARDS	ALACRITIES
AGRONOMY	AIERY	AIRHEADS	AIRWAVE	ALACRITY
AGROUND	AIGLET	AIRHOLE	AIRWAVES	ALAE
AGRYZE	AIGLETS	AIRHOLES	AIRWAY	ALAIMENT
AGRYZED	AIGRETTE	AIRIER	AIRWAYS	ALAIMENTS
AGRYZES	AIGRETTES	AIRIEST	AIRWOMAN	ALALAGMOI
AGRYZING	AIGUILLE	AIRILY	AIRWOMEN	ALALAGMOS
AGUACATE	AIGUILLES	AIRINESS	AIRWORTHY	ALALIA
AGUACATES	AIKIDO	AIRINESSES	AIRY	ALALIAS
AGUE	AIKIDOS	AIRING	AIS	ALAMEDA
AGUED	AIKONA	AIRINGS	AISLE	ALAMEDAS
AGUES	AIL	AIRLESS	AISLED	ALAMODE
AGUISE	AILANTHUS	AIRLIFT	AISLES	ALAMODES
AGUISED	AILANTHUSES	AIRLIFTED	AISLING	ALAMORT
AGUISES	AILANTO	AIRLIFTING	AISLINGS	ALAND
AGUISH	AILANTOS	AIRLIFTS	AIT	ALANG
AGUISHLY	AILED	AIRLINE	AITCH	ALANGS
AGUISING	AILERON	AIRLINER	AITCHBONE	ALANINE
AGUIZE	AILERONS	AIRLINERS	AITCHBONES	ALANINES
AGUIZED	AILETTE	AIRLINES	AITCHES	ALANNAH
AGUIZES	AILETTES	AIRLOCK	AITS	ALANNAHS
AGUIZING	AILING	AIRLOCKS	AITU	ALAP
AGUTI	AILMENT	AIRMAIL	AITUS	ALAPA
AGUTIS	AILMENTS	AIRMAILED	AIZLE	ALAPAS
AH	AILS	AIRMAILING	AIZLES	ALAPS
AHA	AIM	AIRMAILS	AJAR	ALAR
AHEAD	AIMED	AIRMAN	AJEE	ALARM
AHEAP	AIMING	AIRMEN	AJOWAN	ALARMED
AHED	AIMLESS	AIRN	AJOWANS	ALARMEDLY
AHEIGHT	AIMLESSLY	AIRNED	AJUTAGE	ALARMING
AHEM	AIMS	AIRNING	AJUTAGES	ALARMISM
AHENT	AIN	AIRNS	AJWAN	ALARMISMS
AHIGH	AINE	AIRPLANE	AJWANS	ALARMIST
AHIMSA	AINEE	AIRPLANES	AKARYOTE	ALARMISTS
AHIMSAS	AIOLI	AIRPORT	AKARYOTES	ALARMS
AHIND	AIOLIS	AIRPORTS	AKE	ALARUM
AHING	AIR	AIRS	AKED	ALARUMED
AHINT	AIRBASE	AIRSCREW	AKEDAH	ALARUMING
AHOLD	AIRBASES	AIRSCREWS	AKEDAHS	ALARUMS
AHORSE	AIRBORNE	AIRSHAFT	AKEE	ALARY
AHOY	AIRBURST	AIRSHAFTS	AKEES	ALAS
AHS	AIRBURSTS	AIRSHIP	AKENE	ALASTRIM
AHULL	AIRBUSSES	AIRSHIPS	AKENES	ALASTRIMS
AHUNGERED	AIRCRAFT	AIRSICK	AKES	ALATE
AHUNGRY	AIRDRAWN	AIRSIDE	AKIMBO	ALATED
AI	AIRDROME	AIRSIDES	AKIN	ALAY
AIA	AIRDROMES	AIRSPACE	AKINESES	ALAYED
AIAS	AIRED	AIRSPACES	AKINESIA	ALAYING
AIBLINS	AIRER	AIRSPEED	AKINESIAS	ALAYS
AID	AIRERS	AIRSPEEDS	AKINESIS	ALB
AIDANCE	AIRFIELD	AIRSTOP	AKING	ALBACORE
AIDANCES	AIRFIELDS	AIRSTOPS	AKKAS	ALBACORES
AIDANT	AIRFLOW	AIRSTREAM	AKOLUTHOS	ALBARELLI

The Chambers Dictionary is the authority for many longer words; see *OSW* Introduction, page xii

ALBARELLO	ALCARRAZA	ALEGGES	ALGARROBO	ALIENISMS
ALBARELLOS	ALCARRAZAS	ALEGGING	ALGARROBOS	ALIENIST
ALBATA	ALCATRAS	ALEMBIC	ALGATE	ALIENISTS
ALBATAS	ALCATRASES	ALEMBICS	ALGATES	ALIENOR
ALBATROSS	ALCAYDE	ALEMBROTH	ALGEBRA	ALIENORS
ALBATROSSES	ALCAYDES	ALEMBROTHS	ALGEBRAIC	ALIENS
ALBE	ALCAZAR	ALENGTH	ALGEBRAS	ALIFORM
ALBEDO	ALCAZARS	ALEPH	ALGERINE	ALIGARTA
ALBEDOS	ALCHEMIC	ALEPHS	ALGERINES	ALIGARTAS
ALBEE	ALCHEMIES	ALEPINE	ALGESES	ALIGHT
ALBEIT	ALCHEMISE	ALEPINES	ALGESIA	ALIGHTED
ALBERGHI	ALCHEMISED	ALERCE	ALGESIAS	ALIGHTING
ALBERGO	ALCHEMISES	ALERCES	ALGESIS	ALIGHTS
ALBERT	ALCHEMISING	ALERION	ALGICIDE	ALIGN
ALBERTITE	ALCHEMIST	ALERIONS	ALGICIDES	ALIGNED
ALBERTITES	ALCHEMISTS	ALERT	ALGID	ALIGNING
ALBERTS	ALCHEMIZE	ALERTED	ALGIDITIES	ALIGNMENT
ALBESCENT	ALCHEMIZED	ALERTER	ALGIDITY	ALIGNMENTS
ALBESPINE	ALCHEMIZES	ALERTEST	ALGIN	ALIGNS
ALBESPINES	ALCHEMIZING	ALERTING	ALGINATE	ALIKE
ALBESPYNE	ALCHEMY	ALERTLY	ALGINATES	ALIMENT
ALBESPYNES	ALCHERA	ALERTNESS	ALGINIC	ALIMENTAL
ALBICORE	ALCHERAS	ALERTNESSES	ALGINS	ALIMENTED
ALBICORES	ALCHYMIES	ALERTS	ALGOID	ALIMENTING
ALBINESS	ALCHYMY	ALES	ALGOLOGIES	ALIMENTS
ALBINESSES	ALCOHOL	ALETHIC	ALGOLOGY	ALIMONIES
ALBINIC	ALCOHOLIC	ALEURON	ALGORISM	ALIMONY
ALBINISM	ALCOHOLICS	ALEURONE	ALGORISMS	ALINE
ALBINISMS	ALCOHOLS	ALEURONES	ALGORITHM	ALINED
ALBINO	ALCOPOP	ALEURONS	ALGORITHMS	ALINEMENT
ALBINOISM	ALCOPOPS	ALEVIN	ALGUACIL	ALINEMENTS
ALBINOISMS	ALCORZA	ALEVINS	ALGUACILS	ALINES
ALBINOS	ALCORZAS	ALEW	ALGUAZIL	ALINING
ALBINOTIC	ALCOVE	ALEWASHED	ALGUAZILS	ALIPED
ALBITE	ALCOVES	ALEWIFE	ALGUM	ALIPEDS
ALBITES	ALDEA	ALEWIVES	ALGUMS	ALIPHATIC
ALBITIC	ALDEAS	ALEWS	ALIAS	ALIQUANT
ALBITISE	ALDEHYDE	ALEXIA	ALIASES	ALIQUOT
ALBITISED	ALDEHYDES	ALEXIAS	ALIASING	ALISMA
ALBITISES	ALDER	ALEXIC	ALIASINGS	ALISMAS
ALBITISING	ALDERMAN	ALEXIN	ALIBI	ALIT
ALBITIZE	ALDERMEN	ALEXINS	ALIBIS	ALITERACIES
ALBITIZED	ALDERN	ALEYE	ALICANT	ALITERACY
ALBITIZES	ALDERS	ALEYED	ALICANTS	ALITERATE
ALBITIZING	ALDOSE	ALEYES	ALICYCLIC	ALIUNDE
ALBRICIAS	ALDOSES	ALEYING	ALIDAD	ALIVE
ALBS	ALDRIN	ALFA	ALIDADE	ALIVENESS
ALBUGO	ALDRINS	ALFALFA	ALIDADES	ALIVENESSES
ALBUGOS	ALE	ALFALFAS	ALIDADS	ALIYA
ALBUM	ALEATORIC	ALFAQUI	ALIEN	ALIYAH
ALBUMEN	ALEATORIES	ALFAQUIS	ALIENABLE	ALIYAHS
ALBUMENS	ALEATORY	ALFAS	ALIENAGE	ALIYAS
ALBUMIN	ALEBENCH	ALFERECES	ALIENAGES	ALIYOT
ALBUMINS	ALEBENCHES	ALFEREZ	ALIENATE	ALIYOTH
ALBUMS	ALECOST	ALFORJA	ALIENATED	ALIZARI
ALBURNOUS	ALECOSTS	ALFORJAS	ALIENATES	ALIZARIN
ALBURNUM	ALECTRYON	ALFRESCO	ALIENATING	ALIZARINE
ALBURNUMS	ALECTRYONS	ALGA	ALIENATOR	ALIZARINES
ALCAHEST	ALEE	ALGAE	ALIENATORS	ALIZARINS
ALCAHESTS	ALEFT	ALGAL	ALIENED	ALIZARIS
ALCAIDE	ALEGAR	ALGAROBA	ALIENEE	ALKAHEST
ALCAIDES	ALEGARS	ALGAROBAS	ALIENEES	ALKAHESTS
ALCALDE	ALEGGE	ALGARROBA	ALIENING	ALKALI
ALCALDES	ALEGGED	ALGARROBAS	ALIENISM	ALKALIES

ALKALIFIED	ALLEGGED	ALLNESS	ALLOWEDLY	ALMUCES
ALKALIFIES	ALLEGGES	ALLNESSES	ALLOWING	ALMUG
ALKALIFY	ALLEGGING	ALLNIGHT	ALLOWS	ALMUGS
ALKALIFYING	ALLEGIANT	ALLOCABLE	ALLOY	ALNAGE
ALKALINE	ALLEGING	ALLOCARPIES	ALLOYED	ALNAGER
ALKALIS	ALLEGORIC	ALLOCARPY	ALLOYING	ALNAGERS
ALKALISE	ALLEGORIES	ALLOCATE	ALLOYS	ALNAGES
ALKALISED	ALLEGORY	ALLOCATED	ALLS	ALOD
ALKALISES	ALLEGRO	ALLOCATES	ALLSEED	ALODIAL
ALKALISING	ALLEGROS	ALLOCATING	ALLSEEDS	ALODIUM
ALKALIZE	ALLEL	ALLOD	ALLSORTS	ALODIUMS
ALKALIZED	ALLELE	ALLODIAL	ALLSPICE	ALODS
ALKALIZES	ALLELES	ALLODIUM	ALLSPICES	ALOE
ALKALIZING	ALLELS	ALLODIUMS	ALLUDE	ALOED
ALKALOID	ALLELUIA	ALLODS	ALLUDED	ALOES
ALKALOIDS	ALLELUIAH	ALLOGAMIES	ALLUDES	ALOETIC
ALKALOSES	ALLELUIAHS	ALLOGAMY	ALLUDING	ALOETICS
ALKALOSIS	ALLELUIAS	ALLOGRAFT	ALLURE	ALOFT
ALKANE	ALLEMANDE	ALLOGRAFTS	ALLURED	ALOGIA
ALKANES	ALLEMANDES	ALLOGRAPH	ALLURER	ALOGIAS
ALKANET	ALLENARLY	ALLOGRAPHS	ALLURERS	ALOGICAL
ALKANETS	ALLERGEN	ALLOMETRIES	ALLURES	ALOHA
ALKENE	ALLERGENS	ALLOMETRY	ALLURING	ALONE
ALKENES	ALLERGIC	ALLOMORPH	ALLUSION	ALONELY
ALKIE	ALLERGICS	ALLOMORPHS	ALLUSIONS	ALONENESS
ALKIES	ALLERGIES	ALLONGE	ALLUSIVE	ALONENESSES
ALKY	ALLERGIST	ALLONGES	ALLUVIA	ALONG
ALKYD	ALLERGISTS	ALLONS	ALLUVIAL	ALONGSIDE
ALKYDS	ALLERGY	ALLONYM	ALLUVION	ALONGST
ALKYL	ALLERION	ALLONYMS	ALLUVIONS	ALOOF
ALKYLS	ALLERIONS	ALLOPATH	ALLUVIUM	ALOOFLY
ALKYNE	ALLEVIATE	ALLOPATHIES	ALLY	ALOOFNESS
ALKYNES	ALLEVIATED	ALLOPATHS	ALLYING	ALOOFNESSES
ALL	ALLEVIATES	ALLOPATHY	ALLYL	ALOPECIA
ALLANTOIC	ALLEVIATING	ALLOPHONE	ALLYLS	ALOPECIAS
ALLANTOID	ALLEY	ALLOPHONES	ALMA	ALOPECOID
ALLANTOIDS	ALLEYCAT	ALLOPLASM	ALMAH	ALOUD
ALLANTOIS	ALLEYCATS	ALLOPLASMS	ALMAHS	ALOW
ALLANTOISES	ALLEYED	ALLOSAUR	ALMAIN	ALOWE
ALLATIVE	ALLEYS	ALLOSAURS	ALMAINS	ALP
ALLATIVES	ALLEYWAY	ALLOSTERIES	ALMANAC	ALPACA
ALLAY	ALLEYWAYS	ALLOSTERY	ALMANACS	ALPACAS
ALLAYED	ALLHEAL	ALLOT	ALMANDINE	ALPARGATA
ALLAYER	ALLHEALS	ALLOTMENT	ALMANDINES	ALPARGATAS
ALLAYERS	ALLIANCE	ALLOTMENTS	ALMAS	ALPEEN
ALLAYING	ALLIANCES	ALLOTROPE	ALME	ALPEENS
ALLAYINGS	ALLICE	ALLOTROPES	ALMEH	ALPENHORN
ALLAYMENT	ALLICES	ALLOTROPIES	ALMEHS	ALPENHORNS
ALLAYMENTS	ALLICHOLIES	ALLOTROPY	ALMERIES	ALPHA
ALLAYS	ALLICHOLY	ALLOTS	ALMERY	ALPHABET
ALLCOMERS	ALLIED	ALLOTTED	ALMES	ALPHABETED
ALLEDGE	ALLIES	ALLOTTEE	ALMIGHTY	ALPHABETING
ALLEDGED	ALLIGARTA	ALLOTTEES	ALMIRAH	ALPHABETS
ALLEDGES	ALLIGARTAS	ALLOTTERIES	ALMIRAHS	ALPHAS
ALLEDGING	ALLIGATE	ALLOTTERY	ALMOND	ALPHASORT
ALLEE	ALLIGATED	ALLOTTING	ALMONDS	ALPHASORTED
ALLEES	ALLIGATES	ALLOW	ALMONER	ALPHASORTING
ALLEGE	ALLIGATING	ALLOWABLE	ALMONERS	ALPHASORTS
ALLEGED	ALLIGATOR	ALLOWABLY	ALMONRIES	ALPHORN
ALLEGEDLY	ALLIGATORS	ALLOWANCE	ALMONRY	ALPHORNS
ALLEGER	ALLIS	ALLOWANCED	ALMOST	ALPINE
ALLEGERS	ALLISES	ALLOWANCES	ALMOUS	ALPINES
ALLEGES	ALLIUM	ALLOWANCING	ALMS	ALPINISM
ALLEGGE	ALLIUMS	ALLOWED	ALMUCE	ALPINISMS

The Chambers Dictionary is the authority for many longer words; see *OSW* Introduction, page xii

ALPINIST	ALTRICIAL	AMALGAMS	AMBATCH	AMBULATORS
ALPINISTS	ALTRUISM	AMANDINE	AMBATCHES	AMBUSCADE
ALPS	ALTRUISMS	AMANDINES	AMBER	AMBUSCADED
ALREADY	ALTRUIST	AMANITA	AMBERED	AMBUSCADES
ALRIGHT	ALTRUISTS	AMANITAS	AMBERGRIS	AMBUSCADING
ALS	ALTS	AMARACUS	AMBERGRISES	AMBUSCADO
ALSIKE	ALUDEL	AMARACUSES	AMBERITE	AMBUSCADOES
ALSIKES	ALUDELS	AMARANT	AMBERITES	AMBUSCADOS
ALSO	ALULA	AMARANTH	AMBERJACK	AMBUSH
ALSOON	ALULAE	AMARANTHS	AMBERJACKS	AMBUSHED
ALSOONE	ALUM	AMARANTIN	AMBEROID	AMBUSHES
ALT	ALUMINA	AMARANTS	AMBEROIDS	AMBUSHING
ALTAR	ALUMINAS	AMARETTO	AMBEROUS	AMEARST
ALTARAGE	ALUMINATE	AMARETTOS	AMBERS	AMEBA
ALTARAGES	ALUMINATES	AMARYLLID	AMBERY	AMEBAE
ALTARS	ALUMINISE	AMARYLLIDS	AMBIANCE	AMEBAS
ALTARWISE	ALUMINISED	AMARYLLIS	AMBIANCES	AMEBIC
ALTER	ALUMINISES	AMARYLLISES	AMBIENCE	AMEER
ALTERABLE	ALUMINISING	AMASS	AMBIENCES	AMEERS
ALTERANT	ALUMINIUM	AMASSABLE	AMBIENT	AMEIOSES
ALTERANTS	ALUMINIUMS	AMASSED	AMBIENTS	AMEIOSIS
ALTERCATE	ALUMINIZE	AMASSES	AMBIGUITIES	AMELCORN
ALTERCATED	ALUMINIZED	AMASSING	AMBIGUITY	AMELCORNS
ALTERCATES	ALUMINIZES	AMASSMENT	AMBIGUOUS	AMELIA
ALTERCATING	ALUMINIZING	AMASSMENTS	AMBIT	AMELIAS
ALTERED	ALUMINOUS	AMATE	AMBITION	AMEN
ALTERING	ALUMINUM	AMATED	AMBITIONS	AMENABLE
ALTERITIES	ALUMINUMS	AMATES	AMBITIOUS	AMENABLY
ALTERITY	ALUMISH	AMATEUR	AMBITS	AMENAGE
ALTERN	ALUMIUM	AMATEURS	AMBITTY	AMENAGED
ALTERNANT	ALUMIUMS	AMATING	AMBIVERT	AMENAGES
ALTERNANTS	ALUMNA	AMATION	AMBIVERTS	AMENAGING
ALTERNAT	ALUMNAE	AMATIONS	AMBLE	AMENAUNCE
ALTERNATE	ALUMNI	AMATIVE	AMBLED	AMENAUNCES
ALTERNATED	ALUMNUS	AMATOL	AMBLER	AMEND
ALTERNATES	ALUMS	AMATOLS	AMBLERS	AMENDABLE
ALTERNATING	ALUNITE	AMATORIAL	AMBLES	AMENDE
ALTERNATS	ALUNITES	AMATORIAN	AMBLING	AMENDED
ALTERNE	ALURE	AMATORY	AMBLINGS	AMENDER
ALTERNES	ALURES	AMAUROSES	AMBLYOPIA	AMENDERS
ALTERS	ALVEARIES	AMAUROSIS	AMBLYOPIAS	AMENDES
ALTESSE	ALVEARY	AMAUROTIC	AMBO	AMENDING
ALTESSES	ALVEATED	AMAZE	AMBONES	AMENDMENT
ALTEZA	ALVEOLAR	AMAZED	AMBOS	AMENDMENTS
ALTEZAS	ALVEOLATE	AMAZEDLY	AMBRIES	AMENDS
ALTEZZA	ALVEOLE	AMAZEMENT	AMBROID	AMENE
ALTEZZAS	ALVEOLES	AMAZEMENTS	AMBROIDS	AMENED
ALTHAEA	ALVEOLI	AMAZES	AMBROSIA	AMENING
ALTHAEAS	ALVEOLUS	AMAZING	AMBROSIAL	AMENITIES
ALTHEA	ALVINE	AMAZINGLY	AMBROSIAN	AMENITY
ALTHEAS	ALWAY	AMAZON	AMBROSIAS	AMENS
ALTHORN	ALWAYS	AMAZONIAN	AMBROTYPE	AMENT
ALTHORNS	ALYSSUM	AMAZONITE	AMBROTYPES	AMENTA
ALTHOUGH	ALYSSUMS	AMAZONITES	AMBRY	AMENTAL
ALTIMETER	AM	AMAZONS	AMBULACRA	AMENTIA
ALTIMETERS	AMABILE	AMBAGE	AMBULANCE	AMENTIAS
ALTIMETRIES	AMADAVAT	AMBAGES	AMBULANCES	AMENTS
ALTIMETRY	AMADAVATS	AMBAGIOUS	AMBULANT	AMENTUM
ALTISSIMO	AMADOU	AMBAN	AMBULANTS	AMERCE
ALTITUDE	AMADOUS	AMBANS	AMBULATE	AMERCED
ALTITUDES	AMAH	AMBASSAGE	AMBULATED	AMERCES
ALTO	AMAHS	AMBASSAGES	AMBULATES	AMERCING
ALTOS	AMAIN	AMBASSIES	AMBULATING	AMERICIUM
ALTRICES	AMALGAM	AMBASSY	AMBULATOR	AMERICIUMS

AMETHYST	AMNESIAC	AMORTISE	AMPLOSOME	AMYLOPSIN
AMETHYSTS	AMNESIACS	AMORTISED	AMPLOSOMES	AMYLOPSINS
AMI	AMNESIAS	AMORTISES	AMPLY	AMYLS
AMIABLE	AMNESIC	AMORTISING	AMPOULE	AMYLUM
AMIABLY	AMNESICS	AMORTIZE	AMPOULES	AMYLUMS
AMIANTHUS	AMNESTIED	AMORTIZED	AMPS	AMYTAL
AMIANTHUSES	AMNESTIES	AMORTIZES	AMPUL	AMYTALS
AMIANTUS	AMNESTY	AMORTIZING	AMPULE	AN
AMIANTUSES	AMNESTYING	AMOSITE	AMPULES	ANA
AMICABLE	AMNIA	AMOSITES	AMPULLA	ANABAS
AMICABLY	AMNIO	AMOUNT	AMPULLAE	ANABASES
AMICE	AMNION	AMOUNTED	AMPULS	ANABASIS
AMICES	AMNIOS	AMOUNTING	AMPUTATE	ANABATIC
AMID	AMNIOTIC	AMOUNTS	AMPUTATED	ANABIOSES
AMIDE	AMNIOTOMIES	AMOUR	AMPUTATES	ANABIOSIS
AMIDES	AMNIOTOMY	AMOURETTE	AMPUTATING	ANABIOTIC
AMIDMOST	AMOEBA	AMOURETTES	AMPUTATOR	ANABLEPS
AMIDSHIPS	AMOEBAE	AMOURS	AMPUTATORS	ANABLEPSES
AMIDST	AMOEBAEAN	AMOVE	AMPUTEE	ANABOLIC
AMIE	AMOEBAS	AMOVED	AMPUTEES	ANABOLISM
AMIES	AMOEBIC	AMOVES	AMRIT	ANABOLISMS
AMIGO	AMOEBOID	AMOVING	AMRITA	ANABOLITE
AMIGOS	AMOK	AMP	AMRITAS	ANABOLITES
AMILDAR	AMOMUM	AMPASSIES	AMRITS	ANABRANCH
AMILDARS	AMOMUMS	AMPASSY	AMTMAN	ANABRANCHES
AMINE	AMONG	AMPERAGE	AMTMANS	ANACHARIS
AMINES	AMONGST	AMPERAGES	AMTRACK	ANACHARISES
AMIR	AMOOVE	AMPERE	AMTRACKS	ANACONDA
AMIRS	AMOOVED	AMPERES	AMUCK	ANACONDAS
AMIS	AMOOVES	AMPERSAND	AMULET	ANACRUSES
AMISES	AMOOVING	AMPERSANDS	AMULETIC	ANACRUSIS
AMISS	AMORAL	AMPERZAND	AMULETS	ANADEM
AMISSES	AMORALISM	AMPERZANDS	AMUSABLE	ANADEMS
AMISSIBLE	AMORALISMS	AMPHIBIAN	AMUSE	ANAEMIA
AMISSING	AMORALIST	AMPHIBIANS	AMUSED	ANAEMIAS
AMITIES	AMORALISTS	AMPHIBOLE	AMUSEDLY	ANAEMIC
AMITOSES	AMORANCE	AMPHIBOLES	AMUSEMENT	ANAEROBE
AMITOSIS	AMORANCES	AMPHIBOLIES	AMUSEMENTS	ANAEROBES
AMITOTIC	AMORANT	AMPHIBOLY	AMUSER	ANAEROBIC
AMITY	AMORCE	AMPHIGORIES	AMUSERS	ANAGLYPH
AMLA	AMORCES	AMPHIGORY	AMUSES	ANAGLYPHS
AMLAS	AMORET	AMPHIOXUS	AMUSETTE	ANAGOGE
AMMAN	AMORETS	AMPHIOXUSES	AMUSETTES	ANAGOGES
AMMANS	AMORETTI	AMPHIPOD	AMUSING	ANAGOGIC
AMMETER	AMORETTO	AMPHIPODS	AMUSINGLY	ANAGOGIES
AMMETERS	AMORINI	AMPHOLYTE	AMUSIVE	ANAGOGY
AMMIRAL	AMORINO	AMPHOLYTES	AMYGDAL	ANAGRAM
AMMIRALS	AMORISM	AMPHORA	AMYGDALA	ANAGRAMMED
AMMO	AMORISMS	AMPHORAE	AMYGDALAS	ANAGRAMMING
AMMON	AMORIST	AMPHORIC	AMYGDALES	ANAGRAMS
AMMONAL	AMORISTS	AMPLE	AMYGDALIN	ANAL
AMMONALS	AMORNINGS	AMPLENESS	AMYGDALINS	ANALCIME
AMMONIA	AMOROSA	AMPLENESSES	AMYGDALS	ANALCIMES
AMMONIAC	AMOROSAS	AMPLER	AMYGDULE	ANALCITE
AMMONIAS	AMOROSITIES	AMPLEST	AMYGDULES	ANALCITES
AMMONITE	AMOROSITY	AMPLEXUS	AMYL	ANALECTA
AMMONITES	AMOROSO	AMPLIFIED	AMYLASE	ANALECTIC
AMMONIUM	AMOROSOS	AMPLIFIER	AMYLASES	ANALECTS
AMMONIUMS	AMOROUS	AMPLIFIERS	AMYLENE	ANALEMMA
AMMONOID	AMOROUSLY	AMPLIFIES	AMYLENES	ANALEMMAS
AMMONOIDS	AMORPHISM	AMPLIFY	AMYLOID	ANALEMMATA
AMMONS	AMORPHISMS	AMPLIFYING	AMYLOIDAL	ANALEPTIC
AMMOS	AMORPHOUS	AMPLITUDE	AMYLOIDS	ANALEPTICS
AMNESIA	AMORT	AMPLITUDES	AMYLOIDS	ANALGESIA

The Chambers Dictionary is the authority for many longer words; see *OSW* Introduction, page xii

ANALGESIAS	ANAPLASTY	ANCHORESS	ANEAR	ANGERS
ANALGESIC	ANAPTYXES	ANCHORESSES	ANEARED	ANGICO
ANALGESICS	ANAPTYXIS	ANCHORET	ANEARING	ANGICOS
ANALLY	ANARCH	ANCHORETS	ANEARS	ANGINA
ANALOG	ANARCHAL	ANCHORING	ANEATH	ANGINAL
ANALOGA	ANARCHIAL	ANCHORITE	ANECDOTAL	ANGINAS
ANALOGIC	ANARCHIC	ANCHORITES	ANECDOTE	ANGIOGRAM
ANALOGIES	ANARCHIES	ANCHORS	ANECDOTES	ANGIOGRAMS
ANALOGISE	ANARCHISE	ANCHOVETA	ANECHOIC	ANGIOMA
ANALOGISED	ANARCHISED	ANCHOVETAS	ANELACE	ANGIOMAS
ANALOGISES	ANARCHISES	ANCHOVIES	ANELACES	ANGIOMATA
ANALOGISING	ANARCHISING	ANCHOVY	ANELE	ANGKLUNG
ANALOGIST	ANARCHISM	ANCHYLOSE	ANELED	ANGKLUNGS
ANALOGISTS	ANARCHISMS	ANCHYLOSED	ANELES	ANGLE
ANALOGIZE	ANARCHIST	ANCHYLOSES	ANELING	ANGLED
ANALOGIZED	ANARCHISTS	ANCHYLOSING	ANEMIA	ANGLER
ANALOGIZES	ANARCHIZE	ANCIENT	ANEMIAS	ANGLERS
ANALOGIZING	ANARCHIZED	ANCIENTLY	ANEMIC	ANGLES
ANALOGON	ANARCHIZES	ANCIENTRIES	ANEMOGRAM	ANGLESITE
ANALOGONS	ANARCHIZING	ANCIENTRY	ANEMOGRAMS	ANGLESITES
ANALOGOUS	ANARCHS	ANCIENTS	ANEMOLOGIES	ANGLEWISE
ANALOGS	ANARCHY	ANCILE	ANEMOLOGY	ANGLEWORM
ANALOGUE	ANAS	ANCILIA	ANEMONE	ANGLEWORMS
ANALOGUES	ANASARCA	ANCILLARIES	ANEMONES	ANGLICE
ANALOGY	ANASARCAS	ANCILLARY	ANENT	ANGLICISE
ANALYSAND	ANASTASES	ANCIPITAL	ANERLY	ANGLICISED
ANALYSANDS	ANASTASIS	ANCLE	ANEROID	ANGLICISES
ANALYSE	ANASTATIC	ANCLES	ANEROIDS	ANGLICISING
ANALYSED	ANATASE	ANCOME	ANES	ANGLICISM
ANALYSER	ANATASES	ANCOMES	ANESTRA	ANGLICISMS
ANALYSERS	ANATHEMA	ANCON	ANESTRI	ANGLICIST
ANALYSES	ANATHEMAS	ANCONES	ANESTRUM	ANGLICISTS
ANALYSING	ANATOMIC	ANCORA	ANESTRUS	ANGLICIZE
ANALYSIS	ANATOMIES	ANCRESS	ANETIC	ANGLICIZED
ANALYST	ANATOMISE	ANCRESSES	ANEUPLOID	ANGLICIZES
ANALYSTS	ANATOMISED	AND	ANEUPLOIDS	ANGLICIZING
ANALYTIC	ANATOMISES	ANDANTE	ANEURIN	ANGLIFIED
ANALYTICS	ANATOMISING	ANDANTES	ANEURINS	ANGLIFIES
ANALYZE	ANATOMIST	ANDANTINO	ANEURISM	ANGLIFY
ANALYZED	ANATOMISTS	ANDANTINOS	ANEURISMS	ANGLIFYING
ANALYZER	ANATOMIZE	ANDESINE	ANEURYSM	ANGLING
ANALYZERS	ANATOMIZED	ANDESINES	ANEURYSMS	ANGLINGS
ANALYZES	ANATOMIZES	ANDESITE	ANEW	ANGLIST
ANALYZING	ANATOMIZING	ANDESITES	ANGARIES	ANGLISTS
ANAMNESES	ANATOMY	ANDESITIC	ANGARY	ANGLOPHIL
ANAMNESIS	ANATROPIES	ANDIRON	ANGEKKOK	ANGLOPHILS
ANAN	ANATROPY	ANDIRONS	ANGEKKOKS	ANGOLA
ANANA	ANATTA	ANDROECIA	ANGEKOK	ANGOPHORA
ANANAS	ANATTAS	ANDROGEN	ANGEKOKS	ANGOPHORAS
ANANASES	ANATTO	ANDROGENS	ANGEL	ANGORA
ANANDROUS	ANATTOS	ANDROGYNE	ANGELHOOD	ANGORAS
ANANKE	ANAXIAL	ANDROGYNES	ANGELHOODS	ANGRIER
ANANKES	ANBURIES	ANDROGYNIES	ANGELIC	ANGRIES
ANANTHOUS	ANBURY	ANDROGYNY	ANGELICA	ANGRIEST
ANAPAEST	ANCE	ANDROID	ANGELICAL	ANGRILY
ANAPAESTS	ANCESTOR	ANDROIDS	ANGELICAS	ANGRINESS
ANAPEST	ANCESTORS	ANDROLOGIES	ANGELS	ANGRINESSES
ANAPESTS	ANCESTRAL	ANDROLOGY	ANGELUS	ANGRY
ANAPHASE	ANCESTRIES	ANDROMEDA	ANGELUSES	ANGST
ANAPHASES	ANCESTRY	ANDROMEDAS	ANGER	ANGSTROM
ANAPHORA	ANCHOR	ANDS	ANGERED	ANGSTROMS
ANAPHORAS	ANCHORAGE	ANDVILE	ANGERING	ANGSTS
ANAPHORIC	ANCHORAGES	ANDVILES	ANGERLESS	ANGUIFORM
ANAPLASTIES	ANCHORED	ANE	ANGERLY	ANGUINE

ANGUIPED	ANIMATION	ANNALIZED	ANNUALIZES	ANONYMISE
ANGUIPEDE	ANIMATIONS	ANNALIZES	ANNUALIZING	ANONYMISED
ANGUISH	ANIMATISM	ANNALIZING	ANNUALLY	ANONYMISES
ANGUISHED	ANIMATISMS	ANNALS	ANNUALS	ANONYMISING
ANGUISHES	ANIMATOR	ANNAS	ANNUITANT	ANONYMITIES
ANGUISHING	ANIMATORS	ANNAT	ANNUITANTS	ANONYMITY
ANGULAR	ANIME	ANNATES	ANNUITIES	ANONYMIZE
ANGULATE	ANIMES	ANNATS	ANNUITY	ANONYMIZED
ANGULATED	ANIMISM	ANNATTA	ANNUL	ANONYMIZES
ANHEDONIA	ANIMISMS	ANNATTAS	ANNULAR	ANONYMIZING
ANHEDONIAS	ANIMIST	ANNATTO	ANNULARS	ANONYMOUS
ANHEDONIC	ANIMISTIC	ANNATTOS	ANNULATE	ANONYMS
ANHEDRAL	ANIMISTS	ANNEAL	ANNULATED	ANOPHELES
ANHUNGRED	ANIMOSITIES	ANNEALED	ANNULATES	ANORAK
ANHYDRIDE	ANIMOSITY	ANNEALER	ANNULET	ANORAKS
ANHYDRIDES	ANIMUS	ANNEALERS	ANNULETS	ANORECTAL
ANHYDRITE	ANIMUSES	ANNEALING	ANNULI	ANORECTIC
ANHYDRITES	ANION	ANNEALINGS	ANNULLED	ANORECTICS
ANHYDROUS	ANIONIC	ANNEALS	ANNULLING	ANORETIC
ANI	ANIONS	ANNECTENT	ANNULMENT	ANORETICS
ANICONIC	ANIS	ANNELID	ANNULMENTS	ANOREXIA
ANICONISM	ANISE	ANNELIDS	ANNULOSE	ANOREXIAS
ANICONISMS	ANISEED	ANNEX	ANNULS	ANOREXIC
ANICONIST	ANISEEDS	ANNEXE	ANNULUS	ANOREXICS
ANICONISTS	ANISES	ANNEXED	ANOA	ANOREXIES
ANICUT	ANISETTE	ANNEXES	ANOAS	ANOREXY
ANICUTS	ANISETTES	ANNEXING	ANODAL	ANORTHIC
ANIGH	ANKER	ANNEXION	ANODE	ANORTHITE
ANIGHT	ANKERITE	ANNEXIONS	ANODES	ANORTHITES
ANIL	ANKERITES	ANNEXMENT	ANODIC	ANOSMIA
ANILE	ANKERS	ANNEXMENTS	ANODISE	ANOSMIAS
ANILINE	ANKH	ANNEXURE	ANODISED	ANOTHER
ANILINES	ANKHS	ANNEXURES	ANODISES	ANOUGH
ANILITIES	ANKLE	ANNICUT	ANODISING	ANOUROUS
ANILITY	ANKLED	ANNICUTS	ANODIZE	ANOVULANT
ANILS	ANKLES	ANNO	ANODIZED	ANOVULANTS
ANIMA	ANKLET	ANNOTATE	ANODIZES	ANOW
ANIMAL	ANKLETS	ANNOTATED	ANODIZING	ANOXIA
ANIMALIC	ANKLONG	ANNOTATES	ANODYNE	ANOXIAS
ANIMALISE	ANKLONGS	ANNOTATING	ANODYNES	ANOXIC
ANIMALISED	ANKLUNG	ANNOTATOR	ANOESES	ANSATE
ANIMALISES	ANKLUNGS	ANNOTATORS	ANOESIS	ANSATED
ANIMALISING	ANKUS	ANNOUNCE	ANOESTRA	ANSERINE
ANIMALISM	ANKUSES	ANNOUNCED	ANOESTRI	ANSWER
ANIMALISMS	ANKYLOSE	ANNOUNCER	ANOESTRUM	ANSWERED
ANIMALIST	ANKYLOSED	ANNOUNCERS	ANOESTRUS	ANSWERER
ANIMALISTS	ANKYLOSES	ANNOUNCES	ANOETIC	ANSWERERS
ANIMALITIES	ANKYLOSING	ANNOUNCING	ANOINT	ANSWERING
ANIMALITY	ANKYLOSIS	ANNOY	ANOINTED	ANSWERS
ANIMALIZE	ANLACE	ANNOYANCE	ANOINTER	ANT
ANIMALIZED	ANLACES	ANNOYANCES	ANOINTERS	ANTA
ANIMALIZES	ANLAGE	ANNOYED	ANOINTING	ANTACID
ANIMALIZING	ANLAGEN	ANNOYER	ANOINTS	ANTACIDS
ANIMALLY	ANLAGES	ANNOYERS	ANOMALIES	ANTAE
ANIMALS	ANN	ANNOYING	ANOMALOUS	ANTAR
ANIMAS	ANNA	ANNOYS	ANOMALY	ANTARA
ANIMATE	ANNAL	ANNS	ANOMIC	ANTARAS
ANIMATED	ANNALISE	ANNUAL	ANOMIE	ANTARS
ANIMATER	ANNALISED	ANNUALISE	ANOMIES	ANTAS
ANIMATERS	ANNALISES	ANNUALISED	ANOMY	ANTBEAR
ANIMATES	ANNALISING	ANNUALISES	ANON	ANTBEARS
ANIMATIC	ANNALIST	ANNUALISING	ANONYM	ANTBIRD
ANIMATICS	ANNALISTS	ANNUALIZE	ANONYMA	ANTBIRDS
ANIMATING	ANNALIZE	ANNUALIZED	ANONYMAS	ANTE

The Chambers Dictionary is the authority for many longer words; see *OSW* Introduction, page xii

ANTEATER	ANTHRAXES	ANTIPHONY	ANTLIONS	APAID
ANTEATERS	ANTHROPIC	ANTIPODAL	ANTONYM	APANAGE
ANTECEDE	ANTHURIUM	ANTIPODE	ANTONYMIC	APANAGED
ANTECEDED	ANTHURIUMS	ANTIPODES	ANTONYMIES	APANAGES
ANTECEDES	ANTI	ANTIPOLE	ANTONYMS	APART
ANTECEDING	ANTIAR	ANTIPOLES	ANTONYMY	APARTHEID
ANTECHOIR	ANTIARS	ANTIPOPE	ANTRA	APARTHEIDS
ANTECHOIRS	ANTIBODIES	ANTIPOPES	ANTRE	APARTMENT
ANTED	ANTIBODY	ANTIQUARIES	ANTRES	APARTMENTS
ANTEDATE	ANTIC	ANTIQUARK	ANTRORSE	APARTNESS
ANTEDATED	ANTICHLOR	ANTIQUARKS	ANTRUM	APARTNESSES
ANTEDATES	ANTICHLORS	ANTIQUARY	ANTS	APATETIC
ANTEDATING	ANTICIVIC	ANTIQUATE	ANTSIER	APATHATON
ANTEFIX	ANTICIZE	ANTIQUATED	ANTSIEST	APATHATONS
ANTEFIXA	ANTICIZED	ANTIQUATES	ANTSY	APATHETIC
ANTEFIXAL	ANTICIZES	ANTIQUATING	ANUCLEATE	APATHIES
ANTEFIXES	ANTICIZING	ANTIQUE	ANURIA	APATHY
ANTEING	ANTICK	ANTIQUED	ANURIAS	APATITE
ANTELOPE	ANTICKE	ANTIQUELY	ANUROUS	APATITES
ANTELOPES	ANTICKED	ANTIQUES	ANUS	APAY
ANTELUCAN	ANTICKING	ANTIQUING	ANUSES	APAYD
ANTENATAL	ANTICLINE	ANTIQUITIES	ANVIL	APAYING
ANTENATI	ANTICLINES	ANTIQUITY	ANVILS	APAYS
ANTENNA	ANTICOUS	ANTIRIOT	ANXIETIES	APE
ANTENNAE	ANTICS	ANTIRUST	ANXIETY	APEAK
ANTENNAL	ANTIDOTAL	ANTIS	ANXIOUS	APED
ANTENNARY	ANTIDOTE	ANTISCIAN	ANXIOUSLY	APEDOM
ANTENNAS	ANTIDOTES	ANTISCIANS	ANY	APEDOMS
ANTENNULE	ANTIENT	ANTISERA	ANYBODIES	APEEK
ANTENNULES	ANTIENTS	ANTISERUM	ANYBODY	APEHOOD
ANTEPAST	ANTIGAY	ANTISERUMS	ANYHOW	APEHOODS
ANTEPASTS	ANTIGEN	ANTISHIP	ANYONE	APEMAN
ANTERIOR	ANTIGENIC	ANTISKID	ANYONES	APEMEN
ANTEROOM	ANTIGENS	ANTISPAST	ANYROAD	APEPSIA
ANTEROOMS	ANTIHELICES	ANTISPASTS	ANYTHING	APEPSIAS
ANTES	ANTIHELIX	ANTISTAT	ANYTHINGS	APEPSIES
ANTEVERT	ANTIKNOCK	ANTISTATS	ANYTIME	APEPSY
ANTEVERTED	ANTIKNOCKS	ANTITANK	ANYWAY	APERCU
ANTEVERTING	ANTILOG	ANTITHEFT	ANYWAYS	APERCUS
ANTEVERTS	ANTILOGIES	ANTITHET	ANYWHEN	APERIENT
ANTHELIA	ANTILOGS	ANTITHETS	ANYWHERE	APERIENTS
ANTHELICES	ANTILOGY	ANTITOXIC	ANYWISE	APERIES
ANTHELION	ANTIMASK	ANTITOXIN	ANZIANI	APERIODIC
ANTHELIX	ANTIMASKS	ANTITOXINS	AORIST	APERITIF
ANTHEM	ANTIMONIC	ANTITRADE	AORISTIC	APERITIFS
ANTHEMED	ANTIMONIES	ANTITRADES	AORISTS	APERITIVE
ANTHEMIA	ANTIMONY	ANTITRAGI	AORTA	APERITIVES
ANTHEMIC	ANTING	ANTITRUST	AORTAE	APERT
ANTHEMING	ANTINGS	ANTITYPAL	AORTAL	APERTNESS
ANTHEMION	ANTINODAL	ANTITYPE	AORTAS	APERTNESSES
ANTHEMS	ANTINODE	ANTITYPES	AORTIC	APERTURE
ANTHER	ANTINODES	ANTITYPIC	AORTITIS	APERTURES
ANTHERS	ANTINOISE	ANTIVENIN	AORTITISES	APERY
ANTHESES	ANTINOMIC	ANTIVENINS	AOUDAD	APES
ANTHESIS	ANTINOMIES	ANTIVIRAL	AOUDADS	APETALIES
ANTHOCARP	ANTINOMY	ANTIVIRUS	APACE	APETALOUS
ANTHOCARPS	ANTIPAPAL	ANTIWAR	APACHE	APETALY
ANTHOCYAN	ANTIPASTO	ANTLER	APACHES	APEX
ANTHOCYANS	ANTIPASTOS	ANTLERED	APADANA	APEXES
ANTHOID	ANTIPATHIES	ANTLERS	APADANAS	APHAGIA
ANTHOLOGIES	ANTIPATHY	ANTLIA	APAGE	APHAGIAS
ANTHOLOGY	ANTIPHON	ANTLIAE	APAGOGE	APHANITE
ANTHRACIC	ANTIPHONIES	ANTLIATE	APAGOGES	APHANITES
ANTHRAX	ANTIPHONS	ANTLION	APAGOGIC	APHASIA

The Chambers Dictionary is the authority for many longer words; see *OSW* Introduction, page xii

APHASIAC	APICAL	APOLLOS	APPAID	APPENDING
APHASIACS	APICALLY	APOLOGIA	APPAIR	APPENDIX
APHASIAS	APICES	APOLOGIAS	APPAIRED	APPENDIXES
APHASIC	APICIAN	APOLOGIES	APPAIRING	APPENDS
APHELIA	APICULATE	APOLOGISE	APPAIRS	APPERIL
APHELIAN	APIECE	APOLOGISED	APPAL	APPERILL
APHELION	APING	APOLOGISES	APPALLED	APPERILLS
APHERESES	APIOL	APOLOGISING	APPALLING	APPERILS
APHERESIS	APIOLS	APOLOGIST	APPALS	APPERTAIN
APHESES	APISH	APOLOGISTS	APPALTI	APPERTAINED
APHESIS	APISHLY	APOLOGIZE	APPALTO	APPERTAINING
APHETIC	APISHNESS	APOLOGIZED	APPANAGE	APPERTAINS
APHETISE	APISHNESSES	APOLOGIZES	APPANAGED	APPESTAT
APHETISED	APISM	APOLOGIZING	APPANAGES	APPESTATS
APHETISES	APISMS	APOLOGUE	APPARAT	APPETENCE
APHETISING	APIVOROUS	APOLOGUES	APPARATS	APPETENCES
APHETIZE	APLANAT	APOLOGY	APPARATUS	APPETENCIES
APHETIZED	APLANATIC	APOMICTIC	APPARATUSES	APPETENCY
APHETIZES	APLANATS	APOMIXES	APPAREL	APPETENT
APHETIZING	APLASIA	APOMIXIS	APPARELLED	APPETIBLE
APHICIDE	APLASIAS	APOOP	APPARELLING	APPETISE
APHICIDES	APLASTIC	APOPHASES	APPARELS	APPETISED
APHID	APLENTY	APOPHASIS	APPARENCIES	APPETISER
APHIDES	APLITE	APOPHATIC	APPARENCY	APPETISERS
APHIDIAN	APLITES	APOPHYGE	APPARENT	APPETISES
APHIDIANS	APLOMB	APOPHYGES	APPARENTS	APPETISING
APHIDIOUS	APLOMBS	APOPHYSES	APPARITOR	APPETITE
APHIDS	APLUSTRE	APOPHYSIS	APPARITORS	APPETITES
APHIS	APLUSTRES	APOPLEX	APPAY	APPETIZE
APHONIA	APNEA	APOPLEXED	APPAYD	APPETIZED
APHONIAS	APNEAS	APOPLEXES	APPAYING	APPETIZER
APHONIC	APNOEA	APOPLEXIES	APPAYS	APPETIZERS
APHONIES	APNOEAS	APOPLEXING	APPEACH	APPETIZES
APHONOUS	APOCOPATE	APOPLEXY	APPEACHED	APPETIZING
APHONY	APOCOPATED	APOPTOSES	APPEACHES	APPLAUD
APHORISE	APOCOPATES	APOPTOSIS	APPEACHING	APPLAUDED
APHORISED	APOCOPATING	APOPTOTIC	APPEAL	APPLAUDER
APHORISER	APOCOPE	APORIA	APPEALED	APPLAUDERS
APHORISERS	APOCOPES	APORIAS	APPEALING	APPLAUDING
APHORISES	APOCRINE	APORT	APPEALS	APPLAUDS
APHORISING	APOCRYPHA	APOSITIA	APPEAR	APPLAUSE
APHORISM	APOD	APOSITIAS	APPEARED	APPLAUSES
APHORISMS	APODAL	APOSITIC	APPEARER	APPLE
APHORIST	APODE	APOSPORIES	APPEARERS	APPLES
APHORISTS	APODES	APOSPORY	APPEARING	APPLET
APHORIZE	APODICTIC	APOSTASIES	APPEARS	APPLETS
APHORIZED	APODOSES	APOSTASY	APPEASE	APPLIABLE
APHORIZER	APODOSIS	APOSTATE	APPEASED	APPLIANCE
APHORIZERS	APODOUS	APOSTATES	APPEASER	APPLIANCES
APHORIZES	APODS	APOSTATIC	APPEASERS	APPLICANT
APHORIZING	APOENZYME	APOSTIL	APPEASES	APPLICANTS
APHOTIC	APOENZYMES	APOSTILLE	APPEASING	APPLICATE
APHTHA	APOGAEIC	APOSTILLES	APPEL	APPLIED
APHTHAE	APOGAMIC	APOSTILS	APPELLANT	APPLIER
APHTHOUS	APOGAMIES	APOSTLE	APPELLANTS	APPLIERS
APHYLLIES	APOGAMOUS	APOSTLES	APPELLATE	APPLIES
APHYLLOUS	APOGAMY	APOSTOLIC	APPELS	APPLIQUE
APHYLLY	APOGEAL	APOTHECIA	APPEND	APPLIQUES
APIAN	APOGEAN	APOTHEGM	APPENDAGE	APPLY
APIARIAN	APOGEE	APOTHEGMS	APPENDAGES	APPLYING
APIARIES	APOGEES	APOTHEM	APPENDANT	APPOINT
APIARIST	APOGRAPH	APOTHEMS	APPENDANTS	APPOINTED
APIARISTS	APOGRAPHS	APOZEM	APPENDED	APPOINTEE
APIARY	APOLLO	APOZEMS	APPENDICES	APPOINTEES

APPOINTING	APPROVERS	APTOTES	AR	ARBALISTS
APPOINTOR	APPROVES	APTOTIC	ARABA	ARBAS
APPOINTORS	APPROVING	APTS	ARABAS	ARBITER
APPOINTS	APPUI	APYRETIC	ARABESQUE	ARBITERS
APPORT	APPUIED	APYREXIA	ARABESQUES	ARBITRAGE
APPORTION	APPUIS	APYREXIAS	ARABICA	ARBITRAGED
APPORTIONED	APPULSE	AQUA	ARABICAS	ARBITRAGES
APPORTIONING	APPULSES	AQUABATIC	ARABIN	ARBITRAGING
APPORTIONS	APPUY	AQUABATICS	ARABINOSE	ARBITRAL
APPORTS	APPUYED	AQUABOARD	ARABINOSES	ARBITRARY
APPOSE	APPUYING	AQUABOARDS	ARABINS	ARBITRATE
APPOSED	APPUYS	AQUACADE	ARABIS	ARBITRATED
APPOSER	APRAXIA	AQUACADES	ARABISE	ARBITRATES
APPOSERS	APRAXIAS	AQUADROME	ARABISED	ARBITRATING
APPOSES	APRES	AQUADROMES	ARABISES	ARBITRESS
APPOSING	APRICATE	AQUAE	ARABISING	ARBITRESSES
APPOSITE	APRICATED	AQUAFER	ARABIZE	ARBITRIUM
APPRAISAL	APRICATES	AQUAFERS	ARABIZED	ARBITRIUMS
APPRAISALS	APRICATING	AQUALUNG	ARABIZES	ARBLAST
APPRAISE	APRICOCK	AQUALUNGS	ARABIZING	ARBLASTER
APPRAISED	APRICOCKS	AQUANAUT	ARABLE	ARBLASTERS
APPRAISEE	APRICOT	AQUANAUTS	ARACEOUS	ARBLASTS
APPRAISEES	APRICOTS	AQUAPHOBE	ARACHIS	ARBOR
APPRAISER	APRIORISM	AQUAPHOBES	ARACHISES	ARBOREAL
APPRAISERS	APRIORISMS	AQUAPLANE	ARACHNID	ARBOREOUS
APPRAISES	APRIORIST	AQUAPLANED	ARACHNIDS	ARBORES
APPRAISING	APRIORISTS	AQUAPLANES	ARACHNOID	ARBORET
APPREHEND	APRIORITIES	AQUAPLANING	ARACHNOIDS	ARBORETA
APPREHENDED	APRIORITY	AQUAPLANINGS	ARAGONITE	ARBORETS
APPREHENDING	APRON	AQUARELLE	ARAGONITES	ARBORETUM
APPREHENDS	APRONED	AQUARELLES	ARAISE	ARBORIST
APPRESS	APRONFUL	AQUARIA	ARAISED	ARBORISTS
APPRESSED	APRONFULS	AQUARIAN	ARAISES	ARBOROUS
APPRESSES	APRONING	AQUARIANS	ARAISING	ARBORS
APPRESSING	APRONS	AQUARIIST	ARAK	ARBOUR
APPRISE	APROPOS	AQUARIISTS	ARAKS	ARBOURED
APPRISED	APSARAS	AQUARIST	ARALIA	ARBOURS
APPRISER	APSARASES	AQUARISTS	ARALIAS	ARBOVIRUS
APPRISERS	APSE	AQUARIUM	ARAME	ARBOVIRUSES
APPRISES	APSES	AQUARIUMS	ARAMES	ARBS
APPRISING	APSIDAL	AQUAROBIC	ARANEID	ARBUTE
APPRISINGS	APSIDES	AQUAROBICS	ARANEIDS	ARBUTES
APPRIZE	APSIDIOLE	AQUAS	ARANEOUS	ARBUTUS
APPRIZED	APSIDIOLES	AQUATIC	ARAPAIMA	ARBUTUSES
APPRIZER	APSIS	AQUATICS	ARAPAIMAS	ARC
APPRIZERS	APT	AQUATINT	ARAPONGA	ARCADE
APPRIZES	APTED	AQUATINTA	ARAPONGAS	ARCADED
APPRIZING	APTER	AQUATINTAS	ARAPUNGA	ARCADES
APPRIZINGS	APTERAL	AQUATINTED	ARAPUNGAS	ARCADING
APPROACH	APTERIA	AQUATINTING	ARAR	ARCADINGS
APPROACHED	APTERISM	AQUATINTS	ARAROBA	ARCANA
APPROACHES	APTERISMS	AQUAVIT	ARAROBAS	ARCANE
APPROACHING	APTERIUM	AQUAVITS	ARARS	ARCANELY
APPROBATE	APTEROUS	AQUEDUCT	ARAUCARIA	ARCANIST
APPROBATED	APTERYX	AQUEDUCTS	ARAUCARIAS	ARCANISTS
APPROBATES	APTERYXES	AQUEOUS	ARAYSE	ARCANUM
APPROBATING	APTEST	AQUIFER	ARAYSED	ARCCOS
APPROOF	APTING	AQUIFERS	ARAYSES	ARCCOSES
APPROOFS	APTITUDE	AQUILEGIA	ARAYSING	ARCED
APPROVAL	APTITUDES	AQUILEGIAS	ARB	ARCH
APPROVALS	APTLY	AQUILINE	ARBA	ARCHAEI
APPROVE	APTNESS	AQUILON	ARBALEST	ARCHAEUS
APPROVED	APTNESSES	AQUILONS	ARBALESTS	ARCHAIC
APPROVER	APTOTE	AQUIVER	ARBALIST	ARCHAISE

ARCHAISED	ARCHOLOGIES	AREAR	ARGILS	ARILLATE
ARCHAISER	ARCHOLOGY	AREAS	ARGININE	ARILLATED
ARCHAISERS	ARCHON	AREAWAY	ARGININES	ARILLI
ARCHAISES	ARCHONS	AREAWAYS	ARGOL	ARILLODE
ARCHAISING	ARCHONTIC	ARECA	ARGOLS	ARILLODES
ARCHAISM	ARCHWAY	ARECAS	ARGON	ARILLOID
ARCHAISMS	ARCHWAYS	ARED	ARGONAUT	ARILLUS
ARCHAIST	ARCHWISE	AREDD	ARGONAUTS	ARILS
ARCHAISTS	ARCING	AREDE	ARGONS	ARIOSI
ARCHAIZE	ARCINGS	AREDES	ARGOSIES	ARIOSO
ARCHAIZED	ARCKED	AREDING	ARGOSY	ARIOSOS
ARCHAIZER	ARCKING	AREFIED	ARGOT	ARIOT
ARCHAIZERS	ARCKINGS	AREFIES	ARGOTS	ARIPPLE
ARCHAIZES	ARCO	AREFY	ARGUABLE	ARIS
ARCHAIZING	ARCOLOGIES	AREFYING	ARGUABLY	ARISE
ARCHANGEL	ARCOLOGY	AREG	ARGUE	ARISEN
ARCHANGELS	ARCS	ARENA	ARGUED	ARISES
ARCHDUCAL	ARCSECOND	ARENAS	ARGUER	ARISH
ARCHDUCHIES	ARCSECONDS	ARENATION	ARGUERS	ARISHES
ARCHDUCHY	ARCSIN	ARENATIONS	ARGUES	ARISING
ARCHDUKE	ARCSINS	AREOLA	ARGUFIED	ARISTA
ARCHDUKES	ARCTAN	AREOLAE	ARGUFIER	ARISTAE
ARCHED	ARCTANS	AREOLAR	ARGUFIERS	ARISTAS
ARCHEI	ARCTIC	AREOLATE	ARGUFIES	ARISTATE
ARCHER	ARCTICS	AREOLATED	ARGUFY	ARISTO
ARCHERESS	ARCTIID	AREOLE	ARGUFYING	ARISTOS
ARCHERESSES	ARCTIIDS	AREOLES	ARGUING	ARK
ARCHERIES	ARCTOID	AREOMETER	ARGULI	ARKED
ARCHERS	ARCTOPHIL	AREOMETERS	ARGULUS	ARKING
ARCHERY	ARCTOPHILS	AREOSTYLE	ARGUMENT	ARKITE
ARCHES	ARCUATE	AREOSTYLES	ARGUMENTA	ARKITES
ARCHEST	ARCUATED	ARERE	ARGUMENTS	ARKOSE
ARCHETYPE	ARCUATION	ARES	ARGUS	ARKOSES
ARCHETYPES	ARCUATIONS	ARET	ARGUSES	ARKS
ARCHEUS	ARCUS	ARETE	ARGUTE	ARLE
ARCHIL	ARCUSES	ARETES	ARGUTELY	ARLED
ARCHILOWE	ARD	ARETS	ARGYLE	ARLES
ARCHILOWES	ARDEB	ARETT	ARGYLES	ARLING
ARCHILS	ARDEBS	ARETTED	ARGYRIA	ARM
ARCHIMAGE	ARDENCIES	ARETTING	ARGYRIAS	ARMADA
ARCHIMAGES	ARDENCY	ARETTS	ARGYRITE	ARMADAS
ARCHING	ARDENT	AREW	ARGYRITES	ARMADILLO
ARCHITECT	ARDENTLY	ARGAL	ARHYTHMIA	ARMADILLOS
ARCHITECTED	ARDOR	ARGALA	ARHYTHMIAS	ARMAMENT
ARCHITECTING	ARDORS	ARGALAS	ARHYTHMIC	ARMAMENTS
ARCHITECTS	ARDOUR	ARGALI	ARIA	ARMATURE
ARCHITYPE	ARDOURS	ARGALIS	ARIAS	ARMATURES
ARCHITYPES	ARDRI	ARGAN	ARID	ARMBAND
ARCHIVAL	ARDRIGH	ARGAND	ARIDER	ARMBANDS
ARCHIVE	ARDRIGHS	ARGANDS	ARIDEST	ARMCHAIR
ARCHIVED	ARDRIS	ARGANS	ARIDITIES	ARMCHAIRS
ARCHIVES	ARDS	ARGEMONE	ARIDITY	ARMED
ARCHIVING	ARDUOUS	ARGEMONES	ARIDLY	ARMET
ARCHIVIST	ARDUOUSLY	ARGENT	ARIDNESS	ARMETS
ARCHIVISTS	ARE	ARGENTINE	ARIDNESSES	ARMFUL
ARCHIVOLT	AREA	ARGENTINES	ARIEL	ARMFULS
ARCHIVOLTS	AREACH	ARGENTITE	ARIELS	ARMGAUNT
ARCHLET	AREACHED	ARGENTITES	ARIETTA	ARMHOLE
ARCHLETS	AREACHES	ARGENTS	ARIETTAS	ARMHOLES
ARCHLUTE	AREACHING	ARGHAN	ARIETTE	ARMIES
ARCHLUTES	AREAD	ARGHANS	ARIETTES	ARMIGER
ARCHLY	AREADING	ARGIL	ARIGHT	ARMIGERAL
ARCHNESS	AREADS	ARGILLITE	ARIL	ARMIGERO
ARCHNESSES	AREAL	ARGILLITES	ARILLARY	ARMIGEROS

ARMIGERS	AROMATIC	ARRAYERS	ARROWING	ARTHRITISES
ARMIL	AROMATICS	ARRAYING	ARROWROOT	ARTHROPOD
ARMILLA	AROMATISE	ARRAYMENT	ARROWROOTS	ARTHROPODS
ARMILLAE	AROMATISED	ARRAYMENTS	ARROWS	ARTHROSES
ARMILLARY	AROMATISES	ARRAYS	ARROWWOOD	ARTHROSIS
ARMILLAS	AROMATISING	ARREAR	ARROWWOODS	ARTIC
ARMILS	AROMATIZE	ARREARAGE	ARROWY	ARTICHOKE
ARMING	AROMATIZED	ARREARAGES	ARROYO	ARTICHOKES
ARMISTICE	AROMATIZES	ARREARS	ARROYOS	ARTICLE
ARMISTICES	AROMATIZING	ARRECT	ARS	ARTICLED
ARMLESS	AROSE	ARREEDE	ARSE	ARTICLES
ARMLET	AROUND	ARREEDES	ARSEHOLE	ARTICLING
ARMLETS	AROUSAL	ARREEDING	ARSEHOLES	ARTICS
ARMLOCK	AROUSALS	ARREST	ARSENAL	ARTICULAR
ARMLOCKED	AROUSE	ARRESTED	ARSENALS	ARTIER
ARMLOCKING	AROUSED	ARRESTEE	ARSENATE	ARTIES
ARMLOCKS	AROUSER	ARRESTEES	ARSENATES	ARTIEST
ARMOIRE	AROUSERS	ARRESTER	ARSENIATE	ARTIFACT
ARMOIRES	AROUSES	ARRESTERS	ARSENIATES	ARTIFACTS
ARMOR	AROUSING	ARRESTING	ARSENIC	ARTIFICE
ARMORIAL	AROW	ARRESTIVE	ARSENICAL	ARTIFICER
ARMORIALS	AROYNT	ARRESTOR	ARSENICS	ARTIFICERS
ARMORIES	AROYNTED	ARRESTORS	ARSENIDE	ARTIFICES
ARMORIST	AROYNTING	ARRESTS	ARSENIDES	ARTILLERIES
ARMORISTS	AROYNTS	ARRET	ARSENIOUS	ARTILLERY
ARMORS	ARPEGGIO	ARRETS	ARSENITE	ARTINESS
ARMORY	ARPEGGIOS	ARRIAGE	ARSENITES	ARTINESSES
ARMOUR	ARPENT	ARRIAGES	ARSES	ARTISAN
ARMOURED	ARPENTS	ARRIDE	ARSHEEN	ARTISANAL
ARMOURER	ARPILLERA	ARRIDED	ARSHEENS	ARTISANS
ARMOURERS	ARPILLERAS	ARRIDES	ARSHIN	ARTIST
ARMOURIES	ARQUEBUS	ARRIDING	ARSHINE	ARTISTE
ARMOURS	ARQUEBUSES	ARRIERE	ARSHINES	ARTISTES
ARMOURY	ARRACACHA	ARRIERO	ARSHINS	ARTISTIC
ARMOZEEN	ARRACACHAS	ARRIEROS	ARSINE	ARTISTRIES
ARMOZEENS	ARRACK	ARRIS	ARSINES	ARTISTRY
ARMOZINE	ARRACKS	ARRISES	ARSIS	ARTISTS
ARMOZINES	ARRAH	ARRISH	ARSON	ARTLESS
ARMPIT	ARRAIGN	ARRISHES	ARSONIST	ARTLESSLY
ARMPITS	ARRAIGNED	ARRIVAL	ARSONISTS	ARTS
ARMS	ARRAIGNER	ARRIVALS	ARSONITE	ARTSIER
ARMURE	ARRAIGNERS	ARRIVANCE	ARSONITES	ARTSIES
ARMURES	ARRAIGNING	ARRIVANCES	ARSONS	ARTSIEST
ARMY	ARRAIGNINGS	ARRIVANCIES	ART	ARTSMAN
ARNA	ARRAIGNS	ARRIVANCY	ARTAL	ARTSMEN
ARNAS	ARRANGE	ARRIVE	ARTEFACT	ARTSY
ARNICA	ARRANGED	ARRIVED	ARTEFACTS	ARTWORK
ARNICAS	ARRANGER	ARRIVES	ARTEL	ARTWORKS
ARNOTTO	ARRANGERS	ARRIVING	ARTELS	ARTY
ARNOTTOS	ARRANGES	ARRIVISME	ARTEMISIA	ARUGULA
ARNUT	ARRANGING	ARRIVISMES	ARTEMISIAS	ARUGULAS
ARNUTS	ARRANT	ARRIVISTE	ARTERIAL	ARUM
AROBA	ARRANTLY	ARRIVISTES	ARTERIES	ARUMS
AROBAS	ARRAS	ARROBA	ARTERIOLE	ARVAL
AROID	ARRASED	ARROBAS	ARTERIOLES	ARVICOLE
AROIDS	ARRASENE	ARROGANCE	ARTERITIS	ARVICOLES
AROINT	ARRASENES	ARROGANCES	ARTERITISES	ARVO
AROINTED	ARRASES	ARROGANT	ARTERY	ARVOS
AROINTING	ARRAUGHT	ARROGATE	ARTESIAN	ARY
AROINTS	ARRAY	ARROGATED	ARTFUL	ARYBALLOS
AROLLA	ARRAYAL	ARROGATES	ARTFULLY	ARYBALLOSES
AROLLAS	ARRAYALS	ARROGATING	ARTHRITIC	ARYL
AROMA	ARRAYED	ARROW	ARTHRITICS	ARYLS
AROMAS	ARRAYER	ARROWED	ARTHRITIS	ARYTENOID

ARYTENOIDS	ASCRIBE	ASKANTED	ASPHALT	ASSAILERS
AS	ASCRIBED	ASKANTING	ASPHALTED	ASSAILING
ASAFETIDA	ASCRIBES	ASKANTS	ASPHALTER	ASSAILS
ASAFETIDAS	ASCRIBING	ASKARI	ASPHALTERS	ASSAIS
ASANA	ASCUS	ASKARIS	ASPHALTIC	ASSART
ASANAS	ASEISMIC	ASKED	ASPHALTING	ASSARTED
ASAR	ASEITIES	ASKER	ASPHALTS	ASSARTING
ASARUM	ASEITY	ASKERS	ASPHALTUM	ASSARTS
ASARUMS	ASEPALOUS	ASKESES	ASPHALTUMS	ASSASSIN
ASBESTIC	ASEPSES	ASKESIS	ASPHERIC	ASSASSINS
ASBESTINE	ASEPSIS	ASKEW	ASPHODEL	ASSAULT
ASBESTOS	ASEPTATE	ASKING	ASPHODELS	ASSAULTED
ASBESTOSES	ASEPTIC	ASKLENT	ASPHYXIA	ASSAULTER
ASBESTOUS	ASEPTICS	ASKS	ASPHYXIAL	ASSAULTERS
ASCARID	ASEXUAL	ASLAKE	ASPHYXIAS	ASSAULTING
ASCARIDES	ASEXUALLY	ASLAKED	ASPHYXIES	ASSAULTS
ASCARIDS	ASH	ASLAKES	ASPHYXY	ASSAY
ASCARIS	ASHAKE	ASLAKING	ASPIC	ASSAYABLE
ASCAUNT	ASHAME	ASLANT	ASPICK	ASSAYED
ASCEND	ASHAMED	ASLEEP	ASPICKS	ASSAYER
ASCENDANT	ASHAMEDLY	ASLOPE	ASPICS	ASSAYERS
ASCENDANTS	ASHAMES	ASMEAR	ASPIDIA	ASSAYING
ASCENDED	ASHAMING	ASMOULDER	ASPIDIOID	ASSAYINGS
ASCENDENT	ASHEN	ASOCIAL	ASPIDIUM	ASSAYS
ASCENDENTS	ASHERIES	ASP	ASPINE	ASSEGAAI
ASCENDER	ASHERY	ASPARAGUS	ASPINES	ASSEGAAIED
ASCENDERS	ASHES	ASPARAGUSES	ASPIRANT	ASSEGAAIING
ASCENDING	ASHET	ASPARTAME	ASPIRANTS	ASSEGAAIS
ASCENDS	ASHETS	ASPARTAMES	ASPIRATE	ASSEGAI
ASCENSION	ASHIER	ASPECT	ASPIRATED	ASSEGAIED
ASCENSIONS	ASHIEST	ASPECTED	ASPIRATES	ASSEGAIING
ASCENSIVE	ASHINE	ASPECTING	ASPIRATING	ASSEGAIS
ASCENT	ASHIVER	ASPECTS	ASPIRATOR	ASSEMBLE
ASCENTS	ASHLAR	ASPECTUAL	ASPIRATORS	ASSEMBLED
ASCERTAIN	ASHLARED	ASPEN	ASPIRE	ASSEMBLER
ASCERTAINED	ASHLARING	ASPENS	ASPIRED	ASSEMBLERS
ASCERTAINING	ASHLARINGS	ASPER	ASPIRES	ASSEMBLES
ASCERTAINS	ASHLARS	ASPERATE	ASPIRIN	ASSEMBLIES
ASCESES	ASHLER	ASPERATED	ASPIRING	ASSEMBLING
ASCESIS	ASHLERED	ASPERATES	ASPIRINS	ASSEMBLY
ASCETIC	ASHLERING	ASPERATING	ASPLENIUM	ASSENT
ASCETICAL	ASHLERINGS	ASPERGE	ASPLENIUMS	ASSENTED
ASCETICS	ASHLERS	ASPERGED	ASPORT	ASSENTER
ASCI	ASHORE	ASPERGER	ASPORTED	ASSENTERS
ASCIAN	ASHRAM	ASPERGERS	ASPORTING	ASSENTING
ASCIANS	ASHRAMA	ASPERGES	ASPORTS	ASSENTIVE
ASCIDIA	ASHRAMAS	ASPERGILL	ASPOUT	ASSENTOR
ASCIDIAN	ASHRAMITE	ASPERGILLS	ASPRAWL	ASSENTORS
ASCIDIANS	ASHRAMITES	ASPERGING	ASPREAD	ASSENTS
ASCIDIUM	ASHRAMS	ASPERITIES	ASPROUT	ASSERT
ASCITES	ASHY	ASPERITY	ASPS	ASSERTED
ASCITIC	ASIDE	ASPEROUS	ASQUAT	ASSERTER
ASCITICAL	ASIDES	ASPERS	ASQUINT	ASSERTERS
ASCLEPIAD	ASINICO	ASPERSE	ASS	ASSERTING
ASCLEPIADS	ASINICOS	ASPERSED	ASSAGAI	ASSERTION
ASCLEPIAS	ASININE	ASPERSES	ASSAGAIED	ASSERTIONS
ASCLEPIASES	ASININITIES	ASPERSING	ASSAGAIING	ASSERTIVE
ASCONCE	ASININITY	ASPERSION	ASSAGAIS	ASSERTOR
ASCORBATE	ASK	ASPERSIONS	ASSAI	ASSERTORS
ASCORBATES	ASKANCE	ASPERSIVE	ASSAIL	ASSERTORY
ASCOSPORE	ASKANCED	ASPERSOIR	ASSAILANT	ASSERTS
ASCOSPORES	ASKANCES	ASPERSOIRS	ASSAILANTS	ASSES
ASCOT	ASKANCING	ASPERSORIES	ASSAILED	ASSESS
ASCOTS	ASKANT	ASPERSORY	ASSAILER	ASSESSED

ASSESSES	ASSORTER	ASTERISK	ASTRINGED	ATABEK
ASSESSING	ASSORTERS	ASTERISKED	ASTRINGER	ATABEKS
ASSESSOR	ASSORTING	ASTERISKING	ASTRINGERS	ATABRIN
ASSESSORS	ASSORTS	ASTERISKS	ASTRINGES	ATABRINS
ASSET	ASSOT	ASTERISM	ASTRINGING	ATACAMITE
ASSETS	ASSOTS	ASTERISMS	ASTROCYTE	ATACAMITES
ASSEVER	ASSOTT	ASTERN	ASTROCYTES	ATACTIC
ASSEVERED	ASSOTTED	ASTEROID	ASTRODOME	ATAGHAN
ASSEVERING	ASSOTTING	ASTEROIDS	ASTRODOMES	ATAGHANS
ASSEVERS	ASSUAGE	ASTERS	ASTROFELL	ATALAYA
ASSHOLE	ASSUAGED	ASTERT	ASTROFELLS	ATALAYAS
ASSHOLES	ASSUAGES	ASTERTED	ASTROID	ATAMAN
ASSIDUITIES	ASSUAGING	ASTERTING	ASTROIDS	ATAMANS
ASSIDUITY	ASSUAGINGS	ASTERTS	ASTROLABE	ATAP
ASSIDUOUS	ASSUASIVE	ASTHENIA	ASTROLABES	ATAPS
ASSIEGE	ASSUETUDE	ASTHENIAS	ASTROLOGIES	ATARACTIC
ASSIEGED	ASSUETUDES	ASTHENIC	ASTROLOGY	ATARACTICS
ASSIEGES	ASSUMABLE	ASTHENICS	ASTRONAUT	ATARAXIA
ASSIEGING	ASSUMABLY	ASTHMA	ASTRONAUTS	ATARAXIAS
ASSIENTO	ASSUME	ASTHMAS	ASTRONOMIES	ATARAXIC
ASSIENTOS	ASSUMED	ASTHMATIC	ASTRONOMY	ATARAXICS
ASSIGN	ASSUMEDLY	ASTHORE	ASTROPHEL	ATARAXIES
ASSIGNAT	ASSUMES	ASTHORES	ASTROPHELS	ATARAXY
ASSIGNATS	ASSUMING	ASTICHOUS	ASTRUT	ATAVISM
ASSIGNED	ASSUMINGS	ASTIGMIA	ASTUCIOUS	ATAVISMS
ASSIGNEE	ASSUMPSIT	ASTIGMIAS	ASTUCITIES	ATAVISTIC
ASSIGNEES	ASSUMPSITS	ASTILBE	ASTUCITY	ATAXIA
ASSIGNING	ASSURABLE	ASTILBES	ASTUN	ATAXIAS
ASSIGNOR	ASSURANCE	ASTIR	ASTUNNED	ATAXIC
ASSIGNORS	ASSURANCES	ASTOMOUS	ASTUNNING	ATAXIES
ASSIGNS	ASSURE	ASTONE	ASTUNS	ATAXY
ASSIST	ASSURED	ASTONED	ASTUTE	ATCHIEVE
ASSISTANT	ASSUREDLY	ASTONES	ASTUTELY	ATCHIEVED
ASSISTANTS	ASSUREDS	ASTONIED	ASTUTER	ATCHIEVES
ASSISTED	ASSURER	ASTONIES	ASTUTEST	ATCHIEVING
ASSISTING	ASSURERS	ASTONING	ASTYLAR	ATE
ASSISTS	ASSURES	ASTONISH	ASUDDEN	ATEBRIN
ASSIZE	ASSURGENT	ASTONISHED	ASUNDER	ATEBRINS
ASSIZED	ASSURING	ASTONISHES	ASWARM	ATELIER
ASSIZER	ASSWAGE	ASTONISHING	ASWAY	ATELIERS
ASSIZERS	ASSWAGED	ASTONY	ASWIM	ATHANASIES
ASSIZES	ASSWAGES	ASTONYING	ASWING	ATHANASY
ASSIZING	ASSWAGING	ASTOOP	ASWIRL	ATHANOR
ASSOCIATE	ASTABLE	ASTOUND	ASWOON	ATHANORS
ASSOCIATED	ASTARE	ASTOUNDED	ASYLUM	ATHEISE
ASSOCIATES	ASTART	ASTOUNDING	ASYLUMS	ATHEISED
ASSOCIATING	ASTARTED	ASTOUNDS	ASYMMETRIES	ATHEISES
ASSOIL	ASTARTING	ASTRADDLE	ASYMMETRY	ATHEISING
ASSOILED	ASTARTS	ASTRAGAL	ASYMPTOTE	ATHEISM
ASSOILING	ASTATIC	ASTRAGALI	ASYMPTOTES	ATHEISMS
ASSOILS	ASTATINE	ASTRAGALS	ASYNDETIC	ATHEIST
ASSOILZIE	ASTATINES	ASTRAKHAN	ASYNDETON	ATHEISTIC
ASSOILZIED	ASTATKI	ASTRAKHANS	ASYNDETONS	ATHEISTS
ASSOILZIEING	ASTATKIS	ASTRAL	ASYNERGIA	ATHEIZE
ASSOILZIES	ASTEISM	ASTRAND	ASYNERGIAS	ATHEIZED
ASSONANCE	ASTEISMS	ASTRANTIA	ASYNERGIES	ATHEIZES
ASSONANCES	ASTELIC	ASTRANTIAS	ASYNERGY	ATHEIZING
ASSONANT	ASTELIES	ASTRAY	ASYSTOLE	ATHELING
ASSONATE	ASTELY	ASTRICT	ASYSTOLES	ATHELINGS
ASSONATED	ASTER	ASTRICTED	AT	ATHEMATIC
ASSONATES	ASTERIA	ASTRICTING	ATABAL	ATHEOLOGIES
ASSONATING	ASTERIAS	ASTRICTS	ATABALS	ATHEOLOGY
ASSORT	ASTERID	ASTRIDE	ATABEG	ATHEOUS
ASSORTED	ASTERIDS	ASTRINGE	ATABEGS	ATHERINE

ATHERINES	ATOKOUS	ATRIUM	ATTENDEES	ATTRIBUTE
ATHEROMA	ATOKS	ATRIUMS	ATTENDER	ATTRIBUTED
ATHEROMAS	ATOLL	ATROCIOUS	ATTENDERS	ATTRIBUTES
ATHEROMATA	ATOLLS	ATROCITIES	ATTENDING	ATTRIBUTING
ATHETESES	ATOM	ATROCITY	ATTENDS	ATTRIST
ATHETESIS	ATOMIC	ATROPHIED	ATTENT	ATTRISTED
ATHETISE	ATOMICAL	ATROPHIES	ATTENTAT	ATTRISTING
ATHETISED	ATOMICITIES	ATROPHY	ATTENTATS	ATTRISTS
ATHETISES	ATOMICITY	ATROPHYING	ATTENTION	ATTRIT
ATHETISING	ATOMIES	ATROPIA	ATTENTIONS	ATTRITE
ATHETIZE	ATOMISE	ATROPIAS	ATTENTIVE	ATTRITED
ATHETIZED	ATOMISED	ATROPIN	ATTENTS	ATTRITES
ATHETIZES	ATOMISER	ATROPINE	ATTENUANT	ATTRITING
ATHETIZING	ATOMISERS	ATROPINES	ATTENUANTS	ATTRITION
ATHETOID	ATOMISES	ATROPINS	ATTENUATE	ATTRITIONS
ATHETOSES	ATOMISING	ATROPISM	ATTENUATED	ATTRITS
ATHETOSIC	ATOMISM	ATROPISMS	ATTENUATES	ATTRITTED
ATHETOSIS	ATOMISMS	ATROPOUS	ATTENUATING	ATTRITTING
ATHETOTIC	ATOMIST	ATTABOY	ATTERCOP	ATTUENT
ATHIRST	ATOMISTIC	ATTACH	ATTERCOPS	ATTUITE
ATHLETA	ATOMISTS	ATTACHE	ATTEST	ATTUITED
ATHLETAS	ATOMIZE	ATTACHED	ATTESTED	ATTUITES
ATHLETE	ATOMIZED	ATTACHES	ATTESTER	ATTUITING
ATHLETES	ATOMIZER	ATTACHING	ATTESTERS	ATTUITION
ATHLETIC	ATOMIZERS	ATTACK	ATTESTING	ATTUITIONS
ATHLETICS	ATOMIZES	ATTACKED	ATTESTOR	ATTUITIVE
ATHRILL	ATOMIZING	ATTACKER	ATTESTORS	ATTUNE
ATHROB	ATOMS	ATTACKERS	ATTESTS	ATTUNED
ATHROCYTE	ATOMY	ATTACKING	ATTIC	ATTUNES
ATHROCYTES	ATONAL	ATTACKS	ATTICS	ATTUNING
ATHWART	ATONALISM	ATTAIN	ATTIRE	ATWAIN
ATILT	ATONALISMS	ATTAINDER	ATTIRED	ATWEEL
ATIMIES	ATONALIST	ATTAINDERS	ATTIRES	ATWEEN
ATIMY	ATONALISTS	ATTAINED	ATTIRING	ATWITTER
ATINGLE	ATONALITIES	ATTAINING	ATTIRINGS	ATWIXT
ATISHOO	ATONALITY	ATTAINS	ATTITUDE	ATYPICAL
ATISHOOS	ATONE	ATTAINT	ATTITUDES	AUBADE
ATLAS	ATONED	ATTAINTED	ATTOLLENS	AUBADES
ATLASES	ATONEMENT	ATTAINTING	ATTOLLENT	AUBERGE
ATLATL	ATONEMENTS	ATTAINTS	ATTOLLENTS	AUBERGES
ATLATLS	ATONER	ATTAP	ATTONCE	AUBERGINE
ATMAN	ATONERS	ATTAPS	ATTONE	AUBERGINES
ATMANS	ATONES	ATTAR	ATTONES	AUBRETIA
ATMOLOGIES	ATONIC	ATTARS	ATTORN	AUBRETIAS
ATMOLOGY	ATONICITIES	ATTASK	ATTORNED	AUBRIETA
ATMOLYSE	ATONICITY	ATTASKED	ATTORNEY	AUBRIETAS
ATMOLYSED	ATONIES	ATTASKING	ATTORNEYED	AUBRIETIA
ATMOLYSES	ATONING	ATTASKS	ATTORNEYING	AUBRIETIAS
ATMOLYSING	ATONINGLY	ATTASKT	ATTORNEYS	AUBURN
ATMOLYSIS	ATONY	ATTEMPER	ATTORNING	AUCEPS
ATMOLYZE	ATOP	ATTEMPERED	ATTORNS	AUCEPSES
ATMOLYZED	ATOPIC	ATTEMPERING	ATTRACT	AUCTION
ATMOLYZES	ATOPIES	ATTEMPERS	ATTRACTED	AUCTIONED
ATMOLYZING	ATOPY	ATTEMPT	ATTRACTING	AUCTIONING
ATMOMETER	ATRAMENT	ATTEMPTED	ATTRACTOR	AUCTIONS
ATMOMETERS	ATRAMENTS	ATTEMPTER	ATTRACTORS	AUCTORIAL
ATOC	ATRAZINE	ATTEMPTERS	ATTRACTS	AUCUBA
ATOCIA	ATRAZINES	ATTEMPTING	ATTRAHENS	AUCUBAS
ATOCIAS	ATREMBLE	ATTEMPTS	ATTRAHENT	AUDACIOUS
ATOCS	ATRESIA	ATTEND	ATTRAHENTS	AUDACITIES
ATOK	ATRESIAS	ATTENDANT	ATTRAP	AUDACITY
ATOKAL	ATRIA	ATTENDANTS	ATTRAPPED	AUDIBLE
ATOKE	ATRIAL	ATTENDED	ATTRAPPING	AUDIBLES
ATOKES	ATRIP	ATTENDEE	ATTRAPS	AUDIBLY

AUDIENCE	AUGURSHIPS	AUREOLAS	AUTHORING	AUTOGRAFTING
AUDIENCES	AUGURY	AUREOLE	AUTHORINGS	AUTOGRAFTS
AUDIENCIA	AUGUST	AUREOLED	AUTHORISE	AUTOGRAPH
AUDIENCIAS	AUGUSTE	AUREOLES	AUTHORISED	AUTOGRAPHED
AUDIENT	AUGUSTER	AUREUS	AUTHORISES	AUTOGRAPHING
AUDIENTS	AUGUSTES	AURIC	AUTHORISH	AUTOGRAPHS
AUDILE	AUGUSTEST	AURICLE	AUTHORISING	AUTOGUIDE
AUDILES	AUGUSTLY	AURICLED	AUTHORISM	AUTOGUIDES
AUDIO	AUGUSTS	AURICLES	AUTHORISMS	AUTOGYRO
AUDIOGRAM	AUK	AURICULA	AUTHORITIES	AUTOGYROS
AUDIOGRAMS	AUKLET	AURICULAR	AUTHORITY	AUTOHARP
AUDIOLOGIES	AUKLETS	AURICULAS	AUTHORIZE	AUTOHARPS
AUDIOLOGY	AUKS	AURIFIED	AUTHORIZED	AUTOLATRIES
AUDIOPHIL	AULA	AURIFIES	AUTHORIZES	AUTOLATRY
AUDIOPHILS	AULARIAN	AURIFORM	AUTHORIZING	AUTOLOGIES
AUDIOS	AULARIANS	AURIFY	AUTHORS	AUTOLOGY
AUDIOTAPE	AULAS	AURIFYING	AUTISM	AUTOLYSE
AUDIOTAPES	AULD	AURISCOPE	AUTISMS	AUTOLYSED
AUDIPHONE	AULDER	AURISCOPES	AUTISTIC	AUTOLYSES
AUDIPHONES	AULDEST	AURIST	AUTISTICS	AUTOLYSING
AUDIT	AULIC	AURISTS	AUTO	AUTOLYSIS
AUDITED	AULNAGE	AUROCHS	AUTOBAHN	AUTOLYTIC
AUDITING	AULNAGER	AUROCHSES	AUTOBAHNS	AUTOLYZE
AUDITION	AULNAGERS	AURORA	AUTOBUS	AUTOLYZED
AUDITIONED	AULNAGES	AURORAE	AUTOBUSES	AUTOLYZES
AUDITIONING	AULOI	AURORAL	AUTOBUSSES	AUTOLYZING
AUDITIONS	AULOS	AURORALLY	AUTOCADE	AUTOMAT
AUDITIVE	AUMAIL	AURORAS	AUTOCADES	AUTOMATA
AUDITOR	AUMAILED	AUROREAN	AUTOCAR	AUTOMATE
AUDITORIA	AUMAILING	AUROUS	AUTOCARP	AUTOMATED
AUDITORIES	AUMAILS	AUSPICATE	AUTOCARPS	AUTOMATES
AUDITORS	AUMBRIES	AUSPICATED	AUTOCARS	AUTOMATIC
AUDITORY	AUMBRY	AUSPICATES	AUTOCLAVE	AUTOMATICS
AUDITRESS	AUMIL	AUSPICATING	AUTOCLAVED	AUTOMATING
AUDITRESSES	AUMILS	AUSPICE	AUTOCLAVES	AUTOMATON
AUDITS	AUNE	AUSPICES	AUTOCLAVING	AUTOMATONS
AUF	AUNES	AUSTENITE	AUTOCRACIES	AUTOMATS
AUFGABE	AUNT	AUSTENITES	AUTOCRACY	AUTONOMIC
AUFGABES	AUNTER	AUSTERE	AUTOCRAT	AUTONOMICS
AUFS	AUNTERS	AUSTERELY	AUTOCRATS	AUTONOMIES
AUGER	AUNTIE	AUSTERER	AUTOCRIME	AUTONOMY
AUGERS	AUNTIES	AUSTEREST	AUTOCRIMES	AUTONYM
AUGHT	AUNTLIER	AUSTERITIES	AUTOCROSS	AUTONYMS
AUGHTS	AUNTLIEST	AUSTERITY	AUTOCROSSES	AUTOPHAGIES
AUGITE	AUNTLY	AUSTRAL	AUTOCUE	AUTOPHAGY
AUGITES	AUNTS	AUSTRALES	AUTOCUES	AUTOPHOBIES
AUGITIC	AUNTY	AUTACOID	AUTOCYCLE	AUTOPHOBY
AUGMENT	AURA	AUTACOIDS	AUTOCYCLES	AUTOPHONIES
AUGMENTED	AURAE	AUTARCHIC	AUTODYNE	AUTOPHONY
AUGMENTER	AURAL	AUTARCHIES	AUTOFLARE	AUTOPILOT
AUGMENTERS	AURALLY	AUTARCHY	AUTOFLARES	AUTOPILOTS
AUGMENTING	AURAS	AUTARKIC	AUTOFOCUS	AUTOPISTA
AUGMENTOR	AURATE	AUTARKIES	AUTOFOCUSES	AUTOPISTAS
AUGMENTORS	AURATED	AUTARKIST	AUTOGAMIC	AUTOPOINT
AUGMENTS	AURATES	AUTARKISTS	AUTOGAMIES	AUTOPOINTS
AUGUR	AUREATE	AUTARKY	AUTOGAMY	AUTOPSIA
AUGURAL	AUREI	AUTEUR	AUTOGENIC	AUTOPSIAS
AUGURED	AUREITIES	AUTEURS	AUTOGENICS	AUTOPSIED
AUGURER	AUREITY	AUTHENTIC	AUTOGENIES	AUTOPSIES
AUGURERS	AURELIA	AUTHOR	AUTOGENY	AUTOPSY
AUGURIES	AURELIAN	AUTHORED	AUTOGIRO	AUTOPSYING
AUGURING	AURELIANS	AUTHORESS	AUTOGIROS	AUTOPTIC
AUGURS	AURELIAS	AUTHORESSES	AUTOGRAFT	AUTOROUTE
AUGURSHIP	AUREOLA	AUTHORIAL	AUTOGRAFTED	AUTOROUTES

AUTOS	AVAS	AVIATED	AVOISION	AWARENESSES
AUTOSCOPIES	AVASCULAR	AVIATES	AVOISIONS	AWARER
AUTOSCOPY	AVAST	AVIATING	AVOSET	AWAREST
AUTOSOMAL	AVATAR	AVIATION	AVOSETS	AWARN
AUTOSOME	AVATARS	AVIATIONS	AVOUCH	AWARNED
AUTOSOMES	AVAUNT	AVIATOR	AVOUCHED	AWARNING
AUTOTELIC	AVAUNTED	AVIATORS	AVOUCHES	AWARNS
AUTOTIMER	AVAUNTING	AVIATRESS	AVOUCHING	AWASH
AUTOTIMERS	AVAUNTS	AVIATRESSES	AVOURE	AWATCH
AUTOTOMIES	AVE	AVIATRICES	AVOURES	AWAVE
AUTOTOMY	AVENGE	AVIATRIX	AVOUTERER	AWAY
AUTOTOXIN	AVENGED	AVIATRIXES	AVOUTERERS	AWAYES
AUTOTOXINS	AVENGEFUL	AVID	AVOUTRER	AWAYS
AUTOTROPH	AVENGER	AVIDER	AVOUTRERS	AWDL
AUTOTROPHS	AVENGERS	AVIDEST	AVOUTRIES	AWDLS
AUTOTYPE	AVENGES	AVIDIN	AVOUTRY	AWE
AUTOTYPED	AVENGING	AVIDINS	AVOW	AWEARIED
AUTOTYPES	AVENIR	AVIDITIES	AVOWABLE	AWEARY
AUTOTYPING	AVENIRS	AVIDITY	AVOWAL	AWED
AUTOVAC	AVENS	AVIDLY	AVOWALS	AWEEL
AUTOVACS	AVENSES	AVIDNESS	AVOWED	AWEIGH
AUTUMN	AVENTAIL	AVIDNESSES	AVOWEDLY	AWELESS
AUTUMNAL	AVENTAILE	AVIETTE	AVOWER	AWES
AUTUMNS	AVENTAILES	AVIETTES	AVOWERS	AWESOME
AUTUMNY	AVENTAILS	AVIFAUNA	AVOWING	AWESOMELY
AUTUNITE	AVENTRE	AVIFAUNAE	AVOWRIES	AWESTRIKE
AUTUNITES	AVENTRED	AVIFAUNAS	AVOWRY	AWESTRIKES
AUXESES	AVENTRES	AVIFORM	AVOWS	AWESTRIKING
AUXESIS	AVENTRING	AVINE	AVOYER	AWESTRUCK
AUXETIC	AVENTURE	AVION	AVOYERS	AWETO
AUXETICS	AVENTURES	AVIONIC	AVULSE	AWETOS
AUXILIAR	AVENUE	AVIONICS	AVULSED	AWFUL
AUXILIARIES	AVENUES	AVIONS	AVULSES	AWFULLER
AUXILIARS	AVER	AVISANDUM	AVULSING	AWFULLEST
AUXILIARY	AVERAGE	AVISANDUMS	AVULSION	AWFULLY
AUXIN	AVERAGED	AVISE	AVULSIONS	AWFULNESS
AUXINS	AVERAGES	AVISED	AVUNCULAR	AWFULNESSES
AUXOMETER	AVERAGING	AVISEMENT	AVYZE	AWHAPE
AUXOMETERS	AVERMENT	AVISEMENTS	AVYZED	AWHAPED
AVA	AVERMENTS	AVISES	AVYZES	AWHAPES
AVADAVAT	AVERRED	AVISING	AVYZING	AWHAPING
AVADAVATS	AVERRING	AVISO	AW	AWHEEL
AVAIL	AVERS	AVISOS	AWA	AWHEELS
AVAILABLE	AVERSE	AVITAL	AWAIT	AWHILE
AVAILABLY	AVERSELY	AVIZANDUM	AWAITED	AWING
AVAILE	AVERSION	AVIZANDUMS	AWAITING	AWKWARD
AVAILED	AVERSIONS	AVIZE	AWAITS	AWKWARDER
AVAILES	AVERSIVE	AVIZED	AWAKE	AWKWARDEST
AVAILFUL	AVERT	AVIZEFULL	AWAKED	AWKWARDLY
AVAILING	AVERTABLE	AVIZES	AWAKEN	AWL
AVAILS	AVERTED	AVIZING	AWAKENED	AWLBIRD
AVAL	AVERTEDLY	AVOCADO	AWAKENING	AWLBIRDS
AVALANCHE	AVERTIBLE	AVOCADOS	AWAKENINGS	AWLS
AVALANCHED	AVERTING	AVOCATION	AWAKENS	AWMOUS
AVALANCHES	AVERTS	AVOCATIONS	AWAKES	AWMRIE
AVALANCHING	AVES	AVOCET	AWAKING	AWMRIES
AVALE	AVGAS	AVOCETS	AWAKINGS	AWMRY
AVALED	AVGASES	AVOID	AWANTING	AWN
AVALES	AVIAN	AVOIDABLE	AWARD	AWNED
AVALING	AVIARIES	AVOIDANCE	AWARDED	AWNER
AVANT	AVIARIST	AVOIDANCES	AWARDING	AWNERS
AVANTI	AVIARISTS	AVOIDED	AWARDS	AWNIER
AVARICE	AVIARY	AVOIDING	AWARE	AWNIEST
AVARICES	AVIATE	AVOIDS	AWARENESS	AWNING

The Chambers Dictionary is the authority for many longer words; see *OSW* Introduction, page xii

AWNINGS	AXILLARY	AYAHUASCO	AZEOTROPES	AZOTOUS
AWNLESS	AXILS	AYAHUASCOS	AZIDE	AZOTURIA
AWNS	AXING	AYATOLLAH	AZIDES	AZOTURIAS
AWNY	AXINITE	AYATOLLAHS	AZIMUTH	AZULEJO
AWOKE	AXINITES	AYE	AZIMUTHAL	AZULEJOS
AWOKEN	AXIOLOGIES	AYELP	AZIMUTHS	AZURE
AWORK	AXIOLOGY	AYENBITE	AZINE	AZUREAN
AWRACK	AXIOM	AYENBITES	AZINES	AZURES
AWRONG	AXIOMATIC	AYES	AZIONE	AZURINE
AWRY	AXIOMATICS	AYGRE	AZIONES	AZURINES
AWSOME	AXIOMS	AYONT	AZOIC	AZURITE
AX	AXIS	AYRE	AZOLLA	AZURITES
AXE	AXISES	AYRES	AZOLLAS	AZURN
AXED	AXLE	AYRIE	AZONAL	AZURY
AXEL	AXLES	AYRIES	AZONIC	AZYGIES
AXELS	AXMAN	AYS	AZOTE	AZYGOS
AXEMAN	AXMEN	AYU	AZOTES	AZYGOSES
AXEMEN	AXOID	AYURVEDA	AZOTH	AZYGOUS
AXES	AXOIDS	AYURVEDAS	AZOTHS	AZYGY
AXIAL	AXOLOTL	AYURVEDIC	AZOTIC	AZYM
AXIALITIES	AXOLOTLS	AYUS	AZOTISE	AZYME
AXIALITY	AXON	AYWORD	AZOTISED	AZYMES
AXIALLY	AXONS	AYWORDS	AZOTISES	AZYMITE
AXIL	AXOPLASM	AZALEA	AZOTISING	AZYMITES
AXILE	AXOPLASMS	AZALEAS	AZOTIZE	AZYMOUS
AXILLA	AY	AZAN	AZOTIZED	AZYMS
AXILLAE	AYAH	AZANS	AZOTIZES	
AXILLAR	AYAHS	AZEOTROPE	AZOTIZING	

B

BA
BAA
BAAED
BAAING
BAAINGS
BAAS
BAASES
BAASSKAP
BAASSKAPS
BABA
BABACO
BABACOOTE
BABACOOTES
BABACOS
BABAS
BABASSU
BABASSUS
BABBITT
BABBITTED
BABBITTING
BABBITTS
BABBLE
BABBLED
BABBLER
BABBLERS
BABBLES
BABBLIER
BABBLIEST
BABBLING
BABBLINGS
BABBLY
BABE
BABEL
BABELDOM
BABELDOMS
BABELISH
BABELISM
BABELISMS
BABELS
BABES
BABICHE
BABICHES
BABIED
BABIER
BABIES
BABIEST
BABIRUSA
BABIRUSAS
BABIRUSSA
BABIRUSSAS
BABLAH
BABLAHS
BABOO
BABOON

BABOONERIES
BABOONERY
BABOONISH
BABOONS
BABOOS
BABOOSH
BABOOSHES
BABOUCHE
BABOUCHES
BABU
BABUCHE
BABUCHES
BABUDOM
BABUDOMS
BABUISM
BABUISMS
BABUL
BABULS
BABUS
BABUSHKA
BABUSHKAS
BABY
BABYFOOD
BABYFOODS
BABYHOOD
BABYHOODS
BABYING
BABYISH
BAC
BACCA
BACCAE
BACCARA
BACCARAS
BACCARAT
BACCARATS
BACCARE
BACCAS
BACCATE
BACCHANAL
BACCHANALS
BACCHANT
BACCHANTE
BACCHANTES
BACCHANTS
BACCHIAC
BACCHIAN
BACCHIC
BACCHII
BACCHIUS
BACCIES
BACCIFORM
BACCO
BACCOES
BACCOS

BACCY
BACH
BACHARACH
BACHARACHS
BACHED
BACHELOR
BACHELORS
BACHES
BACHING
BACHS
BACILLAR
BACILLARY
BACILLI
BACILLUS
BACK
BACKACHE
BACKACHES
BACKARE
BACKBAND
BACKBANDS
BACKBEAT
BACKBEATS
BACKBIT
BACKBITE
BACKBITER
BACKBITERS
BACKBITES
BACKBITING
BACKBITINGS
BACKBITTEN
BACKBOND
BACKBONDS
BACKBONE
BACKBONED
BACKBONES
BACKCHAT
BACKCHATS
BACKCHATTED
BACKCHATTING
BACKCOURT
BACKCOURTS
BACKDOWN
BACKDOWNS
BACKDROP
BACKDROPS
BACKED
BACKER
BACKERS
BACKET
BACKETS
BACKFALL
BACKFALLS
BACKFIELD
BACKFILE

BACKFILES
BACKFILL
BACKFILLED
BACKFILLING
BACKFILLS
BACKFIRE
BACKFIRED
BACKFIRES
BACKFIRING
BACKFISCH
BACKFISCHES
BACKHAND
BACKHANDS
BACKHOE
BACKHOES
BACKING
BACKINGS
BACKLAND
BACKLANDS
BACKLASH
BACKLASHES
BACKLIFT
BACKLIFTS
BACKLIST
BACKLISTS
BACKLOG
BACKLOGS
BACKLOT
BACKLOTS
BACKMOST
BACKPACK
BACKPACKED
BACKPACKING
BACKPACKINGS
BACKPACKS
BACKPAY
BACKPAYS
BACKPIECE
BACKPIECES
BACKRA
BACKRAS
BACKROOM
BACKS
BACKSAW
BACKSAWS
BACKSET
BACKSETS
BACKSEY
BACKSEYS
BACKSHISH
BACKSHISHED
BACKSHISHES
BACKSHISHING
BACKSIDE

BACKSIDES
BACKSIGHT
BACKSIGHTS
BACKSLASH
BACKSLASHES
BACKSLID
BACKSLIDE
BACKSLIDES
BACKSLIDING
BACKSLIDINGS
BACKSPACE
BACKSPACED
BACKSPACES
BACKSPACING
BACKSPEER
BACKSPEERED
BACKSPEERING
BACKSPEERS
BACKSPEIR
BACKSPEIRED
BACKSPEIRING
BACKSPEIRS
BACKSPIN
BACKSPINS
BACKSTAGE
BACKSTALL
BACKSTALLS
BACKSTAYS
BACKSTOP
BACKSTOPS
BACKSWING
BACKSWINGS
BACKSWORD
BACKSWORDS
BACKTRACK
BACKTRACKED
BACKTRACKING
BACKTRACKINGS
BACKTRACKS
BACKVELD
BACKVELDS
BACKWARD
BACKWARDS
BACKWASH
BACKWASHED
BACKWASHES
BACKWASHING
BACKWATER
BACKWATERS
BACKWOODS
BACKWORD
BACKWORDS
BACKWORK
BACKWORKS

BACKYARD	BADNESSES	BAGWIG	BAITS	BALANITISES
BACKYARDS	BADS	BAGWIGS	BAIZE	BALAS
BACLAVA	BAEL	BAH	BAIZED	BALASES
BACLAVAS	BAELS	BAHADA	BAIZES	BALATA
BACON	BAETYL	BAHADAS	BAIZING	BALATAS
BACONER	BAETYLS	BAHT	BAJADA	BALBOA
BACONERS	BAFF	BAHTS	BAJADAS	BALBOAS
BACONS	BAFFED	BAHUT	BAJAN	BALCONET
BACS	BAFFIES	BAHUTS	BAJANS	BALCONETS
BACTERIA	BAFFING	BAHUVRIHI	BAJRA	BALCONIED
BACTERIAL	BAFFLE	BAHUVRIHIS	BAJRAS	BALCONIES
BACTERIAN	BAFFLED	BAIGNOIRE	BAJREE	BALCONY
BACTERIC	BAFFLEGAB	BAIGNOIRES	BAJREES	BALD
BACTERISE	BAFFLEGABS	BAIL	BAJRI	BALDACHIN
BACTERISED	BAFFLER	BAILABLE	BAJRIS	BALDACHINS
BACTERISES	BAFFLERS	BAILBOND	BAJU	BALDAQUIN
BACTERISING	BAFFLES	BAILBONDS	BAJUS	BALDAQUINS
BACTERIUM	BAFFLING	BAILED	BAKE	BALDER
BACTERIZE	BAFFS	BAILEE	BAKEAPPLE	BALDEST
BACTERIZED	BAFFY	BAILEES	BAKEAPPLES	BALDICOOT
BACTERIZES	BAFT	BAILER	BAKEBOARD	BALDICOOTS
BACTERIZING	BAFTS	BAILERS	BAKEBOARDS	BALDIER
BACTEROID	BAG	BAILEY	BAKED	BALDIES
BACTEROIDS	BAGARRE	BAILEYS	BAKEHOUSE	BALDIEST
BACULA	BAGARRES	BAILIE	BAKEHOUSES	BALDING
BACULINE	BAGASSE	BAILIES	BAKEMEAT	BALDISH
BACULITE	BAGASSES	BAILIFF	BAKEMEATS	BALDLY
BACULITES	BAGATELLE	BAILIFFS	BAKEN	BALDMONEY
BACULUM	BAGATELLES	BAILING	BAKER	BALDMONEYS
BACULUMS	BAGEL	BAILIWICK	BAKERIES	BALDNESS
BAD	BAGELS	BAILIWICKS	BAKERS	BALDNESSES
BADASS	BAGFUL	BAILLI	BAKERY	BALDPATE
BADASSED	BAGFULS	BAILLIAGE	BAKES	BALDPATED
BADASSES	BAGGAGE	BAILLIAGES	BAKESTONE	BALDPATES
BADDIE	BAGGAGES	BAILLIE	BAKESTONES	BALDRIC
BADDIES	BAGGED	BAILLIES	BAKEWARE	BALDRICK
BADDISH	BAGGIER	BAILLIS	BAKEWARES	BALDRICKS
BADDY	BAGGIES	BAILMENT	BAKHSHISH	BALDRICS
BADE	BAGGIEST	BAILMENTS	BAKHSHISHED	BALDY
BADGE	BAGGILY	BAILOR	BAKHSHISHES	BALE
BADGED	BAGGINESS	BAILORS	BAKHSHISHING	BALECTION
BADGER	BAGGINESSES	BAILS	BAKING	BALECTIONS
BADGERED	BAGGING	BAILSMAN	BAKINGS	BALED
BADGERING	BAGGINGS	BAILSMEN	BAKLAVA	BALEEN
BADGERLY	BAGGIT	BAININ	BAKLAVAS	BALEENS
BADGERS	BAGGITS	BAININS	BAKSHEESH	BALEFUL
BADGES	BAGGY	BAINITE	BAKSHEESHED	BALEFULLY
BADGING	BAGMAN	BAINITES	BAKSHEESHES	BALER
BADINAGE	BAGMEN	BAIRN	BAKSHEESHING	BALERS
BADINAGES	BAGNIO	BAIRNLIER	BALACLAVA	BALES
BADIOUS	BAGNIOS	BAIRNLIEST	BALACLAVAS	BALING
BADLANDS	BAGPIPE	BAIRNLIKE	BALADIN	BALISTA
BADLY	BAGPIPER	BAIRNLY	BALADINE	BALISTAE
BADMAN	BAGPIPERS	BAIRNS	BALADINES	BALISTAS
BADMASH	BAGPIPES	BAISEMAIN	BALADINS	BALK
BADMASHES	BAGPIPING	BAISEMAINS	BALALAIKA	BALKANISE
BADMEN	BAGPIPINGS	BAIT	BALALAIKAS	BALKANISED
BADMINTON	BAGS	BAITED	BALANCE	BALKANISES
BADMINTONS	BAGUETTE	BAITER	BALANCED	BALKANISING
BADMOUTH	BAGUETTES	BAITERS	BALANCER	BALKANIZE
BADMOUTHED	BAGUIO	BAITFISH	BALANCERS	BALKANIZED
BADMOUTHING	BAGUIOS	BAITFISHES	BALANCES	BALKANIZES
BADMOUTHS	BAGWASH	BAITING	BALANCING	BALKANIZING
BADNESS	BAGWASHES	BAITINGS	BALANITIS	BALKED

BALKER	BALLISTA	BALNEARY	BANCS	BANDONIONS
BALKERS	BALLISTAE	BALONEY	BAND	BANDOOK
BALKIER	BALLISTAS	BALONEYS	BANDA	BANDOOKS
BALKIEST	BALLISTIC	BALOO	BANDAGE	BANDORA
BALKINESS	BALLISTICS	BALOOS	BANDAGED	BANDORAS
BALKINESSES	BALLIUM	BALSA	BANDAGES	BANDORE
BALKING	BALLIUMS	BALSAM	BANDAGING	BANDORES
BALKINGLY	BALLOCKS	BALSAMED	BANDALORE	BANDROL
BALKINGS	BALLOCKSED	BALSAMIC	BANDALORES	BANDROLS
BALKLINE	BALLOCKSES	BALSAMING	BANDANA	BANDS
BALKLINES	BALLOCKSING	BALSAMS	BANDANAS	BANDSMAN
BALKS	BALLON	BALSAMY	BANDANNA	BANDSMEN
BALKY	BALLONET	BALSAS	BANDANNAS	BANDSTAND
BALL	BALLONETS	BALSAWOOD	BANDAR	BANDSTANDS
BALLABILE	BALLONS	BALSAWOODS	BANDARS	BANDSTER
BALLABILES	BALLOON	BALTHASAR	BANDAS	BANDSTERS
BALLABILI	BALLOONED	BALTHASARS	BANDBRAKE	BANDURA
BALLAD	BALLOONING	BALTHAZAR	BANDBRAKES	BANDURAS
BALLADE	BALLOONINGS	BALTHAZARS	BANDEAU	BANDWAGON
BALLADED	BALLOONS	BALU	BANDEAUX	BANDWAGONS
BALLADEER	BALLOT	BALUS	BANDED	BANDWIDTH
BALLADEERED	BALLOTED	BALUSTER	BANDELET	BANDWIDTHS
BALLADEERING	BALLOTEE	BALUSTERS	BANDELETS	BANDY
BALLADEERS	BALLOTEES	BALZARINE	BANDELIER	BANDYING
BALLADES	BALLOTING	BALZARINES	BANDELIERS	BANDYINGS
BALLADIN	BALLOTS	BAM	BANDEROL	BANDYMAN
BALLADINE	BALLOW	BAMBINI	BANDEROLE	BANDYMEN
BALLADINES	BALLOWS	BAMBINO	BANDEROLES	BANE
BALLADING	BALLPARK	BAMBINOS	BANDEROLS	BANEBERRIES
BALLADINS	BALLPOINT	BAMBOO	BANDICOOT	BANEBERRY
BALLADIST	BALLPOINTS	BAMBOOS	BANDICOOTED	BANED
BALLADISTS	BALLROOM	BAMBOOZLE	BANDICOOTING	BANEFUL
BALLADRIES	BALLROOMS	BAMBOOZLED	BANDICOOTS	BANEFULLY
BALLADRY	BALLS	BAMBOOZLES	BANDIED	BANES
BALLADS	BALLSIER	BAMBOOZLING	BANDIER	BANG
BALLAN	BALLSIEST	BAMMED	BANDIES	BANGED
BALLANS	BALLSY	BAMMER	BANDIEST	BANGER
BALLANT	BALLUP	BAMMERS	BANDING	BANGERS
BALLANTED	BALLUPS	BAMMING	BANDINGS	BANGING
BALLANTING	BALLY	BAMPOT	BANDIT	BANGINGS
BALLANTS	BALLYHOO	BAMPOTS	BANDITRIES	BANGLE
BALLAST	BALLYHOOED	BAMS	BANDITRY	BANGLED
BALLASTED	BALLYHOOING	BAN	BANDITS	BANGLES
BALLASTING	BALLYHOOS	BANAL	BANDITTI	BANGS
BALLASTS	BALLYRAG	BANALER	BANDITTIS	BANGSRING
BALLAT	BALLYRAGGED	BANALEST	BANDOBAST	BANGSRINGS
BALLATED	BALLYRAGGING	BANALISE	BANDOBASTS	BANGSTER
BALLATING	BALLYRAGS	BANALISED	BANDOG	BANGSTERS
BALLATS	BALM	BANALISES	BANDOGS	BANI
BALLCLAY	BALMACAAN	BANALISING	BANDOLEER	BANIA
BALLCLAYS	BALMACAANS	BANALITIES	BANDOLEERS	BANIAN
BALLCOCK	BALMED	BANALITY	BANDOLEON	BANIANS
BALLCOCKS	BALMIER	BANALIZE	BANDOLEONS	BANIAS
BALLED	BALMIEST	BANALIZED	BANDOLERO	BANING
BALLERINA	BALMILY	BANALIZES	BANDOLEROS	BANISH
BALLERINAS	BALMINESS	BANALIZING	BANDOLIER	BANISHED
BALLERINE	BALMINESSES	BANALLY	BANDOLIERS	BANISHES
BALLET	BALMING	BANANA	BANDOLINE	BANISHING
BALLETED	BALMORAL	BANANAS	BANDOLINED	BANISTER
BALLETIC	BALMORALS	BANAUSIAN	BANDOLINES	BANISTERS
BALLETING	BALMS	BANAUSIC	BANDOLINING	BANJAX
BALLETS	BALMY	BANC	BANDONEON	BANJAXED
BALLING	BALNEAL	BANCO	BANDONEONS	BANJAXES
BALLINGS	BALNEARIES	BANCOS	BANDONION	BANJAXING

BANJO	BANTENG	BARBARISM	BARD	BARGESTS
BANJOES	BANTENGS	BARBARISMS	BARDASH	BARGHAIST
BANJOIST	BANTER	BARBARITIES	BARDASHES	BARGHAISTS
BANJOISTS	BANTERED	BARBARITY	BARDED	BARGHEST
BANJOS	BANTERER	BARBARIZE	BARDIC	BARGHESTS
BANJULELE	BANTERERS	BARBARIZED	BARDIER	BARGING
BANJULELES	BANTERING	BARBARIZES	BARDIEST	BARGOOSE
BANK	BANTERINGS	BARBARIZING	BARDING	BARIC
BANKABLE	BANTERS	BARBAROUS	BARDLING	BARILLA
BANKED	BANTING	BARBASCO	BARDLINGS	BARILLAS
BANKER	BANTINGS	BARBASCOS	BARDO	BARING
BANKERLY	BANTLING	BARBASTEL	BARDOS	BARISH
BANKERS	BANTLINGS	BARBASTELS	BARDS	BARITE
BANKET	BANTS	BARBATE	BARDSHIP	BARITES
BANKETS	BANTU	BARBATED	BARDSHIPS	BARITONE
BANKING	BANTUS	BARBE	BARDY	BARITONES
BANKINGS	BANXRING	BARBECUE	BARE	BARIUM
BANKROLL	BANXRINGS	BARBECUED	BAREBACK	BARIUMS
BANKROLLED	BANYAN	BARBECUES	BAREBOAT	BARK
BANKROLLING	BANYANS	BARBECUING	BAREBONE	BARKAN
BANKROLLS	BANZAI	BARBED	BAREBONES	BARKANS
BANKRUPT	BANZAIS	BARBEL	BARED	BARKED
BANKRUPTED	BAOBAB	BARBELS	BAREFACED	BARKEEPER
BANKRUPTING	BAOBABS	BARBEQUE	BAREFOOT	BARKEEPERS
BANKRUPTS	BAP	BARBEQUED	BAREGE	BARKEN
BANKS	BAPS	BARBEQUES	BAREGES	BARKENED
BANKSIA	BAPTISE	BARBEQUING	BAREGINE	BARKENING
BANKSIAS	BAPTISED	BARBER	BAREGINES	BARKENS
BANKSMAN	BAPTISES	BARBERED	BARELY	BARKER
BANKSMEN	BAPTISING	BARBERING	BARENESS	BARKERS
BANLIEUE	BAPTISM	BARBERRIES	BARENESSES	BARKHAN
BANLIEUES	BAPTISMAL	BARBERRY	BARER	BARKHANS
BANNED	BAPTISMS	BARBERS	BARES	BARKIER
BANNER	BAPTIST	BARBES	BARESARK	BARKIEST
BANNERALL	BAPTISTRIES	BARBET	BARESARKS	BARKING
BANNERALLS	BAPTISTRY	BARBETS	BAREST	BARKLESS
BANNERED	BAPTISTS	BARBETTE	BARF	BARKS
BANNERET	BAPTIZE	BARBETTES	BARFED	BARKY
BANNERETS	BAPTIZED	BARBICAN	BARFING	BARLEY
BANNEROL	BAPTIZES	BARBICANS	BARFLIES	BARLEYS
BANNEROLS	BAPTIZING	BARBICEL	BARFLY	BARM
BANNERS	BAPU	BARBICELS	BARFS	BARMAID
BANNING	BAPUS	BARBIE	BARFUL	BARMAIDS
BANNISTER	BAR	BARBIES	BARGAIN	BARMAN
BANNISTERS	BARACAN	BARBING	BARGAINED	BARMBRACK
BANNOCK	BARACANS	BARBITAL	BARGAINER	BARMBRACKS
BANNOCKS	BARAGOUIN	BARBITALS	BARGAINERS	BARMEN
BANNS	BARAGOUINS	BARBITONE	BARGAINING	BARMIER
BANQUET	BARASINGA	BARBITONES	BARGAINS	BARMIEST
BANQUETED	BARASINGAS	BARBOLA	BARGANDER	BARMINESS
BANQUETER	BARATHEA	BARBOLAS	BARGANDERS	BARMINESSES
BANQUETERS	BARATHEAS	BARBOTINE	BARGE	BARMKIN
BANQUETING	BARATHRUM	BARBOTINES	BARGED	BARMKINS
BANQUETINGS	BARATHRUMS	BARBS	BARGEE	BARMS
BANQUETS	BARAZA	BARBULE	BARGEES	BARMY
BANQUETTE	BARAZAS	BARBULES	BARGEESE	BARN
BANQUETTES	BARB	BARCA	BARGELLO	BARNACLE
BANS	BARBARIAN	BARCAROLE	BARGELLOS	BARNACLED
BANSHEE	BARBARIANS	BARCAROLES	BARGEMAN	BARNACLES
BANSHEES	BARBARIC	BARCAS	BARGEMEN	BARNED
BANT	BARBARISE	BARCHAN	BARGEPOLE	BARNEY
BANTAM	BARBARISED	BARCHANE	BARGEPOLES	BARNEYS
BANTAMS	BARBARISES	BARCHANES	BARGES	BARNING
BANTED	BARBARISING	BARCHANS	BARGEST	BARNS

BARNSTORM	BARRACOONS	BARTENDERS	BASH	BASOPHILS
BARNSTORMED	BARRACUDA	BARTER	BASHAW	BASQUE
BARNSTORMING	BARRACUDAS	BARTERED	BASHAWISM	BASQUED
BARNSTORMINGS	BARRAGE	BARTERER	BASHAWISMS	BASQUES
BARNSTORMS	BARRAGES	BARTERERS	BASHAWS	BASQUINE
BARNYARD	BARRANCA	BARTERING	BASHED	BASQUINES
BARNYARDS	BARRANCAS	BARTERS	BASHER	BASS
BAROCCO	BARRANCO	BARTISAN	BASHERS	BASSE
BAROCCOS	BARRANCOS	BARTISANS	BASHES	BASSED
BAROCK	BARRAT	BARTIZAN	BASHFUL	BASSER
BAROCKS	BARRATOR	BARTIZANS	BASHFULLY	BASSES
BAROGRAM	BARRATORS	BARTON	BASHING	BASSEST
BAROGRAMS	BARRATRIES	BARTONS	BASHINGS	BASSET
BAROGRAPH	BARRATRY	BARWOOD	BASHLESS	BASSETED
BAROGRAPHS	BARRATS	BARWOODS	BASHLIK	BASSETING
BAROMETER	BARRE	BARYE	BASHLIKS	BASSETS
BAROMETERS	BARRED	BARYES	BASHO	BASSI
BAROMETRIES	BARREFULL	BARYON	BASIC	BASSIER
BAROMETRY	BARREL	BARYONS	BASICALLY	BASSIEST
BAROMETZ	BARRELAGE	BARYTA	BASICITIES	BASSINET
BAROMETZES	BARRELAGES	BARYTAS	BASICITY	BASSINETS
BARON	BARRELFUL	BARYTES	BASICS	BASSING
BARONAGE	BARRELFULS	BARYTIC	BASIDIA	BASSIST
BARONAGES	BARRELLED	BARYTON	BASIDIAL	BASSISTS
BARONESS	BARRELLING	BARYTONE	BASIDIUM	BASSO
BARONESSES	BARRELS	BARYTONES	BASIFIXED	BASSOON
BARONET	BARREN	BARYTONS	BASIFUGAL	BASSOONS
BARONETCIES	BARRENER	BAS	BASIL	BASSOS
BARONETCY	BARRENEST	BASAL	BASILAR	BASSWOOD
BARONETS	BARRES	BASALT	BASILICA	BASSWOODS
BARONG	BARRET	BASALTIC	BASILICAL	BASSY
BARONGS	BARRETS	BASALTS	BASILICAN	BAST
BARONIAL	BARRETTE	BASAN	BASILICAS	BASTA
BARONIES	BARRETTER	BASANITE	BASILICON	BASTARD
BARONNE	BARRETTERS	BASANITES	BASILICONS	BASTARDIES
BARONNES	BARRETTES	BASANS	BASILISK	BASTARDLY
BARONS	BARRICADE	BASCULE	BASILISKS	BASTARDS
BARONY	BARRICADED	BASCULES	BASILS	BASTARDY
BAROQUE	BARRICADES	BASE	BASIN	BASTE
BAROQUES	BARRICADING	BASEBALL	BASINET	BASTED
BAROSCOPE	BARRICADO	BASEBALLS	BASINETS	BASTER
BAROSCOPES	BARRICADOED	BASEBAND	BASINFUL	BASTERS
BAROSTAT	BARRICADOES	BASEBOARD	BASINFULS	BASTES
BAROSTATS	BARRICADOING	BASEBOARDS	BASING	BASTIDE
BAROUCHE	BARRICADOS	BASED	BASINS	BASTIDES
BAROUCHES	BARRICO	BASELARD	BASIPETAL	BASTILLE
BARP	BARRICOES	BASELARDS	BASIS	BASTILLES
BARPERSON	BARRICOS	BASELESS	BASK	BASTINADE
BARPERSONS	BARRIER	BASELINER	BASKED	BASTINADED
BARPS	BARRIERED	BASELINERS	BASKET	BASTINADES
BARQUE	BARRIERING	BASELY	BASKETFUL	BASTINADING
BARQUES	BARRIERS	BASEMAN	BASKETFULS	BASTINADO
BARRACAN	BARRING	BASEMEN	BASKETRIES	BASTINADOED
BARRACANS	BARRINGS	BASEMENT	BASKETRY	BASTINADOES
BARRACE	BARRIO	BASEMENTS	BASKETS	BASTINADOING
BARRACES	BARRIOS	BASENESS	BASKING	BASTING
BARRACK	BARRISTER	BASENESSES	BASKS	BASTINGS
BARRACKED	BARRISTERS	BASENJI	BASNET	BASTION
BARRACKER	BARROW	BASENJIS	BASNETS	BASTIONED
BARRACKERS	BARROWS	BASEPLATE	BASOCHE	BASTIONS
BARRACKING	BARRULET	BASEPLATES	BASOCHES	BASTLE
BARRACKINGS	BARRULETS	BASER	BASON	BASTLES
BARRACKS	BARS	BASES	BASONS	BASTO
BARRACOON	BARTENDER	BASEST	BASOPHIL	BASTOS

BASTS	BATISTE	BATTILLS	BAWBEES	BAZOOKAS
BASUCO	BATISTES	BATTING	BAWBLE	BAZOUKI
BASUCOS	BATLER	BATTINGS	BAWBLES	BAZOUKIS
BAT	BATLERS	BATTLE	BAWCOCK	BDELLIUM
BATABLE	BATLET	BATTLEBUS	BAWCOCKS	BDELLIUMS
BATATA	BATLETS	BATTLEBUSES	BAWD	BE
BATATAS	BATMAN	BATTLEBUSSES	BAWDIER	BEACH
BATCH	BATMEN	BATTLED	BAWDIES	BEACHED
BATCHED	BATOLOGIES	BATTLER	BAWDIEST	BEACHES
BATCHES	BATOLOGY	BATTLERS	BAWDILY	BEACHHEAD
BATCHING	BATON	BATTLES	BAWDINESS	BEACHHEADS
BATCHINGS	BATONED	BATTLING	BAWDINESSES	BEACHIER
BATE	BATONING	BATTOLOGIES	BAWDKIN	BEACHIEST
BATEAU	BATONS	BATTOLOGY	BAWDKINS	BEACHING
BATEAUX	BATOON	BATTS	BAWDRIES	BEACHY
BATED	BATOONED	BATTUE	BAWDRY	BEACON
BATELESS	BATOONING	BATTUES	BAWDS	BEACONED
BATELEUR	BATOONS	BATTUTA	BAWDY	BEACONING
BATELEURS	BATRACHIA	BATTUTAS	BAWL	BEACONS
BATEMENT	BATS	BATTY	BAWLED	BEAD
BATEMENTS	BATSMAN	BATWOMAN	BAWLER	BEADED
BATES	BATSMEN	BATWOMEN	BAWLERS	BEADIER
BATFISH	BATSWING	BAUBLE	BAWLEY	BEADIEST
BATFISHES	BATSWOMAN	BAUBLES	BAWLEYS	BEADING
BATH	BATSWOMEN	BAUBLING	BAWLING	BEADINGS
BATHCUBE	BATT	BAUCHLE	BAWLINGS	BEADLE
BATHCUBES	BATTA	BAUCHLED	BAWLS	BEADLEDOM
BATHE	BATTALIA	BAUCHLES	BAWN	BEADLEDOMS
BATHED	BATTALIAS	BAUCHLING	BAWNS	BEADLES
BATHER	BATTALION	BAUD	BAWR	BEADMAN
BATHERS	BATTALIONS	BAUDEKIN	BAWRS	BEADMEN
BATHES	BATTAS	BAUDEKINS	BAXTER	BEADS
BATHETIC	BATTED	BAUDRIC	BAXTERS	BEADSMAN
BATHHOUSE	BATTEL	BAUDRICK	BAY	BEADSMEN
BATHHOUSES	BATTELED	BAUDRICKE	BAYADERE	BEADY
BATHING	BATTELER	BAUDRICKES	BAYADERES	BEAGLE
BATHMIC	BATTELERS	BAUDRICKS	BAYARD	BEAGLED
BATHMISM	BATTELING	BAUDRICS	BAYARDS	BEAGLER
BATHMISMS	BATTELLED	BAUDRONS	BAYBERRIES	BEAGLERS
BATHOLITE	BATTELLING	BAUDRONSES	BAYBERRY	BEAGLES
BATHOLITES	BATTELS	BAUDS	BAYE	BEAGLING
BATHOLITH	BATTEMENT	BAUERA	BAYED	BEAGLINGS
BATHOLITHS	BATTEMENTS	BAUERAS	BAYES	BEAK
BATHORSE	BATTEN	BAUHINIA	BAYING	BEAKED
BATHORSES	BATTENED	BAUHINIAS	BAYLE	BEAKER
BATHOS	BATTENING	BAUK	BAYLES	BEAKERS
BATHOSES	BATTENINGS	BAUKED	BAYONET	BEAKIER
BATHROBE	BATTENS	BAUKING	BAYONETED	BEAKIEST
BATHROBES	BATTER	BAUKS	BAYONETING	BEAKS
BATHROOM	BATTERED	BAULK	BAYONETS	BEAKY
BATHROOMS	BATTERER	BAULKED	BAYOU	BEAM
BATHS	BATTERERS	BAULKING	BAYOUS	BEAMED
BATHTUB	BATTERIE	BAULKS	BAYS	BEAMER
BATHTUBS	BATTERIES	BAUR	BAYT	BEAMERS
BATHYAL	BATTERING	BAURS	BAYTED	BEAMIER
BATHYBIUS	BATTERO	BAUSOND	BAYTING	BEAMIEST
BATHYBIUSES	BATTEROS	BAUXITE	BAYTS	BEAMILY
BATHYLITE	BATTERS	BAUXITES	BAZAAR	BEAMINESS
BATHYLITES	BATTERY	BAUXITIC	BAZAARS	BEAMINESSES
BATHYLITH	BATTIER	BAVARDAGE	BAZAR	BEAMING
BATHYLITHS	BATTIEST	BAVARDAGES	BAZARS	BEAMINGLY
BATIK	BATTILL	BAVIN	BAZAZZ	BEAMINGS
BATIKS	BATTILLED	BAVINS	BAZAZZES	BEAMISH
BATING	BATTILLING	BAWBEE	BAZOOKA	BEAMLESS

BEAMLET	BEATEN	BECALMS	BEDAUBING	BEDIMMINGS
BEAMLETS	BEATER	BECAME	BEDAUBS	BEDIMS
BEAMS	BEATERS	BECASSE	BEDAWIN	BEDIZEN
BEAMY	BEATH	BECASSES	BEDAWINS	BEDIZENED
BEAN	BEATHED	BECAUSE	BEDAZE	BEDIZENING
BEANBAG	BEATHING	BECCACCIA	BEDAZED	BEDIZENS
BEANBAGS	BEATHS	BECCACCIAS	BEDAZES	BEDLAM
BEANED	BEATIFIC	BECCAFICO	BEDAZING	BEDLAMISM
BEANERIES	BEATIFIED	BECCAFICOS	BEDAZZLE	BEDLAMISMS
BEANERY	BEATIFIES	BECHAMEL	BEDAZZLED	BEDLAMITE
BEANFEAST	BEATIFY	BECHAMELS	BEDAZZLES	BEDLAMITES
BEANFEASTS	BEATIFYING	BECHANCE	BEDAZZLING	BEDLAMS
BEANIE	BEATING	BECHANCED	BEDBUG	BEDMAKER
BEANIES	BEATINGS	BECHANCES	BEDBUGS	BEDMAKERS
BEANING	BEATITUDE	BECHANCING	BEDCOVER	BEDOUIN
BEANO	BEATITUDES	BECHARM	BEDCOVERS	BEDOUINS
BEANOS	BEATNIK	BECHARMED	BEDDABLE	BEDPAN
BEANPOLE	BEATNIKS	BECHARMING	BEDDED	BEDPANS
BEANPOLES	BEATS	BECHARMS	BEDDER	BEDPOST
BEANS	BEAU	BECK	BEDDERS	BEDPOSTS
BEANSTALK	BEAUFET	BECKE	BEDDING	BEDRAGGLE
BEANSTALKS	BEAUFETS	BECKED	BEDDINGS	BEDRAGGLED
BEAR	BEAUFFET	BECKES	BEDE	BEDRAGGLES
BEARABLE	BEAUFFETS	BECKET	BEDEAFEN	BEDRAGGLING
BEARABLY	BEAUFIN	BECKETS	BEDEAFENED	BEDRAL
BEARBINE	BEAUFINS	BECKING	BEDEAFENING	BEDRALS
BEARBINES	BEAUISH	BECKON	BEDEAFENS	BEDRENCH
BEARD	BEAUT	BECKONED	BEDECK	BEDRENCHED
BEARDED	BEAUTEOUS	BECKONING	BEDECKED	BEDRENCHES
BEARDIE	BEAUTIED	BECKONS	BEDECKING	BEDRENCHING
BEARDIES	BEAUTIES	BECKS	BEDECKS	BEDRID
BEARDING	BEAUTIFIED	BECLOUD	BEDEGUAR	BEDRIDDEN
BEARDLESS	BEAUTIFIES	BECLOUDED	BEDEGUARS	BEDRIGHT
BEARDS	BEAUTIFUL	BECLOUDING	BEDEL	BEDRIGHTS
BEARE	BEAUTIFY	BECLOUDS	BEDELL	BEDROCK
BEARED	BEAUTIFYING	BECOME	BEDELLS	BEDROCKS
BEARER	BEAUTS	BECOMES	BEDELS	BEDROOM
BEARERS	BEAUTY	BECOMING	BEDELSHIP	BEDROOMS
BEARES	BEAUTYING	BECQUEREL	BEDELSHIPS	BEDROP
BEARING	BEAUX	BECQUERELS	BEDEMAN	BEDROPPED
BEARINGS	BEAUXITE	BECURL	BEDEMEN	BEDROPPING
BEARISH	BEAUXITES	BECURLED	BEDERAL	BEDROPS
BEARISHLY	BEAVER	BECURLING	BEDERALS	BEDROPT
BEARNAISE	BEAVERED	BECURLS	BEDES	BEDS
BEARNAISES	BEAVERIES	BED	BEDESMAN	BEDSIDE
BEARS	BEAVERS	BEDABBLE	BEDESMEN	BEDSIDES
BEARSKIN	BEAVERY	BEDABBLED	BEDEVIL	BEDSOCKS
BEARSKINS	BEBEERINE	BEDABBLES	BEDEVILLED	BEDSORE
BEARWARD	BEBEERINES	BEDABBLING	BEDEVILLING	BEDSORES
BEARWARDS	BEBEERU	BEDAD	BEDEVILS	BEDSPREAD
BEAST	BEBEERUS	BEDAGGLE	BEDEW	BEDSPREADS
BEASTHOOD	BEBOP	BEDAGGLED	BEDEWED	BEDSTEAD
BEASTHOODS	BEBOPPED	BEDAGGLES	BEDEWING	BEDSTEADS
BEASTIE	BEBOPPING	BEDAGGLING	BEDEWS	BEDSTRAW
BEASTIES	BEBOPS	BEDARKEN	BEDFAST	BEDSTRAWS
BEASTILY	BEBUNG	BEDARKENED	BEDFELLOW	BEDTICK
BEASTINGS	BEBUNGS	BEDARKENING	BEDFELLOWS	BEDTICKS
BEASTLIER	BECALL	BEDARKENS	BEDIDE	BEDTIME
BEASTLIEST	BECALLED	BEDASH	BEDIGHT	BEDTIMES
BEASTLIKE	BECALLING	BEDASHED	BEDIGHTING	BEDUCK
BEASTLY	BECALLS	BEDASHES	BEDIGHTS	BEDUCKED
BEASTS	BECALM	BEDASHING	BEDIM	BEDUCKING
BEAT	BECALMED	BEDAUB	BEDIMMED	BEDUCKS
BEATABLE	BECALMING	BEDAUBED	BEDIMMING	BEDUIN

BEDUINS	BEERINESS	BEFOUL	BEGIRDED	BEHAVE
BEDUNG	BEERINESSES	BEFOULED	BEGIRDING	BEHAVED
BEDUNGED	BEERS	BEFOULING	BEGIRDS	BEHAVES
BEDUNGING	BEERY	BEFOULS	BEGIRT	BEHAVING
BEDUNGS	BEES	BEFRIEND	BEGLAMOUR	BEHAVIOR
BEDUST	BEESOME	BEFRIENDED	BEGLAMOURED	BEHAVIORS
BEDUSTED	BEESTINGS	BEFRIENDING	BEGLAMOURING	BEHAVIOUR
BEDUSTING	BEESWAX	BEFRIENDS	BEGLAMOURS	BEHAVIOURS
BEDUSTS	BEESWAXED	BEFRINGE	BEGLERBEG	BEHEAD
BEDWARD	BEESWAXES	BEFRINGED	BEGLERBEGS	BEHEADAL
BEDWARDS	BEESWAXING	BEFRINGES	BEGLOOM	BEHEADALS
BEDWARF	BEESWING	BEFRINGING	BEGLOOMED	BEHEADED
BEDWARFED	BEESWINGS	BEFUDDLE	BEGLOOMING	BEHEADING
BEDWARFING	BEET	BEFUDDLED	BEGLOOMS	BEHEADINGS
BEDWARFS	BEETED	BEFUDDLES	BEGNAW	BEHEADS
BEDYDE	BEETING	BEFUDDLING	BEGNAWED	BEHELD
BEDYE	BEETLE	BEG	BEGNAWING	BEHEMOTH
BEDYED	BEETLED	BEGAD	BEGNAWS	BEHEMOTHS
BEDYEING	BEETLES	BEGAN	BEGO	BEHEST
BEDYES	BEETLING	BEGAR	BEGOES	BEHESTS
BEE	BEETROOT	BEGARS	BEGOING	BEHIGHT
BEECH	BEETROOTS	BEGAT	BEGONE	BEHIGHTING
BEECHEN	BEETS	BEGEM	BEGONIA	BEHIGHTS
BEECHES	BEEVES	BEGEMMED	BEGONIAS	BEHIND
BEEF	BEFALL	BEGEMMING	BEGORED	BEHINDS
BEEFALO	BEFALLEN	BEGEMS	BEGORRA	BEHOLD
BEEFALOES	BEFALLING	BEGET	BEGORRAH	BEHOLDEN
BEEFALOS	BEFALLS	BEGETS	BEGOT	BEHOLDER
BEEFCAKE	BEFANA	BEGETTER	BEGOTTEN	BEHOLDERS
BEEFCAKES	BEFANAS	BEGETTERS	BEGRIME	BEHOLDING
BEEFEATER	BEFELD	BEGETTING	BEGRIMED	BEHOLDINGS
BEEFEATERS	BEFELL	BEGGAR	BEGRIMES	BEHOLDS
BEEFED	BEFFANA	BEGGARDOM	BEGRIMING	BEHOOF
BEEFIER	BEFFANAS	BEGGARDOMS	BEGRUDGE	BEHOOFS
BEEFIEST	BEFINNED	BEGGARED	BEGRUDGED	BEHOOVE
BEEFING	BEFIT	BEGGARIES	BEGRUDGES	BEHOOVED
BEEFS	BEFITS	BEGGARING	BEGRUDGING	BEHOOVES
BEEFSTEAK	BEFITTED	BEGGARLY	BEGS	BEHOOVING
BEEFSTEAKS	BEFITTING	BEGGARS	BEGUILE	BEHOTE
BEEFY	BEFLOWER	BEGGARY	BEGUILED	BEHOTES
BEEGAH	BEFLOWERED	BEGGED	BEGUILER	BEHOTING
BEEGAHS	BEFLOWERING	BEGGING	BEGUILERS	BEHOVE
BEEHIVE	BEFLOWERS	BEGGINGLY	BEGUILES	BEHOVED
BEEHIVES	BEFLUM	BEGGINGS	BEGUILING	BEHOVEFUL
BEEKEEPER	BEFLUMMED	BEGHARD	BEGUIN	BEHOVELY
BEEKEEPERS	BEFLUMMING	BEGHARDS	BEGUINAGE	BEHOVES
BEELINE	BEFLUMS	BEGIFT	BEGUINAGES	BEHOVING
BEELINES	BEFOAM	BEGIFTED	BEGUINE	BEHOWL
BEEN	BEFOAMED	BEGIFTING	BEGUINES	BEHOWLED
BEENAH	BEFOAMING	BEGIFTS	BEGUINS	BEHOWLING
BEENAHS	BEFOAMS	BEGILD	BEGUM	BEHOWLS
BEEP	BEFOG	BEGILDED	BEGUMS	BEIGE
BEEPED	BEFOGGED	BEGILDING	BEGUN	BEIGEL
BEEPER	BEFOGGING	BEGILDS	BEGUNK	BEIGELS
BEEPERS	BEFOGS	BEGILT	BEGUNKED	BEIGES
BEEPING	BEFOOL	BEGIN	BEGUNKING	BEIGNET
BEEPS	BEFOOLED	BEGINNE	BEGUNKS	BEIGNETS
BEER	BEFOOLING	BEGINNER	BEHALF	BEIN
BEERAGE	BEFOOLS	BEGINNERS	BEHALVES	BEING
BEERAGES	BEFORE	BEGINNES	BEHAPPEN	BEINGLESS
BEERHALL	BEFORTUNE	BEGINNING	BEHAPPENED	BEINGNESS
BEERHALLS	BEFORTUNED	BEGINNINGS	BEHAPPENING	BEINGNESSES
BEERIER	BEFORTUNES	BEGINS	BEHAPPENS	BEINGS
BEERIEST	BEFORTUNING	BEGIRD	BEHATTED	BEINKED

The Chambers Dictionary is the authority for many longer words; see *OSW* Introduction, page xii

BEINNESS	BELCHES	BELLOWER	BEMEANING	BENCHING
BEINNESSES	BELCHING	BELLOWERS	BEMEANS	BENCHMARK
BEJABERS	BELDAM	BELLOWING	BEMEANT	BENCHMARKS
BEJADE	BELDAME	BELLOWS	BEMEDAL	BEND
BEJADED	BELDAMES	BELLPUSH	BEMEDALLED	BENDED
BEJADES	BELDAMS	BELLPUSHES	BEMEDALLING	BENDEE
BEJADING	BELEAGUER	BELLS	BEMEDALS	BENDER
BEJANT	BELEAGUERED	BELLWORT	BEMETE	BENDERS
BEJANTS	BELEAGUERING	BELLWORTS	BEMETED	BENDIER
BEJESUIT	BELEAGUERS	BELLY	BEMETES	BENDIEST
BEJESUITED	BELEE	BELLYFUL	BEMETING	BENDING
BEJESUITING	BELEED	BELLYFULS	BEMIRE	BENDINGLY
BEJESUITS	BELEEING	BELLYING	BEMIRED	BENDINGS
BEJEWEL	BELEES	BELLYINGS	BEMIRES	BENDLET
BEJEWELLED	BELEMNITE	BELOMANCIES	BEMIRING	BENDLETS
BEJEWELLING	BELEMNITES	BELOMANCY	BEMOAN	BENDS
BEJEWELS	BELFRIED	BELONG	BEMOANED	BENDWISE
BEKAH	BELFRIES	BELONGED	BEMOANER	BENDY
BEKAHS	BELFRY	BELONGER	BEMOANERS	BENE
BEKISS	BELGA	BELONGERS	BEMOANING	BENEATH
BEKISSED	BELGARD	BELONGING	BEMOANINGS	BENEDICT
BEKISSES	BELGARDS	BELONGINGS	BEMOANS	BENEDIGHT
BEKISSING	BELGAS	BELONGS	BEMOCK	BENEFACT
BEKNAVE	BELIE	BELOVE	BEMOCKED	BENEFACTED
BEKNAVED	BELIED	BELOVED	BEMOCKING	BENEFACTING
BEKNAVES	BELIEF	BELOVEDS	BEMOCKS	BENEFACTS
BEKNAVING	BELIEFS	BELOVES	BEMOIL	BENEFIC
BEKNOWN	BELIER	BELOVING	BEMOILED	BENEFICE
BEL	BELIERS	BELOW	BEMOILING	BENEFICED
BELABOR	BELIES	BELS	BEMOILS	BENEFICES
BELABORED	BELIEVE	BELT	BEMONSTER	BENEFIT
BELABORING	BELIEVED	BELTED	BEMONSTERED	BENEFITED
BELABORS	BELIEVER	BELTER	BEMONSTERING	BENEFITING
BELABOUR	BELIEVERS	BELTERS	BEMONSTERS	BENEFITS
BELABOURED	BELIEVES	BELTING	BEMOUTH	BENEFITTED
BELABOURING	BELIEVING	BELTINGS	BEMOUTHED	BENEFITTING
BELABOURS	BELIKE	BELTMAN	BEMOUTHING	BENEMPT
BELACE	BELITTLE	BELTMEN	BEMOUTHS	BENES
BELACED	BELITTLED	BELTS	BEMUD	BENET
BELACES	BELITTLES	BELTWAY	BEMUDDED	BENETS
BELACING	BELITTLING	BELTWAYS	BEMUDDING	BENETTED
BELAH	BELIVE	BELUGA	BEMUDDLE	BENETTING
BELAHS	BELL	BELUGAS	BEMUDDLED	BENGALINE
BELAMIES	BELLBIND	BELVEDERE	BEMUDDLES	BENGALINES
BELAMOURE	BELLBINDS	BELVEDERES	BEMUDDLING	BENI
BELAMOURES	BELLCOTE	BELYING	BEMUDS	BENIGHT
BELAMY	BELLCOTES	BEMA	BEMUFFLE	BENIGHTED
BELATE	BELLE	BEMAD	BEMUFFLED	BENIGHTEN
BELATED	BELLED	BEMADDED	BEMUFFLES	BENIGHTENED
BELATEDLY	BELLES	BEMADDING	BEMUFFLING	BENIGHTENING
BELATES	BELLETER	BEMADS	BEMUSE	BENIGHTENINGS
BELATING	BELLETERS	BEMAS	BEMUSED	BENIGHTENS
BELAUD	BELLHOP	BEMATA	BEMUSES	BENIGHTER
BELAUDED	BELLHOPS	BEMAUL	BEMUSING	BENIGHTERS
BELAUDING	BELLIBONE	BEMAULED	BEN	BENIGHTING
BELAUDS	BELLIBONES	BEMAULING	BENAME	BENIGHTINGS
BELAY	BELLICOSE	BEMAULS	BENAMED	BENIGHTS
BELAYED	BELLIED	BEMAZED	BENAMES	BENIGN
BELAYING	BELLIES	BEMBEX	BENAMING	BENIGNANT
BELAYS	BELLING	BEMBEXES	BENCH	BENIGNER
BELCH	BELLMAN	BEMBIX	BENCHED	BENIGNEST
BELCHED	BELLMEN	BEMBIXES	BENCHER	BENIGNITIES
BELCHER	BELLOW	BEMEAN	BENCHERS	BENIGNITY
BELCHERS	BELLOWED	BEMEANED	BENCHES	BENIGNLY

BENIS	BEPAINTED	BERAYED	BEROBBED	BESEEMING
BENISEED	BEPAINTING	BERAYING	BEROBBING	BESEEMINGS
BENISEEDS	BEPAINTS	BERAYS	BEROBS	BESEEMLY
BENISON	BEPAT	BERBERINE	BERRET	BESEEMS
BENISONS	BEPATCHED	BERBERINES	BERRETS	BESEEN
BENITIER	BEPATS	BERBERIS	BERRIED	BESEES
BENITIERS	BEPATTED	BERBERISES	BERRIES	BESET
BENJ	BEPATTING	BERCEAU	BERRY	BESETMENT
BENJAMIN	BEPEARL	BERCEAUX	BERRYING	BESETMENTS
BENJAMINS	BEPEARLED	BERCEUSE	BERRYINGS	BESETS
BENJES	BEPEARLING	BERCEUSES	BERSERK	BESETTER
BENNE	BEPEARLS	BERDACHE	BERSERKER	BESETTERS
BENNES	BEPELT	BERDACHES	BERSERKERS	BESETTING
BENNET	BEPELTED	BERDASH	BERSERKLY	BESHADOW
BENNETS	BEPELTING	BERDASHES	BERSERKS	BESHADOWED
BENNI	BEPELTS	BERE	BERTH	BESHADOWING
BENNIES	BEPEPPER	BEREAVE	BERTHA	BESHADOWS
BENNIS	BEPEPPERED	BEREAVED	BERTHAGE	BESHAME
BENNY	BEPEPPERING	BEREAVEN	BERTHAGES	BESHAMED
BENS	BEPEPPERS	BEREAVES	BERTHAS	BESHAMES
BENT	BEPESTER	BEREAVING	BERTHE	BESHAMING
BENTHIC	BEPESTERED	BEREFT	BERTHED	BESHINE
BENTHOAL	BEPESTERING	BERES	BERTHES	BESHINES
BENTHONIC	BEPESTERS	BERET	BERTHING	BESHINING
BENTHOS	BEPITIED	BERETS	BERTHS	BESHONE
BENTHOSES	BEPITIES	BERG	BERYL	BESHREW
BENTIER	BEPITY	BERGAMA	BERYLLIA	BESHREWED
BENTIEST	BEPITYING	BERGAMAS	BERYLLIAS	BESHREWING
BENTONITE	BEPLASTER	BERGAMASK	BERYLLIUM	BESHREWS
BENTONITES	BEPLASTERED	BERGAMASKS	BERYLLIUMS	BESIDE
BENTS	BEPLASTERING	BERGAMOT	BERYLS	BESIDES
BENTWOOD	BEPLASTERS	BERGAMOTS	BESAINT	BESIEGE
BENTWOODS	BEPLUMED	BERGANDER	BESAINTED	BESIEGED
BENTY	BEPOMMEL	BERGANDERS	BESAINTING	BESIEGER
BENUMB	BEPOMMELLED	BERGENIA	BESAINTS	BESIEGERS
BENUMBED	BEPOMMELLING	BERGENIAS	BESANG	BESIEGES
BENUMBING	BEPOMMELS	BERGERE	BESAT	BESIEGING
BENUMBS	BEPOWDER	BERGERES	BESAW	BESIEGINGS
BENZAL	BEPOWDERED	BERGFALL	BESCATTER	BESIGH
BENZALS	BEPOWDERING	BERGFALLS	BESCATTERED	BESIGHED
BENZENE	BEPOWDERS	BERGHAAN	BESCATTERING	BESIGHING
BENZENES	BEPRAISE	BERGHAANS	BESCATTERS	BESIGHS
BENZIDINE	BEPRAISED	BERGMEHL	BESCRAWL	BESING
BENZIDINES	BEPRAISES	BERGMEHLS	BESCRAWLED	BESINGING
BENZIL	BEPRAISING	BERGOMASK	BESCRAWLING	BESINGS
BENZILS	BEPROSE	BERGOMASKS	BESCRAWLS	BESIT
BENZINE	BEPROSED	BERGS	BESCREEN	BESITS
BENZINES	BEPROSES	BERGYLT	BESCREENED	BESITTING
BENZOATE	BEPROSING	BERGYLTS	BESCREENING	BESLAVE
BENZOATES	BEPUFF	BERIBERI	BESCREENS	BESLAVED
BENZOIC	BEPUFFED	BERIBERIS	BESEE	BESLAVER
BENZOIN	BEPUFFING	BERK	BESEECH	BESLAVERED
BENZOINS	BEPUFFS	BERKELIUM	BESEECHED	BESLAVERING
BENZOL	BEQUEATH	BERKELIUMS	BESEECHER	BESLAVERS
BENZOLE	BEQUEATHED	BERKS	BESEECHERS	BESLAVES
BENZOLES	BEQUEATHING	BERLEY	BESEECHES	BESLAVING
BENZOLINE	BEQUEATHS	BERLEYS	BESEECHING	BESLOBBER
BENZOLINES	BEQUEST	BERLIN	BESEECHINGS	BESLOBBERED
BENZOLS	BEQUESTS	BERLINE	BESEEING	BESLOBBERING
BENZOYL	BERATE	BERLINES	BESEEKE	BESLOBBERS
BENZOYLS	BERATED	BERLINS	BESEEKES	BESLUBBER
BENZYL	BERATES	BERM	BESEEKING	BESLUBBERED
BENZYLS	BERATING	BERMS	BESEEM	BESLUBBERING
BEPAINT	BERAY	BEROB	BESEEMED	BESLUBBERS

BESMEAR	BESPITTING	BESTREAKED	BETHUMBED	BETROTHALS
BESMEARED	BESPOKE	BESTREAKING	BETHUMBING	BETROTHED
BESMEARING	BESPOKEN	BESTREAKS	BETHUMBS	BETROTHEDS
BESMEARS	BESPORT	BESTREW	BETHUMP	BETROTHING
BESMIRCH	BESPORTED	BESTREWED	BETHUMPED	BETROTHS
BESMIRCHED	BESPORTING	BESTREWING	BETHUMPING	BETS
BESMIRCHES	BESPORTS	BESTREWN	BETHUMPS	BETTED
BESMIRCHING	BESPOT	BESTREWS	BETHWACK	BETTER
BESMUT	BESPOTS	BESTRID	BETHWACKED	BETTERED
BESMUTCH	BESPOTTED	BESTRIDDEN	BETHWACKING	BETTERING
BESMUTCHED	BESPOTTING	BESTRIDE	BETHWACKS	BETTERINGS
BESMUTCHES	BESPOUT	BESTRIDES	BETID	BETTERS
BESMUTCHING	BESPOUTED	BESTRIDING	BETIDE	BETTIES
BESMUTS	BESPOUTING	BESTRODE	BETIDED	BETTING
BESMUTTED	BESPOUTS	BESTROWN	BETIDES	BETTINGS
BESMUTTING	BESPREAD	BESTS	BETIDING	BETTOR
BESOGNIO	BESPREADING	BESTUCK	BETIGHT	BETTORS
BESOGNIOS	BESPREADS	BESTUD	BETIME	BETTY
BESOIN	BESPRENT	BESTUDDED	BETIMED	BETUMBLED
BESOINS	BEST	BESTUDDING	BETIMES	BETWEEN
BESOM	BESTAD	BESTUDS	BETIMING	BETWEENS
BESOMED	BESTADDE	BESUITED	BETING	BETWIXT
BESOMING	BESTAIN	BESUNG	BETISE	BEURRE
BESOMS	BESTAINED	BET	BETISES	BEURRES
BESONIAN	BESTAINING	BETA	BETITLE	BEVATRON
BESONIANS	BESTAINS	BETACISM	BETITLED	BEVATRONS
BESORT	BESTAR	BETACISMS	BETITLES	BEVEL
BESORTED	BESTARRED	BETAINE	BETITLING	BEVELLED
BESORTING	BESTARRING	BETAINES	BETOIL	BEVELLER
BESORTS	BESTARS	BETAKE	BETOILED	BEVELLERS
BESOT	BESTEAD	BETAKEN	BETOILING	BEVELLING
BESOTS	BESTEADED	BETAKES	BETOILS	BEVELLINGS
BESOTTED	BESTEADING	BETAKING	BETOKEN	BEVELMENT
BESOTTING	BESTEADS	BETAS	BETOKENED	BEVELMENTS
BESOUGHT	BESTED	BETATRON	BETOKENING	BEVELS
BESOULED	BESTIAL	BETATRONS	BETOKENS	BEVER
BESPAKE	BESTIALS	BETE	BETON	BEVERAGE
BESPANGLE	BESTIARIES	BETED	BETONIES	BEVERAGES
BESPANGLED	BESTIARY	BETEEM	BETONS	BEVERS
BESPANGLES	BESTICK	BETEEME	BETONY	BEVIES
BESPANGLING	BESTICKING	BETEEMED	BETOOK	BEVUE
BESPAT	BESTICKS	BETEEMES	BETOSS	BEVUES
BESPATE	BESTILL	BETEEMING	BETOSSED	BEVVIED
BESPATTER	BESTILLED	BETEEMS	BETOSSES	BEVVIES
BESPATTERED	BESTILLING	BETEL	BETOSSING	BEVVY
BESPATTERING	BESTILLS	BETELS	BETRAY	BEVY
BESPATTERS	BESTING	BETES	BETRAYAL	BEWAIL
BESPEAK	BESTIR	BETH	BETRAYALS	BEWAILED
BESPEAKING	BESTIRRED	BETHANKIT	BETRAYED	BEWAILING
BESPEAKS	BESTIRRING	BETHANKITS	BETRAYER	BEWAILINGS
BESPECKLE	BESTIRS	BETHEL	BETRAYERS	BEWAILS
BESPECKLED	BESTORM	BETHELS	BETRAYING	BEWARE
BESPECKLES	BESTORMED	BETHESDA	BETRAYS	BEWARED
BESPECKLING	BESTORMING	BETHESDAS	BETREAD	BEWARES
BESPED	BESTORMS	BETHINK	BETREADING	BEWARING
BESPEED	BESTOW	BETHINKING	BETREADS	BEWEEP
BESPEEDING	BESTOWAL	BETHINKS	BETRIM	BEWEEPING
BESPEEDS	BESTOWALS	BETHOUGHT	BETRIMMED	BEWEEPS
BESPICE	BESTOWED	BETHRALL	BETRIMMING	BEWENT
BESPICED	BESTOWER	BETHRALLED	BETRIMS	BEWEPT
BESPICES	BESTOWERS	BETHRALLING	BETROD	BEWET
BESPICING	BESTOWING	BETHRALLS	BETRODDEN	BEWETS
BESPIT	BESTOWS	BETHS	BETROTH	BEWETTED
BESPITS	BESTREAK	BETHUMB	BETROTHAL	BEWETTING

BEWHORE	BHISTEE	BICORNES	BIFURCATE	BIKES
BEWHORED	BHISTEES	BICORNS	BIFURCATED	BIKEWAY
BEWHORES	BHISTI	BICUSPID	BIFURCATES	BIKEWAYS
BEWHORING	BHISTIS	BICUSPIDS	BIFURCATING	BIKIE
BEWIG	BI	BICYCLE	BIG	BIKIES
BEWIGGED	BIANNUAL	BICYCLED	BIGA	BIKING
BEWIGGING	BIANNUALS	BICYCLES	BIGAE	BIKINGS
BEWIGS	BIAS	BICYCLING	BIGAMIES	BIKINI
BEWILDER	BIASED	BICYCLIST	BIGAMIST	BIKINIS
BEWILDERED	BIASES	BICYCLISTS	BIGAMISTS	BILABIAL
BEWILDERING	BIASING	BID	BIGAMOUS	BILABIALS
BEWILDERS	BIASINGS	BIDARKA	BIGAMY	BILABIATE
BEWITCH	BIASSED	BIDARKAS	BIGARADE	BILANDER
BEWITCHED	BIASSES	BIDDABLE	BIGARADES	BILANDERS
BEWITCHES	BIASSING	BIDDEN	BIGENER	BILATERAL
BEWITCHING	BIATHLETE	BIDDER	BIGENERIC	BILBERRIES
BEWRAY	BIATHLETES	BIDDERS	BIGENERS	BILBERRY
BEWRAYED	BIATHLON	BIDDIES	BIGFEET	BILBO
BEWRAYING	BIATHLONS	BIDDING	BIGFOOT	BILBOES
BEWRAYS	BIAXAL	BIDDINGS	BIGG	BILBOS
BEY	BIAXIAL	BIDDY	BIGGED	BILE
BEYOND	BIB	BIDE	BIGGER	BILES
BEYONDS	BIBACIOUS	BIDED	BIGGEST	BILGE
BEYS	BIBATION	BIDENT	BIGGIE	BILGED
BEZ	BIBATIONS	BIDENTAL	BIGGIES	BILGES
BEZANT	BIBBED	BIDENTALS	BIGGIN	BILGIER
BEZANTS	BIBBER	BIDENTATE	BIGGING	BILGIEST
BEZAZZ	BIBBERS	BIDENTS	BIGGINS	BILGING
BEZAZZES	BIBBING	BIDES	BIGGISH	BILGY
BEZEL	BIBCOCK	BIDET	BIGGS	BILHARZIA
BEZELS	BIBCOCKS	BIDETS	BIGGY	BILHARZIAS
BEZES	BIBELOT	BIDING	BIGHA	BILIAN
BEZIQUE	BIBELOTS	BIDINGS	BIGHAS	BILIANS
BEZIQUES	BIBLE	BIDON	BIGHEADED	BILIARIES
BEZOAR	BIBLES	BIDONS	BIGHORN	BILIARY
BEZOARDIC	BIBLICAL	BIDS	BIGHORNS	BILIMBI
BEZOARS	BIBLICISM	BIELD	BIGHT	BILIMBING
BEZONIAN	BIBLICISMS	BIELDED	BIGHTS	BILIMBINGS
BEZONIANS	BIBLICIST	BIELDIER	BIGMOUTH	BILIMBIS
BEZZLE	BIBLICISTS	BIELDIEST	BIGMOUTHS	BILINGUAL
BEZZLED	BIBLIST	BIELDING	BIGNESS	BILIOUS
BEZZLES	BIBLISTS	BIELDS	BIGNESSES	BILIOUSLY
BEZZLING	BIBS	BIELDY	BIGNONIA	BILIRUBIN
BHAGEE	BIBULOUS	BIEN	BIGNONIAS	BILIRUBINS
BHAGEES	BICAMERAL	BIENNIAL	BIGOT	BILITERAL
BHAJAN	BICARB	BIENNIALS	BIGOTED	BILK
BHAJANS	BICARBS	BIER	BIGOTRIES	BILKED
BHAJEE	BICCIES	BIERS	BIGOTRY	BILKER
BHAJEES	BICCY	BIESTINGS	BIGOTS	BILKERS
BHAKTI	BICE	BIFACIAL	BIGS	BILKING
BHAKTIS	BICEPS	BIFARIOUS	BIGUANIDE	BILKS
BHANG	BICEPSES	BIFF	BIGUANIDES	BILL
BHANGRA	BICES	BIFFED	BIGWIG	BILLABONG
BHANGRAS	BICHORD	BIFFIN	BIGWIGS	BILLABONGS
BHANGS	BICIPITAL	BIFFING	BIJECTION	BILLBOARD
BHARAL	BICKER	BIFFINS	BIJECTIONS	BILLBOARDS
BHARALS	BICKERED	BIFFS	BIJOU	BILLBOOK
BHEESTIE	BICKERING	BIFID	BIJOUX	BILLBOOKS
BHEESTIES	BICKERS	BIFILAR	BIJWONER	BILLED
BHEESTY	BICOASTAL	BIFOCAL	BIJWONERS	BILLET
BHEL	BICONCAVE	BIFOCALS	BIKE	BILLETED
BHELS	BICONVEX	BIFOLD	BIKED	BILLETING
BHINDI	BICORN	BIFOLIATE	BIKER	BILLETS
BHINDIS	BICORNE	BIFORM	BIKERS	BILLFOLD

BILLFOLDS	BINDWEEDS	BIOGRAPHIES	BIOTYPES	BIRL
BILLHEAD	BINE	BIOGRAPHING	BIPAROUS	BIRLE
BILLHEADS	BINERVATE	BIOGRAPHS	BIPARTITE	BIRLED
BILLHOOK	BINES	BIOGRAPHY	BIPED	BIRLER
BILLHOOKS	BING	BIOGS	BIPEDAL	BIRLERS
BILLIARD	BINGE	BIOHAZARD	BIPEDS	BIRLES
BILLIARDS	BINGED	BIOHAZARDS	BIPHASIC	BIRLIEMAN
BILLIE	BINGEING	BIOLOGIES	BIPHENYL	BIRLIEMEN
BILLIES	BINGER	BIOLOGIST	BIPHENYLS	BIRLING
BILLING	BINGERS	BIOLOGISTS	BIPINNATE	BIRLINGS
BILLINGS	BINGES	BIOLOGY	BIPLANE	BIRLINN
BILLION	BINGHI	BIOLYSES	BIPLANES	BIRLINNS
BILLIONS	BINGHIS	BIOLYSIS	BIPOD	BIRLS
BILLIONTH	BINGIES	BIOMASS	BIPODS	BIRR
BILLIONTHS	BINGING	BIOMASSES	BIPOLAR	BIRRED
BILLMAN	BINGLE	BIOME	BIPYRAMID	BIRRING
BILLMEN	BINGLED	BIOMES	BIPYRAMIDS	BIRRS
BILLON	BINGLES	BIOMETRIC	BIRAMOUS	BIRSE
BILLONS	BINGLING	BIOMETRICS	BIRCH	BIRSES
BILLOW	BINGO	BIOMETRIES	BIRCHED	BIRSIER
BILLOWED	BINGOS	BIOMETRY	BIRCHEN	BIRSIEST
BILLOWIER	BINGS	BIOMINING	BIRCHES	BIRSLE
BILLOWIEST	BINGY	BIOMININGS	BIRCHING	BIRSLED
BILLOWING	BINK	BIOMORPH	BIRD	BIRSLES
BILLOWS	BINKS	BIOMORPHS	BIRDBATH	BIRSLING
BILLOWY	BINMAN	BIONIC	BIRDBATHS	BIRSY
BILLS	BINMEN	BIONICS	BIRDCAGE	BIRTH
BILLY	BINNACLE	BIONOMIC	BIRDCAGES	BIRTHDAY
BILLYBOY	BINNACLES	BIONOMICS	BIRDCALL	BIRTHDAYS
BILLYBOYS	BINNED	BIONT	BIRDCALLS	BIRTHDOM
BILLYCOCK	BINNING	BIONTIC	BIRDED	BIRTHDOMS
BILLYCOCKS	BINOCLE	BIONTS	BIRDER	BIRTHED
BILOBAR	BINOCLES	BIOPARENT	BIRDERS	BIRTHING
BILOBATE	BINOCULAR	BIOPARENTS	BIRDIE	BIRTHINGS
BILOBED	BINOCULARS	BIOPHOR	BIRDIED	BIRTHMARK
BILOBULAR	BINOMIAL	BIOPHORE	BIRDIEING	BIRTHMARKS
BILOCULAR	BINOMIALS	BIOPHORES	BIRDIES	BIRTHS
BILTONG	BINOMINAL	BIOPHORS	BIRDING	BIRTHWORT
BILTONGS	BINS	BIOPIC	BIRDINGS	BIRTHWORTS
BIMANAL	BINT	BIOPICS	BIRDLIKE	BIRYANI
BIMANOUS	BINTS	BIOPLASM	BIRDMAN	BIRYANIS
BIMANUAL	BINTURONG	BIOPLASMS	BIRDMEN	BIS
BIMBASHI	BINTURONGS	BIOPLAST	BIRDS	BISCACHA
BIMBASHIS	BIO	BIOPLASTS	BIRDSEED	BISCACHAS
BIMBETTE	BIOASSAY	BIOPSIES	BIRDSEEDS	BISCUIT
BIMBETTES	BIOASSAYS	BIOPSY	BIRDSHOT	BISCUITS
BIMBO	BIOBLAST	BIOS	BIRDSHOTS	BISCUITY
BIMBOS	BIOBLASTS	BIOSCOPE	BIRDSONG	BISE
BIMODAL	BIOCIDAL	BIOSCOPES	BIRDSONGS	BISECT
BIMONTHLY	BIOCIDE	BIOSENSOR	BIRDWING	BISECTED
BIN	BIOCIDES	BIOSENSORS	BIRDWINGS	BISECTING
BINARIES	BIODATA	BIOSPHERE	BIREME	BISECTION
BINARY	BIOETHICS	BIOSPHERES	BIREMES	BISECTIONS
BINATE	BIOG	BIOSTABLE	BIRETTA	BISECTOR
BINAURAL	BIOGAS	BIOTA	BIRETTAS	BISECTORS
BIND	BIOGASES	BIOTAS	BIRIYANI	BISECTS
BINDER	BIOGEN	BIOTIC	BIRIYANIS	BISERIAL
BINDERIES	BIOGENIC	BIOTIN	BIRK	BISERRATE
BINDERS	BIOGENIES	BIOTINS	BIRKEN	BISES
BINDERY	BIOGENOUS	BIOTITE	BIRKIE	BISEXUAL
BINDING	BIOGENS	BIOTITES	BIRKIER	BISEXUALS
BINDINGS	BIOGENY	BIOTOPE	BIRKIES	BISH
BINDS	BIOGRAPH	BIOTOPES	BIRKIEST	BISHES
BINDWEED	BIOGRAPHED	BIOTYPE	BIRKS	BISHOP

BISHOPDOM	BITTACLES	BLABBED	BLACKOUT	BLAND
BISHOPDOMS	BITTE	BLABBER	BLACKOUTS	BLANDER
BISHOPED	BITTED	BLABBERS	BLACKS	BLANDEST
BISHOPESS	BITTEN	BLABBING	BLACKTOP	BLANDISH
BISHOPESSES	BITTER	BLABBINGS	BLACKTOPS	BLANDISHED
BISHOPING	BITTERER	BLABS	BLACKWASH	BLANDISHES
BISHOPRIC	BITTEREST	BLACK	BLACKWASHES	BLANDISHING
BISHOPRICS	BITTERISH	BLACKBALL	BLACKWOOD	BLANDLY
BISHOPS	BITTERLY	BLACKBALLED	BLACKWOODS	BLANDNESS
BISK	BITTERN	BLACKBALLING	BLAD	BLANDNESSES
BISKS	BITTERNS	BLACKBALLINGS	BLADDED	BLANDS
BISMAR	BITTERS	BLACKBALLS	BLADDER	BLANK
BISMARS	BITTIE	BLACKBAND	BLADDERED	BLANKED
BISMILLAH	BITTIER	BLACKBANDS	BLADDERS	BLANKER
BISMUTH	BITTIES	BLACKBIRD	BLADDERY	BLANKEST
BISMUTHS	BITTIEST	BLACKBIRDS	BLADDING	BLANKET
BISON	BITTING	BLACKBOY	BLADE	BLANKETED
BISONS	BITTOCK	BLACKBOYS	BLADED	BLANKETIES
BISQUE	BITTOCKS	BLACKBUCK	BLADES	BLANKETING
BISQUES	BITTOR	BLACKBUCKS	BLADEWORK	BLANKETINGS
BISSON	BITTORS	BLACKCAP	BLADEWORKS	BLANKETS
BISTABLE	BITTOUR	BLACKCAPS	BLADS	BLANKETY
BISTER	BITTOURS	BLACKCOCK	BLAE	BLANKIES
BISTERS	BITTS	BLACKCOCKS	BLAEBERRIES	BLANKING
BISTORT	BITTUR	BLACKED	BLAEBERRY	BLANKINGS
BISTORTS	BITTURS	BLACKEN	BLAER	BLANKLY
BISTOURIES	BITTY	BLACKENED	BLAES	BLANKNESS
BISTOURY	BITUMED	BLACKENING	BLAEST	BLANKNESSES
BISTRE	BITUMEN	BLACKENS	BLAG	BLANKS
BISTRED	BITUMENS	BLACKER	BLAGGED	BLANKY
BISTRES	BIVALENCE	BLACKEST	BLAGGER	BLANQUET
BISTRO	BIVALENCES	BLACKFACE	BLAGGERS	BLANQUETS
BISTROS	BIVALENCIES	BLACKFACES	BLAGGING	BLARE
BISULCATE	BIVALENCY	BLACKFISH	BLAGS	BLARED
BIT	BIVALENT	BLACKFISHES	BLAGUE	BLARES
BITCH	BIVALENTS	BLACKGAME	BLAGUES	BLARING
BITCHED	BIVALVE	BLACKGAMES	BLAGUEUR	BLARNEY
BITCHERIES	BIVALVES	BLACKHEAD	BLAGUEURS	BLARNEYED
BITCHERY	BIVARIANT	BLACKHEADS	BLAH	BLARNEYING
BITCHES	BIVARIANTS	BLACKING	BLAHED	BLARNEYS
BITCHIER	BIVARIATE	BLACKINGS	BLAHING	BLASE
BITCHIEST	BIVARIATES	BLACKISH	BLAHS	BLASH
BITCHILY	BIVIA	BLACKJACK	BLAIN	BLASHES
BITCHING	BIVIOUS	BLACKJACKED	BLAINS	BLASHIER
BITCHY	BIVIUM	BLACKJACKING	BLAISE	BLASHIEST
BITE	BIVOUAC	BLACKJACKS	BLAIZE	BLASHY
BITER	BIVOUACKED	BLACKLEAD	BLAMABLE	BLASPHEME
BITERS	BIVOUACKING	BLACKLEADS	BLAMABLY	BLASPHEMED
BITES	BIVOUACS	BLACKLEG	BLAME	BLASPHEMES
BITESIZE	BIVVIED	BLACKLEGGED	BLAMEABLE	BLASPHEMIES
BITING	BIVVIES	BLACKLEGGING	BLAMEABLY	BLASPHEMING
BITINGS	BIVVY	BLACKLEGS	BLAMED	BLASPHEMY
BITLESS	BIVVYING	BLACKLIST	BLAMEFUL	BLAST
BITMAP	BIZ	BLACKLISTED	BLAMELESS	BLASTED
BITMAPS	BIZARRE	BLACKLISTING	BLAMES	BLASTEMA
BITO	BIZAZZ	BLACKLISTINGS	BLAMING	BLASTEMAS
BITONAL	BIZAZZES	BLACKLISTS	BLANCH	BLASTEMATA
BITOS	BIZCACHA	BLACKLY	BLANCHED	BLASTER
BITS	BIZCACHAS	BLACKMAIL	BLANCHES	BLASTERS
BITSIER	BIZONAL	BLACKMAILED	BLANCHING	BLASTING
BITSIEST	BIZONE	BLACKMAILING	BLANCO	BLASTINGS
BITSY	BIZONES	BLACKMAILS	BLANCOED	BLASTMENT
BITT	BIZZES	BLACKNESS	BLANCOING	BLASTMENTS
BITTACLE	BLAB	BLACKNESSES	BLANCOS	BLASTOID

BLASTOIDS	BLEAKEST	BLESSED	BLINDWORM	BLOBBING
BLASTS	BLEAKLY	BLESSEDER	BLINDWORMS	BLOBS
BLASTULA	BLEAKNESS	BLESSEDEST	BLINI	BLOC
BLASTULAE	BLEAKNESSES	BLESSEDLY	BLINIS	BLOCK
BLASTULAR	BLEAKS	BLESSES	BLINK	BLOCKADE
BLASTULAS	BLEAKY	BLESSING	BLINKARD	BLOCKADED
BLAT	BLEAR	BLESSINGS	BLINKARDS	BLOCKADES
BLATANT	BLEARED	BLEST	BLINKED	BLOCKADING
BLATANTLY	BLEARER	BLET	BLINKER	BLOCKAGE
BLATE	BLEAREST	BLETHER	BLINKERED	BLOCKAGES
BLATER	BLEAREYED	BLETHERED	BLINKERING	BLOCKED
BLATEST	BLEARIER	BLETHERER	BLINKERS	BLOCKER
BLATHER	BLEARIEST	BLETHERERS	BLINKING	BLOCKERS
BLATHERED	BLEARILY	BLETHERING	BLINKS	BLOCKHEAD
BLATHERER	BLEARING	BLETHERINGS	BLINNED	BLOCKHEADS
BLATHERERS	BLEARS	BLETHERS	BLINNING	BLOCKHOLE
BLATHERING	BLEARY	BLETS	BLINS	BLOCKHOLES
BLATHERS	BLEAT	BLETTED	BLINTZ	BLOCKIER
BLATS	BLEATED	BLETTING	BLINTZE	BLOCKIEST
BLATT	BLEATER	BLEUATRE	BLINTZES	BLOCKING
BLATTANT	BLEATERS	BLEW	BLIP	BLOCKINGS
BLATTED	BLEATING	BLEWART	BLIPPED	BLOCKISH
BLATTER	BLEATINGS	BLEWARTS	BLIPPING	BLOCKS
BLATTERED	BLEATS	BLEWITS	BLIPS	BLOCKWORK
BLATTERING	BLEB	BLEWITSES	BLISS	BLOCKWORKS
BLATTERS	BLEBS	BLEY	BLISSES	BLOCKY
BLATTING	BLED	BLEYS	BLISSFUL	BLOCS
BLATTS	BLEE	BLIGHT	BLISSLESS	BLOKE
BLAUBOK	BLEED	BLIGHTED	BLIST	BLOKEDOM
BLAUBOKS	BLEEDER	BLIGHTER	BLISTER	BLOKEDOMS
BLAUD	BLEEDERS	BLIGHTERS	BLISTERED	BLOKEISH
BLAUDED	BLEEDING	BLIGHTIES	BLISTERIER	BLOKES
BLAUDING	BLEEDINGS	BLIGHTING	BLISTERIEST	BLOKEY
BLAUDS	BLEEDS	BLIGHTINGS	BLISTERING	BLOKIER
BLAWORT	BLEEP	BLIGHTS	BLISTERS	BLOKIEST
BLAWORTS	BLEEPED	BLIGHTY	BLISTERY	BLONCKET
BLAY	BLEEPER	BLIMBING	BLITE	BLOND
BLAYS	BLEEPERS	BLIMBINGS	BLITES	BLONDE
BLAZE	BLEEPING	BLIMEY	BLITHE	BLONDER
BLAZED	BLEEPS	BLIMP	BLITHELY	BLONDES
BLAZER	BLEES	BLIMPISH	BLITHER	BLONDEST
BLAZERED	BLEMISH	BLIMPS	BLITHERED	BLONDS
BLAZERS	BLEMISHED	BLIMY	BLITHERING	BLOOD
BLAZES	BLEMISHES	BLIN	BLITHERS	BLOODED
BLAZING	BLEMISHING	BLIND	BLITHEST	BLOODHEAT
BLAZON	BLENCH	BLINDAGE	BLITZ	BLOODHEATS
BLAZONED	BLENCHED	BLINDAGES	BLITZED	BLOODIED
BLAZONER	BLENCHES	BLINDED	BLITZES	BLOODIER
BLAZONERS	BLENCHING	BLINDER	BLITZING	BLOODIES
BLAZONING	BLEND	BLINDERS	BLIVE	BLOODIEST
BLAZONRIES	BLENDE	BLINDEST	BLIZZARD	BLOODILY
BLAZONRY	BLENDED	BLINDFISH	BLIZZARDS	BLOODING
BLAZONS	BLENDER	BLINDFISHES	BLIZZARDY	BLOODLESS
BLEACH	BLENDERS	BLINDFOLD	BLOAT	BLOODLUST
BLEACHED	BLENDES	BLINDFOLDED	BLOATED	BLOODLUSTS
BLEACHER	BLENDING	BLINDFOLDING	BLOATER	BLOODROOT
BLEACHERIES	BLENDINGS	BLINDFOLDS	BLOATERS	BLOODROOTS
BLEACHERS	BLENDS	BLINDING	BLOATING	BLOODS
BLEACHERY	BLENNIES	BLINDINGS	BLOATINGS	BLOODSHED
BLEACHES	BLENNY	BLINDLESS	BLOATS	BLOODSHEDS
BLEACHING	BLENT	BLINDLY	BLOATWARE	BLOODSHOT
BLEACHINGS	BLESBOK	BLINDNESS	BLOATWARES	BLOODWOOD
BLEAK	BLESBOKS	BLINDNESSES	BLOB	BLOODWOODS
BLEAKER	BLESS	BLINDS	BLOBBED	BLOODY

The Chambers Dictionary is the authority for many longer words; see *OSW* Introduction, page xii

BLOODYING	BLOWER	BLUDIEST	BLUGGIEST	BLUSHLESS
BLOOM	BLOWERS	BLUDY	BLUGGY	BLUSTER
BLOOMED	BLOWFISH	BLUE	BLUID	BLUSTERED
BLOOMER	BLOWFISHES	BLUEBACK	BLUIDIER	BLUSTERER
BLOOMERIES	BLOWFLIES	BLUEBACKS	BLUIDIEST	BLUSTERERS
BLOOMERS	BLOWFLY	BLUEBEARD	BLUIDS	BLUSTERIER
BLOOMERY	BLOWGUN	BLUEBEARDS	BLUIDY	BLUSTERIEST
BLOOMIER	BLOWGUNS	BLUEBELL	BLUIER	BLUSTERING
BLOOMIEST	BLOWHARD	BLUEBELLS	BLUIEST	BLUSTERINGS
BLOOMING	BLOWHARDS	BLUEBERRIES	BLUING	BLUSTERS
BLOOMLESS	BLOWHOLE	BLUEBERRY	BLUINGS	BLUSTERY
BLOOMS	BLOWHOLES	BLUEBIRD	BLUISH	BLUSTROUS
BLOOMY	BLOWIE	BLUEBIRDS	BLUNDER	BLUTWURST
BLOOP	BLOWIER	BLUEBUCK	BLUNDERED	BLUTWURSTS
BLOOPED	BLOWIES	BLUEBUCKS	BLUNDERER	BO
BLOOPER	BLOWIEST	BLUECAP	BLUNDERERS	BOA
BLOOPERS	BLOWING	BLUECAPS	BLUNDERING	BOAK
BLOOPING	BLOWJOB	BLUECOAT	BLUNDERINGS	BOAKED
BLOOPS	BLOWJOBS	BLUECOATS	BLUNDERS	BOAKING
BLOOSME	BLOWLAMP	BLUED	BLUNGE	BOAKS
BLOOSMED	BLOWLAMPS	BLUEFISH	BLUNGED	BOAR
BLOOSMES	BLOWN	BLUEFISHES	BLUNGER	BOARD
BLOOSMING	BLOWPIPE	BLUEGOWN	BLUNGERS	BOARDED
BLORE	BLOWPIPES	BLUEGOWNS	BLUNGES	BOARDER
BLORES	BLOWS	BLUEGRASS	BLUNGING	BOARDERS
BLOSSOM	BLOWSE	BLUEGRASSES	BLUNK	BOARDING
BLOSSOMED	BLOWSED	BLUEING	BLUNKED	BOARDINGS
BLOSSOMING	BLOWSES	BLUEINGS	BLUNKER	BOARDROOM
BLOSSOMINGS	BLOWSIER	BLUELY	BLUNKERS	BOARDROOMS
BLOSSOMS	BLOWSIEST	BLUENESS	BLUNKING	BOARDS
BLOSSOMY	BLOWSY	BLUENESSES	BLUNKS	BOARDWALK
BLOT	BLOWTORCH	BLUENOSE	BLUNT	BOARDWALKS
BLOTCH	BLOWTORCHES	BLUENOSES	BLUNTED	BOARFISH
BLOTCHED	BLOWY	BLUEPRINT	BLUNTER	BOARFISHES
BLOTCHES	BLOWZE	BLUEPRINTED	BLUNTEST	BOARISH
BLOTCHIER	BLOWZED	BLUEPRINTING	BLUNTING	BOARS
BLOTCHIEST	BLOWZES	BLUEPRINTS	BLUNTISH	BOART
BLOTCHING	BLOWZIER	BLUER	BLUNTLY	BOARTS
BLOTCHINGS	BLOWZIEST	BLUES	BLUNTNESS	BOAS
BLOTCHY	BLOWZY	BLUESIER	BLUNTNESSES	BOAST
BLOTS	BLUB	BLUESIEST	BLUNTS	BOASTED
BLOTTED	BLUBBED	BLUEST	BLUR	BOASTER
BLOTTER	BLUBBER	BLUESTONE	BLURB	BOASTERS
BLOTTERS	BLUBBERED	BLUESTONES	BLURBED	BOASTFUL
BLOTTIER	BLUBBERING	BLUESY	BLURBING	BOASTING
BLOTTIEST	BLUBBERS	BLUETTE	BLURBS	BOASTINGS
BLOTTING	BLUBBING	BLUETTES	BLURRED	BOASTLESS
BLOTTINGS	BLUBS	BLUEWEED	BLURRING	BOASTS
BLOTTO	BLUCHER	BLUEWEEDS	BLURS	BOAT
BLOTTY	BLUCHERS	BLUEWING	BLURT	BOATBILL
BLOUBOK	BLUDE	BLUEWINGS	BLURTED	BOATBILLS
BLOUBOKS	BLUDES	BLUEY	BLURTING	BOATED
BLOUSE	BLUDGE	BLUEYS	BLURTINGS	BOATEL
BLOUSED	BLUDGED	BLUFF	BLURTS	BOATELS
BLOUSES	BLUDGEON	BLUFFED	BLUSH	BOATER
BLOUSING	BLUDGEONED	BLUFFER	BLUSHED	BOATERS
BLOUSON	BLUDGEONING	BLUFFERS	BLUSHER	BOATHOUSE
BLOUSONS	BLUDGEONS	BLUFFEST	BLUSHERS	BOATHOUSES
BLOW	BLUDGER	BLUFFING	BLUSHES	BOATIE
BLOWBALL	BLUDGERS	BLUFFLY	BLUSHET	BOATIES
BLOWBALLS	BLUDGES	BLUFFNESS	BLUSHETS	BOATING
BLOWDOWN	BLUDGING	BLUFFNESSES	BLUSHFUL	BOATINGS
BLOWDOWNS	BLUDIE	BLUFFS	BLUSHING	BOATMAN
BLOWED	BLUDIER	BLUGGIER	BLUSHINGS	BOATMEN

BOATS
BOATSWAIN
BOATSWAINS
BOATTAIL
BOATTAILS
BOB
BOBA
BOBAC
BOBACS
BOBAK
BOBAKS
BOBAS
BOBBED
BOBBERIES
BOBBERY
BOBBIES
BOBBIN
BOBBINET
BOBBINETS
BOBBING
BOBBINS
BOBBISH
BOBBITT
BOBBITTED
BOBBITTING
BOBBITTS
BOBBLE
BOBBLED
BOBBLES
BOBBLIER
BOBBLIEST
BOBBLING
BOBBLY
BOBBY
BOBBYSOCK
BOBBYSOCKS
BOBCAT
BOBCATS
BOBOLINK
BOBOLINKS
BOBS
BOBSLED
BOBSLEDS
BOBSLEIGH
BOBSLEIGHS
BOBSTAYS
BOBTAIL
BOBTAILED
BOBTAILING
BOBTAILS
BOBWHEEL
BOBWHEELS
BOBWIG
BOBWIGS
BOCAGE
BOCAGES
BOCCA
BOCCAS
BOCHE
BOCHES
BOCK
BOCKED
BOCKING
BOCKS

BOD
BODACH
BODACHS
BODACIOUS
BODDLE
BODDLES
BODE
BODED
BODEFUL
BODEGA
BODEGAS
BODEGUERO
BODEGUEROS
BODEMENT
BODEMENTS
BODES
BODGE
BODGED
BODGER
BODGERS
BODGES
BODGIE
BODGIER
BODGIES
BODGIEST
BODGING
BODHRAN
BODHRANS
BODICE
BODICES
BODIED
BODIES
BODIKIN
BODIKINS
BODILESS
BODILY
BODING
BODINGS
BODKIN
BODKINS
BODLE
BODLES
BODRAG
BODRAGS
BODS
BODY
BODYGUARD
BODYGUARDS
BODYING
BODYLINE
BODYLINES
BODYSHELL
BODYSHELLS
BODYSUIT
BODYSUITS
BODYWORK
BODYWORKS
BOEREWORS
BOEREWORSES
BOFF
BOFFED
BOFFIN
BOFFING
BOFFINS

BOFFS
BOG
BOGAN
BOGANS
BOGBEAN
BOGBEANS
BOGEY
BOGEYED
BOGEYING
BOGEYISM
BOGEYISMS
BOGEYS
BOGGARD
BOGGARDS
BOGGART
BOGGARTS
BOGGED
BOGGIER
BOGGIEST
BOGGINESS
BOGGINESSES
BOGGING
BOGGLE
BOGGLED
BOGGLER
BOGGLERS
BOGGLES
BOGGLING
BOGGY
BOGIE
BOGIES
BOGLAND
BOGLANDS
BOGLE
BOGLES
BOGOAK
BOGOAKS
BOGONG
BOGONGS
BOGS
BOGUS
BOGY
BOGYISM
BOGYISMS
BOH
BOHEA
BOHEAS
BOHS
BOHUNK
BOHUNKS
BOIL
BOILED
BOILER
BOILERIES
BOILERS
BOILERY
BOILING
BOILINGS
BOILS
BOING
BOINGED
BOINGING
BOINGS
BOINK

BOINKED
BOINKING
BOINKS
BOK
BOKE
BOKED
BOKES
BOKING
BOKO
BOKOS
BOKS
BOLAS
BOLASES
BOLD
BOLDEN
BOLDENED
BOLDENING
BOLDENS
BOLDER
BOLDEST
BOLDLY
BOLDNESS
BOLDNESSES
BOLDS
BOLE
BOLECTION
BOLECTIONS
BOLERO
BOLEROS
BOLES
BOLETI
BOLETUS
BOLETUSES
BOLIDE
BOLIDES
BOLIVAR
BOLIVARES
BOLIVARS
BOLIVIANO
BOLIVIANOS
BOLIX
BOLIXED
BOLIXES
BOLIXING
BOLL
BOLLARD
BOLLARDS
BOLLED
BOLLEN
BOLLETRIE
BOLLETRIES
BOLLING
BOLLIX
BOLLIXED
BOLLIXES
BOLLIXING
BOLLOCK
BOLLOCKED
BOLLOCKING
BOLLOCKINGS
BOLLOCKS
BOLLOCKSED
BOLLOCKSES
BOLLOCKSING

BOLLS
BOLO
BOLOMETER
BOLOMETERS
BOLOMETRIES
BOLOMETRY
BOLONEY
BOLONEYS
BOLOS
BOLSHEVIK
BOLSHEVIKS
BOLSHIE
BOLSHIER
BOLSHIES
BOLSHIEST
BOLSHY
BOLSTER
BOLSTERED
BOLSTERING
BOLSTERINGS
BOLSTERS
BOLT
BOLTED
BOLTER
BOLTERS
BOLTHEAD
BOLTHEADS
BOLTHOLE
BOLTHOLES
BOLTING
BOLTINGS
BOLTS
BOLUS
BOLUSES
BOMA
BOMAS
BOMB
BOMBARD
BOMBARDED
BOMBARDING
BOMBARDON
BOMBARDONS
BOMBARDS
BOMBASINE
BOMBASINES
BOMBAST
BOMBASTED
BOMBASTIC
BOMBASTING
BOMBASTS
BOMBAX
BOMBAXES
BOMBAZINE
BOMBAZINES
BOMBE
BOMBED
BOMBER
BOMBERS
BOMBES
BOMBILATE
BOMBILATED
BOMBILATES
BOMBILATING
BOMBINATE

BOMBINATED	BONESET	BONSOIR	BOOKLORE	BOORS
BOMBINATES	BONESETS	BONSPIEL	BOOKLORES	BOORTREE
BOMBINATING	BONEYARD	BONSPIELS	BOOKLOUSE	BOORTREES
BOMBING	BONEYARDS	BONTEBOK	BOOKMAKER	BOOS
BOMBLET	BONFIRE	BONTEBOKS	BOOKMAKERS	BOOSE
BOMBLETS	BONFIRES	BONUS	BOOKMAN	BOOSED
BOMBO	BONG	BONUSES	BOOKMARK	BOOSES
BOMBORA	BONGED	BONXIE	BOOKMARKS	BOOSING
BOMBORAS	BONGING	BONXIES	BOOKMEN	BOOST
BOMBOS	BONGO	BONY	BOOKPLATE	BOOSTED
BOMBS	BONGOS	BONZA	BOOKPLATES	BOOSTER
BOMBSHELL	BONGRACE	BONZE	BOOKREST	BOOSTERS
BOMBSHELLS	BONGRACES	BONZER	BOOKRESTS	BOOSTING
BOMBSITE	BONGS	BONZES	BOOKS	BOOSTS
BOMBSITES	BONHOMIE	BOO	BOOKSHELF	BOOT
BOMBYCID	BONHOMIES	BOOB	BOOKSHELVES	BOOTABLE
BOMBYCIDS	BONHOMMIE	BOOBED	BOOKSHOP	BOOTBLACK
BON	BONHOMMIES	BOOBIES	BOOKSHOPS	BOOTBLACKS
BONA	BONHOMOUS	BOOBING	BOOKSIE	BOOTED
BONAMANI	BONIBELL	BOOBOO	BOOKSIER	BOOTEE
BONAMANO	BONIBELLS	BOOBOOK	BOOKSIEST	BOOTEES
BONAMIA	BONIE	BOOBOOKS	BOOKSTALL	BOOTH
BONAMIAS	BONIER	BOOBOOS	BOOKSTALLS	BOOTHOSE
BONANZA	BONIEST	BOOBS	BOOKSTAND	BOOTHS
BONANZAS	BONIFACE	BOOBY	BOOKSTANDS	BOOTIES
BONASSUS	BONIFACES	BOOBYISH	BOOKSTORE	BOOTIKIN
BONASSUSES	BONILASSE	BOOBYISM	BOOKSTORES	BOOTIKINS
BONASUS	BONILASSES	BOOBYISMS	BOOKSY	BOOTING
BONASUSES	BONINESS	BOODIE	BOOKWORK	BOOTLACE
BONBON	BONINESSES	BOODIED	BOOKWORKS	BOOTLACES
BONBONS	BONING	BOODIES	BOOKWORM	BOOTLAST
BONCE	BONINGS	BOODLE	BOOKWORMS	BOOTLASTS
BONCES	BONISM	BOODLES	BOOKY	BOOTLEG
BOND	BONISMS	BOODY	BOOL	BOOTLEGGED
BONDAGE	BONIST	BOODYING	BOOLS	BOOTLEGGING
BONDAGER	BONISTS	BOOED	BOOM	BOOTLEGGINGS
BONDAGERS	BONITO	BOOGIE	BOOMED	BOOTLEGS
BONDAGES	BONITOS	BOOGIED	BOOMER	BOOTLESS
BONDED	BONJOUR	BOOGIEING	BOOMERANG	BOOTLICK
BONDER	BONK	BOOGIES	BOOMERANGED	BOOTLICKED
BONDERS	BONKED	BOOH	BOOMERANGING	BOOTLICKING
BONDING	BONKERS	BOOHED	BOOMERANGS	BOOTLICKINGS
BONDINGS	BONKING	BOOHING	BOOMERS	BOOTLICKS
BONDMAID	BONKS	BOOHS	BOOMING	BOOTMAKER
BONDMAIDS	BONNE	BOOING	BOOMINGS	BOOTMAKERS
BONDMAN	BONNES	BOOK	BOOMLET	BOOTS
BONDMEN	BONNET	BOOKABLE	BOOMLETS	BOOTSTRAP
BONDS	BONNETED	BOOKCASE	BOOMS	BOOTSTRAPPED
BONDSMAN	BONNETING	BOOKCASES	BOOMSLANG	BOOTSTRAPPING
BONDSMEN	BONNETS	BOOKED	BOOMSLANGS	BOOTSTRAPS
BONDSTONE	BONNIBELL	BOOKFUL	BOON	BOOTY
BONDSTONES	BONNIBELLS	BOOKIE	BOONDOCKS	BOOZE
BONDUC	BONNIE	BOOKIER	BOONG	BOOZED
BONDUCS	BONNIER	BOOKIES	BOONGS	BOOZER
BONDWOMAN	BONNIES	BOOKIEST	BOONS	BOOZERS
BONDWOMEN	BONNIEST	BOOKING	BOOR	BOOZES
BONE	BONNILY	BOOKINGS	BOORD	BOOZEY
BONED	BONNINESS	BOOKISH	BOORDE	BOOZIER
BONEHEAD	BONNINESSES	BOOKLAND	BOORDES	BOOZIEST
BONEHEADS	BONNY	BOOKLANDS	BOORDS	BOOZILY
BONELESS	BONSAI	BOOKLESS	BOORISH	BOOZINESS
BONER	BONSAIS	BOOKLET	BOORISHLY	BOOZINESSES
BONERS	BONSELLA	BOOKLETS	BOORKA	BOOZING
BONES	BONSELLAS	BOOKLICE	BOORKAS	BOOZY

BOP	BORGHETTOS	BOSKIER	BOTCHIEST	BOUDOIRS
BOPPED	BORGO	BOSKIEST	BOTCHING	BOUFFANT
BOPPER	BORGOS	BOSKINESS	BOTCHINGS	BOUGE
BOPPERS	BORIC	BOSKINESSES	BOTCHY	BOUGED
BOPPING	BORIDE	BOSKS	BOTEL	BOUGES
BOPS	BORIDES	BOSKY	BOTELS	BOUGET
BOR	BORING	BOSOM	BOTFLIES	BOUGETS
BORA	BORINGLY	BOSOMED	BOTFLY	BOUGH
BORACHIO	BORINGS	BOSOMIER	BOTH	BOUGHPOT
BORACHIOS	BORN	BOSOMIEST	BOTHAN	BOUGHPOTS
BORACIC	BORNE	BOSOMING	BOTHANS	BOUGHS
BORACITE	BORNITE	BOSOMS	BOTHER	BOUGHT
BORACITES	BORNITES	BOSOMY	BOTHERED	BOUGHTEN
BORAGE	BORON	BOSON	BOTHERING	BOUGHTS
BORAGES	BORONIA	BOSONS	BOTHERS	BOUGIE
BORAK	BORONIAS	BOSQUET	BOTHIE	BOUGIES
BORAKS	BORONS	BOSQUETS	BOTHIES	BOUGING
BORANE	BOROUGH	BOSS	BOTHOLE	BOUILLI
BORANES	BOROUGHS	BOSSED	BOTHOLES	BOUILLIS
BORAS	BORREL	BOSSER	BOTHY	BOUILLON
BORATE	BORRELL	BOSSES	BOTHYMAN	BOUILLONS
BORATES	BORROW	BOSSEST	BOTHYMEN	BOUK
BORAX	BORROWED	BOSSIER	BOTONE	BOUKS
BORAXES	BORROWER	BOSSIEST	BOTRYOID	BOULDER
BORAZON	BORROWERS	BOSSILY	BOTRYOSE	BOULDERS
BORAZONS	BORROWING	BOSSINESS	BOTS	BOULE
BORD	BORROWINGS	BOSSINESSES	BOTT	BOULES
BORDAR	BORROWS	BOSSING	BOTTE	BOULEVARD
BORDARS	BORS	BOSSY	BOTTED	BOULEVARDS
BORDE	BORSCH	BOSTANGI	BOTTEGA	BOULLE
BORDEL	BORSCHES	BOSTANGIS	BOTTEGAS	BOULLES
BORDELLO	BORSCHT	BOSTON	BOTTES	BOULT
BORDELLOS	BORSCHTS	BOSTONS	BOTTIES	BOULTED
BORDELS	BORSTAL	BOSTRYX	BOTTINE	BOULTER
BORDER	BORSTALL	BOSTRYXES	BOTTINES	BOULTERS
BORDEREAU	BORSTALLS	BOSUN	BOTTING	BOULTING
BORDEREAUX	BORSTALS	BOSUNS	BOTTLE	BOULTINGS
BORDERED	BORT	BOT	BOTTLED	BOULTS
BORDERER	BORTS	BOTANIC	BOTTLEFUL	BOUN
BORDERERS	BORTSCH	BOTANICAL	BOTTLEFULS	BOUNCE
BORDERING	BORTSCHES	BOTANICALS	BOTTLER	BOUNCED
BORDERS	BORZOI	BOTANIES	BOTTLERS	BOUNCER
BORDES	BORZOIS	BOTANISE	BOTTLES	BOUNCERS
BORDS	BOS	BOTANISED	BOTTLING	BOUNCES
BORDURE	BOSBOK	BOTANISES	BOTTOM	BOUNCIER
BORDURES	BOSBOKS	BOTANISING	BOTTOMED	BOUNCIEST
BORE	BOSCAGE	BOTANIST	BOTTOMING	BOUNCILY
BOREAL	BOSCAGES	BOTANISTS	BOTTOMRIES	BOUNCING
BORECOLE	BOSCHBOK	BOTANIZE	BOTTOMRY	BOUNCY
BORECOLES	BOSCHBOKS	BOTANIZED	BOTTOMS	BOUND
BORED	BOSCHE	BOTANIZES	BOTTONY	BOUNDARIES
BOREDOM	BOSCHES	BOTANIZING	BOTTS	BOUNDARY
BOREDOMS	BOSCHVELD	BOTANY	BOTTY	BOUNDED
BOREE	BOSCHVELDS	BOTARGO	BOTULISM	BOUNDEN
BOREEN	BOSH	BOTARGOES	BOTULISMS	BOUNDER
BOREENS	BOSHES	BOTARGOS	BOUCHE	BOUNDERS
BOREES	BOSHTA	BOTCH	BOUCHEE	BOUNDING
BOREHOLE	BOSHTER	BOTCHED	BOUCHEES	BOUNDLESS
BOREHOLES	BOSK	BOTCHER	BOUCHES	BOUNDS
BOREL	BOSKAGE	BOTCHERIES	BOUCLE	BOUNED
BORER	BOSKAGES	BOTCHERS	BOUCLES	BOUNING
BORERS	BOSKER	BOTCHERY	BOUDERIE	BOUNS
BORES	BOSKET	BOTCHES	BOUDERIES	BOUNTEOUS
BORGHETTO	BOSKETS	BOTCHIER	BOUDOIR	BOUNTIES

The Chambers Dictionary is the authority for many longer words; see *OSW* Introduction, page xii

BOUNTIFUL	BOVIDS	BOWSHOTS	BOYOS	BRAGS
BOUNTREE	BOVINE	BOWSING	BOYS	BRAID
BOUNTREES	BOVINELY	BOWSPRIT	BOZO	BRAIDE
BOUNTY	BOVINES	BOWSPRITS	BOZOS	BRAIDED
BOUNTYHED	BOVVER	BOWSTRING	BOZZETTI	BRAIDER
BOUNTYHEDS	BOVVERS	BOWSTRINGED	BOZZETTO	BRAIDEST
BOUQUET	BOW	BOWSTRINGING	BRA	BRAIDING
BOUQUETS	BOWAT	BOWSTRINGS	BRABBLE	BRAIDINGS
BOURASQUE	BOWATS	BOWSTRUNG	BRABBLED	BRAIDS
BOURASQUES	BOWBENT	BOWWOW	BRABBLES	BRAIL
BOURBON	BOWED	BOWWOWS	BRABBLING	BRAILED
BOURBONS	BOWEL	BOWYANG	BRACCATE	BRAILING
BOURD	BOWELLED	BOWYANGS	BRACCIA	BRAILLER
BOURDER	BOWELLING	BOWYER	BRACCIO	BRAILLERS
BOURDERS	BOWELS	BOWYERS	BRACE	BRAILS
BOURDON	BOWER	BOX	BRACED	BRAIN
BOURDONS	BOWERED	BOXCAR	BRACELET	BRAINBOX
BOURDS	BOWERIES	BOXCARS	BRACELETS	BRAINBOXES
BOURG	BOWERING	BOXED	BRACER	BRAINCASE
BOURGEOIS	BOWERS	BOXEN	BRACERS	BRAINCASES
BOURGEOISES	BOWERY	BOXER	BRACES	BRAINED
BOURGEON	BOWES	BOXERCISE	BRACH	BRAINIER
BOURGEONED	BOWET	BOXERCISES	BRACHES	BRAINIEST
BOURGEONING	BOWETS	BOXERS	BRACHET	BRAINING
BOURGEONS	BOWFIN	BOXES	BRACHETS	BRAINISH
BOURGS	BOWFINS	BOXFUL	BRACHIA	BRAINLESS
BOURKHA	BOWGET	BOXFULS	BRACHIAL	BRAINPAN
BOURKHAS	BOWGETS	BOXIER	BRACHIATE	BRAINPANS
BOURLAW	BOWHEAD	BOXIEST	BRACHIATED	BRAINS
BOURLAWS	BOWHEADS	BOXINESS	BRACHIATES	BRAINSICK
BOURN	BOWING	BOXINESSES	BRACHIATING	BRAINWASH
BOURNE	BOWINGS	BOXING	BRACHIUM	BRAINWASHED
BOURNES	BOWKNOT	BOXINGS	BRACING	BRAINWASHES
BOURNS	BOWKNOTS	BOXKEEPER	BRACK	BRAINWASHING
BOURREE	BOWL	BOXKEEPERS	BRACKEN	BRAINWASHINGS
BOURREES	BOWLDER	BOXROOM	BRACKENS	BRAINY
BOURSE	BOWLDERS	BOXROOMS	BRACKET	BRAIRD
BOURSES	BOWLED	BOXWALLAH	BRACKETED	BRAIRDED
BOURSIER	BOWLER	BOXWALLAHS	BRACKETING	BRAIRDING
BOURSIERS	BOWLERS	BOXWOOD	BRACKETS	BRAIRDS
BOURTREE	BOWLFUL	BOXWOODS	BRACKISH	BRAISE
BOURTREES	BOWLFULS	BOXY	BRACKS	BRAISED
BOUSE	BOWLINE	BOY	BRACT	BRAISES
BOUSED	BOWLINES	BOYAR	BRACTEAL	BRAISING
BOUSES	BOWLING	BOYARS	BRACTEATE	BRAIZE
BOUSIER	BOWLINGS	BOYAU	BRACTEATES	BRAIZES
BOUSIEST	BOWLS	BOYAUX	BRACTEOLE	BRAKE
BOUSING	BOWMAN	BOYCOTT	BRACTEOLES	BRAKED
BOUSY	BOWMEN	BOYCOTTED	BRACTLESS	BRAKELESS
BOUT	BOWNE	BOYCOTTER	BRACTLET	BRAKEMAN
BOUTADE	BOWNED	BOYCOTTERS	BRACTLETS	BRAKEMEN
BOUTADES	BOWNES	BOYCOTTING	BRACTS	BRAKES
BOUTIQUE	BOWNING	BOYCOTTS	BRAD	BRAKIER
BOUTIQUES	BOWPOT	BOYED	BRADAWL	BRAKIEST
BOUTON	BOWPOTS	BOYFRIEND	BRADAWLS	BRAKING
BOUTONNE	BOWR	BOYFRIENDS	BRADS	BRAKY
BOUTONNEE	BOWRS	BOYG	BRAE	BRALESS
BOUTONS	BOWS	BOYGS	BRAES	BRAMBLE
BOUTS	BOWSE	BOYHOOD	BRAG	BRAMBLED
BOUZOUKI	BOWSED	BOYHOODS	BRAGGART	BRAMBLES
BOUZOUKIS	BOWSER	BOYING	BRAGGARTS	BRAMBLIER
BOVATE	BOWSERS	BOYISH	BRAGGED	BRAMBLIEST
BOVATES	BOWSES	BOYISHLY	BRAGGING	BRAMBLING
BOVID	BOWSHOT	BOYO	BRAGLY	BRAMBLINGS

The Chambers Dictionary is the authority for many longer words; see *OSW* Introduction, page xii

BRAMBLY	BRANSLE	BRATTLING	BRAZENED	BREARE
BRAME	BRANSLES	BRATTLINGS	BRAZENING	BREARES
BRAMES	BRANTLE	BRATTY	BRAZENLY	BREASKIT
BRAN	BRANTLES	BRATWURST	BRAZENRIES	BREASKITS
BRANCARD	BRAS	BRATWURSTS	BRAZENRY	BREAST
BRANCARDS	BRASERO	BRAUNCH	BRAZENS	BREASTED
BRANCH	BRASEROS	BRAUNCHED	BRAZES	BREASTING
BRANCHED	BRASES	BRAUNCHES	BRAZIER	BREASTPIN
BRANCHER	BRASH	BRAUNCHING	BRAZIERS	BREASTPINS
BRANCHERIES	BRASHED	BRAUNITE	BRAZIL	BREASTS
BRANCHERS	BRASHER	BRAUNITES	BRAZILEIN	BREATH
BRANCHERY	BRASHES	BRAVA	BRAZILEINS	BREATHE
BRANCHES	BRASHEST	BRAVADO	BRAZILIN	BREATHED
BRANCHIA	BRASHIER	BRAVADOED	BRAZILINS	BREATHER
BRANCHIAE	BRASHIEST	BRAVADOES	BRAZILS	BREATHERS
BRANCHIAL	BRASHING	BRAVADOING	BRAZING	BREATHES
BRANCHIER	BRASHY	BRAVADOS	BREACH	BREATHFUL
BRANCHIEST	BRASIER	BRAVE	BREACHED	BREATHIER
BRANCHING	BRASIERS	BRAVED	BREACHES	BREATHIEST
BRANCHINGS	BRASS	BRAVELY	BREACHING	BREATHILY
BRANCHLET	BRASSARD	BRAVER	BREAD	BREATHING
BRANCHLETS	BRASSARDS	BRAVERIES	BREADED	BREATHINGS
BRANCHY	BRASSART	BRAVERY	BREADHEAD	BREATHS
BRAND	BRASSARTS	BRAVES	BREADHEADS	BREATHY
BRANDADE	BRASSERIE	BRAVEST	BREADING	BRECCIA
BRANDADES	BRASSERIES	BRAVI	BREADLINE	BRECCIAS
BRANDED	BRASSES	BRAVING	BREADLINES	BRECHAM
BRANDER	BRASSET	BRAVO	BREADNUT	BRECHAMS
BRANDERED	BRASSETS	BRAVOES	BREADNUTS	BRED
BRANDERING	BRASSICA	BRAVOS	BREADROOM	BREDE
BRANDERS	BRASSICAS	BRAVURA	BREADROOMS	BREDED
BRANDIED	BRASSIE	BRAVURAS	BREADROOT	BREDES
BRANDIES	BRASSIER	BRAW	BREADROOTS	BREDING
BRANDING	BRASSIERE	BRAWER	BREADS	BREE
BRANDISE	BRASSIERES	BRAWEST	BREADTH	BREECH
BRANDISES	BRASSIES	BRAWL	BREADTHS	BREECHED
BRANDISH	BRASSIEST	BRAWLED	BREAK	BREECHES
BRANDISHED	BRASSILY	BRAWLER	BREAKABLE	BREECHING
BRANDISHES	BRASSY	BRAWLERS	BREAKABLES	BREECHINGS
BRANDISHING	BRAST	BRAWLIER	BREAKAGE	BREED
BRANDLING	BRASTING	BRAWLIEST	BREAKAGES	BREEDER
BRANDLINGS	BRASTS	BRAWLING	BREAKAWAY	BREEDERS
BRANDRETH	BRAT	BRAWLINGS	BREAKAWAYS	BREEDING
BRANDRETHS	BRATCHET	BRAWLS	BREAKBACK	BREEDINGS
BRANDS	BRATCHETS	BRAWLY	BREAKBEAT	BREEDS
BRANDY	BRATLING	BRAWN	BREAKBEATS	BREEKS
BRANGLE	BRATLINGS	BRAWNED	BREAKDOWN	BREEM
BRANGLED	BRATPACK	BRAWNIER	BREAKDOWNS	BREER
BRANGLES	BRATS	BRAWNIEST	BREAKER	BREERED
BRANGLING	BRATTICE	BRAWNS	BREAKERS	BREERING
BRANGLINGS	BRATTICED	BRAWNY	BREAKFAST	BREERS
BRANK	BRATTICES	BRAWS	BREAKFASTED	BREES
BRANKED	BRATTICING	BRAXIES	BREAKFASTING	BREESE
BRANKIER	BRATTICINGS	BRAXY	BREAKFASTS	BREESES
BRANKIEST	BRATTIER	BRAY	BREAKING	BREEZE
BRANKING	BRATTIEST	BRAYED	BREAKINGS	BREEZED
BRANKS	BRATTISH	BRAYER	BREAKNECK	BREEZES
BRANKY	BRATTISHED	BRAYERS	BREAKS	BREEZEWAY
BRANLE	BRATTISHES	BRAYING	BREAKTIME	BREEZEWAYS
BRANLES	BRATTISHING	BRAYS	BREAKTIMES	BREEZIER
BRANNIER	BRATTISHINGS	BRAZE	BREAM	BREEZIEST
BRANNIEST	BRATTLE	BRAZED	BREAMED	BREEZILY
BRANNY	BRATTLED	BRAZELESS	BREAMING	BREEZING
BRANS	BRATTLES	BRAZEN	BREAMS	BREEZY

The Chambers Dictionary is the authority for many longer words; see *OSW* Introduction, page xii

BREGMA
BREGMATA
BREGMATIC
BREHON
BREHONS
BRELOQUE
BRELOQUES
BREME
BREN
BRENNE
BRENNES
BRENNING
BRENS
BRENT
BRENTER
BRENTEST
BRER
BRERE
BRERES
BRERS
BRETASCHE
BRETASCHES
BRETESSE
BRETESSES
BRETHREN
BRETON
BRETONS
BRETTICE
BRETTICED
BRETTICES
BRETTICING
BREVE
BREVES
BREVET
BREVETE
BREVETED
BREVETING
BREVETS
BREVETTED
BREVETTING
BREVIARIES
BREVIARY
BREVIATE
BREVIATES
BREVIER
BREVIERS
BREVITIES
BREVITY
BREW
BREWAGE
BREWAGES
BREWED
BREWER
BREWERIES
BREWERS
BREWERY
BREWING
BREWINGS
BREWIS
BREWISES
BREWPUB
BREWPUBS
BREWS
BREWSTER

BREWSTERS
BRIAR
BRIARED
BRIARS
BRIBE
BRIBED
BRIBER
BRIBERIES
BRIBERS
BRIBERY
BRIBES
BRIBING
BRICABRAC
BRICABRACS
BRICK
BRICKBAT
BRICKBATS
BRICKCLAY
BRICKCLAYS
BRICKED
BRICKEN
BRICKIE
BRICKIER
BRICKIES
BRICKIEST
BRICKING
BRICKINGS
BRICKLE
BRICKS
BRICKWALL
BRICKWALLS
BRICKWORK
BRICKWORKS
BRICKY
BRICKYARD
BRICKYARDS
BRICOLE
BRICOLES
BRIDAL
BRIDALS
BRIDE
BRIDECAKE
BRIDECAKES
BRIDED
BRIDEMAID
BRIDEMAIDS
BRIDEMAN
BRIDEMEN
BRIDES
BRIDESMAN
BRIDESMEN
BRIDEWELL
BRIDEWELLS
BRIDGABLE
BRIDGE
BRIDGED
BRIDGES
BRIDGING
BRIDGINGS
BRIDIE
BRIDIES
BRIDING
BRIDLE
BRIDLED

BRIDLER
BRIDLERS
BRIDLES
BRIDLING
BRIDOON
BRIDOONS
BRIEF
BRIEFCASE
BRIEFCASES
BRIEFED
BRIEFER
BRIEFEST
BRIEFING
BRIEFINGS
BRIEFLESS
BRIEFLY
BRIEFNESS
BRIEFNESSES
BRIEFS
BRIER
BRIERED
BRIERIER
BRIERIEST
BRIERS
BRIERY
BRIG
BRIGADE
BRIGADED
BRIGADES
BRIGADIER
BRIGADIERS
BRIGADING
BRIGALOW
BRIGALOWS
BRIGAND
BRIGANDRIES
BRIGANDRY
BRIGANDS
BRIGHT
BRIGHTEN
BRIGHTENED
BRIGHTENING
BRIGHTENS
BRIGHTER
BRIGHTEST
BRIGHTLY
BRIGS
BRIGUE
BRIGUED
BRIGUES
BRIGUING
BRIGUINGS
BRILL
BRILLER
BRILLEST
BRILLIANT
BRILLIANTED
BRILLIANTING
BRILLIANTS
BRILLS
BRIM
BRIMFUL
BRIMING
BRIMINGS

BRIMLESS
BRIMMED
BRIMMER
BRIMMERS
BRIMMING
BRIMS
BRIMSTONE
BRIMSTONES
BRIMSTONY
BRINDED
BRINDISI
BRINDISIS
BRINDLE
BRINDLED
BRINDLES
BRINE
BRINED
BRINES
BRING
BRINGER
BRINGERS
BRINGING
BRINGINGS
BRINGS
BRINIER
BRINIEST
BRININESS
BRININESSES
BRINING
BRINISH
BRINJAL
BRINJALS
BRINJARRIES
BRINJARRY
BRINK
BRINKMAN
BRINKMEN
BRINKS
BRINY
BRIO
BRIOCHE
BRIOCHES
BRIONIES
BRIONY
BRIOS
BRIQUET
BRIQUETS
BRIQUETTE
BRIQUETTED
BRIQUETTES
BRIQUETTING
BRISE
BRISES
BRISK
BRISKED
BRISKEN
BRISKENED
BRISKENING
BRISKENS
BRISKER
BRISKEST
BRISKET
BRISKETS
BRISKING

BRISKISH
BRISKLY
BRISKNESS
BRISKNESSES
BRISKS
BRISKY
BRISLING
BRISLINGS
BRISTLE
BRISTLED
BRISTLES
BRISTLIER
BRISTLIEST
BRISTLING
BRISTLY
BRISTOLS
BRISURE
BRISURES
BRIT
BRITCHES
BRITS
BRITSCHKA
BRITSCHKAS
BRITSKA
BRITSKAS
BRITTLE
BRITTLELY
BRITTLER
BRITTLES
BRITTLEST
BRITTLY
BRITZKA
BRITZKAS
BRITZSKA
BRITZSKAS
BRIZE
BRIZES
BRO
BROACH
BROACHED
BROACHER
BROACHERS
BROACHES
BROACHING
BROAD
BROADBAND
BROADBILL
BROADBILLS
BROADCAST
BROADCASTED
BROADCASTING
BROADCASTINGS
BROADCASTS
BROADEN
BROADENED
BROADENING
BROADENS
BROADER
BROADEST
BROADISH
BROADLOOM
BROADLY
BROADNESS
BROADNESSES

BROADS	BROIDERERS	BRONCOS	BROS	BRUCITES
BROADSIDE	BROIDERIES	BROND	BROSE	BRUCKLE
BROADSIDES	BROIDERING	BRONDS	BROSES	BRUHAHA
BROADTAIL	BROIDERINGS	BRONDYRON	BROTH	BRUHAHAS
BROADTAILS	BROIDERS	BRONDYRONS	BROTHEL	BRUILZIE
BROADWAY	BROIDERY	BRONZE	BROTHELS	BRUILZIES
BROADWAYS	BROIL	BRONZED	BROTHER	BRUISE
BROADWISE	BROILED	BRONZEN	BROTHERLY	BRUISED
BROCADE	BROILER	BRONZER	BROTHERS	BRUISER
BROCADED	BROILERS	BRONZERS	BROTHS	BRUISERS
BROCADES	BROILING	BRONZES	BROUGH	BRUISES
BROCAGE	BROILS	BRONZIER	BROUGHAM	BRUISING
BROCAGES	BROKAGE	BRONZIEST	BROUGHAMS	BRUISINGS
BROCARD	BROKAGES	BRONZIFIED	BROUGHS	BRUIT
BROCARDS	BROKE	BRONZIFIES	BROUGHT	BRUITED
BROCATEL	BROKED	BRONZIFY	BROUHAHA	BRUITING
BROCATELS	BROKEN	BRONZIFYING	BROUHAHAS	BRUITS
BROCCOLI	BROKENLY	BRONZING	BROUZE	BRULE
BROCCOLIS	BROKER	BRONZINGS	BROUZES	BRULYIE
BROCH	BROKERAGE	BRONZITE	BROW	BRULYIES
BROCHAN	BROKERAGES	BRONZITES	BROWBAND	BRULZIE
BROCHANS	BROKERED	BRONZY	BROWBANDS	BRULZIES
BROCHE	BROKERIES	BROO	BROWBEAT	BRUMAL
BROCHED	BROKERING	BROOCH	BROWBEATEN	BRUMBIES
BROCHES	BROKERS	BROOCHED	BROWBEATING	BRUMBY
BROCHETTE	BROKERY	BROOCHES	BROWBEATINGS	BRUME
BROCHETTES	BROKES	BROOCHING	BROWBEATS	BRUMES
BROCHING	BROKING	BROOD	BROWLESS	BRUMMAGEM
BROCHS	BROKINGS	BROODED	BROWN	BRUMMAGEMS
BROCHURE	BROLGA	BROODER	BROWNED	BRUMMER
BROCHURES	BROLGAS	BROODERS	BROWNER	BRUMMERS
BROCK	BROLLIES	BROODIER	BROWNEST	BRUMOUS
BROCKAGE	BROLLY	BROODIEST	BROWNIE	BRUNCH
BROCKAGES	BROMATE	BROODING	BROWNIER	BRUNCHES
BROCKED	BROMATES	BROODS	BROWNIES	BRUNET
BROCKET	BROMELAIN	BROODY	BROWNIEST	BRUNETS
BROCKETS	BROMELAINS	BROOK	BROWNING	BRUNETTE
BROCKIT	BROMELIA	BROOKED	BROWNINGS	BRUNETTES
BROCKRAM	BROMELIAD	BROOKING	BROWNISH	BRUNT
BROCKRAMS	BROMELIADS	BROOKITE	BROWNNESS	BRUNTED
BROCKS	BROMELIAS	BROOKITES	BROWNNESSES	BRUNTING
BROD	BROMELIN	BROOKLET	BROWNOUT	BRUNTS
BRODDED	BROMELINS	BROOKLETS	BROWNOUTS	BRUSH
BRODDING	BROMIC	BROOKLIME	BROWNS	BRUSHED
BRODEKIN	BROMIDE	BROOKLIMES	BROWNY	BRUSHER
BRODEKINS	BROMIDES	BROOKS	BROWS	BRUSHERS
BRODKIN	BROMIDIC	BROOKWEED	BROWSE	BRUSHES
BRODKINS	BROMINE	BROOKWEEDS	BROWSED	BRUSHIER
BRODS	BROMINES	BROOL	BROWSER	BRUSHIEST
BROG	BROMINISM	BROOLS	BROWSERS	BRUSHING
BROGAN	BROMINISMS	BROOM	BROWSES	BRUSHINGS
BROGANS	BROMISM	BROOMBALL	BROWSIER	BRUSHWOOD
BROGGED	BROMISMS	BROOMBALLS	BROWSIEST	BRUSHWOODS
BROGGING	BROMMER	BROOMED	BROWSING	BRUSHWORK
BROGH	BROMMERS	BROOMIER	BROWSINGS	BRUSHWORKS
BROGHS	BROMOFORM	BROOMIEST	BROWST	BRUSHY
BROGS	BROMOFORMS	BROOMING	BROWSTS	BRUSQUE
BROGUE	BRONCHI	BROOMRAPE	BROWSY	BRUSQUELY
BROGUEISH	BRONCHIA	BROOMRAPES	BRRR	BRUSQUER
BROGUES	BRONCHIAL	BROOMS	BRUCHID	BRUSQUEST
BROGUISH	BRONCHO	BROOMY	BRUCHIDS	BRUST
BROIDER	BRONCHOS	BROOS	BRUCINE	BRUSTING
BROIDERED	BRONCHUS	BROOSE	BRUCINES	BRUSTS
BROIDERER	BRONCO	BROOSES	BRUCITE	BRUT

BRUTAL	BUBO	BUCKO	BUDGETED	BUGGINS
BRUTALISE	BUBOES	BUCKOES	BUDGETING	BUGGY
BRUTALISED	BUBONIC	BUCKRA	BUDGETS	BUGHOUSE
BRUTALISES	BUBS	BUCKRAKE	BUDGIE	BUGHOUSES
BRUTALISING	BUBUKLE	BUCKRAKES	BUDGIES	BUGLE
BRUTALISM	BUBUKLES	BUCKRAM	BUDGING	BUGLED
BRUTALISMS	BUCCAL	BUCKRAMED	BUDLESS	BUGLER
BRUTALIST	BUCCANEER	BUCKRAMING	BUDMASH	BUGLERS
BRUTALISTS	BUCCANEERED	BUCKRAMS	BUDMASHES	BUGLES
BRUTALITIES	BUCCANEERING	BUCKRAS	BUDO	BUGLET
BRUTALITY	BUCCANEERINGS	BUCKS	BUDOS	BUGLETS
BRUTALIZE	BUCCANEERS	BUCKSAW	BUDS	BUGLING
BRUTALIZED	BUCCANIER	BUCKSAWS	BUDWORM	BUGLOSS
BRUTALIZES	BUCCANIERED	BUCKSHEE	BUDWORMS	BUGLOSSES
BRUTALIZING	BUCCANIERING	BUCKSHISH	BUFF	BUGONG
BRUTALLY	BUCCANIERS	BUCKSHISHED	BUFFA	BUGONGS
BRUTE	BUCCINA	BUCKSHISHES	BUFFALO	BUGS
BRUTED	BUCCINAS	BUCKSHISHING	BUFFALOED	BUGWORT
BRUTELIKE	BUCELLAS	BUCKSHOT	BUFFALOES	BUGWORTS
BRUTENESS	BUCELLASES	BUCKSHOTS	BUFFALOING	BUHL
BRUTENESSES	BUCHU	BUCKSKIN	BUFFE	BUHLS
BRUTER	BUCHUS	BUCKSKINS	BUFFED	BUHRSTONE
BRUTERS	BUCK	BUCKSOM	BUFFER	BUHRSTONES
BRUTES	BUCKAROO	BUCKTEETH	BUFFERED	BUIK
BRUTIFIED	BUCKAROOS	BUCKTHORN	BUFFERING	BUIKS
BRUTIFIES	BUCKAYRO	BUCKTHORNS	BUFFERS	BUILD
BRUTIFY	BUCKAYROS	BUCKTOOTH	BUFFET	BUILDED
BRUTIFYING	BUCKBEAN	BUCKU	BUFFETED	BUILDER
BRUTING	BUCKBEANS	BUCKUS	BUFFETING	BUILDERS
BRUTINGS	BUCKBOARD	BUCKWHEAT	BUFFETINGS	BUILDING
BRUTISH	BUCKBOARDS	BUCKWHEATS	BUFFETS	BUILDINGS
BRUTISHLY	BUCKED	BUCKYBALL	BUFFI	BUILDS
BRUXISM	BUCKEEN	BUCKYBALLS	BUFFING	BUILT
BRUXISMS	BUCKEENS	BUCOLIC	BUFFINGS	BUIRDLIER
BRYOLOGIES	BUCKER	BUCOLICAL	BUFFO	BUIRDLIEST
BRYOLOGY	BUCKEROO	BUCOLICS	BUFFOON	BUIRDLY
BRYONIES	BUCKEROOS	BUD	BUFFOONS	BUIST
BRYONY	BUCKERS	BUDDED	BUFFS	BUISTED
BRYOPHYTE	BUCKET	BUDDHA	BUFO	BUISTING
BRYOPHYTES	BUCKETED	BUDDHAS	BUFOS	BUISTS
BUAT	BUCKETFUL	BUDDIER	BUG	BUKE
BUATS	BUCKETFULS	BUDDIES	BUGABOO	BUKES
BUAZE	BUCKETING	BUDDIEST	BUGABOOS	BUKSHEE
BUAZES	BUCKETINGS	BUDDING	BUGBANE	BUKSHEES
BUB	BUCKETS	BUDDINGS	BUGBANES	BUKSHI
BUBA	BUCKHORN	BUDDLE	BUGBEAR	BUKSHIS
BUBAL	BUCKHORNS	BUDDLED	BUGBEARS	BULB
BUBALINE	BUCKHOUND	BUDDLEIA	BUGGAN	BULBAR
BUBALIS	BUCKHOUNDS	BUDDLEIAS	BUGGANE	BULBED
BUBALISES	BUCKIE	BUDDLES	BUGGANES	BULBEL
BUBALS	BUCKIES	BUDDLING	BUGGANS	BULBELS
BUBAS	BUCKING	BUDDY	BUGGED	BULBIL
BUBBIES	BUCKINGS	BUDGE	BUGGER	BULBILS
BUBBLE	BUCKISH	BUDGED	BUGGERED	BULBING
BUBBLED	BUCKISHLY	BUDGER	BUGGERIES	BULBOSITIES
BUBBLES	BUCKLE	BUDGEREE	BUGGERING	BULBOSITY
BUBBLIER	BUCKLED	BUDGERO	BUGGERS	BULBOUS
BUBBLIES	BUCKLER	BUDGEROS	BUGGERY	BULBOUSLY
BUBBLIEST	BUCKLERED	BUDGEROW	BUGGIER	BULBS
BUBBLING	BUCKLERING	BUDGEROWS	BUGGIES	BULBUL
BUBBLY	BUCKLERS	BUDGERS	BUGGIEST	BULBULS
BUBBY	BUCKLES	BUDGES	BUGGIN	BULGE
BUBINGA	BUCKLING	BUDGET	BUGGING	BULGED
BUBINGAS	BUCKLINGS	BUDGETARY	BUGGINGS	BULGER

BULGERS	BULLERING	BULWARKED	BUMPTIOUS	BUNGY
BULGES	BULLERS	BULWARKING	BUMPY	BUNIA
BULGHUR	BULLET	BULWARKS	BUMS	BUNIAS
BULGHURS	BULLETIN	BUM	BUMSUCKER	BUNION
BULGIER	BULLETINS	BUMALO	BUMSUCKERS	BUNIONS
BULGIEST	BULLETRIE	BUMALOTI	BUN	BUNJE
BULGINE	BULLETRIES	BUMALOTIS	BUNA	BUNJEE
BULGINES	BULLETS	BUMBAG	BUNAS	BUNJEES
BULGINESS	BULLFIGHT	BUMBAGS	BUNCE	BUNJES
BULGINESSES	BULLFIGHTS	BUMBAZE	BUNCED	BUNJIE
BULGING	BULLFINCH	BUMBAZED	BUNCES	BUNJIES
BULGINGLY	BULLFINCHES	BUMBAZES	BUNCH	BUNJY
BULGUR	BULLFROG	BUMBAZING	BUNCHED	BUNK
BULGURS	BULLFROGS	BUMBLE	BUNCHES	BUNKED
BULGY	BULLGINE	BUMBLED	BUNCHIER	BUNKER
BULIMIA	BULLGINES	BUMBLER	BUNCHIEST	BUNKERED
BULIMIAS	BULLHEAD	BUMBLERS	BUNCHING	BUNKERING
BULIMIC	BULLHEADS	BUMBLES	BUNCHINGS	BUNKERS
BULIMICS	BULLIED	BUMBLING	BUNCHY	BUNKHOUSE
BULIMIES	BULLIER	BUMBLINGS	BUNCING	BUNKHOUSES
BULIMUS	BULLIES	BUMBO	BUNCO	BUNKING
BULIMUSES	BULLIEST	BUMBOS	BUNCOED	BUNKO
BULIMY	BULLING	BUMF	BUNCOING	BUNKOED
BULK	BULLINGS	BUMFS	BUNCOMBE	BUNKOING
BULKED	BULLION	BUMKIN	BUNCOMBES	BUNKOS
BULKER	BULLIONS	BUMKINS	BUNCOS	BUNKS
BULKERS	BULLISH	BUMMALO	BUND	BUNKUM
BULKHEAD	BULLISHLY	BUMMALOTI	BUNDED	BUNKUMS
BULKHEADS	BULLNOSE	BUMMALOTIS	BUNDING	BUNNIA
BULKIER	BULLNOSES	BUMMAREE	BUNDLE	BUNNIAS
BULKIEST	BULLOCK	BUMMAREES	BUNDLED	BUNNIES
BULKILY	BULLOCKED	BUMMED	BUNDLES	BUNNY
BULKINESS	BULLOCKIES	BUMMEL	BUNDLING	BUNODONT
BULKINESSES	BULLOCKING	BUMMELS	BUNDLINGS	BUNRAKU
BULKING	BULLOCKS	BUMMER	BUNDOBUST	BUNRAKUS
BULKS	BULLOCKY	BUMMERS	BUNDOBUSTS	BUNS
BULKY	BULLS	BUMMEST	BUNDOOK	BUNSEN
BULL	BULLSHIT	BUMMING	BUNDOOKS	BUNSENS
BULLA	BULLSHITS	BUMMLE	BUNDS	BUNT
BULLACE	BULLSHITTED	BUMMLED	BUNDU	BUNTAL
BULLACES	BULLSHITTING	BUMMLES	BUNDUS	BUNTALS
BULLAE	BULLSHITTINGS	BUMMLING	BUNG	BUNTED
BULLARIES	BULLWHACK	BUMMOCK	BUNGALOID	BUNTER
BULLARY	BULLWHACKED	BUMMOCKS	BUNGALOIDS	BUNTERS
BULLATE	BULLWHACKING	BUMP	BUNGALOW	BUNTIER
BULLBAR	BULLWHACKS	BUMPED	BUNGALOWS	BUNTIEST
BULLBARS	BULLWHIP	BUMPER	BUNGED	BUNTING
BULLBAT	BULLWHIPPED	BUMPERED	BUNGEE	BUNTINGS
BULLBATS	BULLWHIPPING	BUMPERING	BUNGEES	BUNTLINE
BULLDOG	BULLWHIPS	BUMPERS	BUNGEY	BUNTLINES
BULLDOGGED	BULLY	BUMPH	BUNGEYS	BUNTS
BULLDOGGING	BULLYING	BUMPHS	BUNGHOLE	BUNTY
BULLDOGS	BULLYISM	BUMPIER	BUNGHOLES	BUNYA
BULLDOZE	BULLYISMS	BUMPIEST	BUNGIE	BUNYAS
BULLDOZED	BULLYRAG	BUMPILY	BUNGIES	BUNYIP
BULLDOZER	BULLYRAGGED	BUMPINESS	BUNGING	BUNYIPS
BULLDOZERS	BULLYRAGGING	BUMPINESSES	BUNGLE	BUONAMANI
BULLDOZES	BULLYRAGS	BUMPING	BUNGLED	BUONAMANO
BULLDOZING	BULRUSH	BUMPINGS	BUNGLER	BUOY
BULLDUST	BULRUSHES	BUMPKIN	BUNGLERS	BUOYAGE
BULLDUSTS	BULRUSHY	BUMPKINS	BUNGLES	BUOYAGES
BULLED	BULSE	BUMPOLOGIES	BUNGLING	BUOYANCE
BULLER	BULSES	BUMPOLOGY	BUNGLINGS	BUOYANCES
BULLERED	BULWARK	BUMPS	BUNGS	BUOYANCIES

The Chambers Dictionary is the authority for many longer words; see *OSW* Introduction, page xii

BUOYANCY	BURGHULS	BURNERS	BURSIFORM	BUSHWHACKED
BUOYANT	BURGLAR	BURNET	BURSITIS	BUSHWHACKING
BUOYED	BURGLARED	BURNETS	BURSITISES	BUSHWHACKINGS
BUOYING	BURGLARIES	BURNING	BURST	BUSHWHACKS
BUOYS	BURGLARING	BURNINGLY	BURSTED	BUSHWOMAN
BUPLEVER	BURGLARS	BURNINGS	BURSTEN	BUSHWOMEN
BUPLEVERS	BURGLARY	BURNISH	BURSTER	BUSHY
BUPPIES	BURGLE	BURNISHED	BURSTERS	BUSIED
BUPPY	BURGLED	BURNISHER	BURSTING	BUSIER
BUPRESTID	BURGLES	BURNISHERS	BURSTS	BUSIES
BUPRESTIDS	BURGLING	BURNISHES	BURTHEN	BUSIEST
BUR	BURGONET	BURNISHING	BURTHENED	BUSILY
BURAN	BURGONETS	BURNISHINGS	BURTHENING	BUSINESS
BURANS	BURGOO	BURNOUS	BURTHENS	BUSINESSES
BURBLE	BURGOOS	BURNOUSE	BURTON	BUSING
BURBLED	BURGRAVE	BURNOUSES	BURTONS	BUSINGS
BURBLER	BURGRAVES	BURNS	BURWEED	BUSK
BURBLERS	BURGS	BURNSIDE	BURWEEDS	BUSKED
BURBLES	BURGUNDIES	BURNSIDES	BURY	BUSKER
BURBLING	BURGUNDY	BURNT	BURYING	BUSKERS
BURBLINGS	BURHEL	BUROO	BUS	BUSKET
BURBOT	BURHELS	BUROOS	BUSBIES	BUSKETS
BURBOTS	BURIAL	BURP	BUSBOY	BUSKIN
BURD	BURIALS	BURPED	BUSBOYS	BUSKINED
BURDASH	BURIED	BURPING	BUSBY	BUSKING
BURDASHES	BURIES	BURPS	BUSED	BUSKINGS
BURDEN	BURIN	BURQA	BUSES	BUSKINS
BURDENED	BURINIST	BURQAS	BUSGIRL	BUSKS
BURDENING	BURINISTS	BURR	BUSGIRLS	BUSKY
BURDENOUS	BURINS	BURRAWANG	BUSH	BUSMAN
BURDENS	BURITI	BURRAWANGS	BUSHCRAFT	BUSMEN
BURDIE	BURITIS	BURRED	BUSHCRAFTS	BUSS
BURDIES	BURK	BURREL	BUSHED	BUSSED
BURDOCK	BURKA	BURRELL	BUSHEL	BUSSES
BURDOCKS	BURKAS	BURRELLS	BUSHELLED	BUSSING
BURDS	BURKE	BURRELS	BUSHELLER	BUSSINGS
BUREAU	BURKED	BURRHEL	BUSHELLERS	BUSSU
BUREAUS	BURKES	BURRHELS	BUSHELLING	BUSSUS
BUREAUX	BURKING	BURRIER	BUSHELLINGS	BUST
BURET	BURKS	BURRIEST	BUSHELMAN	BUSTARD
BURETS	BURL	BURRING	BUSHELMEN	BUSTARDS
BURETTE	BURLAP	BURRITO	BUSHELS	BUSTED
BURETTES	BURLAPS	BURRITOS	BUSHES	BUSTEE
BURG	BURLED	BURRO	BUSHFIRE	BUSTEES
BURGAGE	BURLER	BURROS	BUSHFIRES	BUSTER
BURGAGES	BURLERS	BURROW	BUSHIDO	BUSTERS
BURGANET	BURLESQUE	BURROWED	BUSHIDOS	BUSTIER
BURGANETS	BURLESQUED	BURROWING	BUSHIER	BUSTIERS
BURGEE	BURLESQUES	BURROWS	BUSHIES	BUSTIEST
BURGEES	BURLESQUING	BURRS	BUSHIEST	BUSTING
BURGEON	BURLETTA	BURRSTONE	BUSHINESS	BUSTINGS
BURGEONED	BURLETTAS	BURRSTONES	BUSHINESSES	BUSTLE
BURGEONING	BURLEY	BURRY	BUSHING	BUSTLED
BURGEONS	BURLEYS	BURS	BUSHINGS	BUSTLER
BURGER	BURLIER	BURSA	BUSHMAN	BUSTLERS
BURGERS	BURLIEST	BURSAE	BUSHMEN	BUSTLES
BURGESS	BURLINESS	BURSAL	BUSHVELD	BUSTLING
BURGESSES	BURLINESSES	BURSAR	BUSHVELDS	BUSTS
BURGH	BURLING	BURSARIAL	BUSHWALK	BUSTY
BURGHAL	BURLS	BURSARIES	BUSHWALKED	BUSY
BURGHER	BURLY	BURSARS	BUSHWALKING	BUSYBODIED
BURGHERS	BURN	BURSARY	BUSHWALKINGS	BUSYBODIES
BURGHS	BURNED	BURSE	BUSHWALKS	BUSYBODY
BURGHUL	BURNER	BURSES	BUSHWHACK	BUSYBODYING

BUSYING	BUTTE	BUTTRESSING	BUZZWORDS	BYREMEN
BUSYNESS	BUTTED	BUTTS	BUZZY	BYRES
BUSYNESSES	BUTTER	BUTTY	BWANA	BYREWOMAN
BUT	BUTTERBUR	BUTTYMAN	BWANAS	BYREWOMEN
BUTADIENE	BUTTERBURS	BUTTYMEN	BWAZI	BYRLADY
BUTADIENES	BUTTERCUP	BUTYL	BWAZIS	BYRLAKIN
BUTANE	BUTTERCUPS	BUTYLENE	BY	BYRLAW
BUTANES	BUTTERED	BUTYLENES	BYCATCH	BYRLAWS
BUTANOL	BUTTERFLIES	BUTYLS	BYCATCHES	BYRNIE
BUTANOLS	BUTTERFLY	BUTYRATE	BYCOKET	BYRNIES
BUTCH	BUTTERIER	BUTYRATES	BYCOKETS	BYROAD
BUTCHER	BUTTERIES	BUTYRIC	BYE	BYROADS
BUTCHERED	BUTTERIEST	BUVETTE	BYES	BYROOM
BUTCHERIES	BUTTERINE	BUVETTES	BYGONE	BYROOMS
BUTCHERING	BUTTERINES	BUXOM	BYGONES	BYS
BUTCHERINGS	BUTTERING	BUXOMER	BYKE	BYSSAL
BUTCHERLY	BUTTERNUT	BUXOMEST	BYKED	BYSSI
BUTCHERS	BUTTERNUTS	BUXOMNESS	BYKES	BYSSINE
BUTCHERY	BUTTERS	BUXOMNESSES	BYKING	BYSSOID
BUTCHES	BUTTERY	BUY	BYLANDER	BYSSUS
BUTCHEST	BUTTES	BUYABLE	BYLANDERS	BYSSUSES
BUTCHING	BUTTIES	BUYABLES	BYLAW	BYSTANDER
BUTCHINGS	BUTTING	BUYER	BYLAWS	BYSTANDERS
BUTE	BUTTLE	BUYERS	BYLINE	BYTE
BUTENE	BUTTLED	BUYING	BYLINES	BYTES
BUTENES	BUTTLES	BUYS	BYLIVE	BYTOWNITE
BUTES	BUTTLING	BUZZ	BYNAME	BYTOWNITES
BUTLER	BUTTOCK	BUZZARD	BYNAMES	BYWAY
BUTLERAGE	BUTTOCKED	BUZZARDS	BYNEMPT	BYWAYS
BUTLERAGES	BUTTOCKING	BUZZED	BYPASS	BYWONER
BUTLERED	BUTTOCKS	BUZZER	BYPASSED	BYWONERS
BUTLERIES	BUTTON	BUZZERS	BYPASSES	BYWORD
BUTLERING	BUTTONED	BUZZES	BYPASSING	BYWORDS
BUTLERS	BUTTONING	BUZZIER	BYPATH	BYZANT
BUTLERY	BUTTONS	BUZZIEST	BYPATHS	BYZANTS
BUTMENT	BUTTONY	BUZZING	BYPLACE	
BUTMENTS	BUTTRESS	BUZZINGLY	BYPLACES	
BUTS	BUTTRESSED	BUZZINGS	BYRE	
BUTT	BUTTRESSES	BUZZWORD	BYREMAN	

C

CAATINGA
CAATINGAS
CAB
CABA
CABAL
CABALA
CABALAS
CABALETTA
CABALETTAS
CABALETTE
CABALISM
CABALISMS
CABALIST
CABALISTS
CABALLED
CABALLER
CABALLERO
CABALLEROS
CABALLERS
CABALLINE
CABALLING
CABALS
CABANA
CABANAS
CABARET
CABARETS
CABAS
CABBAGE
CABBAGED
CABBAGES
CABBAGING
CABBAGY
CABBALA
CABBALAS
CABBALISM
CABBALISMS
CABBALIST
CABBALISTS
CABBIE
CABBIES
CABBY
CABER
CABERS
CABIN
CABINED
CABINET
CABINETS
CABINING
CABINS
CABLE
CABLED
CABLEGRAM
CABLEGRAMS
CABLES

CABLET
CABLETS
CABLEWAY
CABLEWAYS
CABLING
CABLINGS
CABMAN
CABMEN
CABOB
CABOBBED
CABOBBING
CABOBS
CABOC
CABOCEER
CABOCEERS
CABOCHED
CABOCHON
CABOCHONS
CABOCS
CABOODLE
CABOODLES
CABOOSE
CABOOSES
CABOSHED
CABOTAGE
CABOTAGES
CABRE
CABRETTA
CABRETTAS
CABRIE
CABRIES
CABRIOLE
CABRIOLES
CABRIOLET
CABRIOLETS
CABRIT
CABRITS
CABS
CACAFOGO
CACAFOGOS
CACAFUEGO
CACAFUEGOS
CACAO
CACAOS
CACHAEMIA
CACHAEMIAS
CACHAEMIC
CACHALOT
CACHALOTS
CACHE
CACHECTIC
CACHED
CACHEPOT
CACHEPOTS

CACHES
CACHET
CACHETS
CACHEXIA
CACHEXIAS
CACHEXIES
CACHEXY
CACHING
CACHOLONG
CACHOLONGS
CACHOLOT
CACHOLOTS
CACHOU
CACHOUS
CACHUCHA
CACHUCHAS
CACIQUE
CACIQUES
CACIQUISM
CACIQUISMS
CACKLE
CACKLED
CACKLER
CACKLERS
CACKLES
CACKLING
CACODEMON
CACODEMONS
CACODOXIES
CACODOXY
CACODYL
CACODYLIC
CACODYLS
CACOEPIES
CACOEPY
CACOETHES
CACOLET
CACOLETS
CACOLOGIES
CACOLOGY
CACOMIXL
CACOMIXLS
CACOON
CACOONS
CACOPHONIES
CACOPHONY
CACOTOPIA
CACOTOPIAS
CACTI
CACTIFORM
CACTUS
CACTUSES
CACUMEN
CACUMINA

CACUMINAL
CAD
CADASTRAL
CADASTRE
CADASTRES
CADAVER
CADAVERIC
CADAVERS
CADDICE
CADDICES
CADDIE
CADDIED
CADDIES
CADDIS
CADDISES
CADDISH
CADDY
CADDYING
CADDYSS
CADDYSSES
CADE
CADEAU
CADEAUX
CADEE
CADEES
CADELLE
CADELLES
CADENCE
CADENCED
CADENCES
CADENCIES
CADENCY
CADENT
CADENTIAL
CADENZA
CADENZAS
CADES
CADET
CADETS
CADETSHIP
CADETSHIPS
CADGE
CADGED
CADGER
CADGERS
CADGES
CADGIER
CADGIEST
CADGING
CADGY
CADI
CADIE
CADIES
CADIS

CADMIUM
CADMIUMS
CADRANS
CADRANSES
CADRE
CADRES
CADS
CADUAC
CADUACS
CADUCEAN
CADUCEI
CADUCEUS
CADUCITIES
CADUCITY
CADUCOUS
CAECA
CAECAL
CAECILIAN
CAECILIANS
CAECITIS
CAECITISES
CAECUM
CAERULE
CAERULEAN
CAESAR
CAESARS
CAESE
CAESIOUS
CAESIUM
CAESIUMS
CAESTUS
CAESTUSES
CAESURA
CAESURAE
CAESURAL
CAESURAS
CAFARD
CAFARDS
CAFE
CAFES
CAFETERIA
CAFETERIAS
CAFETIERE
CAFETIERES
CAFF
CAFFEIN
CAFFEINE
CAFFEINES
CAFFEINS
CAFFEISM
CAFFEISMS
CAFFILA
CAFFILAS
CAFFS

CAFILA	CAITIVE	CALAVANCES	CALEFIES	CALIOLOGY
CAFILAS	CAITIVES	CALCANEA	CALEFY	CALIPASH
CAFTAN	CAJEPUT	CALCANEAL	CALEFYING	CALIPASHES
CAFTANS	CAJEPUTS	CALCANEAN	CALEMBOUR	CALIPEE
CAGE	CAJOLE	CALCANEI	CALEMBOURS	CALIPEES
CAGEBIRD	CAJOLED	CALCANEUM	CALENDAR	CALIPER
CAGEBIRDS	CAJOLER	CALCANEUS	CALENDARED	CALIPERS
CAGED	CAJOLERIES	CALCAR	CALENDARING	CALIPH
CAGELING	CAJOLERS	CALCARATE	CALENDARS	CALIPHAL
CAGELINGS	CAJOLERY	CALCARIA	CALENDER	CALIPHATE
CAGES	CAJOLES	CALCARINE	CALENDERED	CALIPHATES
CAGEWORK	CAJOLING	CALCARS	CALENDERING	CALIPHS
CAGEWORKS	CAJUN	CALCEATE	CALENDERINGS	CALISAYA
CAGEY	CAJUPUT	CALCEATED	CALENDERS	CALISAYAS
CAGEYNESS	CAJUPUTS	CALCEATES	CALENDRER	CALIVER
CAGEYNESSES	CAKE	CALCEATING	CALENDRERS	CALIVERS
CAGIER	CAKED	CALCED	CALENDRIC	CALIX
CAGIEST	CAKES	CALCEDONIES	CALENDRIES	CALK
CAGILY	CAKEWALK	CALCEDONY	CALENDRY	CALKED
CAGINESS	CAKEWALKED	CALCES	CALENDS	CALKER
CAGINESSES	CAKEWALKING	CALCIC	CALENDULA	CALKERS
CAGING	CAKEWALKS	CALCICOLE	CALENDULAS	CALKIN
CAGOT	CAKEY	CALCICOLES	CALENTURE	CALKING
CAGOTS	CAKIER	CALCIFIC	CALENTURES	CALKINS
CAGOUL	CAKIEST	CALCIFIED	CALF	CALKS
CAGOULE	CAKING	CALCIFIES	CALFDOZER	CALL
CAGOULES	CAKINGS	CALCIFUGE	CALFDOZERS	CALLA
CAGOULS	CAKY	CALCIFUGES	CALFLESS	CALLAN
CAGY	CALABASH	CALCIFY	CALFLICK	CALLANS
CAGYNESS	CALABASHES	CALCIFYING	CALFLICKS	CALLANT
CAGYNESSES	CALABOOSE	CALCIMINE	CALFS	CALLANTS
CAHIER	CALABOOSES	CALCIMINED	CALFSKIN	CALLAS
CAHIERS	CALABRESE	CALCIMINES	CALFSKINS	CALLED
CAHOOT	CALABRESES	CALCIMINING	CALIATOUR	CALLER
CAHOOTS	CALADIUM	CALCINE	CALIATOURS	CALLERS
CAILLACH	CALADIUMS	CALCINED	CALIBER	CALLET
CAILLACHS	CALAMANCO	CALCINES	CALIBERED	CALLETS
CAILLE	CALAMANCOES	CALCINING	CALIBERS	CALLID
CAILLEACH	CALAMANCOS	CALCITE	CALIBRATE	CALLIDITIES
CAILLEACHS	CALAMARI	CALCITES	CALIBRATED	CALLIDITY
CAILLES	CALAMARIES	CALCIUM	CALIBRATES	CALLIGRAM
CAILLIACH	CALAMARY	CALCIUMS	CALIBRATING	CALLIGRAMS
CAILLIACHS	CALAMI	CALCRETE	CALIBRE	CALLING
CAIMAC	CALAMINE	CALCRETES	CALIBRED	CALLINGS
CAIMACAM	CALAMINES	CALCSPAR	CALIBRES	CALLIOPE
CAIMACAMS	CALAMINT	CALCSPARS	CALICES	CALLIOPES
CAIMACS	CALAMINTS	CALCULAR	CALICHE	CALLIPER
CAIMAN	CALAMITE	CALCULARY	CALICHES	CALLIPERED
CAIMANS	CALAMITES	CALCULATE	CALICLE	CALLIPERING
CAIN	CALAMITIES	CALCULATED	CALICLES	CALLIPERS
CAINS	CALAMITY	CALCULATES	CALICO	CALLOSITIES
CAIQUE	CALAMUS	CALCULATING	CALICOES	CALLOSITY
CAIQUES	CALANDO	CALCULI	CALICOS	CALLOUS
CAIRD	CALANDRIA	CALCULOSE	CALID	CALLOUSLY
CAIRDS	CALANDRIAS	CALCULOUS	CALIDITIES	CALLOW
CAIRN	CALANTHE	CALCULUS	CALIDITY	CALLOWER
CAIRNED	CALANTHES	CALCULUSES	CALIF	CALLOWEST
CAIRNGORM	CALASH	CALDARIA	CALIFS	CALLOWS
CAIRNGORMS	CALASHES	CALDARIUM	CALIGO	CALLS
CAIRNS	CALATHEA	CALDERA	CALIGOES	CALLUNA
CAISSON	CALATHEAS	CALDERAS	CALIGOS	CALLUNAS
CAISSONS	CALATHI	CALDRON	CALIMA	CALLUS
CAITIFF	CALATHUS	CALDRONS	CALIMAS	CALLUSES
CAITIFFS	CALAVANCE	CALEFIED	CALIOLOGIES	CALM

The Chambers Dictionary is the authority for many longer words; see *OSW* Introduction, page xii

CALMANT	CALVARY	CAMBISTS	CAMORRA	CAMPSITE
CALMANTS	CALVE	CAMBIUM	CAMORRAS	CAMPSITES
CALMATIVE	CALVED	CAMBIUMS	CAMOTE	CAMPUS
CALMATIVES	CALVER	CAMBOGE	CAMOTES	CAMPUSES
CALMED	CALVERED	CAMBOGES	CAMOUFLET	CAMPY
CALMER	CALVERING	CAMBREL	CAMOUFLETS	CAMS
CALMEST	CALVERS	CAMBRELS	CAMP	CAMSHAFT
CALMIER	CALVES	CAMBRIC	CAMPAGNA	CAMSHAFTS
CALMIEST	CALVING	CAMBRICS	CAMPAGNAS	CAMSHEUGH
CALMING	CALVITIES	CAMCORDER	CAMPAIGN	CAMSHO
CALMLY	CALX	CAMCORDERS	CAMPAIGNED	CAMSHOCH
CALMNESS	CALXES	CAME	CAMPAIGNING	CAMSTAIRY
CALMNESSES	CALYCES	CAMEL	CAMPAIGNS	CAMSTANE
CALMS	CALYCINAL	CAMELBACK	CAMPANA	CAMSTANES
CALMSTONE	CALYCINE	CAMELBACKS	CAMPANAS	CAMSTEARY
CALMSTONES	CALYCLE	CAMELEER	CAMPANERO	CAMSTONE
CALMY	CALYCLED	CAMELEERS	CAMPANEROS	CAMSTONES
CALOMEL	CALYCLES	CAMELEON	CAMPANILE	CAMUS
CALOMELS	CALYCOID	CAMELEONS	CAMPANILES	CAMUSES
CALORIC	CALYCULE	CAMELID	CAMPANILI	CAMWOOD
CALORICS	CALYCULES	CAMELIDS	CAMPANIST	CAMWOODS
CALORIE	CALYCULI	CAMELINE	CAMPANISTS	CAN
CALORIES	CALYCULUS	CAMELINES	CAMPANULA	CANADA
CALORIFIC	CALYPSO	CAMELISH	CAMPANULAS	CANADAS
CALORIST	CALYPSOS	CAMELLIA	CAMPEADOR	CANAIGRE
CALORISTS	CALYPTERA	CAMELLIAS	CAMPEADORS	CANAIGRES
CALORY	CALYPTERAS	CAMELOID	CAMPED	CANAILLE
CALOTTE	CALYPTRA	CAMELOIDS	CAMPER	CANAILLES
CALOTTES	CALYPTRAS	CAMELOT	CAMPERS	CANAKIN
CALOTYPE	CALYX	CAMELOTS	CAMPESINO	CANAKINS
CALOTYPES	CALYXES	CAMELRIES	CAMPESINOS	CANAL
CALOYER	CALZONE	CAMELRY	CAMPEST	CANALISE
CALOYERS	CALZONES	CAMELS	CAMPFIRE	CANALISED
CALP	CALZONI	CAMEO	CAMPFIRES	CANALISES
CALPA	CAM	CAMEOS	CAMPHANE	CANALISING
CALPAC	CAMAIEU	CAMERA	CAMPHANES	CANALIZE
CALPACK	CAMAIEUX	CAMERAE	CAMPHENE	CANALIZED
CALPACKS	CAMAN	CAMERAL	CAMPHENES	CANALIZES
CALPACS	CAMANACHD	CAMERAMAN	CAMPHINE	CANALIZING
CALPAS	CAMANACHDS	CAMERAMEN	CAMPHINES	CANALS
CALPS	CAMANS	CAMERAS	CAMPHIRE	CANAPE
CALQUE	CAMARILLA	CAMERATED	CAMPHIRES	CANAPES
CALQUED	CAMARILLAS	CAMES	CAMPHOR	CANARD
CALQUES	CAMARON	CAMESE	CAMPHORIC	CANARDS
CALQUING	CAMARONS	CAMESES	CAMPHORS	CANARIED
CALTHA	CAMAS	CAMION	CAMPIER	CANARIES
CALTHAS	CAMASES	CAMIONS	CAMPIEST	CANARY
CALTHROP	CAMASH	CAMIS	CAMPING	CANARYING
CALTHROPS	CAMASHES	CAMISADE	CAMPION	CANASTA
CALTRAP	CAMASS	CAMISADES	CAMPIONS	CANASTAS
CALTRAPS	CAMASSES	CAMISADO	CAMPLE	CANASTER
CALTROP	CAMBER	CAMISADOS	CAMPLED	CANASTERS
CALTROPS	CAMBERED	CAMISE	CAMPLES	CANBANK
CALUMBA	CAMBERING	CAMISES	CAMPLING	CANBANKS
CALUMBAS	CAMBERINGS	CAMISOLE	CAMPLY	CANCAN
CALUMET	CAMBERS	CAMISOLES	CAMPNESS	CANCANS
CALUMETS	CAMBIA	CAMLET	CAMPNESSES	CANCEL
CALUMNIES	CAMBIAL	CAMLETS	CAMPO	CANCELEER
CALUMNY	CAMBIFORM	CAMMED	CAMPODEID	CANCELEERED
CALUTRON	CAMBISM	CAMMING	CAMPODEIDS	CANCELEERING
CALUTRONS	CAMBISMS	CAMOGIE	CAMPOREE	CANCELEERS
CALVARIA	CAMBIST	CAMOGIES	CAMPOREES	CANCELIER
CALVARIAS	CAMBISTRIES	CAMOMILE	CAMPOS	CANCELIERED
CALVARIES	CAMBISTRY	CAMOMILES	CAMPS	CANCELIERING

CANCELIERS	CANEPHORS	CANNIKINS	CANSTICK	CANTLET
CANCELLED	CANES	CANNILY	CANSTICKS	CANTLETS
CANCELLI	CANESCENT	CANNINESS	CANT	CANTLING
CANCELLING	CANFIELD	CANNINESSES	CANTABANK	CANTO
CANCELS	CANFIELDS	CANNING	CANTABANKS	CANTON
CANCER	CANFUL	CANNON	CANTABILE	CANTONAL
CANCERATE	CANFULS	CANNONADE	CANTABILES	CANTONED
CANCERATED	CANG	CANNONADED	CANTALA	CANTONING
CANCERATES	CANGLE	CANNONADES	CANTALAS	CANTONISE
CANCERATING	CANGLED	CANNONADING	CANTALOUP	CANTONISED
CANCEROUS	CANGLES	CANNONED	CANTALOUPS	CANTONISES
CANCERS	CANGLING	CANNONEER	CANTAR	CANTONISING
CANCRINE	CANGS	CANNONEERS	CANTARS	CANTONIZE
CANCROID	CANGUE	CANNONIER	CANTATA	CANTONIZED
CANCROIDS	CANGUES	CANNONIERS	CANTATAS	CANTONIZES
CANDELA	CANICULAR	CANNONING	CANTATE	CANTONIZING
CANDELAS	CANID	CANNONRIES	CANTATES	CANTONS
CANDENT	CANIDS	CANNONRY	CANTDOG	CANTOR
CANDID	CANIER	CANNONS	CANTDOGS	CANTORIAL
CANDIDA	CANIEST	CANNOT	CANTED	CANTORIS
CANDIDACIES	CANIKIN	CANNS	CANTEEN	CANTORS
CANDIDACY	CANIKINS	CANNULA	CANTEENS	CANTOS
CANDIDAL	CANINE	CANNULAE	CANTER	CANTRED
CANDIDAS	CANINES	CANNULAR	CANTERED	CANTREDS
CANDIDATE	CANING	CANNULAS	CANTERING	CANTREF
CANDIDATES	CANINGS	CANNULATE	CANTERS	CANTREFS
CANDIDER	CANINITIES	CANNY	CANTEST	CANTRIP
CANDIDEST	CANINITY	CANOE	CANTHARI	CANTRIPS
CANDIDLY	CANISTER	CANOED	CANTHARID	CANTS
CANDIE	CANISTERED	CANOEING	CANTHARIDES	CANTUS
CANDIED	CANISTERING	CANOEINGS	CANTHARIDS	CANTY
CANDIES	CANISTERS	CANOEIST	CANTHARIS	CANULA
CANDLE	CANITIES	CANOEISTS	CANTHARUS	CANULAE
CANDLED	CANKER	CANOES	CANTHI	CANULAS
CANDLENUT	CANKERED	CANON	CANTHOOK	CANVAS
CANDLENUTS	CANKERING	CANONESS	CANTHOOKS	CANVASED
CANDLES	CANKEROUS	CANONESSES	CANTHUS	CANVASES
CANDLING	CANKERS	CANONIC	CANTICLE	CANVASING
CANDOCK	CANKERY	CANONICAL	CANTICLES	CANVASS
CANDOCKS	CANN	CANONICALS	CANTICO	CANVASSED
CANDOR	CANNA	CANONISE	CANTICOED	CANVASSER
CANDORS	CANNABIC	CANONISED	CANTICOING	CANVASSERS
CANDOUR	CANNABIN	CANONISES	CANTICOS	CANVASSES
CANDOURS	CANNABINS	CANONISING	CANTICOY	CANVASSING
CANDY	CANNABIS	CANONIST	CANTICOYED	CANY
CANDYING	CANNABISES	CANONISTS	CANTICOYING	CANYON
CANDYTUFT	CANNACH	CANONIZE	CANTICOYS	CANYONS
CANDYTUFTS	CANNACHS	CANONIZED	CANTICUM	CANZONA
CANE	CANNAE	CANONIZES	CANTICUMS	CANZONAS
CANEBRAKE	CANNAS	CANONIZING	CANTIER	CANZONE
CANEBRAKES	CANNED	CANONRIES	CANTIEST	CANZONET
CANED	CANNEL	CANONRY	CANTILENA	CANZONETS
CANEFRUIT	CANNELS	CANONS	CANTILENAS	CANZONI
CANEFRUITS	CANNELURE	CANOODLE	CANTINA	CAP
CANEH	CANNELURES	CANOODLED	CANTINAS	CAPA
CANEHS	CANNER	CANOODLES	CANTINESS	CAPABLE
CANELLA	CANNERIES	CANOODLING	CANTINESSES	CAPABLER
CANELLAS	CANNERS	CANOPIED	CANTING	CAPABLEST
CANELLINI	CANNERY	CANOPIES	CANTINGS	CAPABLY
CANEPHOR	CANNIBAL	CANOPY	CANTION	CAPACIOUS
CANEPHORA	CANNIBALS	CANOPYING	CANTIONS	CAPACITIES
CANEPHORAS	CANNIER	CANOROUS	CANTLE	CAPACITOR
CANEPHORE	CANNIEST	CANS	CANTLED	CAPACITORS
CANEPHORES	CANNIKIN	CANST	CANTLES	CAPACITY

The Chambers Dictionary is the authority for many longer words; see *OSW* Introduction, page xii

CAPARISON	CAPON	CAPS	CAPUCCIOS	CARAT
CAPARISONED	CAPONIER	CAPSAICIN	CAPUCHE	CARATS
CAPARISONING	CAPONIERE	CAPSAICINS	CAPUCHES	CARAUNA
CAPARISONS	CAPONIERES	CAPSICUM	CAPUCHIN	CARAUNAS
CAPAS	CAPONIERS	CAPSICUMS	CAPUCHINS	CARAVAN
CAPE	CAPONISE	CAPSID	CAPUERA	CARAVANCE
CAPED	CAPONISED	CAPSIDS	CAPUERAS	CARAVANCES
CAPELET	CAPONISES	CAPSIZAL	CAPUL	CARAVANED
CAPELETS	CAPONISING	CAPSIZALS	CAPULS	CARAVANER
CAPELIN	CAPONIZE	CAPSIZE	CAPUT	CARAVANERS
CAPELINE	CAPONIZED	CAPSIZED	CAPYBARA	CARAVANING
CAPELINES	CAPONIZES	CAPSIZES	CAPYBARAS	CARAVANNED
CAPELINS	CAPONIZING	CAPSIZING	CAR	CARAVANNING
CAPELLET	CAPONS	CAPSTAN	CARABAO	CARAVANS
CAPELLETS	CAPORAL	CAPSTANS	CARABAOS	CARAVEL
CAPELLINE	CAPORALS	CAPSTONE	CARABID	CARAVELS
CAPELLINES	CAPOS	CAPSTONES	CARABIDS	CARAWAY
CAPER	CAPOT	CAPSULAR	CARABIN	CARAWAYS
CAPERED	CAPOTASTO	CAPSULARY	CARABINE	CARB
CAPERER	CAPOTASTOS	CAPSULATE	CARABINER	CARBACHOL
CAPERERS	CAPOTE	CAPSULE	CARABINERS	CARBACHOLS
CAPERING	CAPOTES	CAPSULES	CARABINES	CARBAMATE
CAPERS	CAPOTS	CAPSULISE	CARABINS	CARBAMATES
CAPES	CAPOTTED	CAPSULISED	CARACAL	CARBAMIDE
CAPESKIN	CAPOTTING	CAPSULISES	CARACALS	CARBAMIDES
CAPESKINS	CAPOUCH	CAPSULISING	CARACARA	CARBANION
CAPEWORK	CAPOUCHES	CAPSULIZE	CARACARAS	CARBANIONS
CAPEWORKS	CAPPED	CAPSULIZED	CARACK	CARBARYL
CAPI	CAPPER	CAPSULIZES	CARACKS	CARBARYLS
CAPIAS	CAPPERS	CAPSULIZING	CARACOL	CARBAZOLE
CAPIASES	CAPPING	CAPTAIN	CARACOLE	CARBAZOLES
CAPILLARIES	CAPPINGS	CAPTAINCIES	CARACOLED	CARBIDE
CAPILLARY	CAPRATE	CAPTAINCY	CARACOLES	CARBIDES
CAPING	CAPRATES	CAPTAINED	CARACOLING	CARBIES
CAPITA	CAPRIC	CAPTAINING	CARACOLLED	CARBINE
CAPITAL	CAPRICCI	CAPTAINRIES	CARACOLLING	CARBINEER
CAPITALLY	CAPRICCIO	CAPTAINRY	CARACOLS	CARBINEERS
CAPITALS	CAPRICCIOS	CAPTAINS	CARACT	CARBINES
CAPITAN	CAPRICE	CAPTAN	CARACTS	CARBINIER
CAPITANI	CAPRICES	CAPTANS	CARACUL	CARBINIERS
CAPITANO	CAPRID	CAPTION	CARACULS	CARBOLIC
CAPITANOS	CAPRIDS	CAPTIONED	CARAFE	CARBOLICS
CAPITANS	CAPRIFIED	CAPTIONING	CARAFES	CARBON
CAPITATE	CAPRIFIES	CAPTIONS	CARAMBA	CARBONADE
CAPITAYN	CAPRIFIG	CAPTIOUS	CARAMBOLA	CARBONADES
CAPITAYNS	CAPRIFIGS	CAPTIVATE	CARAMBOLAS	CARBONADO
CAPITELLA	CAPRIFOIL	CAPTIVATED	CARAMBOLE	CARBONADOED
CAPITULA	CAPRIFOILS	CAPTIVATES	CARAMBOLED	CARBONADOES
CAPITULAR	CAPRIFOLE	CAPTIVATING	CARAMBOLES	CARBONADOING
CAPITULARS	CAPRIFOLES	CAPTIVE	CARAMBOLING	CARBONADOS
CAPITULUM	CAPRIFORM	CAPTIVED	CARAMEL	CARBONARA
CAPIZ	CAPRIFY	CAPTIVES	CARAMELLED	CARBONARAS
CAPIZES	CAPRIFYING	CAPTIVING	CARAMELLING	CARBONATE
CAPLE	CAPRINE	CAPTIVITIES	CARAMELS	CARBONATED
CAPLES	CAPRIOLE	CAPTIVITY	CARANGID	CARBONATES
CAPLET	CAPRIOLED	CAPTOR	CARANGIDS	CARBONATING
CAPLETS	CAPRIOLES	CAPTORS	CARANGOID	CARBONIC
CAPLIN	CAPRIOLING	CAPTURE	CARANGOIDS	CARBONISE
CAPLINS	CAPROATE	CAPTURED	CARANNA	CARBONISED
CAPO	CAPROATES	CAPTURER	CARANNAS	CARBONISES
CAPOCCHIA	CAPROIC	CAPTURERS	CARAP	CARBONISING
CAPOCCHIAS	CAPRYLATE	CAPTURES	CARAPACE	CARBONIZE
CAPOEIRA	CAPRYLATES	CAPTURING	CARAPACES	CARBONIZED
CAPOEIRAS	CAPRYLIC	CAPUCCIO	CARAPS	CARBONIZES

CARBONIZING	CARDER	CARETAKERS	CARL	CARNIFYING
CARBONS	CARDERS	CARETAKES	CARLINE	CARNIVAL
CARBONYL	CARDI	CARETAKING	CARLINES	CARNIVALS
CARBONYLS	CARDIAC	CARETOOK	CARLING	CARNIVORE
CARBOXYL	CARDIACAL	CARETS	CARLINGS	CARNIVORES
CARBOXYLS	CARDIACS	CAREWORN	CARLISH	CARNOSE
CARBOY	CARDIALGIES	CAREX	CARLOAD	CARNOSITIES
CARBOYS	CARDIALGY	CARFARE	CARLOADS	CARNOSITY
CARBS	CARDIES	CARFARES	CARLOCK	CARNOTITE
CARBUNCLE	CARDIGAN	CARFAX	CARLOCKS	CARNOTITES
CARBUNCLES	CARDIGANS	CARFAXES	CARLOT	CARNY
CARBURATE	CARDINAL	CARFOX	CARLOTS	CARNYING
CARBURATED	CARDINALS	CARFOXES	CARLS	CAROB
CARBURATES	CARDING	CARFUFFLE	CARMAN	CAROBS
CARBURATING	CARDIOID	CARFUFFLED	CARMELITE	CAROCHE
CARBURET	CARDIOIDS	CARFUFFLES	CARMELITES	CAROCHES
CARBURETS	CARDIS	CARFUFFLING	CARMEN	CAROL
CARBURETTED	CARDITIS	CARGEESE	CARMINE	CAROLI
CARBURETTING	CARDITISES	CARGO	CARMINES	CAROLLED
CARBURISE	CARDOON	CARGOED	CARNAGE	CAROLLER
CARBURISED	CARDOONS	CARGOES	CARNAGES	CAROLLERS
CARBURISES	CARDPHONE	CARGOING	CARNAHUBA	CAROLLING
CARBURISING	CARDPHONES	CARGOOSE	CARNAHUBAS	CAROLS
CARBURIZE	CARDPUNCH	CARIACOU	CARNAL	CAROLUS
CARBURIZED	CARDPUNCHES	CARIACOUS	CARNALISE	CAROLUSES
CARBURIZES	CARDS	CARIAMA	CARNALISED	CAROM
CARBURIZING	CARDUUS	CARIAMAS	CARNALISES	CAROMED
CARBY	CARDUUSES	CARIBE	CARNALISING	CAROMEL
CARCAJOU	CARDY	CARIBES	CARNALISM	CAROMELLED
CARCAJOUS	CARE	CARIBOU	CARNALISMS	CAROMELLING
CARCAKE	CARED	CARIBOUS	CARNALIST	CAROMELS
CARCAKES	CAREEN	CARICES	CARNALISTS	CAROMING
CARCANET	CAREENAGE	CARIERE	CARNALITIES	CAROMS
CARCANETS	CAREENAGES	CARIERES	CARNALITY	CAROTENE
CARCASE	CAREENED	CARIES	CARNALIZE	CAROTENES
CARCASED	CAREENING	CARILLON	CARNALIZED	CAROTID
CARCASES	CAREENS	CARILLONED	CARNALIZES	CAROTIN
CARCASING	CAREER	CARILLONING	CARNALIZING	CAROTINS
CARCASS	CAREERED	CARILLONS	CARNALLED	CAROUSAL
CARCASSED	CAREERING	CARINA	CARNALLING	CAROUSALS
CARCASSES	CAREERISM	CARINAE	CARNALLY	CAROUSE
CARCASSING	CAREERISMS	CARINAS	CARNALS	CAROUSED
CARCERAL	CAREERIST	CARINATE	CARNATION	CAROUSEL
CARCINOMA	CAREERISTS	CARING	CARNATIONS	CAROUSELS
CARCINOMAS	CAREERS	CARIOCA	CARNAUBA	CAROUSER
CARCINOMATA	CAREFREE	CARIOCAS	CARNAUBAS	CAROUSERS
CARD	CAREFUL	CARIOLE	CARNELIAN	CAROUSES
CARDAMINE	CAREFULLY	CARIOLES	CARNELIANS	CAROUSING
CARDAMINES	CARELESS	CARIOUS	CARNEOUS	CARP
CARDAMOM	CAREME	CARITAS	CARNET	CARPACCIO
CARDAMOMS	CAREMES	CARITATES	CARNETS	CARPACCIOS
CARDAMON	CARER	CARJACK	CARNEY	CARPAL
CARDAMONS	CARERS	CARJACKED	CARNEYED	CARPALS
CARDAMUM	CARES	CARJACKER	CARNEYING	CARPARK
CARDAMUMS	CARESS	CARJACKERS	CARNEYS	CARPARKS
CARDBOARD	CARESSED	CARJACKING	CARNIED	CARPED
CARDBOARDS	CARESSES	CARJACKINGS	CARNIER	CARPEL
CARDCASE	CARESSING	CARJACKS	CARNIES	CARPELS
CARDCASES	CARESSINGS	CARJACOU	CARNIEST	CARPENTER
CARDECU	CARESSIVE	CARJACOUS	CARNIFEX	CARPENTERED
CARDECUE	CARET	CARK	CARNIFEXES	CARPENTERING
CARDECUES	CARETAKE	CARKED	CARNIFIED	CARPENTERS
CARDECUS	CARETAKEN	CARKING	CARNIFIES	CARPENTRIES
CARDED	CARETAKER	CARKS	CARNIFY	CARPENTRY

The Chambers Dictionary is the authority for many longer words; see *OSW* Introduction, page xii

CARPER	CARRYTALE	CARTWHEELING	CASEMENT	CASSIMERE
CARPERS	CARRYTALES	CARTWHEELS	CASEMENTS	CASSIMERES
CARPET	CARS	CARUCAGE	CASEOUS	CASSINGLE
CARPETBAG	CARSE	CARUCAGES	CASERN	CASSINGLES
CARPETBAGS	CARSES	CARUCATE	CASERNE	CASSINO
CARPETED	CARSEY	CARUCATES	CASERNES	CASSINOS
CARPETING	CARSEYS	CARUNCLE	CASERNS	CASSIS
CARPETINGS	CART	CARUNCLES	CASES	CASSISES
CARPETS	CARTA	CARVACROL	CASEWORK	CASSOCK
CARPI	CARTAGE	CARVACROLS	CASEWORKS	CASSOCKED
CARPING	CARTAGES	CARVE	CASH	CASSOCKS
CARPINGLY	CARTAS	CARVED	CASHAW	CASSONADE
CARPINGS	CARTE	CARVEL	CASHAWS	CASSONADES
CARPOLOGIES	CARTED	CARVELS	CASHED	CASSONE
CARPOLOGY	CARTEL	CARVEN	CASHES	CASSONES
CARPORT	CARTELISE	CARVER	CASHEW	CASSOULET
CARPORTS	CARTELISED	CARVERIES	CASHEWS	CASSOULETS
CARPS	CARTELISES	CARVERS	CASHIER	CASSOWARIES
CARPUS	CARTELISING	CARVERY	CASHIERED	CASSOWARY
CARR	CARTELISM	CARVES	CASHIERER	CAST
CARRACK	CARTELISMS	CARVIES	CASHIERERS	CASTANET
CARRACKS	CARTELIST	CARVING	CASHIERING	CASTANETS
CARRACT	CARTELISTS	CARVINGS	CASHIERINGS	CASTAWAY
CARRACTS	CARTELIZE	CARVY	CASHIERS	CASTAWAYS
CARRAGEEN	CARTELIZED	CARYATIC	CASHING	CASTE
CARRAGEENS	CARTELIZES	CARYATID	CASHLESS	CASTED
CARRAT	CARTELIZING	CARYATIDES	CASHMERE	CASTELESS
CARRATS	CARTELS	CARYATIDS	CASHMERES	CASTELLA
CARRAWAY	CARTER	CARYOPSES	CASHPOINT	CASTELLAN
CARRAWAYS	CARTERS	CARYOPSIDES	CASHPOINTS	CASTELLANS
CARRECT	CARTES	CARYOPSIS	CASIMERE	CASTELLUM
CARRECTS	CARTILAGE	CASA	CASIMERES	CASTELLUMS
CARREL	CARTILAGES	CASAS	CASING	CASTER
CARRELL	CARTING	CASBAH	CASINGS	CASTERS
CARRELLS	CARTLOAD	CASBAHS	CASINO	CASTES
CARRELS	CARTLOADS	CASCABEL	CASINOS	CASTIGATE
CARRIAGE	CARTOGRAM	CASCABELS	CASK	CASTIGATED
CARRIAGES	CARTOGRAMS	CASCADE	CASKED	CASTIGATES
CARRIED	CARTOLOGIES	CASCADED	CASKET	CASTIGATING
CARRIER	CARTOLOGY	CASCADES	CASKETS	CASTING
CARRIERS	CARTON	CASCADING	CASKING	CASTINGS
CARRIES	CARTONAGE	CASCADURA	CASKS	CASTLE
CARRIOLE	CARTONAGES	CASCADURAS	CASKSTAND	CASTLED
CARRIOLES	CARTONED	CASCARA	CASKSTANDS	CASTLES
CARRION	CARTONING	CASCARAS	CASQUE	CASTLING
CARRIONS	CARTONS	CASCHROM	CASQUES	CASTOCK
CARRITCH	CARTOON	CASCHROMS	CASSAREEP	CASTOCKS
CARRITCHES	CARTOONED	CASCO	CASSAREEPS	CASTOR
CARRONADE	CARTOONING	CASCOS	CASSARIPE	CASTOREUM
CARRONADES	CARTOONS	CASE	CASSARIPES	CASTOREUMS
CARROT	CARTOUCH	CASEATION	CASSATA	CASTORIES
CARROTIER	CARTOUCHE	CASEATIONS	CASSATAS	CASTORS
CARROTIEST	CARTOUCHES	CASEBOOK	CASSATION	CASTORY
CARROTS	CARTRIDGE	CASEBOOKS	CASSATIONS	CASTRAL
CARROTY	CARTRIDGES	CASED	CASSAVA	CASTRATE
CARROUSEL	CARTROAD	CASEIN	CASSAVAS	CASTRATED
CARROUSELS	CARTROADS	CASEINS	CASSEROLE	CASTRATES
CARRS	CARTS	CASEMAKER	CASSEROLED	CASTRATI
CARRY	CARTULARIES	CASEMAKERS	CASSEROLES	CASTRATING
CARRYALL	CARTULARY	CASEMAN	CASSEROLING	CASTRATO
CARRYALLS	CARTWAY	CASEMATE	CASSETTE	CASTS
CARRYCOT	CARTWAYS	CASEMATED	CASSETTES	CASUAL
CARRYCOTS	CARTWHEEL	CASEMATES	CASSIA	CASUALISE
CARRYING	CARTWHEELED	CASEMEN	CASSIAS	CASUALISED

CASUALISES	CATALYZER	CATCHPOLL	CATGUT	CATTABU
CASUALISING	CATALYZERS	CATCHPOLLS	CATGUTS	CATTABUS
CASUALISM	CATALYZES	CATCHT	CATHARISE	CATTALO
CASUALISMS	CATALYZING	CATCHUP	CATHARISED	CATTALOES
CASUALIZE	CATAMARAN	CATCHUPS	CATHARISES	CATTALOS
CASUALIZED	CATAMARANS	CATCHWEED	CATHARISING	CATTED
CASUALIZES	CATAMENIA	CATCHWEEDS	CATHARIZE	CATTERIES
CASUALIZING	CATAMITE	CATCHWORD	CATHARIZED	CATTERY
CASUALLY	CATAMITES	CATCHWORDS	CATHARIZES	CATTIER
CASUALS	CATAMOUNT	CATCHY	CATHARIZING	CATTIES
CASUALTIES	CATAMOUNTS	CATE	CATHARSES	CATTIEST
CASUALTY	CATAPAN	CATECHISE	CATHARSIS	CATTILY
CASUARINA	CATAPANS	CATECHISED	CATHARTIC	CATTINESS
CASUARINAS	CATAPHYLL	CATECHISES	CATHARTICS	CATTINESSES
CASUIST	CATAPHYLLS	CATECHISING	CATHEAD	CATTING
CASUISTIC	CATAPLASM	CATECHISINGS	CATHEADS	CATTISH
CASUISTRIES	CATAPLASMS	CATECHISM	CATHECTIC	CATTISHLY
CASUISTRY	CATAPLEXIES	CATECHISMS	CATHEDRA	CATTLE
CASUISTS	CATAPLEXY	CATECHIST	CATHEDRAL	CATTLEMAN
CAT	CATAPULT	CATECHISTS	CATHEDRALS	CATTLEMEN
CATABASES	CATAPULTED	CATECHIZE	CATHEDRAS	CATTLEYA
CATABASIS	CATAPULTING	CATECHIZED	CATHETER	CATTLEYAS
CATABOLIC	CATAPULTS	CATECHIZES	CATHETERS	CATTY
CATACLASM	CATARACT	CATECHIZING	CATHETUS	CATWORKS
CATACLASMS	CATARACTS	CATECHIZINGS	CATHEXES	CATWORM
CATACLYSM	CATARHINE	CATECHOL	CATHEXIS	CATWORMS
CATACLYSMS	CATARRH	CATECHOLS	CATHISMA	CAUCHEMAR
CATACOMB	CATARRHAL	CATECHU	CATHISMAS	CAUCHEMARS
CATACOMBS	CATARRHS	CATECHUS	CATHODAL	CAUCUS
CATAFALCO	CATASTA	CATEGORIC	CATHODE	CAUCUSED
CATAFALCOES	CATASTAS	CATEGORIES	CATHODES	CAUCUSES
CATALASE	CATATONIA	CATEGORY	CATHODIC	CAUCUSING
CATALASES	CATATONIAS	CATELOG	CATHOLE	CAUDAD
CATALEPSIES	CATATONIC	CATELOGS	CATHOLES	CAUDAL
CATALEPSY	CATATONICS	CATENA	CATHOLIC	CAUDATE
CATALEXES	CATATONIES	CATENAE	CATHOOD	CAUDATED
CATALEXIS	CATATONY	CATENANE	CATHOODS	CAUDEX
CATALO	CATAWBA	CATENANES	CATHOUSE	CAUDEXES
CATALOES	CATAWBAS	CATENARIES	CATHOUSES	CAUDICES
CATALOG	CATBIRD	CATENARY	CATION	CAUDICLE
CATALOGED	CATBIRDS	CATENAS	CATIONS	CAUDICLES
CATALOGER	CATBOAT	CATENATE	CATKIN	CAUDILLO
CATALOGERS	CATBOATS	CATENATED	CATKINS	CAUDILLOS
CATALOGING	CATCALL	CATENATES	CATLIKE	CAUDLE
CATALOGS	CATCALLED	CATENATING	CATLING	CAUDLED
CATALOGUE	CATCALLING	CATER	CATLINGS	CAUDLES
CATALOGUED	CATCALLS	CATERAN	CATMINT	CAUDLING
CATALOGUES	CATCH	CATERANS	CATMINTS	CAUDRON
CATALOGUING	CATCHABLE	CATERED	CATNAP	CAUDRONS
CATALOS	CATCHED	CATERER	CATNAPS	CAUF
CATALPA	CATCHEN	CATERERS	CATNEP	CAUGHT
CATALPAS	CATCHER	CATERESS	CATNEPS	CAUK
CATALYSE	CATCHERS	CATERESSES	CATNIP	CAUKER
CATALYSED	CATCHES	CATERING	CATNIPS	CAUKERS
CATALYSER	CATCHFLIES	CATERINGS	CATOPTRIC	CAUKS
CATALYSERS	CATCHFLY	CATERS	CATOPTRICS	CAUL
CATALYSES	CATCHIER	CATERWAUL	CATS	CAULD
CATALYSING	CATCHIEST	CATERWAULED	CATSKIN	CAULDER
CATALYSIS	CATCHING	CATERWAULING	CATSKINS	CAULDEST
CATALYST	CATCHINGS	CATERWAULINGS	CATSUIT	CAULDRIFE
CATALYSTS	CATCHMENT	CATERWAULS	CATSUITS	CAULDRON
CATALYTIC	CATCHMENTS	CATES	CATSUP	CAULDRONS
CATALYZE	CATCHPOLE	CATFISH	CATSUPS	CAULDS
CATALYZED	CATCHPOLES	CATFISHES		CAULES

CAULICLE	CAUTERISM	CAVICORN	CECA	CELESTE
CAULICLES	CAUTERISMS	CAVICORNS	CECAL	CELESTES
CAULICULI	CAUTERIZE	CAVIE	CECILS	CELESTIAL
CAULIFORM	CAUTERIZED	CAVIER	CECITIES	CELESTIALS
CAULINARY	CAUTERIZES	CAVIERS	CECITIS	CELESTINE
CAULINE	CAUTERIZING	CAVIES	CECITISES	CELESTINES
CAULIS	CAUTERS	CAVIL	CECITY	CELESTITE
CAULK	CAUTERY	CAVILLED	CECROPIA	CELESTITES
CAULKED	CAUTION	CAVILLER	CECROPIAS	CELIAC
CAULKER	CAUTIONED	CAVILLERS	CECUM	CELIACS
CAULKERS	CAUTIONER	CAVILLING	CEDAR	CELIBACIES
CAULKING	CAUTIONERS	CAVILLINGS	CEDARED	CELIBACY
CAULKINGS	CAUTIONING	CAVILS	CEDARN	CELIBATE
CAULKS	CAUTIONRIES	CAVING	CEDARS	CELIBATES
CAULOME	CAUTIONRY	CAVINGS	CEDARWOOD	CELL
CAULOMES	CAUTIONS	CAVITATE	CEDARWOODS	CELLA
CAULS	CAUTIOUS	CAVITATED	CEDE	CELLAE
CAUM	CAUVES	CAVITATES	CEDED	CELLAR
CAUMED	CAVALCADE	CAVITATING	CEDES	CELLARAGE
CAUMING	CAVALCADED	CAVITIED	CEDI	CELLARAGES
CAUMS	CAVALCADES	CAVITIES	CEDILLA	CELLARED
CAUMSTONE	CAVALCADING	CAVITY	CEDILLAS	CELLARER
CAUMSTONES	CAVALIER	CAVORT	CEDING	CELLARERS
CAUP	CAVALIERED	CAVORTED	CEDIS	CELLARET
CAUPS	CAVALIERING	CAVORTING	CEDRATE	CELLARETS
CAUSA	CAVALIERS	CAVORTS	CEDRATES	CELLARING
CAUSAE	CAVALLA	CAVY	CEDRINE	CELLARIST
CAUSAL	CAVALLAS	CAW	CEDULA	CELLARISTS
CAUSALITIES	CAVALLIES	CAWED	CEDULAS	CELLARMAN
CAUSALITY	CAVALLY	CAWING	CEE	CELLARMEN
CAUSALLY	CAVALRIES	CAWINGS	CEES	CELLAROUS
CAUSATION	CAVALRY	CAWK	CEIL	CELLARS
CAUSATIONS	CAVASS	CAWKER	CEILED	CELLED
CAUSATIVE	CAVASSES	CAWKERS	CEILI	CELLIST
CAUSATIVES	CAVATINA	CAWKS	CEILIDH	CELLISTS
CAUSE	CAVATINAS	CAWS	CEILIDHS	CELLO
CAUSED	CAVE	CAXON	CEILING	CELLOS
CAUSELESS	CAVEAT	CAXONS	CEILINGED	CELLOSE
CAUSEN	CAVEATS	CAY	CEILINGS	CELLOSES
CAUSER	CAVED	CAYENNE	CEILIS	CELLPHONE
CAUSERIE	CAVEL	CAYENNED	CEILS	CELLPHONES
CAUSERIES	CAVELS	CAYENNES	CEINTURE	CELLS
CAUSERS	CAVEMAN	CAYMAN	CEINTURES	CELLULAR
CAUSES	CAVEMEN	CAYMANS	CEL	CELLULASE
CAUSEWAY	CAVENDISH	CAYS	CELADON	CELLULASES
CAUSEWAYED	CAVENDISHES	CAYUSE	CELADONS	CELLULE
CAUSEWAYS	CAVER	CAYUSES	CELANDINE	CELLULES
CAUSEY	CAVERN	CAZIQUE	CELANDINES	CELLULITE
CAUSEYED	CAVERNED	CAZIQUES	CELEBRANT	CELLULITES
CAUSEYS	CAVERNING	CEANOTHUS	CELEBRANTS	CELLULOID®
CAUSING	CAVERNOUS	CEANOTHUSES	CELEBRATE	CELLULOIDS
CAUSTIC	CAVERNS	CEAS	CELEBRATED	CELLULOSE
CAUSTICS	CAVERS	CEASE	CELEBRATES	CELLULOSES
CAUTEL	CAVES	CEASED	CELEBRATING	CELOM
CAUTELOUS	CAVESSON	CEASELESS	CELEBRITIES	CELOMS
CAUTELS	CAVESSONS	CEASES	CELEBRITY	CELS
CAUTER	CAVETTI	CEASING	CELERIAC	CELSITUDE
CAUTERANT	CAVETTO	CEASINGS	CELERIACS	CELSITUDES
CAUTERANTS	CAVIAR	CEAZE	CELERIES	CELT
CAUTERIES	CAVIARE	CEAZED	CELERITIES	CELTS
CAUTERISE	CAVIARES	CEAZES	CELERITY	CEMBALI
CAUTERISED	CAVIARIE	CEAZING	CELERY	CEMBALIST
CAUTERISES	CAVIARIES	CEBADILLA	CELESTA	CEMBALISTS
CAUTERISING	CAVIARS	CEBADILLAS	CELESTAS	CEMBALO

CEMBALOS	CENTENARY	CENTRUMS	CEREBRATE	CERTIFIES
CEMBRA	CENTENIER	CENTRY	CEREBRATED	CERTIFY
CEMBRAS	CENTENIERS	CENTS	CEREBRATES	CERTIFYING
CEMENT	CENTER	CENTUM	CEREBRATING	CERTITUDE
CEMENTA	CENTERED	CENTUMS	CEREBRIC	CERTITUDES
CEMENTED	CENTERING	CENTUMVIR	CEREBRUM	CERTS
CEMENTER	CENTERINGS	CENTUMVIRI	CEREBRUMS	CERULE
CEMENTERS	CENTERS	CENTUPLE	CERECLOTH	CERULEAN
CEMENTING	CENTESES	CENTUPLED	CERECLOTHS	CERULEIN
CEMENTITE	CENTESIMO	CENTUPLES	CERED	CERULEINS
CEMENTITES	CENTESIMOS	CENTUPLING	CEREMENT	CERULEOUS
CEMENTS	CENTESIS	CENTURIAL	CEREMENTS	CERUMEN
CEMENTUM	CENTIARE	CENTURIES	CEREMONIES	CERUMENS
CEMETERIES	CENTIARES	CENTURION	CEREMONY	CERUSE
CEMETERY	CENTIGRAM	CENTURIONS	CEREOUS	CERUSES
CEMITARE	CENTIGRAMS	CENTURY	CERES	CERUSITE
CEMITARES	CENTIME	CEORL	CERESIN	CERUSITES
CENACLE	CENTIMES	CEORLS	CERESINE	CERUSSITE
CENACLES	CENTIMO	CEP	CERESINES	CERUSSITES
CENDRE	CENTIMOS	CEPACEOUS	CERESINS	CERVELAT
CENOBITE	CENTINEL	CEPHALAD	CEREUS	CERVELATS
CENOBITES	CENTINELL	CEPHALATE	CEREUSES	CERVICAL
CENOTAPH	CENTINELLS	CEPHALIC	CERGE	CERVICES
CENOTAPHS	CENTINELS	CEPHALICS	CERGES	CERVID
CENOTE	CENTIPEDE	CEPHALIN	CERIA	CERVIDS
CENOTES	CENTIPEDES	CEPHALINS	CERIAS	CERVINE
CENS	CENTNER	CEPHALOUS	CERIC	CERVIX
CENSE	CENTNERS	CEPS	CERING	CERVIXES
CENSED	CENTO	CERACEOUS	CERIPH	CESAREVNA
CENSER	CENTOIST	CERAMAL	CERIPHS	CESAREVNAS
CENSERS	CENTOISTS	CERAMALS	CERISE	CESIUM
CENSES	CENTONATE	CERAMIC	CERISES	CESIUMS
CENSING	CENTONEL	CERAMICS	CERITE	CESPITOSE
CENSOR	CENTONELL	CERAMIST	CERITES	CESS
CENSORED	CENTONELLS	CERAMISTS	CERIUM	CESSATION
CENSORIAL	CENTONELS	CERASIN	CERIUMS	CESSATIONS
CENSORIAN	CENTONES	CERASINS	CERMET	CESSE
CENSORING	CENTONIST	CERASTES	CERMETS	CESSED
CENSORS	CENTONISTS	CERASTIUM	CERNE	CESSER
CENSUAL	CENTOS	CERASTIUMS	CERNED	CESSERS
CENSURE	CENTRA	CERATE	CERNES	CESSES
CENSURED	CENTRAL	CERATED	CERNING	CESSING
CENSURES	CENTRALLY	CERATES	CERNUOUS	CESSION
CENSURING	CENTRE	CERATITIS	CEROGRAPH	CESSIONS
CENSUS	CENTRED	CERATITISES	CEROGRAPHS	CESSPIT
CENSUSED	CENTREING	CERATODUS	CEROMANCIES	CESSPITS
CENSUSES	CENTREINGS	CERATODUSES	CEROMANCY	CESSPOOL
CENSUSING	CENTRES	CERATOID	CEROON	CESSPOOLS
CENT	CENTRIC	CERBEREAN	CEROONS	CESTI
CENTAGE	CENTRICAL	CERBERIAN	CEROTYPE	CESTODE
CENTAGES	CENTRIES	CERCAL	CEROTYPES	CESTODES
CENTAL	CENTRING	CERCARIA	CEROUS	CESTOID
CENTALS	CENTRINGS	CERCARIAE	CERRIAL	CESTOIDS
CENTARE	CENTRIOLE	CERCARIAN	CERRIS	CESTOS
CENTARES	CENTRIOLES	CERCI	CERRISES	CESTOSES
CENTAUR	CENTRISM	CERCUS	CERT	CESTUI
CENTAUREA	CENTRISMS	CERE	CERTAIN	CESTUIS
CENTAUREAS	CENTRIST	CEREAL	CERTAINLY	CESTUS
CENTAURIES	CENTRISTS	CEREALIST	CERTAINTIES	CESURA
CENTAURS	CENTRODE	CEREALISTS	CERTAINTY	CESURAE
CENTAURY	CENTRODES	CEREALS	CERTES	CESURAL
CENTAVO	CENTROID	CEREBELLA	CERTIFIED	CESURAS
CENTAVOS	CENTROIDS	CEREBRA	CERTIFIER	CESURE
CENTENARIES	CENTRUM	CEREBRAL	CERTIFIERS	CESURES

The Chambers Dictionary is the authority for many longer words; see *OSW* Introduction, page xii

CETACEAN
CETACEANS
CETACEOUS
CETANE
CETANES
CETE
CETERACH
CETERACHS
CETES
CETOLOGIES
CETOLOGY
CETYL
CETYLS
CETYWALL
CETYWALLS
CEVADILLA
CEVADILLAS
CEVAPCICI
CEVICHE
CEVICHES
CEYLANITE
CEYLANITES
CEYLONITE
CEYLONITES
CH
CHA
CHABAZITE
CHABAZITES
CHABOUK
CHABOUKS
CHACE
CHACED
CHACES
CHACING
CHACK
CHACKED
CHACKING
CHACKS
CHACMA
CHACMAS
CHACO
CHACOES
CHACONNE
CHACONNES
CHACOS
CHAD
CHADAR
CHADARS
CHADDAR
CHADDARS
CHADDOR
CHADDORS
CHADOR
CHADORS
CHADS
CHAETA
CHAETAE
CHAETODON
CHAETODONS
CHAETOPOD
CHAETOPODS
CHAFE
CHAFED
CHAFER

CHAFERS
CHAFES
CHAFF
CHAFFED
CHAFFER
CHAFFERED
CHAFFERER
CHAFFERERS
CHAFFERIES
CHAFFERING
CHAFFERS
CHAFFERY
CHAFFIER
CHAFFIEST
CHAFFINCH
CHAFFINCHES
CHAFFING
CHAFFINGS
CHAFFRON
CHAFFRONS
CHAFFS
CHAFFY
CHAFING
CHAFT
CHAFTS
CHAGAN
CHAGANS
CHAGRIN
CHAGRINED
CHAGRINING
CHAGRINS
CHAI
CHAIN
CHAINE
CHAINED
CHAINES
CHAINING
CHAINLESS
CHAINLET
CHAINLETS
CHAINMAN
CHAINMEN
CHAINS
CHAINSAW
CHAINSAWS
CHAINSHOT
CHAINSHOTS
CHAINWORK
CHAINWORKS
CHAIR
CHAIRDAYS
CHAIRED
CHAIRING
CHAIRLIFT
CHAIRLIFTS
CHAIRMAN
CHAIRMEN
CHAIRS
CHAIS
CHAISE
CHAISES
CHAKRA
CHAKRAS
CHAL

CHALAN
CHALANED
CHALANING
CHALANS
CHALAZA
CHALAZAE
CHALAZAS
CHALAZIA
CHALAZION
CHALCID
CHALCIDS
CHALDER
CHALDERS
CHALDRON
CHALDRONS
CHALET
CHALETS
CHALICE
CHALICED
CHALICES
CHALK
CHALKED
CHALKFACE
CHALKFACES
CHALKIER
CHALKIEST
CHALKING
CHALKPIT
CHALKPITS
CHALKS
CHALKY
CHALLAH
CHALLAHS
CHALLAN
CHALLANED
CHALLANING
CHALLANS
CHALLENGE
CHALLENGED
CHALLENGES
CHALLENGING
CHALLIE
CHALLIES
CHALLIS
CHALLISES
CHALONE
CHALONES
CHALONIC
CHALS
CHALUMEAU
CHALUMEAUX
CHALUTZ
CHALUTZES
CHALUTZIM
CHALYBEAN
CHALYBITE
CHALYBITES
CHAM
CHAMADE
CHAMADES
CHAMBER
CHAMBERED
CHAMBERER
CHAMBERERS

CHAMBERING
CHAMBERINGS
CHAMBERS
CHAMBRAY
CHAMBRAYS
CHAMBRE
CHAMELEON
CHAMELEONS
CHAMELOT
CHAMELOTS
CHAMFER
CHAMFERED
CHAMFERING
CHAMFERS
CHAMFRAIN
CHAMFRAINS
CHAMFRON
CHAMFRONS
CHAMISAL
CHAMISALS
CHAMISE
CHAMISES
CHAMISO
CHAMISOS
CHAMLET
CHAMLETS
CHAMMIES
CHAMMY
CHAMOIS
CHAMOMILE
CHAMOMILES
CHAMP
CHAMPAC
CHAMPACS
CHAMPAGNE
CHAMPAGNES
CHAMPAIGN
CHAMPAIGNS
CHAMPAK
CHAMPAKS
CHAMPART
CHAMPARTS
CHAMPED
CHAMPERS
CHAMPERTIES
CHAMPERTY
CHAMPING
CHAMPION
CHAMPIONED
CHAMPIONING
CHAMPIONS
CHAMPLEVE
CHAMPLEVES
CHAMPS
CHAMS
CHANCE
CHANCED
CHANCEFUL
CHANCEL
CHANCELS
CHANCER
CHANCERIES
CHANCERS
CHANCERY

CHANCES
CHANCEY
CHANCIER
CHANCIEST
CHANCING
CHANCRE
CHANCRES
CHANCROID
CHANCROIDS
CHANCROUS
CHANCY
CHANDELLE
CHANDELLED
CHANDELLES
CHANDELLING
CHANDLER
CHANDLERIES
CHANDLERS
CHANDLERY
CHANGE
CHANGED
CHANGEFUL
CHANGER
CHANGERS
CHANGES
CHANGING
CHANK
CHANKS
CHANNEL
CHANNELER
CHANNELERS
CHANNELLED
CHANNELLING
CHANNELS
CHANNER
CHANNERS
CHANOYU
CHANOYUS
CHANSON
CHANSONS
CHANT
CHANTAGE
CHANTAGES
CHANTED
CHANTER
CHANTERS
CHANTEUSE
CHANTEUSES
CHANTEY
CHANTEYS
CHANTIE
CHANTIES
CHANTING
CHANTOR
CHANTORS
CHANTRESS
CHANTRESSES
CHANTRIES
CHANTRY
CHANTS
CHANTY
CHAOLOGIES
CHAOLOGY
CHAOS

The Chambers Dictionary is the authority for many longer words; see *OSW* Introduction, page xii

CHAOSES	CHAR	CHARK	CHARTISMS	CHATTA
CHAOTIC	CHARA	CHARKA	CHARTIST	CHATTAS
CHAP	CHARABANC	CHARKAS	CHARTISTS	CHATTED
CHAPARRAL	CHARABANCS	CHARKED	CHARTLESS	CHATTEL
CHAPARRALS	CHARACID	CHARKHA	CHARTS	CHATTELS
CHAPATI	CHARACIDS	CHARKHAS	CHARWOMAN	CHATTER
CHAPATIS	CHARACIN	CHARKING	CHARWOMEN	CHATTERED
CHAPATTI	CHARACINS	CHARKS	CHARY	CHATTERER
CHAPATTIS	CHARACT	CHARLADIES	CHAS	CHATTERERS
CHAPBOOK	CHARACTER	CHARLADY	CHASE	CHATTERING
CHAPBOOKS	CHARACTERED	CHARLATAN	CHASED	CHATTERINGS
CHAPE	CHARACTERING	CHARLATANS	CHASEPORT	CHATTERS
CHAPEAU	CHARACTERS	CHARLEY	CHASEPORTS	CHATTI
CHAPEAUX	CHARACTS	CHARLEYS	CHASER	CHATTIER
CHAPEL	CHARADE	CHARLIE	CHASERS	CHATTIES
CHAPELESS	CHARADES	CHARLIES	CHASES	CHATTIEST
CHAPELRIES	CHARANGO	CHARLOCK	CHASING	CHATTING
CHAPELRY	CHARANGOS	CHARLOCKS	CHASINGS	CHATTIS
CHAPELS	CHARAS	CHARLOTTE	CHASM	CHATTY
CHAPERON	CHARASES	CHARLOTTES	CHASMAL	CHAUFE
CHAPERONE	CHARBROIL	CHARM	CHASMED	CHAUFED
CHAPERONED	CHARBROILED	CHARMED	CHASMIC	CHAUFER
CHAPERONES	CHARBROILING	CHARMER	CHASMIER	CHAUFERS
CHAPERONING	CHARBROILS	CHARMERS	CHASMIEST	CHAUFES
CHAPERONS	CHARCOAL	CHARMEUSE	CHASMS	CHAUFF
CHAPES	CHARCOALED	CHARMEUSES	CHASMY	CHAUFFED
CHAPESS	CHARCOALING	CHARMFUL	CHASSE	CHAUFFER
CHAPESSES	CHARCOALS	CHARMING	CHASSEED	CHAUFFERS
CHAPITER	CHARD	CHARMLESS	CHASSEING	CHAUFFEUR
CHAPITERS	CHARDS	CHARMS	CHASSEPOT	CHAUFFEURED
CHAPKA	CHARE	CHARNECO	CHASSEPOTS	CHAUFFEURING
CHAPKAS	CHARED	CHARNECOS	CHASSES	CHAUFFEURS
CHAPLAIN	CHARES	CHARNEL	CHASSEUR	CHAUFFING
CHAPLAINS	CHARET	CHARNELS	CHASSEURS	CHAUFFS
CHAPLESS	CHARETS	CHAROSET	CHASSIS	CHAUFING
CHAPLET	CHARGE	CHAROSETH	CHASTE	CHAUMER
CHAPLETED	CHARGED	CHAROSETHS	CHASTELY	CHAUMERS
CHAPLETS	CHARGEFUL	CHAROSETS	CHASTEN	CHAUNCE
CHAPMAN	CHARGER	CHARPIE	CHASTENED	CHAUNCED
CHAPMEN	CHARGERS	CHARPIES	CHASTENER	CHAUNCES
CHAPPAL	CHARGES	CHARPOY	CHASTENERS	CHAUNCING
CHAPPALS	CHARGING	CHARPOYS	CHASTENING	CHAUNGE
CHAPPED	CHARGRILL	CHARQUI	CHASTENS	CHAUNGED
CHAPPESS	CHARGRILLED	CHARQUIS	CHASTER	CHAUNGES
CHAPPESSES	CHARGRILLING	CHARR	CHASTEST	CHAUNGING
CHAPPIE	CHARGRILLS	CHARRED	CHASTISE	CHAUNT
CHAPPIER	CHARIER	CHARRIER	CHASTISED	CHAUNTED
CHAPPIES	CHARIEST	CHARRIEST	CHASTISES	CHAUNTER
CHAPPIEST	CHARILY	CHARRING	CHASTISING	CHAUNTERS
CHAPPING	CHARINESS	CHARRS	CHASTITIES	CHAUNTING
CHAPPY	CHARINESSES	CHARRY	CHASTITY	CHAUNTRIES
CHAPRASSI	CHARING	CHARS	CHASUBLE	CHAUNTRY
CHAPRASSIES	CHARIOT	CHART	CHASUBLES	CHAUNTS
CHAPRASSIS	CHARIOTED	CHARTA	CHAT	CHAUSSES
CHAPRASSY	CHARIOTING	CHARTAS	CHATEAU	CHAUVIN
CHAPS	CHARIOTS	CHARTED	CHATEAUX	CHAUVINS
CHAPSTICK	CHARISM	CHARTER	CHATELAIN	CHAVE
CHAPSTICKS	CHARISMA	CHARTERED	CHATELAINS	CHAVENDER
CHAPTER	CHARISMAS	CHARTERER	CHATLINE	CHAVENDERS
CHAPTERED	CHARISMS	CHARTERERS	CHATLINES	CHAW
CHAPTERING	CHARITIES	CHARTERING	CHATON	CHAWBACON
CHAPTERS	CHARITY	CHARTERS	CHATONS	CHAWBACONS
CHAPTREL	CHARIVARI	CHARTING	CHATOYANT	CHAWDRON
CHAPTRELS	CHARIVARIS	CHARTISM	CHATS	CHAWDRONS

The Chambers Dictionary is the authority for many longer words; see *OSW* Introduction, page xii

CHAWED	CHECKOUT	CHEFS	CHENIXES	CHESTIER
CHAWING	CHECKOUTS	CHEILITIS	CHENOPOD	CHESTIEST
CHAWS	CHECKRAIL	CHEILITISES	CHENOPODS	CHESTING
CHAY	CHECKRAILS	CHEKA	CHEONGSAM	CHESTNUT
CHAYA	CHECKREIN	CHEKAS	CHEONGSAMS	CHESTNUTS
CHAYAS	CHECKREINS	CHEKIST	CHEQUE	CHESTS
CHAYOTE	CHECKROOM	CHEKISTS	CHEQUER	CHESTY
CHAYOTES	CHECKROOMS	CHELA	CHEQUERED	CHETAH
CHAYROOT	CHECKS	CHELAE	CHEQUERING	CHETAHS
CHAYROOTS	CHECKSUM	CHELAS	CHEQUERS	CHETNIK
CHAYS	CHECKSUMS	CHELASHIP	CHEQUES	CHETNIKS
CHAZAN	CHECKY	CHELASHIPS	CHEQUY	CHEVALET
CHAZANIM	CHEDDITE	CHELATE	CHER	CHEVALETS
CHAZANS	CHEDDITES	CHELATED	CHERALITE	CHEVALIER
CHE	CHEECHAKO	CHELATES	CHERALITES	CHEVALIERS
CHEAP	CHEECHAKOES	CHELATING	CHERE	CHEVELURE
CHEAPEN	CHEECHAKOS	CHELATION	CHERIMOYA	CHEVELURES
CHEAPENED	CHEEK	CHELATIONS	CHERIMOYAS	CHEVEN
CHEAPENER	CHEEKBONE	CHELATOR	CHERISH	CHEVENS
CHEAPENERS	CHEEKBONES	CHELATORS	CHERISHED	CHEVEREL
CHEAPENING	CHEEKED	CHELICERA	CHERISHES	CHEVERELS
CHEAPENS	CHEEKIER	CHELICERAE	CHERISHING	CHEVERIL
CHEAPER	CHEEKIEST	CHELIFORM	CHERNOZEM	CHEVERILS
CHEAPEST	CHEEKILY	CHELIPED	CHERNOZEMS	CHEVERON
CHEAPIE	CHEEKING	CHELIPEDS	CHEROOT	CHEVERONS
CHEAPIES	CHEEKS	CHELOID	CHEROOTS	CHEVERYE
CHEAPLY	CHEEKY	CHELOIDAL	CHERRIED	CHEVERYES
CHEAPNESS	CHEEP	CHELOIDS	CHERRIER	CHEVET
CHEAPNESSES	CHEEPED	CHELONE	CHERRIES	CHEVETS
CHEAPO	CHEEPER	CHELONES	CHERRIEST	CHEVIED
CHEAPS	CHEEPERS	CHELONIAN	CHERRY	CHEVIES
CHEAPY	CHEEPING	CHELONIANS	CHERRYING	CHEVILLE
CHEAT	CHEEPS	CHEMIC	CHERT	CHEVILLES
CHEATED	CHEER	CHEMICAL	CHERTIER	CHEVIN
CHEATER	CHEERED	CHEMICALS	CHERTIEST	CHEVINS
CHEATERIES	CHEERER	CHEMICKED	CHERTS	CHEVRE
CHEATERS	CHEERERS	CHEMICKING	CHERTY	CHEVRES
CHEATERY	CHEERFUL	CHEMICS	CHERUB	CHEVRETTE
CHEATING	CHEERFULLER	CHEMISE	CHERUBIC	CHEVRETTES
CHEATINGS	CHEERFULLEST	CHEMISES	CHERUBIM	CHEVRON
CHEATS	CHEERIER	CHEMISM	CHERUBIMS	CHEVRONED
CHECHAKO	CHEERIEST	CHEMISMS	CHERUBIN	CHEVRONS
CHECHAKOES	CHEERILY	CHEMIST	CHERUBINS	CHEVRONY
CHECHAKOS	CHEERING	CHEMISTRIES	CHERUBS	CHEVY
CHECHAQUA	CHEERIO	CHEMISTRY	CHERUP	CHEVYING
CHECHAQUAS	CHEERIOS	CHEMISTS	CHERUPED	CHEW
CHECHAQUO	CHEERLESS	CHEMITYPE	CHERUPING	CHEWABLE
CHECHAQUOS	CHEERLY	CHEMITYPES	CHERUPS	CHEWED
CHECHIA	CHEERS	CHEMITYPIES	CHERVIL	CHEWER
CHECHIAS	CHEERY	CHEMITYPY	CHERVILS	CHEWERS
CHECK	CHEESE	CHEMMIES	CHESIL	CHEWET
CHECKBOOK	CHEESED	CHEMMY	CHESILS	CHEWETS
CHECKBOOKS	CHEESES	CHEMOSTAT	CHESNUT	CHEWIE
CHECKED	CHEESEVAT	CHEMOSTATS	CHESNUTS	CHEWIER
CHECKER	CHEESEVATS	CHEMURGIC	CHESS	CHEWIES
CHECKERED	CHEESIER	CHEMURGIES	CHESSEL	CHEWIEST
CHECKERS	CHEESIEST	CHEMURGY	CHESSELS	CHEWING
CHECKING	CHEESING	CHENAR	CHESSES	CHEWINK
CHECKLIST	CHEESY	CHENARS	CHESSMAN	CHEWINKS
CHECKLISTS	CHEETAH	CHENET	CHESSMEN	CHEWS
CHECKMATE	CHEETAHS	CHENETS	CHEST	CHEWY
CHECKMATED	CHEEWINK	CHENILLE	CHESTED	CHEZ
CHECKMATES	CHEEWINKS	CHENILLES	CHESTFUL	CHI
CHECKMATING	CHEF	CHENIX	CHESTFULS	CHIACK

CHIACKED	CHICKS	CHIKOR	CHIMBS	CHINNING
CHIACKING	CHICKWEED	CHIKORS	CHIME	CHINO
CHIACKINGS	CHICKWEEDS	CHIKS	CHIMED	CHINOOK
CHIACKS	CHICLE	CHILBLAIN	CHIMER	CHINOOKS
CHIAO	CHICLES	CHILBLAINS	CHIMERA	CHINOS
CHIAREZZA	CHICLY	CHILD	CHIMERAS	CHINOVNIK
CHIAREZZE	CHICO	CHILDBED	CHIMERE	CHINOVNIKS
CHIASM	CHICON	CHILDBEDS	CHIMERES	CHINS
CHIASMA	CHICONS	CHILDE	CHIMERIC	CHINSTRAP
CHIASMAS	CHICORIES	CHILDED	CHIMERID	CHINSTRAPS
CHIASMATA	CHICORY	CHILDER	CHIMERIDS	CHINTZ
CHIASMI	CHICOS	CHILDHOOD	CHIMERISM	CHINTZES
CHIASMS	CHICS	CHILDHOODS	CHIMERISMS	CHINTZIER
CHIASMUS	CHID	CHILDING	CHIMERS	CHINTZIEST
CHIASTIC	CHIDDEN	CHILDISH	CHIMES	CHINTZY
CHIAUS	CHIDE	CHILDLESS	CHIMING	CHINWAG
CHIAUSED	CHIDED	CHILDLIKE	CHIMLEY	CHINWAGGED
CHIAUSES	CHIDER	CHILDLY	CHIMLEYS	CHINWAGGING
CHIAUSING	CHIDERS	CHILDNESS	CHIMNEY	CHINWAGS
CHIBOL	CHIDES	CHILDNESSES	CHIMNEYED	CHIP
CHIBOLS	CHIDING	CHILDREN	CHIMNEYING	CHIPBOARD
CHIBOUK	CHIDINGS	CHILDS	CHIMNEYS	CHIPBOARDS
CHIBOUKS	CHIDLINGS	CHILE	CHIMO	CHIPMUCK
CHIBOUQUE	CHIEF	CHILES	CHIMP	CHIPMUCKS
CHIBOUQUES	CHIEFDOM	CHILI	CHIMPS	CHIPMUNK
CHIC	CHIEFDOMS	CHILIAD	CHIN	CHIPMUNKS
CHICA	CHIEFER	CHILIADS	CHINA	CHIPOCHIA
CHICANA	CHIEFERIES	CHILIAGON	CHINAMPA	CHIPOCHIAS
CHICANAS	CHIEFERY	CHILIAGONS	CHINAMPAS	CHIPOLATA
CHICANE	CHIEFESS	CHILIARCH	CHINAR	CHIPOLATAS
CHICANED	CHIEFESSES	CHILIARCHS	CHINAROOT	CHIPPED
CHICANER	CHIEFEST	CHILIASM	CHINAROOTS	CHIPPER
CHICANERIES	CHIEFLESS	CHILIASMS	CHINARS	CHIPPERS
CHICANERS	CHIEFLING	CHILIAST	CHINAS	CHIPPIE
CHICANERY	CHIEFLINGS	CHILIASTS	CHINAWARE	CHIPPIER
CHICANES	CHIEFLY	CHILIOI	CHINAWARES	CHIPPIES
CHICANING	CHIEFRIES	CHILIOIS	CHINCAPIN	CHIPPIEST
CHICANINGS	CHIEFRY	CHILIS	CHINCAPINS	CHIPPING
CHICANO	CHIEFS	CHILL	CHINCH	CHIPPINGS
CHICANOS	CHIEFSHIP	CHILLADA	CHINCHES	CHIPPY
CHICAS	CHIEFSHIPS	CHILLADAS	CHINCOUGH	CHIPS
CHICCORIES	CHIEFTAIN	CHILLED	CHINCOUGHS	CHIPSET
CHICCORY	CHIEFTAINS	CHILLER	CHINDIT	CHIPSETS
CHICER	CHIEL	CHILLERS	CHINDITS	CHIRAGRA
CHICEST	CHIELD	CHILLEST	CHINE	CHIRAGRAS
CHICH	CHIELDS	CHILLI	CHINED	CHIRAGRIC
CHICHA	CHIELS	CHILLIER	CHINES	CHIRAL
CHICHAS	CHIFFON	CHILLIES	CHINESE	CHIRALITIES
CHICHES	CHIFFONS	CHILLIEST	CHINING	CHIRALITY
CHICHI	CHIGGER	CHILLILY	CHINK	CHIRIMOYA
CHICHIS	CHIGGERS	CHILLING	CHINKAPIN	CHIRIMOYAS
CHICK	CHIGNON	CHILLINGS	CHINKAPINS	CHIRK
CHICKADEE	CHIGNONS	CHILLIS	CHINKARA	CHIRKED
CHICKADEES	CHIGOE	CHILLNESS	CHINKARAS	CHIRKING
CHICKAREE	CHIGOES	CHILLNESSES	CHINKED	CHIRKS
CHICKAREES	CHIGRE	CHILLS	CHINKIE	CHIRL
CHICKEN	CHIGRES	CHILLUM	CHINKIER	CHIRLED
CHICKENED	CHIHUAHUA	CHILLUMS	CHINKIES	CHIRLING
CHICKENING	CHIHUAHUAS	CHILLY	CHINKIEST	CHIRLS
CHICKENS	CHIK	CHILOPOD	CHINKING	CHIRM
CHICKLING	CHIKARA	CHILOPODS	CHINKS	CHIRMED
CHICKLINGS	CHIKARAS	CHIMAERA	CHINKY	CHIRMING
CHICKPEA	CHIKHOR	CHIMAERAS	CHINLESS	CHIRMS
CHICKPEAS	CHIKHORS	CHIMB	CHINNED	CHIROLOGIES

The Chambers Dictionary is the authority for many longer words; see *OSW* Introduction, page xii

CHIROLOGY	CHIV	CHOBDARS	CHOKOS	CHOOSE
CHIRONOMIES	CHIVALRIC	CHOC	CHOKRA	CHOOSER
CHIRONOMY	CHIVALRIES	CHOCCIER	CHOKRAS	CHOOSERS
CHIROPODIES	CHIVALRY	CHOCCIES	CHOKRI	CHOOSES
CHIROPODY	CHIVAREE	CHOCCIEST	CHOKRIS	CHOOSEY
CHIRP	CHIVAREES	CHOCCY	CHOKY	CHOOSIER
CHIRPED	CHIVE	CHOCHO	CHOLAEMIA	CHOOSIEST
CHIRPER	CHIVED	CHOCHOS	CHOLAEMIAS	CHOOSING
CHIRPERS	CHIVES	CHOCK	CHOLAEMIC	CHOOSY
CHIRPIER	CHIVIED	CHOCKED	CHOLECYST	CHOP
CHIRPIEST	CHIVIES	CHOCKER	CHOLECYSTS	CHOPHOUSE
CHIRPILY	CHIVING	CHOCKING	CHOLELITH	CHOPHOUSES
CHIRPING	CHIVS	CHOCKO	CHOLELITHS	CHOPIN
CHIRPS	CHIVVED	CHOCKOS	CHOLEMIA	CHOPINE
CHIRPY	CHIVVIED	CHOCKS	CHOLEMIAS	CHOPINES
CHIRR	CHIVVIES	CHOCO	CHOLENT	CHOPINS
CHIRRE	CHIVVING	CHOCOLATE	CHOLENTS	CHOPLOGIC
CHIRRED	CHIVVY	CHOCOLATES	CHOLER	CHOPLOGICS
CHIRRES	CHIVVYING	CHOCOLATIER	CHOLERA	CHOPPED
CHIRRING	CHIVY	CHOCOLATIEST	CHOLERAIC	CHOPPER
CHIRRS	CHIVYING	CHOCOLATY	CHOLERAS	CHOPPERS
CHIRRUP	CHIYOGAMI	CHOCOS	CHOLERIC	CHOPPIER
CHIRRUPED	CHIYOGAMIS	CHOCS	CHOLERS	CHOPPIEST
CHIRRUPING	CHIZ	CHOCTAW	CHOLI	CHOPPING
CHIRRUPS	CHIZZ	CHOCTAWS	CHOLIAMB	CHOPPINGS
CHIRRUPY	CHIZZED	CHODE	CHOLIAMBS	CHOPPY
CHIRT	CHIZZES	CHOENIX	CHOLIC	CHOPS
CHIRTED	CHIZZING	CHOENIXES	CHOLINE	CHOPSTICK
CHIRTING	CHLAMYDES	CHOICE	CHOLINES	CHOPSTICKS
CHIRTS	CHLAMYDIA	CHOICEFUL	CHOLIS	CHORAGI
CHIS	CHLAMYDIAS	CHOICELY	CHOLTRIES	CHORAGIC
CHISEL	CHLAMYS	CHOICER	CHOLTRY	CHORAGUS
CHISELLED	CHLAMYSES	CHOICES	CHOMP	CHORAGUSES
CHISELLER	CHLOASMA	CHOICEST	CHOMPED	CHORAL
CHISELLERS	CHLOASMATA	CHOIR	CHOMPING	CHORALE
CHISELLING	CHLORACNE	CHOIRBOY	CHOMPS	CHORALES
CHISELLINGS	CHLORACNES	CHOIRBOYS	CHON	CHORALIST
CHISELS	CHLORAL	CHOIRED	CHONDRAL	CHORALISTS
CHIT	CHLORALS	CHOIRGIRL	CHONDRE	CHORALLY
CHITAL	CHLORATE	CHOIRGIRLS	CHONDRES	CHORALS
CHITALS	CHLORATES	CHOIRING	CHONDRI	CHORD
CHITCHAT	CHLORDAN	CHOIRMAN	CHONDRIFIED	CHORDA
CHITCHATS	CHLORDANE	CHOIRMEN	CHONDRIFIES	CHORDAE
CHITCHATTED	CHLORDANES	CHOIRS	CHONDRIFY	CHORDAL
CHITCHATTING	CHLORDANS	CHOKE	CHONDRIFYING	CHORDATE
CHITIN	CHLORELLA	CHOKEBORE	CHONDRIN	CHORDATES
CHITINOID	CHLORELLAS	CHOKEBORES	CHONDRINS	CHORDEE
CHITINOUS	CHLORIC	CHOKECOIL	CHONDRITE	CHORDEES
CHITINS	CHLORIDE	CHOKECOILS	CHONDRITES	CHORDING
CHITLINGS	CHLORIDES	CHOKED	CHONDROID	CHORDINGS
CHITON	CHLORIN	CHOKEDAMP	CHONDRULE	CHORDS
CHITONS	CHLORINE	CHOKEDAMPS	CHONDRULES	CHORE
CHITS	CHLORINES	CHOKER	CHONDRUS	CHOREA
CHITTED	CHLORINS	CHOKERS	CHONS	CHOREAS
CHITTER	CHLORITE	CHOKES	CHOOF	CHOREE
CHITTERED	CHLORITES	CHOKEY	CHOOFED	CHOREES
CHITTERING	CHLORITIC	CHOKEYS	CHOOFING	CHOREGI
CHITTERINGS	CHLOROSES	CHOKIDAR	CHOOFS	CHOREGIC
CHITTERS	CHLOROSIS	CHOKIDARS	CHOOK	CHOREGUS
CHITTIER	CHLOROTIC	CHOKIER	CHOOKIE	CHOREGUSES
CHITTIES	CHLOROUS	CHOKIES	CHOOKIES	CHOREIC
CHITTIEST	CHOANA	CHOKIEST	CHOOKS	CHORES
CHITTING	CHOANAE	CHOKING	CHOOM	CHOREUS
CHITTY	CHOBDAR	CHOKO	CHOOMS	CHOREUSES

The Chambers Dictionary is the authority for many longer words; see *OSW* Introduction, page xii

CHORIA	CHOWRIES	CHRYSALIS	CHUMPINGS	CHURRING
CHORIAL	CHOWRIS	CHRYSALISES	CHUMPS	CHURRS
CHORIAMB	CHOWRY	CHRYSANTH	CHUMS	CHURRUS
CHORIAMBI	CHOWS	CHRYSANTHS	CHUNDER	CHURRUSES
CHORIAMBS	CHRISM	CHTHONIAN	CHUNDERED	CHUSE
CHORIC	CHRISMAL	CHTHONIC	CHUNDERING	CHUSES
CHORINE	CHRISMALS	CHUB	CHUNDERS	CHUSING
CHORINES	CHRISMS	CHUBBIER	CHUNK	CHUT
CHORIOID	CHRISOM	CHUBBIEST	CHUNKIER	CHUTE
CHORIOIDS	CHRISOMS	CHUBBY	CHUNKIEST	CHUTES
CHORION	CHRISTEN	CHUBS	CHUNKING	CHUTIST
CHORIONIC	CHRISTENED	CHUCK	CHUNKINGS	CHUTISTS
CHORISES	CHRISTENING	CHUCKED	CHUNKS	CHUTNEY
CHORISIS	CHRISTENINGS	CHUCKHOLE	CHUNKY	CHUTNEYS
CHORISM	CHRISTENS	CHUCKHOLES	CHUNNEL	CHUTZPAH
CHORISMS	CHRISTIE	CHUCKIE	CHUNNELS	CHUTZPAHS
CHORIST	CHRISTIES	CHUCKIES	CHUNNER	CHYACK
CHORISTER	CHRISTOM	CHUCKING	CHUNNERED	CHYACKED
CHORISTERS	CHRISTOMS	CHUCKLE	CHUNNERING	CHYACKING
CHORISTS	CHRISTY	CHUCKLED	CHUNNERS	CHYACKS
CHORIZO	CHROMA	CHUCKLES	CHUNTER	CHYLDE
CHORIZONT	CHROMAKEY	CHUCKLING	CHUNTERED	CHYLE
CHORIZONTS	CHROMAKEYS	CHUCKLINGS	CHUNTERING	CHYLES
CHORIZOS	CHROMAS	CHUCKS	CHUNTERS	CHYLIFIED
CHOROID	CHROMATE	CHUDDAH	CHUPATI	CHYLIFIES
CHOROIDS	CHROMATES	CHUDDAHS	CHUPATIS	CHYLIFY
CHOROLOGIES	CHROMATIC	CHUDDAR	CHUPATTI	CHYLIFYING
CHOROLOGY	CHROMATICS	CHUDDARS	CHUPATTIS	CHYLURIA
CHORTLE	CHROMATID	CHUDDIES	CHUPPAH	CHYLURIAS
CHORTLED	CHROMATIDS	CHUDDY	CHUPPAHS	CHYME
CHORTLES	CHROMATIN	CHUFA	CHUPRASSIES	CHYMES
CHORTLING	CHROMATINS	CHUFAS	CHUPRASSY	CHYMIFIED
CHORUS	CHROME	CHUFF	CHURCH	CHYMIFIES
CHORUSED	CHROMED	CHUFFED	CHURCHED	CHYMIFY
CHORUSES	CHROMEL	CHUFFIER	CHURCHES	CHYMIFYING
CHORUSING	CHROMELS	CHUFFIEST	CHURCHIER	CHYMISTRIES
CHOSE	CHROMENE	CHUFFING	CHURCHIEST	CHYMISTRY
CHOSEN	CHROMENES	CHUFFS	CHURCHING	CHYMOUS
CHOSES	CHROMES	CHUFFY	CHURCHINGS	CHYND
CHOTA	CHROMIC	CHUG	CHURCHISM	CHYPRE
CHOTT	CHROMIDIA	CHUGGED	CHURCHISMS	CHYPRES
CHOTTS	CHROMING	CHUGGING	CHURCHLIER	CIABATTA
CHOU	CHROMITE	CHUGS	CHURCHLIEST	CIABATTAS
CHOUGH	CHROMITES	CHUKAR	CHURCHLY	CIABATTE
CHOUGHS	CHROMIUM	CHUKARS	CHURCHMAN	CIAO
CHOULTRIES	CHROMIUMS	CHUKKA	CHURCHMEN	CIAOS
CHOULTRY	CHROMO	CHUKKAS	CHURCHWAY	CIBATION
CHOUNTER	CHROMOGEN	CHUKKER	CHURCHWAYS	CIBATIONS
CHOUNTERED	CHROMOGENS	CHUKKERS	CHURCHY	CIBOL
CHOUNTERING	CHROMOS	CHUKOR	CHURIDARS	CIBOLS
CHOUNTERS	CHRONAXIE	CHUKORS	CHURINGA	CIBORIA
CHOUSE	CHRONAXIES	CHUM	CHURINGAS	CIBORIUM
CHOUSED	CHRONIC	CHUMLEY	CHURL	CICADA
CHOUSES	CHRONICAL	CHUMLEYS	CHURLISH	CICADAS
CHOUSING	CHRONICLE	CHUMMAGE	CHURLS	CICALA
CHOUT	CHRONICLED	CHUMMAGES	CHURN	CICALAS
CHOUTS	CHRONICLES	CHUMMED	CHURNED	CICATRICE
CHOUX	CHRONICLING	CHUMMIER	CHURNING	CICATRICES
CHOW	CHRONICS	CHUMMIES	CHURNINGS	CICATRISE
CHOWDER	CHRONON	CHUMMIEST	CHURNMILK	CICATRISED
CHOWDERS	CHRONONS	CHUMMING	CHURNMILKS	CICATRISES
CHOWKIDAR	CHRYSALID	CHUMMY	CHURNS	CICATRISING
CHOWKIDARS	CHRYSALIDES	CHUMP	CHURR	CICATRIX
CHOWRI	CHRYSALIDS	CHUMPING	CHURRED	CICATRIXES

CICATRIZE	CILICES	CINERIN	CIRES	CITE
CICATRIZED	CILICIOUS	CINERINS	CIRL	CITEABLE
CICATRIZES	CILIOLATE	CINGULA	CIRLS	CITED
CICATRIZING	CILIUM	CINGULUM	CIRQUE	CITER
CICELIES	CILL	CINNABAR	CIRQUES	CITERS
CICELY	CILLS	CINNABARS	CIRRATE	CITES
CICERO	CIMAR	CINNAMIC	CIRRHOPOD	CITESS
CICERONE	CIMARS	CINNAMON	CIRRHOPODS	CITESSES
CICERONED	CIMBALOM	CINNAMONS	CIRRHOSES	CITHARA
CICERONEING	CIMBALOMS	CINQUAIN	CIRRHOSIS	CITHARAS
CICERONES	CIMELIA	CINQUAINS	CIRRHOTIC	CITHARIST
CICERONI	CIMEX	CINQUE	CIRRI	CITHARISTS
CICEROS	CIMICES	CINQUES	CIRRIFORM	CITHER
CICHLID	CIMIER	CION	CIRRIPED	CITHERN
CICHLIDS	CIMIERS	CIONS	CIRRIPEDE	CITHERNS
CICHLOID	CIMINITE	CIPHER	CIRRIPEDES	CITHERS
CICINNUS	CIMINITES	CIPHERED	CIRRIPEDS	CITIES
CICINNUSES	CIMOLITE	CIPHERING	CIRROSE	CITIFIED
CICISBEI	CIMOLITES	CIPHERINGS	CIRROUS	CITIFIES
CICISBEO	CINCH	CIPHERS	CIRRUS	CITIFY
CICLATON	CINCHED	CIPOLIN	CIRSOID	CITIFYING
CICLATONS	CINCHES	CIPOLINS	CISALPINE	CITIGRADE
CICLATOUN	CINCHING	CIPOLLINO	CISCO	CITING
CICLATOUNS	CINCHINGS	CIPOLLINOS	CISCOES	CITIZEN
CICUTA	CINCHONA	CIPPI	CISCOS	CITIZENRIES
CICUTAS	CINCHONAS	CIPPUS	CISELEUR	CITIZENRY
CID	CINCHONIC	CIRCA	CISELEURS	CITIZENS
CIDARIS	CINCINNUS	CIRCADIAN	CISELURE	CITO
CIDARISES	CINCINNUSES	CIRCAR	CISELURES	CITOLE
CIDE	CINCT	CIRCARS	CISLUNAR	CITOLES
CIDED	CINCTURE	CIRCINATE	CISPADANE	CITRANGE
CIDER	CINCTURED	CIRCITER	CISPLATIN	CITRANGES
CIDERKIN	CINCTURES	CIRCLE	CISPLATINS	CITRATE
CIDERKINS	CINCTURING	CIRCLED	CISSIER	CITRATES
CIDERS	CINDER	CIRCLER	CISSIES	CITREOUS
CIDERY	CINDERED	CIRCLERS	CISSIEST	CITRIC
CIDES	CINDERING	CIRCLES	CISSOID	CITRIN
CIDING	CINDERS	CIRCLET	CISSOIDS	CITRINE
CIDS	CINDERY	CIRCLETS	CISSUS	CITRINES
CIEL	CINEAST	CIRCLING	CISSUSES	CITRINS
CIELED	CINEASTE	CIRCLINGS	CISSY	CITRON
CIELING	CINEASTES	CIRCLIP	CIST	CITRONS
CIELINGS	CINEASTS	CIRCLIPS	CISTED	CITROUS
CIELS	CINEMA	CIRCS	CISTERN	CITRUS
CIERGE	CINEMAS	CIRCUIT	CISTERNA	CITRUSES
CIERGES	CINEMATIC	CIRCUITED	CISTERNAE	CITS
CIG	CINEOL	CIRCUITIES	CISTERNS	CITTERN
CIGAR	CINEOLE	CIRCUITING	CISTIC	CITTERNS
CIGARETTE	CINEOLES	CIRCUITRIES	CISTRON	CITY
CIGARETTES	CINEOLS	CIRCUITRY	CISTRONS	CITYFIED
CIGARILLO	CINEPHILE	CIRCUITS	CISTS	CITYFIES
CIGARILLOS	CINEPHILES	CIRCUITY	CISTUS	CITYFY
CIGARS	CINEPLEX	CIRCULAR	CISTUSES	CITYFYING
CIGGIE	CINEPLEXES	CIRCULARS	CISTVAEN	CITYSCAPE
CIGGIES	CINERAMIC	CIRCULATE	CISTVAENS	CITYSCAPES
CIGGY	CINERARIA	CIRCULATED	CIT	CIVE
CIGS	CINERARIAS	CIRCULATES	CITABLE	CIVES
CILANTRO	CINERARY	CIRCULATING	CITADEL	CIVET
CILANTROS	CINERATOR	CIRCULATINGS	CITADELS	CIVETS
CILIA	CINERATORS	CIRCUS	CITAL	CIVIC
CILIARY	CINEREA	CIRCUSES	CITALS	CIVICALLY
CILIATE	CINEREAL	CIRCUSSY	CITATION	CIVICS
CILIATES	CINEREAS	CIRCUSY	CITATIONS	CIVIL
CILICE	CINEREOUS	CIRE	CITATORY	CIVILIAN

CIVILIANS	CLAIM	CLANGORING	CLARION	CLASTS
CIVILISE	CLAIMABLE	CLANGORS	CLARIONET	CLAT
CIVILISED	CLAIMANT	CLANGOUR	CLARIONETS	CLATCH
CIVILISER	CLAIMANTS	CLANGOURED	CLARIONS	CLATCHED
CIVILISERS	CLAIMED	CLANGOURING	CLARITIES	CLATCHES
CIVILISES	CLAIMER	CLANGOURS	CLARITY	CLATCHING
CIVILISING	CLAIMERS	CLANGS	CLARKIA	CLATHRATE
CIVILIST	CLAIMING	CLANK	CLARKIAS	CLATS
CIVILISTS	CLAIMS	CLANKED	CLARO	CLATTED
CIVILITIES	CLAM	CLANKING	CLAROES	CLATTER
CIVILITY	CLAMANCIES	CLANKINGS	CLAROS	CLATTERED
CIVILIZE	CLAMANCY	CLANKS	CLARSACH	CLATTERER
CIVILIZED	CLAMANT	CLANNISH	CLARSACHS	CLATTERERS
CIVILIZER	CLAMANTLY	CLANS	CLART	CLATTERING
CIVILIZERS	CLAMBAKE	CLANSHIP	CLARTED	CLATTERS
CIVILIZES	CLAMBAKES	CLANSHIPS	CLARTIER	CLATTERY
CIVILIZING	CLAMBE	CLANSMAN	CLARTIEST	CLATTING
CIVILLY	CLAMBER	CLANSMEN	CLARTING	CLAUCHT
CIVISM	CLAMBERED	CLAP	CLARTS	CLAUCHTED
CIVISMS	CLAMBERING	CLAPBOARD	CLARTY	CLAUCHTING
CIVVIES	CLAMBERS	CLAPBOARDS	CLARY	CLAUCHTS
CIVVY	CLAME	CLAPBREAD	CLASH	CLAUGHT
CIZERS	CLAMES	CLAPBREADS	CLASHED	CLAUGHTED
CLABBER	CLAMMED	CLAPDISH	CLASHER	CLAUGHTING
CLABBERS	CLAMMIER	CLAPDISHES	CLASHERS	CLAUGHTS
CLACHAN	CLAMMIEST	CLAPNET	CLASHES	CLAUSAL
CLACHANS	CLAMMILY	CLAPNETS	CLASHING	CLAUSE
CLACK	CLAMMING	CLAPPED	CLASHINGS	CLAUSES
CLACKBOX	CLAMMY	CLAPPER	CLASP	CLAUSTRA
CLACKBOXES	CLAMOR	CLAPPERED	CLASPED	CLAUSTRAL
CLACKDISH	CLAMORED	CLAPPERING	CLASPER	CLAUSTRUM
CLACKDISHES	CLAMORING	CLAPPERINGS	CLASPERS	CLAUSULA
CLACKED	CLAMOROUS	CLAPPERS	CLASPING	CLAUSULAE
CLACKER	CLAMORS	CLAPPING	CLASPINGS	CLAUSULAR
CLACKERS	CLAMOUR	CLAPPINGS	CLASPS	CLAUT
CLACKING	CLAMOURED	CLAPS	CLASS	CLAUTED
CLACKS	CLAMOURER	CLAPTRAP	CLASSABLE	CLAUTING
CLAD	CLAMOURERS	CLAPTRAPS	CLASSED	CLAUTS
CLADDED	CLAMOURING	CLAQUE	CLASSES	CLAVATE
CLADDER	CLAMOURS	CLAQUES	CLASSIBLE	CLAVATED
CLADDERS	CLAMP	CLAQUEUR	CLASSIC	CLAVATION
CLADDING	CLAMPDOWN	CLAQUEURS	CLASSICAL	CLAVATIONS
CLADDINGS	CLAMPDOWNS	CLARAIN	CLASSICS	CLAVE
CLADE	CLAMPED	CLARAINS	CLASSIER	CLAVECIN
CLADES	CLAMPER	CLARENCE	CLASSIEST	CLAVECINS
CLADISM	CLAMPERED	CLARENCES	CLASSIFIC	CLAVER
CLADISMS	CLAMPERING	CLARENDON	CLASSIFIED	CLAVERED
CLADIST	CLAMPERS	CLARENDONS	CLASSIFIES	CLAVERING
CLADISTIC	CLAMPING	CLARET	CLASSIFY	CLAVERS
CLADISTICS	CLAMPS	CLARETED	CLASSIFYING	CLAVES
CLADISTS	CLAMS	CLARETING	CLASSING	CLAVICLE
CLADODE	CLAMSHELL	CLARETS	CLASSIS	CLAVICLES
CLADODES	CLAMSHELLS	CLARIES	CLASSISM	CLAVICORN
CLADOGRAM	CLAN	CLARIFIED	CLASSISMS	CLAVICORNS
CLADOGRAMS	CLANG	CLARIFIER	CLASSIST	CLAVICULA
CLADS	CLANGBOX	CLARIFIERS	CLASSLESS	CLAVICULAE
CLAES	CLANGBOXES	CLARIFIES	CLASSMAN	CLAVIE
CLAG	CLANGED	CLARIFY	CLASSMATE	CLAVIER
CLAGGED	CLANGER	CLARIFYING	CLASSMATES	CLAVIERS
CLAGGIER	CLANGERS	CLARINET	CLASSMEN	CLAVIES
CLAGGIEST	CLANGING	CLARINETS	CLASSROOM	CLAVIFORM
CLAGGING	CLANGINGS	CLARINI	CLASSROOMS	CLAVIGER
CLAGGY	CLANGOR	CLARINO	CLASSY	CLAVIGERS
CLAGS	CLANGORED	CLARINOS	CLASTIC	CLAVIS

CLAVULATE	CLEARWAYS	CLERGIES	CLICKERS	CLIMES
CLAW	CLEARWING	CLERGY	CLICKET	CLINAMEN
CLAWBACK	CLEARWINGS	CLERGYMAN	CLICKETED	CLINAMENS
CLAWBACKS	CLEAT	CLERGYMEN	CLICKETING	CLINCH
CLAWED	CLEATED	CLERIC	CLICKETS	CLINCHED
CLAWING	CLEATING	CLERICAL	CLICKING	CLINCHER
CLAWLESS	CLEATS	CLERICALS	CLICKINGS	CLINCHERS
CLAWS	CLEAVABLE	CLERICATE	CLICKS	CLINCHES
CLAY	CLEAVAGE	CLERICATES	CLIED	CLINCHING
CLAYED	CLEAVAGES	CLERICITIES	CLIENT	CLINE
CLAYEY	CLEAVE	CLERICITY	CLIENTAGE	CLINES
CLAYIER	CLEAVED	CLERICS	CLIENTAGES	CLING
CLAYIEST	CLEAVER	CLERIHEW	CLIENTAL	CLINGER
CLAYING	CLEAVERS	CLERIHEWS	CLIENTELE	CLINGERS
CLAYISH	CLEAVES	CLERISIES	CLIENTELES	CLINGFILM
CLAYMORE	CLEAVING	CLERISY	CLIENTS	CLINGFILMS
CLAYMORES	CLEAVINGS	CLERK	CLIES	CLINGIER
CLAYPAN	CLECHE	CLERKDOM	CLIFF	CLINGIEST
CLAYPANS	CLECK	CLERKDOMS	CLIFFED	CLINGING
CLAYS	CLECKED	CLERKED	CLIFFHANG	CLINGS
CLAYTONIA	CLECKING	CLERKESS	CLIFFHANGING	CLINGY
CLAYTONIAS	CLECKINGS	CLERKESSES	CLIFFHANGINGS	CLINIC
CLEAN	CLECKS	CLERKING	CLIFFHANGS	CLINICAL
CLEANED	CLEEK	CLERKISH	CLIFFHUNG	CLINICIAN
CLEANER	CLEEKED	CLERKLIKE	CLIFFIER	CLINICIANS
CLEANERS	CLEEKING	CLERKLING	CLIFFIEST	CLINICS
CLEANEST	CLEEKIT	CLERKLINGS	CLIFFS	CLINIQUE
CLEANING	CLEEKS	CLERKLY	CLIFFY	CLINIQUES
CLEANINGS	CLEEP	CLERKS	CLIFT	CLINK
CLEANLIER	CLEEPED	CLERKSHIP	CLIFTED	CLINKED
CLEANLIEST	CLEEPING	CLERKSHIPS	CLIFTIER	CLINKER
CLEANLY	CLEEPS	CLERUCH	CLIFTIEST	CLINKERS
CLEANNESS	CLEEVE	CLERUCHIA	CLIFTS	CLINKING
CLEANNESSES	CLEEVES	CLERUCHIAS	CLIFTY	CLINKS
CLEANS	CLEF	CLERUCHIES	CLIMACTIC	CLINOAXES
CLEANSE	CLEFS	CLERUCHS	CLIMATAL	CLINOAXIS
CLEANSED	CLEFT	CLERUCHY	CLIMATE	CLINQUANT
CLEANSER	CLEFTS	CLEUCH	CLIMATED	CLINQUANTS
CLEANSERS	CLEG	CLEUCHS	CLIMATES	CLINT
CLEANSES	CLEGS	CLEUGH	CLIMATIC	CLINTS
CLEANSING	CLEIDOIC	CLEUGHS	CLIMATING	CLIP
CLEANSINGS	CLEITHRAL	CLEVE	CLIMATISE	CLIPART
CLEANSKIN	CLEM	CLEVEITE	CLIMATISED	CLIPARTS
CLEANSKINS	CLEMATIS	CLEVEITES	CLIMATISES	CLIPBOARD
CLEAR	CLEMATISES	CLEVER	CLIMATISING	CLIPBOARDS
CLEARAGE	CLEMENCIES	CLEVERER	CLIMATIZE	CLIPE
CLEARAGES	CLEMENCY	CLEVEREST	CLIMATIZED	CLIPED
CLEARANCE	CLEMENT	CLEVERISH	CLIMATIZES	CLIPES
CLEARANCES	CLEMENTLY	CLEVERLY	CLIMATIZING	CLIPING
CLEARCOLE	CLEMMED	CLEVES	CLIMATURE	CLIPPED
CLEARCOLES	CLEMMING	CLEVIS	CLIMATURES	CLIPPER
CLEARED	CLEMS	CLEVISES	CLIMAX	CLIPPERS
CLEARER	CLENCH	CLEW	CLIMAXED	CLIPPIE
CLEARERS	CLENCHED	CLEWED	CLIMAXES	CLIPPIES
CLEAREST	CLENCHES	CLEWING	CLIMAXING	CLIPPING
CLEARING	CLENCHING	CLEWS	CLIMB	CLIPPINGS
CLEARINGS	CLEPE	CLIANTHUS	CLIMBABLE	CLIPS
CLEARLY	CLEPED	CLIANTHUSES	CLIMBED	CLIPT
CLEARNESS	CLEPES	CLICHE	CLIMBER	CLIQUE
CLEARNESSES	CLEPING	CLICHEED	CLIMBERS	CLIQUES
CLEARS	CLEPSYDRA	CLICHES	CLIMBING	CLIQUEY
CLEARSKIN	CLEPSYDRAS	CLICK	CLIMBINGS	CLIQUIER
CLEARSKINS	CLERECOLE	CLICKED	CLIMBS	CLIQUIEST
CLEARWAY	CLERECOLES	CLICKER	CLIME	CLIQUISH

The Chambers Dictionary is the authority for many longer words; see *OSW* Introduction, page xii

CLIQUISM	CLODPOLLS	CLOSELY	CLOUDLETS	CLUBBIST
CLIQUISMS	CLODS	CLOSENESS	CLOUDS	CLUBBISTS
CLIQUY	CLOFF	CLOSENESSES	CLOUDTOWN	CLUBBY
CLITELLA	CLOFFS	CLOSER	CLOUDTOWNS	CLUBHOUSE
CLITELLAR	CLOG	CLOSERS	CLOUDY	CLUBHOUSES
CLITELLUM	CLOGDANCE	CLOSES	CLOUGH	CLUBLAND
CLITHRAL	CLOGDANCES	CLOSEST	CLOUGHS	CLUBLANDS
CLITIC	CLOGGED	CLOSET	CLOUR	CLUBMAN
CLITICS	CLOGGER	CLOSETED	CLOURED	CLUBMEN
CLITORAL	CLOGGERS	CLOSETING	CLOURING	CLUBROOM
CLITORIS	CLOGGIER	CLOSETS	CLOURS	CLUBROOMS
CLITORISES	CLOGGIEST	CLOSING	CLOUS	CLUBROOT
CLITTER	CLOGGING	CLOSINGS	CLOUT	CLUBROOTS
CLITTERED	CLOGGY	CLOSURE	CLOUTED	CLUBRUSH
CLITTERING	CLOGS	CLOSURED	CLOUTER	CLUBRUSHES
CLITTERS	CLOISON	CLOSURES	CLOUTERLY	CLUBS
CLIVERS	CLOISONNE	CLOSURING	CLOUTERS	CLUBWOMAN
CLIVIA	CLOISONNES	CLOT	CLOUTING	CLUBWOMEN
CLIVIAS	CLOISONS	CLOTBUR	CLOUTS	CLUCK
CLOACA	CLOISTER	CLOTBURS	CLOVE	CLUCKED
CLOACAE	CLOISTERED	CLOTE	CLOVEN	CLUCKIER
CLOACAL	CLOISTERING	CLOTEBUR	CLOVEPINK	CLUCKIEST
CLOACALIN	CLOISTERS	CLOTEBURS	CLOVEPINKS	CLUCKING
CLOACINAL	CLOISTRAL	CLOTES	CLOVER	CLUCKS
CLOAK	CLOKE	CLOTH	CLOVERED	CLUCKY
CLOAKED	CLOKED	CLOTHE	CLOVERS	CLUDGIE
CLOAKING	CLOKES	CLOTHED	CLOVERY	CLUDGIES
CLOAKROOM	CLOKING	CLOTHES	CLOVES	CLUE
CLOAKROOMS	CLOMB	CLOTHIER	CLOW	CLUED
CLOAKS	CLOMP	CLOTHIERS	CLOWDER	CLUEING
CLOAM	CLOMPED	CLOTHING	CLOWDERS	CLUELESS
CLOAMS	CLOMPING	CLOTHINGS	CLOWN	CLUES
CLOBBER	CLOMPS	CLOTHS	CLOWNED	CLUING
CLOBBERED	CLONAL	CLOTPOLL	CLOWNERIES	CLUMBER
CLOBBERING	CLONALLY	CLOTPOLLS	CLOWNERY	CLUMBERS
CLOBBERS	CLONE	CLOTS	CLOWNING	CLUMP
CLOCHARD	CLONED	CLOTTED	CLOWNINGS	CLUMPED
CLOCHARDS	CLONES	CLOTTER	CLOWNISH	CLUMPER
CLOCHE	CLONIC	CLOTTERED	CLOWNS	CLUMPERS
CLOCHES	CLONICITIES	CLOTTERING	CLOWS	CLUMPIER
CLOCK	CLONICITY	CLOTTERS	CLOY	CLUMPIEST
CLOCKED	CLONING	CLOTTIER	CLOYE	CLUMPING
CLOCKER	CLONK	CLOTTIEST	CLOYED	CLUMPS
CLOCKERS	CLONKED	CLOTTING	CLOYES	CLUMPY
CLOCKING	CLONKING	CLOTTINGS	CLOYING	CLUMSIER
CLOCKINGS	CLONKS	CLOTTY	CLOYLESS	CLUMSIEST
CLOCKS	CLONUS	CLOTURE	CLOYMENT	CLUMSILY
CLOCKWISE	CLONUSES	CLOTURED	CLOYMENTS	CLUMSY
CLOCKWORK	CLOOP	CLOTURES	CLOYS	CLUNCH
CLOCKWORKS	CLOOPS	CLOTURING	CLOYSOME	CLUNCHES
CLOD	CLOOT	CLOU	CLOZE	CLUNG
CLODDED	CLOOTS	CLOUD	CLUB	CLUNK
CLODDIER	CLOP	CLOUDAGE	CLUBABLE	CLUNKED
CLODDIEST	CLOPPED	CLOUDAGES	CLUBBABLE	CLUNKIER
CLODDING	CLOPPING	CLOUDED	CLUBBED	CLUNKIEST
CLODDISH	CLOPS	CLOUDIER	CLUBBER	CLUNKING
CLODDY	CLOQUE	CLOUDIEST	CLUBBERS	CLUNKS
CLODLY	CLOQUES	CLOUDILY	CLUBBIER	CLUNKY
CLODPATE	CLOSE	CLOUDING	CLUBBIEST	CLUPEID
CLODPATED	CLOSED	CLOUDINGS	CLUBBING	CLUPEIDS
CLODPATES	CLOSEDOWN	CLOUDLAND	CLUBBINGS	CLUPEOID
CLODPOLE	CLOSEDOWNS	CLOUDLANDS	CLUBBISH	CLUPEOIDS
CLODPOLES	CLOSEHEAD	CLOUDLESS	CLUBBISM	CLUSIA
CLODPOLL	CLOSEHEADS	CLOUDLET	CLUBBISMS	CLUSIAS

CLUSTER	COADJUTORS	COAPTING	COBALTS	COCCIDS
CLUSTERED	COADUNATE	COAPTS	COBB	COCCO
CLUSTERING	COADUNATED	COARB	COBBED	COCCOID
CLUSTERS	COADUNATES	COARBS	COBBER	COCCOLITE
CLUSTERY	COADUNATING	COARCTATE	COBBERS	COCCOLITES
CLUTCH	COAGULA	COARCTATED	COBBIER	COCCOLITH
CLUTCHED	COAGULANT	COARCTATES	COBBIEST	COCCOLITHS
CLUTCHES	COAGULANTS	COARCTATING	COBBING	COCCOS
CLUTCHING	COAGULASE	COARSE	COBBLE	COCCUS
CLUTTER	COAGULASES	COARSELY	COBBLED	COCCYGEAL
CLUTTERED	COAGULATE	COARSEN	COBBLER	COCCYGES
CLUTTERING	COAGULATED	COARSENED	COBBLERIES	COCCYGIAN
CLUTTERS	COAGULATES	COARSENING	COBBLERS	COCCYX
CLY	COAGULATING	COARSENS	COBBLERY	COCH
CLYING	COAGULUM	COARSER	COBBLES	COCHES
CLYPE	COAITA	COARSEST	COBBLING	COCHINEAL
CLYPEAL	COAITAS	COARSISH	COBBLINGS	COCHINEALS
CLYPEATE	COAL	COAST	COBBS	COCHLEA
CLYPED	COALBALL	COASTAL	COBBY	COCHLEAE
CLYPEI	COALBALLS	COASTED	COBIA	COCHLEAR
CLYPES	COALED	COASTER	COBIAS	COCHLEARE
CLYPEUS	COALER	COASTERS	COBLE	COCHLEARES
CLYPING	COALERS	COASTING	COBLES	COCHLEARS
CLYSTER	COALESCE	COASTINGS	COBLOAF	COCHLEATE
CLYSTERS	COALESCED	COASTLINE	COBLOAVES	COCK
CNEMIAL	COALESCES	COASTLINES	COBNUT	COCKADE
CNIDA	COALESCING	COASTS	COBNUTS	COCKADES
CNIDAE	COALFACE	COASTWARD	COBRA	COCKATEEL
CNIDARIAN	COALFACES	COASTWARDS	COBRAS	COCKATEELS
CNIDARIANS	COALFIELD	COASTWISE	COBRIC	COCKATIEL
COACH	COALFIELDS	COAT	COBRIFORM	COCKATIELS
COACHDOG	COALFISH	COATE	COBS	COCKATOO
COACHDOGS	COALFISHES	COATED	COBURG	COCKATOOS
COACHED	COALHOUSE	COATEE	COBURGS	COCKBIRD
COACHEE	COALHOUSES	COATEES	COBWEB	COCKBIRDS
COACHEES	COALIER	COATER	COBWEBBED	COCKBOAT
COACHER	COALIEST	COATERS	COBWEBBIER	COCKBOATS
COACHERS	COALING	COATES	COBWEBBIEST	COCKED
COACHES	COALISE	COATI	COBWEBBING	COCKER
COACHIES	COALISED	COATING	COBWEBBY	COCKERED
COACHING	COALISES	COATINGS	COBWEBS	COCKEREL
COACHINGS	COALISING	COATIS	COBZA	COCKERELS
COACHLINE	COALITION	COATLESS	COBZAS	COCKERING
COACHLINES	COALITIONS	COATRACK	COCA	COCKERS
COACHLOAD	COALIZE	COATRACKS	COCAINE	COCKET
COACHLOADS	COALIZED	COATS	COCAINES	COCKETS
COACHMAN	COALIZES	COATSTAND	COCAINISE	COCKEYE
COACHMEN	COALIZING	COATSTANDS	COCAINISED	COCKEYED
COACHWHIP	COALMAN	COAX	COCAINISES	COCKEYES
COACHWHIPS	COALMEN	COAXED	COCAINISING	COCKFIGHT
COACHWOOD	COALMINE	COAXER	COCAINISM	COCKFIGHTS
COACHWOODS	COALMINER	COAXERS	COCAINISMS	COCKHORSE
COACHWORK	COALMINERS	COAXES	COCAINIST	COCKHORSES
COACHWORKS	COALMINES	COAXIAL	COCAINISTS	COCKIER
COACHY	COALPIT	COAXIALLY	COCAINIZE	COCKIES
COACT	COALPITS	COAXING	COCAINIZED	COCKIEST
COACTED	COALS	COAXINGLY	COCAINIZES	COCKILY
COACTING	COALTAR	COB	COCAINIZING	COCKINESS
COACTION	COALTARS	COBALAMIN	COCAS	COCKINESSES
COACTIONS	COALY	COBALAMINS	COCCAL	COCKING
COACTIVE	COAMING	COBALT	COCCI	COCKLAIRD
COACTS	COAMINGS	COBALTIC	COCCID	COCKLAIRDS
COADAPTED	COAPT	COBALTINE	COCCIDIA	COCKLE
COADJUTOR	COAPTED	COBALTITES	COCCIDIUM	COCKLEBUR

COCKLEBURS	COCOPLUM	CODPIECE	COFFERED	COGNOMENS
COCKLED	COCOPLUMS	CODPIECES	COFFERING	COGNOMINA
COCKLEMAN	COCOS	CODS	COFFERS	COGNOSCE
COCKLEMEN	COCOTTE	COED	COFFIN	COGNOSCED
COCKLES	COCOTTES	COEDS	COFFINED	COGNOSCES
COCKLING	COCTILE	COEHORN	COFFING	COGNOSCING
COCKLOFT	COCTION	COEHORNS	COFFINING	COGNOVIT
COCKLOFTS	COCTIONS	COELIAC	COFFINITE	COGNOVITS
COCKMATCH	COCULTURE	COELIACS	COFFINITES	COGS
COCKMATCHES	COCULTURED	COELOM	COFFINS	COGUE
COCKNEY	COCULTURES	COELOMATE	COFFLE	COGUES
COCKNEYFIED	COCULTURING	COELOMATES	COFFLES	COGWHEEL
COCKNEYFIES	COCUSWOOD	COELOME	COFFRET	COGWHEELS
COCKNEYFY	COCUSWOODS	COELOMES	COFFRETS	COHAB
COCKNEYFYING	COD	COELOMIC	COFFS	COHABIT
COCKNEYS	CODA	COELOMS	COFT	COHABITED
COCKNIFIED	CODAS	COELOSTAT	COG	COHABITEE
COCKNIFIES	CODDED	COELOSTATS	COGENCE	COHABITEES
COCKNIFY	CODDER	COEMPTION	COGENCES	COHABITING
COCKNIFYING	CODDERS	COEMPTIONS	COGENCIES	COHABITOR
COCKPIT	CODDING	COENOBIA	COGENCY	COHABITORS
COCKPITS	CODDLE	COENOBITE	COGENER	COHABITS
COCKROACH	CODDLED	COENOBITES	COGENERS	COHABS
COCKROACHES	CODDLES	COENOBIUM	COGENT	COHEIR
COCKS	CODDLING	COENOCYTE	COGENTLY	COHEIRESS
COCKSCOMB	CODE	COENOCYTES	COGGED	COHEIRESSES
COCKSCOMBS	CODEBOOK	COENOSARC	COGGER	COHEIRS
COCKSFOOT	CODEBOOKS	COENOSARCS	COGGERS	COHERE
COCKSFOOTS	CODED	COENURI	COGGIE	COHERED
COCKSHIES	CODEINE	COENURUS	COGGIES	COHERENCE
COCKSHOT	CODEINES	COENZYME	COGGING	COHERENCES
COCKSHOTS	CODER	COENZYMES	COGGINGS	COHERENCIES
COCKSHUT	CODERS	COEQUAL	COGGLE	COHERENCY
COCKSHUTS	CODES	COEQUALLY	COGGLED	COHERENT
COCKSHY	CODETTA	COEQUALS	COGGLES	COHERER
COCKSIER	CODETTAS	COERCE	COGGLIER	COHERERS
COCKSIEST	CODEX	COERCED	COGGLIEST	COHERES
COCKSPUR	CODFISH	COERCES	COGGLING	COHERING
COCKSPURS	CODFISHES	COERCIBLE	COGGLY	COHERITOR
COCKSURE	CODGER	COERCIBLY	COGIE	COHERITORS
COCKSWAIN	CODGERS	COERCING	COGIES	COHESIBLE
COCKSWAINED	CODICES	COERCION	COGITABLE	COHESION
COCKSWAINING	CODICIL	COERCIONS	COGITATE	COHESIONS
COCKSWAINS	CODICILS	COERCIVE	COGITATED	COHESIVE
COCKSY	CODIFIED	COETERNAL	COGITATES	COHIBIT
COCKTAIL	CODIFIER	COEVAL	COGITATING	COHIBITED
COCKTAILS	CODIFIERS	COEVALS	COGNATE	COHIBITING
COCKY	CODIFIES	COEXIST	COGNATES	COHIBITS
COCO	CODIFY	COEXISTED	COGNATION	COHO
COCOA	CODIFYING	COEXISTING	COGNATIONS	COHOBATE
COCOANUT	CODILLA	COEXISTS	COGNISANT	COHOBATED
COCOANUTS	CODILLAS	COEXTEND	COGNISE	COHOBATES
COCOAS	CODILLE	COEXTENDED	COGNISED	COHOBATING
COCONUT	CODILLES	COEXTENDING	COGNISES	COHOE
COCONUTS	CODING	COEXTENDS	COGNISING	COHOES
COCOON	CODINGS	COFACTOR	COGNITION	COHOG
COCOONED	CODIST	COFACTORS	COGNITIONS	COHOGS
COCOONERIES	CODISTS	COFF	COGNITIVE	COHORN
COCOONERY	CODLIN	COFFED	COGNIZANT	COHORNS
COCOONING	CODLING	COFFEE	COGNIZE	COHORT
COCOONINGS	CODLINGS	COFFEES	COGNIZED	COHORTS
COCOONS	CODLINS	COFFER	COGNIZES	COHOS
COCOPAN	CODON	COFFERDAM	COGNIZING	COHUNE
COCOPANS	CODONS	COFFERDAMS	COGNOMEN	COHUNES

The Chambers Dictionary is the authority for many longer words; see *OSW* Introduction, page xii

COHYPONYM	COKERNUTS	COLLAGES	COLLIGATE	COLOCYNTHS
COHYPONYMS	COKES	COLLAGIST	COLLIGATED	COLOG
COIF	COKESES	COLLAGISTS	COLLIGATES	COLOGNE
COIFED	COKIER	COLLAPSAR	COLLIGATING	COLOGNES
COIFFEUR	COKIEST	COLLAPSARS	COLLIMATE	COLOGS
COIFFEURS	COKING	COLLAPSE	COLLIMATED	COLON
COIFFEUSE	COKY	COLLAPSED	COLLIMATES	COLONEL
COIFFEUSES	COL	COLLAPSES	COLLIMATING	COLONELCIES
COIFFURE	COLA	COLLAPSING	COLLINEAR	COLONELCY
COIFFURED	COLANDER	COLLAR	COLLING	COLONELS
COIFFURES	COLANDERS	COLLARD	COLLINGS	COLONES
COIFFURING	COLAS	COLLARDS	COLLINS	COLONIAL
COIFING	COLCANNON	COLLARED	COLLINSES	COLONIALS
COIFS	COLCANNONS	COLLARING	COLLISION	COLONIC
COIGN	COLCHICA	COLLARS	COLLISIONS	COLONICS
COIGNE	COLCHICUM	COLLATE	COLLOCATE	COLONIES
COIGNED	COLCHICUMS	COLLATED	COLLOCATED	COLONISE
COIGNES	COLCOTHAR	COLLATES	COLLOCATES	COLONISED
COIGNING	COLCOTHARS	COLLATING	COLLOCATING	COLONISES
COIGNS	COLD	COLLATION	COLLODION	COLONISING
COIL	COLDBLOOD	COLLATIONS	COLLODIONS	COLONIST
COILED	COLDBLOODS	COLLATIVE	COLLOGUE	COLONISTS
COILING	COLDER	COLLATOR	COLLOGUED	COLONITIS
COILS	COLDEST	COLLATORS	COLLOGUES	COLONITISES
COIN	COLDHOUSE	COLLEAGUE	COLLOGUING	COLONIZE
COINAGE	COLDHOUSES	COLLEAGUED	COLLOID	COLONIZED
COINAGES	COLDISH	COLLEAGUES	COLLOIDAL	COLONIZES
COINCIDE	COLDLY	COLLEAGUING	COLLOIDS	COLONIZING
COINCIDED	COLDNESS	COLLECT	COLLOP	COLONNADE
COINCIDES	COLDNESSES	COLLECTED	COLLOPS	COLONNADES
COINCIDING	COLDS	COLLECTING	COLLOQUE	COLONS
COINED	COLE	COLLECTINGS	COLLOQUED	COLONY
COINER	COLECTOMIES	COLLECTOR	COLLOQUES	COLOPHON
COINERS	COLECTOMY	COLLECTORS	COLLOQUIA	COLOPHONIES
COINHERE	COLES	COLLECTS	COLLOQUIED	COLOPHONS
COINHERED	COLESEED	COLLED	COLLOQUIES	COLOPHONY
COINHERES	COLESEEDS	COLLEEN	COLLOQUING	COLOR
COINHERING	COLESLAW	COLLEENS	COLLOQUY	COLORANT
COINING	COLESLAWS	COLLEGE	COLLOQUYING	COLORANTS
COININGS	COLEUS	COLLEGER	COLLOTYPE	COLORED
COINS	COLEUSES	COLLEGERS	COLLOTYPES	COLORIFIC
COIR	COLEWORT	COLLEGES	COLLS	COLORING
COIRS	COLEWORTS	COLLEGIA	COLLUDE	COLORS
COISTREL	COLEY	COLLEGIAL	COLLUDED	COLOSSAL
COISTRELS	COLEYS	COLLEGIAN	COLLUDER	COLOSSEUM
COISTRIL	COLIBRI	COLLEGIANS	COLLUDERS	COLOSSEUMS
COISTRILS	COLIBRIS	COLLEGIUM	COLLUDES	COLOSSI
COIT	COLIC	COLLEGIUMS	COLLUDING	COLOSSUS
COITAL	COLICKIER	COLLET	COLLUSION	COLOSSUSES
COITION	COLICKIEST	COLLETS	COLLUSIONS	COLOSTOMIES
COITIONS	COLICKY	COLLICULI	COLLUSIVE	COLOSTOMY
COITS	COLICS	COLLIDE	COLLUVIES	COLOSTRIC
COITUS	COLIFORM	COLLIDED	COLLY	COLOSTRUM
COITUSES	COLIFORMS	COLLIDER	COLLYING	COLOSTRUMS
COJOIN	COLIN	COLLIDERS	COLLYRIA	COLOTOMIES
COJOINED	COLINS	COLLIDES	COLLYRIUM	COLOTOMY
COJOINING	COLISEUM	COLLIDING	COLLYRIUMS	COLOUR
COJOINS	COLISEUMS	COLLIE	COLOBI	COLOURANT
COJONES	COLITIS	COLLIED	COLOBID	COLOURANTS
COKE	COLITISES	COLLIER	COLOBOMA	COLOURED
COKED	COLL	COLLIERIES	COLOBOMATA	COLOUREDS
COKEHEAD	COLLAGE	COLLIERS	COLOBUS	COLOURER
COKEHEADS	COLLAGEN	COLLIERY	COLOBUSES	COLOURERS
COKERNUT	COLLAGENS	COLLIES	COLOCYNTH	COLOURFUL

The Chambers Dictionary is the authority for many longer words; see *OSW* Introduction, page xii

COLOURING	COMAE	COMEDO	COMMEND	COMMODITIES
COLOURINGS	COMAL	COMEDOS	COMMENDAM	COMMODITY
COLOURISE	COMARB	COMEDOWN	COMMENDAMS	COMMODO
COLOURISED	COMARBS	COMEDOWNS	COMMENDED	COMMODORE
COLOURISES	COMART	COMEDY	COMMENDING	COMMODORES
COLOURISING	COMARTS	COMELIER	COMMENDS	COMMON
COLOURIST	COMAS	COMELIEST	COMMENSAL	COMMONAGE
COLOURISTS	COMATE	COMELY	COMMENSALS	COMMONAGES
COLOURIZE	COMATES	COMER	COMMENT	COMMONED
COLOURIZED	COMATOSE	COMERS	COMMENTED	COMMONER
COLOURIZES	COMATULID	COMES	COMMENTER	COMMONERS
COLOURIZING	COMATULIDS	COMET	COMMENTERS	COMMONEST
COLOURMAN	COMB	COMETARY	COMMENTING	COMMONEY
COLOURMEN	COMBAT	COMETHER	COMMENTOR	COMMONEYS
COLOURS	COMBATANT	COMETHERS	COMMENTORS	COMMONING
COLOURWAY	COMBATANTS	COMETIC	COMMENTS	COMMONINGS
COLOURWAYS	COMBATED	COMETS	COMMER	COMMONLY
COLOURY	COMBATING	COMFIER	COMMERCE	COMMONS
COLS	COMBATIVE	COMFIEST	COMMERCED	COMMORANT
COLT	COMBATS	COMFIT	COMMERCES	COMMORANTS
COLTED	COMBE	COMFITS	COMMERCING	COMMOS
COLTER	COMBED	COMFITURE	COMMERE	COMMOT
COLTERS	COMBER	COMFITURES	COMMERES	COMMOTE
COLTING	COMBERS	COMFORT	COMMERGE	COMMOTES
COLTISH	COMBES	COMFORTED	COMMERGED	COMMOTION
COLTS	COMBI	COMFORTER	COMMERGES	COMMOTIONS
COLTSFOOT	COMBIER	COMFORTERS	COMMERGING	COMMOTS
COLTSFOOTS	COMBIES	COMFORTING	COMMERS	COMMOVE
COLTWOOD	COMBIEST	COMFORTS	COMMIE	COMMOVED
COLTWOODS	COMBINATE	COMFREY	COMMIES	COMMOVES
COLUBRIAD	COMBINE	COMFREYS	COMMINATE	COMMOVING
COLUBRIADS	COMBINED	COMFY	COMMINATED	COMMUNAL
COLUBRID	COMBINES	COMIC	COMMINATES	COMMUNARD
COLUBRIDS	COMBING	COMICAL	COMMINATING	COMMUNARDS
COLUBRINE	COMBINGS	COMICALLY	COMMINGLE	COMMUNE
COLUGO	COMBINING	COMICE	COMMINGLED	COMMUNED
COLUGOS	COMBIS	COMICES	COMMINGLES	COMMUNES
COLUMBARIES	COMBLE	COMICS	COMMINGLING	COMMUNING
COLUMBARY	COMBLES	COMING	COMMINUTE	COMMUNINGS
COLUMBATE	COMBLESS	COMINGS	COMMINUTED	COMMUNION
COLUMBATES	COMBO	COMIQUE	COMMINUTES	COMMUNIONS
COLUMBIC	COMBOS	COMIQUES	COMMINUTING	COMMUNISE
COLUMBINE	COMBRETUM	COMITADJI	COMMIS	COMMUNISED
COLUMBINES	COMBRETUMS	COMITADJIS	COMMISSAR	COMMUNISES
COLUMBITE	COMBS	COMITAL	COMMISSARS	COMMUNISING
COLUMBITES	COMBUST	COMITATUS	COMMIT	COMMUNISM
COLUMBIUM	COMBUSTED	COMITATUSES	COMMITS	COMMUNISMS
COLUMBIUMS	COMBUSTING	COMITIA	COMMITTAL	COMMUNIST
COLUMEL	COMBUSTOR	COMITIES	COMMITTALS	COMMUNISTS
COLUMELLA	COMBUSTORS	COMITY	COMMITTED	COMMUNITIES
COLUMELLAE	COMBUSTS	COMMA	COMMITTEE	COMMUNITY
COLUMELS	COMBWISE	COMMAND	COMMITTEES	COMMUNIZE
COLUMN	COMBY	COMMANDED	COMMITTING	COMMUNIZED
COLUMNAL	COME	COMMANDER	COMMIX	COMMUNIZES
COLUMNAR	COMEBACK	COMMANDERS	COMMIXED	COMMUNIZING
COLUMNED	COMEBACKS	COMMANDING	COMMIXES	COMMUTATE
COLUMNIST	COMEDDLE	COMMANDO	COMMIXING	COMMUTATED
COLUMNISTS	COMEDDLED	COMMANDOS	COMMO	COMMUTATES
COLUMNS	COMEDDLES	COMMANDS	COMMODE	COMMUTATING
COLURE	COMEDDLING	COMMAS	COMMODES	COMMUTE
COLURES	COMEDIAN	COMMENCE	COMMODIFIED	COMMUTED
COLZA	COMEDIANS	COMMENCED	COMMODIFIES	COMMUTER
COLZAS	COMEDIC	COMMENCES	COMMODIFY	COMMUTERS
COMA	COMEDIES	COMMENCING	COMMODIFYING	COMMUTES

COMMUTING	COMPELLING	COMPLINE	COMPRISE	CONCEDE
COMMUTUAL	COMPELS	COMPLINES	COMPRISED	CONCEDED
COMMY	COMPEND	COMPLINS	COMPRISES	CONCEDER
COMODO	COMPENDIA	COMPLISH	COMPRISING	CONCEDERS
COMOSE	COMPENDS	COMPLISHED	COMPS	CONCEDES
COMOUS	COMPER	COMPLISHES	COMPT	CONCEDING
COMP	COMPERE	COMPLISHING	COMPTABLE	CONCEDO
COMPACT	COMPERED	COMPLOT	COMPTED	CONCEIT
COMPACTED	COMPERES	COMPLOTS	COMPTER	CONCEITED
COMPACTER	COMPERING	COMPLOTTED	COMPTERS	CONCEITING
COMPACTEST	COMPERS	COMPLOTTING	COMPTIBLE	CONCEITS
COMPACTING	COMPESCE	COMPLUVIA	COMPTING	CONCEITY
COMPACTLY	COMPESCED	COMPLY	COMPTROLL	CONCEIVE
COMPACTOR	COMPESCES	COMPLYING	COMPTROLLED	CONCEIVED
COMPACTORS	COMPESCING	COMPO	COMPTROLLING	CONCEIVES
COMPACTS	COMPETE	COMPONE	COMPTROLLS	CONCEIVING
COMPADRE	COMPETED	COMPONENT	COMPTS	CONCENT
COMPADRES	COMPETENT	COMPONENTS	COMPULSE	CONCENTER
COMPAGE	COMPETES	COMPONY	COMPULSED	CONCENTERED
COMPAGES	COMPETING	COMPORT	COMPULSES	CONCENTERING
COMPAND	COMPILE	COMPORTED	COMPULSING	CONCENTERS
COMPANDED	COMPILED	COMPORTING	COMPUTANT	CONCENTRE
COMPANDER	COMPILER	COMPORTS	COMPUTANTS	CONCENTRED
COMPANDERS	COMPILERS	COMPOS	COMPUTE	CONCENTRES
COMPANDING	COMPILES	COMPOSE	COMPUTED	CONCENTRING
COMPANDOR	COMPILING	COMPOSED	COMPUTER	CONCENTS
COMPANDORS	COMPING	COMPOSER	COMPUTERS	CONCENTUS
COMPANDS	COMPINGS	COMPOSERS	COMPUTES	CONCEPT
COMPANIED	COMPITAL	COMPOSES	COMPUTING	CONCEPTI
COMPANIES	COMPLAIN	COMPOSING	COMPUTIST	CONCEPTS
COMPANING	COMPLAINED	COMPOSITE	COMPUTISTS	CONCEPTUS
COMPANION	COMPLAINING	COMPOSITED	COMRADE	CONCEPTUSES
COMPANIONED	COMPLAININGS	COMPOSITES	COMRADELY	CONCERN
COMPANIONING	COMPLAINS	COMPOSITING	COMRADES	CONCERNED
COMPANIONS	COMPLAINT	COMPOST	COMS	CONCERNING
COMPANY	COMPLAINTS	COMPOSTED	COMUS	CONCERNS
COMPANYING	COMPLEAT	COMPOSTER	COMUSES	CONCERT
COMPARE	COMPLECT	COMPOSTERS	CON	CONCERTED
COMPARED	COMPLECTED	COMPOSTING	CONACRE	CONCERTI
COMPARES	COMPLECTING	COMPOSTS	CONACRED	CONCERTING
COMPARING	COMPLECTS	COMPOSURE	CONACRES	CONCERTO
COMPART	COMPLETE	COMPOSURES	CONACRING	CONCERTOS
COMPARTED	COMPLETED	COMPOT	CONARIA	CONCERTS
COMPARTING	COMPLETER	COMPOTE	CONARIAL	CONCETTI
COMPARTS	COMPLETES	COMPOTES	CONARIUM	CONCETTO
COMPASS	COMPLETEST	COMPOTIER	CONATION	CONCH
COMPASSED	COMPLETING	COMPOTIERS	CONATIONS	CONCHA
COMPASSES	COMPLEX	COMPOTS	CONATIVE	CONCHAE
COMPASSING	COMPLEXED	COMPOUND	CONATUS	CONCHAL
COMPASSINGS	COMPLEXER	COMPOUNDED	CONCAUSE	CONCHATE
COMPAST	COMPLEXES	COMPOUNDING	CONCAUSES	CONCHE
COMPEAR	COMPLEXEST	COMPOUNDS	CONCAVE	CONCHED
COMPEARED	COMPLEXING	COMPRADOR	CONCAVED	CONCHES
COMPEARING	COMPLEXLY	COMPRADORS	CONCAVELY	CONCHIE
COMPEARS	COMPLEXUS	COMPRESS	CONCAVES	CONCHIES
COMPED	COMPLEXUSES	COMPRESSED	CONCAVING	CONCHING
COMPEER	COMPLIANT	COMPRESSES	CONCAVITIES	CONCHITIS
COMPEERED	COMPLICE	COMPRESSING	CONCAVITY	CONCHITISES
COMPEERING	COMPLICES	COMPRINT	CONCEAL	CONCHOID
COMPEERS	COMPLIED	COMPRINTED	CONCEALED	CONCHOIDS
COMPEL	COMPLIER	COMPRINTING	CONCEALER	CONCHS
COMPELLED	COMPLIERS	COMPRINTS	CONCEALERS	CONCHY
COMPELLER	COMPLIES	COMPRISAL	CONCEALING	CONCIERGE
COMPELLERS	COMPLIN	COMPRISALS	CONCEALS	CONCIERGES

The Chambers Dictionary is the authority for many longer words; see *OSW* Introduction, page xii

CONCILIAR
CONCISE
CONCISED
CONCISELY
CONCISER
CONCISES
CONCISEST
CONCISING
CONCISION
CONCISIONS
CONCLAVE
CONCLAVES
CONCLUDE
CONCLUDED
CONCLUDES
CONCLUDING
CONCOCT
CONCOCTED
CONCOCTER
CONCOCTERS
CONCOCTING
CONCOCTOR
CONCOCTORS
CONCOCTS
CONCOLOR
CONCORD
CONCORDAT
CONCORDATS
CONCORDED
CONCORDING
CONCORDS
CONCOURS
CONCOURSE
CONCOURSES
CONCREATE
CONCREATED
CONCREATES
CONCREATING
CONCRETE
CONCRETED
CONCRETES
CONCRETING
CONCREW
CONCREWED
CONCREWING
CONCREWS
CONCUBINE
CONCUBINES
CONCUPIES
CONCUPY
CONCUR
CONCURRED
CONCURRING
CONCURS
CONCUSS
CONCUSSED
CONCUSSES
CONCUSSING
CONCYCLIC
COND
CONDEMN
CONDEMNED
CONDEMNING
CONDEMNS

CONDENSE
CONDENSED
CONDENSER
CONDENSERS
CONDENSES
CONDENSING
CONDER
CONDERS
CONDIDDLE
CONDIDDLED
CONDIDDLES
CONDIDDLING
CONDIE
CONDIES
CONDIGN
CONDIGNLY
CONDIMENT
CONDIMENTED
CONDIMENTING
CONDIMENTS
CONDITION
CONDITIONED
CONDITIONING
CONDITIONINGS
CONDITIONS
CONDO
CONDOLE
CONDOLED
CONDOLENT
CONDOLES
CONDOLING
CONDOM
CONDOMS
CONDONE
CONDONED
CONDONES
CONDONING
CONDOR
CONDORS
CONDOS
CONDUCE
CONDUCED
CONDUCES
CONDUCING
CONDUCIVE
CONDUCT
CONDUCTED
CONDUCTI
CONDUCTING
CONDUCTOR
CONDUCTORS
CONDUCTS
CONDUCTUS
CONDUIT
CONDUITS
CONDYLAR
CONDYLE
CONDYLES
CONDYLOID
CONDYLOMA
CONDYLOMAS
CONDYLOMATA
CONE
CONED

CONES
CONEY
CONEYS
CONF
CONFAB
CONFABBED
CONFABBING
CONFABS
CONFECT
CONFECTED
CONFECTING
CONFECTS
CONFER
CONFEREE
CONFEREES
CONFERRED
CONFERRER
CONFERRERS
CONFERRING
CONFERS
CONFERVA
CONFERVAE
CONFERVAS
CONFESS
CONFESSED
CONFESSES
CONFESSING
CONFESSOR
CONFESSORS
CONFEST
CONFESTLY
CONFETTI
CONFIDANT
CONFIDANTS
CONFIDE
CONFIDED
CONFIDENT
CONFIDENTS
CONFIDER
CONFIDERS
CONFIDES
CONFIDING
CONFIGURE
CONFIGURED
CONFIGURES
CONFIGURING
CONFINE
CONFINED
CONFINER
CONFINERS
CONFINES
CONFINING
CONFIRM
CONFIRMED
CONFIRMEE
CONFIRMEES
CONFIRMER
CONFIRMERS
CONFIRMING
CONFIRMINGS
CONFIRMOR
CONFIRMORS
CONFIRMS
CONFISEUR

CONFISEURS
CONFIT
CONFITEOR
CONFITEORS
CONFITS
CONFITURE
CONFITURES
CONFIX
CONFIXED
CONFIXES
CONFIXING
CONFLATE
CONFLATED
CONFLATES
CONFLATING
CONFLICT
CONFLICTED
CONFLICTING
CONFLICTS
CONFLUENT
CONFLUENTS
CONFLUX
CONFLUXES
CONFOCAL
CONFORM
CONFORMAL
CONFORMED
CONFORMER
CONFORMERS
CONFORMING
CONFORMS
CONFOUND
CONFOUNDED
CONFOUNDING
CONFOUNDS
CONFRERE
CONFRERES
CONFRERIE
CONFRERIES
CONFRONT
CONFRONTE
CONFRONTED
CONFRONTING
CONFRONTS
CONFS
CONFUSE
CONFUSED
CONFUSES
CONFUSING
CONFUSION
CONFUSIONS
CONFUTE
CONFUTED
CONFUTES
CONFUTING
CONGA
CONGAED
CONGAING
CONGAS
CONGE
CONGEAL
CONGEALED
CONGEALING
CONGEALS

CONGED
CONGEE
CONGEED
CONGEEING
CONGEES
CONGEING
CONGENER
CONGENERS
CONGENIAL
CONGENIC
CONGER
CONGERIES
CONGERS
CONGES
CONGEST
CONGESTED
CONGESTING
CONGESTS
CONGIARIES
CONGIARY
CONGII
CONGIUS
CONGLOBE
CONGLOBED
CONGLOBES
CONGLOBING
CONGO
CONGOS
CONGOU
CONGOUS
CONGRATS
CONGREE
CONGREED
CONGREEING
CONGREES
CONGREET
CONGREETED
CONGREETING
CONGREETS
CONGRESS
CONGRESSED
CONGRESSES
CONGRESSING
CONGRUE
CONGRUED
CONGRUENT
CONGRUES
CONGRUING
CONGRUITIES
CONGRUITY
CONGRUOUS
CONIA
CONIAS
CONIC
CONICAL
CONICALLY
CONICS
CONIDIA
CONIDIAL
CONIDIUM
CONIES
CONIFER
CONIFERS
CONIFORM

CONIINE	CONNECTORS	CONSERVED	CONSTER	CONTAGIONS
CONIINES	CONNECTS	CONSERVER	CONSTERED	CONTAGIUM
CONIMA	CONNED	CONSERVERS	CONSTERING	CONTAIN
CONIMAS	CONNER	CONSERVES	CONSTERS	CONTAINED
CONIN	CONNERS	CONSERVING	CONSTRAIN	CONTAINER
CONINE	CONNES	CONSIDER	CONSTRAINED	CONTAINERS
CONINES	CONNEXION	CONSIDERED	CONSTRAINING	CONTAINING
CONING	CONNEXIONS	CONSIDERING	CONSTRAINS	CONTAINS
CONINS	CONNEXIVE	CONSIDERS	CONSTRICT	CONTANGO
CONJECT	CONNING	CONSIGN	CONSTRICTED	CONTANGOED
CONJECTED	CONNINGS	CONSIGNED	CONSTRICTING	CONTANGOING
CONJECTING	CONNIVE	CONSIGNEE	CONSTRICTS	CONTANGOS
CONJECTS	CONNIVED	CONSIGNEES	CONSTRUCT	CONTE
CONJEE	CONNIVENT	CONSIGNER	CONSTRUCTED	CONTECK
CONJEED	CONNIVER	CONSIGNERS	CONSTRUCTING	CONTECKS
CONJEEING	CONNIVERS	CONSIGNING	CONSTRUCTS	CONTEMN
CONJEES	CONNIVES	CONSIGNOR	CONSTRUE	CONTEMNED
CONJOIN	CONNIVING	CONSIGNORS	CONSTRUED	CONTEMNER
CONJOINED	CONNOTATE	CONSIGNS	CONSTRUER	CONTEMNERS
CONJOINING	CONNOTATED	CONSIST	CONSTRUERS	CONTEMNING
CONJOINS	CONNOTATES	CONSISTED	CONSTRUES	CONTEMNOR
CONJOINT	CONNOTATING	CONSISTING	CONSTRUING	CONTEMNORS
CONJUGAL	CONNOTE	CONSISTS	CONSUL	CONTEMNS
CONJUGANT	CONNOTED	CONSOCIES	CONSULAGE	CONTEMPER
CONJUGANTS	CONNOTES	CONSOLATE	CONSULAGES	CONTEMPERED
CONJUGATE	CONNOTING	CONSOLATED	CONSULAR	CONTEMPERING
CONJUGATED	CONNOTIVE	CONSOLATES	CONSULARS	CONTEMPERS
CONJUGATES	CONNS	CONSOLATING	CONSULATE	CONTEMPT
CONJUGATING	CONNUBIAL	CONSOLE	CONSULATES	CONTEMPTS
CONJUGATINGS	CONODONT	CONSOLED	CONSULS	CONTEND
CONJUNCT	CONODONTS	CONSOLER	CONSULT	CONTENDED
CONJURE	CONOID	CONSOLERS	CONSULTA	CONTENDER
CONJURED	CONOIDAL	CONSOLES	CONSULTAS	CONTENDERS
CONJURER	CONOIDIC	CONSOLING	CONSULTED	CONTENDING
CONJURERS	CONOIDS	CONSOLS	CONSULTEE	CONTENDINGS
CONJURES	CONQUER	CONSOLUTE	CONSULTEES	CONTENDS
CONJURIES	CONQUERED	CONSOMME	CONSULTER	CONTENT
CONJURING	CONQUERING	CONSOMMES	CONSULTERS	CONTENTED
CONJURINGS	CONQUEROR	CONSONANT	CONSULTING	CONTENTING
CONJUROR	CONQUERORS	CONSONANTS	CONSULTOR	CONTENTS
CONJURORS	CONQUERS	CONSONOUS	CONSULTORS	CONTES
CONJURY	CONQUEST	CONSORT	CONSULTS	CONTESSA
CONK	CONQUESTS	CONSORTED	CONSUME	CONTESSAS
CONKED	CONS	CONSORTER	CONSUMED	CONTEST
CONKER	CONSCIENT	CONSORTERS	CONSUMER	CONTESTED
CONKERS	CONSCIOUS	CONSORTIA	CONSUMERS	CONTESTER
CONKIER	CONSCIOUSES	CONSORTING	CONSUMES	CONTESTERS
CONKIEST	CONSCRIBE	CONSORTS	CONSUMING	CONTESTING
CONKING	CONSCRIBED	CONSPIRE	CONSUMINGS	CONTESTS
CONKS	CONSCRIBES	CONSPIRED	CONSUMPT	CONTEXT
CONKY	CONSCRIBING	CONSPIRER	CONSUMPTS	CONTEXTS
CONN	CONSCRIPT	CONSPIRERS	CONTACT	CONTICENT
CONNATE	CONSCRIPTED	CONSPIRES	CONTACTED	CONTINENT
CONNATION	CONSCRIPTING	CONSPIRING	CONTACTING	CONTINENTS
CONNATIONS	CONSCRIPTS	CONSTABLE	CONTACTOR	CONTINUA
CONNATURE	CONSEIL	CONSTABLES	CONTACTORS	CONTINUAL
CONNATURES	CONSEILS	CONSTANCIES	CONTACTS	CONTINUE
CONNE	CONSENSUS	CONSTANCY	CONTADINA	CONTINUED
CONNECT	CONSENSUSES	CONSTANT	CONTADINAS	CONTINUER
CONNECTED	CONSENT	CONSTANTS	CONTADINE	CONTINUERS
CONNECTER	CONSENTED	CONSTATE	CONTADINI	CONTINUES
CONNECTERS	CONSENTING	CONSTATED	CONTADINO	CONTINUING
CONNECTING	CONSENTS	CONSTATES	CONTAGIA	CONTINUO
CONNECTOR	CONSERVE	CONSTATING	CONTAGION	CONTINUOS

CONTINUUM	CONTUND	CONVICT	COOKIES	COOP
CONTINUUMS	CONTUNDED	CONVICTED	COOKING	COOPED
CONTLINE	CONTUNDING	CONVICTING	COOKMAID	COOPER
CONTLINES	CONTUNDS	CONVICTS	COOKMAIDS	COOPERAGE
CONTO	CONTUSE	CONVINCE	COOKOUT	COOPERAGES
CONTORNO	CONTUSED	CONVINCED	COOKOUTS	COOPERATE
CONTORNOS	CONTUSES	CONVINCES	COOKROOM	COOPERATED
CONTORT	CONTUSING	CONVINCING	COOKROOMS	COOPERATES
CONTORTED	CONTUSION	CONVIVE	COOKS	COOPERATING
CONTORTING	CONTUSIONS	CONVIVED	COOKWARE	COOPERED
CONTORTS	CONTUSIVE	CONVIVES	COOKWARES	COOPERIES
CONTOS	CONUNDRUM	CONVIVIAL	COOKY	COOPERING
CONTOUR	CONUNDRUMS	CONVIVING	COOL	COOPERINGS
CONTOURED	CONURBAN	CONVO	COOLABAH	COOPERS
CONTOURING	CONURBIA	CONVOCATE	COOLABAHS	COOPERY
CONTOURS	CONURBIAS	CONVOCATED	COOLAMON	COOPING
CONTRA	CONURE	CONVOCATES	COOLAMONS	COOPS
CONTRACT	CONURES	CONVOCATING	COOLANT	COOPT
CONTRACTED	CONVECTOR	CONVOKE	COOLANTS	COOPTED
CONTRACTING	CONVECTORS	CONVOKED	COOLED	COOPTING
CONTRACTS	CONVENE	CONVOKES	COOLER	COOPTS
CONTRAIL	CONVENED	CONVOKING	COOLERS	COORDINAL
CONTRAILS	CONVENER	CONVOLUTE	COOLEST	COOS
CONTRAIR	CONVENERS	CONVOLVE	COOLHOUSE	COOSEN
CONTRALTI	CONVENES	CONVOLVED	COOLHOUSES	COOSENED
CONTRALTO	CONVENING	CONVOLVES	COOLIBAH	COOSENING
CONTRALTOS	CONVENOR	CONVOLVING	COOLIBAHS	COOSENS
CONTRARIED	CONVENORS	CONVOS	COOLIBAR	COOSER
CONTRARIES	CONVENT	CONVOY	COOLIBARS	COOSERS
CONTRARY	CONVENTED	CONVOYED	COOLIE	COOSIN
CONTRARYING	CONVENTING	CONVOYING	COOLIES	COOSINED
CONTRAS	CONVENTS	CONVOYS	COOLING	COOSINING
CONTRAST	CONVERGE	CONVULSE	COOLISH	COOSINS
CONTRASTED	CONVERGED	CONVULSED	COOLLY	COOST
CONTRASTING	CONVERGES	CONVULSES	COOLNESS	COOT
CONTRASTS	CONVERGING	CONVULSING	COOLNESSES	COOTIE
CONTRASTY	CONVERSE	CONY	COOLS	COOTIES
CONTRAT	CONVERSED	COO	COOLTH	COOTIKIN
CONTRATE	CONVERSES	COOED	COOLTHS	COOTIKINS
CONTRATS	CONVERSING	COOEE	COOLY	COOTS
CONTRIST	CONVERT	COOEED	COOM	COP
CONTRISTED	CONVERTED	COOEEING	COOMB	COPACETIC
CONTRISTING	CONVERTER	COOEES	COOMBE	COPAIBA
CONTRISTS	CONVERTERS	COOEY	COOMBES	COPAIBAS
CONTRITE	CONVERTING	COOEYED	COOMBS	COPAIVA
CONTRIVE	CONVERTOR	COOEYING	COOMED	COPAIVAS
CONTRIVED	CONVERTORS	COOEYS	COOMIER	COPAL
CONTRIVER	CONVERTS	COOF	COOMIEST	COPALS
CONTRIVERS	CONVEX	COOFS	COOMING	COPARTNER
CONTRIVES	CONVEXED	COOING	COOMS	COPARTNERS
CONTRIVING	CONVEXES	COOINGLY	COOMY	COPATAINE
CONTROL	CONVEXITIES	COOINGS	COON	COPATRIOT
CONTROLE	CONVEXITY	COOK	COONCAN	COPATRIOTS
CONTROLLED	CONVEXLY	COOKABLE	COONCANS	COPE
CONTROLLING	CONVEY	COOKBOOK	COONDOG	COPECK
CONTROLS	CONVEYAL	COOKBOOKS	COONDOGS	COPECKS
CONTROUL	CONVEYALS	COOKED	COONHOUND	COPED
CONTROULED	CONVEYED	COOKER	COONHOUNDS	COPEMATE
CONTROULING	CONVEYER	COOKERIES	COONS	COPEMATES
CONTROULS	CONVEYERS	COOKERS	COONSKIN	COPEPOD
CONTUMACIES	CONVEYING	COOKERY	COONSKINS	COPEPODS
CONTUMACY	CONVEYOR	COOKHOUSE	COONTIE	COPER
CONTUMELIES	CONVEYORS	COOKHOUSES	COONTIES	COPERED
CONTUMELY	CONVEYS	COOKIE	COONTY	COPERING

The Chambers Dictionary is the authority for many longer words; see *OSW* Introduction, page xii

COPERS	COPSY	CORALROOTS	CORDUROYS	CORKWOOD
COPES	COPTER	CORALS	CORDWAIN	CORKWOODS
COPESTONE	COPTERS	CORALWORT	CORDWAINS	CORKY
COPESTONES	COPULA	CORALWORTS	CORDWOOD	CORM
COPIED	COPULAR	CORAM	CORDWOODS	CORMEL
COPIER	COPULAS	CORAMINE	CORDYLINE	CORMELS
COPIERS	COPULATE	CORAMINES	CORDYLINES	CORMIDIA
COPIES	COPULATED	CORANACH	CORE	CORMIDIUM
COPILOT	COPULATES	CORANACHS	CORED	CORMORANT
COPILOTS	COPULATING	CORANTO	COREGENT	CORMORANTS
COPING	COPY	CORANTOES	COREGENTS	CORMOUS
COPINGS	COPYBOOK	CORANTOS	CORELESS	CORMS
COPIOUS	COPYBOOKS	CORBAN	CORELLA	CORMUS
COPIOUSLY	COPYCAT	CORBANS	CORELLAS	CORMUSES
COPITA	COPYCATS	CORBE	COREOPSIS	CORN
COPITAS	COPYCATTED	CORBEAU	COREOPSISES	CORNACRE
COPLANAR	COPYCATTING	CORBEAUS	CORER	CORNACRES
COPOLYMER	COPYHOLD	CORBEIL	CORERS	CORNAGE
COPOLYMERS	COPYHOLDS	CORBEILLE	CORES	CORNAGES
COPPED	COPYING	CORBEILLES	COREY	CORNBALL
COPPER	COPYISM	CORBEILS	COREYS	CORNBALLS
COPPERAS	COPYISMS	CORBEL	CORF	CORNBORER
COPPERASES	COPYIST	CORBELED	CORFHOUSE	CORNBORERS
COPPERED	COPYISTS	CORBELING	CORFHOUSES	CORNBRAKE
COPPERING	COPYREAD	CORBELINGS	CORGI	CORNBRAKES
COPPERINGS	COPYREADING	CORBELLED	CORGIS	CORNBRASH
COPPERISH	COPYREADINGS	CORBELLING	CORIA	CORNBRASHES
COPPERS	COPYREADS	CORBELLINGS	CORIANDER	CORNBREAD
COPPERY	COPYRIGHT	CORBELS	CORIANDERS	CORNBREADS
COPPICE	COPYRIGHTED	CORBES	CORIES	CORNCRAKE
COPPICED	COPYRIGHTING	CORBICULA	CORING	CORNCRAKES
COPPICES	COPYRIGHTS	CORBICULAE	CORIOUS	CORNEA
COPPICING	COQUET	CORBIE	CORIUM	CORNEAL
COPPICINGS	COQUETRIES	CORBIES	CORIUMS	CORNEAS
COPPIES	COQUETRY	CORCASS	CORIVAL	CORNED
COPPIN	COQUETS	CORCASSES	CORIVALLED	CORNEL
COPPING	COQUETTE	CORD	CORIVALLING	CORNELIAN
COPPINS	COQUETTED	CORDAGE	CORIVALRIES	CORNELIANS
COPPLE	COQUETTES	CORDAGES	CORIVALRY	CORNELS
COPPLES	COQUETTING	CORDATE	CORIVALS	CORNEMUSE
COPPY	COQUILLA	CORDED	CORK	CORNEMUSES
COPRA	COQUILLAS	CORDIAL	CORKAGE	CORNEOUS
COPRAS	COQUILLE	CORDIALLY	CORKAGES	CORNER
COPRESENT	COQUILLES	CORDIALS	CORKBOARD	CORNERED
COPROLITE	COQUINA	CORDIFORM	CORKBOARDS	CORNERING
COPROLITES	COQUINAS	CORDINER	CORKBORER	CORNERS
COPROLITH	COQUITO	CORDINERS	CORKBORERS	CORNET
COPROLITHS	COQUITOS	CORDING	CORKED	CORNETCIES
COPROLOGIES	COR	CORDINGS	CORKER	CORNETCY
COPROLOGY	CORACLE	CORDITE	CORKERS	CORNETIST
COPROSMA	CORACLES	CORDITES	CORKIER	CORNETISTS
COPROSMAS	CORACOID	CORDLESS	CORKIEST	CORNETS
COPROZOIC	CORACOIDS	CORDOBA	CORKINESS	CORNETT
COPS	CORAGGIO	CORDOBAS	CORKINESSES	CORNETTI
COPSE	CORAGGIOS	CORDON	CORKING	CORNETTO
COPSED	CORAL	CORDONED	CORKIR	CORNETTS
COPSES	CORALLA	CORDONING	CORKIRS	CORNFIELD
COPSEWOOD	CORALLINE	CORDONS	CORKS	CORNFIELDS
COPSEWOODS	CORALLINES	CORDOTOMIES	CORKSCREW	CORNFLAG
COPSHOP	CORALLITE	CORDOTOMY	CORKSCREWED	CORNFLAGS
COPSHOPS	CORALLITES	CORDOVAN	CORKSCREWING	CORNFLAKE
COPSIER	CORALLOID	CORDOVANS	CORKSCREWS	CORNFLAKES
COPSIEST	CORALLUM	CORDS	CORKTREE	CORNFLIES
COPSING	CORALROOT	CORDUROY	CORKTREES	CORNFLOUR

The Chambers Dictionary is the authority for many longer words; see *OSW* Introduction, page xii

CORNFLOURS	COROLLAS	CORRECTORS	CORSLETED	COS
CORNFLY	COROLLINE	CORRECTS	CORSLETS	COSE
CORNHUSK	CORONA	CORRELATE	CORSNED	COSEC
CORNHUSKS	CORONACH	CORRELATED	CORSNEDS	COSECANT
CORNI	CORONACHS	CORRELATES	CORSO	COSECANTS
CORNICE	CORONAE	CORRELATING	CORSOS	COSECH
CORNICED	CORONAL	CORRIDA	CORTEGE	COSECHS
CORNICES	CORONALS	CORRIDAS	CORTEGES	COSECS
CORNICHE	CORONARIES	CORRIDOR	CORTEX	COSED
CORNICHES	CORONARY	CORRIDORS	CORTEXES	COSEISMAL
CORNICING	CORONAS	CORRIE	CORTICAL	COSEISMIC
CORNICLE	CORONATE	CORRIES	CORTICATE	COSES
CORNICLES	CORONATED	CORRIGENT	CORTICES	COSET
CORNICULA	CORONER	CORRIGENTS	CORTICOID	COSETS
CORNIER	CORONERS	CORRIVAL	CORTICOIDS	COSH
CORNIEST	CORONET	CORRIVALLED	CORTILE	COSHED
CORNIFIC	CORONETED	CORRIVALLING	CORTILI	COSHER
CORNIFORM	CORONETS	CORRIVALS	CORTISOL	COSHERED
CORNING	CORONIS	CORRODE	CORTISOLS	COSHERER
CORNIST	CORONISES	CORRODED	CORTISONE	COSHERERS
CORNISTS	CORONIUM	CORRODENT	CORTISONES	COSHERIES
CORNLAND	CORONIUMS	CORRODENTS	CORUNDUM	COSHERING
CORNLANDS	CORONOID	CORRODES	CORUNDUMS	COSHERINGS
CORNLOFT	COROZO	CORRODIES	CORUSCANT	COSHERS
CORNLOFTS	COROZOS	CORRODING	CORUSCATE	COSHERY
CORNMILL	CORPORA	CORRODY	CORUSCATED	COSHES
CORNMILLS	CORPORAL	CORROSION	CORUSCATES	COSHING
CORNMOTH	CORPORALS	CORROSIONS	CORUSCATING	COSIER
CORNMOTHS	CORPORAS	CORROSIVE	CORVEE	COSIERS
CORNO	CORPORASES	CORROSIVES	CORVEES	COSIES
CORNOPEAN	CORPORATE	CORRUGATE	CORVES	COSIEST
CORNOPEANS	CORPOREAL	CORRUGATED	CORVET	COSILY
CORNPIPE	CORPORIFIED	CORRUGATES	CORVETED	COSINE
CORNPIPES	CORPORIFIES	CORRUGATING	CORVETING	COSINES
CORNRENT	CORPORIFY	CORRUPT	CORVETS	COSINESS
CORNRENTS	CORPORIFYING	CORRUPTED	CORVETTE	COSINESSES
CORNROW	CORPOSANT	CORRUPTER	CORVETTED	COSING
CORNROWS	CORPOSANTS	CORRUPTERS	CORVETTES	COSMEA
CORNS	CORPS	CORRUPTEST	CORVETTING	COSMEAS
CORNSTALK	CORPSE	CORRUPTING	CORVID	COSMESES
CORNSTALKS	CORPSED	CORRUPTLY	CORVIDS	COSMESIS
CORNSTONE	CORPSES	CORRUPTS	CORVINE	COSMETIC
CORNSTONES	CORPSING	CORS	CORVUS	COSMETICS
CORNU	CORPULENT	CORSAC	CORVUSES	COSMIC
CORNUA	CORPUS	CORSACS	CORY	COSMICAL
CORNUAL	CORPUSCLE	CORSAGE	CORYBANT	COSMISM
CORNUAL	CORPUSCLES	CORSAGES	CORYBANTES	COSMISMS
CORNUTE	CORRADE	CORSAIR	CORYBANTS	COSMIST
CORNUTED	CORRADED	CORSAIRS	CORYDALIS	COSMISTS
CORNUTES	CORRADES	CORSE	CORYDALISES	COSMOCRAT
CORNUTING	CORRADING	CORSELET	CORYLUS	COSMOCRATS
CORNUTO	CORRAL	CORSELETS	CORYLUSES	COSMOGENIES
CORNUTOS	CORRALLED	CORSES	CORYMB	COSMOGENY
CORNWORM	CORRALLING	CORSET	CORYMBOSE	COSMOGONIES
CORNWORMS	CORRALS	CORSETED	CORYMBS	COSMOGONY
CORNY	CORRASION	CORSETIER	CORYPHAEI	COSMOLOGIES
COROCORE	CORRASIONS	CORSETIERS	CORYPHE	COSMOLOGY
COROCORES	CORRECT	CORSETING	CORYPHEE	COSMONAUT
COROCORO	CORRECTED	CORSETRIES	CORYPHEES	COSMONAUTS
COROCOROS	CORRECTER	CORSETRY	CORYPHENE	COSMORAMA
CORODIES	CORRECTEST	CORSETS	CORYPHENES	COSMORAMAS
CORODY	CORRECTING	CORSIVE	CORYPHES	COSMOS
COROLLA	CORRECTLY	CORSIVES	CORYZA	COSMOSES
COROLLARIES	CORRECTOR	CORSLET	CORYZAS	COSMOTRON
COROLLARY				

COSMOTRONS	COTELETTE	COTTONING	COUNSELOR	COURBETTES
COSPHERED	COTELETTES	COTTONS	COUNSELORS	COURBING
COSPONSOR	COTELINE	COTTONY	COUNSELS	COURBS
COSPONSORED	COTELINES	COTTOWN	COUNT	COURD
COSPONSORING	COTENANT	COTTOWNS	COUNTABLE	COURE
COSPONSORS	COTENANTS	COTTS	COUNTED	COURED
COSS	COTERIE	COTTUS	COUNTER	COURES
COSSES	COTERIES	COTTUSES	COUNTERED	COURGETTE
COSSET	COTES	COTWAL	COUNTERING	COURGETTES
COSSETED	COTH	COTWALS	COUNTERS	COURIER
COSSETING	COTHS	COTYLAE	COUNTESS	COURIERS
COSSETS	COTHURN	COTYLE	COUNTESSES	COURING
COSSIE	COTHURNI	COTYLEDON	COUNTIES	COURLAN
COSSIES	COTHURNS	COTYLEDONS	COUNTING	COURLANS
COST	COTHURNUS	COTYLES	COUNTLESS	COURS
COSTA	COTICULAR	COTYLOID	COUNTLINE	COURSE
COSTAE	COTIDAL	COUCAL	COUNTLINES	COURSED
COSTAL	COTILLION	COUCALS	COUNTRIES	COURSER
COSTALGIA	COTILLIONS	COUCH	COUNTROL	COURSERS
COSTALGIAS	COTILLON	COUCHANT	COUNTROLLED	COURSES
COSTALS	COTILLONS	COUCHE	COUNTROLLING	COURSING
COSTARD	COTING	COUCHED	COUNTROLS	COURSINGS
COSTARDS	COTINGA	COUCHEE	COUNTRY	COURT
COSTATE	COTINGAS	COUCHEES	COUNTS	COURTED
COSTATED	COTISE	COUCHES	COUNTSHIP	COURTEOUS
COSTE	COTISED	COUCHETTE	COUNTSHIPS	COURTESAN
COSTEAN	COTISES	COUCHETTES	COUNTY	COURTESANS
COSTEANED	COTISING	COUCHING	COUP	COURTESIED
COSTEANING	COTLAND	COUCHINGS	COUPE	COURTESIES
COSTEANINGS	COTLANDS	COUDE	COUPED	COURTESY
COSTEANS	COTQUEAN	COUGAR	COUPEE	COURTESYING
COSTED	COTQUEANS	COUGARS	COUPEES	COURTEZAN
COSTER	COTS	COUGH	COUPER	COURTEZANS
COSTERS	COTT	COUGHED	COUPERS	COURTIER
COSTES	COTTA	COUGHER	COUPES	COURTIERS
COSTING	COTTABUS	COUGHERS	COUPING	COURTING
COSTIVE	COTTABUSES	COUGHING	COUPLE	COURTINGS
COSTIVELY	COTTAGE	COUGHINGS	COUPLED	COURTLET
COSTLIER	COTTAGED	COUGHS	COUPLEDOM	COURTLETS
COSTLIEST	COTTAGER	COUGUAR	COUPLEDOMS	COURTLIER
COSTLY	COTTAGERS	COUGUARS	COUPLER	COURTLIEST
COSTMARIES	COTTAGES	COULD	COUPLERS	COURTLIKE
COSTMARY	COTTAGEY	COULEE	COUPLES	COURTLING
COSTREL	COTTAGING	COULEES	COUPLET	COURTLINGS
COSTRELS	COTTAGINGS	COULIS	COUPLETS	COURTLY
COSTS	COTTAR	COULISSE	COUPLING	COURTROOM
COSTUME	COTTARS	COULISSES	COUPLINGS	COURTROOMS
COSTUMED	COTTAS	COULOIR	COUPON	COURTS
COSTUMER	COTTED	COULOIRS	COUPONS	COURTSHIP
COSTUMERS	COTTER	COULOMB	COUPS	COURTSHIPS
COSTUMES	COTTERS	COULOMBS	COUPURE	COURTYARD
COSTUMIER	COTTID	COULTER	COUPURES	COURTYARDS
COSTUMIERS	COTTIDS	COULTERS	COUR	COUSCOUS
COSTUMING	COTTIER	COUMARIC	COURAGE	COUSCOUSES
COSTUS	COTTIERS	COUMARIN	COURAGES	COUSIN
COSTUSES	COTTISE	COUMARINS	COURANT	COUSINAGE
COSY	COTTISED	COUNCIL	COURANTE	COUSINAGES
COT	COTTISES	COUNCILOR	COURANTES	COUSINLY
COTANGENT	COTTISING	COUNCILORS	COURANTS	COUSINRIES
COTANGENTS	COTTOID	COUNCILS	COURB	COUSINRY
COTE	COTTON	COUNSEL	COURBARIL	COUSINS
COTEAU	COTTONADE	COUNSELLED	COURBARILS	COUTER
COTEAUX	COTTONADES	COUNSELLING	COURBED	COUTERS
COTED	COTTONED	COUNSELLINGS	COURBETTE	COUTH

COUTHER	COVETED	COWHERB	COXSWAINED	CRACKHEAD
COUTHEST	COVETING	COWHERBS	COXSWAINING	CRACKHEADS
COUTHIE	COVETISE	COWHERD	COXSWAINS	CRACKING
COUTHIER	COVETISES	COWHERDS	COXY	CRACKJAW
COUTHIEST	COVETOUS	COWHIDE	COY	CRACKLE
COUTHY	COVETS	COWHIDED	COYED	CRACKLED
COUTIL	COVEY	COWHIDES	COYER	CRACKLES
COUTILLE	COVEYS	COWHIDING	COYEST	CRACKLIER
COUTILLES	COVIN	COWHOUSE	COYING	CRACKLIEST
COUTILS	COVING	COWHOUSES	COYISH	CRACKLING
COUTURE	COVINGS	COWING	COYISHLY	CRACKLINGS
COUTURES	COVINOUS	COWISH	COYLY	CRACKLY
COUTURIER	COVINS	COWITCH	COYNESS	CRACKNEL
COUTURIERS	COVYNE	COWITCHES	COYNESSES	CRACKNELS
COUVADE	COVYNES	COWL	COYOTE	CRACKPOT
COUVADES	COW	COWLED	COYOTES	CRACKPOTS
COUVERT	COWAGE	COWLICK	COYOTILLO	CRACKS
COUVERTS	COWAGES	COWLICKS	COYOTILLOS	CRACKSMAN
COVALENCIES	COWAL	COWLING	COYPU	CRACKSMEN
COVALENCY	COWALS	COWLINGS	COYPUS	CRACOWE
COVALENT	COWAN	COWLS	COYSTREL	CRACOWES
COVARIANT	COWANS	COWMAN	COYSTRELS	CRADLE
COVARIANTS	COWARD	COWMEN	COYSTRIL	CRADLED
COVARIED	COWARDED	COWP	COYSTRILS	CRADLES
COVARIES	COWARDICE	COWPAT	COZ	CRADLING
COVARY	COWARDICES	COWPATS	COZE	CRADLINGS
COVARYING	COWARDING	COWPEA	COZED	CRAFT
COVE	COWARDLY	COWPEAS	COZEN	CRAFTED
COVED	COWARDREE	COWPED	COZENAGE	CRAFTIER
COVELET	COWARDREES	COWPING	COZENAGES	CRAFTIEST
COVELETS	COWARDRIES	COWPOKE	COZENED	CRAFTILY
COVELLITE	COWARDRY	COWPOKES	COZENER	CRAFTING
COVELLITES	COWARDS	COWPOX	COZENERS	CRAFTLESS
COVEN	COWBANE	COWPOXES	COZENING	CRAFTS
COVENANT	COWBANES	COWPS	COZENS	CRAFTSMAN
COVENANTED	COWBELL	COWRIE	COZES	CRAFTSMEN
COVENANTING	COWBELLS	COWRIES	COZIER	CRAFTWORK
COVENANTS	COWBERRIES	COWRY	COZIERS	CRAFTWORKS
COVENS	COWBERRY	COWS	COZIES	CRAFTY
COVENT	COWBIRD	COWSHED	COZIEST	CRAG
COVENTS	COWBIRDS	COWSHEDS	COZING	CRAGFAST
COVER	COWBOY	COWSLIP	COZY	CRAGGED
COVERAGE	COWBOYS	COWSLIPS	COZZES	CRAGGIER
COVERAGES	COWED	COWTREE	CRAB	CRAGGIEST
COVERALL	COWER	COWTREES	CRABBED	CRAGGY
COVERALLS	COWERED	COX	CRABBEDLY	CRAGS
COVERED	COWERING	COXA	CRABBER	CRAGSMAN
COVERING	COWERS	COXAE	CRABBERS	CRAGSMEN
COVERINGS	COWFEEDER	COXAL	CRABBIER	CRAIG
COVERLET	COWFEEDERS	COXALGIA	CRABBIEST	CRAIGS
COVERLETS	COWFISH	COXALGIAS	CRABBILY	CRAKE
COVERLID	COWFISHES	COXCOMB	CRABBING	CRAKED
COVERLIDS	COWGIRL	COXCOMBIC	CRABBY	CRAKES
COVERS	COWGIRLS	COXCOMBRIES	CRABLIKE	CRAKING
COVERSLIP	COWGRASS	COXCOMBRY	CRABS	CRAM
COVERSLIPS	COWGRASSES	COXCOMBS	CRABSTICK	CRAMBO
COVERT	COWHAGE	COXED	CRABSTICKS	CRAMBOES
COVERTLY	COWHAGES	COXES	CRABWISE	CRAME
COVERTS	COWHAND	COXIER	CRACK	CRAMES
COVERTURE	COWHANDS	COXIEST	CRACKDOWN	CRAMESIES
COVERTURES	COWHEARD	COXINESS	CRACKDOWNS	CRAMESY
COVES	COWHEARDS	COXINESSES	CRACKED	CRAMMABLE
COVET	COWHEEL	COXING	CRACKER	CRAMMED
COVETABLE	COWHEELS	COXSWAIN	CRACKERS	CRAMMER

CRAMMERS
CRAMMING
CRAMOISIES
CRAMOISY
CRAMP
CRAMPBARK
CRAMPBARKS
CRAMPED
CRAMPET
CRAMPETS
CRAMPIER
CRAMPIEST
CRAMPING
CRAMPIT
CRAMPITS
CRAMPON
CRAMPONS
CRAMPS
CRAMPY
CRAMS
CRAN
CRANAGE
CRANAGES
CRANBERRIES
CRANBERRY
CRANCH
CRANCHED
CRANCHES
CRANCHING
CRANE
CRANED
CRANEFLIES
CRANEFLY
CRANES
CRANIA
CRANIAL
CRANING
CRANIUM
CRANIUMS
CRANK
CRANKCASE
CRANKCASES
CRANKED
CRANKIER
CRANKIEST
CRANKILY
CRANKING
CRANKLE
CRANKLED
CRANKLES
CRANKLING
CRANKNESS
CRANKNESSES
CRANKS
CRANKY
CRANNIED
CRANNIES
CRANNOG
CRANNOGS
CRANNY
CRANNYING
CRANREUCH
CRANREUCHS
CRANS

CRANTS
CRANTSES
CRAP
CRAPE
CRAPES
CRAPIER
CRAPIEST
CRAPLE
CRAPLES
CRAPPED
CRAPPIER
CRAPPIEST
CRAPPING
CRAPPY
CRAPS
CRAPULENT
CRAPULOUS
CRAPY
CRARE
CRARES
CRASES
CRASH
CRASHED
CRASHES
CRASHING
CRASHLAND
CRASHLANDED
CRASHLANDING
CRASHLANDS
CRASHPAD
CRASHPADS
CRASIS
CRASS
CRASSER
CRASSEST
CRASSLY
CRASSNESS
CRASSNESSES
CRATCH
CRATCHES
CRATE
CRATED
CRATER
CRATERED
CRATERING
CRATEROUS
CRATERS
CRATES
CRATING
CRATON
CRATONS
CRATUR
CRATURS
CRAUNCH
CRAUNCHED
CRAUNCHES
CRAUNCHING
CRAVAT
CRAVATS
CRAVATTED
CRAVATTING
CRAVE
CRAVED
CRAVEN

CRAVENED
CRAVENING
CRAVENLY
CRAVENS
CRAVER
CRAVERS
CRAVES
CRAVING
CRAVINGS
CRAW
CRAWFISH
CRAWFISHED
CRAWFISHES
CRAWFISHING
CRAWL
CRAWLED
CRAWLER
CRAWLERS
CRAWLIER
CRAWLIEST
CRAWLING
CRAWLINGS
CRAWLS
CRAWLY
CRAWS
CRAYER
CRAYERS
CRAYFISH
CRAYFISHES
CRAYON
CRAYONED
CRAYONING
CRAYONS
CRAZE
CRAZED
CRAZES
CRAZIER
CRAZIES
CRAZIEST
CRAZILY
CRAZINESS
CRAZINESSES
CRAZING
CRAZY
CREACH
CREACHS
CREAGH
CREAGHS
CREAK
CREAKED
CREAKIER
CREAKIEST
CREAKILY
CREAKING
CREAKS
CREAKY
CREAM
CREAMED
CREAMER
CREAMERIES
CREAMERS
CREAMERY
CREAMIER
CREAMIEST

CREAMING
CREAMLAID
CREAMS
CREAMWARE
CREAMWARES
CREAMWOVE
CREAMY
CREANCE
CREANCES
CREANT
CREASE
CREASED
CREASER
CREASERS
CREASES
CREASIER
CREASIEST
CREASING
CREASOTE
CREASOTED
CREASOTES
CREASOTING
CREASY
CREATABLE
CREATE
CREATED
CREATES
CREATIC
CREATIN
CREATINE
CREATINES
CREATING
CREATINS
CREATION
CREATIONS
CREATIVE
CREATOR
CREATORS
CREATRESS
CREATRESSES
CREATRIX
CREATRIXES
CREATURAL
CREATURE
CREATURES
CRECHE
CRECHES
CRED
CREDAL
CREDENCE
CREDENCES
CREDENDA
CREDENDUM
CREDENT
CREDENZA
CREDENZAS
CREDIBLE
CREDIBLY
CREDIT
CREDITED
CREDITING
CREDITOR
CREDITORS
CREDITS

CREDO
CREDOS
CREDS
CREDULITIES
CREDULITY
CREDULOUS
CREE
CREED
CREEDAL
CREEDS
CREEING
CREEK
CREEKIER
CREEKIEST
CREEKS
CREEKY
CREEL
CREELS
CREEP
CREEPER
CREEPERED
CREEPERS
CREEPIE
CREEPIER
CREEPIES
CREEPIEST
CREEPING
CREEPS
CREEPY
CREES
CREESE
CREESED
CREESES
CREESH
CREESHED
CREESHES
CREESHIER
CREESHIEST
CREESHING
CREESHY
CREESING
CREMASTER
CREMASTERS
CREMATE
CREMATED
CREMATES
CREMATING
CREMATION
CREMATIONS
CREMATOR
CREMATORIES
CREMATORS
CREMATORY
CREME
CREMES
CREMOCARP
CREMOCARPS
CREMONA
CREMONAS
CREMOR
CREMORNE
CREMORNES
CREMORS
CREMOSIN

The Chambers Dictionary is the authority for many longer words; see *OSW* Introduction, page xii

CREMSIN	CRESCENT	CRIBBED	CRIMPING	CRISPIEST
CRENA	CRESCENTS	CRIBBING	CRIMPLE	CRISPIN
CRENAS	CRESCIVE	CRIBBLE	CRIMPLED	CRISPING
CRENATE	CRESOL	CRIBBLED	CRIMPLES	CRISPINS
CRENATED	CRESOLS	CRIBBLES	CRIMPLING	CRISPLY
CRENATION	CRESS	CRIBBLING	CRIMPS	CRISPNESS
CRENATIONS	CRESSES	CRIBELLA	CRIMPY	CRISPNESSES
CRENATURE	CRESSET	CRIBELLAR	CRIMS	CRISPS
CRENATURES	CRESSETS	CRIBELLUM	CRIMSON	CRISPY
CRENEL	CREST	CRIBLE	CRIMSONED	CRISSA
CRENELATE	CRESTED	CRIBRATE	CRIMSONING	CRISSUM
CRENELATED	CRESTING	CRIBROSE	CRIMSONS	CRISTA
CRENELATES	CRESTLESS	CRIBROUS	CRINAL	CRISTAE
CRENELATING	CRESTON	CRIBS	CRINATE	CRISTATE
CRENELLE	CRESTONS	CRIBWORK	CRINATED	CRIT
CRENELLED	CRESTS	CRIBWORKS	CRINE	CRITERIA
CRENELLES	CRESYLIC	CRICETID	CRINED	CRITERION
CRENELLING	CRETIC	CRICETIDS	CRINES	CRITH
CRENELS	CRETICS	CRICK	CRINGE	CRITHS
CRENULATE	CRETIN	CRICKED	CRINGED	CRITIC
CREODONT	CRETINISE	CRICKET	CRINGER	CRITICAL
CREODONTS	CRETINISED	CRICKETED	CRINGERS	CRITICISE
CREOLE	CRETINISES	CRICKETER	CRINGES	CRITICISED
CREOLES	CRETINISING	CRICKETERS	CRINGING	CRITICISES
CREOLIAN	CRETINISM	CRICKETING	CRINGINGS	CRITICISING
CREOLIANS	CRETINISMS	CRICKETINGS	CRINGLE	CRITICISM
CREOLIST	CRETINIZE	CRICKETS	CRINGLES	CRITICISMS
CREOLISTS	CRETINIZED	CRICKEY	CRINING	CRITICIZE
CREOSOL	CRETINIZES	CRICKING	CRINITE	CRITICIZED
CREOSOLS	CRETINIZING	CRICKS	CRINITES	CRITICIZES
CREOSOTE	CRETINOID	CRICKY	CRINKLE	CRITICIZING
CREOSOTED	CRETINOIDS	CRICOID	CRINKLED	CRITICS
CREOSOTES	CRETINOUS	CRICOIDS	CRINKLES	CRITIQUE
CREOSOTING	CRETINS	CRIED	CRINKLIER	CRITIQUED
CREPANCE	CRETISM	CRIER	CRINKLIES	CRITIQUES
CREPANCES	CRETISMS	CRIERS	CRINKLIEST	CRITIQUING
CREPE	CRETONNE	CRIES	CRINKLING	CRITS
CREPERIE	CRETONNES	CRIKEY	CRINKLY	CRITTER
CREPERIES	CREUTZER	CRIM	CRINOID	CRITTERS
CREPES	CREUTZERS	CRIME	CRINOIDAL	CRITTUR
CREPEY	CREVASSE	CRIMED	CRINOIDS	CRITTURS
CREPIER	CREVASSED	CRIMEFUL	CRINOLINE	CRIVENS
CREPIEST	CREVASSES	CRIMELESS	CRINOLINES	CRIVVENS
CREPINESS	CREVASSING	CRIMEN	CRINOSE	CROAK
CREPINESSES	CREVETTE	CRIMES	CRINUM	CROAKED
CREPITANT	CREVETTES	CRIMINA	CRINUMS	CROAKER
CREPITATE	CREVICE	CRIMINAL	CRIOLLO	CROAKERS
CREPITATED	CREVICES	CRIMINALS	CRIOLLOS	CROAKIER
CREPITATES	CREW	CRIMINATE	CRIPES	CROAKIEST
CREPITATING	CREWE	CRIMINATED	CRIPPLE	CROAKILY
CREPITUS	CREWED	CRIMINATES	CRIPPLED	CROAKING
CREPITUSES	CREWEL	CRIMINATING	CRIPPLES	CROAKINGS
CREPOLINE	CREWELIST	CRIMINE	CRIPPLING	CROAKS
CREPOLINES	CREWELISTS	CRIMING	CRIPPLINGS	CROAKY
CREPON	CREWELLED	CRIMINI	CRISE	CROC
CREPONS	CREWELLING	CRIMINOUS	CRISES	CROCEATE
CREPT	CREWELS	CRIMMER	CRISIS	CROCEIN
CREPUSCLE	CREWES	CRIMMERS	CRISP	CROCEINS
CREPUSCLES	CREWING	CRIMP	CRISPATE	CROCEOUS
CREPY	CREWS	CRIMPED	CRISPED	CROCHE
CRESCENDO	CRIANT	CRIMPER	CRISPER	CROCHES
CRESCENDOED	CRIB	CRIMPERS	CRISPERS	CROCHET
CRESCENDOING	CRIBBAGE	CRIMPIER	CRISPEST	CROCHETED
CRESCENDOS	CRIBBAGES	CRIMPIEST	CRISPIER	CROCHETING

CROCHETINGS
CROCHETS
CROCK
CROCKED
CROCKERIES
CROCKERY
CROCKET
CROCKETS
CROCKING
CROCKS
CROCODILE
CROCODILES
CROCOITE
CROCOITES
CROCOSMIA
CROCOSMIAS
CROCS
CROCUS
CROCUSES
CROFT
CROFTER
CROFTERS
CROFTING
CROFTINGS
CROFTS
CROISSANT
CROISSANTS
CROMACK
CROMACKS
CROMB
CROMBED
CROMBING
CROMBS
CROME
CROMED
CROMES
CROMING
CROMLECH
CROMLECHS
CROMORNA
CROMORNAS
CROMORNE
CROMORNES
CRONE
CRONES
CRONET
CRONETS
CRONIES
CRONK
CRONKER
CRONKEST
CRONY
CRONYISM
CRONYISMS
CROODLE
CROODLED
CROODLES
CROODLING
CROOK
CROOKBACK
CROOKBACKS
CROOKED
CROOKEDER
CROOKEDEST

CROOKEDLY
CROOKER
CROOKEST
CROOKING
CROOKS
CROON
CROONED
CROONER
CROONERS
CROONING
CROONINGS
CROONS
CROOVE
CROOVES
CROP
CROPBOUND
CROPFUL
CROPFULL
CROPFULS
CROPLAND
CROPLANDS
CROPPED
CROPPER
CROPPERS
CROPPIES
CROPPING
CROPPINGS
CROPPY
CROPS
CROPSICK
CROQUANTE
CROQUANTES
CROQUET
CROQUETED
CROQUETING
CROQUETS
CROQUETTE
CROQUETTES
CROQUIS
CRORE
CRORES
CROSIER
CROSIERED
CROSIERS
CROSS
CROSSBAND
CROSSBANDS
CROSSBAR
CROSSBARS
CROSSBEAM
CROSSBEAMS
CROSSBILL
CROSSBILLS
CROSSBIT
CROSSBITE
CROSSBITES
CROSSBITING
CROSSBITTEN
CROSSBOW
CROSSBOWS
CROSSBRED
CROSSBUCK
CROSSBUCKS
CROSSCUT

CROSSCUTS
CROSSCUTTING
CROSSCUTTINGS
CROSSE
CROSSED
CROSSER
CROSSES
CROSSEST
CROSSETTE
CROSSETTES
CROSSFALL
CROSSFALLS
CROSSFIRE
CROSSFIRES
CROSSFISH
CROSSFISHES
CROSSHEAD
CROSSHEADS
CROSSING
CROSSINGS
CROSSISH
CROSSJACK
CROSSJACKS
CROSSLET
CROSSLETS
CROSSLY
CROSSNESS
CROSSNESSES
CROSSOVER
CROSSOVERS
CROSSROAD
CROSSROADS
CROSSTIE
CROSSTIES
CROSSTOWN
CROSSTREE
CROSSTREES
CROSSWALK
CROSSWALKS
CROSSWAY
CROSSWAYS
CROSSWIND
CROSSWINDS
CROSSWISE
CROSSWORD
CROSSWORDS
CROSSWORT
CROSSWORTS
CROST
CROSTINI
CROSTINIS
CROTAL
CROTALA
CROTALINE
CROTALISM
CROTALISMS
CROTALS
CROTALUM
CROTCH
CROTCHED
CROTCHES
CROTCHET
CROTCHETIER
CROTCHETIEST

CROTCHETS
CROTCHETY
CROTON
CROTONS
CROTTLE
CROTTLES
CROUCH
CROUCHED
CROUCHES
CROUCHING
CROUP
CROUPADE
CROUPADES
CROUPE
CROUPED
CROUPER
CROUPERS
CROUPES
CROUPIER
CROUPIERS
CROUPIEST
CROUPING
CROUPON
CROUPONS
CROUPOUS
CROUPS
CROUPY
CROUSE
CROUSELY
CROUSTADE
CROUSTADES
CROUT
CROUTE
CROUTES
CROUTON
CROUTONS
CROUTS
CROW
CROWBAR
CROWBARS
CROWBERRIES
CROWBERRY
CROWD
CROWDED
CROWDER
CROWDERS
CROWDIE
CROWDIES
CROWDING
CROWDS
CROWED
CROWFOOT
CROWFOOTS
CROWING
CROWN
CROWNED
CROWNER
CROWNERS
CROWNET
CROWNETS
CROWNING
CROWNINGS
CROWNLESS
CROWNLET

CROWNLETS
CROWNS
CROWNWORK
CROWNWORKS
CROWS
CROZE
CROZES
CROZIER
CROZIERS
CRU
CRUBEEN
CRUBEENS
CRUCES
CRUCIAL
CRUCIAN
CRUCIANS
CRUCIATE
CRUCIBLE
CRUCIBLES
CRUCIFER
CRUCIFERS
CRUCIFIED
CRUCIFIER
CRUCIFIERS
CRUCIFIES
CRUCIFIX
CRUCIFIXES
CRUCIFORM
CRUCIFY
CRUCIFYING
CRUCK
CRUCKS
CRUD
CRUDDED
CRUDDIER
CRUDDIEST
CRUDDING
CRUDDLE
CRUDDLED
CRUDDLES
CRUDDLING
CRUDDY
CRUDE
CRUDELY
CRUDENESS
CRUDENESSES
CRUDER
CRUDES
CRUDEST
CRUDITES
CRUDITIES
CRUDITY
CRUDS
CRUDY
CRUE
CRUEL
CRUELLER
CRUELLEST
CRUELLS
CRUELLY
CRUELNESS
CRUELNESSES
CRUELS
CRUELTIES

The Chambers Dictionary is the authority for many longer words; see *OSW* Introduction, page xii

CRUELTY	CRUNCHED	CRUZADOES	CUBBING	CUDDLED
CRUES	CRUNCHES	CRUZADOS	CUBBINGS	CUDDLES
CRUET	CRUNCHIER	CRUZEIRO	CUBBISH	CUDDLIER
CRUETS	CRUNCHIEST	CRUZEIROS	CUBBY	CUDDLIEST
CRUISE	CRUNCHING	CRWTH	CUBE	CUDDLING
CRUISED	CRUNCHY	CRWTHS	CUBEB	CUDDLY
CRUISER	CRUNKLE	CRY	CUBEBS	CUDDY
CRUISERS	CRUNKLED	CRYBABIES	CUBED	CUDGEL
CRUISES	CRUNKLES	CRYBABY	CUBES	CUDGELLED
CRUISEWAY	CRUNKLING	CRYING	CUBHOOD	CUDGELLER
CRUISEWAYS	CRUOR	CRYINGS	CUBHOODS	CUDGELLERS
CRUISIE	CRUORES	CRYOGEN	CUBIC	CUDGELLING
CRUISIES	CRUPPER	CRYOGENIC	CUBICA	CUDGELLINGS
CRUISING	CRUPPERS	CRYOGENICS	CUBICAL	CUDGELS
CRUIVE	CRURAL	CRYOGENIES	CUBICALLY	CUDS
CRUIVES	CRUS	CRYOGENS	CUBICAS	CUDWEED
CRULLER	CRUSADE	CRYOGENY	CUBICLE	CUDWEEDS
CRULLERS	CRUSADED	CRYOLITE	CUBICLES	CUE
CRUMB	CRUSADER	CRYOLITES	CUBICS	CUED
CRUMBED	CRUSADERS	CRYOMETER	CUBIFORM	CUEING
CRUMBIER	CRUSADES	CRYOMETERS	CUBING	CUEIST
CRUMBIEST	CRUSADING	CRYONIC	CUBISM	CUEISTS
CRUMBING	CRUSADO	CRYONICS	CUBISMS	CUES
CRUMBLE	CRUSADOS	CRYOPROBE	CUBIST	CUESTA
CRUMBLED	CRUSE	CRYOPROBES	CUBISTIC	CUESTAS
CRUMBLES	CRUSES	CRYOSCOPE	CUBISTS	CUFF
CRUMBLIER	CRUSET	CRYOSCOPES	CUBIT	CUFFED
CRUMBLIES	CRUSETS	CRYOSCOPIES	CUBITAL	CUFFIN
CRUMBLIEST	CRUSH	CRYOSCOPY	CUBITS	CUFFING
CRUMBLING	CRUSHABLE	CRYOSTAT	CUBITUS	CUFFINS
CRUMBLY	CRUSHED	CRYOSTATS	CUBITUSES	CUFFLE
CRUMBS	CRUSHER	CRYOTRON	CUBLESS	CUFFLED
CRUMBY	CRUSHERS	CRYOTRONS	CUBOID	CUFFLES
CRUMEN	CRUSHES	CRYPT	CUBOIDAL	CUFFLING
CRUMENAL	CRUSHING	CRYPTADIA	CUBOIDS	CUFFO
CRUMENALS	CRUSIAN	CRYPTAL	CUBS	CUFFS
CRUMENS	CRUSIANS	CRYPTIC	CUCKOLD	CUFFUFFLE
CRUMHORN	CRUSIE	CRYPTICAL	CUCKOLDED	CUFFUFFLES
CRUMHORNS	CRUSIES	CRYPTO	CUCKOLDING	CUIF
CRUMMACK	CRUST	CRYPTOGAM	CUCKOLDLY	CUIFS
CRUMMACKS	CRUSTA	CRYPTOGAMS	CUCKOLDOM	CUING
CRUMMIER	CRUSTAE	CRYPTON	CUCKOLDOMS	CUIRASS
CRUMMIES	CRUSTAL	CRYPTONS	CUCKOLDRIES	CUIRASSED
CRUMMIEST	CRUSTATE	CRYPTONYM	CUCKOLDRY	CUIRASSES
CRUMMOCK	CRUSTATED	CRYPTONYMS	CUCKOLDS	CUIRASSING
CRUMMOCKS	CRUSTED	CRYPTOS	CUCKOO	CUISH
CRUMMY	CRUSTIER	CRYPTS	CUCKOOS	CUISHES
CRUMP	CRUSTIES	CRYSTAL	CUCULLATE	CUISINE
CRUMPED	CRUSTIEST	CRYSTALS	CUCUMBER	CUISINES
CRUMPER	CRUSTILY	CSARDAS	CUCUMBERS	CUISINIER
CRUMPEST	CRUSTING	CSARDASES	CUCURBIT	CUISINIERS
CRUMPET	CRUSTLESS	CTENE	CUCURBITS	CUISSE
CRUMPETS	CRUSTS	CTENES	CUD	CUISSER
CRUMPIER	CRUSTY	CTENIFORM	CUDBEAR	CUISSERS
CRUMPIEST	CRUSY	CTENOID	CUDBEARS	CUISSES
CRUMPING	CRUTCH	CUADRILLA	CUDDEEHIH	CUIT
CRUMPLE	CRUTCHED	CUADRILLAS	CUDDEEHIHS	CUITER
CRUMPLED	CRUTCHES	CUB	CUDDEN	CUITERED
CRUMPLES	CRUTCHING	CUBAGE	CUDDENS	CUITERING
CRUMPLING	CRUVE	CUBAGES	CUDDIE	CUITERS
CRUMPLINGS	CRUVES	CUBATURE	CUDDIES	CUITIKIN
CRUMPS	CRUX	CUBATURES	CUDDIN	CUITIKINS
CRUMPY	CRUXES	CUBBED	CUDDINS	CUITS
CRUNCH	CRUZADO	CUBBIES	CUDDLE	CUITTLE

The Chambers Dictionary is the authority for many longer words; see *OSW* Introduction, page xii

CUITTLED	CULTISH	CUNDIES	CUPROUS	CURDIER
CUITTLES	CULTISM	CUNDY	CUPS	CURDIEST
CUITTLING	CULTISMS	CUNEAL	CUPULAR	CURDINESS
CULCH	CULTIST	CUNEATE	CUPULATE	CURDINESSES
CULCHES	CULTISTS	CUNEATIC	CUPULE	CURDING
CULCHIE	CULTIVAR	CUNEIFORM	CUPULES	CURDLE
CULCHIES	CULTIVARS	CUNEIFORMS	CUR	CURDLED
CULET	CULTIVATE	CUNETTE	CURABLE	CURDLES
CULETS	CULTIVATED	CUNETTES	CURACAO	CURDLING
CULEX	CULTIVATES	CUNJEVOI	CURACAOS	CURDS
CULICES	CULTIVATING	CUNJEVOIS	CURACIES	CURDY
CULICID	CULTRATE	CUNNER	CURACOA	CURE
CULICIDS	CULTRATED	CUNNERS	CURACOAS	CURED
CULICINE	CULTS	CUNNING	CURACY	CURELESS
CULICINES	CULTURAL	CUNNINGER	CURARA	CURER
CULINARY	CULTURE	CUNNINGEST	CURARAS	CURERS
CULL	CULTURED	CUNNINGLY	CURARE	CURES
CULLED	CULTURES	CUNNINGS	CURARES	CURETTAGE
CULLENDER	CULTURING	CUNT	CURARI	CURETTAGES
CULLENDERS	CULTURIST	CUNTS	CURARINE	CURETTE
CULLER	CULTURISTS	CUP	CURARINES	CURETTED
CULLERS	CULTUS	CUPBEARER	CURARIS	CURETTES
CULLET	CULTUSES	CUPBEARERS	CURARISE	CURETTING
CULLETS	CULVER	CUPBOARD	CURARISED	CURFEW
CULLIED	CULVERIN	CUPBOARDED	CURARISES	CURFEWS
CULLIES	CULVERINS	CUPBOARDING	CURARISING	CURFUFFLE
CULLING	CULVERS	CUPBOARDS	CURARIZE	CURFUFFLED
CULLINGS	CULVERT	CUPCAKE	CURARIZED	CURFUFFLES
CULLION	CULVERTS	CUPCAKES	CURARIZES	CURFUFFLING
CULLIONLY	CUM	CUPEL	CURARIZING	CURIA
CULLIONS	CUMARIN	CUPELED	CURASSOW	CURIAE
CULLIS	CUMARINS	CUPELING	CURASSOWS	CURIALISM
CULLISES	CUMBENT	CUPELLED	CURAT	CURIALISMS
CULLS	CUMBER	CUPELLING	CURATE	CURIALIST
CULLY	CUMBERED	CUPELS	CURATED	CURIALISTS
CULLYING	CUMBERER	CUPFUL	CURATES	CURIAS
CULLYISM	CUMBERERS	CUPFULS	CURATING	CURIE
CULLYISMS	CUMBERING	CUPGALL	CURATIVE	CURIES
CULM	CUMBERS	CUPGALLS	CURATOR	CURIET
CULMED	CUMBRANCE	CUPHEAD	CURATORS	CURIETS
CULMEN	CUMBRANCES	CUPHEADS	CURATORY	CURING
CULMENS	CUMBROUS	CUPID	CURATRIX	CURIO
CULMINANT	CUMEC	CUPIDITIES	CURATRIXES	CURIOS
CULMINATE	CUMECS	CUPIDITY	CURATS	CURIOSA
CULMINATED	CUMIN	CUPIDS	CURB	CURIOSITIES
CULMINATES	CUMINS	CUPMAN	CURBABLE	CURIOSITY
CULMINATING	CUMMER	CUPMEN	CURBED	CURIOUS
CULMING	CUMMERS	CUPOLA	CURBING	CURIOUSER
CULMS	CUMMIN	CUPOLAED	CURBLESS	CURIOUSLY
CULOTTE	CUMMINS	CUPOLAING	CURBS	CURIUM
CULOTTES	CUMQUAT	CUPOLAR	CURBSTONE	CURIUMS
CULPABLE	CUMQUATS	CUPOLAS	CURBSTONES	CURL
CULPABLY	CUMSHAW	CUPOLATED	CURCH	CURLED
CULPATORY	CUMSHAWS	CUPPA	CURCHES	CURLER
CULPRIT	CUMULATE	CUPPAS	CURCULIO	CURLERS
CULPRITS	CUMULATED	CUPPED	CURCULIOS	CURLEW
CULT	CUMULATES	CUPPER	CURCUMA	CURLEWS
CULTCH	CUMULATING	CUPPERS	CURCUMAS	CURLICUE
CULTCHES	CUMULI	CUPPING	CURCUMIN	CURLICUES
CULTER	CUMULOSE	CUPPINGS	CURCUMINE	CURLIER
CULTERS	CUMULUS	CUPREOUS	CURCUMINES	CURLIEST
CULTIC	CUNABULA	CUPRIC	CURCUMINS	CURLINESS
CULTIGEN	CUNCTATOR	CUPRITE	CURD	CURLINESSES
CULTIGENS	CUNCTATORS	CUPRITES	CURDED	CURLING

The Chambers Dictionary is the authority for many longer words; see *OSW* Introduction, page xii

CURLINGS	CURSITOR	CURVES	CUSTODIAL	CUTINISING
CURLPAPER	CURSITORS	CURVESOME	CUSTODIAN	CUTINIZE
CURLPAPERS	CURSITORY	CURVET	CUSTODIANS	CUTINIZED
CURLS	CURSIVE	CURVETED	CUSTODIER	CUTINIZES
CURLY	CURSIVELY	CURVETING	CUSTODIERS	CUTINIZING
CURN	CURSOR	CURVETS	CUSTODIES	CUTINS
CURNEY	CURSORARY	CURVETTED	CUSTODY	CUTIS
CURNIER	CURSORES	CURVETTING	CUSTOM	CUTISES
CURNIEST	CURSORIAL	CURVIER	CUSTOMARIES	CUTLASS
CURNS	CURSORILY	CURVIEST	CUSTOMARY	CUTLASSES
CURNY	CURSORS	CURVIFORM	CUSTOMED	CUTLER
CURPEL	CURSORY	CURVING	CUSTOMER	CUTLERIES
CURPELS	CURST	CURVITAL	CUSTOMERS	CUTLERS
CURR	CURSTNESS	CURVITIES	CUSTOMISE	CUTLERY
CURRACH	CURSTNESSES	CURVITY	CUSTOMISED	CUTLET
CURRACHS	CURSUS	CURVY	CUSTOMISES	CUTLETS
CURRAGH	CURT	CUSCUS	CUSTOMISING	CUTLINE
CURRAGHS	CURTAIL	CUSCUSES	CUSTOMIZE	CUTLINES
CURRAJONG	CURTAILED	CUSEC	CUSTOMIZED	CUTPURSE
CURRAJONGS	CURTAILING	CUSECS	CUSTOMIZES	CUTPURSES
CURRANT	CURTAILS	CUSH	CUSTOMIZING	CUTS
CURRANTIER	CURTAIN	CUSHAT	CUSTOMS	CUTTER
CURRANTIEST	CURTAINED	CUSHATS	CUSTOS	CUTTERS
CURRANTS	CURTAINING	CUSHAW	CUSTREL	CUTTIER
CURRANTY	CURTAINS	CUSHAWS	CUSTRELS	CUTTIES
CURRAWONG	CURTAL	CUSHES	CUSTUMARIES	CUTTIEST
CURRAWONGS	CURTALAX	CUSHIER	CUSTUMARY	CUTTING
CURRED	CURTALAXE	CUSHIEST	CUT	CUTTINGS
CURRENCIES	CURTALAXES	CUSHION	CUTANEOUS	CUTTLE
CURRENCY	CURTALS	CUSHIONED	CUTAWAY	CUTTLES
CURRENT	CURTANA	CUSHIONET	CUTAWAYS	CUTTO
CURRENTLY	CURTANAS	CUSHIONETS	CUTBACK	CUTTOE
CURRENTS	CURTATE	CUSHIONING	CUTBACKS	CUTTOES
CURRICLE	CURTATION	CUSHIONS	CUTCH	CUTTY
CURRICLES	CURTATIONS	CUSHIONY	CUTCHA	CUTWORK
CURRICULA	CURTAXE	CUSHY	CUTCHERIES	CUTWORKS
CURRIE	CURTAXES	CUSK	CUTCHERRIES	CUTWORM
CURRIED	CURTER	CUSKS	CUTCHERRY	CUTWORMS
CURRIER	CURTESIES	CUSP	CUTCHERY	CUVEE
CURRIERS	CURTEST	CUSPATE	CUTCHES	CUVEES
CURRIES	CURTESY	CUSPED	CUTE	CUVETTE
CURRING	CURTILAGE	CUSPID	CUTELY	CUVETTES
CURRISH	CURTILAGES	CUSPIDAL	CUTENESS	CUZ
CURRISHLY	CURTLY	CUSPIDATE	CUTENESSES	CUZZES
CURRS	CURTNESS	CUSPIDOR	CUTER	CWM
CURRY	CURTNESSES	CUSPIDORE	CUTES	CWMS
CURRYCOMB	CURTSEY	CUSPIDORES	CUTESIER	CYAN
CURRYCOMBS	CURTSEYED	CUSPIDORS	CUTESIEST	CYANAMIDE
CURRYING	CURTSEYING	CUSPIDS	CUTEST	CYANAMIDES
CURRYINGS	CURTSEYS	CUSPS	CUTESY	CYANATE
CURS	CURTSIED	CUSS	CUTEY	CYANATES
CURSAL	CURTSIES	CUSSED	CUTEYS	CYANIC
CURSE	CURTSY	CUSSER	CUTGLASS	CYANIDE
CURSED	CURTSYING	CUSSERS	CUTICLE	CYANIDED
CURSEDER	CURULE	CUSSES	CUTICLES	CYANIDES
CURSEDEST	CURVATE	CUSSING	CUTICULAR	CYANIDING
CURSEDLY	CURVATED	CUSSWORD	CUTIE	CYANIDINGS
CURSENARY	CURVATION	CUSSWORDS	CUTIES	CYANIN
CURSER	CURVATIONS	CUSTARD	CUTIKIN	CYANINE
CURSERS	CURVATIVE	CUSTARDS	CUTIKINS	CYANINES
CURSES	CURVATURE	CUSTOCK	CUTIN	CYANINS
CURSI	CURVATURES	CUSTOCKS	CUTINISE	CYANISE
CURSING	CURVE	CUSTODE	CUTINISED	CYANISED
CURSINGS	CURVED	CUSTODES	CUTINISES	CYANISES

CYANISING	CYCLES	CYLINDERS	CYPRESS	CYTODE
CYANITE	CYCLEWAY	CYLINDRIC	CYPRESSES	CYTODES
CYANITES	CYCLEWAYS	CYLIX	CYPRIAN	CYTOID
CYANIZE	CYCLIC	CYMA	CYPRIANS	CYTOKINE
CYANIZED	CYCLICAL	CYMAGRAPH	CYPRID	CYTOKINES
CYANIZES	CYCLICISM	CYMAGRAPHS	CYPRIDES	CYTOKININ
CYANIZING	CYCLICISMS	CYMAR	CYPRIDS	CYTOKININS
CYANOGEN	CYCLICITIES	CYMARS	CYPRINE	CYTOLOGIES
CYANOGENS	CYCLICITY	CYMAS	CYPRINID	CYTOLOGY
CYANOSED	CYCLING	CYMATIA	CYPRINIDS	CYTOLYSES
CYANOSES	CYCLINGS	CYMATICS	CYPRINOID	CYTOLYSIS
CYANOSIS	CYCLIST	CYMATIUM	CYPRIS	CYTOMETER
CYANOTIC	CYCLISTS	CYMBAL	CYPRUS	CYTOMETERS
CYANOTYPE	CYCLIZINE	CYMBALIST	CYPRUSES	CYTOMETRIES
CYANOTYPES	CYCLIZINES	CYMBALISTS	CYPSELA	CYTOMETRY
CYANS	CYCLO	CYMBALO	CYPSELAE	CYTON
CYANURET	CYCLOID	CYMBALOES	CYST	CYTONS
CYANURETS	CYCLOIDAL	CYMBALOS	CYSTEINE	CYTOPENIA
CYATHI	CYCLOIDS	CYMBALS	CYSTEINES	CYTOPENIAS
CYATHIA	CYCLOLITH	CYMBIDIA	CYSTIC	CYTOPLASM
CYATHIUM	CYCLOLITHS	CYMBIDIUM	CYSTID	CYTOPLASMS
CYATHUS	CYCLONE	CYMBIDIUMS	CYSTIDEAN	CYTOSINE
CYBERCAFE	CYCLONES	CYMBIFORM	CYSTIDEANS	CYTOSINES
CYBERCAFES	CYCLONIC	CYME	CYSTIDS	CYTOSOME
CYBERNATE	CYCLONITE	CYMES	CYSTIFORM	CYTOSOMES
CYBERNATED	CYCLONITES	CYMOGRAPH	CYSTINE	CYTOTOXIC
CYBERNATES	CYCLOPEAN	CYMOGRAPHS	CYSTINES	CYTOTOXIN
CYBERNATING	CYCLOPES	CYMOID	CYSTITIS	CYTOTOXINS
CYBERPET	CYCLOPIAN	CYMOPHANE	CYSTITISES	CZAPKA
CYBERPETS	CYCLOPIC	CYMOPHANES	CYSTOCARP	CZAPKAS
CYBERPUNK	CYCLOPS	CYMOSE	CYSTOCARPS	CZAR
CYBERPUNKS	CYCLORAMA	CYMOUS	CYSTOCELE	CZARDAS
CYBERSEX	CYCLORAMAS	CYNANCHE	CYSTOCELES	CZARDASES
CYBERSEXES	CYCLOS	CYNANCHES	CYSTOID	CZARDOM
CYBORG	CYCLOSES	CYNEGETIC	CYSTOIDS	CZARDOMS
CYBORGS	CYCLOSIS	CYNIC	CYSTOLITH	CZAREVICH
CYBRID	CYCLOTRON	CYNICAL	CYSTOLITHS	CZAREVICHES
CYBRIDS	CYCLOTRONS	CYNICALLY	CYSTOTOMIES	CZAREVNA
CYCAD	CYCLUS	CYNICISM	CYSTOTOMY	CZAREVNAS
CYCADS	CYCLUSES	CYNICISMS	CYSTS	CZARINA
CYCLAMATE	CYDER	CYNICS	CYTASE	CZARINAS
CYCLAMATES	CYDERS	CYNOMOLGI	CYTASES	CZARISM
CYCLAMEN	CYESES	CYNOSURE	CYTE	CZARISMS
CYCLAMENS	CYESIS	CYNOSURES	CYTES	CZARIST
CYCLE	CYGNET	CYPHER	CYTISI	CZARISTS
CYCLED	CYGNETS	CYPHERED	CYTISINE	CZARITSA
CYCLER	CYLICES	CYPHERING	CYTISINES	CZARITSAS
CYCLERS	CYLINDER	CYPHERS	CYTISUS	CZARS

D

DA
DAB
DABBED
DABBER
DABBERS
DABBING
DABBITIES
DABBITY
DABBLE
DABBLED
DABBLER
DABBLERS
DABBLES
DABBLING
DABBLINGS
DABCHICK
DABCHICKS
DABS
DABSTER
DABSTERS
DACE
DACES
DACHA
DACHAS
DACHSHUND
DACHSHUNDS
DACITE
DACITES
DACKER
DACKERED
DACKERING
DACKERS
DACOIT
DACOITAGE
DACOITAGES
DACOITIES
DACOITS
DACOITY
DACTYL
DACTYLAR
DACTYLIC
DACTYLIST
DACTYLISTS
DACTYLS
DAD
DADDED
DADDIES
DADDING
DADDLE
DADDLED
DADDLES
DADDLING
DADDOCK
DADDOCKS

DADDY
DADO
DADOED
DADOES
DADOING
DADOS
DADS
DAE
DAEDAL
DAEDALIAN
DAEDALIC
DAEING
DAEMON
DAEMONIC
DAEMONS
DAES
DAFF
DAFFED
DAFFIER
DAFFIES
DAFFIEST
DAFFING
DAFFINGS
DAFFODIL
DAFFODILS
DAFFS
DAFFY
DAFTAR
DAFTARS
DAFTER
DAFTEST
DAFTIE
DAFTIES
DAFTLY
DAFTNESS
DAFTNESSES
DAG
DAGABA
DAGABAS
DAGGA
DAGGAS
DAGGED
DAGGER
DAGGERS
DAGGIER
DAGGIEST
DAGGING
DAGGINGS
DAGGLE
DAGGLED
DAGGLES
DAGGLING
DAGGY

DAGLOCK
DAGLOCKS
DAGO
DAGOBA
DAGOBAS
DAGOES
DAGOS
DAGS
DAGWOOD
DAGWOODS
DAH
DAHABEEAH
DAHABEEAHS
DAHABIEH
DAHABIEHS
DAHABIYAH
DAHABIYAHS
DAHABIYEH
DAHABIYEHS
DAHL
DAHLIA
DAHLIAS
DAHLS
DAHS
DAIDLE
DAIDLED
DAIDLES
DAIDLING
DAIKER
DAIKERED
DAIKERING
DAIKERS
DAIKON
DAIKONS
DAILIES
DAILY
DAIMEN
DAIMIO
DAIMIOS
DAIMON
DAIMONIC
DAIMONS
DAINE
DAINED
DAINES
DAINING
DAINT
DAINTIER
DAINTIES
DAINTIEST
DAINTILY
DAINTY
DAIQUIRI
DAIQUIRIS

DAIRIES
DAIRY
DAIRYING
DAIRYINGS
DAIRYMAID
DAIRYMAIDS
DAIRYMAN
DAIRYMEN
DAIS
DAISES
DAISIED
DAISIES
DAISY
DAK
DAKER
DAKERED
DAKERING
DAKERS
DAKOIT
DAKOITI
DAKOITIS
DAKOITS
DAKS
DAL
DALE
DALES
DALESMAN
DALESMEN
DALI
DALIS
DALLE
DALLES
DALLIANCE
DALLIANCES
DALLIED
DALLIER
DALLIERS
DALLIES
DALLOP
DALLOPS
DALLY
DALLYING
DALMAHOY
DALMAHOYS
DALMATIC
DALMATICS
DALS
DALT
DALTON
DALTONISM
DALTONISMS
DALTONS
DALTS
DAM

DAMAGE
DAMAGED
DAMAGES
DAMAGING
DAMAN
DAMANS
DAMAR
DAMARS
DAMASCENE
DAMASCENED
DAMASCENES
DAMASCENING
DAMASCENINGS
DAMASK
DAMASKED
DAMASKEEN
DAMASKEENED
DAMASKEENING
DAMASKEENS
DAMASKIN
DAMASKINED
DAMASKING
DAMASKINING
DAMASKINS
DAMASKS
DAMASQUIN
DAMASQUINED
DAMASQUINING
DAMASQUINS
DAMASSIN
DAMASSINS
DAMBOARD
DAMBOARDS
DAMBROD
DAMBRODS
DAME
DAMES
DAMFOOL
DAMMAR
DAMMARS
DAMME
DAMMED
DAMMER
DAMMERS
DAMMING
DAMMIT
DAMN
DAMNABLE
DAMNABLY
DAMNATION
DAMNATIONS
DAMNATORY
DAMNED
DAMNEDER

DAMNEDEST	DANDIFY	DANSEUSE	DARKEYS	DARTLING
DAMNIFIED	DANDIFYING	DANSEUSES	DARKIE	DARTRE
DAMNIFIES	DANDILY	DANT	DARKIES	DARTRES
DAMNIFY	DANDIPRAT	DANTED	DARKISH	DARTROUS
DAMNIFYING	DANDIPRATS	DANTING	DARKLE	DARTS
DAMNING	DANDLE	DANTON	DARKLED	DARZI
DAMNS	DANDLED	DANTONED	DARKLES	DARZIS
DAMOISEL	DANDLER	DANTONING	DARKLING	DAS
DAMOISELS	DANDLERS	DANTONS	DARKLINGS	DASH
DAMOSEL	DANDLES	DANTS	DARKLY	DASHBOARD
DAMOSELS	DANDLING	DAP	DARKMANS	DASHBOARDS
DAMOZEL	DANDRIFF	DAPHNE	DARKNESS	DASHED
DAMOZELS	DANDRIFFS	DAPHNES	DARKNESSES	DASHEEN
DAMP	DANDRUFF	DAPHNID	DARKROOM	DASHEENS
DAMPED	DANDRUFFS	DAPHNIDS	DARKROOMS	DASHEKI
DAMPEN	DANDY	DAPPED	DARKS	DASHEKIS
DAMPENED	DANDYFUNK	DAPPER	DARKSOME	DASHER
DAMPENING	DANDYFUNKS	DAPPERER	DARKY	DASHERS
DAMPENS	DANDYISH	DAPPEREST	DARLING	DASHES
DAMPER	DANDYISM	DAPPERLY	DARLINGS	DASHIKI
DAMPERS	DANDYISMS	DAPPERS	DARN	DASHIKIS
DAMPEST	DANDYPRAT	DAPPING	DARNED	DASHING
DAMPIER	DANDYPRATS	DAPPLE	DARNEDER	DASHINGLY
DAMPIEST	DANEGELD	DAPPLED	DARNEDEST	DASSIE
DAMPING	DANEGELDS	DAPPLES	DARNEL	DASSIES
DAMPINGS	DANEGELT	DAPPLING	DARNELS	DASTARD
DAMPISH	DANEGELTS	DAPS	DARNER	DASTARDIES
DAMPLY	DANELAGH	DAPSONE	DARNERS	DASTARDLY
DAMPNESS	DANELAGHS	DAPSONES	DARNING	DASTARDS
DAMPNESSES	DANELAW	DAQUIRI	DARNINGS	DASTARDY
DAMPS	DANELAWS	DAQUIRIS	DARNS	DASYPOD
DAMPY	DANG	DARAF	DARRAIGN	DASYPODS
DAMS	DANGED	DARAFS	DARRAIGNE	DASYURE
DAMSEL	DANGER	DARBIES	DARRAIGNED	DASYURES
DAMSELFLIES	DANGERED	DARCIES	DARRAIGNES	DATA
DAMSELFLY	DANGERING	DARCY	DARRAIGNING	DATABANK
DAMSELS	DANGEROUS	DARCYS	DARRAIGNS	DATABANKS
DAMSON	DANGERS	DARE	DARRAIN	DATABASE
DAMSONS	DANGING	DARED	DARRAINE	DATABASES
DAN	DANGLE	DAREFUL	DARRAINED	DATABLE
DANCE	DANGLED	DARES	DARRAINES	DATABUS
DANCEABLE	DANGLER	DARG	DARRAINING	DATABUSES
DANCED	DANGLERS	DARGA	DARRAINS	DATABUSSES
DANCER	DANGLES	DARGAS	DARRAYN	DATACOMMS
DANCERS	DANGLIER	DARGLE	DARRAYNED	DATAGLOVE
DANCES	DANGLIEST	DARGLES	DARRAYNING	DATAGLOVES
DANCETTE	DANGLING	DARGS	DARRAYNS	DATAL
DANCETTEE	DANGLINGS	DARI	DARRE	DATALLER
DANCETTES	DANGLY	DARIC	DARRED	DATALLERS
DANCETTY	DANGS	DARICS	DARRES	DATALS
DANCING	DANIO	DARING	DARRING	DATARIA
DANCINGS	DANIOS	DARINGLY	DARSHAN	DATARIAS
DANDELION	DANK	DARINGS	DARSHANS	DATARIES
DANDELIONS	DANKER	DARIOLE	DART	DATARY
DANDER	DANKEST	DARIOLES	DARTBOARD	DATE
DANDERED	DANKISH	DARIS	DARTBOARDS	DATEABLE
DANDERING	DANKNESS	DARK	DARTED	DATED
DANDERS	DANKNESSES	DARKEN	DARTER	DATELESS
DANDIACAL	DANKS	DARKENED	DARTERS	DATER
DANDIER	DANNEBROG	DARKENING	DARTING	DATERS
DANDIES	DANNEBROGS	DARKENS	DARTINGLY	DATES
DANDIEST	DANS	DARKER	DARTLE	DATING
DANDIFIED	DANSEUR	DARKEST	DARTLED	DATINGS
DANDIFIES	DANSEURS	DARKEY	DARTLES	DATIVAL

DATIVE	DAVEN	DAYSMAN	DEADS	DEATHLESS
DATIVES	DAVENED	DAYSMEN	DEADSTOCK	DEATHLIER
DATOLITE	DAVENING	DAYSPRING	DEADSTOCKS	DEATHLIEST
DATOLITES	DAVENPORT	DAYSPRINGS	DEAF	DEATHLIKE
DATUM	DAVENPORTS	DAYSTAR	DEAFEN	DEATHLY
DATURA	DAVENS	DAYSTARS	DEAFENED	DEATHS
DATURAS	DAVIDIA	DAYTALE	DEAFENING	DEATHSMAN
DATURINE	DAVIDIAS	DAYTALER	DEAFENINGS	DEATHSMEN
DATURINES	DAVIT	DAYTALERS	DEAFENS	DEATHWARD
DAUB	DAVITS	DAYTALES	DEAFER	DEATHWARDS
DAUBE	DAW	DAYTIME	DEAFEST	DEATHY
DAUBED	DAWBRIES	DAYTIMES	DEAFLY	DEAVE
DAUBER	DAWBRY	DAZE	DEAFNESS	DEAVED
DAUBERIES	DAWCOCK	DAZED	DEAFNESSES	DEAVES
DAUBERS	DAWCOCKS	DAZEDLY	DEAL	DEAVING
DAUBERY	DAWD	DAZER	DEALBATE	DEAW
DAUBES	DAWDED	DAZERS	DEALER	DEAWIE
DAUBIER	DAWDING	DAZES	DEALERS	DEAWS
DAUBIEST	DAWDLE	DAZING	DEALFISH	DEAWY
DAUBING	DAWDLED	DAZZLE	DEALFISHES	DEB
DAUBINGS	DAWDLER	DAZZLED	DEALING	DEBACLE
DAUBS	DAWDLERS	DAZZLER	DEALINGS	DEBACLES
DAUBY	DAWDLES	DAZZLERS	DEALS	DEBAG
DAUD	DAWDLING	DAZZLES	DEALT	DEBAGGED
DAUDED	DAWDS	DAZZLING	DEAN	DEBAGGING
DAUDING	DAWED	DAZZLINGS	DEANER	DEBAGGINGS
DAUDS	DAWING	DEACON	DEANERIES	DEBAGS
DAUGHTER	DAWISH	DEACONESS	DEANERS	DEBAR
DAUGHTERS	DAWK	DEACONESSES	DEANERY	DEBARK
DAULT	DAWKS	DEACONRIES	DEANS	DEBARKED
DAULTS	DAWN	DEACONRY	DEANSHIP	DEBARKING
DAUNDER	DAWNED	DEACONS	DEANSHIPS	DEBARKS
DAUNDERED	DAWNER	DEAD	DEAR	DEBARMENT
DAUNDERING	DAWNERED	DEADED	DEARE	DEBARMENTS
DAUNDERS	DAWNERING	DEADEN	DEARED	DEBARRASS
DAUNER	DAWNERS	DEADENED	DEARER	DEBARRASSED
DAUNERED	DAWNING	DEADENER	DEARES	DEBARRASSES
DAUNERING	DAWNINGS	DEADENERS	DEAREST	DEBARRASSING
DAUNERS	DAWNS	DEADENING	DEARIE	DEBARRED
DAUNT	DAWS	DEADENINGS	DEARIES	DEBARRING
DAUNTED	DAWT	DEADENS	DEARING	DEBARS
DAUNTER	DAWTED	DEADER	DEARLING	DEBASE
DAUNTERS	DAWTIE	DEADERS	DEARLINGS	DEBASED
DAUNTING	DAWTIES	DEADEST	DEARLY	DEBASER
DAUNTLESS	DAWTING	DEADHEAD	DEARN	DEBASERS
DAUNTON	DAWTS	DEADHEADED	DEARNESS	DEBASES
DAUNTONED	DAY	DEADHEADING	DEARNESSES	DEBASING
DAUNTONING	DAYBREAK	DEADHEADS	DEARNFUL	DEBATABLE
DAUNTONS	DAYBREAKS	DEADHOUSE	DEARNLY	DEBATE
DAUNTS	DAYDREAM	DEADHOUSES	DEARNS	DEBATED
DAUPHIN	DAYDREAMED	DEADING	DEARS	DEBATEFUL
DAUPHINE	DAYDREAMING	DEADLIER	DEARTH	DEBATER
DAUPHINES	DAYDREAMS	DEADLIEST	DEARTHS	DEBATERS
DAUPHINS	DAYDREAMT	DEADLINE	DEARY	DEBATES
DAUR	DAYGLO	DEADLINES	DEASIL	DEBATING
DAURED	DAYLIGHT	DEADLOCK	DEASILS	DEBAUCH
DAURING	DAYLIGHTS	DEADLOCKED	DEASIUL	DEBAUCHED
DAURS	DAYLONG	DEADLOCKING	DEASIULS	DEBAUCHEE
DAUT	DAYMARK	DEADLOCKS	DEASOIL	DEBAUCHEES
DAUTED	DAYMARKS	DEADLY	DEASOILS	DEBAUCHER
DAUTIE	DAYNT	DEADNESS	DEATH	DEBAUCHERS
DAUTIES	DAYS	DEADNESSES	DEATHFUL	DEBAUCHES
DAUTING	DAYSACK	DEADPAN	DEATHIER	DEBAUCHING
DAUTS	DAYSACKS	DEADPANS	DEATHIEST	DEBBIER

The Chambers Dictionary is the authority for many longer words; see *OSW* Introduction, page xii

DEBBIES	DEBUTANT	DECARBING	DECIARE	DECKO
DEBBIEST	DEBUTANTE	DECARBS	DECIARES	DECKOED
DEBBY	DEBUTANTES	DECARE	DECIBEL	DECKOING
DEBEL	DEBUTANTS	DECARES	DECIBELS	DECKOS
DEBELLED	DEBUTED	DECASTERE	DECIDABLE	DECKS
DEBELLING	DEBUTING	DECASTERES	DECIDE	DECLAIM
DEBELS	DEBUTS	DECASTICH	DECIDED	DECLAIMED
DEBENTURE	DECACHORD	DECASTICHS	DECIDEDLY	DECLAIMER
DEBENTURES	DECACHORDS	DECASTYLE	DECIDER	DECLAIMERS
DEBILE	DECAD	DECASTYLES	DECIDERS	DECLAIMING
DEBILITIES	DECADAL	DECATHLON	DECIDES	DECLAIMINGS
DEBILITY	DECADE	DECATHLONS	DECIDING	DECLAIMS
DEBIT	DECADENCE	DECAUDATE	DECIDUA	DECLARANT
DEBITED	DECADENCES	DECAUDATED	DECIDUAE	DECLARANTS
DEBITING	DECADENCIES	DECAUDATES	DECIDUAL	DECLARE
DEBITOR	DECADENCY	DECAUDATING	DECIDUAS	DECLARED
DEBITORS	DECADENT	DECAY	DECIDUATE	DECLARER
DEBITS	DECADENTS	DECAYED	DECIDUOUS	DECLARERS
DEBONAIR	DECADES	DECAYING	DECIGRAM	DECLARES
DEBOSH	DECADS	DECAYS	DECIGRAMS	DECLARING
DEBOSHED	DECAFF	DECCIE	DECILITER	DECLASS
DEBOSHES	DECAFFS	DECCIES	DECILITERS	DECLASSE
DEBOSHING	DECAGON	DECEASE	DECILITRE	DECLASSED
DEBOSS	DECAGONAL	DECEASED	DECILITRES	DECLASSEE
DEBOSSED	DECAGONS	DECEASES	DECILLION	DECLASSES
DEBOSSES	DECAGRAM	DECEASING	DECILLIONS	DECLASSING
DEBOSSING	DECAGRAMS	DECEDENT	DECIMAL	DECLINAL
DEBOUCH	DECAHEDRA	DECEDENTS	DECIMALLY	DECLINANT
DEBOUCHE	DECAL	DECEIT	DECIMALS	DECLINATE
DEBOUCHED	DECALCIFIED	DECEITFUL	DECIMATE	DECLINE
DEBOUCHES	DECALCIFIES	DECEITS	DECIMATED	DECLINED
DEBOUCHING	DECALCIFY	DECEIVE	DECIMATES	DECLINES
DEBRIDE	DECALCIFYING	DECEIVED	DECIMATING	DECLINING
DEBRIDED	DECALITRE	DECEIVER	DECIMATOR	DECLIVITIES
DEBRIDES	DECALITRES	DECEIVERS	DECIMATORS	DECLIVITY
DEBRIDING	DECALOGUE	DECEIVES	DECIME	DECLIVOUS
DEBRIEF	DECALOGUES	DECEIVING	DECIMES	DECLUTCH
DEBRIEFED	DECALS	DECEMVIR	DECIMETER	DECLUTCHED
DEBRIEFING	DECAMETRE	DECEMVIRI	DECIMETERS	DECLUTCHES
DEBRIEFINGS	DECAMETRES	DECEMVIRS	DECIMETRE	DECLUTCHING
DEBRIEFS	DECAMP	DECENCIES	DECIMETRES	DECO
DEBRIS	DECAMPED	DECENCY	DECIPHER	DECOCT
DEBRUISED	DECAMPING	DECENNARIES	DECIPHERED	DECOCTED
DEBS	DECAMPS	DECENNARY	DECIPHERING	DECOCTING
DEBT	DECANAL	DECENNIA	DECIPHERS	DECOCTION
DEBTED	DECANE	DECENNIAL	DECISION	DECOCTIONS
DEBTEE	DECANES	DECENNIUM	DECISIONS	DECOCTIVE
DEBTEES	DECANI	DECENNIUMS	DECISIVE	DECOCTS
DEBTOR	DECANT	DECENT	DECISORY	DECOCTURE
DEBTORS	DECANTATE	DECENTER	DECISTERE	DECOCTURES
DEBTS	DECANTATED	DECENTEST	DECISTERES	DECODE
DEBUG	DECANTATES	DECENTLY	DECK	DECODED
DEBUGGED	DECANTATING	DECEPTION	DECKCHAIR	DECODER
DEBUGGING	DECANTED	DECEPTIONS	DECKCHAIRS	DECODERS
DEBUGS	DECANTER	DECEPTIVE	DECKED	DECODES
DEBUNK	DECANTERS	DECEPTORY	DECKER	DECODING
DEBUNKED	DECANTING	DECERN	DECKERS	DECOHERER
DEBUNKING	DECANTS	DECERNED	DECKHOUSE	DECOHERERS
DEBUNKS	DECAPOD	DECERNING	DECKHOUSES	DECOKE
DEBUS	DECAPODAL	DECERNS	DECKING	DECOKED
DEBUSSED	DECAPODAN	DECESSION	DECKINGS	DECOKES
DEBUSSES	DECAPODS	DECESSIONS	DECKLE	DECOKING
DEBUSSING	DECARB	DECHEANCE	DECKLED	DECOLLATE
DEBUT	DECARBED	DECHEANCES	DECKLES	DECOLLATED

DECOLLATES
DECOLLATING
DECOLLETE
DECOLOR
DECOLORED
DECOLORING
DECOLORS
DECOLOUR
DECOLOURED
DECOLOURING
DECOLOURS
DECOMPLEX
DECOMPOSE
DECOMPOSED
DECOMPOSES
DECOMPOSING
DECONGEST
DECONGESTED
DECONGESTING
DECONGESTS
DECONTROL
DECONTROLLED
DECONTROLLING
DECONTROLS
DECOR
DECORATE
DECORATED
DECORATES
DECORATING
DECORATOR
DECORATORS
DECOROUS
DECORS
DECORUM
DECORUMS
DECOUPAGE
DECOUPAGES
DECOUPLE
DECOUPLED
DECOUPLES
DECOUPLING
DECOUPLINGS
DECOY
DECOYED
DECOYING
DECOYS
DECREASE
DECREASED
DECREASES
DECREASING
DECREE
DECREED
DECREEING
DECREES
DECREET
DECREETS
DECREMENT
DECREMENTED
DECREMENTING
DECREMENTS
DECREPIT
DECRETAL
DECRETALS
DECRETIST

DECRETISTS
DECRETIVE
DECRETORY
DECREW
DECREWED
DECREWING
DECREWS
DECRIAL
DECRIALS
DECRIED
DECRIER
DECRIERS
DECRIES
DECROWN
DECROWNED
DECROWNING
DECROWNS
DECRY
DECRYING
DECRYPT
DECRYPTED
DECRYPTING
DECRYPTS
DECTET
DECTETS
DECUBITI
DECUBITUS
DECUMAN
DECUMANS
DECUMBENT
DECUPLE
DECUPLED
DECUPLES
DECUPLING
DECURIA
DECURIAS
DECURIES
DECURION
DECURIONS
DECURRENT
DECURSION
DECURSIONS
DECURSIVE
DECURVE
DECURVED
DECURVES
DECURVING
DECURY
DECUSSATE
DECUSSATED
DECUSSATES
DECUSSATING
DEDAL
DEDALIAN
DEDANS
DEDICANT
DEDICANTS
DEDICATE
DEDICATED
DEDICATEE
DEDICATEES
DEDICATES
DEDICATING
DEDICATOR

DEDICATORS
DEDIMUS
DEDIMUSES
DEDUCE
DEDUCED
DEDUCES
DEDUCIBLE
DEDUCING
DEDUCT
DEDUCTED
DEDUCTING
DEDUCTION
DEDUCTIONS
DEDUCTIVE
DEDUCTS
DEE
DEED
DEEDED
DEEDER
DEEDEST
DEEDFUL
DEEDIER
DEEDIEST
DEEDILY
DEEDING
DEEDLESS
DEEDS
DEEDY
DEEING
DEEJAY
DEEJAYED
DEEJAYING
DEEJAYS
DEEK
DEEM
DEEMED
DEEMING
DEEMS
DEEMSTER
DEEMSTERS
DEEN
DEENS
DEEP
DEEPEN
DEEPENED
DEEPENING
DEEPENS
DEEPER
DEEPEST
DEEPFELT
DEEPIE
DEEPIES
DEEPLY
DEEPMOST
DEEPNESS
DEEPNESSES
DEEPS
DEER
DEERBERRIES
DEERBERRY
DEERE
DEERHORN
DEERHORNS
DEERLET

DEERLETS
DEERSKIN
DEERSKINS
DEES
DEEV
DEEVE
DEEVED
DEEVES
DEEVING
DEEVS
DEF
DEFACE
DEFACED
DEFACER
DEFACERS
DEFACES
DEFACING
DEFAECATE
DEFAECATED
DEFAECATES
DEFAECATING
DEFALCATE
DEFALCATED
DEFALCATES
DEFALCATING
DEFAME
DEFAMED
DEFAMES
DEFAMING
DEFAMINGS
DEFAST
DEFASTE
DEFAT
DEFATS
DEFATTED
DEFATTING
DEFAULT
DEFAULTED
DEFAULTER
DEFAULTERS
DEFAULTING
DEFAULTS
DEFEAT
DEFEATED
DEFEATING
DEFEATISM
DEFEATISMS
DEFEATIST
DEFEATISTS
DEFEATS
DEFEATURE
DEFEATURED
DEFEATURES
DEFEATURING
DEFECATE
DEFECATED
DEFECATES
DEFECATING
DEFECATOR
DEFECATORS
DEFECT
DEFECTED
DEFECTING
DEFECTION

DEFECTIONS
DEFECTIVE
DEFECTIVES
DEFECTOR
DEFECTORS
DEFECTS
DEFENCE
DEFENCED
DEFENCES
DEFEND
DEFENDANT
DEFENDANTS
DEFENDED
DEFENDER
DEFENDERS
DEFENDING
DEFENDS
DEFENSE
DEFENSES
DEFENSIVE
DEFENSIVES
DEFER
DEFERABLE
DEFERENCE
DEFERENCES
DEFERENT
DEFERENTS
DEFERMENT
DEFERMENTS
DEFERRAL
DEFERRALS
DEFERRED
DEFERRER
DEFERRERS
DEFERRING
DEFERS
DEFFER
DEFFEST
DEFFLY
DEFIANCE
DEFIANCES
DEFIANT
DEFIANTLY
DEFICIENT
DEFICIENTS
DEFICIT
DEFICITS
DEFIED
DEFIER
DEFIERS
DEFIES
DEFILADE
DEFILADED
DEFILADES
DEFILADING
DEFILE
DEFILED
DEFILER
DEFILERS
DEFILES
DEFILING
DEFINABLE
DEFINABLY
DEFINE

DEFINED	DEFORMS	DEGASSING	DEIDS	DELATION
DEFINER	DEFOUL	DEGAUSS	DEIFIC	DELATIONS
DEFINERS	DEFOULED	DEGAUSSED	DEIFICAL	DELATOR
DEFINES	DEFOULING	DEGAUSSES	DEIFIED	DELATORS
DEFINIENS	DEFOULS	DEGAUSSING	DEIFIER	DELAY
DEFINIENTIA	DEFRAG	DEGENDER	DEIFIERS	DELAYED
DEFINING	DEFRAGGED	DEGENDERED	DEIFIES	DELAYER
DEFINITE	DEFRAGGING	DEGENDERING	DEIFORM	DELAYERS
DEFLATE	DEFRAGS	DEGENDERS	DEIFY	DELAYING
DEFLATED	DEFRAUD	DEGOUT	DEIFYING	DELAYS
DEFLATER	DEFRAUDED	DEGOUTS	DEIGN	DELE
DEFLATERS	DEFRAUDER	DEGRADE	DEIGNED	DELEBLE
DEFLATES	DEFRAUDERS	DEGRADED	DEIGNING	DELED
DEFLATING	DEFRAUDING	DEGRADES	DEIGNS	DELEGABLE
DEFLATION	DEFRAUDS	DEGRADING	DEIL	DELEGACIES
DEFLATIONS	DEFRAY	DEGRAS	DEILS	DELEGACY
DEFLATOR	DEFRAYAL	DEGREASE	DEINOSAUR	DELEGATE
DEFLATORS	DEFRAYALS	DEGREASED	DEINOSAURS	DELEGATED
DEFLECT	DEFRAYED	DEGREASES	DEIPAROUS	DELEGATES
DEFLECTED	DEFRAYER	DEGREASING	DEISEAL	DELEGATING
DEFLECTING	DEFRAYERS	DEGREE	DEISEALS	DELEING
DEFLECTOR	DEFRAYING	DEGREES	DEISHEAL	DELENDA
DEFLECTORS	DEFRAYS	DEGUM	DEISHEALS	DELES
DEFLECTS	DEFREEZE	DEGUMMED	DEISM	DELETE
DEFLEX	DEFREEZES	DEGUMMING	DEISMS	DELETED
DEFLEXED	DEFREEZING	DEGUMS	DEIST	DELETES
DEFLEXES	DEFROCK	DEGUST	DEISTIC	DELETING
DEFLEXING	DEFROCKED	DEGUSTATE	DEISTICAL	DELETION
DEFLEXION	DEFROCKING	DEGUSTATED	DEISTS	DELETIONS
DEFLEXIONS	DEFROCKS	DEGUSTATES	DEITIES	DELETIVE
DEFLEXURE	DEFROST	DEGUSTATING	DEITY	DELETORY
DEFLEXURES	DEFROSTED	DEGUSTED	DEIXES	DELF
DEFLORATE	DEFROSTER	DEGUSTING	DEIXIS	DELFS
DEFLORATED	DEFROSTERS	DEGUSTS	DEJECT	DELFT
DEFLORATES	DEFROSTING	DEHISCE	DEJECTA	DELFTS
DEFLORATING	DEFROSTS	DEHISCED	DEJECTED	DELI
DEFLOWER	DEFROZE	DEHISCENT	DEJECTING	DELIBATE
DEFLOWERED	DEFROZEN	DEHISCES	DEJECTION	DELIBATED
DEFLOWERING	DEFT	DEHISCING	DEJECTIONS	DELIBATES
DEFLOWERS	DEFTER	DEHORN	DEJECTORY	DELIBATING
DEFLUENT	DEFTEST	DEHORNED	DEJECTS	DELIBLE
DEFLUXION	DEFTLY	DEHORNER	DEJEUNE	DELICACIES
DEFLUXIONS	DEFTNESS	DEHORNERS	DEJEUNER	DELICACY
DEFOLIANT	DEFTNESSES	DEHORNING	DEJEUNERS	DELICATE
DEFOLIANTS	DEFUNCT	DEHORNS	DEJEUNES	DELICATES
DEFOLIATE	DEFUNCTS	DEHORT	DEKALOGIES	DELICE
DEFOLIATED	DEFUSE	DEHORTED	DEKALOGY	DELICES
DEFOLIATES	DEFUSED	DEHORTER	DEKKO	DELICIOUS
DEFOLIATING	DEFUSES	DEHORTERS	DEKKOED	DELICT
DEFORCE	DEFUSING	DEHORTING	DEKKOING	DELICTS
DEFORCED	DEFUZE	DEHORTS	DEKKOS	DELIGHT
DEFORCES	DEFUZED	DEHYDRATE	DEL	DELIGHTED
DEFORCING	DEFUZES	DEHYDRATED	DELAINE	DELIGHTING
DEFOREST	DEFUZING	DEHYDRATES	DELAINES	DELIGHTS
DEFORESTED	DEFY	DEHYDRATING	DELAPSE	DELIMIT
DEFORESTING	DEFYING	DEI	DELAPSED	DELIMITED
DEFORESTS	DEGAGE	DEICIDAL	DELAPSES	DELIMITER
DEFORM	DEGARNISH	DEICIDE	DELAPSING	DELIMITERS
DEFORMED	DEGARNISHED	DEICIDES	DELAPSION	DELIMITING
DEFORMER	DEGARNISHES	DEICTIC	DELAPSIONS	DELIMITS
DEFORMERS	DEGARNISHING	DEICTICS	DELATE	DELINEATE
DEFORMING	DEGAS	DEID	DELATED	DELINEATED
DEFORMITIES	DEGASSED	DEIDER	DELATES	DELINEATES
DEFORMITY	DEGASSES	DEIDEST	DELATING	DELINEATING

DELIQUIUM
DELIQUIUMS
DELIRIA
DELIRIANT
DELIRIOUS
DELIRIUM
DELIRIUMS
DELIS
DELIVER
DELIVERED
DELIVERER
DELIVERERS
DELIVERIES
DELIVERING
DELIVERLY
DELIVERS
DELIVERY
DELL
DELLS
DELOPE
DELOPED
DELOPES
DELOPING
DELOUSE
DELOUSED
DELOUSES
DELOUSING
DELPH
DELPHIC
DELPHIN
DELPHINIA
DELPHS
DELS
DELT
DELTA
DELTAIC
DELTAS
DELTOID
DELTOIDS
DELTS
DELUBRUM
DELUBRUMS
DELUDABLE
DELUDE
DELUDED
DELUDER
DELUDERS
DELUDES
DELUDING
DELUGE
DELUGED
DELUGES
DELUGING
DELUNDUNG
DELUNDUNGS
DELUSION
DELUSIONS
DELUSIVE
DELUSORY
DELVE
DELVED
DELVER
DELVERS
DELVES

DELVING
DEMAGOGIC
DEMAGOGIES
DEMAGOGUE
DEMAGOGUES
DEMAGOGY
DEMAIN
DEMAINE
DEMAINES
DEMAINS
DEMAN
DEMAND
DEMANDANT
DEMANDANTS
DEMANDED
DEMANDER
DEMANDERS
DEMANDING
DEMANDS
DEMANNED
DEMANNING
DEMANNINGS
DEMANS
DEMARCATE
DEMARCATED
DEMARCATES
DEMARCATING
DEMARCHE
DEMARCHES
DEMARK
DEMARKED
DEMARKING
DEMARKS
DEMAYNE
DEMAYNES
DEME
DEMEAN
DEMEANE
DEMEANED
DEMEANES
DEMEANING
DEMEANOR
DEMEANORS
DEMEANOUR
DEMEANOURS
DEMEANS
DEMENT
DEMENTATE
DEMENTATED
DEMENTATES
DEMENTATING
DEMENTED
DEMENTI
DEMENTIA
DEMENTIAS
DEMENTING
DEMENTIS
DEMENTS
DEMERARA
DEMERARAS
DEMERGE
DEMERGED
DEMERGER
DEMERGERS

DEMERGES
DEMERGING
DEMERIT
DEMERITS
DEMERSAL
DEMERSE
DEMERSED
DEMERSES
DEMERSING
DEMERSION
DEMERSIONS
DEMES
DEMESNE
DEMESNES
DEMIC
DEMIES
DEMIGOD
DEMIGODS
DEMIJOHN
DEMIJOHNS
DEMIPIQUE
DEMIPIQUES
DEMIREP
DEMIREPS
DEMISABLE
DEMISE
DEMISED
DEMISES
DEMISING
DEMISS
DEMISSION
DEMISSIONS
DEMISSIVE
DEMISSLY
DEMIST
DEMISTED
DEMISTER
DEMISTERS
DEMISTING
DEMISTS
DEMIT
DEMITASSE
DEMITASSES
DEMITS
DEMITTED
DEMITTING
DEMIURGE
DEMIURGES
DEMIURGIC
DEMIURGUS
DEMIURGUSES
DEMO
DEMOB
DEMOBBED
DEMOBBING
DEMOBS
DEMOCRACIES
DEMOCRACY
DEMOCRAT
DEMOCRATIES
DEMOCRATS
DEMOCRATY
DEMODE
DEMODED

DEMOLISH
DEMOLISHED
DEMOLISHES
DEMOLISHING
DEMOLOGIES
DEMOLOGY
DEMON
DEMONESS
DEMONESSES
DEMONIAC
DEMONIACS
DEMONIAN
DEMONIC
DEMONISE
DEMONISED
DEMONISES
DEMONISING
DEMONISM
DEMONISMS
DEMONIST
DEMONISTS
DEMONIZE
DEMONIZED
DEMONIZES
DEMONIZING
DEMONRIES
DEMONRY
DEMONS
DEMOS
DEMOSES
DEMOTE
DEMOTED
DEMOTES
DEMOTIC
DEMOTING
DEMOTION
DEMOTIONS
DEMOTIST
DEMOTISTS
DEMOUNT
DEMOUNTED
DEMOUNTING
DEMOUNTS
DEMPSTER
DEMPSTERS
DEMPT
DEMULCENT
DEMULCENTS
DEMULSIFIED
DEMULSIFIES
DEMULSIFY
DEMULSIFYING
DEMUR
DEMURE
DEMURED
DEMURELY
DEMURER
DEMURES
DEMUREST
DEMURING
DEMURRAGE
DEMURRAGES
DEMURRAL
DEMURRALS

DEMURRED
DEMURRER
DEMURRERS
DEMURRING
DEMURS
DEMY
DEMYSHIP
DEMYSHIPS
DEMYSTIFIED
DEMYSTIFIES
DEMYSTIFY
DEMYSTIFYING
DEN
DENARIES
DENARII
DENARIUS
DENARY
DENATURE
DENATURED
DENATURES
DENATURING
DENAY
DENAYED
DENAYING
DENAYS
DENAZIFIED
DENAZIFIES
DENAZIFY
DENAZIFYING
DENDRITE
DENDRITES
DENDRITIC
DENDROID
DENDRON
DENDRONS
DENE
DENES
DENET
DENETS
DENETTED
DENETTING
DENGUE
DENGUES
DENIABLE
DENIABLY
DENIAL
DENIALS
DENIED
DENIER
DENIERS
DENIES
DENIGRATE
DENIGRATED
DENIGRATES
DENIGRATING
DENIM
DENIMS
DENITRATE
DENITRATED
DENITRATES
DENITRATING
DENITRIFIED
DENITRIFIES
DENITRIFY

DENITRIFYING	DENTILS	DEPARTERS	DEPLOYS	DEPROGRAM
DENIZEN	DENTIN	DEPARTING	DEPLUME	DEPROGRAMMED
DENIZENED	DENTINE	DEPARTINGS	DEPLUMED	DEPROGRAMMING
DENIZENING	DENTINES	DEPARTS	DEPLUMES	DEPROGRAMS
DENIZENS	DENTING	DEPARTURE	DEPLUMING	DEPSIDE
DENNED	DENTINS	DEPARTURES	DEPONE	DEPSIDES
DENNET	DENTIST	DEPASTURE	DEPONED	DEPTH
DENNETS	DENTISTRIES	DEPASTURED	DEPONENT	DEPTHLESS
DENNING	DENTISTRY	DEPASTURES	DEPONENTS	DEPTHS
DENOTABLE	DENTISTS	DEPASTURING	DEPONES	DEPURANT
DENOTATE	DENTITION	DEPECHE	DEPONING	DEPURANTS
DENOTATED	DENTITIONS	DEPECHES	DEPORT	DEPURATE
DENOTATES	DENTOID	DEPEINCT	DEPORTED	DEPURATED
DENOTATING	DENTS	DEPEINCTED	DEPORTEE	DEPURATES
DENOTE	DENTURE	DEPEINCTING	DEPORTEES	DEPURATING
DENOTED	DENTURES	DEPEINCTS	DEPORTING	DEPURATOR
DENOTES	DENUDATE	DEPEND	DEPORTS	DEPURATORS
DENOTING	DENUDATED	DEPENDANT	DEPOSABLE	DEPUTE
DENOUNCE	DENUDATES	DEPENDANTS	DEPOSAL	DEPUTED
DENOUNCED	DENUDATING	DEPENDED	DEPOSALS	DEPUTES
DENOUNCER	DENUDE	DEPENDENT	DEPOSE	DEPUTIES
DENOUNCERS	DENUDED	DEPENDENTS	DEPOSED	DEPUTING
DENOUNCES	DENUDES	DEPENDING	DEPOSER	DEPUTISE
DENOUNCING	DENUDING	DEPENDS	DEPOSERS	DEPUTISED
DENS	DENY	DEPICT	DEPOSES	DEPUTISES
DENSE	DENYING	DEPICTED	DEPOSING	DEPUTISING
DENSELY	DENYINGLY	DEPICTER	DEPOSIT	DEPUTIZE
DENSENESS	DEODAND	DEPICTERS	DEPOSITED	DEPUTIZED
DENSENESSES	DEODANDS	DEPICTING	DEPOSITING	DEPUTIZES
DENSER	DEODAR	DEPICTION	DEPOSITOR	DEPUTIZING
DENSEST	DEODARS	DEPICTIONS	DEPOSITORS	DEPUTY
DENSIFIED	DEODATE	DEPICTIVE	DEPOSITS	DERACINE
DENSIFIER	DEODATES	DEPICTOR	DEPOT	DERAIGN
DENSIFIERS	DEODORANT	DEPICTORS	DEPOTS	DERAIGNED
DENSIFIES	DEODORANTS	DEPICTS	DEPRAVE	DERAIGNING
DENSIFY	DEODORISE	DEPICTURE	DEPRAVED	DERAIGNS
DENSIFYING	DEODORISED	DEPICTURED	DEPRAVES	DERAIL
DENSITIES	DEODORISES	DEPICTURES	DEPRAVING	DERAILED
DENSITY	DEODORISING	DEPICTURING	DEPRAVITIES	DERAILER
DENT	DEODORIZE	DEPILATE	DEPRAVITY	DERAILERS
DENTAL	DEODORIZED	DEPILATED	DEPRECATE	DERAILING
DENTALIA	DEODORIZES	DEPILATES	DEPRECATED	DERAILS
DENTALIUM	DEODORIZING	DEPILATING	DEPRECATES	DERANGE
DENTALIUMS	DEONTIC	DEPILATOR	DEPRECATING	DERANGED
DENTALS	DEONTICS	DEPILATORS	DEPREDATE	DERANGES
DENTARIA	DEOXIDATE	DEPLANE	DEPREDATED	DERANGING
DENTARIAS	DEOXIDATED	DEPLANED	DEPREDATES	DERATE
DENTARIES	DEOXIDATES	DEPLANES	DEPREDATING	DERATED
DENTARY	DEOXIDATING	DEPLANING	DEPREHEND	DERATES
DENTATE	DEOXIDISE	DEPLETE	DEPREHENDED	DERATING
DENTATED	DEOXIDISES	DEPLETED	DEPREHENDING	DERATINGS
DENTATION	DEOXIDISES	DEPLETES	DEPREHENDS	DERATION
DENTATIONS	DEOXIDISING	DEPLETING	DEPRESS	DERATIONED
DENTED	DEOXIDIZE	DEPLETION	DEPRESSED	DERATIONING
DENTEL	DEOXIDIZED	DEPLETIONS	DEPRESSES	DERATIONS
DENTELLE	DEOXIDIZES	DEPLETIVE	DEPRESSING	DERAY
DENTELLES	DEOXIDIZING	DEPLETORY	DEPRESSOR	DERAYED
DENTELS	DEPAINT	DEPLORE	DEPRESSORS	DERAYING
DENTEX	DEPAINTED	DEPLORED	DEPRIVAL	DERAYS
DENTEXES	DEPAINTING	DEPLORES	DEPRIVALS	DERBIES
DENTICLE	DEPAINTS	DEPLORING	DEPRIVE	DERBY
DENTICLES	DEPART	DEPLOY	DEPRIVED	DERE
DENTIFORM	DEPARTED	DEPLOYED	DEPRIVES	DERED
DENTIL	DEPARTER	DEPLOYING	DEPRIVING	DERELICT

DERELICTS	DERTHS	DESERVER	DESMIDS	DESPOTISMS
DERES	DERV	DESERVERS	DESMINE	DESPOTS
DERHAM	DERVISH	DESERVES	DESMINES	DESPUMATE
DERHAMS	DERVISHES	DESERVING	DESMODIUM	DESPUMATED
DERIDE	DERVS	DESEX	DESMODIUMS	DESPUMATES
DERIDED	DESALT	DESEXED	DESMOID	DESPUMATING
DERIDER	DESALTED	DESEXES	DESMOIDS	DESSE
DERIDERS	DESALTING	DESEXING	DESMOSOME	DESSERT
DERIDES	DESALTINGS	DESICCANT	DESMOSOMES	DESSERTS
DERIDING	DESALTS	DESICCANTS	DESOEUVRE	DESSES
DERIG	DESCALE	DESICCATE	DESOLATE	DESTEMPER
DERIGGED	DESCALED	DESICCATED	DESOLATED	DESTEMPERED
DERIGGING	DESCALES	DESICCATES	DESOLATER	DESTEMPERING
DERIGS	DESCALING	DESICCATING	DESOLATERS	DESTEMPERS
DERING	DESCANT	DESIGN	DESOLATES	DESTINATE
DERISIBLE	DESCANTED	DESIGNATE	DESOLATING	DESTINATED
DERISION	DESCANTING	DESIGNATED	DESOLATOR	DESTINATES
DERISIONS	DESCANTS	DESIGNATES	DESOLATORS	DESTINATING
DERISIVE	DESCEND	DESIGNATING	DESORB	DESTINE
DERISORY	DESCENDED	DESIGNED	DESORBED	DESTINED
DERIVABLE	DESCENDER	DESIGNER	DESORBING	DESTINES
DERIVABLY	DESCENDERS	DESIGNERS	DESORBS	DESTINIES
DERIVATE	DESCENDING	DESIGNFUL	DESPAIR	DESTINING
DERIVATES	DESCENDINGS	DESIGNING	DESPAIRED	DESTINY
DERIVE	DESCENDS	DESIGNINGS	DESPAIRING	DESTITUTE
DERIVED	DESCENT	DESIGNS	DESPAIRS	DESTITUTED
DERIVES	DESCENTS	DESILVER	DESPATCH	DESTITUTES
DERIVING	DESCHOOL	DESILVERED	DESPATCHED	DESTITUTING
DERM	DESCHOOLED	DESILVERING	DESPATCHES	DESTRIER
DERMA	DESCHOOLING	DESILVERS	DESPATCHING	DESTRIERS
DERMAL	DESCHOOLINGS	DESINE	DESPERADO	DESTROY
DERMAS	DESCHOOLS	DESINED	DESPERADOES	DESTROYED
DERMATIC	DESCRIBE	DESINENCE	DESPERADOS	DESTROYER
DERMATOID	DESCRIBED	DESINENCES	DESPERATE	DESTROYERS
DERMATOME	DESCRIBER	DESINENT	DESPIGHT	DESTROYING
DERMATOMES	DESCRIBERS	DESINES	DESPIGHTS	DESTROYS
DERMIC	DESCRIBES	DESINING	DESPISAL	DESTRUCT
DERMIS	DESCRIBING	DESIPIENT	DESPISALS	DESTRUCTED
DERMISES	DESCRIED	DESIRABLE	DESPISE	DESTRUCTING
DERMOID	DESCRIES	DESIRABLES	DESPISED	DESTRUCTS
DERMOIDS	DESCRIVE	DESIRABLY	DESPISER	DESUETUDE
DERMS	DESCRIVED	DESIRE	DESPISERS	DESUETUDES
DERN	DESCRIVES	DESIRED	DESPISES	DESULPHUR
DERNFUL	DESCRIVING	DESIRER	DESPISING	DESULPHURED
DERNIER	DESCRY	DESIRERS	DESPITE	DESULPHURING
DERNLY	DESCRYING	DESIRES	DESPITES	DESULPHURS
DERNS	DESECRATE	DESIRING	DESPOIL	DESULTORY
DEROGATE	DESECRATED	DESIROUS	DESPOILED	DESYATIN
DEROGATED	DESECRATES	DESIST	DESPOILER	DESYATINS
DEROGATES	DESECRATING	DESISTED	DESPOILERS	DESYNE
DEROGATING	DESELECT	DESISTING	DESPOILING	DESYNED
DERRICK	DESELECTED	DESISTS	DESPOILS	DESYNES
DERRICKED	DESELECTING	DESK	DESPOND	DESYNING
DERRICKING	DESELECTS	DESKBOUND	DESPONDED	DETACH
DERRICKS	DESERT	DESKILL	DESPONDING	DETACHED
DERRIERE	DESERTED	DESKILLED	DESPONDINGS	DETACHES
DERRIERES	DESERTER	DESKILLING	DESPONDS	DETACHING
DERRIES	DESERTERS	DESKILLS	DESPOT	DETAIL
DERRINGER	DESERTING	DESKS	DESPOTAT	DETAILED
DERRINGERS	DESERTION	DESKTOP	DESPOTATE	DETAILING
DERRIS	DESERTIONS	DESKTOPS	DESPOTATES	DETAILS
DERRISES	DESERTS	DESMAN	DESPOTATS	DETAIN
DERRY	DESERVE	DESMANS	DESPOTIC	DETAINED
DERTH	DESERVED	DESMID	DESPOTISM	DETAINEE

DETAINEES	DETONATOR	DEUTERIDE	DEVILESS	DEVOTING
DETAINER	DETONATORS	DEUTERIDES	DEVILESSES	DEVOTION
DETAINERS	DETORSION	DEUTERIUM	DEVILET	DEVOTIONS
DETAINING	DETORSIONS	DEUTERIUMS	DEVILETS	DEVOTS
DETAINS	DETORT	DEUTERON	DEVILING	DEVOUR
DETECT	DETORTED	DEUTERONS	DEVILINGS	DEVOURED
DETECTED	DETORTING	DEUTON	DEVILISH	DEVOURER
DETECTING	DETORTION	DEUTONS	DEVILISM	DEVOURERS
DETECTION	DETORTIONS	DEVA	DEVILISMS	DEVOURING
DETECTIONS	DETORTS	DEVALL	DEVILKIN	DEVOURS
DETECTIVE	DETOUR	DEVALLED	DEVILKINS	DEVOUT
DETECTIVES	DETOURED	DEVALLING	DEVILLED	DEVOUTER
DETECTOR	DETOURING	DEVALLS	DEVILLING	DEVOUTEST
DETECTORS	DETOURS	DEVALUATE	DEVILMENT	DEVOUTLY
DETECTS	DETOX	DEVALUATED	DEVILMENTS	DEVVEL
DETENT	DETOXED	DEVALUATES	DEVILRIES	DEVVELLED
DETENTE	DETOXES	DEVALUATING	DEVILRY	DEVVELLING
DETENTES	DETOXIFIED	DEVALUE	DEVILS	DEVVELS
DETENTION	DETOXIFIES	DEVALUED	DEVILSHIP	DEW
DETENTIONS	DETOXIFY	DEVALUES	DEVILSHIPS	DEWAN
DETENTS	DETOXIFYING	DEVALUING	DEVILTRIES	DEWANI
DETENU	DETOXING	DEVAS	DEVILTRY	DEWANIS
DETENUE	DETRACT	DEVASTATE	DEVIOUS	DEWANNIES
DETENUES	DETRACTED	DEVASTATED	DEVIOUSLY	DEWANNY
DETENUS	DETRACTING	DEVASTATES	DEVISABLE	DEWANS
DETER	DETRACTINGS	DEVASTATING	DEVISAL	DEWAR
DETERGE	DETRACTOR	DEVEL	DEVISALS	DEWARS
DETERGED	DETRACTORS	DEVELLED	DEVISE	DEWATER
DETERGENT	DETRACTS	DEVELLING	DEVISED	DEWATERED
DETERGENTS	DETRAIN	DEVELOP	DEVISEE	DEWATERING
DETERGES	DETRAINED	DEVELOPE	DEVISEES	DEWATERINGS
DETERGING	DETRAINING	DEVELOPED	DEVISER	DEWATERS
DETERMENT	DETRAINS	DEVELOPER	DEVISERS	DEWED
DETERMENTS	DETRAQUE	DEVELOPERS	DEVISES	DEWFULL
DETERMINE	DETRAQUEE	DEVELOPES	DEVISING	DEWIER
DETERMINED	DETRAQUEES	DEVELOPING	DEVISOR	DEWIEST
DETERMINES	DETRAQUES	DEVELOPS	DEVISORS	DEWILY
DETERMINING	DETRIMENT	DEVELS	DEVITRIFIED	DEWINESS
DETERRED	DETRIMENTS	DEVEST	DEVITRIFIES	DEWINESSES
DETERRENT	DETRITAL	DEVESTED	DEVITRIFY	DEWING
DETERRENTS	DETRITION	DEVESTING	DEVITRIFYING	DEWITT
DETERRING	DETRITIONS	DEVESTS	DEVLING	DEWITTED
DETERS	DETRITUS	DEVIANCE	DEVLINGS	DEWITTING
DETERSION	DETRUDE	DEVIANCES	DEVOICE	DEWITTS
DETERSIONS	DETRUDED	DEVIANCIES	DEVOICED	DEWLAP
DETERSIVE	DETRUDES	DEVIANCY	DEVOICES	DEWLAPPED
DETERSIVES	DETRUDING	DEVIANT	DEVOICING	DEWLAPS
DETEST	DETRUSION	DEVIANTS	DEVOID	DEWLAPT
DETESTED	DETRUSIONS	DEVIATE	DEVOIR	DEWPOINT
DETESTING	DETUNE	DEVIATED	DEVOIRS	DEWPOINTS
DETESTS	DETUNED	DEVIATES	DEVOLVE	DEWS
DETHRONE	DETUNES	DEVIATING	DEVOLVED	DEWY
DETHRONED	DETUNING	DEVIATION	DEVOLVES	DEXTER
DETHRONER	DEUCE	DEVIATIONS	DEVOLVING	DEXTERITIES
DETHRONERS	DEUCED	DEVIATOR	DEVONPORT	DEXTERITY
DETHRONES	DEUCEDLY	DEVIATORS	DEVONPORTS	DEXTEROUS
DETHRONING	DEUCES	DEVIATORY	DEVORE	DEXTERS
DETHRONINGS	DEUDDARN	DEVICE	DEVOT	DEXTRAL
DETINUE	DEUDDARNS	DEVICEFUL	DEVOTE	DEXTRALLY
DETINUES	DEUS	DEVICES	DEVOTED	DEXTRAN
DETONATE	DEUTERATE	DEVIL	DEVOTEDLY	DEXTRANS
DETONATED	DEUTERATED	DEVILDOM	DEVOTEE	DEXTRIN
DETONATES	DEUTERATES	DEVILDOMS	DEVOTEES	DEXTRINE
DETONATING	DEUTERATING	DEVILED	DEVOTES	DEXTRINES

The Chambers Dictionary is the authority for many longer words; see *OSW* Introduction, page xii

DEXTRINS	DIABOLOGY	DIALOGING	DIAPERS	DIATHESIS
DEXTRORSE	DIABOLOS	DIALOGISE	DIAPHONE	DIATHETIC
DEXTROSE	DIACHYLON	DIALOGISED	DIAPHONES	DIATOM
DEXTROSES	DIACHYLONS	DIALOGISES	DIAPHRAGM	DIATOMIC
DEXTROUS	DIACHYLUM	DIALOGISING	DIAPHRAGMS	DIATOMIST
DEY	DIACHYLUMS	DIALOGIST	DIAPHYSES	DIATOMISTS
DEYS	DIACID	DIALOGISTS	DIAPHYSIS	DIATOMITE
DHAK	DIACODION	DIALOGITE	DIAPIR	DIATOMITES
DHAKS	DIACODIONS	DIALOGITES	DIAPIRIC	DIATOMS
DHAL	DIACODIUM	DIALOGIZE	DIAPIRISM	DIATONIC
DHALS	DIACODIUMS	DIALOGIZED	DIAPIRISMS	DIATRETUM
DHARMA	DIACONAL	DIALOGIZES	DIAPIRS	DIATRETUMS
DHARMAS	DIACONATE	DIALOGIZING	DIAPYESES	DIATRIBE
DHARMSALA	DIACONATES	DIALOGS	DIAPYESIS	DIATRIBES
DHARMSALAS	DIACRITIC	DIALOGUE	DIAPYETIC	DIATROPIC
DHARNA	DIACRITICS	DIALOGUED	DIAPYETICS	DIAXON
DHARNAS	DIACT	DIALOGUES	DIARCH	DIAXONS
DHOBI	DIACTINAL	DIALOGUING	DIARCHAL	DIAZEPAM
DHOBIS	DIACTINE	DIALS	DIARCHIC	DIAZEPAMS
DHOL	DIACTINIC	DIALYSE	DIARCHIES	DIAZEUXES
DHOLE	DIADEM	DIALYSED	DIARCHY	DIAZEUXIS
DHOLES	DIADEMED	DIALYSER	DIARIAL	DIAZO
DHOLL	DIADEMS	DIALYSERS	DIARIAN	DIAZOES
DHOLLS	DIADOCHI	DIALYSES	DIARIES	DIAZOS
DHOLS	DIADROM	DIALYSING	DIARISE	DIB
DHOOLIES	DIADROMS	DIALYSIS	DIARISED	DIBASIC
DHOOLY	DIAERESES	DIALYTIC	DIARISES	DIBBED
DHOOTI	DIAERESIS	DIALYZE	DIARISING	DIBBER
DHOOTIS	DIAGLYPH	DIALYZED	DIARIST	DIBBERS
DHOTI	DIAGLYPHS	DIALYZER	DIARISTS	DIBBING
DHOTIS	DIAGNOSE	DIALYZERS	DIARIZE	DIBBLE
DHOW	DIAGNOSED	DIALYZES	DIARIZED	DIBBLED
DHOWS	DIAGNOSES	DIALYZING	DIARIZES	DIBBLER
DHURRA	DIAGNOSING	DIAMAGNET	DIARIZING	DIBBLERS
DHURRAS	DIAGNOSIS	DIAMAGNETS	DIARRHEA	DIBBLES
DHURRIE	DIAGONAL	DIAMANTE	DIARRHEAL	DIBBLING
DHURRIES	DIAGONALS	DIAMANTES	DIARRHEAS	DIBBS
DI	DIAGRAM	DIAMETER	DIARRHEIC	DIBS
DIABASE	DIAGRAMS	DIAMETERS	DIARRHOEA	DIBUTYL
DIABASES	DIAGRAPH	DIAMETRAL	DIARRHOEAS	DICACIOUS
DIABASIC	DIAGRAPHS	DIAMETRIC	DIARY	DICACITIES
DIABETES	DIAGRID	DIAMOND	DIASCOPE	DICACITY
DIABETIC	DIAGRIDS	DIAMONDED	DIASCOPES	DICAST
DIABETICS	DIAL	DIAMONDS	DIASPORA	DICASTERIES
DIABLE	DIALECT	DIAMYL	DIASPORAS	DICASTERY
DIABLERIE	DIALECTAL	DIANDRIES	DIASPORE	DICASTIC
DIABLERIES	DIALECTIC	DIANDROUS	DIASPORES	DICASTS
DIABLERY	DIALECTICS	DIANDRY	DIASTASE	DICE
DIABLES	DIALECTS	DIANODAL	DIASTASES	DICED
DIABOLIC	DIALED	DIANOETIC	DIASTASIC	DICENTRA
DIABOLISE	DIALING	DIANTHUS	DIASTASIS	DICENTRAS
DIABOLISED	DIALIST	DIANTHUSES	DIASTATIC	DICER
DIABOLISES	DIALISTS	DIAPASE	DIASTEMA	DICERS
DIABOLISING	DIALLAGE	DIAPASES	DIASTEMATA	DICES
DIABOLISM	DIALLAGES	DIAPASON	DIASTER	DICEY
DIABOLISMS	DIALLAGIC	DIAPASONS	DIASTERS	DICH
DIABOLIST	DIALLED	DIAPAUSE	DIASTOLE	DICHASIA
DIABOLISTS	DIALLER	DIAPAUSES	DIASTOLES	DICHASIAL
DIABOLIZE	DIALLERS	DIAPENTE	DIASTOLIC	DICHASIUM
DIABOLIZED	DIALLING	DIAPENTES	DIASTYLE	DICHOGAMIES
DIABOLIZES	DIALLINGS	DIAPER	DIASTYLES	DICHOGAMY
DIABOLIZING	DIALOG	DIAPERED	DIATHERMIES	DICHORD
DIABOLO	DIALOGED	DIAPERING	DIATHERMY	DICHORDS
DIABOLOGIES	DIALOGIC	DIAPERINGS	DIATHESES	DICHOTOMIES

The Chambers Dictionary is the authority for many longer words; see *OSW* Introduction, page xii

DICHOTOMY	DICTION	DIEGESIS	DIFFUSES	DIGNITARIES
DICHROIC	DICTIONS	DIELDRIN	DIFFUSING	DIGNITARY
DICHROISM	DICTS	DIELDRINS	DIFFUSION	DIGNITIES
DICHROISMS	DICTUM	DIELYTRA	DIFFUSIONS	DIGNITY
DICHROITE	DICTY	DIELYTRAS	DIFFUSIVE	DIGONAL
DICHROITES	DICTYOGEN	DIENE	DIG	DIGRAPH
DICHROMAT	DICTYOGENS	DIENES	DIGAMIES	DIGRAPHS
DICHROMATS	DICYCLIC	DIERESES	DIGAMIST	DIGRESS
DICHROMIC	DID	DIERESIS	DIGAMISTS	DIGRESSED
DICHT	DIDACTIC	DIES	DIGAMMA	DIGRESSES
DICHTED	DIDACTICS	DIESEL	DIGAMMAS	DIGRESSING
DICHTING	DIDACTYL	DIESELISE	DIGAMOUS	DIGS
DICHTS	DIDACTYLS	DIESELISED	DIGAMY	DIGYNIAN
DICIER	DIDAKAI	DIESELISES	DIGASTRIC	DIGYNOUS
DICIEST	DIDAKAIS	DIESELISING	DIGEST	DIHEDRA
DICING	DIDAKEI	DIESELIZE	DIGESTED	DIHEDRAL
DICINGS	DIDAKEIS	DIESELIZED	DIGESTER	DIHEDRALS
DICK	DIDAPPER	DIESELIZES	DIGESTERS	DIHEDRON
DICKENS	DIDAPPERS	DIESELIZING	DIGESTING	DIHEDRONS
DICKER	DIDDER	DIESELS	DIGESTION	DIHYBRID
DICKERED	DIDDERED	DIESES	DIGESTIONS	DIHYBRIDS
DICKERING	DIDDERING	DIESIS	DIGESTIVE	DIHYDRIC
DICKERS	DIDDERS	DIESTRUS	DIGESTIVES	DIKA
DICKEY	DIDDICOY	DIESTRUSES	DIGESTS	DIKAS
DICKEYS	DIDDICOYS	DIET	DIGGABLE	DIKAST
DICKHEAD	DIDDIER	DIETARIAN	DIGGED	DIKASTS
DICKHEADS	DIDDIES	DIETARIANS	DIGGER	DIKE
DICKIE	DIDDIEST	DIETARIES	DIGGERS	DIKED
DICKIER	DIDDLE	DIETARY	DIGGING	DIKER
DICKIES	DIDDLED	DIETED	DIGGINGS	DIKERS
DICKIEST	DIDDLER	DIETER	DIGHT	DIKES
DICKS	DIDDLERS	DIETERS	DIGHTED	DIKEY
DICKTIER	DIDDLES	DIETETIC	DIGHTING	DIKIER
DICKTIEST	DIDDLING	DIETETICS	DIGHTS	DIKIEST
DICKTY	DIDDY	DIETHYL	DIGIT	DIKING
DICKY	DIDELPHIC	DIETICIAN	DIGITAL	DIKKOP
DICLINISM	DIDELPHID	DIETICIANS	DIGITALIN	DIKKOPS
DICLINISMS	DIDELPHIDS	DIETINE	DIGITALINS	DIKTAT
DICLINOUS	DIDICOI	DIETINES	DIGITALIS	DIKTATS
DICOT	DIDICOIS	DIETING	DIGITALISES	DILATABLE
DICOTS	DIDICOY	DIETIST	DIGITALS	DILATANCIES
DICROTIC	DIDICOYS	DIETISTS	DIGITATE	DILATANCY
DICROTISM	DIDO	DIETITIAN	DIGITATED	DILATANT
DICROTISMS	DIDOES	DIETITIANS	DIGITISE	DILATATOR
DICROTOUS	DIDOS	DIETS	DIGITISED	DILATATORS
DICT	DIDRACHM	DIFFER	DIGITISER	DILATE
DICTA	DIDRACHMA	DIFFERED	DIGITISERS	DILATED
DICTATE	DIDRACHMAS	DIFFERENT	DIGITISES	DILATER
DICTATED	DIDRACHMS	DIFFERING	DIGITISING	DILATERS
DICTATES	DIDST	DIFFERS	DIGITIZE	DILATES
DICTATING	DIDYMIUM	DIFFICILE	DIGITIZED	DILATING
DICTATION	DIDYMIUMS	DIFFICULT	DIGITIZER	DILATION
DICTATIONS	DIDYMOUS	DIFFIDENT	DIGITIZERS	DILATIONS
DICTATOR	DIE	DIFFLUENT	DIGITIZES	DILATIVE
DICTATORS	DIEB	DIFFORM	DIGITIZING	DILATOR
DICTATORY	DIEBACK	DIFFRACT	DIGITS	DILATORS
DICTATRIX	DIEBACKS	DIFFRACTED	DIGLOT	DILATORY
DICTATRIXES	DIEBS	DIFFRACTING	DIGLOTS	DILDO
DICTATURE	DIED	DIFFRACTS	DIGLYPH	DILDOE
DICTATURES	DIEDRAL	DIFFUSE	DIGLYPHS	DILDOES
DICTED	DIEDRALS	DIFFUSED	DIGNIFIED	DILDOS
DICTIER	DIEDRE	DIFFUSELY	DIGNIFIES	DILEMMA
DICTIEST	DIEDRES	DIFFUSER	DIGNIFY	DILEMMAS
DICTING	DIEGESES	DIFFUSERS	DIGNIFYING	DILIGENCE

DILIGENCES	DIMIDIATED	DINGIER	DIOPSIDE	DIPLOMATES
DILIGENT	DIMIDIATES	DINGIES	DIOPSIDES	DIPLOMATING
DILL	DIMIDIATING	DINGIEST	DIOPTASE	DIPLOMATS
DILLI	DIMINISH	DINGINESS	DIOPTASES	DIPLON
DILLIER	DIMINISHED	DINGINESSES	DIOPTER	DIPLONS
DILLIES	DIMINISHES	DINGING	DIOPTERS	DIPLONT
DILLIEST	DIMINISHING	DINGLE	DIOPTRATE	DIPLONTS
DILLING	DIMINISHINGS	DINGLES	DIOPTRE	DIPLOPIA
DILLINGS	DIMISSORY	DINGO	DIOPTRES	DIPLOPIAS
DILLIS	DIMITIES	DINGOES	DIOPTRIC	DIPLOZOA
DILLS	DIMITY	DINGS	DIOPTRICS	DIPLOZOON
DILLY	DIMLY	DINGUS	DIORAMA	DIPNOAN
DILUENT	DIMMED	DINGUSES	DIORAMAS	DIPNOANS
DILUENTS	DIMMER	DINGY	DIORAMIC	DIPNOOUS
DILUTABLE	DIMMERS	DINIC	DIORISM	DIPODIES
DILUTABLES	DIMMEST	DINICS	DIORISMS	DIPODY
DILUTE	DIMMING	DINING	DIORISTIC	DIPOLAR
DILUTED	DIMMISH	DINK	DIORITE	DIPOLE
DILUTEE	DIMNESS	DINKED	DIORITES	DIPOLES
DILUTEES	DIMNESSES	DINKER	DIORITIC	DIPPED
DILUTER	DIMORPH	DINKEST	DIOSGENIN	DIPPER
DILUTERS	DIMORPHIC	DINKIER	DIOSGENINS	DIPPERS
DILUTES	DIMORPHS	DINKIES	DIOTA	DIPPIER
DILUTING	DIMPLE	DINKIEST	DIOTAS	DIPPIEST
DILUTION	DIMPLED	DINKING	DIOXAN	DIPPING
DILUTIONS	DIMPLES	DINKS	DIOXANE	DIPPINGS
DILUTOR	DIMPLIER	DINKUM	DIOXANES	DIPPY
DILUTORS	DIMPLIEST	DINKY	DIOXANS	DIPS
DILUVIA	DIMPLING	DINMONT	DIOXIDE	DIPSADES
DILUVIAL	DIMPLY	DINMONTS	DIOXIDES	DIPSAS
DILUVIAN	DIMS	DINNED	DIOXIN	DIPSO
DILUVION	DIMWIT	DINNER	DIOXINS	DIPSOS
DILUVIONS	DIMWITS	DINNERED	DIP	DIPSTICK
DILUVIUM	DIMYARIAN	DINNERING	DIPCHICK	DIPSTICKS
DILUVIUMS	DIN	DINNERS	DIPCHICKS	DIPTERA
DIM	DINAR	DINNING	DIPEPTIDE	DIPTERAL
DIMBLE	DINARCHIES	DINNLE	DIPEPTIDES	DIPTERAN
DIMBLES	DINARCHY	DINNLED	DIPHENYL	DIPTERANS
DIME	DINARS	DINNLES	DIPHENYLS	DIPTERAS
DIMENSION	DINDLE	DINNLING	DIPHONE	DIPTERIST
DIMENSIONED	DINDLED	DINO	DIPHONES	DIPTERISTS
DIMENSIONING	DINDLES	DINOMANIA	DIPHTHONG	DIPTEROI
DIMENSIONS	DINDLING	DINOMANIAS	DIPHTHONGS	DIPTEROS
DIMER	DINE	DINOS	DIPHYSITE	DIPTEROSES
DIMERIC	DINED	DINOSAUR	DIPHYSITES	DIPTEROUS
DIMERISE	DINER	DINOSAURS	DIPLEGIA	DIPTYCH
DIMERISED	DINERS	DINOTHERE	DIPLEGIAS	DIPTYCHS
DIMERISES	DINES	DINOTHERES	DIPLEX	DIRDAM
DIMERISING	DINETTE	DINS	DIPLOE	DIRDAMS
DIMERISM	DINETTES	DINT	DIPLOES	DIRDUM
DIMERISMS	DINFUL	DINTED	DIPLOGEN	DIRDUMS
DIMERIZE	DING	DINTING	DIPLOGENS	DIRE
DIMERIZED	DINGBAT	DINTS	DIPLOID	DIRECT
DIMERIZES	DINGBATS	DIOCESAN	DIPLOIDIES	DIRECTED
DIMERIZING	DINGE	DIOCESANS	DIPLOIDY	DIRECTER
DIMEROUS	DINGED	DIOCESE	DIPLOMA	DIRECTEST
DIMERS	DINGER	DIOCESES	DIPLOMACIES	DIRECTING
DIMES	DINGERS	DIODE	DIPLOMACY	DIRECTION
DIMETER	DINGES	DIODES	DIPLOMAED	DIRECTIONS
DIMETERS	DINGESES	DIOECIOUS	DIPLOMAING	DIRECTIVE
DIMETHYL	DINGEY	DIOECISM	DIPLOMAS	DIRECTIVES
DIMETHYLS	DINGEYS	DIOECISMS	DIPLOMAT	DIRECTLY
DIMETRIC	DINGHIES	DIOESTRUS	DIPLOMATE	DIRECTOR
DIMIDIATE	DINGHY	DIOESTRUSES	DIPLOMATED	DIRECTORIES

The Chambers Dictionary is the authority for many longer words; see *OSW* Introduction, page xii

DIRECTORS	DISABUSED	DISARRAYING	DISBURSE	DISCLAIMING
DIRECTORY	DISABUSES	DISARRAYS	DISBURSED	DISCLAIMS
DIRECTRICES	DISABUSING	DISAS	DISBURSES	DISCLOSE
DIRECTRIX	DISACCORD	DISASTER	DISBURSING	DISCLOSED
DIRECTRIXES	DISACCORDED	DISASTERS	DISC	DISCLOSES
DIRECTS	DISACCORDING	DISATTIRE	DISCAGE	DISCLOSING
DIREFUL	DISACCORDS	DISATTIRED	DISCAGED	DISCLOST
DIREFULLY	DISADORN	DISATTIRES	DISCAGES	DISCO
DIREMPT	DISADORNED	DISATTIRING	DISCAGING	DISCOBOLI
DIREMPTED	DISADORNING	DISATTUNE	DISCAL	DISCOED
DIREMPTING	DISADORNS	DISATTUNED	DISCALCED	DISCOER
DIREMPTS	DISAFFECT	DISATTUNES	DISCANDIE	DISCOERS
DIRENESS	DISAFFECTED	DISATTUNING	DISCANDIED	DISCOID
DIRENESSES	DISAFFECTING	DISAVOUCH	DISCANDIES	DISCOIDAL
DIRER	DISAFFECTS	DISAVOUCHED	DISCANDY	DISCOING
DIREST	DISAFFIRM	DISAVOUCHES	DISCANDYING	DISCOLOR
DIRGE	DISAFFIRMED	DISAVOUCHING	DISCANDYINGS	DISCOLORED
DIRGES	DISAFFIRMING	DISAVOW	DISCANT	DISCOLORING
DIRHAM	DISAFFIRMS	DISAVOWAL	DISCANTED	DISCOLORS
DIRHAMS	DISAGREE	DISAVOWALS	DISCANTING	DISCOLOUR
DIRHEM	DISAGREED	DISAVOWED	DISCANTS	DISCOLOURED
DIRHEMS	DISAGREEING	DISAVOWING	DISCARD	DISCOLOURING
DIRIGE	DISAGREES	DISAVOWS	DISCARDED	DISCOLOURS
DIRIGENT	DISALLIED	DISBAND	DISCARDING	DISCOMFIT
DIRIGES	DISALLIES	DISBANDED	DISCARDS	DISCOMFITED
DIRIGIBLE	DISALLOW	DISBANDING	DISCASE	DISCOMFITING
DIRIGIBLES	DISALLOWED	DISBANDS	DISCASED	DISCOMFITS
DIRIGISM	DISALLOWING	DISBAR	DISCASES	DISCOMMON
DIRIGISME	DISALLOWS	DISBARK	DISCASING	DISCOMMONED
DIRIGISMES	DISALLY	DISBARKED	DISCED	DISCOMMONING
DIRIGISMS	DISALLYING	DISBARKING	DISCEPT	DISCOMMONS
DIRIGISTE	DISANCHOR	DISBARKS	DISCEPTED	DISCORD
DIRIMENT	DISANCHORED	DISBARRED	DISCEPTING	DISCORDED
DIRK	DISANCHORING	DISBARRING	DISCEPTS	DISCORDING
DIRKE	DISANCHORS	DISBARS	DISCERN	DISCORDS
DIRKED	DISANNEX	DISBELIEF	DISCERNED	DISCOS
DIRKES	DISANNEXED	DISBELIEFS	DISCERNER	DISCOUNT
DIRKING	DISANNEXES	DISBENCH	DISCERNERS	DISCOUNTED
DIRKS	DISANNEXING	DISBENCHED	DISCERNING	DISCOUNTING
DIRL	DISANNUL	DISBENCHES	DISCERNS	DISCOUNTS
DIRLED	DISANNULLED	DISBENCHING	DISCERP	DISCOURE
DIRLING	DISANNULLING	DISBODIED	DISCERPED	DISCOURED
DIRLS	DISANNULLINGS	DISBOSOM	DISCERPING	DISCOURES
DIRNDL	DISANNULS	DISBOSOMED	DISCERPS	DISCOURING
DIRNDLS	DISANOINT	DISBOSOMING	DISCHARGE	DISCOURSE
DIRT	DISANOINTED	DISBOSOMS	DISCHARGED	DISCOURSED
DIRTED	DISANOINTING	DISBOWEL	DISCHARGES	DISCOURSES
DIRTIED	DISANOINTS	DISBOWELLED	DISCHARGING	DISCOURSING
DIRTIER	DISAPPEAR	DISBOWELLING	DISCHURCH	DISCOVER
DIRTIES	DISAPPEARED	DISBOWELS	DISCHURCHED	DISCOVERED
DIRTIEST	DISAPPEARING	DISBRANCH	DISCHURCHES	DISCOVERIES
DIRTILY	DISAPPEARS	DISBRANCHED	DISCHURCHING	DISCOVERING
DIRTINESS	DISAPPLIED	DISBRANCHES	DISCIDE	DISCOVERS
DIRTINESSES	DISAPPLIES	DISBRANCHING	DISCIDED	DISCOVERT
DIRTING	DISAPPLY	DISBUD	DISCIDES	DISCOVERY
DIRTS	DISAPPLYING	DISBUDDED	DISCIDING	DISCREDIT
DIRTY	DISARM	DISBUDDING	DISCINCT	DISCREDITED
DIRTYING	DISARMED	DISBUDS	DISCING	DISCREDITING
DISA	DISARMER	DISBURDEN	DISCIPLE	DISCREDITS
DISABLE	DISARMERS	DISBURDENED	DISCIPLED	DISCREET
DISABLED	DISARMING	DISBURDENING	DISCIPLES	DISCREETER
DISABLES	DISARMS	DISBURDENS	DISCIPLING	DISCREETEST
DISABLING	DISARRAY	DISBURSAL	DISCLAIM	DISCRETE
DISABUSE	DISARRAYED	DISBURSALS	DISCLAIMED	DISCRETER

DISCRETEST	DISENTAILING	DISGRACER	DISHONOURS	DISJOINTED
DISCROWN	DISENTAILS	DISGRACERS	DISHORN	DISJOINTING
DISCROWNED	DISENTOMB	DISGRACES	DISHORNED	DISJOINTS
DISCROWNING	DISENTOMBED	DISGRACING	DISHORNING	DISJUNCT
DISCROWNS	DISENTOMBING	DISGRADE	DISHORNS	DISJUNCTS
DISCS	DISENTOMBS	DISGRADED	DISHORSE	DISJUNE
DISCUMBER	DISESTEEM	DISGRADES	DISHORSED	DISJUNES
DISCUMBERED	DISESTEEMED	DISGRADING	DISHORSES	DISK
DISCUMBERING	DISESTEEMING	DISGUISE	DISHORSING	DISKED
DISCUMBERS	DISESTEEMS	DISGUISED	DISHOUSE	DISKETTE
DISCURE	DISEUR	DISGUISER	DISHOUSED	DISKETTES
DISCURED	DISEURS	DISGUISERS	DISHOUSES	DISKING
DISCURES	DISEUSE	DISGUISES	DISHOUSING	DISKLESS
DISCURING	DISEUSES	DISGUISING	DISHTOWEL	DISKS
DISCURSUS	DISFAME	DISGUISINGS	DISHTOWELS	DISLEAF
DISCURSUSES	DISFAMES	DISGUST	DISHUMOUR	DISLEAFED
DISCUS	DISFAVOR	DISGUSTED	DISHUMOURED	DISLEAFING
DISCUSES	DISFAVORED	DISGUSTING	DISHUMOURING	DISLEAFS
DISCUSS	DISFAVORING	DISGUSTS	DISHUMOURS	DISLEAL
DISCUSSED	DISFAVORS	DISH	DISHWATER	DISLEAVE
DISCUSSES	DISFAVOUR	DISHABIT	DISHWATERS	DISLEAVED
DISCUSSING	DISFAVOURED	DISHABITED	DISHY	DISLEAVES
DISDAIN	DISFAVOURING	DISHABITING	DISILLUDE	DISLEAVING
DISDAINED	DISFAVOURS	DISHABITS	DISILLUDED	DISLIKE
DISDAINING	DISFIGURE	DISHABLE	DISILLUDES	DISLIKED
DISDAINS	DISFIGURED	DISHABLED	DISILLUDING	DISLIKEN
DISEASE	DISFIGURES	DISHABLES	DISIMMURE	DISLIKENED
DISEASED	DISFIGURING	DISHABLING	DISIMMURED	DISLIKENING
DISEASES	DISFLESH	DISHALLOW	DISIMMURES	DISLIKENS
DISEASING	DISFLESHED	DISHALLOWED	DISIMMURING	DISLIKES
DISEDGE	DISFLESHES	DISHALLOWING	DISINFECT	DISLIKING
DISEDGED	DISFLESHING	DISHALLOWS	DISINFECTED	DISLIMB
DISEDGES	DISFLUENT	DISHED	DISINFECTING	DISLIMBED
DISEDGING	DISFOREST	DISHELM	DISINFECTS	DISLIMBING
DISEMBARK	DISFORESTED	DISHELMED	DISINFEST	DISLIMBS
DISEMBARKED	DISFORESTING	DISHELMING	DISINFESTED	DISLIMN
DISEMBARKING	DISFORESTS	DISHELMS	DISINFESTING	DISLIMNING
DISEMBARKS	DISFORM	DISHERIT	DISINFESTS	DISLIMNS
DISEMBODIED	DISFORMED	DISHERITED	DISINHUME	DISLINK
DISEMBODIES	DISFORMING	DISHERITING	DISINHUMED	DISLINKED
DISEMBODY	DISFORMS	DISHERITS	DISINHUMES	DISLINKING
DISEMBODYING	DISFROCK	DISHES	DISINHUMING	DISLINKS
DISEMPLOY	DISFROCKED	DISHEVEL	DISINTER	DISLOAD
DISEMPLOYED	DISFROCKING	DISHEVELLED	DISINTERRED	DISLOADED
DISEMPLOYING	DISFROCKS	DISHEVELLING	DISINTERRING	DISLOADING
DISEMPLOYS	DISGAVEL	DISHEVELS	DISINTERS	DISLOADS
DISENABLE	DISGAVELLED	DISHFUL	DISINURE	DISLOCATE
DISENABLED	DISGAVELLING	DISHFULS	DISINURED	DISLOCATED
DISENABLES	DISGAVELS	DISHIER	DISINURES	DISLOCATES
DISENABLING	DISGEST	DISHIEST	DISINURING	DISLOCATING
DISENDOW	DISGESTED	DISHING	DISINVEST	DISLODGE
DISENDOWED	DISGESTING	DISHINGS	DISINVESTED	DISLODGED
DISENDOWING	DISGESTS	DISHOME	DISINVESTING	DISLODGES
DISENDOWS	DISGODDED	DISHOMED	DISINVESTS	DISLODGING
DISENGAGE	DISGORGE	DISHOMES	DISJASKIT	DISLOIGN
DISENGAGED	DISGORGED	DISHOMING	DISJECT	DISLOIGNED
DISENGAGES	DISGORGES	DISHONEST	DISJECTED	DISLOIGNING
DISENGAGING	DISGORGING	DISHONOR	DISJECTING	DISLOIGNS
DISENROL	DISGOWN	DISHONORED	DISJECTS	DISLOYAL
DISENROLLED	DISGOWNED	DISHONORING	DISJOIN	DISLUSTRE
DISENROLLING	DISGOWNING	DISHONORS	DISJOINED	DISLUSTRED
DISENROLS	DISGOWNS	DISHONOUR	DISJOINING	DISLUSTRES
DISENTAIL	DISGRACE	DISHONOURED	DISJOINS	DISLUSTRING
DISENTAILED	DISGRACED	DISHONOURING	DISJOINT	

The Chambers Dictionary is the authority for many longer words; see *OSW* Introduction, page xii

DISMAL	DISORDERED	DISPEOPLED	DISPOSALS	DISPUTED
DISMALITIES	DISORDERING	DISPEOPLES	DISPOSE	DISPUTER
DISMALITY	DISORDERS	DISPEOPLING	DISPOSED	DISPUTERS
DISMALLER	DISORIENT	DISPERSAL	DISPOSER	DISPUTES
DISMALLEST	DISORIENTED	DISPERSALS	DISPOSERS	DISPUTING
DISMALLY	DISORIENTING	DISPERSE	DISPOSES	DISQUIET
DISMALS	DISORIENTS	DISPERSED	DISPOSING	DISQUIETED
DISMAN	DISOWN	DISPERSER	DISPOSINGS	DISQUIETING
DISMANNED	DISOWNED	DISPERSERS	DISPOST	DISQUIETS
DISMANNING	DISOWNER	DISPERSES	DISPOSTED	DISRANK
DISMANS	DISOWNERS	DISPERSING	DISPOSTING	DISRANKED
DISMANTLE	DISOWNING	DISPIRIT	DISPOSTS	DISRANKING
DISMANTLED	DISOWNS	DISPIRITED	DISPOSURE	DISRANKS
DISMANTLES	DISPACE	DISPIRITING	DISPOSURES	DISRATE
DISMANTLING	DISPACED	DISPIRITS	DISPRAD	DISRATED
DISMASK	DISPACES	DISPLACE	DISPRAISE	DISRATES
DISMASKED	DISPACING	DISPLACED	DISPRAISED	DISRATING
DISMASKING	DISPARAGE	DISPLACES	DISPRAISES	DISREGARD
DISMASKS	DISPARAGED	DISPLACING	DISPRAISING	DISREGARDED
DISMAST	DISPARAGES	DISPLANT	DISPREAD	DISREGARDING
DISMASTED	DISPARAGING	DISPLANTED	DISPREADING	DISREGARDS
DISMASTING	DISPARATE	DISPLANTING	DISPREADS	DISRELISH
DISMASTS	DISPARATES	DISPLANTS	DISPRED	DISRELISHED
DISMAY	DISPARITIES	DISPLAY	DISPREDDEN	DISRELISHES
DISMAYD	DISPARITY	DISPLAYED	DISPREDDING	DISRELISHING
DISMAYED	DISPARK	DISPLAYER	DISPREDS	DISREPAIR
DISMAYFUL	DISPARKED	DISPLAYERS	DISPRISON	DISREPAIRS
DISMAYING	DISPARKING	DISPLAYING	DISPRISONED	DISREPUTE
DISMAYL	DISPARKS	DISPLAYS	DISPRISONING	DISREPUTES
DISMAYLED	DISPART	DISPLE	DISPRISONS	DISROBE
DISMAYLING	DISPARTED	DISPLEASE	DISPRIZE	DISROBED
DISMAYLS	DISPARTING	DISPLEASED	DISPRIZED	DISROBES
DISMAYS	DISPARTS	DISPLEASES	DISPRIZES	DISROBING
DISME	DISPATCH	DISPLEASING	DISPRIZING	DISROOT
DISMEMBER	DISPATCHED	DISPLED	DISPROFIT	DISROOTED
DISMEMBERED	DISPATCHES	DISPLES	DISPROFITS	DISROOTING
DISMEMBERING	DISPATCHING	DISPLING	DISPROOF	DISROOTS
DISMEMBERS	DISPATHIES	DISPLODE	DISPROOFS	DISRUPT
DISMES	DISPATHY	DISPLODED	DISPROOVE	DISRUPTED
DISMISS	DISPAUPER	DISPLODES	DISPROOVED	DISRUPTER
DISMISSAL	DISPAUPERED	DISPLODING	DISPROOVES	DISRUPTERS
DISMISSALS	DISPAUPERING	DISPLUME	DISPROOVING	DISRUPTING
DISMISSED	DISPAUPERS	DISPLUMED	DISPROVAL	DISRUPTOR
DISMISSES	DISPEACE	DISPLUMES	DISPROVALS	DISRUPTORS
DISMISSING	DISPEACES	DISPLUMING	DISPROVE	DISRUPTS
DISMODED	DISPEL	DISPONDEE	DISPROVED	DISS
DISMOUNT	DISPELLED	DISPONDEES	DISPROVEN	DISSAVING
DISMOUNTED	DISPELLING	DISPONE	DISPROVES	DISSAVINGS
DISMOUNTING	DISPELS	DISPONED	DISPROVING	DISSEAT
DISMOUNTS	DISPENCE	DISPONEE	DISPUNGE	DISSEATED
DISNEST	DISPENCED	DISPONEES	DISPUNGED	DISSEATING
DISNESTED	DISPENCES	DISPONER	DISPUNGES	DISSEATS
DISNESTING	DISPENCING	DISPONERS	DISPUNGING	DISSECT
DISNESTS	DISPEND	DISPONES	DISPURSE	DISSECTED
DISOBEY	DISPENDED	DISPONGE	DISPURSED	DISSECTING
DISOBEYED	DISPENDING	DISPONGED	DISPURSES	DISSECTINGS
DISOBEYING	DISPENDS	DISPONGES	DISPURSING	DISSECTOR
DISOBEYS	DISPENSE	DISPONGING	DISPURVEY	DISSECTORS
DISOBLIGE	DISPENSED	DISPONING	DISPURVEYED	DISSECTS
DISOBLIGED	DISPENSER	DISPORT	DISPURVEYING	DISSED
DISOBLIGES	DISPENSERS	DISPORTED	DISPURVEYS	DISSEISE
DISOBLIGING	DISPENSES	DISPORTING	DISPUTANT	DISSEISED
DISORBED	DISPENSING	DISPORTS	DISPUTANTS	DISSEISES
DISORDER	DISPEOPLE	DISPOSAL	DISPUTE	DISSEISIN

The Chambers Dictionary is the authority for many longer words; see *OSW* Introduction, page xii

DISSEISING	DISSUADER	DISTRACTS	DITALS	DITZIEST
DISSEISINS	DISSUADERS	DISTRAIL	DITAS	DITZY
DISSEISOR	DISSUADES	DISTRAILS	DITCH	DIURESES
DISSEISORS	DISSUADING	DISTRAIN	DITCHED	DIURESIS
DISSEIZE	DISSUNDER	DISTRAINED	DITCHER	DIURETIC
DISSEIZED	DISSUNDERED	DISTRAINING	DITCHERS	DIURETICS
DISSEIZES	DISSUNDERING	DISTRAINS	DITCHES	DIURNAL
DISSEIZIN	DISSUNDERS	DISTRAINT	DITCHING	DIURNALLY
DISSEIZING	DISTAFF	DISTRAINTS	DITE	DIURNALS
DISSEIZINS	DISTAFFS	DISTRAIT	DITED	DIUTURNAL
DISSEIZOR	DISTAIN	DISTRAITE	DITES	DIV
DISSEIZORS	DISTAINED	DISTRESS	DITHECAL	DIVA
DISSEMBLE	DISTAINING	DISTRESSED	DITHECOUS	DIVAGATE
DISSEMBLED	DISTAINS	DISTRESSES	DITHEISM	DIVAGATED
DISSEMBLES	DISTAL	DISTRESSING	DITHEISMS	DIVAGATES
DISSEMBLIES	DISTALLY	DISTRICT	DITHEIST	DIVAGATING
DISSEMBLING	DISTANCE	DISTRICTED	DITHEISTS	DIVALENCIES
DISSEMBLINGS	DISTANCED	DISTRICTING	DITHELETE	DIVALENCY
DISSEMBLY	DISTANCES	DISTRICTS	DITHELETES	DIVALENT
DISSENT	DISTANCING	DISTRUST	DITHELISM	DIVALENTS
DISSENTED	DISTANT	DISTRUSTED	DITHELISMS	DIVAN
DISSENTER	DISTANTLY	DISTRUSTING	DITHER	DIVANS
DISSENTERS	DISTASTE	DISTRUSTS	DITHERED	DIVAS
DISSENTING	DISTASTED	DISTUNE	DITHERER	DIVE
DISSENTS	DISTASTES	DISTUNED	DITHERERS	DIVED
DISSERT	DISTASTING	DISTUNES	DITHERIER	DIVELLENT
DISSERTED	DISTEMPER	DISTUNING	DITHERIEST	DIVER
DISSERTING	DISTEMPERED	DISTURB	DITHERING	DIVERGE
DISSERTS	DISTEMPERING	DISTURBED	DITHERS	DIVERGED
DISSERVE	DISTEMPERS	DISTURBER	DITHERY	DIVERGENT
DISSERVED	DISTEND	DISTURBERS	DITHYRAMB	DIVERGES
DISSERVES	DISTENDED	DISTURBING	DITHYRAMBS	DIVERGING
DISSERVING	DISTENDING	DISTURBS	DITING	DIVERS
DISSES	DISTENDS	DISTYLE	DITOKOUS	DIVERSE
DISSEVER	DISTENT	DISTYLES	DITONE	DIVERSED
DISSEVERED	DISTHENE	DISUNION	DITONES	DIVERSELY
DISSEVERING	DISTHENES	DISUNIONS	DITROCHEE	DIVERSES
DISSEVERS	DISTHRONE	DISUNITE	DITROCHEES	DIVERSIFIED
DISSHIVER	DISTHRONED	DISUNITED	DITS	DIVERSIFIES
DISSHIVERED	DISTHRONES	DISUNITES	DITSIER	DIVERSIFY
DISSHIVERING	DISTHRONING	DISUNITIES	DITSIEST	DIVERSIFYING
DISSHIVERS	DISTICH	DISUNITING	DITSY	DIVERSING
DISSIDENT	DISTICHAL	DISUNITY	DITT	DIVERSION
DISSIDENTS	DISTICHS	DISUSAGE	DITTANDER	DIVERSIONS
DISSIGHT	DISTIL	DISUSAGES	DITTANDERS	DIVERSITIES
DISSIGHTS	DISTILL	DISUSE	DITTANIES	DIVERSITY
DISSIMILE	DISTILLED	DISUSED	DITTANY	DIVERSLY
DISSIMILES	DISTILLER	DISUSES	DITTAY	DIVERT
DISSING	DISTILLERS	DISUSING	DITTAYS	DIVERTED
DISSIPATE	DISTILLING	DISVALUE	DITTED	DIVERTING
DISSIPATED	DISTILLINGS	DISVALUED	DITTIED	DIVERTIVE
DISSIPATES	DISTILLS	DISVALUES	DITTIES	DIVERTS
DISSIPATING	DISTILS	DISVALUING	DITTING	DIVES
DISSOCIAL	DISTINCT	DISVOUCH	DITTIT	DIVEST
DISSOLUTE	DISTINCTER	DISVOUCHED	DITTO	DIVESTED
DISSOLUTES	DISTINCTEST	DISVOUCHES	DITTOED	DIVESTING
DISSOLVE	DISTINGUE	DISVOUCHING	DITTOING	DIVESTS
DISSOLVED	DISTORT	DISYOKE	DITTOLOGIES	DIVESTURE
DISSOLVES	DISTORTED	DISYOKED	DITTOLOGY	DIVESTURES
DISSOLVING	DISTORTING	DISYOKES	DITTOS	DIVI
DISSOLVINGS	DISTORTS	DISYOKING	DITTS	DIVIDABLE
DISSONANT	DISTRACT	DIT	DITTY	DIVIDANT
DISSUADE	DISTRACTED	DITA	DITTYING	DIVIDE
DISSUADED	DISTRACTING	DITAL	DITZIER	DIVIDED

DIVIDEDLY	DIVULGED	DOBCHICKS	DOCTORESSES	DOEKS
DIVIDEND	DIVULGES	DOBHASH	DOCTORIAL	DOEN
DIVIDENDS	DIVULGING	DOBHASHES	DOCTORING	DOER
DIVIDER	DIVULSION	DOBS	DOCTORLY	DOERS
DIVIDERS	DIVULSIONS	DOC	DOCTORS	DOES
DIVIDES	DIVULSIVE	DOCENT	DOCTRESS	DOEST
DIVIDING	DIVVIES	DOCENTS	DOCTRESSES	DOETH
DIVIDINGS	DIVVY	DOCHMIAC	DOCTRINAL	DOFF
DIVIDIVI	DIWAN	DOCHMII	DOCTRINE	DOFFED
DIVIDIVIS	DIWANS	DOCHMIUS	DOCTRINES	DOFFER
DIVIDUAL	DIXI	DOCHMIUSES	DOCUDRAMA	DOFFERS
DIVIDUOUS	DIXIE	DOCHT	DOCUDRAMAS	DOFFING
DIVINATOR	DIXIES	DOCIBLE	DOCUMENT	DOFFS
DIVINATORS	DIXY	DOCILE	DOCUMENTED	DOG
DIVINE	DIZAIN	DOCILER	DOCUMENTING	DOGARESSA
DIVINED	DIZAINS	DOCILEST	DOCUMENTS	DOGARESSAS
DIVINELY	DIZEN	DOCILITIES	DOD	DOGATE
DIVINER	DIZENED	DOCILITY	DODDARD	DOGATES
DIVINERS	DIZENING	DOCIMASIES	DODDED	DOGBANE
DIVINES	DIZENS	DOCIMASY	DODDER	DOGBANES
DIVINEST	DIZYGOTIC	DOCK	DODDERED	DOGBERRIES
DIVING	DIZZARD	DOCKAGE	DODDERER	DOGBERRY
DIVINGS	DIZZARDS	DOCKAGES	DODDERERS	DOGBOLT
DIVINIFIED	DIZZIED	DOCKED	DODDERIER	DOGBOLTS
DIVINIFIES	DIZZIER	DOCKEN	DODDERIEST	DOGCART
DIVINIFY	DIZZIES	DOCKENS	DODDERING	DOGCARTS
DIVINIFYING	DIZZIEST	DOCKER	DODDERS	DOGDAYS
DIVINING	DIZZILY	DOCKERS	DODDERY	DOGE
DIVINISE	DIZZINESS	DOCKET	DODDIER	DOGEATE
DIVINISED	DIZZINESSES	DOCKETED	DODDIES	DOGEATES
DIVINISES	DIZZY	DOCKETING	DODDIEST	DOGES
DIVINISING	DIZZYING	DOCKETS	DODDING	DOGESHIP
DIVINITIES	DJEBEL	DOCKING	DODDIPOLL	DOGESHIPS
DIVINITY	DJEBELS	DOCKINGS	DODDIPOLLS	DOGFIGHT
DIVINIZE	DJELLABA	DOCKISE	DODDLE	DOGFIGHTS
DIVINIZED	DJELLABAH	DOCKISED	DODDLES	DOGFISH
DIVINIZES	DJELLABAHS	DOCKISES	DODDY	DOGFISHES
DIVINIZING	DJELLABAS	DOCKISING	DODDYPOLL	DOGFOX
DIVIS	DJIBBAH	DOCKIZE	DODDYPOLLS	DOGFOXES
DIVISIBLE	DJIBBAHS	DOCKIZED	DODECAGON	DOGGED
DIVISIBLY	DJINN	DOCKIZES	DODECAGONS	DOGGEDER
DIVISIM	DJINNI	DOCKIZING	DODGE	DOGGEDEST
DIVISION	DO	DOCKLAND	DODGED	DOGGEDLY
DIVISIONS	DOAB	DOCKLANDS	DODGEMS	DOGGER
DIVISIVE	DOABLE	DOCKS	DODGER	DOGGEREL
DIVISOR	DOABS	DOCKSIDE	DODGERIES	DOGGERELS
DIVISORS	DOAT	DOCKSIDES	DODGERS	DOGGERIES
DIVORCE	DOATED	DOCKYARD	DODGERY	DOGGERMAN
DIVORCED	DOATER	DOCKYARDS	DODGES	DOGGERMEN
DIVORCEE	DOATERS	DOCQUET	DODGIER	DOGGERS
DIVORCEES	DOATING	DOCQUETED	DODGIEST	DOGGERY
DIVORCER	DOATINGS	DOCQUETING	DODGING	DOGGESS
DIVORCERS	DOATS	DOCQUETS	DODGINGS	DOGGESSES
DIVORCES	DOB	DOCS	DODGY	DOGGIE
DIVORCING	DOBBED	DOCTOR	DODKIN	DOGGIER
DIVORCIVE	DOBBER	DOCTORAL	DODKINS	DOGGIES
DIVOT	DOBBERS	DOCTORAND	DODMAN	DOGGIEST
DIVOTS	DOBBIE	DOCTORANDS	DODMANS	DOGGINESS
DIVS	DOBBIES	DOCTORATE	DODO	DOGGINESSES
DIVULGATE	DOBBIN	DOCTORATED	DODOES	DOGGING
DIVULGATED	DOBBING	DOCTORATES	DODOS	DOGGINGS
DIVULGATES	DOBBINS	DOCTORATING	DODS	DOGGISH
DIVULGATING	DOBBY	DOCTORED	DOE	DOGGISHLY
DIVULGE	DOBCHICK	DOCTORESS	DOEK	DOGGO

DOGGONE	DOINGS	DOLOR	DOMINOS	DONNOT
DOGGONED	DOIT	DOLORIFIC	DOMY	DONNOTS
DOGGONEDER	DOITED	DOLOROSO	DON	DONOR
DOGGONEDEST	DOITIT	DOLOROUS	DONA	DONORS
DOGGONER	DOITKIN	DOLORS	DONAH	DONS
DOGGONEST	DOITKINS	DOLOUR	DONAHS	DONSHIP
DOGGREL	DOITS	DOLOURS	DONARIES	DONSHIPS
DOGGRELS	DOJO	DOLPHIN	DONARY	DONSIE
DOGGY	DOJOS	DOLPHINET	DONAS	DONSIER
DOGHOLE	DOLCE	DOLPHINETS	DONATARIES	DONSIEST
DOGHOLES	DOLCES	DOLPHINS	DONATARY	DONUT
DOGIE	DOLDRUMS	DOLT	DONATE	DONUTS
DOGIES	DOLE	DOLTISH	DONATED	DONUTTED
DOGMA	DOLED	DOLTISHLY	DONATES	DONUTTING
DOGMAS	DOLEFUL	DOLTS	DONATING	DONZEL
DOGMATIC	DOLEFULLY	DOMAIN	DONATION	DONZELS
DOGMATICS	DOLENT	DOMAINAL	DONATIONS	DOO
DOGMATISE	DOLERITE	DOMAINS	DONATISM	DOOB
DOGMATISED	DOLERITES	DOMAL	DONATISMS	DOOBS
DOGMATISES	DOLERITIC	DOMANIAL	DONATIVE	DOOCOT
DOGMATISING	DOLES	DOMATIA	DONATIVES	DOOCOTS
DOGMATISM	DOLESOME	DOMATIUM	DONATOR	DOODAD
DOGMATISMS	DOLIA	DOME	DONATORIES	DOODADS
DOGMATIST	DOLICHOS	DOMED	DONATORS	DOODAH
DOGMATISTS	DOLICHOSES	DOMES	DONATORY	DOODAHS
DOGMATIZE	DOLICHURI	DOMESTIC	DONDER	DOODLE
DOGMATIZED	DOLINA	DOMESTICS	DONDERED	DOODLEBUG
DOGMATIZES	DOLINAS	DOMETT	DONDERING	DOODLEBUGS
DOGMATIZING	DOLINE	DOMETTS	DONDERS	DOODLED
DOGMATORY	DOLINES	DOMICAL	DONE	DOODLER
DOGS	DOLING	DOMICIL	DONEE	DOODLERS
DOGSBODIES	DOLIUM	DOMICILE	DONEES	DOODLES
DOGSBODY	DOLL	DOMICILED	DONENESS	DOODLING
DOGSHIP	DOLLAR	DOMICILES	DONENESSES	DOOFER
DOGSHIPS	DOLLARED	DOMICILING	DONG	DOOFERS
DOGSHORES	DOLLARS	DOMICILS	DONGA	DOOK
DOGSKIN	DOLLDOM	DOMIER	DONGAS	DOOKED
DOGSKINS	DOLLDOMS	DOMIEST	DONGED	DOOKET
DOGSLED	DOLLED	DOMINANCE	DONGING	DOOKETS
DOGSLEDS	DOLLHOOD	DOMINANCES	DONGLE	DOOKING
DOGSLEEP	DOLLHOODS	DOMINANCIES	DONGLES	DOOKS
DOGSLEEPS	DOLLIED	DOMINANCY	DONGS	DOOL
DOGTEETH	DOLLIER	DOMINANT	DONING	DOOLALLY
DOGTOOTH	DOLLIERS	DOMINANTS	DONINGS	DOOLE
DOGTOWN	DOLLIES	DOMINATE	DONJON	DOOLES
DOGTOWNS	DOLLINESS	DOMINATED	DONJONS	DOOLIE
DOGTROT	DOLLINESSES	DOMINATES	DONKEY	DOOLIES
DOGTROTS	DOLLING	DOMINATING	DONKEYS	DOOLS
DOGVANE	DOLLISH	DOMINATOR	DONNARD	DOOM
DOGVANES	DOLLOP	DOMINATORS	DONNART	DOOMED
DOGWOOD	DOLLOPS	DOMINEE	DONNAT	DOOMFUL
DOGWOODS	DOLLS	DOMINEER	DONNATS	DOOMIER
DOGY	DOLLY	DOMINEERED	DONNE	DOOMIEST
DOH	DOLLYING	DOMINEERING	DONNED	DOOMING
DOHS	DOLMA	DOMINEERS	DONNEE	DOOMS
DOHYO	DOLMADES	DOMINEES	DONNEES	DOOMSAYER
DOHYOS	DOLMAN	DOMING	DONNERD	DOOMSAYERS
DOILED	DOLMANS	DOMINICAL	DONNERED	DOOMSDAY
DOILIES	DOLMAS	DOMINIE	DONNERT	DOOMSDAYS
DOILT	DOLMEN	DOMINIES	DONNES	DOOMSMAN
DOILTER	DOLMENS	DOMINION	DONNING	DOOMSMEN
DOILTEST	DOLOMITE	DOMINIONS	DONNISH	DOOMSTER
DOILY	DOLOMITES	DOMINO	DONNISM	DOOMSTERS
DOING	DOLOMITIC	DOMINOES	DONNISMS	DOOMWATCH

DOOMWATCHED	DOPPIES	DORSALLY	DOTARD	DOUBTINGS
DOOMWATCHES	DOPPING	DORSALS	DOTARDS	DOUBTLESS
DOOMWATCHING	DOPPINGS	DORSE	DOTATION	DOUBTS
DOOMWATCHINGS	DOPS	DORSEL	DOTATIONS	DOUC
DOOMY	DOPY	DORSELS	DOTE	DOUCE
DOONA	DOR	DORSER	DOTED	DOUCELY
DOONAS	DORAD	DORSERS	DOTER	DOUCENESS
DOOR	DORADO	DORSES	DOTERS	DOUCENESSES
DOORBELL	DORADOS	DORSIFLEX	DOTES	DOUCEPERE
DOORBELLS	DORADS	DORSUM	DOTH	DOUCEPERES
DOORKNOB	DOREE	DORT	DOTIER	DOUCER
DOORKNOBS	DOREES	DORTED	DOTIEST	DOUCEST
DOORKNOCK	DORHAWK	DORTER	DOTING	DOUCET
DOORKNOCKED	DORHAWKS	DORTERS	DOTINGLY	DOUCETS
DOORKNOCKING	DORIDOID	DORTIER	DOTINGS	DOUCEUR
DOORKNOCKS	DORIDOIDS	DORTIEST	DOTISH	DOUCEURS
DOORMAT	DORIES	DORTING	DOTS	DOUCHE
DOORMATS	DORISE	DORTOUR	DOTTED	DOUCHED
DOORN	DORISED	DORTOURS	DOTTEREL	DOUCHES
DOORNAIL	DORISES	DORTS	DOTTERELS	DOUCHING
DOORNAILS	DORISING	DORTY	DOTTIER	DOUCINE
DOORNS	DORIZE	DORY	DOTTIEST	DOUCINES
DOORPOST	DORIZED	DOS	DOTTINESS	DOUCS
DOORPOSTS	DORIZES	DOSAGE	DOTTINESSES	DOUGH
DOORS	DORIZING	DOSAGES	DOTTING	DOUGHIER
DOORSMAN	DORK	DOSE	DOTTIPOLL	DOUGHIEST
DOORSMEN	DORKIER	DOSED	DOTTIPOLLS	DOUGHNUT
DOORSTEP	DORKIEST	DOSEH	DOTTLE	DOUGHNUTS
DOORSTEPPED	DORKS	DOSEHS	DOTTLED	DOUGHNUTTED
DOORSTEPPING	DORKY	DOSES	DOTTLER	DOUGHNUTTING
DOORSTEPPINGS	DORLACH	DOSH	DOTTLES	DOUGHNUTTINGS
DOORSTEPS	DORLACHS	DOSHES	DOTTLEST	DOUGHS
DOORSTONE	DORM	DOSIMETER	DOTTREL	DOUGHT
DOORSTONES	DORMANCIES	DOSIMETERS	DOTTRELS	DOUGHTIER
DOORSTOP	DORMANCY	DOSIMETRIES	DOTTY	DOUGHTIEST
DOORSTOPS	DORMANT	DOSIMETRY	DOTY	DOUGHTILY
DOORWAY	DORMANTS	DOSING	DOUANE	DOUGHTY
DOORWAYS	DORMER	DOSIOLOGIES	DOUANES	DOUGHY
DOOS	DORMERS	DOSIOLOGY	DOUANIER	DOULEIA
DOP	DORMICE	DOSOLOGIES	DOUANIERS	DOULEIAS
DOPA	DORMIE	DOSOLOGY	DOUAR	DOUMA
DOPAMINE	DORMIENT	DOSS	DOUARS	DOUMAS
DOPAMINES	DORMITION	DOSSAL	DOUBLE	DOUP
DOPANT	DORMITIONS	DOSSALS	DOUBLED	DOUPS
DOPANTS	DORMITIVE	DOSSED	DOUBLER	DOUR
DOPAS	DORMITIVES	DOSSEL	DOUBLERS	DOURA
DOPATTA	DORMITORIES	DOSSELS	DOUBLES	DOURAS
DOPATTAS	DORMITORY	DOSSER	DOUBLET	DOURER
DOPE	DORMOUSE	DOSSERS	DOUBLETON	DOUREST
DOPED	DORMS	DOSSES	DOUBLETONS	DOURINE
DOPER	DORMY	DOSSHOUSE	DOUBLETS	DOURINES
DOPERS	DORNICK	DOSSHOUSES	DOUBLING	DOURLY
DOPES	DORNICKS	DOSSIER	DOUBLINGS	DOURNESS
DOPEY	DORONICUM	DOSSIERS	DOUBLOON	DOURNESSES
DOPIER	DORONICUMS	DOSSIL	DOUBLOONS	DOUSE
DOPIEST	DORP	DOSSILS	DOUBLY	DOUSED
DOPINESS	DORPS	DOSSING	DOUBT	DOUSER
DOPINESSES	DORR	DOST	DOUBTABLE	DOUSERS
DOPING	DORRED	DOT	DOUBTED	DOUSES
DOPINGS	DORRING	DOTAGE	DOUBTER	DOUSING
DOPPED	DORRS	DOTAGES	DOUBTERS	DOUT
DOPPER	DORS	DOTAL	DOUBTFUL	DOUTED
DOPPERS	DORSA	DOTANT	DOUBTFULS	DOUTER
DOPPIE	DORSAL	DOTANTS	DOUBTING	DOUTERS

The Chambers Dictionary is the authority for many longer words; see *OSW* Introduction, page xii

DOUTING	DOWING	DOWNSHIFTING	DOZIEST	DRAFTSMEN
DOUTS	DOWITCHER	DOWNSHIFTS	DOZINESS	DRAFTY
DOUZEPER	DOWITCHERS	DOWNSIDE	DOZINESSES	DRAG
DOUZEPERS	DOWL	DOWNSIDES	DOZING	DRAGEE
DOVE	DOWLAS	DOWNSIZE	DOZINGS	DRAGEES
DOVECOT	DOWLASES	DOWNSIZED	DOZY	DRAGGED
DOVECOTS	DOWLE	DOWNSIZES	DRAB	DRAGGIER
DOVED	DOWLES	DOWNSIZING	DRABBED	DRAGGIEST
DOVEISH	DOWLNE	DOWNSPOUT	DRABBER	DRAGGING
DOVEKIE	DOWLNES	DOWNSPOUTS	DRABBERS	DRAGGLE
DOVEKIES	DOWLNEY	DOWNSTAGE	DRABBEST	DRAGGLED
DOVELET	DOWLS	DOWNSTAIR	DRABBET	DRAGGLES
DOVELETS	DOWN	DOWNSTAIRS	DRABBETS	DRAGGLING
DOVELIKE	DOWNA	DOWNSWING	DRABBIER	DRAGGY
DOVER	DOWNBEAT	DOWNSWINGS	DRABBIEST	DRAGHOUND
DOVERED	DOWNBEATS	DOWNTIME	DRABBING	DRAGHOUNDS
DOVERING	DOWNBOW	DOWNTIMES	DRABBISH	DRAGLINE
DOVERS	DOWNBOWS	DOWNTREND	DRABBLE	DRAGLINES
DOVES	DOWNBURST	DOWNTRENDS	DRABBLED	DRAGNET
DOVETAIL	DOWNBURSTS	DOWNTURN	DRABBLER	DRAGNETS
DOVETAILED	DOWNCAST	DOWNTURNS	DRABBLERS	DRAGOMAN
DOVETAILING	DOWNCASTS	DOWNWARD	DRABBLES	DRAGOMANS
DOVETAILINGS	DOWNED	DOWNWARDS	DRABBLING	DRAGON
DOVETAILS	DOWNER	DOWNWIND	DRABBLINGS	DRAGONESS
DOVIE	DOWNERS	DOWNY	DRABBY	DRAGONESSES
DOVIER	DOWNFALL	DOWP	DRABETTE	DRAGONET
DOVIEST	DOWNFALLS	DOWPS	DRABETTES	DRAGONETS
DOVING	DOWNFLOW	DOWRIES	DRABLER	DRAGONFLIES
DOVISH	DOWNFLOWS	DOWRY	DRABLERS	DRAGONFLY
DOW	DOWNFORCE	DOWS	DRABLY	DRAGONISE
DOWABLE	DOWNFORCES	DOWSE	DRABNESS	DRAGONISED
DOWAGER	DOWNGRADE	DOWSED	DRABNESSES	DRAGONISES
DOWAGERS	DOWNGRADED	DOWSER	DRABS	DRAGONISH
DOWAR	DOWNGRADES	DOWSERS	DRACHM	DRAGONISING
DOWARS	DOWNGRADING	DOWSES	DRACHMA	DRAGONISM
DOWD	DOWNHILL	DOWSET	DRACHMAE	DRAGONISMS
DOWDIER	DOWNHILLS	DOWSETS	DRACHMAI	DRAGONIZE
DOWDIES	DOWNHOLE	DOWSING	DRACHMAS	DRAGONIZED
DOWDIEST	DOWNIER	DOWT	DRACHMS	DRAGONIZES
DOWDILY	DOWNIEST	DOWTS	DRACONE	DRAGONIZING
DOWDINESS	DOWNINESS	DOXIES	DRACONES	DRAGONNE
DOWDINESSES	DOWNINESSES	DOXOLOGIES	DRACONIAN	DRAGONS
DOWDS	DOWNING	DOXOLOGY	DRACONIC	DRAGOON
DOWDY	DOWNLAND	DOXY	DRACONISM	DRAGOONED
DOWDYISH	DOWNLANDS	DOYEN	DRACONISMS	DRAGOONING
DOWDYISM	DOWNLOAD	DOYENNE	DRACONTIC	DRAGOONS
DOWDYISMS	DOWNLOADED	DOYENNES	DRAD	DRAGS
DOWED	DOWNLOADING	DOYENS	DRAFF	DRAGSMAN
DOWEL	DOWNLOADS	DOYLEY	DRAFFIER	DRAGSMEN
DOWELLED	DOWNMOST	DOYLEYS	DRAFFIEST	DRAGSTER
DOWELLING	DOWNPIPE	DOYLIES	DRAFFISH	DRAGSTERS
DOWELLINGS	DOWNPIPES	DOYLY	DRAFFS	DRAIL
DOWELS	DOWNPLAY	DOZE	DRAFFY	DRAILED
DOWER	DOWNPLAYED	DOZED	DRAFT	DRAILING
DOWERED	DOWNPLAYING	DOZEN	DRAFTED	DRAILS
DOWERING	DOWNPLAYS	DOZENED	DRAFTEE	DRAIN
DOWERLESS	DOWNPOUR	DOZENING	DRAFTEES	DRAINABLE
DOWERS	DOWNPOURS	DOZENS	DRAFTER	DRAINAGE
DOWF	DOWNRIGHT	DOZENTH	DRAFTERS	DRAINAGES
DOWFNESS	DOWNRUSH	DOZENTHS	DRAFTIER	DRAINED
DOWFNESSES	DOWNRUSHES	DOZER	DRAFTIEST	DRAINER
DOWIE	DOWNS	DOZERS	DRAFTING	DRAINERS
DOWIER	DOWNSHIFT	DOZES	DRAFTS	DRAINING
DOWIEST	DOWNSHIFTED	DOZIER	DRAFTSMAN	DRAINPIPE

The Chambers Dictionary is the authority for many longer words; see *OSW* Introduction, page xii

DRAINPIPES	DRAUGHT	DREAMILY	DRESSERS	DRILLED
DRAINS	DRAUGHTED	DREAMING	DRESSES	DRILLER
DRAISENE	DRAUGHTER	DREAMINGS	DRESSIER	DRILLERS
DRAISENES	DRAUGHTERS	DREAMLESS	DRESSIEST	DRILLING
DRAISINE	DRAUGHTIER	DREAMS	DRESSING	DRILLINGS
DRAISINES	DRAUGHTIEST	DREAMT	DRESSINGS	DRILLS
DRAKE	DRAUGHTING	DREAMTIME	DRESSMADE	DRILLSHIP
DRAKES	DRAUGHTS	DREAMTIMES	DRESSMAKE	DRILLSHIPS
DRAM	DRAUGHTY	DREAMY	DRESSMAKES	DRILY
DRAMA	DRAUNT	DREAR	DRESSMAKING	DRINK
DRAMAS	DRAUNTED	DREARE	DRESSMAKINGS	DRINKABLE
DRAMATIC	DRAUNTING	DREARER	DRESSY	DRINKER
DRAMATICS	DRAUNTS	DREARES	DREST	DRINKERS
DRAMATISE	DRAVE	DREAREST	DREVILL	DRINKING
DRAMATISED	DRAW	DREARIER	DREVILLS	DRINKINGS
DRAMATISES	DRAWABLE	DREARIEST	DREW	DRINKS
DRAMATISING	DRAWBACK	DREARILY	DREY	DRIP
DRAMATIST	DRAWBACKS	DREARING	DREYS	DRIPPED
DRAMATISTS	DRAWBAR	DREARINGS	DRIB	DRIPPIER
DRAMATIZE	DRAWBARS	DREARS	DRIBBED	DRIPPIEST
DRAMATIZED	DRAWEE	DREARY	DRIBBER	DRIPPING
DRAMATIZES	DRAWEES	DRECK	DRIBBERS	DRIPPINGS
DRAMATIZING	DRAWER	DRECKIER	DRIBBING	DRIPPY
DRAMATURG	DRAWERS	DRECKIEST	DRIBBLE	DRIPS
DRAMATURGS	DRAWING	DRECKS	DRIBBLED	DRISHEEN
DRAMMACH	DRAWINGS	DRECKY	DRIBBLER	DRISHEENS
DRAMMACHS	DRAWL	DREDGE	DRIBBLERS	DRIVABLE
DRAMMED	DRAWLED	DREDGED	DRIBBLES	DRIVE
DRAMMING	DRAWLER	DREDGER	DRIBBLET	DRIVEABLE
DRAMMOCK	DRAWLERS	DREDGERS	DRIBBLETS	DRIVEL
DRAMMOCKS	DRAWLING	DREDGES	DRIBBLIER	DRIVELLED
DRAMS	DRAWLS	DREDGING	DRIBBLIEST	DRIVELLER
DRANK	DRAWN	DREE	DRIBBLING	DRIVELLERS
DRANT	DRAWS	DREED	DRIBBLY	DRIVELLING
DRANTED	DRAY	DREEING	DRIBLET	DRIVELS
DRANTING	DRAYAGE	DREES	DRIBLETS	DRIVEN
DRANTS	DRAYAGES	DREG	DRIBS	DRIVER
DRAP	DRAYMAN	DREGGIER	DRICE	DRIVERS
DRAPE	DRAYMEN	DREGGIEST	DRICES	DRIVES
DRAPED	DRAYS	DREGGY	DRICKSIE	DRIVEWAY
DRAPER	DRAZEL	DREGS	DRICKSIER	DRIVEWAYS
DRAPERIED	DRAZELS	DREICH	DRICKSIEST	DRIVING
DRAPERIES	DREAD	DREICHER	DRIED	DRIZZLE
DRAPERS	DREADED	DREICHEST	DRIER	DRIZZLED
DRAPERY	DREADER	DREK	DRIERS	DRIZZLES
DRAPERYING	DREADERS	DREKS	DRIES	DRIZZLIER
DRAPES	DREADFUL	DRENCH	DRIEST	DRIZZLIEST
DRAPET	DREADING	DRENCHED	DRIFT	DRIZZLING
DRAPETS	DREADLESS	DRENCHER	DRIFTAGE	DRIZZLY
DRAPIER	DREADLY	DRENCHERS	DRIFTAGES	DROGER
DRAPIERS	DREADS	DRENCHES	DRIFTED	DROGERS
DRAPING	DREAM	DRENCHING	DRIFTER	DROGHER
DRAPPED	DREAMBOAT	DRENT	DRIFTERS	DROGHERS
DRAPPIE	DREAMBOATS	DREPANIUM	DRIFTIER	DROGUE
DRAPPIES	DREAMED	DREPANIUMS	DRIFTIEST	DROGUES
DRAPPING	DREAMER	DRERE	DRIFTING	DROGUET
DRAPPY	DREAMERIES	DRERES	DRIFTLESS	DROGUETS
DRAPS	DREAMERS	DRERIHEAD	DRIFTPIN	DROICH
DRASTIC	DREAMERY	DRERIHEADS	DRIFTPINS	DROICHIER
DRASTICS	DREAMFUL	DRESS	DRIFTS	DROICHIEST
DRAT	DREAMHOLE	DRESSAGE	DRIFTWOOD	DROICHS
DRATCHELL	DREAMHOLES	DRESSAGES	DRIFTWOODS	DROICHY
DRATCHELLS	DREAMIER	DRESSED	DRIFTY	DROIL
DRATTED	DREAMIEST	DRESSER	DRILL	DROILED

The Chambers Dictionary is the authority for many longer words; see *OSW* Introduction, page xii

DROILING	DROOPED	DROVINGS	DRUMBLED	DRYSALTER
DROILS	DROOPIER	DROW	DRUMBLES	DRYSALTERS
DROIT	DROOPIEST	DROWN	DRUMBLING	DSO
DROITS	DROOPILY	DROWNDED	DRUMFIRE	DSOBO
DROLE	DROOPING	DROWNED	DRUMFIRES	DSOBOS
DROLER	DROOPS	DROWNER	DRUMFISH	DSOMO
DROLES	DROOPY	DROWNERS	DRUMFISHES	DSOMOS
DROLEST	DROP	DROWNING	DRUMHEAD	DSOS
DROLL	DROPFLIES	DROWNINGS	DRUMHEADS	DUAD
DROLLED	DROPFLY	DROWNS	DRUMLIER	DUADS
DROLLER	DROPLET	DROWS	DRUMLIEST	DUAL
DROLLERIES	DROPLETS	DROWSE	DRUMLIN	DUALIN
DROLLERY	DROPOUT	DROWSED	DRUMLINS	DUALINS
DROLLEST	DROPOUTS	DROWSES	DRUMLY	DUALISM
DROLLING	DROPPED	DROWSIER	DRUMMED	DUALISMS
DROLLINGS	DROPPER	DROWSIEST	DRUMMER	DUALIST
DROLLISH	DROPPERS	DROWSIHED	DRUMMERS	DUALISTIC
DROLLNESS	DROPPING	DROWSIHEDS	DRUMMING	DUALISTS
DROLLNESSES	DROPPINGS	DROWSILY	DRUMMOCK	DUALITIES
DROLLS	DROPPLE	DROWSING	DRUMMOCKS	DUALITY
DROLLY	DROPPLES	DROWSY	DRUMS	DUALLED
DROME	DROPS	DRUB	DRUMSTICK	DUALLING
DROMEDARE	DROPSICAL	DRUBBED	DRUMSTICKS	DUALLY
DROMEDARES	DROPSIED	DRUBBING	DRUNK	DUALS
DROMEDARIES	DROPSIES	DRUBBINGS	DRUNKARD	DUAN
DROMEDARY	DROPSTONE	DRUBS	DRUNKARDS	DUANS
DROMES	DROPSTONES	DRUCKEN	DRUNKEN	DUAR
DROMIC	DROPSY	DRUDGE	DRUNKENLY	DUARCHIES
DROMICAL	DROPWISE	DRUDGED	DRUNKER	DUARCHY
DROMOI	DROSERA	DRUDGER	DRUNKEST	DUARS
DROMON	DROSERAS	DRUDGERIES	DRUNKS	DUB
DROMOND	DROSHKIES	DRUDGERS	DRUPE	DUBBED
DROMONDS	DROSHKY	DRUDGERY	DRUPEL	DUBBIN
DROMONS	DROSKIES	DRUDGES	DRUPELET	DUBBING
DROMOS	DROSKY	DRUDGING	DRUPELETS	DUBBINGS
DRONE	DROSS	DRUDGISM	DRUPELS	DUBBINS
DRONED	DROSSES	DRUDGISMS	DRUPES	DUBIETIES
DRONES	DROSSIER	DRUG	DRUSE	DUBIETY
DRONGO	DROSSIEST	DRUGGED	DRUSES	DUBIOSITIES
DRONGOES	DROSSY	DRUGGER	DRUSIER	DUBIOSITY
DRONGOS	DROSTDIES	DRUGGERS	DRUSIEST	DUBIOUS
DRONIER	DROSTDY	DRUGGET	DRUSY	DUBIOUSLY
DRONIEST	DROSTDYS	DRUGGETS	DRUTHERS	DUBITABLE
DRONING	DROUGHT	DRUGGIE	DRUXIER	DUBITABLY
DRONINGLY	DROUGHTIER	DRUGGIER	DRUXIEST	DUBITANCIES
DRONISH	DROUGHTIEST	DRUGGIES	DRUXY	DUBITANCY
DRONISHLY	DROUGHTS	DRUGGIEST	DRY	DUBITATE
DRONY	DROUGHTY	DRUGGING	DRYAD	DUBITATED
DROOG	DROUK	DRUGGIST	DRYADES	DUBITATES
DROOGISH	DROUKED	DRUGGISTS	DRYADS	DUBITATING
DROOGS	DROUKING	DRUGGY	DRYBEAT	DUBS
DROOK	DROUKINGS	DRUGS	DRYBEATEN	DUCAL
DROOKED	DROUKIT	DRUID	DRYBEATING	DUCALLY
DROOKING	DROUKS	DRUIDESS	DRYBEATS	DUCAT
DROOKINGS	DROUTH	DRUIDESSES	DRYER	DUCATOON
DROOKIT	DROUTHIER	DRUIDIC	DRYERS	DUCATOONS
DROOKS	DROUTHIEST	DRUIDICAL	DRYING	DUCATS
DROOL	DROUTHS	DRUIDISM	DRYINGS	DUCDAME
DROOLED	DROUTHY	DRUIDISMS	DRYISH	DUCE
DROOLING	DROVE	DRUIDS	DRYLY	DUCES
DROOLS	DROVER	DRUM	DRYMOUTH	DUCHESS
DROOME	DROVERS	DRUMBEAT	DRYMOUTHS	DUCHESSE
DROOMES	DROVES	DRUMBEATS	DRYNESS	DUCHESSES
DROOP	DROVING	DRUMBLE	DRYNESSES	DUCHIES

DUCHY	DUELLO	DULCIANAS	DUMDUMS	DUNGEONED
DUCK	DUELLOS	DULCIANS	DUMFOUND	DUNGEONER
DUCKBILL	DUELS	DULCIFIED	DUMFOUNDED	DUNGEONERS
DUCKBILLS	DUELSOME	DULCIFIES	DUMFOUNDING	DUNGEONING
DUCKED	DUENDE	DULCIFY	DUMFOUNDS	DUNGEONS
DUCKER	DUENDES	DULCIFYING	DUMKA	DUNGIER
DUCKERS	DUENNA	DULCIMER	DUMKY	DUNGIEST
DUCKIER	DUENNAS	DULCIMERS	DUMMERER	DUNGING
DUCKIES	DUES	DULCITE	DUMMERERS	DUNGMERE
DUCKIEST	DUET	DULCITES	DUMMIED	DUNGMERES
DUCKING	DUETS	DULCITOL	DUMMIER	DUNGS
DUCKINGS	DUETT	DULCITOLS	DUMMIES	DUNGY
DUCKLING	DUETTED	DULCITUDE	DUMMIEST	DUNITE
DUCKLINGS	DUETTI	DULCITUDES	DUMMINESS	DUNITES
DUCKMOLE	DUETTING	DULCOSE	DUMMINESSES	DUNK
DUCKMOLES	DUETTINO	DULCOSES	DUMMY	DUNKED
DUCKS	DUETTINOS	DULE	DUMMYING	DUNKER
DUCKSHOVE	DUETTIST	DULES	DUMOSE	DUNKERS
DUCKSHOVED	DUETTISTS	DULIA	DUMOSITIES	DUNKING
DUCKSHOVES	DUETTO	DULIAS	DUMOSITY	DUNKS
DUCKSHOVING	DUETTOS	DULL	DUMOUS	DUNLIN
DUCKWEED	DUETTS	DULLARD	DUMP	DUNLINS
DUCKWEEDS	DUFF	DULLARDS	DUMPBIN	DUNNAGE
DUCKY	DUFFED	DULLED	DUMPBINS	DUNNAGES
DUCT	DUFFEL	DULLER	DUMPED	DUNNAKIN
DUCTED	DUFFELS	DULLEST	DUMPER	DUNNAKINS
DUCTILE	DUFFER	DULLIER	DUMPERS	DUNNART
DUCTILITIES	DUFFERDOM	DULLIEST	DUMPIER	DUNNARTS
DUCTILITY	DUFFERDOMS	DULLING	DUMPIES	DUNNED
DUCTING	DUFFERISM	DULLISH	DUMPIEST	DUNNER
DUCTLESS	DUFFERISMS	DULLNESS	DUMPINESS	DUNNEST
DUCTS	DUFFERS	DULLNESSES	DUMPINESSES	DUNNIER
DUD	DUFFEST	DULLS	DUMPING	DUNNIES
DUDDER	DUFFING	DULLY	DUMPISH	DUNNIEST
DUDDERIES	DUFFINGS	DULNESS	DUMPISHLY	DUNNING
DUDDERS	DUFFLE	DULNESSES	DUMPLE	DUNNINGS
DUDDERY	DUFFLES	DULOCRACIES	DUMPLED	DUNNISH
DUDDIE	DUFFS	DULOCRACY	DUMPLES	DUNNITE
DUDDIER	DUG	DULOSES	DUMPLING	DUNNITES
DUDDIEST	DUGONG	DULOSIS	DUMPLINGS	DUNNO
DUDDY	DUGONGS	DULOTIC	DUMPS	DUNNOCK
DUDE	DUGOUT	DULSE	DUMPSTER	DUNNOCKS
DUDEEN	DUGOUTS	DULSES	DUMPSTERS	DUNNY
DUDEENS	DUGS	DULY	DUMPY	DUNS
DUDES	DUIKER	DUMA	DUN	DUNSH
DUDGEON	DUIKERS	DUMAIST	DUNCE	DUNSHED
DUDGEONS	DUING	DUMAISTS	DUNCEDOM	DUNSHES
DUDHEEN	DUKE	DUMAS	DUNCEDOMS	DUNSHING
DUDHEENS	DUKED	DUMB	DUNCERIES	DUNT
DUDISH	DUKEDOM	DUMBED	DUNCERY	DUNTED
DUDISM	DUKEDOMS	DUMBER	DUNCES	DUNTING
DUDISMS	DUKELING	DUMBEST	DUNCH	DUNTS
DUDS	DUKELINGS	DUMBFOUND	DUNCHED	DUO
DUE	DUKERIES	DUMBFOUNDED	DUNCHES	DUODECIMO
DUED	DUKERY	DUMBFOUNDING	DUNCHING	DUODECIMOS
DUEFUL	DUKES	DUMBFOUNDS	DUNDER	DUODENA
DUEL	DUKESHIP	DUMBING	DUNDERS	DUODENAL
DUELLED	DUKESHIPS	DUMBLY	DUNE	DUODENARY
DUELLER	DUKING	DUMBNESS	DUNES	DUODENUM
DUELLERS	DULCAMARA	DUMBNESSES	DUNG	DUOLOGUE
DUELLING	DULCAMARAS	DUMBO	DUNGAREE	DUOLOGUES
DUELLINGS	DULCET	DUMBOS	DUNGAREES	DUOMI
DUELLIST	DULCIAN	DUMBS	DUNGED	DUOMO
DUELLISTS	DULCIANA	DUMDUM	DUNGEON	DUOMOS

DUOPOLIES	DURDUM	DUSTCART	DWARFER	DYKIER
DUOPOLY	DURDUMS	DUSTCARTS	DWARFEST	DYKIEST
DUOS	DURE	DUSTED	DWARFING	DYKING
DUOTONE	DURED	DUSTER	DWARFISH	DYNAMIC
DUOTONES	DUREFUL	DUSTERS	DWARFISM	DYNAMICAL
DUP	DURES	DUSTIER	DWARFISMS	DYNAMICS
DUPABLE	DURESS	DUSTIEST	DWARFS	DYNAMISE
DUPATTA	DURESSE	DUSTILY	DWARVES	DYNAMISED
DUPATTAS	DURESSES	DUSTINESS	DWAUM	DYNAMISES
DUPE	DURGAN	DUSTINESSES	DWAUMED	DYNAMISING
DUPED	DURGANS	DUSTING	DWAUMING	DYNAMISM
DUPER	DURGIER	DUSTLESS	DWAUMS	DYNAMISMS
DUPERIES	DURGIEST	DUSTMAN	DWEEB	DYNAMIST
DUPERS	DURGY	DUSTMEN	DWEEBS	DYNAMISTS
DUPERY	DURIAN	DUSTPROOF	DWELL	DYNAMITE
DUPES	DURIANS	DUSTS	DWELLED	DYNAMITED
DUPING	DURING	DUSTSHEET	DWELLER	DYNAMITER
DUPION	DURION	DUSTSHEETS	DWELLERS	DYNAMITERS
DUPIONS	DURIONS	DUSTY	DWELLING	DYNAMITES
DUPLE	DURMAST	DUTCH	DWELLINGS	DYNAMITING
DUPLET	DURMASTS	DUTCHES	DWELLS	DYNAMIZE
DUPLETS	DURN	DUTEOUS	DWELT	DYNAMIZED
DUPLEX	DURNS	DUTEOUSLY	DWILE	DYNAMIZES
DUPLEXER	DURO	DUTIABLE	DWILES	DYNAMIZING
DUPLEXERS	DUROS	DUTIED	DWINDLE	DYNAMO
DUPLEXES	DUROY	DUTIES	DWINDLED	DYNAMOS
DUPLICAND	DUROYS	DUTIFUL	DWINDLES	DYNAMOTOR
DUPLICANDS	DURRA	DUTIFULLY	DWINDLING	DYNAMOTORS
DUPLICATE	DURRAS	DUTY	DWINE	DYNAST
DUPLICATED	DURRIE	DUUMVIR	DWINED	DYNASTIC
DUPLICATES	DURRIES	DUUMVIRAL	DWINES	DYNASTIES
DUPLICATING	DURST	DUUMVIRI	DWINING	DYNASTS
DUPLICITIES	DURUKULI	DUUMVIRS	DYABLE	DYNASTY
DUPLICITY	DURUKULIS	DUVET	DYAD	DYNATRON
DUPLIED	DURUM	DUVETINE	DYADIC	DYNATRONS
DUPLIES	DURUMS	DUVETINES	DYADS	DYNE
DUPLY	DUSH	DUVETS	DYARCHIES	DYNES
DUPLYING	DUSHED	DUVETYN	DYARCHY	DYNODE
DUPONDII	DUSHES	DUVETYNE	DYBBUK	DYNODES
DUPONDIUS	DUSHING	DUVETYNES	DYBBUKIM	DYSCHROA
DUPPED	DUSK	DUVETYNS	DYBBUKS	DYSCHROAS
DUPPIES	DUSKED	DUX	DYE	DYSCHROIA
DUPPING	DUSKEN	DUXELLES	DYEABLE	DYSCHROIAS
DUPPY	DUSKENED	DUXES	DYED	DYSCRASIA
DUPS	DUSKENING	DUYKER	DYEING	DYSCRASIAS
DURA	DUSKENS	DUYKERS	DYEINGS	DYSENTERIES
DURABLE	DUSKER	DVANDVA	DYELINE	DYSENTERY
DURABLES	DUSKEST	DVANDVAS	DYELINES	DYSGENIC
DURABLY	DUSKIER	DVORNIK	DYER	DYSGENICS
DURAL	DUSKIEST	DVORNIKS	DYERS	DYSLECTIC
DURALS	DUSKILY	DWALE	DYES	DYSLECTICS
DURALUMIN	DUSKINESS	DWALES	DYESTER	DYSLEXIA
DURALUMINS	DUSKINESSES	DWALM	DYESTERS	DYSLEXIAS
DURAMEN	DUSKING	DWALMED	DYESTUFF	DYSLEXIC
DURAMENS	DUSKISH	DWALMING	DYESTUFFS	DYSLEXICS
DURANCE	DUSKISHLY	DWALMS	DYING	DYSLOGIES
DURANCES	DUSKLY	DWAM	DYINGLY	DYSLOGY
DURANT	DUSKNESS	DWAMMED	DYINGNESS	DYSMELIA
DURANTS	DUSKNESSES	DWAMMING	DYINGNESSES	DYSMELIAS
DURAS	DUSKS	DWAMS	DYINGS	DYSMELIC
DURATION	DUSKY	DWANG	DYKE	DYSODIL
DURATIONS	DUST	DWANGS	DYKED	DYSODILE
DURBAR	DUSTBIN	DWARF	DYKES	DYSODILES
DURBARS	DUSTBINS	DWARFED	DYKEY	DYSODILS

The Chambers Dictionary is the authority for many longer words; see *OSW* Introduction, page xii

DYSODYLE
DYSODYLES
DYSPATHIES
DYSPATHY
DYSPEPSIA
DYSPEPSIAS
DYSPEPSIES
DYSPEPSY
DYSPEPTIC
DYSPEPTICS
DYSPHAGIA
DYSPHAGIAS
DYSPHAGIC
DYSPHAGIES
DYSPHAGY

DYSPHASIA
DYSPHASIAS
DYSPHONIA
DYSPHONIAS
DYSPHONIC
DYSPHORIA
DYSPHORIAS
DYSPHORIC
DYSPLASIA
DYSPLASIAS
DYSPNEA
DYSPNEAL
DYSPNEAS
DYSPNEIC
DYSPNOEA

DYSPNOEAL
DYSPNOEAS
DYSPNOEIC
DYSPRAXIA
DYSPRAXIAS
DYSTECTIC
DYSTHESIA
DYSTHESIAS
DYSTHETIC
DYSTHYMIA
DYSTHYMIAS
DYSTHYMIC
DYSTOCIA
DYSTOCIAS
DYSTONIA

DYSTONIAS
DYSTONIC
DYSTOPIA
DYSTOPIAN
DYSTOPIAS
DYSTROPHIES
DYSTROPHY
DYSURIA
DYSURIAS
DYSURIC
DYSURIES
DYSURY
DYTISCID
DYTISCIDS
DYVOUR

DYVOURIES
DYVOURS
DYVOURY
DZEREN
DZERENS
DZHO
DZHOS
DZIGGETAI
DZIGGETAIS
DZO
DZOS

E

EA
EACH
EACHWHERE
EADISH
EADISHES
EAGER
EAGERER
EAGEREST
EAGERLY
EAGERNESS
EAGERNESSES
EAGERS
EAGLE
EAGLES
EAGLET
EAGLETS
EAGLEWOOD
EAGLEWOODS
EAGRE
EAGRES
EALDORMAN
EALDORMEN
EALE
EALES
EAN
EANED
EANING
EANLING
EANLINGS
EANS
EAR
EARACHE
EARACHES
EARBASH
EARBASHED
EARBASHES
EARBASHING
EARBOB
EARBOBS
EARCON
EARCONS
EARD
EARDED
EARDING
EARDROP
EARDROPS
EARDRUM
EARDRUMS
EARDS
EARED
EARFLAP
EARFLAPS
EARFUL
EARFULS

EARING
EARINGS
EARL
EARLAP
EARLAPS
EARLDOM
EARLDOMS
EARLESS
EARLIER
EARLIES
EARLIEST
EARLINESS
EARLINESSES
EARLOBE
EARLOBES
EARLOCK
EARLOCKS
EARLS
EARLY
EARMARK
EARMARKED
EARMARKING
EARMARKS
EARMUFFS
EARN
EARNED
EARNER
EARNERS
EARNEST
EARNESTLY
EARNESTS
EARNING
EARNINGS
EARNS
EARPHONE
EARPHONES
EARPICK
EARPICKS
EARPIECE
EARPIECES
EARPLUG
EARPLUGS
EARRING
EARRINGS
EARS
EARSHOT
EARSHOTS
EARST
EARTH
EARTHBORN
EARTHED
EARTHEN
EARTHFALL
EARTHFALLS

EARTHFAST
EARTHFLAX
EARTHFLAXES
EARTHIER
EARTHIEST
EARTHING
EARTHLIER
EARTHLIES
EARTHLIEST
EARTHLING
EARTHLINGS
EARTHLY
EARTHMAN
EARTHMEN
EARTHS
EARTHWARD
EARTHWARDS
EARTHWAX
EARTHWAXES
EARTHWOLF
EARTHWOLVES
EARTHWORK
EARTHWORKS
EARTHWORM
EARTHWORMS
EARTHY
EARWAX
EARWAXES
EARWIG
EARWIGGED
EARWIGGING
EARWIGGY
EARWIGS
EAS
EASE
EASED
EASEFUL
EASEL
EASELESS
EASELS
EASEMENT
EASEMENTS
EASES
EASIER
EASIEST
EASILY
EASINESS
EASINESSES
EASING
EASLE
EASLES
EASSEL
EASSIL
EAST

EASTBOUND
EASTED
EASTER
EASTERLIES
EASTERLY
EASTERN
EASTERNER
EASTERNERS
EASTING
EASTINGS
EASTLAND
EASTLIN
EASTLING
EASTLINGS
EASTLINS
EASTMOST
EASTS
EASTWARD
EASTWARDS
EASY
EAT
EATABLE
EATABLES
EATAGE
EATAGES
EATCHE
EATCHES
EATEN
EATER
EATERIES
EATERS
EATERY
EATH
EATHE
EATHLY
EATING
EATINGS
EATS
EAU
EAUS
EAUX
EAVES
EAVESDRIP
EAVESDRIPS
EAVESDROP
EAVESDROPPED
EAVESDROPPING
EAVESDROPPINGS
EAVESDROPS
EBAUCHE
EBAUCHES
EBB
EBBED
EBBING

EBBLESS
EBBS
EBBTIDE
EBBTIDES
EBENEZER
EBENEZERS
EBENISTE
EBENISTES
EBIONISE
EBIONISED
EBIONISES
EBIONISING
EBIONISM
EBIONISMS
EBIONITIC
EBIONIZE
EBIONIZED
EBIONIZES
EBIONIZING
EBON
EBONICS
EBONIES
EBONISE
EBONISED
EBONISES
EBONISING
EBONIST
EBONISTS
EBONITE
EBONITES
EBONIZE
EBONIZED
EBONIZES
EBONIZING
EBONS
EBONY
EBRIATE
EBRIATED
EBRIETIES
EBRIETY
EBRILLADE
EBRILLADES
EBRIOSE
EBRIOSITIES
EBRIOSITY
EBULLIENT
EBURNEAN
EBURNEOUS
ECAD
ECADS
ECARTE
ECARTES
ECAUDATE
ECBOLE

ECBOLES	ECHOLESS	ECOSSAISES	ECTROPIONS	EDICTAL
ECBOLIC	ECHT	ECOSTATE	ECTROPIUM	EDICTALLY
ECBOLICS	ECLAIR	ECOSYSTEM	ECTROPIUMS	EDICTS
ECCE	ECLAIRS	ECOSYSTEMS	ECTYPAL	EDIFICE
ECCENTRIC	ECLAMPSIA	ECOTOXIC	ECTYPE	EDIFICES
ECCENTRICS	ECLAMPSIAS	ECOTYPE	ECTYPES	EDIFICIAL
ECCLESIA	ECLAMPSIES	ECOTYPES	ECU	EDIFIED
ECCLESIAE	ECLAMPSY	ECRASEUR	ECUELLE	EDIFIER
ECCLESIAL	ECLAMPTIC	ECRASEURS	ECUELLES	EDIFIERS
ECCO	ECLAT	ECRITOIRE	ECUMENIC	EDIFIES
ECCRINE	ECLATS	ECRITOIRES	ECUMENICS	EDIFY
ECCRISES	ECLECTIC	ECRU	ECUMENISM	EDIFYING
ECCRISIS	ECLECTICS	ECRUS	ECUMENISMS	EDILE
ECCRITIC	ECLIPSE	ECSTASES	ECURIE	EDILES
ECCRITICS	ECLIPSED	ECSTASIED	ECURIES	EDIT
ECDYSES	ECLIPSES	ECSTASIES	ECUS	EDITED
ECDYSIAST	ECLIPSING	ECSTASIS	ECZEMA	EDITING
ECDYSIASTS	ECLIPTIC	ECSTASISE	ECZEMAS	EDITION
ECDYSIS	ECLIPTICS	ECSTASISED	EDACIOUS	EDITIONS
ECH	ECLOGITE	ECSTASISES	EDACITIES	EDITOR
ECHAPPE	ECLOGITES	ECSTASISING	EDACITY	EDITORIAL
ECHAPPES	ECLOGUE	ECSTASIZE	EDAPHIC	EDITORIALS
ECHE	ECLOGUES	ECSTASIZED	EDDIED	EDITORS
ECHED	ECLOSE	ECSTASIZES	EDDIES	EDITRESS
ECHELON	ECLOSED	ECSTASIZING	EDDISH	EDITRESSES
ECHELONS	ECLOSES	ECSTASY	EDDISHES	EDITS
ECHES	ECLOSING	ECSTASYING	EDDO	EDUCABLE
ECHEVERIA	ECLOSION	ECSTATIC	EDDOES	EDUCATE
ECHEVERIAS	ECLOSIONS	ECSTATICS	EDDY	EDUCATED
ECHIDNA	ECOCIDE	ECTASES	EDDYING	EDUCATES
ECHIDNAS	ECOCIDES	ECTASIS	EDELWEISS	EDUCATING
ECHIDNINE	ECOD	ECTHYMA	EDELWEISSES	EDUCATION
ECHIDNINES	ECOFREAK	ECTHYMAS	EDEMA	EDUCATIONS
ECHINATE	ECOFREAKS	ECTOBLAST	EDEMAS	EDUCATIVE
ECHINATED	ECOLOGIC	ECTOBLASTS	EDEMATA	EDUCATOR
ECHING	ECOLOGIES	ECTOCRINE	EDEMATOSE	EDUCATORS
ECHINI	ECOLOGIST	ECTOCRINES	EDEMATOUS	EDUCATORY
ECHINOID	ECOLOGISTS	ECTODERM	EDENTAL	EDUCE
ECHINOIDS	ECOLOGY	ECTODERMS	EDENTATE	EDUCED
ECHINUS	ECONOMIC	ECTOGENIC	EDENTATES	EDUCEMENT
ECHINUSES	ECONOMICS	ECTOGENIES	EDGE	EDUCEMENTS
ECHO	ECONOMIES	ECTOGENY	EDGEBONE	EDUCES
ECHOED	ECONOMISE	ECTOMORPH	EDGEBONES	EDUCIBLE
ECHOER	ECONOMISED	ECTOMORPHS	EDGED	EDUCING
ECHOERS	ECONOMISES	ECTOPHYTE	EDGELESS	EDUCT
ECHOES	ECONOMISING	ECTOPHYTES	EDGER	EDUCTION
ECHOGRAM	ECONOMISM	ECTOPIA	EDGERS	EDUCTIONS
ECHOGRAMS	ECONOMISMS	ECTOPIAS	EDGES	EDUCTOR
ECHOIC	ECONOMIST	ECTOPIC	EDGEWAYS	EDUCTORS
ECHOING	ECONOMISTS	ECTOPIES	EDGEWISE	EDUCTS
ECHOISE	ECONOMIZE	ECTOPLASM	EDGIER	EDUSKUNTA
ECHOISED	ECONOMIZED	ECTOPLASMS	EDGIEST	EDUSKUNTAS
ECHOISES	ECONOMIZES	ECTOPY	EDGINESS	EE
ECHOISING	ECONOMIZING	ECTOSARC	EDGINESSES	EECH
ECHOISM	ECONOMY	ECTOSARCS	EDGING	EECHED
ECHOISMS	ECONUT	ECTOTHERM	EDGINGS	EECHES
ECHOIST	ECONUTS	ECTOTHERMS	EDGY	EECHING
ECHOISTS	ECOPHOBIA	ECTOZOA	EDH	EEK
ECHOIZE	ECOPHOBIAS	ECTOZOAN	EDHS	EEL
ECHOIZED	ECORCHE	ECTOZOANS	EDIBILITIES	EELFARE
ECHOIZES	ECORCHES	ECTOZOIC	EDIBILITY	EELFARES
ECHOIZING	ECOSPHERE	ECTOZOON	EDIBLE	EELGRASS
ECHOLALIA	ECOSPHERES	ECTROPIC	EDIBLES	EELGRASSES
ECHOLALIAS	ECOSSAISE	ECTROPION	EDICT	EELIER

EELIEST	EFFIERCING	EGG	EGRESS	EISELS
EELPOUT	EFFIGIES	EGGAR	EGRESSES	EITHER
EELPOUTS	EFFIGY	EGGARS	EGRESSION	EJACULATE
EELS	EFFING	EGGCUP	EGRESSIONS	EJACULATED
EELWORM	EFFLUENCE	EGGCUPS	EGRET	EJACULATES
EELWORMS	EFFLUENCES	EGGED	EGRETS	EJACULATING
EELWRACK	EFFLUENT	EGGER	EH	EJECT
EELWRACKS	EFFLUENTS	EGGERIES	EHED	EJECTA
EELY	EFFLUVIA	EGGERS	EHING	EJECTED
EEN	EFFLUVIAL	EGGERY	EHS	EJECTING
EERIE	EFFLUVIUM	EGGHEAD	EIDENT	EJECTION
EERIER	EFFLUX	EGGHEADS	EIDER	EJECTIONS
EERIEST	EFFLUXES	EGGIER	EIDERDOWN	EJECTIVE
EERILY	EFFLUXION	EGGIEST	EIDERDOWNS	EJECTMENT
EERINESS	EFFLUXIONS	EGGING	EIDERS	EJECTMENTS
EERINESSES	EFFORCE	EGGLER	EIDETIC	EJECTOR
EERY	EFFORCED	EGGLERS	EIDETICS	EJECTORS
EEVEN	EFFORCES	EGGMASS	EIDOGRAPH	EJECTS
EEVENS	EFFORCING	EGGMASSES	EIDOGRAPHS	EKE
EEVN	EFFORT	EGGNOG	EIDOLA	EKED
EEVNING	EFFORTFUL	EGGNOGS	EIDOLON	EKES
EEVNINGS	EFFORTS	EGGS	EIGENTONE	EKING
EEVNS	EFFRAIDE	EGGSHELL	EIGENTONES	EKISTIC
EF	EFFRAY	EGGSHELLS	EIGHT	EKISTICS
EFF	EFFRAYS	EGGWASH	EIGHTEEN	EKKA
EFFABLE	EFFS	EGGWASHES	EIGHTEENS	EKKAS
EFFACE	EFFULGE	EGGY	EIGHTFOIL	EKLOGITE
EFFACED	EFFULGED	EGIS	EIGHTFOILS	EKLOGITES
EFFACES	EFFULGENT	EGISES	EIGHTFOLD	EKPHRASES
EFFACING	EFFULGES	EGLANTINE	EIGHTFOOT	EKPHRASIS
EFFECT	EFFULGING	EGLANTINES	EIGHTH	EKPWELE
EFFECTED	EFFUSE	EGLATERE	EIGHTHLY	EKPWELES
EFFECTER	EFFUSED	EGLATERES	EIGHTHS	EKUELE
EFFECTERS	EFFUSES	EGMA	EIGHTIES	EL
EFFECTING	EFFUSING	EGMAS	EIGHTIETH	ELABORATE
EFFECTIVE	EFFUSION	EGO	EIGHTIETHS	ELABORATED
EFFECTIVES	EFFUSIONS	EGOISM	EIGHTS	ELABORATES
EFFECTOR	EFFUSIVE	EGOISMS	EIGHTSMAN	ELABORATING
EFFECTORS	EFS	EGOIST	EIGHTSMEN	ELAEOLITE
EFFECTS	EFT	EGOISTIC	EIGHTSOME	ELAEOLITES
EFFECTUAL	EFTEST	EGOISTS	EIGHTSOMES	ELAN
EFFED	EFTS	EGOITIES	EIGHTVO	ELANCE
EFFEIR	EFTSOONS	EGOITY	EIGHTVOS	ELANCED
EFFEIRED	EGAD	EGOMANIA	EIGHTY	ELANCES
EFFEIRING	EGAL	EGOMANIAC	EIGNE	ELANCING
EFFEIRS	EGALITIES	EGOMANIACS	EIK	ELAND
EFFENDI	EGALITY	EGOMANIAS	EIKED	ELANDS
EFFENDIS	EGALLY	EGOS	EIKING	ELANET
EFFERE	EGAREMENT	EGOTHEISM	EIKON	ELANETS
EFFERED	EGAREMENTS	EGOTHEISMS	EIKONS	ELANS
EFFERENCE	EGENCE	EGOTISE	EIKS	ELAPHINE
EFFERENCES	EGENCES	EGOTISED	EILD	ELAPSE
EFFERENT	EGENCIES	EGOTISES	EILDING	ELAPSED
EFFERES	EGENCY	EGOTISING	EILDINGS	ELAPSES
EFFERING	EGER	EGOTISM	EILDS	ELAPSING
EFFETE	EGERS	EGOTISMS	EINE	ELASTANCE
EFFETELY	EGEST	EGOTIST	EIRACK	ELASTANCES
EFFICACIES	EGESTA	EGOTISTIC	EIRACKS	ELASTASE
EFFICACY	EGESTED	EGOTISTS	EIRENIC	ELASTASES
EFFICIENT	EGESTING	EGOTIZE	EIRENICON	ELASTIC
EFFICIENTS	EGESTION	EGOTIZED	EIRENICONS	ELASTICS
EFFIERCE	EGESTIONS	EGOTIZES	EISEL	ELASTIN
EFFIERCED	EGESTIVE	EGOTIZING	EISELL	ELASTINS
EFFIERCES	EGESTS	EGREGIOUS	EISELLS	ELASTOMER

The Chambers Dictionary is the authority for many longer words; see *OSW* Introduction, page xii

ELASTOMERS	ELECTRISING	ELEVEN	ELLS	ELSHINS
ELATE	ELECTRIZE	ELEVENS	ELLWAND	ELSIN
ELATED	ELECTRIZED	ELEVENSES	ELLWANDS	ELSINS
ELATEDLY	ELECTRIZES	ELEVENTH	ELM	ELT
ELATER	ELECTRIZING	ELEVENTHS	ELMEN	ELTCHI
ELATERIN	ELECTRO	ELEVON	ELMIER	ELTCHIS
ELATERINS	ELECTRODE	ELEVONS	ELMIEST	ELTS
ELATERITE	ELECTRODES	ELF	ELMS	ELUANT
ELATERITES	ELECTRON	ELFED	ELMWOOD	ELUANTS
ELATERIUM	ELECTRONS	ELFHOOD	ELMWOODS	ELUATE
ELATERIUMS	ELECTROS	ELFHOODS	ELMY	ELUATES
ELATERS	ELECTRUM	ELFIN	ELOCUTE	ELUCIDATE
ELATES	ELECTRUMS	ELFING	ELOCUTED	ELUCIDATED
ELATING	ELECTS	ELFINS	ELOCUTES	ELUCIDATES
ELATION	ELECTUARIES	ELFISH	ELOCUTING	ELUCIDATING
ELATIONS	ELECTUARY	ELFLAND	ELOCUTION	ELUDE
ELATIVE	ELEGANCE	ELFLANDS	ELOCUTIONS	ELUDED
ELATIVES	ELEGANCES	ELFLOCKS	ELOCUTORY	ELUDER
ELBOW	ELEGANCIES	ELFS	ELOGE	ELUDERS
ELBOWED	ELEGANCY	ELIAD	ELOGES	ELUDES
ELBOWING	ELEGANT	ELIADS	ELOGIES	ELUDIBLE
ELBOWS	ELEGANTLY	ELICIT	ELOGIST	ELUDING
ELCHEE	ELEGIAC	ELICITED	ELOGISTS	ELUENT
ELCHEES	ELEGIACAL	ELICITING	ELOGIUM	ELUENTS
ELCHI	ELEGIACS	ELICITOR	ELOGIUMS	ELUSION
ELCHIS	ELEGIAST	ELICITORS	ELOGY	ELUSIONS
ELD	ELEGIASTS	ELICITS	ELOIGN	ELUSIVE
ELDER	ELEGIES	ELIDE	ELOIGNED	ELUSIVELY
ELDERLIES	ELEGISE	ELIDED	ELOIGNER	ELUSORY
ELDERLY	ELEGISED	ELIDES	ELOIGNERS	ELUTE
ELDERS	ELEGISES	ELIDING	ELOIGNING	ELUTED
ELDERSHIP	ELEGISING	ELIGIBLE	ELOIGNS	ELUTES
ELDERSHIPS	ELEGIST	ELIGIBLES	ELOIN	ELUTING
ELDEST	ELEGISTS	ELIGIBLY	ELOINED	ELUTION
ELDIN	ELEGIT	ELIMINANT	ELOINER	ELUTIONS
ELDING	ELEGITS	ELIMINANTS	ELOINERS	ELUTOR
ELDINGS	ELEGIZE	ELIMINATE	ELOINING	ELUTORS
ELDINS	ELEGIZED	ELIMINATED	ELOINMENT	ELUTRIATE
ELDRITCH	ELEGIZES	ELIMINATES	ELOINMENTS	ELUTRIATED
ELDS	ELEGIZING	ELIMINATING	ELOINS	ELUTRIATES
ELECT	ELEGY	ELISION	ELONGATE	ELUTRIATING
ELECTABLE	ELEMENT	ELISIONS	ELONGATED	ELUVIA
ELECTED	ELEMENTAL	ELITE	ELONGATES	ELUVIAL
ELECTING	ELEMENTALS	ELITES	ELONGATING	ELUVIUM
ELECTION	ELEMENTS	ELITISM	ELOPE	ELUVIUMS
ELECTIONS	ELEMI	ELITISMS	ELOPED	ELVAN
ELECTIVE	ELEMIS	ELITIST	ELOPEMENT	ELVANITE
ELECTIVES	ELENCH	ELITISTS	ELOPEMENTS	ELVANITES
ELECTOR	ELENCHI	ELIXIR	ELOPER	ELVANS
ELECTORAL	ELENCHS	ELIXIRS	ELOPERS	ELVER
ELECTORS	ELENCHUS	ELK	ELOPES	ELVERS
ELECTRESS	ELENCTIC	ELKHOUND	ELOPING	ELVES
ELECTRESSES	ELEPHANT	ELKHOUNDS	ELOPS	ELVISH
ELECTRET	ELEPHANTS	ELKS	ELOPSES	ELYTRA
ELECTRETS	ELEUTHERI	ELL	ELOQUENCE	ELYTRAL
ELECTRIC	ELEVATE	ELLAGIC	ELOQUENCES	ELYTRON
ELECTRICS	ELEVATED	ELLIPSE	ELOQUENT	ELYTRUM
ELECTRIFIED	ELEVATES	ELLIPSES	ELPEE	EM
ELECTRIFIES	ELEVATING	ELLIPSIS	ELPEES	EMACIATE
ELECTRIFY	ELEVATION	ELLIPSOID	ELS	EMACIATED
ELECTRIFYING	ELEVATIONS	ELLIPSOIDS	ELSE	EMACIATES
ELECTRISE	ELEVATOR	ELLIPTIC	ELSEWHERE	EMACIATING
ELECTRISED	ELEVATORS	ELLOPS	ELSEWISE	EMAIL
ELECTRISES	ELEVATORY	ELLOPSES	ELSHIN	EMAILED

EMAILING	EMBASSADE	EMBLEMIZED	EMBOWED	EMBROGLIO
EMAILS	EMBASSADES	EMBLEMIZES	EMBOWEL	EMBROGLIOS
EMALANGENI	EMBASSAGE	EMBLEMIZING	EMBOWELLED	EMBROIDER
EMANANT	EMBASSAGES	EMBLEMS	EMBOWELLING	EMBROIDERED
EMANATE	EMBASSIES	EMBLIC	EMBOWELS	EMBROIDERING
EMANATED	EMBASSY	EMBLICS	EMBOWER	EMBROIDERS
EMANATES	EMBASTE	EMBLOOM	EMBOWERED	EMBROIL
EMANATING	EMBATHE	EMBLOOMED	EMBOWERING	EMBROILED
EMANATION	EMBATHED	EMBLOOMING	EMBOWERS	EMBROILING
EMANATIONS	EMBATHES	EMBLOOMS	EMBOWING	EMBROILS
EMANATIST	EMBATHING	EMBLOSSOM	EMBOWS	EMBROWN
EMANATISTS	EMBATTLE	EMBLOSSOMED	EMBOX	EMBROWNED
EMANATIVE	EMBATTLED	EMBLOSSOMING	EMBOXED	EMBROWNING
EMANATORY	EMBATTLES	EMBLOSSOMS	EMBOXES	EMBROWNS
EMBACE	EMBATTLING	EMBODIED	EMBOXING	EMBRUE
EMBACES	EMBAY	EMBODIES	EMBRACE	EMBRUED
EMBACING	EMBAYED	EMBODY	EMBRACED	EMBRUES
EMBAIL	EMBAYING	EMBODYING	EMBRACEOR	EMBRUING
EMBAILED	EMBAYLD	EMBOG	EMBRACEORS	EMBRUTE
EMBAILING	EMBAYMENT	EMBOGGED	EMBRACER	EMBRUTED
EMBAILS	EMBAYMENTS	EMBOGGING	EMBRACERIES	EMBRUTES
EMBALE	EMBAYS	EMBOGS	EMBRACERS	EMBRUTING
EMBALED	EMBED	EMBOGUE	EMBRACERY	EMBRYO
EMBALES	EMBEDDED	EMBOGUED	EMBRACES	EMBRYOID
EMBALING	EMBEDDING	EMBOGUES	EMBRACING	EMBRYOIDS
EMBALL	EMBEDDINGS	EMBOGUING	EMBRACIVE	EMBRYON
EMBALLED	EMBEDMENT	EMBOIL	EMBRAID	EMBRYONAL
EMBALLING	EMBEDMENTS	EMBOILED	EMBRAIDED	EMBRYONIC
EMBALLINGS	EMBEDS	EMBOILING	EMBRAIDING	EMBRYONS
EMBALLS	EMBELLISH	EMBOILS	EMBRAIDS	EMBRYOS
EMBALM	EMBELLISHED	EMBOLDEN	EMBRANGLE	EMBRYOTIC
EMBALMED	EMBELLISHES	EMBOLDENED	EMBRANGLED	EMBUS
EMBALMER	EMBELLISHING	EMBOLDENING	EMBRANGLES	EMBUSIED
EMBALMERS	EMBER	EMBOLDENS	EMBRANGLING	EMBUSIES
EMBALMING	EMBERS	EMBOLI	EMBRASOR	EMBUSQUE
EMBALMINGS	EMBEZZLE	EMBOLIC	EMBRASORS	EMBUSQUES
EMBALMS	EMBEZZLED	EMBOLIES	EMBRASURE	EMBUSSED
EMBANK	EMBEZZLER	EMBOLISM	EMBRASURES	EMBUSSES
EMBANKED	EMBEZZLERS	EMBOLISMS	EMBRAVE	EMBUSSING
EMBANKER	EMBEZZLES	EMBOLUS	EMBRAVED	EMBUSY
EMBANKERS	EMBEZZLING	EMBOLUSES	EMBRAVES	EMBUSYING
EMBANKING	EMBITTER	EMBOLY	EMBRAVING	EMCEE
EMBANKS	EMBITTERED	EMBORDER	EMBRAZURE	EMCEED
EMBAR	EMBITTERING	EMBORDERED	EMBRAZURES	EMCEEING
EMBARGO	EMBITTERINGS	EMBORDERING	EMBREAD	EMCEES
EMBARGOED	EMBITTERS	EMBORDERS	EMBREADED	EME
EMBARGOES	EMBLAZE	EMBOSCATA	EMBREADING	EMEER
EMBARGOING	EMBLAZED	EMBOSCATAS	EMBREADS	EMEERS
EMBARK	EMBLAZES	EMBOSOM	EMBREATHE	EMEND
EMBARKED	EMBLAZING	EMBOSOMED	EMBREATHED	EMENDABLE
EMBARKING	EMBLAZON	EMBOSOMING	EMBREATHES	EMENDALS
EMBARKS	EMBLAZONED	EMBOSOMS	EMBREATHING	EMENDATE
EMBARRASS	EMBLAZONING	EMBOSS	EMBREWE	EMENDATED
EMBARRASSED	EMBLAZONS	EMBOSSED	EMBREWED	EMENDATES
EMBARRASSES	EMBLEM	EMBOSSER	EMBREWES	EMENDATING
EMBARRASSING	EMBLEMA	EMBOSSERS	EMBREWING	EMENDATOR
EMBARRED	EMBLEMATA	EMBOSSES	EMBRITTLE	EMENDATORS
EMBARRING	EMBLEMED	EMBOSSING	EMBRITTLED	EMENDED
EMBARRINGS	EMBLEMING	EMBOST	EMBRITTLES	EMENDING
EMBARS	EMBLEMISE	EMBOUND	EMBRITTLING	EMENDS
EMBASE	EMBLEMISED	EMBOUNDED	EMBROCATE	EMERALD
EMBASED	EMBLEMISES	EMBOUNDING	EMBROCATED	EMERALDS
EMBASES	EMBLEMISING	EMBOUNDS	EMBROCATES	EMERAUDE
EMBASING	EMBLEMIZE	EMBOW	EMBROCATING	EMERAUDES

The Chambers Dictionary is the authority for many longer words; see *OSW* Introduction, page xii

EMERGE	EMISSION	EMPACKETS	EMPERISE	EMPLONGES
EMERGED	EMISSIONS	EMPAESTIC	EMPERISED	EMPLONGING
EMERGENCE	EMISSIVE	EMPAIRE	EMPERISES	EMPLOY
EMERGENCES	EMIT	EMPAIRED	EMPERISH	EMPLOYED
EMERGENCIES	EMITS	EMPAIRES	EMPERISHED	EMPLOYEE
EMERGENCY	EMITTED	EMPAIRING	EMPERISHES	EMPLOYEES
EMERGENT	EMITTER	EMPALE	EMPERISHING	EMPLOYER
EMERGES	EMITTERS	EMPALED	EMPERISING	EMPLOYERS
EMERGING	EMITTING	EMPALES	EMPERIZE	EMPLOYING
EMERIED	EMMA	EMPALING	EMPERIZED	EMPLOYS
EMERIES	EMMARBLE	EMPANEL	EMPERIZES	EMPLUME
EMERITI	EMMARBLED	EMPANELLED	EMPERIZING	EMPLUMED
EMERITUS	EMMARBLES	EMPANELLING	EMPEROR	EMPLUMES
EMERODS	EMMARBLING	EMPANELS	EMPERORS	EMPLUMING
EMERSED	EMMAS	EMPANOPLIED	EMPERY	EMPOISON
EMERSION	EMMER	EMPANOPLIES	EMPHASES	EMPOISONED
EMERSIONS	EMMERS	EMPANOPLY	EMPHASIS	EMPOISONING
EMERY	EMMESH	EMPANOPLYING	EMPHASISE	EMPOISONS
EMERYING	EMMESHED	EMPARE	EMPHASISED	EMPOLDER
EMES	EMMESHES	EMPARED	EMPHASISES	EMPOLDERED
EMESES	EMMESHING	EMPARES	EMPHASISING	EMPOLDERING
EMESIS	EMMET	EMPARING	EMPHASIZE	EMPOLDERS
EMETIC	EMMETROPE	EMPARL	EMPHASIZED	EMPORIA
EMETICAL	EMMETROPES	EMPARLED	EMPHASIZES	EMPORIUM
EMETICS	EMMETS	EMPARLING	EMPHASIZING	EMPORIUMS
EMETIN	EMMEW	EMPARLS	EMPHATIC	EMPOWER
EMETINE	EMMEWED	EMPART	EMPHLYSES	EMPOWERED
EMETINES	EMMEWING	EMPARTED	EMPHLYSIS	EMPOWERING
EMETINS	EMMEWS	EMPARTING	EMPHYSEMA	EMPOWERS
EMEU	EMMOVE	EMPARTS	EMPHYSEMAS	EMPRESS
EMEUS	EMMOVED	EMPATHIC	EMPIERCE	EMPRESSE
EMEUTE	EMMOVES	EMPATHIES	EMPIERCED	EMPRESSES
EMEUTES	EMMOVING	EMPATHISE	EMPIERCES	EMPRISE
EMICANT	EMOLLIATE	EMPATHISED	EMPIERCING	EMPRISES
EMICATE	EMOLLIATED	EMPATHISES	EMPIGHT	EMPTIED
EMICATED	EMOLLIATES	EMPATHISING	EMPIRE	EMPTIER
EMICATES	EMOLLIATING	EMPATHIZE	EMPIRES	EMPTIERS
EMICATING	EMOLLIENT	EMPATHIZED	EMPIRIC	EMPTIES
EMICATION	EMOLLIENTS	EMPATHIZES	EMPIRICAL	EMPTIEST
EMICATIONS	EMOLUMENT	EMPATHIZING	EMPIRICS	EMPTILY
EMICTION	EMOLUMENTS	EMPATHY	EMPLACE	EMPTINESS
EMICTIONS	EMONG	EMPATRON	EMPLACED	EMPTINESSES
EMICTORY	EMONGES	EMPATRONED	EMPLACES	EMPTION
EMIGRANT	EMONGEST	EMPATRONING	EMPLACING	EMPTIONAL
EMIGRANTS	EMONGST	EMPATRONS	EMPLANE	EMPTIONS
EMIGRATE	EMOTE	EMPAYRE	EMPLANED	EMPTY
EMIGRATED	EMOTED	EMPAYRED	EMPLANES	EMPTYING
EMIGRATES	EMOTES	EMPAYRES	EMPLANING	EMPTYINGS
EMIGRATING	EMOTICON	EMPAYRING	EMPLASTER	EMPTYSES
EMIGRE	EMOTICONS	EMPEACH	EMPLASTERED	EMPTYSIS
EMIGRES	EMOTING	EMPEACHED	EMPLASTERING	EMPURPLE
EMINENCE	EMOTION	EMPEACHES	EMPLASTERS	EMPURPLED
EMINENCES	EMOTIONAL	EMPEACHING	EMPLASTIC	EMPURPLES
EMINENCIES	EMOTIONS	EMPENNAGE	EMPLASTICS	EMPURPLING
EMINENCY	EMOTIVE	EMPENNAGES	EMPLEACH	EMPUSA
EMINENT	EMOTIVISM	EMPEOPLE	EMPLEACHED	EMPUSAS
EMINENTLY	EMOTIVISMS	EMPEOPLED	EMPLEACHES	EMPUSE
EMIR	EMOVE	EMPEOPLES	EMPLEACHING	EMPUSES
EMIRATE	EMOVED	EMPEOPLING	EMPLECTON	EMPYEMA
EMIRATES	EMOVES	EMPERCE	EMPLECTONS	EMPYEMAS
EMIRS	EMOVING	EMPERCED	EMPLECTUM	EMPYEMATA
EMISSARIES	EMPACKET	EMPERCES	EMPLECTUMS	EMPYEMIC
EMISSARY	EMPACKETED	EMPERCING	EMPLONGE	EMPYESES
EMISSILE	EMPACKETING	EMPERIES	EMPLONGED	EMPYESIS

EMPYREAL	ENACT	ENCASES	ENCLASPS	ENCRADLES
EMPYREAN	ENACTED	ENCASH	ENCLAVE	ENCRADLING
EMPYREANS	ENACTING	ENCASHED	ENCLAVED	ENCRATIES
EMPYREUMA	ENACTION	ENCASHES	ENCLAVES	ENCRATY
EMPYREUMATA	ENACTIONS	ENCASHING	ENCLAVING	ENCREASE
EMS	ENACTIVE	ENCASING	ENCLISES	ENCREASED
EMU	ENACTMENT	ENCAUSTIC	ENCLISIS	ENCREASES
EMULATE	ENACTMENTS	ENCAUSTICS	ENCLITIC	ENCREASING
EMULATED	ENACTOR	ENCAVE	ENCLITICS	ENCRIMSON
EMULATES	ENACTORS	ENCAVED	ENCLOSE	ENCRIMSONED
EMULATING	ENACTS	ENCAVES	ENCLOSED	ENCRIMSONING
EMULATION	ENACTURE	ENCAVING	ENCLOSER	ENCRIMSONS
EMULATIONS	ENACTURES	ENCEINTE	ENCLOSERS	ENCRINAL
EMULATIVE	ENALLAGE	ENCEINTES	ENCLOSES	ENCRINIC
EMULATOR	ENALLAGES	ENCHAFE	ENCLOSING	ENCRINITE
EMULATORS	ENAMEL	ENCHAFED	ENCLOSURE	ENCRINITES
EMULE	ENAMELLED	ENCHAFES	ENCLOSURES	ENCROACH
EMULED	ENAMELLER	ENCHAFING	ENCLOTHE	ENCROACHED
EMULES	ENAMELLERS	ENCHAIN	ENCLOTHED	ENCROACHES
EMULGE	ENAMELLING	ENCHAINED	ENCLOTHES	ENCROACHING
EMULGED	ENAMELLINGS	ENCHAINING	ENCLOTHING	ENCRUST
EMULGENCE	ENAMELS	ENCHAINS	ENCLOUD	ENCRUSTED
EMULGENCES	ENAMOR	ENCHANT	ENCLOUDED	ENCRUSTING
EMULGENT	ENAMORADO	ENCHANTED	ENCLOUDING	ENCRUSTS
EMULGES	ENAMORADOS	ENCHANTER	ENCLOUDS	ENCRYPT
EMULGING	ENAMORED	ENCHANTERS	ENCODE	ENCRYPTED
EMULING	ENAMORING	ENCHANTING	ENCODED	ENCRYPTING
EMULOUS	ENAMORS	ENCHANTS	ENCODES	ENCRYPTS
EMULOUSLY	ENAMOUR	ENCHARGE	ENCODING	ENCUMBER
EMULSIFIED	ENAMOURED	ENCHARGED	ENCOLOUR	ENCUMBERED
EMULSIFIES	ENAMOURING	ENCHARGES	ENCOLOURED	ENCUMBERING
EMULSIFY	ENAMOURS	ENCHARGING	ENCOLOURING	ENCUMBERS
EMULSIFYING	ENARCH	ENCHARM	ENCOLOURS	ENCURTAIN
EMULSIN	ENARCHED	ENCHARMED	ENCOLPION	ENCURTAINED
EMULSINS	ENARCHES	ENCHARMING	ENCOLPIONS	ENCURTAINING
EMULSION	ENARCHING	ENCHARMS	ENCOLPIUM	ENCURTAINS
EMULSIONS	ENARM	ENCHASE	ENCOLPIUMS	ENCYCLIC
EMULSIVE	ENARMED	ENCHASED	ENCOLURE	ENCYST
EMULSOID	ENARMING	ENCHASES	ENCOLURES	ENCYSTED
EMULSOIDS	ENARMS	ENCHASING	ENCOMIA	ENCYSTING
EMULSOR	ENATE	ENCHEASON	ENCOMIAST	ENCYSTS
EMULSORS	ENATION	ENCHEASONS	ENCOMIASTS	END
EMUNCTION	ENATIONS	ENCHEER	ENCOMION	ENDAMAGE
EMUNCTIONS	ENAUNTER	ENCHEERED	ENCOMIUM	ENDAMAGED
EMUNCTORIES	ENCAENIA	ENCHEERING	ENCOMIUMS	ENDAMAGES
EMUNCTORY	ENCAENIAS	ENCHEERS	ENCOMPASS	ENDAMAGING
EMUNGE	ENCAGE	ENCHILADA	ENCOMPASSED	ENDAMOEBA
EMUNGED	ENCAGED	ENCHILADAS	ENCOMPASSES	ENDAMOEBAE
EMUNGES	ENCAGES	ENCHORIAL	ENCOMPASSING	ENDAMOEBAS
EMUNGING	ENCAGING	ENCHORIC	ENCORE	ENDANGER
EMURE	ENCALM	ENCIERRO	ENCORED	ENDANGERED
EMURED	ENCALMED	ENCIERROS	ENCORES	ENDANGERING
EMURES	ENCALMING	ENCIPHER	ENCORING	ENDANGERS
EMURING	ENCALMS	ENCIPHERED	ENCOUNTER	ENDARCH
EMUS	ENCAMP	ENCIPHERING	ENCOUNTERED	ENDART
EMYDES	ENCAMPED	ENCIPHERS	ENCOUNTERING	ENDARTED
EMYS	ENCAMPING	ENCIRCLE	ENCOUNTERS	ENDARTING
EN	ENCAMPS	ENCIRCLED	ENCOURAGE	ENDARTS
ENABLE	ENCANTHIS	ENCIRCLES	ENCOURAGED	ENDEAR
ENABLED	ENCANTHISES	ENCIRCLING	ENCOURAGES	ENDEARED
ENABLER	ENCARPUS	ENCIRCLINGS	ENCOURAGING	ENDEARING
ENABLERS	ENCARPUSES	ENCLASP	ENCOURAGINGS	ENDEARS
ENABLES	ENCASE	ENCLASPED	ENCRADLE	ENDEAVOR
ENABLING	ENCASED	ENCLASPING	ENCRADLED	ENDEAVORED

ENDEAVORING	ENDOLYMPH	ENDURABLE	ENFELON	ENFREE
ENDEAVORS	ENDOLYMPHS	ENDURABLY	ENFELONED	ENFREED
ENDEAVOUR	ENDOMIXES	ENDURANCE	ENFELONING	ENFREEDOM
ENDEAVOURED	ENDOMIXIS	ENDURANCES	ENFELONS	ENFREEDOMED
ENDEAVOURING	ENDOMIXISES	ENDURE	ENFEOFF	ENFREEDOMING
ENDEAVOURS	ENDOMORPH	ENDURED	ENFEOFFED	ENFREEDOMS
ENDECAGON	ENDOMORPHS	ENDURER	ENFEOFFING	ENFREEING
ENDECAGONS	ENDOPHAGIES	ENDURERS	ENFEOFFS	ENFREES
ENDED	ENDOPHAGY	ENDURES	ENFESTED	ENFREEZE
ENDEICTIC	ENDOPHYTE	ENDURING	ENFETTER	ENFREEZES
ENDEIXES	ENDOPHYTES	ENDURO	ENFETTERED	ENFREEZING
ENDEIXIS	ENDOPLASM	ENDUROS	ENFETTERING	ENFROSEN
ENDEIXISES	ENDOPLASMS	ENDWAYS	ENFETTERS	ENFROZE
ENDEMIAL	ENDORPHIN	ENDWISE	ENFIERCE	ENFROZEN
ENDEMIC	ENDORPHINS	ENE	ENFIERCED	ENG
ENDEMICAL	ENDORSE	ENEMA	ENFIERCES	ENGAGE
ENDEMICS	ENDORSED	ENEMAS	ENFIERCING	ENGAGED
ENDEMISM	ENDORSEE	ENEMATA	ENFILADE	ENGAGER
ENDEMISMS	ENDORSEES	ENEMIES	ENFILADED	ENGAGERS
ENDENIZEN	ENDORSER	ENEMY	ENFILADES	ENGAGES
ENDENIZENED	ENDORSERS	ENERGETIC	ENFILADING	ENGAGING
ENDENIZENING	ENDORSES	ENERGETICS	ENFILED	ENGAOL
ENDENIZENS	ENDORSING	ENERGIC	ENFIRE	ENGAOLED
ENDERMIC	ENDOSARC	ENERGID	ENFIRED	ENGAOLING
ENDERON	ENDOSARCS	ENERGIDS	ENFIRES	ENGAOLS
ENDERONS	ENDOSCOPE	ENERGIES	ENFIRING	ENGARLAND
ENDEW	ENDOSCOPES	ENERGISE	ENFIX	ENGARLANDED
ENDEWED	ENDOSCOPIES	ENERGISED	ENFIXED	ENGARLANDING
ENDEWING	ENDOSCOPY	ENERGISER	ENFIXES	ENGARLANDS
ENDEWS	ENDOSMOSE	ENERGISERS	ENFIXING	ENGENDER
ENDGAME	ENDOSMOSES	ENERGISES	ENFLAME	ENGENDERED
ENDGAMES	ENDOSPERM	ENERGISING	ENFLAMED	ENGENDERING
ENDING	ENDOSPERMS	ENERGIZE	ENFLAMES	ENGENDERS
ENDINGS	ENDOSPORE	ENERGIZED	ENFLAMING	ENGENDURE
ENDIRON	ENDOSPORES	ENERGIZER	ENFLESH	ENGENDURES
ENDIRONS	ENDOSS	ENERGIZERS	ENFLESHED	ENGILD
ENDITE	ENDOSSED	ENERGIZES	ENFLESHES	ENGILDED
ENDITED	ENDOSSES	ENERGIZING	ENFLESHING	ENGILDING
ENDITES	ENDOSSING	ENERGUMEN	ENFLOWER	ENGILDS
ENDITING	ENDOSTEA	ENERGUMENS	ENFLOWERED	ENGILT
ENDIVE	ENDOSTEAL	ENERGY	ENFLOWERING	ENGINE
ENDIVES	ENDOSTEUM	ENERVATE	ENFLOWERS	ENGINED
ENDLANG	ENDOW	ENERVATED	ENFOLD	ENGINEER
ENDLESS	ENDOWED	ENERVATES	ENFOLDED	ENGINEERED
ENDLESSLY	ENDOWER	ENERVATING	ENFOLDING	ENGINEERING
ENDLONG	ENDOWERS	ENERVE	ENFOLDS	ENGINEERINGS
ENDMOST	ENDOWING	ENERVED	ENFORCE	ENGINEERS
ENDOBLAST	ENDOWMENT	ENERVES	ENFORCED	ENGINER
ENDOBLASTS	ENDOWMENTS	ENERVING	ENFORCER	ENGINERIES
ENDOCARP	ENDOWS	ENES	ENFORCERS	ENGINERS
ENDOCARPS	ENDOZOA	ENEW	ENFORCES	ENGINERY
ENDOCRINE	ENDOZOIC	ENEWED	ENFORCING	ENGINES
ENDOCRINES	ENDOZOON	ENEWING	ENFOREST	ENGINING
ENDODERM	ENDS	ENEWS	ENFORESTED	ENGIRD
ENDODERMS	ENDSHIP	ENFACE	ENFORESTING	ENGIRDING
ENDODYNE	ENDSHIPS	ENFACED	ENFORESTS	ENGIRDLE
ENDOGAMIC	ENDUE	ENFACES	ENFORM	ENGIRDLED
ENDOGAMIES	ENDUED	ENFACING	ENFORMED	ENGIRDLES
ENDOGAMY	ENDUES	ENFANT	ENFORMING	ENGIRDLING
ENDOGEN	ENDUING	ENFANTS	ENFORMS	ENGIRDS
ENDOGENIC	ENDUNGEON	ENFEEBLE	ENFRAME	ENGIRT
ENDOGENIES	ENDUNGEONED	ENFEEBLED	ENFRAMED	ENGISCOPE
ENDOGENS	ENDUNGEONING	ENFEEBLES	ENFRAMES	ENGISCOPES
ENDOGENY	ENDUNGEONS	ENFEEBLING	ENFRAMING	ENGLOBE

ENGLOBED	ENGRENAGE	ENIGMATIC	ENLIST	ENOUNCE
ENGLOBES	ENGRENAGES	ENISLE	ENLISTED	ENOUNCED
ENGLOBING	ENGRIEVE	ENISLED	ENLISTING	ENOUNCES
ENGLOOM	ENGRIEVED	ENISLES	ENLISTS	ENOUNCING
ENGLOOMED	ENGRIEVES	ENISLING	ENLIT	ENOW
ENGLOOMING	ENGRIEVING	ENJAMB	ENLIVEN	ENPLANE
ENGLOOMS	ENGROOVE	ENJAMBED	ENLIVENED	ENPLANED
ENGLUT	ENGROOVED	ENJAMBING	ENLIVENER	ENPLANES
ENGLUTS	ENGROOVES	ENJAMBS	ENLIVENERS	ENPLANING
ENGLUTTED	ENGROOVING	ENJOIN	ENLIVENING	ENPRINT
ENGLUTTING	ENGROSS	ENJOINED	ENLIVENS	ENPRINTS
ENGOBE	ENGROSSED	ENJOINER	ENLOCK	ENQUIRE
ENGOBES	ENGROSSER	ENJOINERS	ENLOCKED	ENQUIRED
ENGORE	ENGROSSERS	ENJOINING	ENLOCKING	ENQUIRER
ENGORED	ENGROSSES	ENJOINS	ENLOCKS	ENQUIRERS
ENGORES	ENGROSSING	ENJOY	ENLUMINE	ENQUIRES
ENGORGE	ENGS	ENJOYABLE	ENLUMINED	ENQUIRIES
ENGORGED	ENGUARD	ENJOYABLY	ENLUMINES	ENQUIRING
ENGORGES	ENGUARDED	ENJOYED	ENLUMINING	ENQUIRY
ENGORGING	ENGUARDING	ENJOYER	ENMESH	ENRACE
ENGORING	ENGUARDS	ENJOYERS	ENMESHED	ENRACED
ENGOULED	ENGULF	ENJOYING	ENMESHES	ENRACES
ENGOUMENT	ENGULFED	ENJOYMENT	ENMESHING	ENRACING
ENGOUMENTS	ENGULFING	ENJOYMENTS	ENMEW	ENRAGE
ENGRACE	ENGULFS	ENJOYS	ENMEWED	ENRAGED
ENGRACED	ENGULPH	ENKERNEL	ENMEWING	ENRAGES
ENGRACES	ENGULPHED	ENKERNELLED	ENMEWS	ENRAGING
ENGRACING	ENGULPHING	ENKERNELLING	ENMITIES	ENRANCKLE
ENGRAFF	ENGULPHS	ENKERNELS	ENMITY	ENRANCKLED
ENGRAFFED	ENGYSCOPE	ENKINDLE	ENMOSSED	ENRANCKLES
ENGRAFFING	ENGYSCOPES	ENKINDLED	ENMOVE	ENRANCKLING
ENGRAFFS	ENHALO	ENKINDLES	ENMOVED	ENRANGE
ENGRAFT	ENHALOED	ENKINDLING	ENMOVES	ENRANGED
ENGRAFTED	ENHALOES	ENLACE	ENMOVING	ENRANGES
ENGRAFTING	ENHALOING	ENLACED	ENNAGE	ENRANGING
ENGRAFTS	ENHALOS	ENLACES	ENNAGES	ENRANK
ENGRAIL	ENHANCE	ENLACING	ENNEAD	ENRANKED
ENGRAILED	ENHANCED	ENLARD	ENNEADIC	ENRANKING
ENGRAILING	ENHANCER	ENLARDED	ENNEADS	ENRANKS
ENGRAILS	ENHANCERS	ENLARDING	ENNEAGON	ENRAPT
ENGRAIN	ENHANCES	ENLARDS	ENNEAGONS	ENRAPTURE
ENGRAINED	ENHANCING	ENLARGE	ENNOBLE	ENRAPTURED
ENGRAINER	ENHANCIVE	ENLARGED	ENNOBLED	ENRAPTURES
ENGRAINERS	ENHEARSE	ENLARGEN	ENNOBLES	ENRAPTURING
ENGRAINING	ENHEARSED	ENLARGENED	ENNOBLING	ENRAUNGE
ENGRAINS	ENHEARSES	ENLARGENING	ENNUI	ENRAUNGED
ENGRAM	ENHEARSING	ENLARGENS	ENNUIED	ENRAUNGES
ENGRAMMA	ENHEARTEN	ENLARGER	ENNUIS	ENRAUNGING
ENGRAMMAS	ENHEARTENED	ENLARGERS	ENNUYE	ENRAVISH
ENGRAMS	ENHEARTENING	ENLARGES	ENNUYED	ENRAVISHED
ENGRASP	ENHEARTENS	ENLARGING	ENNUYING	ENRAVISHES
ENGRASPED	ENHUNGER	ENLEVE	ENODAL	ENRAVISHING
ENGRASPING	ENHUNGERED	ENLIGHT	ENOKI	ENRHEUM
ENGRASPS	ENHUNGERING	ENLIGHTED	ENOKIS	ENRHEUMED
ENGRAVE	ENHUNGERS	ENLIGHTEN	ENOMOTIES	ENRHEUMING
ENGRAVED	ENHYDRITE	ENLIGHTENED	ENOMOTY	ENRHEUMS
ENGRAVEN	ENHYDRITES	ENLIGHTENING	ENORM	ENRICH
ENGRAVER	ENHYDROS	ENLIGHTENS	ENORMITIES	ENRICHED
ENGRAVERIES	ENHYDROSES	ENLIGHTING	ENORMITY	ENRICHES
ENGRAVERS	ENHYDROUS	ENLIGHTS	ENORMOUS	ENRICHING
ENGRAVERY	ENIAC	ENLINK	ENOSES	ENRIDGED
ENGRAVES	ENIACS	ENLINKED	ENOSIS	ENRING
ENGRAVING	ENIGMA	ENLINKING	ENOUGH	ENRINGED
ENGRAVINGS	ENIGMAS	ENLINKS	ENOUGHS	ENRINGING

ENRINGS	ENSHELLING	ENSTAMP	ENTENTES	ENTITLES
ENRIVEN	ENSHELLS	ENSTAMPED	ENTER	ENTITLING
ENROBE	ENSHELTER	ENSTAMPING	ENTERA	ENTITY
ENROBED	ENSHELTERED	ENSTAMPS	ENTERABLE	ENTOBLAST
ENROBES	ENSHELTERING	ENSTATITE	ENTERAL	ENTOBLASTS
ENROBING	ENSHELTERS	ENSTATITES	ENTERATE	ENTODERM
ENROL	ENSHIELD	ENSTEEP	ENTERED	ENTODERMS
ENROLL	ENSHIELDED	ENSTEEPED	ENTERER	ENTOIL
ENROLLED	ENSHIELDING	ENSTEEPING	ENTERERS	ENTOILED
ENROLLER	ENSHIELDS	ENSTEEPS	ENTERIC	ENTOILING
ENROLLERS	ENSHRINE	ENSTYLE	ENTERICS	ENTOILS
ENROLLING	ENSHRINED	ENSTYLED	ENTERING	ENTOMB
ENROLLS	ENSHRINES	ENSTYLES	ENTERINGS	ENTOMBED
ENROLMENT	ENSHRINING	ENSTYLING	ENTERITIS	ENTOMBING
ENROLMENTS	ENSHROUD	ENSUE	ENTERITISES	ENTOMBS
ENROLS	ENSHROUDED	ENSUED	ENTERON	ENTOMIC
ENROOT	ENSHROUDING	ENSUES	ENTERS	ENTOPHYTE
ENROOTED	ENSHROUDS	ENSUING	ENTERTAIN	ENTOPHYTES
ENROOTING	ENSIFORM	ENSURE	ENTERTAINED	ENTOPIC
ENROOTS	ENSIGN	ENSURED	ENTERTAINING	ENTOPTIC
ENROUGH	ENSIGNCIES	ENSURER	ENTERTAININGS	ENTOPTICS
ENROUGHED	ENSIGNCY	ENSURERS	ENTERTAINS	ENTOTIC
ENROUGHING	ENSIGNED	ENSURES	ENTERTAKE	ENTOURAGE
ENROUGHS	ENSIGNING	ENSURING	ENTERTAKEN	ENTOURAGES
ENROUND	ENSIGNS	ENSWATHE	ENTERTAKES	ENTOZOA
ENROUNDED	ENSILAGE	ENSWATHED	ENTERTAKING	ENTOZOAL
ENROUNDING	ENSILAGED	ENSWATHES	ENTERTOOK	ENTOZOIC
ENROUNDS	ENSILAGEING	ENSWATHING	ENTETE	ENTOZOON
ENS	ENSILAGES	ENSWEEP	ENTETEE	ENTRAIL
ENSAMPLE	ENSILAGING	ENSWEEPING	ENTHALPIES	ENTRAILED
ENSAMPLED	ENSILE	ENSWEEPS	ENTHALPY	ENTRAILING
ENSAMPLES	ENSILED	ENSWEPT	ENTHETIC	ENTRAILS
ENSAMPLING	ENSILES	ENTAIL	ENTHRAL	ENTRAIN
ENSATE	ENSILING	ENTAILED	ENTHRALL	ENTRAINED
ENSCONCE	ENSKIED	ENTAILER	ENTHRALLED	ENTRAINING
ENSCONCED	ENSKIES	ENTAILERS	ENTHRALLING	ENTRAINS
ENSCONCES	ENSKY	ENTAILING	ENTHRALLS	ENTRALL
ENSCONCING	ENSKYING	ENTAILS	ENTHRALS	ENTRALLES
ENSEAL	ENSLAVE	ENTAME	ENTHRONE	ENTRAMMEL
ENSEALED	ENSLAVED	ENTAMED	ENTHRONED	ENTRAMMELLED
ENSEALING	ENSLAVER	ENTAMES	ENTHRONES	ENTRAMMELLING
ENSEALS	ENSLAVERS	ENTAMING	ENTHRONING	ENTRAMMELS
ENSEAM	ENSLAVES	ENTAMOEBA	ENTHUSE	ENTRANCE
ENSEAMED	ENSLAVING	ENTAMOEBAE	ENTHUSED	ENTRANCED
ENSEAMING	ENSNARE	ENTAMOEBAS	ENTHUSES	ENTRANCES
ENSEAMS	ENSNARED	ENTANGLE	ENTHUSING	ENTRANCING
ENSEAR	ENSNARES	ENTANGLED	ENTHYMEME	ENTRANT
ENSEARED	ENSNARING	ENTANGLES	ENTHYMEMES	ENTRANTS
ENSEARING	ENSNARL	ENTANGLING	ENTIA	ENTRAP
ENSEARS	ENSNARLED	ENTASES	ENTICE	ENTRAPPED
ENSEMBLE	ENSNARLING	ENTASIS	ENTICED	ENTRAPPER
ENSEMBLES	ENSNARLS	ENTAYLE	ENTICER	ENTRAPPERS
ENSEW	ENSORCELL	ENTAYLED	ENTICERS	ENTRAPPING
ENSEWED	ENSORCELLED	ENTAYLES	ENTICES	ENTRAPS
ENSEWING	ENSORCELLING	ENTAYLING	ENTICING	ENTREAT
ENSEWS	ENSORCELLS	ENTELECHIES	ENTICINGS	ENTREATED
ENSHEATH	ENSOUL	ENTELECHY	ENTIRE	ENTREATIES
ENSHEATHE	ENSOULED	ENTELLUS	ENTIRELY	ENTREATING
ENSHEATHED	ENSOULING	ENTELLUSES	ENTIRES	ENTREATS
ENSHEATHES	ENSOULS	ENTENDER	ENTIRETIES	ENTREATY
ENSHEATHING	ENSPHERE	ENTENDERED	ENTIRETY	ENTRECHAT
ENSHEATHS	ENSPHERED	ENTENDERING	ENTITIES	ENTRECHATS
ENSHELL	ENSPHERES	ENTENDERS	ENTITLE	ENTRECOTE
ENSHELLED	ENSPHERING	ENTENTE	ENTITLED	ENTRECOTES

The Chambers Dictionary is the authority for many longer words; see *OSW* Introduction, page xii

ENTREE	ENURING	ENWHEEL	EPARCHATE	EPICALYCES
ENTREES	ENVASSAL	ENWHEELED	EPARCHATES	EPICALYX
ENTREMES	ENVASSALLED	ENWHEELING	EPARCHIES	EPICALYXES
ENTREMETS	ENVASSALLING	ENWHEELS	EPARCHS	EPICANTHI
ENTRENCH	ENVASSALS	ENWIND	EPARCHY	EPICARP
ENTRENCHED	ENVAULT	ENWINDING	EPATANT	EPICARPS
ENTRENCHES	ENVAULTED	ENWINDS	EPAULE	EPICEDE
ENTRENCHING	ENVAULTING	ENWOMB	EPAULES	EPICEDES
ENTREPOT	ENVAULTS	ENWOMBED	EPAULET	EPICEDIA
ENTREPOTS	ENVEIGLE	ENWOMBING	EPAULETS	EPICEDIAL
ENTRESOL	ENVEIGLED	ENWOMBS	EPAULETTE	EPICEDIAN
ENTRESOLS	ENVEIGLES	ENWOUND	EPAULETTES	EPICEDIUM
ENTREZ	ENVEIGLING	ENWRAP	EPAXIAL	EPICENE
ENTRIES	ENVELOP	ENWRAPPED	EPEDAPHIC	EPICENES
ENTRISM	ENVELOPE	ENWRAPPING	EPEE	EPICENTER
ENTRISMS	ENVELOPED	ENWRAPPINGS	EPEES	EPICENTERS
ENTRIST	ENVELOPES	ENWRAPS	EPEIRA	EPICENTRE
ENTRISTS	ENVELOPING	ENWREATHE	EPEIRAS	EPICENTRES
ENTROLD	ENVELOPS	ENWREATHED	EPEIRID	EPICIER
ENTROPIC	ENVENOM	ENWREATHES	EPEIRIDS	EPICIERS
ENTROPIES	ENVENOMED	ENWREATHING	EPEOLATRIES	EPICISM
ENTROPION	ENVENOMING	ENZIAN	EPEOLATRY	EPICISMS
ENTROPIONS	ENVENOMS	ENZIANS	EPERDU	EPICIST
ENTROPIUM	ENVERMEIL	ENZONE	EPERDUE	EPICISTS
ENTROPIUMS	ENVERMEILED	ENZONED	EPERGNE	EPICLESES
ENTROPY	ENVERMEILING	ENZONES	EPERGNES	EPICLESIS
ENTRUST	ENVERMEILS	ENZONING	EPHA	EPICOTYL
ENTRUSTED	ENVIABLE	ENZOOTIC	EPHAH	EPICOTYLS
ENTRUSTING	ENVIABLY	ENZOOTICS	EPHAHS	EPICRITIC
ENTRUSTS	ENVIED	ENZYMATIC	EPHAS	EPICS
ENTRY	ENVIER	ENZYME	EPHEBE	EPICURE
ENTRYISM	ENVIERS	ENZYMES	EPHEBES	EPICUREAN
ENTRYISMS	ENVIES	ENZYMIC	EPHEBI	EPICUREANS
ENTRYIST	ENVIOUS	EOAN	EPHEBIC	EPICURES
ENTRYISTS	ENVIOUSLY	EOLIENNE	EPHEBOS	EPICURISE
ENTWINE	ENVIRON	EOLIENNES	EPHEBUS	EPICURISED
ENTWINED	ENVIRONED	EOLIPILE	EPHEDRA	EPICURISES
ENTWINES	ENVIRONING	EOLIPILES	EPHEDRAS	EPICURISING
ENTWINING	ENVIRONS	EOLITH	EPHEDRINE	EPICURISM
ENTWIST	ENVISAGE	EOLITHIC	EPHEDRINES	EPICURISMS
ENTWISTED	ENVISAGED	EOLITHS	EPHELIDES	EPICURIZE
ENTWISTING	ENVISAGES	EON	EPHELIS	EPICURIZED
ENTWISTS	ENVISAGING	EONISM	EPHEMERA	EPICURIZES
ENUCLEATE	ENVISION	EONISMS	EPHEMERAE	EPICURIZING
ENUCLEATED	ENVISIONED	EONS	EPHEMERAL	EPICYCLE
ENUCLEATES	ENVISIONING	EORL	EPHEMERALS	EPICYCLES
ENUCLEATING	ENVISIONS	EORLS	EPHEMERAS	EPICYCLIC
ENUMERATE	ENVOI	EOSIN	EPHEMERID	EPIDEMIC
ENUMERATED	ENVOIS	EOSINS	EPHEMERIDES	EPIDEMICS
ENUMERATES	ENVOY	EOTHEN	EPHEMERIDS	EPIDERMAL
ENUMERATING	ENVOYS	EPACRID	EPHEMERIS	EPIDERMIC
ENUNCIATE	ENVOYSHIP	EPACRIDS	EPHEMERON	EPIDERMIS
ENUNCIATED	ENVOYSHIPS	EPACRIS	EPHIALTES	EPIDERMISES
ENUNCIATES	ENVY	EPACRISES	EPHOD	EPIDOSITE
ENUNCIATING	ENVYING	EPACT	EPHODS	EPIDOSITES
ENURE	ENVYINGS	EPACTS	EPHOR	EPIDOTE
ENURED	ENWALL	EPAENETIC	EPHORALTIES	EPIDOTES
ENUREMENT	ENWALLED	EPAGOGE	EPHORALTY	EPIDOTIC
ENUREMENTS	ENWALLING	EPAGOGES	EPHORS	EPIDURAL
ENURES	ENWALLOW	EPAGOGIC	EPIBLAST	EPIDURALS
ENURESES	ENWALLOWED	EPAINETIC	EPIBLASTS	EPIFAUNA
ENURESIS	ENWALLOWING	EPANODOS	EPIC	EPIFAUNAE
ENURETIC	ENWALLOWS	EPANODOSES	EPICAL	EPIFAUNAS
ENURETICS	ENWALLS	EPARCH	EPICALLY	EPIFOCAL

The Chambers Dictionary is the authority for many longer words; see *OSW* Introduction, page xii

EPIGAEAL
EPIGAEAN
EPIGAEOUS
EPIGAMIC
EPIGEAL
EPIGEAN
EPIGENE
EPIGEOUS
EPIGON
EPIGONE
EPIGONES
EPIGONI
EPIGONS
EPIGRAM
EPIGRAMS
EPIGRAPH
EPIGRAPHED
EPIGRAPHIES
EPIGRAPHING
EPIGRAPHS
EPIGRAPHY
EPIGYNIES
EPIGYNOUS
EPIGYNY
EPILATE
EPILATED
EPILATES
EPILATING
EPILATION
EPILATIONS
EPILATOR
EPILATORS
EPILEPSIES
EPILEPSY
EPILEPTIC
EPILEPTICS
EPILOBIUM
EPILOBIUMS
EPILOG
EPILOGIC
EPILOGISE
EPILOGISED
EPILOGISES
EPILOGISING
EPILOGIST
EPILOGISTS
EPILOGIZE
EPILOGIZED
EPILOGIZES
EPILOGIZING
EPILOGS
EPILOGUE
EPILOGUES
EPIMER
EPIMERIC
EPIMERS
EPINASTIC
EPINASTIES
EPINASTY
EPINEURAL
EPINICIAN
EPINICION
EPINICIONS
EPINIKIAN

EPINIKION
EPINIKIONS
EPINOSIC
EPIPHANIC
EPIPHRAGM
EPIPHRAGMS
EPIPHYSES
EPIPHYSIS
EPIPHYTAL
EPIPHYTE
EPIPHYTES
EPIPHYTIC
EPIPLOIC
EPIPLOON
EPIPLOONS
EPIPOLIC
EPIPOLISM
EPIPOLISMS
EPIRRHEMA
EPIRRHEMAS
EPISCOPAL
EPISCOPE
EPISCOPES
EPISCOPIES
EPISCOPY
EPISEMON
EPISEMONS
EPISODAL
EPISODE
EPISODES
EPISODIAL
EPISODIC
EPISOME
EPISOMES
EPISPERM
EPISPERMS
EPISPORE
EPISPORES
EPISTASES
EPISTASIS
EPISTATIC
EPISTAXES
EPISTAXIS
EPISTAXISES
EPISTEMIC
EPISTEMICS
EPISTERNA
EPISTLE
EPISTLED
EPISTLER
EPISTLERS
EPISTLES
EPISTLING
EPISTOLER
EPISTOLERS
EPISTOLET
EPISTOLETS
EPISTOLIC
EPISTYLE
EPISTYLES
EPITAPH
EPITAPHED
EPITAPHER
EPITAPHERS

EPITAPHIC
EPITAPHING
EPITAPHS
EPITASES
EPITASIS
EPITAXIAL
EPITAXIES
EPITAXY
EPITHELIA
EPITHEM
EPITHEMA
EPITHEMATA
EPITHEMS
EPITHESES
EPITHESIS
EPITHET
EPITHETED
EPITHETIC
EPITHETING
EPITHETON
EPITHETONS
EPITHETS
EPITOME
EPITOMES
EPITOMIC
EPITOMISE
EPITOMISED
EPITOMISES
EPITOMISING
EPITOMIST
EPITOMISTS
EPITOMIZE
EPITOMIZED
EPITOMIZES
EPITOMIZING
EPITONIC
EPITOPE
EPITOPES
EPITRITE
EPITRITES
EPIZEUXES
EPIZEUXIS
EPIZEUXISES
EPIZOA
EPIZOAN
EPIZOANS
EPIZOIC
EPIZOON
EPIZOOTIC
EPIZOOTICS
EPOCH
EPOCHA
EPOCHAL
EPOCHAS
EPOCHS
EPODE
EPODES
EPODIC
EPONYM
EPONYMIC
EPONYMOUS
EPONYMS
EPOPEE
EPOPEES

EPOPOEIA
EPOPOEIAS
EPOPT
EPOPTS
EPOS
EPOSES
EPOXIDE
EPOXIDES
EPOXIES
EPOXY
EPRIS
EPRISE
EPROM
EPROMS
EPSILON
EPSILONS
EPSOMITE
EPSOMITES
EPUISE
EPUISEE
EPULARY
EPULATION
EPULATIONS
EPULIDES
EPULIS
EPULISES
EPULOTIC
EPULOTICS
EPURATE
EPURATED
EPURATES
EPURATING
EPURATION
EPURATIONS
EPYLLION
EPYLLIONS
EQUABLE
EQUABLY
EQUAL
EQUALISE
EQUALISED
EQUALISER
EQUALISERS
EQUALISES
EQUALISING
EQUALITIES
EQUALITY
EQUALIZE
EQUALIZED
EQUALIZER
EQUALIZERS
EQUALIZES
EQUALIZING
EQUALLED
EQUALLING
EQUALLY
EQUALNESS
EQUALNESSES
EQUALS
EQUANT
EQUANTS
EQUATE
EQUATED
EQUATES

EQUATING
EQUATION
EQUATIONS
EQUATOR
EQUATORS
EQUERRIES
EQUERRY
EQUID
EQUIDS
EQUINAL
EQUINE
EQUINIA
EQUINIAS
EQUINITIES
EQUINITY
EQUINOX
EQUINOXES
EQUIP
EQUIPAGE
EQUIPAGED
EQUIPAGES
EQUIPAGING
EQUIPE
EQUIPES
EQUIPMENT
EQUIPMENTS
EQUIPOISE
EQUIPOISED
EQUIPOISES
EQUIPOISING
EQUIPPED
EQUIPPING
EQUIPS
EQUISETA
EQUISETIC
EQUISETUM
EQUISETUMS
EQUITABLE
EQUITABLY
EQUITANT
EQUITIES
EQUITY
EQUIVALVE
EQUIVOCAL
EQUIVOKE
EQUIVOKES
EQUIVOQUE
EQUIVOQUES
ER
ERA
ERADIATE
ERADIATED
ERADIATES
ERADIATING
ERADICATE
ERADICATED
ERADICATES
ERADICATING
ERAS
ERASABLE
ERASE
ERASED
ERASEMENT
ERASEMENTS

ERASER	ERGOMETERS	EROGENOUS	ERUCT	ESCAPADO
ERASERS	ERGON	EROSE	ERUCTATE	ESCAPADOES
ERASES	ERGONOMIC	EROSION	ERUCTATED	ESCAPE
ERASING	ERGONOMICS	EROSIONS	ERUCTATES	ESCAPED
ERASION	ERGONS	EROSIVE	ERUCTATING	ESCAPEE
ERASIONS	ERGOT	EROSTRATE	ERUCTED	ESCAPEES
ERASURE	ERGOTISE	EROTEMA	ERUCTING	ESCAPER
ERASURES	ERGOTISED	EROTEMAS	ERUCTS	ESCAPERS
ERATHEM	ERGOTISES	EROTEME	ERUDITE	ESCAPES
ERATHEMS	ERGOTISING	EROTEMES	ERUDITELY	ESCAPING
ERBIA	ERGOTISM	EROTESES	ERUDITES	ESCAPISM
ERBIAS	ERGOTISMS	EROTESIS	ERUDITION	ESCAPISMS
ERBIUM	ERGOTIZE	EROTETIC	ERUDITIONS	ESCAPIST
ERBIUMS	ERGOTIZED	EROTIC	ERUMPENT	ESCAPISTS
ERE	ERGOTIZES	EROTICA	ERUPT	ESCARGOT
ERECT	ERGOTIZING	EROTICAL	ERUPTED	ESCARGOTS
ERECTED	ERGOTS	EROTICISE	ERUPTING	ESCAROLE
ERECTER	ERGS	EROTICISED	ERUPTION	ESCAROLES
ERECTERS	ERIACH	EROTICISES	ERUPTIONS	ESCARP
ERECTILE	ERIACHS	EROTICISING	ERUPTIVE	ESCARPED
ERECTING	ERIC	EROTICISM	ERUPTS	ESCARPING
ERECTION	ERICA	EROTICISMS	ERVALENTA	ESCARPS
ERECTIONS	ERICAS	EROTICIST	ERVALENTAS	ESCHALOT
ERECTIVE	ERICK	EROTICISTS	ERVEN	ESCHALOTS
ERECTLY	ERICKS	EROTICIZE	ERYNGIUM	ESCHAR
ERECTNESS	ERICOID	EROTICIZED	ERYNGIUMS	ESCHARS
ERECTNESSES	ERICS	EROTICIZES	ERYNGO	ESCHEAT
ERECTOR	ERIGERON	EROTICIZING	ERYNGOES	ESCHEATED
ERECTORS	ERIGERONS	EROTICS	ERYNGOS	ESCHEATING
ERECTS	ERING	EROTISM	ERYTHEMA	ESCHEATOR
ERED	ERINGO	EROTISMS	ERYTHEMAL	ESCHEATORS
ERELONG	ERINGOES	ERR	ERYTHEMAS	ESCHEATS
EREMIC	ERINGOS	ERRABLE	ERYTHRINA	ESCHEW
EREMITAL	ERINITE	ERRAND	ERYTHRINAS	ESCHEWAL
EREMITE	ERINITES	ERRANDS	ERYTHRISM	ESCHEWALS
EREMITES	ERIOMETER	ERRANT	ERYTHRISMS	ESCHEWED
EREMITIC	ERIOMETERS	ERRANTLY	ERYTHRITE	ESCHEWER
EREMITISM	ERIONITE	ERRANTRIES	ERYTHRITES	ESCHEWERS
EREMITISMS	ERIONITES	ERRANTRY	ES	ESCHEWING
ERENOW	ERISTIC	ERRANTS	ESCALADE	ESCHEWS
EREPSIN	ERISTICAL	ERRATA	ESCALADED	ESCLANDRE
EREPSINS	ERK	ERRATIC	ESCALADES	ESCLANDRES
ERES	ERKS	ERRATICAL	ESCALADING	ESCOLAR
ERETHISM	ERMELIN	ERRATICS	ESCALADO	ESCOLARS
ERETHISMS	ERMELINS	ERRATUM	ESCALADOES	ESCOPETTE
ERETHITIC	ERMINE	ERRED	ESCALATE	ESCOPETTES
EREWHILE	ERMINED	ERRHINE	ESCALATED	ESCORT
ERF	ERMINES	ERRHINES	ESCALATES	ESCORTAGE
ERG	ERN	ERRING	ESCALATING	ESCORTAGES
ERGATANER	ERNE	ERRINGLY	ESCALATOR	ESCORTED
ERGATANERS	ERNED	ERRINGS	ESCALATORS	ESCORTING
ERGATE	ERNES	ERRONEOUS	ESCALIER	ESCORTS
ERGATES	ERNING	ERROR	ESCALIERS	ESCOT
ERGATIVE	ERNS	ERRORIST	ESCALLOP	ESCOTS
ERGATOID	ERODE	ERRORISTS	ESCALLOPS	ESCOTTED
ERGO	ERODED	ERRORS	ESCALOP	ESCOTTING
ERGODIC	ERODENT	ERRS	ESCALOPE	ESCRIBANO
ERGOGRAM	ERODENTS	ERS	ESCALOPED	ESCRIBANOS
ERGOGRAMS	ERODES	ERSATZ	ESCALOPES	ESCRIBE
ERGOGRAPH	ERODIBLE	ERSATZES	ESCALOPING	ESCRIBED
ERGOGRAPHS	ERODING	ERSES	ESCALOPS	ESCRIBES
ERGOMANIA	ERODIUM	ERST	ESCAPABLE	ESCRIBING
ERGOMANIAS	ERODIUMS	ERSTWHILE	ESCAPADE	ESCROC
ERGOMETER	EROGENIC	ERUCIFORM	ESCAPADES	ESCROCS

ESCROL	ESPLANADE	ESTANCIAS	ESTREATED	ETCHING
ESCROLL	ESPLANADES	ESTATE	ESTREATING	ETCHINGS
ESCROLLS	ESPOUSAL	ESTATED	ESTREATS	ETEN
ESCROLS	ESPOUSALS	ESTATES	ESTREPE	ETENS
ESCROW	ESPOUSE	ESTATING	ESTREPED	ETERNAL
ESCROWED	ESPOUSED	ESTEEM	ESTREPES	ETERNALLY
ESCROWING	ESPOUSER	ESTEEMED	ESTREPING	ETERNE
ESCROWS	ESPOUSERS	ESTEEMING	ESTRICH	ETERNISE
ESCUAGE	ESPOUSES	ESTEEMS	ESTRICHES	ETERNISED
ESCUAGES	ESPOUSING	ESTER	ESTRIDGE	ETERNISES
ESCUDO	ESPRESSO	ESTERIFIED	ESTRIDGES	ETERNISING
ESCUDOS	ESPRESSOS	ESTERIFIES	ESTRILDID	ETERNITIES
ESCULENT	ESPRIT	ESTERIFY	ESTRILDIDS	ETERNITY
ESCULENTS	ESPRITS	ESTERIFYING	ESTRO	ETERNIZE
ESEMPLASIES	ESPUMOSO	ESTERS	ESTROGEN	ETERNIZED
ESEMPLASY	ESPUMOSOS	ESTHESIA	ESTROGENS	ETERNIZES
ESILE	ESPY	ESTHESIAS	ESTROS	ETERNIZING
ESILES	ESPYING	ESTHETE	ESTROUS	ETESIAN
ESKAR	ESQUIRE	ESTHETES	ESTRUM	ETH
ESKARS	ESQUIRES	ESTIMABLE	ESTRUMS	ETHAL
ESKER	ESQUIRESS	ESTIMABLY	ESTRUS	ETHALS
ESKERS	ESQUIRESSES	ESTIMATE	ESTRUSES	ETHANE
ESKIES	ESQUISSE	ESTIMATED	ESTS	ETHANES
ESKY®	ESQUISSES	ESTIMATES	ESTUARIAL	ETHANOL
ESLOIN	ESS	ESTIMATING	ESTUARIAN	ETHANOLS
ESLOINED	ESSAY	ESTIMATOR	ESTUARIES	ETHE
ESLOINING	ESSAYED	ESTIMATORS	ESTUARINE	ETHENE
ESLOINS	ESSAYER	ESTIVAL	ESTUARY	ETHENES
ESLOYNE	ESSAYERS	ESTIVATE	ESURIENCE	ETHER
ESLOYNED	ESSAYETTE	ESTIVATED	ESURIENCES	ETHERCAP
ESLOYNES	ESSAYETTES	ESTIVATES	ESURIENCIES	ETHERCAPS
ESLOYNING	ESSAYING	ESTIVATING	ESURIENCY	ETHEREAL
ESNE	ESSAYISH	ESTOC	ESURIENT	ETHEREOUS
ESNECIES	ESSAYIST	ESTOCS	ETA	ETHERIAL
ESNECY	ESSAYISTS	ESTOILE	ETACISM	ETHERIC
ESNES	ESSAYS	ESTOILES	ETACISMS	ETHERICAL
ESOPHAGI	ESSE	ESTOP	ETAERIO	ETHERIFIED
ESOPHAGUS	ESSENCE	ESTOPPAGE	ETAERIOS	ETHERIFIES
ESOTERIC	ESSENCES	ESTOPPAGES	ETAGE	ETHERIFY
ESOTERICA	ESSENTIAL	ESTOPPED	ETAGERE	ETHERIFYING
ESOTERIES	ESSENTIALS	ESTOPPEL	ETAGERES	ETHERION
ESOTERISM	ESSES	ESTOPPELS	ETAGES	ETHERIONS
ESOTERISMS	ESSIVE	ESTOPPING	ETALAGE	ETHERISE
ESOTERY	ESSIVES	ESTOPS	ETALAGES	ETHERISED
ESPADA	ESSOIN	ESTOVER	ETALON	ETHERISES
ESPADAS	ESSOINER	ESTOVERS	ETALONS	ETHERISING
ESPAGNOLE	ESSOINERS	ESTRADE	ETAPE	ETHERISM
ESPAGNOLES	ESSOINS	ESTRADES	ETAPES	ETHERISMS
ESPALIER	ESSONITE	ESTRADIOL	ETAS	ETHERIST
ESPALIERED	ESSONITES	ESTRADIOLS	ETAT	ETHERISTS
ESPALIERING	ESSOYNE	ESTRAL	ETATISME	ETHERIZE
ESPALIERS	ESSOYNES	ESTRANGE	ETATISMES	ETHERIZED
ESPARTO	EST	ESTRANGED	ETATISTE	ETHERIZES
ESPARTOS	ESTABLISH	ESTRANGER	ETATISTES	ETHERIZING
ESPECIAL	ESTABLISHED	ESTRANGERS	ETATS	ETHERS
ESPERANCE	ESTABLISHES	ESTRANGES	ETCETERA	ETHIC
ESPERANCES	ESTABLISHING	ESTRANGING	ETCETERAS	ETHICAL
ESPIAL	ESTACADE	ESTRAPADE	ETCH	ETHICALLY
ESPIALS	ESTACADES	ESTRAPADES	ETCHANT	ETHICALS
ESPIED	ESTAFETTE	ESTRAY	ETCHANTS	ETHICISE
ESPIEGLE	ESTAFETTES	ESTRAYED	ETCHED	ETHICISED
ESPIES	ESTAMINET	ESTRAYING	ETCHER	ETHICISES
ESPIONAGE	ESTAMINETS	ESTRAYS	ETCHERS	ETHICISING
ESPIONAGES	ESTANCIA	ESTREAT	ETCHES	ETHICISM

ETHICISMS	ETRENNES	EUGENIST	EUPATRIDAE	EUREKA
ETHICIST	ETRIER	EUGENISTS	EUPATRIDS	EUREKAS
ETHICISTS	ETRIERS	EUGENOL	EUPEPSIA	EURHYTHMIES
ETHICIZE	ETTERCAP	EUGENOLS	EUPEPSIAS	EURHYTHMY
ETHICIZED	ETTERCAPS	EUGH	EUPEPSIES	EURIPI
ETHICIZES	ETTIN	EUGHEN	EUPEPSY	EURIPUS
ETHICIZING	ETTINS	EUGHS	EUPEPTIC	EURIPUSES
ETHICS	ETTLE	EUK	EUPHAUSID	EURO
ETHIOPS	ETTLED	EUKARYON	EUPHAUSIDS	EUROPIUM
ETHIOPSES	ETTLES	EUKARYONS	EUPHEMISE	EUROPIUMS
ETHMOID	ETTLING	EUKARYOT	EUPHEMISED	EUROS
ETHMOIDAL	ETUDE	EUKARYOTE	EUPHEMISES	EURYTHERM
ETHNARCH	ETUDES	EUKARYOTES	EUPHEMISING	EURYTHERMS
ETHNARCHIES	ETUI	EUKARYOTS	EUPHEMISM	EURYTHMIES
ETHNARCHS	ETUIS	EUKED	EUPHEMISMS	EURYTHMY
ETHNARCHY	ETWEE	EUKING	EUPHEMIZE	EUSOL
ETHNIC	ETWEES	EUKS	EUPHEMIZED	EUSOLS
ETHNICAL	ETYMA	EULACHAN	EUPHEMIZES	EUSTACIES
ETHNICISM	ETYMIC	EULACHANS	EUPHEMIZING	EUSTACY
ETHNICISMS	ETYMOLOGIES	EULACHON	EUPHENICS	EUSTASIES
ETHNICITIES	ETYMOLOGY	EULACHONS	EUPHOBIA	EUSTASY
ETHNICITY	ETYMON	EULOGIA	EUPHOBIAS	EUSTATIC
ETHNICS	ETYMONS	EULOGIES	EUPHON	EUSTYLE
ETHNOCIDE	ETYPIC	EULOGISE	EUPHONIA	EUSTYLES
ETHNOCIDES	ETYPICAL	EULOGISED	EUPHONIAS	EUTAXIES
ETHNOLOGIES	EUCAIN	EULOGISES	EUPHONIC	EUTAXITE
ETHNOLOGY	EUCAINE	EULOGISING	EUPHONIES	EUTAXITES
ETHOLOGIC	EUCAINES	EULOGIST	EUPHONISE	EUTAXITIC
ETHOLOGIES	EUCAINS	EULOGISTS	EUPHONISED	EUTAXY
ETHOLOGY	EUCALYPT	EULOGIUM	EUPHONISES	EUTECTIC
ETHOS	EUCALYPTI	EULOGIUMS	EUPHONISING	EUTECTICS
ETHOSES	EUCALYPTS	EULOGIZE	EUPHONISM	EUTECTOID
ETHS	EUCARYON	EULOGIZED	EUPHONISMS	EUTECTOIDS
ETHYL	EUCARYONS	EULOGIZES	EUPHONIUM	EUTEXIA
ETHYLATE	EUCARYOT	EULOGIZING	EUPHONIUMS	EUTEXIAS
ETHYLATED	EUCARYOTE	EUMELANIN	EUPHONIZE	EUTHANASIES
ETHYLATES	EUCARYOTES	EUMELANINS	EUPHONIZED	EUTHANASY
ETHYLATING	EUCARYOTS	EUMERISM	EUPHONIZES	EUTHENICS
ETHYLENE	EUCHARIS	EUMERISMS	EUPHONIZING	EUTHENIST
ETHYLENES	EUCHARISES	EUNUCH	EUPHONS	EUTHENISTS
ETHYLS	EUCHLORIC	EUNUCHISE	EUPHONY	EUTHERIAN
ETHYNE	EUCHOLOGIES	EUNUCHISED	EUPHORBIA	EUTHERIANS
ETHYNES	EUCHOLOGY	EUNUCHISES	EUPHORBIAS	EUTRAPELIES
ETIOLATE	EUCHRE	EUNUCHISING	EUPHORIA	EUTRAPELY
ETIOLATED	EUCHRED	EUNUCHISM	EUPHORIAS	EUTROPHIC
ETIOLATES	EUCHRES	EUNUCHISMS	EUPHORIC	EUTROPHIES
ETIOLATING	EUCHRING	EUNUCHIZE	EUPHORIES	EUTROPHY
ETIOLIN	EUCLASE	EUNUCHIZED	EUPHORY	EUTROPIC
ETIOLINS	EUCLASES	EUNUCHIZES	EUPHRASIES	EUTROPIES
ETIOLOGIES	EUCRITE	EUNUCHIZING	EUPHRASY	EUTROPOUS
ETIOLOGY	EUCRITES	EUNUCHOID	EUPHROE	EUTROPY
ETIQUETTE	EUCRITIC	EUNUCHOIDS	EUPHROES	EUXENITE
ETIQUETTES	EUCYCLIC	EUNUCHS	EUPHUISE	EUXENITES
ETNA	EUDAEMONIES	EUOI	EUPHUISED	EVACUANT
ETNAS	EUDAEMONY	EUONYMIN	EUPHUISES	EVACUANTS
ETOILE	EUDIALYTE	EUONYMINS	EUPHUISING	EVACUATE
ETOILES	EUDIALYTES	EUONYMUS	EUPHUISM	EVACUATED
ETOURDI	EUGE	EUONYMUSES	EUPHUISMS	EVACUATES
ETOURDIE	EUGENIA	EUOUAE	EUPHUIST	EVACUATING
ETRANGER	EUGENIAS	EUOUAES	EUPHUISTS	EVACUATOR
ETRANGERE	EUGENIC	EUPAD	EUPHUIZE	EVACUATORS
ETRANGERES	EUGENICS	EUPADS	EUPHUIZED	EVACUEE
ETRANGERS	EUGENISM	EUPATRID	EUPHUIZES	EVACUEES
ETRENNE	EUGENISMS	EUPATRIDS	EUPHUIZING	EVADABLE

EVADE	EVENT	EVILLEST	EVOVAE	EXAMINER
EVADED	EVENTED	EVILLY	EVOVAES	EXAMINERS
EVADER	EVENTER	EVILNESS	EVULGATE	EXAMINES
EVADERS	EVENTERS	EVILNESSES	EVULGATED	EXAMINING
EVADES	EVENTFUL	EVILS	EVULGATES	EXAMPLAR
EVADING	EVENTIDE	EVINCE	EVULGATING	EXAMPLARS
EVAGATION	EVENTIDES	EVINCED	EVULSE	EXAMPLE
EVAGATIONS	EVENTING	EVINCES	EVULSED	EXAMPLED
EVAGINATE	EVENTINGS	EVINCIBLE	EVULSES	EXAMPLES
EVAGINATED	EVENTRATE	EVINCIBLY	EVULSING	EXAMPLING
EVAGINATES	EVENTRATED	EVINCING	EVULSION	EXAMS
EVAGINATING	EVENTRATES	EVINCIVE	EVULSIONS	EXANIMATE
EVALUATE	EVENTRATING	EVIRATE	EVZONE	EXANTHEM
EVALUATED	EVENTS	EVIRATED	EVZONES	EXANTHEMA
EVALUATES	EVENTUAL	EVIRATES	EWE	EXANTHEMATA
EVALUATING	EVENTUATE	EVIRATING	EWER	EXANTHEMS
EVANESCE	EVENTUATED	EVITABLE	EWERS	EXARATE
EVANESCED	EVENTUATES	EVITATE	EWES	EXARATION
EVANESCES	EVENTUATING	EVITATED	EWEST	EXARATIONS
EVANESCING	EVER	EVITATES	EWFTES	EXARCH
EVANGEL	EVERGLADE	EVITATING	EWGHEN	EXARCHAL
EVANGELIC	EVERGLADES	EVITATION	EWHOW	EXARCHATE
EVANGELIES	EVERGREEN	EVITATIONS	EWK	EXARCHATES
EVANGELS	EVERGREENS	EVITE	EWKED	EXARCHIES
EVANGELY	EVERMORE	EVITED	EWKING	EXARCHIST
EVANISH	EVERSIBLE	EVITERNAL	EWKS	EXARCHISTS
EVANISHED	EVERSION	EVITES	EWT	EXARCHS
EVANISHES	EVERSIONS	EVITING	EWTS	EXARCHY
EVANISHING	EVERT	EVOCABLE	EX	EXCAMB
EVANITION	EVERTED	EVOCATE	EXACT	EXCAMBED
EVANITIONS	EVERTING	EVOCATED	EXACTABLE	EXCAMBING
EVAPORATE	EVERTOR	EVOCATES	EXACTED	EXCAMBION
EVAPORATED	EVERTORS	EVOCATING	EXACTER	EXCAMBIONS
EVAPORATES	EVERTS	EVOCATION	EXACTERS	EXCAMBIUM
EVAPORATING	EVERY	EVOCATIONS	EXACTEST	EXCAMBIUMS
EVAPORITE	EVERYBODY	EVOCATIVE	EXACTING	EXCAMBS
EVAPORITES	EVERYDAY	EVOCATOR	EXACTION	EXCARNATE
EVASIBLE	EVERYDAYS	EVOCATORS	EXACTIONS	EXCARNATED
EVASION	EVERYMAN	EVOCATORY	EXACTLY	EXCARNATES
EVASIONS	EVERYMEN	EVOE	EXACTMENT	EXCARNATING
EVASIVE	EVERYONE	EVOHE	EXACTMENTS	EXCAUDATE
EVASIVELY	EVERYWAY	EVOKE	EXACTNESS	EXCAVATE
EVE	EVERYWHEN	EVOKED	EXACTNESSES	EXCAVATED
EVECTION	EVES	EVOKER	EXACTOR	EXCAVATES
EVECTIONS	EVET	EVOKERS	EXACTORS	EXCAVATING
EVEJAR	EVETS	EVOKES	EXACTRESS	EXCAVATOR
EVEJARS	EVHOE	EVOKING	EXACTRESSES	EXCAVATORS
EVEN	EVICT	EVOLUE	EXACTS	EXCEED
EVENED	EVICTED	EVOLUES	EXALT	EXCEEDED
EVENEMENT	EVICTING	EVOLUTE	EXALTED	EXCEEDING
EVENEMENTS	EVICTION	EVOLUTED	EXALTEDLY	EXCEEDS
EVENER	EVICTIONS	EVOLUTES	EXALTING	EXCEL
EVENERS	EVICTOR	EVOLUTING	EXALTS	EXCELLED
EVENEST	EVICTORS	EVOLUTION	EXAM	EXCELLENT
EVENFALL	EVICTS	EVOLUTIONS	EXAMEN	EXCELLING
EVENFALLS	EVIDENCE	EVOLUTIVE	EXAMENS	EXCELS
EVENING	EVIDENCED	EVOLVABLE	EXAMINANT	EXCELSIOR
EVENINGS	EVIDENCES	EVOLVE	EXAMINANTS	EXCELSIORS
EVENLY	EVIDENCING	EVOLVED	EXAMINATE	EXCENTRIC
EVENNESS	EVIDENT	EVOLVENT	EXAMINATES	EXCENTRICS
EVENNESSES	EVIDENTLY	EVOLVER	EXAMINE	EXCEPT
EVENS	EVIDENTS	EVOLVERS	EXAMINED	EXCEPTANT
EVENSONG	EVIL	EVOLVES	EXAMINEE	EXCEPTANTS
EVENSONGS	EVILLER	EVOLVING	EXAMINEES	EXCEPTED

EXCEPTING	EXCLAIMING	EXCUSES	EXEMPTIONS	EXHUMED
EXCEPTION	EXCLAIMS	EXCUSING	EXEMPTS	EXHUMER
EXCEPTIONS	EXCLAVE	EXCUSIVE	EXEQUATUR	EXHUMERS
EXCEPTIVE	EXCLAVES	EXEAT	EXEQUATURS	EXHUMES
EXCEPTOR	EXCLOSURE	EXEATS	EXEQUIAL	EXHUMING
EXCEPTORS	EXCLOSURES	EXECRABLE	EXEQUIES	EXIES
EXCEPTS	EXCLUDE	EXECRABLY	EXEQUY	EXIGEANT
EXCERPT	EXCLUDED	EXECRATE	EXERCISE	EXIGEANTE
EXCERPTA	EXCLUDEE	EXECRATED	EXERCISED	EXIGENCE
EXCERPTED	EXCLUDEES	EXECRATES	EXERCISER	EXIGENCES
EXCERPTING	EXCLUDER	EXECRATING	EXERCISERS	EXIGENCIES
EXCERPTINGS	EXCLUDERS	EXECUTANT	EXERCISES	EXIGENCY
EXCERPTOR	EXCLUDES	EXECUTANTS	EXERCISING	EXIGENT
EXCERPTORS	EXCLUDING	EXECUTE	EXERGONIC	EXIGENTLY
EXCERPTS	EXCLUSION	EXECUTED	EXERGUAL	EXIGENTS
EXCERPTUM	EXCLUSIONS	EXECUTER	EXERGUE	EXIGIBLE
EXCESS	EXCLUSIVE	EXECUTERS	EXERGUES	EXIGUITIES
EXCESSES	EXCLUSIVES	EXECUTES	EXERT	EXIGUITY
EXCESSIVE	EXCLUSORY	EXECUTING	EXERTED	EXIGUOUS
EXCHANGE	EXCORIATE	EXECUTION	EXERTING	EXILE
EXCHANGED	EXCORIATED	EXECUTIONS	EXERTION	EXILED
EXCHANGER	EXCORIATES	EXECUTIVE	EXERTIONS	EXILEMENT
EXCHANGERS	EXCORIATING	EXECUTIVES	EXERTIVE	EXILEMENTS
EXCHANGES	EXCREMENT	EXECUTOR	EXERTS	EXILES
EXCHANGING	EXCREMENTS	EXECUTORS	EXES	EXILIAN
EXCHEAT	EXCRETA	EXECUTORY	EXEUNT	EXILIC
EXCHEATS	EXCRETAL	EXECUTRICES	EXFOLIATE	EXILING
EXCHEQUER	EXCRETE	EXECUTRIES	EXFOLIATED	EXILITIES
EXCHEQUERED	EXCRETED	EXECUTRIX	EXFOLIATES	EXILITY
EXCHEQUERING	EXCRETER	EXECUTRIXES	EXFOLIATING	EXIMIOUS
EXCHEQUERS	EXCRETERS	EXECUTRY	EXHALABLE	EXINE
EXCIDE	EXCRETES	EXEDRA	EXHALANT	EXINES
EXCIDED	EXCRETING	EXEDRAE	EXHALANTS	EXIST
EXCIDES	EXCRETION	EXEEM	EXHALE	EXISTED
EXCIDING	EXCRETIONS	EXEEMED	EXHALED	EXISTENCE
EXCIPIENT	EXCRETIVE	EXEEMING	EXHALES	EXISTENCES
EXCIPIENTS	EXCRETORIES	EXEEMS	EXHALING	EXISTENT
EXCISABLE	EXCRETORY	EXEGESES	EXHAUST	EXISTING
EXCISE	EXCUBANT	EXEGESIS	EXHAUSTED	EXISTS
EXCISED	EXCUDIT	EXEGETE	EXHAUSTER	EXIT
EXCISEMAN	EXCULPATE	EXEGETES	EXHAUSTERS	EXITANCE
EXCISEMEN	EXCULPATED	EXEGETIC	EXHAUSTING	EXITANCES
EXCISES	EXCULPATES	EXEGETICS	EXHAUSTS	EXITED
EXCISING	EXCULPATING	EXEGETIST	EXHEDRA	EXITING
EXCISION	EXCURRENT	EXEGETISTS	EXHEDRAE	EXITS
EXCISIONS	EXCURSE	EXEME	EXHIBIT	EXOCARP
EXCITABLE	EXCURSED	EXEMED	EXHIBITED	EXOCARPS
EXCITANCIES	EXCURSES	EXEMES	EXHIBITER	EXOCRINE
EXCITANCY	EXCURSING	EXEMING	EXHIBITERS	EXOCRINES
EXCITANT	EXCURSION	EXEMPLA	EXHIBITING	EXODE
EXCITANTS	EXCURSIONED	EXEMPLAR	EXHIBITOR	EXODERM
EXCITE	EXCURSIONING	EXEMPLARS	EXHIBITORS	EXODERMAL
EXCITED	EXCURSIONS	EXEMPLARY	EXHIBITS	EXODERMIS
EXCITEDLY	EXCURSIVE	EXEMPLE	EXHORT	EXODERMISES
EXCITER	EXCURSUS	EXEMPLES	EXHORTED	EXODERMS
EXCITERS	EXCURSUSES	EXEMPLIFIED	EXHORTER	EXODES
EXCITES	EXCUSABLE	EXEMPLIFIES	EXHORTERS	EXODIC
EXCITING	EXCUSABLY	EXEMPLIFY	EXHORTING	EXODIST
EXCITON	EXCUSAL	EXEMPLIFYING	EXHORTS	EXODISTS
EXCITONS	EXCUSALS	EXEMPLUM	EXHUMATE	EXODUS
EXCITOR	EXCUSE	EXEMPT	EXHUMATED	EXODUSES
EXCITORS	EXCUSED	EXEMPTED	EXHUMATES	EXOENZYME
EXCLAIM	EXCUSER	EXEMPTING	EXHUMATING	EXOENZYMES
EXCLAIMED	EXCUSERS	EXEMPTION	EXHUME	EXOERGIC

The Chambers Dictionary is the authority for many longer words; see *OSW* Introduction, page xii

EXOGAMIC	EXOTICA	EXPENSIVE	EXPLOITER	EXPUNCT
EXOGAMIES	EXOTICISM	EXPERT	EXPLOITERS	EXPUNCTED
EXOGAMOUS	EXOTICISMS	EXPERTED	EXPLOITING	EXPUNCTING
EXOGAMY	EXOTICS	EXPERTING	EXPLOITS	EXPUNCTS
EXOGEN	EXOTOXIC	EXPERTISE	EXPLORE	EXPUNGE
EXOGENOUS	EXOTOXIN	EXPERTISED	EXPLORED	EXPUNGED
EXOGENS	EXOTOXINS	EXPERTISES	EXPLORER	EXPUNGER
EXOMION	EXPAND	EXPERTISING	EXPLORERS	EXPUNGERS
EXOMIONS	EXPANDED	EXPERTIZE	EXPLORES	EXPUNGES
EXOMIS	EXPANDER	EXPERTIZED	EXPLORING	EXPUNGING
EXOMISES	EXPANDERS	EXPERTIZES	EXPLOSION	EXPURGATE
EXON	EXPANDING	EXPERTIZING	EXPLOSIONS	EXPURGATED
EXONERATE	EXPANDOR	EXPERTLY	EXPLOSIVE	EXPURGATES
EXONERATED	EXPANDORS	EXPERTS	EXPLOSIVES	EXPURGATING
EXONERATES	EXPANDS	EXPIABLE	EXPO	EXPURGE
EXONERATING	EXPANSE	EXPIATE	EXPONENT	EXPURGED
EXONIC	EXPANSES	EXPIATED	EXPONENTS	EXPURGES
EXONS	EXPANSILE	EXPIATES	EXPONIBLE	EXPURGING
EXONYM	EXPANSION	EXPIATING	EXPORT	EXQUISITE
EXONYMS	EXPANSIONS	EXPIATION	EXPORTED	EXQUISITES
EXOPHAGIES	EXPANSIVE	EXPIATIONS	EXPORTER	EXSCIND
EXOPHAGY	EXPAT	EXPIATOR	EXPORTERS	EXSCINDED
EXOPLASM	EXPATIATE	EXPIATORS	EXPORTING	EXSCINDING
EXOPLASMS	EXPATIATED	EXPIATORY	EXPORTS	EXSCINDS
EXOPOD	EXPATIATES	EXPIRABLE	EXPOS	EXSECT
EXOPODITE	EXPATIATING	EXPIRANT	EXPOSABLE	EXSECTED
EXOPODITES	EXPATS	EXPIRANTS	EXPOSAL	EXSECTING
EXOPODS	EXPECT	EXPIRE	EXPOSALS	EXSECTION
EXORABLE	EXPECTANT	EXPIRED	EXPOSE	EXSECTIONS
EXORATION	EXPECTANTS	EXPIRES	EXPOSED	EXSECTS
EXORATIONS	EXPECTED	EXPIRIES	EXPOSER	EXSERT
EXORCISE	EXPECTER	EXPIRING	EXPOSERS	EXSERTED
EXORCISED	EXPECTERS	EXPIRY	EXPOSES	EXSERTILE
EXORCISER	EXPECTING	EXPISCATE	EXPOSING	EXSERTING
EXORCISERS	EXPECTINGS	EXPISCATED	EXPOSITOR	EXSERTION
EXORCISES	EXPECTS	EXPISCATES	EXPOSITORS	EXSERTIONS
EXORCISING	EXPEDIENT	EXPISCATING	EXPOSTURE	EXSERTS
EXORCISM	EXPEDIENTS	EXPLAIN	EXPOSTURES	EXSICCANT
EXORCISMS	EXPEDITE	EXPLAINED	EXPOSURE	EXSICCATE
EXORCIST	EXPEDITED	EXPLAINER	EXPOSURES	EXSICCATED
EXORCISTS	EXPEDITER	EXPLAINERS	EXPOUND	EXSICCATES
EXORCIZE	EXPEDITERS	EXPLAINING	EXPOUNDED	EXSICCATING
EXORCIZED	EXPEDITES	EXPLAINS	EXPOUNDER	EXSUCCOUS
EXORCIZER	EXPEDITING	EXPLANT	EXPOUNDERS	EXTANT
EXORCIZERS	EXPEDITOR	EXPLANTED	EXPOUNDING	EXTASIES
EXORCIZES	EXPEDITORS	EXPLANTING	EXPOUNDS	EXTASY
EXORCIZING	EXPEL	EXPLANTS	EXPRESS	EXTATIC
EXORDIA	EXPELLANT	EXPLETIVE	EXPRESSED	EXTEMPORE
EXORDIAL	EXPELLANTS	EXPLETIVES	EXPRESSES	EXTEMPORES
EXORDIUM	EXPELLED	EXPLETORY	EXPRESSING	EXTEND
EXORDIUMS	EXPELLEE	EXPLICATE	EXPRESSLY	EXTENDANT
EXOSMOSE	EXPELLEES	EXPLICATED	EXPRESSO	EXTENDED
EXOSMOSES	EXPELLENT	EXPLICATES	EXPRESSOS	EXTENDER
EXOSMOSIS	EXPELLENTS	EXPLICATING	EXPUGN	EXTENDERS
EXOSMOTIC	EXPELLING	EXPLICIT	EXPUGNED	EXTENDING
EXOSPHERE	EXPELS	EXPLICITS	EXPUGNING	EXTENDS
EXOSPHERES	EXPEND	EXPLODE	EXPUGNS	EXTENSE
EXOSPORAL	EXPENDED	EXPLODED	EXPULSE	EXTENSILE
EXOSPORE	EXPENDER	EXPLODER	EXPULSED	EXTENSION
EXOSPORES	EXPENDERS	EXPLODERS	EXPULSES	EXTENSIONS
EXOSTOSES	EXPENDING	EXPLODES	EXPULSING	EXTENSITIES
EXOSTOSIS	EXPENDS	EXPLODING	EXPULSION	EXTENSITY
EXOTERIC	EXPENSE	EXPLOIT	EXPULSIONS	EXTENSIVE
EXOTIC	EXPENSES	EXPLOITED	EXPULSIVE	EXTENSOR

The Chambers Dictionary is the authority for many longer words; see *OSW* Introduction, page xii

EXTENSORS
EXTENT
EXTENTS
EXTENUATE
EXTENUATED
EXTENUATES
EXTENUATING
EXTENUATINGS
EXTERIOR
EXTERIORS
EXTERMINE
EXTERMINED
EXTERMINES
EXTERMINING
EXTERN
EXTERNAL
EXTERNALS
EXTERNAT
EXTERNATS
EXTERNE
EXTERNES
EXTERNS
EXTINCT
EXTINCTED
EXTINE
EXTINES
EXTIRP
EXTIRPATE
EXTIRPATED
EXTIRPATES
EXTIRPATING
EXTIRPED
EXTIRPING
EXTIRPS
EXTOL
EXTOLD
EXTOLLED
EXTOLLER
EXTOLLERS
EXTOLLING
EXTOLMENT
EXTOLMENTS
EXTOLS

EXTORSIVE
EXTORT
EXTORTED
EXTORTING
EXTORTION
EXTORTIONS
EXTORTIVE
EXTORTS
EXTRA
EXTRACT
EXTRACTED
EXTRACTING
EXTRACTOR
EXTRACTORS
EXTRACTS
EXTRADITE
EXTRADITED
EXTRADITES
EXTRADITING
EXTRADOS
EXTRADOSES
EXTRAIT
EXTRAITS
EXTRANET
EXTRANETS
EXTRAPOSE
EXTRAPOSED
EXTRAPOSES
EXTRAPOSING
EXTRAS
EXTRAUGHT
EXTRAVERT
EXTRAVERTED
EXTRAVERTING
EXTRAVERTS
EXTREAT
EXTREATS
EXTREME
EXTREMELY
EXTREMER
EXTREMES
EXTREMEST
EXTREMISM

EXTREMISMS
EXTREMIST
EXTREMISTS
EXTREMITIES
EXTREMITY
EXTRICATE
EXTRICATED
EXTRICATES
EXTRICATING
EXTRINSIC
EXTRORSAL
EXTRORSE
EXTROVERT
EXTROVERTED
EXTROVERTING
EXTROVERTS
EXTRUDE
EXTRUDED
EXTRUDER
EXTRUDERS
EXTRUDES
EXTRUDING
EXTRUSION
EXTRUSIONS
EXTRUSIVE
EXTRUSORY
EXUBERANT
EXUBERATE
EXUBERATED
EXUBERATES
EXUBERATING
EXUDATE
EXUDATES
EXUDATION
EXUDATIONS
EXUDATIVE
EXUDE
EXUDED
EXUDES
EXUDING
EXUL
EXULS
EXULT

EXULTANCE
EXULTANCES
EXULTANCIES
EXULTANCY
EXULTANT
EXULTED
EXULTING
EXULTS
EXURB
EXURBAN
EXURBIA
EXURBIAS
EXURBS
EXUVIAE
EXUVIAL
EXUVIATE
EXUVIATED
EXUVIATES
EXUVIATING
EYALET
EYALETS
EYAS
EYASES
EYE
EYEBALL
EYEBALLED
EYEBALLING
EYEBALLS
EYEBOLT
EYEBOLTS
EYEBRIGHT
EYEBRIGHTS
EYEBROW
EYEBROWED
EYEBROWING
EYEBROWS
EYED
EYEFUL
EYEFULS
EYEGLASS
EYEGLASSES
EYEHOOK
EYEHOOKS

EYEING
EYELASH
EYELASHES
EYELESS
EYELET
EYELETED
EYELETEER
EYELETEERS
EYELETING
EYELETS
EYELIAD
EYELIADS
EYELID
EYELIDS
EYELINER
EYELINERS
EYES
EYESHADE
EYESHADES
EYESHADOW
EYESHADOWS
EYESIGHT
EYESIGHTS
EYESORE
EYESORES
EYESTALK
EYESTALKS
EYESTRAIN
EYESTRAINS
EYING
EYLIAD
EYLIADS
EYNE
EYOT
EYOTS
EYRA
EYRAS
EYRE
EYRES
EYRIE
EYRIES
EYRY

F

FA	FACETS	FACTOTUMS	FADY	FAILLES
FAB	FACIA	FACTS	FAECAL	FAILS
FABACEOUS	FACIAL	FACTUAL	FAECES	FAILURE
FABBER	FACIALLY	FACTUM	FAERIE	FAILURES
FABBEST	FACIALS	FACTUMS	FAERIES	FAIN
FABLE	FACIAS	FACTURE	FAERY	FAINE
FABLED	FACIES	FACTURES	FAFF	FAINEANCE
FABLER	FACILE	FACULA	FAFFED	FAINEANCES
FABLERS	FACILELY	FACULAE	FAFFING	FAINEANCIES
FABLES	FACILITIES	FACULAR	FAFFS	FAINEANCY
FABLIAU	FACILITY	FACULTIES	FAG	FAINEANT
FABLIAUX	FACING	FACULTY	FAGACEOUS	FAINEANTS
FABLING	FACINGS	FACUNDITIES	FAGGED	FAINED
FABLINGS	FACONNE	FACUNDITY	FAGGERIES	FAINER
FABRIC	FACONNES	FAD	FAGGERY	FAINES
FABRICANT	FACSIMILE	FADABLE	FAGGING	FAINEST
FABRICANTS	FACSIMILED	FADAISE	FAGGINGS	FAINING
FABRICATE	FACSIMILEING	FADAISES	FAGGOT	FAINITES
FABRICATED	FACSIMILES	FADDIER	FAGGOTED	FAINLY
FABRICATES	FACT	FADDIEST	FAGGOTING	FAINNESS
FABRICATING	FACTICE	FADDINESS	FAGGOTINGS	FAINNESSES
FABRICKED	FACTICES	FADDINESSES	FAGGOTS	FAINS
FABRICKING	FACTICITIES	FADDISH	FAGOT	FAINT
FABRICS	FACTICITY	FADDISM	FAGOTED	FAINTED
FABULAR	FACTION	FADDISMS	FAGOTING	FAINTER
FABULISE	FACTIONAL	FADDIST	FAGOTINGS	FAINTEST
FABULISED	FACTIONS	FADDISTS	FAGOTS	FAINTIER
FABULISES	FACTIOUS	FADDLE	FAGOTTI	FAINTIEST
FABULISING	FACTIS	FADDLED	FAGOTTIST	FAINTING
FABULIST	FACTISES	FADDLES	FAGOTTISTS	FAINTINGS
FABULISTS	FACTITIVE	FADDLING	FAGOTTO	FAINTISH
FABULIZE	FACTIVE	FADDY	FAGS	FAINTLY
FABULIZED	FACTOID	FADE	FAH	FAINTNESS
FABULIZES	FACTOIDS	FADED	FAHLBAND	FAINTNESSES
FABULIZING	FACTOR	FADEDLY	FAHLBANDS	FAINTS
FABULOUS	FACTORAGE	FADEDNESS	FAHLERZ	FAINTY
FABURDEN	FACTORAGES	FADEDNESSES	FAHLERZES	FAIR
FABURDENS	FACTORED	FADELESS	FAHLORE	FAIRED
FACADE	FACTORIAL	FADER	FAHLORES	FAIRER
FACADES	FACTORIALS	FADERS	FAHS	FAIREST
FACE	FACTORIES	FADES	FAIBLE	FAIRIES
FACED	FACTORING	FADEUR	FAIBLES	FAIRILY
FACELESS	FACTORINGS	FADEURS	FAIENCE	FAIRING
FACEMAN	FACTORISE	FADGE	FAIENCES	FAIRINGS
FACEMEN	FACTORISED	FADGED	FAIK	FAIRISH
FACER	FACTORISES	FADGES	FAIKED	FAIRLY
FACERS	FACTORISING	FADGING	FAIKES	FAIRNESS
FACES	FACTORIZE	FADIER	FAIKING	FAIRNESSES
FACET	FACTORIZED	FADIEST	FAIKS	FAIRS
FACETE	FACTORIZES	FADING	FAIL	FAIRWAY
FACETED	FACTORIZING	FADINGS	FAILED	FAIRWAYS
FACETIAE	FACTORS	FADO	FAILING	FAIRY
FACETING	FACTORY	FADOS	FAILINGS	FAIRYDOM
FACETIOUS	FACTOTUM	FADS	FAILLE	FAIRYDOMS

The Chambers Dictionary is the authority for many longer words; see *OSW* Introduction, page xii

FAIRYHOOD	FALCONS	FALTBOATS	FANFARADES	FANTASM
FAIRYHOODS	FALCULA	FALTER	FANFARE	FANTASMS
FAIRYISM	FALCULAS	FALTERED	FANFARED	FANTASQUE
FAIRYISMS	FALCULATE	FALTERING	FANFARES	FANTASQUES
FAIRYLAND	FALDAGE	FALTERINGS	FANFARING	FANTAST
FAIRYLANDS	FALDAGES	FALTERS	FANFARON	FANTASTIC
FAIRYLIKE	FALDERAL	FALX	FANFARONA	FANTASTICS
FAIRYTALE	FALDERALS	FAME	FANFARONAS	FANTASTRIES
FAIRYTALES	FALDETTA	FAMED	FANFARONS	FANTASTRY
FAITH	FALDETTAS	FAMELESS	FANFOLD	FANTASTS
FAITHCURE	FALDSTOOL	FAMES	FANG	FANTASY
FAITHCURES	FALDSTOOLS	FAMILIAL	FANGED	FANTASYING
FAITHED	FALL	FAMILIAR	FANGING	FANTEEG
FAITHFUL	FALLACIES	FAMILIARS	FANGLE	FANTEEGS
FAITHING	FALLACY	FAMILIES	FANGLED	FANTIGUE
FAITHLESS	FALLAL	FAMILISM	FANGLES	FANTIGUES
FAITHS	FALLALERIES	FAMILISMS	FANGLESS	FANTOD
FAITOR	FALLALERY	FAMILY	FANGLING	FANTODS
FAITORS	FALLALS	FAMINE	FANGO	FANTOM
FAITOUR	FALLEN	FAMINES	FANGOS	FANTOMS
FAITOURS	FALLER	FAMING	FANGS	FANTOOSH
FAIX	FALLERS	FAMISH	FANION	FANZINE
FAJITAS	FALLIBLE	FAMISHED	FANIONS	FANZINES
FAKE	FALLIBLY	FAMISHES	FANK	FAP
FAKED	FALLING	FAMISHING	FANKLE	FAQUIR
FAKEMENT	FALLINGS	FAMOUS	FANKLED	FAQUIRS
FAKEMENTS	FALLOUT	FAMOUSED	FANKLES	FAR
FAKER	FALLOUTS	FAMOUSES	FANKLING	FARAD
FAKERIES	FALLOW	FAMOUSING	FANKS	FARADAY
FAKERS	FALLOWED	FAMOUSLY	FANLIGHT	FARADAYS
FAKERY	FALLOWER	FAMULUS	FANLIGHTS	FARADIC
FAKES	FALLOWEST	FAMULUSES	FANNED	FARADISE
FAKING	FALLOWING	FAN	FANNEL	FARADISED
FAKIR	FALLOWS	FANAL	FANNELL	FARADISES
FAKIRISM	FALLS	FANALS	FANNELLS	FARADISING
FAKIRISMS	FALSE	FANATIC	FANNELS	FARADISM
FAKIRS	FALSED	FANATICAL	FANNER	FARADISMS
FALAFEL	FALSEHOOD	FANATICS	FANNERS	FARADIZE
FALAFELS	FALSEHOODS	FANCIABLE	FANNIES	FARADIZED
FALAJ	FALSELY	FANCIED	FANNING	FARADIZES
FALANGISM	FALSENESS	FANCIER	FANNINGS	FARADIZING
FALANGISMS	FALSENESSES	FANCIERS	FANNY	FARADS
FALANGIST	FALSER	FANCIES	FANON	FARAND
FALANGISTS	FALSERS	FANCIEST	FANONS	FARANDINE
FALBALA	FALSES	FANCIFUL	FANS	FARANDINES
FALBALAS	FALSEST	FANCILESS	FANTAD	FARANDOLE
FALCADE	FALSETTO	FANCY	FANTADS	FARANDOLES
FALCADES	FALSETTOS	FANCYING	FANTAIL	FARAWAY
FALCATE	FALSEWORK	FANCYWORK	FANTAILED	FARAWAYS
FALCATED	FALSEWORKS	FANCYWORKS	FANTAILS	FARCE
FALCATION	FALSIES	FAND	FANTASIA	FARCED
FALCATIONS	FALSIFIED	FANDANGLE	FANTASIAS	FARCES
FALCES	FALSIFIER	FANDANGLES	FANTASIED	FARCEUR
FALCHION	FALSIFIERS	FANDANGO	FANTASIES	FARCEURS
FALCHIONS	FALSIFIES	FANDANGOES	FANTASISE	FARCEUSE
FALCIFORM	FALSIFY	FANDANGOS	FANTASISED	FARCEUSES
FALCON	FALSIFYING	FANDED	FANTASISES	FARCI
FALCONER	FALSING	FANDING	FANTASISING	FARCICAL
FALCONERS	FALSISH	FANDOM	FANTASIST	FARCIED
FALCONET	FALSISM	FANDOMS	FANTASISTS	FARCIES
FALCONETS	FALSISMS	FANDS	FANTASIZE	FARCIFIED
FALCONINE	FALSITIES	FANE	FANTASIZED	FARCIFIES
FALCONRIES	FALSITY	FANES	FANTASIZES	FARCIFY
FALCONRY	FALTBOAT	FANFARADE	FANTASIZING	FARCIFYING

The Chambers Dictionary is the authority for many longer words; see *OSW* Introduction, page xii

FARCIN	FARRIERIES	FASHERY	FATIGATES	FAUCHONS
FARCING	FARRIERS	FASHES	FATIGATING	FAUCIAL
FARCINGS	FARRIERY	FASHING	FATIGUE	FAUGH
FARCINS	FARRING	FASHION	FATIGUED	FAULCHIN
FARCY	FARROW	FASHIONED	FATIGUES	FAULCHINS
FARD	FARROWED	FASHIONER	FATIGUING	FAULCHION
FARDAGE	FARROWING	FASHIONERS	FATISCENT	FAULCHIONS
FARDAGES	FARROWS	FASHIONING	FATLING	FAULT
FARDED	FARRUCA	FASHIONS	FATLINGS	FAULTED
FARDEL	FARRUCAS	FASHIOUS	FATLY	FAULTFUL
FARDELS	FARS	FAST	FATNESS	FAULTIER
FARDEN	FARSE	FASTBACK	FATNESSES	FAULTIEST
FARDENS	FARSED	FASTBACKS	FATS	FAULTILY
FARDING	FARSES	FASTBALL	FATSIA	FAULTING
FARDINGS	FARSING	FASTBALLS	FATSIAS	FAULTLESS
FARDS	FART	FASTED	FATSO	FAULTS
FARE	FARTED	FASTEN	FATSOES	FAULTY
FARED	FARTHEL	FASTENED	FATSOS	FAUN
FARES	FARTHELS	FASTENER	FATSTOCK	FAUNA
FAREWELL	FARTHER	FASTENERS	FATSTOCKS	FAUNAE
FAREWELLS	FARTHEST	FASTENING	FATTED	FAUNAL
FARFET	FARTHING	FASTENINGS	FATTEN	FAUNAS
FARINA	FARTHINGS	FASTENS	FATTENED	FAUNIST
FARINAS	FARTING	FASTER	FATTENER	FAUNISTIC
FARING	FARTLEK	FASTERS	FATTENERS	FAUNISTS
FARINOSE	FARTLEKS	FASTEST	FATTENING	FAUNS
FARL	FARTS	FASTI	FATTENINGS	FAURD
FARLE	FAS	FASTIGIUM	FATTENS	FAUSTIAN
FARLES	FASCES	FASTIGIUMS	FATTER	FAUTEUIL
FARLS	FASCI	FASTING	FATTEST	FAUTEUILS
FARM	FASCIA	FASTINGS	FATTIER	FAUTOR
FARMED	FASCIAL	FASTISH	FATTIES	FAUTORS
FARMER	FASCIAS	FASTLY	FATTIEST	FAUVETTE
FARMERESS	FASCIATE	FASTNESS	FATTINESS	FAUVETTES
FARMERESSES	FASCIATED	FASTNESSES	FATTINESSES	FAUX
FARMERIES	FASCICLE	FASTS	FATTING	FAVE
FARMERS	FASCICLED	FASTUOUS	FATTISH	FAVEL
FARMERY	FASCICLES	FAT	FATTISM	FAVELA
FARMHOUSE	FASCICULE	FATAL	FATTISMS	FAVELAS
FARMHOUSES	FASCICULES	FATALISM	FATTIST	FAVELL
FARMING	FASCICULI	FATALISMS	FATTISTS	FAVEOLATE
FARMINGS	FASCINATE	FATALIST	FATTRELS	FAVER
FARMOST	FASCINATED	FATALISTS	FATTY	FAVEST
FARMS	FASCINATES	FATALITIES	FATUITIES	FAVISM
FARMSTEAD	FASCINATING	FATALITY	FATUITOUS	FAVISMS
FARMSTEADS	FASCINE	FATALLY	FATUITY	FAVOR
FARMYARD	FASCINES	FATE	FATUOUS	FAVORABLE
FARMYARDS	FASCIO	FATED	FATWA	FAVORABLY
FARNESOL	FASCIOLA	FATEFUL	FATWAED	FAVORED
FARNESOLS	FASCIOLAS	FATEFULLY	FATWAH	FAVORER
FARNESS	FASCIOLE	FATES	FATWAHED	FAVORERS
FARNESSES	FASCIOLES	FATHER	FATWAHING	FAVORING
FARO	FASCISM	FATHERED	FATWAHS	FAVORITE
FAROS	FASCISMI	FATHERING	FATWAING	FAVORITES
FAROUCHE	FASCISMO	FATHERLY	FATWAS	FAVORLESS
FARRAGO	FASCISMS	FATHERS	FAUBOURG	FAVORS
FARRAGOES	FASCIST	FATHOM	FAUBOURGS	FAVOSE
FARRAGOS	FASCISTA	FATHOMED	FAUCAL	FAVOUR
FARRAND	FASCISTI	FATHOMING	FAUCES	FAVOURED
FARRANT	FASCISTIC	FATHOMS	FAUCET	FAVOURER
FARRED	FASCISTS	FATIDICAL	FAUCETS	FAVOURERS
FARREN	FASH	FATIGABLE	FAUCHION	FAVOURING
FARRENS	FASHED	FATIGATE	FAUCHIONS	FAVOURITE
FARRIER	FASHERIES	FATIGATED	FAUCHON	FAVOURITES

FAVOURS	FEAST	FECUNDATE	FEERIE	FELINITY
FAVOUS	FEASTED	FECUNDATED	FEERIES	FELL
FAVRILE	FEASTER	FECUNDATES	FEERIN	FELLA
FAVRILES	FEASTERS	FECUNDATING	FEERING	FELLABLE
FAVUS	FEASTFUL	FECUNDITIES	FEERINGS	FELLAH
FAVUSES	FEASTING	FECUNDITY	FEERINS	FELLAHEEN
FAW	FEASTINGS	FED	FEERS	FELLAHIN
FAWN	FEASTS	FEDARIE	FEES	FELLAHS
FAWNED	FEAT	FEDARIES	FEESE	FELLAS
FAWNER	FEATED	FEDAYEE	FEESED	FELLATE
FAWNERS	FEATEOUS	FEDAYEEN	FEESES	FELLATED
FAWNING	FEATHER	FEDELINI	FEESING	FELLATES
FAWNINGLY	FEATHERED	FEDELINIS	FEET	FELLATING
FAWNINGS	FEATHERIER	FEDERACIES	FEETLESS	FELLATIO
FAWNS	FEATHERIEST	FEDERACY	FEEZE	FELLATION
FAWS	FEATHERING	FEDERAL	FEEZED	FELLATIONS
FAX	FEATHERINGS	FEDERALS	FEEZES	FELLATIOS
FAXED	FEATHERS	FEDERARIE	FEEZING	FELLED
FAXES	FEATHERY	FEDERARIES	FEGARIES	FELLER
FAXING	FEATING	FEDERARY	FEGARY	FELLERS
FAY	FEATLY	FEDERATE	FEGS	FELLEST
FAYALITE	FEATOUS	FEDERATED	FEHM	FELLIES
FAYALITES	FEATS	FEDERATES	FEHME	FELLING
FAYED	FEATUOUS	FEDERATING	FEHMIC	FELLNESS
FAYENCE	FEATURE	FEDORA	FEIGN	FELLNESSES
FAYENCES	FEATURED	FEDORAS	FEIGNED	FELLOE
FAYER	FEATURELY	FEDS	FEIGNEDLY	FELLOES
FAYEST	FEATURES	FEE	FEIGNING	FELLOW
FAYING	FEATURING	FEEBLE	FEIGNINGS	FELLOWLY
FAYNE	FEBLESSE	FEEBLED	FEIGNS	FELLOWS
FAYNED	FEBLESSES	FEEBLER	FEIJOA	FELLS
FAYNES	FEBRICITIES	FEEBLES	FEIJOAS	FELLY
FAYNING	FEBRICITY	FEEBLEST	FEINT	FELON
FAYRE	FEBRICULA	FEEBLING	FEINTED	FELONIES
FAYRES	FEBRICULAS	FEEBLISH	FEINTER	FELONIOUS
FAYS	FEBRICULE	FEEBLY	FEINTEST	FELONOUS
FAZE	FEBRICULES	FEED	FEINTING	FELONRIES
FAZED	FEBRIFIC	FEEDBACK	FEINTS	FELONRY
FAZENDA	FEBRIFUGE	FEEDBACKS	FEIS	FELONS
FAZENDAS	FEBRIFUGES	FEEDER	FEISEANNA	FELONY
FAZES	FEBRILE	FEEDERS	FEISTIER	FELSIC
FAZING	FEBRILITIES	FEEDING	FEISTIEST	FELSITE
FEAGUE	FEBRILITY	FEEDINGS	FEISTY	FELSITES
FEAGUED	FECAL	FEEDLOT	FELAFEL	FELSITIC
FEAGUES	FECES	FEEDLOTS	FELAFELS	FELSPAR
FEAGUING	FECHT	FEEDS	FELDGRAU	FELSPARS
FEAL	FECHTER	FEEDSTOCK	FELDGRAUS	FELSTONE
FEALED	FECHTERS	FEEDSTOCKS	FELDSHER	FELSTONES
FEALING	FECHTING	FEEDSTUFF	FELDSHERS	FELT
FEALS	FECHTS	FEEDSTUFFS	FELDSPAR	FELTED
FEALTIES	FECIAL	FEEING	FELDSPARS	FELTER
FEALTY	FECIT	FEEL	FELDSPATH	FELTERED
FEAR	FECK	FEELBAD	FELDSPATHS	FELTERING
FEARE	FECKLESS	FEELBADS	FELICIA	FELTERS
FEARED	FECKLY	FEELER	FELICIAS	FELTIER
FEARES	FECKS	FEELERS	FELICIFIC	FELTIEST
FEARFUL	FECULA	FEELGOOD	FELICITER	FELTING
FEARFULLY	FECULAS	FEELGOODS	FELICITIES	FELTINGS
FEARING	FECULENCE	FEELING	FELICITY	FELTS
FEARLESS	FECULENCES	FEELINGLY	FELID	FELTY
FEARS	FECULENCIES	FEELINGS	FELIDS	FELUCCA
FEARSOME	FECULENCY	FEELS	FELINE	FELUCCAS
FEASIBLE	FECULENT	FEER	FELINES	FELWORT
FEASIBLY	FECUND	FEERED	FELINITIES	FELWORTS

FIGURES	FILFOT	FILMISH	FINALLY	FINICKETY
FIGURINE	FILFOTS	FILMLAND	FINALS	FINICKIER
FIGURINES	FILIAL	FILMLANDS	FINANCE	FINICKIEST
FIGURING	FILIALLY	FILMS	FINANCED	FINICKING
FIGURIST	FILIATE	FILMSET	FINANCES	FINICKINGS
FIGURISTS	FILIATED	FILMSETS	FINANCIAL	FINICKY
FIGWORT	FILIATES	FILMSETTING	FINANCIER	FINIKIN
FIGWORTS	FILIATING	FILMSETTINGS	FINANCIERED	FINING
FIKE	FILIATION	FILMY	FINANCIERING	FININGS
FIKED	FILIATIONS	FILO	FINANCIERS	FINIS
FIKERIES	FILIBEG	FILOPLUME	FINANCING	FINISH
FIKERY	FILIBEGS	FILOPLUMES	FINBACK	FINISHED
FIKES	FILICIDE	FILOPODIA	FINBACKS	FINISHER
FIKIER	FILICIDES	FILOS	FINCH	FINISHERS
FIKIEST	FILIFORM	FILOSE	FINCHED	FINISHES
FIKING	FILIGRAIN	FILOSELLE	FINCHES	FINISHING
FIKISH	FILIGRAINS	FILOSELLES	FIND	FINISHINGS
FIKY	FILIGRANE	FILS	FINDER	FINITE
FIL	FILIGRANES	FILTER	FINDERS	FINITELY
FILABEG	FILIGREE	FILTERED	FINDING	FINITUDE
FILABEGS	FILIGREED	FILTERING	FINDINGS	FINITUDES
FILACEOUS	FILIGREES	FILTERS	FINDRAM	FINJAN
FILACER	FILING	FILTH	FINDRAMS	FINJANS
FILACERS	FILINGS	FILTHIER	FINDS	FINK
FILAGREE	FILIOQUE	FILTHIEST	FINE	FINKED
FILAGREES	FILIOQUES	FILTHILY	FINED	FINKING
FILAMENT	FILL	FILTHS	FINEER	FINKS
FILAMENTS	FILLE	FILTHY	FINEERED	FINLESS
FILANDER	FILLED	FILTRABLE	FINEERING	FINNAC
FILANDERS	FILLER	FILTRATE	FINEERS	FINNACK
FILAR	FILLERS	FILTRATED	FINEISH	FINNACKS
FILARIA	FILLES	FILTRATES	FINELESS	FINNACS
FILARIAL	FILLET	FILTRATING	FINELY	FINNAN
FILARIAS	FILLETED	FIMBLE	FINENESS	FINNANS
FILASSE	FILLETING	FIMBLES	FINENESSES	FINNED
FILASSES	FILLETS	FIMBRIA	FINER	FINNER
FILATORIES	FILLIBEG	FIMBRIAE	FINERIES	FINNERS
FILATORY	FILLIBEGS	FIMBRIATE	FINERS	FINNESKO
FILATURE	FILLIES	FIMBRIATED	FINERY	FINNIER
FILATURES	FILLING	FIMBRIATES	FINES	FINNIEST
FILAZER	FILLINGS	FIMBRIATING	FINESSE	FINNOCHIO
FILAZERS	FILLIP	FIN	FINESSED	FINNOCHIOS
FILBERD	FILLIPED	FINABLE	FINESSER	FINNOCK
FILBERDS	FILLIPEEN	FINAGLE	FINESSERS	FINNOCKS
FILBERT	FILLIPEENS	FINAGLED	FINESSES	FINNSKO
FILBERTS	FILLIPING	FINAGLES	FINESSING	FINNY
FILCH	FILLIPS	FINAGLING	FINESSINGS	FINO
FILCHED	FILLISTER	FINAL	FINEST	FINOCCHIO
FILCHER	FILLISTERS	FINALE	FINGAN	FINOCCHIOS
FILCHERS	FILLS	FINALES	FINGANS	FINOCHIO
FILCHES	FILLY	FINALISE	FINGER	FINOCHIOS
FILCHING	FILM	FINALISED	FINGERED	FINOS
FILCHINGS	FILMABLE	FINALISES	FINGERING	FINS
FILE	FILMDOM	FINALISING	FINGERINGS	FINSKO
FILED	FILMDOMS	FINALISM	FINGERS	FIORD
FILEMOT	FILMED	FINALISMS	FINGERTIP	FIORDS
FILEMOTS	FILMGOER	FINALIST	FINGERTIPS	FIORIN
FILENAME	FILMGOERS	FINALISTS	FINI	FIORINS
FILENAMES	FILMIC	FINALITIES	FINIAL	FIORITURA
FILER	FILMIER	FINALITY	FINIALS	FIORITURE
FILERS	FILMIEST	FINALIZE	FINICAL	FIPPENCE
FILES	FILMINESS	FINALIZED	FINICALLY	FIPPENCES
FILET	FILMINESSES	FINALIZES	FINICKETIER	FIPPLE
FILETS	FILMING	FINALIZING	FINICKETIEST	FIPPLES

FIR	FIREWEED	FISHER	FISTING	FIXED
FIRE	FIREWEEDS	FISHERIES	FISTMELE	FIXEDLY
FIREARM	FIREWOMAN	FISHERMAN	FISTMELES	FIXEDNESS
FIREARMS	FIREWOMEN	FISHERMEN	FISTS	FIXEDNESSES
FIREBALL	FIREWOOD	FISHERY	FISTULA	FIXER
FIREBALLS	FIREWOODS	FISHES	FISTULAE	FIXERS
FIREBOX	FIREWORK	FISHEYE	FISTULAR	FIXES
FIREBOXES	FIREWORKS	FISHEYES	FISTULAS	FIXING
FIREBRAND	FIREWORM	FISHFUL	FISTULOSE	FIXINGS
FIREBRANDS	FIREWORMS	FISHGIG	FISTULOUS	FIXITIES
FIREBRAT	FIRING	FISHGIGS	FISTY	FIXITY
FIREBRATS	FIRINGS	FISHIER	FIT	FIXIVE
FIREBRICK	FIRK	FISHIEST	FITCH	FIXTURE
FIREBRICKS	FIRKED	FISHIFIED	FITCHE	FIXTURES
FIREBUG	FIRKIN	FISHIFIES	FITCHEE	FIXURE
FIREBUGS	FIRKING	FISHIFY	FITCHES	FIXURES
FIRECREST	FIRKINS	FISHIFYING	FITCHET	FIZ
FIRECRESTS	FIRKS	FISHINESS	FITCHETS	FIZGIG
FIRED	FIRLOT	FISHINESSES	FITCHEW	FIZGIGS
FIREDAMP	FIRLOTS	FISHING	FITCHEWS	FIZZ
FIREDAMPS	FIRM	FISHINGS	FITCHY	FIZZED
FIREDOG	FIRMAMENT	FISHSKIN	FITFUL	FIZZEN
FIREDOGS	FIRMAMENTS	FISHSKINS	FITFULLY	FIZZENS
FIREFLIES	FIRMAN	FISHWIFE	FITLIER	FIZZER
FIREFLOAT	FIRMANS	FISHWIVES	FITLIEST	FIZZERS
FIREFLOATS	FIRMED	FISHY	FITLY	FIZZES
FIREFLY	FIRMER	FISHYBACK	FITMENT	FIZZGIG
FIREGUARD	FIRMERS	FISHYBACKS	FITMENTS	FIZZGIGS
FIREGUARDS	FIRMEST	FISK	FITNESS	FIZZIER
FIREHOUSE	FIRMING	FISKED	FITNESSES	FIZZIEST
FIREHOUSES	FIRMLESS	FISKING	FITS	FIZZING
FIRELESS	FIRMLY	FISKS	FITT	FIZZINGS
FIRELIGHT	FIRMNESS	FISNOMIE	FITTE	FIZZLE
FIRELIGHTS	FIRMNESSES	FISNOMIES	FITTED	FIZZLED
FIRELOCK	FIRMS	FISSILE	FITTER	FIZZLES
FIRELOCKS	FIRMWARE	FISSILITIES	FITTERS	FIZZLING
FIREMAN	FIRMWARES	FISSILITY	FITTES	FIZZY
FIREMARK	FIRN	FISSION	FITTEST	FJORD
FIREMARKS	FIRNS	FISSIONS	FITTING	FJORDS
FIREMEN	FIRRIER	FISSIPED	FITTINGLY	FLAB
FIREPAN	FIRRIEST	FISSIPEDE	FITTINGS	FLABBIER
FIREPANS	FIRRING	FISSIPEDES	FITTS	FLABBIEST
FIREPLACE	FIRRINGS	FISSIPEDS	FIVE	FLABBILY
FIREPLACES	FIRRY	FISSIVE	FIVEFOLD	FLABBY
FIREPOT	FIRS	FISSLE	FIVEPENCE	FLABELLA
FIREPOTS	FIRST	FISSLED	FIVEPENCES	FLABELLUM
FIREPROOF	FIRSTLING	FISSLES	FIVEPENNY	FLABELLUMS
FIREPROOFED	FIRSTLINGS	FISSLING	FIVEPIN	FLABS
FIREPROOFING	FIRSTLY	FISSURE	FIVEPINS	FLACCID
FIREPROOFINGS	FIRSTS	FISSURED	FIVER	FLACCIDER
FIREPROOFS	FIRTH	FISSURES	FIVERS	FLACCIDEST
FIRER	FIRTHS	FISSURING	FIVES	FLACCIDLY
FIRERS	FISC	FIST	FIX	FLACK
FIRES	FISCAL	FISTED	FIXABLE	FLACKER
FIRESHIP	FISCALLY	FISTFUL	FIXATE	FLACKERED
FIRESHIPS	FISCALS	FISTFULS	FIXATED	FLACKERING
FIRESIDE	FISCS	FISTIANA	FIXATES	FLACKERS
FIRESIDES	FISGIG	FISTIC	FIXATING	FLACKET
FIRESTONE	FISGIGS	FISTICAL	FIXATION	FLACKETS
FIRESTONES	FISH	FISTICUFF	FIXATIONS	FLACKS
FIRETHORN	FISHABLE	FISTICUFFS	FIXATIVE	FLACON
FIRETHORNS	FISHBALL	FISTIER	FIXATIVES	FLACONS
FIREWALL	FISHBALLS	FISTIEST	FIXATURE	FLAFF
FIREWALLS	FISHED	FISTIEST	FIXATURES	FLAFFED

FLAFFER	FLAMED	FLAPPED	FLATLONG	FLAUTIST
FLAFFERED	FLAMELESS	FLAPPER	FLATLY	FLAUTISTS
FLAFFERING	FLAMELET	FLAPPERS	FLATMATE	FLAVIN
FLAFFERS	FLAMELETS	FLAPPIER	FLATMATES	FLAVINE
FLAFFING	FLAMEN	FLAPPIEST	FLATNESS	FLAVINES
FLAFFS	FLAMENCO	FLAPPING	FLATNESSES	FLAVINS
FLAG	FLAMENCOS	FLAPPINGS	FLATPACK	FLAVONE
FLAGELLA	FLAMENS	FLAPPY	FLATPACKS	FLAVONES
FLAGELLUM	FLAMEOUT	FLAPS	FLATS	FLAVOR
FLAGEOLET	FLAMEOUTS	FLAPTRACK	FLATSHARE	FLAVORED
FLAGEOLETS	FLAMES	FLAPTRACKS	FLATSHARES	FLAVORING
FLAGGED	FLAMFEW	FLARE	FLATTED	FLAVORINGS
FLAGGIER	FLAMFEWS	FLARED	FLATTEN	FLAVOROUS
FLAGGIEST	FLAMIER	FLARES	FLATTENED	FLAVORS
FLAGGING	FLAMIEST	FLARIER	FLATTENING	FLAVOUR
FLAGGINGS	FLAMINES	FLARIEST	FLATTENS	FLAVOURED
FLAGGY	FLAMING	FLARING	FLATTER	FLAVOURING
FLAGITATE	FLAMINGLY	FLARINGLY	FLATTERED	FLAVOURINGS
FLAGITATED	FLAMINGO	FLARY	FLATTERER	FLAVOURS
FLAGITATES	FLAMINGOES	FLASER	FLATTERERS	FLAW
FLAGITATING	FLAMINGOS	FLASERS	FLATTERIES	FLAWED
FLAGON	FLAMM	FLASH	FLATTERING	FLAWIER
FLAGONS	FLAMMABLE	FLASHBACK	FLATTERS	FLAWIEST
FLAGPOLE	FLAMMED	FLASHBACKED	FLATTERY	FLAWING
FLAGPOLES	FLAMMING	FLASHBACKING	FLATTEST	FLAWLESS
FLAGRANCE	FLAMMS	FLASHBACKS	FLATTIES	FLAWN
FLAGRANCES	FLAMMULE	FLASHBULB	FLATTING	FLAWNS
FLAGRANCIES	FLAMMULES	FLASHBULBS	FLATTINGS	FLAWS
FLAGRANCY	FLAMS	FLASHCUBE	FLATTISH	FLAWY
FLAGRANT	FLAMY	FLASHCUBES	FLATTY	FLAX
FLAGS	FLAN	FLASHED	FLATULENT	FLAXEN
FLAGSHIP	FLANCH	FLASHER	FLATUOUS	FLAXES
FLAGSHIPS	FLANCHED	FLASHERS	FLATUS	FLAXIER
FLAGSTAFF	FLANCHES	FLASHES	FLATUSES	FLAXIEST
FLAGSTAFFS	FLANCHING	FLASHEST	FLATWARE	FLAXY
FLAGSTICK	FLANCHINGS	FLASHGUN	FLATWARES	FLAY
FLAGSTICKS	FLANERIE	FLASHGUNS	FLATWAYS	FLAYED
FLAGSTONE	FLANERIES	FLASHIER	FLATWISE	FLAYER
FLAGSTONES	FLANEUR	FLASHIEST	FLATWORM	FLAYERS
FLAIL	FLANEURS	FLASHILY	FLATWORMS	FLAYING
FLAILED	FLANGE	FLASHING	FLAUGHT	FLAYS
FLAILING	FLANGED	FLASHINGS	FLAUGHTED	FLEA
FLAILS	FLANGES	FLASHY	FLAUGHTER	FLEAM
FLAIR	FLANGING	FLASK	FLAUGHTERED	FLEAMS
FLAIRS	FLANK	FLASKET	FLAUGHTERING	FLEAPIT
FLAK	FLANKED	FLASKETS	FLAUGHTERS	FLEAPITS
FLAKE	FLANKER	FLASKS	FLAUGHTING	FLEAS
FLAKED	FLANKERED	FLAT	FLAUGHTS	FLEASOME
FLAKES	FLANKERING	FLATBACK	FLAUNCH	FLEAWORT
FLAKIER	FLANKERS	FLATBACKS	FLAUNCHED	FLEAWORTS
FLAKIES	FLANKING	FLATBED	FLAUNCHES	FLECHE
FLAKIEST	FLANKS	FLATBEDS	FLAUNCHING	FLECHES
FLAKINESS	FLANNEL	FLATBOAT	FLAUNCHINGS	FLECHETTE
FLAKINESSES	FLANNELLED	FLATBOATS	FLAUNE	FLECHETTES
FLAKING	FLANNELLING	FLATFISH	FLAUNES	FLECK
FLAKS	FLANNELLY	FLATFISHES	FLAUNT	FLECKED
FLAKY	FLANNELS	FLATHEAD	FLAUNTED	FLECKER
FLAM	FLANNEN	FLATHEADS	FLAUNTER	FLECKERED
FLAMBE	FLANNENS	FLATIRON	FLAUNTERS	FLECKERING
FLAMBEAU	FLANS	FLATIRONS	FLAUNTIER	FLECKERS
FLAMBEAUS	FLAP	FLATLET	FLAUNTIEST	FLECKING
FLAMBEAUX	FLAPJACK	FLATLETS	FLAUNTING	FLECKLESS
FLAMBEED	FLAPJACKS	FLATLING	FLAUNTS	FLECKS
FLAME	FLAPPABLE	FLATLINGS	FLAUNTY	FLECTION

The Chambers Dictionary is the authority for many longer words; see *OSW* Introduction, page xii

FLECTIONS	FLESH	FLICHTERED	FLIPPER	FLOCCULAR
FLED	FLESHED	FLICHTERING	FLIPPERS	FLOCCULE
FLEDGE	FLESHER	FLICHTERS	FLIPPEST	FLOCCULES
FLEDGED	FLESHERS	FLICK	FLIPPING	FLOCCULI
FLEDGES	FLESHES	FLICKED	FLIPS	FLOCCULUS
FLEDGIER	FLESHHOOD	FLICKER	FLIRT	FLOCCUS
FLEDGIEST	FLESHHOODS	FLICKERED	FLIRTED	FLOCK
FLEDGING	FLESHIER	FLICKERING	FLIRTIER	FLOCKED
FLEDGLING	FLESHIEST	FLICKERS	FLIRTIEST	FLOCKING
FLEDGLINGS	FLESHING	FLICKING	FLIRTING	FLOCKS
FLEDGY	FLESHINGS	FLICKS	FLIRTINGS	FLOE
FLEE	FLESHLESS	FLICS	FLIRTISH	FLOES
FLEECE	FLESHLIER	FLIER	FLIRTS	FLOG
FLEECED	FLESHLIEST	FLIERS	FLIRTY	FLOGGED
FLEECER	FLESHLING	FLIES	FLISK	FLOGGING
FLEECERS	FLESHLINGS	FLIEST	FLISKED	FLOGGINGS
FLEECES	FLESHLY	FLIGHT	FLISKIER	FLOGS
FLEECH	FLESHMENT	FLIGHTED	FLISKIEST	FLOKATI
FLEECHED	FLESHMENTS	FLIGHTIER	FLISKING	FLOKATIS
FLEECHES	FLESHWORM	FLIGHTIEST	FLISKS	FLONG
FLEECHING	FLESHWORMS	FLIGHTILY	FLISKY	FLONGS
FLEECHINGS	FLESHY	FLIGHTING	FLIT	FLOOD
FLEECIER	FLETCH	FLIGHTS	FLITCH	FLOODED
FLEECIEST	FLETCHED	FLIGHTY	FLITCHES	FLOODGATE
FLEECING	FLETCHER	FLIMP	FLITE	FLOODGATES
FLEECY	FLETCHERS	FLIMPED	FLITED	FLOODING
FLEEING	FLETCHES	FLIMPING	FLITES	FLOODINGS
FLEER	FLETCHING	FLIMPS	FLITING	FLOODLIT
FLEERED	FLETTON	FLIMSIER	FLITS	FLOODMARK
FLEERER	FLETTONS	FLIMSIES	FLITT	FLOODMARKS
FLEERERS	FLEURET	FLIMSIEST	FLITTED	FLOODS
FLEERING	FLEURETS	FLIMSILY	FLITTER	FLOODTIDE
FLEERINGS	FLEURETTE	FLIMSY	FLITTERED	FLOODTIDES
FLEERS	FLEURETTES	FLINCH	FLITTERING	FLOODWALL
FLEES	FLEURON	FLINCHED	FLITTERN	FLOODWALLS
FLEET	FLEURONS	FLINCHER	FLITTERNS	FLOODWAY
FLEETED	FLEURY	FLINCHERS	FLITTERS	FLOODWAYS
FLEETER	FLEW	FLINCHES	FLITTING	FLOOR
FLEETEST	FLEWED	FLINCHING	FLITTINGS	FLOORED
FLEETING	FLEWS	FLINCHINGS	FLIVVER	FLOORER
FLEETLY	FLEX	FLINDER	FLIVVERS	FLOORERS
FLEETNESS	FLEXED	FLINDERS	FLIX	FLOORHEAD
FLEETNESSES	FLEXES	FLING	FLIXED	FLOORHEADS
FLEETS	FLEXIBLE	FLINGER	FLIXES	FLOORING
FLEG	FLEXIBLY	FLINGERS	FLIXING	FLOORINGS
FLEGGED	FLEXILE	FLINGING	FLOAT	FLOORS
FLEGGING	FLEXING	FLINGS	FLOATABLE	FLOOSIE
FLEGS	FLEXION	FLINT	FLOATAGE	FLOOSIES
FLEME	FLEXIONS	FLINTIER	FLOATAGES	FLOOSY
FLEMES	FLEXITIME	FLINTIEST	FLOATANT	FLOOZIE
FLEMING	FLEXITIMES	FLINTIFIED	FLOATANTS	FLOOZIES
FLEMISH	FLEXOR	FLINTIFIES	FLOATED	FLOOZY
FLEMISHED	FLEXORS	FLINTIFY	FLOATEL	FLOP
FLEMISHES	FLEXUOSE	FLINTIFYING	FLOATELS	FLOPHOUSE
FLEMISHING	FLEXUOUS	FLINTILY	FLOATER	FLOPHOUSES
FLEMIT	FLEXURAL	FLINTLOCK	FLOATERS	FLOPPED
FLENCH	FLEXURE	FLINTLOCKS	FLOATIER	FLOPPIER
FLENCHED	FLEXURES	FLINTS	FLOATIEST	FLOPPIES
FLENCHES	FLEY	FLINTY	FLOATING	FLOPPIEST
FLENCHING	FLEYED	FLIP	FLOATINGS	FLOPPILY
FLENSE	FLEYING	FLIPPANCIES	FLOATS	FLOPPING
FLENSED	FLEYS	FLIPPANCY	FLOATY	FLOPPY
FLENSES	FLIC	FLIPPANT	FLOCCI	FLOPS
FLENSING	FLICHTER	FLIPPED	FLOCCOSE	FLOPTICAL

The Chambers Dictionary is the authority for many longer words; see OSW Introduction, page xii

FLOR	FLOTILLA	FLOWN	FLUKES	FLUSHNESSES
FLORA	FLOTILLAS	FLOWS	FLUKEY	FLUSHY
FLORAE	FLOTSAM	FLU	FLUKIER	FLUSTER
FLORAL	FLOTSAMS	FLUATE	FLUKIEST	FLUSTERED
FLORALLY	FLOUNCE	FLUATES	FLUKING	FLUSTERING
FLORAS	FLOUNCED	FLUB	FLUKY	FLUSTERS
FLOREAT	FLOUNCES	FLUBBED	FLUME	FLUSTERY
FLOREATED	FLOUNCIER	FLUBBING	FLUMES	FLUSTRATE
FLORENCE	FLOUNCIEST	FLUBS	FLUMMERIES	FLUSTRATED
FLORENCES	FLOUNCING	FLUCTUANT	FLUMMERY	FLUSTRATES
FLORET	FLOUNCINGS	FLUCTUATE	FLUMMOX	FLUSTRATING
FLORETS	FLOUNCY	FLUCTUATED	FLUMMOXED	FLUTE
FLORIATED	FLOUNDER	FLUCTUATES	FLUMMOXES	FLUTED
FLORID	FLOUNDERED	FLUCTUATING	FLUMMOXING	FLUTER
FLORIDEAN	FLOUNDERING	FLUE	FLUMP	FLUTERS
FLORIDEANS	FLOUNDERS	FLUELLIN	FLUMPED	FLUTES
FLORIDER	FLOUR	FLUELLINS	FLUMPING	FLUTIER
FLORIDEST	FLOURED	FLUENCE	FLUMPS	FLUTIEST
FLORIDITIES	FLOURIER	FLUENCES	FLUNG	FLUTINA
FLORIDITY	FLOURIEST	FLUENCIES	FLUNK	FLUTINAS
FLORIDLY	FLOURING	FLUENCY	FLUNKED	FLUTING
FLORIER	FLOURISH	FLUENT	FLUNKEY	FLUTINGS
FLORIEST	FLOURISHED	FLUENTLY	FLUNKEYS	FLUTIST
FLORIFORM	FLOURISHES	FLUENTS	FLUNKIES	FLUTISTS
FLORIGEN	FLOURISHING	FLUES	FLUNKING	FLUTTER
FLORIGENS	FLOURISHY	FLUEWORK	FLUNKS	FLUTTERED
FLORIN	FLOURS	FLUEWORKS	FLUNKY	FLUTTERING
FLORINS	FLOURY	FLUEY	FLUOR	FLUTTERS
FLORIST	FLOUSE	FLUFF	FLUORESCE	FLUTY
FLORISTIC	FLOUSED	FLUFFED	FLUORESCED	FLUVIAL
FLORISTICS	FLOUSES	FLUFFIER	FLUORESCES	FLUVIATIC
FLORISTRIES	FLOUSH	FLUFFIEST	FLUORESCING	FLUX
FLORISTRY	FLOUSHED	FLUFFING	FLUORIC	FLUXED
FLORISTS	FLOUSHES	FLUFFS	FLUORIDE	FLUXES
FLORS	FLOUSHING	FLUFFY	FLUORIDES	FLUXING
FLORUIT	FLOUSING	FLUGEL	FLUORINE	FLUXION
FLORUITED	FLOUT	FLUGELMAN	FLUORINES	FLUXIONAL
FLORUITING	FLOUTED	FLUGELMEN	FLUORITE	FLUXIONS
FLORUITS	FLOUTING	FLUGELS	FLUORITES	FLUXIVE
FLORY	FLOUTS	FLUID	FLUOROSES	FLY
FLOSCULAR	FLOW	FLUIDAL	FLUOROSIS	FLYABLE
FLOSCULE	FLOWAGE	FLUIDIC	FLUORS	FLYAWAY
FLOSCULES	FLOWAGES	FLUIDICS	FLUORSPAR	FLYBANE
FLOSH	FLOWED	FLUIDIFIED	FLUORSPARS	FLYBANES
FLOSHES	FLOWER	FLUIDIFIES	FLURR	FLYBELT
FLOSS	FLOWERAGE	FLUIDIFY	FLURRED	FLYBELTS
FLOSSED	FLOWERAGES	FLUIDIFYING	FLURRIED	FLYBLOW
FLOSSES	FLOWERED	FLUIDISE	FLURRIES	FLYBLOWS
FLOSSIER	FLOWERER	FLUIDISED	FLURRING	FLYBOAT
FLOSSIEST	FLOWERERS	FLUIDISES	FLURRS	FLYBOATS
FLOSSING	FLOWERET	FLUIDISING	FLURRY	FLYBOOK
FLOSSINGS	FLOWERETS	FLUIDITIES	FLURRYING	FLYBOOKS
FLOSSY	FLOWERIER	FLUIDITY	FLUS	FLYER
FLOTA	FLOWERIEST	FLUIDIZE	FLUSH	FLYERS
FLOTAGE	FLOWERING	FLUIDIZED	FLUSHED	FLYEST
FLOTAGES	FLOWERINGS	FLUIDIZES	FLUSHER	FLYING
FLOTANT	FLOWERPOT	FLUIDIZING	FLUSHERS	FLYINGS
FLOTAS	FLOWERPOTS	FLUIDNESS	FLUSHES	FLYLEAF
FLOTATION	FLOWERS	FLUIDNESSES	FLUSHEST	FLYLEAVES
FLOTATIONS	FLOWERY	FLUIDS	FLUSHIER	FLYMAKER
FLOTE	FLOWING	FLUIER	FLUSHIEST	FLYMAKERS
FLOTEL	FLOWINGLY	FLUIEST	FLUSHING	FLYOVER
FLOTELS	FLOWMETER	FLUKE	FLUSHINGS	FLYOVERS
FLOTES	FLOWMETERS	FLUKED	FLUSHNESS	FLYPAPER

The Chambers Dictionary is the authority for many longer words; see *OSW* Introduction, page xii

FLYPAPERS	FOCUSINGS	FOGRAMITES	FOLIATION	FONDLED
FLYPE	FOCUSSED	FOGRAMITIES	FOLIATIONS	FONDLER
FLYPED	FOCUSSES	FOGRAMITY	FOLIATURE	FONDLERS
FLYPES	FOCUSSING	FOGRAMS	FOLIATURES	FONDLES
FLYPING	FODDER	FOGS	FOLIE	FONDLING
FLYPITCH	FODDERED	FOGY	FOLIES	FONDLINGS
FLYPITCHES	FODDERER	FOGYDOM	FOLIO	FONDLY
FLYSCH	FODDERERS	FOGYDOMS	FOLIOED	FONDNESS
FLYSCHES	FODDERING	FOGYISH	FOLIOING	FONDNESSES
FLYTE	FODDERINGS	FOGYISM	FOLIOLATE	FONDS
FLYTED	FODDERS	FOGYISMS	FOLIOLE	FONDUE
FLYTES	FOE	FOH	FOLIOLES	FONDUES
FLYTING	FOEDARIE	FOHN	FOLIOLOSE	FONE
FLYTINGS	FOEDARIES	FOHNS	FOLIOS	FONLY
FLYTRAP	FOEDERATI	FOHS	FOLIOSE	FONNED
FLYTRAPS	FOEHN	FOIBLE	FOLIUM	FONNING
FLYWAY	FOEHNS	FOIBLES	FOLK	FONS
FLYWAYS	FOEMAN	FOID	FOLKIE	FONT
FLYWEIGHT	FOEMEN	FOIDS	FOLKIES	FONTAL
FLYWEIGHTS	FOEN	FOIL	FOLKLAND	FONTANEL
FLYWHEEL	FOES	FOILBORNE	FOLKLANDS	FONTANELS
FLYWHEELS	FOETAL	FOILED	FOLKLORE	FONTANGE
FOAL	FOETICIDE	FOILING	FOLKLORES	FONTANGES
FOALED	FOETICIDES	FOILINGS	FOLKLORIC	FONTICULI
FOALFOOT	FOETID	FOILS	FOLKMOOT	FONTLET
FOALFOOTS	FOETIDER	FOIN	FOLKMOOTS	FONTLETS
FOALING	FOETIDEST	FOINED	FOLKS	FONTS
FOALS	FOETOR	FOINING	FOLKSIER	FOOD
FOAM	FOETORS	FOININGLY	FOLKSIEST	FOODFUL
FOAMED	FOETUS	FOINS	FOLKSY	FOODIE
FOAMIER	FOETUSES	FOISON	FOLKWAY	FOODIES
FOAMIEST	FOG	FOISONS	FOLKWAYS	FOODISM
FOAMILY	FOGASH	FOIST	FOLLICLE	FOODISMS
FOAMINESS	FOGASHES	FOISTED	FOLLICLES	FOODLESS
FOAMINESSES	FOGBOUND	FOISTER	FOLLIED	FOODS
FOAMING	FOGEY	FOISTERS	FOLLIES	FOODSTUFF
FOAMINGLY	FOGEYDOM	FOISTING	FOLLOW	FOODSTUFFS
FOAMINGS	FOGEYDOMS	FOISTS	FOLLOWED	FOODY
FOAMLESS	FOGEYISH	FOLACIN	FOLLOWER	FOOL
FOAMS	FOGEYISM	FOLACINS	FOLLOWERS	FOOLED
FOAMY	FOGEYISMS	FOLATE	FOLLOWING	FOOLERIES
FOB	FOGEYS	FOLATES	FOLLOWINGS	FOOLERY
FOBBED	FOGGAGE	FOLD	FOLLOWS	FOOLHARDIER
FOBBING	FOGGAGES	FOLDABLE	FOLLY	FOOLHARDIEST
FOBS	FOGGED	FOLDAWAY	FOLLYING	FOOLHARDY
FOCACCIA	FOGGER	FOLDBOAT	FOMENT	FOOLING
FOCACCIAS	FOGGERS	FOLDBOATS	FOMENTED	FOOLINGS
FOCAL	FOGGIER	FOLDED	FOMENTER	FOOLISH
FOCALISE	FOGGIEST	FOLDER	FOMENTERS	FOOLISHER
FOCALISED	FOGGILY	FOLDEROL	FOMENTING	FOOLISHEST
FOCALISES	FOGGINESS	FOLDEROLS	FOMENTS	FOOLISHLY
FOCALISING	FOGGINESSES	FOLDERS	FOMES	FOOLPROOF
FOCALIZE	FOGGING	FOLDING	FOMITES	FOOLS
FOCALIZED	FOGGY	FOLDINGS	FON	FOOLSCAP
FOCALIZES	FOGHORN	FOLDS	FOND	FOOLSCAPS
FOCALIZING	FOGHORNS	FOLIA	FONDA	FOOT
FOCALLY	FOGIES	FOLIAGE	FONDANT	FOOTAGE
FOCI	FOGLE	FOLIAGED	FONDANTS	FOOTAGES
FOCIMETER	FOGLES	FOLIAGES	FONDAS	FOOTBALL
FOCIMETERS	FOGLESS	FOLIAR	FONDED	FOOTBALLS
FOCUS	FOGMAN	FOLIATE	FONDER	FOOTBAR
FOCUSED	FOGMEN	FOLIATED	FONDEST	FOOTBARS
FOCUSES	FOGRAM	FOLIATES	FONDING	FOOTBOARD
FOCUSING	FOGRAMITE	FOLIATING	FONDLE	FOOTBOARDS

FOOTBOY	FOOTS	FORBIDDAL	FORECABIN	FOREKNOWN
FOOTBOYS	FOOTSLOG	FORBIDDALS	FORECABINS	FOREKNOWS
FOOTCLOTH	FOOTSLOGGED	FORBIDDEN	FORECAR	FOREL
FOOTCLOTHS	FOOTSLOGGING	FORBIDDER	FORECARS	FORELAID
FOOTED	FOOTSLOGGINGS	FORBIDDERS	FORECAST	FORELAIN
FOOTER	FOOTSLOGS	FORBIDDING	FORECASTED	FORELAND
FOOTERS	FOOTSORE	FORBIDDINGS	FORECASTING	FORELANDS
FOOTFALL	FOOTSTALK	FORBIDS	FORECASTS	FORELAY
FOOTFALLS	FOOTSTALKS	FORBODE	FORECLOSE	FORELAYING
FOOTFAULT	FOOTSTEP	FORBODES	FORECLOSED	FORELAYS
FOOTFAULTED	FOOTSTEPS	FORBORE	FORECLOSES	FORELEG
FOOTFAULTING	FOOTSTOOL	FORBORNE	FORECLOSING	FORELEGS
FOOTFAULTS	FOOTSTOOLS	FORBS	FORECLOTH	FORELEND
FOOTGEAR	FOOTWAY	FORBY	FORECLOTHS	FORELENDING
FOOTGEARS	FOOTWAYS	FORBYE	FORECOURT	FORELENDS
FOOTHILL	FOOTWEAR	FORCAT	FORECOURTS	FORELENT
FOOTHILLS	FOOTWEARS	FORCATS	FOREDATE	FORELIE
FOOTHOLD	FOOTWELL	FORCE	FOREDATED	FORELIES
FOOTHOLDS	FOOTWELLS	FORCED	FOREDATES	FORELIFT
FOOTIE	FOOTWORK	FORCEDLY	FOREDATING	FORELIFTED
FOOTIER	FOOTWORKS	FORCEFUL	FOREDECK	FORELIFTING
FOOTIES	FOOTWORN	FORCELESS	FOREDECKS	FORELIFTS
FOOTIEST	FOOTY	FORCEMEAT	FOREDOOM	FORELIMB
FOOTING	FOOZLE	FORCEMEATS	FOREDOOMED	FORELIMBS
FOOTINGS	FOOZLED	FORCEPS	FOREDOOMING	FORELOCK
FOOTLE	FOOZLER	FORCEPSES	FOREDOOMS	FORELOCKS
FOOTLED	FOOZLERS	FORCER	FOREFEEL	FORELS
FOOTLES	FOOZLES	FORCERS	FOREFEELING	FORELYING
FOOTLESS	FOOZLING	FORCES	FOREFEELS	FOREMAN
FOOTLIGHT	FOOZLINGS	FORCIBLE	FOREFEET	FOREMAST
FOOTLIGHTS	FOP	FORCIBLY	FOREFELT	FOREMASTS
FOOTLING	FOPLING	FORCING	FOREFOOT	FOREMEAN
FOOTLINGS	FOPLINGS	FORCIPATE	FOREFRONT	FOREMEANING
FOOTLOOSE	FOPPERIES	FORCIPES	FOREFRONTS	FOREMEANS
FOOTMAN	FOPPERY	FORD	FOREGLEAM	FOREMEANT
FOOTMARK	FOPPISH	FORDABLE	FOREGLEAMS	FOREMEN
FOOTMARKS	FOPPISHLY	FORDED	FOREGO	FOREMOST
FOOTMEN	FOPS	FORDID	FOREGOER	FORENAME
FOOTMUFF	FOR	FORDING	FOREGOERS	FORENAMED
FOOTMUFFS	FORA	FORDO	FOREGOES	FORENAMES
FOOTNOTE	FORAGE	FORDOES	FOREGOING	FORENIGHT
FOOTNOTES	FORAGED	FORDOING	FOREGOINGS	FORENIGHTS
FOOTPACE	FORAGER	FORDONE	FOREGONE	FORENOON
FOOTPACES	FORAGERS	FORDS	FOREGUT	FORENOONS
FOOTPAD	FORAGES	FORE	FOREGUTS	FORENSIC
FOOTPADS	FORAGING	FOREANENT	FOREHAND	FORENSICS
FOOTPAGE	FORAMEN	FOREARM	FOREHANDS	FOREPART
FOOTPAGES	FORAMINA	FOREARMED	FOREHEAD	FOREPARTS
FOOTPATH	FORAMINAL	FOREARMING	FOREHEADS	FOREPAST
FOOTPATHS	FORANE	FOREARMS	FOREHENT	FOREPAW
FOOTPLATE	FORASMUCH	FOREBEAR	FOREHENTING	FOREPAWS
FOOTPLATES	FORAY	FOREBEARS	FOREHENTS	FOREPEAK
FOOTPOST	FORAYED	FOREBITT	FOREIGN	FOREPEAKS
FOOTPOSTS	FORAYER	FOREBITTS	FOREIGNER	FOREPLAN
FOOTPRINT	FORAYERS	FOREBODE	FOREIGNERS	FOREPLANNED
FOOTPRINTS	FORAYING	FOREBODED	FOREJUDGE	FOREPLANNING
FOOTRA	FORAYS	FOREBODER	FOREJUDGED	FOREPLANS
FOOTRAS	FORB	FOREBODERS	FOREJUDGES	FOREPLAY
FOOTREST	FORBAD	FOREBODES	FOREJUDGING	FOREPLAYS
FOOTRESTS	FORBADE	FOREBODING	FOREKING	FOREPOINT
FOOTROT	FORBEAR	FOREBODINGS	FOREKINGS	FOREPOINTED
FOOTROTS	FORBEARING	FOREBRAIN	FOREKNEW	FOREPOINTING
FOOTRULE	FORBEARS	FOREBRAINS	FOREKNOW	FOREPOINTS
FOOTRULES	FORBID	FOREBY	FOREKNOWING	FORERAN

FOREREACH	FOREST	FOREWIND	FORGOT	FORMABLE
FOREREACHED	FORESTAGE	FOREWINDS	FORGOTTEN	FORMAL
FOREREACHES	FORESTAGES	FOREWING	FORHAILE	FORMALIN
FOREREACHING	FORESTAIR	FOREWINGS	FORHAILED	FORMALINS
FOREREAD	FORESTAIRS	FOREWOMAN	FORHAILES	FORMALISE
FOREREADING	FORESTAL	FOREWOMEN	FORHAILING	FORMALISED
FOREREADINGS	FORESTALL	FOREWORD	FORHENT	FORMALISES
FOREREADS	FORESTALLED	FOREWORDS	FORHENTING	FORMALISING
FORERUN	FORESTALLING	FORFAIR	FORHENTS	FORMALISM
FORERUNNING	FORESTALLINGS	FORFAIRED	FORHOO	FORMALISMS
FORERUNS	FORESTALLS	FORFAIRING	FORHOOED	FORMALIST
FORES	FORESTAY	FORFAIRN	FORHOOIE	FORMALISTS
FORESAID	FORESTAYS	FORFAIRS	FORHOOIED	FORMALITIES
FORESAIL	FORESTEAL	FORFAITER	FORHOOIEING	FORMALITY
FORESAILS	FORESTED	FORFAITERS	FORHOOIES	FORMALIZE
FORESAW	FORESTER	FORFAULT	FORHOOING	FORMALIZED
FORESAY	FORESTERS	FORFAULTS	FORHOOS	FORMALIZES
FORESAYING	FORESTINE	FORFEIT	FORHOW	FORMALIZING
FORESAYS	FORESTING	FORFEITED	FORHOWED	FORMALLY
FORESEE	FORESTRIES	FORFEITER	FORHOWING	FORMANT
FORESEEING	FORESTRY	FORFEITERS	FORHOWS	FORMANTS
FORESEEN	FORESTS	FORFEITING	FORINSEC	FORMAT
FORESEES	FORETASTE	FORFEITS	FORINT	FORMATE
FORESHEW	FORETASTED	FORFEND	FORINTS	FORMATED
FORESHEWED	FORETASTES	FORFENDED	FORJASKIT	FORMATES
FORESHEWING	FORETASTING	FORFENDING	FORJESKIT	FORMATING
FORESHEWN	FORETAUGHT	FORFENDS	FORJUDGE	FORMATION
FORESHEWS	FORETEACH	FORFEX	FORJUDGED	FORMATIONS
FORESHIP	FORETEACHES	FORFEXES	FORJUDGES	FORMATIVE
FORESHIPS	FORETEACHING	FORFICATE	FORJUDGING	FORMATIVES
FORESHOCK	FORETEETH	FORGAT	FORK	FORMATS
FORESHOCKS	FORETELL	FORGATHER	FORKED	FORMATTED
FORESHORE	FORETELLING	FORGATHERED	FORKEDLY	FORMATTER
FORESHORES	FORETELLS	FORGATHERING	FORKER	FORMATTERS
FORESHOW	FORETHINK	FORGATHERS	FORKERS	FORMATTING
FORESHOWED	FORETHINKING	FORGAVE	FORKFUL	FORME
FORESHOWING	FORETHINKS	FORGE	FORKFULS	FORMED
FORESHOWN	FORETHOUGHT	FORGEABLE	FORKHEAD	FORMER
FORESHOWS	FORETHOUGHTS	FORGED	FORKHEADS	FORMERLY
FORESIDE	FORETIME	FORGEMAN	FORKIER	FORMERS
FORESIDES	FORETIMES	FORGEMEN	FORKIEST	FORMES
FORESIGHT	FORETOKEN	FORGER	FORKINESS	FORMIATE
FORESIGHTS	FORETOKENED	FORGERIES	FORKINESSES	FORMIATES
FORESKIN	FORETOKENING	FORGERS	FORKING	FORMIC
FORESKINS	FORETOKENINGS	FORGERY	FORKS	FORMICANT
FORESKIRT	FORETOKENS	FORGES	FORKTAIL	FORMICARIES
FORESKIRTS	FORETOLD	FORGET	FORKTAILS	FORMICARY
FORESLACK	FORETOOTH	FORGETFUL	FORKY	FORMICATE
FORESLACKED	FORETOP	FORGETIVE	FORLANA	FORMING
FORESLACKING	FORETOPS	FORGETS	FORLANAS	FORMINGS
FORESLACKS	FOREVER	FORGETTER	FORLEND	FORMLESS
FORESLOW	FOREVERS	FORGETTERS	FORLENDING	FORMOL
FORESLOWED	FOREWARD	FORGETTING	FORLENDS	FORMOLS
FORESLOWING	FOREWARDS	FORGETTINGS	FORLENT	FORMS
FORESLOWS	FOREWARN	FORGING	FORLESE	FORMULA
FORESPEAK	FOREWARNED	FORGINGS	FORLESES	FORMULAE
FORESPEAKING	FOREWARNING	FORGIVE	FORLESING	FORMULAIC
FORESPEAKS	FOREWARNINGS	FORGIVEN	FORLORE	FORMULAR
FORESPEND	FOREWARNS	FORGIVES	FORLORN	FORMULARIES
FORESPENDING	FOREWEIGH	FORGIVING	FORLORNER	FORMULARY
FORESPENDS	FOREWEIGHED	FORGO	FORLORNEST	FORMULAS
FORESPENT	FOREWEIGHING	FORGOES	FORLORNLY	FORMULATE
FORESPOKE	FOREWEIGHS	FORGOING	FORLORNS	FORMULATED
FORESPOKEN	FOREWENT	FORGONE	FORM	FORMULATES

The Chambers Dictionary is the authority for many longer words; see *OSW* Introduction, page xii

FORMULATING	FORSPEAKING	FORTUITY	FOSSIL	FOULEST
FORMULISE	FORSPEAKS	FORTUNATE	FOSSILISE	FOULING
FORMULISED	FORSPEND	FORTUNE	FOSSILISED	FOULLY
FORMULISES	FORSPENDING	FORTUNED	FOSSILISES	FOULMART
FORMULISING	FORSPENDS	FORTUNES	FOSSILISING	FOULMARTS
FORMULISM	FORSPENT	FORTUNING	FOSSILIZE	FOULNESS
FORMULISMS	FORSPOKE	FORTUNIZE	FOSSILIZED	FOULNESSES
FORMULIST	FORSPOKEN	FORTUNIZED	FOSSILIZES	FOULS
FORMULISTS	FORSWATT	FORTUNIZES	FOSSILIZING	FOUMART
FORMULIZE	FORSWEAR	FORTUNIZING	FOSSILS	FOUMARTS
FORMULIZED	FORSWEARING	FORTY	FOSSOR	FOUND
FORMULIZES	FORSWEARS	FORTYISH	FOSSORIAL	FOUNDED
FORMULIZING	FORSWINK	FORUM	FOSSORS	FOUNDER
FORMWORK	FORSWINKED	FORUMS	FOSSULA	FOUNDERED
FORMWORKS	FORSWINKING	FORWANDER	FOSSULAE	FOUNDERING
FORNENST	FORSWINKS	FORWANDERED	FOSSULATE	FOUNDERS
FORNENT	FORSWONCK	FORWANDERING	FOSTER	FOUNDING
FORNICAL	FORSWORE	FORWANDERS	FOSTERAGE	FOUNDINGS
FORNICATE	FORSWORN	FORWARD	FOSTERAGES	FOUNDLING
FORNICATED	FORSWUNK	FORWARDED	FOSTERED	FOUNDLINGS
FORNICATES	FORSYTHIA	FORWARDER	FOSTERER	FOUNDRESS
FORNICATING	FORSYTHIAS	FORWARDERS	FOSTERERS	FOUNDRESSES
FORNICES	FORT	FORWARDEST	FOSTERING	FOUNDRIES
FORNIX	FORTALICE	FORWARDING	FOSTERINGS	FOUNDRY
FORPET	FORTALICES	FORWARDINGS	FOSTERS	FOUNDS
FORPETS	FORTE	FORWARDLY	FOSTRESS	FOUNT
FORPINE	FORTED	FORWARDS	FOSTRESSES	FOUNTAIN
FORPINED	FORTES	FORWARN	FOTHER	FOUNTAINED
FORPINES	FORTH	FORWARNED	FOTHERED	FOUNTAINING
FORPINING	FORTHCAME	FORWARNING	FOTHERING	FOUNTAINS
FORPIT	FORTHCOME	FORWARNS	FOTHERS	FOUNTFUL
FORPITS	FORTHCOMES	FORWASTE	FOU	FOUNTS
FORRAD	FORTHCOMING	FORWASTED	FOUAT	FOUR
FORRADER	FORTHINK	FORWASTES	FOUATS	FOURFOLD
FORRAY	FORTHINKING	FORWASTING	FOUD	FOURGON
FORRAYED	FORTHINKS	FORWEARIED	FOUDRIE	FOURGONS
FORRAYING	FORTHOUGHT	FORWEARIES	FOUDRIES	FOURPENCE
FORRAYS	FORTHWITH	FORWEARY	FOUDS	FOURPENCES
FORREN	FORTHY	FORWEARYING	FOUER	FOURPENNIES
FORRIT	FORTIES	FORWENT	FOUEST	FOURPENNY
FORSAID	FORTIETH	FORWHY	FOUET	FOURS
FORSAKE	FORTIETHS	FORWORN	FOUETS	FOURSCORE
FORSAKEN	FORTIFIED	FORZANDI	FOUETTE	FOURSES
FORSAKES	FORTIFIER	FORZANDO	FOUETTES	FOURSOME
FORSAKING	FORTIFIERS	FORZANDOS	FOUGADE	FOURSOMES
FORSAKINGS	FORTIFIES	FORZATI	FOUGADES	FOURTEEN
FORSAY	FORTIFY	FORZATO	FOUGASSE	FOURTEENS
FORSAYING	FORTIFYING	FORZATOS	FOUGASSES	FOURTH
FORSAYS	FORTILAGE	FOSS	FOUGHT	FOURTHLY
FORSLACK	FORTILAGES	FOSSA	FOUGHTEN	FOURTHS
FORSLACKED	FORTING	FOSSAE	FOUGHTIER	FOUS
FORSLACKING	FORTIS	FOSSAS	FOUGHTIEST	FOUSSA
FORSLACKS	FORTITUDE	FOSSE	FOUGHTY	FOUSSAS
FORSLOE	FORTITUDES	FOSSED	FOUL	FOUSTIER
FORSLOED	FORTLET	FOSSES	FOULARD	FOUSTIEST
FORSLOEING	FORTLETS	FOSSETTE	FOULARDS	FOUSTY
FORSLOES	FORTNIGHT	FOSSETTES	FOULDER	FOUTER
FORSLOW	FORTNIGHTS	FOSSICK	FOULDERED	FOUTERED
FORSLOWED	FORTRESS	FOSSICKED	FOULDERING	FOUTERING
FORSLOWING	FORTRESSED	FOSSICKER	FOULDERS	FOUTERS
FORSLOWS	FORTRESSES	FOSSICKERS	FOULE	FOUTH
FORSOOK	FORTRESSING	FOSSICKING	FOULED	FOUTHS
FORSOOTH	FORTS	FOSSICKINGS	FOULER	FOUTRA
FORSPEAK	FORTUITIES	FOSSICKS	FOULES	FOUTRAS

FOUTRE	FOZY	FRAILTY	FRATCHES	FREE
FOUTRED	FRA	FRAIM	FRATCHETY	FREEBASE
FOUTRES	FRAB	FRAIMS	FRATCHIER	FREEBASED
FOUTRING	FRABBED	FRAISE	FRATCHIEST	FREEBASES
FOVEA	FRABBING	FRAISED	FRATCHING	FREEBASING
FOVEAE	FRABBIT	FRAISES	FRATCHY	FREEBEE
FOVEAL	FRABJOUS	FRAISING	FRATE	FREEBEES
FOVEATE	FRABS	FRAME	FRATER	FREEBIE
FOVEOLA	FRACAS	FRAMED	FRATERIES	FREEBIES
FOVEOLAE	FRACK	FRAMER	FRATERNAL	FREEBOOTIES
FOVEOLAS	FRACKING	FRAMERS	FRATERS	FREEBOOTY
FOVEOLE	FRACKINGS	FRAMES	FRATERY	FREEBORN
FOVEOLES	FRACT	FRAMEWORK	FRATI	FREED
FOWL	FRACTAL	FRAMEWORKS	FRATRIES	FREEDMAN
FOWLED	FRACTALS	FRAMING	FRATRY	FREEDMEN
FOWLER	FRACTED	FRAMINGS	FRAU	FREEDOM
FOWLERS	FRACTING	FRAMPAL	FRAUD	FREEDOMS
FOWLING	FRACTION	FRAMPLER	FRAUDFUL	FREEHAND
FOWLINGS	FRACTIONS	FRAMPLERS	FRAUDS	FREEHOLD
FOWLS	FRACTIOUS	FRAMPOLD	FRAUDSMAN	FREEHOLDS
FOWTH	FRACTS	FRANC	FRAUDSMEN	FREEING
FOWTHS	FRACTURE	FRANCHISE	FRAUDSTER	FREELANCE
FOX	FRACTURED	FRANCHISED	FRAUDSTERS	FREELANCED
FOXBERRIES	FRACTURES	FRANCHISES	FRAUGHT	FREELANCES
FOXBERRY	FRACTURING	FRANCHISING	FRAUGHTED	FREELANCING
FOXED	FRAE	FRANCIUM	FRAUGHTER	FREELOAD
FOXES	FRAENA	FRANCIUMS	FRAUGHTEST	FREELOADED
FOXGLOVE	FRAENUM	FRANCO	FRAUGHTING	FREELOADING
FOXGLOVES	FRAG	FRANCOLIN	FRAUGHTS	FREELOADINGS
FOXHOLE	FRAGGED	FRANCOLINS	FRAULEIN	FREELOADS
FOXHOLES	FRAGGING	FRANCS	FRAULEINS	FREELY
FOXHOUND	FRAGILE	FRANGIBLE	FRAUS	FREEMAN
FOXHOUNDS	FRAGILELY	FRANION	FRAUTAGE	FREEMASON
FOXIER	FRAGILER	FRANIONS	FRAUTAGES	FREEMASONS
FOXIEST	FRAGILEST	FRANK	FRAY	FREEMEN
FOXINESS	FRAGILITIES	FRANKED	FRAYED	FREENESS
FOXINESSES	FRAGILITY	FRANKER	FRAYING	FREENESSES
FOXING	FRAGMENT	FRANKEST	FRAYINGS	FREEPHONE
FOXINGS	FRAGMENTED	FRANKING	FRAYS	FREEPHONES
FOXSHARK	FRAGMENTING	FRANKLIN	FRAZIL	FREER
FOXSHARKS	FRAGMENTS	FRANKLINS	FRAZILS	FREERS
FOXSHIP	FRAGOR	FRANKLY	FRAZZLE	FREES
FOXSHIPS	FRAGORS	FRANKNESS	FRAZZLED	FREESHEET
FOXTROT	FRAGRANCE	FRANKNESSES	FRAZZLES	FREESHEETS
FOXTROTS	FRAGRANCED	FRANKS	FRAZZLING	FREESIA
FOXTROTTED	FRAGRANCES	FRANTIC	FREAK	FREESIAS
FOXTROTTING	FRAGRANCIES	FRANTICLY	FREAKED	FREEST
FOXY	FRAGRANCING	FRANZIER	FREAKFUL	FREESTONE
FOY	FRAGRANCY	FRANZIEST	FREAKIER	FREESTONES
FOYER	FRAGRANT	FRANZY	FREAKIEST	FREESTYLE
FOYERS	FRAGS	FRAP	FREAKING	FREESTYLES
FOYLE	FRAICHEUR	FRAPPANT	FREAKISH	FREET
FOYLED	FRAICHEURS	FRAPPE	FREAKS	FREETIER
FOYLES	FRAIL	FRAPPED	FREAKY	FREETIEST
FOYLING	FRAILER	FRAPPEE	FRECKLE	FREETS
FOYNE	FRAILEST	FRAPPES	FRECKLED	FREETY
FOYNED	FRAILISH	FRAPPING	FRECKLES	FREEWARE
FOYNES	FRAILLY	FRAPS	FRECKLIER	FREEWARES
FOYNING	FRAILNESS	FRAS	FRECKLIEST	FREEWAY
FOYS	FRAILNESSES	FRASCATI	FRECKLING	FREEWAYS
FOZIER	FRAILS	FRASCATIS	FRECKLINGS	FREEWHEEL
FOZIEST	FRAILTEE	FRASS	FRECKLY	FREEWHEELED
FOZINESS	FRAILTEES	FRASSES	FREDAINE	FREEWHEELING
FOZINESSES	FRAILTIES	FRATCH	FREDAINES	FREEWHEELINGS

The Chambers Dictionary is the authority for many longer words; see *OSW* Introduction, page xii

FREEWHEELS	FRESCOIST	FRICASSEES	FRIKKADEL	FRITHGILD
FREEWOMAN	FRESCOISTS	FRICATIVE	FRIKKADELS	FRITHGILDS
FREEWOMEN	FRESCOS	FRICATIVES	FRILL	FRITHS
FREEZABLE	FRESH	FRICHT	FRILLED	FRITS
FREEZE	FRESHED	FRICHTED	FRILLIER	FRITTED
FREEZER	FRESHEN	FRICHTING	FRILLIES	FRITTER
FREEZERS	FRESHENED	FRICHTS	FRILLIEST	FRITTERED
FREEZES	FRESHENER	FRICTION	FRILLING	FRITTERER
FREEZING	FRESHENERS	FRICTIONS	FRILLINGS	FRITTERERS
FREEZINGS	FRESHENING	FRIDGE	FRILLS	FRITTERING
FREIGHT	FRESHENS	FRIDGED	FRILLY	FRITTERS
FREIGHTED	FRESHER	FRIDGES	FRINGE	FRITTING
FREIGHTER	FRESHERS	FRIDGING	FRINGED	FRITURE
FREIGHTERS	FRESHES	FRIED	FRINGES	FRITURES
FREIGHTING	FRESHEST	FRIEDCAKE	FRINGIER	FRIVOL
FREIGHTS	FRESHET	FRIEDCAKES	FRINGIEST	FRIVOLITIES
FREIT	FRESHETS	FRIEND	FRINGING	FRIVOLITY
FREITIER	FRESHING	FRIENDED	FRINGY	FRIVOLLED
FREITIEST	FRESHISH	FRIENDING	FRIPON	FRIVOLLING
FREITS	FRESHLY	FRIENDINGS	FRIPONS	FRIVOLOUS
FREITY	FRESHMAN	FRIENDLIER	FRIPPER	FRIVOLS
FREMD	FRESHMEN	FRIENDLIES	FRIPPERER	FRIZ
FREMDS	FRESHNESS	FRIENDLIEST	FRIPPERERS	FRIZE
FREMIT	FRESHNESSES	FRIENDLY	FRIPPERIES	FRIZES
FREMITS	FRESNEL	FRIENDS	FRIPPERS	FRIZING
FREMITUS	FRESNELS	FRIER	FRIPPERY	FRIZZ
FREMITUSES	FRET	FRIERS	FRIS	FRIZZANTE
FRENA	FRETFUL	FRIES	FRISEE	FRIZZED
FRENCH	FRETFULLY	FRIEZE	FRISEES	FRIZZES
FRENETIC	FRETS	FRIEZED	FRISES	FRIZZIER
FRENETICS	FRETSAW	FRIEZES	FRISETTE	FRIZZIEST
FRENNE	FRETSAWS	FRIEZING	FRISETTES	FRIZZING
FRENULA	FRETTED	FRIG	FRISEUR	FRIZZLE
FRENULUM	FRETTIER	FRIGATE	FRISEURS	FRIZZLED
FRENUM	FRETTIEST	FRIGATES	FRISK	FRIZZLES
FRENZICAL	FRETTING	FRIGATOON	FRISKA	FRIZZLIER
FRENZIED	FRETTINGS	FRIGATOONS	FRISKAS	FRIZZLIEST
FRENZIES	FRETTY	FRIGES	FRISKED	FRIZZLING
FRENZY	FRETWORK	FRIGGED	FRISKER	FRIZZLY
FRENZYING	FRETWORKS	FRIGGER	FRISKERS	FRIZZY
FREON	FRIABLE	FRIGGERS	FRISKET	FRO
FREONS	FRIAND	FRIGGING	FRISKETS	FROCK
FREQUENCE	FRIANDE	FRIGGINGS	FRISKFUL	FROCKED
FREQUENCES	FRIANDES	FRIGHT	FRISKIER	FROCKING
FREQUENCIES	FRIANDS	FRIGHTED	FRISKIEST	FROCKINGS
FREQUENCY	FRIAR	FRIGHTEN	FRISKILY	FROCKLESS
FREQUENT	FRIARBIRD	FRIGHTENED	FRISKING	FROCKS
FREQUENTED	FRIARBIRDS	FRIGHTENING	FRISKINGS	FROG
FREQUENTER	FRIARIES	FRIGHTENS	FRISKS	FROGBIT
FREQUENTERS	FRIARLY	FRIGHTFUL	FRISKY	FROGBITS
FREQUENTEST	FRIARS	FRIGHTING	FRISSON	FROGGED
FREQUENTING	FRIARY	FRIGHTS	FRISSONS	FROGGERIES
FREQUENTS	FRIBBLE	FRIGID	FRIST	FROGGERY
FRERE	FRIBBLED	FRIGIDER	FRISTED	FROGGIER
FRERES	FRIBBLER	FRIGIDEST	FRISTING	FROGGIEST
FRESCADE	FRIBBLERS	FRIGIDITIES	FRISTS	FROGGING
FRESCADES	FRIBBLES	FRIGIDITY	FRISURE	FROGGINGS
FRESCO	FRIBBLING	FRIGIDLY	FRISURES	FROGGY
FRESCOED	FRIBBLISH	FRIGOT	FRIT	FROGLET
FRESCOER	FRICADEL	FRIGOTS	FRITFLIES	FROGLETS
FRESCOERS	FRICADELS	FRIGS	FRITFLY	FROGLING
FRESCOES	FRICASSEE	FRIJOL	FRITH	FROGLINGS
FRESCOING	FRICASSEED	FRIJOLE	FRITHBORH	FROGMAN
FRESCOINGS	FRICASSEEING	FRIJOLES	FRITHBORHS	FROGMARCH

FROGMARCHED	FROSTBITTEN	FROZEN	FRUMPS	FUDDLER
FROGMARCHES	FROSTED	FRUCTANS	FRUMPY	FUDDLERS
FROGMARCHING	FROSTIER	FRUCTED	FRUSH	FUDDLES
FROGMEN	FROSTIEST	FRUCTIFIED	FRUSHED	FUDDLING
FROGMOUTH	FROSTILY	FRUCTIFIES	FRUSHES	FUDDLINGS
FROGMOUTHS	FROSTING	FRUCTIFY	FRUSHING	FUDGE
FROGS	FROSTINGS	FRUCTIFYING	FRUST	FUDGED
FROIDEUR	FROSTLESS	FRUCTIVE	FRUSTA	FUDGES
FROIDEURS	FROSTLIKE	FRUCTOSE	FRUSTRATE	FUDGING
FROISE	FROSTS	FRUCTOSES	FRUSTRATED	FUDS
FROISES	FROSTWORK	FRUCTUARIES	FRUSTRATES	FUEL
FROLIC	FROSTWORKS	FRUCTUARY	FRUSTRATING	FUELLED
FROLICKED	FROSTY	FRUCTUATE	FRUSTS	FUELLER
FROLICKING	FROTH	FRUCTUATED	FRUSTULE	FUELLERS
FROLICS	FROTHED	FRUCTUATES	FRUSTULES	FUELLING
FROM	FROTHERIES	FRUCTUATING	FRUSTUM	FUELS
FROMENTIES	FROTHERY	FRUCTUOUS	FRUSTUMS	FUERO
FROMENTY	FROTHIER	FRUGAL	FRUTEX	FUEROS
FROND	FROTHIEST	FRUGALIST	FRUTICES	FUFF
FRONDAGE	FROTHILY	FRUGALISTS	FRUTICOSE	FUFFED
FRONDAGES	FROTHING	FRUGALITIES	FRUTIFIED	FUFFIER
FRONDED	FROTHLESS	FRUGALITY	FRUTIFIES	FUFFIEST
FRONDENT	FROTHS	FRUGALLY	FRUTIFY	FUFFING
FRONDEUR	FROTHY	FRUICT	FRUTIFYING	FUFFS
FRONDEURS	FROTTAGE	FRUICTS	FRY	FUFFY
FRONDOSE	FROTTAGES	FRUIT	FRYER	FUG
FRONDS	FROTTEUR	FRUITAGE	FRYERS	FUGACIOUS
FRONT	FROTTEURS	FRUITAGES	FRYING	FUGACITIES
FRONTAGE	FROUGHIER	FRUITCAKE	FRYINGS	FUGACITY
FRONTAGER	FROUGHIEST	FRUITCAKES	FUB	FUGAL
FRONTAGERS	FROUGHY	FRUITED	FUBBED	FUGALLY
FRONTAGES	FROUNCE	FRUITER	FUBBERIES	FUGATO
FRONTAL	FROUNCED	FRUITERER	FUBBERY	FUGATOS
FRONTALS	FROUNCES	FRUITERERS	FUBBIER	FUGGED
FRONTED	FROUNCING	FRUITERIES	FUBBIEST	FUGGIER
FRONTIER	FROW	FRUITERS	FUBBING	FUGGIEST
FRONTIERED	FROWARD	FRUITERY	FUBBY	FUGGING
FRONTIERING	FROWARDLY	FRUITFUL	FUBS	FUGGY
FRONTIERS	FROWARDS	FRUITIER	FUBSIER	FUGHETTA
FRONTING	FROWIE	FRUITIEST	FUBSIEST	FUGHETTAS
FRONTLESS	FROWIER	FRUITING	FUBSY	FUGIE
FRONTLET	FROWIEST	FRUITINGS	FUCHSIA	FUGIES
FRONTLETS	FROWN	FRUITION	FUCHSIAS	FUGITIVE
FRONTMAN	FROWNED	FRUITIONS	FUCHSINE	FUGITIVES
FRONTMEN	FROWNING	FRUITIVE	FUCHSINES	FUGLE
FRONTON	FROWNS	FRUITLESS	FUCHSITE	FUGLED
FRONTONS	FROWS	FRUITLET	FUCHSITES	FUGLEMAN
FRONTOON	FROWSIER	FRUITLETS	FUCI	FUGLEMEN
FRONTOONS	FROWSIEST	FRUITS	FUCK	FUGLES
FRONTS	FROWST	FRUITWOOD	FUCKED	FUGLING
FRONTWARD	FROWSTED	FRUITWOODS	FUCKER	FUGS
FRONTWARDS	FROWSTER	FRUITY	FUCKERS	FUGUE
FRONTWAYS	FROWSTERS	FRUMENTIES	FUCKING	FUGUES
FRONTWISE	FROWSTIER	FRUMENTY	FUCKINGS	FUGUIST
FRORE	FROWSTIEST	FRUMP	FUCKS	FUGUISTS
FROREN	FROWSTING	FRUMPED	FUCOID	FULCRA
FRORN	FROWSTS	FRUMPIER	FUCOIDAL	FULCRATE
FRORNE	FROWSTY	FRUMPIEST	FUCOIDS	FULCRUM
FRORY	FROWSY	FRUMPING	FUCUS	FULCRUMS
FROST	FROWY	FRUMPISH	FUCUSED	FULFIL
FROSTBIT	FROWZIER	FRUMPLE	FUCUSES	FULFILL
FROSTBITE	FROWZIEST	FRUMPLED	FUD	FULFILLED
FROSTBITES	FROWZY	FRUMPLES	FUDDLE	FULFILLER
FROSTBITING	FROZE	FRUMPLING	FUDDLED	FULFILLERS

The Chambers Dictionary is the authority for many longer words; see *OSW* Introduction, page xii

FULFILLING	FULSOMEST	FUNDI	FUNNINESS	FURLONG
FULFILLINGS	FULVID	FUNDIE	FUNNINESSES	FURLONGS
FULFILLS	FULVOUS	FUNDIES	FUNNING	FURLOUGH
FULFILS	FUM	FUNDING	FUNNY	FURLOUGHED
FULGENCIES	FUMADO	FUNDINGS	FUNS	FURLOUGHING
FULGENCY	FUMADOES	FUNDIS	FUNSTER	FURLOUGHS
FULGENT	FUMADOS	FUNDLESS	FUNSTERS	FURLS
FULGENTLY	FUMAGE	FUNDS	FUR	FURMENTIES
FULGID	FUMAGES	FUNDUS	FURACIOUS	FURMENTY
FULGOR	FUMAROLE	FUNDY	FURACITIES	FURMETIES
FULGOROUS	FUMAROLES	FUNEBRAL	FURACITY	FURMETY
FULGORS	FUMAROLIC	FUNEBRE	FURAL	FURMITIES
FULGOUR	FUMATORIA	FUNEBRIAL	FURALS	FURMITY
FULGOURS	FUMATORIES	FUNERAL	FURAN	FURNACE
FULGURAL	FUMATORY	FUNERALS	FURANE	FURNACED
FULGURANT	FUMBLE	FUNERARY	FURANES	FURNACES
FULGURATE	FUMBLED	FUNEREAL	FURANS	FURNACING
FULGURATED	FUMBLER	FUNEST	FURBELOW	FURNIMENT
FULGURATES	FUMBLERS	FUNFAIR	FURBELOWED	FURNIMENTS
FULGURATING	FUMBLES	FUNFAIRS	FURBELOWING	FURNISH
FULGURITE	FUMBLING	FUNG	FURBELOWS	FURNISHED
FULGURITES	FUME	FUNGAL	FURBISH	FURNISHER
FULGUROUS	FUMED	FUNGI	FURBISHED	FURNISHERS
FULHAM	FUMEROLE	FUNGIBLES	FURBISHER	FURNISHES
FULHAMS	FUMEROLES	FUNGICIDE	FURBISHERS	FURNISHING
FULL	FUMES	FUNGICIDES	FURBISHES	FURNISHINGS
FULLAGE	FUMET	FUNGIFORM	FURBISHING	FURNITURE
FULLAGES	FUMETS	FUNGOID	FURCAL	FURNITURES
FULLAM	FUMETTE	FUNGOIDAL	FURCATE	FUROL
FULLAMS	FUMETTES	FUNGOSITIES	FURCATED	FUROLE
FULLAN	FUMETTI	FUNGOSITY	FURCATION	FUROLES
FULLANS	FUMETTO	FUNGOUS	FURCATIONS	FUROLS
FULLBACK	FUMIER	FUNGS	FURCULA	FUROR
FULLBACKS	FUMIEST	FUNGUS	FURCULAE	FURORE
FULLED	FUMIGANT	FUNGUSES	FURCULAR	FURORES
FULLER	FUMIGANTS	FUNICLE	FURDER	FURORS
FULLERENE	FUMIGATE	FUNICLES	FUREUR	FURPHIES
FULLERENES	FUMIGATED	FUNICULAR	FUREURS	FURPHY
FULLERS	FUMIGATES	FUNICULI	FURFAIR	FURR
FULLEST	FUMIGATING	FUNICULUS	FURFAIRS	FURRED
FULLING	FUMIGATOR	FUNK	FURFUR	FURRIER
FULLISH	FUMIGATORS	FUNKED	FURFURAL	FURRIERIES
FULLNESS	FUMING	FUNKHOLE	FURFURALS	FURRIERS
FULLNESSES	FUMITORIES	FUNKHOLES	FURFURAN	FURRIERY
FULLS	FUMITORY	FUNKIA	FURFURANS	FURRIES
FULLY	FUMOSITIES	FUNKIAS	FURFUROL	FURRIEST
FULMAR	FUMOSITY	FUNKIER	FURFUROLE	FURRINESS
FULMARS	FUMOUS	FUNKIEST	FURFUROLES	FURRINESSES
FULMINANT	FUMS	FUNKINESS	FURFUROLS	FURRING
FULMINANTS	FUMY	FUNKINESSES	FURFUROUS	FURRINGS
FULMINATE	FUN	FUNKING	FURFURS	FURROW
FULMINATED	FUNBOARD	FUNKS	FURIBUND	FURROWED
FULMINATES	FUNBOARDS	FUNKY	FURIES	FURROWING
FULMINATING	FUNCTION	FUNNED	FURIOSITIES	FURROWS
FULMINE	FUNCTIONED	FUNNEL	FURIOSITY	FURROWY
FULMINED	FUNCTIONING	FUNNELLED	FURIOSO	FURRS
FULMINES	FUNCTIONS	FUNNELLING	FURIOSOS	FURRY
FULMINING	FUND	FUNNELS	FURIOUS	FURS
FULMINOUS	FUNDABLE	FUNNER	FURIOUSLY	FURTH
FULNESS	FUNDAMENT	FUNNEST	FURL	FURTHER
FULNESSES	FUNDAMENTS	FUNNIER	FURLANA	FURTHERED
FULSOME	FUNDED	FUNNIES	FURLANAS	FURTHERER
FULSOMELY	FUNDER	FUNNIEST	FURLED	FURTHERERS
FULSOMER	FUNDERS	FUNNILY	FURLING	FURTHERING

FURTHERS	FUSIBLE	FUSSING	FUTHORC	FUZZIER
FURTHEST	FUSIFORM	FUSSY	FUTHORCS	FUZZIEST
FURTIVE	FUSIL	FUST	FUTHORK	FUZZILY
FURTIVELY	FUSILE	FUSTED	FUTHORKS	FUZZINESS
FURUNCLE	FUSILEER	FUSTET	FUTILE	FUZZINESSES
FURUNCLES	FUSILEERS	FUSTETS	FUTILELY	FUZZING
FURY	FUSILIER	FUSTIAN	FUTILER	FUZZLE
FURZE	FUSILIERS	FUSTIANS	FUTILEST	FUZZLED
FURZES	FUSILLADE	FUSTIC	FUTILITIES	FUZZLES
FURZIER	FUSILLADES	FUSTICS	FUTILITY	FUZZLING
FURZIEST	FUSILLI	FUSTIER	FUTON	FUZZY
FURZY	FUSILS	FUSTIEST	FUTONS	FY
FUSAIN	FUSING	FUSTIGATE	FUTTOCK	FYKE
FUSAINS	FUSION	FUSTIGATED	FUTTOCKS	FYKED
FUSAROL	FUSIONISM	FUSTIGATES	FUTURE	FYKES
FUSAROLE	FUSIONISMS	FUSTIGATING	FUTURES	FYKING
FUSAROLES	FUSIONIST	FUSTILUGS	FUTURISM	FYLE
FUSAROLS	FUSIONISTS	FUSTILY	FUTURISMS	FYLES
FUSC	FUSIONS	FUSTINESS	FUTURIST	FYLFOT
FUSCOUS	FUSS	FUSTINESSES	FUTURISTS	FYLFOTS
FUSE	FUSSED	FUSTING	FUTURITIES	FYNBOS
FUSED	FUSSER	FUSTOC	FUTURITY	FYNBOSES
FUSEE	FUSSERS	FUSTOCS	FUZE	FYRD
FUSEES	FUSSES	FUSTS	FUZEE	FYRDS
FUSELAGE	FUSSIER	FUSTY	FUZEES	FYTTE
FUSELAGES	FUSSIEST	FUTCHEL	FUZES	FYTTES
FUSES	FUSSILY	FUTCHELS	FUZZ	
FUSHION	FUSSINESS	FUTHARK	FUZZED	
FUSHIONS	FUSSINESSES	FUTHARKS	FUZZES	

G

GAB
GABARDINE
GABARDINES
GABBARD
GABBARDS
GABBART
GABBARTS
GABBED
GABBER
GABBERS
GABBIER
GABBIEST
GABBING
GABBLE
GABBLED
GABBLER
GABBLERS
GABBLES
GABBLING
GABBLINGS
GABBRO
GABBROIC
GABBROID
GABBROS
GABBY
GABELLE
GABELLER
GABELLERS
GABELLES
GABERDINE
GABERDINES
GABFEST
GABFESTS
GABIES
GABION
GABIONADE
GABIONADES
GABIONAGE
GABIONAGES
GABIONED
GABIONS
GABLE
GABLED
GABLES
GABLET
GABLETS
GABNASH
GABNASHES
GABS
GABY
GAD
GADABOUT
GADABOUTS
GADDED

GADDER
GADDERS
GADDING
GADE
GADES
GADFLIES
GADFLY
GADGE
GADGES
GADGET
GADGETEER
GADGETEERS
GADGETRIES
GADGETRY
GADGETS
GADGIE
GADGIES
GADI
GADIS
GADJE
GADJES
GADLING
GADLINGS
GADOID
GADOIDS
GADROON
GADROONED
GADROONS
GADS
GADSMAN
GADSMEN
GADSO
GADSOS
GADWALL
GADWALLS
GADZOOKS
GAE
GAED
GAELICISE
GAELICISED
GAELICISES
GAELICISING
GAELICISM
GAELICISMS
GAELICIZE
GAELICIZED
GAELICIZES
GAELICIZING
GAES
GAFF
GAFFE
GAFFED
GAFFER
GAFFERS

GAFFES
GAFFING
GAFFINGS
GAFFS
GAG
GAGA
GAGAKU
GAGAKUS
GAGE
GAGED
GAGES
GAGGED
GAGGER
GAGGERS
GAGGING
GAGGLE
GAGGLED
GAGGLES
GAGGLING
GAGGLINGS
GAGING
GAGMAN
GAGMEN
GAGS
GAGSTER
GAGSTERS
GAHNITE
GAHNITES
GAID
GAIDS
GAIETIES
GAIETY
GAIJIN
GAILLARD
GAILLARDE
GAILY
GAIN
GAINABLE
GAINED
GAINER
GAINERS
GAINEST
GAINFUL
GAINFULLY
GAINING
GAININGS
GAINLESS
GAINLIER
GAINLIEST
GAINLY
GAINS
GAINSAID
GAINSAY
GAINSAYER

GAINSAYERS
GAINSAYING
GAINSAYINGS
GAINSAYS
GAIR
GAIRFOWL
GAIRFOWLS
GAIRS
GAIT
GAITED
GAITER
GAITERS
GAITING
GAITS
GAITT
GAITTS
GAJO
GAJOS
GAL
GALA
GALABEA
GALABEAH
GALABEAHS
GALABEAS
GALABIA
GALABIAH
GALABIAHS
GALABIAS
GALACTIC
GALACTOSE
GALACTOSES
GALAGE
GALAGES
GALAGO
GALAGOS
GALAH
GALAHS
GALANGA
GALANGAL
GALANGALS
GALANGAS
GALANT
GALANTINE
GALANTINES
GALAPAGO
GALAPAGOS
GALAS
GALATEA
GALATEAS
GALAXIES
GALAXY
GALBANUM
GALBANUMS
GALDRAGON

GALDRAGONS
GALE
GALEA
GALEAE
GALEAS
GALEATE
GALEATED
GALENA
GALENAS
GALENGALE
GALENGALES
GALENITE
GALENITES
GALENOID
GALERE
GALERES
GALES
GALETTE
GALETTES
GALILEE
GALILEES
GALINGALE
GALINGALES
GALIONGEE
GALIONGEES
GALIOT
GALIOTS
GALIPOT
GALIPOTS
GALL
GALLABEA
GALLABEAH
GALLABEAHS
GALLABEAS
GALLABIA
GALLABIAH
GALLABIAHS
GALLABIAS
GALLABIEH
GALLABIEHS
GALLABIYA
GALLABIYAS
GALLANT
GALLANTER
GALLANTEST
GALLANTLY
GALLANTRIES
GALLANTRY
GALLANTS
GALLATE
GALLATES
GALLEASS
GALLEASSES
GALLED

GALLEON	GALLIWASPS	GALS	GAMBOGES	GAMMOCKED
GALLEONS	GALLIZE	GALTONIA	GAMBOGIAN	GAMMOCKING
GALLERIA	GALLIZED	GALTONIAS	GAMBOGIC	GAMMOCKS
GALLERIAS	GALLIZES	GALUMPH	GAMBOL	GAMMON
GALLERIED	GALLIZING	GALUMPHED	GAMBOLLED	GAMMONED
GALLERIES	GALLNUT	GALUMPHER	GAMBOLLING	GAMMONER
GALLERY	GALLNUTS	GALUMPHERS	GAMBOLS	GAMMONERS
GALLERYING	GALLON	GALUMPHING	GAMBOS	GAMMONING
GALLET	GALLONAGE	GALUMPHS	GAMBREL	GAMMONINGS
GALLETED	GALLONAGES	GALUT	GAMBRELS	GAMMONS
GALLETING	GALLONS	GALUTH	GAMBROON	GAMMY
GALLETS	GALLOON	GALUTHS	GAMBROONS	GAMP
GALLEY	GALLOONED	GALUTS	GAMBS	GAMPISH
GALLEYS	GALLOONS	GALVANIC	GAME	GAMPS
GALLFLIES	GALLOP	GALVANISE	GAMECOCK	GAMS
GALLFLY	GALLOPADE	GALVANISED	GAMECOCKS	GAMUT
GALLIARD	GALLOPADED	GALVANISES	GAMED	GAMUTS
GALLIARDS	GALLOPADES	GALVANISING	GAMELAN	GAMY
GALLIASS	GALLOPADING	GALVANISM	GAMELANS	GAMYNESS
GALLIASSES	GALLOPED	GALVANISMS	GAMELY	GAMYNESSES
GALLIC	GALLOPER	GALVANIST	GAMENESS	GAN
GALLICISE	GALLOPERS	GALVANISTS	GAMENESSES	GANCH
GALLICISED	GALLOPING	GALVANIZE	GAMER	GANCHED
GALLICISES	GALLOPS	GALVANIZED	GAMES	GANCHES
GALLICISING	GALLOW	GALVANIZES	GAMESIER	GANCHING
GALLICISM	GALLOWED	GALVANIZING	GAMESIEST	GANDER
GALLICISMS	GALLOWING	GAM	GAMESOME	GANDERISM
GALLICIZE	GALLOWS	GAMASH	GAMEST	GANDERISMS
GALLICIZED	GALLOWSES	GAMASHES	GAMESTER	GANDERS
GALLICIZES	GALLS	GAMAY	GAMESTERS	GANE
GALLICIZING	GALLSTONE	GAMAYS	GAMESY	GANG
GALLIED	GALLSTONES	GAMB	GAMETAL	GANGBOARD
GALLIES	GALLUMPH	GAMBA	GAMETE	GANGBOARDS
GALLINAZO	GALLUMPHED	GAMBADO	GAMETES	GANGED
GALLINAZOS	GALLUMPHING	GAMBADOED	GAMETIC	GANGER
GALLING	GALLUMPHS	GAMBADOES	GAMEY	GANGERS
GALLINGLY	GALLUS	GAMBADOING	GAMIC	GANGING
GALLINULE	GALLUSES	GAMBADOS	GAMIER	GANGINGS
GALLINULES	GALLY	GAMBAS	GAMIEST	GANGLAND
GALLIOT	GALLYING	GAMBESON	GAMIN	GANGLANDS
GALLIOTS	GALOCHE	GAMBESONS	GAMINE	GANGLIA
GALLIPOT	GALOCHED	GAMBET	GAMINERIE	GANGLIAR
GALLIPOTS	GALOCHES	GAMBETS	GAMINERIES	GANGLIATE
GALLISE	GALOCHING	GAMBETTA	GAMINES	GANGLIER
GALLISED	GALOOT	GAMBETTAS	GAMINESS	GANGLIEST
GALLISES	GALOOTS	GAMBIER	GAMINESSES	GANGLING
GALLISING	GALOP	GAMBIERS	GAMING	GANGLION
GALLISISE	GALOPED	GAMBIR	GAMINGS	GANGLIONS
GALLISISED	GALOPIN	GAMBIRS	GAMINS	GANGLY
GALLISISES	GALOPING	GAMBIST	GAMMA	GANGPLANK
GALLISISING	GALOPINS	GAMBISTS	GAMMADIA	GANGPLANKS
GALLISIZE	GALOPPED	GAMBIT	GAMMADION	GANGREL
GALLISIZED	GALOPPING	GAMBITED	GAMMAS	GANGRELS
GALLISIZES	GALOPS	GAMBITING	GAMMATIA	GANGRENE
GALLISIZING	GALORE	GAMBITS	GAMMATION	GANGRENED
GALLIUM	GALOSH	GAMBLE	GAMME	GANGRENES
GALLIUMS	GALOSHED	GAMBLED	GAMMED	GANGRENING
GALLIVANT	GALOSHES	GAMBLER	GAMMER	GANGS
GALLIVANTED	GALOSHING	GAMBLERS	GAMMERS	GANGSMAN
GALLIVANTING	GALOWSES	GAMBLES	GAMMES	GANGSMEN
GALLIVANTS	GALRAVAGE	GAMBLING	GAMMIER	GANGSTA
GALLIVAT	GALRAVAGED	GAMBLINGS	GAMMIEST	GANGSTAS
GALLIVATS	GALRAVAGES	GAMBO	GAMMING	GANGSTER
GALLIWASP	GALRAVAGING	GAMBOGE	GAMMOCK	GANGSTERS

The Chambers Dictionary is the authority for many longer words; see *OSW* Introduction, page xii

GANGUE	GARAGE	GARGARISE	GARNISHINGS	GARUMS
GANGUES	GARAGED	GARGARISED	GARNISHRIES	GARVIE
GANGWAY	GARAGES	GARGARISES	GARNISHRY	GARVIES
GANGWAYS	GARAGING	GARGARISING	GARNITURE	GARVOCK
GANISTER	GARAGINGS	GARGARISM	GARNITURES	GARVOCKS
GANISTERS	GARAGIST	GARGARISMS	GAROTTE	GAS
GANJA	GARAGISTE	GARGARIZE	GAROTTED	GASAHOL
GANJAS	GARAGISTES	GARGARIZED	GAROTTER	GASAHOLS
GANNET	GARAGISTS	GARGARIZES	GAROTTERS	GASALIER
GANNETRIES	GARB	GARGARIZING	GAROTTES	GASALIERS
GANNETRY	GARBAGE	GARGET	GAROTTING	GASBAG
GANNETS	GARBAGES	GARGETS	GAROTTINGS	GASBAGS
GANNISTER	GARBANZO	GARGETY	GARPIKE	GASCON
GANNISTERS	GARBANZOS	GARGLE	GARPIKES	GASCONADE
GANOID	GARBE	GARGLED	GARRAN	GASCONADED
GANOIDS	GARBED	GARGLES	GARRANS	GASCONADES
GANOIN	GARBES	GARGLING	GARRE	GASCONADING
GANOINE	GARBING	GARGOYLE	GARRED	GASCONISM
GANOINES	GARBLE	GARGOYLES	GARRES	GASCONISMS
GANOINS	GARBLED	GARIAL	GARRET	GASCONS
GANSEY	GARBLER	GARIALS	GARRETED	GASEITIES
GANSEYS	GARBLERS	GARIBALDI	GARRETEER	GASEITY
GANT	GARBLES	GARIBALDIS	GARRETEERS	GASELIER
GANTED	GARBLING	GARIGUE	GARRETS	GASELIERS
GANTING	GARBLINGS	GARIGUES	GARRIGUE	GASEOUS
GANTLET	GARBO	GARISH	GARRIGUES	GASES
GANTLETS	GARBOARD	GARISHED	GARRING	GASFIELD
GANTLINE	GARBOARDS	GARISHES	GARRISON	GASFIELDS
GANTLINES	GARBOIL	GARISHING	GARRISONED	GASH
GANTLOPE	GARBOILS	GARISHLY	GARRISONING	GASHED
GANTLOPES	GARBOLOGIES	GARJAN	GARRISONS	GASHER
GANTRIES	GARBOLOGY	GARJANS	GARRON	GASHES
GANTRY	GARBOS	GARLAND	GARRONS	GASHEST
GANTS	GARBS	GARLANDED	GARROT	GASHFUL
GAOL	GARBURE	GARLANDING	GARROTE	GASHING
GAOLED	GARBURES	GARLANDRIES	GARROTED	GASHLY
GAOLER	GARCINIA	GARLANDRY	GARROTES	GASHOLDER
GAOLERESS	GARCINIAS	GARLANDS	GARROTING	GASHOLDERS
GAOLERESSES	GARCON	GARLIC	GARROTS	GASIFIED
GAOLERS	GARCONS	GARLICKIER	GARROTTE	GASIFIER
GAOLING	GARDA	GARLICKIEST	GARROTTED	GASIFIERS
GAOLS	GARDAI	GARLICKY	GARROTTER	GASIFIES
GAP	GARDANT	GARLICS	GARROTTERS	GASIFORM
GAPE	GARDANTS	GARMENT	GARROTTES	GASIFY
GAPED	GARDEN	GARMENTED	GARROTTING	GASIFYING
GAPER	GARDENED	GARMENTING	GARROTTINGS	GASKET
GAPERS	GARDENER	GARMENTS	GARRULITIES	GASKETS
GAPES	GARDENERS	GARNER	GARRULITY	GASKIN
GAPESEED	GARDENIA	GARNERED	GARRULOUS	GASKINS
GAPESEEDS	GARDENIAS	GARNERING	GARRYA	GASLIGHT
GAPEWORM	GARDENING	GARNERS	GARRYAS	GASLIGHTS
GAPEWORMS	GARDENINGS	GARNET	GARRYOWEN	GASLIT
GAPING	GARDENS	GARNETS	GARRYOWENS	GASMAN
GAPINGLY	GARDEROBE	GARNI	GARS	GASMEN
GAPINGS	GARDEROBES	GARNISH	GART	GASOGENE
GAPO	GARDYLOO	GARNISHED	GARTER	GASOGENES
GAPOS	GARDYLOOS	GARNISHEE	GARTERED	GASOHOL
GAPPED	GARE	GARNISHEED	GARTERING	GASOHOLS
GAPPIER	GAREFOWL	GARNISHEEING	GARTERS	GASOLENE
GAPPIEST	GAREFOWLS	GARNISHEES	GARTH	GASOLENES
GAPPING	GARFISH	GARNISHER	GARTHS	GASOLIER
GAPPY	GARFISHES	GARNISHERS	GARUDA	GASOLIERS
GAPS	GARGANEY	GARNISHES	GARUDAS	GASOLINE
GAR	GARGANEYS	GARNISHING	GARUM	GASOLINES

The Chambers Dictionary is the authority for many longer words; see *OSW* Introduction, page xii

GASOMETER	GATEFOLD	GAUGE	GAUZY	GAZEBOS
GASOMETERS	GATEFOLDS	GAUGEABLE	GAVAGE	GAZED
GASOMETRIES	GATEHOUSE	GAUGED	GAVAGES	GAZEFUL
GASOMETRY	GATEHOUSES	GAUGER	GAVE	GAZELLE
GASP	GATELEG	GAUGERS	GAVEL	GAZELLES
GASPED	GATELESS	GAUGES	GAVELKIND	GAZEMENT
GASPER	GATEMAN	GAUGING	GAVELKINDS	GAZEMENTS
GASPEREAU	GATEMEN	GAUGINGS	GAVELMAN	GAZER
GASPEREAUS	GATEPOST	GAUJE	GAVELMEN	GAZERS
GASPERS	GATEPOSTS	GAUJES	GAVELOCK	GAZES
GASPIER	GATES	GAULEITER	GAVELOCKS	GAZETTE
GASPIEST	GATEWAY	GAULEITERS	GAVELS	GAZETTED
GASPINESS	GATEWAYS	GAULT	GAVIAL	GAZETTEER
GASPINESSES	GATH	GAULTER	GAVIALS	GAZETTEERED
GASPING	GATHER	GAULTERS	GAVOTTE	GAZETTEERING
GASPINGLY	GATHERED	GAULTS	GAVOTTES	GAZETTEERS
GASPINGS	GATHERER	GAUM	GAWCIER	GAZETTES
GASPS	GATHERERS	GAUMED	GAWCIEST	GAZETTING
GASPY	GATHERING	GAUMIER	GAWCY	GAZIER
GASSED	GATHERINGS	GAUMIEST	GAWD	GAZIEST
GASSER	GATHERS	GAUMING	GAWDS	GAZING
GASSERS	GATHS	GAUMLESS	GAWK	GAZOGENE
GASSES	GATING	GAUMS	GAWKED	GAZOGENES
GASSIER	GATINGS	GAUMY	GAWKER	GAZON
GASSIEST	GATS	GAUN	GAWKERS	GAZONS
GASSINESS	GAU	GAUNCH	GAWKIER	GAZOO
GASSINESSES	GAUCHE	GAUNCHED	GAWKIES	GAZOOKA
GASSING	GAUCHER	GAUNCHES	GAWKIEST	GAZOOKAS
GASSINGS	GAUCHERIE	GAUNCHING	GAWKIHOOD	GAZOON
GASSY	GAUCHERIES	GAUNT	GAWKIHOODS	GAZOONS
GAST	GAUCHESCO	GAUNTED	GAWKINESS	GAZOOS
GASTED	GAUCHEST	GAUNTER	GAWKINESSES	GAZPACHO
GASTER	GAUCHO	GAUNTEST	GAWKING	GAZPACHOS
GASTERS	GAUCHOS	GAUNTING	GAWKS	GAZUMP
GASTFULL	GAUCIE	GAUNTLET	GAWKY	GAZUMPED
GASTING	GAUCIER	GAUNTLETS	GAWP	GAZUMPING
GASTNESS	GAUCIEST	GAUNTLY	GAWPED	GAZUMPS
GASTNESSE	GAUCY	GAUNTNESS	GAWPER	GAZUNDER
GASTNESSES	GAUD	GAUNTNESSES	GAWPERS	GAZUNDERED
GASTRAEA	GAUDEAMUS	GAUNTREE	GAWPING	GAZUNDERING
GASTRAEAS	GAUDEAMUSES	GAUNTREES	GAWPS	GAZUNDERS
GASTRAEUM	GAUDED	GAUNTRIES	GAWPUS	GAZY
GASTRAEUMS	GAUDERIES	GAUNTRY	GAWPUSES	GEAL
GASTRIC	GAUDERY	GAUNTS	GAWSIER	GEALED
GASTRIN	GAUDGIE	GAUP	GAWSIEST	GEALING
GASTRINS	GAUDGIES	GAUPED	GAWSY	GEALOUS
GASTRITIS	GAUDIER	GAUPER	GAY	GEALOUSIES
GASTRITISES	GAUDIES	GAUPERS	GAYAL	GEALOUSY
GASTROPOD	GAUDIEST	GAUPING	GAYALS	GEALS
GASTROPODS	GAUDILY	GAUPS	GAYER	GEAN
GASTRULA	GAUDINESS	GAUPUS	GAYEST	GEANS
GASTRULAE	GAUDINESSES	GAUPUSES	GAYNESS	GEAR
GASTRULAS	GAUDING	GAUR	GAYNESSES	GEARBOX
GASTS	GAUDS	GAURS	GAYS	GEARBOXES
GAT	GAUDY	GAUS	GAYSOME	GEARE
GATE	GAUFER	GAUSS	GAZAL	GEARED
GATEAU	GAUFERS	GAUSSES	GAZALS	GEARES
GATEAUS	GAUFFER	GAUSSIAN	GAZANIA	GEARING
GATEAUX	GAUFFERED	GAUZE	GAZANIAS	GEARINGS
GATECRASH	GAUFFERING	GAUZES	GAZAR	GEARLESS
GATECRASHED	GAUFFERINGS	GAUZIER	GAZARS	GEARS
GATECRASHES	GAUFFERS	GAUZIEST	GAZE	GEARSHIFT
GATECRASHING	GAUFRE	GAUZINESS	GAZEBO	GEARSHIFTS
GATED	GAUFRES	GAUZINESSES	GAZEBOES	GEARWHEEL

GEARWHEELS	GELDS	GEMONY	GENIALISED	GENTEELLY
GEASON	GELID	GEMOT	GENIALISES	GENTES
GEAT	GELIDER	GEMOTS	GENIALISING	GENTIAN
GEATS	GELIDEST	GEMS	GENIALITIES	GENTIANS
GEBUR	GELIDITIES	GEMSBOK	GENIALITY	GENTIER
GEBURS	GELIDITY	GEMSBOKS	GENIALIZE	GENTIEST
GECK	GELIDLY	GEMSHORN	GENIALIZED	GENTILE
GECKED	GELIDNESS	GEMSHORNS	GENIALIZES	GENTILES
GECKING	GELIDNESSES	GEMSTONE	GENIALIZING	GENTILIC
GECKO	GELIGNITE	GEMSTONES	GENIALLY	GENTILISE
GECKOES	GELIGNITES	GEMUTLICH	GENIC	GENTILISED
GECKOS	GELLED	GEN	GENIE	GENTILISES
GECKS	GELLIES	GENA	GENIES	GENTILISH
GED	GELLING	GENAL	GENII	GENTILISING
GEDDIT	GELLY	GENAPPE	GENIP	GENTILISM
GEDS	GELOSIES	GENAPPES	GENIPAP	GENTILISMS
GEE	GELOSY	GENAS	GENIPAPS	GENTILITIES
GEEBUNG	GELS	GENDARME	GENIPS	GENTILITY
GEEBUNGS	GELSEMINE	GENDARMES	GENISTA	GENTILIZE
GEECHEE	GELSEMINES	GENDER	GENISTAS	GENTILIZED
GEECHEES	GELSEMIUM	GENDERED	GENITAL	GENTILIZES
GEED	GELSEMIUMS	GENDERING	GENITALIA	GENTILIZING
GEEGAW	GELT	GENDERS	GENITALIC	GENTLE
GEEGAWS	GELTS	GENE	GENITALS	GENTLED
GEEING	GEM	GENEALOGIES	GENITIVAL	GENTLEMAN
GEEK	GEMATRIA	GENEALOGY	GENITIVE	GENTLEMEN
GEEKIER	GEMATRIAS	GENERA	GENITIVES	GENTLER
GEEKIEST	GEMEL	GENERABLE	GENITOR	GENTLES
GEEKS	GEMELS	GENERAL	GENITORS	GENTLEST
GEEKY	GEMFISH	GENERALE	GENITRICES	GENTLING
GEEP	GEMFISHES	GENERALIA	GENITRIX	GENTLY
GEEPS	GEMINATE	GENERALLED	GENITRIXES	GENTOO
GEES	GEMINATED	GENERALLING	GENITURE	GENTOOS
GEESE	GEMINATES	GENERALLY	GENITURES	GENTRICE
GEEZER	GEMINATING	GENERALS	GENIUS	GENTRICES
GEEZERS	GEMINI	GENERANT	GENIUSES	GENTRIES
GEFUFFLE	GEMINIES	GENERANTS	GENIZAH	GENTRIFIED
GEFUFFLED	GEMINOUS	GENERATE	GENIZAHS	GENTRIFIES
GEFUFFLES	GEMINY	GENERATED	GENLOCK	GENTRIFY
GEFUFFLING	GEMMA	GENERATES	GENLOCKS	GENTRIFYING
GEISHA	GEMMAE	GENERATING	GENNEL	GENTRY
GEISHAS	GEMMAN	GENERATOR	GENNELS	GENTS
GEIST	GEMMATE	GENERATORS	GENNET	GENTY
GEISTS	GEMMATED	GENERIC	GENNETS	GENU
GEIT	GEMMATES	GENERICAL	GENOA	GENUFLECT
GEITS	GEMMATING	GENERICS	GENOAS	GENUFLECTED
GEL	GEMMATION	GENEROUS	GENOCIDAL	GENUFLECTING
GELADA	GEMMATIONS	GENES	GENOCIDE	GENUFLECTS
GELADAS	GEMMATIVE	GENESES	GENOCIDES	GENUINE
GELASTIC	GEMMED	GENESIS	GENOM	GENUINELY
GELATI	GEMMEN	GENET	GENOME	GENUS
GELATIN	GEMMEOUS	GENETIC	GENOMES	GENUSES
GELATINE	GEMMERIES	GENETICAL	GENOMS	GEO
GELATINES	GEMMERY	GENETICS	GENOTYPE	GEOCARPIC
GELATINS	GEMMIER	GENETRICES	GENOTYPES	GEOCARPIES
GELATION	GEMMIEST	GENETRIX	GENOTYPIC	GEOCARPY
GELATIONS	GEMMING	GENETRIXES	GENRE	GEODE
GELATO	GEMMOLOGIES	GENETS	GENRES	GEODES
GELD	GEMMOLOGY	GENETTE	GENS	GEODESIC
GELDED	GEMMULE	GENETTES	GENSDARMES	GEODESICS
GELDER	GEMMULES	GENEVA	GENT	GEODESIES
GELDERS	GEMMY	GENEVAS	GENTEEL	GEODESIST
GELDING	GEMOLOGIES	GENIAL	GENTEELER	GEODESISTS
GELDINGS	GEMOLOGY	GENIALISE	GENTEELEST	GEODESY

The Chambers Dictionary is the authority for many longer words; see *OSW* Introduction, page xii

GEODETIC	GEOPONICS	GERMINATING	GEUM	GHILGAI
GEODETICS	GEORGETTE	GERMING	GEUMS	GHILGAIS
GEODIC	GEORGETTES	GERMINS	GEWGAW	GHILLIE
GEOFACT	GEORGIC	GERMS	GEWGAWS	GHILLIED
GEOFACTS	GEORGICS	GERNE	GEY	GHILLIES
GEOGENIES	GEOS	GERNED	GEYAN	GHILLYING
GEOGENY	GEOSPHERE	GERNES	GEYER	GHIS
GEOGNOSES	GEOSPHERES	GERNING	GEYEST	GHOST
GEOGNOSIES	GEOSTATIC	GERONTIC	GEYSER	GHOSTED
GEOGNOSIS	GEOSTATICS	GEROPIGA	GEYSERITE	GHOSTIER
GEOGNOST	GEOTACTIC	GEROPIGAS	GEYSERITES	GHOSTIEST
GEOGNOSTS	GEOTAXES	GERTCHA	GEYSERS	GHOSTING
GEOGNOSY	GEOTAXIS	GERUND	GHARIAL	GHOSTINGS
GEOGONIC	GEOTROPIC	GERUNDIAL	GHARIALS	GHOSTLIER
GEOGONIES	GERAH	GERUNDIVE	GHARRI	GHOSTLIEST
GEOGONY	GERAHS	GERUNDIVES	GHARRIES	GHOSTLIKE
GEOGRAPHIES	GERANIOL	GERUNDS	GHARRIS	GHOSTLY
GEOGRAPHY	GERANIOLS	GESNERIA	GHARRY	GHOSTS
GEOID	GERANIUM	GESNERIAS	GHAST	GHOSTY
GEOIDAL	GERANIUMS	GESSAMINE	GHASTED	GHOUL
GEOIDS	GERBE	GESSAMINES	GHASTFUL	GHOULISH
GEOLATRIES	GERBERA	GESSE	GHASTFULL	GHOULS
GEOLATRY	GERBERAS	GESSED	GHASTING	GHYLL
GEOLOGER	GERBES	GESSES	GHASTLIER	GHYLLS
GEOLOGERS	GERBIL	GESSING	GHASTLIEST	GI
GEOLOGIAN	GERBILLE	GESSO	GHASTLY	GIAMBEUX
GEOLOGIANS	GERBILLES	GESSOES	GHASTNESS	GIANT
GEOLOGIC	GERBILS	GEST	GHASTNESSES	GIANTESS
GEOLOGIES	GERE	GESTALT	GHASTS	GIANTESSES
GEOLOGISE	GERENT	GESTALTS	GHAT	GIANTHOOD
GEOLOGISED	GERENTS	GESTANT	GHATS	GIANTHOODS
GEOLOGISES	GERENUK	GESTAPO	GHAUT	GIANTISM
GEOLOGISING	GERENUKS	GESTAPOS	GHAUTS	GIANTISMS
GEOLOGIST	GERES	GESTATE	GHAZAL	GIANTLIER
GEOLOGISTS	GERFALCON	GESTATED	GHAZALS	GIANTLIEST
GEOLOGIZE	GERFALCONS	GESTATES	GHAZEL	GIANTLY
GEOLOGIZED	GERIATRIC	GESTATING	GHAZELS	GIANTRIES
GEOLOGIZES	GERIATRICS	GESTATION	GHAZI	GIANTRY
GEOLOGIZING	GERLE	GESTATIONS	GHAZIS	GIANTS
GEOLOGY	GERLES	GESTATIVE	GHEE	GIANTSHIP
GEOMANCER	GERM	GESTATORY	GHEES	GIANTSHIPS
GEOMANCERS	GERMAIN	GESTE	GHERAO	GIAOUR
GEOMANCIES	GERMAINE	GESTES	GHERAOED	GIAOURS
GEOMANCY	GERMAINES	GESTIC	GHERAOING	GIB
GEOMANT	GERMAINS	GESTS	GHERAOS	GIBBED
GEOMANTIC	GERMAN	GESTURAL	GHERKIN	GIBBER
GEOMANTS	GERMANDER	GESTURE	GHERKINS	GIBBERED
GEOMETER	GERMANDERS	GESTURED	GHESSE	GIBBERING
GEOMETERS	GERMANE	GESTURES	GHESSED	GIBBERISH
GEOMETRIC	GERMANELY	GESTURING	GHESSES	GIBBERISHES
GEOMETRID	GERMANIUM	GET	GHESSING	GIBBERS
GEOMETRIDS	GERMANIUMS	GETA	GHEST	GIBBET
GEOMETRIES	GERMANS	GETAS	GHETTO	GIBBETED
GEOMETRY	GERMED	GETAWAY	GHETTOES	GIBBETING
GEOMYOID	GERMEN	GETAWAYS	GHETTOISE	GIBBETS
GEOPHAGIES	GERMENS	GETS	GHETTOISED	GIBBING
GEOPHAGY	GERMICIDE	GETTABLE	GHETTOISES	GIBBON
GEOPHILIC	GERMICIDES	GETTER	GHETTOISING	GIBBONS
GEOPHONE	GERMIN	GETTERED	GHETTOIZE	GIBBOSE
GEOPHONES	GERMINAL	GETTERING	GHETTOIZED	GIBBOSITIES
GEOPHYTE	GERMINANT	GETTERINGS	GHETTOIZES	GIBBOSITY
GEOPHYTES	GERMINATE	GETTERS	GHETTOIZING	GIBBOUS
GEOPHYTIC	GERMINATED	GETTING	GHETTOS	GIBBOUSLY
GEOPONIC	GERMINATES	GETTINGS	GHI	GIBBSITE

The Chambers Dictionary is the authority for many longer words; see *OSW* Introduction, page xii

GIBBSITES	GIGGITING	GILLYVOR	GINGEROUS	GIRASOLE
GIBE	GIGGITS	GILLYVORS	GINGERS	GIRASOLES
GIBED	GIGGLE	GILPEY	GINGERY	GIRASOLS
GIBEL	GIGGLED	GILPEYS	GINGHAM	GIRD
GIBELS	GIGGLER	GILPIES	GINGHAMS	GIRDED
GIBER	GIGGLERS	GILPY	GINGILI	GIRDER
GIBERS	GIGGLES	GILRAVAGE	GINGILIS	GIRDERS
GIBES	GIGGLIER	GILRAVAGED	GINGIVAL	GIRDING
GIBING	GIGGLIEST	GILRAVAGES	GINGKO	GIRDINGS
GIBINGLY	GIGGLING	GILRAVAGING	GINGKOES	GIRDLE
GIBLET	GIGGLINGS	GILSONITE	GINGLE	GIRDLED
GIBLETS	GIGGLY	GILSONITES	GINGLES	GIRDLER
GIBS	GIGLET	GILT	GINGLYMI	GIRDLERS
GIBUS	GIGLETS	GILTCUP	GINGLYMUS	GIRDLES
GIBUSES	GIGLOT	GILTCUPS	GINGS	GIRDLING
GID	GIGLOTS	GILTS	GINHOUSE	GIRDS
GIDDAP	GIGMAN	GILTWOOD	GINHOUSES	GIRKIN
GIDDIED	GIGMANITIES	GIMBAL	GINK	GIRKINS
GIDDIER	GIGMANITY	GIMBALS	GINKGO	GIRL
GIDDIES	GIGMEN	GIMCRACK	GINKGOES	GIRLHOOD
GIDDIEST	GIGOLO	GIMCRACKS	GINKS	GIRLHOODS
GIDDILY	GIGOLOS	GIMLET	GINN	GIRLIE
GIDDINESS	GIGOT	GIMLETED	GINNED	GIRLIES
GIDDINESSES	GIGOTS	GIMLETING	GINNEL	GIRLISH
GIDDUP	GIGS	GIMLETS	GINNELS	GIRLISHLY
GIDDY	GIGUE	GIMMAL	GINNER	GIRLOND
GIDDYING	GIGUES	GIMMALLED	GINNERIES	GIRLONDS
GIDGEE	GILA	GIMMALS	GINNERS	GIRLS
GIDGEES	GILAS	GIMME	GINNERY	GIRLY
GIDJEE	GILBERT	GIMMER	GINNIER	GIRN
GIDJEES	GILBERTS	GIMMERS	GINNIEST	GIRNED
GIDS	GILCUP	GIMMES	GINNING	GIRNEL
GIE	GILCUPS	GIMMICK	GINNY	GIRNELS
GIED	GILD	GIMMICKED	GINORMOUS	GIRNER
GIEING	GILDED	GIMMICKIER	GINS	GIRNERS
GIEN	GILDEN	GIMMICKIEST	GINSENG	GIRNIE
GIES	GILDER	GIMMICKING	GINSENGS	GIRNIER
GIF	GILDERS	GIMMICKRIES	GINSHOP	GIRNIEST
GIFT	GILDING	GIMMICKRY	GINSHOPS	GIRNING
GIFTED	GILDINGS	GIMMICKS	GIO	GIRNS
GIFTEDLY	GILDS	GIMMICKY	GIOCOSO	GIRO
GIFTING	GILET	GIMMOR	GIOS	GIRON
GIFTS	GILETS	GIMMORS	GIP	GIRONIC
GIFTSHOP	GILGAI	GIMP	GIPPIES	GIRONS
GIFTSHOPS	GILGAIS	GIMPED	GIPPO	GIROS
GIG	GILGIE	GIMPIER	GIPPOS	GIROSOL
GIGA	GILGIES	GIMPIEST	GIPPY	GIROSOLS
GIGABYTE	GILL	GIMPING	GIPS	GIRR
GIGABYTES	GILLAROO	GIMPS	GIPSEN	GIRRS
GIGAFLOP	GILLAROOS	GIMPY	GIPSENS	GIRT
GIGAFLOPS	GILLED	GIN	GIPSIED	GIRTED
GIGAHERTZ	GILLET	GING	GIPSIES	GIRTH
GIGAHERTZES	GILLETS	GINGAL	GIPSY	GIRTHED
GIGANTEAN	GILLFLIRT	GINGALL	GIPSYING	GIRTHING
GIGANTIC	GILLFLIRTS	GINGALLS	GIRAFFE	GIRTHLINE
GIGANTISM	GILLIE	GINGALS	GIRAFFES	GIRTHLINES
GIGANTISMS	GILLIED	GINGELLIES	GIRAFFID	GIRTHS
GIGAS	GILLIES	GINGELLY	GIRAFFINE	GIRTING
GIGAWATT	GILLING	GINGER	GIRAFFOID	GIRTLINE
GIGAWATTS	GILLION	GINGERADE	GIRANDOLA	GIRTLINES
GIGGED	GILLIONS	GINGERADES	GIRANDOLAS	GIRTS
GIGGING	GILLS	GINGERED	GIRANDOLE	GIS
GIGGIT	GILLY	GINGERING	GIRANDOLES	GISARME
GIGGITED	GILLYING	GINGERLY	GIRASOL	GISARMES

The Chambers Dictionary is the authority for many longer words; see *OSW* Introduction, page xii

GISM	GLACIATES	GLAMORISING	GLAUCOMA	GLEES
GISMO	GLACIATING	GLAMORIZE	GLAUCOMAS	GLEESOME
GISMOLOGIES	GLACIER	GLAMORIZED	GLAUCOUS	GLEET
GISMOLOGY	GLACIERS	GLAMORIZES	GLAUM	GLEETED
GISMOS	GLACIS	GLAMORIZING	GLAUMED	GLEETIER
GISMS	GLACISES	GLAMOROUS	GLAUMING	GLEETIEST
GIST	GLAD	GLAMORS	GLAUMS	GLEETING
GISTS	GLADDED	GLAMOUR	GLAUR	GLEETS
GIT	GLADDEN	GLAMOURED	GLAURIER	GLEETY
GITANA	GLADDENED	GLAMOURING	GLAURIEST	GLEG
GITANAS	GLADDENING	GLAMOURS	GLAURS	GLEGGER
GITANO	GLADDENS	GLAMS	GLAURY	GLEGGEST
GITANOS	GLADDER	GLANCE	GLAZE	GLEI
GITE	GLADDEST	GLANCED	GLAZED	GLEIS
GITES	GLADDIE	GLANCES	GLAZEN	GLEN
GITS	GLADDIES	GLANCING	GLAZER	GLENGARRIES
GITTERN	GLADDING	GLANCINGS	GLAZERS	GLENGARRY
GITTERNED	GLADDON	GLAND	GLAZES	GLENOID
GITTERNING	GLADDONS	GLANDERED	GLAZIER	GLENOIDAL
GITTERNS	GLADE	GLANDERS	GLAZIERS	GLENOIDS
GIUST	GLADES	GLANDES	GLAZIEST	GLENS
GIUSTED	GLADFUL	GLANDS	GLAZING	GLENT
GIUSTING	GLADIATE	GLANDULAR	GLAZINGS	GLENTED
GIUSTO	GLADIATOR	GLANDULE	GLAZY	GLENTING
GIUSTS	GLADIATORS	GLANDULES	GLEAM	GLENTS
GIVE	GLADIER	GLANS	GLEAMED	GLEY
GIVEAWAY	GLADIEST	GLARE	GLEAMIER	GLEYED
GIVEAWAYS	GLADIOLE	GLAREAL	GLEAMIEST	GLEYING
GIVED	GLADIOLES	GLARED	GLEAMING	GLEYS
GIVEN	GLADIOLI	GLAREOUS	GLEAMINGS	GLIA
GIVENNESS	GLADIOLUS	GLARES	GLEAMS	GLIADIN
GIVENNESSES	GLADIOLUSES	GLARIER	GLEAMY	GLIADINE
GIVER	GLADIUS	GLARIEST	GLEAN	GLIADINES
GIVERS	GLADIUSES	GLARING	GLEANED	GLIADINS
GIVES	GLADLY	GLARINGLY	GLEANER	GLIAL
GIVING	GLADNESS	GLARY	GLEANERS	GLIAS
GIVINGS	GLADNESSES	GLASNOST	GLEANING	GLIB
GIZMO	GLADS	GLASNOSTS	GLEANINGS	GLIBBED
GIZMOLOGIES	GLADSOME	GLASS	GLEANS	GLIBBER
GIZMOLOGY	GLADY	GLASSED	GLEAVE	GLIBBERY
GIZMOS	GLAIK	GLASSEN	GLEAVES	GLIBBEST
GIZZ	GLAIKET	GLASSES	GLEBE	GLIBBING
GIZZARD	GLAIKIT	GLASSFUL	GLEBES	GLIBLY
GIZZARDS	GLAIKS	GLASSFULS	GLEBOUS	GLIBNESS
GIZZEN	GLAIR	GLASSIER	GLEBY	GLIBNESSES
GIZZENED	GLAIRED	GLASSIEST	GLED	GLIBS
GIZZENING	GLAIREOUS	GLASSIFIED	GLEDE	GLID
GIZZENS	GLAIRIER	GLASSIFIES	GLEDES	GLIDDER
GIZZES	GLAIRIEST	GLASSIFY	GLEDGE	GLIDDERY
GJU	GLAIRIN	GLASSIFYING	GLEDGED	GLIDDEST
GJUS	GLAIRING	GLASSILY	GLEDGES	GLIDE
GLABELLA	GLAIRINS	GLASSINE	GLEDGING	GLIDED
GLABELLAE	GLAIRS	GLASSINES	GLEDS	GLIDER
GLABELLAR	GLAIRY	GLASSING	GLEE	GLIDERS
GLABRATE	GLAIVE	GLASSLIKE	GLEED	GLIDES
GLABROUS	GLAIVED	GLASSMAN	GLEEDS	GLIDING
GLACE	GLAIVES	GLASSMEN	GLEEFUL	GLIDINGLY
GLACEED	GLAM	GLASSWARE	GLEEING	GLIDINGS
GLACEING	GLAMOR	GLASSWARES	GLEEK	GLIFF
GLACES	GLAMORED	GLASSWORK	GLEEKED	GLIFFING
GLACIAL	GLAMORING	GLASSWORKS	GLEEKING	GLIFFINGS
GLACIALS	GLAMORISE	GLASSWORT	GLEEKS	GLIFFS
GLACIATE	GLAMORISED	GLASSWORTS	GLEEMAN	GLIFT
GLACIATED	GLAMORISES	GLASSY	GLEEMEN	GLIFTS

The Chambers Dictionary is the authority for many longer words; see *OSW* Introduction, page xii

GLIKE	GLOATING	GLOOMED	GLOUTED	GLUMLY
GLIKES	GLOATS	GLOOMFUL	GLOUTING	GLUMMER
GLIM	GLOB	GLOOMIER	GLOUTS	GLUMMEST
GLIMMER	GLOBAL	GLOOMIEST	GLOVE	GLUMNESS
GLIMMERED	GLOBALISE	GLOOMILY	GLOVED	GLUMNESSES
GLIMMERING	GLOBALISED	GLOOMING	GLOVER	GLUMPIER
GLIMMERINGS	GLOBALISES	GLOOMINGS	GLOVERS	GLUMPIEST
GLIMMERS	GLOBALISING	GLOOMS	GLOVES	GLUMPISH
GLIMMERY	GLOBALISM	GLOOMY	GLOVING	GLUMPS
GLIMPSE	GLOBALISMS	GLOOP	GLOVINGS	GLUMPY
GLIMPSED	GLOBALIZE	GLOOPED	GLOW	GLUON
GLIMPSES	GLOBALIZED	GLOOPIER	GLOWED	GLUONS
GLIMPSING	GLOBALIZES	GLOOPIEST	GLOWER	GLUT
GLIMS	GLOBALIZING	GLOOPING	GLOWERED	GLUTAEAL
GLINT	GLOBALLY	GLOOPS	GLOWERING	GLUTAEI
GLINTED	GLOBATE	GLOOPY	GLOWERS	GLUTAEUS
GLINTING	GLOBATED	GLOP	GLOWING	GLUTAMATE
GLINTS	GLOBBIER	GLOPS	GLOWINGLY	GLUTAMATES
GLIOMA	GLOBBIEST	GLORIA	GLOWLAMP	GLUTAMINE
GLIOMAS	GLOBBY	GLORIAS	GLOWLAMPS	GLUTAMINES
GLIOMATA	GLOBE	GLORIED	GLOWS	GLUTEAL
GLIOSES	GLOBED	GLORIES	GLOXINIA	GLUTEI
GLIOSIS	GLOBES	GLORIFIED	GLOXINIAS	GLUTELIN
GLISK	GLOBIN	GLORIFIES	GLOZE	GLUTELINS
GLISKS	GLOBING	GLORIFY	GLOZED	GLUTEN
GLISSADE	GLOBINS	GLORIFYING	GLOZES	GLUTENOUS
GLISSADED	GLOBOID	GLORIOLE	GLOZING	GLUTENS
GLISSADES	GLOBOIDS	GLORIOLES	GLOZINGS	GLUTEUS
GLISSADING	GLOBOSE	GLORIOSA	GLUCAGON	GLUTINOUS
GLISSANDI	GLOBOSES	GLORIOSAS	GLUCAGONS	GLUTS
GLISSANDO	GLOBOSITIES	GLORIOUS	GLUCINA	GLUTTED
GLISSANDOS	GLOBOSITY	GLORY	GLUCINAS	GLUTTING
GLISTEN	GLOBOUS	GLORYING	GLUCINIUM	GLUTTON
GLISTENED	GLOBS	GLOSS	GLUCINIUMS	GLUTTONIES
GLISTENING	GLOBULAR	GLOSSA	GLUCINUM	GLUTTONS
GLISTENS	GLOBULE	GLOSSAE	GLUCINUMS	GLUTTONY
GLISTER	GLOBULES	GLOSSAL	GLUCOSE	GLYCERIA
GLISTERED	GLOBULET	GLOSSARIES	GLUCOSES	GLYCERIAS
GLISTERING	GLOBULETS	GLOSSARY	GLUCOSIC	GLYCERIC
GLISTERS	GLOBULIN	GLOSSAS	GLUCOSIDE	GLYCERIDE
GLIT	GLOBULINS	GLOSSATOR	GLUCOSIDES	GLYCERIDES
GLITCH	GLOBULITE	GLOSSATORS	GLUE	GLYCERIN
GLITCHES	GLOBULITES	GLOSSED	GLUED	GLYCERINE
GLITS	GLOBULOUS	GLOSSEME	GLUER	GLYCERINES
GLITTER	GLOBY	GLOSSEMES	GLUERS	GLYCERINS
GLITTERED	GLODE	GLOSSER	GLUES	GLYCEROL
GLITTERIER	GLOGG	GLOSSERS	GLUEY	GLYCEROLS
GLITTERIEST	GLOGGS	GLOSSES	GLUEYNESS	GLYCERYL
GLITTERING	GLOIRE	GLOSSIER	GLUEYNESSES	GLYCERYLS
GLITTERINGS	GLOIRES	GLOSSIES	GLUG	GLYCIN
GLITTERS	GLOM	GLOSSIEST	GLUGGED	GLYCINE
GLITTERY	GLOMERATE	GLOSSILY	GLUGGING	GLYCINES
GLITZ	GLOMERATED	GLOSSINA	GLUGS	GLYCINS
GLITZES	GLOMERATES	GLOSSINAS	GLUHWEIN	GLYCOCOLL
GLITZIER	GLOMERATING	GLOSSING	GLUHWEINS	GLYCOCOLLS
GLITZIEST	GLOMERULE	GLOSSITIS	GLUIER	GLYCOGEN
GLITZILY	GLOMERULES	GLOSSITISES	GLUIEST	GLYCOGENS
GLITZY	GLOMERULI	GLOSSY	GLUING	GLYCOL
GLOAMING	GLOMMED	GLOTTAL	GLUISH	GLYCOLIC
GLOAMINGS	GLOMMING	GLOTTIC	GLUM	GLYCOLLIC
GLOAT	GLOMS	GLOTTIDES	GLUME	GLYCOLS
GLOATED	GLONOIN	GLOTTIS	GLUMELLA	GLYCONIC
GLOATER	GLONOINS	GLOTTISES	GLUMELLAS	GLYCONICS
GLOATERS	GLOOM	GLOUT	GLUMES	GLYCOSE

The Chambers Dictionary is the authority for many longer words; see *OSW* Introduction, page xii

GLYCOSES	GNOMONS	GOBBING	GODPARENTS	GOITROUS
GLYCOSIDE	GNOSES	GOBBLE	GODROON	GOLD
GLYCOSIDES	GNOSIS	GOBBLED	GODROONED	GOLDARN
GLYCOSYL	GNOSTIC	GOBBLER	GODROONS	GOLDCREST
GLYCOSYLS	GNOSTICAL	GOBBLERS	GODS	GOLDCRESTS
GLYPH	GNU	GOBBLES	GODSEND	GOLDEN
GLYPHIC	GNUS	GOBBLING	GODSENDS	GOLDENED
GLYPHS	GO	GOBBO	GODSHIP	GOLDENER
GLYPTIC	GOA	GOBIES	GODSHIPS	GOLDENEST
GLYPTICS	GOAD	GOBIID	GODSO	GOLDENING
GMELINITE	GOADED	GOBIIDS	GODSON	GOLDENLY
GMELINITES	GOADING	GOBIOID	GODSONS	GOLDENROD
GNAR	GOADS	GOBLET	GODSOS	GOLDENRODS
GNARL	GOADSMAN	GOBLETS	GODSPEED	GOLDENS
GNARLED	GOADSMEN	GOBLIN	GODSPEEDS	GOLDER
GNARLIER	GOADSTER	GOBLINS	GODWARD	GOLDEST
GNARLIEST	GOADSTERS	GOBO	GODWARDS	GOLDEYE
GNARLING	GOAF	GOBOES	GODWIT	GOLDEYES
GNARLS	GOAFS	GOBONY	GODWITS	GOLDFIELD
GNARLY	GOAL	GOBOS	GOE	GOLDFIELDS
GNARR	GOALBALL	GOBS	GOEL	GOLDFINCH
GNARRED	GOALBALLS	GOBSHITE	GOELS	GOLDFINCHES
GNARRING	GOALED	GOBSHITES	GOER	GOLDFINNIES
GNARRS	GOALIE	GOBURRA	GOERS	GOLDFINNY
GNARS	GOALIES	GOBURRAS	GOES	GOLDFISH
GNASH	GOALING	GOBY	GOETHITE	GOLDFISHES
GNASHED	GOALLESS	GOD	GOETHITES	GOLDIER
GNASHER	GOALMOUTH	GODCHILD	GOETIC	GOLDIEST
GNASHERS	GOALMOUTHS	GODCHILDREN	GOETIES	GOLDISH
GNASHES	GOALPOST	GODDAM	GOETY	GOLDLESS
GNASHING	GOALPOSTS	GODDAMN	GOEY	GOLDMINER
GNAT	GOALS	GODDAMNED	GOFER	GOLDMINERS
GNATHAL	GOANNA	GODDED	GOFERS	GOLDS
GNATHIC	GOANNAS	GODDEN	GOFF	GOLDSINNIES
GNATHITE	GOARY	GODDENS	GOFFED	GOLDSINNY
GNATHITES	GOAS	GODDESS	GOFFER	GOLDSIZE
GNATHONIC	GOAT	GODDESSES	GOFFERED	GOLDSIZES
GNATLING	GOATEE	GODDING	GOFFERING	GOLDSMITH
GNATLINGS	GOATEED	GODET	GOFFERINGS	GOLDSMITHS
GNATS	GOATEES	GODETIA	GOFFERS	GOLDSPINK
GNAW	GOATFISH	GODETIAS	GOFFING	GOLDSPINKS
GNAWED	GOATFISHES	GODETS	GOFFS	GOLDSTICK
GNAWER	GOATHERD	GODFATHER	GOGGLE	GOLDSTICKS
GNAWERS	GOATHERDS	GODFATHERS	GOGGLED	GOLDSTONE
GNAWING	GOATIER	GODHEAD	GOGGLER	GOLDSTONES
GNAWN	GOATIEST	GODHEADS	GOGGLERS	GOLDY
GNAWS	GOATISH	GODHOOD	GOGGLES	GOLE
GNEISS	GOATLING	GODHOODS	GOGGLIER	GOLEM
GNEISSES	GOATLINGS	GODLESS	GOGGLIEST	GOLEMS
GNEISSIC	GOATS	GODLESSLY	GOGGLING	GOLES
GNEISSOID	GOATSKIN	GODLIER	GOGGLINGS	GOLF
GNEISSOSE	GOATSKINS	GODLIEST	GOGGLY	GOLFED
GNOCCHI	GOATWEED	GODLIKE	GOGLET	GOLFER
GNOCCHIS	GOATWEEDS	GODLILY	GOGLETS	GOLFERS
GNOMAE	GOATY	GODLINESS	GOGO	GOLFIANA
GNOME	GOB	GODLINESSES	GOIER	GOLFIANAS
GNOMES	GOBANG	GODLING	GOIEST	GOLFING
GNOMIC	GOBANGS	GODLINGS	GOING	GOLFINGS
GNOMISH	GOBBED	GODLY	GOINGS	GOLFS
GNOMIST	GOBBELINE	GODMOTHER	GOITER	GOLIARD
GNOMISTS	GOBBELINES	GODMOTHERS	GOITERS	GOLIARDIC
GNOMON	GOBBET	GODOWN	GOITRE	GOLIARDIES
GNOMONIC	GOBBETS	GODOWNS	GOITRED	GOLIARDS
GNOMONICS	GOBBI	GODPARENT	GOITRES	GOLIARDY

The Chambers Dictionary is the authority for many longer words; see *OSW* Introduction, page xii

GOLIAS	GONDELAYS	GOODSIRES	GOOSEFOOTS	GORGONIZING
GOLIASED	GONDOLA	GOODTIME	GOOSEGOB	GORGONS
GOLIASES	GONDOLAS	GOODWIFE	GOOSEGOBS	GORIER
GOLIASING	GONDOLIER	GOODWILL	GOOSEGOG	GORIEST
GOLLAN	GONDOLIERS	GOODWILLS	GOOSEGOGS	GORILLA
GOLLAND	GONE	GOODWIVES	GOOSEHERD	GORILLAS
GOLLANDS	GONENESS	GOODY	GOOSEHERDS	GORILLIAN
GOLLANS	GONENESSES	GOODYEAR	GOOSERIES	GORILLINE
GOLLAR	GONER	GOODYEARS	GOOSERY	GORILLOID
GOLLARED	GONERS	GOOEY	GOOSES	GORILY
GOLLARING	GONFALON	GOOF	GOOSEY	GORINESS
GOLLARS	GONFALONS	GOOFBALL	GOOSEYS	GORINESSES
GOLLER	GONFANON	GOOFBALLS	GOOSIER	GORING
GOLLERED	GONFANONS	GOOFED	GOOSIES	GORINGS
GOLLERING	GONG	GOOFIER	GOOSIEST	GORM
GOLLERS	GONGED	GOOFIEST	GOOSING	GORMAND
GOLLIES	GONGING	GOOFILY	GOOSY	GORMANDS
GOLLIWOG	GONGS	GOOFINESS	GOPAK	GORMED
GOLLIWOGS	GONGSTER	GOOFINESSES	GOPAKS	GORMIER
GOLLOP	GONGSTERS	GOOFING	GOPHER	GORMIEST
GOLLOPED	GONIA	GOOFS	GOPHERED	GORMING
GOLLOPING	GONIATITE	GOOFY	GOPHERING	GORMLESS
GOLLOPS	GONIATITES	GOOGLE	GOPHERS	GORMS
GOLLY	GONIDIA	GOOGLED	GOPURA	GORMY
GOLLYWOG	GONIDIAL	GOOGLES	GOPURAM	GORP
GOLLYWOGS	GONIDIC	GOOGLIES	GOPURAMS	GORPED
GOLOMYNKA	GONIDIUM	GOOGLING	GOPURAS	GORPING
GOLOMYNKAS	GONION	GOOGLY	GORAL	GORPS
GOLOSH	GONK	GOOGOL	GORALS	GORSE
GOLOSHED	GONKS	GOOGOLS	GORAMIES	GORSEDD
GOLOSHES	GONNA	GOOIER	GORAMY	GORSEDDS
GOLOSHING	GONOCOCCI	GOOIEST	GORBLIMEY	GORSES
GOLOSHOES	GONOCYTE	GOOK	GORBLIMY	GORSIER
GOLP	GONOCYTES	GOOKS	GORCOCK	GORSIEST
GOLPE	GONOPHORE	GOOL	GORCOCKS	GORSOON
GOLPES	GONOPHORES	GOOLD	GORCROW	GORSOONS
GOLPS	GONORRHEA	GOOLDS	GORCROWS	GORSY
GOMBEEN	GONORRHEAS	GOOLEY	GORE	GORY
GOMBEENS	GONS	GOOLEYS	GORED	GOS
GOMBO	GONYS	GOOLIE	GORES	GOSH
GOMBOS	GONYSES	GOOLIES	GORGE	GOSHAWK
GOMBRO	GONZO	GOOLS	GORGED	GOSHAWKS
GOMBROS	GOO	GOOLY	GORGEOUS	GOSHT
GOMERAL	GOOBER	GOON	GORGERIN	GOSHTS
GOMERALS	GOOBERS	GOONDA	GORGERINS	GOSLARITE
GOMERIL	GOOD	GOONDAS	GORGES	GOSLARITES
GOMERILS	GOODFACED	GOONEY	GORGET	GOSLET
GOMOKU	GOODIER	GOONEYS	GORGETS	GOSLETS
GOMOKUS	GOODIES	GOONS	GORGIA	GOSLING
GOMPA	GOODIEST	GOOP	GORGIAS	GOSLINGS
GOMPAS	GOODINESS	GOOPIER	GORGING	GOSPEL
GOMPHOSES	GOODINESSES	GOOPIEST	GORGIO	GOSPELISE
GOMPHOSIS	GOODISH	GOOPS	GORGIOS	GOSPELISED
GOMUTI	GOODLIER	GOOPY	GORGON	GOSPELISES
GOMUTIS	GOODLIEST	GOOR	GORGONEIA	GOSPELISING
GOMUTO	GOODLY	GOOROO	GORGONIAN	GOSPELIZE
GOMUTOS	GOODMAN	GOOROOS	GORGONIANS	GOSPELIZED
GON	GOODMEN	GOORS	GORGONISE	GOSPELIZES
GONAD	GOODNESS	GOOS	GORGONISED	GOSPELIZING
GONADAL	GOODNESSES	GOOSANDER	GORGONISES	GOSPELLED
GONADIAL	GOODNIGHT	GOOSANDERS	GORGONISING	GOSPELLER
GONADIC	GOODNIGHTS	GOOSE	GORGONIZE	GOSPELLERS
GONADS	GOODS	GOOSED	GORGONIZED	GOSPELLING
GONDELAY	GOODSIRE	GOOSEFOOT	GORGONIZES	GOSPELS

The Chambers Dictionary is the authority for many longer words; see *OSW* Introduction, page xii

GOSPODAR	GOURMANDS	GOWNBOYS	GRADDANS	GRAITH
GOSPODARS	GOURMET	GOWNED	GRADE	GRAITHED
GOSSAMER	GOURMETS	GOWNING	GRADED	GRAITHING
GOSSAMERS	GOUSTIER	GOWNMAN	GRADELY	GRAITHLY
GOSSAMERY	GOUSTIEST	GOWNMEN	GRADER	GRAITHS
GOSSAN	GOUSTROUS	GOWNS	GRADERS	GRAKLE
GOSSANS	GOUSTY	GOWNSMAN	GRADES	GRAKLES
GOSSE	GOUT	GOWNSMEN	GRADIENT	GRALLOCH
GOSSES	GOUTFLIES	GOWPEN	GRADIENTS	GRALLOCHED
GOSSIB	GOUTFLY	GOWPENFUL	GRADIN	GRALLOCHING
GOSSIBS	GOUTIER	GOWPENFULS	GRADINE	GRALLOCHS
GOSSIP	GOUTIEST	GOWPENS	GRADINES	GRAM
GOSSIPED	GOUTINESS	GOY	GRADING	GRAMA
GOSSIPING	GOUTINESSES	GOYIM	GRADINI	GRAMARIES
GOSSIPINGS	GOUTS	GOYISCH	GRADINO	GRAMARY
GOSSIPRIES	GOUTTE	GOYISH	GRADINS	GRAMARYE
GOSSIPRY	GOUTTES	GOYS	GRADS	GRAMARYES
GOSSIPS	GOUTWEED	GOZZAN	GRADUAL	GRAMAS
GOSSIPY	GOUTWEEDS	GOZZANS	GRADUALLY	GRAMASH
GOSSOON	GOUTWORT	GRAAL	GRADUALS	GRAMASHES
GOSSOONS	GOUTWORTS	GRAALS	GRADUAND	GRAME
GOSSYPINE	GOUTY	GRAB	GRADUANDS	GRAMERCIES
GOSSYPOL	GOV	GRABBED	GRADUATE	GRAMERCY
GOSSYPOLS	GOVERN	GRABBER	GRADUATED	GRAMES
GOT	GOVERNALL	GRABBERS	GRADUATES	GRAMMA
GOTHIC	GOVERNALLS	GRABBING	GRADUATING	GRAMMAR
GOTHICISE	GOVERNED	GRABBLE	GRADUATOR	GRAMMARS
GOTHICISED	GOVERNESS	GRABBLED	GRADUATORS	GRAMMAS
GOTHICISES	GOVERNESSED	GRABBLER	GRADUS	GRAMMATIC
GOTHICISING	GOVERNESSES	GRABBLERS	GRADUSES	GRAMME
GOTHICIZE	GOVERNESSING	GRABBLES	GRAFF	GRAMMES
GOTHICIZED	GOVERNING	GRABBLING	GRAFFED	GRAMOCHE
GOTHICIZES	GOVERNOR	GRABEN	GRAFFING	GRAMOCHES
GOTHICIZING	GOVERNORS	GRABENS	GRAFFITI	GRAMPUS
GOTHITE	GOVERNS	GRABS	GRAFFITIS	GRAMPUSES
GOTHITES	GOVS	GRACE	GRAFFITO	GRAMS
GOTTA	GOWAN	GRACED	GRAFFS	GRAN
GOTTEN	GOWANED	GRACEFUL	GRAFT	GRANARIES
GOUACHE	GOWANS	GRACELESS	GRAFTED	GRANARY
GOUACHES	GOWANY	GRACES	GRAFTER	GRAND
GOUGE	GOWD	GRACILE	GRAFTERS	GRANDAD
GOUGED	GOWDER	GRACILITIES	GRAFTING	GRANDADDIES
GOUGERE	GOWDEST	GRACILITY	GRAFTINGS	GRANDADDY
GOUGERES	GOWDS	GRACING	GRAFTS	GRANDADS
GOUGES	GOWDSPINK	GRACIOSO	GRAIL	GRANDAM
GOUGING	GOWDSPINKS	GRACIOSOS	GRAILE	GRANDAMS
GOUJEERS	GOWF	GRACIOUS	GRAILES	GRANDDAD
GOUJONS	GOWFED	GRACIOUSES	GRAILS	GRANDDADS
GOUK	GOWFER	GRACKLE	GRAIN	GRANDE
GOUKS	GOWFERS	GRACKLES	GRAINAGE	GRANDEE
GOULASH	GOWFING	GRAD	GRAINAGES	GRANDEES
GOULASHES	GOWFS	GRADABLE	GRAINE	GRANDER
GOURA	GOWK	GRADABLES	GRAINED	GRANDEST
GOURAMI	GOWKS	GRADATE	GRAINER	GRANDEUR
GOURAMIS	GOWL	GRADATED	GRAINERS	GRANDEURS
GOURAS	GOWLAN	GRADATES	GRAINES	GRANDIOSE
GOURD	GOWLAND	GRADATIM	GRAINIER	GRANDLY
GOURDE	GOWLANDS	GRADATING	GRAINIEST	GRANDMA
GOURDES	GOWLANS	GRADATION	GRAINING	GRANDMAMA
GOURDIER	GOWLED	GRADATIONS	GRAININGS	GRANDMAMAS
GOURDIEST	GOWLING	GRADATORY	GRAINS	GRANDMAS
GOURDS	GOWLS	GRADDAN	GRAINY	GRANDNESS
GOURDY	GOWN	GRADDANED	GRAIP	GRANDNESSES
GOURMAND	GOWNBOY	GRADDANING	GRAIPS	GRANDPA

The Chambers Dictionary is the authority for many longer words; see OSW Introduction, page xii

GRANDPAPA	GRANULOMA	GRASSHOOK	GRAVEL	GREASERS
GRANDPAPAS	GRANULOMAS	GRASSHOOKS	GRAVELESS	GREASES
GRANDPAS	GRANULOMATA	GRASSIER	GRAVELLED	GREASIER
GRANDS	GRANULOSE	GRASSIEST	GRAVELLING	GREASIES
GRANDSIRE	GRANULOUS	GRASSING	GRAVELLY	GREASIEST
GRANDSIRES	GRAPE	GRASSINGS	GRAVELS	GREASILY
GRANDSON	GRAPED	GRASSLAND	GRAVELY	GREASING
GRANDSONS	GRAPELESS	GRASSLANDS	GRAVEN	GREASY
GRANFER	GRAPERIES	GRASSUM	GRAVENESS	GREAT
GRANFERS	GRAPERY	GRASSUMS	GRAVENESSES	GREATCOAT
GRANGE	GRAPES	GRASSY	GRAVER	GREATCOATS
GRANGER	GRAPESEED	GRASTE	GRAVERS	GREATEN
GRANGERS	GRAPESEEDS	GRAT	GRAVES	GREATENED
GRANGES	GRAPESHOT	GRATE	GRAVEST	GREATENING
GRANITA	GRAPESHOTS	GRATED	GRAVEYARD	GREATENS
GRANITAS	GRAPETREE	GRATEFUL	GRAVEYARDS	GREATER
GRANITE	GRAPETREES	GRATER	GRAVID	GREATEST
GRANITES	GRAPEVINE	GRATERS	GRAVIDITIES	GREATLY
GRANITIC	GRAPEVINES	GRATES	GRAVIDITY	GREATNESS
GRANITISE	GRAPEY	GRATICULE	GRAVIES	GREATNESSES
GRANITISED	GRAPH	GRATICULES	GRAVING	GREATS
GRANITISES	GRAPHED	GRATIFIED	GRAVINGS	GREAVE
GRANITISING	GRAPHEME	GRATIFIER	GRAVITAS	GREAVED
GRANITITE	GRAPHEMES	GRATIFIERS	GRAVITASES	GREAVES
GRANITITES	GRAPHEMIC	GRATIFIES	GRAVITATE	GREAVING
GRANITIZE	GRAPHEMICS	GRATIFY	GRAVITATED	GREBE
GRANITIZED	GRAPHIC	GRATIFYING	GRAVITATES	GREBES
GRANITIZES	GRAPHICAL	GRATIN	GRAVITATING	GRECE
GRANITIZING	GRAPHICLY	GRATINATE	GRAVITIES	GRECES
GRANITOID	GRAPHICS	GRATINATED	GRAVITON	GRECIAN
GRANIVORE	GRAPHING	GRATINATES	GRAVITONS	GRECIANS
GRANIVORES	GRAPHITE	GRATINATING	GRAVITY	GRECQUE
GRANNAM	GRAPHITES	GRATINE	GRAVLAX	GRECQUES
GRANNAMS	GRAPHITIC	GRATINEE	GRAVLAXES	GREE
GRANNIE	GRAPHIUM	GRATING	GRAVURE	GREECE
GRANNIED	GRAPHIUMS	GRATINGLY	GRAVURES	GREECES
GRANNIEING	GRAPHS	GRATINGS	GRAVY	GREED
GRANNIES	GRAPIER	GRATINS	GRAY	GREEDIER
GRANNY	GRAPIEST	GRATIS	GRAYED	GREEDIEST
GRANNYING	GRAPING	GRATITUDE	GRAYER	GREEDILY
GRANOLA	GRAPLE	GRATITUDES	GRAYEST	GREEDS
GRANOLAS	GRAPLES	GRATTOIR	GRAYFLIES	GREEDY
GRANS	GRAPNEL	GRATTOIRS	GRAYFLY	GREEGREE
GRANT	GRAPNELS	GRATUITIES	GRAYING	GREEGREES
GRANTABLE	GRAPPA	GRATUITY	GRAYLE	GREEING
GRANTED	GRAPPAS	GRATULANT	GRAYLES	GREEKING
GRANTEE	GRAPPLE	GRATULATE	GRAYLING	GREEKINGS
GRANTEES	GRAPPLED	GRATULATED	GRAYLINGS	GREEN
GRANTER	GRAPPLES	GRATULATES	GRAYS	GREENBACK
GRANTERS	GRAPPLING	GRATULATING	GRAYWACKE	GREENBACKS
GRANTING	GRAPY	GRAUNCH	GRAYWACKES	GREENED
GRANTOR	GRASP	GRAUNCHED	GRAZE	GREENER
GRANTORS	GRASPABLE	GRAUNCHER	GRAZED	GREENERIES
GRANTS	GRASPED	GRAUNCHERS	GRAZER	GREENERS
GRANULAR	GRASPER	GRAUNCHES	GRAZERS	GREENERY
GRANULARY	GRASPERS	GRAUNCHING	GRAZES	GREENEST
GRANULATE	GRASPING	GRAUPEL	GRAZIER	GREENFLIES
GRANULATED	GRASPLESS	GRAUPELS	GRAZIERS	GREENFLY
GRANULATES	GRASPS	GRAVADLAX	GRAZING	GREENGAGE
GRANULATING	GRASS	GRAVADLAXES	GRAZINGS	GREENGAGES
GRANULE	GRASSED	GRAVAMEN	GRAZIOSO	GREENHAND
GRANULES	GRASSER	GRAVAMINA	GREASE	GREENHANDS
GRANULITE	GRASSERS	GRAVE	GREASED	GREENHORN
GRANULITES	GRASSES	GRAVED	GREASER	GREENHORNS

The Chambers Dictionary is the authority for many longer words; see *OSW* Introduction, page xii

GREENIE	GREMIALS	GRIDELINS	GRILSE	GRIPPY
GREENIER	GREMLIN	GRIDES	GRILSES	GRIPS
GREENIES	GREMLINS	GRIDING	GRIM	GRIPSACK
GREENIEST	GREMOLATA	GRIDIRON	GRIMACE	GRIPSACKS
GREENING	GREMOLATAS	GRIDIRONED	GRIMACED	GRIPTAPE
GREENINGS	GREN	GRIDIRONING	GRIMACES	GRIPTAPES
GREENISH	GRENADE	GRIDIRONS	GRIMACING	GRIS
GREENLET	GRENADES	GRIDLOCK	GRIMALKIN	GRISAILLE
GREENLETS	GRENADIER	GRIDLOCKS	GRIMALKINS	GRISAILLES
GREENLY	GRENADIERS	GRIDS	GRIME	GRISE
GREENMAIL	GRENADINE	GRIECE	GRIMED	GRISED
GREENMAILS	GRENADINES	GRIECED	GRIMES	GRISELY
GREENNESS	GRENNED	GRIECES	GRIMIER	GRISEOUS
GREENNESSES	GRENNING	GRIEF	GRIMIEST	GRISES
GREENROOM	GRENS	GRIEFFUL	GRIMILY	GRISETTE
GREENROOMS	GRESE	GRIEFLESS	GRIMINESS	GRISETTES
GREENS	GRESES	GRIEFS	GRIMINESSES	GRISGRIS
GREENSAND	GRESSING	GRIESIE	GRIMING	GRISING
GREENSANDS	GRESSINGS	GRIESY	GRIMLY	GRISKIN
GREENTH	GREVE	GRIESLY	GRIMMER	GRISKINS
GREENTHS	GREVES	GRIESY	GRIMMEST	GRISLED
GREENWASH	GREW	GRIEVANCE	GRIMNESS	GRISLIER
GREENWASHED	GREWED	GRIEVANCES	GRIMNESSES	GRISLIEST
GREENWASHES	GREWHOUND	GRIEVE	GRIMOIRE	GRISLY
GREENWASHING	GREWHOUNDS	GRIEVED	GRIMOIRES	GRISON
GREENWEED	GREWING	GRIEVER	GRIMY	GRISONS
GREENWEEDS	GREWS	GRIEVERS	GRIN	GRIST
GREENWOOD	GREY	GRIEVES	GRIND	GRISTLE
GREENWOODS	GREYBEARD	GRIEVING	GRINDED	GRISTLES
GREENY	GREYBEARDS	GRIEVOUS	GRINDER	GRISTLIER
GREES	GREYED	GRIFF	GRINDERIES	GRISTLIEST
GREESE	GREYER	GRIFFE	GRINDERS	GRISTLY
GREESES	GREYEST	GRIFFES	GRINDERY	GRISTS
GREESING	GREYHEN	GRIFFIN	GRINDING	GRISY
GREESINGS	GREYHENS	GRIFFINS	GRINDINGS	GRIT
GREET	GREYHOUND	GRIFFON	GRINDS	GRITH
GREETE	GREYHOUNDS	GRIFFONS	GRINGO	GRITHS
GREETED	GREYING	GRIFFS	GRINGOS	GRITS
GREETER	GREYINGS	GRIFT	GRINNED	GRITSTONE
GREETERS	GREYISH	GRIFTED	GRINNER	GRITSTONES
GREETES	GREYLY	GRIFTER	GRINNERS	GRITTED
GREETING	GREYNESS	GRIFTERS	GRINNING	GRITTER
GREETINGS	GREYNESSES	GRIFTING	GRINS	GRITTERS
GREETS	GREYS	GRIFTS	GRIOT	GRITTEST
GREFFIER	GREYSTONE	GRIG	GRIOTS	GRITTIER
GREFFIERS	GREYSTONES	GRIGGED	GRIP	GRITTIEST
GREGALE	GREYWACKE	GRIGGING	GRIPE	GRITTING
GREGALES	GREYWACKES	GRIGRI	GRIPED	GRITTY
GREGARIAN	GRIBBLE	GRIGRIS	GRIPER	GRIVET
GREGARINE	GRIBBLES	GRIGS	GRIPERS	GRIVETS
GREGARINES	GRICE	GRIKE	GRIPES	GRIZE
GREGATIM	GRICER	GRIKES	GRIPING	GRIZES
GREGE	GRICERS	GRILL	GRIPINGLY	GRIZZLE
GREGO	GRICES	GRILLADE	GRIPLE	GRIZZLED
GREGOS	GRICING	GRILLADES	GRIPPE	GRIZZLER
GREIGE	GRICINGS	GRILLAGE	GRIPPED	GRIZZLERS
GREIN	GRID	GRILLAGES	GRIPPER	GRIZZLES
GREINED	GRIDDER	GRILLE	GRIPPERS	GRIZZLIER
GREINING	GRIDDERS	GRILLED	GRIPPES	GRIZZLIES
GREINS	GRIDDLE	GRILLES	GRIPPIER	GRIZZLIEST
GREISEN	GRIDDLES	GRILLING	GRIPPIEST	GRIZZLING
GREISENS	GRIDE	GRILLINGS	GRIPPING	GRIZZLY
GREISLY	GRIDED	GRILLS	GRIPPLE	GROAN
GREMIAL	GRIDELIN	GRILLWORK	GRIPPLES	GROANED

The Chambers Dictionary is the authority for many longer words; see *OSW* Introduction, page xii

GROANER
GROANERS
GROANFUL
GROANING
GROANINGS
GROANS
GROAT
GROATS
GROCER
GROCERIES
GROCERS
GROCERY
GROCKLE
GROCKLES
GRODIER
GRODIEST
GRODY
GROG
GROGGED
GROGGERIES
GROGGERY
GROGGIER
GROGGIEST
GROGGING
GROGGY
GROGRAM
GROGRAMS
GROGS
GROIN
GROINED
GROINING
GROININGS
GROINS
GROMA
GROMAS
GROMET
GROMETS
GROMMET
GROMMETS
GROMWELL
GROMWELLS
GRONE
GRONED
GRONEFULL
GRONES
GRONING
GROOF
GROOFS
GROOLIER
GROOLIEST
GROOLY
GROOM
GROOMED
GROOMING
GROOMS
GROOMSMAN
GROOMSMEN
GROOVE
GROOVED
GROOVER
GROOVERS
GROOVES
GROOVIER
GROOVIEST

GROOVING
GROOVY
GROPE
GROPED
GROPER
GROPERS
GROPES
GROPING
GROPINGLY
GROSBEAK
GROSBEAKS
GROSCHEN
GROSCHENS
GROSER
GROSERS
GROSERT
GROSERTS
GROSET
GROSETS
GROSGRAIN
GROSGRAINS
GROSS
GROSSART
GROSSARTS
GROSSED
GROSSER
GROSSES
GROSSEST
GROSSING
GROSSLY
GROSSNESS
GROSSNESSES
GROSSULAR
GROSSULARS
GROT
GROTESQUE
GROTESQUER
GROTESQUES
GROTESQUEST
GROTS
GROTTIER
GROTTIEST
GROTTO
GROTTOES
GROTTOS
GROTTY
GROUCH
GROUCHED
GROUCHES
GROUCHIER
GROUCHIEST
GROUCHILY
GROUCHING
GROUCHY
GROUF
GROUFS
GROUGH
GROUGHS
GROUND
GROUNDAGE
GROUNDAGES
GROUNDED
GROUNDEN
GROUNDER

GROUNDERS
GROUNDHOG
GROUNDHOGS
GROUNDING
GROUNDINGS
GROUNDMAN
GROUNDMEN
GROUNDNUT
GROUNDNUTS
GROUNDS
GROUNDSEL
GROUNDSELS
GROUP
GROUPABLE
GROUPAGE
GROUPAGES
GROUPED
GROUPER
GROUPERS
GROUPIE
GROUPIES
GROUPING
GROUPINGS
GROUPIST
GROUPISTS
GROUPLET
GROUPLETS
GROUPS
GROUPWARE
GROUPWARES
GROUPY
GROUSE
GROUSED
GROUSER
GROUSERS
GROUSES
GROUSEST
GROUSING
GROUT
GROUTED
GROUTER
GROUTERS
GROUTIER
GROUTIEST
GROUTING
GROUTINGS
GROUTS
GROUTY
GROVE
GROVEL
GROVELED
GROVELER
GROVELERS
GROVELING
GROVELLED
GROVELLER
GROVELLERS
GROVELLING
GROVELS
GROVES
GROVET
GROVETS
GROW
GROWABLE

GROWER
GROWERS
GROWING
GROWINGS
GROWL
GROWLED
GROWLER
GROWLERIES
GROWLERS
GROWLERY
GROWLIER
GROWLIEST
GROWLING
GROWLINGS
GROWLS
GROWLY
GROWN
GROWS
GROWTH
GROWTHIST
GROWTHISTS
GROWTHS
GROYNE
GROYNES
GRUB
GRUBBED
GRUBBER
GRUBBERS
GRUBBIER
GRUBBIEST
GRUBBING
GRUBBLE
GRUBBLED
GRUBBLES
GRUBBLING
GRUBBY
GRUBS
GRUBSTAKE
GRUBSTAKED
GRUBSTAKES
GRUBSTAKING
GRUDGE
GRUDGED
GRUDGEFUL
GRUDGES
GRUDGING
GRUDGINGS
GRUE
GRUED
GRUEING
GRUEL
GRUELING
GRUELINGS
GRUELLED
GRUELLING
GRUELLINGS
GRUELS
GRUES
GRUESOME
GRUESOMER
GRUESOMEST
GRUFE
GRUFES
GRUFF

GRUFFER
GRUFFEST
GRUFFISH
GRUFFLY
GRUFFNESS
GRUFFNESSES
GRUFTED
GRUING
GRUM
GRUMBLE
GRUMBLED
GRUMBLER
GRUMBLERS
GRUMBLES
GRUMBLIER
GRUMBLIEST
GRUMBLING
GRUMBLINGS
GRUMBLY
GRUME
GRUMES
GRUMLY
GRUMMER
GRUMMEST
GRUMMET
GRUMMETS
GRUMNESS
GRUMNESSES
GRUMOSE
GRUMOUS
GRUMP
GRUMPED
GRUMPH
GRUMPHED
GRUMPHIE
GRUMPHIES
GRUMPHING
GRUMPHS
GRUMPIER
GRUMPIEST
GRUMPILY
GRUMPING
GRUMPS
GRUMPY
GRUNGE
GRUNGES
GRUNGIER
GRUNGIEST
GRUNGY
GRUNION
GRUNIONS
GRUNT
GRUNTED
GRUNTER
GRUNTERS
GRUNTING
GRUNTINGS
GRUNTLE
GRUNTLED
GRUNTLES
GRUNTLING
GRUNTS
GRUPPETTI
GRUPPETTO

The Chambers Dictionary is the authority for many longer words; see *OSW* Introduction, page xii

GRUTCH	GUARANTYING	GUERDONED	GUIDEPOST	GUITAR
GRUTCHED	GUARD	GUERDONING	GUIDEPOSTS	GUITARIST
GRUTCHES	GUARDABLE	GUERDONS	GUIDER	GUITARISTS
GRUTCHING	GUARDAGE	GUEREZA	GUIDERS	GUITARS
GRUTTEN	GUARDAGES	GUEREZAS	GUIDES	GUIZER
GRYCE	GUARDANT	GUERIDON	GUIDESHIP	GUIZERS
GRYCES	GUARDANTS	GUERIDONS	GUIDESHIPS	GULA
GRYDE	GUARDED	GUERILLA	GUIDING	GULAG
GRYDED	GUARDEDLY	GUERILLAS	GUIDINGS	GULAGS
GRYDES	GUARDEE	GUERITE	GUIDON	GULAR
GRYDING	GUARDEES	GUERITES	GUIDONS	GULAS
GRYESLY	GUARDIAN	GUERNSEY	GUIDS	GULCH
GRYESY	GUARDIANS	GUERNSEYS	GUILD	GULCHED
GRYFON	GUARDING	GUERRILLA	GUILDER	GULCHES
GRYFONS	GUARDLESS	GUERRILLAS	GUILDERS	GULCHING
GRYKE	GUARDRAIL	GUES	GUILDHALL	GULDEN
GRYKES	GUARDRAILS	GUESS	GUILDHALLS	GULDENS
GRYPE	GUARDROOM	GUESSABLE	GUILDRIES	GULE
GRYPES	GUARDROOMS	GUESSED	GUILDRY	GULES
GRYPHON	GUARDS	GUESSER	GUILDS	GULF
GRYPHONS	GUARDSHIP	GUESSERS	GUILDSMAN	GULFED
GRYPT	GUARDSHIPS	GUESSES	GUILDSMEN	GULFIER
GRYSBOK	GUARDSMAN	GUESSING	GUILE	GULFIEST
GRYSBOKS	GUARDSMEN	GUESSINGS	GUILED	GULFING
GRYSELY	GUARISH	GUESSWORK	GUILEFUL	GULFS
GRYSIE	GUARISHED	GUESSWORKS	GUILELESS	GULFWEED
GU	GUARISHES	GUEST	GUILER	GULFWEEDS
GUACAMOLE	GUARISHING	GUESTED	GUILERS	GULFY
GUACAMOLES	GUARS	GUESTEN	GUILES	GULL
GUACHARO	GUAVA	GUESTENED	GUILING	GULLABLE
GUACHAROS	GUAVAS	GUESTENING	GUILLEMOT	GULLED
GUACO	GUAYULE	GUESTENS	GUILLEMOTS	GULLER
GUACOS	GUAYULES	GUESTING	GUILLOCHE	GULLERIES
GUAIACUM	GUB	GUESTS	GUILLOCHED	GULLERS
GUAIACUMS	GUBBAH	GUESTWISE	GUILLOCHES	GULLERY
GUAN	GUBBAHS	GUFF	GUILLOCHING	GULLET
GUANA	GUBBINS	GUFFAW	GUILT	GULLETS
GUANACO	GUBBINSES	GUFFAWED	GUILTIER	GULLEY
GUANACOS	GUBS	GUFFAWING	GUILTIEST	GULLEYED
GUANAS	GUCK	GUFFAWS	GUILTILY	GULLEYING
GUANAZOLO	GUCKIER	GUFFIE	GUILTLESS	GULLEYS
GUANAZOLOS	GUCKIEST	GUFFIES	GUILTS	GULLIBLE
GUANGO	GUCKS	GUFFS	GUILTY	GULLIED
GUANGOS	GUCKY	GUGA	GUIMBARD	GULLIES
GUANINE	GUDDLE	GUGAS	GUIMBARDS	GULLING
GUANINES	GUDDLED	GUGGLE	GUIMP	GULLISH
GUANO	GUDDLES	GUGGLED	GUIMPED	GULLS
GUANOS	GUDDLING	GUGGLES	GUIMPING	GULLY
GUANS	GUDE	GUGGLING	GUIMPS	GULLYING
GUAR	GUDEMAN	GUICHET	GUINEA	GULOSITIES
GUARANA	GUDEMEN	GUICHETS	GUINEAS	GULOSITY
GUARANAS	GUDES	GUID	GUIPURE	GULP
GUARANI	GUDESIRE	GUIDABLE	GUIPURES	GULPED
GUARANIES	GUDESIRES	GUIDAGE	GUIRO	GULPER
GUARANIS	GUDEWIFE	GUIDAGES	GUIROS	GULPERS
GUARANTEE	GUDEWIVES	GUIDANCE	GUISARD	GULPH
GUARANTEED	GUDGEON	GUIDANCES	GUISARDS	GULPHS
GUARANTEEING	GUDGEONED	GUIDE	GUISE	GULPING
GUARANTEES	GUDGEONING	GUIDEBOOK	GUISED	GULPS
GUARANTIED	GUDGEONS	GUIDEBOOKS	GUISER	GULY
GUARANTIES	GUE	GUIDED	GUISERS	GUM
GUARANTOR	GUENON	GUIDELESS	GUISES	GUMBO
GUARANTORS	GUENONS	GUIDELINE	GUISING	GUMBOIL
GUARANTY	GUERDON	GUIDELINES	GUISINGS	GUMBOILS

GUMBOOT	GUNITES	GUPPY	GUSLE	GUTTERING
GUMBOOTS	GUNK	GUPS	GUSLES	GUTTERINGS
GUMBOS	GUNKS	GUR	GUSLI	GUTTERS
GUMDROP	GUNLAYER	GURAMI	GUSLIS	GUTTIER
GUMDROPS	GUNLAYERS	GURAMIS	GUSSET	GUTTIES
GUMMA	GUNLESS	GURDWARA	GUSSETED	GUTTIEST
GUMMATA	GUNLOCK	GURDWARAS	GUSSETING	GUTTING
GUMMATOUS	GUNLOCKS	GURGE	GUSSETS	GUTTLE
GUMMED	GUNMAKER	GURGES	GUSSIE	GUTTLED
GUMMIER	GUNMAKERS	GURGLE	GUSSIES	GUTTLES
GUMMIEST	GUNMAN	GURGLED	GUST	GUTTLING
GUMMINESS	GUNMEN	GURGLES	GUSTABLE	GUTTURAL
GUMMINESSES	GUNMETAL	GURGLING	GUSTABLES	GUTTURALS
GUMMING	GUNMETALS	GURGOYLE	GUSTATION	GUTTY
GUMMINGS	GUNNAGE	GURGOYLES	GUSTATIONS	GUTZER
GUMMITE	GUNNAGES	GURJUN	GUSTATIVE	GUTZERS
GUMMITES	GUNNED	GURJUNS	GUSTATORY	GUV
GUMMOSES	GUNNEL	GURL	GUSTED	GUVS
GUMMOSIS	GUNNELS	GURLED	GUSTFUL	GUY
GUMMOSITIES	GUNNER	GURLET	GUSTIE	GUYED
GUMMOSITY	GUNNERA	GURLETS	GUSTIER	GUYING
GUMMOUS	GUNNERAS	GURLIER	GUSTIEST	GUYLE
GUMMY	GUNNERIES	GURLIEST	GUSTINESS	GUYLED
GUMNUT	GUNNERS	GURLING	GUSTINESSES	GUYLER
GUMNUTS	GUNNERY	GURLS	GUSTING	GUYLERS
GUMP	GUNNIES	GURLY	GUSTO	GUYLES
GUMPED	GUNNING	GURN	GUSTOS	GUYLING
GUMPHION	GUNNINGS	GURNARD	GUSTS	GUYOT
GUMPHIONS	GUNNY	GURNARDS	GUSTY	GUYOTS
GUMPING	GUNPLAY	GURNED	GUT	GUYS
GUMPS	GUNPLAYS	GURNET	GUTBUCKET	GUYSE
GUMPTION	GUNPOINT	GURNETS	GUTBUCKETS	GUYSES
GUMPTIONS	GUNPOINTS	GURNEY	GUTCHER	GUZZLE
GUMPTIOUS	GUNPORT	GURNEYS	GUTCHERS	GUZZLED
GUMS	GUNPORTS	GURNING	GUTFUL	GUZZLER
GUMSHIELD	GUNPOWDER	GURNS	GUTFULS	GUZZLERS
GUMSHIELDS	GUNPOWDERS	GURRAH	GUTLESS	GUZZLES
GUMSHOE	GUNROOM	GURRAHS	GUTROT	GUZZLING
GUMSHOED	GUNROOMS	GURRIES	GUTROTS	GWINIAD
GUMSHOEING	GUNRUNNER	GURRY	GUTS	GWINIADS
GUMSHOES	GUNRUNNERS	GURS	GUTSED	GWYNIAD
GUN	GUNS	GURU	GUTSER	GWYNIADS
GUNBOAT	GUNSEL	GURUDOM	GUTSERS	GYAL
GUNBOATS	GUNSELS	GURUDOMS	GUTSES	GYALS
GUNCOTTON	GUNSHIP	GURUISM	GUTSFUL	GYBE
GUNCOTTONS	GUNSHIPS	GURUISMS	GUTSFULS	GYBED
GUNDIES	GUNSHOT	GURUS	GUTSIER	GYBES
GUNDY	GUNSHOTS	GURUSHIP	GUTSIEST	GYBING
GUNFIGHT	GUNSMITH	GURUSHIPS	GUTSINESS	GYELD
GUNFIGHTING	GUNSMITHS	GUS	GUTSINESSES	GYELDS
GUNFIGHTS	GUNSTICK	GUSH	GUTSING	GYLDEN
GUNFIRE	GUNSTICKS	GUSHED	GUTSY	GYM
GUNFIRES	GUNSTOCK	GUSHER	GUTTA	GYMBAL
GUNFLINT	GUNSTOCKS	GUSHERS	GUTTAE	GYMBALS
GUNFLINTS	GUNSTONE	GUSHES	GUTTAS	GYMKHANA
GUNFOUGHT	GUNSTONES	GUSHIER	GUTTATE	GYMKHANAS
GUNGE	GUNTER	GUSHIEST	GUTTATED	GYMMAL
GUNGES	GUNTERS	GUSHING	GUTTATES	GYMMALS
GUNGIER	GUNWALE	GUSHINGLY	GUTTATING	GYMNASIA
GUNGIEST	GUNWALES	GUSHY	GUTTATION	GYMNASIAL
GUNGY	GUNYAH	GUSLA	GUTTATIONS	GYMNASIC
GUNHOUSE	GUNYAHS	GUSLAR	GUTTED	GYMNASIEN
GUNHOUSES	GUP	GUSLARS	GUTTER	GYMNASIUM
GUNITE	GUPPIES	GUSLAS	GUTTERED	GYMNASIUMS

GYMNAST	GYNECIUM	GYPS	GYRATIONS	GYRONS
GYMNASTIC	GYNIE	GYPSEOUS	GYRATORY	GYROPLANE
GYMNASTICS	GYNIES	GYPSIED	GYRE	GYROPLANES
GYMNASTS	GYNNEY	GYPSIES	GYRED	GYROS
GYMNIC	GYNNEYS	GYPSUM	GYRES	GYROSCOPE
GYMNOSOPH	GYNNIES	GYPSUMS	GYRFALCON	GYROSCOPES
GYMNOSOPHS	GYNNY	GYPSY	GYRFALCONS	GYROSE
GYMP	GYNOCRACIES	GYPSYDOM	GYRI	GYROSTAT
GYMPED	GYNOCRACY	GYPSYDOMS	GYRING	GYROSTATS
GYMPING	GYNOECIA	GYPSYING	GYRO	GYROUS
GYMPS	GYNOECIUM	GYPSYISM	GYROCAR	GYROVAGUE
GYMS	GYNOPHORE	GYPSYISMS	GYROCARS	GYROVAGUES
GYNAE	GYNOPHORES	GYPSYWORT	GYRODYNE	GYRUS
GYNAECEUM	GYNY	GYPSYWORTS	GYRODYNES	GYRUSES
GYNAECEUMS	GYP	GYRAL	GYROIDAL	GYTE
GYNAECIA	GYPPED	GYRALLY	GYROLITE	GYTES
GYNAECIUM	GYPPIE	GYRANT	GYROLITES	GYTRASH
GYNAECOID	GYPPIES	GYRATE	GYROMANCIES	GYTRASHES
GYNAES	GYPPING	GYRATED	GYROMANCY	GYVE
GYNANDRIES	GYPPO	GYRATES	GYRON	GYVED
GYNANDRY	GYPPOS	GYRATING	GYRONIC	GYVES
GYNECIA	GYPPY	GYRATION	GYRONNY	GYVING

H

HA	HACKBERRY	HADRONS	HAGBUTS	HAILSTONE
HAAF	HACKBOLT	HADROSAUR	HAGDEN	HAILSTONES
HAAFS	HACKBOLTS	HADROSAURS	HAGDENS	HAILY
HAANEPOOT	HACKBUT	HADS	HAGDON	HAIN
HAANEPOOTS	HACKBUTS	HADST	HAGDONS	HAINCH
HAAR	HACKED	HAE	HAGDOWN	HAINCHED
HAARS	HACKEE	HAECCEITIES	HAGDOWNS	HAINCHES
HABANERA	HACKEES	HAECCEITY	HAGFISH	HAINCHING
HABANERAS	HACKER	HAEING	HAGFISHES	HAINED
HABDABS	HACKERIES	HAEM	HAGG	HAINING
HABERDINE	HACKERS	HAEMAL	HAGGARD	HAININGS
HABERDINES	HACKERY	HAEMATIC	HAGGARDLY	HAINS
HABERGEON	HACKETTE	HAEMATIN	HAGGARDS	HAIQUE
HABERGEONS	HACKETTES	HAEMATINS	HAGGED	HAIQUES
HABILABLE	HACKING	HAEMATITE	HAGGING	HAIR
HABILE	HACKINGS	HAEMATITES	HAGGIS	HAIRBELL
HABIT	HACKLE	HAEMATOID	HAGGISES	HAIRBELLS
HABITABLE	HACKLED	HAEMATOMA	HAGGISH	HAIRBRUSH
HABITABLY	HACKLER	HAEMATOMAS	HAGGISHLY	HAIRBRUSHES
HABITANS	HACKLERS	HAEMIC	HAGGLE	HAIRCLOTH
HABITANT	HACKLES	HAEMIN	HAGGLED	HAIRCLOTHS
HABITANTS	HACKLET	HAEMINS	HAGGLER	HAIRCUT
HABITAT	HACKLETS	HAEMOCOEL	HAGGLERS	HAIRCUTS
HABITATS	HACKLIER	HAEMOCOELS	HAGGLES	HAIRDO
HABITED	HACKLIEST	HAEMOCYTE	HAGGLING	HAIRDOS
HABITING	HACKLING	HAEMOCYTES	HAGGS	HAIRDRIER
HABITS	HACKLY	HAEMONIES	HAGIARCHIES	HAIRDRIERS
HABITUAL	HACKNEY	HAEMONY	HAGIARCHY	HAIRDRYER
HABITUALS	HACKNEYED	HAEMOSTAT	HAGIOLOGIES	HAIRDRYERS
HABITUATE	HACKNEYING	HAEMOSTATS	HAGIOLOGY	HAIRED
HABITUATED	HACKNEYS	HAEMS	HAGLET	HAIRGRIP
HABITUATES	HACKS	HAEREMAI	HAGLETS	HAIRGRIPS
HABITUATING	HACQUETON	HAET	HAGS	HAIRIER
HABITUDE	HACQUETONS	HAETS	HAH	HAIRIEST
HABITUDES	HAD	HAFF	HAHNIUM	HAIRINESS
HABITUE	HADAL	HAFFET	HAHNIUMS	HAIRINESSES
HABITUES	HADDEN	HAFFETS	HAICK	HAIRING
HABITUS	HADDIE	HAFFIT	HAICKS	HAIRLESS
HABLE	HADDIES	HAFFITS	HAIDUK	HAIRLIKE
HABOOB	HADDING	HAFFLIN	HAIDUKS	HAIRLINE
HABOOBS	HADDOCK	HAFFLINS	HAIK	HAIRLINES
HACEK	HADDOCKS	HAFFS	HAIKAI	HAIRNET
HACEKS	HADE	HAFNIUM	HAIKS	HAIRNETS
HACHIS	HADED	HAFNIUMS	HAIKU	HAIRPIECE
HACHURE	HADES	HAFT	HAIL	HAIRPIECES
HACHURED	HADING	HAFTED	HAILED	HAIRPIN
HACHURES	HADJ	HAFTING	HAILER	HAIRPINS
HACHURING	HADJES	HAFTS	HAILERS	HAIRS
HACIENDA	HADJI	HAG	HAILIER	HAIRSPRAY
HACIENDAS	HADJIS	HAGBERRIES	HAILIEST	HAIRSPRAYS
HACK	HADROME	HAGBERRY	HAILING	HAIRST
HACKAMORE	HADROMES	HAGBOLT	HAILS	HAIRSTED
HACKAMORES	HADRON	HAGBOLTS	HAILSHOT	HAIRSTING
HACKBERRIES	HADRONIC	HAGBUT	HAILSHOTS	HAIRSTS

The Chambers Dictionary is the authority for many longer words; see *OSW* Introduction, page xii

HAIRSTYLE	HALIDES	HALLUX	HAMADRYADS	HAMULAR
HAIRSTYLES	HALIDOM	HALLWAY	HAMAL	HAMULATE
HAIRY	HALIDOMS	HALLWAYS	HAMALS	HAMULI
HAITH	HALIEUTIC	HALLYON	HAMAMELIS	HAMULUS
HAJ	HALIEUTICS	HALLYONS	HAMAMELISES	HAMZA
HAJES	HALIMOT	HALM	HAMARTIA	HAMZAH
HAJI	HALIMOTE	HALMA	HAMARTIAS	HAMZAHS
HAJIS	HALIMOTES	HALMAS	HAMATE	HAMZAS
HAJJ	HALIMOTS	HALMS	HAMBLE	HAN
HAJJES	HALING	HALO	HAMBLED	HANAP
HAJJI	HALIOTIS	HALOBIONT	HAMBLES	HANAPER
HAJJIS	HALITE	HALOBIONTS	HAMBLING	HANAPERS
HAKA	HALITES	HALOED	HAMBURGER	HANAPS
HAKAM	HALITOSES	HALOES	HAMBURGERS	HANCE
HAKAMS	HALITOSIS	HALOGEN	HAME	HANCES
HAKAS	HALITOTIC	HALOGENS	HAMED	HANCH
HAKE	HALITOUS	HALOID	HAMES	HANCHED
HAKES	HALITUS	HALOIDS	HAMEWITH	HANCHES
HAKIM	HALITUSES	HALOING	HAMFATTER	HANCHING
HAKIMS	HALL	HALON	HAMFATTERED	HAND
HALAL	HALLAL	HALONS	HAMFATTERING	HANDBAG
HALALLED	HALLALI	HALOPHILE	HAMFATTERS	HANDBAGGED
HALALLING	HALLALIS	HALOPHILES	HAMING	HANDBAGGING
HALALS	HALLALLED	HALOPHILIES	HAMLET	HANDBAGGINGS
HALATION	HALLALLING	HALOPHILY	HAMLETS	HANDBAGS
HALATIONS	HALLALOO	HALOPHOBE	HAMMAL	HANDBALL
HALAVAH	HALLALOOS	HALOPHOBES	HAMMALS	HANDBALLS
HALAVAHS	HALLALS	HALOPHYTE	HAMMAM	HANDBELL
HALBERD	HALLAN	HALOPHYTES	HAMMAMS	HANDBELLS
HALBERDS	HALLANS	HALOS	HAMMED	HANDBILL
HALBERT	HALLIAN	HALOTHANE	HAMMER	HANDBILLS
HALBERTS	HALLIANS	HALOTHANES	HAMMERED	HANDBOOK
HALCYON	HALLIARD	HALSE	HAMMERER	HANDBOOKS
HALCYONS	HALLIARDS	HALSED	HAMMERERS	HANDBRAKE
HALE	HALLING	HALSER	HAMMERING	HANDBRAKES
HALED	HALLINGS	HALSERS	HAMMERINGS	HANDCAR
HALENESS	HALLION	HALSES	HAMMERKOP	HANDCARS
HALENESSES	HALLIONS	HALSING	HAMMERKOPS	HANDCART
HALER	HALLMARK	HALT	HAMMERMAN	HANDCARTS
HALERS	HALLMARKED	HALTED	HAMMERMEN	HANDCLAP
HALES	HALLMARKING	HALTER	HAMMERS	HANDCLAPS
HALEST	HALLMARKS	HALTERED	HAMMIER	HANDCLASP
HALF	HALLO	HALTERES	HAMMIEST	HANDCLASPS
HALFA	HALLOA	HALTERING	HAMMILY	HANDCRAFT
HALFAS	HALLOAED	HALTERS	HAMMING	HANDCRAFTS
HALFEN	HALLOAING	HALTING	HAMMOCK	HANDCUFF
HALFLIN	HALLOAS	HALTINGLY	HAMMOCKS	HANDCUFFED
HALFLING	HALLOED	HALTINGS	HAMMY	HANDCUFFING
HALFLINGS	HALLOING	HALTS	HAMOSE	HANDCUFFS
HALFLINS	HALLOO	HALVA	HAMOUS	HANDED
HALFPACE	HALLOOED	HALVAH	HAMPER	HANDER
HALFPACES	HALLOOING	HALVAHS	HAMPERED	HANDERS
HALFPENCE	HALLOOS	HALVAS	HAMPERING	HANDFAST
HALFPENNIES	HALLOS	HALVE	HAMPERS	HANDFASTED
HALFPENNY	HALLOUMI	HALVED	HAMPSTER	HANDFASTING
HALFS	HALLOUMIS	HALVER	HAMPSTERS	HANDFASTINGS
HALFWAY	HALLOW	HALVERS	HAMS	HANDFASTS
HALFWIT	HALLOWED	HALVES	HAMSTER	HANDFUL
HALFWITS	HALLOWING	HALVING	HAMSTERS	HANDFULS
HALIBUT	HALLOWS	HALYARD	HAMSTRING	HANDGRIP
HALIBUTS	HALLS	HALYARDS	HAMSTRINGED	HANDGRIPS
HALICORE	HALLSTAND	HAM	HAMSTRINGING	HANDGUN
HALICORES	HALLSTANDS	HAMADRYAD	HAMSTRINGS	HANDGUNS
HALIDE	HALLUCES	HAMADRYADES	HAMSTRUNG	HANDHOLD

The Chambers Dictionary is the authority for many longer words; see *OSW* Introduction, page xii

HANDHOLDS	HANDWORKS	HAPLESSLY	HARBOURERS	HARDWARES
HANDICAP	HANDY	HAPLOID	HARBOURING	HARDWOOD
HANDICAPPED	HANDYMAN	HAPLOIDIES	HARBOURS	HARDWOODS
HANDICAPPING	HANDYMEN	HAPLOIDY	HARD	HARDY
HANDICAPS	HANDYWORK	HAPLOLOGIES	HARDBACK	HARE
HANDIER	HANDYWORKS	HAPLOLOGY	HARDBACKS	HAREBELL
HANDIEST	HANEPOOT	HAPLY	HARDBAG	HAREBELLS
HANDILY	HANEPOOTS	HAPPED	HARDBAGS	HARED
HANDINESS	HANG	HAPPEN	HARDBAKE	HAREEM
HANDINESSES	HANGABLE	HAPPENED	HARDBAKES	HAREEMS
HANDING	HANGAR	HAPPENING	HARDBALL	HARELD
HANDIWORK	HANGARS	HAPPENINGS	HARDBALLS	HARELDS
HANDIWORKS	HANGBIRD	HAPPENS	HARDBEAM	HAREM
HANDJAR	HANGBIRDS	HAPPIED	HARDBEAMS	HAREMS
HANDJARS	HANGDOG	HAPPIER	HARDBOARD	HARES
HANDLE	HANGDOGS	HAPPIES	HARDBOARDS	HAREWOOD
HANDLEBAR	HANGED	HAPPIEST	HARDEN	HAREWOODS
HANDLEBARS	HANGER	HAPPILY	HARDENED	HARICOT
HANDLED	HANGERS	HAPPINESS	HARDENER	HARICOTS
HANDLER	HANGFIRE	HAPPINESSES	HARDENERS	HARIGALDS
HANDLERS	HANGFIRES	HAPPING	HARDENING	HARIGALS
HANDLES	HANGING	HAPPY	HARDENINGS	HARIM
HANDLESS	HANGINGS	HAPPYING	HARDENS	HARIMS
HANDLING	HANGMAN	HAPS	HARDER	HARING
HANDLINGS	HANGMEN	HAPTEN	HARDEST	HARIOLATE
HANDLIST	HANGNAIL	HAPTENS	HARDFACE	HARIOLATED
HANDLISTS	HANGNAILS	HAPTERON	HARDFACES	HARIOLATES
HANDMADE	HANGNEST	HAPTERONS	HARDGRASS	HARIOLATING
HANDMAID	HANGNESTS	HAPTIC	HARDGRASSES	HARISH
HANDMAIDS	HANGOUT	HAPTICS	HARDHACK	HARK
HANDOUT	HANGOUTS	HAQUETON	HARDHACKS	HARKED
HANDOUTS	HANGOVER	HAQUETONS	HARDHEAD	HARKEN
HANDOVER	HANGOVERS	HARAM	HARDHEADS	HARKENED
HANDOVERS	HANGS	HARAMBEE	HARDIER	HARKENING
HANDPLAY	HANJAR	HARAMBEES	HARDIEST	HARKENS
HANDPLAYS	HANJARS	HARAMS	HARDIHEAD	HARKING
HANDRAIL	HANK	HARANGUE	HARDIHEADS	HARKS
HANDRAILS	HANKED	HARANGUED	HARDIHOOD	HARL
HANDS	HANKER	HARANGUER	HARDIHOODS	HARLED
HANDSAW	HANKERED	HARANGUERS	HARDILY	HARLEQUIN
HANDSAWS	HANKERING	HARANGUES	HARDIMENT	HARLEQUINED
HANDSEL	HANKERINGS	HARANGUING	HARDIMENTS	HARLEQUINING
HANDSELLED	HANKERS	HARASS	HARDINESS	HARLEQUINS
HANDSELLING	HANKIE	HARASSED	HARDINESSES	HARLING
HANDSELS	HANKIES	HARASSER	HARDISH	HARLINGS
HANDSET	HANKING	HARASSERS	HARDLINE	HARLOT
HANDSETS	HANKS	HARASSES	HARDLINER	HARLOTRIES
HANDSHAKE	HANKY	HARASSING	HARDLINERS	HARLOTRY
HANDSHAKES	HANSEL	HARASSINGS	HARDLY	HARLOTS
HANDSOME	HANSELLED	HARBINGER	HARDNESS	HARLS
HANDSOMER	HANSELLING	HARBINGERED	HARDNESSES	HARM
HANDSOMEST	HANSELS	HARBINGERING	HARDNOSED	HARMALA
HANDSPIKE	HANSOM	HARBINGERS	HARDOKE	HARMALAS
HANDSPIKES	HANSOMS	HARBOR	HARDOKES	HARMALIN
HANDSTAFF	HANTLE	HARBORAGE	HARDPARTS	HARMALINE
HANDSTAFFS	HANTLES	HARBORAGES	HARDS	HARMALINES
HANDSTAND	HANUMAN	HARBORED	HARDSHELL	HARMALINS
HANDSTANDS	HANUMANS	HARBORER	HARDSHIP	HARMAN
HANDSTAVES	HAOMA	HARBORERS	HARDSHIPS	HARMANS
HANDSTURN	HAOMAS	HARBORING	HARDTACK	HARMATTAN
HANDSTURNS	HAP	HARBORS	HARDTACKS	HARMATTANS
HANDTOWEL	HAPHAZARD	HARBOUR	HARDTOP	HARMDOING
HANDTOWELS	HAPHAZARDS	HARBOURED	HARDTOPS	HARMDOINGS
HANDWORK	HAPLESS	HARBOURER	HARDWARE	HARMED

The Chambers Dictionary is the authority for many longer words; see *OSW* Introduction, page xii

HARMEL	HARQUEBUS	HASHISHES	HATCHETS	HAULDS
HARMELS	HARQUEBUSES	HASHMARK	HATCHETY	HAULED
HARMFUL	HARRIDAN	HASHMARKS	HATCHING	HAULER
HARMFULLY	HARRIDANS	HASHY	HATCHINGS	HAULERS
HARMIN	HARRIED	HASK	HATCHLING	HAULIER
HARMINE	HARRIER	HASKS	HATCHLINGS	HAULIERS
HARMINES	HARRIERS	HASLET	HATCHMENT	HAULING
HARMING	HARRIES	HASLETS	HATCHMENTS	HAULM
HARMINS	HARROW	HASP	HATCHWAY	HAULMS
HARMLESS	HARROWED	HASPED	HATCHWAYS	HAULS
HARMONIC	HARROWING	HASPING	HATE	HAULST
HARMONICA	HARROWS	HASPS	HATEABLE	HAULT
HARMONICAS	HARRUMPH	HASSAR	HATED	HAUNCH
HARMONICS	HARRUMPHED	HASSARS	HATEFUL	HAUNCHED
HARMONIES	HARRUMPHING	HASSLE	HATEFULLY	HAUNCHES
HARMONISE	HARRUMPHS	HASSLED	HATELESS	HAUNCHING
HARMONISED	HARRY	HASSLES	HATER	HAUNT
HARMONISES	HARRYING	HASSLING	HATERENT	HAUNTED
HARMONISING	HARSH	HASSOCK	HATERENTS	HAUNTER
HARMONIST	HARSHEN	HASSOCKS	HATERS	HAUNTERS
HARMONISTS	HARSHENED	HASSOCKY	HATES	HAUNTING
HARMONIUM	HARSHENING	HAST	HATFUL	HAUNTINGS
HARMONIUMS	HARSHENS	HASTA	HATFULS	HAUNTS
HARMONIZE	HARSHER	HASTATE	HATGUARD	HAURIANT
HARMONIZED	HARSHEST	HASTATED	HATGUARDS	HAURIENT
HARMONIZES	HARSHLY	HASTE	HATH	HAUSE
HARMONIZING	HARSHNESS	HASTED	HATING	HAUSED
HARMONY	HARSHNESSES	HASTEN	HATLESS	HAUSES
HARMOST	HARSLET	HASTENED	HATPEG	HAUSFRAU
HARMOSTIES	HARSLETS	HASTENER	HATPEGS	HAUSFRAUS
HARMOSTS	HART	HASTENERS	HATPIN	HAUSING
HARMOSTY	HARTAL	HASTENING	HATPINS	HAUSTELLA
HARMOTOME	HARTALS	HASTENS	HATRACK	HAUSTORIA
HARMOTOMES	HARTBEES	HASTES	HATRACKS	HAUT
HARMS	HARTBEESES	HASTIER	HATRED	HAUTBOIS
HARN	HARTELY	HASTIEST	HATREDS	HAUTBOY
HARNESS	HARTEN	HASTILY	HATS	HAUTBOYS
HARNESSED	HARTENED	HASTINESS	HATSTAND	HAUTE
HARNESSES	HARTENING	HASTINESSES	HATSTANDS	HAUTEUR
HARNESSING	HARTENS	HASTING	HATTED	HAUTEURS
HARNS	HARTLESSE	HASTINGS	HATTER	HAUYNE
HARO	HARTS	HASTY	HATTERED	HAUYNES
HAROS	HARTSHORN	HAT	HATTERING	HAVE
HAROSET	HARTSHORNS	HATABLE	HATTERS	HAVELOCK
HAROSETH	HARUSPEX	HATBAND	HATTING	HAVELOCKS
HAROSETHS	HARUSPICES	HATBANDS	HATTINGS	HAVEN
HAROSETS	HARUSPICIES	HATBOX	HATTOCK	HAVENED
HARP	HARUSPICY	HATBOXES	HATTOCKS	HAVENING
HARPED	HARVEST	HATBRUSH	HAUBERK	HAVENS
HARPER	HARVESTED	HATBRUSHES	HAUBERKS	HAVEOUR
HARPERS	HARVESTER	HATCH	HAUD	HAVEOURS
HARPIES	HARVESTERS	HATCHBACK	HAUDING	HAVER
HARPING	HARVESTING	HATCHBACKS	HAUDS	HAVERED
HARPINGS	HARVESTS	HATCHED	HAUGH	HAVEREL
HARPIST	HAS	HATCHEL	HAUGHS	HAVERELS
HARPISTS	HASH	HATCHELLED	HAUGHT	HAVERING
HARPOON	HASHED	HATCHELLING	HAUGHTIER	HAVERINGS
HARPOONED	HASHEESH	HATCHELS	HAUGHTIEST	HAVERS
HARPOONER	HASHEESHES	HATCHER	HAUGHTILY	HAVERSACK
HARPOONERS	HASHES	HATCHERIES	HAUGHTY	HAVERSACKS
HARPOONING	HASHIER	HATCHERS	HAUL	HAVERSINE
HARPOONS	HASHIEST	HATCHERY	HAULAGE	HAVERSINES
HARPS	HASHING	HATCHES	HAULAGES	HAVES
HARPY	HASHISH	HATCHET	HAULD	HAVILDAR

HAVILDARS	HAYFIELD	HE	HEADMOST	HEALING
HAVING	HAYFIELDS	HEAD	HEADNOTE	HEALINGLY
HAVINGS	HAYFORK	HEADACHE	HEADNOTES	HEALINGS
HAVIOUR	HAYFORKS	HEADACHES	HEADPEACE	HEALS
HAVIOURS	HAYING	HEADACHIER	HEADPEACES	HEALSOME
HAVOC	HAYINGS	HEADACHIEST	HEADPHONE	HEALTH
HAVOCKED	HAYLE	HEADACHY	HEADPHONES	HEALTHFUL
HAVOCKING	HAYLES	HEADAGE	HEADPIECE	HEALTHIER
HAVOCS	HAYLOFT	HEADAGES	HEADPIECES	HEALTHIEST
HAW	HAYLOFTS	HEADBAND	HEADRACE	HEALTHILY
HAWBUCK	HAYMAKER	HEADBANDS	HEADRACES	HEALTHS
HAWBUCKS	HAYMAKERS	HEADBOARD	HEADRAIL	HEALTHY
HAWED	HAYMAKING	HEADBOARDS	HEADRAILS	HEAME
HAWFINCH	HAYMAKINGS	HEADCASE	HEADREACH	HEAP
HAWFINCHES	HAYMOW	HEADCASES	HEADREACHED	HEAPED
HAWING	HAYMOWS	HEADCHAIR	HEADREACHES	HEAPIER
HAWK	HAYRICK	HEADCHAIRS	HEADREACHING	HEAPIEST
HAWKBELL	HAYRICKS	HEADCLOTH	HEADREST	HEAPING
HAWKBELLS	HAYRIDE	HEADCLOTHS	HEADRESTS	HEAPS
HAWKBIT	HAYRIDES	HEADDRESS	HEADRIG	HEAPSTEAD
HAWKBITS	HAYS	HEADDRESSES	HEADRIGS	HEAPSTEADS
HAWKED	HAYSEED	HEADED	HEADRING	HEAPY
HAWKER	HAYSEEDS	HEADER	HEADRINGS	HEAR
HAWKERS	HAYSEL	HEADERS	HEADROOM	HEARD
HAWKEY	HAYSELS	HEADFAST	HEADROOMS	HEARDS
HAWKEYS	HAYSTACK	HEADFASTS	HEADROPE	HEARE
HAWKIE	HAYSTACKS	HEADFRAME	HEADROPES	HEARER
HAWKIES	HAYWARD	HEADFRAMES	HEADS	HEARERS
HAWKING	HAYWARDS	HEADGEAR	HEADSCARF	HEARES
HAWKINGS	HAYWIRE	HEADGEARS	HEADSCARVES	HEARIE
HAWKISH	HAYWIRES	HEADHUNT	HEADSET	HEARING
HAWKISHLY	HAZAN	HEADHUNTED	HEADSETS	HEARINGS
HAWKIT	HAZANIM	HEADHUNTING	HEADSHAKE	HEARKEN
HAWKLIKE	HAZANS	HEADHUNTINGS	HEADSHAKES	HEARKENED
HAWKS	HAZARD	HEADHUNTS	HEADSHIP	HEARKENER
HAWKSBILL	HAZARDED	HEADIER	HEADSHIPS	HEARKENERS
HAWKSBILLS	HAZARDING	HEADIEST	HEADSHOT	HEARKENING
HAWKWEED	HAZARDIZE	HEADILY	HEADSHOTS	HEARKENS
HAWKWEEDS	HAZARDIZES	HEADINESS	HEADSMAN	HEARS
HAWM	HAZARDOUS	HEADINESSES	HEADSMEN	HEARSAY
HAWMED	HAZARDRIES	HEADING	HEADSTALL	HEARSAYS
HAWMING	HAZARDRY	HEADINGS	HEADSTALLS	HEARSE
HAWMS	HAZARDS	HEADLAMP	HEADSTICK	HEARSED
HAWS	HAZE	HEADLAMPS	HEADSTICKS	HEARSES
HAWSE	HAZED	HEADLAND	HEADSTOCK	HEARSIER
HAWSED	HAZEL	HEADLANDS	HEADSTOCKS	HEARSIEST
HAWSEHOLE	HAZELLY	HEADLEASE	HEADSTONE	HEARSING
HAWSEHOLES	HAZELNUT	HEADLEASES	HEADSTONES	HEARSY
HAWSEPIPE	HAZELNUTS	HEADLESS	HEADWAY	HEART
HAWSEPIPES	HAZELS	HEADLIGHT	HEADWAYS	HEARTACHE
HAWSER	HAZER	HEADLIGHTS	HEADWORD	HEARTACHES
HAWSERS	HAZERS	HEADLINE	HEADWORDS	HEARTBEAT
HAWSES	HAZES	HEADLINED	HEADWORK	HEARTBEATS
HAWSING	HAZIER	HEADLINER	HEADWORKS	HEARTBURN
HAWTHORN	HAZIEST	HEADLINERS	HEADY	HEARTBURNS
HAWTHORNS	HAZILY	HEADLINES	HEAL	HEARTED
HAY	HAZINESS	HEADLINING	HEALABLE	HEARTEN
HAYBAND	HAZINESSES	HEADLOCK	HEALD	HEARTENED
HAYBANDS	HAZING	HEADLOCKS	HEALDED	HEARTENING
HAYBOX	HAZINGS	HEADLONG	HEALDING	HEARTENS
HAYBOXES	HAZY	HEADMAN	HEALDS	HEARTFELT
HAYCOCK	HAZZAN	HEADMARK	HEALED	HEARTH
HAYCOCKS	HAZZANIM	HEADMARKS	HEALER	HEARTHS
HAYED	HAZZANS	HEADMEN	HEALERS	HEARTIER

The Chambers Dictionary is the authority for many longer words; see *OSW* Introduction, page xii

HEARTIES	HEAVERS	HEDDLES	HEFTINESSES	HELICOID
HEARTIEST	HEAVES	HEDDLING	HEFTING	HELICON
HEARTIKIN	HEAVIER	HEDERAL	HEFTS	HELICONS
HEARTIKINS	HEAVIES	HEDERATED	HEFTY	HELICTITE
HEARTILY	HEAVIEST	HEDGE	HEGEMONIC	HELICTITES
HEARTING	HEAVILY	HEDGEBILL	HEGEMONIES	HELIDECK
HEARTLAND	HEAVINESS	HEDGEBILLS	HEGEMONY	HELIDECKS
HEARTLANDS	HEAVINESSES	HEDGED	HEGIRA	HELIDROME
HEARTLESS	HEAVING	HEDGEHOG	HEGIRAS	HELIDROMES
HEARTLET	HEAVINGS	HEDGEHOGS	HEID	HELIMAN
HEARTLETS	HEAVY	HEDGEPIG	HEIDS	HELIMEN
HEARTLING	HEBDOMAD	HEDGEPIGS	HEIFER	HELING
HEARTLINGS	HEBDOMADS	HEDGER	HEIFERS	HELIODOR
HEARTLY	HEBE	HEDGEROW	HEIGH	HELIODORS
HEARTPEA	HEBEN	HEDGEROWS	HEIGHT	HELIOLOGIES
HEARTPEAS	HEBENON	HEDGERS	HEIGHTEN	HELIOLOGY
HEARTS	HEBENONS	HEDGES	HEIGHTENED	HELIOSES
HEARTSEED	HEBENS	HEDGIER	HEIGHTENING	HELIOSIS
HEARTSEEDS	HEBES	HEDGIEST	HEIGHTENS	HELIOSTAT
HEARTSOME	HEBETANT	HEDGING	HEIGHTS	HELIOSTATS
HEARTWOOD	HEBETATE	HEDGINGS	HEIL	HELIOTYPE
HEARTWOODS	HEBETATED	HEDGY	HEINOUS	HELIOTYPES
HEARTY	HEBETATES	HEDONIC	HEINOUSLY	HELIOTYPIES
HEAST	HEBETATING	HEDONICS	HEIR	HELIOTYPY
HEASTE	HEBETUDE	HEDONISM	HEIRDOM	HELIOZOAN
HEASTES	HEBETUDES	HEDONISMS	HEIRDOMS	HELIOZOANS
HEASTS	HEBONA	HEDONIST	HEIRED	HELIOZOIC
HEAT	HEBONAS	HEDONISTS	HEIRESS	HELIPAD
HEATED	HECATOMB	HEDYPHANE	HEIRESSES	HELIPADS
HEATER	HECATOMBS	HEDYPHANES	HEIRING	HELIPILOT
HEATERS	HECH	HEED	HEIRLESS	HELIPILOTS
HEATH	HECHT	HEEDED	HEIRLOOM	HELIPORT
HEATHBIRD	HECHTING	HEEDFUL	HEIRLOOMS	HELIPORTS
HEATHBIRDS	HECHTS	HEEDFULLY	HEIRS	HELISCOOP
HEATHCOCK	HECK	HEEDINESS	HEIRSHIP	HELISCOOPS
HEATHCOCKS	HECKLE	HEEDINESSES	HEIRSHIPS	HELISTOP
HEATHEN	HECKLED	HEEDING	HEIST	HELISTOPS
HEATHENRIES	HECKLER	HEEDLESS	HEISTED	HELIUM
HEATHENRY	HECKLERS	HEEDS	HEISTER	HELIUMS
HEATHENS	HECKLES	HEEDY	HEISTERS	HELIX
HEATHER	HECKLING	HEEHAW	HEISTING	HELIXES
HEATHERIER	HECKLINGS	HEEHAWED	HEISTS	HELL
HEATHERIEST	HECKS	HEEHAWING	HEJAB	HELLEBORE
HEATHERS	HECOGENIN	HEEHAWS	HEJABS	HELLEBORES
HEATHERY	HECOGENINS	HEEL	HEJIRA	HELLED
HEATHIER	HECTARE	HEELED	HEJIRAS	HELLENISE
HEATHIEST	HECTARES	HEELER	HEJRA	HELLENISED
HEATHS	HECTIC	HEELERS	HEJRAS	HELLENISES
HEATHY	HECTICAL	HEELING	HELCOID	HELLENISING
HEATING	HECTICS	HEELINGS	HELD	HELLENIZE
HEATINGS	HECTOGRAM	HEELS	HELE	HELLENIZED
HEATS	HECTOGRAMS	HEEZE	HELED	HELLENIZES
HEATSPOT	HECTOR	HEEZED	HELENIUM	HELLENIZING
HEATSPOTS	HECTORED	HEEZES	HELENIUMS	HELLER
HEAUME	HECTORER	HEEZIE	HELES	HELLERS
HEAUMES	HECTORERS	HEEZIES	HELIAC	HELLFIRE
HEAVE	HECTORING	HEEZING	HELIACAL	HELLFIRES
HEAVED	HECTORINGS	HEFT	HELIBORNE	HELLHOUND
HEAVEN	HECTORISM	HEFTE	HELIBUS	HELLHOUNDS
HEAVENLIER	HECTORISMS	HEFTED	HELIBUSES	HELLICAT
HEAVENLIEST	HECTORLY	HEFTIER	HELIBUSSES	HELLICATS
HEAVENLY	HECTORS	HEFTIEST	HELICAL	HELLIER
HEAVENS	HEDDLE	HEFTILY	HELICALLY	HELLIERS
HEAVER	HEDDLED	HEFTINESS	HELICES	HELLING

HELLION	HEMICYCLES	HENNERY	HERALDING	HERDESS
HELLIONS	HEMIHEDRIES	HENNIER	HERALDRIES	HERDESSES
HELLISH	HEMIHEDRY	HENNIES	HERALDRY	HERDIC
HELLISHLY	HEMINA	HENNIEST	HERALDS	HERDICS
HELLO	HEMINAS	HENNIN	HERB	HERDING
HELLOED	HEMIOLA	HENNING	HERBAGE	HERDMAN
HELLOING	HEMIOLAS	HENNINS	HERBAGED	HERDMEN
HELLOS	HEMIOLIA	HENNY	HERBAGES	HERDS
HELLOVA	HEMIOLIAS	HENOTIC	HERBAL	HERDSMAN
HELLS	HEMIOLIC	HENPECK	HERBALISM	HERDSMEN
HELLUVA	HEMIONE	HENPECKED	HERBALISMS	HERDWICK
HELLWARD	HEMIONES	HENPECKING	HERBALIST	HERDWICKS
HELLWARDS	HEMIONUS	HENPECKS	HERBALISTS	HERE
HELM	HEMIONUSES	HENRIES	HERBALS	HEREABOUT
HELMED	HEMIOPIA	HENRY	HERBAR	HEREABOUTS
HELMET	HEMIOPIAS	HENRYS	HERBARIA	HEREAFTER
HELMETED	HEMIOPIC	HENS	HERBARIAN	HEREAFTERS
HELMETS	HEMIOPSIA	HENT	HERBARIANS	HEREAT
HELMING	HEMIOPSIAS	HENTING	HERBARIES	HEREAWAY
HELMINTH	HEMISPACE	HENTS	HERBARIUM	HEREBY
HELMINTHS	HEMISPACES	HEP	HERBARIUMS	HEREDITIES
HELMLESS	HEMISTICH	HEPAR	HERBARS	HEREDITY
HELMS	HEMISTICHS	HEPARIN	HERBARY	HEREFROM
HELMSMAN	HEMITROPE	HEPARINS	HERBELET	HEREIN
HELMSMEN	HEMITROPES	HEPARS	HERBELETS	HERENESS
HELOT	HEMLOCK	HEPATIC	HERBICIDE	HERENESSES
HELOTAGE	HEMLOCKS	HEPATICAL	HERBICIDES	HEREOF
HELOTAGES	HEMMED	HEPATICS	HERBIER	HEREON
HELOTISM	HEMMING	HEPATISE	HERBIEST	HERESIES
HELOTISMS	HEMP	HEPATISED	HERBIST	HERESY
HELOTRIES	HEMPEN	HEPATISES	HERBISTS	HERETIC
HELOTRY	HEMPIER	HEPATISING	HERBIVORA	HERETICAL
HELOTS	HEMPIES	HEPATITE	HERBIVORE	HERETICS
HELP	HEMPIEST	HEPATITES	HERBIVORES	HERETO
HELPABLE	HEMPS	HEPATITIS	HERBIVORIES	HEREUNDER
HELPDESK	HEMPY	HEPATITISES	HERBIVORY	HEREUNTO
HELPDESKS	HEMS	HEPATIZE	HERBLESS	HEREUPON
HELPED	HEN	HEPATIZED	HERBLET	HEREWITH
HELPER	HENBANE	HEPATIZES	HERBLETS	HERIED
HELPERS	HENBANES	HEPATIZING	HERBORISE	HERIES
HELPFUL	HENCE	HEPPER	HERBORISED	HERIOT
HELPING	HENCHMAN	HEPPEST	HERBORISES	HERIOTS
HELPINGS	HENCHMEN	HEPS	HERBORISING	HERISSE
HELPLESS	HEND	HEPSTER	HERBORIST	HERISSON
HELPLINE	HENDED	HEPSTERS	HERBORISTS	HERISSONS
HELPLINES	HENDIADYS	HEPT	HERBORIZE	HERITABLE
HELPMATE	HENDIADYSES	HEPTAD	HERBORIZED	HERITABLY
HELPMATES	HENDING	HEPTADS	HERBORIZES	HERITAGE
HELPMEET	HENDS	HEPTAGLOT	HERBORIZING	HERITAGES
HELPMEETS	HENEQUEN	HEPTAGLOTS	HERBOSE	HERITOR
HELPS	HENEQUENS	HEPTAGON	HERBOUS	HERITORS
HELVE	HENEQUIN	HEPTAGONS	HERBS	HERITRESS
HELVED	HENEQUINS	HEPTANE	HERBY	HERITRESSES
HELVES	HENGE	HEPTANES	HERCOGAMIES	HERITRICES
HELVETIUM	HENGES	HEPTAPODIES	HERCOGAMY	HERITRIX
HELVETIUMS	HENIQUIN	HEPTAPODY	HERCULEAN	HERITRIXES
HELVING	HENIQUINS	HEPTARCH	HERCYNITE	HERKOGAMIES
HEM	HENNA	HEPTARCHIES	HERCYNITES	HERKOGAMY
HEMAL	HENNAED	HEPTARCHS	HERD	HERL
HEME	HENNAS	HEPTARCHY	HERDBOY	HERLING
HEMES	HENNED	HER	HERDBOYS	HERLINGS
HEMIALGIA	HENNER	HERALD	HERDED	HERLS
HEMIALGIAS	HENNERIES	HERALDED	HERDEN	HERM
HEMICYCLE	HENNERS	HERALDIC	HERDENS	HERMA

HERMAE	HERRINGERS	HETERO	HEXAPLAS	HICCUPS
HERMANDAD	HERRINGS	HETERODOX	HEXAPLOID	HICCUPY
HERMANDADS	HERRY	HETERONYM	HEXAPLOIDS	HICK
HERMETIC	HERRYING	HETERONYMS	HEXAPOD	HICKEY
HERMETICS	HERRYMENT	HETEROPOD	HEXAPODIES	HICKEYS
HERMIT	HERRYMENTS	HETEROPODS	HEXAPODS	HICKORIES
HERMITAGE	HERS	HETEROS	HEXAPODY	HICKORY
HERMITAGES	HERSALL	HETEROSES	HEXARCH	HICKS
HERMITESS	HERSALLS	HETEROSIS	HEXASTICH	HICKWALL
HERMITESSES	HERSE	HETEROTIC	HEXASTICHS	HICKWALLS
HERMITS	HERSED	HETES	HEXASTYLE	HID
HERMS	HERSELF	HETHER	HEXASTYLES	HIDAGE
HERN	HERSES	HETING	HEXED	HIDAGES
HERNIA	HERSHIP	HETMAN	HEXENE	HIDALGA
HERNIAE	HERSHIPS	HETMANATE	HEXENES	HIDALGAS
HERNIAL	HERSTORIES	HETMANATES	HEXES	HIDALGO
HERNIAS	HERSTORY	HETMANS	HEXING	HIDALGOS
HERNIATED	HERTZ	HETS	HEXINGS	HIDDEN
HERNS	HERTZES	HEUCH	HEXOSE	HIDDENITE
HERNSHAW	HERY	HEUCHS	HEXOSES	HIDDENITES
HERNSHAWS	HERYE	HEUGH	HEXYLENE	HIDDENLY
HERO	HERYED	HEUGHS	HEXYLENES	HIDDER
HEROE	HERYES	HEUREKA	HEY	HIDDERS
HEROES	HERYING	HEUREKAS	HEYDAY	HIDE
HEROIC	HES	HEURETIC	HEYDAYS	HIDED
HEROICAL	HESITANCE	HEURETICS	HEYDUCK	HIDEOSITIES
HEROICLY	HESITANCES	HEURISM	HEYDUCKS	HIDEOSITY
HEROICS	HESITANCIES	HEURISMS	HEYED	HIDEOUS
HEROIN	HESITANCY	HEURISTIC	HEYING	HIDEOUSLY
HEROINE	HESITANT	HEURISTICS	HEYS	HIDEOUT
HEROINES	HESITATE	HEVEA	HI	HIDEOUTS
HEROINS	HESITATED	HEVEAS	HIANT	HIDER
HEROISE	HESITATES	HEW	HIATUS	HIDERS
HEROISED	HESITATING	HEWED	HIATUSES	HIDES
HEROISES	HESITATOR	HEWER	HIBACHI	HIDING
HEROISING	HESITATORS	HEWERS	HIBACHIS	HIDINGS
HEROISM	HESP	HEWGH	HIBAKUSHA	HIDLING
HEROISMS	HESPED	HEWING	HIBERNAL	HIDLINGS
HEROIZE	HESPERID	HEWINGS	HIBERNATE	HIDLINS
HEROIZED	HESPERIDS	HEWN	HIBERNATED	HIDROSES
HEROIZES	HESPING	HEWS	HIBERNATES	HIDROSIS
HEROIZING	HESPS	HEX	HIBERNATING	HIDROTIC
HERON	HESSIAN	HEXACHORD	HIBERNISE	HIDROTICS
HERONRIES	HESSIANS	HEXACHORDS	HIBERNISED	HIE
HERONRY	HESSONITE	HEXACT	HIBERNISES	HIED
HERONS	HESSONITES	HEXACTS	HIBERNISING	HIEING
HERONSEW	HEST	HEXAD	HIBERNIZE	HIELAMAN
HERONSEWS	HESTERNAL	HEXADIC	HIBERNIZED	HIELAMANS
HERONSHAW	HESTS	HEXADS	HIBERNIZES	HIEMAL
HERONSHAWS	HET	HEXAFOIL	HIBERNIZING	HIEMS
HEROON	HETAERA	HEXAFOILS	HIBISCUS	HIERACIUM
HEROONS	HETAERAE	HEXAGLOT	HIBISCUSES	HIERACIUMS
HEROSHIP	HETAERISM	HEXAGON	HIC	HIERARCH
HEROSHIPS	HETAERISMS	HEXAGONAL	HICATEE	HIERARCHIES
HERPES	HETAIRA	HEXAGONS	HICATEES	HIERARCHS
HERPESES	HETAIRAI	HEXAGRAM	HICCATEE	HIERARCHY
HERPETIC	HETAIRAS	HEXAGRAMS	HICCATEES	HIERATIC
HERPETOID	HETAIRIA	HEXAHEDRA	HICCOUGH	HIERATICA
HERRIED	HETAIRIAS	HEXAMETER	HICCOUGHED	HIERATICAS
HERRIES	HETAIRISM	HEXAMETERS	HICCOUGHING	HIEROCRAT
HERRIMENT	HETAIRISMS	HEXANE	HICCOUGHS	HIEROCRATS
HERRIMENTS	HETAIRIST	HEXANES	HICCUP	HIERODULE
HERRING	HETAIRISTS	HEXAPLA	HICCUPED	HIERODULES
HERRINGER	HETE	HEXAPLAR	HICCUPING	HIEROGRAM

HIEROGRAMS	HIJACK	HIMSELF	HIPPING	HIRUDIN
HIEROLOGIES	HIJACKED	HIN	HIPPINGS	HIRUDINS
HIEROLOGY	HIJACKER	HIND	HIPPINS	HIRUNDINE
HIERURGIES	HIJACKERS	HINDBERRIES	HIPPISH	HIS
HIERURGY	HIJACKING	HINDBERRY	HIPPO	HISH
HIES	HIJACKS	HINDBRAIN	HIPPOCRAS	HISHED
HIGGLE	HIJINKS	HINDBRAINS	HIPPOCRASES	HISHES
HIGGLED	HIJRA	HINDER	HIPPODAME	HISHING
HIGGLER	HIJRAH	HINDERED	HIPPODAMES	HISN
HIGGLERS	HIJRAHS	HINDERER	HIPPOLOGIES	HISPID
HIGGLES	HIJRAS	HINDERERS	HIPPOLOGY	HISPIDITIES
HIGGLING	HIKE	HINDERING	HIPPOS	HISPIDITY
HIGGLINGS	HIKED	HINDERS	HIPPURIC	HISS
HIGH	HIKER	HINDFEET	HIPPURITE	HISSED
HIGHBALL	HIKERS	HINDFOOT	HIPPURITES	HISSES
HIGHBALLED	HIKES	HINDHEAD	HIPPUS	HISSING
HIGHBALLING	HIKING	HINDHEADS	HIPPUSES	HISSINGLY
HIGHBALLS	HILA	HINDLEG	HIPPY	HISSINGS
HIGHBOY	HILAR	HINDLEGS	HIPPYDOM	HIST
HIGHBOYS	HILARIOUS	HINDMOST	HIPPYDOMS	HISTAMINE
HIGHBROW	HILARITIES	HINDRANCE	HIPS	HISTAMINES
HIGHBROWS	HILARITY	HINDRANCES	HIPSTER	HISTED
HIGHCHAIR	HILCH	HINDS	HIPSTERS	HISTIDINE
HIGHCHAIRS	HILCHED	HINDSIGHT	HIPT	HISTIDINES
HIGHED	HILCHES	HINDSIGHTS	HIRABLE	HISTIE
HIGHER	HILCHING	HINDWARD	HIRAGANA	HISTING
HIGHERED	HILD	HINDWING	HIRAGANAS	HISTIOID
HIGHERING	HILDING	HINDWINGS	HIRAGE	HISTOGEN
HIGHERS	HILDINGS	HING	HIRAGES	HISTOGENIES
HIGHEST	HILI	HINGE	HIRCINE	HISTOGENS
HIGHING	HILL	HINGED	HIRCOSITIES	HISTOGENY
HIGHISH	HILLED	HINGES	HIRCOSITY	HISTOGRAM
HIGHJACK	HILLFOLK	HINGING	HIRE	HISTOGRAMS
HIGHJACKED	HILLIER	HINGS	HIREABLE	HISTOID
HIGHJACKING	HILLIEST	HINNIED	HIREAGE	HISTOLOGIES
HIGHJACKS	HILLINESS	HINNIES	HIREAGES	HISTOLOGY
HIGHLAND	HILLINESSES	HINNY	HIRED	HISTONE
HIGHLANDS	HILLING	HINNYING	HIRELING	HISTONES
HIGHLIGHT	HILLMEN	HINS	HIRELINGS	HISTORIAN
HIGHLIGHTED	HILLO	HINT	HIRER	HISTORIANS
HIGHLIGHTING	HILLOCK	HINTED	HIRERS	HISTORIC
HIGHLIGHTS	HILLOCKS	HINTING	HIRES	HISTORIED
HIGHLY	HILLOCKY	HINTINGLY	HIRING	HISTORIES
HIGHMAN	HILLOED	HINTS	HIRINGS	HISTORIFIED
HIGHMEN	HILLOING	HIP	HIRLING	HISTORIFIES
HIGHMOST	HILLOS	HIPNESS	HIRLINGS	HISTORIFY
HIGHNESS	HILLS	HIPNESSES	HIRPLE	HISTORIFYING
HIGHNESSES	HILLSIDE	HIPPARCH	HIRPLED	HISTORISM
HIGHROAD	HILLSIDES	HIPPARCHS	HIRPLES	HISTORISMS
HIGHROADS	HILLTOP	HIPPED	HIRPLING	HISTORY
HIGHS	HILLTOPS	HIPPEN	HIRRIENT	HISTORYING
HIGHT	HILLY	HIPPENS	HIRRIENTS	HISTRIO
HIGHTAIL	HILT	HIPPER	HIRSEL	HISTRION
HIGHTAILED	HILTED	HIPPEST	HIRSELLED	HISTRIONS
HIGHTAILING	HILTING	HIPPIATRIES	HIRSELLING	HISTRIOS
HIGHTAILS	HILTS	HIPPIATRY	HIRSELS	HISTS
HIGHTH	HILUM	HIPPIC	HIRSLE	HIT
HIGHTHS	HILUS	HIPPIE	HIRSLED	HITCH
HIGHTING	HIM	HIPPIEDOM	HIRSLES	HITCHED
HIGHTS	HIMATIA	HIPPIEDOMS	HIRSLING	HITCHER
HIGHWAY	HIMATION	HIPPIER	HIRSTIE	HITCHERS
HIGHWAYS	HIMATIONS	HIPPIES	HIRSUTE	HITCHES
HIJAB	HIMBO	HIPPIEST	HIRSUTISM	HITCHIER
HIJABS	HIMBOS	HIPPIN	HIRSUTISMS	HITCHIEST

The Chambers Dictionary is the authority for many longer words; see *OSW* Introduction, page xii

HITCHILY	HOARSEST	HOBOING	HOGGEREL	HOISTWAYS
HITCHING	HOARY	HOBOISM	HOGGERELS	HOKE
HITCHY	HOAS	HOBOISMS	HOGGERIES	HOKED
HITHE	HOAST	HOBOS	HOGGERS	HOKES
HITHER	HOASTED	HOBS	HOGGERY	HOKEY
HITHERED	HOASTING	HOC	HOGGET	HOKI
HITHERING	HOASTMAN	HOCK	HOGGETS	HOKIER
HITHERS	HOASTMEN	HOCKED	HOGGIN	HOKIEST
HITHERTO	HOASTS	HOCKER	HOGGING	HOKING
HITHES	HOATZIN	HOCKERS	HOGGINGS	HOKIS
HITS	HOATZINS	HOCKEY	HOGGINS	HOKKU
HITTER	HOAX	HOCKEYS	HOGGISH	HOKUM
HITTERS	HOAXED	HOCKING	HOGGISHLY	HOKUMS
HITTING	HOAXER	HOCKS	HOGGS	HOLD
HIVE	HOAXERS	HOCUS	HOGH	HOLDBACK
HIVED	HOAXES	HOCUSED	HOGHOOD	HOLDBACKS
HIVELESS	HOAXING	HOCUSES	HOGHOODS	HOLDEN
HIVELIKE	HOB	HOCUSING	HOGHS	HOLDER
HIVER	HOBBIES	HOCUSSED	HOGS	HOLDERBAT
HIVERS	HOBBISH	HOCUSSES	HOGSHEAD	HOLDERBATS
HIVES	HOBBIT	HOCUSSING	HOGSHEADS	HOLDERS
HIVEWARD	HOBBITRIES	HOD	HOGTIE	HOLDFAST
HIVEWARDS	HOBBITRY	HODDED	HOGTIED	HOLDFASTS
HIVING	HOBBITS	HODDEN	HOGTIES	HOLDING
HIYA	HOBBLE	HODDENS	HOGTYING	HOLDINGS
HIZEN	HOBBLED	HODDING	HOGWARD	HOLDOUT
HIZENS	HOBBLER	HODDLE	HOGWARDS	HOLDOUTS
HIZZ	HOBBLERS	HODDLED	HOGWASH	HOLDOVER
HIZZED	HOBBLES	HODDLES	HOGWASHES	HOLDOVERS
HIZZES	HOBBLING	HODDLING	HOGWEED	HOLDS
HIZZING	HOBBLINGS	HODIERNAL	HOGWEEDS	HOLE
HO	HOBBY	HODJA	HOH	HOLED
HOA	HOBBYISM	HODJAS	HOHED	HOLES
HOACTZIN	HOBBYISMS	HODMAN	HOHING	HOLESOM
HOACTZINS	HOBBYIST	HODMANDOD	HOHS	HOLESOME
HOAED	HOBBYISTS	HODMANDODS	HOI	HOLEY
HOAING	HOBBYLESS	HODMEN	HOICK	HOLIBUT
HOAR	HOBDAY	HODOGRAPH	HOICKED	HOLIBUTS
HOARD	HOBDAYED	HODOGRAPHS	HOICKING	HOLIDAY
HOARDED	HOBDAYING	HODOMETER	HOICKS	HOLIDAYED
HOARDER	HOBDAYS	HODOMETERS	HOICKSED	HOLIDAYING
HOARDERS	HOBGOBLIN	HODOMETRIES	HOICKSES	HOLIDAYS
HOARDING	HOBGOBLINS	HODOMETRY	HOICKSING	HOLIER
HOARDINGS	HOBJOB	HODOSCOPE	HOIDEN	HOLIES
HOARDS	HOBJOBBED	HODOSCOPES	HOIDENS	HOLIEST
HOARED	HOBJOBBER	HODS	HOIK	HOLILY
HOARHEAD	HOBJOBBERS	HOE	HOIKED	HOLINESS
HOARHEADS	HOBJOBBING	HOED	HOIKING	HOLINESSES
HOARHOUND	HOBJOBBINGS	HOEDOWN	HOIKS	HOLING
HOARHOUNDS	HOBJOBS	HOEDOWNS	HOING	HOLINGS
HOARIER	HOBNAIL	HOEING	HOISE	HOLISM
HOARIEST	HOBNAILED	HOER	HOISED	HOLISMS
HOARILY	HOBNAILING	HOERS	HOISES	HOLIST
HOARINESS	HOBNAILS	HOES	HOISING	HOLISTIC
HOARINESSES	HOBNOB	HOG	HOIST	HOLISTS
HOARING	HOBNOBBED	HOGAN	HOISTED	HOLLA
HOARS	HOBNOBBING	HOGANS	HOISTER	HOLLAND
HOARSE	HOBNOBBY	HOGBACK	HOISTERS	HOLLANDS
HOARSELY	HOBNOBS	HOGBACKS	HOISTING	HOLLAS
HOARSEN	HOBO	HOGEN	HOISTINGS	HOLLER
HOARSENED	HOBODOM	HOGENS	HOISTMAN	HOLLERED
HOARSENING	HOBODOMS	HOGG	HOISTMEN	HOLLERING
HOARSENS	HOBOED	HOGGED	HOISTS	HOLLERS
HOARSER	HOBOES	HOGGER	HOISTWAY	HOLLIDAM

The Chambers Dictionary is the authority for many longer words; see *OSW* Introduction, page xii

HOLLIDAMS	HOLYSTONES	HOMILETIC	HOMOTONIC	HONKIE
HOLLIES	HOLYSTONING	HOMILETICS	HOMOTONIES	HONKIES
HOLLO	HOMAGE	HOMILIES	HOMOTONY	HONKING
HOLLOA	HOMAGED	HOMILIST	HOMOTYPAL	HONKS
HOLLOAED	HOMAGER	HOMILISTS	HOMOTYPE	HONKY
HOLLOAING	HOMAGERS	HOMILY	HOMOTYPES	HONOR
HOLLOAS	HOMAGES	HOMING	HOMOTYPIC	HONORAND
HOLLOED	HOMAGING	HOMINGS	HOMOTYPIES	HONORANDS
HOLLOES	HOMALOID	HOMINID	HOMOTYPY	HONORARIA
HOLLOING	HOMALOIDS	HOMINIDS	HOMOUSIAN	HONORARIES
HOLLOS	HOMBRE	HOMINIES	HOMOUSIANS	HONORARY
HOLLOW	HOMBRES	HOMINOID	HOMUNCLE	HONORED
HOLLOWARE	HOME	HOMINOIDS	HOMUNCLES	HONORIFIC
HOLLOWARES	HOMEBOUND	HOMINY	HOMUNCULE	HONORIFICS
HOLLOWED	HOMEBOY	HOMME	HOMUNCULES	HONORING
HOLLOWER	HOMEBOYS	HOMMES	HOMUNCULI	HONORS
HOLLOWEST	HOMEBUYER	HOMMOCK	HOMY	HONOUR
HOLLOWING	HOMEBUYERS	HOMMOCKS	HON	HONOURED
HOLLOWLY	HOMECRAFT	HOMO	HONCHO	HONOURER
HOLLOWS	HOMECRAFTS	HOMODONT	HONCHOS	HONOURERS
HOLLY	HOMED	HOMODYNE	HOND	HONOURING
HOLLYHOCK	HOMEFELT	HOMOEOBOX	HONDS	HONOURS
HOLLYHOCKS	HOMELAND	HOMOEOSES	HONE	HONS
HOLM	HOMELANDS	HOMOEOSIS	HONED	HOO
HOLMIA	HOMELESS	HOMOEOTIC	HONER	HOOCH
HOLMIAS	HOMELIER	HOMOGAMIC	HONERS	HOOCHES
HOLMIC	HOMELIEST	HOMOGAMIES	HONES	HOOD
HOLMIUM	HOMELIKE	HOMOGAMY	HONEST	HOODED
HOLMIUMS	HOMELILY	HOMOGENIES	HONESTER	HOODIE
HOLMS	HOMELY	HOMOGENY	HONESTEST	HOODIES
HOLOCAUST	HOMELYN	HOMOGRAFT	HONESTIES	HOODING
HOLOCAUSTS	HOMELYNS	HOMOGRAFTS	HONESTLY	HOODLESS
HOLOCRINE	HOMEMAKER	HOMOGRAPH	HONESTY	HOODLUM
HOLOGRAM	HOMEMAKERS	HOMOGRAPHS	HONEWORT	HOODLUMS
HOLOGRAMS	HOMEOBOX	HOMOLOG	HONEWORTS	HOODMAN
HOLOGRAPH	HOMEOMERIES	HOMOLOGIES	HONEY	HOODMEN
HOLOGRAPHED	HOMEOMERY	HOMOLOGS	HONEYBUN	HOODOO
HOLOGRAPHING	HOMEOPATH	HOMOLOGUE	HONEYBUNS	HOODOOED
HOLOGRAPHS	HOMEOPATHS	HOMOLOGUES	HONEYCOMB	HOODOOING
HOLOHEDRA	HOMEOSES	HOMOLOGY	HONEYCOMBED	HOODOOS
HOLOPHOTE	HOMEOSIS	HOMOMORPH	HONEYCOMBING	HOODS
HOLOPHOTES	HOMEOTIC	HOMOMORPHS	HONEYCOMBINGS	HOODWINK
HOLOPHYTE	HOMEOWNER	HOMONYM	HONEYCOMBS	HOODWINKED
HOLOPHYTES	HOMEOWNERS	HOMONYMIC	HONEYED	HOODWINKING
HOLOPTIC	HOMER	HOMONYMIES	HONEYING	HOODWINKS
HOLOTYPE	HOMERS	HOMONYMS	HONEYLESS	HOOEY
HOLOTYPES	HOMES	HOMONYMY	HONEYMOON	HOOEYS
HOLOTYPIC	HOMESICK	HOMOPHILE	HONEYMOONED	HOOF
HOLOZOIC	HOMESPUN	HOMOPHILES	HONEYMOONING	HOOFBEAT
HOLP	HOMESPUNS	HOMOPHOBE	HONEYMOONS	HOOFBEATS
HOLPEN	HOMESTALL	HOMOPHOBES	HONEYPOT	HOOFED
HOLS	HOMESTALLS	HOMOPHONE	HONEYPOTS	HOOFER
HOLSTER	HOMESTEAD	HOMOPHONES	HONEYS	HOOFERS
HOLSTERED	HOMESTEADS	HOMOPHONIES	HONG	HOOFING
HOLSTERS	HOMEWARD	HOMOPHONY	HONGI	HOOFLESS
HOLT	HOMEWARDS	HOMOPHYLIES	HONGING	HOOFPRINT
HOLTS	HOMEWORK	HOMOPHYLY	HONGIS	HOOFPRINTS
HOLY	HOMEWORKS	HOMOPLASIES	HONGS	HOOFROT
HOLYDAM	HOMEY	HOMOPLASY	HONIED	HOOFROTS
HOLYDAME	HOMICIDAL	HOMOPOLAR	HONING	HOOFS
HOLYDAMES	HOMICIDE	HOMOS	HONK	HOOK
HOLYDAMS	HOMICIDES	HOMOTAXES	HONKED	HOOKA
HOLYSTONE	HOMIER	HOMOTAXIC	HONKER	HOOKAH
HOLYSTONED	HOMIEST	HOMOTAXIS	HONKERS	HOOKAHS

The Chambers Dictionary is the authority for many longer words; see *OSW* Introduction, page xii

HOOKAS	HOOVE	HORIZONS	HOROLOGERS	HORSINESSES
HOOKED	HOOVED	HORKEY	HOROLOGES	HORSING
HOOKER	HOOVEN	HORKEYS	HOROLOGIC	HORSINGS
HOOKERS	HOOVER	HORME	HOROLOGIES	HORSON
HOOKEY	HOOVERED	HORMES	HOROLOGY	HORSONS
HOOKEYS	HOOVERING	HORMONAL	HOROMETRIES	HORST
HOOKIER	HOOVERS	HORMONE	HOROMETRY	HORSTS
HOOKIES	HOOVES	HORMONES	HOROSCOPE	HORSY
HOOKIEST	HOOVING	HORMONIC	HOROSCOPES	HORTATION
HOOKING	HOP	HORN	HOROSCOPIES	HORTATIONS
HOOKS	HOPBIND	HORNBEAK	HOROSCOPY	HORTATIVE
HOOKY	HOPBINDS	HORNBEAKS	HORRENT	HORTATORY
HOOLACHAN	HOPBINE	HORNBEAM	HORRIBLE	HOS
HOOLACHANS	HOPBINES	HORNBEAMS	HORRIBLY	HOSANNA
HOOLEY	HOPDOG	HORNBILL	HORRID	HOSANNAS
HOOLEYS	HOPDOGS	HORNBILLS	HORRIDEST	HOSE
HOOLICAN	HOPE	HORNBOOK	HORRIDLY	HOSED
HOOLICANS	HOPED	HORNBOOKS	HORRIFIC	HOSEMAN
HOOLIER	HOPEFUL	HORNBUG	HORRIFIED	HOSEMEN
HOOLIEST	HOPEFULLY	HORNBUGS	HORRIFIES	HOSEN
HOOLIGAN	HOPEFULS	HORNED	HORRIFY	HOSEPIPE
HOOLIGANS	HOPELESS	HORNER	HORRIFYING	HOSEPIPES
HOOLOCK	HOPER	HORNERS	HORROR	HOSES
HOOLOCKS	HOPERS	HORNET	HORRORS	HOSIER
HOOLY	HOPES	HORNETS	HORS	HOSIERIES
HOON	HOPING	HORNFELS	HORSE	HOSIERS
HOONS	HOPINGLY	HORNFUL	HORSEBACK	HOSIERY
HOOP	HOPLITE	HORNFULS	HORSEBACKS	HOSING
HOOPED	HOPLITES	HORNGELD	HORSECAR	HOSPICE
HOOPER	HOPLOLOGIES	HORNGELDS	HORSECARS	HOSPICES
HOOPERS	HOPLOLOGY	HORNIER	HORSED	HOSPITAGE
HOOPING	HOPPED	HORNIEST	HORSEFLIES	HOSPITAGES
HOOPOE	HOPPER	HORNINESS	HORSEFLY	HOSPITAL
HOOPOES	HOPPERS	HORNINESSES	HORSEHAIR	HOSPITALE
HOOPS	HOPPIER	HORNING	HORSEHAIRS	HOSPITALES
HOORAH	HOPPIEST	HORNINGS	HORSEHIDE	HOSPITALS
HOORAHED	HOPPING	HORNISH	HORSEHIDES	HOSPITIA
HOORAHING	HOPPINGS	HORNIST	HORSELESS	HOSPITIUM
HOORAHS	HOPPLE	HORNISTS	HORSEMAN	HOSPODAR
HOORAY	HOPPLED	HORNITO	HORSEMEAT	HOSPODARS
HOORAYED	HOPPLES	HORNITOS	HORSEMEATS	HOSS
HOORAYING	HOPPLING	HORNLESS	HORSEMEN	HOSSES
HOORAYS	HOPPY	HORNLET	HORSEMINT	HOST
HOORD	HOPS	HORNLETS	HORSEMINTS	HOSTA
HOORDS	HOPSACK	HORNPIPE	HORSEPLAY	HOSTAGE
HOOROO	HOPSACKS	HORNPIPES	HORSEPLAYS	HOSTAGES
HOOSEGOW	HOPSCOTCH	HORNS	HORSEPOND	HOSTAS
HOOSEGOWS	HOPSCOTCHES	HORNSTONE	HORSEPONDS	HOSTED
HOOSGOW	HORAL	HORNSTONES	HORSES	HOSTEL
HOOSGOWS	HORARY	HORNTAIL	HORSESHOE	HOSTELER
HOOSH	HORDE	HORNTAILS	HORSESHOES	HOSTELERS
HOOSHED	HORDED	HORNWORK	HORSETAIL	HOSTELLER
HOOSHES	HORDEIN	HORNWORKS	HORSETAILS	HOSTELLERS
HOOSHING	HORDEINS	HORNWORM	HORSEWAY	HOSTELRIES
HOOT	HORDEOLA	HORNWORMS	HORSEWAYS	HOSTELRY
HOOTCH	HORDEOLUM	HORNWORT	HORSEWHIP	HOSTELS
HOOTCHES	HORDES	HORNWORTS	HORSEWHIPPED	HOSTESS
HOOTED	HORDING	HORNWRACK	HORSEWHIPPING	HOSTESSED
HOOTER	HORDOCK	HORNWRACKS	HORSEWHIPS	HOSTESSES
HOOTERS	HORDOCKS	HORNY	HORSEY	HOSTESSING
HOOTING	HORE	HORNYHEAD	HORSIER	HOSTILE
HOOTNANNIES	HOREHOUND	HORNYHEADS	HORSIEST	HOSTILELY
HOOTNANNY	HOREHOUNDS	HOROLOGE	HORSINESS	HOSTILITIES
HOOTS	HORIZON	HOROLOGER		HOSTILITY

The Chambers Dictionary is the authority for many longer words; see *OSW* Introduction, page xii

HOSTING	HOUGH	HOVE	HOXED	HUFFKINS
HOSTINGS	HOUGHED	HOVED	HOXES	HUFFS
HOSTLER	HOUGHING	HOVEL	HOXING	HUFFY
HOSTLERS	HOUGHS	HOVELED	HOY	HUG
HOSTLESSE	HOUMMOS	HOVELING	HOYA	HUGE
HOSTRIES	HOUMMOSES	HOVELLED	HOYAS	HUGELY
HOSTRY	HOUMUS	HOVELLER	HOYDEN	HUGENESS
HOSTS	HOUMUSES	HOVELLERS	HOYDENISH	HUGENESSES
HOT	HOUND	HOVELLING	HOYDENISM	HUGEOUS
HOTBED	HOUNDED	HOVELS	HOYDENISMS	HUGEOUSLY
HOTBEDS	HOUNDING	HOVEN	HOYDENS	HUGER
HOTCH	HOUNDS	HOVER	HOYED	HUGEST
HOTCHED	HOUR	HOVERED	HOYING	HUGGABLE
HOTCHES	HOURI	HOVERING	HOYS	HUGGED
HOTCHING	HOURIS	HOVERPORT	HUANACO	HUGGING
HOTCHPOT	HOURLONG	HOVERPORTS	HUANACOS	HUGS
HOTCHPOTS	HOURLY	HOVERS	HUAQUERO	HUGY
HOTE	HOURPLATE	HOVES	HUAQUEROS	HUH
HOTEL	HOURPLATES	HOVING	HUB	HUI
HOTELIER	HOURS	HOW	HUBBIES	HUIA
HOTELIERS	HOUSE	HOWBE	HUBBUB	HUIAS
HOTELS	HOUSEBOAT	HOWBEIT	HUBBUBOO	HUIS
HOTEN	HOUSEBOATS	HOWDAH	HUBBUBOOS	HUISSIER
HOTFOOT	HOUSEBOY	HOWDAHS	HUBBUBS	HUISSIERS
HOTHEAD	HOUSEBOYS	HOWDIE	HUBBY	HUITAIN
HOTHEADED	HOUSECOAT	HOWDIES	HUBRIS	HUITAINS
HOTHEADS	HOUSECOATS	HOWDY	HUBRISES	HULA
HOTHOUSE	HOUSED	HOWE	HUBRISTIC	HULAS
HOTHOUSES	HOUSEFLIES	HOWES	HUBS	HULE
HOTLINE	HOUSEFLY	HOWEVER	HUCK	HULES
HOTLINES	HOUSEFUL	HOWF	HUCKABACK	HULK
HOTLY	HOUSEFULS	HOWFED	HUCKABACKS	HULKIER
HOTNESS	HOUSEHOLD	HOWFF	HUCKLE	HULKIEST
HOTNESSES	HOUSEHOLDS	HOWFFED	HUCKLES	HULKING
HOTPOT	HOUSEL	HOWFFING	HUCKS	HULKS
HOTPOTS	HOUSELESS	HOWFFS	HUCKSTER	HULKY
HOTS	HOUSELLED	HOWFING	HUCKSTERED	HULL
HOTSHOT	HOUSELLING	HOWFS	HUCKSTERIES	HULLED
HOTSHOTS	HOUSELLINGS	HOWITZER	HUCKSTERING	HULLIER
HOTTED	HOUSELS	HOWITZERS	HUCKSTERS	HULLIEST
HOTTENTOT	HOUSEMAID	HOWK	HUCKSTERY	HULLING
HOTTENTOTS	HOUSEMAIDS	HOWKED	HUDDEN	HULLO
HOTTER	HOUSEMAN	HOWKER	HUDDLE	HULLOED
HOTTERED	HOUSEMEN	HOWKERS	HUDDLED	HULLOING
HOTTERING	HOUSEROOM	HOWKING	HUDDLES	HULLOS
HOTTERS	HOUSEROOMS	HOWKS	HUDDLING	HULLS
HOTTEST	HOUSES	HOWL	HUDDUP	HULLY
HOTTIE	HOUSETOP	HOWLED	HUE	HUM
HOTTIES	HOUSETOPS	HOWLER	HUED	HUMA
HOTTING	HOUSEWIFE	HOWLERS	HUELESS	HUMAN
HOTTINGS	HOUSEWIVES	HOWLET	HUER	HUMANE
HOTTISH	HOUSEWORK	HOWLETS	HUERS	HUMANELY
HOUDAH	HOUSEWORKS	HOWLING	HUES	HUMANER
HOUDAHS	HOUSEY	HOWLINGS	HUFF	HUMANEST
HOUDAN	HOUSIER	HOWLS	HUFFED	HUMANISE
HOUDANS	HOUSIEST	HOWRE	HUFFIER	HUMANISED
HOUF	HOUSING	HOWRES	HUFFIEST	HUMANISES
HOUFED	HOUSINGS	HOWS	HUFFILY	HUMANISING
HOUFF	HOUSLING	HOWSO	HUFFINESS	HUMANISM
HOUFFED	HOUT	HOWSOEVER	HUFFINESSES	HUMANISMS
HOUFFING	HOUTED	HOWTOWDIE	HUFFING	HUMANIST
HOUFFS	HOUTING	HOWTOWDIES	HUFFISH	HUMANISTS
HOUFING	HOUTINGS	HOWZAT	HUFFISHLY	HUMANITIES
HOUFS	HOUTS	HOX	HUFFKIN	HUMANITY

HUMANIZE	HUMIDER	HUMORS	HUNKIES	HURRIED
HUMANIZED	HUMIDEST	HUMOUR	HUNKIEST	HURRIEDLY
HUMANIZES	HUMIDIFIED	HUMOURED	HUNKS	HURRIES
HUMANIZING	HUMIDIFIES	HUMOURING	HUNKSES	HURRY
HUMANKIND	HUMIDIFY	HUMOURS	HUNKY	HURRYING
HUMANKINDS	HUMIDIFYING	HUMOUS	HUNT	HURRYINGS
HUMANLIKE	HUMIDITIES	HUMP	HUNTED	HURST
HUMANLY	HUMIDITY	HUMPBACK	HUNTER	HURSTS
HUMANNESS	HUMIDLY	HUMPBACKS	HUNTERS	HURT
HUMANNESSES	HUMIDNESS	HUMPED	HUNTING	HURTER
HUMANOID	HUMIDNESSES	HUMPEN	HUNTINGS	HURTERS
HUMANOIDS	HUMIDOR	HUMPENS	HUNTRESS	HURTFUL
HUMANS	HUMIDORS	HUMPER	HUNTRESSES	HURTFULLY
HUMAS	HUMIFIED	HUMPERS	HUNTS	HURTING
HUMBLE	HUMIFIES	HUMPH	HUNTSMAN	HURTLE
HUMBLED	HUMIFY	HUMPHED	HUNTSMEN	HURTLED
HUMBLER	HUMIFYING	HUMPHING	HUP	HURTLES
HUMBLES	HUMILIANT	HUMPHS	HUPPAH	HURTLESS
HUMBLESSE	HUMILIATE	HUMPIER	HUPPAHS	HURTLING
HUMBLESSES	HUMILIATED	HUMPIES	HUPPED	HURTS
HUMBLEST	HUMILIATES	HUMPIEST	HUPPING	HUSBAND
HUMBLING	HUMILIATING	HUMPING	HUPS	HUSBANDED
HUMBLINGS	HUMILITIES	HUMPS	HURCHEON	HUSBANDING
HUMBLY	HUMILITY	HUMPTIES	HURCHEONS	HUSBANDLY
HUMBUG	HUMITE	HUMPTY	HURDEN	HUSBANDRIES
HUMBUGGED	HUMITES	HUMPY	HURDENS	HUSBANDRY
HUMBUGGER	HUMLIE	HUMS	HURDIES	HUSBANDS
HUMBUGGERS	HUMLIES	HUMSTRUM	HURDLE	HUSH
HUMBUGGING	HUMMABLE	HUMSTRUMS	HURDLED	HUSHABIED
HUMBUGS	HUMMAUM	HUMUNGOUS	HURDLER	HUSHABIES
HUMBUZZ	HUMMAUMS	HUMUS	HURDLERS	HUSHABY
HUMBUZZES	HUMMED	HUMUSES	HURDLES	HUSHABYING
HUMDINGER	HUMMEL	HUMUSY	HURDLING	HUSHED
HUMDINGERS	HUMMELLED	HUNCH	HURDLINGS	HUSHER
HUMDRUM	HUMMELLER	HUNCHBACK	HURDS	HUSHERED
HUMDRUMS	HUMMELLERS	HUNCHBACKS	HURL	HUSHERING
HUMECT	HUMMELLING	HUNCHED	HURLBAT	HUSHERS
HUMECTANT	HUMMELS	HUNCHES	HURLBATS	HUSHES
HUMECTANTS	HUMMER	HUNCHING	HURLED	HUSHIER
HUMECTATE	HUMMERS	HUNDRED	HURLER	HUSHIEST
HUMECTATED	HUMMING	HUNDREDER	HURLERS	HUSHING
HUMECTATES	HUMMINGS	HUNDREDERS	HURLEY	HUSHY
HUMECTATING	HUMMOCK	HUNDREDOR	HURLEYS	HUSK
HUMECTED	HUMMOCKED	HUNDREDORS	HURLIES	HUSKED
HUMECTING	HUMMOCKS	HUNDREDS	HURLING	HUSKER
HUMECTIVE	HUMMOCKY	HUNDREDTH	HURLINGS	HUSKERS
HUMECTIVES	HUMMUM	HUNDREDTHS	HURLS	HUSKIER
HUMECTS	HUMMUMS	HUNG	HURLY	HUSKIES
HUMEFIED	HUMMUS	HUNGER	HURRA	HUSKIEST
HUMEFIES	HUMMUSES	HUNGERED	HURRAED	HUSKILY
HUMEFY	HUMOGEN	HUNGERFUL	HURRAH	HUSKINESS
HUMEFYING	HUMOGENS	HUNGERING	HURRAHED	HUSKINESSES
HUMERAL	HUMONGOUS	HUNGERLY	HURRAHING	HUSKING
HUMERALS	HUMOR	HUNGERS	HURRAHS	HUSKINGS
HUMERI	HUMORAL	HUNGRIER	HURRAING	HUSKS
HUMERUS	HUMORALLY	HUNGRIEST	HURRAS	HUSKY
HUMF	HUMORED	HUNGRILY	HURRAY	HUSO
HUMFED	HUMORESK	HUNGRY	HURRAYED	HUSOS
HUMFING	HUMORESKS	HUNK	HURRAYING	HUSS
HUMFS	HUMORING	HUNKER	HURRAYS	HUSSAR
HUMHUM	HUMORIST	HUNKERED	HURRICANE	HUSSARS
HUMHUMS	HUMORISTS	HUNKERING	HURRICANES	HUSSES
HUMIC	HUMORLESS	HUNKERS	HURRICANO	HUSSIES
HUMID	HUMOROUS	HUNKIER	HURRICANOES	HUSSIF

The Chambers Dictionary is the authority for many longer words; see *OSW* Introduction, page xii

HUSSIFS	HYBRIDISMS	HYDROLYTES	HYING	HYPALGIAS
HUSSY	HYBRIDITIES	HYDROLYZE	HYKE	HYPALLAGE
HUSTINGS	HYBRIDITY	HYDROLYZED	HYKES	HYPALLAGES
HUSTLE	HYBRIDIZE	HYDROLYZES	HYLDING	HYPANTHIA
HUSTLED	HYBRIDIZED	HYDROLYZING	HYLDINGS	HYPATE
HUSTLER	HYBRIDIZES	HYDROMEL	HYLE	HYPATES
HUSTLERS	HYBRIDIZING	HYDROMELS	HYLEG	HYPE
HUSTLES	HYBRIDOMA	HYDRONAUT	HYLEGS	HYPED
HUSTLING	HYBRIDOMAS	HYDRONAUTS	HYLES	HYPER
HUSTLINGS	HYBRIDOUS	HYDROPIC	HYLIC	HYPERBOLA
HUSWIFE	HYBRIDS	HYDROPSIES	HYLICISM	HYPERBOLAS
HUSWIVES	HYBRIS	HYDROPSY	HYLICISMS	HYPERBOLE
HUT	HYBRISES	HYDROPTIC	HYLICIST	HYPERBOLES
HUTCH	HYDATHODE	HYDROPULT	HYLICISTS	HYPERCUBE
HUTCHED	HYDATHODES	HYDROPULTS	HYLISM	HYPERCUBES
HUTCHES	HYDATID	HYDROS	HYLISMS	HYPEREMIA
HUTCHING	HYDATIDS	HYDROSKI	HYLIST	HYPEREMIAS
HUTIA	HYDATOID	HYDROSKIS	HYLISTS	HYPEREMIC
HUTIAS	HYDRA	HYDROSOMA	HYLOBATE	HYPERGAMIES
HUTMENT	HYDRAEMIA	HYDROSOMATA	HYLOBATES	HYPERGAMY
HUTMENTS	HYDRAEMIAS	HYDROSOME	HYLOIST	HYPERLINK
HUTS	HYDRANGEA	HYDROSOMES	HYLOISTS	HYPERLINKS
HUTTED	HYDRANGEAS	HYDROSTAT	HYLOPHYTE	HYPERMART
HUTTING	HYDRANT	HYDROSTATS	HYLOPHYTES	HYPERMARTS
HUTTINGS	HYDRANTH	HYDROUS	HYLOZOISM	HYPERNYM
HUTZPAH	HYDRANTHS	HYDROVANE	HYLOZOISMS	HYPERNYMIES
HUTZPAHS	HYDRANTS	HYDROVANES	HYLOZOIST	HYPERNYMS
HUZOOR	HYDRAS	HYDROXIDE	HYLOZOISTS	HYPERNYMY
HUZOORS	HYDRATE	HYDROXIDES	HYMEN	HYPERON
HUZZA	HYDRATED	HYDROXY	HYMENAEAL	HYPERONS
HUZZAED	HYDRATES	HYDROXYL	HYMENAEAN	HYPEROPIA
HUZZAING	HYDRATING	HYDROXYLS	HYMENAL	HYPEROPIAS
HUZZAS	HYDRATION	HYDROZOA	HYMENEAL	HYPERS
HUZZIES	HYDRATIONS	HYDROZOAN	HYMENEALS	HYPERTEXT
HUZZY	HYDRAULIC	HYDROZOANS	HYMENEAN	HYPERTEXTS
HWYL	HYDRAULICKED	HYDROZOON	HYMENIA	HYPES
HWYLS	HYDRAULICKING	HYDYNE	HYMENIAL	HYPHA
HYACINE	HYDRAULICS	HYDYNES	HYMENIUM	HYPHAE
HYACINES	HYDRAZINE	HYE	HYMENIUMS	HYPHAL
HYACINTH	HYDRAZINES	HYED	HYMENS	HYPHEN
HYACINTHS	HYDREMIA	HYEING	HYMN	HYPHENATE
HYAENA	HYDREMIAS	HYEN	HYMNAL	HYPHENATED
HYAENAS	HYDRIA	HYENA	HYMNALS	HYPHENATES
HYALINE	HYDRIAE	HYENAS	HYMNARIES	HYPHENATING
HYALINES	HYDRIC	HYENS	HYMNARY	HYPHENED
HYALINISE	HYDRIDE	HYES	HYMNED	HYPHENIC
HYALINISED	HYDRIDES	HYETAL	HYMNIC	HYPHENING
HYALINISES	HYDRIODIC	HYETOLOGIES	HYMNING	HYPHENISE
HYALINISING	HYDRO	HYETOLOGY	HYMNIST	HYPHENISED
HYALINIZE	HYDROCELE	HYGIENE	HYMNISTS	HYPHENISES
HYALINIZED	HYDROCELES	HYGIENES	HYMNODIES	HYPHENISING
HYALINIZES	HYDROFOIL	HYGIENIC	HYMNODIST	HYPHENISM
HYALINIZING	HYDROFOILS	HYGIENICS	HYMNODISTS	HYPHENISMS
HYALITE	HYDROGEN	HYGIENIST	HYMNODY	HYPHENIZE
HYALITES	HYDROGENS	HYGIENISTS	HYMNOLOGIES	HYPHENIZED
HYALOID	HYDROID	HYGRISTOR	HYMNOLOGY	HYPHENIZES
HYALONEMA	HYDROIDS	HYGRISTORS	HYMNS	HYPHENIZING
HYALONEMAS	HYDROLOGIES	HYGRODEIK	HYNDE	HYPHENS
HYBRID	HYDROLOGY	HYGRODEIKS	HYNDES	HYPING
HYBRIDISE	HYDROLYSE	HYGROLOGIES	HYOID	HYPINOSES
HYBRIDISED	HYDROLYSED	HYGROLOGY	HYOSCINE	HYPINOSIS
HYBRIDISES	HYDROLYSES	HYGROPHIL	HYOSCINES	HYPNIC
HYBRIDISING	HYDROLYSING	HYGROSTAT	HYP	HYPNICS
HYBRIDISM	HYDROLYTE	HYGROSTATS	HYPALGIA	HYPNOGENIES

The Chambers Dictionary is the authority for many longer words; see *OSW* Introduction, page xii

HYPNOGENY
HYPNOID
HYPNOIDAL
HYPNOLOGIES
HYPNOLOGY
HYPNONE
HYPNONES
HYPNOSES
HYPNOSIS
HYPNOTEE
HYPNOTEES
HYPNOTIC
HYPNOTICS
HYPNOTISE
HYPNOTISED
HYPNOTISES
HYPNOTISING
HYPNOTISM
HYPNOTISMS
HYPNOTIST
HYPNOTISTS

HYPNOTIZE
HYPNOTIZED
HYPNOTIZES
HYPNOTIZING
HYPNOTOID
HYPNUM
HYPNUMS
HYPO
HYPOBLAST
HYPOBLASTS
HYPOBOLE
HYPOBOLES
HYPOCAUST
HYPOCAUSTS
HYPOCIST
HYPOCISTS
HYPOCOTYL
HYPOCOTYLS
HYPOCRISIES
HYPOCRISY
HYPOCRITE

HYPOCRITES
HYPODERM
HYPODERMA
HYPODERMAS
HYPODERMS
HYPOGAEA
HYPOGAEAL
HYPOGAEAN
HYPOGAEUM
HYPOGEA
HYPOGEAL
HYPOGEAN
HYPOGENE
HYPOGEOUS
HYPOGEUM
HYPOGYNIES
HYPOGYNY
HYPOID
HYPOMANIA
HYPOMANIAS
HYPOMANIC

HYPONASTIES
HYPONASTY
HYPONYM
HYPONYMIES
HYPONYMS
HYPONYMY
HYPOS
HYPOSTYLE
HYPOSTYLES
HYPOTAXES
HYPOTAXIS
HYPOTHEC
HYPOTHECS
HYPOTONIA
HYPOTONIAS
HYPOTONIC
HYPOXEMIA
HYPOXEMIAS
HYPOXEMIC
HYPOXIA
HYPOXIAS

HYPOXIC
HYPPED
HYPPING
HYPS
HYPURAL
HYRACES
HYRACOID
HYRAX
HYRAXES
HYSON
HYSONS
HYSSOP
HYSSOPS
HYSTERIA
HYSTERIAS
HYSTERIC
HYSTERICS
HYSTEROID
HYTHE
HYTHES

I

IAMB	ICHNITES	ICTERINE	IDENTIFYING	IDLES
IAMBI	ICHNOLITE	ICTERUS	IDENTIKIT	IDLESSE
IAMBIC	ICHNOLITES	ICTERUSES	IDENTIKITS	IDLESSES
IAMBICS	ICHNOLOGIES	ICTIC	IDENTITIES	IDLEST
IAMBIST	ICHNOLOGY	ICTUS	IDENTITY	IDLING
IAMBISTS	ICHOR	ICTUSES	IDEOGRAM	IDLY
IAMBS	ICHOROUS	ICY	IDEOGRAMS	IDOCRASE
IAMBUS	ICHORS	ID	IDEOGRAPH	IDOCRASES
IAMBUSES	ICHTHIC	IDANT	IDEOGRAPHS	IDOL
IANTHINE	ICHTHYIC	IDANTS	IDEOLOGIC	IDOLA
IATROGENIES	ICHTHYOID	IDE	IDEOLOGIES	IDOLATER
IATROGENY	ICHTHYOIDS	IDEA	IDEOLOGUE	IDOLATERS
IBERIS	ICHTHYS	IDEAED	IDEOLOGUES	IDOLATOR
IBERISES	ICHTHYSES	IDEAL	IDEOLOGY	IDOLATORS
IBEX	ICICLE	IDEALESS	IDEOMOTOR	IDOLATRIES
IBEXES	ICICLES	IDEALISE	IDEOPHONE	IDOLATRY
IBICES	ICIER	IDEALISED	IDEOPHONES	IDOLISE
IBIDEM	ICIEST	IDEALISER	IDES	IDOLISED
IBIS	ICILY	IDEALISERS	IDIOBLAST	IDOLISER
IBISES	ICINESS	IDEALISES	IDIOBLASTS	IDOLISERS
IBUPROFEN	ICINESSES	IDEALISING	IDIOCIES	IDOLISES
IBUPROFENS	ICING	IDEALISM	IDIOCY	IDOLISING
ICE	ICINGS	IDEALISMS	IDIOGRAPH	IDOLISM
ICEBALL	ICKER	IDEALIST	IDIOGRAPHS	IDOLISMS
ICEBALLS	ICKERS	IDEALISTS	IDIOLECT	IDOLIST
ICEBERG	ICKIER	IDEALITIES	IDIOLECTS	IDOLISTS
ICEBERGS	ICKIEST	IDEALITY	IDIOM	IDOLIZE
ICEBLINK	ICKY	IDEALIZE	IDIOMATIC	IDOLIZED
ICEBLINKS	ICON	IDEALIZED	IDIOMS	IDOLIZER
ICEBOAT	ICONIC	IDEALIZER	IDIOPATHIES	IDOLIZERS
ICEBOATS	ICONIFIED	IDEALIZERS	IDIOPATHY	IDOLIZES
ICEBOUND	ICONIFIES	IDEALIZES	IDIOPHONE	IDOLIZING
ICEBOX	ICONIFY	IDEALIZING	IDIOPHONES	IDOLS
ICEBOXES	ICONIFYING	IDEALLESS	IDIOPLASM	IDOLUM
ICECAP	ICONISE	IDEALLY	IDIOPLASMS	IDS
ICECAPS	ICONISED	IDEALOGUE	IDIOT	IDYL
ICED	ICONISES	IDEALOGUES	IDIOTCIES	IDYLL
ICEFIELD	ICONISING	IDEALS	IDIOTCY	IDYLLIAN
ICEFIELDS	ICONIZE	IDEAS	IDIOTIC	IDYLLIC
ICEPACK	ICONIZED	IDEATE	IDIOTICAL	IDYLLIST
ICEPACKS	ICONIZES	IDEATED	IDIOTICON	IDYLLISTS
ICER	ICONIZING	IDEATES	IDIOTICONS	IDYLLS
ICERS	ICONOLOGIES	IDEATING	IDIOTISH	IDYLS
ICES	ICONOLOGY	IDEATION	IDIOTISM	IF
ICESTONE	ICONOSTAS	IDEATIONS	IDIOTISMS	IFF
ICESTONES	ICONOSTASES	IDEATIVE	IDIOTS	IFFIER
ICH	ICONS	IDEE	IDLE	IFFIEST
ICHABOD	ICTAL	IDEES	IDLED	IFFINESS
ICHED	ICTERIC	IDEM	IDLEHOOD	IFFINESSES
ICHES	ICTERICAL	IDENTIC	IDLEHOODS	IFFY
ICHING	ICTERICALS	IDENTICAL	IDLENESS	IFS
ICHNEUMON	ICTERICS	IDENTIFIED	IDLENESSES	IGAD
ICHNEUMONS	ICTERID	IDENTIFIES	IDLER	IGAPO
ICHNITE	ICTERIDS	IDENTIFY	IDLERS	IGAPOS

The Chambers Dictionary is the authority for many longer words; see *OSW* Introduction, page xii

IGARAPE	ILEOSTOMY	ILLUMINES	IMBASE	IMBROWNING
IGARAPES	ILEUM	ILLUMING	IMBASED	IMBROWNS
IGLOO	ILEUS	ILLUMINING	IMBASES	IMBRUE
IGLOOS	ILEUSES	ILLUPI	IMBASING	IMBRUED
IGNARO	ILEX	ILLUPIS	IMBATHE	IMBRUES
IGNAROES	ILEXES	ILLUSION	IMBATHED	IMBRUING
IGNAROS	ILIA	ILLUSIONS	IMBATHES	IMBRUTE
IGNEOUS	ILIAC	ILLUSIVE	IMBATHING	IMBRUTED
IGNESCENT	ILIACUS	ILLUSORY	IMBECILE	IMBRUTES
IGNESCENTS	ILIACUSES	ILLUVIA	IMBECILES	IMBRUTING
IGNITABLE	ILICES	ILLUVIAL	IMBECILIC	IMBUE
IGNITE	ILIUM	ILLUVIUM	IMBED	IMBUED
IGNITED	ILK	ILLUVIUMS	IMBEDDED	IMBUES
IGNITER	ILKA	ILLY	IMBEDDING	IMBUING
IGNITERS	ILKADAY	ILMENITE	IMBEDS	IMBURSE
IGNITES	ILKADAYS	ILMENITES	IMBIBE	IMBURSED
IGNITIBLE	ILKS	IMAGE	IMBIBED	IMBURSES
IGNITING	ILL	IMAGEABLE	IMBIBER	IMBURSING
IGNITION	ILLAPSE	IMAGED	IMBIBERS	IMIDAZOLE
IGNITIONS	ILLAPSED	IMAGELESS	IMBIBES	IMIDAZOLES
IGNITRON	ILLAPSES	IMAGERIES	IMBIBING	IMIDE
IGNITRONS	ILLAPSING	IMAGERY	IMBITTER	IMIDES
IGNOBLE	ILLATION	IMAGES	IMBITTERED	IMIDIC
IGNOBLER	ILLATIONS	IMAGINAL	IMBITTERING	IMINE
IGNOBLEST	ILLATIVE	IMAGINARY	IMBITTERS	IMINES
IGNOBLY	ILLATIVES	IMAGINE	IMBODIED	IMITABLE
IGNOMIES	ILLEGAL	IMAGINED	IMBODIES	IMITANCIES
IGNOMINIES	ILLEGALLY	IMAGINER	IMBODY	IMITANCY
IGNOMINY	ILLEGIBLE	IMAGINERS	IMBODYING	IMITANT
IGNOMY	ILLEGIBLY	IMAGINES	IMBORDER	IMITANTS
IGNORABLE	ILLIAD	IMAGING	IMBORDERED	IMITATE
IGNORAMUS	ILLIADS	IMAGINGS	IMBORDERING	IMITATED
IGNORAMUSES	ILLIBERAL	IMAGINING	IMBORDERS	IMITATES
IGNORANCE	ILLICIT	IMAGININGS	IMBOSK	IMITATING
IGNORANCES	ILLICITLY	IMAGINIST	IMBOSKED	IMITATION
IGNORANT	ILLIMITED	IMAGINISTS	IMBOSKING	IMITATIONS
IGNORANTS	ILLINIUM	IMAGISM	IMBOSKS	IMITATIVE
IGNORE	ILLINIUMS	IMAGISMS	IMBOSOM	IMITATOR
IGNORED	ILLIPE	IMAGIST	IMBOSOMED	IMITATORS
IGNORER	ILLIPES	IMAGISTIC	IMBOSOMING	IMMANACLE
IGNORERS	ILLIQUID	IMAGISTS	IMBOSOMS	IMMANACLED
IGNORES	ILLISION	IMAGO	IMBOSS	IMMANACLES
IGNORING	ILLISIONS	IMAGOES	IMBOSSED	IMMANACLING
IGUANA	ILLITE	IMAGOS	IMBOSSES	IMMANE
IGUANAS	ILLITES	IMAM	IMBOSSING	IMMANELY
IGUANID	ILLNESS	IMAMATE	IMBOWER	IMMANENCE
IGUANIDS	ILLNESSES	IMAMATES	IMBOWERED	IMMANENCES
IGUANODON	ILLOGIC	IMAMS	IMBOWERING	IMMANENCIES
IGUANODONS	ILLOGICAL	IMARET	IMBOWERS	IMMANENCY
IHRAM	ILLOGICS	IMARETS	IMBRANGLE	IMMANENT
IHRAMS	ILLS	IMARI	IMBRANGLED	IMMANITIES
IJTIHAD	ILLTH	IMARIS	IMBRANGLES	IMMANITY
IJTIHADS	ILLTHS	IMAUM	IMBRANGLING	IMMANTLE
IKAT	ILLUDE	IMAUMS	IMBRAST	IMMANTLED
IKATS	ILLUDED	IMBALANCE	IMBREX	IMMANTLES
IKEBANA	ILLUDES	IMBALANCES	IMBRICATE	IMMANTLING
IKEBANAS	ILLUDING	IMBAR	IMBRICATED	IMMASK
IKON	ILLUME	IMBARK	IMBRICATES	IMMASKED
IKONS	ILLUMED	IMBARKED	IMBRICATING	IMMASKING
ILEA	ILLUMES	IMBARKING	IMBRICES	IMMASKS
ILEAC	ILLUMINE	IMBARKS	IMBROGLIO	IMMATURE
ILEITIS	ILLUMINED	IMBARRED	IMBROGLIOS	IMMEDIACIES
ILEITISES	ILLUMINER	IMBARRING	IMBROWN	IMMEDIACY
ILEOSTOMIES	ILLUMINERS	IMBARS	IMBROWNED	IMMEDIATE

IMMENSE	IMMORALLY	IMPARITY	IMPELLER	IMPLEAD
IMMENSELY	IMMORTAL	IMPARK	IMPELLERS	IMPLEADED
IMMENSER	IMMORTALS	IMPARKED	IMPELLING	IMPLEADER
IMMENSEST	IMMOVABLE	IMPARKING	IMPELS	IMPLEADERS
IMMENSITIES	IMMOVABLES	IMPARKS	IMPEND	IMPLEADING
IMMENSITY	IMMOVABLY	IMPARL	IMPENDED	IMPLEADS
IMMERGE	IMMUNE	IMPARLED	IMPENDENT	IMPLEDGE
IMMERGED	IMMUNES	IMPARLING	IMPENDING	IMPLEDGED
IMMERGES	IMMUNISE	IMPARLS	IMPENDS	IMPLEDGES
IMMERGING	IMMUNISED	IMPART	IMPENNATE	IMPLEDGING
IMMERSE	IMMUNISES	IMPARTED	IMPERATOR	IMPLEMENT
IMMERSED	IMMUNISING	IMPARTER	IMPERATORS	IMPLEMENTED
IMMERSES	IMMUNITIES	IMPARTERS	IMPERFECT	IMPLEMENTING
IMMERSING	IMMUNITY	IMPARTIAL	IMPERFECTS	IMPLEMENTS
IMMERSION	IMMUNIZE	IMPARTING	IMPERIA	IMPLETE
IMMERSIONS	IMMUNIZED	IMPARTS	IMPERIAL	IMPLETED
IMMESH	IMMUNIZES	IMPASSE	IMPERIALS	IMPLETES
IMMESHED	IMMUNIZING	IMPASSES	IMPERIL	IMPLETING
IMMESHES	IMMUNOGEN	IMPASSION	IMPERILLED	IMPLETION
IMMESHING	IMMUNOGENS	IMPASSIONED	IMPERILLING	IMPLETIONS
IMMEW	IMMURE	IMPASSIONING	IMPERILS	IMPLEX
IMMEWED	IMMURED	IMPASSIONS	IMPERIOUS	IMPLEXES
IMMEWING	IMMURES	IMPASSIVE	IMPERIUM	IMPLEXION
IMMEWS	IMMURING	IMPASTE	IMPETICOS	IMPLEXIONS
IMMIGRANT	IMMUTABLE	IMPASTED	IMPETICOSSED	IMPLICATE
IMMIGRANTS	IMMUTABLY	IMPASTES	IMPETICOSSES	IMPLICATED
IMMIGRATE	IMP	IMPASTING	IMPETICOSSING	IMPLICATES
IMMIGRATED	IMPACABLE	IMPASTO	IMPETIGINES	IMPLICATING
IMMIGRATES	IMPACT	IMPASTOED	IMPETIGO	IMPLICIT
IMMIGRATING	IMPACTED	IMPASTOS	IMPETIGOS	IMPLIED
IMMINENCE	IMPACTING	IMPATIENS	IMPETRATE	IMPLIEDLY
IMMINENCES	IMPACTION	IMPATIENT	IMPETRATED	IMPLIES
IMMINENCIES	IMPACTIONS	IMPAVE	IMPETRATES	IMPLODE
IMMINENCY	IMPACTITE	IMPAVED	IMPETRATING	IMPLODED
IMMINENT	IMPACTITES	IMPAVES	IMPETUOUS	IMPLODENT
IMMINGLE	IMPACTIVE	IMPAVID	IMPETUS	IMPLODENTS
IMMINGLED	IMPACTS	IMPAVIDLY	IMPETUSES	IMPLODES
IMMINGLES	IMPAINT	IMPAVING	IMPI	IMPLODING
IMMINGLING	IMPAINTED	IMPAWN	IMPIES	IMPLORE
IMMINUTE	IMPAINTING	IMPAWNED	IMPIETIES	IMPLORED
IMMISSION	IMPAINTS	IMPAWNING	IMPIETY	IMPLORER
IMMISSIONS	IMPAIR	IMPAWNS	IMPING	IMPLORERS
IMMIT	IMPAIRED	IMPEACH	IMPINGE	IMPLORES
IMMITS	IMPAIRER	IMPEACHED	IMPINGED	IMPLORING
IMMITTED	IMPAIRERS	IMPEACHER	IMPINGENT	IMPLOSION
IMMITTING	IMPAIRING	IMPEACHERS	IMPINGES	IMPLOSIONS
IMMIX	IMPAIRINGS	IMPEACHES	IMPINGING	IMPLOSIVE
IMMIXED	IMPAIRS	IMPEACHING	IMPIOUS	IMPLOSIVES
IMMIXES	IMPALA	IMPEARL	IMPIOUSLY	IMPLUNGE
IMMIXING	IMPALAS	IMPEARLED	IMPIS	IMPLUNGED
IMMIXTURE	IMPALE	IMPEARLING	IMPISH	IMPLUNGES
IMMIXTURES	IMPALED	IMPEARLS	IMPISHLY	IMPLUNGING
IMMOBILE	IMPALES	IMPECCANT	IMPLANT	IMPLUVIA
IMMODEST	IMPALING	IMPED	IMPLANTED	IMPLUVIUM
IMMODESTIES	IMPANATE	IMPEDANCE	IMPLANTING	IMPLY
IMMODESTY	IMPANEL	IMPEDANCES	IMPLANTS	IMPLYING
IMMOLATE	IMPANELLED	IMPEDE	IMPLATE	IMPOCKET
IMMOLATED	IMPANELLING	IMPEDED	IMPLATED	IMPOCKETED
IMMOLATES	IMPANELS	IMPEDES	IMPLATES	IMPOCKETING
IMMOLATING	IMPANNEL	IMPEDING	IMPLATING	IMPOCKETS
IMMOLATOR	IMPANNELLED	IMPEL	IMPLEACH	IMPOLDER
IMMOLATORS	IMPANNELLING	IMPELLED	IMPLEACHED	IMPOLDERED
IMMOMENT	IMPANNELS	IMPELLENT	IMPLEACHES	IMPOLDERING
IMMORAL	IMPARITIES	IMPELLENTS	IMPLEACHING	IMPOLDERS

IMPOLICIES	IMPRESARI	IMPURER	INBREAK	INCEPTING
IMPOLICY	IMPRESAS	IMPUREST	INBREAKS	INCEPTION
IMPOLITE	IMPRESE	IMPURITIES	INBREATHE	INCEPTIONS
IMPOLITER	IMPRESES	IMPURITY	INBREATHED	INCEPTIVE
IMPOLITEST	IMPRESS	IMPURPLE	INBREATHES	INCEPTIVES
IMPOLITIC	IMPRESSE	IMPURPLED	INBREATHING	INCEPTOR
IMPONE	IMPRESSED	IMPURPLES	INBRED	INCEPTORS
IMPONED	IMPRESSES	IMPURPLING	INBREED	INCEPTS
IMPONENT	IMPRESSING	IMPUTABLE	INBREEDING	INCERTAIN
IMPONENTS	IMPREST	IMPUTABLY	INBREEDINGS	INCESSANT
IMPONES	IMPRESTS	IMPUTE	INBREEDS	INCEST
IMPONING	IMPRIMIS	IMPUTED	INBRING	INCESTS
IMPORT	IMPRINT	IMPUTER	INBRINGING	INCH
IMPORTANT	IMPRINTED	IMPUTERS	INBRINGINGS	INCHASE
IMPORTED	IMPRINTING	IMPUTES	INBRINGS	INCHASED
IMPORTER	IMPRINTINGS	IMPUTING	INBROUGHT	INCHASES
IMPORTERS	IMPRINTS	IMSHI	INBURNING	INCHASING
IMPORTING	IMPRISON	IMSHY	INBURST	INCHED
IMPORTS	IMPRISONED	IN	INBURSTS	INCHES
IMPORTUNE	IMPRISONING	INABILITIES	INBY	INCHING
IMPORTUNED	IMPRISONS	INABILITY	INBYE	INCHMEAL
IMPORTUNES	IMPROBITIES	INACTION	INCAGE	INCHOATE
IMPORTUNING	IMPROBITY	INACTIONS	INCAGED	INCHOATED
IMPORTUNINGS	IMPROMPTU	INACTIVE	INCAGES	INCHOATES
IMPOSABLE	IMPROMPTUS	INAIDABLE	INCAGING	INCHOATING
IMPOSE	IMPROPER	INAMORATA	INCAPABLE	INCHPIN
IMPOSED	IMPROV	INAMORATAS	INCAPABLES	INCHPINS
IMPOSER	IMPROVE	INAMORATO	INCAPABLY	INCIDENCE
IMPOSERS	IMPROVED	INAMORATOS	INCARNATE	INCIDENCES
IMPOSES	IMPROVER	INANE	INCARNATED	INCIDENT
IMPOSING	IMPROVERS	INANELY	INCARNATES	INCIDENTS
IMPOST	IMPROVES	INANENESS	INCARNATING	INCIPIENT
IMPOSTER	IMPROVING	INANENESSES	INCASE	INCIPIT
IMPOSTERS	IMPROVISE	INANER	INCASED	INCISE
IMPOSTOR	IMPROVISED	INANEST	INCASES	INCISED
IMPOSTORS	IMPROVISES	INANIMATE	INCASING	INCISES
IMPOSTS	IMPROVISING	INANITIES	INCAUTION	INCISING
IMPOSTUME	IMPROVS	INANITION	INCAUTIONS	INCISION
IMPOSTUMES	IMPRUDENT	INANITIONS	INCAVE	INCISIONS
IMPOSTURE	IMPS	INANITY	INCAVED	INCISIVE
IMPOSTURES	IMPSONITE	INAPT	INCAVES	INCISOR
IMPOT	IMPSONITES	INAPTLY	INCAVI	INCISORS
IMPOTENCE	IMPUDENCE	INAPTNESS	INCAVING	INCISORY
IMPOTENCES	IMPUDENCES	INAPTNESSES	INCAVO	INCISURE
IMPOTENCIES	IMPUDENT	INARABLE	INCEDE	INCISURES
IMPOTENCY	IMPUGN	INARCH	INCEDED	INCITANT
IMPOTENT	IMPUGNED	INARCHED	INCEDES	INCITANTS
IMPOTS	IMPUGNER	INARCHES	INCEDING	INCITE
IMPOUND	IMPUGNERS	INARCHING	INCENSE	INCITED
IMPOUNDED	IMPUGNING	INARM	INCENSED	INCITER
IMPOUNDER	IMPUGNS	INARMED	INCENSER	INCITERS
IMPOUNDERS	IMPULSE	INARMING	INCENSERS	INCITES
IMPOUNDING	IMPULSED	INARMS	INCENSES	INCITING
IMPOUNDS	IMPULSES	INAUDIBLE	INCENSING	INCIVIL
IMPRECATE	IMPULSING	INAUDIBLY	INCENSOR	INCIVISM
IMPRECATED	IMPULSION	INAUGURAL	INCENSORIES	INCIVISMS
IMPRECATES	IMPULSIONS	INAUGURALS	INCENSORS	INCLASP
IMPRECATING	IMPULSIVE	INAURATE	INCENSORY	INCLASPED
IMPRECISE	IMPUNDULU	INBEING	INCENTIVE	INCLASPING
IMPREGN	IMPUNDULUS	INBEINGS	INCENTIVES	INCLASPS
IMPREGNED	IMPUNITIES	INBENT	INCENTRE	INCLE
IMPREGNING	IMPUNITY	INBOARD	INCENTRES	INCLEMENT
IMPREGNS	IMPURE	INBORN	INCEPT	INCLES
IMPRESA	IMPURELY	INBOUND	INCEPTED	INCLINE

The Chambers Dictionary is the authority for many longer words; see *OSW* Introduction, page xii

INCLINED	INCRETION	INDAGATE	INDICATING	INDOLENT
INCLINES	INCRETIONS	INDAGATED	INDICATOR	INDOLES
INCLINING	INCROSS	INDAGATES	INDICATORS	INDOLS
INCLININGS	INCROSSED	INDAGATING	INDICES	INDOOR
INCLIP	INCROSSES	INDAGATOR	INDICIA	INDOORS
INCLIPPED	INCROSSING	INDAGATORS	INDICIAL	INDORSE
INCLIPPING	INCRUST	INDAMINE	INDICIUM	INDORSED
INCLIPS	INCRUSTED	INDAMINES	INDICT	INDORSES
INCLOSE	INCRUSTING	INDART	INDICTED	INDORSING
INCLOSED	INCRUSTS	INDARTED	INDICTEE	INDOXYL
INCLOSER	INCUBATE	INDARTING	INDICTEES	INDOXYLS
INCLOSERS	INCUBATED	INDARTS	INDICTING	INDRAFT
INCLOSES	INCUBATES	INDEBTED	INDICTION	INDRAFTS
INCLOSING	INCUBATING	INDECENCIES	INDICTIONS	INDRAUGHT
INCLOSURE	INCUBATOR	INDECENCY	INDICTS	INDRAUGHTS
INCLOSURES	INCUBATORS	INDECENT	INDIE	INDRAWN
INCLUDE	INCUBI	INDECENTER	INDIES	INDRENCH
INCLUDED	INCUBOUS	INDECENTEST	INDIGENCE	INDRENCHED
INCLUDES	INCUBUS	INDECORUM	INDIGENCES	INDRENCHES
INCLUDING	INCUBUSES	INDECORUMS	INDIGENCIES	INDRENCHING
INCLUSION	INCUDES	INDEED	INDIGENCY	INDRI
INCLUSIONS	INCULCATE	INDELIBLE	INDIGENE	INDRIS
INCLUSIVE	INCULCATED	INDELIBLY	INDIGENES	INDRISES
INCOGNITO	INCULCATES	INDEMNIFIED	INDIGENT	INDUBIOUS
INCOGNITOS	INCULCATING	INDEMNIFIES	INDIGENTS	INDUCE
INCOME	INCULPATE	INDEMNIFY	INDIGEST	INDUCED
INCOMER	INCULPATED	INDEMNIFYING	INDIGESTS	INDUCER
INCOMERS	INCULPATES	INDEMNITIES	INDIGN	INDUCERS
INCOMES	INCULPATING	INDEMNITY	INDIGNANT	INDUCES
INCOMING	INCULT	INDENE	INDIGNIFIED	INDUCIAE
INCOMINGS	INCUMBENT	INDENES	INDIGNIFIES	INDUCIBLE
INCOMMODE	INCUMBENTS	INDENT	INDIGNIFY	INDUCING
INCOMMODED	INCUNABLE	INDENTED	INDIGNIFYING	INDUCT
INCOMMODES	INCUNABLES	INDENTER	INDIGNITIES	INDUCTED
INCOMMODING	INCUR	INDENTERS	INDIGNITY	INDUCTEE
INCONDITE	INCURABLE	INDENTING	INDIGO	INDUCTEES
INCONIE	INCURABLES	INDENTION	INDIGOES	INDUCTILE
INCONNU	INCURABLY	INDENTIONS	INDIGOS	INDUCTING
INCONNUE	INCURIOUS	INDENTS	INDIGOTIN	INDUCTION
INCONNUES	INCURRED	INDENTURE	INDIGOTINS	INDUCTIONS
INCONNUS	INCURRENT	INDENTURED	INDIRECT	INDUCTIVE
INCONY	INCURRING	INDENTURES	INDIRUBIN	INDUCTOR
INCORPSE	INCURS	INDENTURING	INDIRUBINS	INDUCTORS
INCORPSED	INCURSION	INDEW	INDISPOSE	INDUCTS
INCORPSES	INCURSIONS	INDEWED	INDISPOSED	INDUE
INCORPSING	INCURSIVE	INDEWING	INDISPOSES	INDUED
INCORRECT	INCURVATE	INDEWS	INDISPOSING	INDUES
INCORRUPT	INCURVATED	INDEX	INDITE	INDUING
INCREASE	INCURVATES	INDEXAL	INDITED	INDULGE
INCREASED	INCURVATING	INDEXED	INDITER	INDULGED
INCREASER	INCURVE	INDEXER	INDITERS	INDULGENT
INCREASERS	INCURVED	INDEXERS	INDITES	INDULGER
INCREASES	INCURVES	INDEXES	INDITING	INDULGERS
INCREASING	INCURVING	INDEXICAL	INDIUM	INDULGES
INCREASINGS	INCURVITIES	INDEXING	INDIUMS	INDULGING
INCREATE	INCURVITY	INDEXINGS	INDIVIDUA	INDULIN
INCREMATE	INCUS	INDEXLESS	INDOCIBLE	INDULINE
INCREMATED	INCUSE	INDICAN	INDOCILE	INDULINES
INCREMATES	INCUSED	INDICANS	INDOL	INDULINS
INCREMATING	INCUSES	INDICANT	INDOLE	INDULT
INCREMENT	INCUSING	INDICANTS	INDOLENCE	INDULTS
INCREMENTED	INCUT	INDICATE	INDOLENCES	INDUMENTA
INCREMENTING	INDABA	INDICATED	INDOLENCIES	INDUNA
INCREMENTS	INDABAS	INDICATES	INDOLENCY	INDUNAS

The Chambers Dictionary is the authority for many longer words; see *OSW* Introduction, page xii

INDURATE	INERUDITE	INFERABLE	INFLATUSES	INFRACTORS
INDURATED	INESSIVE	INFERE	INFLECT	INFRACTS
INDURATES	INESSIVES	INFERENCE	INFLECTED	INFRARED
INDURATING	INEXACT	INFERENCES	INFLECTING	INFRAREDS
INDUSIA	INEXACTLY	INFERIAE	INFLECTS	INFRINGE
INDUSIAL	INEXPERT	INFERIOR	INFLEXED	INFRINGED
INDUSIATE	INFALL	INFERIORS	INFLEXION	INFRINGES
INDUSIUM	INFALLS	INFERNAL	INFLEXIONS	INFRINGING
INDUSTRIES	INFAME	INFERNO	INFLEXURE	INFULA
INDUSTRY	INFAMED	INFERNOS	INFLEXURES	INFULAE
INDUVIAE	INFAMES	INFERRED	INFLICT	INFURIATE
INDUVIAL	INFAMIES	INFERRING	INFLICTED	INFURIATED
INDUVIATE	INFAMING	INFERS	INFLICTER	INFURIATES
INDWELL	INFAMISE	INFERTILE	INFLICTERS	INFURIATING
INDWELLER	INFAMISED	INFEST	INFLICTING	INFUSCATE
INDWELLERS	INFAMISES	INFESTED	INFLICTOR	INFUSE
INDWELLING	INFAMISING	INFESTING	INFLICTORS	INFUSED
INDWELLINGS	INFAMIZE	INFESTS	INFLICTS	INFUSER
INDWELLS	INFAMIZED	INFICETE	INFLOW	INFUSERS
INDWELT	INFAMIZES	INFIDEL	INFLOWING	INFUSES
INEARTH	INFAMIZING	INFIDELS	INFLOWINGS	INFUSIBLE
INEARTHED	INFAMOUS	INFIELD	INFLOWS	INFUSING
INEARTHING	INFAMY	INFIELDER	INFLUENCE	INFUSION
INEARTHS	INFANCIES	INFIELDERS	INFLUENCED	INFUSIONS
INEBRIANT	INFANCY	INFIELDS	INFLUENCES	INFUSIVE
INEBRIANTS	INFANT	INFILL	INFLUENCING	INFUSORIA
INEBRIATE	INFANTA	INFILLED	INFLUENT	INFUSORY
INEBRIATED	INFANTAS	INFILLING	INFLUENTS	INGAN
INEBRIATES	INFANTE	INFILLINGS	INFLUENZA	INGANS
INEBRIATING	INFANTES	INFILLS	INFLUENZAS	INGATE
INEBRIETIES	INFANTILE	INFIMUM	INFLUX	INGATES
INEBRIETY	INFANTINE	INFIMUMS	INFLUXES	INGATHER
INEBRIOUS	INFANTRIES	INFINITE	INFLUXION	INGATHERED
INEDIBLE	INFANTRY	INFINITES	INFLUXIONS	INGATHERING
INEDITED	INFANTS	INFINITIES	INFO	INGATHERINGS
INEFFABLE	INFARCT	INFINITY	INFOBAHN	INGATHERS
INEFFABLY	INFARCTS	INFIRM	INFOBAHNS	INGENER
INELASTIC	INFARE	INFIRMARIES	INFOLD	INGENERS
INELEGANT	INFARES	INFIRMARY	INFOLDED	INGENIOUS
INEPT	INFATUATE	INFIRMER	INFOLDING	INGENIUM
INEPTER	INFATUATED	INFIRMEST	INFOLDS	INGENIUMS
INEPTEST	INFATUATES	INFIRMITIES	INFOMANIA	INGENU
INEPTLY	INFATUATING	INFIRMITY	INFOMANIAS	INGENUE
INEPTNESS	INFAUNA	INFIRMLY	INFORCE	INGENUES
INEPTNESSES	INFAUNAE	INFIX	INFORCED	INGENUITIES
INEQUABLE	INFAUNAL	INFIXED	INFORCES	INGENUITY
INEQUITIES	INFAUNAS	INFIXES	INFORCING	INGENUOUS
INEQUITY	INFAUST	INFIXING	INFORM	INGENUS
INERM	INFECT	INFLAME	INFORMAL	INGEST
INERMOUS	INFECTED	INFLAMED	INFORMANT	INGESTA
INERRABLE	INFECTING	INFLAMER	INFORMANTS	INGESTED
INERRABLY	INFECTION	INFLAMERS	INFORMED	INGESTING
INERRANCIES	INFECTIONS	INFLAMES	INFORMER	INGESTION
INERRANCY	INFECTIVE	INFLAMING	INFORMERS	INGESTIONS
INERRANT	INFECTOR	INFLATE	INFORMING	INGESTIVE
INERT	INFECTORS	INFLATED	INFORMS	INGESTS
INERTER	INFECTS	INFLATES	INFORTUNE	INGINE
INERTEST	INFECUND	INFLATING	INFORTUNES	INGINES
INERTIA	INFEFT	INFLATION	INFOS	INGLE
INERTIAL	INFEFTED	INFLATIONS	INFRA	INGLENEUK
INERTIAS	INFEFTING	INFLATIVE	INFRACT	INGLENEUKS
INERTLY	INFEFTS	INFLATOR	INFRACTED	INGLENOOK
INERTNESS	INFELT	INFLATORS	INFRACTING	INGLENOOKS
INERTNESSES	INFER	INFLATUS	INFRACTOR	INGLES

The Chambers Dictionary is the authority for many longer words; see OSW Introduction, page xii

INGLOBE
INGLOBED
INGLOBES
INGLOBING
INGLUVIAL
INGLUVIES
INGO
INGOES
INGOING
INGOINGS
INGOT
INGOTS
INGRAFT
INGRAFTED
INGRAFTING
INGRAFTS
INGRAIN
INGRAINED
INGRAINING
INGRAINS
INGRAM
INGRATE
INGRATELY
INGRATES
INGRESS
INGRESSES
INGROOVE
INGROOVED
INGROOVES
INGROOVING
INGROSS
INGROSSED
INGROSSES
INGROSSING
INGROUP
INGROUPS
INGROWING
INGROWN
INGROWTH
INGROWTHS
INGRUM
INGUINAL
INGULF
INGULFED
INGULFING
INGULFS
INGULPH
INGULPHED
INGULPHING
INGULPHS
INHABIT
INHABITED
INHABITER
INHABITERS
INHABITING
INHABITOR
INHABITORS
INHABITS
INHALANT
INHALANTS
INHALATOR
INHALATORS
INHALE
INHALED

INHALER
INHALERS
INHALES
INHALING
INHARMONIES
INHARMONY
INHAUL
INHAULER
INHAULERS
INHAULS
INHAUST
INHAUSTED
INHAUSTING
INHAUSTS
INHEARSE
INHEARSED
INHEARSES
INHEARSING
INHERCE
INHERCED
INHERCES
INHERCING
INHERE
INHERED
INHERENCE
INHERENCES
INHERENCIES
INHERENCY
INHERENT
INHERES
INHERING
INHERIT
INHERITED
INHERITING
INHERITOR
INHERITORS
INHERITS
INHESION
INHESIONS
INHIBIT
INHIBITED
INHIBITER
INHIBITERS
INHIBITING
INHIBITOR
INHIBITORS
INHIBITS
INHOLDER
INHOLDERS
INHOOP
INHOOPED
INHOOPING
INHOOPS
INHUMAN
INHUMANE
INHUMANLY
INHUMATE
INHUMATED
INHUMATES
INHUMATING
INHUME
INHUMED
INHUMER
INHUMERS

INHUMES
INHUMING
INIA
INIMICAL
INION
INIQUITIES
INIQUITY
INISLE
INISLED
INISLES
INISLING
INITIAL
INITIALED
INITIALING
INITIALLED
INITIALLING
INITIALLY
INITIALS
INITIATE
INITIATED
INITIATES
INITIATING
INITIATOR
INITIATORS
INJECT
INJECTED
INJECTING
INJECTION
INJECTIONS
INJECTOR
INJECTORS
INJECTS
INJELLIED
INJELLIES
INJELLY
INJELLYING
INJERA
INJERAS
INJOINT
INJOINTED
INJOINTING
INJOINTS
INJUNCT
INJUNCTED
INJUNCTING
INJUNCTS
INJURE
INJURED
INJURER
INJURERS
INJURES
INJURIES
INJURING
INJURIOUS
INJURY
INJUSTICE
INJUSTICES
INK
INKBERRIES
INKBERRY
INKED
INKER
INKERS
INKHOLDER

INKHOLDERS
INKHORN
INKHORNS
INKIER
INKIEST
INKINESS
INKINESSES
INKING
INKLE
INKLED
INKLES
INKLING
INKLINGS
INKPOT
INKPOTS
INKS
INKSPOT
INKSPOTS
INKSTAND
INKSTANDS
INKSTONE
INKSTONES
INKWELL
INKWELLS
INKY
INLACE
INLACED
INLACES
INLACING
INLAID
INLAND
INLANDER
INLANDERS
INLANDS
INLAY
INLAYER
INLAYERS
INLAYING
INLAYINGS
INLAYS
INLET
INLETS
INLIER
INLIERS
INLOCK
INLOCKED
INLOCKING
INLOCKS
INLY
INLYING
INMATE
INMATES
INMESH
INMESHED
INMESHES
INMESHING
INMOST
INN
INNARDS
INNATE
INNATELY
INNATIVE
INNED
INNER

INNERMOST
INNERS
INNERVATE
INNERVATED
INNERVATES
INNERVATING
INNERVE
INNERVED
INNERVES
INNERVING
INNERWEAR
INNERWEARS
INNING
INNINGS
INNKEEPER
INNKEEPERS
INNOCENCE
INNOCENCES
INNOCENCIES
INNOCENCY
INNOCENT
INNOCENTS
INNOCUITIES
INNOCUITY
INNOCUOUS
INNOVATE
INNOVATED
INNOVATES
INNOVATING
INNOVATOR
INNOVATORS
INNOXIOUS
INNS
INNUENDO
INNUENDOED
INNUENDOES
INNUENDOING
INNUENDOS
INNYARD
INNYARDS
INOCULA
INOCULATE
INOCULATED
INOCULATES
INOCULATING
INOCULUM
INOCULUMS
INODOROUS
INOPINATE
INORB
INORBED
INORBING
INORBS
INORGANIC
INORNATE
INOSITOL
INOSITOLS
INOTROPIC
INPAYMENT
INPAYMENTS
INPHASE
INPOURING
INPOURINGS
INPUT

INPUTS	INSCRIBES	INSIDER	INSPHERED	INSUCKEN
INPUTTER	INSCRIBING	INSIDERS	INSPHERES	INSULA
INPUTTERS	INSCROLL	INSIDES	INSPHERING	INSULAE
INPUTTING	INSCROLLED	INSIDIOUS	INSPIRE	INSULAR
INQILAB	INSCROLLING	INSIGHT	INSPIRED	INSULARLY
INQILABS	INSCROLLS	INSIGHTS	INSPIRER	INSULAS
INQUERE	INSCULP	INSIGNE	INSPIRERS	INSULATE
INQUERED	INSCULPED	INSIGNIA	INSPIRES	INSULATED
INQUERES	INSCULPING	INSIGNIAS	INSPIRING	INSULATES
INQUERING	INSCULPS	INSINCERE	INSPIRIT	INSULATING
INQUEST	INSCULPT	INSINEW	INSPIRITED	INSULATOR
INQUESTS	INSEAM	INSINEWED	INSPIRITING	INSULATORS
INQUIET	INSEAMED	INSINEWING	INSPIRITS	INSULIN
INQUIETED	INSEAMING	INSINEWS	INSTABLE	INSULINS
INQUIETING	INSEAMS	INSINUATE	INSTAL	INSULSE
INQUIETLY	INSECT	INSINUATED	INSTALL	INSULSITIES
INQUIETS	INSECTARIES	INSINUATES	INSTALLED	INSULSITY
INQUILINE	INSECTARY	INSINUATING	INSTALLING	INSULT
INQUILINES	INSECTILE	INSIPID	INSTALLS	INSULTANT
INQUINATE	INSECTION	INSIPIDLY	INSTALS	INSULTED
INQUINATED	INSECTIONS	INSIPIENT	INSTANCE	INSULTER
INQUINATES	INSECTS	INSIST	INSTANCED	INSULTERS
INQUINATING	INSECURE	INSISTED	INSTANCES	INSULTING
INQUIRE	INSEEM	INSISTENT	INSTANCIES	INSULTS
INQUIRED	INSEEMED	INSISTING	INSTANCING	INSURABLE
INQUIRER	INSEEMING	INSISTS	INSTANCY	INSURANCE
INQUIRERS	INSEEMS	INSNARE	INSTANT	INSURANCES
INQUIRES	INSELBERG	INSNARED	INSTANTLY	INSURANT
INQUIRIES	INSELBERGE	INSNARES	INSTANTS	INSURANTS
INQUIRING	INSENSATE	INSNARING	INSTAR	INSURE
INQUIRY	INSERT	INSOLATE	INSTARRED	INSURED
INQUORATE	INSERTED	INSOLATED	INSTARRING	INSUREDS
INRO	INSERTER	INSOLATES	INSTARS	INSURER
INROAD	INSERTERS	INSOLATING	INSTATE	INSURERS
INROADS	INSERTING	INSOLE	INSTATED	INSURES
INRUSH	INSERTION	INSOLENCE	INSTATES	INSURGENT
INRUSHES	INSERTIONS	INSOLENCES	INSTATING	INSURGENTS
INRUSHING	INSERTS	INSOLENT	INSTEAD	INSURING
INRUSHINGS	INSET	INSOLES	INSTEP	INSWATHE
INS	INSETS	INSOLUBLE	INSTEPS	INSWATHED
INSANE	INSETTING	INSOLUBLY	INSTIGATE	INSWATHES
INSANELY	INSHALLAH	INSOLVENT	INSTIGATED	INSWATHING
INSANER	INSHEATHE	INSOLVENTS	INSTIGATES	INSWING
INSANEST	INSHEATHED	INSOMNIA	INSTIGATING	INSWINGER
INSANIE	INSHEATHES	INSOMNIAC	INSTIL	INSWINGERS
INSANIES	INSHEATHING	INSOMNIACS	INSTILL	INSWINGS
INSANITIES	INSHELL	INSOMNIAS	INSTILLED	INTACT
INSANITY	INSHELLED	INSOMUCH	INSTILLING	INTAGLIO
INSATIATE	INSHELLING	INSOOTH	INSTILLS	INTAGLIOED
INSATIETIES	INSHELLS	INSOUL	INSTILS	INTAGLIOING
INSATIETY	INSHELTER	INSOULED	INSTINCT	INTAGLIOS
INSCAPE	INSHELTERED	INSOULING	INSTINCTS	INTAKE
INSCAPES	INSHELTERING	INSOULS	INSTITUTE	INTAKES
INSCIENCE	INSHELTERS	INSPAN	INSTITUTED	INTARSIA
INSCIENCES	INSHIP	INSPANNED	INSTITUTES	INTARSIAS
INSCIENT	INSHIPPED	INSPANNING	INSTITUTING	INTEGER
INSCONCE	INSHIPPING	INSPANS	INSTRESS	INTEGERS
INSCONCED	INSHIPS	INSPECT	INSTRESSED	INTEGRAL
INSCONCES	INSHORE	INSPECTED	INSTRESSES	INTEGRALS
INSCONCING	INSHRINE	INSPECTING	INSTRESSING	INTEGRAND
INSCRIBE	INSHRINED	INSPECTOR	INSTRUCT	INTEGRANDS
INSCRIBED	INSHRINES	INSPECTORS	INSTRUCTED	INTEGRANT
INSCRIBER	INSHRINING	INSPECTS	INSTRUCTING	INTEGRATE
INSCRIBERS	INSIDE	INSPHERE	INSTRUCTS	INTEGRATED

The Chambers Dictionary is the authority for many longer words; see *OSW* Introduction, page xii

INTEGRATES	INTERCROPS	INTERJOINED	INTERNING	INTERVIEW
INTEGRATING	INTERCUT	INTERJOINING	INTERNIST	INTERVIEWED
INTEGRITIES	INTERCUTS	INTERJOINS	INTERNISTS	INTERVIEWING
INTEGRITY	INTERCUTTING	INTERKNIT	INTERNODE	INTERVIEWS
INTELLECT	INTERDASH	INTERKNITS	INTERNODES	INTERWAR
INTELLECTS	INTERDASHED	INTERKNITTED	INTERNS	INTERWIND
INTENABLE	INTERDASHES	INTERKNITTING	INTERPAGE	INTERWINDING
INTEND	INTERDASHING	INTERLACE	INTERPAGED	INTERWINDS
INTENDANT	INTERDEAL	INTERLACED	INTERPAGES	INTERWORK
INTENDANTS	INTERDEALING	INTERLACES	INTERPAGING	INTERWORKED
INTENDED	INTERDEALS	INTERLACING	INTERPLAY	INTERWORKING
INTENDEDS	INTERDEALT	INTERLAID	INTERPLAYS	INTERWORKS
INTENDER	INTERDICT	INTERLARD	INTERPLED	INTERWOUND
INTENDERED	INTERDICTED	INTERLARDED	INTERPONE	INTERWOVE
INTENDERING	INTERDICTING	INTERLARDING	INTERPONED	INTERZONE
INTENDERS	INTERDICTS	INTERLARDS	INTERPONES	INTERZONES
INTENDING	INTERDINE	INTERLAY	INTERPONING	INTESTACIES
INTENDS	INTERDINED	INTERLAYING	INTERPOSE	INTESTACY
INTENIBLE	INTERDINES	INTERLAYS	INTERPOSED	INTESTATE
INTENSATE	INTERDINING	INTERLEAF	INTERPOSES	INTESTATES
INTENSATED	INTERESS	INTERLEAVES	INTERPOSING	INTESTINE
INTENSATES	INTERESSE	INTERLINE	INTERPRET	INTESTINES
INTENSATING	INTERESSED	INTERLINED	INTERPRETED	INTHRAL
INTENSE	INTERESSES	INTERLINES	INTERPRETING	INTHRALL
INTENSELY	INTERESSING	INTERLINING	INTERPRETS	INTHRALLED
INTENSER	INTEREST	INTERLININGS	INTERRAIL	INTHRALLING
INTENSEST	INTERESTED	INTERLINK	INTERRAILED	INTHRALLS
INTENSIFIED	INTERESTING	INTERLINKED	INTERRAILING	INTHRALS
INTENSIFIES	INTERESTS	INTERLINKING	INTERRAILS	INTI
INTENSIFY	INTERFACE	INTERLINKS	INTERRED	INTIFADA
INTENSIFYING	INTERFACED	INTERLOCK	INTERREGES	INTIFADAS
INTENSION	INTERFACES	INTERLOCKED	INTERREX	INTIL
INTENSIONS	INTERFACING	INTERLOCKING	INTERRING	INTIMA
INTENSITIES	INTERFACINGS	INTERLOCKS	INTERRUPT	INTIMACIES
INTENSITY	INTERFERE	INTERLOPE	INTERRUPTED	INTIMACY
INTENSIVE	INTERFERED	INTERLOPED	INTERRUPTING	INTIMAE
INTENSIVES	INTERFERES	INTERLOPES	INTERRUPTS	INTIMATE
INTENT	INTERFERING	INTERLOPING	INTERS	INTIMATED
INTENTION	INTERFLOW	INTERLUDE	INTERSECT	INTIMATES
INTENTIONS	INTERFLOWED	INTERLUDED	INTERSECTED	INTIMATING
INTENTIVE	INTERFLOWING	INTERLUDES	INTERSECTING	INTIME
INTENTLY	INTERFLOWS	INTERLUDING	INTERSECTS	INTIMISM
INTENTS	INTERFOLD	INTERMENT	INTERSERT	INTIMISMS
INTER	INTERFOLDED	INTERMENTS	INTERSERTED	INTIMIST
INTERACT	INTERFOLDING	INTERMIT	INTERSERTING	INTIMISTE
INTERACTED	INTERFOLDS	INTERMITS	INTERSERTS	INTIMISTES
INTERACTING	INTERFUSE	INTERMITTED	INTERSEX	INTIMISTS
INTERACTS	INTERFUSED	INTERMITTING	INTERSEXES	INTIMITIES
INTERBANK	INTERFUSES	INTERMIX	INTERTEXT	INTIMITY
INTERBRED	INTERFUSING	INTERMIXED	INTERTEXTS	INTINE
INTERCEDE	INTERGREW	INTERMIXES	INTERTIE	INTINES
INTERCEDED	INTERGROW	INTERMIXING	INTERTIES	INTIRE
INTERCEDES	INTERGROWING	INTERMURE	INTERVAL	INTIS
INTERCEDING	INTERGROWN	INTERMURED	INTERVALE	INTITULE
INTERCEPT	INTERGROWS	INTERMURES	INTERVALES	INTITULED
INTERCEPTED	INTERIM	INTERMURING	INTERVALS	INTITULES
INTERCEPTING	INTERIMS	INTERN	INTERVEIN	INTITULING
INTERCEPTS	INTERIOR	INTERNAL	INTERVEINED	INTO
INTERCITY	INTERIORS	INTERNALS	INTERVEINING	INTOED
INTERCOM	INTERJECT	INTERNE	INTERVEINS	INTOMB
INTERCOMS	INTERJECTED	INTERNED	INTERVENE	INTOMBED
INTERCROP	INTERJECTING	INTERNEE	INTERVENED	INTOMBING
INTERCROPPED	INTERJECTS	INTERNEES	INTERVENES	INTOMBS
INTERCROPPING	INTERJOIN	INTERNES	INTERVENING	INTONACO

INTONACOS	INTROLD	INUNDANT	INVENTOR	INVOLUTING
INTONATE	INTROMIT	INUNDATE	INVENTORIED	INVOLVE
INTONATED	INTROMITS	INUNDATED	INVENTORIES	INVOLVED
INTONATES	INTROMITTED	INUNDATES	INVENTORS	INVOLVES
INTONATING	INTROMITTING	INUNDATING	INVENTORY	INVOLVING
INTONATOR	INTRON	INURBANE	INVENTORYING	INWALL
INTONATORS	INTRONS	INURE	INVENTS	INWALLED
INTONE	INTRORSE	INURED	INVERSE	INWALLING
INTONED	INTROS	INUREMENT	INVERSELY	INWALLS
INTONER	INTROVERT	INUREMENTS	INVERSES	INWARD
INTONERS	INTROVERTED	INURES	INVERSION	INWARDLY
INTONES	INTROVERTING	INURING	INVERSIONS	INWARDS
INTONING	INTROVERTS	INURN	INVERSIVE	INWEAVE
INTONINGS	INTRUDE	INURNED	INVERT	INWEAVES
INTORSION	INTRUDED	INURNING	INVERTASE	INWEAVING
INTORSIONS	INTRUDER	INURNS	INVERTASES	INWICK
INTORTED	INTRUDERS	INUSITATE	INVERTED	INWICKED
INTORTION	INTRUDES	INUST	INVERTER	INWICKING
INTORTIONS	INTRUDING	INUSTION	INVERTERS	INWICKS
INTOWN	INTRUSION	INUSTIONS	INVERTIN	INWIND
INTRA	INTRUSIONS	INUTILITIES	INVERTING	INWINDING
INTRADA	INTRUSIVE	INUTILITY	INVERTINS	INWINDS
INTRADAS	INTRUSIVES	INVADE	INVERTOR	INWIT
INTRADOS	INTRUST	INVADED	INVERTORS	INWITH
INTRADOSES	INTRUSTED	INVADER	INVERTS	INWITS
INTRANET	INTRUSTING	INVADERS	INVEST	INWORK
INTRANETS	INTRUSTS	INVADES	INVESTED	INWORKED
INTRANT	INTUBATE	INVADING	INVESTING	INWORKING
INTRANTS	INTUBATED	INVALID	INVESTOR	INWORKINGS
INTREAT	INTUBATES	INVALIDED	INVESTORS	INWORKS
INTREATED	INTUBATING	INVALIDING	INVESTS	INWORN
INTREATING	INTUIT	INVALIDINGS	INVEXED	INWOUND
INTREATS	INTUITED	INVALIDLY	INVIABLE	INWOVE
INTRENCH	INTUITING	INVALIDS	INVIDIOUS	INWOVEN
INTRENCHED	INTUITION	INVARIANT	INVIOLATE	INWRAP
INTRENCHES	INTUITIONS	INVARIANTS	INVIOUS	INWRAPPED
INTRENCHING	INTUITIVE	INVASION	INVISIBLE	INWRAPPING
INTREPID	INTUITS	INVASIONS	INVISIBLES	INWRAPS
INTRICACIES	INTUMESCE	INVASIVE	INVISIBLY	INWREATHE
INTRICACY	INTUMESCED	INVEAGLE	INVITE	INWREATHED
INTRICATE	INTUMESCES	INVEAGLED	INVITED	INWREATHES
INTRIGANT	INTUMESCING	INVEAGLES	INVITEE	INWREATHING
INTRIGANTS	INTUSE	INVEAGLING	INVITEES	INWROUGHT
INTRIGUE	INTUSES	INVECKED	INVITER	INYALA
INTRIGUED	INTWINE	INVECTED	INVITERS	INYALAS
INTRIGUER	INTWINED	INVECTIVE	INVITES	IO
INTRIGUERS	INTWINES	INVECTIVES	INVITING	IODATE
INTRIGUES	INTWINING	INVEIGH	INVITINGS	IODATES
INTRIGUING	INTWIST	INVEIGHED	INVOICE	IODIC
INTRINCE	INTWISTED	INVEIGHING	INVOICED	IODIDE
INTRINSIC	INTWISTING	INVEIGHS	INVOICES	IODIDES
INTRO	INTWISTS	INVEIGLE	INVOICING	IODINE
INTRODUCE	INULA	INVEIGLED	INVOKE	IODINES
INTRODUCED	INULAS	INVEIGLER	INVOKED	IODISE
INTRODUCES	INULASE	INVEIGLERS	INVOKES	IODISED
INTRODUCING	INULASES	INVEIGLES	INVOKING	IODISES
INTROIT	INULIN	INVEIGLING	INVOLUCEL	IODISING
INTROITS	INULINS	INVENIT	INVOLUCELS	IODISM
INTROITUS	INUMBRATE	INVENT	INVOLUCRA	IODISMS
INTROITUSES	INUMBRATED	INVENTED	INVOLUCRE	IODIZE
INTROJECT	INUMBRATES	INVENTING	INVOLUCRES	IODIZED
INTROJECTED	INUMBRATING	INVENTION	INVOLUTE	IODIZES
INTROJECTING	INUNCTION	INVENTIONS	INVOLUTED	IODIZING
INTROJECTS	INUNCTIONS	INVENTIVE	INVOLUTES	IODOFORM

IODOFORMS	IRENOLOGIES	IRONIST	ISAGOGES	ISOCHIMAL
IODOPHILE	IRENOLOGY	IRONISTS	ISAGOGIC	ISOCHIMALS
IODOUS	IRES	IRONIZE	ISAGOGICS	ISOCHIME
IODURET	IRID	IRONIZED	ISALLOBAR	ISOCHIMES
IODURETS	IRIDAL	IRONIZES	ISALLOBARS	ISOCHOR
IODYRITE	IRIDEAL	IRONIZING	ISATIN	ISOCHORE
IODYRITES	IRIDES	IRONS	ISATINE	ISOCHORES
IOLITE	IRIDIAL	IRONSMITH	ISATINES	ISOCHORIC
IOLITES	IRIDIAN	IRONSMITHS	ISATINS	ISOCHORS
ION	IRIDIC	IRONSTONE	ISCHAEMIA	ISOCHRONE
IONIC	IRIDISE	IRONSTONES	ISCHAEMIAS	ISOCHRONES
IONISE	IRIDISED	IRONWARE	ISCHAEMIC	ISOCLINAL
IONISED	IRIDISES	IRONWARES	ISCHEMIA	ISOCLINALS
IONISER	IRIDISING	IRONWOOD	ISCHEMIAS	ISOCLINE
IONISERS	IRIDIUM	IRONWOODS	ISCHEMIC	ISOCLINES
IONISES	IRIDIUMS	IRONWORK	ISCHIA	ISOCLINIC
IONISING	IRIDIZE	IRONWORKS	ISCHIADIC	ISOCLINICS
IONIUM	IRIDIZED	IRONY	ISCHIAL	ISOCRACIES
IONIUMS	IRIDIZES	IRRADIANT	ISCHIATIC	ISOCRACY
IONIZE	IRIDIZING	IRRADIATE	ISCHIUM	ISOCRATIC
IONIZED	IRIDOLOGIES	IRRADIATED	ISCHURIA	ISOCRYMAL
IONIZER	IRIDOLOGY	IRRADIATES	ISCHURIAS	ISOCRYMALS
IONIZERS	IRIDOTOMIES	IRRADIATING	ISENERGIC	ISOCRYME
IONIZES	IRIDOTOMY	IRREALITIES	ISH	ISOCRYMES
IONIZING	IRIDS	IRREALITY	ISHES	ISOCYCLIC
IONOMER	IRIS	IRREGULAR	ISINGLASS	ISODICA
IONOMERS	IRISATE	IRREGULARS	ISINGLASSES	ISODICON
IONONE	IRISATED	IRRELATED	ISLAND	ISODOMA
IONONES	IRISATES	IRRIGABLE	ISLANDED	ISODOMON
IONOPAUSE	IRISATING	IRRIGATE	ISLANDER	ISODOMONS
IONOPAUSES	IRISATION	IRRIGATED	ISLANDERS	ISODOMOUS
IONOPHORE	IRISATIONS	IRRIGATES	ISLANDING	ISODOMUM
IONOPHORES	IRISCOPE	IRRIGATING	ISLANDS	ISODONT
IONS	IRISCOPES	IRRIGATOR	ISLE	ISODONTAL
IOS	IRISED	IRRIGATORS	ISLED	ISODONTALS
IOTA	IRISES	IRRIGUOUS	ISLEMAN	ISODONTS
IOTAS	IRITIC	IRRISION	ISLEMEN	ISOETES
IPECAC	IRITIS	IRRISIONS	ISLES	ISOGAMETE
IPECACS	IRITISES	IRRISORY	ISLESMAN	ISOGAMETES
IPOMOEA	IRK	IRRITABLE	ISLESMEN	ISOGAMIC
IPOMOEAS	IRKED	IRRITABLY	ISLET	ISOGAMIES
IPPON	IRKING	IRRITANCIES	ISLETS	ISOGAMOUS
IPPONS	IRKS	IRRITANCY	ISLING	ISOGAMY
IPRINDOLE	IRKSOME	IRRITANT	ISM	ISOGENIES
IPRINDOLES	IRKSOMELY	IRRITANTS	ISMATIC	ISOGENOUS
IRACUND	IROKO	IRRITATE	ISMATICAL	ISOGENY
IRADE	IROKOS	IRRITATED	ISMS	ISOGLOSS
IRADES	IRON	IRRITATES	ISO	ISOGLOSSES
IRASCIBLE	IRONBARK	IRRITATING	ISOBAR	ISOGON
IRASCIBLY	IRONBARKS	IRRITATOR	ISOBARE	ISOGONAL
IRATE	IRONED	IRRITATORS	ISOBARES	ISOGONALS
IRATELY	IRONER	IRRUPT	ISOBARIC	ISOGONIC
IRATER	IRONERS	IRRUPTED	ISOBARS	ISOGONICS
IRATEST	IRONIC	IRRUPTING	ISOBASE	ISOGONS
IRE	IRONICAL	IRRUPTION	ISOBASES	ISOGRAM
IREFUL	IRONIER	IRRUPTIONS	ISOBATH	ISOGRAMS
IREFULLY	IRONIES	IRRUPTIVE	ISOBATHIC	ISOHEL
IRENIC	IRONIEST	IRRUPTS	ISOBATHS	ISOHELS
IRENICAL	IRONING	IS	ISOBRONT	ISOHYET
IRENICISM	IRONINGS	ISABEL	ISOBRONTS	ISOHYETAL
IRENICISMS	IRONISE	ISABELLA	ISOCHASM	ISOHYETALS
IRENICON	IRONISED	ISABELLAS	ISOCHASMS	ISOHYETS
IRENICONS	IRONISES	ISABELS	ISOCHEIM	ISOKONT
IRENICS	IRONISING	ISAGOGE	ISOCHEIMS	ISOKONTAN

ISOKONTANS	ISOMORPHS	ISOTOPES	ITALICIZED	ITINERACY
ISOKONTS	ISONIAZID	ISOTOPIC	ITALICIZES	ITINERANT
ISOLABLE	ISONIAZIDS	ISOTOPIES	ITALICIZING	ITINERANTS
ISOLATE	ISONOMIC	ISOTOPY	ITALICS	ITINERARIES
ISOLATED	ISONOMIES	ISOTRON	ITAS	ITINERARY
ISOLATES	ISONOMOUS	ISOTRONS	ITCH	ITINERATE
ISOLATING	ISONOMY	ISOTROPIC	ITCHED	ITINERATED
ISOLATION	ISOPLETH	ISOTROPIES	ITCHES	ITINERATES
ISOLATIONS	ISOPLETHS	ISOTROPY	ITCHIER	ITINERATING
ISOLATIVE	ISOPOD	ISOTYPE	ITCHIEST	ITS
ISOLATOR	ISOPODAN	ISOTYPES	ITCHINESS	ITSELF
ISOLATORS	ISOPODOUS	ISSEI	ITCHINESSES	IURE
ISOLINE	ISOPODS	ISSEIS	ITCHING	IVIED
ISOLINES	ISOPOLITIES	ISSUABLE	ITCHWEED	IVIES
ISOLOGOUS	ISOPOLITY	ISSUABLY	ITCHWEEDS	IVORIED
ISOLOGUE	ISOPRENE	ISSUANCE	ITCHY	IVORIES
ISOLOGUES	ISOPRENES	ISSUANCES	ITEM	IVORIST
ISOMER	ISOPROPYL	ISSUANT	ITEMED	IVORISTS
ISOMERASE	ISOPROPYLS	ISSUE	ITEMING	IVORY
ISOMERASES	ISOS	ISSUED	ITEMISE	IVRESSE
ISOMERE	ISOSCELES	ISSUELESS	ITEMISED	IVRESSES
ISOMERES	ISOSPIN	ISSUER	ITEMISES	IVY
ISOMERIC	ISOSPINS	ISSUERS	ITEMISING	IWIS
ISOMERISE	ISOSPORIES	ISSUES	ITEMIZE	IXIA
ISOMERISED	ISOSPORY	ISSUING	ITEMIZED	IXIAS
ISOMERISES	ISOSTASIES	ISTHMIAN	ITEMIZES	IXODIASES
ISOMERISING	ISOSTASY	ISTHMUS	ITEMIZING	IXODIASIS
ISOMERISM	ISOSTATIC	ISTHMUSES	ITEMS	IXTLE
ISOMERISMS	ISOSTERIC	ISTLE	ITERANCE	IXTLES
ISOMERIZE	ISOTACTIC	ISTLES	ITERANCES	IZARD
ISOMERIZED	ISOTHERAL	IT	ITERANT	IZARDS
ISOMERIZES	ISOTHERALS	ITA	ITERATE	IZVESTIA
ISOMERIZING	ISOTHERE	ITACISM	ITERATED	IZVESTIAS
ISOMEROUS	ISOTHERES	ITACISMS	ITERATES	IZVESTIYA
ISOMERS	ISOTHERM	ITALIC	ITERATING	IZVESTIYAS
ISOMETRIC	ISOTHERMS	ITALICISE	ITERATION	IZZARD
ISOMETRICS	ISOTONE	ITALICISED	ITERATIONS	IZZARDS
ISOMETRIES	ISOTONES	ITALICISES	ITERATIVE	IZZAT
ISOMETRY	ISOTONIC	ITALICISING	ITERUM	IZZATS
ISOMORPH	ISOTOPE	ITALICIZE	ITINERACIES	

J

JAB
JABBED
JABBER
JABBERED
JABBERER
JABBERERS
JABBERING
JABBERINGS
JABBERS
JABBING
JABBLE
JABBLED
JABBLES
JABBLING
JABERS
JABIRU
JABIRUS
JABORANDI
JABORANDIS
JABOT
JABOTS
JABS
JACAMAR
JACAMARS
JACANA
JACANAS
JACARANDA
JACARANDAS
JACCHUS
JACCHUSES
JACENT
JACINTH
JACINTHS
JACK
JACKAL
JACKALLED
JACKALLING
JACKALS
JACKAROO
JACKAROOED
JACKAROOING
JACKAROOS
JACKASS
JACKASSES
JACKBOOT
JACKBOOTED
JACKBOOTING
JACKBOOTS
JACKDAW
JACKDAWS
JACKED
JACKEEN
JACKEENS
JACKEROO

JACKEROOED
JACKEROOING
JACKEROOS
JACKET
JACKETED
JACKETING
JACKETS
JACKING
JACKKNIFE
JACKKNIFED
JACKKNIFES
JACKKNIFING
JACKKNIVES
JACKMAN
JACKMEN
JACKPOT
JACKPOTS
JACKS
JACKSHAFT
JACKSHAFTS
JACKSIE
JACKSIES
JACKSMITH
JACKSMITHS
JACKSY
JACOBIN
JACOBINS
JACOBUS
JACOBUSES
JACONET
JACONETS
JACQUARD
JACQUARDS
JACTATION
JACTATIONS
JACULATE
JACULATED
JACULATES
JACULATING
JACULATOR
JACULATORS
JACUZZI
JACUZZIS
JADE
JADED
JADEDLY
JADEITE
JADEITES
JADERIES
JADERY
JADES
JADING
JADISH
JAEGER

JAEGERS
JAG
JAGER
JAGERS
JAGGED
JAGGEDER
JAGGEDEST
JAGGEDLY
JAGGER
JAGGERIES
JAGGERY
JAGGIER
JAGGIEST
JAGGING
JAGGY
JAGHIR
JAGHIRDAR
JAGHIRDARS
JAGHIRE
JAGHIRES
JAGHIRS
JAGIR
JAGIRS
JAGS
JAGUAR
JAGUARS
JAIL
JAILED
JAILER
JAILERESS
JAILERESSES
JAILERS
JAILHOUSE
JAILHOUSES
JAILING
JAILOR
JAILORESS
JAILORESSES
JAILORS
JAILS
JAK
JAKE
JAKES
JAKESES
JAKS
JALAP
JALAPENO
JALAPENOS
JALAPIC
JALAPIN
JALAPINS
JALAPS
JALOPIES

JALOPPIES
JALOPPY
JALOPY
JALOUSE
JALOUSED
JALOUSES
JALOUSIE
JALOUSIED
JALOUSIES
JALOUSING
JAM
JAMADAR
JAMADARS
JAMB
JAMBALAYA
JAMBALAYAS
JAMBE
JAMBEAU
JAMBEAUX
JAMBEE
JAMBEES
JAMBER
JAMBERS
JAMBES
JAMBEUX
JAMBIER
JAMBIERS
JAMBIYA
JAMBIYAH
JAMBIYAHS
JAMBIYAS
JAMBO
JAMBOK
JAMBOKKED
JAMBOKKING
JAMBOKS
JAMBOLAN
JAMBOLANA
JAMBOLANAS
JAMBOLANS
JAMBONE
JAMBONES
JAMBOOL
JAMBOOLS
JAMBOREE
JAMBOREES
JAMBOS
JAMBS
JAMBU
JAMBUL
JAMBULS
JAMBUS
JAMDANI
JAMDANIS

JAMES
JAMESES
JAMJAR
JAMJARS
JAMMED
JAMMER
JAMMERS
JAMMIER
JAMMIEST
JAMMING
JAMMY
JAMPAN
JAMPANEE
JAMPANEES
JAMPANI
JAMPANIS
JAMPANS
JAMPOT
JAMPOTS
JAMS
JANDAL®
JANDALS
JANE
JANES
JANGLE
JANGLED
JANGLER
JANGLERS
JANGLES
JANGLIER
JANGLIEST
JANGLING
JANGLINGS
JANGLY
JANISSARIES
JANISSARY
JANITOR
JANITORS
JANITRESS
JANITRESSES
JANITRIX
JANITRIXES
JANIZAR
JANIZARIES
JANIZARS
JANIZARY
JANKER
JANKERS
JANN
JANNOCK
JANNOCKS
JANNS
JANSKY
JANSKYS

JANTEE	JARRINGS	JAUP	JEALOUSY	JELLYBEAN
JANTIER	JARS	JAUPED	JEAN	JELLYBEANS
JANTIES	JARTA	JAUPING	JEANETTE	JELLYFISH
JANTIEST	JARTAS	JAUPS	JEANETTES	JELLYFISHES
JANTY	JARUL	JAVEL	JEANS	JELLYING
JAP	JARULS	JAVELIN	JEAT	JELUTONG
JAPAN	JARVEY	JAVELINS	JEATS	JELUTONGS
JAPANNED	JARVEYS	JAVELS	JEBEL	JEMADAR
JAPANNER	JARVIE	JAW	JEBELS	JEMADARS
JAPANNERS	JARVIES	JAWAN	JEE	JEMIDAR
JAPANNING	JASEY	JAWANS	JEED	JEMIDARS
JAPANS	JASEYS	JAWARI	JEEING	JEMIMA
JAPE	JASIES	JAWARIS	JEEL	JEMIMAS
JAPED	JASMINE	JAWBATION	JEELED	JEMMIED
JAPER	JASMINES	JAWBATIONS	JEELIE	JEMMIER
JAPERS	JASP	JAWBONE	JEELIED	JEMMIES
JAPES	JASPE	JAWBONED	JEELIEING	JEMMIEST
JAPING	JASPER	JAWBONES	JEELIES	JEMMINESS
JAPINGS	JASPERISE	JAWBONING	JEELING	JEMMINESSES
JAPONICA	JASPERISED	JAWBONINGS	JEELS	JEMMY
JAPONICAS	JASPERISES	JAWBOX	JEELY	JEMMYING
JAPPED	JASPERISING	JAWBOXES	JEELYING	JENNET
JAPPING	JASPERIZE	JAWED	JEEPERS	JENNETING
JAPS	JASPERIZED	JAWFALL	JEEPNEY	JENNETINGS
JAR	JASPERIZES	JAWFALLS	JEEPNEYS	JENNETS
JARARACA	JASPERIZING	JAWHOLE	JEER	JENNIES
JARARACAS	JASPEROUS	JAWHOLES	JEERED	JENNY
JARARAKA	JASPERS	JAWING	JEERER	JEOFAIL
JARARAKAS	JASPERY	JAWINGS	JEERERS	JEOFAILS
JARFUL	JASPES	JAWS	JEERING	JEOPARD
JARFULS	JASPIDEAN	JAY	JEERINGLY	JEOPARDED
JARGON	JASPIS	JAYS	JEERINGS	JEOPARDER
JARGONED	JASPISES	JAYWALK	JEERS	JEOPARDERS
JARGONEER	JASPS	JAYWALKED	JEES	JEOPARDIED
JARGONEERS	JASS	JAYWALKER	JEFF	JEOPARDIES
JARGONING	JASSES	JAYWALKERS	JEFFED	JEOPARDING
JARGONISE	JASY	JAYWALKING	JEFFING	JEOPARDS
JARGONISED	JATAKA	JAYWALKINGS	JEFFS	JEOPARDY
JARGONISES	JATAKAS	JAYWALKS	JEHAD	JEOPARDYING
JARGONISING	JATO	JAZERANT	JEHADS	JEQUIRITIES
JARGONIST	JATOS	JAZERANTS	JEJUNA	JEQUIRITY
JARGONISTS	JAUNCE	JAZIES	JEJUNE	JERBIL
JARGONIZE	JAUNCED	JAZY	JEJUNELY	JERBILS
JARGONIZED	JAUNCES	JAZZ	JEJUNITIES	JERBOA
JARGONIZES	JAUNCING	JAZZED	JEJUNITY	JERBOAS
JARGONIZING	JAUNDICE	JAZZER	JEJUNUM	JEREED
JARGONS	JAUNDICED	JAZZERS	JELAB	JEREEDS
JARGOON	JAUNDICES	JAZZES	JELABS	JEREMIAD
JARGOONS	JAUNDICING	JAZZIER	JELL	JEREMIADS
JARK	JAUNSE	JAZZIEST	JELLABA	JERFALCON
JARKMAN	JAUNSED	JAZZILY	JELLABAS	JERFALCONS
JARKMEN	JAUNSES	JAZZINESS	JELLED	JERID
JARKS	JAUNSING	JAZZINESSES	JELLIED	JERIDS
JARL	JAUNT	JAZZING	JELLIES	JERK
JARLS	JAUNTED	JAZZMAN	JELLIFIED	JERKED
JAROOL	JAUNTEE	JAZZMEN	JELLIFIES	JERKER
JAROOLS	JAUNTIE	JAZZY	JELLIFORM	JERKERS
JAROSITE	JAUNTIER	JEALOUS	JELLIFY	JERKIER
JAROSITES	JAUNTIES	JEALOUSE	JELLIFYING	JERKIES
JARRAH	JAUNTIEST	JEALOUSED	JELLING	JERKIEST
JARRAHS	JAUNTILY	JEALOUSES	JELLO	JERKIN
JARRED	JAUNTING	JEALOUSIES	JELLOS	JERKINESS
JARRING	JAUNTS	JEALOUSING	JELLS	JERKINESSES
JARRINGLY	JAUNTY	JEALOUSLY	JELLY	JERKING

JERKINGS	JETSOMS	JIBES	JILT	JIRBLES
JERKINS	JETSON	JIBING	JILTED	JIRBLING
JERKS	JETSONS	JIBS	JILTING	JIRD
JERKWATER	JETSTREAM	JICKAJOG	JILTS	JIRDS
JERKWATERS	JETSTREAMS	JICKAJOGGED	JIMCRACK	JIRGA
JERKY	JETTATURA	JICKAJOGGING	JIMCRACKS	JIRGAS
JEROBOAM	JETTATURAS	JICKAJOGS	JIMINY	JIRKINET
JEROBOAMS	JETTED	JIFF	JIMJAM	JIRKINETS
JERQUE	JETTIED	JIFFIES	JIMJAMS	JISM
JERQUED	JETTIER	JIFFS	JIMMIED	JISMS
JERQUER	JETTIES	JIFFY	JIMMIES	JISSOM
JERQUERS	JETTIEST	JIG	JIMMY	JISSOMS
JERQUES	JETTINESS	JIGAJIG	JIMMYING	JITNEY
JERQUING	JETTINESSES	JIGAJIGGED	JIMP	JITNEYS
JERQUINGS	JETTING	JIGAJIGGING	JIMPER	JITTER
JERRICAN	JETTISON	JIGAJIGS	JIMPEST	JITTERBUG
JERRICANS	JETTISONED	JIGAJOG	JIMPIER	JITTERBUGGED
JERRIES	JETTISONING	JIGAJOGGED	JIMPIEST	JITTERBUGGING
JERRY	JETTISONS	JIGAJOGGING	JIMPLY	JITTERBUGS
JERRYCAN	JETTON	JIGAJOGS	JIMPNESS	JITTERED
JERRYCANS	JETTONS	JIGAMAREE	JIMPNESSES	JITTERIER
JERSEY	JETTY	JIGAMAREES	JIMPY	JITTERIEST
JERSEYS	JETTYING	JIGGED	JINGAL	JITTERING
JESS	JEU	JIGGER	JINGALS	JITTERS
JESSAMIES	JEUNE	JIGGERED	JINGBANG	JITTERY
JESSAMINE	JEUX	JIGGERING	JINGBANGS	JIVE
JESSAMINES	JEW	JIGGERS	JINGLE	JIVED
JESSAMY	JEWED	JIGGING	JINGLED	JIVER
JESSANT	JEWEL	JIGGINGS	JINGLER	JIVERS
JESSED	JEWELFISH	JIGGISH	JINGLERS	JIVES
JESSERANT	JEWELFISHES	JIGGLE	JINGLES	JIVING
JESSERANTS	JEWELLED	JIGGLED	JINGLET	JIZ
JESSES	JEWELLER	JIGGLES	JINGLETS	JIZZ
JESSIE	JEWELLERIES	JIGGLIER	JINGLIER	JIZZES
JESSIES	JEWELLERS	JIGGLIEST	JINGLIEST	JNANA
JEST	JEWELLERY	JIGGLING	JINGLING	JNANAS
JESTBOOK	JEWELLING	JIGGLY	JINGLY	JO
JESTBOOKS	JEWELRIES	JIGGUMBOB	JINGO	JOANNA
JESTED	JEWELRY	JIGGUMBOBS	JINGOES	JOANNAS
JESTEE	JEWELS	JIGJIG	JINGOISH	JOANNES
JESTEES	JEWFISH	JIGJIGGED	JINGOISM	JOANNESES
JESTER	JEWFISHES	JIGJIGGING	JINGOISMS	JOB
JESTERS	JEWING	JIGJIGS	JINGOIST	JOBATION
JESTFUL	JEWS	JIGOT	JINGOISTS	JOBATIONS
JESTING	JEZAIL	JIGOTS	JINJILI	JOBBED
JESTINGLY	JEZAILS	JIGS	JINJILIS	JOBBER
JESTINGS	JHALA	JIGSAW	JINK	JOBBERIES
JESTS	JHALAS	JIGSAWED	JINKED	JOBBERS
JESUS	JIAO	JIGSAWING	JINKER	JOBBERY
JET	JIAOS	JIGSAWS	JINKERS	JOBBIE
JETE	JIB	JIHAD	JINKING	JOBBIES
JETES	JIBBAH	JIHADS	JINKS	JOBBING
JETFOIL	JIBBAHS	JILGIE	JINN	JOBBINGS
JETFOILS	JIBBED	JILGIES	JINNEE	JOBCENTRE
JETLINER	JIBBER	JILL	JINNI	JOBCENTRES
JETLINERS	JIBBERED	JILLAROO	JINNS	JOBE
JETON	JIBBERING	JILLAROOS	JINX	JOBED
JETONS	JIBBERS	JILLET	JINXED	JOBERNOWL
JETPLANE	JIBBING	JILLETS	JINXES	JOBERNOWLS
JETPLANES	JIBBINGS	JILLFLIRT	JINXING	JOBES
JETS	JIBE	JILLFLIRTS	JIPYAPA	JOBING
JETSAM	JIBED	JILLION	JIPYAPAS	JOBLESS
JETSAMS	JIBER	JILLIONS	JIRBLE	JOBS
JETSOM	JIBERS	JILLS	JIRBLED	JOBSHARE

JOBSHARES	JOIN	JOLLIES	JOSH	JOUSTED
JOBSWORTH	JOINDER	JOLLIEST	JOSHED	JOUSTER
JOBSWORTHS	JOINDERS	JOLLIFIED	JOSHER	JOUSTERS
JOCK	JOINED	JOLLIFIES	JOSHERS	JOUSTING
JOCKETTE	JOINER	JOLLIFY	JOSHES	JOUSTS
JOCKETTES	JOINERIES	JOLLIFYING	JOSHING	JOVIAL
JOCKEY	JOINERS	JOLLILY	JOSKIN	JOVIALITIES
JOCKEYED	JOINERY	JOLLIMENT	JOSKINS	JOVIALITY
JOCKEYING	JOINING	JOLLIMENTS	JOSS	JOVIALLY
JOCKEYISM	JOININGS	JOLLINESS	JOSSER	JOW
JOCKEYISMS	JOINS	JOLLINESSES	JOSSERS	JOWAR
JOCKEYS	JOINT	JOLLING	JOSSES	JOWARI
JOCKNEY	JOINTED	JOLLITIES	JOSTLE	JOWARIS
JOCKNEYS	JOINTER	JOLLITY	JOSTLED	JOWARS
JOCKO	JOINTERS	JOLLS	JOSTLES	JOWED
JOCKOS	JOINTING	JOLLY	JOSTLING	JOWING
JOCKS	JOINTLESS	JOLLYBOAT	JOSTLINGS	JOWL
JOCKSTRAP	JOINTLY	JOLLYBOATS	JOT	JOWLED
JOCKSTRAPS	JOINTNESS	JOLLYER	JOTA	JOWLER
JOCKTELEG	JOINTNESSES	JOLLYERS	JOTAS	JOWLERS
JOCKTELEGS	JOINTRESS	JOLLYHEAD	JOTS	JOWLIER
JOCO	JOINTRESSES	JOLLYHEADS	JOTTED	JOWLIEST
JOCOSE	JOINTS	JOLLYING	JOTTER	JOWLING
JOCOSELY	JOINTURE	JOLLYINGS	JOTTERS	JOWLS
JOCOSITIES	JOINTURED	JOLT	JOTTING	JOWLY
JOCOSITY	JOINTURES	JOLTED	JOTTINGS	JOWS
JOCULAR	JOINTURING	JOLTER	JOTUN	JOY
JOCULARLY	JOINTWORM	JOLTERS	JOTUNN	JOYANCE
JOCULATOR	JOINTWORMS	JOLTHEAD	JOTUNNS	JOYANCES
JOCULATORS	JOIST	JOLTHEADS	JOTUNS	JOYED
JOCUND	JOISTED	JOLTIER	JOUAL	JOYFUL
JOCUNDITIES	JOISTING	JOLTIEST	JOUALS	JOYFULLER
JOCUNDITY	JOISTS	JOLTING	JOUGS	JOYFULLEST
JOCUNDLY	JOJOBA	JOLTINGLY	JOUISANCE	JOYFULLY
JODEL	JOJOBAS	JOLTS	JOUISANCES	JOYING
JODELLED	JOKE	JOLTY	JOUK	JOYLESS
JODELLING	JOKED	JOMO	JOUKED	JOYLESSLY
JODELS	JOKER	JOMOS	JOUKERIES	JOYOUS
JODHPURS	JOKERS	JONCANOE	JOUKERY	JOYOUSLY
JOE	JOKES	JONCANOES	JOUKING	JOYS
JOES	JOKESMITH	JONGLEUR	JOUKS	JUBA
JOEY	JOKESMITHS	JONGLEURS	JOULE	JUBAS
JOEYS	JOKESOME	JONQUIL	JOULED	JUBATE
JOG	JOKEY	JONQUILS	JOULES	JUBBAH
JOGGED	JOKIER	JONTIES	JOULING	JUBBAHS
JOGGER	JOKIEST	JONTY	JOUNCE	JUBE
JOGGERS	JOKING	JOOK	JOUNCED	JUBES
JOGGING	JOKINGLY	JOOKED	JOUNCES	JUBILANCE
JOGGINGS	JOKOL	JOOKERIES	JOUNCING	JUBILANCES
JOGGLE	JOKY	JOOKERY	JOUR	JUBILANCIES
JOGGLED	JOLE	JOOKING	JOURNAL	JUBILANCY
JOGGLES	JOLED	JOOKS	JOURNALLED	JUBILANT
JOGGLING	JOLES	JOR	JOURNALLING	JUBILATE
JOGPANTS	JOLING	JORAM	JOURNALS	JUBILATED
JOGS	JOLL	JORAMS	JOURNEY	JUBILATES
JOGTROT	JOLLED	JORDAN	JOURNEYED	JUBILATING
JOGTROTS	JOLLEY	JORDANS	JOURNEYER	JUBILEE
JOHANNES	JOLLEYER	JORDELOO	JOURNEYERS	JUBILEES
JOHANNESES	JOLLEYERS	JORDELOOS	JOURNEYING	JUD
JOHN	JOLLEYING	JORS	JOURNEYS	JUDAS
JOHNNIE	JOLLEYINGS	JORUM	JOURNO	JUDASES
JOHNNIES	JOLLEYS	JORUMS	JOURNOS	JUDDER
JOHNNY	JOLLIED	JOSEPH	JOURS	JUDDERED
JOHNS	JOLLIER	JOSEPHS	JOUST	JUDDERING

The Chambers Dictionary is the authority for many longer words; see *OSW* Introduction, page xii

JUDDERS	JUGULAR	JUMBOISE	JUNK	JURYWOMEN
JUDGE	JUGULARS	JUMBOISED	JUNKANOO	JUS
JUDGED	JUGULATE	JUMBOISES	JUNKANOOS	JUSSIVE
JUDGEMENT	JUGULATED	JUMBOISING	JUNKED	JUSSIVES
JUDGEMENTS	JUGULATES	JUMBOIZE	JUNKER	JUST
JUDGES	JUGULATING	JUMBOIZED	JUNKERS	JUSTED
JUDGESHIP	JUGUM	JUMBOIZES	JUNKET	JUSTER
JUDGESHIPS	JUICE	JUMBOIZING	JUNKETED	JUSTEST
JUDGING	JUICED	JUMBOS	JUNKETEER	JUSTICE
JUDGMENT	JUICELESS	JUMBUCK	JUNKETEERS	JUSTICER
JUDGMENTS	JUICER	JUMBUCKS	JUNKETING	JUSTICERS
JUDICABLE	JUICERS	JUMBY	JUNKETINGS	JUSTICES
JUDICATOR	JUICES	JUMELLE	JUNKETS	JUSTICIAR
JUDICATORS	JUICIER	JUMELLES	JUNKIE	JUSTICIARS
JUDICIAL	JUICIEST	JUMP	JUNKIER	JUSTIFIED
JUDICIARIES	JUICINESS	JUMPABLE	JUNKIES	JUSTIFIER
JUDICIARY	JUICINESSES	JUMPED	JUNKIEST	JUSTIFIERS
JUDICIOUS	JUICING	JUMPER	JUNKINESS	JUSTIFIES
JUDIES	JUICY	JUMPERS	JUNKINESSES	JUSTIFY
JUDO	JUJU	JUMPIER	JUNKING	JUSTIFYING
JUDOGI	JUJUBE	JUMPIEST	JUNKMAN	JUSTING
JUDOGIS	JUJUBES	JUMPILY	JUNKMEN	JUSTLE
JUDOIST	JUJUS	JUMPINESS	JUNKS	JUSTLED
JUDOISTS	JUKE	JUMPINESSES	JUNKY	JUSTLES
JUDOKA	JUKED	JUMPING	JUNTA	JUSTLING
JUDOKAS	JUKES	JUMPS	JUNTAS	JUSTLY
JUDOS	JUKING	JUMPY	JUNTO	JUSTNESS
JUDS	JUKSKEI	JUNCATE	JUNTOS	JUSTNESSES
JUDY	JUKSKEIS	JUNCATES	JUPATI	JUSTS
JUG	JULEP	JUNCO	JUPATIS	JUT
JUGA	JULEPS	JUNCOES	JUPON	JUTE
JUGAL	JULIENNE	JUNCOS	JUPONS	JUTES
JUGALS	JULIENNED	JUNCTION	JURA	JUTS
JUGATE	JULIENNES	JUNCTIONS	JURAL	JUTTED
JUGFUL	JULIENNING	JUNCTURE	JURALLY	JUTTIED
JUGFULS	JUMAR	JUNCTURES	JURANT	JUTTIES
JUGGED	JUMARRED	JUNCUS	JURANTS	JUTTING
JUGGING	JUMARRING	JUNCUSES	JURAT	JUTTINGLY
JUGGINGS	JUMARS	JUNEATING	JURATORY	JUTTY
JUGGINS	JUMART	JUNEATINGS	JURATS	JUTTYING
JUGGINSES	JUMARTS	JUNGLE	JURE	JUVE
JUGGLE	JUMBAL	JUNGLES	JURIDIC	JUVENAL
JUGGLED	JUMBALS	JUNGLI	JURIDICAL	JUVENALS
JUGGLER	JUMBIE	JUNGLIER	JURIES	JUVENILE
JUGGLERIES	JUMBIES	JUNGLIEST	JURIST	JUVENILES
JUGGLERS	JUMBLE	JUNGLIS	JURISTIC	JUVENILIA
JUGGLERY	JUMBLED	JUNGLIST	JURISTS	JUVES
JUGGLES	JUMBLER	JUNGLISTS	JUROR	JUXTAPOSE
JUGGLING	JUMBLERS	JUNGLY	JURORS	JUXTAPOSED
JUGGLINGS	JUMBLES	JUNIOR	JURY	JUXTAPOSES
JUGHEAD	JUMBLIER	JUNIORITIES	JURYMAN	JUXTAPOSING
JUGHEADS	JUMBLIEST	JUNIORITY	JURYMAST	JYMOLD
JUGLET	JUMBLING	JUNIORS	JURYMASTS	JYNX
JUGLETS	JUMBLY	JUNIPER	JURYMEN	JYNXES
JUGS	JUMBO	JUNIPERS	JURYWOMAN	

K

KA
KAAMA
KAAMAS
KABAB
KABABBED
KABABBING
KABABS
KABADDI
KABADDIS
KABALA
KABALAS
KABAYA
KABAYAS
KABBALA
KABBALAH
KABBALAHS
KABBALAS
KABELE
KABELES
KABELJOU
KABELJOUS
KABELJOUW
KABELJOUWS
KABOB
KABOBBED
KABOBBING
KABOBS
KABUKI
KABUKIS
KACCHA
KACCHAS
KACHAHRI
KACHAHRIS
KACHCHA
KACHERI
KACHERIS
KACHINA
KACHINAS
KADE
KADES
KADI
KADIS
KAE
KAED
KAEING
KAES
KAFFIYEH
KAFFIYEHS
KAFILA
KAFILAS
KAFTAN
KAFTANS
KAGO

KAGOOL
KAGOOLS
KAGOS
KAGOUL
KAGOULE
KAGOULES
KAGOULS
KAHAL
KAHALS
KAHAWAI
KAHAWAIS
KAI
KAIAK
KAIAKED
KAIAKING
KAIAKS
KAID
KAIDS
KAIE
KAIES
KAIF
KAIFS
KAIKAI
KAIKAIS
KAIL
KAILS
KAILYAIRD
KAILYAIRDS
KAILYARD
KAILYARDS
KAIM
KAIMAKAM
KAIMAKAMS
KAIMS
KAIN
KAING
KAINITE
KAINITES
KAINS
KAIS
KAISER
KAISERDOM
KAISERDOMS
KAISERIN
KAISERINS
KAISERISM
KAISERISMS
KAISERS
KAIZEN
KAIZENS
KAJAWAH
KAJAWAHS
KAKA
KAKAPO

KAKAPOS
KAKAS
KAKEMONO
KAKEMONOS
KAKI
KAKIEMON
KAKIEMONS
KAKIS
KAKODYL
KAKODYLS
KALAMDAN
KALAMDANS
KALAMKARI
KALAMKARIS
KALANCHOE
KALANCHOES
KALE
KALENDAR
KALENDARED
KALENDARING
KALENDARS
KALENDS
KALES
KALI
KALIAN
KALIANS
KALIF
KALIFS
KALINITE
KALINITES
KALIS
KALIUM
KALIUMS
KALLITYPE
KALLITYPES
KALMIA
KALMIAS
KALONG
KALONGS
KALOTYPE
KALOTYPES
KALPA
KALPAK
KALPAKS
KALPAS
KALPIS
KALPISES
KALSOMINE®
KALSOMINED
KALSOMINES
KALSOMINING
KALUMPIT
KALUMPITS
KALYPTRA

KALYPTRAS
KAM
KAMA
KAMACITE
KAMACITES
KAMALA
KAMALAS
KAMAS
KAME
KAMEES
KAMEESES
KAMEEZ
KAMEEZES
KAMELA
KAMELAS
KAMERAD
KAMERADED
KAMERADING
KAMERADS
KAMES
KAMI
KAMICHI
KAMICHIS
KAMIK
KAMIKAZE
KAMIKAZES
KAMIKS
KAMILA
KAMILAS
KAMIS
KAMISES
KAMME
KAMPONG
KAMPONGS
KAMSEEN
KAMSEENS
KAMSIN
KAMSINS
KANA
KANAKA
KANAKAS
KANAS
KANDIES
KANDY
KANEH
KANEHS
KANG
KANGA
KANGAROO
KANGAROOED
KANGAROOING
KANGAROOS
KANGAS
KANGHA

KANGHAS
KANGS
KANJI
KANJIS
KANS
KANSES
KANT
KANTAR
KANTARS
KANTED
KANTELA
KANTELAS
KANTELE
KANTELES
KANTEN
KANTENS
KANTHA
KANTHAS
KANTIKOY
KANTIKOYED
KANTIKOYING
KANTIKOYS
KANTING
KANTS
KANZU
KANZUS
KAOLIANG
KAOLIANGS
KAOLIN
KAOLINE
KAOLINES
KAOLINISE
KAOLINISED
KAOLINISES
KAOLINISING
KAOLINITE
KAOLINITES
KAOLINIZE
KAOLINIZED
KAOLINIZES
KAOLINIZING
KAOLINS
KAON
KAONS
KAPOK
KAPOKS
KAPPA
KAPPAS
KAPUT
KAPUTT
KARA
KARABINER
KARABINERS
KARAISM

The Chambers Dictionary is the authority for many longer words; see *OSW* Introduction, page xii

KARAISMS	KARZIES	KAYLES	KEDGIER	KEEVE
KARAIT	KARZY	KAYO	KEDGIEST	KEEVES
KARAITS	KAS	KAYOED	KEDGING	KEF
KARAKA	KASBAH	KAYOES	KEDGY	KEFFEL
KARAKAS	KASBAHS	KAYOING	KEDS	KEFFELS
KARAKUL	KASHA	KAYOINGS	KEECH	KEFFIYEH
KARAKULS	KASHAS	KAYOS	KEECHES	KEFFIYEHS
KARAOKE	KASHMIR	KAYS	KEEK	KEFIR
KARAOKES	KASHMIRS	KAZATZKA	KEEKED	KEFIRS
KARAS	KASHRUS	KAZATZKAS	KEEKER	KEFS
KARAT	KASHRUSES	KAZI	KEEKERS	KEFUFFLE
KARATE	KASHRUT	KAZIS	KEEKING	KEFUFFLED
KARATEIST	KASHRUTH	KAZOO	KEEKS	KEFUFFLES
KARATEISTS	KASHRUTHS	KAZOOS	KEEL	KEFUFFLING
KARATEKA	KASHRUTS	KEA	KEELAGE	KEG
KARATEKAS	KAT	KEAS	KEELAGES	KEGS
KARATES	KATA	KEASAR	KEELBOAT	KEIGHT
KARATS	KATABASES	KEASARS	KEELBOATS	KEIR
KARITE	KATABASIS	KEAVIE	KEELED	KEIRS
KARITES	KATABATIC	KEAVIES	KEELER	KEISTER
KARK	KATAKANA	KEB	KEELERS	KEISTERS
KARKED	KATAKANAS	KEBAB	KEELHAUL	KEITLOA
KARKING	KATANA	KEBABBED	KEELHAULED	KEITLOAS
KARKS	KATANAS	KEBABBING	KEELHAULING	KEKS
KARMA	KATAS	KEBABS	KEELHAULINGS	KEKSYE
KARMAS	KATHAK	KEBBED	KEELHAULS	KEKSYES
KARMIC	KATHAKALI	KEBBIE	KEELIE	KELIM
KAROSS	KATHAKALIS	KEBBIES	KEELIES	KELIMS
KAROSSES	KATHAKS	KEBBING	KEELING	KELL
KARRI	KATHARSES	KEBBOCK	KEELINGS	KELLAUT
KARRIS	KATHARSIS	KEBBOCKS	KEELIVINE	KELLAUTS
KARSEY	KATHODE	KEBBUCK	KEELIVINES	KELLIES
KARSEYS	KATHODES	KEBBUCKS	KEELMAN	KELLS
KARSIES	KATI	KEBELE	KEELMEN	KELLY
KARST	KATION	KEBELES	KEELS	KELOID
KARSTIC	KATIONS	KEBLAH	KEELSON	KELOIDAL
KARSTIFIED	KATIPO	KEBLAHS	KEELSONS	KELOIDS
KARSTIFIES	KATIPOS	KEBOB	KEELYVINE	KELP
KARSTIFY	KATIS	KEBOBBED	KEELYVINES	KELPER
KARSTIFYING	KATORGA	KEBOBBING	KEEN	KELPERS
KARSTS	KATORGAS	KEBOBS	KEENED	KELPIE
KARSY	KATS	KEBS	KEENER	KELPIES
KART	KATTI	KECK	KEENERS	KELPS
KARTER	KATTIS	KECKED	KEENEST	KELPY
KARTERS	KATYDID	KECKING	KEENING	KELSON
KARTING	KATYDIDS	KECKLE	KEENINGS	KELSONS
KARTINGS	KAUGH	KECKLED	KEENLY	KELT
KARTS	KAUGHS	KECKLES	KEENNESS	KELTER
KARYOGAMIES	KAURI	KECKLING	KEENNESSES	KELTERS
KARYOGAMY	KAURIS	KECKLINGS	KEENS	KELTIE
KARYOGRAM	KAVA	KECKS	KEEP	KELTIES
KARYOGRAMS	KAVAS	KECKSES	KEEPER	KELTS
KARYOLOGIES	KAVASS	KECKSIES	KEEPERS	KELTY
KARYOLOGY	KAVASSES	KECKSY	KEEPING	KELVIN
KARYON	KAW	KED	KEEPINGS	KELVINS
KARYONS	KAWED	KEDDAH	KEEPNET	KEMB
KARYOSOME	KAWING	KEDDAHS	KEEPNETS	KEMBED
KARYOSOMES	KAWS	KEDGE	KEEPS	KEMBING
KARYOTIN	KAY	KEDGED	KEEPSAKE	KEMBO
KARYOTINS	KAYAK	KEDGER	KEEPSAKES	KEMBOED
KARYOTYPE	KAYAKED	KEDGEREE	KEEPSAKY	KEMBOING
KARYOTYPED	KAYAKING	KEDGEREES	KEESHOND	KEMBOS
KARYOTYPES	KAYAKS	KEDGERS	KEESHONDEN	KEMBS
KARYOTYPING	KAYLE	KEDGES	KEESHONDS	KEMP

The Chambers Dictionary is the authority for many longer words; see *OSW* Introduction, page xii

KEMPED	KERBS	KETA	KHAKI	KHURTA
KEMPER	KERBSIDE	KETAMINE	KHAKIS	KHURTAS
KEMPERS	KERBSIDES	KETAMINES	KHALAT	KHUSKHUS
KEMPING	KERBSTONE	KETAS	KHALATS	KHUSKHUSES
KEMPINGS	KERBSTONES	KETCH	KHALIF	KHUTBAH
KEMPLE	KERCHIEF	KETCHES	KHALIFA	KHUTBAHS
KEMPLES	KERCHIEFED	KETCHING	KHALIFAH	KIANG
KEMPS	KERCHIEFING	KETCHUP	KHALIFAHS	KIANGS
KEMPT	KERCHIEFS	KETCHUPS	KHALIFAS	KIAUGH
KEN	KERF	KETONE	KHALIFAT	KIAUGHS
KENAF	KERFS	KETONES	KHALIFATE	KIBBLE
KENAFS	KERFUFFLE	KETONURIA	KHALIFATES	KIBBLED
KENDO	KERFUFFLED	KETONURIAS	KHALIFATS	KIBBLES
KENDOS	KERFUFFLES	KETOSE	KHALIFS	KIBBLING
KENNED	KERFUFFLING	KETOSES	KHAMSIN	KIBBUTZ
KENNEL	KERMES	KETOSIS	KHAMSINS	KIBBUTZIM
KENNELLED	KERMESITE	KETS	KHAN	KIBE
KENNELLING	KERMESITES	KETTLE	KHANATE	KIBES
KENNELS	KERMESSE	KETTLEFUL	KHANATES	KIBITKA
KENNER	KERMESSES	KETTLEFULS	KHANGA	KIBITKAS
KENNERS	KERMIS	KETTLES	KHANGAS	KIBITZ
KENNET	KERMISES	KEVEL	KHANJAR	KIBITZED
KENNETS	KERN	KEVELS	KHANJARS	KIBITZER
KENNING	KERNE	KEX	KHANS	KIBITZERS
KENNINGS	KERNED	KEXES	KHANSAMA	KIBITZES
KENO	KERNEL	KEY	KHANSAMAH	KIBITZING
KENOS	KERNELLED	KEYBOARD	KHANSAMAHS	KIBLAH
KENOSES	KERNELLING	KEYBOARDED	KHANSAMAS	KIBLAHS
KENOSIS	KERNELLY	KEYBOARDING	KHANUM	KIBOSH
KENOTIC	KERNELS	KEYBOARDS	KHANUMS	KIBOSHED
KENS	KERNES	KEYBUGLE	KHARIF	KIBOSHES
KENSPECK	KERNING	KEYBUGLES	KHARIFS	KIBOSHING
KENT	KERNINGS	KEYED	KHAT	KICK
KENTED	KERNISH	KEYHOLE	KHATS	KICKABLE
KENTIA	KERNITE	KEYHOLES	KHAYA	KICKBACK
KENTIAS	KERNITES	KEYING	KHAYAS	KICKBACKS
KENTING	KERNS	KEYLESS	KHEDA	KICKBALL
KENTLEDGE	KEROGEN	KEYLINE	KHEDAS	KICKBALLS
KENTLEDGES	KEROGENS	KEYLINES	KHEDIVA	KICKDOWN
KENTS	KEROSENE	KEYNOTE	KHEDIVAL	KICKDOWNS
KEP	KEROSENES	KEYNOTED	KHEDIVAS	KICKED
KEPHALIC	KEROSINE	KEYNOTES	KHEDIVATE	KICKER
KEPHALICS	KEROSINES	KEYNOTING	KHEDIVATES	KICKERS
KEPHALIN	KERRIA	KEYPAD	KHEDIVE	KICKING
KEPHALINS	KERRIAS	KEYPADS	KHEDIVES	KICKS
KEPHIR	KERSEY	KEYPUNCH	KHEDIVIAL	KICKSHAW
KEPHIRS	KERSEYS	KEYPUNCHED	KHILAFAT	KICKSHAWS
KEPI	KERVE	KEYPUNCHES	KHILAFATS	KICKSHAWSES
KEPIS	KERVED	KEYPUNCHING	KHILAT	KICKSTAND
KEPPING	KERVES	KEYS	KHILATS	KICKSTANDS
KEPPIT	KERVING	KEYSTONE	KHILIM	KID
KEPS	KERYGMA	KEYSTONED	KHILIMS	KIDDED
KEPT	KERYGMAS	KEYSTONES	KHODJA	KIDDER
KERAMIC	KERYGMATA	KEYSTONING	KHODJAS	KIDDERS
KERAMICS	KESAR	KEYSTROKE	KHOJA	KIDDIED
KERATIN	KESARS	KEYSTROKES	KHOJAS	KIDDIER
KERATINS	KESH	KEYWORD	KHOR	KIDDIERS
KERATITIS	KESHES	KEYWORDS	KHORS	KIDDIES
KERATITISES	KEST	KGOTLA	KHOTBAH	KIDDING
KERATOID	KESTING	KGOTLAS	KHOTBAHS	KIDDLE
KERATOSE	KESTREL	KHADDAR	KHOTBEH	KIDDLES
KERATOSES	KESTRELS	KHADDARS	KHOTBEHS	KIDDO
KERATOSIS	KESTS	KHADI	KHUD	KIDDOS
KERB	KET	KHADIS	KHUDS	KIDDUSH

KIDDUSHES	KILLADARS	KILTERS	KINETICAL	KINSHIPS
KIDDY	KILLAS	KILTIE	KINETICS	KINSMAN
KIDDYING	KILLASES	KILTIES	KINFOLK	KINSMEN
KIDDYWINK	KILLCOW	KILTING	KINFOLKS	KINSWOMAN
KIDDYWINKS	KILLCOWS	KILTS	KING	KINSWOMEN
KIDEL	KILLCROP	KILTY	KINGCRAFT	KINTLEDGE
KIDELS	KILLCROPS	KIMBO	KINGCRAFTS	KINTLEDGES
KIDGE	KILLDEE	KIMBOED	KINGCUP	KIOSK
KIDGIE	KILLDEER	KIMBOING	KINGCUPS	KIOSKS
KIDGIER	KILLDEERS	KIMBOS	KINGDOM	KIP
KIDGIEST	KILLDEES	KIMCHI	KINGDOMED	KIPE
KIDLET	KILLED	KIMCHIS	KINGDOMS	KIPES
KIDLETS	KILLER	KIMMER	KINGED	KIPP
KIDLING	KILLERS	KIMMERS	KINGFISH	KIPPA
KIDLINGS	KILLICK	KIMONO	KINGFISHES	KIPPAGE
KIDNAP	KILLICKS	KIMONOS	KINGHOOD	KIPPAGES
KIDNAPPED	KILLIFISH	KIN	KINGHOODS	KIPPAS
KIDNAPPER	KILLIFISHES	KINA	KINGING	KIPPED
KIDNAPPERS	KILLING	KINAKINA	KINGKLIP	KIPPER
KIDNAPPING	KILLINGS	KINAKINAS	KINGKLIPS	KIPPERED
KIDNAPS	KILLJOY	KINAS	KINGLE	KIPPERER
KIDNEY	KILLJOYS	KINASE	KINGLES	KIPPERERS
KIDNEYS	KILLOCK	KINASES	KINGLESS	KIPPERING
KIDOLOGIES	KILLOCKS	KINCHIN	KINGLET	KIPPERS
KIDOLOGY	KILLOGIE	KINCHINS	KINGLETS	KIPPING
KIDS	KILLOGIES	KINCOB	KINGLIER	KIPPS
KIDSKIN	KILLS	KINCOBS	KINGLIEST	KIPS
KIDSKINS	KILLUT	KIND	KINGLING	KIR
KIDSTAKES	KILLUTS	KINDA	KINGLINGS	KIRBEH
KIDULT	KILN	KINDED	KINGLY	KIRBEHS
KIDULTS	KILNED	KINDER	KINGMAKER	KIRBIGRIP
KIDVID	KILNING	KINDERS	KINGMAKERS	KIRBIGRIPS
KIDVIDS	KILNS	KINDEST	KINGPOST	KIRIMON
KIER	KILO	KINDIES	KINGPOSTS	KIRIMONS
KIERIE	KILOBAR	KINDING	KINGS	KIRK
KIERIES	KILOBARS	KINDLE	KINGSHIP	KIRKED
KIERS	KILOBIT	KINDLED	KINGSHIPS	KIRKING
KIESERITE	KILOBITS	KINDLER	KINGWOOD	KIRKINGS
KIESERITES	KILOBYTE	KINDLERS	KINGWOODS	KIRKS
KIEVE	KILOBYTES	KINDLES	KININ	KIRKTON
KIEVES	KILOCYCLE	KINDLESS	KININS	KIRKTONS
KIF	KILOCYCLES	KINDLIER	KINK	KIRKWARD
KIFS	KILOGRAM	KINDLIEST	KINKAJOU	KIRKYAIRD
KIGHT	KILOGRAMS	KINDLILY	KINKAJOUS	KIRKYAIRDS
KIGHTS	KILOGRAY	KINDLING	KINKED	KIRKYARD
KIKE	KILOGRAYS	KINDLINGS	KINKIER	KIRKYARDS
KIKES	KILOHERTZ	KINDLY	KINKIEST	KIRMESS
KIKOI	KILOHERTZES	KINDNESS	KINKILY	KIRMESSES
KIKOIS	KILOJOULE	KINDNESSES	KINKING	KIRN
KIKUMON	KILOJOULES	KINDRED	KINKLE	KIRNS
KIKUMONS	KILOMETRE	KINDREDS	KINKLES	KIRPAN
KIKUYU	KILOMETRES	KINDS	KINKS	KIRPANS
KIKUYUS	KILOS	KINDY	KINKY	KIRRI
KILD	KILOTON	KINE	KINLESS	KIRRIS
KILDERKIN	KILOTONS	KINEMA	KINO	KIRS
KILDERKINS	KILOVOLT	KINEMAS	KINONE	KIRSCH
KILERG	KILOVOLTS	KINEMATIC	KINONES	KIRSCHES
KILERGS	KILOWATT	KINEMATICS	KINOS	KIRTLE
KILEY	KILOWATTS	KINESCOPE	KINRED	KIRTLED
KILEYS	KILP	KINESCOPES	KINREDS	KIRTLES
KILIM	KILPS	KINESES	KINS	KISAN
KILIMS	KILT	KINESICS	KINSFOLK	KISANS
KILL	KILTED	KINESIS	KINSFOLKS	KISH
KILLADAR	KILTER	KINETIC	KINSHIP	KISHES

The Chambers Dictionary is the authority for many longer words; see *OSW* Introduction, page xii

KISHKE	KITTIWAKES	KLUDGE	KNEADERS	KNITTLES
KISHKES	KITTLE	KLUDGES	KNEADING	KNITWEAR
KISMET	KITTLED	KLUTZ	KNEADS	KNITWEARS
KISMETS	KITTLER	KLUTZES	KNEE	KNIVE
KISS	KITTLES	KLYSTRON	KNEECAP	KNIVED
KISSABLE	KITTLEST	KLYSTRONS	KNEECAPPED	KNIVES
KISSAGRAM	KITTLIER	KNACK	KNEECAPPING	KNIVING
KISSAGRAMS	KITTLIEST	KNACKER	KNEECAPPINGS	KNOB
KISSED	KITTLING	KNACKERED	KNEECAPS	KNOBBED
KISSEL	KITTLY	KNACKERIES	KNEED	KNOBBER
KISSELS	KITTUL	KNACKERING	KNEEHOLE	KNOBBERS
KISSER	KITTULS	KNACKERS	KNEEHOLES	KNOBBIER
KISSERS	KITTY	KNACKERY	KNEEING	KNOBBIEST
KISSES	KIVA	KNACKIER	KNEEL	KNOBBLE
KISSING	KIVAS	KNACKIEST	KNEELED	KNOBBLED
KISSOGRAM	KIWI	KNACKISH	KNEELER	KNOBBLES
KISSOGRAMS	KIWIS	KNACKS	KNEELERS	KNOBBLIER
KIST	KLANG	KNACKY	KNEELING	KNOBBLIEST
KISTED	KLANGS	KNAG	KNEELS	KNOBBLING
KISTING	KLATCH	KNAGGIER	KNEES	KNOBBLY
KISTS	KLATCHES	KNAGGIEST	KNEIDLACH	KNOBBY
KISTVAEN	KLATSCH	KNAGGY	KNELL	KNOBS
KISTVAENS	KLATSCHES	KNAGS	KNELLED	KNOCK
KIT	KLAVIER	KNAIDEL	KNELLING	KNOCKED
KITCHEN	KLAVIERS	KNAIDLOCH	KNELLS	KNOCKER
KITCHENED	KLAXON	KNAP	KNELT	KNOCKERS
KITCHENER	KLAXONED	KNAPPED	KNEVELL	KNOCKING
KITCHENERS	KLAXONING	KNAPPER	KNEVELLED	KNOCKINGS
KITCHENING	KLAXONS	KNAPPERS	KNEVELLING	KNOCKOUT
KITCHENS	KLENDUSIC	KNAPPING	KNEVELLS	KNOCKOUTS
KITE	KLEPHT	KNAPPLE	KNEW	KNOCKS
KITED	KLEPHTIC	KNAPPLED	KNICKER	KNOLL
KITENGE	KLEPHTISM	KNAPPLES	KNICKERED	KNOLLED
KITENGES	KLEPHTISMS	KNAPPLING	KNICKERS	KNOLLING
KITES	KLEPHTS	KNAPS	KNICKS	KNOLLS
KITH	KLEZMER	KNAPSACK	KNIFE	KNOP
KITHARA	KLEZMORIM	KNAPSACKS	KNIFED	KNOPS
KITHARAS	KLINKER	KNAPSCAL	KNIFELESS	KNOSP
KITHE	KLINKERS	KNAPSCALS	KNIFES	KNOSPS
KITHED	KLINOSTAT	KNAPSCULL	KNIFING	KNOT
KITHES	KLINOSTATS	KNAPSCULLS	KNIFINGS	KNOTGRASS
KITHING	KLIPDAS	KNAPSKULL	KNIGHT	KNOTGRASSES
KITHS	KLIPDASES	KNAPSKULLS	KNIGHTAGE	KNOTLESS
KITING	KLONDIKE	KNAPWEED	KNIGHTAGES	KNOTS
KITINGS	KLONDIKED	KNAPWEEDS	KNIGHTED	KNOTTED
KITLING	KLONDIKER	KNAR	KNIGHTING	KNOTTER
KITLINGS	KLONDIKERS	KNARL	KNIGHTLIER	KNOTTERS
KITS	KLONDIKES	KNARLS	KNIGHTLIEST	KNOTTIER
KITSCH	KLONDIKING	KNARRED	KNIGHTLY	KNOTTIEST
KITSCHES	KLONDYKE	KNARRING	KNIGHTS	KNOTTING
KITSCHIER	KLONDYKED	KNARS	KNIPHOFIA	KNOTTINGS
KITSCHIEST	KLONDYKER	KNAVE	KNIPHOFIAS	KNOTTY
KITSCHILY	KLONDYKERS	KNAVERIES	KNISH	KNOTWEED
KITSCHY	KLONDYKES	KNAVERY	KNISHES	KNOTWEEDS
KITTED	KLONDYKING	KNAVES	KNIT	KNOTWORK
KITTEN	KLOOCH	KNAVESHIP	KNITCH	KNOTWORKS
KITTENED	KLOOCHES	KNAVESHIPS	KNITCHES	KNOUT
KITTENING	KLOOCHMAN	KNAVISH	KNITS	KNOUTED
KITTENISH	KLOOCHMANS	KNAVISHLY	KNITTED	KNOUTING
KITTENS	KLOOCHMEN	KNAWEL	KNITTER	KNOUTS
KITTENY	KLOOF	KNAWELS	KNITTERS	KNOW
KITTIES	KLOOFS	KNEAD	KNITTING	KNOWABLE
KITTING	KLOOTCH	KNEADED	KNITTINGS	KNOWE
KITTIWAKE	KLOOTCHES	KNEADER	KNITTLE	KNOWER

The Chambers Dictionary is the authority for many longer words; see *OSW* Introduction, page xii

KNOWERS	KOFTAS	KOOLAH	KOUROS	KRIS
KNOWES	KOFTGAR	KOOLAHS	KOUSKOUS	KRISED
KNOWHOW	KOFTGARI	KOORI	KOUSKOUSES	KRISES
KNOWHOWS	KOFTGARIS	KOORIS	KOW	KRISING
KNOWING	KOFTGARS	KOP	KOWHAI	KROMESKIES
KNOWINGLY	KOFTWORK	KOPASETIC	KOWHAIS	KROMESKY
KNOWLEDGE	KOFTWORKS	KOPECK	KOWS	KRONA
KNOWLEDGED	KOHL	KOPECKS	KOWTOW	KRONE
KNOWLEDGES	KOHLRABI	KOPH	KOWTOWED	KRONEN
KNOWLEDGING	KOHLRABIS	KOPHS	KOWTOWING	KRONER
KNOWN	KOHLS	KOPJE	KOWTOWS	KRONOR
KNOWNS	KOI	KOPJES	KRAAL	KRONUR
KNOWS	KOINE	KOPPA	KRAALED	KRULLER
KNUB	KOINES	KOPPAS	KRAALING	KRULLERS
KNUBBIER	KOKANEE	KOPPIE	KRAALS	KRUMHORN
KNUBBIEST	KOKANEES	KOPPIES	KRAB	KRUMHORNS
KNUBBLE	KOKER	KOPS	KRABS	KRUMMHORN
KNUBBLED	KOKERS	KORA	KRAFT	KRUMMHORNS
KNUBBLES	KOKRA	KORAS	KRAFTS	KRYOMETER
KNUBBLIER	KOKRAS	KORE	KRAIT	KRYOMETERS
KNUBBLIEST	KOKUM	KORERO	KRAITS	KRYPSES
KNUBBLING	KOKUMS	KOREROS	KRAKEN	KRYPSIS
KNUBBLY	KOLA	KORES	KRAKENS	KRYPTON
KNUBBY	KOLAS	KORFBALL	KRAKOWIAK	KRYPTONS
KNUBS	KOLINSKIES	KORFBALLS	KRAKOWIAKS	KRYTRON
KNUCKLE	KOLINSKY	KORKIR	KRAMERIA	KRYTRONS
KNUCKLED	KOLKHOZ	KORKIRS	KRAMERIAS	KSAR
KNUCKLES	KOLKHOZES	KORMA	KRANG	KSARS
KNUCKLIER	KOLO	KORMAS	KRANGS	KUCHCHA
KNUCKLIEST	KOLOS	KORORA	KRANS	KUDOS
KNUCKLING	KOMATIK	KORORAS	KRANSES	KUDOSES
KNUCKLY	KOMATIKS	KORUNA	KRANTZ	KUDU
KNUR	KOMBU	KORUNAS	KRANTZES	KUDUS
KNURL	KOMBUS	KOS	KRANZ	KUDZU
KNURLED	KOMISSAR	KOSES	KRANZES	KUDZUS
KNURLIER	KOMISSARS	KOSHER	KRATER	KUFIYAH
KNURLIEST	KOMITAJI	KOSHERED	KRATERS	KUFIYAHS
KNURLING	KOMITAJIS	KOSHERING	KRAUT	KUKRI
KNURLINGS	KON	KOSHERS	KRAUTS	KUKRIS
KNURLS	KOND	KOSMOS	KREASOTE	KUKU
KNURLY	KONFYT	KOSMOSES	KREASOTED	KUKUS
KNURR	KONFYTS	KOSS	KREASOTES	KULAK
KNURRS	KONIMETER	KOSSES	KREASOTING	KULAKS
KNURS	KONIMETERS	KOTO	KREATINE	KULAN
KNUT	KONIOLOGIES	KOTOS	KREATINES	KULANS
KNUTS	KONIOLOGY	KOTOW	KREESE	KUMARA
KO	KONISCOPE	KOTOWED	KREESED	KUMARAS
KOA	KONISCOPES	KOTOWING	KREESES	KUMARI
KOALA	KONK	KOTOWS	KREESING	KUMARIS
KOALAS	KONKED	KOTTABOS	KREMLIN	KUMISS
KOAN	KONKING	KOTTABOSES	KREMLINS	KUMISSES
KOANS	KONKS	KOTWAL	KRENG	KUMMEL
KOAS	KONNING	KOTWALS	KRENGS	KUMMELS
KOB	KONS	KOULAN	KREOSOTE	KUMQUAT
KOBAN	KOODOO	KOULANS	KREOSOTED	KUMQUATS
KOBANG	KOODOOS	KOUMISS	KREOSOTES	KUNKAR
KOBANGS	KOOK	KOUMISSES	KREOSOTING	KUNKARS
KOBANS	KOOKED	KOUPREY	KREPLACH	KUNKUR
KOBOLD	KOOKIE	KOUPREYS	KREUTZER	KUNKURS
KOBOLDS	KOOKIER	KOURBASH	KREUTZERS	KUNZITE
KOBS	KOOKIEST	KOURBASHED	KRILL	KUNZITES
KOFF	KOOKING	KOURBASHES	KRILLS	KURBASH
KOFFS	KOOKS	KOURBASHING	KRIMMER	KURBASHED
KOFTA	KOOKY	KOUROI	KRIMMERS	KURBASHES

KURBASHING
KURGAN
KURGANS
KURI
KURIS
KURRAJONG
KURRAJONGS
KURRE
KURRES
KURSAAL
KURSAALS
KURTA
KURTAS
KURTOSES
KURTOSIS
KURU
KURUS
KURVEY
KURVEYED
KURVEYING
KURVEYOR

KURVEYORS
KURVEYS
KUTCH
KUTCHA
KUTCHES
KUZU
KUZUS
KVASS
KVASSES
KVETCH
KVETCHED
KVETCHER
KVETCHERS
KVETCHES
KVETCHING
KWACHA
KWACHAS
KWANZA
KWANZAS
KWELA
KWELAS

KY
KYANG
KYANGS
KYANISE
KYANISED
KYANISES
KYANISING
KYANITE
KYANITES
KYANIZE
KYANIZED
KYANIZES
KYANIZING
KYAT
KYATS
KYBOSH
KYBOSHED
KYBOSHES
KYBOSHING
KYDST
KYE

KYLE
KYLES
KYLICES
KYLIE
KYLIES
KYLIN
KYLINS
KYLIX
KYLLOSES
KYLLOSIS
KYLOE
KYLOES
KYMOGRAM
KYMOGRAMS
KYMOGRAPH
KYMOGRAPHS
KYND
KYNDE
KYNDED
KYNDES
KYNDING

KYNDS
KYNE
KYOGEN
KYOGENS
KYPHOSES
KYPHOSIS
KYPHOTIC
KYRIELLE
KYRIELLES
KYTE
KYTES
KYTHE
KYTHED
KYTHES
KYTHING
KYU
KYUS

L

LA
LAAGER
LAAGERED
LAAGERING
LAAGERS
LAB
LABARA
LABARUM
LABARUMS
LABDA
LABDACISM
LABDACISMS
LABDANUM
LABDANUMS
LABDAS
LABEL
LABELLA
LABELLED
LABELLING
LABELLOID
LABELLUM
LABELS
LABIA
LABIAL
LABIALISE
LABIALISED
LABIALISES
LABIALISING
LABIALISM
LABIALISMS
LABIALIZE
LABIALIZED
LABIALIZES
LABIALIZING
LABIALLY
LABIALS
LABIATE
LABIATES
LABILE
LABILITIES
LABILITY
LABIS
LABISES
LABIUM
LABLAB
LABLABS
LABOR
LABORED
LABORING
LABORIOUS
LABORS
LABOUR
LABOURED
LABOURER

LABOURERS
LABOURING
LABOURISM
LABOURISMS
LABOURIST
LABOURISTS
LABOURS
LABRA
LABRET
LABRETS
LABRID
LABRIDS
LABROID
LABROIDS
LABROSE
LABRUM
LABRYS
LABRYSES
LABS
LABURNUM
LABURNUMS
LABYRINTH
LABYRINTHS
LAC
LACCOLITE
LACCOLITES
LACCOLITH
LACCOLITHS
LACE
LACEBARK
LACEBARKS
LACED
LACERABLE
LACERANT
LACERATE
LACERATED
LACERATES
LACERATING
LACERTIAN
LACERTINE
LACES
LACET
LACETS
LACEWING
LACEWINGS
LACEY
LACHES
LACHESES
LACHRYMAL
LACHRYMALS
LACIER
LACIEST
LACING
LACINGS

LACINIA
LACINIAE
LACINIATE
LACK
LACKADAY
LACKED
LACKER
LACKERED
LACKERING
LACKERS
LACKEY
LACKEYED
LACKEYING
LACKEYS
LACKING
LACKLAND
LACKLANDS
LACKS
LACMUS
LACMUSES
LACONIC
LACONICAL
LACONISM
LACONISMS
LACQUER
LACQUERED
LACQUERER
LACQUERERS
LACQUERING
LACQUERINGS
LACQUERS
LACQUEY
LACQUEYED
LACQUEYING
LACQUEYS
LACRIMAL
LACRIMALS
LACRIMOSO
LACROSSE
LACROSSES
LACRYMAL
LACRYMALS
LACS
LACTARIAN
LACTARIANS
LACTASE
LACTASES
LACTATE
LACTATED
LACTATES
LACTATING
LACTATION
LACTATIONS
LACTEAL

LACTEALS
LACTEOUS
LACTIC
LACTIFIC
LACTONE
LACTONES
LACTOSE
LACTOSES
LACUNA
LACUNAE
LACUNAL
LACUNAR
LACUNARIA
LACUNARS
LACUNARY
LACUNATE
LACUNOSE
LACY
LAD
LADANUM
LADANUMS
LADDER
LADDERED
LADDERING
LADDERS
LADDERY
LADDIE
LADDIES
LADDISH
LADE
LADED
LADEN
LADES
LADETTE
LADETTES
LADIES
LADIFIED
LADIFIES
LADIFY
LADIFYING
LADING
LADINGS
LADLE
LADLED
LADLEFUL
LADLEFULS
LADLES
LADLING
LADRONE
LADRONES
LADS
LADY
LADYBIRD
LADYBIRDS

LADYBUG
LADYBUGS
LADYCOW
LADYCOWS
LADYFIED
LADYFIES
LADYFLIES
LADYFLY
LADYFY
LADYFYING
LADYHOOD
LADYHOODS
LADYISH
LADYISM
LADYISMS
LADYKIN
LADYKINS
LADYLIKE
LADYSHIP
LADYSHIPS
LAER
LAERED
LAERING
LAERS
LAESIE
LAETARE
LAETARES
LAEVIGATE
LAEVIGATED
LAEVIGATES
LAEVIGATING
LAEVULOSE
LAEVULOSES
LAG
LAGAN
LAGANS
LAGENA
LAGENAS
LAGER
LAGERS
LAGGARD
LAGGARDS
LAGGED
LAGGEN
LAGGENS
LAGGER
LAGGERS
LAGGIN
LAGGING
LAGGINGLY
LAGGINGS
LAGGINS
LAGNAPPE
LAGNAPPES

LAGNIAPPE	LAIRIZING	LAMBDA	LAMINGTONS	LANCEGAY
LAGNIAPPES	LAIRS	LAMBDAS	LAMINITIS	LANCEGAYS
LAGOMORPH	LAIRY	LAMBDOID	LAMINITISES	LANCELET
LAGOMORPHS	LAISSE	LAMBED	LAMINOSE	LANCELETS
LAGOON	LAISSES	LAMBENCIES	LAMISH	LANCEOLAR
LAGOONAL	LAITANCE	LAMBENCY	LAMITER	LANCER
LAGOONS	LAITANCES	LAMBENT	LAMITERS	LANCERS
LAGRIMOSO	LAITH	LAMBENTLY	LAMMED	LANCES
LAGS	LAITIES	LAMBER	LAMMER	LANCET
LAGUNE	LAITY	LAMBERS	LAMMERS	LANCETED
LAGUNES	LAKE	LAMBERT	LAMMIE	LANCETS
LAH	LAKED	LAMBERTS	LAMMIES	LANCH
LAHAR	LAKELAND	LAMBIE	LAMMIGER	LANCHED
LAHARS	LAKELANDS	LAMBIES	LAMMIGERS	LANCHES
LAHS	LAKELET	LAMBING	LAMMING	LANCHING
LAIC	LAKELETS	LAMBITIVE	LAMMINGS	LANCIFORM
LAICAL	LAKER	LAMBITIVES	LAMMY	LANCINATE
LAICISE	LAKERS	LAMBKIN	LAMP	LANCINATED
LAICISED	LAKES	LAMBKINS	LAMPAD	LANCINATES
LAICISES	LAKESIDE	LAMBLING	LAMPADARIES	LANCINATING
LAICISING	LAKESIDES	LAMBLINGS	LAMPADARY	LANCING
LAICITIES	LAKH	LAMBOYS	LAMPADIST	LAND
LAICITY	LAKHS	LAMBS	LAMPADISTS	LANDAMMAN
LAICIZE	LAKIER	LAMBSKIN	LAMPADS	LANDAMMANS
LAICIZED	LAKIEST	LAMBSKINS	LAMPAS	LANDAU
LAICIZES	LAKIN	LAME	LAMPASES	LANDAULET
LAICIZING	LAKING	LAMED	LAMPASSE	LANDAULETS
LAICS	LAKINS	LAMELLA	LAMPASSES	LANDAUS
LAID	LAKISH	LAMELLAE	LAMPED	LANDDAMNE
LAIDED	LAKY	LAMELLAR	LAMPERN	LANDDAMNED
LAIDING	LALANG	LAMELLATE	LAMPERNS	LANDDAMNES
LAIDLY	LALANGS	LAMELLOID	LAMPERS	LANDDAMNING
LAIDS	LALDIE	LAMELLOSE	LAMPERSES	LANDDROS
LAIGH	LALDIES	LAMELY	LAMPHOLE	LANDDROSES
LAIGHER	LALDY	LAMENESS	LAMPHOLES	LANDDROST
LAIGHEST	LALLAN	LAMENESSES	LAMPING	LANDDROSTS
LAIGHS	LALLANS	LAMENT	LAMPINGS	LANDE
LAIK	LALLATION	LAMENTED	LAMPION	LANDED
LAIKA	LALLATIONS	LAMENTING	LAMPIONS	LANDER
LAIKAS	LALLING	LAMENTINGS	LAMPLIGHT	LANDERS
LAIKED	LALLINGS	LAMENTS	LAMPLIGHTS	LANDES
LAIKER	LALLYGAG	LAMER	LAMPOON	LANDFALL
LAIKERS	LALLYGAGGED	LAMES	LAMPOONED	LANDFALLS
LAIKING	LALLYGAGGING	LAMEST	LAMPOONER	LANDFILL
LAIKS	LALLYGAGS	LAMETER	LAMPOONERS	LANDFILLS
LAIN	LAM	LAMETERS	LAMPOONING	LANDFORCE
LAIR	LAMA	LAMIA	LAMPOONS	LANDFORCES
LAIRAGE	LAMAISTIC	LAMIAE	LAMPPOST	LANDFORM
LAIRAGES	LAMANTIN	LAMIAS	LAMPPOSTS	LANDFORMS
LAIRD	LAMANTINS	LAMIGER	LAMPREY	LANDGRAVE
LAIRDS	LAMAS	LAMIGERS	LAMPREYS	LANDGRAVES
LAIRDSHIP	LAMASERAI	LAMINA	LAMPS	LANDING
LAIRDSHIPS	LAMASERAIS	LAMINABLE	LAMPSHADE	LANDINGS
LAIRED	LAMASERIES	LAMINAE	LAMPSHADES	LANDLADIES
LAIRIER	LAMASERY	LAMINAR	LAMPUKA	LANDLADY
LAIRIEST	LAMB	LAMINARY	LAMPUKAS	LANDLER
LAIRING	LAMBADA	LAMINATE	LAMPUKI	LANDLERS
LAIRISE	LAMBADAS	LAMINATED	LAMPUKIS	LANDLESS
LAIRISED	LAMBAST	LAMINATES	LAMS	LANDLOPER
LAIRISES	LAMBASTE	LAMINATING	LANA	LANDLOPERS
LAIRISING	LAMBASTED	LAMINATOR	LANAS	LANDLORD
LAIRIZE	LAMBASTES	LAMINATORS	LANATE	LANDLORDS
LAIRIZED	LAMBASTING	LAMING	LANCE	LANDMAN
LAIRIZES	LAMBASTS	LAMINGTON	LANCED	LANDMARK

LANDMARKS	LANGUETTES	LAPELLED	LARCENIST	LARMIER
LANDMASS	LANGUID	LAPELS	LARCENISTS	LARMIERS
LANDMASSES	LANGUIDLY	LAPFUL	LARCENOUS	LARN
LANDMEN	LANGUISH	LAPFULS	LARCENY	LARNAKES
LANDOWNER	LANGUISHED	LAPHELD	LARCH	LARNAX
LANDOWNERS	LANGUISHES	LAPIDARIES	LARCHEN	LARNED
LANDRACE	LANGUISHING	LAPIDARY	LARCHES	LARNING
LANDRACES	LANGUISHINGS	LAPIDATE	LARD	LARNS
LANDRAIL	LANGUOR	LAPIDATED	LARDALITE	LAROID
LANDRAILS	LANGUORS	LAPIDATES	LARDALITES	LARRIGAN
LANDS	LANGUR	LAPIDATING	LARDED	LARRIGANS
LANDSCAPE	LANGURS	LAPIDEOUS	LARDER	LARRIKIN
LANDSCAPED	LANIARD	LAPIDIFIC	LARDERER	LARRIKINS
LANDSCAPES	LANIARDS	LAPIDIFIED	LARDERERS	LARRUP
LANDSCAPING	LANIARY	LAPIDIFIES	LARDERS	LARRUPED
LANDSIDE	LANK	LAPIDIFY	LARDIER	LARRUPING
LANDSIDES	LANKED	LAPIDIFYING	LARDIEST	LARRUPS
LANDSKIP	LANKER	LAPILLI	LARDING	LARUM
LANDSKIPPED	LANKEST	LAPIS	LARDON	LARUMS
LANDSKIPPING	LANKIER	LAPISES	LARDONS	LARVA
LANDSKIPS	LANKIEST	LAPJE	LARDOON	LARVAE
LANDSLIDE	LANKILY	LAPJES	LARDOONS	LARVAL
LANDSLIDES	LANKINESS	LAPPED	LARDS	LARVATE
LANDSLIP	LANKINESSES	LAPPEL	LARDY	LARVATED
LANDSLIPS	LANKING	LAPPELS	LARE	LARVICIDE
LANDSMAN	LANKLY	LAPPER	LARES	LARVICIDES
LANDSMEN	LANKNESS	LAPPERED	LARGE	LARVIFORM
LANDWARD	LANKNESSES	LAPPERING	LARGELY	LARVIKITE
LANDWARDS	LANKS	LAPPERS	LARGEN	LARVIKITES
LANDWIND	LANKY	LAPPET	LARGENED	LARYNGAL
LANDWINDS	LANNER	LAPPETED	LARGENESS	LARYNGEAL
LANE	LANNERET	LAPPETS	LARGENESSES	LARYNGES
LANES	LANNERETS	LAPPIE	LARGENING	LARYNX
LANEWAY	LANNERS	LAPPIES	LARGENS	LARYNXES
LANEWAYS	LANOLIN	LAPPING	LARGER	LAS
LANG	LANOLINE	LAPPINGS	LARGES	LASAGNA
LANGAHA	LANOLINES	LAPS	LARGESS	LASAGNAS
LANGAHAS	LANOLINS	LAPSABLE	LARGESSE	LASAGNE
LANGER	LANOSE	LAPSANG	LARGESSES	LASAGNES
LANGEST	LANT	LAPSANGS	LARGEST	LASCAR
LANGLAUF	LANTANA	LAPSE	LARGHETTO	LASCARS
LANGLAUFS	LANTANAS	LAPSED	LARGHETTOS	LASE
LANGOUSTE	LANTERLOO	LAPSES	LARGISH	LASED
LANGOUSTES	LANTERLOOS	LAPSING	LARGITION	LASER
LANGRAGE	LANTERN	LAPSTONE	LARGITIONS	LASERS
LANGRAGES	LANTERNED	LAPSTONES	LARGO	LASERWORT
LANGREL	LANTERNING	LAPSTRAKE	LARGOS	LASERWORTS
LANGRELS	LANTERNS	LAPSTRAKES	LARIAT	LASES
LANGRIDGE	LANTHANUM	LAPSTREAK	LARIATS	LASH
LANGRIDGES	LANTHANUMS	LAPSTREAKS	LARINE	LASHED
LANGSPEL	LANTHORN	LAPSUS	LARK	LASHER
LANGSPELS	LANTHORNS	LAPTOP	LARKED	LASHERS
LANGSPIEL	LANTS	LAPTOPS	LARKER	LASHES
LANGSPIELS	LANTSKIP	LAPWING	LARKERS	LASHING
LANGUAGE	LANTSKIPS	LAPWINGS	LARKIER	LASHINGS
LANGUAGED	LANUGO	LAPWORK	LARKIEST	LASHKAR
LANGUAGES	LANUGOS	LAPWORKS	LARKINESS	LASHKARS
LANGUAGING	LANX	LAQUEARIA	LARKINESSES	LASING
LANGUE	LANYARD	LAR	LARKING	LASINGS
LANGUED	LANYARDS	LARBOARD	LARKISH	LASKET
LANGUES	LAP	LARBOARDS	LARKS	LASKETS
LANGUET	LAPDOG	LARCENER	LARKSPUR	LASQUE
LANGUETS	LAPDOGS	LARCENERS	LARKSPURS	LASQUES
LANGUETTE	LAPEL	LARCENIES	LARKY	LASS

LASSES	LATEWAKE	LATTICING	LAUREATE	LAW
LASSI	LATEWAKES	LATTICINI	LAUREATED	LAWED
LASSIE	LATEX	LATTICINO	LAUREATES	LAWER
LASSIES	LATEXES	LAUCH	LAUREATING	LAWEST
LASSIS	LATH	LAUCHING	LAUREL	LAWFUL
LASSITUDE	LATHE	LAUCHS	LAURELLED	LAWFULLY
LASSITUDES	LATHED	LAUD	LAURELS	LAWIN
LASSLORN	LATHEE	LAUDABLE	LAUWINE	LAWING
LASSO	LATHEES	LAUDABLY	LAUWINES	LAWINGS
LASSOCK	LATHEN	LAUDANUM	LAV	LAWINS
LASSOCKS	LATHER	LAUDANUMS	LAVA	LAWK
LASSOED	LATHERED	LAUDATION	LAVABO	LAWKS
LASSOES	LATHERIER	LAUDATIONS	LAVABOES	LAWLAND
LASSOING	LATHERIEST	LAUDATIVE	LAVABOS	LAWLANDS
LASSOS	LATHERING	LAUDATIVES	LAVAFORM	LAWLESS
LASSU	LATHERS	LAUDATORIES	LAVAGE	LAWLESSLY
LASSUS	LATHERY	LAUDATORY	LAVAGES	LAWMAN
LAST	LATHES	LAUDED	LAVALIERE	LAWMEN
LASTAGE	LATHI	LAUDER	LAVALIERES	LAWMONGER
LASTAGES	LATHIER	LAUDERS	LAVAS	LAWMONGERS
LASTED	LATHIEST	LAUDING	LAVATERA	LAWN
LASTER	LATHING	LAUDS	LAVATERAS	LAWNIER
LASTERS	LATHINGS	LAUF	LAVATION	LAWNIEST
LASTING	LATHIS	LAUFS	LAVATIONS	LAWNMOWER
LASTINGLY	LATHLIKE	LAUGH	LAVATORIES	LAWNMOWERS
LASTINGS	LATHS	LAUGHABLE	LAVATORY	LAWNS
LASTLY	LATHY	LAUGHABLY	LAVE	LAWNY
LASTS	LATHYRISM	LAUGHED	LAVED	LAWS
LAT	LATHYRISMS	LAUGHER	LAVEER	LAWSUIT
LATCH	LATHYRUS	LAUGHERS	LAVEERED	LAWSUITS
LATCHED	LATHYRUSES	LAUGHFUL	LAVEERING	LAWYER
LATCHES	LATICES	LAUGHIER	LAVEERS	LAWYERLY
LATCHET	LATICLAVE	LAUGHIEST	LAVEMENT	LAWYERS
LATCHETS	LATICLAVES	LAUGHING	LAVEMENTS	LAX
LATCHING	LATIFONDI	LAUGHINGS	LAVENDER	LAXATIVE
LATCHKEY	LATISH	LAUGHS	LAVENDERED	LAXATIVES
LATCHKEYS	LATITANCIES	LAUGHSOME	LAVENDERING	LAXATOR
LATE	LATITANCY	LAUGHTER	LAVENDERS	LAXATORS
LATED	LATITANT	LAUGHTERS	LAVER	LAXER
LATEEN	LATITAT	LAUGHY	LAVEROCK	LAXES
LATEENS	LATITATS	LAUNCE	LAVEROCKED	LAXEST
LATELY	LATITUDE	LAUNCED	LAVEROCKING	LAXISM
LATEN	LATITUDES	LAUNCES	LAVEROCKS	LAXISMS
LATENCE	LATKE	LAUNCH	LAVERS	LAXIST
LATENCES	LATKES	LAUNCHED	LAVES	LAXISTS
LATENCIES	LATRANT	LAUNCHER	LAVING	LAXITIES
LATENCY	LATRATION	LAUNCHERS	LAVISH	LAXITY
LATENED	LATRATIONS	LAUNCHES	LAVISHED	LAXLY
LATENESS	LATRIA	LAUNCHING	LAVISHER	LAXNESS
LATENESSES	LATRIAS	LAUNCING	LAVISHES	LAXNESSES
LATENING	LATRINE	LAUND	LAVISHEST	LAY
LATENS	LATRINES	LAUNDER	LAVISHING	LAYABOUT
LATENT	LATROCINIES	LAUNDERED	LAVISHLY	LAYABOUTS
LATENTLY	LATROCINY	LAUNDERER	LAVOLT	LAYAWAY
LATER	LATRON	LAUNDERERS	LAVOLTA	LAYAWAYS
LATERAL	LATRONS	LAUNDERING	LAVOLTAED	LAYBACK
LATERALLY	LATS	LAUNDERS	LAVOLTAING	LAYBACKED
LATERALS	LATTEN	LAUNDRESS	LAVOLTAS	LAYBACKING
LATERITE	LATTENS	LAUNDRESSES	LAVOLTED	LAYBACKS
LATERITES	LATTER	LAUNDRIES	LAVOLTING	LAYER
LATERITIC	LATTERLY	LAUNDRY	LAVOLTS	LAYERED
LATESCENT	LATTICE	LAUNDS	LAVRA	LAYERING
LATEST	LATTICED	LAURA	LAVRAS	LAYERINGS
LATESTS	LATTICES	LAURAS	LAVS	LAYERS

LAYETTE	LEADED	LEALLY	LEASINGS	LECTINS
LAYETTES	LEADEN	LEALTIES	LEASOW	LECTION
LAYING	LEADENED	LEALTY	LEASOWE	LECTIONS
LAYINGS	LEADENING	LEAM	LEASOWED	LECTOR
LAYLOCK	LEADENLY	LEAMED	LEASOWES	LECTORATE
LAYLOCKS	LEADENS	LEAMING	LEASOWING	LECTORATES
LAYMAN	LEADER	LEAMS	LEASOWS	LECTORS
LAYMEN	LEADERENE	LEAN	LEAST	LECTRESS
LAYOUT	LEADERENES	LEANED	LEASTS	LECTRESSES
LAYOUTS	LEADERS	LEANER	LEASTWAYS	LECTURE
LAYPERSON	LEADIER	LEANEST	LEASTWISE	LECTURED
LAYPERSONS	LEADIEST	LEANING	LEASURE	LECTURER
LAYS	LEADING	LEANINGS	LEASURES	LECTURERS
LAYSTALL	LEADINGS	LEANLY	LEAT	LECTURES
LAYSTALLS	LEADLESS	LEANNESS	LEATHER	LECTURING
LAYTIME	LEADS	LEANNESSES	LEATHERED	LECTURN
LAYTIMES	LEADSMAN	LEANS	LEATHERIER	LECTURNS
LAYWOMAN	LEADSMEN	LEANT	LEATHERIEST	LECYTHI
LAYWOMEN	LEADY	LEANY	LEATHERING	LECYTHUS
LAZAR	LEAF	LEAP	LEATHERINGS	LED
LAZARET	LEAFAGE	LEAPED	LEATHERN	LEDDEN
LAZARETS	LEAFAGES	LEAPER	LEATHERS	LEDDENS
LAZARETTO	LEAFBUD	LEAPEROUS	LEATHERY	LEDGE
LAZARETTOS	LEAFBUDS	LEAPERS	LEATS	LEDGER
LAZARS	LEAFED	LEAPING	LEAVE	LEDGERED
LAZE	LEAFERIES	LEAPOROUS	LEAVED	LEDGERING
LAZED	LEAFERY	LEAPROUS	LEAVEN	LEDGERS
LAZES	LEAFIER	LEAPS	LEAVENED	LEDGES
LAZIER	LEAFIEST	LEAPT	LEAVENING	LEDGIER
LAZIEST	LEAFINESS	LEAR	LEAVENINGS	LEDGIEST
LAZILY	LEAFINESSES	LEARE	LEAVENOUS	LEDGY
LAZINESS	LEAFING	LEARED	LEAVENS	LEDUM
LAZINESSES	LEAFLESS	LEARES	LEAVER	LEDUMS
LAZING	LEAFLET	LEARIER	LEAVERS	LEE
LAZO	LEAFLETED	LEARIEST	LEAVES	LEEAR
LAZOED	LEAFLETING	LEARING	LEAVIER	LEEARS
LAZOES	LEAFLETS	LEARN	LEAVIEST	LEECH
LAZOING	LEAFLETTED	LEARNABLE	LEAVING	LEECHDOM
LAZOS	LEAFLETTING	LEARNED	LEAVINGS	LEECHDOMS
LAZULITE	LEAFLIKE	LEARNEDLY	LEAVY	LEECHED
LAZULITES	LEAFS	LEARNER	LEAZE	LEECHEE
LAZURITE	LEAFY	LEARNERS	LEAZES	LEECHEES
LAZURITES	LEAGUE	LEARNING	LEBBEK	LEECHES
LAZY	LEAGUED	LEARNINGS	LEBBEKS	LEECHING
LAZZARONE	LEAGUER	LEARNS	LECANORA	LEED
LAZZARONI	LEAGUERED	LEARNT	LECANORAS	LEEING
LAZZI	LEAGUERING	LEARS	LECH	LEEK
LAZZO	LEAGUERS	LEARY	LECHED	LEEKS
LEA	LEAGUES	LEAS	LECHER	LEEP
LEACH	LEAGUING	LEASABLE	LECHERED	LEEPED
LEACHATE	LEAK	LEASE	LECHERIES	LEEPING
LEACHATES	LEAKAGE	LEASEBACK	LECHERING	LEEPS
LEACHED	LEAKAGES	LEASEBACKS	LECHEROUS	LEER
LEACHES	LEAKED	LEASED	LECHERS	LEERED
LEACHIER	LEAKER	LEASEHOLD	LECHERY	LEERIER
LEACHIEST	LEAKERS	LEASEHOLDS	LECHES	LEERIEST
LEACHING	LEAKIER	LEASER	LECHING	LEERING
LEACHINGS	LEAKIEST	LEASERS	LECHWE	LEERINGLY
LEACHOUR	LEAKINESS	LEASES	LECHWES	LEERINGS
LEACHOURS	LEAKINESSES	LEASH	LECITHIN	LEERS
LEACHTUB	LEAKING	LEASHED	LECITHINS	LEERY
LEACHTUBS	LEAKS	LEASHES	LECTERN	LEES
LEACHY	LEAKY	LEASHING	LECTERNS	LEESE
LEAD	LEAL	LEASING	LECTIN	LEESES

The Chambers Dictionary is the authority for many longer words; see *OSW* Introduction, page xii

LEESING	LEGENDRIES	LEHRS	LEMONFISH	LENSMAN
LEET	LEGENDRY	LEI	LEMONFISHES	LENSMEN
LEETLE	LEGENDS	LEIDGER	LEMONIER	LENT
LEETS	LEGER	LEIDGERS	LEMONIEST	LENTANDO
LEEWARD	LEGERING	LEIGER	LEMONING	LENTEN
LEEWARDS	LEGERINGS	LEIGERS	LEMONS	LENTI
LEEWAY	LEGERITIES	LEIPOA	LEMONY	LENTIC
LEEWAYS	LEGERITY	LEIPOAS	LEMPIRA	LENTICEL
LEFT	LEGERS	LEIR	LEMPIRAS	LENTICELS
LEFTE	LEGES	LEIRED	LEMUR	LENTICLE
LEFTER	LEGGE	LEIRING	LEMURES	LENTICLES
LEFTEST	LEGGED	LEIRS	LEMURIAN	LENTIFORM
LEFTIE	LEGGER	LEIS	LEMURIANS	LENTIGINES
LEFTIES	LEGGERS	LEISH	LEMURINE	LENTIGO
LEFTISH	LEGGES	LEISHER	LEMURINES	LENTIL
LEFTISM	LEGGIER	LEISHEST	LEMUROID	LENTILS
LEFTISMS	LEGGIEST	LEISLER	LEMUROIDS	LENTISK
LEFTIST	LEGGINESS	LEISLERS	LEMURS	LENTISKS
LEFTISTS	LEGGINESSES	LEISTER	LEND	LENTO
LEFTOVER	LEGGING	LEISTERED	LENDER	LENTOID
LEFTOVERS	LEGGINGS	LEISTERING	LENDERS	LENTOR
LEFTS	LEGGISM	LEISTERS	LENDING	LENTORS
LEFTWARD	LEGGISMS	LEISURE	LENDINGS	LENTOS
LEFTWARDS	LEGGY	LEISURED	LENDS	LENTOUS
LEFTY	LEGHORN	LEISURELY	LENES	LENVOY
LEG	LEGHORNS	LEISURES	LENG	LENVOYS
LEGACIES	LEGIBLE	LEISURING	LENGED	LEONE
LEGACY	LEGIBLY	LEITMOTIF	LENGER	LEONES
LEGAL	LEGION	LEITMOTIFS	LENGEST	LEONINE
LEGALESE	LEGIONARIES	LEITMOTIV	LENGING	LEOPARD
LEGALESES	LEGIONARY	LEITMOTIVS	LENGS	LEOPARDS
LEGALISE	LEGIONED	LEK	LENGTH	LEOTARD
LEGALISED	LEGIONS	LEKE	LENGTHEN	LEOTARDS
LEGALISES	LEGISLATE	LEKKED	LENGTHENED	LEP
LEGALISING	LEGISLATED	LEKKING	LENGTHENING	LEPER
LEGALISM	LEGISLATES	LEKKINGS	LENGTHENS	LEPERS
LEGALISMS	LEGISLATING	LEKS	LENGTHFUL	LEPID
LEGALIST	LEGIST	LEKYTHOI	LENGTHIER	LEPIDOTE
LEGALISTS	LEGISTS	LEKYTHOS	LENGTHIEST	LEPORINE
LEGALITIES	LEGIT	LEMAN	LENGTHILY	LEPPED
LEGALITY	LEGITIM	LEMANS	LENGTHS	LEPPING
LEGALIZE	LEGITIMS	LEME	LENGTHY	LEPRA
LEGALIZED	LEGLAN	LEMED	LENIENCE	LEPRAS
LEGALIZES	LEGLANS	LEMEL	LENIENCES	LEPROSE
LEGALIZING	LEGLEN	LEMELS	LENIENCIES	LEPROSERIES
LEGALLY	LEGLENS	LEMES	LENIENCY	LEPROSERY
LEGATARIES	LEGLESS	LEMING	LENIENT	LEPROSIES
LEGATARY	LEGLET	LEMMA	LENIENTLY	LEPROSITIES
LEGATE	LEGLETS	LEMMAS	LENIENTS	LEPROSITY
LEGATEE	LEGLIN	LEMMATA	LENIFIED	LEPROSY
LEGATEES	LEGLINS	LEMMATISE	LENIFIES	LEPROUS
LEGATES	LEGROOM	LEMMATISED	LENIFY	LEPS
LEGATINE	LEGROOMS	LEMMATISES	LENIFYING	LEPTA
LEGATION	LEGS	LEMMATISING	LENIS	LEPTOME
LEGATIONS	LEGUME	LEMMATIZE	LENITIES	LEPTOMES
LEGATO	LEGUMES	LEMMATIZED	LENITION	LEPTON
LEGATOR	LEGUMIN	LEMMATIZES	LENITIONS	LEPTONIC
LEGATORS	LEGUMINS	LEMMATIZING	LENITIVE	LEPTONS
LEGATOS	LEGWEAR	LEMMING	LENITIVES	LEPTOSOME
LEGEND	LEGWEARS	LEMMINGS	LENITY	LEPTOSOMES
LEGENDARIES	LEGWORK	LEMON	LENO	LEPTOTENE
LEGENDARY	LEGWORKS	LEMONADE	LENOS	LEPTOTENES
LEGENDIST	LEHR	LEMONADES	LENS	LERE
LEGENDISTS	LEHRJAHRE	LEMONED	LENSES	LERED

The Chambers Dictionary is the authority for many longer words; see *OSW* Introduction, page xii

LERES	LETTERNS	LEVERAGED	LEXIGRAM	LIBELLANTS
LERING	LETTERS	LEVERAGES	LEXIGRAMS	LIBELLED
LERNAEAN	LETTING	LEVERAGING	LEXIS	LIBELLEE
LERNEAN	LETTINGS	LEVERED	LEXISES	LIBELLEES
LERP	LETTRE	LEVERET	LEY	LIBELLER
LERPS	LETTRES	LEVERETS	LEYS	LIBELLERS
LES	LETTUCE	LEVERING	LEZ	LIBELLING
LESBIAN	LETTUCES	LEVERS	LEZES	LIBELLINGS
LESBIANS	LEU	LEVIABLE	LEZZ	LIBELLOUS
LESBIC	LEUCAEMIA	LEVIATHAN	LEZZES	LIBELOUS
LESBO	LEUCAEMIAS	LEVIATHANS	LEZZIES	LIBELS
LESBOS	LEUCAEMIC	LEVIED	LEZZY	LIBER
LESES	LEUCH	LEVIES	LI	LIBERAL
LESION	LEUCHEN	LEVIGABLE	LIABILITIES	LIBERALLY
LESIONS	LEUCIN	LEVIGATE	LIABILITY	LIBERALS
LESS	LEUCINE	LEVIGATED	LIABLE	LIBERATE
LESSEE	LEUCINES	LEVIGATES	LIAISE	LIBERATED
LESSEES	LEUCINS	LEVIGATING	LIAISED	LIBERATES
LESSEN	LEUCITE	LEVIN	LIAISES	LIBERATING
LESSENED	LEUCITES	LEVINS	LIAISING	LIBERATOR
LESSENING	LEUCITIC	LEVIRATE	LIAISON	LIBERATORS
LESSENS	LEUCOCYTE	LEVIRATES	LIAISONS	LIBERO
LESSER	LEUCOCYTES	LEVIS	LIANA	LIBEROS
LESSES	LEUCOMA	LEVITATE	LIANAS	LIBERS
LESSON	LEUCOMAS	LEVITATED	LIANE	LIBERTIES
LESSONED	LEUCOSIN	LEVITATES	LIANES	LIBERTINE
LESSONING	LEUCOSINS	LEVITATING	LIANG	LIBERTINES
LESSONINGS	LEUCOTOME	LEVITE	LIANGS	LIBERTY
LESSONS	LEUCOTOMES	LEVITES	LIANOID	LIBIDINAL
LESSOR	LEUCOTOMIES	LEVITIC	LIAR	LIBIDO
LESSORS	LEUCOTOMY	LEVITICAL	LIARD	LIBIDOS
LEST	LEUGH	LEVITIES	LIARDS	LIBKEN
LESTED	LEUGHEN	LEVITY	LIARS	LIBKENS
LESTING	LEUKAEMIA	LEVULOSE	LIART	LIBRA
LESTS	LEUKAEMIAS	LEVULOSES	LIB	LIBRAE
LET	LEUKEMIA	LEVY	LIBANT	LIBRAIRE
LETCH	LEUKEMIAS	LEVYING	LIBATE	LIBRAIRES
LETCHED	LEV	LEW	LIBATED	LIBRAIRIE
LETCHES	LEVA	LEWD	LIBATES	LIBRAIRIES
LETCHING	LEVANT	LEWDER	LIBATING	LIBRARIAN
LETCHINGS	LEVANTED	LEWDEST	LIBATION	LIBRARIANS
LETHAL	LEVANTER	LEWDLY	LIBATIONS	LIBRARIES
LETHALITIES	LEVANTERS	LEWDNESS	LIBATORY	LIBRARY
LETHALITY	LEVANTINE	LEWDNESSES	LIBBARD	LIBRAS
LETHALLY	LEVANTINES	LEWDSBIES	LIBBARDS	LIBRATE
LETHARGIC	LEVANTING	LEWDSBY	LIBBED	LIBRATED
LETHARGIES	LEVANTS	LEWDSTER	LIBBER	LIBRATES
LETHARGY	LEVATOR	LEWDSTERS	LIBBERS	LIBRATING
LETHEAN	LEVATORS	LEWIS	LIBBING	LIBRATION
LETHEE	LEVE	LEWISES	LIBECCHIO	LIBRATIONS
LETHEES	LEVEE	LEWISIA	LIBECCHIOS	LIBRATORY
LETHIED	LEVEED	LEWISIAS	LIBECCIO	LIBRETTI
LETS	LEVEEING	LEWISITE	LIBECCIOS	LIBRETTO
LETTABLE	LEVEES	LEWISITES	LIBEL	LIBRETTOS
LETTED	LEVEL	LEWISSON	LIBELANT	LIBS
LETTER	LEVELLED	LEWISSONS	LIBELANTS	LICE
LETTERBOX	LEVELLER	LEX	LIBELED	LICENCE
LETTERBOXES	LEVELLERS	LEXEME	LIBELEE	LICENCED
LETTERED	LEVELLEST	LEXEMES	LIBELEES	LICENCES
LETTERER	LEVELLING	LEXES	LIBELER	LICENCING
LETTERERS	LEVELLINGS	LEXICAL	LIBELERS	LICENSE
LETTERING	LEVELS	LEXICALLY	LIBELING	LICENSED
LETTERINGS	LEVER	LEXICON	LIBELINGS	LICENSEE
LETTERN	LEVERAGE	LEXICONS	LIBELLANT	LICENSEES

LICENSER	LIDLESS	LIFTABLE	LIGHTSOME	LILL
LICENSERS	LIDO	LIFTBACK	LIGNAGE	LILLED
LICENSES	LIDOCAINE	LIFTBACKS	LIGNAGES	LILLING
LICENSING	LIDOCAINES	LIFTED	LIGNALOES	LILLS
LICENSOR	LIDOS	LIFTER	LIGNE	LILO
LICENSORS	LIDS	LIFTERS	LIGNEOUS	LILOS
LICENSURE	LIE	LIFTING	LIGNES	LILT
LICENSURES	LIED	LIFTS	LIGNIFIED	LILTED
LICH	LIEDER	LIFULL	LIGNIFIES	LILTING
LICHANOS	LIEF	LIG	LIGNIFORM	LILTS
LICHANOSES	LIEFER	LIGAMENT	LIGNIFY	LILY
LICHEE	LIEFEST	LIGAMENTS	LIGNIFYING	LIMA
LICHEES	LIEFS	LIGAN	LIGNIN	LIMACEL
LICHEN	LIEGE	LIGAND	LIGNINS	LIMACELS
LICHENED	LIEGEDOM	LIGANDS	LIGNITE	LIMACEOUS
LICHENIN	LIEGEDOMS	LIGANS	LIGNITES	LIMACES
LICHENINS	LIEGELESS	LIGASE	LIGNITIC	LIMACINE
LICHENISM	LIEGEMAN	LIGASES	LIGNOSE	LIMACON
LICHENISMS	LIEGEMEN	LIGATE	LIGNOSES	LIMACONS
LICHENIST	LIEGER	LIGATED	LIGNUM	LIMAIL
LICHENISTS	LIEGERS	LIGATES	LIGNUMS	LIMAILS
LICHENOID	LIEGES	LIGATING	LIGROIN	LIMAS
LICHENOSE	LIEN	LIGATION	LIGROINS	LIMATION
LICHENOUS	LIENAL	LIGATIONS	LIGS	LIMATIONS
LICHENS	LIENS	LIGATURE	LIGULA	LIMAX
LICHES	LIENTERIC	LIGATURED	LIGULAE	LIMB
LICHGATE	LIENTERIES	LIGATURES	LIGULAR	LIMBATE
LICHGATES	LIENTERY	LIGATURING	LIGULAS	LIMBEC
LICHI	LIER	LIGER	LIGULATE	LIMBECK
LICHIS	LIERNE	LIGERS	LIGULE	LIMBECKS
LICHT	LIERNES	LIGGE	LIGULES	LIMBECS
LICHTED	LIERS	LIGGED	LIGULOID	LIMBED
LICHTER	LIES	LIGGEN	LIGURE	LIMBER
LICHTEST	LIEU	LIGGER	LIGURES	LIMBERED
LICHTING	LIEUS	LIGGERS	LIKABLE	LIMBERING
LICHTLIED	LIEVE	LIGGES	LIKE	LIMBERS
LICHTLIES	LIEVER	LIGGING	LIKEABLE	LIMBIC
LICHTLY	LIEVEST	LIGGINGS	LIKED	LIMBING
LICHTLYING	LIFE	LIGHT	LIKELIER	LIMBLESS
LICHTS	LIFEBELT	LIGHTED	LIKELIEST	LIMBMEAL
LICHWAKE	LIFEBELTS	LIGHTEN	LIKELY	LIMBO
LICHWAKES	LIFEBOAT	LIGHTENED	LIKEN	LIMBOS
LICHWAY	LIFEBOATS	LIGHTENING	LIKENED	LIMBOUS
LICHWAYS	LIFEBUOY	LIGHTENINGS	LIKENESS	LIMBS
LICIT	LIFEBUOYS	LIGHTENS	LIKENESSES	LIME
LICITLY	LIFEFUL	LIGHTER	LIKENING	LIMEADE
LICK	LIFEGUARD	LIGHTERS	LIKENS	LIMEADES
LICKED	LIFEGUARDS	LIGHTEST	LIKER	LIMED
LICKER	LIFEHOLD	LIGHTFUL	LIKERS	LIMEKILN
LICKERISH	LIFELESS	LIGHTING	LIKES	LIMEKILNS
LICKERS	LIFELIKE	LIGHTINGS	LIKEWAKE	LIMELIGHT
LICKING	LIFELINE	LIGHTISH	LIKEWAKES	LIMELIGHTED
LICKINGS	LIFELINES	LIGHTLESS	LIKEWALK	LIMELIGHTING
LICKPENNIES	LIFELONG	LIGHTLIED	LIKEWALKS	LIMELIGHTS
LICKPENNY	LIFER	LIGHTLIES	LIKEWISE	LIMELIT
LICKS	LIFERS	LIGHTLY	LIKIN	LIMEN
LICORICE	LIFESOME	LIGHTLYING	LIKING	LIMENS
LICORICES	LIFESPAN	LIGHTNESS	LIKINGS	LIMEPIT
LICTOR	LIFESPANS	LIGHTNESSES	LIKINS	LIMEPITS
LICTORS	LIFESTYLE	LIGHTNING	LILAC	LIMERICK
LID	LIFESTYLES	LIGHTNINGS	LILACS	LIMERICKS
LIDDED	LIFETIME	LIGHTS	LILANGENI	LIMES
LIDGER	LIFETIMES	LIGHTSHIP	LILIED	LIMESTONE
LIDGERS	LIFT	LIGHTSHIPS	LILIES	LIMESTONES

LIMEWASH	LIMPKIN	LINESMEN	LINKAGES	LIONELS
LIMEWASHES	LIMPKINS	LINEY	LINKBOY	LIONESS
LIMEWATER	LIMPLY	LING	LINKBOYS	LIONESSES
LIMEWATERS	LIMPNESS	LINGA	LINKED	LIONET
LIMEY	LIMPNESSES	LINGAM	LINKER	LIONETS
LIMEYS	LIMPS	LINGAMS	LINKERS	LIONISE
LIMIER	LIMULI	LINGAS	LINKING	LIONISED
LIMIEST	LIMULUS	LINGEL	LINKMAN	LIONISES
LIMINAL	LIMULUSES	LINGELS	LINKMEN	LIONISING
LIMINESS	LIMY	LINGER	LINKS	LIONISM
LIMINESSES	LIN	LINGERED	LINKSTER	LIONISMS
LIMING	LINAC	LINGERER	LINKSTERS	LIONIZE
LIMINGS	LINACS	LINGERERS	LINKWORK	LIONIZED
LIMIT	LINAGE	LINGERIE	LINKWORKS	LIONIZES
LIMITABLE	LINAGES	LINGERIES	LINN	LIONIZING
LIMITARY	LINALOOL	LINGERING	LINNED	LIONLIKE
LIMITED	LINALOOLS	LINGERINGS	LINNET	LIONLY
LIMITEDLY	LINCH	LINGERS	LINNETS	LIONS
LIMITEDS	LINCHES	LINGIER	LINNEY	LIP
LIMITER	LINCHET	LINGIEST	LINNEYS	LIPARITE
LIMITERS	LINCHETS	LINGLE	LINNIES	LIPARITES
LIMITES	LINCHPIN	LINGLES	LINNING	LIPASE
LIMITING	LINCHPINS	LINGO	LINNS	LIPASES
LIMITINGS	LINCRUSTA	LINGOES	LINNY	LIPECTOMIES
LIMITLESS	LINCRUSTAS	LINGOT	LINO	LIPECTOMY
LIMITS	LINCTURE	LINGOTS	LINOCUT	LIPID
LIMMA	LINCTURES	LINGS	LINOCUTS	LIPIDE
LIMMAS	LINCTUS	LINGSTER	LINOLEUM	LIPIDES
LIMMER	LINCTUSES	LINGSTERS	LINOLEUMS	LIPIDS
LIMMERS	LIND	LINGUA	LINOS	LIPLESS
LIMN	LINDANE	LINGUAE	LINS	LIPLIKE
LIMNAEID	LINDANES	LINGUAL	LINSANG	LIPOGRAM
LIMNAEIDS	LINDEN	LINGUALLY	LINSANGS	LIPOGRAMS
LIMNED	LINDENS	LINGUAS	LINSEED	LIPOID
LIMNER	LINDS	LINGUINE	LINSEEDS	LIPOIDS
LIMNERS	LINDWORM	LINGUINI	LINSEY	LIPOMA
LIMNETIC	LINDWORMS	LINGUIST	LINSEYS	LIPOMATA
LIMNING	LINE	LINGUISTS	LINSTOCK	LIPOSOMAL
LIMNOLOGIES	LINEAGE	LINGULA	LINSTOCKS	LIPOSOME
LIMNOLOGY	LINEAGES	LINGULAE	LINT	LIPOSOMES
LIMNS	LINEAL	LINGULAR	LINTEL	LIPPED
LIMO	LINEALITIES	LINGULAS	LINTELLED	LIPPEN
LIMONITE	LINEALITY	LINGULATE	LINTELS	LIPPENED
LIMONITES	LINEALLY	LINGY	LINTER	LIPPENING
LIMONITIC	LINEAMENT	LINHAY	LINTERS	LIPPENS
LIMOS	LINEAMENTS	LINHAYS	LINTIE	LIPPIE
LIMOSES	LINEAR	LINIER	LINTIER	LIPPIER
LIMOSIS	LINEARITIES	LINIEST	LINTIES	LIPPIES
LIMOUS	LINEARITY	LINIMENT	LINTIEST	LIPPIEST
LIMOUSINE	LINEARLY	LINIMENTS	LINTS	LIPPING
LIMOUSINES	LINEATE	LININ	LINTSEED	LIPPITUDE
LIMP	LINEATED	LINING	LINTSEEDS	LIPPITUDES
LIMPED	LINEATION	LININGS	LINTSTOCK	LIPPY
LIMPER	LINEATIONS	LININS	LINTSTOCKS	LIPS
LIMPEST	LINED	LINISH	LINTWHITE	LIPSTICK
LIMPET	LINEMAN	LINISHED	LINTWHITES	LIPSTICKED
LIMPETS	LINEMEN	LINISHER	LINTY	LIPSTICKING
LIMPID	LINEN	LINISHERS	LINY	LIPSTICKS
LIMPIDITIES	LINENS	LINISHES	LION	LIQUABLE
LIMPIDITY	LINEOLATE	LINISHING	LIONCEL	LIQUATE
LIMPIDLY	LINER	LINISHINGS	LIONCELLE	LIQUATED
LIMPING	LINERS	LINK	LIONCELLES	LIQUATES
LIMPINGLY	LINES	LINKABLE	LIONCELS	LIQUATING
LIMPINGS	LINESMAN	LINKAGE	LIONEL	LIQUATION

LIQUATIONS
LIQUEFIED
LIQUEFIER
LIQUEFIERS
LIQUEFIES
LIQUEFY
LIQUEFYING
LIQUESCE
LIQUESCED
LIQUESCES
LIQUESCING
LIQUEUR
LIQUEURED
LIQUEURING
LIQUEURS
LIQUID
LIQUIDATE
LIQUIDATED
LIQUIDATES
LIQUIDATING
LIQUIDISE
LIQUIDISED
LIQUIDISES
LIQUIDISING
LIQUIDITIES
LIQUIDITY
LIQUIDIZE
LIQUIDIZED
LIQUIDIZES
LIQUIDIZING
LIQUIDLY
LIQUIDS
LIQUIDUS
LIQUIDUSES
LIQUOR
LIQUORED
LIQUORICE
LIQUORICES
LIQUORING
LIQUORISH
LIQUORS
LIRA
LIRAS
LIRE
LIRIPIPE
LIRIPIPES
LIRIPOOP
LIRIPOOPS
LIRK
LIRKED
LIRKING
LIRKS
LIS
LISK
LISKS
LISLE
LISLES
LISP
LISPED
LISPER
LISPERS
LISPING
LISPINGLY
LISPINGS

LISPOUND
LISPOUNDS
LISPS
LISPUND
LISPUNDS
LISSES
LISSOM
LISSOME
LISSOMELY
LISSOMLY
LIST
LISTED
LISTEL
LISTELS
LISTEN
LISTENED
LISTENER
LISTENERS
LISTENING
LISTENS
LISTER
LISTERIA
LISTERIAS
LISTERS
LISTETH
LISTFUL
LISTING
LISTINGS
LISTLESS
LISTS
LIT
LITANIES
LITANY
LITCHI
LITCHIS
LITE
LITED
LITER
LITERACIES
LITERACY
LITERAL
LITERALLY
LITERALS
LITERARY
LITERATE
LITERATES
LITERATI
LITERATIM
LITERATO
LITERATOR
LITERATORS
LITERATUS
LITEROSE
LITERS
LITES
LITH
LITHARGE
LITHARGES
LITHATE
LITHATES
LITHE
LITHED
LITHELY
LITHENESS

LITHENESSES
LITHER
LITHERLY
LITHES
LITHESOME
LITHEST
LITHIA
LITHIAS
LITHIASES
LITHIASIS
LITHIC
LITHING
LITHISTID
LITHISTIDS
LITHITE
LITHITES
LITHIUM
LITHIUMS
LITHO
LITHOCYST
LITHOCYSTS
LITHOID
LITHOIDAL
LITHOLOGIES
LITHOLOGY
LITHOPONE
LITHOPONES
LITHOS
LITHOTOME
LITHOTOMES
LITHOTOMIES
LITHOTOMY
LITHS
LITIGABLE
LITIGANT
LITIGANTS
LITIGATE
LITIGATED
LITIGATES
LITIGATING
LITIGIOUS
LITING
LITMUS
LITMUSES
LITOTES
LITRE
LITRES
LITTEN
LITTER
LITTERED
LITTERING
LITTERS
LITTERY
LITTLE
LITTLEANE
LITTLEANES
LITTLER
LITTLES
LITTLEST
LITTLIN
LITTLING
LITTLINGS
LITTLINS
LITTORAL

LITTORALS
LITURGIC
LITURGICS
LITURGIES
LITURGIST
LITURGISTS
LITURGY
LITUUS
LITUUSES
LIVABLE
LIVE
LIVEABLE
LIVED
LIVELIER
LIVELIEST
LIVELILY
LIVELOD
LIVELODS
LIVELONG
LIVELONGS
LIVELOOD
LIVELOODS
LIVELY
LIVEN
LIVENED
LIVENER
LIVENERS
LIVENING
LIVENS
LIVER
LIVERIED
LIVERIES
LIVERISH
LIVERS
LIVERWING
LIVERWINGS
LIVERWORT
LIVERWORTS
LIVERY
LIVERYMAN
LIVERYMEN
LIVES
LIVEST
LIVESTOCK
LIVESTOCKS
LIVEWARE
LIVEWARES
LIVID
LIVIDER
LIVIDEST
LIVIDITIES
LIVIDITY
LIVIDLY
LIVIDNESS
LIVIDNESSES
LIVING
LIVINGS
LIVOR
LIVORS
LIVRAISON
LIVRAISONS
LIVRE
LIVRES
LIXIVIA

LIXIVIAL
LIXIVIATE
LIXIVIATED
LIXIVIATES
LIXIVIATING
LIXIVIOUS
LIXIVIUM
LIXIVIUMS
LIZARD
LIZARDS
LLAMA
LLAMAS
LLANERO
LLANEROS
LLANO
LLANOS
LO
LOACH
LOACHES
LOAD
LOADED
LOADEN
LOADENED
LOADENING
LOADENS
LOADER
LOADERS
LOADING
LOADINGS
LOADS
LOADSTAR
LOADSTARS
LOADSTONE
LOADSTONES
LOAF
LOAFED
LOAFER
LOAFERISH
LOAFERS
LOAFING
LOAFINGS
LOAFS
LOAM
LOAMED
LOAMIER
LOAMIEST
LOAMINESS
LOAMINESSES
LOAMING
LOAMS
LOAMY
LOAN
LOANABLE
LOANBACK
LOANBACKS
LOANED
LOANING
LOANINGS
LOANS
LOAST
LOATH
LOATHE
LOATHED
LOATHER

LOATHERS	LOBWORM	LOCKOUTS	LODGEMENTS	LOGICISMS
LOATHES	LOBWORMS	LOCKPICK	LODGEPOLE	LOGICIST
LOATHEST	LOCAL	LOCKPICKS	LODGEPOLES	LOGICISTS
LOATHFUL	LOCALE	LOCKRAM	LODGER	LOGICIZE
LOATHING	LOCALES	LOCKRAMS	LODGERS	LOGICIZED
LOATHINGS	LOCALISE	LOCKS	LODGES	LOGICIZES
LOATHLY	LOCALISED	LOCKSMAN	LODGING	LOGICIZING
LOATHSOME	LOCALISER	LOCKSMEN	LODGINGS	LOGICS
LOATHY	LOCALISERS	LOCKSMITH	LODGMENT	LOGIE
LOAVE	LOCALISES	LOCKSMITHS	LODGMENTS	LOGIER
LOAVED	LOCALISING	LOCKSTEP	LODICULA	LOGIES
LOAVES	LOCALISM	LOCKSTEPS	LODICULAE	LOGIEST
LOAVING	LOCALISMS	LOCO	LODICULE	LOGIN
LOB	LOCALIST	LOCOED	LODICULES	LOGINS
LOBAR	LOCALISTS	LOCOES	LODS	LOGION
LOBATE	LOCALITIES	LOCOFOCO	LOESS	LOGISTIC
LOBATION	LOCALITY	LOCOFOCOS	LOESSES	LOGISTICS
LOBATIONS	LOCALIZE	LOCOMAN	LOFT	LOGJUICE
LOBBED	LOCALIZED	LOCOMEN	LOFTED	LOGJUICES
LOBBIED	LOCALIZER	LOCOMOTE	LOFTER	LOGLINE
LOBBIES	LOCALIZERS	LOCOMOTED	LOFTERS	LOGLINES
LOBBING	LOCALIZES	LOCOMOTES	LOFTIER	LOGLOG
LOBBY	LOCALIZING	LOCOMOTING	LOFTIEST	LOGLOGS
LOBBYER	LOCALLY	LOCOMOTOR	LOFTILY	LOGO
LOBBYERS	LOCALS	LOCOMOTORS	LOFTINESS	LOGOFF
LOBBYING	LOCATABLE	LOCOPLANT	LOFTINESSES	LOGOFFS
LOBBYINGS	LOCATE	LOCOPLANTS	LOFTING	LOGOGRAM
LOBBYIST	LOCATED	LOCOS	LOFTS	LOGOGRAMS
LOBBYISTS	LOCATES	LOCOWEED	LOFTY	LOGOGRAPH
LOBE	LOCATING	LOCOWEEDS	LOG	LOGOGRAPHS
LOBECTOMIES	LOCATION	LOCULAR	LOGAN	LOGOGRIPH
LOBECTOMY	LOCATIONS	LOCULATE	LOGANIA	LOGOGRIPHS
LOBED	LOCATIVE	LOCULE	LOGANIAS	LOGOMACHIES
LOBELET	LOCATIVES	LOCULES	LOGANS	LOGOMACHY
LOBELETS	LOCELLATE	LOCULI	LOGAOEDIC	LOGON
LOBELIA	LOCH	LOCULUS	LOGARITHM	LOGONS
LOBELIAS	LOCHAN	LOCUM	LOGARITHMS	LOGOPEDIC
LOBELINE	LOCHANS	LOCUMS	LOGBOARD	LOGOPHILE
LOBELINES	LOCHIA	LOCUPLETE	LOGBOARDS	LOGOPHILES
LOBES	LOCHIAL	LOCUS	LOGBOOK	LOGORRHEA
LOBI	LOCHS	LOCUST	LOGBOOKS	LOGORRHEAS
LOBING	LOCI	LOCUSTA	LOGE	LOGOS
LOBINGS	LOCK	LOCUSTAE	LOGES	LOGOTHETE
LOBIPED	LOCKABLE	LOCUSTED	LOGGAT	LOGOTHETES
LOBLOLLIES	LOCKAGE	LOCUSTING	LOGGATS	LOGOTYPE
LOBLOLLY	LOCKAGES	LOCUSTS	LOGGED	LOGOTYPES
LOBO	LOCKAWAY	LOCUTION	LOGGER	LOGOUT
LOBOS	LOCKAWAYS	LOCUTIONS	LOGGERS	LOGOUTS
LOBOSE	LOCKED	LOCUTORIES	LOGGIA	LOGS
LOBOTOMIES	LOCKER	LOCUTORY	LOGGIAS	LOGWOOD
LOBOTOMY	LOCKERS	LOD	LOGGIE	LOGWOODS
LOBS	LOCKET	LODE	LOGGING	LOGY
LOBSCOUSE	LOCKETS	LODEN	LOGGINGS	LOID
LOBSCOUSES	LOCKFAST	LODENS	LOGIA	LOIDED
LOBSTER	LOCKFUL	LODES	LOGIC	LOIDING
LOBSTERS	LOCKFULS	LODESMAN	LOGICAL	LOIDS
LOBULAR	LOCKHOUSE	LODESMEN	LOGICALLY	LOIN
LOBULATE	LOCKHOUSES	LODESTAR	LOGICIAN	LOINCLOTH
LOBULATED	LOCKING	LODESTARS	LOGICIANS	LOINCLOTHS
LOBULE	LOCKJAW	LODESTONE	LOGICISE	LOINS
LOBULES	LOCKJAWS	LODESTONES	LOGICISED	LOIPE
LOBULI	LOCKMAN	LODGE	LOGICISES	LOIPEN
LOBULUS	LOCKMEN	LODGED	LOGICISING	LOIR
LOBUS	LOCKOUT	LODGEMENT	LOGICISM	LOIRS

LOITER	LONGBOATS	LOOKED	LOOTS	LORIC
LOITERED	LONGBOW	LOOKER	LOOVES	LORICA
LOITERER	LONGBOWS	LOOKERS	LOP	LORICAE
LOITERERS	LONGCLOTH	LOOKING	LOPE	LORICATE
LOITERING	LONGCLOTHS	LOOKISM	LOPED	LORICATED
LOITERINGS	LONGE	LOOKISMS	LOPER	LORICATES
LOITERS	LONGED	LOOKOUT	LOPERS	LORICATING
LOKE	LONGEING	LOOKOUTS	LOPES	LORICS
LOKES	LONGER	LOOKS	LOPGRASS	LORIES
LOKSHEN	LONGERON	LOOM	LOPGRASSES	LORIKEET
LOLIGO	LONGERONS	LOOMED	LOPHODONT	LORIKEETS
LOLIGOS	LONGES	LOOMING	LOPING	LORIMER
LOLIUM	LONGEST	LOOMS	LOPPED	LORIMERS
LOLIUMS	LONGEVAL	LOON	LOPPER	LORINER
LOLL	LONGEVITIES	LOONIE	LOPPERED	LORINERS
LOLLED	LONGEVITY	LOONIER	LOPPERING	LORING
LOLLER	LONGEVOUS	LOONIES	LOPPERS	LORINGS
LOLLERS	LONGHAND	LOONIEST	LOPPING	LORIOT
LOLLIES	LONGHANDS	LOONINESS	LOPPINGS	LORIOTS
LOLLING	LONGHORN	LOONINESSES	LOPS	LORIS
LOLLINGLY	LONGHORNS	LOONING	LOPSIDED	LORISES
LOLLIPOP	LONGHOUSE	LOONINGS	LOQUACITIES	LORN
LOLLIPOPS	LONGHOUSES	LOONS	LOQUACITY	LORRELL
LOLLOP	LONGICORN	LOONY	LOQUAT	LORRELLS
LOLLOPED	LONGICORNS	LOOP	LOQUATS	LORRIES
LOLLOPING	LONGING	LOOPED	LOQUITUR	LORRY
LOLLOPS	LONGINGLY	LOOPER	LOR	LORY
LOLLS	LONGINGS	LOOPERS	LORAL	LOS
LOLLY	LONGISH	LOOPHOLE	LORAN	LOSABLE
LOLLYGAG	LONGITUDE	LOOPHOLED	LORANS	LOSE
LOLLYGAGGED	LONGITUDES	LOOPHOLES	LORATE	LOSED
LOLLYGAGGING	LONGLY	LOOPHOLING	LORAZEPAM	LOSEL
LOLLYGAGS	LONGNESS	LOOPIER	LORAZEPAMS	LOSELS
LOLOG	LONGNESSES	LOOPIEST	LORCHA	LOSEN
LOLOGS	LONGS	LOOPING	LORCHAS	LOSER
LOMA	LONGSHIP	LOOPINGS	LORD	LOSERS
LOMAS	LONGSHIPS	LOOPS	LORDED	LOSES
LOMATA	LONGSHORE	LOOPY	LORDING	LOSH
LOME	LONGSOME	LOOR	LORDINGS	LOSING
LOMED	LONGUEUR	LOORD	LORDKIN	LOSINGLY
LOMENT	LONGUEURS	LOORDS	LORDKINS	LOSINGS
LOMENTA	LONGWALL	LOOS	LORDLESS	LOSS
LOMENTS	LONGWALLS	LOOSE	LORDLIER	LOSSES
LOMENTUM	LONGWAYS	LOOSED	LORDLIEST	LOSSIER
LOMES	LONGWISE	LOOSELY	LORDLING	LOSSIEST
LOMING	LONICERA	LOOSEN	LORDLINGS	LOSSMAKER
LOMPISH	LONICERAS	LOOSENED	LORDLY	LOSSMAKERS
LONE	LOO	LOOSENER	LORDOSES	LOSSY
LONELIER	LOOBIER	LOOSENERS	LORDOSIS	LOST
LONELIEST	LOOBIES	LOOSENESS	LORDOTIC	LOT
LONELY	LOOBIEST	LOOSENESSES	LORDS	LOTA
LONENESS	LOOBILY	LOOSENING	LORDSHIP	LOTAH
LONENESSES	LOOBY	LOOSENS	LORDSHIPS	LOTAHS
LONER	LOOED	LOOSER	LORDY	LOTAS
LONERS	LOOF	LOOSES	LORE	LOTE
LONESOME	LOOFA	LOOSEST	LOREL	LOTES
LONESOMES	LOOFAH	LOOSING	LORELS	LOTH
LONG	LOOFAHS	LOOT	LORES	LOTHEFULL
LONGA	LOOFAS	LOOTED	LORETTE	LOTHER
LONGAEVAL	LOOFFUL	LOOTEN	LORETTES	LOTHEST
LONGAN	LOOFFULS	LOOTER	LORGNETTE	LOTHFULL
LONGANS	LOOFS	LOOTERS	LORGNETTES	LOTIC
LONGAS	LOOING	LOOTING	LORGNON	LOTION
LONGBOAT	LOOK	LOOTINGS	LORGNONS	LOTIONS

The Chambers Dictionary is the authority for many longer words; see *OSW* Introduction, page xii

LOTO	LOURING	LOVINGS	LOXODROME	LUCIDNESSES
LOTOS	LOURINGLY	LOW	LOXODROMES	LUCIFER
LOTOSES	LOURINGS	LOWAN	LOXODROMIES	LUCIFERIN
LOTS	LOURS	LOWANS	LOXODROMY	LUCIFERINS
LOTTED	LOURY	LOWBOY	LOXYGEN	LUCIFERS
LOTTERIES	LOUSE	LOWBOYS	LOXYGENS	LUCIGEN
LOTTERY	LOUSED	LOWE	LOY	LUCIGENS
LOTTING	LOUSES	LOWED	LOYAL	LUCK
LOTTO	LOUSIER	LOWER	LOYALIST	LUCKEN
LOTTOS	LOUSIEST	LOWERED	LOYALISTS	LUCKIE
LOTUS	LOUSILY	LOWERIER	LOYALLER	LUCKIER
LOTUSES	LOUSINESS	LOWERIEST	LOYALLEST	LUCKIES
LOUCHE	LOUSINESSES	LOWERING	LOYALLY	LUCKIEST
LOUCHELY	LOUSING	LOWERINGS	LOYALTIES	LUCKILY
LOUD	LOUSY	LOWERMOST	LOYALTY	LUCKINESS
LOUDEN	LOUT	LOWERS	LOYS	LUCKINESSES
LOUDENED	LOUTED	LOWERY	LOZELL	LUCKLESS
LOUDENING	LOUTING	LOWES	LOZELLS	LUCKS
LOUDENS	LOUTISH	LOWEST	LOZEN	LUCKY
LOUDER	LOUTISHLY	LOWING	LOZENGE	LUCRATIVE
LOUDEST	LOUTS	LOWINGS	LOZENGED	LUCRE
LOUDISH	LOUVER	LOWLAND	LOZENGES	LUCRES
LOUDLY	LOUVERED	LOWLANDER	LOZENGY	LUCTATION
LOUDMOUTH	LOUVERS	LOWLANDERS	LOZENS	LUCTATIONS
LOUDMOUTHS	LOUVRE	LOWLANDS	LUAU	LUCUBRATE
LOUDNESS	LOUVRED	LOWLIER	LUAUS	LUCUBRATED
LOUDNESSES	LOUVRES	LOWLIEST	LUBBARD	LUCUBRATES
LOUGH	LOVABLE	LOWLIGHT	LUBBARDS	LUCUBRATING
LOUGHS	LOVAGE	LOWLIGHTED	LUBBER	LUCULENT
LOUIS	LOVAGES	LOWLIGHTING	LUBBERLY	LUCUMA
LOUN	LOVAT	LOWLIGHTS	LUBBERS	LUCUMAS
LOUND	LOVATS	LOWLIHEAD	LUBFISH	LUCUMO
LOUNDED	LOVE	LOWLIHEADS	LUBFISHES	LUCUMONES
LOUNDER	LOVEABLE	LOWLILY	LUBRA	LUCUMOS
LOUNDERED	LOVEBIRD	LOWLINESS	LUBRAS	LUD
LOUNDERING	LOVEBIRDS	LOWLINESSES	LUBRIC	LUDIC
LOUNDERINGS	LOVEBITE	LOWLY	LUBRICAL	LUDICALLY
LOUNDERS	LOVEBITES	LOWN	LUBRICANT	LUDICROUS
LOUNDING	LOVED	LOWND	LUBRICANTS	LUDO
LOUNDS	LOVELESS	LOWNDED	LUBRICATE	LUDOS
LOUNED	LOVELIER	LOWNDING	LUBRICATED	LUDS
LOUNGE	LOVELIES	LOWNDS	LUBRICATES	LUDSHIP
LOUNGED	LOVELIEST	LOWNE	LUBRICATING	LUDSHIPS
LOUNGER	LOVELIGHT	LOWNED	LUBRICITIES	LUES
LOUNGERS	LOVELIGHTS	LOWNES	LUBRICITY	LUETIC
LOUNGES	LOVELILY	LOWNESS	LUBRICOUS	LUFF
LOUNGING	LOVELOCK	LOWNESSES	LUCARNE	LUFFA
LOUNGINGS	LOVELOCKS	LOWNING	LUCARNES	LUFFAS
LOUNING	LOVELORN	LOWNS	LUCE	LUFFED
LOUNS	LOVELY	LOWS	LUCENCIES	LUFFING
LOUP	LOVEMAKER	LOWSE	LUCENCY	LUFFS
LOUPE	LOVEMAKERS	LOWSER	LUCENT	LUG
LOUPED	LOVER	LOWSES	LUCERN	LUGE
LOUPEN	LOVERED	LOWSEST	LUCERNE	LUGED
LOUPES	LOVERLESS	LOWSING	LUCERNES	LUGEING
LOUPING	LOVERLY	LOWSIT	LUCERNS	LUGEINGS
LOUPIT	LOVERS	LOWT	LUCES	LUGER
LOUPS	LOVES	LOWTED	LUCID	LUGERS
LOUR	LOVESICK	LOWTING	LUCIDER	LUGES
LOURE	LOVESOME	LOWTS	LUCIDEST	LUGGABLE
LOURED	LOVEY	LOWVELD	LUCIDITIES	LUGGABLES
LOURES	LOVEYS	LOWVELDS	LUCIDITY	LUGGAGE
LOURIER	LOVING	LOX	LUCIDLY	LUGGAGES
LOURIEST	LOVINGLY	LOXES	LUCIDNESS	LUGGED

LUGGER	LUMINE	LUNCHEONING	LURDANES	LUSTILY
LUGGERS	LUMINED	LUNCHEONS	LURDANS	LUSTINESS
LUGGIE	LUMINES	LUNCHER	LURDEN	LUSTINESSES
LUGGIES	LUMINESCE	LUNCHERS	LURDENS	LUSTING
LUGGING	LUMINESCED	LUNCHES	LURE	LUSTIQUE
LUGHOLE	LUMINESCES	LUNCHING	LURED	LUSTLESS
LUGHOLES	LUMINESCING	LUNE	LURES	LUSTRA
LUGING	LUMINING	LUNES	LURGI	LUSTRAL
LUGINGS	LUMINIST	LUNETTE	LURGIES	LUSTRATE
LUGS	LUMINISTS	LUNETTES	LURGIS	LUSTRATED
LUGSAIL	LUMINOUS	LUNG	LURGY	LUSTRATES
LUGSAILS	LUMME	LUNGE	LURID	LUSTRATING
LUGWORM	LUMMIER	LUNGED	LURIDER	LUSTRE
LUGWORMS	LUMMIEST	LUNGEING	LURIDEST	LUSTRED
LUIT	LUMMOX	LUNGES	LURIDLY	LUSTRES
LUITEN	LUMMOXES	LUNGFUL	LURIDNESS	LUSTRINE
LUKE	LUMMY	LUNGFULS	LURIDNESSES	LUSTRINES
LUKEWARM	LUMP	LUNGI	LURING	LUSTRING
LULIBUB	LUMPED	LUNGIE	LURK	LUSTRINGS
LULIBUBS	LUMPEN	LUNGIES	LURKED	LUSTROUS
LULL	LUMPENLY	LUNGING	LURKER	LUSTRUM
LULLABIED	LUMPER	LUNGIS	LURKERS	LUSTRUMS
LULLABIES	LUMPERS	LUNGS	LURKING	LUSTS
LULLABY	LUMPFISH	LUNGWORT	LURKINGS	LUSTY
LULLABYING	LUMPFISHES	LUNGWORTS	LURKS	LUTANIST
LULLED	LUMPIER	LUNISOLAR	LURRIES	LUTANISTS
LULLING	LUMPIEST	LUNITIDAL	LURRY	LUTE
LULLS	LUMPILY	LUNKER	LURS	LUTEAL
LULU	LUMPINESS	LUNKERS	LURVE	LUTECIUM
LULUS	LUMPINESSES	LUNKHEAD	LURVES	LUTECIUMS
LUM	LUMPING	LUNKHEADS	LUSCIOUS	LUTED
LUMBAGO	LUMPISH	LUNT	LUSH	LUTEIN
LUMBAGOS	LUMPISHLY	LUNTED	LUSHED	LUTEINISE
LUMBANG	LUMPKIN	LUNTING	LUSHER	LUTEINISED
LUMBANGS	LUMPKINS	LUNTS	LUSHERS	LUTEINISES
LUMBAR	LUMPS	LUNULA	LUSHES	LUTEINISING
LUMBER	LUMPY	LUNULAE	LUSHEST	LUTEINIZE
LUMBERED	LUMS	LUNULAR	LUSHIER	LUTEINIZED
LUMBERER	LUNA	LUNULATE	LUSHIEST	LUTEINIZES
LUMBERERS	LUNACIES	LUNULATED	LUSHING	LUTEINIZING
LUMBERING	LUNACY	LUNULE	LUSHLY	LUTEINS
LUMBERINGS	LUNANAUT	LUNULES	LUSHNESS	LUTENIST
LUMBERLY	LUNANAUTS	LUNYIE	LUSHNESSES	LUTENISTS
LUMBERMAN	LUNAR	LUNYIES	LUSHY	LUTEOLIN
LUMBERMEN	LUNARIAN	LUPIN	LUSK	LUTEOLINS
LUMBERS	LUNARIANS	LUPINE	LUSKED	LUTEOLOUS
LUMBRICAL	LUNARIES	LUPINES	LUSKING	LUTEOUS
LUMBRICALS	LUNARIST	LUPINS	LUSKISH	LUTER
LUMBRICI	LUNARISTS	LUPPEN	LUSKS	LUTERS
LUMBRICUS	LUNARNAUT	LUPULIN	LUST	LUTES
LUMBRICUSES	LUNARNAUTS	LUPULINE	LUSTED	LUTESCENT
LUMEN	LUNARS	LUPULINIC	LUSTER	LUTETIUM
LUMENAL	LUNARY	LUPULINS	LUSTERED	LUTETIUMS
LUMENS	LUNAS	LUPUS	LUSTERING	LUTHERN
LUMINA	LUNATE	LUPUSES	LUSTERS	LUTHERNS
LUMINAIRE	LUNATED	LUR	LUSTFUL	LUTHIER
LUMINAIRES	LUNATIC	LURCH	LUSTFULLY	LUTHIERS
LUMINAL	LUNATICS	LURCHED	LUSTICK	LUTING
LUMINANCE	LUNATION	LURCHER	LUSTIER	LUTINGS
LUMINANCES	LUNATIONS	LURCHERS	LUSTIEST	LUTIST
LUMINANT	LUNCH	LURCHES	LUSTIHEAD	LUTISTS
LUMINANTS	LUNCHED	LURCHING	LUSTIHEADS	LUTTEN
LUMINARIES	LUNCHEON	LURDAN	LUSTIHOOD	LUTZ
LUMINARY	LUNCHEONED	LURDANE	LUSTIHOODS	LUTZES

LUV	LUZZES	LYME	LYNXES	LYSERGIDE
LUVS	LYAM	LYMES	LYOMEROUS	LYSERGIDES
LUVVIE	LYAMS	LYMITER	LYONNAISE	LYSES
LUVVIES	LYART	LYMITERS	LYOPHIL	LYSIGENIC
LUVVY	LYCEE	LYMPH	LYOPHILE	LYSIMETER
LUX	LYCEES	LYMPHAD	LYOPHILIC	LYSIMETERS
LUXATE	LYCEUM	LYMPHADS	LYOPHOBE	LYSIN
LUXATED	LYCEUMS	LYMPHATIC	LYOPHOBIC	LYSINE
LUXATES	LYCHEE	LYMPHATICS	LYRATE	LYSINES
LUXATING	LYCHEES	LYMPHOID	LYRATED	LYSING
LUXATION	LYCHGATE	LYMPHOMA	LYRE	LYSINS
LUXATIONS	LYCHGATES	LYMPHOMAS	LYRES	LYSIS
LUXE	LYCHNIS	LYMPHOMATA	LYRIC	LYSOL
LUXES	LYCHNISES	LYMPHS	LYRICAL	LYSOLS
LUXMETER	LYCOPOD	LYMS	LYRICALLY	LYSOSOME
LUXMETERS	LYCOPODS	LYNAGE	LYRICISM	LYSOSOMES
LUXURIANT	LYDDITE	LYNAGES	LYRICISMS	LYSOZYME
LUXURIATE	LYDDITES	LYNCEAN	LYRICIST	LYSOZYMES
LUXURIATED	LYE	LYNCH	LYRICISTS	LYSSA
LUXURIATES	LYES	LYNCHED	LYRICON	LYSSAS
LUXURIATING	LYFULL	LYNCHES	LYRICONS	LYTE
LUXURIES	LYING	LYNCHET	LYRICS	LYTED
LUXURIOUS	LYINGLY	LYNCHETS	LYRIFORM	LYTES
LUXURIST	LYINGS	LYNCHING	LYRISM	LYTHE
LUXURISTS	LYKEWAKE	LYNCHPIN	LYRISMS	LYTHES
LUXURY	LYKEWAKES	LYNCHPINS	LYRIST	LYTING
LUZ	LYKEWALK	LYNE	LYRISTS	LYTTA
LUZERN	LYKEWALKS	LYNES	LYSE	LYTTAE
LUZERNS	LYM	LYNX	LYSED	LYTTAS

M

MA	MACERATORS	MACRAMIS	MADDING	MADWOMAN
MAA	MACERS	MACRO	MADDINGLY	MADWOMEN
MAAED	MACES	MACROBIAN	MADDOCK	MADWORT
MAAING	MACHAIR	MACROCODE	MADDOCKS	MADWORTS
MAAR	MACHAIRS	MACROCODES	MADE	MADZOON
MAARS	MACHAN	MACROCOPIES	MADEFIED	MADZOONS
MAAS	MACHANS	MACROCOPY	MADEFIES	MAE
MAATJES	MACHETE	MACROCOSM	MADEFY	MAELID
MAC	MACHETES	MACROCOSMS	MADEFYING	MAELIDS
MACABRE	MACHINATE	MACROCYTE	MADELEINE	MAELSTROM
MACACO	MACHINATED	MACROCYTES	MADELEINES	MAELSTROMS
MACACOS	MACHINATES	MACRODOME	MADERISE	MAENAD
MACADAM	MACHINATING	MACRODOMES	MADERISED	MAENADIC
MACADAMIA	MACHINE	MACROLOGIES	MADERISES	MAENADS
MACADAMIAS	MACHINED	MACROLOGY	MADERISING	MAESTOSO
MACADAMS	MACHINERIES	MACRON	MADERIZE	MAESTRI
MACAHUBA	MACHINERY	MACRONS	MADERIZED	MAESTRO
MACAHUBAS	MACHINES	MACROPOD	MADERIZES	MAESTROS
MACALLUM	MACHINING	MACROPODS	MADERIZING	MAFFIA
MACALLUMS	MACHINIST	MACROS	MADGE	MAFFIAS
MACAQUE	MACHINISTS	MACRURAL	MADGES	MAFFICK
MACAQUES	MACHISMO	MACRUROUS	MADHOUSE	MAFFICKED
MACARISE	MACHISMOS	MACS	MADHOUSES	MAFFICKER
MACARISED	MACHMETER	MACTATION	MADID	MAFFICKERS
MACARISES	MACHMETERS	MACTATIONS	MADLING	MAFFICKING
MACARISING	MACHO	MACULA	MADLINGS	MAFFICKINGS
MACARISM	MACHOS	MACULAE	MADLY	MAFFICKS
MACARISMS	MACHREE	MACULAR	MADMAN	MAFFLED
MACARIZE	MACHREES	MACULATE	MADMEN	MAFFLIN
MACARIZED	MACHZOR	MACULATED	MADNESS	MAFFLING
MACARIZES	MACHZORIM	MACULATES	MADNESSES	MAFFLINGS
MACARIZING	MACING	MACULATING	MADOQUA	MAFFLINS
MACARONI	MACINTOSH	MACULE	MADOQUAS	MAFIA
MACARONIC	MACINTOSHES	MACULES	MADRAS	MAFIAS
MACARONICS	MACK	MACULOSE	MADRASA	MAFIC
MACARONIES	MACKEREL	MAD	MADRASAH	MAFICS
MACARONIS	MACKERELS	MADAM	MADRASAHS	MAFIOSI
MACAROON	MACKINAW	MADAME	MADRASAS	MAFIOSO
MACAROONS	MACKINAWS	MADAMED	MADRASES	MAG
MACASSAR	MACKLE	MADAMING	MADRASSA	MAGALOG
MACASSARS	MACKLED	MADAMS	MADRASSAH	MAGALOGS
MACAW	MACKLES	MADAROSES	MADRASSAHS	MAGAZINE
MACAWS	MACKLING	MADAROSIS	MADRASSAS	MAGAZINES
MACCHIE	MACKS	MADBRAIN	MADREPORE	MAGDALEN
MACE	MACLE	MADCAP	MADREPORES	MAGDALENE
MACED	MACLED	MADCAPS	MADRIGAL	MAGDALENES
MACEDOINE	MACLES	MADDED	MADRIGALS	MAGDALENS
MACEDOINES	MACON	MADDEN	MADRONA	MAGE
MACER	MACONS	MADDENED	MADRONAS	MAGENTA
MACERATE	MACOYA	MADDENING	MADRONE	MAGENTAS
MACERATED	MACOYAS	MADDENS	MADRONES	MAGES
MACERATES	MACRAME	MADDER	MADRONO	MAGESHIP
MACERATING	MACRAMES	MADDERS	MADRONOS	MAGESHIPS
MACERATOR	MACRAMI	MADDEST	MADS	MAGG

The Chambers Dictionary is the authority for many longer words; see *OSW* Introduction, page xii

MAGGED	MAGNETIZES	MAHSEERS	MAILSHOTS	MAIST
MAGGING	MAGNETIZING	MAHSIR	MAILSHOTTED	MAISTER
MAGGOT	MAGNETO	MAHSIRS	MAILSHOTTING	MAISTERED
MAGGOTIER	MAGNETON	MAHUA	MAILVAN	MAISTERING
MAGGOTIEST	MAGNETONS	MAHUAS	MAILVANS	MAISTERS
MAGGOTS	MAGNETOS	MAHWA	MAIM	MAISTRIES
MAGGOTY	MAGNETRON	MAHWAS	MAIMED	MAISTRING
MAGGS	MAGNETRONS	MAHZOR	MAIMING	MAISTRINGS
MAGI	MAGNETS	MAHZORIM	MAIMINGS	MAISTRY
MAGIAN	MAGNIFIC	MAID	MAIMS	MAIZE
MAGIANISM	MAGNIFICO	MAIDAN	MAIN	MAIZES
MAGIANISMS	MAGNIFICOES	MAIDANS	MAINBOOM	MAJESTIC
MAGIANS	MAGNIFIED	MAIDED	MAINBOOMS	MAJESTIES
MAGIC	MAGNIFIER	MAIDEN	MAINBRACE	MAJESTY
MAGICAL	MAGNIFIERS	MAIDENISH	MAINBRACES	MAJLIS
MAGICALLY	MAGNIFIES	MAIDENLY	MAINDOOR	MAJLISES
MAGICIAN	MAGNIFY	MAIDENS	MAINDOORS	MAJOLICA
MAGICIANS	MAGNIFYING	MAIDHOOD	MAINED	MAJOLICAS
MAGICKED	MAGNITUDE	MAIDHOODS	MAINER	MAJOR
MAGICKING	MAGNITUDES	MAIDING	MAINEST	MAJORAT
MAGICS	MAGNOLIA	MAIDISH	MAINFRAME	MAJORATS
MAGILP	MAGNOLIAS	MAIDISM	MAINFRAMES	MAJORED
MAGILPS	MAGNON	MAIDISMS	MAINING	MAJORETTE
MAGISM	MAGNONS	MAIDLESS	MAINLAND	MAJORETTES
MAGISMS	MAGNOX	MAIDS	MAINLANDS	MAJORING
MAGISTER	MAGNOXES	MAIEUTIC	MAINLINE	MAJORITIES
MAGISTERIES	MAGNUM	MAIEUTICS	MAINLINED	MAJORITY
MAGISTERS	MAGNUMS	MAIGRE	MAINLINER	MAJORS
MAGISTERY	MAGOT	MAIGRES	MAINLINERS	MAJORSHIP
MAGISTRAL	MAGOTS	MAIK	MAINLINES	MAJORSHIPS
MAGISTRALS	MAGPIE	MAIKO	MAINLINING	MAJUSCULE
MAGLEV	MAGPIES	MAIKOS	MAINLININGS	MAJUSCULES
MAGMA	MAGS	MAIKS	MAINLY	MAK
MAGMAS	MAGSMAN	MAIL	MAINMAST	MAKABLE
MAGMATA	MAGSMEN	MAILABLE	MAINMASTS	MAKAR
MAGMATIC	MAGUEY	MAILBAG	MAINOR	MAKARS
MAGNALIUM	MAGUEYS	MAILBAGS	MAINORS	MAKE
MAGNALIUMS	MAGUS	MAILBOX	MAINOUR	MAKEABLE
MAGNATE	MAGYAR	MAILBOXES	MAINOURS	MAKEBATE
MAGNATES	MAHARAJA	MAILE	MAINPRISE	MAKEBATES
MAGNES	MAHARAJAH	MAILED	MAINPRISES	MAKELESS
MAGNESES	MAHARAJAHS	MAILER	MAINS	MAKEOVER
MAGNESIA	MAHARAJAS	MAILERS	MAINSAIL	MAKEOVERS
MAGNESIAN	MAHARANEE	MAILES	MAINSAILS	MAKER
MAGNESIAS	MAHARANEES	MAILGRAM	MAINSHEET	MAKERS
MAGNESITE	MAHARANI	MAILGRAMMED	MAINSHEETS	MAKES
MAGNESITES	MAHARANIS	MAILGRAMMING	MAINSTAY	MAKESHIFT
MAGNESIUM	MAHARISHI	MAILGRAMS	MAINSTAYS	MAKESHIFTS
MAGNESIUMS	MAHARISHIS	MAILING	MAINTAIN	MAKIMONO
MAGNET	MAHATMA	MAILINGS	MAINTAINED	MAKIMONOS
MAGNETIC	MAHATMAS	MAILLOT	MAINTAINING	MAKING
MAGNETICS	MAHLSTICK	MAILLOTS	MAINTAINS	MAKINGS
MAGNETISE	MAHLSTICKS	MAILMAN	MAINTOP	MAKO
MAGNETISED	MAHMAL	MAILMEN	MAINTOPS	MAKOS
MAGNETISES	MAHMALS	MAILMERGE	MAINYARD	MAKS
MAGNETISING	MAHOE	MAILMERGED	MAINYARDS	MAL
MAGNETISM	MAHOES	MAILMERGES	MAIOLICA	MALACHITE
MAGNETISMS	MAHOGANIES	MAILMERGING	MAIOLICAS	MALACHITES
MAGNETIST	MAHOGANY	MAILROOM	MAIR	MALACIA
MAGNETISTS	MAHONIA	MAILROOMS	MAIRE	MALACIAS
MAGNETITE	MAHONIAS	MAILS	MAIRES	MALADIES
MAGNETITES	MAHOUT	MAILSACK	MAIRS	MALADROIT
MAGNETIZE	MAHOUTS	MAILSACKS	MAISE	MALADY
MAGNETIZED	MAHSEER	MAILSHOT	MAISES	MALAGUENA

MALAGUENAS	MALICING	MALMAG	MAMILLAE	MANAGES
MALAISE	MALICIOUS	MALMAGS	MAMILLAR	MANAGING
MALAISES	MALIGN	MALMS	MAMILLARY	MANAKIN
MALAMUTE	MALIGNANT	MALMSEY	MAMILLATE	MANAKINS
MALAMUTES	MALIGNANTS	MALMSEYS	MAMMA	MANANA
MALANDER	MALIGNED	MALMSTONE	MAMMAE	MANANAS
MALANDERS	MALIGNER	MALMSTONES	MAMMAL	MANAS
MALAPERT	MALIGNERS	MALODOUR	MAMMALIAN	MANATEE
MALAR	MALIGNING	MALODOURS	MAMMALOGIES	MANATEES
MALARIA	MALIGNITIES	MALONATE	MAMMALOGY	MANATI
MALARIAL	MALIGNITY	MALONATES	MAMMALS	MANATIS
MALARIAN	MALIGNLY	MALS	MAMMARY	MANCALA
MALARIAS	MALIGNS	MALSTICK	MAMMAS	MANCALAS
MALARIOUS	MALIK	MALSTICKS	MAMMATE	MANCANDO
MALARKEY	MALIKS	MALT	MAMMEE	MANCHE
MALARKEYS	MALINGER	MALTALENT	MAMMEES	MANCHES
MALARKIES	MALINGERED	MALTALENTS	MAMMER	MANCHET
MALARKY	MALINGERIES	MALTASE	MAMMERED	MANCHETS
MALARS	MALINGERING	MALTASES	MAMMERING	MANCIPATE
MALATE	MALINGERS	MALTED	MAMMERS	MANCIPATED
MALATES	MALINGERY	MALTHA	MAMMET	MANCIPATES
MALAX	MALIS	MALTHAS	MAMMETRIES	MANCIPATING
MALAXAGE	MALISM	MALTIER	MAMMETRY	MANCIPLE
MALAXAGES	MALISMS	MALTIEST	MAMMETS	MANCIPLES
MALAXATE	MALISON	MALTING	MAMMIES	MANCUS
MALAXATED	MALISONS	MALTINGS	MAMMIFER	MANCUSES
MALAXATES	MALIST	MALTMAN	MAMMIFERS	MAND
MALAXATING	MALKIN	MALTMEN	MAMMIFORM	MANDALA
MALAXATOR	MALKINS	MALTOSE	MAMMILLA	MANDALAS
MALAXATORS	MALL	MALTOSES	MAMMILLAE	MANDAMUS
MALAXED	MALLAM	MALTREAT	MAMMOCK	MANDAMUSES
MALAXES	MALLAMS	MALTREATED	MAMMOCKED	MANDARIN
MALAXING	MALLANDER	MALTREATING	MAMMOCKING	MANDARINE
MALE	MALLANDERS	MALTREATS	MAMMOCKS	MANDARINES
MALEATE	MALLARD	MALTS	MAMMOGRAM	MANDARINS
MALEATES	MALLARDS	MALTSTER	MAMMOGRAMS	MANDATARIES
MALEDICT	MALLEABLE	MALTSTERS	MAMMON	MANDATARY
MALEDICTED	MALLEATE	MALTWORM	MAMMONISH	MANDATE
MALEDICTING	MALLEATED	MALTWORMS	MAMMONISM	MANDATED
MALEDICTS	MALLEATES	MALTY	MAMMONISMS	MANDATES
MALEFFECT	MALLEATING	MALVA	MAMMONIST	MANDATING
MALEFFECTS	MALLECHO	MALVAS	MAMMONISTS	MANDATOR
MALEFIC	MALLECHOS	MALVASIA	MAMMONITE	MANDATORIES
MALEFICE	MALLED	MALVASIAS	MAMMONITES	MANDATORS
MALEFICES	MALLEE	MALVESIE	MAMMONS	MANDATORY
MALEIC	MALLEES	MALVESIES	MAMMOTH	MANDIBLE
MALEMUTE	MALLEI	MALVOISIE	MAMMOTHS	MANDIBLES
MALEMUTES	MALLEMUCK	MALVOISIES	MAMMY	MANDILION
MALENGINE	MALLEMUCKS	MAM	MAMS	MANDILIONS
MALENGINES	MALLENDER	MAMA	MAMSELLE	MANDIOC
MALES	MALLENDERS	MAMAS	MAMSELLES	MANDIOCA
MALFORMED	MALLEOLAR	MAMBA	MAMZER	MANDIOCAS
MALGRADO	MALLEOLI	MAMBAS	MAMZERIM	MANDIOCCA
MALGRE	MALLEOLUS	MAMBO	MAMZERS	MANDIOCCAS
MALGRED	MALLEOLUSES	MAMBOED	MAN	MANDIOCS
MALGRES	MALLET	MAMBOING	MANA	MANDIR
MALGRING	MALLETS	MAMBOS	MANACLE	MANDIRA
MALI	MALLEUS	MAMEE	MANACLED	MANDIRAS
MALIC	MALLEUSES	MAMEES	MANACLES	MANDIRS
MALICE	MALLING	MAMELON	MANACLING	MANDOLA
MALICED	MALLOW	MAMELONS	MANAGE	MANDOLAS
MALICES	MALLOWS	MAMELUCO	MANAGED	MANDOLIN
MALICHO	MALLS	MAMELUCOS	MANAGER	MANDOLINE
MALICHOS	MALM	MAMILLA	MANAGERS	MANDOLINES

MANDOLINS	MANGIER	MANIKIN	MANOMETRIES	MANTOES
MANDOM	MANGIEST	MANIKINS	MANOMETRY	MANTOS
MANDOMS	MANGINESS	MANILA	MANOR	MANTRA
MANDORA	MANGINESSES	MANILAS	MANORIAL	MANTRAM
MANDORAS	MANGING	MANILLA	MANORS	MANTRAMS
MANDORLA	MANGLE	MANILLAS	MANOS	MANTRAP
MANDORLAS	MANGLED	MANILLE	MANPACK	MANTRAPS
MANDRAKE	MANGLER	MANILLES	MANPACKS	MANTRAS
MANDRAKES	MANGLERS	MANIOC	MANPOWER	MANTUA
MANDREL	MANGLES	MANIOCS	MANPOWERS	MANTUAS
MANDRELS	MANGLING	MANIPLE	MANQUE	MANTY
MANDRIL	MANGO	MANIPLES	MANRED	MANUAL
MANDRILL	MANGOES	MANIPLIES	MANREDS	MANUALLY
MANDRILLS	MANGOLD	MANIPULAR	MANRENT	MANUALS
MANDRILS	MANGOLDS	MANIPULARS	MANRENTS	MANUBRIA
MANDUCATE	MANGONEL	MANIS	MANRIDER	MANUBRIAL
MANDUCATED	MANGONELS	MANITO	MANRIDERS	MANUBRIUM
MANDUCATES	MANGOSTAN	MANITOS	MANRIDING	MANUKA
MANDUCATING	MANGOSTANS	MANITOU	MANS	MANUKAS
MANDYLION	MANGOUSTE	MANITOUS	MANSARD	MANUL
MANDYLIONS	MANGOUSTES	MANJACK	MANSARDS	MANULS
MANE	MANGROVE	MANJACKS	MANSE	MANUMEA
MANED	MANGROVES	MANKIER	MANSES	MANUMEAS
MANEGE	MANGS	MANKIEST	MANSHIFT	MANUMIT
MANEGED	MANGY	MANKIND	MANSHIFTS	MANUMITS
MANEGES	MANHANDLE	MANKINDS	MANSION	MANUMITTED
MANEGING	MANHANDLED	MANKY	MANSIONS	MANUMITTING
MANEH	MANHANDLES	MANLIER	MANSONRIES	MANURANCE
MANEHS	MANHANDLING	MANLIEST	MANSONRY	MANURANCES
MANELESS	MANHOLE	MANLINESS	MANSUETE	MANURE
MANENT	MANHOLES	MANLINESSES	MANSWORN	MANURED
MANES	MANHOOD	MANLY	MANTA	MANURER
MANET	MANHOODS	MANNA	MANTAS	MANURERS
MANEUVER	MANHUNT	MANNAS	MANTEAU	MANURES
MANEUVERED	MANHUNTS	MANNED	MANTEAUS	MANURIAL
MANEUVERING	MANI	MANNEQUIN	MANTEAUX	MANURING
MANEUVERS	MANIA	MANNEQUINS	MANTEEL	MANURINGS
MANFUL	MANIAC	MANNER	MANTEELS	MANUS
MANFULLY	MANIACAL	MANNERED	MANTEL	MANY
MANG	MANIACS	MANNERISM	MANTELET	MANYATA
MANGA	MANIAS	MANNERISMS	MANTELETS	MANYATAS
MANGABEY	MANIC	MANNERIST	MANTELS	MANYATTA
MANGABEYS	MANICALLY	MANNERISTS	MANTIC	MANYATTAS
MANGAL	MANICURE	MANNERLY	MANTICORA	MANYFOLD
MANGALS	MANICURED	MANNERS	MANTICORAS	MANYPLIES
MANGANATE	MANICURES	MANNIKIN	MANTICORE	MANZANITA
MANGANATES	MANICURING	MANNIKINS	MANTICORES	MANZANITAS
MANGANESE	MANIES	MANNING	MANTID	MANZELLO
MANGANESES	MANIFEST	MANNISH	MANTIDS	MANZELLOS
MANGANIC	MANIFESTED	MANNITE	MANTIES	MAORMOR
MANGANITE	MANIFESTING	MANNITES	MANTILLA	MAORMORS
MANGANITES	MANIFESTO	MANNITOL	MANTILLAS	MAP
MANGANOUS	MANIFESTOED	MANNITOLS	MANTIS	MAPLE
MANGAS	MANIFESTOES	MANNOSE	MANTISES	MAPLES
MANGE	MANIFESTOING	MANNOSES	MANTISSA	MAPPED
MANGED	MANIFESTOS	MANO	MANTISSAS	MAPPEMOND
MANGEL	MANIFESTS	MANOAO	MANTLE	MAPPEMONDS
MANGELS	MANIFOLD	MANOAOS	MANTLED	MAPPER
MANGER	MANIFOLDED	MANOEUVRE	MANTLES	MAPPERIES
MANGERS	MANIFOLDING	MANOEUVRED	MANTLET	MAPPERS
MANGES	MANIFOLDS	MANOEUVRES	MANTLETS	MAPPERY
MANGETOUT	MANIFORM	MANOEUVRING	MANTLING	MAPPING
MANGETOUTS	MANIHOC	MANOMETER	MANTLINGS	MAPPINGS
MANGEY	MANIHOCS	MANOMETERS	MANTO	MAPPIST

The Chambers Dictionary is the authority for many longer words; see *OSW* Introduction, page xii

MAPPISTS	MARCHESA	MARIDS	MARKKA	MAROQUIN
MAPS	MARCHESAS	MARIES	MARKKAA	MAROQUINS
MAPSTICK	MARCHESE	MARIGOLD	MARKKAS	MAROR
MAPSTICKS	MARCHESES	MARIGOLDS	MARKMAN	MARORS
MAPWISE	MARCHESI	MARIGRAM	MARKMEN	MARPLOT
MAQUETTE	MARCHING	MARIGRAMS	MARKS	MARPLOTS
MAQUETTES	MARCHMAN	MARIGRAPH	MARKSMAN	MARQUE
MAQUI	MARCHMEN	MARIGRAPHS	MARKSMEN	MARQUEE
MAQUIS	MARCHPANE	MARIHUANA	MARL	MARQUEES
MAQUISARD	MARCHPANES	MARIHUANAS	MARLE	MARQUES
MAQUISARDS	MARCONI	MARIJUANA	MARLED	MARQUESS
MAR	MARCONIED	MARIJUANAS	MARLES	MARQUESSES
MARA	MARCONIING	MARIMBA	MARLIER	MARQUETRIES
MARABOU	MARCONIS	MARIMBAS	MARLIEST	MARQUETRY
MARABOUS	MARCS	MARINA	MARLIN	MARQUIS
MARABOUT	MARD	MARINADE	MARLINE	MARQUISE
MARABOUTS	MARDIED	MARINADED	MARLINES	MARQUISES
MARACA	MARDIER	MARINADES	MARLING	MARRAM
MARACAS	MARDIES	MARINADING	MARLINGS	MARRAMS
MARAE	MARDIEST	MARINAS	MARLINS	MARRED
MARAES	MARDY	MARINATE	MARLS	MARRELS
MARAGING	MARDYING	MARINATED	MARLSTONE	MARRIAGE
MARAGINGS	MARE	MARINATES	MARLSTONES	MARRIAGES
MARAH	MAREMMA	MARINATING	MARLY	MARRIED
MARAHS	MAREMMAS	MARINE	MARM	MARRIER
MARAS	MARES	MARINER	MARMALADE	MARRIERS
MARASMIC	MARESCHAL	MARINERA	MARMALADES	MARRIES
MARASMUS	MARESCHALS	MARINERAS	MARMARISE	MARRING
MARASMUSES	MARG	MARINERS	MARMARISED	MARROW
MARATHON	MARGARIC	MARINES	MARMARISES	MARROWED
MARATHONS	MARGARIN	MARINIERE	MARMARISING	MARROWFAT
MARAUD	MARGARINE	MARIPOSA	MARMARIZE	MARROWFATS
MARAUDED	MARGARINES	MARIPOSAS	MARMARIZED	MARROWING
MARAUDER	MARGARINS	MARISCHAL	MARMARIZES	MARROWISH
MARAUDERS	MARGARITA	MARISCHALLED	MARMARIZING	MARROWS
MARAUDING	MARGARITAS	MARISCHALLING	MARMELISE	MARROWSKIED
MARAUDS	MARGARITE	MARISCHALS	MARMELISED	MARROWSKIES
MARAVEDI	MARGARITES	MARISH	MARMELISES	MARROWSKY
MARAVEDIS	MARGAY	MARISHES	MARMELISING	MARROWSKYING
MARBLE	MARGAYS	MARITAGE	MARMELIZE	MARROWY
MARBLED	MARGE	MARITAGES	MARMELIZED	MARRUM
MARBLER	MARGENT	MARITAL	MARMELIZES	MARRUMS
MARBLERS	MARGENTED	MARITALLY	MARMELIZING	MARRY
MARBLES	MARGENTING	MARITIME	MARMITE	MARRYING
MARBLIER	MARGENTS	MARJORAM	MARMITES	MARRYINGS
MARBLIEST	MARGES	MARJORAMS	MARMOREAL	MARS
MARBLING	MARGIN	MARK	MARMOSE	MARSH
MARBLINGS	MARGINAL	MARKED	MARMOSES	MARSHAL
MARBLY	MARGINALS	MARKEDLY	MARMOSET	MARSHALCIES
MARC	MARGINATE	MARKER	MARMOSETS	MARSHALCY
MARCASITE	MARGINED	MARKERS	MARMOT	MARSHALLED
MARCASITES	MARGINING	MARKET	MARMOTS	MARSHALLING
MARCATO	MARGINS	MARKETED	MARMS	MARSHALLINGS
MARCEL	MARGOSA	MARKETEER	MAROCAIN	MARSHALS
MARCELLA	MARGOSAS	MARKETEERS	MAROCAINS	MARSHES
MARCELLAS	MARGRAVE	MARKETER	MARON	MARSHIER
MARCELLED	MARGRAVES	MARKETERS	MARONS	MARSHIEST
MARCELLING	MARGS	MARKETING	MAROON	MARSHLAND
MARCELS	MARIA	MARKETINGS	MAROONED	MARSHLANDS
MARCH	MARIACHI	MARKETS	MAROONER	MARSHWORT
MARCHED	MARIACHIS	MARKHOR	MAROONERS	MARSHWORTS
MARCHER	MARIALITE	MARKHORS	MAROONING	MARSHY
MARCHERS	MARIALITES	MARKING	MAROONINGS	MARSPORT
MARCHES	MARID	MARKINGS	MAROONS	MARSPORTS

MARSQUAKE	MARZIPANS	MASOCHISMS	MASTERED	MATCHER
MARSQUAKES	MAS	MASOCHIST	MASTERFUL	MATCHERS
MARSUPIA	MASA	MASOCHISTS	MASTERIES	MATCHES
MARSUPIAL	MASALA	MASON	MASTERING	MATCHING
MARSUPIALS	MASALAS	MASONED	MASTERINGS	MATCHLESS
MARSUPIUM	MASAS	MASONIC	MASTERLY	MATCHLOCK
MARSUPIUMS	MASCARA	MASONING	MASTERS	MATCHLOCKS
MART	MASCARAS	MASONRIED	MASTERY	MATCHWOOD
MARTAGON	MASCARON	MASONRIES	MASTFUL	MATCHWOODS
MARTAGONS	MASCARONS	MASONRY	MASTHEAD	MATE
MARTED	MASCLE	MASONS	MASTHEADED	MATED
MARTEL	MASCLED	MASOOLAH	MASTHEADING	MATELASSE
MARTELLED	MASCLES	MASOOLAHS	MASTHEADS	MATELASSES
MARTELLING	MASCON	MASQUE	MASTHOUSE	MATELESS
MARTELLO	MASCONS	MASQUER	MASTHOUSES	MATELOT
MARTELLOS	MASCOT	MASQUERS	MASTIC	MATELOTE
MARTELS	MASCOTS	MASQUES	MASTICATE	MATELOTES
MARTEN	MASCULINE	MASS	MASTICATED	MATELOTS
MARTENS	MASCULINES	MASSA	MASTICATES	MATER
MARTEXT	MASCULY	MASSACRE	MASTICATING	MATERIAL
MARTEXTS	MASE	MASSACRED	MASTICH	MATERIALS
MARTIAL	MASED	MASSACRES	MASTICHS	MATERIEL
MARTIALLY	MASER	MASSACRING	MASTICOT	MATERIELS
MARTIN	MASERS	MASSAGE	MASTICOTS	MATERNAL
MARTINET	MASES	MASSAGED	MASTICS	MATERNITIES
MARTINETS	MASH	MASSAGES	MASTIER	MATERNITY
MARTING	MASHALLAH	MASSAGING	MASTIEST	MATERS
MARTINI	MASHED	MASSAGIST	MASTIFF	MATES
MARTINIS	MASHER	MASSAGISTS	MASTIFFS	MATESHIP
MARTINS	MASHERS	MASSAS	MASTING	MATESHIPS
MARTLET	MASHES	MASSE	MASTITIS	MATEY
MARTLETS	MASHIE	MASSED	MASTITISES	MATEYNESS
MARTS	MASHIER	MASSES	MASTLESS	MATEYNESSES
MARTYR	MASHIES	MASSETER	MASTODON	MATFELON
MARTYRDOM	MASHIEST	MASSETERS	MASTODONS	MATFELONS
MARTYRDOMS	MASHING	MASSEUR	MASTOID	MATGRASS
MARTYRED	MASHINGS	MASSEURS	MASTOIDAL	MATGRASSES
MARTYRIA	MASHLAM	MASSEUSE	MASTOIDS	MATH
MARTYRIES	MASHLAMS	MASSEUSES	MASTS	MATHESES
MARTYRING	MASHLIM	MASSICOT	MASTY	MATHESIS
MARTYRISE	MASHLIMS	MASSICOTS	MASU	MATHS
MARTYRISED	MASHLIN	MASSIER	MASULA	MATICO
MARTYRISES	MASHLINS	MASSIEST	MASULAS	MATICOS
MARTYRISING	MASHLOCH	MASSIF	MASURIUM	MATIER
MARTYRIUM	MASHLOCHS	MASSIFS	MASURIUMS	MATIEST
MARTYRIZE	MASHLUM	MASSINESS	MASUS	MATILY
MARTYRIZED	MASHLUMS	MASSINESSES	MAT	MATIN
MARTYRIZES	MASHMAN	MASSING	MATACHIN	MATINAL
MARTYRIZING	MASHMEN	MASSIVE	MATACHINA	MATINEE
MARTYRS	MASHUA	MASSIVELY	MATACHINAS	MATINEES
MARTYRY	MASHUAS	MASSOOLA	MATACHINI	MATINESS
MARVEL	MASHY	MASSOOLAS	MATADOR	MATINESSES
MARVELLED	MASING	MASSY	MATADORA	MATING
MARVELLING	MASJID	MASSYMORE	MATADORAS	MATINS
MARVELS	MASJIDS	MASSYMORES	MATADORE	MATJES
MARVER	MASK	MAST	MATADORES	MATLO
MARVERED	MASKED	MASTABA	MATADORS	MATLOS
MARVERING	MASKER	MASTABAS	MATAMATA	MATLOW
MARVERS	MASKERS	MASTED	MATAMATAS	MATLOWS
MARXISANT	MASKING	MASTER	MATCH	MATOKE
MARY	MASKS	MASTERATE	MATCHABLE	MATOKES
MARYBUD	MASLIN	MASTERATES	MATCHBOX	MATOOKE
MARYBUDS	MASLINS	MASTERDOM	MATCHBOXES	MATOOKES
MARZIPAN	MASOCHISM	MASTERDOMS	MATCHED	MATRASS

MATRASSES	MATURE	MAUNGIEST	MAXILLULAE	MAZED
MATRIARCH	MATURED	MAUNGY	MAXIM	MAZEFUL
MATRIARCHS	MATURELY	MAUNNA	MAXIMA	MAZELTOV
MATRIC	MATURER	MAUSOLEAN	MAXIMAL	MAZEMENT
MATRICE	MATURES	MAUSOLEUM	MAXIMALLY	MAZEMENTS
MATRICES	MATUREST	MAUSOLEUMS	MAXIMIN	MAZER
MATRICIDE	MATURING	MAUTHER	MAXIMINS	MAZERS
MATRICIDES	MATURITIES	MAUTHERS	MAXIMISE	MAZES
MATRICS	MATURITY	MAUVAIS	MAXIMISED	MAZHBI
MATRICULA	MATUTINAL	MAUVAISE	MAXIMISES	MAZHBIS
MATRICULAS	MATUTINE	MAUVE	MAXIMISING	MAZIER
MATRILINIES	MATWEED	MAUVEIN	MAXIMIST	MAZIEST
MATRILINY	MATWEEDS	MAUVEINE	MAXIMISTS	MAZILY
MATRIMONIES	MATY	MAUVEINES	MAXIMIZE	MAZINESS
MATRIMONY	MATZA	MAUVEINS	MAXIMIZED	MAZINESSES
MATRIX	MATZAH	MAUVER	MAXIMIZES	MAZING
MATRIXES	MATZAHS	MAUVES	MAXIMIZING	MAZOUT
MATRON	MATZAS	MAUVEST	MAXIMS	MAZOUTS
MATRONAGE	MATZO	MAUVIN	MAXIMUM	MAZUMA
MATRONAGES	MATZOH	MAUVINE	MAXIS	MAZUMAS
MATRONAL	MATZOON	MAUVINES	MAXIXE	MAZURKA
MATRONISE	MATZOONS	MAUVINS	MAXIXES	MAZURKAS
MATRONISED	MATZOS	MAVEN	MAXWELL	MAZUT
MATRONISES	MATZOT	MAVENS	MAXWELLS	MAZUTS
MATRONISING	MATZOTH	MAVERICK	MAY	MAZY
MATRONIZE	MAUD	MAVERICKED	MAYA	MAZZARD
MATRONIZED	MAUDLIN	MAVERICKING	MAYAS	MAZZARDS
MATRONIZES	MAUDS	MAVERICKS	MAYBE	MBAQANGA
MATRONIZING	MAUGRE	MAVIN	MAYBES	MBAQANGAS
MATRONLY	MAUGRED	MAVINS	MAYDAY	MBIRA
MATRONS	MAUGRES	MAVIS	MAYDAYS	MBIRAS
MATROSS	MAUGRING	MAVISES	MAYED	ME
MATROSSES	MAUL	MAW	MAYEST	MEACOCK
MATS	MAULED	MAWBOUND	MAYFLIES	MEACOCKS
MATSURI	MAULERS	MAWK	MAYFLOWER	MEAD
MATSURIS	MAULGRE	MAWKIER	MAYFLOWERS	MEADOW
MATT	MAULGRED	MAWKIEST	MAYFLY	MEADOWS
MATTAMORE	MAULGRES	MAWKIN	MAYHAP	MEADOWY
MATTAMORES	MAULGRING	MAWKINS	MAYHEM	MEADS
MATTE	MAULING	MAWKISH	MAYHEMS	MEAGRE
MATTED	MAULS	MAWKISHLY	MAYING	MEAGRELY
MATTER	MAULSTICK	MAWKS	MAYINGS	MEAGRER
MATTERED	MAULSTICKS	MAWKY	MAYOR	MEAGRES
MATTERFUL	MAULVI	MAWMET	MAYORAL	MEAGREST
MATTERING	MAULVIS	MAWMETRIES	MAYORALTIES	MEAL
MATTERS	MAUMET	MAWMETRY	MAYORALTY	MEALED
MATTERY	MAUMETRIES	MAWMETS	MAYORESS	MEALER
MATTES	MAUMETRY	MAWPUS	MAYORESSES	MEALERS
MATTIE	MAUMETS	MAWPUSES	MAYORS	MEALIE
MATTIES	MAUN	MAWR	MAYORSHIP	MEALIER
MATTING	MAUND	MAWRS	MAYORSHIPS	MEALIES
MATTINGS	MAUNDED	MAWS	MAYPOLE	MEALIEST
MATTINS	MAUNDER	MAWSEED	MAYPOLES	MEALINESS
MATTOCK	MAUNDERED	MAWSEEDS	MAYS	MEALINESSES
MATTOCKS	MAUNDERER	MAWTHER	MAYST	MEALING
MATTOID	MAUNDERERS	MAWTHERS	MAYSTER	MEALS
MATTOIDS	MAUNDERING	MAX	MAYSTERS	MEALTIME
MATTRESS	MAUNDERINGS	MAXES	MAYWEED	MEALTIMES
MATTRESSES	MAUNDERS	MAXI	MAYWEEDS	MEALWORM
MATURABLE	MAUNDIES	MAXILLA	MAZARD	MEALWORMS
MATURATE	MAUNDING	MAXILLAE	MAZARDS	MEALY
MATURATED	MAUNDS	MAXILLARIES	MAZARINE	MEAN
MATURATES	MAUNDY	MAXILLARY	MAZARINES	MEANDER
MATURATING	MAUNGIER	MAXILLULA	MAZE	MEANDERED

The Chambers Dictionary is the authority for many longer words; see *OSW* Introduction, page xii

MEANDERING	MEATY	MEDIAEVAL	MEDIUMS	MEGABUCKS
MEANDERS	MEAWES	MEDIAL	MEDIUS	MEGABYTE
MEANDRIAN	MEAZEL	MEDIALLY	MEDIUSES	MEGABYTES
MEANDROUS	MEAZELS	MEDIALS	MEDLAR	MEGACITIES
MEANE	MEBOS	MEDIAN	MEDLARS	MEGACITY
MEANED	MEBOSES	MEDIANS	MEDLE	MEGACURIE
MEANER	MECHANIC	MEDIANT	MEDLED	MEGACURIES
MEANES	MECHANICS	MEDIANTS	MEDLES	MEGACYCLE
MEANEST	MECHANISE	MEDIATE	MEDLEY	MEGACYCLES
MEANIE	MECHANISED	MEDIATED	MEDLEYS	MEGADEATH
MEANIES	MECHANISES	MEDIATELY	MEDLING	MEGADEATHS
MEANING	MECHANISING	MEDIATES	MEDRESSEH	MEGADOSE
MEANINGLY	MECHANISM	MEDIATING	MEDRESSEHS	MEGADOSES
MEANINGS	MECHANISMS	MEDIATION	MEDULLA	MEGADYNE
MEANLY	MECHANIST	MEDIATIONS	MEDULLAE	MEGADYNES
MEANNESS	MECHANISTS	MEDIATISE	MEDULLAR	MEGAFARAD
MEANNESSES	MECHANIZE	MEDIATISED	MEDULLARY	MEGAFARADS
MEANS	MECHANIZED	MEDIATISES	MEDULLAS	MEGAFAUNA
MEANT	MECHANIZES	MEDIATISING	MEDULLATE	MEGAFAUNAE
MEANTIME	MECHANIZING	MEDIATIVE	MEDUSA	MEGAFAUNAS
MEANTIMES	MECONATE	MEDIATIZE	MEDUSAE	MEGAFLOP
MEANWHILE	MECONATES	MEDIATIZED	MEDUSAN	MEGAFLOPS
MEANWHILES	MECONIC	MEDIATIZES	MEDUSANS	MEGAFLORA
MEANY	MECONIN	MEDIATIZING	MEDUSAS	MEGAFLORAE
MEARE	MECONINS	MEDIATOR	MEDUSOID	MEGAFLORAS
MEARES	MECONIUM	MEDIATORS	MEDUSOIDS	MEGAFOG
MEARING	MECONIUMS	MEDIATORY	MEED	MEGAFOGS
MEASE	MEDACCA	MEDIATRICES	MEEDS	MEGAGAUSS
MEASED	MEDACCAS	MEDIATRIX	MEEK	MEGAGAUSSES
MEASES	MEDAEWART	MEDIC	MEEKEN	MEGAHERTZ
MEASING	MEDAEWARTS	MEDICABLE	MEEKENED	MEGAHERTZES
MEASLE	MEDAKA	MEDICAID	MEEKENING	MEGAJOULE
MEASLED	MEDAKAS	MEDICAIDS	MEEKENS	MEGAJOULES
MEASLES	MEDAL	MEDICAL	MEEKER	MEGALITH
MEASLIER	MEDALED	MEDICALLY	MEEKEST	MEGALITHS
MEASLIEST	MEDALET	MEDICALS	MEEKLY	MEGAPHONE
MEASLING	MEDALETS	MEDICARE	MEEKNESS	MEGAPHONED
MEASLY	MEDALING	MEDICARES	MEEKNESSES	MEGAPHONES
MEASURE	MEDALIST	MEDICATE	MEEMIE	MEGAPHONING
MEASURED	MEDALISTS	MEDICATED	MEEMIES	MEGAPODE
MEASURER	MEDALLED	MEDICATES	MEER	MEGAPODES
MEASURERS	MEDALLIC	MEDICATING	MEERCAT	MEGARA
MEASURES	MEDALLING	MEDICINAL	MEERCATS	MEGARAD
MEASURING	MEDALLION	MEDICINE	MEERED	MEGARADS
MEASURINGS	MEDALLIONED	MEDICINED	MEERING	MEGARON
MEAT	MEDALLIONING	MEDICINER	MEERKAT	MEGARONS
MEATAL	MEDALLIONS	MEDICINERS	MEERKATS	MEGASCOPE
MEATBALL	MEDALLIST	MEDICINES	MEERS	MEGASCOPES
MEATBALLS	MEDALLISTS	MEDICINING	MEET	MEGASPORE
MEATH	MEDALS	MEDICK	MEETER	MEGASPORES
MEATHE	MEDCINAL	MEDICKS	MEETEST	MEGASS
MEATHEAD	MEDDLE	MEDICO	MEETING	MEGASSE
MEATHEADS	MEDDLED	MEDICOS	MEETINGS	MEGASSES
MEATHES	MEDDLER	MEDICS	MEETLY	MEGASTAR
MEATHS	MEDDLERS	MEDIEVAL	MEETNESS	MEGASTARS
MEATIER	MEDDLES	MEDII	MEETNESSES	MEGASTORE
MEATIEST	MEDDLING	MEDINA	MEETS	MEGASTORES
MEATILY	MEDDLINGS	MEDINAS	MEG	MEGATON
MEATINESS	MEDFLIES	MEDIOCRE	MEGA	MEGATONS
MEATINESSES	MEDFLY	MEDITATE	MEGABAR	MEGAVOLT
MEATLESS	MEDIA	MEDITATED	MEGABARS	MEGAVOLTS
MEATS	MEDIACIES	MEDITATES	MEGABIT	MEGAWATT
MEATUS	MEDIACY	MEDITATING	MEGABITS	MEGAWATTS
MEATUSES	MEDIAE	MEDIUM	MEGABUCK	MEGILLAH

The Chambers Dictionary is the authority for many longer words; see *OSW* Introduction, page xii

MEGILLAHS	MELAS	MELODISED	MEMORIZE	MENOLOGY
MEGILLOTH	MELATONIN	MELODISES	MEMORIZED	MENOMINEE
MEGILP	MELATONINS	MELODISING	MEMORIZES	MENOMINEES
MEGILPS	MELD	MELODIST	MEMORIZING	MENOMINI
MEGOHM	MELDED	MELODISTS	MEMORY	MENOMINIS
MEGOHMS	MELDER	MELODIZE	MEMOS	MENOPAUSE
MEGRIM	MELDERS	MELODIZED	MEN	MENOPAUSES
MEGRIMS	MELDING	MELODIZES	MENACE	MENOPOME
MEGS	MELDS	MELODIZING	MENACED	MENOPOMES
MEIN	MELEE	MELODRAMA	MENACER	MENORAH
MEINED	MELEES	MELODRAMAS	MENACERS	MENORAHS
MEINEY	MELIC	MELODRAME	MENACES	MENORRHEA
MEINEYS	MELICS	MELODRAMES	MENACING	MENORRHEAS
MEINIE	MELIK	MELODY	MENADIONE	MENSAL
MEINIES	MELIKS	MELOMANIA	MENADIONES	MENSCH
MEINING	MELILITE	MELOMANIAS	MENAGE	MENSCHES
MEINS	MELILITES	MELOMANIC	MENAGED	MENSE
MEINT	MELILOT	MELON	MENAGERIE	MENSED
MEINY	MELILOTS	MELONS	MENAGERIES	MENSEFUL
MEIOFAUNA	MELINITE	MELS	MENAGES	MENSELESS
MEIONITE	MELINITES	MELT	MENAGING	MENSES
MEIONITES	MELIORATE	MELTDOWN	MENARCHE	MENSH
MEIOSES	MELIORATED	MELTDOWNS	MENARCHES	MENSHED
MEIOSIS	MELIORATES	MELTED	MEND	MENSHES
MEIOTIC	MELIORATING	MELTIER	MENDACITIES	MENSHING
MEISHI	MELIORISM	MELTIEST	MENDACITY	MENSING
MEISHIS	MELIORISMS	MELTING	MENDED	MENSTRUA
MEISTER	MELIORIST	MELTINGLY	MENDER	MENSTRUAL
MEISTERS	MELIORISTS	MELTINGS	MENDERS	MENSTRUUM
MEITH	MELIORITIES	MELTITH	MENDICANT	MENSTRUUMS
MEITHS	MELIORITY	MELTITHS	MENDICANTS	MENSUAL
MEJLIS	MELISMA	MELTON	MENDICITIES	MENSURAL
MEJLISES	MELISMAS	MELTONS	MENDICITY	MENSWEAR
MEKOMETER	MELISMATA	MELTS	MENDING	MENSWEARS
MEKOMETERS	MELL	MELTY	MENDINGS	MENT
MEL	MELLAY	MEMBER	MENDS	MENTA
MELA	MELLAYS	MEMBERED	MENE	MENTAL
MELAMINE	MELLED	MEMBERS	MENED	MENTALISM
MELAMINES	MELLING	MEMBRAL	MENEER	MENTALISMS
MELAMPODE	MELLITE	MEMBRANE	MENEERS	MENTALIST
MELAMPODES	MELLITES	MEMBRANES	MENES	MENTALISTS
MELANGE	MELLITIC	MEME	MENFOLK	MENTALITIES
MELANGES	MELLOW	MEMENTO	MENFOLKS	MENTALITY
MELANIC	MELLOWED	MEMENTOES	MENG	MENTALLY
MELANIN	MELLOWER	MEMENTOS	MENGE	MENTATION
MELANINS	MELLOWEST	MEMES	MENGED	MENTATIONS
MELANISM	MELLOWING	MEMO	MENGES	MENTEE
MELANISMS	MELLOWLY	MEMOIR	MENGING	MENTEES
MELANITE	MELLOWS	MEMOIRISM	MENGS	MENTHOL
MELANITES	MELLOWY	MEMOIRISMS	MENHADEN	MENTHOLS
MELANO	MELLS	MEMOIRIST	MENHADENS	MENTICIDE
MELANOMA	MELOCOTON	MEMOIRISTS	MENHIR	MENTICIDES
MELANOMAS	MELOCOTONS	MEMOIRS	MENHIRS	MENTION
MELANOMATA	MELODEON	MEMORABLE	MENIAL	MENTIONED
MELANOS	MELODEONS	MEMORABLY	MENIALS	MENTIONING
MELANOSES	MELODIC	MEMORANDA	MENING	MENTIONS
MELANOSIS	MELODICA	MEMORIAL	MENINGEAL	MENTO
MELANOTIC	MELODICAS	MEMORIALS	MENINGES	MENTOR
MELANOUS	MELODICS	MEMORIES	MENINX	MENTORIAL
MELANURIA	MELODIES	MEMORISE	MENISCI	MENTORING
MELANURIAS	MELODION	MEMORISED	MENISCOID	MENTORINGS
MELANURIC	MELODIONS	MEMORISES	MENISCUS	MENTORS
MELAPHYRE	MELODIOUS	MEMORISING	MENISCUSES	MENTOS
MELAPHYRES	MELODISE	MEMORITER	MENOLOGIES	MENTUM

The Chambers Dictionary is the authority for many longer words; see *OSW* Introduction, page xii

MENU	MERCURISED	MERKINS	MESCALIN	MESONIC
MENUISIER	MERCURISES	MERKS	MESCALINS	MESONS
MENUISIERS	MERCURISING	MERL	MESCALISM	MESOPHYLL
MENUS	MERCURIZE	MERLE	MESCALISMS	MESOPHYLLS
MENYIE	MERCURIZED	MERLES	MESCALS	MESOPHYTE
MENYIES	MERCURIZES	MERLIN	MESCLUM	MESOPHYTES
MEOW	MERCURIZING	MERLING	MESCLUMS	MESOTRON
MEOWED	MERCUROUS	MERLINGS	MESCLUN	MESOTRONS
MEOWING	MERCURY	MERLINS	MESCLUNS	MESPRISE
MEOWS	MERCY	MERLON	MESDAMES	MESPRISES
MEPACRINE	MERE	MERLONS	MESE	MESPRIZE
MEPACRINES	MERED	MERLS	MESEL	MESPRIZES
MEPHITIC	MEREL	MERMAID	MESELED	MESQUIN
MEPHITIS	MERELL	MERMAIDEN	MESELS	MESQUINE
MEPHITISES	MERELLS	MERMAIDENS	MESENTERA	MESQUIT
MEPHITISM	MERELS	MERMAIDS	MESENTERIES	MESQUITE
MEPHITISMS	MERELY	MERMAN	MESENTERY	MESQUITES
MERC	MERENGUE	MERMEN	MESES	MESQUITS
MERCAPTAN	MERENGUES	MEROGONIES	MESETA	MESS
MERCAPTANS	MERER	MEROGONY	MESETAS	MESSAGE
MERCAT	MERES	MEROISTIC	MESH	MESSAGED
MERCATS	MERESMAN	MEROME	MESHED	MESSAGES
MERCENARIES	MERESMEN	MEROMES	MESHES	MESSAGING
MERCENARY	MEREST	MERONYM	MESHIER	MESSAGINGS
MERCER	MERESTONE	MERONYMIES	MESHIEST	MESSAN
MERCERIES	MERESTONES	MERONYMS	MESHING	MESSANS
MERCERISE	MERFOLK	MERONYMY	MESHINGS	MESSED
MERCERISED	MERFOLKS	MEROPIDAN	MESHUGA	MESSENGER
MERCERISES	MERGANSER	MEROPIDANS	MESHUGAAS	MESSENGERED
MERCERISING	MERGANSERS	MEROSOME	MESHUGAASEN	MESSENGERING
MERCERIZE	MERGE	MEROSOMES	MESHUGGA	MESSENGERS
MERCERIZED	MERGED	MEROZOITE	MESHUGGE	MESSES
MERCERIZES	MERGENCE	MEROZOITES	MESHY	MESSIAH
MERCERIZING	MERGENCES	MERPEOPLE	MESIAL	MESSIAHS
MERCERS	MERGER	MERPEOPLES	MESIALLY	MESSIANIC
MERCERY	MERGERS	MERRIER	MESIAN	MESSIAS
MERCHANT	MERGES	MERRIES	MESIC	MESSIASES
MERCHANTED	MERGING	MERRIEST	MESMERIC	MESSIER
MERCHANTING	MERI	MERRILY	MESMERISE	MESSIEST
MERCHANTINGS	MERICARP	MERRIMENT	MESMERISED	MESSIEURS
MERCHANTS	MERICARPS	MERRIMENTS	MESMERISES	MESSILY
MERCHET	MERIDIAN	MERRINESS	MESMERISING	MESSINESS
MERCHETS	MERIDIANS	MERRINESSES	MESMERISM	MESSINESSES
MERCHILD	MERIL	MERRY	MESMERISMS	MESSING
MERCHILDREN	MERILS	MERRYMAN	MESMERIST	MESSMATE
MERCIABLE	MERIMAKE	MERRYMEN	MESMERISTS	MESSMATES
MERCIES	MERIMAKES	MERSALYL	MESMERIZE	MESSUAGE
MERCIFIDE	MERING	MERSALYLS	MESMERIZED	MESSUAGES
MERCIFIED	MERINGUE	MERSE	MESMERIZES	MESSY
MERCIFIES	MERINGUES	MERSES	MESMERIZING	MESTEE
MERCIFUL	MERINO	MERSION	MESNE	MESTEES
MERCIFY	MERINOS	MERSIONS	MESOBLAST	MESTIZA
MERCIFYING	MERIS	MERYCISM	MESOBLASTS	MESTIZAS
MERCILESS	MERISM	MERYCISMS	MESOCARP	MESTIZO
MERCS	MERISMS	MES	MESOCARPS	MESTIZOS
MERCURATE	MERISTEM	MESA	MESODERM	MESTO
MERCURATED	MERISTEMS	MESAIL	MESODERMS	MET
MERCURATES	MERISTIC	MESAILS	MESOGLOEA	METABASES
MERCURATING	MERIT	MESAL	MESOGLOEAS	METABASIS
MERCURIAL	MERITED	MESALLY	MESOLITE	METABATIC
MERCURIALS	MERITING	MESARAIC	MESOLITES	METABOLIC
MERCURIC	MERITS	MESARCH	MESOMORPH	METACARPI
MERCURIES	MERK	MESAS	MESOMORPHS	METAGE
MERCURISE	MERKIN	MESCAL	MESON	METAGES

METAIRIE	METED	METHYSIS	METRONOMES	MIASMAL
METAIRIES	METEOR	METHYSTIC	METROPLEX	MIASMAS
METAL	METEORIC	METIC	METROPLEXES	MIASMATA
METALED	METEORISM	METICAL	METROS	MIASMATIC
METALING	METEORISMS	METICALS	METS	MIASMIC
METALIST	METEORIST	METICS	METTLE	MIASMOUS
METALISTS	METEORISTS	METIER	METTLED	MIASMS
METALIZE	METEORITE	METIERS	METTLES	MIAUL
METALIZED	METEORITES	METIF	MEU	MIAULED
METALIZES	METEOROID	METIFS	MEUNIERE	MIAULING
METALIZING	METEOROIDS	METING	MEUS	MIAULS
METALLED	METEOROUS	METIS	MEUSE	MICA
METALLIC	METEORS	METISSE	MEUSED	MICACEOUS
METALLINE	METER	METISSES	MEUSES	MICAS
METALLING	METERED	METOL	MEUSING	MICATE
METALLINGS	METERING	METOLS	MEVE	MICATED
METALLISE	METERS	METONYM	MEVED	MICATES
METALLISED	METES	METONYMIC	MEVES	MICATING
METALLISES	METESTICK	METONYMIES	MEVING	MICE
METALLISING	METESTICKS	METONYMS	MEW	MICELLA
METALLIST	METEWAND	METONYMY	MEWED	MICELLAE
METALLISTS	METEWANDS	METOPAE	MEWING	MICELLAR
METALLIZE	METEYARD	METOPE	MEWL	MICELLE
METALLIZED	METEYARDS	METOPES	MEWLED	MICELLES
METALLIZES	METHADON	METOPIC	MEWLING	MICHE
METALLIZING	METHADONE	METOPISM	MEWLS	MICHED
METALLOID	METHADONES	METOPISMS	MEWS	MICHER
METALLOIDS	METHADONS	METOPON	MEWSED	MICHERS
METALLY	METHANAL	METOPONS	MEWSES	MICHES
METALS	METHANALS	METOPRYL	MEWSING	MICHING
METALWARE	METHANE	METOPRYLS	MEYNT	MICHINGS
METALWARES	METHANES	METRE	MEZAIL	MICK
METALWORK	METHANOL	METRED	MEZAILS	MICKEY
METALWORKS	METHANOLS	METRES	MEZE	MICKEYED
METAMER	METHEGLIN	METRIC	MEZEREON	MICKEYING
METAMERE	METHEGLINS	METRICAL	MEZEREONS	MICKEYS
METAMERES	METHINK	METRICATE	MEZEREUM	MICKIES
METAMERIC	METHINKETH	METRICATED	MEZEREUMS	MICKLE
METAMERS	METHINKS	METRICATES	MEZES	MICKLES
METANOIA	METHOD	METRICATING	MEZUZA	MICKS
METANOIAS	METHODIC	METRICIAN	MEZUZAH	MICKY
METAPELET	METHODISE	METRICIANS	MEZUZAHS	MICO
METAPHASE	METHODISED	METRICISE	MEZUZOTH	MICOS
METAPHASES	METHODISES	METRICISED	MEZZANINE	MICRA
METAPHOR	METHODISING	METRICISES	MEZZANINES	MICRO
METAPHORS	METHODIST	METRICISING	MEZZE	MICROBAR
METAPLASM	METHODISTS	METRICIST	MEZZES	MICROBARS
METAPLASMS	METHODIZE	METRICISTS	MEZZO	MICROBE
METAPLOT	METHODIZED	METRICIZE	MEZZOS	MICROBES
METATARSI	METHODIZES	METRICIZED	MEZZOTINT	MICROBIAL
METATE	METHODIZING	METRICIZES	MEZZOTINTS	MICROBIAN
METATES	METHODS	METRICIZING	MGANGA	MICROBIC
METAYAGE	METHOUGHT	METRICS	MGANGAS	MICROBUS
METAYAGES	METHS	METRIFIER	MHO	MICROBUSES
METAYER	METHYL	METRIFIERS	MHORR	MICROBUSSES
METAYERS	METHYLATE	METRING	MHORRS	MICROCAR
METAZOA	METHYLATED	METRIST	MHOS	MICROCARD
METAZOAN	METHYLATES	METRISTS	MI	MICROCARDS
METAZOANS	METHYLATING	METRITIS	MIAOW	MICROCARS
METAZOIC	METHYLENE	METRITISES	MIAOWED	MICROCHIP
METAZOON	METHYLENES	METRO	MIAOWING	MICROCHIPS
METCAST	METHYLIC	METROLOGIES	MIAOWS	MICROCODE
METCASTS	METHYLS	METROLOGY	MIASM	MICROCODES
METE	METHYSES	METRONOME	MIASMA	MICROCOPIED

MICROCOPIES	MIDDAY	MIEVE	MILDEWED	MILKWORTS
MICROCOPY	MIDDAYS	MIEVED	MILDEWING	MILKY
MICROCOPYING	MIDDEN	MIEVES	MILDEWS	MILL
MICROCOPYINGS	MIDDENS	MIEVING	MILDEWY	MILLBOARD
MICROCOSM	MIDDEST	MIFF	MILDLY	MILLBOARDS
MICROCOSMS	MIDDIES	MIFFED	MILDNESS	MILLDAM
MICROCYTE	MIDDLE	MIFFIER	MILDNESSES	MILLDAMS
MICROCYTES	MIDDLED	MIFFIEST	MILDS	MILLE
MICRODOT	MIDDLEMAN	MIFFILY	MILE	MILLED
MICRODOTS	MIDDLEMEN	MIFFINESS	MILEAGE	MILLENARIES
MICROFILM	MIDDLES	MIFFINESSES	MILEAGES	MILLENARY
MICROFILMED	MIDDLING	MIFFING	MILER	MILLENNIA
MICROFILMING	MIDDLINGS	MIFFS	MILERS	MILLEPED
MICROFILMS	MIDDY	MIFFY	MILES	MILLEPEDE
MICROFORM	MIDFIELD	MIFTY	MILESTONE	MILLEPEDES
MICROFORMS	MIDFIELDS	MIGHT	MILESTONES	MILLEPEDS
MICROGRAM	MIDGE	MIGHTEST	MILFOIL	MILLEPORE
MICROGRAMS	MIDGES	MIGHTFUL	MILFOILS	MILLEPORES
MICROLITE	MIDGET	MIGHTIER	MILIARIA	MILLER
MICROLITES	MIDGETS	MIGHTIEST	MILIARIAS	MILLERITE
MICROLITH	MIDI	MIGHTILY	MILIARY	MILLERITES
MICROLITHS	MIDINETTE	MIGHTS	MILIEU	MILLERS
MICROLOGIES	MIDINETTES	MIGHTST	MILIEUS	MILLES
MICROLOGY	MIDIRON	MIGHTY	MILIEUX	MILLET
MICROMESH	MIDIRONS	MIGNON	MILITANCIES	MILLETS
MICROMESHES	MIDIS	MIGNONNE	MILITANCY	MILLIARD
MICRON	MIDLAND	MIGRAINE	MILITANT	MILLIARDS
MICRONS	MIDLANDS	MIGRAINES	MILITANTS	MILLIARE
MICROPORE	MIDMOST	MIGRANT	MILITAR	MILLIARES
MICROPORES	MIDMOSTS	MIGRANTS	MILITARIA	MILLIARIES
MICROPSIA	MIDNIGHT	MIGRATE	MILITARIES	MILLIARY
MICROPSIAS	MIDNIGHTS	MIGRATED	MILITARY	MILLIBAR
MICROPUMP	MIDNOON	MIGRATES	MILITATE	MILLIBARS
MICROPUMPS	MIDNOONS	MIGRATING	MILITATED	MILLIEME
MICROPYLE	MIDRIB	MIGRATION	MILITATES	MILLIEMES
MICROPYLES	MIDRIBS	MIGRATIONS	MILITATING	MILLIME
MICROS	MIDRIFF	MIGRATOR	MILITIA	MILLIMES
MICROSOME	MIDRIFFS	MIGRATORS	MILITIAS	MILLIMOLE
MICROSOMES	MIDS	MIGRATORY	MILK	MILLIMOLES
MICROTOME	MIDSHIP	MIHRAB	MILKED	MILLINER
MICROTOMES	MIDSHIPS	MIHRABS	MILKEN	MILLINERIES
MICROTOMIES	MIDSIZE	MIKADO	MILKER	MILLINERS
MICROTOMY	MIDST	MIKADOS	MILKERS	MILLINERY
MICROTONE	MIDSTREAM	MIKE	MILKFISH	MILLING
MICROTONES	MIDSTREAMS	MIKES	MILKFISHES	MILLINGS
MICROWAVE	MIDSTS	MIKRA	MILKIER	MILLION
MICROWAVED	MIDSUMMER	MIKRON	MILKIEST	MILLIONS
MICROWAVES	MIDSUMMERS	MIKRONS	MILKILY	MILLIONTH
MICROWAVING	MIDTERM	MIL	MILKINESS	MILLIONTHS
MICROWIRE	MIDTERMS	MILADI	MILKINESSES	MILLIPED
MICROWIRES	MIDWAY	MILADIES	MILKING	MILLIPEDE
MICRURGIES	MIDWAYS	MILADIS	MILKINGS	MILLIPEDES
MICRURGY	MIDWIFE	MILADY	MILKLESS	MILLIPEDS
MICTION	MIDWIFED	MILAGE	MILKLIKE	MILLIREM
MICTIONS	MIDWIFERIES	MILAGES	MILKMAID	MILLIREMS
MICTURATE	MIDWIFERY	MILCH	MILKMAIDS	MILLOCRAT
MICTURATED	MIDWIFES	MILD	MILKMAN	MILLOCRATS
MICTURATES	MIDWIFING	MILDEN	MILKMEN	MILLPOND
MICTURATING	MIDWIVE	MILDENED	MILKO	MILLPONDS
MID	MIDWIVED	MILDENING	MILKOS	MILLRACE
MIDAIR	MIDWIVES	MILDENS	MILKS	MILLRACES
MIDAIRS	MIDWIVING	MILDER	MILKWOOD	MILLRIND
MIDBRAIN	MIEN	MILDEST	MILKWOODS	MILLRINDS
MIDBRAINS	MIENS	MILDEW	MILKWORT	MILLRUN

The Chambers Dictionary is the authority for many longer words; see *OSW* Introduction, page xii

MILLRUNS	MIMOSAS	MINGED	MINIMISM	MINORITY
MILLS	MIMSEY	MINGES	MINIMISMS	MINORS
MILLSCALE	MIMSIER	MINGIER	MINIMIST	MINORSHIP
MILLSCALES	MIMSIEST	MINGIEST	MINIMISTS	MINORSHIPS
MILLSTONE	MIMSY	MINGIN	MINIMIZE	MINOS
MILLSTONES	MIMULUS	MINGINESS	MINIMIZED	MINSHUKU
MILLTAIL	MIMULUSES	MINGINESSES	MINIMIZES	MINSHUKUS
MILLTAILS	MINA	MINGING	MINIMIZING	MINSTER
MILO	MINACIOUS	MINGLE	MINIMS	MINSTERS
MILOMETER	MINACITIES	MINGLED	MINIMUM	MINSTREL
MILOMETERS	MINACITY	MINGLER	MINIMUS	MINSTRELS
MILOR	MINAE	MINGLERS	MINIMUSES	MINT
MILORD	MINAR	MINGLES	MINING	MINTAGE
MILORDS	MINARET	MINGLING	MININGS	MINTAGES
MILORS	MINARETS	MINGLINGS	MINION	MINTED
MILOS	MINARS	MINGS	MINIONS	MINTER
MILREIS	MINAS	MINGY	MINIPILL	MINTERS
MILS	MINATORY	MINI	MINIPILLS	MINTIER
MILSEY	MINBAR	MINIATE	MINIRUGBIES	MINTIEST
MILSEYS	MINBARS	MINIATED	MINIRUGBY	MINTING
MILT	MINCE	MINIATES	MINIS	MINTS
MILTED	MINCED	MINIATING	MINISCULE	MINTY
MILTER	MINCEMEAT	MINIATION	MINISCULES	MINUEND
MILTERS	MINCEMEATS	MINIATIONS	MINISH	MINUENDS
MILTING	MINCER	MINIATURE	MINISHED	MINUET
MILTONIA	MINCERS	MINIATURED	MINISHES	MINUETS
MILTONIAS	MINCES	MINIATURES	MINISHING	MINUS
MILTS	MINCEUR	MINIATURING	MINISKIRT	MINUSCULE
MILTZ	MINCING	MINIBAR	MINISKIRTS	MINUSCULES
MILTZES	MINCINGLY	MINIBARS	MINISTER	MINUSES
MILVINE	MINCINGS	MINIBIKE	MINISTERED	MINUTE
MIM	MIND	MINIBIKES	MINISTERING	MINUTED
MIMBAR	MINDED	MINIBREAK	MINISTERS	MINUTELY
MIMBARS	MINDER	MINIBREAKS	MINISTRIES	MINUTEMAN
MIME	MINDERS	MINIBUS	MINISTRY	MINUTEMEN
MIMED	MINDFUCK	MINIBUSES	MINIUM	MINUTER
MIMER	MINDFUCKS	MINIBUSSES	MINIUMS	MINUTES
MIMERS	MINDFUL	MINICAB	MINIVER	MINUTEST
MIMES	MINDFULLY	MINICABS	MINIVERS	MINUTIA
MIMESES	MINDING	MINICAM	MINIVET	MINUTIAE
MIMESIS	MINDINGS	MINICAMS	MINIVETS	MINUTING
MIMESTER	MINDLESS	MINIDISK	MINK	MINUTIOSE
MIMESTERS	MINDS	MINIDISKS	MINKE	MINX
MIMETIC	MINDSET	MINIER	MINKES	MINXES
MIMETICAL	MINDSETS	MINIEST	MINKS	MINY
MIMETITE	MINE	MINIFIED	MINNEOLA	MINYAN
MIMETITES	MINED	MINIFIES	MINNEOLAS	MINYANIM
MIMIC	MINEFIELD	MINIFY	MINNICK	MINYANS
MIMICAL	MINEFIELDS	MINIFYING	MINNICKED	MIOMBO
MIMICKED	MINEOLA	MINIKIN	MINNICKING	MIOMBOS
MIMICKER	MINEOLAS	MINIKINS	MINNICKS	MIOSES
MIMICKERS	MINER	MINIM	MINNIE	MIOSIS
MIMICKING	MINERAL	MINIMA	MINNIES	MIOTIC
MIMICRIES	MINERALS	MINIMAL	MINNOCK	MIOTICS
MIMICRY	MINERS	MINIMAX	MINNOCKED	MIR
MIMICS	MINES	MINIMAXED	MINNOCKING	MIRABELLE
MIMING	MINESTONE	MINIMAXES	MINNOCKS	MIRABELLES
MIMMER	MINESTONES	MINIMAXING	MINNOW	MIRABILIA
MIMMEST	MINETTE	MINIMENT	MINNOWS	MIRABILIS
MIMMICK	MINETTES	MINIMENTS	MINO	MIRABILISES
MIMMICKED	MINEVER	MINIMISE	MINOR	MIRABLE
MIMMICKING	MINEVERS	MINIMISED	MINORED	MIRACIDIA
MIMMICKS	MING	MINIMISES	MINORING	MIRACLE
MIMOSA	MINGE	MINIMISING	MINORITIES	MIRACLES

The Chambers Dictionary is the authority for many longer words; see *OSW* Introduction, page xii

MIRADOR	MISALLIES	MISCHANCING	MISDIALED	MISFALLEN
MIRADORS	MISALLOT	MISCHANCY	MISDIALING	MISFALLING
MIRAGE	MISALLOTS	MISCHARGE	MISDIALLED	MISFALLS
MIRAGES	MISALLOTTED	MISCHARGED	MISDIALLING	MISFALNE
MIRBANE	MISALLOTTING	MISCHARGES	MISDIALS	MISFARE
MIRBANES	MISALLY	MISCHARGING	MISDID	MISFARED
MIRE	MISALLYING	MISCHIEF	MISDIET	MISFARES
MIRED	MISANDRIES	MISCHIEFED	MISDIETS	MISFARING
MIREPOIX	MISANDRY	MISCHIEFING	MISDIGHT	MISFARINGS
MIRES	MISAPPLIED	MISCHIEFS	MISDIRECT	MISFEASOR
MIRI	MISAPPLIES	MISCIBLE	MISDIRECTED	MISFEASORS
MIRIER	MISAPPLY	MISCOLOR	MISDIRECTING	MISFED
MIRIEST	MISAPPLYING	MISCOLORED	MISDIRECTS	MISFEED
MIRIFIC	MISARRAY	MISCOLORING	MISDO	MISFEEDING
MIRIFICAL	MISARRAYS	MISCOLORS	MISDOER	MISFEEDS
MIRIN	MISASSIGN	MISCOLOUR	MISDOERS	MISFEIGN
MIRINESS	MISASSIGNED	MISCOLOURED	MISDOES	MISFEIGNED
MIRINESSES	MISASSIGNING	MISCOLOURING	MISDOING	MISFEIGNING
MIRING	MISASSIGNS	MISCOLOURS	MISDOINGS	MISFEIGNS
MIRINS	MISAUNTER	MISCOPIED	MISDONE	MISFELL
MIRITI	MISAUNTERS	MISCOPIES	MISDONNE	MISFIELD
MIRITIS	MISAVISED	MISCOPY	MISDOUBT	MISFIELDED
MIRK	MISBECAME	MISCOPYING	MISDOUBTED	MISFIELDING
MIRKER	MISBECOME	MISCOUNT	MISDOUBTING	MISFIELDS
MIRKEST	MISBECOMES	MISCOUNTED	MISDOUBTS	MISFILE
MIRKS	MISBECOMING	MISCOUNTING	MISDRAW	MISFILED
MIRLIER	MISBEGOT	MISCOUNTS	MISDRAWING	MISFILES
MIRLIEST	MISBEHAVE	MISCREANT	MISDRAWINGS	MISFILING
MIRLIGOES	MISBEHAVED	MISCREANTS	MISDRAWN	MISFIRE
MIRLITON	MISBEHAVES	MISCREATE	MISDRAWS	MISFIRED
MIRLITONS	MISBEHAVING	MISCREDIT	MISDREAD	MISFIRES
MIRLY	MISBELIEF	MISCREDITED	MISDREADS	MISFIRING
MIRROR	MISBELIEFS	MISCREDITING	MISDREW	MISFIT
MIRRORED	MISBESEEM	MISCREDITS	MISE	MISFITS
MIRRORING	MISBESEEMED	MISCREED	MISEASE	MISFITTED
MIRRORS	MISBESEEMING	MISCREEDS	MISEASES	MISFITTING
MIRS	MISBESEEMS	MISCUE	MISEMPLOY	MISFORM
MIRTH	MISBESTOW	MISCUED	MISEMPLOYED	MISFORMED
MIRTHFUL	MISBESTOWED	MISCUEING	MISEMPLOYING	MISFORMING
MIRTHLESS	MISBESTOWING	MISCUES	MISEMPLOYS	MISFORMS
MIRTHS	MISBESTOWS	MISCUING	MISENTRIES	MISGAVE
MIRV	MISBIRTH	MISDATE	MISENTRY	MISGIVE
MIRVED	MISBIRTHS	MISDATED	MISER	MISGIVEN
MIRVING	MISBORN	MISDATES	MISERABLE	MISGIVES
MIRVS	MISCALL	MISDATING	MISERABLES	MISGIVING
MIRY	MISCALLED	MISDEAL	MISERABLY	MISGIVINGS
MIS	MISCALLING	MISDEALING	MISERE	MISGO
MISADVISE	MISCALLS	MISDEALS	MISERERE	MISGOES
MISADVISED	MISCARRIED	MISDEALT	MISERERES	MISGOING
MISADVISES	MISCARRIES	MISDEED	MISERES	MISGONE
MISADVISING	MISCARRY	MISDEEDS	MISERIES	MISGOTTEN
MISAIM	MISCARRYING	MISDEEM	MISERLIER	MISGOVERN
MISAIMED	MISCAST	MISDEEMED	MISERLIEST	MISGOVERNED
MISAIMING	MISCASTING	MISDEEMING	MISERLY	MISGOVERNING
MISAIMS	MISCASTS	MISDEEMINGS	MISERS	MISGOVERNS
MISALIGN	MISCEGEN	MISDEEMS	MISERY	MISGRAFF
MISALIGNED	MISCEGENE	MISDEMEAN	MISES	MISGRAFT
MISALIGNING	MISCEGENES	MISDEMEANED	MISESTEEM	MISGRAFTED
MISALIGNS	MISCEGENS	MISDEMEANING	MISESTEEMED	MISGRAFTING
MISALLEGE	MISCEGINE	MISDEMEANS	MISESTEEMING	MISGRAFTS
MISALLEGED	MISCEGINES	MISDEMPT	MISESTEEMS	MISGROWTH
MISALLEGES	MISCHANCE	MISDESERT	MISFAITH	MISGROWTHS
MISALLEGING	MISCHANCED	MISDESERTS	MISFAITHS	MISGUGGLE
MISALLIED	MISCHANCES	MISDIAL	MISFALL	MISGUGGLED

The Chambers Dictionary is the authority for many longer words; see *OSW* Introduction, page xii

MISGUGGLES	MISKNOW	MISMATING	MISPRISES	MISSEES
MISGUGGLING	MISKNOWING	MISMETRE	MISPRISING	MISSEL
MISGUIDE	MISKNOWN	MISMETRED	MISPRIZE	MISSELS
MISGUIDED	MISKNOWS	MISMETRES	MISPRIZED	MISSEND
MISGUIDER	MISLAID	MISMETRING	MISPRIZES	MISSENDING
MISGUIDERS	MISLAY	MISNAME	MISPRIZING	MISSENDS
MISGUIDES	MISLAYING	MISNAMED	MISPROUD	MISSENT
MISGUIDING	MISLAYS	MISNAMES	MISQUOTE	MISSES
MISHANDLE	MISLEAD	MISNAMING	MISQUOTED	MISSET
MISHANDLED	MISLEADER	MISNOMER	MISQUOTES	MISSETS
MISHANDLES	MISLEADERS	MISNOMERED	MISQUOTING	MISSETTING
MISHANDLING	MISLEADING	MISNOMERING	MISRATE	MISSHAPE
MISHANTER	MISLEADS	MISNOMERS	MISRATED	MISSHAPED
MISHANTERS	MISLEARED	MISO	MISRATES	MISSHAPEN
MISHAP	MISLED	MISOCLERE	MISRATING	MISSHAPES
MISHAPPED	MISLEEKE	MISOGAMIES	MISREAD	MISSHAPING
MISHAPPEN	MISLEEKED	MISOGAMY	MISREADING	MISSHOOD
MISHAPPENED	MISLEEKES	MISOGYNIES	MISREADINGS	MISSHOODS
MISHAPPENING	MISLEEKING	MISOGYNY	MISREADS	MISSIER
MISHAPPENS	MISLETOE	MISOLOGIES	MISRECKON	MISSIES
MISHAPPING	MISLETOES	MISOLOGY	MISRECKONED	MISSIEST
MISHAPS	MISLIGHT	MISONEISM	MISRECKONING	MISSILE
MISHAPT	MISLIGHTED	MISONEISMS	MISRECKONINGS	MISSILERIES
MISHEAR	MISLIGHTING	MISONEIST	MISRECKONS	MISSILERY
MISHEARD	MISLIGHTS	MISONEISTS	MISREGARD	MISSILES
MISHEARING	MISLIKE	MISORDER	MISREGARDS	MISSILRIES
MISHEARS	MISLIKED	MISORDERED	MISRELATE	MISSILRY
MISHEGAAS	MISLIKER	MISORDERING	MISRELATED	MISSING
MISHEGAASEN	MISLIKERS	MISORDERS	MISRELATES	MISSINGLY
MISHIT	MISLIKES	MISOS	MISRELATING	MISSION
MISHITS	MISLIKING	MISPICKEL	MISREPORT	MISSIONED
MISHITTING	MISLIKINGS	MISPICKELS	MISREPORTED	MISSIONER
MISHMASH	MISLIPPEN	MISPLACE	MISREPORTING	MISSIONERS
MISHMASHES	MISLIPPENED	MISPLACED	MISREPORTS	MISSIONING
MISHMEE	MISLIPPENING	MISPLACES	MISROUTE	MISSIONS
MISHMEES	MISLIPPENS	MISPLACING	MISROUTED	MISSIS
MISHMI	MISLIT	MISPLAY	MISROUTEING	MISSISES
MISHMIS	MISLIVE	MISPLAYED	MISROUTES	MISSISH
MISINFORM	MISLIVED	MISPLAYING	MISROUTING	MISSIVE
MISINFORMED	MISLIVES	MISPLAYS	MISRULE	MISSIVES
MISINFORMING	MISLIVING	MISPLEAD	MISRULED	MISSPEAK
MISINFORMS	MISLUCK	MISPLEADED	MISRULES	MISSPEAKING
MISINTEND	MISLUCKED	MISPLEADING	MISRULING	MISSPEAKS
MISINTENDED	MISLUCKING	MISPLEADINGS	MISS	MISSPELL
MISINTENDING	MISLUCKS	MISPLEADS	MISSA	MISSPELLED
MISINTENDS	MISMADE	MISPLEASE	MISSABLE	MISSPELLING
MISJOIN	MISMAKE	MISPLEASED	MISSAE	MISSPELLINGS
MISJOINED	MISMAKES	MISPLEASES	MISSAID	MISSPELLS
MISJOINING	MISMAKING	MISPLEASING	MISSAL	MISSPELT
MISJOINS	MISMANAGE	MISPLED	MISSALS	MISSPEND
MISJUDGE	MISMANAGED	MISPOINT	MISSAW	MISSPENDING
MISJUDGED	MISMANAGES	MISPOINTED	MISSAY	MISSPENDS
MISJUDGES	MISMANAGING	MISPOINTING	MISSAYING	MISSPENT
MISJUDGING	MISMARRIED	MISPOINTS	MISSAYINGS	MISSPOKE
MISKEN	MISMARRIES	MISPRAISE	MISSAYS	MISSPOKEN
MISKENNED	MISMARRY	MISPRAISED	MISSED	MISSTATE
MISKENNING	MISMARRYING	MISPRAISES	MISSEE	MISSTATED
MISKENS	MISMATCH	MISPRAISING	MISSEEING	MISSTATES
MISKENT	MISMATCHED	MISPRINT	MISSEEM	MISSTATING
MISKEY	MISMATCHES	MISPRINTED	MISSEEMED	MISSTEP
MISKEYED	MISMATCHING	MISPRINTING	MISSEEMING	MISSTEPPED
MISKEYING	MISMATE	MISPRINTS	MISSEEMINGS	MISSTEPPING
MISKEYS	MISMATED	MISPRISE	MISSEEMS	MISSTEPS
MISKNEW	MISMATES	MISPRISED	MISSEEN	MISSUIT

The Chambers Dictionary is the authority for many longer words; see *OSW* Introduction, page xii

MISSUITED	MISTLING	MITE	MIXT	MOBILES
MISSUITING	MISTOLD	MITER	MIXTION	MOBILISE
MISSUITS	MISTOOK	MITERED	MIXTIONS	MOBILISED
MISSUS	MISTRAL	MITERING	MIXTURE	MOBILISER
MISSUSES	MISTRALS	MITERS	MIXTURES	MOBILISERS
MISSY	MISTREAT	MITES	MIXY	MOBILISES
MIST	MISTREATED	MITHER	MIZ	MOBILISING
MISTAKE	MISTREATING	MITHERED	MIZEN	MOBILITIES
MISTAKEN	MISTREATS	MITHERING	MIZENS	MOBILITY
MISTAKES	MISTRESS	MITHERS	MIZMAZE	MOBILIZE
MISTAKING	MISTRESSED	MITICIDAL	MIZMAZES	MOBILIZED
MISTAKINGS	MISTRESSES	MITICIDE	MIZZ	MOBILIZER
MISTAUGHT	MISTRESSING	MITICIDES	MIZZEN	MOBILIZERS
MISTEACH	MISTRIAL	MITIER	MIZZENS	MOBILIZES
MISTEACHES	MISTRIALS	MITIEST	MIZZES	MOBILIZING
MISTEACHING	MISTRUST	MITIGABLE	MIZZLE	MOBLE
MISTED	MISTRUSTED	MITIGANT	MIZZLED	MOBLED
MISTELL	MISTRUSTING	MITIGATE	MIZZLES	MOBLES
MISTELLING	MISTRUSTS	MITIGATED	MIZZLIER	MOBLING
MISTELLS	MISTRYST	MITIGATES	MIZZLIEST	MOBOCRACIES
MISTEMPER	MISTRYSTED	MITIGATING	MIZZLING	MOBOCRACY
MISTEMPERED	MISTRYSTING	MITIGATOR	MIZZLINGS	MOBOCRAT
MISTEMPERING	MISTRYSTS	MITIGATORS	MIZZLY	MOBOCRATS
MISTEMPERS	MISTS	MITOGEN	MIZZONITE	MOBS
MISTER	MISTUNE	MITOGENIC	MIZZONITES	MOBSMAN
MISTERED	MISTUNED	MITOGENS	MNA	MOBSMEN
MISTERIES	MISTUNES	MITOSES	MNAS	MOBSTER
MISTERING	MISTUNING	MITOSIS	MNEME	MOBSTERS
MISTERM	MISTY	MITOTIC	MNEMES	MOCASSIN
MISTERMED	MISUSAGE	MITRAILLE	MNEMIC	MOCASSINS
MISTERMING	MISUSAGES	MITRAILLES	MNEMON	MOCCASIN
MISTERMS	MISUSE	MITRAL	MNEMONIC	MOCCASINS
MISTERS	MISUSED	MITRE	MNEMONICS	MOCH
MISTERY	MISUSER	MITRED	MNEMONIST	MOCHA
MISTFUL	MISUSERS	MITRES	MNEMONISTS	MOCHAS
MISTHINK	MISUSES	MITRIFORM	MNEMONS	MOCHELL
MISTHINKING	MISUSING	MITRING	MO	MOCHELLS
MISTHINKS	MISUST	MITT	MOA	MOCHIE
MISTHOUGHT	MISWEEN	MITTEN	MOAN	MOCHIER
MISTHOUGHTS	MISWEENED	MITTENED	MOANED	MOCHIEST
MISTICO	MISWEENING	MITTENS	MOANER	MOCHINESS
MISTICOS	MISWEENS	MITTIMUS	MOANERS	MOCHINESSES
MISTIER	MISWEND	MITTIMUSES	MOANFUL	MOCHS
MISTIEST	MISWENDING	MITTS	MOANFULLY	MOCHY
MISTIGRIS	MISWENDS	MITY	MOANING	MOCK
MISTIGRISES	MISWENT	MITZVAH	MOANS	MOCKABLE
MISTILY	MISWORD	MITZVAHS	MOAS	MOCKADO
MISTIME	MISWORDED	MITZVOTH	MOAT	MOCKADOES
MISTIMED	MISWORDING	MIURUS	MOATED	MOCKAGE
MISTIMES	MISWORDINGS	MIURUSES	MOATING	MOCKAGES
MISTIMING	MISWORDS	MIX	MOATS	MOCKED
MISTINESS	MISWRITE	MIXABLE	MOB	MOCKER
MISTINESSES	MISWRITES	MIXED	MOBBED	MOCKERIES
MISTING	MISWRITING	MIXEDLY	MOBBIE	MOCKERNUT
MISTINGS	MISWRITTEN	MIXEDNESS	MOBBIES	MOCKERNUTS
MISTITLE	MISWROTE	MIXEDNESSES	MOBBING	MOCKERS
MISTITLED	MISYOKE	MIXEN	MOBBINGS	MOCKERY
MISTITLES	MISYOKED	MIXENS	MOBBISH	MOCKING
MISTITLING	MISYOKES	MIXER	MOBBLE	MOCKINGLY
MISTLE	MISYOKING	MIXERS	MOBBLED	MOCKINGS
MISTLED	MITCH	MIXES	MOBBLES	MOCKS
MISTLES	MITCHED	MIXIER	MOBBLING	MOCOCK
MISTLETOE	MITCHES	MIXIEST	MOBBY	MOCOCKS
MISTLETOES	MITCHING	MIXING	MOBILE	MOCUCK

The Chambers Dictionary is the authority for many longer words; see *OSW* Introduction, page xii

MOCUCKS	MODES	MOHAIR	MOKIS	MOLLUSCAN
MOCUDDUM	MODEST	MOHAIRS	MOKO	MOLLUSCS
MOCUDDUMS	MODESTER	MOHAWK	MOKOS	MOLLUSK
MOD	MODESTEST	MOHAWKS	MOLA	MOLLUSKAN
MODAL	MODESTIES	MOHEL	MOLAL	MOLLUSKS
MODALISM	MODESTLY	MOHELS	MOLALITIES	MOLLY
MODALISMS	MODESTY	MOHR	MOLALITY	MOLLYMAWK
MODALIST	MODI	MOHRS	MOLAR	MOLLYMAWKS
MODALISTS	MODICUM	MOHUR	MOLARITIES	MOLOCH
MODALITIES	MODICUMS	MOHURS	MOLARITY	MOLOCHISE
MODALITY	MODIFIED	MOI	MOLARS	MOLOCHISED
MODALLY	MODIFIER	MOIDER	MOLAS	MOLOCHISES
MODALS	MODIFIERS	MOIDERED	MOLASSES	MOLOCHISING
MODE	MODIFIES	MOIDERING	MOLD	MOLOCHIZE
MODEL	MODIFY	MOIDERS	MOLDED	MOLOCHIZED
MODELED	MODIFYING	MOIDORE	MOLDING	MOLOCHIZES
MODELER	MODII	MOIDORES	MOLDS	MOLOCHIZING
MODELERS	MODILLION	MOIETIES	MOLDWARP	MOLOCHS
MODELING	MODILLIONS	MOIETY	MOLDWARPS	MOLOSSI
MODELINGS	MODIOLAR	MOIL	MOLE	MOLOSSUS
MODELLED	MODIOLI	MOILED	MOLECAST	MOLT
MODELLER	MODIOLUS	MOILER	MOLECASTS	MOLTED
MODELLERS	MODIOLUSES	MOILERS	MOLECULAR	MOLTEN
MODELLI	MODISH	MOILING	MOLECULE	MOLTENLY
MODELLING	MODISHLY	MOILS	MOLECULES	MOLTING
MODELLINGS	MODIST	MOINEAU	MOLEHILL	MOLTO
MODELLO	MODISTE	MOINEAUS	MOLEHILLS	MOLTS
MODELLOS	MODISTES	MOIRE	MOLEHUNT	MOLY
MODELS	MODISTS	MOIRES	MOLEHUNTS	MOLYBDATE
MODEM	MODIUS	MOISER	MOLERAT	MOLYBDATES
MODEMED	MODIWORT	MOISERS	MOLERATS	MOLYBDIC
MODEMING	MODIWORTS	MOIST	MOLES	MOLYBDOUS
MODEMS	MODS	MOISTED	MOLESKIN	MOM
MODENA	MODULAR	MOISTEN	MOLESKINS	MOME
MODENAS	MODULATE	MOISTENED	MOLEST	MOMENT
MODER	MODULATED	MOISTENING	MOLESTED	MOMENTA
MODERATE	MODULATES	MOISTENS	MOLESTER	MOMENTANY
MODERATED	MODULATING	MOISTER	MOLESTERS	MOMENTARY
MODERATES	MODULATOR	MOISTEST	MOLESTFUL	MOMENTLY
MODERATING	MODULATORS	MOISTIFIED	MOLESTING	MOMENTOUS
MODERATO	MODULE	MOISTIFIES	MOLESTS	MOMENTS
MODERATOR	MODULES	MOISTIFY	MOLIES	MOMENTUM
MODERATORS	MODULI	MOISTIFYING	MOLIMEN	MOMES
MODERATOS	MODULO	MOISTING	MOLIMENS	MOMMA
MODERN	MODULUS	MOISTLY	MOLINE	MOMMAS
MODERNER	MODUS	MOISTNESS	MOLINES	MOMMET
MODERNEST	MOE	MOISTNESSES	MOLINET	MOMMETS
MODERNISE	MOELLON	MOISTS	MOLINETS	MOMMIES
MODERNISED	MOELLONS	MOISTURE	MOLL	MOMMY
MODERNISES	MOES	MOISTURES	MOLLA	MOMS
MODERNISING	MOFETTE	MOIT	MOLLAH	MOMZER
MODERNISM	MOFETTES	MOITHER	MOLLAHS	MOMZERIM
MODERNISMS	MOFUSSIL	MOITHERED	MOLLAS	MOMZERS
MODERNIST	MOFUSSILS	MOITHERING	MOLLIE	MON
MODERNISTS	MOG	MOITHERS	MOLLIES	MONA
MODERNITIES	MOGGAN	MOITS	MOLLIFIED	MONACHAL
MODERNITY	MOGGANS	MOJO	MOLLIFIER	MONACHISM
MODERNIZE	MOGGIE	MOJOES	MOLLIFIERS	MONACHISMS
MODERNIZED	MOGGIES	MOJOS	MOLLIFIES	MONACHIST
MODERNIZES	MOGGY	MOKADDAM	MOLLIFY	MONACID
MODERNIZING	MOGS	MOKADDAMS	MOLLIFYING	MONACT
MODERNLY	MOGUL	MOKE	MOLLITIES	MONACTINE
MODERNS	MOGULED	MOKES	MOLLS	MONAD
MODERS	MOGULS	MOKI	MOLLUSC	MONADES

The Chambers Dictionary is the authority for many longer words; see OSW Introduction, page xii

MONADIC	MONEYMAN	MONKFISH	MONOGYNIES	MONOSES
MONADICAL	MONEYMEN	MONKFISHES	MONOGYNY	MONOSIES
MONADISM	MONEYS	MONKHOOD	MONOHULL	MONOSIS
MONADISMS	MONEYWORT	MONKHOODS	MONOHULLS	MONOSTICH
MONADNOCK	MONEYWORTS	MONKISH	MONOKINI	MONOSTICHS
MONADNOCKS	MONG	MONKS	MONOKINIS	MONOSTYLE
MONADS	MONGCORN	MONKSHOOD	MONOLATER	MONOSY
MONAL	MONGCORNS	MONKSHOODS	MONOLATERS	MONOTINT
MONALS	MONGER	MONO	MONOLATRIES	MONOTINTS
MONANDRIES	MONGERIES	MONOACID	MONOLATRY	MONOTONE
MONANDRY	MONGERING	MONOAMINE	MONOLAYER	MONOTONED
MONARCH	MONGERINGS	MONOAMINES	MONOLAYERS	MONOTONES
MONARCHAL	MONGERS	MONOBASIC	MONOLITH	MONOTONIC
MONARCHIC	MONGERY	MONOCARP	MONOLITHS	MONOTONIES
MONARCHIES	MONGOL	MONOCARPS	MONOLOGIC	MONOTONING
MONARCHS	MONGOLISM	MONOCEROS	MONOLOGIES	MONOTONY
MONARCHY	MONGOLISMS	MONOCEROSES	MONOLOGUE	MONOTREME
MONARDA	MONGOLOID	MONOCHORD	MONOLOGUES	MONOTREMES
MONARDAS	MONGOLOIDS	MONOCHORDS	MONOLOGY	MONOTROCH
MONAS	MONGOLS	MONOCLE	MONOMACHIES	MONOTROCHS
MONASES	MONGOOSE	MONOCLED	MONOMACHY	MONOTYPE
MONASTERIES	MONGOOSES	MONOCLES	MONOMANIA	MONOTYPES
MONASTERY	MONGREL	MONOCLINE	MONOMANIAS	MONOTYPIC
MONASTIC	MONGRELLY	MONOCLINES	MONOMARK	MONOXIDE
MONASTICS	MONGRELS	MONOCOQUE	MONOMARKS	MONOXIDES
MONATOMIC	MONGS	MONOCOQUES	MONOMER	MONOXYLON
MONAUL	MONIAL	MONOCOT	MONOMERIC	MONOXYLONS
MONAULS	MONIALS	MONOCOTS	MONOMERS	MONSIEUR
MONAURAL	MONICKER	MONOCRACIES	MONOMETER	MONSOON
MONAXIAL	MONICKERS	MONOCRACY	MONOMETERS	MONSOONAL
MONAXON	MONIED	MONOCRAT	MONOMIAL	MONSOONS
MONAXONIC	MONIES	MONOCRATS	MONOMIALS	MONSTER
MONAXONS	MONIKER	MONOCULAR	MONOMODE	MONSTERA
MONAZITE	MONIKERS	MONOCYTE	MONOPHAGIES	MONSTERAS
MONAZITES	MONILIA	MONOCYTES	MONOPHAGY	MONSTERS
MONDAIN	MONILIAS	MONODIC	MONOPHASE	MONSTROUS
MONDAINE	MONIMENT	MONODICAL	MONOPHONIES	MONTAGE
MONDAINES	MONIMENTS	MONODIES	MONOPHONY	MONTAGED
MONDAINS	MONIPLIES	MONODIST	MONOPITCH	MONTAGES
MONDIAL	MONISM	MONODISTS	MONOPLANE	MONTAGING
MONDO	MONISMS	MONODONT	MONOPLANES	MONTANE
MONECIOUS	MONIST	MONODRAMA	MONOPOD	MONTANT
MONER	MONISTIC	MONODRAMAS	MONOPODE	MONTANTO
MONERA	MONISTS	MONODY	MONOPODES	MONTANTOS
MONERGISM	MONITION	MONOECISM	MONOPODIA	MONTANTS
MONERGISMS	MONITIONS	MONOECISMS	MONOPODS	MONTARIA
MONERON	MONITIVE	MONOFIL	MONOPOLE	MONTARIAS
MONETARY	MONITOR	MONOFILS	MONOPOLES	MONTE
MONETH	MONITORED	MONOGAMIC	MONOPOLIES	MONTEITH
MONETHS	MONITORING	MONOGAMIES	MONOPOLY	MONTEITHS
MONETISE	MONITORS	MONOGAMY	MONOPSONIES	MONTEM
MONETISED	MONITORY	MONOGENIC	MONOPSONY	MONTEMS
MONETISES	MONITRESS	MONOGENIES	MONOPTERA	MONTERO
MONETISING	MONITRESSES	MONOGENY	MONOPTOTE	MONTEROS
MONETIZE	MONK	MONOGLOT	MONOPTOTES	MONTES
MONETIZED	MONKERIES	MONOGLOTS	MONOPULSE	MONTH
MONETIZES	MONKERY	MONOGONIES	MONOPULSES	MONTHLIES
MONETIZING	MONKEY	MONOGONY	MONORAIL	MONTHLING
MONEY	MONKEYED	MONOGRAM	MONORAILS	MONTHLINGS
MONEYBAGS	MONKEYING	MONOGRAMS	MONORCHID	MONTHLY
MONEYED	MONKEYISH	MONOGRAPH	MONORHINE	MONTHS
MONEYER	MONKEYISM	MONOGRAPHED	MONORHYME	MONTICLE
MONEYERS	MONKEYISMS	MONOGRAPHING	MONORHYMES	MONTICLES
MONEYLESS	MONKEYS	MONOGRAPHS	MONOS	MONTICULE

MONTICULES	MOONFACES	MOORHEN	MOPPED	MORAYS
MONTIES	MOONIER	MOORHENS	MOPPER	MORBID
MONTRE	MOONIES	MOORIER	MOPPERS	MORBIDER
MONTRES	MOONIEST	MOORIEST	MOPPET	MORBIDEST
MONTURE	MOONING	MOORILL	MOPPETS	MORBIDITIES
MONTURES	MOONISH	MOORILLS	MOPPIER	MORBIDITY
MONTY	MOONLESS	MOORING	MOPPIEST	MORBIDLY
MONUMENT	MOONLET	MOORINGS	MOPPING	MORBIFIC
MONUMENTED	MOONLETS	MOORISH	MOPPY	MORBILLI
MONUMENTING	MOONLIGHT	MOORLAND	MOPS	MORBUS
MONUMENTS	MOONLIGHTED	MOORLANDS	MOPSIES	MORBUSES
MONY	MOONLIGHTING	MOORLOG	MOPSTICK	MORCEAU
MONYPLIES	MOONLIGHTINGS	MOORLOGS	MOPSTICKS	MORCEAUX
MONZONITE	MOONLIGHTS	MOORMAN	MOPSY	MORDACITIES
MONZONITES	MOONLIT	MOORMEN	MOPUS	MORDACITY
MOO	MOONPHASE	MOORS	MOPUSES	MORDANCIES
MOOCH	MOONPHASES	MOORVA	MOPY	MORDANCY
MOOCHED	MOONQUAKE	MOORVAS	MOQUETTE	MORDANT
MOOCHER	MOONQUAKES	MOORY	MOQUETTES	MORDANTED
MOOCHERS	MOONRAKER	MOOS	MOR	MORDANTING
MOOCHES	MOONRAKERS	MOOSE	MORA	MORDANTLY
MOOCHING	MOONRISE	MOOSEYARD	MORACEOUS	MORDANTS
MOOD	MOONRISES	MOOSEYARDS	MORAINAL	MORDENT
MOODIED	MOONROCK	MOOT	MORAINE	MORDENTS
MOODIER	MOONROCKS	MOOTABLE	MORAINES	MORE
MOODIES	MOONROOF	MOOTED	MORAINIC	MOREEN
MOODIEST	MOONROOFS	MOOTER	MORAL	MOREENS
MOODILY	MOONS	MOOTERS	MORALE	MOREISH
MOODINESS	MOONSAIL	MOOTEST	MORALES	MOREL
MOODINESSES	MOONSAILS	MOOTING	MORALISE	MORELLO
MOODS	MOONSCAPE	MOOTINGS	MORALISED	MORELLOS
MOODY	MOONSCAPES	MOOTMAN	MORALISER	MORELS
MOODYING	MOONSEED	MOOTMEN	MORALISERS	MORENDO
MOOED	MOONSEEDS	MOOTS	MORALISES	MOREOVER
MOOI	MOONSET	MOOVE	MORALISING	MOREPORK
MOOING	MOONSETS	MOOVED	MORALISM	MOREPORKS
MOOK	MOONSHEE	MOOVES	MORALISMS	MORES
MOOKS	MOONSHEES	MOOVING	MORALIST	MORGANITE
MOOKTAR	MOONSHINE	MOP	MORALISTS	MORGANITES
MOOKTARS	MOONSHINES	MOPANE	MORALITIES	MORGAY
MOOL	MOONSHINY	MOPANES	MORALITY	MORGAYS
MOOLA	MOONSHOT	MOPANI	MORALIZE	MORGEN
MOOLAH	MOONSHOTS	MOPANIS	MORALIZED	MORGENS
MOOLAHS	MOONSTONE	MOPBOARD	MORALIZER	MORGUE
MOOLAS	MOONSTONES	MOPBOARDS	MORALIZERS	MORGUES
MOOLED	MOONWALK	MOPE	MORALIZES	MORIA
MOOLI	MOONWALKED	MOPED	MORALIZING	MORIAS
MOOLIES	MOONWALKING	MOPEDS	MORALL	MORIBUND
MOOLING	MOONWALKS	MOPEHAWK	MORALLED	MORICHE
MOOLIS	MOONWORT	MOPEHAWKS	MORALLER	MORICHES
MOOLS	MOONWORTS	MOPER	MORALLERS	MORION
MOOLY	MOONY	MOPERS	MORALLING	MORIONS
MOON	MOOP	MOPES	MORALLS	MORISCO
MOONBEAM	MOOPED	MOPEY	MORALLY	MORISCOES
MOONBEAMS	MOOPING	MOPHEAD	MORALS	MORISCOS
MOONBLIND	MOOPS	MOPHEADS	MORAS	MORISH
MOONCALF	MOOR	MOPIER	MORASS	MORKIN
MOONCALVES	MOORAGE	MOPIEST	MORASSES	MORKINS
MOONED	MOORAGES	MOPING	MORASSY	MORLING
MOONER	MOORCOCK	MOPINGLY	MORAT	MORLINGS
MOONERS	MOORCOCKS	MOPISH	MORATORIA	MORMAOR
MOONEYE	MOORED	MOPISHLY	MORATORY	MORMAORS
MOONEYES	MOORFOWL	MOPOKE	MORATS	MORN
MOONFACE	MOORFOWLS	MOPOKES	MORAY	MORNAY

The Chambers Dictionary is the authority for many longer words; see *OSW* Introduction, page xii

MORNAYS	MORSES	MORULA	MOTETS	MOTOCROSSES
MORNE	MORSURE	MORULAE	MOTETT	MOTOR
MORNED	MORSURES	MORULAR	MOTETTIST	MOTORABLE
MORNES	MORT	MORWONG	MOTETTISTS	MOTORAIL
MORNING	MORTAL	MORWONGS	MOTETTS	MOTORAILS
MORNINGS	MORTALISE	MOSAIC	MOTEY	MOTORBIKE
MORNS	MORTALISED	MOSAICISM	MOTH	MOTORBIKES
MOROCCO	MORTALISES	MOSAICISMS	MOTHBALL	MOTORBOAT
MOROCCOS	MORTALISING	MOSAICIST	MOTHBALLED	MOTORBOATS
MORON	MORTALITIES	MOSAICISTS	MOTHBALLING	MOTORCADE
MORONIC	MORTALITY	MOSAICS	MOTHBALLS	MOTORCADES
MORONS	MORTALIZE	MOSCHATEL	MOTHED	MOTORED
MOROSE	MORTALIZED	MOSCHATELS	MOTHER	MOTORIAL
MOROSELY	MORTALIZES	MOSE	MOTHERED	MOTORING
MOROSER	MORTALIZING	MOSED	MOTHERING	MOTORISE
MOROSEST	MORTALLY	MOSES	MOTHERINGS	MOTORISED
MOROSITIES	MORTALS	MOSEY	MOTHERLY	MOTORISES
MOROSITY	MORTAR	MOSEYED	MOTHERS	MOTORISING
MORPH	MORTARED	MOSEYING	MOTHERY	MOTORIST
MORPHEAN	MORTARING	MOSEYS	MOTHIER	MOTORISTS
MORPHED	MORTARS	MOSHAV	MOTHIEST	MOTORIUM
MORPHEME	MORTBELL	MOSHAVIM	MOTHPROOF	MOTORIUMS
MORPHEMES	MORTBELLS	MOSHING	MOTHPROOFED	MOTORIZE
MORPHEMIC	MORTCLOTH	MOSHINGS	MOTHPROOFING	MOTORIZED
MORPHEMICS	MORTCLOTHS	MOSING	MOTHPROOFS	MOTORIZES
MORPHETIC	MORTGAGE	MOSKONFYT	MOTHS	MOTORIZING
MORPHEW	MORTGAGED	MOSKONFYTS	MOTHY	MOTORMAN
MORPHEWS	MORTGAGEE	MOSLINGS	MOTIER	MOTORMEN
MORPHIA	MORTGAGEES	MOSQUE	MOTIEST	MOTORS
MORPHIAS	MORTGAGER	MOSQUES	MOTIF	MOTORWAY
MORPHIC	MORTGAGERS	MOSQUITO	MOTIFS	MOTORWAYS
MORPHINE	MORTGAGES	MOSQUITOES	MOTILE	MOTORY
MORPHINES	MORTGAGING	MOSQUITOS	MOTILES	MOTOSCAFI
MORPHING	MORTGAGOR	MOSS	MOTILITIES	MOTOSCAFO
MORPHINGS	MORTGAGORS	MOSSBACK	MOTILITY	MOTS
MORPHO	MORTICE	MOSSBACKS	MOTION	MOTSER
MORPHOS	MORTICED	MOSSED	MOTIONAL	MOTSERS
MORPHOSES	MORTICER	MOSSES	MOTIONED	MOTT
MORPHOSIS	MORTICERS	MOSSIE	MOTIONING	MOTTE
MORPHOTIC	MORTICES	MOSSIER	MOTIONIST	MOTTES
MORPHS	MORTICIAN	MOSSIES	MOTIONISTS	MOTTIER
MORRA	MORTICIANS	MOSSIEST	MOTIONS	MOTTIEST
MORRAS	MORTICING	MOSSINESS	MOTIVATE	MOTTLE
MORRHUA	MORTIFIC	MOSSINESSES	MOTIVATED	MOTTLED
MORRHUAS	MORTIFIED	MOSSING	MOTIVATES	MOTTLES
MORRICE	MORTIFIER	MOSSLAND	MOTIVATING	MOTTLING
MORRICES	MORTIFIERS	MOSSLANDS	MOTIVATOR	MOTTLINGS
MORRION	MORTIFIES	MOSSPLANT	MOTIVATORS	MOTTO
MORRIONS	MORTIFY	MOSSPLANTS	MOTIVE	MOTTOED
MORRIS	MORTIFYING	MOSSY	MOTIVED	MOTTOES
MORRISED	MORTIFYINGS	MOST	MOTIVES	MOTTS
MORRISES	MORTISE	MOSTLY	MOTIVIC	MOTTY
MORRISING	MORTISED	MOSTS	MOTIVING	MOTU
MORRO	MORTISER	MOSTWHAT	MOTIVITIES	MOTUCA
MORROS	MORTISERS	MOT	MOTIVITY	MOTUCAS
MORROW	MORTISES	MOTE	MOTLEY	MOTUS
MORROWS	MORTISING	MOTED	MOTLEYER	MOTZA
MORS	MORTLING	MOTEL	MOTLEYEST	MOTZAS
MORSAL	MORTLINGS	MOTELIER	MOTLEYS	MOU
MORSE	MORTMAIN	MOTELIERS	MOTLIER	MOUCH
MORSEL	MORTMAINS	MOTELS	MOTLIEST	MOUCHARD
MORSELLED	MORTS	MOTEN	MOTMOT	MOUCHARDS
MORSELLING	MORTUARIES	MOTES	MOTMOTS	MOUCHED
MORSELS	MORTUARY	MOTET	MOTOCROSS	MOUCHER

MOUCHERS	MOUP	MOUTHERS	MOYAS	MUCKHEAP
MOUCHES	MOUPED	MOUTHFEEL	MOYGASHEL	MUCKHEAPS
MOUCHING	MOUPING	MOUTHFEELS	MOYGASHELS	MUCKIER
MOUCHOIR	MOUPS	MOUTHFUL	MOYITIES	MUCKIEST
MOUCHOIRS	MOURN	MOUTHFULS	MOYITY	MUCKINESS
MOUDIWART	MOURNED	MOUTHIER	MOYL	MUCKINESSES
MOUDIWARTS	MOURNER	MOUTHIEST	MOYLE	MUCKING
MOUDIWORT	MOURNERS	MOUTHING	MOYLED	MUCKLE
MOUDIWORTS	MOURNFUL	MOUTHLESS	MOYLES	MUCKLES
MOUE	MOURNING	MOUTHS	MOYLING	MUCKLUCK
MOUES	MOURNINGS	MOUTHWASH	MOYLS	MUCKLUCKS
MOUFFLON	MOURNIVAL	MOUTHWASHES	MOYS	MUCKS
MOUFFLONS	MOURNIVALS	MOUTHY	MOZ	MUCKSWEAT
MOUFLON	MOURNS	MOUTON	MOZE	MUCKSWEATS
MOUFLONS	MOUS	MOUTONS	MOZED	MUCKY
MOUGHT	MOUSAKA	MOVABLE	MOZES	MUCLUC
MOUILLE	MOUSAKAS	MOVABLES	MOZETTA	MUCLUCS
MOUJIK	MOUSE	MOVABLY	MOZETTAS	MUCOID
MOULAGE	MOUSED	MOVE	MOZING	MUCOR
MOULAGES	MOUSEKIN	MOVEABLE	MOZZ	MUCORS
MOULD	MOUSEKINS	MOVEABLES	MOZZES	MUCOSA
MOULDABLE	MOUSER	MOVEABLY	MOZZETTA	MUCOSAE
MOULDED	MOUSERIES	MOVED	MOZZETTAS	MUCOSITIES
MOULDER	MOUSERS	MOVELESS	MOZZIE	MUCOSITY
MOULDERED	MOUSERY	MOVEMENT	MOZZIES	MUCOUS
MOULDERING	MOUSES	MOVEMENTS	MOZZLE	MUCRO
MOULDERS	MOUSEY	MOVER	MOZZLES	MUCRONATE
MOULDIER	MOUSIE	MOVERS	MPRET	MUCRONES
MOULDIEST	MOUSIER	MOVES	MPRETS	MUCROS
MOULDING	MOUSIES	MOVIE	MRIDAMGAM	MUCULENT
MOULDINGS	MOUSIEST	MOVIEGOER	MRIDAMGAMS	MUCUS
MOULDS	MOUSING	MOVIEGOERS	MRIDANG	MUCUSES
MOULDWARP	MOUSINGS	MOVIELAND	MRIDANGA	MUD
MOULDWARPS	MOUSLE	MOVIELANDS	MRIDANGAM	MUDBATH
MOULDY	MOUSLED	MOVIES	MRIDANGAMS	MUDBATHS
MOULIN	MOUSLES	MOVING	MRIDANGAS	MUDCAT
MOULINET	MOUSLING	MOVINGLY	MRIDANGS	MUDCATS
MOULINETS	MOUSME	MOW	MU	MUDDED
MOULINS	MOUSMEE	MOWA	MUCATE	MUDDER
MOULS	MOUSMEES	MOWAS	MUCATES	MUDDERS
MOULT	MOUSMES	MOWBURN	MUCH	MUDDIED
MOULTED	MOUSSAKA	MOWBURNED	MUCHEL	MUDDIER
MOULTEN	MOUSSAKAS	MOWBURNING	MUCHELL	MUDDIES
MOULTING	MOUSSE	MOWBURNS	MUCHELLS	MUDDIEST
MOULTINGS	MOUSSES	MOWBURNT	MUCHELS	MUDDILY
MOULTS	MOUST	MOWDIWART	MUCHES	MUDDINESS
MOUND	MOUSTACHE	MOWDIWARTS	MUCHLY	MUDDINESSES
MOUNDED	MOUSTACHES	MOWDIWORT	MUCHNESS	MUDDING
MOUNDING	MOUSTED	MOWDIWORTS	MUCHNESSES	MUDDLE
MOUNDS	MOUSTING	MOWED	MUCID	MUDDLED
MOUNSEER	MOUSTS	MOWER	MUCIGEN	MUDDLER
MOUNSEERS	MOUSY	MOWERS	MUCIGENS	MUDDLERS
MOUNT	MOUTAN	MOWING	MUCILAGE	MUDDLES
MOUNTAIN	MOUTANS	MOWINGS	MUCILAGES	MUDDLING
MOUNTAINS	MOUTER	MOWN	MUCIN	MUDDY
MOUNTANT	MOUTERED	MOWRA	MUCINS	MUDDYING
MOUNTANTS	MOUTERER	MOWRAS	MUCK	MUDEJAR
MOUNTED	MOUTERERS	MOWS	MUCKED	MUDEJARES
MOUNTER	MOUTERING	MOXA	MUCKENDER	MUDFISH
MOUNTERS	MOUTERS	MOXAS	MUCKENDERS	MUDFISHES
MOUNTING	MOUTH	MOXIE	MUCKER	MUDFLAP
MOUNTINGS	MOUTHABLE	MOXIES	MUCKERED	MUDFLAPS
MOUNTS	MOUTHED	MOY	MUCKERING	MUDFLAT
	MOUTHER	MOYA	MUCKERS	MUDFLATS

MUDGE	MUFLON	MULCTING	MULTIPARAE	MUMPERS
MUDGED	MUFLONS	MULCTS	MULTIPARAS	MUMPING
MUDGER	MUFTI	MULE	MULTIPED	MUMPISH
MUDGERS	MUFTIS	MULES	MULTIPEDE	MUMPISHLY
MUDGES	MUG	MULETEER	MULTIPEDES	MUMPS
MUDGING	MUGEARITE	MULETEERS	MULTIPEDS	MUMPSIMUS
MUDGUARD	MUGEARITES	MULEY	MULTIPLE	MUMPSIMUSES
MUDGUARDS	MUGFUL	MULEYS	MULTIPLES	MUMS
MUDHOLE	MUGFULS	MULGA	MULTIPLET	MUMSIER
MUDHOLES	MUGGED	MULGAS	MULTIPLETS	MUMSIEST
MUDHOOK	MUGGEE	MULISH	MULTIPLEX	MUMSY
MUDHOOKS	MUGGEES	MULISHLY	MULTIPLEXED	MUN
MUDIR	MUGGER	MULL	MULTIPLEXES	MUNCH
MUDIRIA	MUGGERS	MULLAH	MULTIPLEXING	MUNCHED
MUDIRIAS	MUGGIER	MULLAHS	MULTIPLIED	MUNCHER
MUDIRIEH	MUGGIEST	MULLARKIES	MULTIPLIES	MUNCHERS
MUDIRIEHS	MUGGINESS	MULLARKY	MULTIPLY	MUNCHES
MUDIRS	MUGGINESSES	MULLED	MULTIPLYING	MUNCHING
MUDLARK	MUGGING	MULLEIN	MULTITUDE	MUNCHKIN
MUDLARKED	MUGGINGS	MULLEINS	MULTITUDES	MUNCHKINS
MUDLARKING	MUGGINS	MULLER	MULTIUSER	MUNDANE
MUDLARKS	MUGGINSES	MULLERS	MULTUM	MUNDANELY
MUDLOGGER	MUGGISH	MULLET	MULTUMS	MUNDANER
MUDLOGGERS	MUGGY	MULLETS	MULTURE	MUNDANEST
MUDPACK	MUGS	MULLEY	MULTURED	MUNDANITIES
MUDPACKS	MUGSHOT	MULLEYS	MULTURER	MUNDANITY
MUDPUPPIES	MUGSHOTS	MULLIGAN	MULTURERS	MUNDIC
MUDPUPPY	MUGWORT	MULLIGANS	MULTURES	MUNDICS
MUDRA	MUGWORTS	MULLING	MULTURING	MUNDIFIED
MUDRAS	MUGWUMP	MULLION	MUM	MUNDIFIES
MUDS	MUGWUMPS	MULLIONED	MUMBLE	MUNDIFY
MUDSCOW	MUID	MULLIONS	MUMBLED	MUNDIFYING
MUDSCOWS	MUIDS	MULLOCK	MUMBLER	MUNDUNGUS
MUDSLIDE	MUIL	MULLOCKS	MUMBLERS	MUNDUNGUSES
MUDSLIDES	MUILS	MULLOWAY	MUMBLES	MUNGCORN
MUDSTONE	MUIR	MULLOWAYS	MUMBLING	MUNGCORNS
MUDSTONES	MUIRBURN	MULLS	MUMBLINGS	MUNGO
MUDWORT	MUIRBURNS	MULMUL	MUMCHANCE	MUNGOOSE
MUDWORTS	MUIRS	MULMULL	MUMCHANCES	MUNGOOSES
MUEDDIN	MUIST	MULMULLS	MUMM	MUNGOS
MUEDDINS	MUISTED	MULMULS	MUMMED	MUNICIPAL
MUENSTER	MUISTING	MULSE	MUMMER	MUNIFIED
MUENSTERS	MUISTS	MULSES	MUMMERIES	MUNIFIES
MUESLI	MUJAHEDIN	MULSH	MUMMERS	MUNIFY
MUESLIS	MUJAHIDIN	MULSHED	MUMMERY	MUNIFYING
MUEZZIN	MUJIK	MULSHES	MUMMIA	MUNIMENT
MUEZZINS	MUJIKS	MULSHING	MUMMIAS	MUNIMENTS
MUFF	MUKHTAR	MULTEITIES	MUMMIED	MUNITE
MUFFED	MUKHTARS	MULTEITY	MUMMIES	MUNITED
MUFFETTEE	MUKLUK	MULTIFID	MUMMIFIED	MUNITES
MUFFETTEES	MUKLUKS	MULTIFIL	MUMMIFIES	MUNITING
MUFFIN	MULATTA	MULTIFILS	MUMMIFORM	MUNITION
MUFFINEER	MULATTAS	MULTIFOIL	MUMMIFY	MUNITIONED
MUFFINEERS	MULATTO	MULTIFOILS	MUMMIFYING	MUNITIONING
MUFFING	MULATTOES	MULTIFORM	MUMMING	MUNITIONS
MUFFINS	MULATTOS	MULTIFORMS	MUMMINGS	MUNNION
MUFFISH	MULBERRIES	MULTIGYM	MUMMOCK	MUNNIONS
MUFFLE	MULBERRY	MULTIGYMS	MUMMOCKS	MUNSHI
MUFFLED	MULCH	MULTIHULL	MUMMS	MUNSHIS
MUFFLER	MULCHED	MULTIHULLS	MUMMY	MUNSTER
MUFFLERS	MULCHES	MULTIMODE	MUMMYING	MUNSTERS
MUFFLES	MULCHING	MULTIPACK	MUMP	MUNT
MUFFLING	MULCT	MULTIPACKS	MUMPED	MUNTIN
MUFFS	MULCTED	MULTIPARA	MUMPER	MUNTING

The Chambers Dictionary is the authority for many longer words; see *OSW* Introduction, page xii

MUNTINGS	MURKINESSES	MUSACEOUS	MUSHINESSES	MUSOS
MUNTINS	MURKISH	MUSANG	MUSHING	MUSQUASH
MUNTJAC	MURKS	MUSANGS	MUSHMOUTH	MUSQUASHES
MUNTJACS	MURKSOME	MUSCADEL	MUSHMOUTHS	MUSROL
MUNTJAK	MURKY	MUSCADELS	MUSHROOM	MUSROLS
MUNTJAKS	MURL	MUSCADIN	MUSHROOMED	MUSS
MUNTS	MURLAIN	MUSCADINE	MUSHROOMING	MUSSE
MUNTU	MURLAINS	MUSCADINES	MUSHROOMS	MUSSED
MUNTUS	MURLAN	MUSCADINS	MUSHY	MUSSEL
MUON	MURLANS	MUSCARINE	MUSIC	MUSSELLED
MUONIC	MURLED	MUSCARINES	MUSICAL	MUSSELS
MUONIUM	MURLIER	MUSCAT	MUSICALE	MUSSES
MUONIUMS	MURLIEST	MUSCATEL	MUSICALES	MUSSIER
MUONS	MURLIN	MUSCATELS	MUSICALLY	MUSSIEST
MUQADDAM	MURLING	MUSCATS	MUSICALS	MUSSINESS
MUQADDAMS	MURLINS	MUSCID	MUSICIAN	MUSSINESSES
MURAENA	MURLS	MUSCIDS	MUSICIANS	MUSSING
MURAENAS	MURLY	MUSCLE	MUSICKED	MUSSITATE
MURAGE	MURMUR	MUSCLED	MUSICKER	MUSSITATED
MURAGES	MURMURED	MUSCLEMAN	MUSICKERS	MUSSITATES
MURAL	MURMURER	MUSCLEMEN	MUSICKING	MUSSITATING
MURALIST	MURMURERS	MUSCLES	MUSICS	MUSSY
MURALISTS	MURMURING	MUSCLIER	MUSIMON	MUST
MURALS	MURMURINGS	MUSCLIEST	MUSIMONS	MUSTACHE
MURDER	MURMUROUS	MUSCLING	MUSING	MUSTACHES
MURDERED	MURMURS	MUSCLINGS	MUSINGLY	MUSTACHIO
MURDEREE	MURPHIES	MUSCLY	MUSINGS	MUSTACHIOS
MURDEREES	MURPHY	MUSCOID	MUSIT	MUSTANG
MURDERER	MURRA	MUSCOLOGIES	MUSITS	MUSTANGS
MURDERERS	MURRAIN	MUSCOLOGY	MUSIVE	MUSTARD
MURDERESS	MURRAINED	MUSCONE	MUSK	MUSTARDS
MURDERESSES	MURRAINS	MUSCONES	MUSKED	MUSTED
MURDERING	MURRAM	MUSCOSE	MUSKEG	MUSTEE
MURDEROUS	MURRAMS	MUSCOVADO	MUSKEGS	MUSTEES
MURDERS	MURRAS	MUSCOVADOS	MUSKET	MUSTELINE
MURE	MURRAY	MUSCOVITE	MUSKETEER	MUSTELINES
MURED	MURRAYS	MUSCOVITES	MUSKETEERS	MUSTER
MURENA	MURRE	MUSCULAR	MUSKETOON	MUSTERED
MURENAS	MURRELET	MUSCULOUS	MUSKETOONS	MUSTERER
MURES	MURRELETS	MUSE	MUSKETRIES	MUSTERERS
MUREX	MURREN	MUSED	MUSKETRY	MUSTERING
MUREXES	MURRENS	MUSEFUL	MUSKETS	MUSTERS
MURGEON	MURRES	MUSEFULLY	MUSKIER	MUSTH
MURGEONED	MURREY	MUSEOLOGIES	MUSKIEST	MUSTHS
MURGEONING	MURREYS	MUSEOLOGY	MUSKILY	MUSTIER
MURGEONS	MURRHA	MUSER	MUSKINESS	MUSTIEST
MURIATE	MURRHAS	MUSERS	MUSKINESSES	MUSTILY
MURIATED	MURRHINE	MUSES	MUSKING	MUSTINESS
MURIATES	MURRIES	MUSET	MUSKLE	MUSTINESSES
MURIATIC	MURRIN	MUSETS	MUSKLES	MUSTING
MURICATE	MURRINE	MUSETTE	MUSKONE	MUSTS
MURICATED	MURRINS	MUSETTES	MUSKONES	MUSTY
MURICES	MURRION	MUSEUM	MUSKRAT	MUTABLE
MURIFORM	MURRIONS	MUSEUMS	MUSKRATS	MUTABLY
MURINE	MURRY	MUSH	MUSKS	MUTAGEN
MURINES	MURTHER	MUSHA	MUSKY	MUTAGENIC
MURING	MURTHERED	MUSHED	MUSLIN	MUTAGENS
MURK	MURTHERER	MUSHER	MUSLINED	MUTANDA
MURKER	MURTHERERS	MUSHERS	MUSLINET	MUTANDUM
MURKEST	MURTHERING	MUSHES	MUSLINETS	MUTANT
MURKIER	MURTHERS	MUSHIER	MUSLINS	MUTANTS
MURKIEST	MURVA	MUSHIEST	MUSMON	MUTATE
MURKILY	MURVAS	MUSHILY	MUSMONS	MUTATED
MURKINESS	MUS	MUSHINESS	MUSO	MUTATES

MUTATING	MUTUALISING	MYCOSIS	MYOMATA	MYSTIFIER
MUTATION	MUTUALISM	MYCOTIC	MYOPE	MYSTIFIERS
MUTATIONS	MUTUALISMS	MYCOTOXIN	MYOPES	MYSTIFIES
MUTATIVE	MUTUALITIES	MYCOTOXINS	MYOPIA	MYSTIFY
MUTATORY	MUTUALITY	MYDRIASES	MYOPIAS	MYSTIFYING
MUTCH	MUTUALIZE	MYDRIASIS	MYOPIC	MYSTIQUE
MUTCHES	MUTUALIZED	MYDRIATIC	MYOPICS	MYSTIQUES
MUTCHKIN	MUTUALIZES	MYDRIATICS	MYOPS	MYTH
MUTCHKINS	MUTUALIZING	MYELIN	MYOPSES	MYTHI
MUTE	MUTUALLY	MYELINS	MYOSES	MYTHIC
MUTED	MUTUALS	MYELITIS	MYOSIN	MYTHICAL
MUTELY	MUTUCA	MYELITISES	MYOSINS	MYTHICISE
MUTENESS	MUTUCAS	MYELOID	MYOSIS	MYTHICISED
MUTENESSES	MUTULE	MYELOMA	MYOSITIS	MYTHICISES
MUTER	MUTULES	MYELOMAS	MYOSITISES	MYTHICISING
MUTES	MUTUUM	MYELOMATA	MYOSOTE	MYTHICISM
MUTEST	MUTUUMS	MYELON	MYOSOTES	MYTHICISMS
MUTI	MUX	MYELONS	MYOSOTIS	MYTHICIST
MUTICOUS	MUXED	MYGALE	MYOSOTISES	MYTHICISTS
MUTILATE	MUXES	MYGALES	MYOTONIA	MYTHICIZE
MUTILATED	MUXING	MYIASES	MYOTONIAS	MYTHICIZED
MUTILATES	MUZAKY	MYIASIS	MYOTUBE	MYTHICIZES
MUTILATING	MUZHIK	MYLODON	MYOTUBES	MYTHICIZING
MUTILATOR	MUZHIKS	MYLODONS	MYRBANE	MYTHISE
MUTILATORS	MUZZIER	MYLODONT	MYRBANES	MYTHISED
MUTINE	MUZZIEST	MYLODONTS	MYRIAD	MYTHISES
MUTINED	MUZZILY	MYLOHYOID	MYRIADS	MYTHISING
MUTINEER	MUZZINESS	MYLOHYOIDS	MYRIADTH	MYTHISM
MUTINEERED	MUZZINESSES	MYLONITE	MYRIADTHS	MYTHISMS
MUTINEERING	MUZZLE	MYLONITES	MYRIAPOD	MYTHIST
MUTINEERS	MUZZLED	MYLONITIC	MYRIAPODS	MYTHISTS
MUTINES	MUZZLER	MYNA	MYRINGA	MYTHIZE
MUTING	MUZZLERS	MYNAH	MYRINGAS	MYTHIZED
MUTINIED	MUZZLES	MYNAHS	MYRIOPOD	MYTHIZES
MUTINIES	MUZZLING	MYNAS	MYRIOPODS	MYTHIZING
MUTINING	MUZZY	MYNHEER	MYRIORAMA	MYTHOI
MUTINOUS	MVULE	MYNHEERS	MYRIORAMAS	MYTHOLOGIES
MUTINY	MVULES	MYOBLAST	MYRISTIC	MYTHOLOGY
MUTINYING	MY	MYOBLASTS	MYRMECOID	MYTHOMANE
MUTIS	MYAL	MYOFIBRIL	MYRMIDON	MYTHOMANES
MUTISM	MYALGIA	MYOFIBRILS	MYRMIDONS	MYTHOPOET
MUTISMS	MYALGIAS	MYOGEN	MYROBALAN	MYTHOPOETS
MUTON	MYALGIC	MYOGENIC	MYROBALANS	MYTHOS
MUTONS	MYALISM	MYOGENS	MYRRH	MYTHS
MUTOSCOPE	MYALISMS	MYOGLOBIN	MYRRHIC	MYTHUS
MUTOSCOPES	MYALL	MYOGLOBINS	MYRRHINE	MYTILOID
MUTT	MYALLS	MYOGRAM	MYRRHOL	MYXEDEMA
MUTTER	MYCELIA	MYOGRAMS	MYRRHOLS	MYXEDEMAS
MUTTERED	MYCELIAL	MYOGRAPH	MYRRHS	MYXEDEMIC
MUTTERER	MYCELIUM	MYOGRAPHIES	MYRTLE	MYXOEDEMA
MUTTERERS	MYCETES	MYOGRAPHS	MYRTLES	MYXOEDEMAS
MUTTERING	MYCETOMA	MYOGRAPHY	MYSELF	MYXOMA
MUTTERINGS	MYCETOMAS	MYOID	MYSTAGOGIES	MYXOMATA
MUTTERS	MYCETOMATA	MYOLOGIES	MYSTAGOGY	MYXOVIRUS
MUTTON	MYCOLOGIC	MYOLOGIST	MYSTERIES	MYXOVIRUSES
MUTTONS	MYCOLOGIES	MYOLOGISTS	MYSTERY	MZEE
MUTTONY	MYCOLOGY	MYOLOGY	MYSTIC	MZEES
MUTTS	MYCOPHAGIES	MYOMA	MYSTICAL	MZUNGU
MUTUAL	MYCOPHAGY	MYOMANCIES	MYSTICISM	MZUNGUS
MUTUALISE	MYCORHIZA	MYOMANCY	MYSTICISMS	
MUTUALISED	MYCORHIZAS	MYOMANTIC	MYSTICS	
MUTUALISES	MYCOSES	MYOMAS	MYSTIFIED	

N

NA
NAAM
NAAMS
NAAN
NAANS
NAARTJE
NAARTJES
NAB
NABBED
NABBER
NABBERS
NABBING
NABK
NABKS
NABLA
NABLAS
NABOB
NABOBS
NABS
NACARAT
NACARATS
NACELLE
NACELLES
NACH
NACHE
NACHES
NACHO
NACHOS
NACHTMAAL
NACHTMAALS
NACKET
NACKETS
NACRE
NACRED
NACREOUS
NACRES
NACRITE
NACRITES
NACROUS
NADA
NADAS
NADIR
NADIRS
NAE
NAEBODIES
NAEBODY
NAETHING
NAETHINGS
NAEVE
NAEVES
NAEVI
NAEVOID
NAEVUS
NAFF

NAFFING
NAFFLY
NAFFNESS
NAFFNESSES
NAFFS
NAG
NAGA
NAGANA
NAGANAS
NAGAPIE
NAGAPIES
NAGARI
NAGARIS
NAGAS
NAGGED
NAGGER
NAGGERS
NAGGIER
NAGGIEST
NAGGING
NAGGY
NAGMAAL
NAGMAALS
NAGOR
NAGORS
NAGS
NAHAL
NAHALS
NAIAD
NAIADES
NAIADS
NAIANT
NAIF
NAIFER
NAIFEST
NAIK
NAIKS
NAIL
NAILED
NAILER
NAILERIES
NAILERS
NAILERY
NAILING
NAILINGS
NAILLESS
NAILS
NAIN
NAINSELL
NAINSELLS
NAINSOOK
NAINSOOKS
NAIRA
NAIRAS

NAISSANT
NAIVE
NAIVELY
NAIVENESS
NAIVENESSES
NAIVER
NAIVEST
NAIVETE
NAIVETES
NAIVETIES
NAIVETY
NAIVIST
NAKED
NAKEDER
NAKEDEST
NAKEDLY
NAKEDNESS
NAKEDNESSES
NAKER
NAKERS
NALA
NALAS
NALLA
NALLAH
NALLAHS
NALLAS
NALOXONE
NALOXONES
NAM
NAMABLE
NAMASKAR
NAMASKARS
NAMASTE
NAMASTES
NAME
NAMEABLE
NAMED
NAMELESS
NAMELY
NAMER
NAMERS
NAMES
NAMESAKE
NAMESAKES
NAMETAPE
NAMETAPES
NAMING
NAMINGS
NAMS
NAN
NANA
NANAS
NANCE
NANCES

NANCIES
NANCY
NANDINE
NANDINES
NANDOO
NANDOOS
NANDU
NANDUS
NANISM
NANISMS
NANKEEN
NANKEENS
NANKIN
NANKINS
NANNA
NANNAS
NANNIED
NANNIES
NANNY
NANNYGAI
NANNYGAIS
NANNYGHAI
NANNYGHAIS
NANNYING
NANNYISH
NANOGRAM
NANOGRAMS
NANOMETRE
NANOMETRES
NANS
NAOI
NAOS
NAOSES
NAP
NAPA
NAPALM
NAPALMED
NAPALMING
NAPALMS
NAPAS
NAPE
NAPERIES
NAPERY
NAPES
NAPHTHA
NAPHTHAS
NAPHTHENE
NAPHTHENES
NAPHTHOL
NAPHTHOLS
NAPIFORM
NAPKIN
NAPKINS
NAPLESS

NAPOLEON
NAPOLEONS
NAPOO
NAPOOED
NAPOOING
NAPOOS
NAPPA
NAPPAS
NAPPE
NAPPED
NAPPER
NAPPERS
NAPPES
NAPPIER
NAPPIES
NAPPIEST
NAPPINESS
NAPPINESSES
NAPPING
NAPPY
NAPRON
NAPRONS
NAPS
NARAS
NARASES
NARC
NARCEEN
NARCEENS
NARCEINE
NARCEINES
NARCISSI
NARCISSUS
NARCISSUSES
NARCO
NARCOS
NARCOSES
NARCOSIS
NARCOTIC
NARCOTICS
NARCOTINE
NARCOTINES
NARCOTISE
NARCOTISED
NARCOTISES
NARCOTISING
NARCOTISM
NARCOTISMS
NARCOTIST
NARCOTISTS
NARCOTIZE
NARCOTIZED
NARCOTIZES
NARCOTIZING
NARCS

NARD	NASAL	NATIVIST	NAUTCHES	NEAFE
NARDED	NASALISE	NATIVISTS	NAUTIC	NEAFES
NARDING	NASALISED	NATIVITIES	NAUTICAL	NEAFFE
NARDOO	NASALISES	NATIVITY	NAUTICS	NEAFFES
NARDOOS	NASALISING	NATRIUM	NAUTILI	NEAL
NARDS	NASALITIES	NATRIUMS	NAUTILUS	NEALED
NARE	NASALITY	NATROLITE	NAUTILUSES	NEALING
NARES	NASALIZE	NATROLITES	NAVAID	NEALS
NARGHILE	NASALIZED	NATRON	NAVAIDS	NEANIC
NARGHILES	NASALIZES	NATRONS	NAVAL	NEAP
NARGHILIES	NASALIZING	NATS	NAVALISM	NEAPED
NARGHILLIES	NASALLY	NATTER	NAVALISMS	NEAPING
NARGHILY	NASALS	NATTERED	NAVARCH	NEAPS
NARGHILY	NASARD	NATTERER	NAVARCHIES	NEAR
NARGILE	NASARDS	NATTERERS	NAVARCHS	NEARED
NARGILEH	NASCENCE	NATTERING	NAVARCHY	NEARER
NARGILEHS	NASCENCES	NATTERS	NAVARHO	NEAREST
NARGILES	NASCENCIES	NATTERY	NAVARHOS	NEARING
NARGILIES	NASCENCY	NATTIER	NAVARIN	NEARLY
NARGILLIES	NASCENT	NATTIEST	NAVARINS	NEARNESS
NARGILLY	NASEBERRIES	NATTILY	NAVE	NEARNESSES
NARGILY	NASEBERRY	NATTINESS	NAVEL	NEARS
NARIAL	NASHGAB	NATTINESSES	NAVELS	NEARSIDE
NARICORN	NASHGABS	NATTY	NAVELWORT	NEARSIDES
NARICORNS	NASION	NATURA	NAVELWORTS	NEAT
NARINE	NASIONS	NATURAE	NAVES	NEATEN
NARK	NASTALIK	NATURAL	NAVETTE	NEATENED
NARKED	NASTALIKS	NATURALLY	NAVETTES	NEATENING
NARKIER	NASTIC	NATURALS	NAVEW	NEATENS
NARKIEST	NASTIER	NATURE	NAVEWS	NEATER
NARKING	NASTIES	NATURED	NAVICERT	NEATEST
NARKS	NASTIEST	NATURES	NAVICERTS	NEATH
NARKY	NASTILY	NATURING	NAVICULA	NEATLY
NARQUOIS	NASTINESS	NATURISM	NAVICULAR	NEATNESS
NARRAS	NASTINESSES	NATURISMS	NAVICULARS	NEATNESSES
NARRASES	NASTY	NATURIST	NAVICULAS	NEB
NARRATE	NASUTE	NATURISTS	NAVIES	NEBBED
NARRATED	NASUTES	NAUGHT	NAVIGABLE	NEBBICH
NARRATES	NAT	NAUGHTIER	NAVIGABLY	NEBBICHS
NARRATING	NATAL	NAUGHTIES	NAVIGATE	NEBBING
NARRATION	NATALITIES	NAUGHTIEST	NAVIGATED	NEBBISH
NARRATIONS	NATALITY	NAUGHTILY	NAVIGATES	NEBBISHE
NARRATIVE	NATANT	NAUGHTS	NAVIGATING	NEBBISHER
NARRATIVES	NATATION	NAUGHTY	NAVIGATOR	NEBBISHERS
NARRATOR	NATATIONS	NAUMACHIA	NAVIGATORS	NEBBISHES
NARRATORS	NATATORIA	NAUMACHIAE	NAVVIED	NEBBUK
NARRATORY	NATATORY	NAUMACHIAS	NAVVIES	NEBBUKS
NARRE	NATCH	NAUMACHIES	NAVVY	NEBECK
NARROW	NATCHES	NAUMACHY	NAVVYING	NEBECKS
NARROWED	NATES	NAUNT	NAVY	NEBEK
NARROWER	NATHELESS	NAUNTS	NAWAB	NEBEKS
NARROWEST	NATHEMO	NAUPLII	NAWABS	NEBEL
NARROWING	NATHEMORE	NAUPLIOID	NAY	NEBELS
NARROWINGS	NATHLESS	NAUPLIUS	NAYS	NEBISH
NARROWLY	NATIFORM	NAUSEA	NAYTHLES	NEBISHES
NARROWS	NATION	NAUSEANT	NAYWARD	NEBRIS
NARTHEX	NATIONAL	NAUSEANTS	NAYWARDS	NEBRISES
NARTHEXES	NATIONALS	NAUSEAS	NAYWORD	NEBS
NARTJIE	NATIONS	NAUSEATE	NAYWORDS	NEBULA
NARTJIES	NATIVE	NAUSEATED	NAZE	NEBULAE
NARWHAL	NATIVELY	NAUSEATES	NAZES	NEBULAR
NARWHALS	NATIVES	NAUSEATING	NAZIR	NEBULAS
NARY	NATIVISM	NAUSEOUS	NAZIRS	NEBULE
NAS	NATIVISMS	NAUTCH	NE	NEBULES

The Chambers Dictionary is the authority for many longer words; see *OSW* Introduction, page xii

NEBULISE	NECROSIS	NEEMBS	NEGROPHIL	NENUPHARS
NEBULISED	NECROTIC	NEEMS	NEGROPHILS	NEOBLAST
NEBULISER	NECROTISE	NEEP	NEGUS	NEOBLASTS
NEBULISERS	NECROTISED	NEEPS	NEGUSES	NEODYMIUM
NEBULISES	NECROTISES	NEESBERRIES	NEIF	NEODYMIUMS
NEBULISING	NECROTISING	NEESBERRY	NEIFS	NEOLITH
NEBULIUM	NECROTIZE	NEESE	NEIGH	NEOLITHS
NEBULIUMS	NECROTIZED	NEESED	NEIGHBOR	NEOLOGIAN
NEBULIZE	NECROTIZES	NEESES	NEIGHBORED	NEOLOGIANS
NEBULIZED	NECROTIZING	NEESING	NEIGHBORING	NEOLOGIC
NEBULIZER	NECROTOMIES	NEEZE	NEIGHBORS	NEOLOGIES
NEBULIZERS	NECROTOMY	NEEZED	NEIGHBOUR	NEOLOGISE
NEBULIZES	NECTAR	NEEZES	NEIGHBOURED	NEOLOGISED
NEBULIZING	NECTAREAL	NEEZING	NEIGHBOURING	NEOLOGISES
NEBULOUS	NECTAREAN	NEF	NEIGHBOURS	NEOLOGISING
NEBULY	NECTARED	NEFANDOUS	NEIGHED	NEOLOGISM
NECESSARIES	NECTARIAL	NEFARIOUS	NEIGHING	NEOLOGISMS
NECESSARY	NECTARIES	NEFAST	NEIGHS	NEOLOGIST
NECESSITIES	NECTARINE	NEFS	NEIST	NEOLOGISTS
NECESSITY	NECTARINES	NEGATE	NEITHER	NEOLOGIZE
NECK	NECTAROUS	NEGATED	NEIVE	NEOLOGIZED
NECKATEE	NECTARS	NEGATES	NEIVES	NEOLOGIZES
NECKATEES	NECTARY	NEGATING	NEK	NEOLOGIZING
NECKBAND	NED	NEGATION	NEKS	NEOLOGY
NECKBANDS	NEDDIES	NEGATIONS	NEKTON	NEOMYCIN
NECKBEEF	NEDDY	NEGATIVE	NEKTONS	NEOMYCINS
NECKBEEFS	NEDS	NEGATIVED	NELIES	NEON
NECKCLOTH	NEE	NEGATIVES	NELIS	NEONATAL
NECKCLOTHS	NEED	NEGATIVING	NELLIES	NEONATE
NECKED	NEEDED	NEGATORY	NELLY	NEONATES
NECKGEAR	NEEDER	NEGATRON	NELSON	NEONOMIAN
NECKGEARS	NEEDERS	NEGATRONS	NELSONS	NEONOMIANS
NECKING	NEEDFIRE	NEGLECT	NELUMBIUM	NEONS
NECKINGS	NEEDFIRES	NEGLECTED	NELUMBIUMS	NEOPAGAN
NECKLACE	NEEDFUL	NEGLECTER	NELUMBO	NEOPAGANS
NECKLACED	NEEDFULLY	NEGLECTERS	NELUMBOS	NEOPHILE
NECKLACES	NEEDIER	NEGLECTING	NEMATIC	NEOPHILES
NECKLACING	NEEDIEST	NEGLECTS	NEMATODE	NEOPHILIA
NECKLACINGS	NEEDILY	NEGLIGE	NEMATODES	NEOPHILIAS
NECKLET	NEEDINESS	NEGLIGEE	NEMATOID	NEOPHOBE
NECKLETS	NEEDINESSES	NEGLIGEES	NEMERTEAN	NEOPHOBES
NECKLINE	NEEDING	NEGLIGENT	NEMERTEANS	NEOPHOBIA
NECKLINES	NEEDLE	NEGLIGES	NEMERTIAN	NEOPHOBIAS
NECKPIECE	NEEDLED	NEGOCIANT	NEMERTIANS	NEOPHOBIC
NECKPIECES	NEEDLEFUL	NEGOCIANTS	NEMERTINE	NEOPHYTE
NECKS	NEEDLEFULS	NEGOTIANT	NEMERTINES	NEOPHYTES
NECKTIE	NEEDLER	NEGOTIANTS	NEMESES	NEOPHYTIC
NECKTIES	NEEDLERS	NEGOTIATE	NEMESIA	NEOPILINA
NECKVERSE	NEEDLES	NEGOTIATED	NEMESIAS	NEOPILINAS
NECKVERSES	NEEDLESS	NEGOTIATES	NEMESIS	NEOPLASM
NECKWEAR	NEEDLIER	NEGOTIATING	NEMN	NEOPLASMS
NECKWEARS	NEEDLIEST	NEGRESS	NEMNED	NEOPRENE
NECKWEED	NEEDLING	NEGRESSES	NEMNING	NEOPRENES
NECKWEEDS	NEEDLY	NEGRITUDE	NEMNS	NEOTEINIA
NECROLOGIES	NEEDMENT	NEGRITUDES	NEMOPHILA	NEOTEINIAS
NECROLOGY	NEEDMENTS	NEGRO	NEMOPHILAS	NEOTENIC
NECROPHIL	NEEDS	NEGROES	NEMORAL	NEOTENIES
NECROPHILS	NEEDY	NEGROHEAD	NEMOROUS	NEOTENOUS
NECROPSIES	NEELD	NEGROHEADS	NEMPT	NEOTENY
NECROPSY	NEELDS	NEGROID	NENE	NEOTERIC
NECROSE	NEELE	NEGROIDAL	NENES	NEOTERICS
NECROSED	NEELES	NEGROIDS	NENNIGAI	NEOTERISE
NECROSES	NEEM	NEGROISM	NENNIGAIS	NEOTERISED
NECROSING	NEEMB	NEGROISMS	NENUPHAR	NEOTERISES

NEOTERISING	NEREID	NESTLES	NEURITIS	NEWELLED
NEOTERISM	NEREIDES	NESTLIKE	NEURITISES	NEWELLS
NEOTERISMS	NEREIDS	NESTLING	NEUROCHIP	NEWELS
NEOTERIST	NERINE	NESTLINGS	NEUROCHIPS	NEWER
NEOTERISTS	NERINES	NESTS	NEUROGLIA	NEWEST
NEOTERIZE	NERITE	NET	NEUROGLIAS	NEWFANGLE
NEOTERIZED	NERITES	NETBALL	NEUROGRAM	NEWING
NEOTERIZES	NERITIC	NETBALLS	NEUROGRAMS	NEWISH
NEOTERIZING	NERK	NETE	NEUROLOGIES	NEWISHLY
NEOTOXIN	NERKA	NETES	NEUROLOGY	NEWLY
NEOTOXINS	NERKAS	NETFUL	NEUROMA	NEWMARKET
NEP	NERKS	NETFULS	NEUROMAS	NEWMARKETS
NEPENTHE	NEROLI	NETHELESS	NEUROMATA	NEWNESS
NEPENTHES	NEROLIS	NETHER	NEURON	NEWNESSES
NEPER	NERVAL	NETIZEN	NEURONAL	NEWS
NEPERS	NERVATE	NETIZENS	NEURONE	NEWSAGENT
NEPETA	NERVATION	NETS	NEURONES	NEWSAGENTS
NEPETAS	NERVATIONS	NETSUKE	NEURONIC	NEWSBOY
NEPHALISM	NERVATURE	NETSUKES	NEURONS	NEWSBOYS
NEPHALISMS	NERVATURES	NETT	NEUROPATH	NEWSCAST
NEPHALIST	NERVE	NETTED	NEUROPATHS	NEWSCASTS
NEPHALISTS	NERVED	NETTIER	NEUROPIL	NEWSED
NEPHELINE	NERVELESS	NETTIEST	NEUROPILS	NEWSES
NEPHELINES	NERVELET	NETTING	NEUROSES	NEWSFLASH
NEPHELITE	NERVELETS	NETTINGS	NEUROSIS	NEWSFLASHES
NEPHELITES	NERVER	NETTLE	NEUROTIC	NEWSGIRL
NEPHEW	NERVERS	NETTLED	NEUROTICS	NEWSGIRLS
NEPHEWS	NERVES	NETTLES	NEUROTOMIES	NEWSGROUP
NEPHOGRAM	NERVIER	NETTLIER	NEUROTOMY	NEWSGROUPS
NEPHOGRAMS	NERVIEST	NETTLIEST	NEUSTON	NEWSHAWK
NEPHOLOGIES	NERVILY	NETTLING	NEUSTONS	NEWSHAWKS
NEPHOLOGY	NERVINE	NETTLY	NEUTER	NEWSHOUND
NEPHRALGIES	NERVINES	NETTS	NEUTERED	NEWSHOUNDS
NEPHRALGY	NERVINESS	NETTY	NEUTERING	NEWSIER
NEPHRIC	NERVINESSES	NETWORK	NEUTERS	NEWSIES
NEPHRIDIA	NERVING	NETWORKED	NEUTRAL	NEWSIEST
NEPHRITE	NERVOUS	NETWORKER	NEUTRALLY	NEWSINESS
NEPHRITES	NERVOUSLY	NETWORKERS	NEUTRALS	NEWSINESSES
NEPHRITIC	NERVULAR	NETWORKING	NEUTRETTO	NEWSING
NEPHRITICS	NERVULE	NETWORKINGS	NEUTRETTOS	NEWSLESS
NEPHRITIS	NERVULES	NETWORKS	NEUTRINO	NEWSMAN
NEPHRITISES	NERVURE	NEUK	NEUTRINOS	NEWSMEN
NEPHROID	NERVURES	NEUKS	NEUTRON	NEWSPAPER
NEPHRON	NERVY	NEUM	NEUTRONS	NEWSPAPERS
NEPHRONS	NESCIENCE	NEUME	NEVE	NEWSPEAK
NEPHROSES	NESCIENCES	NEUMES	NEVEL	NEWSPEAKS
NEPHROSIS	NESCIENT	NEUMS	NEVELLED	NEWSPRINT
NEPHROTIC	NESH	NEURAL	NEVELLING	NEWSPRINTS
NEPIONIC	NESHER	NEURALGIA	NEVELS	NEWSREEL
NEPIT	NESHEST	NEURALGIAS	NEVER	NEWSREELS
NEPITS	NESHNESS	NEURALGIC	NEVERMORE	NEWSROOM
NEPOTIC	NESHNESSES	NEURALLY	NEVES	NEWSROOMS
NEPOTISM	NESS	NEURATION	NEVI	NEWSTRADE
NEPOTISMS	NESSES	NEURATIONS	NEVUS	NEWSTRADES
NEPOTIST	NEST	NEURILITIES	NEW	NEWSWIRE
NEPOTISTS	NESTED	NEURILITY	NEWBIE	NEWSWIRES
NEPS	NESTER	NEURINE	NEWBIES	NEWSWOMAN
NEPTUNIUM	NESTERS	NEURINES	NEWBORN	NEWSWOMEN
NEPTUNIUMS	NESTFUL	NEURISM	NEWCOME	NEWSY
NERD	NESTFULS	NEURISMS	NEWCOMER	NEWT
NERDIER	NESTING	NEURITE	NEWCOMERS	NEWTON
NERDIEST	NESTINGS	NEURITES	NEWED	NEWTONS
NERDS	NESTLE	NEURITIC	NEWEL	NEWTS
NERDY	NESTLED	NEURITICS	NEWELL	NEXT

The Chambers Dictionary is the authority for many longer words; see *OSW* Introduction, page xii

NEXTLY	NICKELISED	NIDI	NIGGERDOM	NIGRICANT
NEXTNESS	NICKELISES	NIDIFIED	NIGGERDOMS	NIGRIFIED
NEXTNESSES	NICKELISING	NIDIFIES	NIGGERED	NIGRIFIES
NEXTS	NICKELIZE	NIDIFY	NIGGERING	NIGRIFY
NEXUS	NICKELIZED	NIDIFYING	NIGGERISH	NIGRIFYING
NGAIO	NICKELIZES	NIDING	NIGGERISM	NIGRITUDE
NGAIOS	NICKELIZING	NIDINGS	NIGGERISMS	NIGRITUDES
NGANA	NICKELLED	NIDOR	NIGGERS	NIGROSIN
NGANAS	NICKELLING	NIDOROUS	NIGGERY	NIGROSINE
NGULTRUM	NICKELOUS	NIDORS	NIGGLE	NIGROSINES
NGULTRUMS	NICKELS	NIDS	NIGGLED	NIGROSINS
NGWEE	NICKER	NIDUS	NIGGLER	NIHIL
NHANDU	NICKERED	NIE	NIGGLERS	NIHILISM
NHANDUS	NICKERING	NIECE	NIGGLES	NIHILISMS
NIACIN	NICKERS	NIECES	NIGGLIER	NIHILIST
NIACINS	NICKING	NIED	NIGGLIEST	NIHILISTS
NIAISERIE	NICKNAME	NIEF	NIGGLING	NIHILITIES
NIAISERIES	NICKNAMED	NIEFS	NIGGLINGS	NIHILITY
NIB	NICKNAMES	NIELLATED	NIGGLY	NIHILS
NIBBED	NICKNAMING	NIELLI	NIGH	NIHONGA
NIBBING	NICKPOINT	NIELLIST	NIGHED	NIHONGAS
NIBBLE	NICKPOINTS	NIELLISTS	NIGHEST	NIKAU
NIBBLED	NICKS	NIELLO	NIGHING	NIKAUS
NIBBLER	NICKSTICK	NIELLOED	NIGHLY	NIL
NIBBLERS	NICKSTICKS	NIELLOING	NIGHNESS	NILGAI
NIBBLES	NICKUM	NIELLOS	NIGHNESSES	NILGAIS
NIBBLING	NICKUMS	NIES	NIGHS	NILGAU
NIBBLINGS	NICOL	NIEVE	NIGHT	NILGAUS
NIBLICK	NICOLS	NIEVEFUL	NIGHTBIRD	NILL
NIBLICKS	NICOMPOOP	NIEVEFULS	NIGHTBIRDS	NILLED
NIBS	NICOMPOOPS	NIEVES	NIGHTCAP	NILLING
NICAD	NICOTIAN	NIFE	NIGHTCAPS	NILLS
NICADS	NICOTIANA	NIFES	NIGHTCLUB	NILS
NICCOLITE	NICOTIANAS	NIFF	NIGHTCLUBS	NIM
NICCOLITES	NICOTIANS	NIFFED	NIGHTED	NIMB
NICE	NICOTINE	NIFFER	NIGHTFALL	NIMBED
NICEISH	NICOTINED	NIFFERED	NIGHTFALLS	NIMBI
NICELY	NICOTINES	NIFFERING	NIGHTFIRE	NIMBLE
NICENESS	NICOTINIC	NIFFERS	NIGHTFIRES	NIMBLER
NICENESSES	NICTATE	NIFFIER	NIGHTGEAR	NIMBLESSE
NICER	NICTATED	NIFFIEST	NIGHTGEARS	NIMBLESSES
NICEST	NICTATES	NIFFING	NIGHTGOWN	NIMBLEST
NICETIES	NICTATING	NIFFNAFF	NIGHTGOWNS	NIMBLY
NICETY	NICTATION	NIFFNAFFED	NIGHTHAWK	NIMBS
NICHE	NICTATIONS	NIFFNAFFING	NIGHTHAWKS	NIMBUS
NICHED	NICTITATE	NIFFNAFFS	NIGHTIE	NIMBUSED
NICHER	NICTITATED	NIFFS	NIGHTIES	NIMBUSES
NICHERED	NICTITATES	NIFFY	NIGHTJAR	NIMBYISM
NICHERING	NICTITATING	NIFTIER	NIGHTJARS	NIMBYISMS
NICHERS	NID	NIFTIEST	NIGHTLESS	NIMIETIES
NICHES	NIDAL	NIFTILY	NIGHTLIFE	NIMIETY
NICHING	NIDAMENTA	NIFTINESS	NIGHTLIFES	NIMIOUS
NICISH	NIDATION	NIFTINESSES	NIGHTLONG	NIMMED
NICK	NIDATIONS	NIFTY	NIGHTLY	NIMMER
NICKAR	NIDDERING	NIGELLA	NIGHTMARE	NIMMERS
NICKARS	NIDDERINGS	NIGELLAS	NIGHTMARES	NIMMING
NICKED	NIDE	NIGER	NIGHTMARY	NIMONIC
NICKEL	NIDERING	NIGERS	NIGHTS	NIMS
NICKELED	NIDERINGS	NIGGARD	NIGHTSPOT	NINCOM
NICKELIC	NIDERLING	NIGGARDED	NIGHTSPOTS	NINCOMS
NICKELINE	NIDERLINGS	NIGGARDING	NIGHTWARD	NINCUM
NICKELINES	NIDES	NIGGARDLY	NIGHTWEAR	NINCUMS
NICKELING	NIDGET	NIGGARDS	NIGHTWEARS	NINE
NICKELISE	NIDGETS	NIGGER	NIGHTY	NINEFOLD

NINEHOLES	NIRAMIAI	NITROXYL	NOCHEL	NODOSITY
NINEPENCE	NIRAMIAIS	NITROXYLS	NOCHELLED	NODOUS
NINEPENCES	NIRL	NITRY	NOCHELLING	NODS
NINEPENNIES	NIRLED	NITRYL	NOCHELS	NODULAR
NINEPENNY	NIRLIE	NITRYLS	NOCK	NODULATED
NINEPIN	NIRLIER	NITS	NOCKED	NODULE
NINEPINS	NIRLIEST	NITTIER	NOCKET	NODULED
NINES	NIRLING	NITTIEST	NOCKETS	NODULES
NINESCORE	NIRLIT	NITTY	NOCKING	NODULOSE
NINESCORES	NIRLS	NITWIT	NOCKS	NODULOUS
NINETEEN	NIRLY	NITWITS	NOCTILIO	NODUS
NINETEENS	NIRVANA	NITWITTED	NOCTILIOS	NOEL
NINETIES	NIRVANAS	NIVAL	NOCTILUCA	NOELS
NINETIETH	NIS	NIVEOUS	NOCTILUCAE	NOES
NINETIETHS	NISBERRIES	NIX	NOCTUA	NOESES
NINETY	NISBERRY	NIXED	NOCTUARIES	NOESIS
NINJA	NISEI	NIXES	NOCTUARY	NOETIC
NINJAS	NISEIS	NIXIE	NOCTUAS	NOG
NINJITSU	NISI	NIXIES	NOCTUID	NOGAKU
NINJITSUS	NISSE	NIXING	NOCTUIDS	NOGG
NINJUTSU	NISSES	NIXY	NOCTULE	NOGGED
NINJUTSUS	NISUS	NIZAM	NOCTULES	NOGGIN
NINNIES	NIT	NIZAMS	NOCTURN	NOGGING
NINNY	NITE	NO	NOCTURNAL	NOGGINGS
NINON	NITER	NOB	NOCTURNALS	NOGGINS
NINONS	NITERIE	NOBBIER	NOCTURNE	NOGGS
NINTH	NITERIES	NOBBIEST	NOCTURNES	NOGS
NINTHLY	NITERS	NOBBILY	NOCTURNS	NOH
NINTHS	NITERY	NOBBINESS	NOCUOUS	NOHOW
NIOBATE	NITES	NOBBINESSES	NOCUOUSLY	NOHOWISH
NIOBATES	NITHING	NOBBLE	NOD	NOIL
NIOBIC	NITHINGS	NOBBLED	NODAL	NOILS
NIOBITE	NITID	NOBBLER	NODALISE	NOINT
NIOBITES	NITON	NOBBLERS	NODALISED	NOINTED
NIOBIUM	NITONS	NOBBLES	NODALISES	NOINTING
NIOBIUMS	NITRATE	NOBBLING	NODALISING	NOINTS
NIOBOUS	NITRATED	NOBBUT	NODALITIES	NOISE
NIP	NITRATES	NOBBY	NODALITY	NOISED
NIPA	NITRATINE	NOBELIUM	NODALIZE	NOISEFUL
NIPAS	NITRATINES	NOBELIUMS	NODALIZED	NOISELESS
NIPCHEESE	NITRATING	NOBILESSE	NODALIZES	NOISES
NIPCHEESES	NITRATION	NOBILESSES	NODALIZING	NOISETTE
NIPPED	NITRATIONS	NOBILIARY	NODALLY	NOISETTES
NIPPER	NITRE	NOBILITIES	NODATED	NOISIER
NIPPERED	NITRES	NOBILITY	NODATION	NOISIEST
NIPPERING	NITRIC	NOBLE	NODATIONS	NOISILY
NIPPERKIN	NITRIDE	NOBLEMAN	NODDED	NOISINESS
NIPPERKINS	NITRIDED	NOBLEMEN	NODDER	NOISINESSES
NIPPERS	NITRIDES	NOBLENESS	NODDERS	NOISING
NIPPIER	NITRIDING	NOBLENESSES	NODDIES	NOISOME
NIPPIEST	NITRIDINGS	NOBLER	NODDING	NOISOMELY
NIPPILY	NITRIFIED	NOBLES	NODDINGLY	NOISY
NIPPINESS	NITRIFIES	NOBLESSE	NODDINGS	NOLE
NIPPINESSES	NITRIFY	NOBLESSES	NODDLE	NOLES
NIPPING	NITRIFYING	NOBLEST	NODDLED	NOLITION
NIPPINGLY	NITRILE	NOBLY	NODDLES	NOLITIONS
NIPPLE	NITRILES	NOBODIES	NODDLING	NOLL
NIPPLED	NITRITE	NOBODY	NODDY	NOLLS
NIPPLES	NITRITES	NOBS	NODE	NOM
NIPPLING	NITROGEN	NOCAKE	NODES	NOMA
NIPPY	NITROGENS	NOCAKES	NODI	NOMAD
NIPS	NITROSO	NOCENT	NODICAL	NOMADE
NIPTER	NITROSYL	NOCENTLY	NODOSE	NOMADES
NIPTERS	NITROUS	NOCENTS	NODOSITIES	NOMADIC

NOMADIES	NONANES	NOOMETRY	NORSELLING	NOSINESSES
NOMADISE	NONARY	NOON	NORSELS	NOSING
NOMADISED	NONCE	NOONDAY	NORTENA	NOSINGS
NOMADISES	NONCES	NOONDAYS	NORTENAS	NOSODE
NOMADISING	NONE	NOONED	NORTENO	NOSODES
NOMADISM	NONENTITIES	NOONER	NORTENOS	NOSOLOGIES
NOMADISMS	NONENTITY	NOONERS	NORTH	NOSOLOGY
NOMADIZE	NONES	NOONING	NORTHED	NOSTALGIA
NOMADIZED	NONESUCH	NOONINGS	NORTHER	NOSTALGIAS
NOMADIZES	NONESUCHES	NOONS	NORTHERED	NOSTALGIC
NOMADIZING	NONET	NOONTIDE	NORTHERING	NOSTOC
NOMADS	NONETS	NOONTIDES	NORTHERLIES	NOSTOCS
NOMADY	NONETTE	NOONTIME	NORTHERLY	NOSTOI
NOMARCH	NONETTES	NOONTIMES	NORTHERN	NOSTOLOGIES
NOMARCHIES	NONETTI	NOOP	NORTHERNS	NOSTOLOGY
NOMARCHS	NONETTO	NOOPS	NORTHERS	NOSTOS
NOMARCHY	NONETTOS	NOOSE	NORTHING	NOSTRIL
NOMAS	NONG	NOOSED	NORTHINGS	NOSTRILS
NOMBLES	NONGS	NOOSES	NORTHLAND	NOSTRUM
NOMBRIL	NONILLION	NOOSING	NORTHLANDS	NOSTRUMS
NOMBRILS	NONILLIONS	NOOSPHERE	NORTHMOST	NOSY
NOME	NONJURING	NOOSPHERES	NORTHS	NOT
NOMEN	NONJUROR	NOPAL	NORTHWARD	NOTA
NOMES	NONJURORS	NOPALS	NORTHWARDS	NOTABILIA
NOMIC	NONNIES	NOPE	NORWARD	NOTABLE
NOMINA	NONNY	NOR	NORWARDS	NOTABLES
NOMINABLE	NONPAREIL	NORI	NOS	NOTABLY
NOMINAL	NONPAREILS	NORIA	NOSE	NOTAEUM
NOMINALLY	NONPAROUS	NORIAS	NOSEAN	NOTAEUMS
NOMINALS	NONPLUS	NORIMON	NOSEANS	NOTAL
NOMINATE	NONPLUSED	NORIMONS	NOSEBAG	NOTANDA
NOMINATED	NONPLUSES	NORIS	NOSEBAGS	NOTANDUM
NOMINATES	NONPLUSING	NORITE	NOSEBAND	NOTAPHILIES
NOMINATING	NONPLUSSED	NORITES	NOSEBANDS	NOTAPHILY
NOMINATOR	NONPLUSSES	NORK	NOSEBLEED	NOTARIAL
NOMINATORS	NONPLUSSING	NORKS	NOSEBLEEDS	NOTARIES
NOMINEE	NONPOLAR	NORLAND	NOSED	NOTARISE
NOMINEES	NONSENSE	NORLANDS	NOSEDIVE	NOTARISED
NOMISM	NONSENSES	NORM	NOSEDIVED	NOTARISES
NOMISMS	NONSUCH	NORMA	NOSEDIVES	NOTARISING
NOMISTIC	NONSUCHES	NORMAL	NOSEDIVING	NOTARIZE
NOMOCRACIES	NONSUIT	NORMALCIES	NOSEGAY	NOTARIZED
NOMOCRACY	NONSUITED	NORMALCY	NOSEGAYS	NOTARIZES
NOMOGENIES	NONSUITING	NORMALISE	NOSELESS	NOTARIZING
NOMOGENY	NONSUITS	NORMALISED	NOSELITE	NOTARY
NOMOGRAM	NONUPLE	NORMALISES	NOSELITES	NOTATE
NOMOGRAMS	NONUPLET	NORMALISING	NOSER	NOTATED
NOMOGRAPH	NONUPLETS	NORMALITIES	NOSERS	NOTATES
NOMOGRAPHS	NOODLE	NORMALITY	NOSES	NOTATING
NOMOI	NOODLED	NORMALIZE	NOSEY	NOTATION
NOMOLOGIES	NOODLEDOM	NORMALIZED	NOSEYS	NOTATIONS
NOMOLOGY	NOODLEDOMS	NORMALIZES	NOSH	NOTCH
NOMOS	NOODLES	NORMALIZING	NOSHED	NOTCHBACK
NOMOTHETE	NOODLING	NORMALLY	NOSHER	NOTCHBACKS
NOMOTHETES	NOOK	NORMALS	NOSHERIES	NOTCHED
NOMS	NOOKIE	NORMAN	NOSHERS	NOTCHEL
NON	NOOKIER	NORMANS	NOSHERY	NOTCHELLED
NONAGE	NOOKIES	NORMAS	NOSHES	NOTCHELLING
NONAGED	NOOKIEST	NORMATIVE	NOSHING	NOTCHELS
NONAGES	NOOKS	NORMS	NOSIER	NOTCHER
NONAGON	NOOKY	NORSEL	NOSIES	NOTCHERS
NONAGONAL	NOOLOGIES	NORSELLED	NOSIEST	NOTCHES
NONAGONS	NOOLOGY	NORSELLER	NOSILY	NOTCHIER
NONANE	NOOMETRIES	NORSELLERS	NOSINESS	NOTCHIEST

The Chambers Dictionary is the authority for many longer words; see *OSW* Introduction, page xii

NOTCHING	NOUN	NOVELIZES	NOYOUS	NUCLEON
NOTCHINGS	NOUNAL	NOVELIZING	NOYS	NUCLEONS
NOTCHY	NOUNIER	NOVELLA	NOYSOME	NUCLEUS
NOTE	NOUNIEST	NOVELLAE	NOZZER	NUCLIDE
NOTEBOOK	NOUNS	NOVELLAS	NOZZERS	NUCLIDES
NOTEBOOKS	NOUNY	NOVELLE	NOZZLE	NUCULE
NOTECASE	NOUP	NOVELS	NOZZLES	NUCULES
NOTECASES	NOUPS	NOVELTIES	NTH	NUDATION
NOTED	NOURICE	NOVELTY	NU	NUDATIONS
NOTEDLY	NOURICES	NOVENA	NUANCE	NUDE
NOTEDNESS	NOURISH	NOVENARIES	NUANCED	NUDELY
NOTEDNESSES	NOURISHED	NOVENARY	NUANCES	NUDENESS
NOTELESS	NOURISHER	NOVENAS	NUANCING	NUDENESSES
NOTELET	NOURISHERS	NOVENNIAL	NUB	NUDER
NOTELETS	NOURISHES	NOVERCAL	NUBBED	NUDES
NOTEPAPER	NOURISHING	NOVERINT	NUBBIER	NUDEST
NOTEPAPERS	NOURITURE	NOVERINTS	NUBBIEST	NUDGE
NOTER	NOURITURES	NOVICE	NUBBIN	NUDGED
NOTERS	NOURSLE	NOVICES	NUBBING	NUDGER
NOTES	NOURSLED	NOVICIATE	NUBBINS	NUDGERS
NOTHING	NOURSLES	NOVICIATES	NUBBLE	NUDGES
NOTHINGS	NOURSLING	NOVITIATE	NUBBLED	NUDGING
NOTICE	NOUS	NOVITIATES	NUBBLES	NUDICAUL
NOTICED	NOUSELL	NOVITIES	NUBBLIER	NUDIE
NOTICES	NOUSELLED	NOVITY	NUBBLIEST	NUDIES
NOTICING	NOUSELLING	NOVODAMUS	NUBBLING	NUDISM
NOTIFIED	NOUSELLS	NOVODAMUSES	NUBBLY	NUDISMS
NOTIFIER	NOUSES	NOVUM	NUBBY	NUDIST
NOTIFIERS	NOUSLE	NOVUMS	NUBECULA	NUDISTS
NOTIFIES	NOUSLED	NOW	NUBECULAE	NUDITIES
NOTIFY	NOUSLES	NOWADAYS	NUBIA	NUDITY
NOTIFYING	NOUSLING	NOWAY	NUBIAS	NUDNIK
NOTING	NOUT	NOWAYS	NUBIFORM	NUDNIKS
NOTION	NOUVEAU	NOWED	NUBILE	NUFF
NOTIONAL	NOUVELLE	NOWHENCE	NUBILITIES	NUFFIN
NOTIONIST	NOUVELLES	NOWHERE	NUBILITY	NUFFINS
NOTIONISTS	NOVA	NOWHERES	NUBILOUS	NUFFS
NOTIONS	NOVAE	NOWHITHER	NUBS	NUGAE
NOTITIA	NOVALIA	NOWISE	NUCELLAR	NUGATORY
NOTITIAE	NOVAS	NOWL	NUCELLI	NUGGAR
NOTITIAS	NOVATION	NOWLS	NUCELLUS	NUGGARS
NOTOCHORD	NOVATIONS	NOWN	NUCHA	NUGGET
NOTOCHORDS	NOVEL	NOWNESS	NUCHAE	NUGGETS
NOTORIETIES	NOVELDOM	NOWNESSES	NUCHAL	NUGGETY
NOTORIETY	NOVELDOMS	NOWS	NUCLEAL	NUISANCE
NOTORIOUS	NOVELESE	NOWT	NUCLEAR	NUISANCER
NOTORNIS	NOVELESES	NOWTS	NUCLEASE	NUISANCERS
NOTORNISES	NOVELETTE	NOWY	NUCLEASES	NUISANCES
NOTOUR	NOVELETTES	NOX	NUCLEATE	NUKE
NOTT	NOVELISE	NOXAL	NUCLEATED	NUKED
NOTUM	NOVELISED	NOXES	NUCLEATES	NUKES
NOUGAT	NOVELISER	NOXIOUS	NUCLEATING	NUKING
NOUGATS	NOVELISERS	NOXIOUSLY	NUCLEATOR	NULL
NOUGHT	NOVELISES	NOY	NUCLEATORS	NULLA
NOUGHTS	NOVELISH	NOYADE	NUCLEI	NULLAH
NOUL	NOVELISING	NOYADES	NUCLEIDE	NULLAHS
NOULD	NOVELISM	NOYANCE	NUCLEIDES	NULLAS
NOULDE	NOVELISMS	NOYANCES	NUCLEIN	NULLED
NOULE	NOVELIST	NOYAU	NUCLEINS	NULLIFIED
NOULES	NOVELISTS	NOYAUS	NUCLEOLAR	NULLIFIER
NOULS	NOVELIZE	NOYED	NUCLEOLE	NULLIFIERS
NOUMENA	NOVELIZED	NOYES	NUCLEOLES	NULLIFIES
NOUMENAL	NOVELIZER	NOYESES	NUCLEOLI	NULLIFY
NOUMENON	NOVELIZERS	NOYING	NUCLEOLUS	NULLIFYING

NULLING	NUMINA	NURDLING	NUTCASES	NUZZLING
NULLINGS	NUMINOUS	NURDS	NUTGALL	NY
NULLIPARA	NUMINOUSES	NURHAG	NUTGALLS	NYAFF
NULLIPARAE	NUMMARY	NURHAGS	NUTHATCH	NYAFFED
NULLIPARAS	NUMMULAR	NURL	NUTHATCHES	NYAFFING
NULLIPORE	NUMMULARY	NURLED	NUTHOUSE	NYAFFS
NULLIPORES	NUMMULINE	NURLING	NUTHOUSES	NYALA
NULLITIES	NUMMULITE	NURLS	NUTJOBBER	NYALAS
NULLITY	NUMMULITES	NURR	NUTJOBBERS	NYANZA
NULLNESS	NUMNAH	NURRS	NUTLET	NYANZAS
NULLNESSES	NUMNAHS	NURS	NUTLETS	NYAS
NULLS	NUMPTIES	NURSE	NUTLIKE	NYASES
NUMB	NUMPTY	NURSED	NUTMEAL	NYBBLE
NUMBAT	NUMSKULL	NURSELIKE	NUTMEALS	NYBBLES
NUMBATS	NUMSKULLS	NURSELING	NUTMEG	NYCTALOPES
NUMBED	NUN	NURSELINGS	NUTMEGGED	NYCTALOPS
NUMBER	NUNATAK	NURSEMAID	NUTMEGGING	NYE
NUMBERED	NUNATAKER	NURSEMAIDED	NUTMEGGY	NYED
NUMBERER	NUNATAKS	NURSEMAIDING	NUTMEGS	NYES
NUMBERERS	NUNCHAKU	NURSEMAIDS	NUTPECKER	NYING
NUMBERING	NUNCHAKUS	NURSER	NUTPECKERS	NYLGHAU
NUMBERS	NUNCHEON	NURSERIES	NUTRIA	NYLGHAUS
NUMBEST	NUNCHEONS	NURSERS	NUTRIAS	NYLON
NUMBING	NUNCIO	NURSERY	NUTRIENT	NYLONS
NUMBINGLY	NUNCIOS	NURSES	NUTRIENTS	NYMPH
NUMBLES	NUNCLE	NURSING	NUTRIMENT	NYMPHAE
NUMBLY	NUNCLES	NURSINGS	NUTRIMENTS	NYMPHAEA
NUMBNESS	NUNCUPATE	NURSLE	NUTRITION	NYMPHAEUM
NUMBNESSES	NUNCUPATED	NURSLED	NUTRITIONS	NYMPHAEUMS
NUMBS	NUNCUPATES	NURSLES	NUTRITIVE	NYMPHAL
NUMBSKULL	NUNCUPATING	NURSLING	NUTRITIVES	NYMPHALID
NUMBSKULLS	NUNDINAL	NURSLINGS	NUTS	NYMPHALIDS
NUMDAH	NUNDINE	NURTURAL	NUTSHELL	NYMPHEAN
NUMDAHS	NUNDINES	NURTURANT	NUTSHELLS	NYMPHET
NUMEN	NUNHOOD	NURTURE	NUTTED	NYMPHETS
NUMERABLE	NUNHOODS	NURTURED	NUTTER	NYMPHIC
NUMERABLY	NUNNATION	NURTURER	NUTTERIES	NYMPHICAL
NUMERACIES	NUNNATIONS	NURTURERS	NUTTERS	NYMPHISH
NUMERACY	NUNNERIES	NURTURES	NUTTERY	NYMPHLIKE
NUMERAIRE	NUNNERY	NURTURING	NUTTIER	NYMPHLY
NUMERAIRES	NUNNISH	NUS	NUTTIEST	NYMPHO
NUMERAL	NUNS	NUT	NUTTILY	NYMPHOS
NUMERALLY	NUNSHIP	NUTANT	NUTTINESS	NYMPHS
NUMERALS	NUNSHIPS	NUTARIAN	NUTTINESSES	NYS
NUMERARY	NUPTIAL	NUTARIANS	NUTTING	NYSSA
NUMERATE	NUPTIALS	NUTATE	NUTTINGS	NYSSAS
NUMERATED	NUR	NUTATED	NUTTY	NYSTAGMIC
NUMERATES	NURAGHE	NUTATES	NUTWOOD	NYSTAGMUS
NUMERATING	NURAGHI	NUTATING	NUTWOODS	NYSTAGMUSES
NUMERATOR	NURAGHIC	NUTATION	NUZZER	NYSTATIN
NUMERATORS	NURD	NUTATIONS	NUZZERS	NYSTATINS
NUMERIC	NURDLE	NUTBUTTER	NUZZLE	
NUMERICAL	NURDLED	NUTBUTTERS	NUZZLED	
NUMEROUS	NURDLES	NUTCASE	NUZZLES	

O

OAF	OBANG	OBESEST	OBLASTS	OBOVOID
OAFISH	OBANGS	OBESITIES	OBLATE	OBREPTION
OAFS	OBAS	OBESITY	OBLATES	OBREPTIONS
OAK	OBBLIGATI	OBEY	OBLATION	OBS
OAKEN	OBBLIGATO	OBEYED	OBLATIONS	OBSCENE
OAKENSHAW	OBBLIGATOS	OBEYER	OBLATORY	OBSCENELY
OAKENSHAWS	OBCONIC	OBEYERS	OBLIGANT	OBSCENER
OAKER	OBCONICAL	OBEYING	OBLIGANTS	OBSCENEST
OAKERS	OBCORDATE	OBEYS	OBLIGATE	OBSCENITIES
OAKIER	OBDURACIES	OBFUSCATE	OBLIGATED	OBSCENITY
OAKIEST	OBDURACY	OBFUSCATED	OBLIGATES	OBSCURANT
OAKLEAF	OBDURATE	OBFUSCATES	OBLIGATI	OBSCURANTS
OAKLEAVES	OBDURATED	OBFUSCATING	OBLIGATING	OBSCURE
OAKLING	OBDURATES	OBI	OBLIGATO	OBSCURED
OAKLINGS	OBDURATING	OBIA	OBLIGATOS	OBSCURELY
OAKS	OBDURE	OBIAS	OBLIGE	OBSCURER
OAKUM	OBDURED	OBIED	OBLIGED	OBSCURERS
OAKUMS	OBDURES	OBIING	OBLIGEE	OBSCURES
OAKY	OBDURING	OBIISM	OBLIGEES	OBSCUREST
OAR	OBEAH	OBIISMS	OBLIGES	OBSCURING
OARAGE	OBEAHED	OBIIT	OBLIGING	OBSCURITIES
OARAGES	OBEAHING	OBIS	OBLIGOR	OBSCURITY
OARED	OBEAHISM	OBIT	OBLIGORS	OBSECRATE
OARIER	OBEAHISMS	OBITAL	OBLIQUE	OBSECRATED
OARIEST	OBEAHS	OBITER	OBLIQUED	OBSECRATES
OARING	OBECHE	OBITS	OBLIQUELY	OBSECRATING
OARLESS	OBECHES	OBITUAL	OBLIQUER	OBSEQUENT
OARS	OBEDIENCE	OBITUARIES	OBLIQUES	OBSEQUIAL
OARSMAN	OBEDIENCES	OBITUARY	OBLIQUEST	OBSEQUIE
OARSMEN	OBEDIENT	OBJECT	OBLIQUID	OBSEQUIES
OARSWOMAN	OBEISANCE	OBJECTED	OBLIQUING	OBSEQUY
OARSWOMEN	OBEISANCES	OBJECTIFIED	OBLIQUITIES	OBSERVANT
OARWEED	OBEISANT	OBJECTIFIES	OBLIQUITY	OBSERVANTS
OARWEEDS	OBEISM	OBJECTIFY	OBLIVION	OBSERVE
OARY	OBEISMS	OBJECTIFYING	OBLIVIONS	OBSERVED
OASES	OBELI	OBJECTING	OBLIVIOUS	OBSERVER
OASIS	OBELIA	OBJECTION	OBLONG	OBSERVERS
OAST	OBELION	OBJECTIONS	OBLONGS	OBSERVES
OASTS	OBELISCAL	OBJECTIVE	OBLOQUIES	OBSERVING
OAT	OBELISE	OBJECTIVES	OBLOQUY	OBSESS
OATCAKE	OBELISED	OBJECTOR	OBNOXIOUS	OBSESSED
OATCAKES	OBELISES	OBJECTORS	OBO	OBSESSES
OATEN	OBELISING	OBJECTS	OBOE	OBSESSING
OATER	OBELISK	OBJET	OBOES	OBSESSION
OATERS	OBELISKS	OBJETS	OBOIST	OBSESSIONS
OATH	OBELIZE	OBJURE	OBOISTS	OBSESSIVE
OATHABLE	OBELIZED	OBJURED	OBOL	OBSIDIAN
OATHS	OBELIZES	OBJURES	OBOLARY	OBSIDIANS
OATMEAL	OBELIZING	OBJURGATE	OBOLI	OBSIGN
OATMEALS	OBELUS	OBJURGATED	OBOLS	OBSIGNATE
OATS	OBESE	OBJURGATES	OBOLUS	OBSIGNATED
OAVES	OBESENESS	OBJURGATING	OBOS	OBSIGNATES
OB	OBESENESSES	OBJURING	OBOVATE	OBSIGNATING
OBA	OBESER	OBLAST	OBOVATELY	OBSIGNED

OBSIGNING	OBTUSE	OCCLUSORS	OCHREA	OCTETTS
OBSIGNS	OBTUSELY	OCCULT	OCHREAE	OCTILLION
OBSOLESCE	OBTUSER	OCCULTED	OCHREATE	OCTILLIONS
OBSOLESCED	OBTUSEST	OCCULTING	OCHRED	OCTOFID
OBSOLESCES	OBTUSITIES	OCCULTISM	OCHREOUS	OCTOHEDRA
OBSOLESCING	OBTUSITY	OCCULTISMS	OCHRES	OCTONARIES
OBSOLETE	OBUMBRATE	OCCULTIST	OCHREY	OCTONARII
OBSTACLE	OBUMBRATED	OCCULTISTS	OCHRING	OCTONARY
OBSTACLES	OBUMBRATES	OCCULTLY	OCHROID	OCTOPI
OBSTETRIC	OBUMBRATING	OCCULTS	OCHROUS	OCTOPLOID
OBSTETRICS	OBVENTION	OCCUPANCE	OCHRY	OCTOPLOIDS
OBSTINACIES	OBVENTIONS	OCCUPANCES	OCKER	OCTOPOD
OBSTINACY	OBVERSE	OCCUPANCIES	OCKERISM	OCTOPODES
OBSTINATE	OBVERSELY	OCCUPANCY	OCKERISMS	OCTOPODS
OBSTRUCT	OBVERSES	OCCUPANT	OCKERS	OCTOPUS
OBSTRUCTED	OBVERSION	OCCUPANTS	OCOTILLO	OCTOPUSES
OBSTRUCTING	OBVERSIONS	OCCUPATE	OCOTILLOS	OCTOPUSH
OBSTRUCTS	OBVERT	OCCUPATED	OCREA	OCTOPUSHES
OBSTRUENT	OBVERTED	OCCUPATES	OCREAE	OCTOROON
OBSTRUENTS	OBVERTING	OCCUPATING	OCREATE	OCTOROONS
OBTAIN	OBVERTS	OCCUPIED	OCTA	OCTOSTYLE
OBTAINED	OBVIATE	OCCUPIER	OCTACHORD	OCTOSTYLES
OBTAINER	OBVIATED	OCCUPIERS	OCTACHORDS	OCTROI
OBTAINERS	OBVIATES	OCCUPIES	OCTAD	OCTROIS
OBTAINING	OBVIATING	OCCUPY	OCTADIC	OCTUOR
OBTAINS	OBVIATION	OCCUPYING	OCTADS	OCTUORS
OBTECT	OBVIATIONS	OCCUR	OCTAGON	OCTUPLE
OBTECTED	OBVIOUS	OCCURRED	OCTAGONAL	OCTUPLED
OBTEMPER	OBVIOUSLY	OCCURRENT	OCTAGONS	OCTUPLES
OBTEMPERED	OBVOLUTE	OCCURRENTS	OCTAHEDRA	OCTUPLET
OBTEMPERING	OBVOLUTED	OCCURRING	OCTAL	OCTUPLETS
OBTEMPERS	OBVOLVENT	OCCURS	OCTALS	OCTUPLING
OBTEND	OCA	OCEAN	OCTAMETER	OCULAR
OBTENDED	OCARINA	OCEANARIA	OCTAMETERS	OCULARIST
OBTENDING	OCARINAS	OCEANAUT	OCTANE	OCULARISTS
OBTENDS	OCAS	OCEANAUTS	OCTANES	OCULARLY
OBTENTION	OCCAM	OCEANIC	OCTANT	OCULARS
OBTENTIONS	OCCAMIES	OCEANID	OCTANTAL	OCULATE
OBTEST	OCCAMS	OCEANIDES	OCTANTS	OCULATED
OBTESTED	OCCAMY	OCEANIDS	OCTAPLA	OCULI
OBTESTING	OCCASION	OCEANS	OCTAPLAS	OCULIST
OBTESTS	OCCASIONED	OCELLAR	OCTAPLOID	OCULISTS
OBTRUDE	OCCASIONING	OCELLATE	OCTAPLOIDS	OCULUS
OBTRUDED	OCCASIONS	OCELLATED	OCTAPODIC	OD
OBTRUDER	OCCIDENT	OCELLI	OCTAPODIES	ODA
OBTRUDERS	OCCIDENTS	OCELLUS	OCTAPODY	ODAL
OBTRUDES	OCCIPITAL	OCELOID	OCTAROON	ODALIQUE
OBTRUDING	OCCIPITALS	OCELOT	OCTAROONS	ODALIQUES
OBTRUDINGS	OCCIPUT	OCELOTS	OCTAS	ODALISK
OBTRUSION	OCCIPUTS	OCH	OCTASTICH	ODALISKS
OBTRUSIONS	OCCLUDE	OCHE	OCTASTICHS	ODALISQUE
OBTRUSIVE	OCCLUDED	OCHER	OCTASTYLE	ODALISQUES
OBTUND	OCCLUDENT	OCHERED	OCTASTYLES	ODALLER
OBTUNDED	OCCLUDENTS	OCHERING	OCTAVAL	ODALLERS
OBTUNDENT	OCCLUDER	OCHEROUS	OCTAVE	ODALS
OBTUNDENTS	OCCLUDERS	OCHERS	OCTAVES	ODAS
OBTUNDING	OCCLUDES	OCHERY	OCTAVO	ODD
OBTUNDS	OCCLUDING	OCHES	OCTAVOS	ODDBALL
OBTURATE	OCCLUSAL	OCHIDORE	OCTENNIAL	ODDBALLS
OBTURATED	OCCLUSION	OCHIDORES	OCTET	ODDER
OBTURATES	OCCLUSIONS	OCHLOCRAT	OCTETS	ODDEST
OBTURATING	OCCLUSIVE	OCHLOCRATS	OCTETT	ODDISH
OBTURATOR	OCCLUSIVES	OCHONE	OCTETTE	ODDITIES
OBTURATORS	OCCLUSOR	OCHRE	OCTETTES	ODDITY

The Chambers Dictionary is the authority for many longer words; see *OSW* Introduction, page xii

ODDLY	OE	OFFENSES	OFFSIDER	OILCAN
ODDMENT	OECIST	OFFENSIVE	OFFSIDERS	OILCANS
ODDMENTS	OECISTS	OFFENSIVES	OFFSIDES	OILCLOTH
ODDNESS	OECOLOGIES	OFFER	OFFSPRING	OILCLOTHS
ODDNESSES	OECOLOGY	OFFERABLE	OFFSPRINGS	OILED
ODDS	OECUMENIC	OFFERED	OFFTAKE	OILER
ODDSMAN	OEDEMA	OFFEREE	OFFTAKES	OILERIES
ODDSMEN	OEDEMAS	OFFEREES	OFLAG	OILERS
ODE	OEDEMATA	OFFERER	OFLAGS	OILERY
ODEA	OEILLADE	OFFERERS	OFT	OILFIELD
ODEON	OEILLADES	OFFERING	OFTEN	OILFIELDS
ODEONS	OENANTHIC	OFFERINGS	OFTENER	OILIER
ODES	OENOLOGIES	OFFEROR	OFTENEST	OILIEST
ODEUM	OENOLOGY	OFFERORS	OFTENNESS	OILILY
ODEUMS	OENOMANCIES	OFFERS	OFTENNESSES	OILINESS
ODIC	OENOMANCY	OFFERTORIES	OFTTIMES	OILINESSES
ODIOUS	OENOMANIA	OFFERTORY	OGAM	OILING
ODIOUSLY	OENOMANIAS	OFFHAND	OGAMIC	OILLET
ODISM	OENOMEL	OFFHANDED	OGAMS	OILLETS
ODISMS	OENOMELS	OFFICE	OGDOAD	OILMAN
ODIST	OENOMETER	OFFICER	OGDOADS	OILMEN
ODISTS	OENOMETERS	OFFICERED	OGEE	OILNUT
ODIUM	OENOPHIL	OFFICERING	OGEES	OILNUTS
ODIUMS	OENOPHILE	OFFICERS	OGGIN	OILS
ODOGRAPH	OENOPHILES	OFFICES	OGGINS	OILSKIN
ODOGRAPHS	OENOPHILIES	OFFICIAL	OGHAM	OILSKINS
ODOMETER	OENOPHILS	OFFICIALS	OGHAMIC	OILSTONE
ODOMETERS	OENOPHILY	OFFICIANT	OGHAMS	OILSTONES
ODOMETRIES	OERLIKON	OFFICIANTS	OGIVAL	OILY
ODOMETRY	OERLIKONS	OFFICIATE	OGIVE	OINK
ODONATIST	OERSTED	OFFICIATED	OGIVES	OINKED
ODONATISTS	OERSTEDS	OFFICIATES	OGLE	OINKING
ODONTALGIES	OES	OFFICIATING	OGLED	OINKS
ODONTALGY	OESOPHAGI	OFFICINAL	OGLER	OINT
ODONTIC	OESTRAL	OFFICIOUS	OGLERS	OINTED
ODONTIST	OESTROGEN	OFFING	OGLES	OINTING
ODONTISTS	OESTROGENS	OFFINGS	OGLING	OINTMENT
ODONTOID	OESTROUS	OFFISH	OGLINGS	OINTMENTS
ODONTOMA	OESTRUM	OFFLINE	OGMIC	OINTS
ODONTOMAS	OESTRUMS	OFFLOAD	OGRE	OITICICA
ODONTOMATA	OESTRUS	OFFLOADED	OGREISH	OITICICAS
ODOR	OESTRUSES	OFFLOADING	OGRES	OJIME
ODORANT	OEUVRE	OFFLOADS	OGRESS	OJIMES
ODORANTS	OEUVRES	OFFPEAK	OGRESSES	OKAPI
ODORATE	OF	OFFPRINT	OGRISH	OKAPIS
ODOROUS	OFAY	OFFPRINTS	OH	OKAY
ODOROUSLY	OFAYS	OFFPUT	OHM	OKAYED
ODORS	OFF	OFFPUTS	OHMAGE	OKAYING
ODOUR	OFFAL	OFFS	OHMAGES	OKAYS
ODOURED	OFFALS	OFFSADDLE	OHMIC	OKE
ODOURLESS	OFFBEAT	OFFSADDLED	OHMMETER	OKES
ODOURS	OFFBEATS	OFFSADDLES	OHMMETERS	OKIMONO
ODS	OFFCUT	OFFSADDLING	OHMS	OKIMONOS
ODSO	OFFCUTS	OFFSCUM	OHO	OKRA
ODSOS	OFFED	OFFSCUMS	OHONE	OKRAS
ODYL	OFFENCE	OFFSEASON	OHOS	OKTA
ODYLE	OFFENCES	OFFSEASONS	OI	OKTAS
ODYLES	OFFEND	OFFSET	OIDIA	OLD
ODYLISM	OFFENDED	OFFSETS	OIDIUM	OLDEN
ODYLISMS	OFFENDER	OFFSETTING	OIK	OLDENED
ODYLS	OFFENDERS	OFFSHOOT	OIKIST	OLDENING
ODYSSEY	OFFENDING	OFFSHOOTS	OIKISTS	OLDENS
ODYSSEYS	OFFENDS	OFFSHORE	OIKS	OLDER
ODZOOKS	OFFENSE	OFFSIDE	OIL	OLDEST

The Chambers Dictionary is the authority for many longer words; see *OSW* Introduction, page xii

OLDIE	OLIPHANT	OMENTAL	OMS	ONFALL
OLDIES	OLIPHANTS	OMENTUM	ON	ONFALLS
OLDISH	OLITORIES	OMER	ONAGER	ONFLOW
OLDNESS	OLITORY	OMERS	ONAGERS	ONFLOWS
OLDNESSES	OLIVARY	OMERTA	ONANISM	ONGOING
OLDS	OLIVE	OMERTAS	ONANISMS	ONGOINGS
OLDSQUAW	OLIVENITE	OMICRON	ONANIST	ONION
OLDSQUAWS	OLIVENITES	OMICRONS	ONANISTIC	ONIONED
OLDSTER	OLIVER	OMINOUS	ONANISTS	ONIONIER
OLDSTERS	OLIVERS	OMINOUSLY	ONBOARD	ONIONIEST
OLDY	OLIVES	OMISSIBLE	ONCE	ONIONING
OLE	OLIVET	OMISSION	ONCER	ONIONS
OLEACEOUS	OLIVETS	OMISSIONS	ONCERS	ONIONY
OLEANDER	OLIVINE	OMISSIVE	ONCES	ONIRIC
OLEANDERS	OLIVINES	OMIT	ONCIDIUM	ONISCOID
OLEARIA	OLLA	OMITS	ONCIDIUMS	ONKUS
OLEARIAS	OLLAMH	OMITTANCE	ONCOGEN	ONLIEST
OLEASTER	OLLAMHS	OMITTANCES	ONCOGENE	ONLINE
OLEASTERS	OLLAS	OMITTED	ONCOGENES	ONLOOKER
OLEATE	OLLAV	OMITTER	ONCOGENIC	ONLOOKERS
OLEATES	OLLAVS	OMITTERS	ONCOGENS	ONLOOKING
OLECRANAL	OLM	OMITTING	ONCOLOGIES	ONLY
OLECRANON	OLMS	OMLAH	ONCOLOGY	ONNED
OLECRANONS	OLOGIES	OMLAHS	ONCOLYSES	ONNING
OLEFIANT	OLOGY	OMMATEA	ONCOLYSIS	ONOMASTIC
OLEFIN	OLOROSO	OMMATEUM	ONCOLYTIC	ONOMASTICS
OLEFINE	OLOROSOS	OMMATIDIA	ONCOLYTICS	ONRUSH
OLEFINES	OLPAE	OMNEITIES	ONCOME	ONRUSHES
OLEFINS	OLPE	OMNEITY	ONCOMES	ONS
OLEIC	OLPES	OMNIANA	ONCOMETER	ONSET
OLEIN	OLYCOOK	OMNIBUS	ONCOMETERS	ONSETS
OLEINS	OLYCOOKS	OMNIBUSES	ONCOMICE	ONSETTER
OLENT	OLYKOEK	OMNIETIES	ONCOMING	ONSETTERS
OLEO	OLYKOEKS	OMNIETY	ONCOMINGS	ONSETTING
OLEOGRAPH	OLYMPIAD	OMNIFIC	ONCOMOUSE	ONSETTINGS
OLEOGRAPHS	OLYMPIADS	OMNIFIED	ONCOST	ONSHORE
OLEOS	OLYMPICS	OMNIFIES	ONCOSTMAN	ONSIDE
OLEUM	OM	OMNIFORM	ONCOSTMEN	ONSIDES
OLEUMS	OMADHAUN	OMNIFY	ONCOSTS	ONSLAUGHT
OLFACT	OMADHAUNS	OMNIFYING	ONCOTOMIES	ONSLAUGHTS
OLFACTED	OMASA	OMNIUM	ONCOTOMY	ONST
OLFACTING	OMASAL	OMNIUMS	ONCUS	ONSTEAD
OLFACTION	OMASUM	OMNIVORE	ONDATRA	ONSTEADS
OLFACTIONS	OMBRE	OMNIVORES	ONDATRAS	ONTO
OLFACTIVE	OMBRELLA	OMNIVORIES	ONDINE	ONTOGENIC
OLFACTORY	OMBRELLAS	OMNIVORY	ONDINES	ONTOGENIES
OLFACTS	OMBRES	OMOHYOID	ONDING	ONTOGENY
OLIBANUM	OMBROPHIL	OMOHYOIDS	ONDINGS	ONTOLOGIC
OLIBANUMS	OMBROPHILS	OMOPHAGIA	ONE	ONTOLOGIES
OLID	OMBU	OMOPHAGIAS	ONEFOLD	ONTOLOGY
OLIGAEMIA	OMBUDSMAN	OMOPHAGIC	ONEIRIC	ONUS
OLIGAEMIAS	OMBUDSMEN	OMOPHAGIES	ONELY	ONUSES
OLIGARCH	OMBUS	OMOPHAGY	ONENESS	ONWARD
OLIGARCHIES	OMEGA	OMOPHORIA	ONENESSES	ONWARDLY
OLIGARCHS	OMEGAS	OMOPLATE	ONER	ONWARDS
OLIGARCHY	OMELET	OMOPLATES	ONEROUS	ONYCHA
OLIGIST	OMELETS	OMPHACITE	ONEROUSLY	ONYCHAS
OLIGISTS	OMELETTE	OMPHACITES	ONERS	ONYCHIA
OLIGOPOLIES	OMELETTES	OMPHALI	ONES	ONYCHIAS
OLIGOPOLY	OMEN	OMPHALIC	ONESELF	ONYCHITE
OLIGURIA	OMENED	OMPHALOID	ONEYER	ONYCHITES
OLIGURIAS	OMENING	OMPHALOS	ONEYERS	ONYCHITIS
OLIO	OMENS	OMRAH	ONEYRE	ONYCHITISES
OLIOS	OMENTA	OMRAHS	ONEYRES	ONYCHIUM

The Chambers Dictionary is the authority for many longer words; see *OSW* Introduction, page xii

ONYCHIUMS
ONYMOUS
ONYX
ONYXES
OO
OOBIT
OOBITS
OOCYTE
OOCYTES
OODLES
OODLINS
OOF
OOFS
OOFTISH
OOFTISHES
OOGAMIES
OOGAMOUS
OOGAMY
OOGENESES
OOGENESIS
OOGENETIC
OOGENIES
OOGENY
OOGONIA
OOGONIAL
OOGONIUM
OOH
OOHED
OOHING
OOHS
OOIDAL
OOLAKAN
OOLAKANS
OOLITE
OOLITES
OOLITIC
OOLOGIES
OOLOGIST
OOLOGISTS
OOLOGY
OOLONG
OOLONGS
OOM
OOMIAC
OOMIACK
OOMIACKS
OOMIACS
OOMIAK
OOMIAKS
OOMPAH
OOMPAHED
OOMPAHING
OOMPAHS
OOMPH
OOMPHS
OOMS
OON
OONS
OONT
OONTS
OOP
OOPED
OOPHORON
OOPHORONS

OOPHYTE
OOPHYTES
OOPING
OOPS
OOR
OORIAL
OORIALS
OORIE
OORIER
OORIEST
OOS
OOSE
OOSES
OOSIER
OOSIEST
OOSPHERE
OOSPHERES
OOSPORE
OOSPORES
OOSY
OOZE
OOZED
OOZES
OOZIER
OOZIEST
OOZILY
OOZINESS
OOZINESSES
OOZING
OOZY
OP
OPACITIES
OPACITY
OPACOUS
OPAH
OPAHS
OPAL
OPALED
OPALINE
OPALINES
OPALISED
OPALIZED
OPALS
OPAQUE
OPAQUED
OPAQUELY
OPAQUER
OPAQUES
OPAQUEST
OPAQUING
OPCODE
OPCODES
OPE
OPED
OPEN
OPENABLE
OPENED
OPENER
OPENERS
OPENEST
OPENING
OPENINGS
OPENLY
OPENNESS

OPENNESSES
OPENS
OPENWORK
OPENWORKS
OPEPE
OPEPES
OPERA
OPERABLE
OPERAND
OPERANDS
OPERANT
OPERANTS
OPERAS
OPERATE
OPERATED
OPERATES
OPERATIC
OPERATING
OPERATION
OPERATIONS
OPERATIVE
OPERATIVES
OPERATOR
OPERATORS
OPERCULA
OPERCULAR
OPERCULUM
OPERETTA
OPERETTAS
OPERON
OPERONS
OPEROSE
OPEROSELY
OPEROSITIES
OPEROSITY
OPES
OPHIDIAN
OPHIDIANS
OPHIOLITE
OPHIOLITES
OPHIOLOGIES
OPHIOLOGY
OPHITE
OPHITES
OPHITIC
OPHIURA
OPHIURAN
OPHIURANS
OPHIURAS
OPHIURID
OPHIURIDS
OPHIUROID
OPHIUROIDS
OPIATE
OPIATED
OPIATES
OPIATING
OPIFICER
OPIFICERS
OPINABLE
OPINE
OPINED
OPINES
OPING

OPINICUS
OPINICUSES
OPINING
OPINION
OPINIONED
OPINIONS
OPIOID
OPIUM
OPIUMISM
OPIUMISMS
OPIUMS
OPOBALSAM
OPOBALSAMS
OPODELDOC
OPODELDOCS
OPOPANAX
OPOPANAXES
OPORICE
OPORICES
OPOSSUM
OPOSSUMS
OPPIDAN
OPPIDANS
OPPILATE
OPPILATED
OPPILATES
OPPILATING
OPPO
OPPONENCIES
OPPONENCY
OPPONENT
OPPONENTS
OPPORTUNE
OPPOS
OPPOSABLE
OPPOSE
OPPOSED
OPPOSER
OPPOSERS
OPPOSES
OPPOSING
OPPOSITE
OPPOSITES
OPPRESS
OPPRESSED
OPPRESSES
OPPRESSING
OPPRESSOR
OPPRESSORS
OPPUGN
OPPUGNANT
OPPUGNANTS
OPPUGNED
OPPUGNER
OPPUGNERS
OPPUGNING
OPPUGNS
OPS
OPSIMATH
OPSIMATHIES
OPSIMATHS
OPSIMATHY
OPSOMANIA
OPSOMANIAS

OPSONIC
OPSONIN
OPSONINS
OPSONIUM
OPSONIUMS
OPT
OPTANT
OPTANTS
OPTATIVE
OPTATIVES
OPTED
OPTER
OPTERS
OPTIC
OPTICAL
OPTICALLY
OPTICIAN
OPTICIANS
OPTICS
OPTIMA
OPTIMAL
OPTIMALLY
OPTIMATE
OPTIMATES
OPTIME
OPTIMES
OPTIMISE
OPTIMISED
OPTIMISES
OPTIMISING
OPTIMISM
OPTIMISMS
OPTIMIST
OPTIMISTS
OPTIMIZE
OPTIMIZED
OPTIMIZES
OPTIMIZING
OPTIMUM
OPTING
OPTION
OPTIONAL
OPTIONS
OPTOLOGIES
OPTOLOGY
OPTOMETER
OPTOMETERS
OPTOMETRIES
OPTOMETRY
OPTOPHONE
OPTOPHONES
OPTRONICS
OPTS
OPULENCE
OPULENCES
OPULENT
OPULENTLY
OPULUS
OPULUSES
OPUNTIA
OPUNTIAS
OPUS
OPUSCLE
OPUSCLES

OPUSCULA	ORATRIX	ORDAINER	ORES	ORGY
OPUSCULE	ORATRIXES	ORDAINERS	ORESTUNCK	ORIBI
OPUSCULES	ORB	ORDAINING	OREWEED	ORIBIS
OPUSCULUM	ORBED	ORDAINS	OREWEEDS	ORICALCHE
OPUSES	ORBICULAR	ORDALIAN	OREXIS	ORICALCHES
OR	ORBIER	ORDALIUM	OREXISES	ORICHALC
ORACH	ORBIEST	ORDALIUMS	ORF	ORICHALCS
ORACHE	ORBING	ORDEAL	ORFE	ORIEL
ORACHES	ORBIT	ORDEALS	ORFES	ORIELLED
ORACIES	ORBITA	ORDER	ORFS	ORIELS
ORACLE	ORBITAL	ORDERED	ORGAN	ORIENCIES
ORACLED	ORBITALS	ORDERER	ORGANA	ORIENCY
ORACLES	ORBITAS	ORDERERS	ORGANDIE	ORIENT
ORACLING	ORBITED	ORDERING	ORGANDIES	ORIENTAL
ORACULAR	ORBITER	ORDERINGS	ORGANELLE	ORIENTALS
ORACULOUS	ORBITERS	ORDERLESS	ORGANELLES	ORIENTATE
ORACY	ORBITIES	ORDERLIES	ORGANIC	ORIENTATED
ORAGIOUS	ORBITING	ORDERLY	ORGANICAL	ORIENTATES
ORAL	ORBITS	ORDERS	ORGANISE	ORIENTATING
ORALISM	ORBITY	ORDINAIRE	ORGANISED	ORIENTED
ORALISMS	ORBS	ORDINAIRES	ORGANISER	ORIENTEER
ORALITIES	ORBY	ORDINAL	ORGANISERS	ORIENTEERED
ORALITY	ORC	ORDINALS	ORGANISES	ORIENTEERING
ORALLY	ORCA	ORDINANCE	ORGANISING	ORIENTEERINGS
ORALS	ORCAS	ORDINANCES	ORGANISM	ORIENTEERS
ORANG	ORCEIN	ORDINAND	ORGANISMS	ORIENTING
ORANGE	ORCEINS	ORDINANDS	ORGANIST	ORIENTS
ORANGEADE	ORCHARD	ORDINANT	ORGANISTS	ORIFEX
ORANGEADES	ORCHARDS	ORDINANTS	ORGANITIES	ORIFEXES
ORANGER	ORCHAT	ORDINAR	ORGANITY	ORIFICE
ORANGERIES	ORCHATS	ORDINARIES	ORGANIZE	ORIFICES
ORANGERY	ORCHEL	ORDINARS	ORGANIZED	ORIFICIAL
ORANGES	ORCHELLA	ORDINARY	ORGANIZER	ORIFLAMME
ORANGEST	ORCHELLAS	ORDINATE	ORGANIZERS	ORIFLAMMES
ORANGEY	ORCHELS	ORDINATED	ORGANIZES	ORIGAMI
ORANGIER	ORCHESES	ORDINATES	ORGANIZING	ORIGAMIS
ORANGIEST	ORCHESIS	ORDINATING	ORGANON	ORIGAN
ORANGS	ORCHESTIC	ORDINEE	ORGANS	ORIGANE
ORANT	ORCHESTICS	ORDINEES	ORGANUM	ORIGANES
ORANTS	ORCHESTRA	ORDNANCE	ORGANZA	ORIGANS
ORARIA	ORCHESTRAS	ORDNANCES	ORGANZAS	ORIGANUM
ORARIAN	ORCHID	ORDS	ORGANZINE	ORIGANUMS
ORARIANS	ORCHIDIST	ORDURE	ORGANZINES	ORIGIN
ORARION	ORCHIDISTS	ORDURES	ORGASM	ORIGINAL
ORARIONS	ORCHIDS	ORDUROUS	ORGASMED	ORIGINALS
ORARIUM	ORCHIL	ORE	ORGASMIC	ORIGINATE
ORARIUMS	ORCHILLA	OREAD	ORGASMING	ORIGINATED
ORATE	ORCHILLAS	OREADES	ORGASMS	ORIGINATES
ORATED	ORCHILS	OREADS	ORGASTIC	ORIGINATING
ORATES	ORCHIS	ORECROWE	ORGEAT	ORIGINS
ORATING	ORCHISES	ORECROWED	ORGEATS	ORILLION
ORATION	ORCHITIC	ORECROWES	ORGIA	ORILLIONS
ORATIONS	ORCHITIS	ORECROWING	ORGIAS	ORIOLE
ORATOR	ORCHITISES	ORECTIC	ORGIAST	ORIOLES
ORATORIAL	ORCIN	OREGANO	ORGIASTIC	ORISON
ORATORIAN	ORCINE	OREGANOS	ORGIASTS	ORISONS
ORATORIANS	ORCINES	OREIDE	ORGIC	ORLE
ORATORIES	ORCINOL	OREIDES	ORGIES	ORLEANS
ORATORIO	ORCINOLS	OREOLOGIES	ORGILLOUS	ORLEANSES
ORATORIOS	ORCINS	OREOLOGY	ORGONE	ORLES
ORATORS	ORCS	OREPEARCH	ORGONES	ORLOP
ORATORY	ORD	OREPEARCHED	ORGUE	ORLOPS
ORATRESS	ORDAIN	OREPEARCHES	ORGUES	ORMER
ORATRESSES	ORDAINED	OREPEARCHING	ORGULOUS	ORMERS

ORMOLU	ORTHICONS	OSIERIES	OSTEODERM	OTHERNESSES
ORMOLUS	ORTHO	OSIERS	OSTEODERMS	OTHERS
ORNAMENT	ORTHOAXES	OSIERY	OSTEOGEN	OTHERWISE
ORNAMENTED	ORTHOAXIS	OSMATE	OSTEOGENIES	OTIC
ORNAMENTING	ORTHODOX	OSMATES	OSTEOGENS	OTIOSE
ORNAMENTS	ORTHODOXIES	OSMETERIA	OSTEOGENY	OTIOSITIES
ORNATE	ORTHODOXY	OSMIATE	OSTEOID	OTIOSITY
ORNATELY	ORTHOEPIC	OSMIATES	OSTEOLOGIES	OTITIS
ORNATER	ORTHOEPIES	OSMIC	OSTEOLOGY	OTITISES
ORNATEST	ORTHOEPY	OSMIOUS	OSTEOMA	OTOCYST
ORNERY	ORTHOPEDIES	OSMIUM	OSTEOMAS	OTOCYSTS
ORNIS	ORTHOPEDY	OSMIUMS	OSTEOMATA	OTOLITH
ORNISES	ORTHOPOD	OSMOMETER	OSTEOPATH	OTOLITHS
ORNITHIC	ORTHOPODS	OSMOMETERS	OSTEOPATHS	OTOLOGIES
ORNITHOID	ORTHOPTIC	OSMOMETRIES	OSTEOTOME	OTOLOGIST
OROGEN	ORTHOPTICS	OSMOMETRY	OSTEOTOMES	OTOLOGISTS
OROGENIC	ORTHOS	OSMOSE	OSTEOTOMIES	OTOLOGY
OROGENIES	ORTHOSES	OSMOSED	OSTEOTOMY	OTORRHOEA
OROGENS	ORTHOSIS	OSMOSES	OSTIA	OTORRHOEAS
OROGENY	ORTHOTIC	OSMOSING	OSTIAL	OTOSCOPE
OROGRAPHIES	ORTHOTICS	OSMOSIS	OSTIARIES	OTOSCOPES
OROGRAPHY	ORTHOTIST	OSMOTIC	OSTIARY	OTTAR
OROIDE	ORTHOTISTS	OSMOUS	OSTIATE	OTTARS
OROIDES	ORTHOTONE	OSMUND	OSTINATO	OTTAVA
OROLOGIES	ORTHROS	OSMUNDA	OSTINATOS	OTTAVAS
OROLOGIST	ORTHROSES	OSMUNDAS	OSTIOLATE	OTTAVINO
OROLOGISTS	ORTOLAN	OSMUNDS	OSTIOLE	OTTAVINOS
OROLOGY	ORTOLANS	OSNABURG	OSTIOLES	OTTER
OROPESA	ORTS	OSNABURGS	OSTIUM	OTTERED
OROPESAS	ORVAL	OSPREY	OSTLER	OTTERING
OROROTUND	ORVALS	OSPREYS	OSTLERESS	OTTERS
OROTUND	ORYX	OSSA	OSTLERESSES	OTTO
ORPHAN	ORYXES	OSSARIUM	OSTLERS	OTTOMAN
ORPHANAGE	ORZO	OSSARIUMS	OSTRACA	OTTOMANS
ORPHANAGES	ORZOS	OSSEIN	OSTRACEAN	OTTOS
ORPHANED	OS	OSSEINS	OSTRACISE	OTTRELITE
ORPHANING	OSCHEAL	OSSELET	OSTRACISED	OTTRELITES
ORPHANISM	OSCILLATE	OSSELETS	OSTRACISES	OU
ORPHANISMS	OSCILLATED	OSSEOUS	OSTRACISING	OUABAIN
ORPHANS	OSCILLATES	OSSETER	OSTRACISM	OUABAINS
ORPHARION	OSCILLATING	OSSETERS	OSTRACISMS	OUAKARI
ORPHARIONS	OSCINE	OSSIA	OSTRACIZE	OUAKARIS
ORPHREY	OSCININE	OSSICLE	OSTRACIZED	OUBIT
ORPHREYS	OSCITANCIES	OSSICLES	OSTRACIZES	OUBITS
ORPIMENT	OSCITANCY	OSSICULAR	OSTRACIZING	OUBLIETTE
ORPIMENTS	OSCITANT	OSSIFIC	OSTRACOD	OUBLIETTES
ORPIN	OSCITATE	OSSIFIED	OSTRACODS	OUCH
ORPINE	OSCITATED	OSSIFIES	OSTRACON	OUCHES
ORPINES	OSCITATES	OSSIFRAGA	OSTRAKA	OUCHT
ORPINS	OSCITATING	OSSIFRAGAS	OSTRAKON	OUCHTS
ORRA	OSCULA	OSSIFRAGE	OSTREGER	OUD
ORRERIES	OSCULANT	OSSIFRAGES	OSTREGERS	OUDS
ORRERY	OSCULAR	OSSIFY	OSTRICH	OUGHLIED
ORRIS	OSCULATE	OSSIFYING	OSTRICHES	OUGHLIES
ORRISES	OSCULATED	OSSUARIES	OTAKU	OUGHLY
ORS	OSCULATES	OSSUARY	OTALGIA	OUGHLYING
ORSEILLE	OSCULATING	OSTEAL	OTALGIAS	OUGHT
ORSEILLES	OSCULE	OSTEITIS	OTALGIES	OUGHTNESS
ORSELLIC	OSCULES	OSTEITISES	OTALGY	OUGHTNESSES
ORT	OSCULUM	OSTENSIVE	OTARIES	OUGHTS
ORTANIQUE	OSHAC	OSTENSORIES	OTARINE	OUGLIE
ORTANIQUES	OSHACS	OSTENSORY	OTARY	OUGLIED
ORTHIAN	OSIER	OSTENT	OTHER	OUGLIEING
ORTHICON	OSIERED	OSTENTS	OTHERNESS	OUGLIES

OUIJA	OUTBACKERS	OUTCROPPING	OUTFALL	OUTGLARE
OUIJAS	OUTBACKS	OUTCROPS	OUTFALLS	OUTGLARED
OUISTITI	OUTBAR	OUTCROSS	OUTFIELD	OUTGLARES
OUISTITIS	OUTBARRED	OUTCROSSED	OUTFIELDS	OUTGLARING
OUK	OUTBARRING	OUTCROSSES	OUTFIGHT	OUTGO
OUKS	OUTBARS	OUTCROSSING	OUTFIGHTING	OUTGOER
OULACHON	OUTBID	OUTCROSSINGS	OUTFIGHTS	OUTGOERS
OULACHONS	OUTBIDDING	OUTCRY	OUTFIT	OUTGOES
OULAKAN	OUTBIDS	OUTCRYING	OUTFITS	OUTGOING
OULAKANS	OUTBOARD	OUTDANCE	OUTFITTED	OUTGOINGS
OULD	OUTBOUND	OUTDANCED	OUTFITTER	OUTGONE
OULDER	OUTBOUNDS	OUTDANCES	OUTFITTERS	OUTGREW
OULDEST	OUTBOX	OUTDANCING	OUTFITTING	OUTGROW
OULK	OUTBOXED	OUTDARE	OUTFITTINGS	OUTGROWING
OULKS	OUTBOXES	OUTDARED	OUTFLANK	OUTGROWN
OULONG	OUTBOXING	OUTDARES	OUTFLANKED	OUTGROWS
OULONGS	OUTBRAG	OUTDARING	OUTFLANKING	OUTGROWTH
OUNCE	OUTBRAGGED	OUTDATE	OUTFLANKS	OUTGROWTHS
OUNCES	OUTBRAGGING	OUTDATED	OUTFLASH	OUTGUARD
OUNDY	OUTBRAGS	OUTDATES	OUTFLASHED	OUTGUARDS
OUP	OUTBRAVE	OUTDATING	OUTFLASHES	OUTGUN
OUPED	OUTBRAVED	OUTDID	OUTFLASHING	OUTGUNNED
OUPH	OUTBRAVES	OUTDO	OUTFLEW	OUTGUNNING
OUPHE	OUTBRAVING	OUTDOES	OUTFLIES	OUTGUNS
OUPHES	OUTBREAK	OUTDOING	OUTFLING	OUTGUSH
OUPHS	OUTBREAKING	OUTDONE	OUTFLINGS	OUTGUSHED
OUPING	OUTBREAKS	OUTDOOR	OUTFLOW	OUTGUSHES
OUPS	OUTBRED	OUTDOORS	OUTFLOWED	OUTGUSHING
OUR	OUTBREED	OUTDOORSY	OUTFLOWING	OUTHAUL
OURALI	OUTBREEDING	OUTDRANK	OUTFLOWINGS	OUTHAULER
OURALIS	OUTBREEDINGS	OUTDRINK	OUTFLOWN	OUTHAULERS
OURARI	OUTBREEDS	OUTDRINKING	OUTFLOWS	OUTHAULS
OURARIS	OUTBROKE	OUTDRINKS	OUTFLUSH	OUTHER
OUREBI	OUTBROKEN	OUTDRIVE	OUTFLUSHED	OUTHIRE
OUREBIS	OUTBURN	OUTDRIVEN	OUTFLUSHES	OUTHIRED
OURIE	OUTBURNED	OUTDRIVES	OUTFLUSHING	OUTHIRES
OURIER	OUTBURNING	OUTDRIVING	OUTFLY	OUTHIRING
OURIEST	OUTBURNS	OUTDROVE	OUTFLYING	OUTHIT
OURN	OUTBURNT	OUTDRUNK	OUTFOOT	OUTHITS
OUROBOROS	OUTBURST	OUTDURE	OUTFOOTED	OUTHITTING
OUROBOROSES	OUTBURSTING	OUTDURED	OUTFOOTING	OUTHOUSE
OUROLOGIES	OUTBURSTS	OUTDURES	OUTFOOTS	OUTHOUSES
OUROLOGY	OUTBY	OUTDURING	OUTFOUGHT	OUTHYRE
OUROSCOPIES	OUTBYE	OUTDWELL	OUTFOX	OUTHYRED
OUROSCOPY	OUTCAST	OUTDWELLED	OUTFOXED	OUTHYRES
OURS	OUTCASTE	OUTDWELLING	OUTFOXES	OUTHYRING
OURSELF	OUTCASTED	OUTDWELLS	OUTFOXING	OUTING
OURSELVES	OUTCASTES	OUTDWELT	OUTFROWN	OUTINGS
OUSEL	OUTCASTING	OUTEAT	OUTFROWNED	OUTJEST
OUSELS	OUTCASTS	OUTEATEN	OUTFROWNING	OUTJESTED
OUST	OUTCLASS	OUTEATING	OUTFROWNS	OUTJESTING
OUSTED	OUTCLASSED	OUTEATS	OUTGAS	OUTJESTS
OUSTER	OUTCLASSES	OUTED	OUTGASSED	OUTJET
OUSTERS	OUTCLASSING	OUTEDGE	OUTGASSES	OUTJETS
OUSTING	OUTCOME	OUTEDGES	OUTGASSING	OUTJOCKEY
OUSTITI	OUTCOMES	OUTER	OUTGASSINGS	OUTJOCKEYED
OUSTITIS	OUTCRAFTIED	OUTERMOST	OUTGATE	OUTJOCKEYING
OUSTS	OUTCRAFTIES	OUTERS	OUTGATES	OUTJOCKEYS
OUT	OUTCRAFTY	OUTERWEAR	OUTGAVE	OUTJUMP
OUTAGE	OUTCRAFTYING	OUTERWEARS	OUTGIVE	OUTJUMPED
OUTAGES	OUTCRIED	OUTFACE	OUTGIVEN	OUTJUMPING
OUTATE	OUTCRIES	OUTFACED	OUTGIVES	OUTJUMPS
OUTBACK	OUTCROP	OUTFACES	OUTGIVING	OUTJUT
OUTBACKER	OUTCROPPED	OUTFACING	OUTGIVINGS	OUTJUTS

The Chambers Dictionary is the authority for many longer words; see *OSW* Introduction, page xii

OUTLAID	OUTLUSTRING	OUTPLAYS	OUTREDDED	OUTSCORN
OUTLAIN	OUTLYING	OUTPOINT	OUTREDDEN	OUTSCORNED
OUTLAND	OUTMAN	OUTPOINTED	OUTREDDENED	OUTSCORNING
OUTLANDER	OUTMANNED	OUTPOINTING	OUTREDDENING	OUTSCORNS
OUTLANDERS	OUTMANNING	OUTPOINTS	OUTREDDENS	OUTSELL
OUTLANDS	OUTMANS	OUTPORT	OUTREDDING	OUTSELLING
OUTLASH	OUTMANTLE	OUTPORTS	OUTREDS	OUTSELLS
OUTLASHES	OUTMANTLED	OUTPOST	OUTREIGN	OUTSET
OUTLAST	OUTMANTLES	OUTPOSTS	OUTREIGNED	OUTSETS
OUTLASTED	OUTMANTLING	OUTPOUR	OUTREIGNING	OUTSHINE
OUTLASTING	OUTMARCH	OUTPOURED	OUTREIGNS	OUTSHINES
OUTLASTS	OUTMARCHED	OUTPOURER	OUTRELIEF	OUTSHINING
OUTLAUNCE	OUTMARCHES	OUTPOURERS	OUTRELIEFS	OUTSHONE
OUTLAUNCED	OUTMARCHING	OUTPOURING	OUTREMER	OUTSHOOT
OUTLAUNCES	OUTMATCH	OUTPOURINGS	OUTREMERS	OUTSHOOTING
OUTLAUNCH	OUTMATCHED	OUTPOURS	OUTRIDDEN	OUTSHOOTS
OUTLAUNCHED	OUTMATCHES	OUTPOWER	OUTRIDE	OUTSHOT
OUTLAUNCHES	OUTMATCHING	OUTPOWERED	OUTRIDER	OUTSHOTS
OUTLAUNCHING	OUTMODE	OUTPOWERING	OUTRIDERS	OUTSIDE
OUTLAUNCING	OUTMODED	OUTPOWERS	OUTRIDES	OUTSIDER
OUTLAW	OUTMODES	OUTPRAY	OUTRIDING	OUTSIDERS
OUTLAWED	OUTMODING	OUTPRAYED	OUTRIGGER	OUTSIDES
OUTLAWING	OUTMOST	OUTPRAYING	OUTRIGGERS	OUTSIGHT
OUTLAWRIES	OUTMOVE	OUTPRAYS	OUTRIGHT	OUTSIGHTS
OUTLAWRY	OUTMOVED	OUTPRICE	OUTRIVAL	OUTSIT
OUTLAWS	OUTMOVES	OUTPRICED	OUTRIVALLED	OUTSITS
OUTLAY	OUTMOVING	OUTPRICES	OUTRIVALLING	OUTSITTING
OUTLAYING	OUTNAME	OUTPRICING	OUTRIVALS	OUTSIZE
OUTLAYS	OUTNAMED	OUTPRIZE	OUTROAR	OUTSIZED
OUTLEAP	OUTNAMES	OUTPRIZED	OUTROARED	OUTSIZES
OUTLEAPED	OUTNAMING	OUTPRIZES	OUTROARING	OUTSKIRTS
OUTLEAPING	OUTNESS	OUTPRIZING	OUTROARS	OUTSLEEP
OUTLEAPS	OUTNESSES	OUTPUT	OUTRODE	OUTSLEEPING
OUTLEAPT	OUTNIGHT	OUTPUTS	OUTROOP	OUTSLEEPS
OUTLEARN	OUTNIGHTED	OUTPUTTING	OUTROOPER	OUTSLEPT
OUTLEARNED	OUTNIGHTING	OUTRACE	OUTROOPERS	OUTSMART
OUTLEARNING	OUTNIGHTS	OUTRACED	OUTROOPS	OUTSMARTED
OUTLEARNS	OUTNUMBER	OUTRACES	OUTROOT	OUTSMARTING
OUTLEARNT	OUTNUMBERED	OUTRACING	OUTROOTED	OUTSMARTS
OUTLER	OUTNUMBERING	OUTRAGE	OUTROOTING	OUTSOAR
OUTLERS	OUTNUMBERS	OUTRAGED	OUTROOTS	OUTSOARED
OUTLET	OUTPACE	OUTRAGES	OUTROPE	OUTSOARING
OUTLETS	OUTPACED	OUTRAGING	OUTROPER	OUTSOARS
OUTLIE	OUTPACES	OUTRAIGNE	OUTROPERS	OUTSOLD
OUTLIED	OUTPACING	OUTRAIGNED	OUTROPES	OUTSOLE
OUTLIER	OUTPART	OUTRAIGNES	OUTRUN	OUTSOLES
OUTLIERS	OUTPARTS	OUTRAIGNING	OUTRUNNER	OUTSOURCE
OUTLIES	OUTPEEP	OUTRAN	OUTRUNNERS	OUTSOURCED
OUTLINE	OUTPEEPED	OUTRANCE	OUTRUNNING	OUTSOURCES
OUTLINEAR	OUTPEEPING	OUTRANCES	OUTRUNS	OUTSOURCING
OUTLINED	OUTPEEPS	OUTRANK	OUTRUSH	OUTSOURCINGS
OUTLINES	OUTPEER	OUTRANKED	OUTRUSHED	OUTSPAN
OUTLINING	OUTPEERED	OUTRANKING	OUTRUSHES	OUTSPANNED
OUTLIVE	OUTPEERING	OUTRANKS	OUTRUSHING	OUTSPANNING
OUTLIVED	OUTPEERS	OUTRATE	OUTS	OUTSPANS
OUTLIVES	OUTPLACE	OUTRATED	OUTSAIL	OUTSPEAK
OUTLIVING	OUTPLACED	OUTRATES	OUTSAILED	OUTSPEAKING
OUTLOOK	OUTPLACER	OUTRATING	OUTSAILING	OUTSPEAKS
OUTLOOKED	OUTPLACERS	OUTRE	OUTSAILS	OUTSPEND
OUTLOOKING	OUTPLACES	OUTREACH	OUTSAT	OUTSPENDING
OUTLOOKS	OUTPLACING	OUTREACHED	OUTSCOLD	OUTSPENDS
OUTLUSTRE	OUTPLAY	OUTREACHES	OUTSCOLDED	OUTSPENT
OUTLUSTRED	OUTPLAYED	OUTREACHING	OUTSCOLDING	OUTSPOKE
OUTLUSTRES	OUTPLAYING	OUTRED	OUTSCOLDS	OUTSPOKEN

The Chambers Dictionary is the authority for many longer words; see *OSW* Introduction, page xii

OUTSPORT	OUTTAKING	OUTWATCHING	OUVRAGE	OVERBEATS
OUTSPORTED	OUTTALK	OUTWEAR	OUVRAGES	OVERBID
OUTSPORTING	OUTTALKED	OUTWEARIED	OUVRIER	OVERBIDDING
OUTSPORTS	OUTTALKING	OUTWEARIES	OUVRIERE	OVERBIDDINGS
OUTSPRANG	OUTTALKS	OUTWEARING	OUVRIERES	OVERBIDS
OUTSPREAD	OUTTELL	OUTWEARS	OUVRIERS	OVERBITE
OUTSPREADING	OUTTELLING	OUTWEARY	OUZEL	OVERBITES
OUTSPREADS	OUTTELLS	OUTWEARYING	OUZELS	OVERBLEW
OUTSPRING	OUTTHINK	OUTWEED	OUZO	OVERBLOW
OUTSPRINGING	OUTTHINKING	OUTWEEDED	OUZOS	OVERBLOWING
OUTSPRINGS	OUTTHINKS	OUTWEEDING	OVA	OVERBLOWN
OUTSPRUNG	OUTTHOUGHT	OUTWEEDS	OVAL	OVERBLOWS
OUTSTAND	OUTTOLD	OUTWEEP	OVALBUMIN	OVERBOARD
OUTSTANDING	OUTTONGUE	OUTWEEPING	OVALBUMINS	OVERBOIL
OUTSTANDS	OUTTONGUED	OUTWEEPS	OVALLY	OVERBOILED
OUTSTARE	OUTTONGUES	OUTWEIGH	OVALS	OVERBOILING
OUTSTARED	OUTTONGUING	OUTWEIGHED	OVARIAN	OVERBOILS
OUTSTARES	OUTTOOK	OUTWEIGHING	OVARIES	OVERBOLD
OUTSTARING	OUTTOP	OUTWEIGHS	OVARIOLE	OVERBOOK
OUTSTAY	OUTTOPPED	OUTWELL	OVARIOLES	OVERBOOKED
OUTSTAYED	OUTTOPPING	OUTWELLED	OVARIOUS	OVERBOOKING
OUTSTAYING	OUTTOPS	OUTWELLING	OVARITIS	OVERBOOKS
OUTSTAYS	OUTTRAVEL	OUTWELLS	OVARITISES	OVERBORE
OUTSTEP	OUTTRAVELED	OUTWENT	OVARY	OVERBORNE
OUTSTEPPED	OUTTRAVELING	OUTWEPT	OVATE	OVERBOUGHT
OUTSTEPPING	OUTTRAVELLED	OUTWICK	OVATED	OVERBOUND
OUTSTEPS	OUTTRAVELLING	OUTWICKED	OVATES	OVERBOUNDED
OUTSTOOD	OUTTRAVELS	OUTWICKING	OVATING	OVERBOUNDING
OUTSTRAIN	OUTTURN	OUTWICKS	OVATION	OVERBOUNDS
OUTSTRAINED	OUTTURNS	OUTWIN	OVATIONS	OVERBRIM
OUTSTRAINING	OUTVALUE	OUTWIND	OVATOR	OVERBRIMMED
OUTSTRAINS	OUTVALUED	OUTWINDING	OVATORS	OVERBRIMMING
OUTSTRIKE	OUTVALUES	OUTWINDS	OVEN	OVERBRIMS
OUTSTRIKES	OUTVALUING	OUTWING	OVENS	OVERBROW
OUTSTRIKING	OUTVENOM	OUTWINGED	OVENWARE	OVERBROWED
OUTSTRIP	OUTVENOMED	OUTWINGING	OVENWARES	OVERBROWING
OUTSTRIPPED	OUTVENOMING	OUTWINGS	OVENWOOD	OVERBROWS
OUTSTRIPPING	OUTVENOMS	OUTWINNING	OVENWOODS	OVERBUILD
OUTSTRIPS	OUTVIE	OUTWINS	OVER	OVERBUILDING
OUTSTRUCK	OUTVIED	OUTWIT	OVERACT	OVERBUILDS
OUTSUM	OUTVIES	OUTWITH	OVERACTED	OVERBUILT
OUTSUMMED	OUTVOICE	OUTWITS	OVERACTING	OVERBULK
OUTSUMMING	OUTVOICED	OUTWITTED	OVERACTS	OVERBULKED
OUTSUMS	OUTVOICES	OUTWITTING	OVERAGE	OVERBULKING
OUTSWAM	OUTVOICING	OUTWON	OVERAGES	OVERBULKS
OUTSWEAR	OUTVOTE	OUTWORE	OVERALL	OVERBURN
OUTSWEARING	OUTVOTED	OUTWORK	OVERALLED	OVERBURNED
OUTSWEARS	OUTVOTER	OUTWORKER	OVERALLS	OVERBURNING
OUTSWELL	OUTVOTERS	OUTWORKERS	OVERARCH	OVERBURNS
OUTSWELLED	OUTVOTES	OUTWORKING	OVERARCHED	OVERBURNT
OUTSWELLING	OUTVOTING	OUTWORKS	OVERARCHES	OVERBUSIED
OUTSWELLS	OUTVYING	OUTWORN	OVERARCHING	OVERBUSIES
OUTSWIM	OUTWALK	OUTWORTH	OVERARM	OVERBUSY
OUTSWIMMING	OUTWALKED	OUTWORTHED	OVERATE	OVERBUSYING
OUTSWIMS	OUTWALKING	OUTWORTHING	OVERAWE	OVERBUY
OUTSWING	OUTWALKS	OUTWORTHS	OVERAWED	OVERBUYING
OUTSWINGS	OUTWARD	OUTWOUND	OVERAWES	OVERBUYS
OUTSWOLLEN	OUTWARDLY	OUTWREST	OVERAWING	OVERBY
OUTSWORE	OUTWARDS	OUTWRESTED	OVERBEAR	OVERCALL
OUTSWORN	OUTWASH	OUTWRESTING	OVERBEARING	OVERCALLED
OUTSWUM	OUTWASHES	OUTWRESTS	OVERBEARS	OVERCALLING
OUTTAKE	OUTWATCH	OUTWROUGHT	OVERBEAT	OVERCALLS
OUTTAKEN	OUTWATCHED	OUVERT	OVERBEATEN	OVERCAME
OUTTAKES	OUTWATCHES	OUVERTE	OVERBEATING	OVERCARRIED

OVERCARRIES	OVERDONE	OVERFLIES	OVERGRAZE	OVERHYPES
OVERCARRY	OVERDOSE	OVERFLOW	OVERGRAZED	OVERHYPING
OVERCARRYING	OVERDOSED	OVERFLOWED	OVERGRAZES	OVERING
OVERCAST	OVERDOSES	OVERFLOWING	OVERGRAZING	OVERINKED
OVERCASTING	OVERDOSING	OVERFLOWINGS	OVERGRAZINGS	OVERISSUE
OVERCASTINGS	OVERDRAFT	OVERFLOWN	OVERGREAT	OVERISSUED
OVERCASTS	OVERDRAFTS	OVERFLOWS	OVERGREEN	OVERISSUES
OVERCATCH	OVERDRAW	OVERFLUSH	OVERGREENED	OVERISSUING
OVERCATCHES	OVERDRAWING	OVERFLUSHES	OVERGREENING	OVERJOY
OVERCATCHING	OVERDRAWN	OVERFLY	OVERGREENS	OVERJOYED
OVERCAUGHT	OVERDRAWS	OVERFLYING	OVERGREW	OVERJOYING
OVERCHECK	OVERDRESS	OVERFOLD	OVERGROW	OVERJOYS
OVERCHECKS	OVERDRESSED	OVERFOLDED	OVERGROWING	OVERJUMP
OVERCLAD	OVERDRESSES	OVERFOLDING	OVERGROWN	OVERJUMPED
OVERCLOUD	OVERDRESSING	OVERFOLDS	OVERGROWS	OVERJUMPING
OVERCLOUDED	OVERDREW	OVERFOND	OVERHAILE	OVERJUMPS
OVERCLOUDING	OVERDRIVE	OVERFREE	OVERHAILED	OVERKEEP
OVERCLOUDS	OVERDRIVEN	OVERFULL	OVERHAILES	OVERKEEPING
OVERCLOY	OVERDRIVES	OVERFUND	OVERHAILING	OVERKEEPS
OVERCLOYED	OVERDRIVING	OVERFUNDED	OVERHAIR	OVERKEPT
OVERCLOYING	OVERDROVE	OVERFUNDING	OVERHAIRS	OVERKEST
OVERCLOYS	OVERDUE	OVERFUNDINGS	OVERHALE	OVERKILL
OVERCOAT	OVERDUST	OVERFUNDS	OVERHALED	OVERKILLS
OVERCOATS	OVERDUSTED	OVERGALL	OVERHALES	OVERKIND
OVERCOME	OVERDUSTING	OVERGALLED	OVERHALING	OVERKING
OVERCOMES	OVERDUSTS	OVERGALLING	OVERHAND	OVERKINGS
OVERCOMING	OVERDYE	OVERGALLS	OVERHANDED	OVERKNEE
OVERCOOK	OVERDYED	OVERGANG	OVERHANDING	OVERLADE
OVERCOOKED	OVERDYEING	OVERGANGING	OVERHANDS	OVERLADED
OVERCOOKING	OVERDYES	OVERGANGS	OVERHANG	OVERLADEN
OVERCOOKS	OVEREAT	OVERGAVE	OVERHANGING	OVERLADES
OVERCOUNT	OVEREATEN	OVERGET	OVERHANGS	OVERLADING
OVERCOUNTED	OVEREATING	OVERGETS	OVERHAPPY	OVERLAID
OVERCOUNTING	OVEREATS	OVERGETTING	OVERHASTE	OVERLAIN
OVERCOUNTS	OVERED	OVERGIVE	OVERHASTES	OVERLAND
OVERCOVER	OVEREXERT	OVERGIVEN	OVERHASTY	OVERLANDED
OVERCOVERED	OVEREXERTED	OVERGIVES	OVERHAUL	OVERLANDING
OVERCOVERING	OVEREXERTING	OVERGIVING	OVERHAULED	OVERLANDS
OVERCOVERS	OVEREXERTS	OVERGLAZE	OVERHAULING	OVERLAP
OVERCRAW	OVEREYE	OVERGLAZED	OVERHAULS	OVERLAPPED
OVERCRAWED	OVEREYED	OVERGLAZES	OVERHEAD	OVERLAPPING
OVERCRAWING	OVEREYEING	OVERGLAZING	OVERHEADS	OVERLAPS
OVERCRAWS	OVEREYES	OVERGLOOM	OVERHEAR	OVERLARD
OVERCROP	OVEREYING	OVERGLOOMED	OVERHEARD	OVERLARDED
OVERCROPPED	OVERFALL	OVERGLOOMING	OVERHEARING	OVERLARDING
OVERCROPPING	OVERFALLEN	OVERGLOOMS	OVERHEARS	OVERLARDS
OVERCROPS	OVERFALLING	OVERGO	OVERHEAT	OVERLAY
OVERCROW	OVERFALLS	OVERGOES	OVERHEATED	OVERLAYING
OVERCROWD	OVERFAR	OVERGOING	OVERHEATING	OVERLAYINGS
OVERCROWDED	OVERFED	OVERGOINGS	OVERHEATINGS	OVERLAYS
OVERCROWDING	OVERFEED	OVERGONE	OVERHEATS	OVERLEAF
OVERCROWDINGS	OVERFEEDING	OVERGORGE	OVERHELD	OVERLEAP
OVERCROWDS	OVERFEEDS	OVERGORGED	OVERHENT	OVERLEAPED
OVERCROWED	OVERFELL	OVERGORGES	OVERHENTING	OVERLEAPING
OVERCROWING	OVERFILL	OVERGORGING	OVERHENTS	OVERLEAPS
OVERCROWS	OVERFILLED	OVERGOT	OVERHIT	OVERLEAPT
OVERDATED	OVERFILLING	OVERGRAIN	OVERHITS	OVERLEND
OVERDID	OVERFILLS	OVERGRAINED	OVERHITTING	OVERLENDING
OVERDIGHT	OVERFINE	OVERGRAINING	OVERHOLD	OVERLENDS
OVERDO	OVERFISH	OVERGRAINS	OVERHOLDING	OVERLENT
OVERDOER	OVERFISHED	OVERGRASS	OVERHOLDS	OVERLIE
OVERDOERS	OVERFISHES	OVERGRASSED	OVERHUNG	OVERLIER
OVERDOES	OVERFISHING	OVERGRASSES	OVERHYPE	OVERLIERS
OVERDOING	OVERFLEW	OVERGRASSING	OVERHYPED	OVERLIES

OVERLIVE
OVERLIVED
OVERLIVES
OVERLIVING
OVERLOAD
OVERLOADED
OVERLOADING
OVERLOADS
OVERLOCK
OVERLOCKED
OVERLOCKING
OVERLOCKINGS
OVERLOCKS
OVERLONG
OVERLOOK
OVERLOOKED
OVERLOOKING
OVERLOOKS
OVERLORD
OVERLORDED
OVERLORDING
OVERLORDS
OVERLOUD
OVERLUSTY
OVERLY
OVERLYING
OVERMAN
OVERMANNED
OVERMANNING
OVERMANS
OVERMAST
OVERMASTED
OVERMASTING
OVERMASTS
OVERMATCH
OVERMATCHED
OVERMATCHES
OVERMATCHING
OVERMEN
OVERMERRY
OVERMOUNT
OVERMOUNTED
OVERMOUNTING
OVERMOUNTS
OVERMUCH
OVERNAME
OVERNAMED
OVERNAMES
OVERNAMING
OVERNEAT
OVERNET
OVERNETS
OVERNETTED
OVERNETTING
OVERNICE
OVERNIGHT
OVERNIGHTS
OVERPAGE
OVERPAID
OVERPAINT
OVERPAINTED
OVERPAINTING
OVERPAINTS
OVERPART

OVERPARTED
OVERPARTING
OVERPARTS
OVERPASS
OVERPASSED
OVERPASSES
OVERPASSING
OVERPAST
OVERPAY
OVERPAYING
OVERPAYS
OVERPEDAL
OVERPEDALED
OVERPEDALING
OVERPEDALLED
OVERPEDALLING
OVERPEDALS
OVERPEER
OVERPEERED
OVERPEERING
OVERPEERS
OVERPERCH
OVERPERCHED
OVERPERCHES
OVERPERCHING
OVERPITCH
OVERPITCHED
OVERPITCHES
OVERPITCHING
OVERPLAST
OVERPLAY
OVERPLAYED
OVERPLAYING
OVERPLAYS
OVERPLIED
OVERPLIES
OVERPLUS
OVERPLUSES
OVERPLUSSES
OVERPLY
OVERPLYING
OVERPOISE
OVERPOISED
OVERPOISES
OVERPOISING
OVERPOST
OVERPOSTED
OVERPOSTING
OVERPOSTS
OVERPOWER
OVERPOWERED
OVERPOWERING
OVERPOWERS
OVERPRESS
OVERPRESSED
OVERPRESSES
OVERPRESSING
OVERPRICE
OVERPRICED
OVERPRICES
OVERPRICING
OVERPRINT
OVERPRINTED
OVERPRINTING

OVERPRINTS
OVERPRIZE
OVERPRIZED
OVERPRIZES
OVERPRIZING
OVERPROOF
OVERPROUD
OVERRACK
OVERRACKED
OVERRACKING
OVERRACKS
OVERRAKE
OVERRAKED
OVERRAKES
OVERRAKING
OVERRAN
OVERRANK
OVERRASH
OVERRATE
OVERRATED
OVERRATES
OVERRATING
OVERRAUGHT
OVERREACH
OVERREACHED
OVERREACHES
OVERREACHING
OVERREACT
OVERREACTED
OVERREACTING
OVERREACTS
OVERREAD
OVERREADING
OVERREADS
OVERRED
OVERREDDED
OVERREDDING
OVERREDS
OVERREN
OVERRENNING
OVERRENS
OVERRIDDEN
OVERRIDE
OVERRIDER
OVERRIDERS
OVERRIDES
OVERRIDING
OVERRIPE
OVERRIPEN
OVERRIPENED
OVERRIPENING
OVERRIPENS
OVERROAST
OVERROASTED
OVERROASTING
OVERROASTS
OVERRODE
OVERRUFF
OVERRUFFED
OVERRUFFING
OVERRUFFS
OVERRULE
OVERRULED
OVERRULER

OVERRULERS
OVERRULES
OVERRULING
OVERRULINGS
OVERRUN
OVERRUNNING
OVERRUNS
OVERS
OVERSAIL
OVERSAILED
OVERSAILING
OVERSAILS
OVERSAW
OVERSCORE
OVERSCORED
OVERSCORES
OVERSCORING
OVERSEA
OVERSEAS
OVERSEE
OVERSEEING
OVERSEEN
OVERSEER
OVERSEERS
OVERSEES
OVERSELL
OVERSELLING
OVERSELLS
OVERSET
OVERSETS
OVERSETTING
OVERSEW
OVERSEWED
OVERSEWING
OVERSEWN
OVERSEWS
OVERSEXED
OVERSHADE
OVERSHADED
OVERSHADES
OVERSHADING
OVERSHINE
OVERSHINES
OVERSHINING
OVERSHIRT
OVERSHIRTS
OVERSHOE
OVERSHOES
OVERSHONE
OVERSHOOT
OVERSHOOTING
OVERSHOOTS
OVERSHOT
OVERSIDE
OVERSIGHT
OVERSIGHTS
OVERSIZE
OVERSIZED
OVERSIZES
OVERSIZING
OVERSKIP
OVERSKIPPED
OVERSKIPPING
OVERSKIPS

OVERSKIRT
OVERSKIRTS
OVERSLEEP
OVERSLEEPING
OVERSLEEPS
OVERSLEPT
OVERSLIP
OVERSLIPPED
OVERSLIPPING
OVERSLIPS
OVERSMAN
OVERSMEN
OVERSOLD
OVERSOUL
OVERSOULS
OVERSOW
OVERSOWED
OVERSOWING
OVERSOWN
OVERSOWS
OVERSPEND
OVERSPENDING
OVERSPENDS
OVERSPENT
OVERSPILL
OVERSPILLS
OVERSPIN
OVERSPINS
OVERSTAFF
OVERSTAFFED
OVERSTAFFING
OVERSTAFFS
OVERSTAIN
OVERSTAINED
OVERSTAINING
OVERSTAINS
OVERSTAND
OVERSTANDING
OVERSTANDS
OVERSTANK
OVERSTARE
OVERSTARED
OVERSTARES
OVERSTARING
OVERSTATE
OVERSTATED
OVERSTATES
OVERSTATING
OVERSTAY
OVERSTAYED
OVERSTAYING
OVERSTAYS
OVERSTEER
OVERSTEERED
OVERSTEERING
OVERSTEERS
OVERSTEP
OVERSTEPPED
OVERSTEPPING
OVERSTEPS
OVERSTINK
OVERSTINKING
OVERSTINKS
OVERSTOCK

OVERSTOCKED	OVERTIMED	OVERVEILED	OVIBOS	OWLERY
OVERSTOCKING	OVERTIMER	OVERVEILING	OVIBOSES	OWLET
OVERSTOCKS	OVERTIMERS	OVERVEILS	OVIBOVINE	OWLETS
OVERSTOOD	OVERTIMES	OVERVIEW	OVICIDE	OWLIER
OVERSTREW	OVERTIMING	OVERVIEWS	OVICIDES	OWLIEST
OVERSTREWED	OVERTIRE	OVERWASH	OVIDUCAL	OWLING
OVERSTREWING	OVERTIRED	OVERWASHES	OVIDUCT	OWLISH
OVERSTREWN	OVERTIRES	OVERWATCH	OVIDUCTAL	OWLS
OVERSTREWS	OVERTIRING	OVERWATCHED	OVIDUCTS	OWLY
OVERSTUDIED	OVERTLY	OVERWATCHES	OVIFEROUS	OWN
OVERSTUDIES	OVERTOIL	OVERWATCHING	OVIFORM	OWNED
OVERSTUDY	OVERTOILED	OVERWEAR	OVIGEROUS	OWNER
OVERSTUDYING	OVERTOILING	OVERWEARIED	OVINE	OWNERLESS
OVERSTUFF	OVERTOILS	OVERWEARIES	OVIPARITIES	OWNERS
OVERSTUFFED	OVERTONE	OVERWEARING	OVIPARITY	OWNERSHIP
OVERSTUFFING	OVERTONES	OVERWEARS	OVIPAROUS	OWNERSHIPS
OVERSTUFFS	OVERTOOK	OVERWEARY	OVIPOSIT	OWNING
OVERSTUNK	OVERTOP	OVERWEARYING	OVIPOSITED	OWNS
OVERSWAM	OVERTOPPED	OVERWEEN	OVIPOSITING	OWRE
OVERSWAY	OVERTOPPING	OVERWEENED	OVIPOSITS	OWRECOME
OVERSWAYED	OVERTOPS	OVERWEENING	OVIRAPTOR	OWRECOMES
OVERSWAYING	OVERTOWER	OVERWEENINGS	OVIRAPTORS	OWRELAY
OVERSWAYS	OVERTOWERED	OVERWEENS	OVISAC	OWRELAYS
OVERSWEAR	OVERTOWERING	OVERWEIGH	OVISACS	OWRES
OVERSWEARING	OVERTOWERS	OVERWEIGHED	OVIST	OWREWORD
OVERSWEARS	OVERTRAIN	OVERWEIGHING	OVISTS	OWREWORDS
OVERSWELL	OVERTRAINED	OVERWEIGHS	OVOID	OWRIE
OVERSWELLED	OVERTRAINING	OVERWENT	OVOIDAL	OWRIER
OVERSWELLING	OVERTRAINS	OVERWHELM	OVOIDS	OWRIEST
OVERSWELLS	OVERTRICK	OVERWHELMED	OVOLI	OWSEN
OVERSWIM	OVERTRICKS	OVERWHELMING	OVOLO	OWT
OVERSWIMMING	OVERTRIP	OVERWHELMINGS	OVOTESTES	OWTS
OVERSWIMS	OVERTRIPPED	OVERWHELMS	OVOTESTIS	OX
OVERSWOLLEN	OVERTRIPPING	OVERWIND	OVULAR	OXALATE
OVERSWORE	OVERTRIPS	OVERWINDING	OVULATE	OXALATES
OVERSWORN	OVERTRUMP	OVERWINDS	OVULATED	OXALIC
OVERSWUM	OVERTRUMPED	OVERWING	OVULATES	OXALIS
OVERT	OVERTRUMPING	OVERWINGED	OVULATING	OXALISES
OVERTAKE	OVERTRUMPS	OVERWINGING	OVULATION	OXAZINE
OVERTAKEN	OVERTRUST	OVERWINGS	OVULATIONS	OXAZINES
OVERTAKES	OVERTRUSTED	OVERWISE	OVULE	OXBLOOD
OVERTAKING	OVERTRUSTING	OVERWORD	OVULES	OXBLOODS
OVERTALK	OVERTRUSTS	OVERWORDS	OVUM	OXEN
OVERTALKED	OVERTURE	OVERWORE	OW	OXER
OVERTALKING	OVERTURED	OVERWORK	OWCHE	OXERS
OVERTALKS	OVERTURES	OVERWORKED	OWCHES	OXFORD
OVERTASK	OVERTURING	OVERWORKING	OWE	OXFORDS
OVERTASKED	OVERTURN	OVERWORKS	OWED	OXGANG
OVERTASKING	OVERTURNED	OVERWORN	OWELTIES	OXGANGS
OVERTASKS	OVERTURNING	OVERWOUND	OWELTY	OXGATE
OVERTAX	OVERTURNS	OVERWREST	OWER	OXGATES
OVERTAXED	OVERTYPE	OVERWRESTED	OWERBY	OXHEAD
OVERTAXES	OVERTYPED	OVERWRESTING	OWERLOUP	OXHEADS
OVERTAXING	OVERTYPES	OVERWRESTS	OWERLOUPEN	OXIDANT
OVERTEEM	OVERTYPING	OVERWRITE	OWERLOUPING	OXIDANTS
OVERTEEMED	OVERUSE	OVERWRITES	OWERLOUPIT	OXIDASE
OVERTEEMING	OVERUSED	OVERWRITING	OWERLOUPS	OXIDASES
OVERTEEMS	OVERUSES	OVERWRITTEN	OWES	OXIDATE
OVERTHREW	OVERUSING	OVERWROTE	OWING	OXIDATED
OVERTHROW	OVERVALUE	OVERWROUGHT	OWL	OXIDATES
OVERTHROWING	OVERVALUED	OVERYEAR	OWLED	OXIDATING
OVERTHROWN	OVERVALUES	OVERYEARED	OWLER	OXIDATION
OVERTHROWS	OVERVALUING	OVERYEARING	OWLERIES	OXIDATIONS
OVERTIME	OVERVEIL	OVERYEARS	OWLERS	OXIDE

The Chambers Dictionary is the authority for many longer words; see *OSW* Introduction, page xii

OXIDES
OXIDISE
OXIDISED
OXIDISER
OXIDISERS
OXIDISES
OXIDISING
OXIDIZE
OXIDIZED
OXIDIZER
OXIDIZERS
OXIDIZES
OXIDIZING
OXIME
OXIMES
OXIMETER
OXIMETERS
OXLAND
OXLANDS

OXLIP
OXLIPS
OXONIUM
OXONIUMS
OXSLIP
OXSLIPS
OXTAIL
OXTAILS
OXTER
OXTERED
OXTERING
OXTERS
OXYGEN
OXYGENATE
OXYGENATED
OXYGENATES
OXYGENATING
OXYGENISE
OXYGENISED

OXYGENISES
OXYGENISING
OXYGENIZE
OXYGENIZED
OXYGENIZES
OXYGENIZING
OXYGENOUS
OXYGENS
OXYMEL
OXYMELS
OXYMORON
OXYMORONS
OXYTOCIC
OXYTOCICS
OXYTOCIN
OXYTOCINS
OXYTONE
OXYTONES
OY

OYE
OYER
OYERS
OYES
OYESES
OYEZ
OYEZES
OYS
OYSTER
OYSTERS
OYSTRIGE
OYSTRIGES
OZAENA
OZAENAS
OZEKI
OZEKIS
OZOCERITE
OZOCERITES
OZOKERITE

OZOKERITES
OZONATION
OZONATIONS
OZONE
OZONES
OZONISE
OZONISED
OZONISER
OZONISERS
OZONISES
OZONISING
OZONIZE
OZONIZED
OZONIZER
OZONIZERS
OZONIZES
OZONIZING

P

PA
PABOUCHE
PABOUCHES
PABULAR
PABULOUS
PABULUM
PABULUMS
PACA
PACABLE
PACAS
PACATION
PACATIONS
PACE
PACED
PACEMAKER
PACEMAKERS
PACER
PACERS
PACES
PACEY
PACHA
PACHAK
PACHAKS
PACHALIC
PACHALICS
PACHAS
PACHINKO
PACHINKOS
PACHISI
PACHISIS
PACHYDERM
PACHYDERMS
PACIER
PACIEST
PACIFIC
PACIFICAL
PACIFIED
PACIFIER
PACIFIERS
PACIFIES
PACIFISM
PACIFISMS
PACIFIST
PACIFISTS
PACIFY
PACIFYING
PACING
PACK
PACKAGE
PACKAGED
PACKAGER
PACKAGERS
PACKAGES
PACKAGING

PACKAGINGS
PACKED
PACKER
PACKERS
PACKET
PACKETED
PACKETING
PACKETS
PACKFONG
PACKFONGS
PACKING
PACKINGS
PACKMAN
PACKMEN
PACKS
PACKSHEET
PACKSHEETS
PACKSTAFF
PACKSTAFFS
PACKWAY
PACKWAYS
PACO
PACOS
PACT
PACTA
PACTION
PACTIONAL
PACTIONED
PACTIONING
PACTIONS
PACTS
PACTUM
PACY
PAD
PADANG
PADANGS
PADAUK
PADAUKS
PADDED
PADDER
PADDERS
PADDIES
PADDING
PADDINGS
PADDLE
PADDLED
PADDLER
PADDLERS
PADDLES
PADDLING
PADDLINGS
PADDOCK
PADDOCKS
PADDY

PADELLA
PADELLAS
PADEMELON
PADEMELONS
PADERERO
PADEREROES
PADEREROS
PADISHAH
PADISHAHS
PADLE
PADLES
PADLOCK
PADLOCKED
PADLOCKING
PADLOCKS
PADMA
PADMAS
PADOUK
PADOUKS
PADRE
PADRES
PADRONE
PADRONI
PADS
PADSAW
PADSAWS
PADUASOY
PADUASOYS
PADYMELON
PADYMELONS
PAEAN
PAEANS
PAEDERAST
PAEDERASTS
PAEDEUTIC
PAEDEUTICS
PAEDIATRIES
PAEDIATRY
PAEDOLOGIES
PAEDOLOGY
PAELLA
PAELLAS
PAENULA
PAENULAE
PAENULAS
PAEON
PAEONIC
PAEONICS
PAEONIES
PAEONS
PAEONY
PAGAN
PAGANISE
PAGANISED

PAGANISES
PAGANISH
PAGANISING
PAGANISM
PAGANISMS
PAGANIZE
PAGANIZED
PAGANIZES
PAGANIZING
PAGANS
PAGE
PAGEANT
PAGEANTRIES
PAGEANTRY
PAGEANTS
PAGED
PAGEHOOD
PAGEHOODS
PAGER
PAGERS
PAGES
PAGINAL
PAGINATE
PAGINATED
PAGINATES
PAGINATING
PAGING
PAGINGS
PAGLE
PAGLES
PAGOD
PAGODA
PAGODAS
PAGODS
PAGRI
PAGRIS
PAGURIAN
PAGURIANS
PAGURID
PAGURIDS
PAH
PAHOEHOE
PAHOEHOES
PAHS
PAID
PAIDEUTIC
PAIDEUTICS
PAIDLE
PAIDLES
PAIGLE
PAIGLES
PAIK
PAIKED
PAIKING

PAIKS
PAIL
PAILFUL
PAILFULS
PAILLASSE
PAILLASSES
PAILLETTE
PAILLETTES
PAILLON
PAILLONS
PAILS
PAIN
PAINED
PAINFUL
PAINFULLER
PAINFULLEST
PAINFULLY
PAINIM
PAINIMS
PAINING
PAINLESS
PAINS
PAINT
PAINTABLE
PAINTBALL
PAINTBALLS
PAINTED
PAINTER
PAINTERLY
PAINTERS
PAINTIER
PAINTIEST
PAINTING
PAINTINGS
PAINTRESS
PAINTRESSES
PAINTS
PAINTURE
PAINTURES
PAINTY
PAIOCK
PAIOCKE
PAIOCKES
PAIOCKS
PAIR
PAIRE
PAIRED
PAIRES
PAIRIAL
PAIRIALS
PAIRING
PAIRINGS
PAIRS
PAIRWISE

PAIS	PALAVER	PALKEES	PALMETTO	PALSIES
PAISA	PALAVERED	PALKI	PALMETTOES	PALSIEST
PAISANO	PALAVERER	PALKIS	PALMETTOS	PALSTAFF
PAISANOS	PALAVERERS	PALL	PALMFUL	PALSTAFFS
PAISAS	PALAVERING	PALLA	PALMFULS	PALSTAVE
PAISE	PALAVERS	PALLADIC	PALMHOUSE	PALSTAVES
PAISLEY	PALAY	PALLADIUM	PALMHOUSES	PALSY
PAISLEYS	PALAYS	PALLADIUMS	PALMIE	PALSYING
PAITRICK	PALAZZI	PALLADOUS	PALMIER	PALTER
PAITRICKS	PALAZZO	PALLAE	PALMIES	PALTERED
PAJAMAS	PALE	PALLAH	PALMIEST	PALTERER
PAJOCK	PALEA	PALLAHS	PALMIET	PALTERERS
PAJOCKE	PALEAE	PALLED	PALMIETS	PALTERING
PAJOCKES	PALEBUCK	PALLET	PALMING	PALTERS
PAJOCKS	PALEBUCKS	PALLETED	PALMIPED	PALTRIER
PAKAPOO	PALED	PALLETISE	PALMIPEDE	PALTRIEST
PAKAPOOS	PALEFACE	PALLETISED	PALMIPEDES	PALTRILY
PAKEHA	PALEFACES	PALLETISES	PALMIPEDS	PALTRY
PAKEHAS	PALELY	PALLETISING	PALMIST	PALUDAL
PAKFONG	PALEMPORE	PALLETIZE	PALMISTRIES	PALUDIC
PAKFONGS	PALEMPORES	PALLETIZED	PALMISTRY	PALUDINAL
PAKKA	PALENESS	PALLETIZES	PALMISTS	PALUDINE
PAKORA	PALENESSES	PALLETIZING	PALMITATE	PALUDISM
PAKORAS	PALER	PALLETS	PALMITATES	PALUDISMS
PAKTONG	PALES	PALLIA	PALMITIN	PALUDOSE
PAKTONGS	PALEST	PALLIAL	PALMITINS	PALUDOUS
PAL	PALESTRA	PALLIARD	PALMS	PALUSTRAL
PALABRA	PALESTRAE	PALLIARDS	PALMTOP	PALY
PALABRAS	PALESTRAS	PALLIASSE	PALMTOPS	PAM
PALACE	PALET	PALLIASSES	PALMY	PAMPA
PALACES	PALETOT	PALLIATE	PALMYRA	PAMPAS
PALADIN	PALETOTS	PALLIATED	PALMYRAS	PAMPASES
PALADINS	PALETS	PALLIATES	PALOLO	PAMPEAN
PALAESTRA	PALETTE	PALLIATING	PALOLOS	PAMPER
PALAESTRAE	PALETTES	PALLID	PALOMINO	PAMPERED
PALAESTRAS	PALEWISE	PALLIDER	PALOMINOS	PAMPERER
PALAFITTE	PALFREY	PALLIDEST	PALOOKA	PAMPERERS
PALAFITTES	PALFREYED	PALLIDITIES	PALOOKAS	PAMPERING
PALAGI	PALFREYS	PALLIDITY	PALP	PAMPERO
PALAGIS	PALIER	PALLIDLY	PALPABLE	PAMPEROS
PALAMA	PALIEST	PALLIER	PALPABLY	PAMPERS
PALAMAE	PALIFORM	PALLIEST	PALPAL	PAMPHLET
PALAMATE	PALILALIA	PALLING	PALPATE	PAMPHLETS
PALAMINO	PALILALIAS	PALLIUM	PALPATED	PAMS
PALAMINOS	PALILLOGIES	PALLONE	PALPATES	PAN
PALAMPORE	PALILLOGY	PALLONES	PALPATING	PANACEA
PALAMPORES	PALIMONIES	PALLOR	PALPATION	PANACEAN
PALANKEEN	PALIMONY	PALLORS	PALPATIONS	PANACEAS
PALANKEENS	PALING	PALLS	PALPEBRAL	PANACHAEA
PALANQUIN	PALINGS	PALLY	PALPED	PANACHAEAS
PALANQUINS	PALINODE	PALM	PALPI	PANACHE
PALAS	PALINODES	PALMAR	PALPING	PANACHES
PALASES	PALINODIES	PALMARIAN	PALPITANT	PANADA
PALATABLE	PALINODY	PALMARY	PALPITATE	PANADAS
PALATABLY	PALISADE	PALMATE	PALPITATED	PANAMA
PALATAL	PALISADED	PALMATED	PALPITATES	PANAMAS
PALATALS	PALISADES	PALMATELY	PALPITATING	PANARIES
PALATE	PALISADING	PALMATION	PALPS	PANARY
PALATED	PALISADO	PALMATIONS	PALPUS	PANATELLA
PALATES	PALISADOED	PALMED	PALS	PANATELLAS
PALATIAL	PALISADOES	PALMER	PALSGRAVE	PANAX
PALATINE	PALISADOING	PALMERS	PALSGRAVES	PANAXES
PALATINES	PALISH	PALMETTE	PALSIED	PANCAKE
PALATING	PALKEE	PALMETTES	PALSIER	PANCAKED

PANCAKES	PANEGOISM	PANLOGISMS	PANTERS	PAPALIZE
PANCAKING	PANEGOISMS	PANMICTIC	PANTHEISM	PAPALIZED
PANCE	PANEGYRIC	PANMIXIA	PANTHEISMS	PAPALIZES
PANCES	PANEGYRICS	PANMIXIAS	PANTHEIST	PAPALIZING
PANCHAX	PANEGYRIES	PANMIXIS	PANTHEISTS	PAPALLY
PANCHAXES	PANEGYRY	PANMIXISES	PANTHENOL	PAPARAZZI
PANCHAYAT	PANEITIES	PANNAGE	PANTHENOLS	PAPARAZZO
PANCHAYATS	PANEITY	PANNAGES	PANTHER	PAPAS
PANCHEON	PANEL	PANNE	PANTHERS	PAPAW
PANCHEONS	PANELLED	PANNED	PANTIES	PAPAWS
PANCHION	PANELLING	PANNELLED	PANTIHOSE	PAPAYA
PANCHIONS	PANELLINGS	PANNES	PANTILE	PAPAYAS
PANCOSMIC	PANELLIST	PANNICK	PANTILED	PAPE
PANCRATIC	PANELLISTS	PANNICKS	PANTILES	PAPER
PANCREAS	PANELS	PANNICLE	PANTILING	PAPERBACK
PANCREASES	PANES	PANNICLES	PANTILINGS	PAPERBACKED
PAND	PANETTONE	PANNIER	PANTINE	PAPERBACKING
PANDA	PANETTONI	PANNIERED	PANTINES	PAPERBACKS
PANDAR	PANFUL	PANNIERS	PANTING	PAPERED
PANDARED	PANFULS	PANNIKEL	PANTINGLY	PAPERER
PANDARING	PANG	PANNIKELL	PANTINGS	PAPERERS
PANDARS	PANGA	PANNIKELLS	PANTLER	PAPERIER
PANDAS	PANGAMIC	PANNIKELS	PANTLERS	PAPERIEST
PANDATION	PANGAMIES	PANNIKIN	PANTO	PAPERING
PANDATIONS	PANGAMY	PANNIKINS	PANTOFFLE	PAPERINGS
PANDECT	PANGAS	PANNING	PANTOFFLES	PAPERLESS
PANDECTS	PANGED	PANNINGS	PANTOFLE	PAPERS
PANDEMIA	PANGEN	PANNOSE	PANTOFLES	PAPERWARE
PANDEMIAN	PANGENE	PANNUS	PANTOMIME	PAPERWARES
PANDEMIAS	PANGENES	PANNUSES	PANTOMIMES	PAPERWORK
PANDEMIC	PANGENS	PANOCHA	PANTON	PAPERWORKS
PANDEMICS	PANGING	PANOCHAS	PANTONS	PAPERY
PANDER	PANGLESS	PANOISTIC	PANTOS	PAPES
PANDERED	PANGOLIN	PANOPLIED	PANTOUFLE	PAPETERIE
PANDERESS	PANGOLINS	PANOPLIES	PANTOUFLES	PAPETERIES
PANDERESSES	PANGRAM	PANOPLY	PANTOUM	PAPILIO
PANDERING	PANGRAMS	PANOPTIC	PANTOUMS	PAPILIOS
PANDERISM	PANGS	PANORAMA	PANTRIES	PAPILLA
PANDERISMS	PANHANDLE	PANORAMAS	PANTRY	PAPILLAE
PANDERLY	PANHANDLED	PANORAMIC	PANTRYMAN	PAPILLAR
PANDEROUS	PANHANDLES	PANS	PANTRYMEN	PAPILLARY
PANDERS	PANHANDLING	PANSEXUAL	PANTS	PAPILLATE
PANDIED	PANIC	PANSIED	PANTUN	PAPILLOMA
PANDIES	PANICK	PANSIES	PANTUNS	PAPILLOMAS
PANDIT	PANICKED	PANSOPHIC	PANZER	PAPILLOMATA
PANDITS	PANICKIER	PANSOPHIES	PANZERS	PAPILLON
PANDOOR	PANICKIEST	PANSOPHY	PAOLI	PAPILLONS
PANDOORS	PANICKING	PANSPERMIES	PAOLO	PAPILLOSE
PANDORA	PANICKS	PANSPERMY	PAP	PAPILLOTE
PANDORAS	PANICKY	PANSY	PAPA	PAPILLOTES
PANDORE	PANICLE	PANT	PAPABLE	PAPILLOUS
PANDORES	PANICLED	PANTABLE	PAPACIES	PAPILLULE
PANDOUR	PANICLES	PANTABLES	PAPACY	PAPILLULES
PANDOURS	PANICS	PANTAGAMIES	PAPAIN	PAPISH
PANDOWDIES	PANIM	PANTAGAMY	PAPAINS	PAPISHER
PANDOWDY	PANIMS	PANTALEON	PAPAL	PAPISHERS
PANDS	PANING	PANTALEONS	PAPALISE	PAPISHES
PANDURA	PANISC	PANTALETS	PAPALISED	PAPISM
PANDURAS	PANISCS	PANTALON	PAPALISES	PAPISMS
PANDURATE	PANISK	PANTALONS	PAPALISING	PAPIST
PANDY	PANISKS	PANTALOON	PAPALISM	PAPISTIC
PANDYING	PANISLAM	PANTALOONS	PAPALISMS	PAPISTRIES
PANE	PANISLAMS	PANTED	PAPALIST	PAPISTRY
PANED	PANLOGISM	PANTER	PAPALISTS	PAPISTS

The Chambers Dictionary is the authority for many longer words; see *OSW* Introduction, page xii

PAPOOSE	PARADISIC	PARALYSED	PARAS	PARDALISES
PAPOOSES	PARADOR	PARALYSER	PARASANG	PARDALS
PAPPADOM	PARADORES	PARALYSERS	PARASANGS	PARDED
PAPPADOMS	PARADOS	PARALYSES	PARASCEVE	PARDI
PAPPED	PARADOSES	PARALYSING	PARASCEVES	PARDIE
PAPPIER	PARADOX	PARALYSIS	PARASITE	PARDINE
PAPPIES	PARADOXAL	PARALYTIC	PARASITES	PARDNER
PAPPIEST	PARADOXER	PARALYTICS	PARASITIC	PARDNERS
PAPPING	PARADOXERS	PARALYZE	PARASOL	PARDON
PAPPOOSE	PARADOXES	PARALYZED	PARASOLS	PARDONED
PAPPOOSES	PARADOXIES	PARALYZER	PARATAXES	PARDONER
PAPPOSE	PARADOXY	PARALYZERS	PARATAXIS	PARDONERS
PAPPOUS	PARADROP	PARALYZES	PARATHA	PARDONING
PAPPUS	PARADROPS	PARALYZING	PARATHAS	PARDONINGS
PAPPUSES	PARAFFIN	PARAMATTA	PARATONIC	PARDONS
PAPPY	PARAFFINE	PARAMATTAS	PARAVAIL	PARDS
PAPRIKA	PARAFFINED	PARAMECIA	PARAVANE	PARDY
PAPRIKAS	PARAFFINES	PARAMEDIC	PARAVANES	PARE
PAPS	PARAFFINING	PARAMEDICS	PARAVANT	PARECIOUS
PAPULA	PARAFFINS	PARAMENT	PARAVAUNT	PARED
PAPULAE	PARAFFINY	PARAMENTS	PARAZOA	PAREGORIC
PAPULAR	PARAFFLE	PARAMESE	PARAZOAN	PAREGORICS
PAPULE	PARAFFLES	PARAMESES	PARAZOANS	PAREIRA
PAPULES	PARAFLE	PARAMETER	PARAZOON	PAREIRAS
PAPULOSE	PARAFLES	PARAMETERS	PARBOIL	PARELLA
PAPULOUS	PARAFOIL	PARAMO	PARBOILED	PARELLAS
PAPYRI	PARAFOILS	PARAMORPH	PARBOILING	PARELLE
PAPYRUS	PARAGE	PARAMORPHS	PARBOILS	PARELLES
PAR	PARAGES	PARAMOS	PARBREAK	PARENESES
PARA	PARAGOGE	PARAMOUNT	PARBREAKED	PARENESIS
PARABASES	PARAGOGES	PARAMOUNTS	PARBREAKING	PARENT
PARABASIS	PARAGOGIC	PARAMOUR	PARBREAKS	PARENTAGE
PARABEMA	PARAGOGUE	PARAMOURS	PARBUCKLE	PARENTAGES
PARABEMATA	PARAGOGUES	PARANETE	PARBUCKLED	PARENTAL
PARABLE	PARAGON	PARANETES	PARBUCKLES	PARENTED
PARABLED	PARAGONED	PARANG	PARBUCKLING	PARENTING
PARABLES	PARAGONING	PARANGS	PARCEL	PARENTINGS
PARABLING	PARAGONS	PARANOEA	PARCELLED	PARENTS
PARABOLA	PARAGRAM	PARANOEAS	PARCELLING	PAREO
PARABOLAS	PARAGRAMS	PARANOEIC	PARCELS	PAREOS
PARABOLE	PARAGRAPH	PARANOEICS	PARCENARIES	PARER
PARABOLES	PARAGRAPHED	PARANOIA	PARCENARY	PARERGA
PARABOLIC	PARAGRAPHING	PARANOIAC	PARCENER	PARERGON
PARABRAKE	PARAGRAPHS	PARANOIACS	PARCENERS	PARERS
PARABRAKES	PARAKEET	PARANOIAS	PARCH	PARES
PARACHUTE	PARAKEETS	PARANOIC	PARCHED	PARESES
PARACHUTED	PARALALIA	PARANOICS	PARCHEDLY	PARESIS
PARACHUTES	PARALALIAS	PARANOID	PARCHEESI	PARETIC
PARACHUTING	PARALEGAL	PARANYM	PARCHEESIS	PAREU
PARACLETE	PARALEGALS	PARANYMPH	PARCHES	PAREUS
PARACLETES	PARALEXIA	PARANYMPHS	PARCHESI	PARFAIT
PARACME	PARALEXIAS	PARANYMS	PARCHESIS	PARFAITS
PARACMES	PARALLAX	PARAPET	PARCHING	PARFLECHE
PARACUSES	PARALLAXES	PARAPETED	PARCHMENT	PARFLECHES
PARACUSIS	PARALLEL	PARAPETS	PARCHMENTS	PARGANA
PARADE	PARALLELED	PARAPH	PARCIMONIES	PARGANAS
PARADED	PARALLELING	PARAPHED	PARCIMONY	PARGASITE
PARADES	PARALLELINGS	PARAPHING	PARCLOSE	PARGASITES
PARADIGM	PARALLELS	PARAPHS	PARCLOSES	PARGE
PARADIGMS	PARALOGIA	PARAPODIA	PARD	PARGED
PARADING	PARALOGIAS	PARAQUITO	PARDAL	PARGES
PARADISAL	PARALOGIES	PARAQUITOS	PARDALE	PARGET
PARADISE	PARALOGY	PARARHYME	PARDALES	PARGETED
PARADISES	PARALYSE	PARARHYMES	PARDALIS	PARGETER

PARGETERS	PARLANDO	PAROUSIAS	PARSERS	PARTNER
PARGETING	PARLAY	PAROXYSM	PARSES	PARTNERED
PARGETINGS	PARLAYED	PAROXYSMS	PARSIMONIES	PARTNERING
PARGETS	PARLAYING	PARP	PARSIMONY	PARTNERS
PARGETTED	PARLAYS	PARPANE	PARSING	PARTON
PARGETTING	PARLE	PARPANES	PARSINGS	PARTONS
PARGETTINGS	PARLED	PARPED	PARSLEY	PARTOOK
PARGING	PARLES	PARPEN	PARSLEYS	PARTRIDGE
PARHELIA	PARLEY	PARPEND	PARSNEP	PARTRIDGES
PARHELIC	PARLEYED	PARPENDS	PARSNEPS	PARTS
PARHELION	PARLEYING	PARPENS	PARSNIP	PARTURE
PARHYPATE	PARLEYS	PARPENT	PARSNIPS	PARTURES
PARHYPATES	PARLEYVOO	PARPENTS	PARSON	PARTWORK
PARIAH	PARLEYVOOED	PARPING	PARSONAGE	PARTWORKS
PARIAHS	PARLEYVOOING	PARPOINT	PARSONAGES	PARTY
PARIAL	PARLEYVOOS	PARPOINTS	PARSONIC	PARTYGOER
PARIALS	PARLIES	PARPS	PARSONISH	PARTYGOERS
PARIETAL	PARLING	PARQUET	PARSONS	PARTYING
PARIETALS	PARLOR	PARQUETED	PART	PARTYISM
PARING	PARLORS	PARQUETING	PARTAKE	PARTYISMS
PARINGS	PARLOUR	PARQUETRIES	PARTAKEN	PARULIS
PARISCHAN	PARLOURS	PARQUETRY	PARTAKER	PARULISES
PARISCHANS	PARLOUS	PARQUETS	PARTAKERS	PARURE
PARISH	PARLY	PARQUETTED	PARTAKES	PARURES
PARISHEN	PAROCHIAL	PARQUETTING	PARTAKING	PARVENU
PARISHENS	PAROCHIN	PARR	PARTAKINGS	PARVENUS
PARISHES	PAROCHINE	PARRAKEET	PARTAN	PARVIS
PARISON	PAROCHINES	PARRAKEETS	PARTANS	PARVISE
PARISONS	PAROCHINS	PARRAL	PARTED	PARVISES
PARITIES	PARODIC	PARRALS	PARTER	PAS
PARITOR	PARODICAL	PARREL	PARTERRE	PASCAL
PARITORS	PARODIED	PARRELS	PARTERRES	PASCALS
PARITY	PARODIES	PARRHESIA	PARTERS	PASCHAL
PARK	PARODIST	PARRHESIAS	PARTI	PASCUAL
PARKA	PARODISTS	PARRICIDE	PARTIAL	PASEAR
PARKAS	PARODY	PARRICIDES	PARTIALLY	PASEARED
PARKED	PARODYING	PARRIED	PARTIALS	PASEARING
PARKEE	PAROEMIA	PARRIES	PARTIBLE	PASEARS
PARKEES	PAROEMIAC	PARRITCH	PARTICLE	PASEO
PARKER	PAROEMIACS	PARRITCHES	PARTICLES	PASEOS
PARKERS	PAROEMIAL	PARROCK	PARTIED	PASH
PARKI	PAROEMIAS	PARROCKED	PARTIES	PASHA
PARKIE	PAROICOUS	PARROCKING	PARTIM	PASHALIK
PARKIER	PAROL	PARROCKS	PARTING	PASHALIKS
PARKIES	PAROLE	PARROQUET	PARTINGS	PASHAS
PARKIEST	PAROLED	PARROQUETS	PARTIS	PASHED
PARKIN	PAROLEE	PARROT	PARTISAN	PASHES
PARKING	PAROLEES	PARROTED	PARTISANS	PASHIM
PARKINGS	PAROLES	PARROTER	PARTITA	PASHIMS
PARKINS	PAROLING	PARROTERS	PARTITAS	PASHING
PARKIS	PARONYM	PARROTING	PARTITE	PASHM
PARKISH	PARONYMIES	PARROTRIES	PARTITION	PASHMINA
PARKLAND	PARONYMS	PARROTRY	PARTITIONED	PASHMINAS
PARKLANDS	PARONYMY	PARROTS	PARTITIONING	PASHMS
PARKLIKE	PAROQUET	PARROTY	PARTITIONS	PASPALUM
PARKLY	PAROQUETS	PARRS	PARTITIVE	PASPALUMS
PARKS	PAROTIC	PARRY	PARTITIVES	PASPIES
PARKWARD	PAROTID	PARRYING	PARTITURA	PASPY
PARKWARDS	PAROTIDS	PARS	PARTITURAS	PASQUILER
PARKWAY	PAROTIS	PARSE	PARTIZAN	PASQUILERS
PARKWAYS	PAROTISES	PARSEC	PARTIZANS	PASS
PARKY	PAROTITIS	PARSECS	PARTLET	PASSABLE
PARLANCE	PAROTITISES	PARSED	PARTLETS	PASSABLY
PARLANCES	PAROUSIA	PARSER	PARTLY	PASSADE

PASSADES	PASSOUT	PAT	PATES	PATRIMONY
PASSADO	PASSOUTS	PATACA	PATH	PATRIOT
PASSADOES	PASSPORT	PATACAS	PATHED	PATRIOTIC
PASSADOS	PASSPORTS	PATAGIA	PATHETIC	PATRIOTS
PASSAGE	PASSUS	PATAGIAL	PATHETICS	PATRISTIC
PASSAGED	PASSUSES	PATAGIUM	PATHIC	PATRISTICS
PASSAGES	PASSWORD	PATAMAR	PATHICS	PATROL
PASSAGING	PASSWORDS	PATAMARS	PATHING	PATROLLED
PASSAMENT	PAST	PATBALL	PATHLESS	PATROLLER
PASSAMENTED	PASTA	PATBALLS	PATHOGEN	PATROLLERS
PASSAMENTING	PASTANCE	PATCH	PATHOGENIES	PATROLLING
PASSAMENTS	PASTANCES	PATCHABLE	PATHOGENS	PATROLMAN
PASSANT	PASTAS	PATCHED	PATHOGENY	PATROLMEN
PASSATA	PASTE	PATCHER	PATHOLOGIES	PATROLOGIES
PASSATAS	PASTED	PATCHERIES	PATHOLOGY	PATROLOGY
PASSE	PASTEL	PATCHERS	PATHOS	PATROLS
PASSED	PASTELS	PATCHERY	PATHOSES	PATRON
PASSEE	PASTER	PATCHES	PATHS	PATRONAGE
PASSEMENT	PASTERN	PATCHIER	PATHWAY	PATRONAGED
PASSEMENTED	PASTERNS	PATCHIEST	PATHWAYS	PATRONAGES
PASSEMENTING	PASTERS	PATCHILY	PATIBLE	PATRONAGING
PASSEMENTS	PASTES	PATCHING	PATIENCE	PATRONAL
PASSENGER	PASTICCI	PATCHINGS	PATIENCES	PATRONESS
PASSENGERS	PASTICCIO	PATCHOCKE	PATIENT	PATRONESSES
PASSEPIED	PASTICHE	PATCHOCKES	PATIENTED	PATRONISE
PASSEPIEDS	PASTICHES	PATCHOULI	PATIENTER	PATRONISED
PASSER	PASTIER	PATCHOULIES	PATIENTEST	PATRONISES
PASSERINE	PASTIES	PATCHOULIS	PATIENTING	PATRONISING
PASSERINES	PASTIEST	PATCHOULY	PATIENTLY	PATRONIZE
PASSERS	PASTIL	PATCHWORK	PATIENTS	PATRONIZED
PASSES	PASTILLE	PATCHWORKS	PATIN	PATRONIZES
PASSIBLE	PASTILLES	PATCHY	PATINA	PATRONIZING
PASSIBLY	PASTILS	PATE	PATINAS	PATRONNE
PASSIM	PASTIME	PATED	PATINATED	PATRONNES
PASSING	PASTIMES	PATELLA	PATINE	PATRONS
PASSINGS	PASTINESS	PATELLAE	PATINED	PATROON
PASSION	PASTINESSES	PATELLAR	PATINES	PATROONS
PASSIONAL	PASTING	PATELLAS	PATINS	PATS
PASSIONALS	PASTINGS	PATELLATE	PATIO	PATSIES
PASSIONED	PASTIS	PATEN	PATIOS	PATSY
PASSIONING	PASTISES	PATENCIES	PATLY	PATTE
PASSIONS	PASTOR	PATENCY	PATNESS	PATTED
PASSIVATE	PASTORAL	PATENS	PATNESSES	PATTEE
PASSIVATED	PASTORALE	PATENT	PATOIS	PATTEN
PASSIVATES	PASTORALES	PATENTED	PATONCE	PATTENED
PASSIVATING	PASTORALI	PATENTEE	PATRIAL	PATTENING
PASSIVE	PASTORALS	PATENTEES	PATRIALS	PATTENS
PASSIVELY	PASTORATE	PATENTING	PATRIARCH	PATTER
PASSIVES	PASTORATES	PATENTLY	PATRIARCHS	PATTERED
PASSIVISM	PASTORLY	PATENTOR	PATRIATE	PATTERER
PASSIVISMS	PASTORS	PATENTORS	PATRIATED	PATTERERS
PASSIVIST	PASTRAMI	PATENTS	PATRIATES	PATTERING
PASSIVISTS	PASTRAMIS	PATER	PATRIATING	PATTERN
PASSIVITIES	PASTRIES	PATERA	PATRICIAN	PATTERNED
PASSIVITY	PASTRY	PATERAE	PATRICIANS	PATTERNING
PASSKEY	PASTS	PATERCOVE	PATRICIDE	PATTERNS
PASSKEYS	PASTURAGE	PATERCOVES	PATRICIDES	PATTERS
PASSLESS	PASTURAGES	PATERERO	PATRICK	PATTES
PASSMAN	PASTURAL	PATEREROES	PATRICKS	PATTIES
PASSMEN	PASTURE	PATEREROS	PATRICO	PATTING
PASSMENT	PASTURED	PATERNAL	PATRICOES	PATTLE
PASSMENTED	PASTURES	PATERNITIES	PATRILINIES	PATTLES
PASSMENTING	PASTURING	PATERNITY	PATRILINY	PATTY
PASSMENTS	PASTY	PATERS	PATRIMONIES	PATULIN

PATULINS
PATULOUS
PATZER
PATZERS
PAUA
PAUAS
PAUCITIES
PAUCITY
PAUGHTIER
PAUGHTIEST
PAUGHTY
PAUL
PAULDRON
PAULDRONS
PAULOWNIA
PAULOWNIAS
PAULS
PAUNCE
PAUNCES
PAUNCH
PAUNCHED
PAUNCHES
PAUNCHIER
PAUNCHIEST
PAUNCHING
PAUNCHY
PAUPER
PAUPERESS
PAUPERESSES
PAUPERISE
PAUPERISED
PAUPERISES
PAUPERISING
PAUPERISM
PAUPERISMS
PAUPERIZE
PAUPERIZED
PAUPERIZES
PAUPERIZING
PAUPERS
PAUSAL
PAUSE
PAUSED
PAUSEFUL
PAUSELESS
PAUSER
PAUSERS
PAUSES
PAUSING
PAUSINGLY
PAUSINGS
PAVAGE
PAVAGES
PAVAN
PAVANE
PAVANES
PAVANS
PAVE
PAVED
PAVEMENT
PAVEMENTED
PAVEMENTING
PAVEMENTS
PAVEN

PAVENS
PAVER
PAVERS
PAVES
PAVID
PAVILION
PAVILIONED
PAVILIONING
PAVILIONS
PAVIN
PAVING
PAVINGS
PAVINS
PAVIOR
PAVIORS
PAVIOUR
PAVIOURS
PAVIS
PAVISE
PAVISES
PAVLOVA
PAVLOVAS
PAVONAZZO
PAVONAZZOS
PAVONE
PAVONES
PAVONIAN
PAVONINE
PAW
PAWA
PAWAS
PAWAW
PAWAWED
PAWAWING
PAWAWS
PAWED
PAWING
PAWK
PAWKIER
PAWKIEST
PAWKILY
PAWKINESS
PAWKINESSES
PAWKS
PAWKY
PAWL
PAWLS
PAWN
PAWNCE
PAWNCES
PAWNED
PAWNEE
PAWNEES
PAWNER
PAWNERS
PAWNING
PAWNS
PAWNSHOP
PAWNSHOPS
PAWPAW
PAWPAWS
PAWS
PAX
PAXES

PAXIUBA
PAXIUBAS
PAXWAX
PAXWAXES
PAY
PAYABLE
PAYBACK
PAYBACKS
PAYED
PAYEE
PAYEES
PAYER
PAYERS
PAYFONE
PAYFONES
PAYING
PAYINGS
PAYMASTER
PAYMASTERS
PAYMENT
PAYMENTS
PAYNIM
PAYNIMRIES
PAYNIMRY
PAYNIMS
PAYOLA
PAYOLAS
PAYROLL
PAYROLLS
PAYS
PAYSAGE
PAYSAGES
PAYSAGIST
PAYSAGISTS
PAYSD
PAYSLIP
PAYSLIPS
PAZAZZ
PAZAZZES
PEA
PEABERRIES
PEABERRY
PEACE
PEACEABLE
PEACEABLY
PEACED
PEACEFUL
PEACELESS
PEACENIK
PEACENIKS
PEACES
PEACETIME
PEACETIMES
PEACH
PEACHED
PEACHER
PEACHERS
PEACHES
PEACHIER
PEACHIEST
PEACHING
PEACHY
PEACING
PEACOCK

PEACOCKED
PEACOCKING
PEACOCKS
PEACOCKY
PEACOD
PEACODS
PEAFOWL
PEAFOWLS
PEAG
PEAGS
PEAK
PEAKED
PEAKIER
PEAKIEST
PEAKING
PEAKS
PEAKY
PEAL
PEALED
PEALING
PEALS
PEAN
PEANED
PEANING
PEANS
PEANUT
PEANUTS
PEAPOD
PEAPODS
PEAR
PEARCE
PEARCED
PEARCES
PEARCING
PEARE
PEARES
PEARL
PEARLED
PEARLER
PEARLERS
PEARLIER
PEARLIES
PEARLIEST
PEARLIN
PEARLING
PEARLINGS
PEARLINS
PEARLISED
PEARLITE
PEARLITES
PEARLITIC
PEARLIZED
PEARLS
PEARLWORT
PEARLWORTS
PEARLY
PEARMAIN
PEARMAINS
PEARS
PEARST
PEART
PEARTER
PEARTEST
PEARTLY

PEAS
PEASANT
PEASANTRIES
PEASANTRY
PEASANTS
PEASANTY
PEASCOD
PEASCODS
PEASE
PEASECOD
PEASECODS
PEASED
PEASES
PEASEWEEP
PEASEWEEPS
PEASING
PEASON
PEAT
PEATARIES
PEATARY
PEATERIES
PEATERY
PEATIER
PEATIEST
PEATMAN
PEATMEN
PEATS
PEATSHIP
PEATSHIPS
PEATY
PEAVEY
PEAVEYS
PEAVIES
PEAVY
PEAZE
PEAZED
PEAZES
PEAZING
PEBA
PEBAS
PEBBLE
PEBBLED
PEBBLES
PEBBLIER
PEBBLIEST
PEBBLING
PEBBLINGS
PEBBLY
PEBRINE
PEBRINES
PEC
PECAN
PECANS
PECCABLE
PECCANCIES
PECCANCY
PECCANT
PECCANTLY
PECCARIES
PECCARY
PECCAVI
PECCAVIS
PECH
PECHED

PECHING	PEDALLING	PEDIMENT	PEER	PEISHWAHS
PECHS	PEDALLINGS	PEDIMENTS	PEERAGE	PEISHWAS
PECK	PEDALO	PEDIPALP	PEERAGES	PEISING
PECKE	PEDALOES	PEDIPALPI	PEERED	PEIZE
PECKED	PEDALOS	PEDIPALPS	PEERESS	PEIZED
PECKER	PEDALS	PEDLAR	PEERESSES	PEIZES
PECKERS	PEDANT	PEDLARIES	PEERIE	PEIZING
PECKES	PEDANTIC	PEDLARS	PEERIER	PEJORATE
PECKING	PEDANTISE	PEDLARY	PEERIES	PEJORATED
PECKINGS	PEDANTISED	PEDOLOGIES	PEERIEST	PEJORATES
PECKISH	PEDANTISES	PEDOLOGY	PEERING	PEJORATING
PECKS	PEDANTISING	PEDOMETER	PEERLESS	PEKAN
PECS	PEDANTISM	PEDOMETERS	PEERS	PEKANS
PECTEN	PEDANTISMS	PEDRAIL	PEERY	PEKE
PECTIC	PEDANTIZE	PEDRAILS	PEES	PEKES
PECTIN	PEDANTIZED	PEDRERO	PEESWEEP	PEKOE
PECTINAL	PEDANTIZES	PEDREROES	PEESWEEPS	PEKOES
PECTINATE	PEDANTIZING	PEDREROS	PEETWEET	PELA
PECTINEAL	PEDANTRIES	PEDRO	PEETWEETS	PELAGE
PECTINES	PEDANTRY	PEDROS	PEEVE	PELAGES
PECTINS	PEDANTS	PEDS	PEEVED	PELAGIAN
PECTISE	PEDATE	PEDUNCLE	PEEVER	PELAGIANS
PECTISED	PEDATELY	PEDUNCLES	PEEVERS	PELAGIC
PECTISES	PEDATIFID	PEE	PEEVES	PELAS
PECTISING	PEDDER	PEECE	PEEVING	PELE
PECTIZE	PEDDERS	PEECES	PEEVISH	PELERINE
PECTIZED	PEDDLE	PEED	PEEVISHLY	PELERINES
PECTIZES	PEDDLED	PEEING	PEEWEE	PELES
PECTIZING	PEDDLER	PEEK	PEEWEES	PELF
PECTOLITE	PEDDLERS	PEEKABO	PEEWIT	PELFS
PECTOLITES	PEDDLES	PEEKABOO	PEEWITS	PELHAM
PECTORAL	PEDDLING	PEEKABOOS	PEG	PELHAMS
PECTORALS	PEDDLINGS	PEEKABOS	PEGASUS	PELICAN
PECTOSE	PEDERAST	PEEKED	PEGASUSES	PELICANS
PECTOSES	PEDERASTIES	PEEKING	PEGBOARD	PELISSE
PECULATE	PEDERASTS	PEEKS	PEGBOARDS	PELISSES
PECULATED	PEDERASTY	PEEL	PEGGED	PELITE
PECULATES	PEDERERO	PEELED	PEGGIES	PELITES
PECULATING	PEDEREROES	PEELER	PEGGING	PELITIC
PECULATOR	PEDEREROS	PEELERS	PEGGINGS	PELL
PECULATORS	PEDESES	PEELING	PEGGY	PELLACH
PECULIA	PEDESIS	PEELINGS	PEGH	PELLACHS
PECULIAR	PEDESTAL	PEELS	PEGHED	PELLACK
PECULIARS	PEDESTALLED	PEEN	PEGHING	PELLACKS
PECULIUM	PEDESTALLING	PEENED	PEGHS	PELLAGRA
PECUNIARY	PEDESTALS	PEENGE	PEGMATITE	PELLAGRAS
PECUNIOUS	PEDETIC	PEENGED	PEGMATITES	PELLAGRIN
PED	PEDICAB	PEENGEING	PEGS	PELLAGRINS
PEDAGOGIC	PEDICABS	PEENGES	PEIGNOIR	PELLET
PEDAGOGICS	PEDICEL	PEENGING	PEIGNOIRS	PELLETED
PEDAGOGIES	PEDICELS	PEENING	PEIN	PELLETIFIED
PEDAGOGUE	PEDICLE	PEENS	PEINCT	PELLETIFIES
PEDAGOGUED	PEDICLED	PEEOY	PEINCTED	PELLETIFY
PEDAGOGUES	PEDICLES	PEEOYS	PEINCTING	PELLETIFYING
PEDAGOGUING	PEDICULAR	PEEP	PEINCTS	PELLETING
PEDAGOGY	PEDICULI	PEEPE	PEINED	PELLETISE
PEDAL	PEDICULUS	PEEPED	PEINING	PELLETISED
PEDALED	PEDICURE	PEEPER	PEINS	PELLETISES
PEDALIER	PEDICURED	PEEPERS	PEIRASTIC	PELLETISING
PEDALIERS	PEDICURES	PEEPES	PEISE	PELLETIZE
PEDALING	PEDICURING	PEEPING	PEISED	PELLETIZED
PEDALLED	PEDIGREE	PEEPS	PEISES	PELLETIZES
PEDALLER	PEDIGREED	PEEPUL	PEISHWA	PELLETIZING
PEDALLERS	PEDIGREES	PEEPULS	PEISHWAH	PELLETS

PELLICLE
PELLICLES
PELLITORIES
PELLITORY
PELLOCK
PELLOCKS
PELLS
PELLUCID
PELMA
PELMANISM
PELMANISMS
PELMAS
PELMATIC
PELMET
PELMETS
PELOID
PELOIDS
PELOLOGIES
PELOLOGY
PELORIA
PELORIAS
PELORIC
PELORIES
PELORISED
PELORISM
PELORISMS
PELORIZED
PELORUS
PELORUSES
PELORY
PELOTA
PELOTAS
PELT
PELTA
PELTAE
PELTAS
PELTAST
PELTASTS
PELTATE
PELTED
PELTER
PELTERED
PELTERING
PELTERS
PELTING
PELTINGLY
PELTINGS
PELTRIES
PELTRY
PELTS
PELVES
PELVIC
PELVIFORM
PELVIS
PELVISES
PEMBROKE
PEMBROKES
PEMICAN
PEMICANS
PEMMICAN
PEMMICANS
PEMOLINE
PEMOLINES
PEMPHIGUS

PEMPHIGUSES
PEN
PENAL
PENALISE
PENALISED
PENALISES
PENALISING
PENALIZE
PENALIZED
PENALIZES
PENALIZING
PENALLY
PENALTIES
PENALTY
PENANCE
PENANCED
PENANCES
PENANCING
PENATES
PENCE
PENCEL
PENCELS
PENCES
PENCHANT
PENCHANTS
PENCIL
PENCILLED
PENCILLER
PENCILLERS
PENCILLING
PENCILLINGS
PENCILS
PENCRAFT
PENCRAFTS
PEND
PENDANT
PENDANTS
PENDED
PENDENCIES
PENDENCY
PENDENT
PENDENTLY
PENDENTS
PENDICLE
PENDICLER
PENDICLERS
PENDICLES
PENDING
PENDRAGON
PENDRAGONS
PENDS
PENDULAR
PENDULATE
PENDULATED
PENDULATES
PENDULATING
PENDULINE
PENDULOUS
PENDULUM
PENDULUMS
PENE
PENED
PENEPLAIN
PENEPLAINS

PENEPLANE
PENEPLANES
PENES
PENETRANT
PENETRANTS
PENETRATE
PENETRATED
PENETRATES
PENETRATING
PENFOLD
PENFOLDS
PENFUL
PENFULS
PENGUIN
PENGUINRIES
PENGUINRY
PENGUINS
PENHOLDER
PENHOLDERS
PENI
PENIAL
PENIE
PENIES
PENILE
PENILLION
PENING
PENINSULA
PENINSULAS
PENIS
PENISES
PENISTONE
PENISTONES
PENITENCE
PENITENCES
PENITENCIES
PENITENCY
PENITENT
PENITENTS
PENK
PENKNIFE
PENKNIVES
PENKS
PENLIGHT
PENLIGHTS
PENMAN
PENMEN
PENNA
PENNAE
PENNAL
PENNALISM
PENNALISMS
PENNALS
PENNANT
PENNANTS
PENNATE
PENNATULA
PENNATULAE
PENNATULAS
PENNE
PENNED
PENNEECH
PENNEECHS
PENNEECK
PENNEECKS

PENNER
PENNERS
PENNES
PENNIED
PENNIES
PENNIFORM
PENNILESS
PENNILL
PENNINE
PENNINES
PENNING
PENNINITE
PENNINITES
PENNON
PENNONCEL
PENNONCELS
PENNONED
PENNONS
PENNY
PENNYFEE
PENNYFEES
PENNYLAND
PENNYLANDS
PENOLOGIES
PENOLOGY
PENONCEL
PENONCELS
PENS
PENSEE
PENSEES
PENSEL
PENSELS
PENSIL
PENSILE
PENSILITIES
PENSILITY
PENSILS
PENSION
PENSIONED
PENSIONER
PENSIONERS
PENSIONING
PENSIONS
PENSIVE
PENSIVELY
PENSTEMON
PENSTEMONS
PENSTOCK
PENSTOCKS
PENSUM
PENSUMS
PENT
PENTACLE
PENTACLES
PENTACT
PENTACTS
PENTAD
PENTADIC
PENTADS
PENTAGON
PENTAGONS
PENTAGRAM
PENTAGRAMS
PENTALOGIES

PENTALOGY
PENTALPHA
PENTALPHAS
PENTAMERIES
PENTAMERY
PENTANE
PENTANES
PENTANGLE
PENTANGLES
PENTAPODIES
PENTAPODY
PENTARCH
PENTARCHIES
PENTARCHS
PENTARCHY
PENTATHLA
PENTEL®
PENTELS
PENTENE
PENTENES
PENTHIA
PENTHIAS
PENTHOUSE
PENTHOUSED
PENTHOUSES
PENTHOUSING
PENTICE
PENTICED
PENTICES
PENTICING
PENTISE
PENTISED
PENTISES
PENTISING
PENTODE
PENTODES
PENTOMIC
PENTOSAN
PENTOSANE
PENTOSANES
PENTOSANS
PENTOSE
PENTOSES
PENTOXIDE
PENTOXIDES
PENTROOF
PENTROOFS
PENTS
PENTYLENE
PENTYLENES
PENUCHE
PENUCHES
PENUCHI
PENUCHIS
PENUCHLE
PENUCHLES
PENULT
PENULTIMA
PENULTIMAS
PENULTS
PENUMBRA
PENUMBRAL
PENUMBRAS
PENURIES

The Chambers Dictionary is the authority for many longer words; see *OSW* Introduction, page xii

PENURIOUS	PEPTICS	PERCIFORM	PERFECTOS	PERICARPS
PENURY	PEPTIDASE	PERCINE	PERFECTS	PERICLASE
PENWOMAN	PEPTIDASES	PERCING	PERFERVID	PERICLASES
PENWOMEN	PEPTIDE	PERCOCT	PERFERVOR	PERICLINE
PEON	PEPTIDES	PERCOID	PERFERVORS	PERICLINES
PEONAGE	PEPTISE	PERCOLATE	PERFET	PERICON
PEONAGES	PEPTISED	PERCOLATED	PERFIDIES	PERICONES
PEONIES	PEPTISES	PERCOLATES	PERFIDY	PERICOPE
PEONISM	PEPTISING	PERCOLATING	PERFORANS	PERICOPES
PEONISMS	PEPTIZE	PERCOLIN	PERFORANSES	PERICRANIES
PEONS	PEPTIZED	PERCOLINS	PERFORANT	PERICRANY
PEONY	PEPTIZES	PERCUSS	PERFORATE	PERICYCLE
PEOPLE	PEPTIZING	PERCUSSED	PERFORATED	PERICYCLES
PEOPLED	PEPTONE	PERCUSSES	PERFORATES	PERIDERM
PEOPLES	PEPTONES	PERCUSSING	PERFORATING	PERIDERMS
PEOPLING	PEPTONISE	PERCUSSOR	PERFORCE	PERIDIA
PEP	PEPTONISED	PERCUSSORS	PERFORM	PERIDIAL
PEPERINO	PEPTONISES	PERDENDO	PERFORMED	PERIDINIA
PEPERINOS	PEPTONISING	PERDIE	PERFORMER	PERIDIUM
PEPEROMIA	PEPTONIZE	PERDITION	PERFORMERS	PERIDIUMS
PEPEROMIAS	PEPTONIZED	PERDITIONS	PERFORMING	PERIDOT
PEPERONI	PEPTONIZES	PERDU	PERFORMINGS	PERIDOTE
PEPERONIS	PEPTONIZING	PERDUE	PERFORMS	PERIDOTES
PEPFUL	PER	PERDUES	PERFUME	PERIDOTIC
PEPINO	PERACUTE	PERDURE	PERFUMED	PERIDOTS
PEPINOS	PERAEA	PERDURED	PERFUMER	PERIDROME
PEPLA	PERAEON	PERDURES	PERFUMERIES	PERIDROMES
PEPLOS	PERAEONS	PERDURING	PERFUMERS	PERIGEAL
PEPLOSES	PERAEOPOD	PERDUS	PERFUMERY	PERIGEAN
PEPLUM	PERAEOPODS	PERDY	PERFUMES	PERIGEE
PEPLUMS	PERAI	PERE	PERFUMING	PERIGEES
PEPLUS	PERAIS	PEREGAL	PERFUMY	PERIGON
PEPLUSES	PERCALE	PEREGALS	PERFUSATE	PERIGONE
PEPO	PERCALES	PEREGRINE	PERFUSATES	PERIGONES
PEPOS	PERCALINE	PEREGRINES	PERFUSE	PERIGONIA
PEPPED	PERCALINES	PEREIA	PERFUSED	PERIGONS
PEPPER	PERCASE	PEREION	PERFUSES	PERIGYNIES
PEPPERED	PERCE	PEREIOPOD	PERFUSING	PERIGYNY
PEPPERER	PERCEABLE	PEREIOPODS	PERFUSION	PERIHELIA
PEPPERERS	PERCEANT	PEREIRA	PERFUSIONS	PERIKARYA
PEPPERIER	PERCED	PEREIRAS	PERFUSIVE	PERIL
PEPPERIEST	PERCEIVE	PERENNATE	PERGOLA	PERILLED
PEPPERING	PERCEIVED	PERENNATED	PERGOLAS	PERILLING
PEPPERINGS	PERCEIVER	PERENNATES	PERGUNNAH	PERILOUS
PEPPERONI	PERCEIVERS	PERENNATING	PERGUNNAHS	PERILS
PEPPERONIS	PERCEIVES	PERENNIAL	PERHAPS	PERILUNE
PEPPERS	PERCEIVING	PERENNIALS	PERI	PERILUNES
PEPPERY	PERCEIVINGS	PERENNITIES	PERIAGUA	PERILYMPH
PEPPIER	PERCEN	PERENNITY	PERIAGUAS	PERILYMPHS
PEPPIEST	PERCENTAL	PERES	PERIAKTOI	PERIMETER
PEPPING	PERCEPT	PERFAY	PERIAKTOS	PERIMETERS
PEPPY	PERCEPTS	PERFECT	PERIANTH	PERIMETRIES
PEPS	PERCES	PERFECTA	PERIANTHS	PERIMETRY
PEPSIN	PERCH	PERFECTAS	PERIAPT	PERIMORPH
PEPSINATE	PERCHANCE	PERFECTED	PERIAPTS	PERIMORPHS
PEPSINATED	PERCHED	PERFECTER	PERIBLAST	PERINAEUM
PEPSINATES	PERCHER	PERFECTERS	PERIBLASTS	PERINAEUMS
PEPSINATING	PERCHERON	PERFECTEST	PERIBLEM	PERINATAL
PEPSINE	PERCHERONS	PERFECTI	PERIBLEMS	PERINEA
PEPSINES	PERCHERS	PERFECTING	PERIBOLI	PERINEAL
PEPSINS	PERCHERY	PERFECTLY	PERIBOLOI	PERINEUM
PEPTIC	PERCHES	PERFECTO	PERIBOLOS	PERINEUMS
PEPTICITIES	PERCHING	PERFECTOR	PERIBOLUS	PERIOD
PEPTICITY	PERCHINGS	PERFECTORS	PERICARP	PERIODATE

PERIODATES	PERJUROUS	PEROXIDE	PERSONATED	PERTURBS
PERIODED	PERJURY	PEROXIDED	PERSONATES	PERTUSATE
PERIODIC	PERK	PEROXIDES	PERSONATING	PERTUSE
PERIODING	PERKED	PEROXIDING	PERSONATINGS	PERTUSED
PERIODS	PERKIER	PERPEND	PERSONIFIED	PERTUSION
PERIOST	PERKIEST	PERPENDED	PERSONIFIES	PERTUSIONS
PERIOSTEA	PERKILY	PERPENDING	PERSONIFY	PERTUSSAL
PERIOSTS	PERKIN	PERPENDS	PERSONIFYING	PERTUSSIS
PERIOTIC	PERKINESS	PERPENT	PERSONISE	PERTUSSISES
PERIOTICS	PERKINESSES	PERPENTS	PERSONISED	PERUKE
PERIPATUS	PERKING	PERPETUAL	PERSONISES	PERUKED
PERIPATUSES	PERKINS	PERPETUALS	PERSONISING	PERUKES
PERIPETIA	PERKS	PERPLEX	PERSONIZE	PERUSAL
PERIPETIAS	PERKY	PERPLEXED	PERSONIZED	PERUSALS
PERIPETIES	PERLITE	PERPLEXES	PERSONIZES	PERUSE
PERIPETY	PERLITES	PERPLEXING	PERSONIZING	PERUSED
PERIPHERIES	PERLITIC	PERRADIAL	PERSONNEL	PERUSER
PERIPHERY	PERLOUS	PERRADII	PERSONNELS	PERUSERS
PERIPLAST	PERM	PERRADIUS	PERSONS	PERUSES
PERIPLASTS	PERMALLOY	PERRIER	PERSPIRE	PERUSING
PERIPLUS	PERMALLOYS	PERRIERS	PERSPIRED	PERV
PERIPLUSES	PERMANENT	PERRIES	PERSPIRES	PERVADE
PERIPROCT	PERMEABLE	PERRON	PERSPIRING	PERVADED
PERIPROCTS	PERMEABLY	PERRONS	PERST	PERVADES
PERIPTERIES	PERMEANCE	PERRUQUE	PERSUADE	PERVADING
PERIPTERY	PERMEANCES	PERRUQUES	PERSUADED	PERVASION
PERIQUE	PERMEASE	PERRY	PERSUADER	PERVASIONS
PERIQUES	PERMEASES	PERSANT	PERSUADERS	PERVASIVE
PERIS	PERMEATE	PERSAUNT	PERSUADES	PERVE
PERISARC	PERMEATED	PERSE	PERSUADING	PERVED
PERISARCS	PERMEATES	PERSECUTE	PERSUE	PERVERSE
PERISCIAN	PERMEATING	PERSECUTED	PERSUED	PERVERSER
PERISCIANS	PERMED	PERSECUTES	PERSUES	PERVERSEST
PERISCOPE	PERMING	PERSECUTING	PERSUING	PERVERT
PERISCOPES	PERMIT	PERSEITIES	PERSWADE	PERVERTED
PERISH	PERMITS	PERSEITY	PERSWADED	PERVERTER
PERISHED	PERMITTED	PERSELINE	PERSWADES	PERVERTERS
PERISHER	PERMITTER	PERSELINES	PERSWADING	PERVERTING
PERISHERS	PERMITTERS	PERSES	PERT	PERVERTS
PERISHES	PERMITTING	PERSEVERE	PERTAIN	PERVES
PERISHING	PERMS	PERSEVERED	PERTAINED	PERVIATE
PERISPERM	PERMUTATE	PERSEVERES	PERTAINING	PERVIATED
PERISPERMS	PERMUTATED	PERSEVERING	PERTAINS	PERVIATES
PERISTOME	PERMUTATES	PERSICO	PERTAKE	PERVIATING
PERISTOMES	PERMUTATING	PERSICOS	PERTAKEN	PERVICACIES
PERISTYLE	PERMUTE	PERSICOT	PERTAKES	PERVICACY
PERISTYLES	PERMUTED	PERSICOTS	PERTAKING	PERVING
PERITI	PERMUTES	PERSIENNE	PERTER	PERVIOUS
PERITONEA	PERMUTING	PERSIENNES	PERTEST	PERVS
PERITRICH	PERN	PERSIMMON	PERTHITE	PESADE
PERITRICHA	PERNANCIES	PERSIMMONS	PERTHITES	PESADES
PERITUS	PERNANCY	PERSING	PERTHITIC	PESANT
PERIWIG	PERNS	PERSIST	PERTINENT	PESANTE
PERIWIGGED	PERONE	PERSISTED	PERTINENTS	PESANTS
PERIWIGGING	PERONEAL	PERSISTING	PERTLY	PESAUNT
PERIWIGS	PERONES	PERSISTS	PERTNESS	PESAUNTS
PERJINK	PERONEUS	PERSON	PERTNESSES	PESETA
PERJURE	PERONEUSES	PERSONA	PERTOOK	PESETAS
PERJURED	PERORATE	PERSONAE	PERTS	PESEWA
PERJURER	PERORATED	PERSONAGE	PERTURB	PESEWAS
PERJURERS	PERORATES	PERSONAGES	PERTURBED	PESHWA
PERJURES	PERORATING	PERSONAL	PERTURBER	PESHWAS
PERJURIES	PEROVSKIA	PERSONAS	PERTURBERS	PESKIER
PERJURING	PEROVSKIAS	PERSONATE	PERTURBING	PESKIEST

PESKILY	PETCOCK	PETS	PFENNINGS	PHARAONIC
PESKY	PETCOCKS	PETTED	PH	PHARE
PESO	PETECHIA	PETTEDLY	PHACELIA	PHARES
PESOS	PETECHIAE	PETTER	PHACELIAS	PHARISAIC
PESSARIES	PETECHIAL	PETTERS	PHACOID	PHARMACIES
PESSARY	PETER	PETTICOAT	PHACOIDAL	PHARMACY
PESSIMA	PETERED	PETTICOATS	PHACOLITE	PHAROS
PESSIMAL	PETERING	PETTIER	PHACOLITES	PHAROSES
PESSIMISM	PETERMAN	PETTIES	PHACOLITH	PHARYNGAL
PESSIMISMS	PETERMEN	PETTIEST	PHACOLITHS	PHARYNGES
PESSIMIST	PETERS	PETTIFOG	PHAEIC	PHARYNX
PESSIMISTS	PETERSHAM	PETTIFOGGED	PHAEISM	PHARYNXES
PESSIMUM	PETERSHAMS	PETTIFOGGING	PHAEISMS	PHASE
PEST	PETHER	PETTIFOGGINGS	PHAENOGAM	PHASED
PESTER	PETHERS	PETTIFOGS	PHAENOGAMS	PHASELESS
PESTERED	PETHIDINE	PETTILY	PHAETON	PHASEOLIN
PESTERER	PETHIDINES	PETTINESS	PHAETONS	PHASEOLINS
PESTERERS	PETILLANT	PETTINESSES	PHAGE	PHASES
PESTERING	PETIOLAR	PETTING	PHAGEDENA	PHASIC
PESTEROUS	PETIOLATE	PETTINGS	PHAGEDENAS	PHASING
PESTERS	PETIOLE	PETTISH	PHAGES	PHASIS
PESTFUL	PETIOLED	PETTISHLY	PHAGOCYTE	PHASMID
PESTHOUSE	PETIOLES	PETTITOES	PHAGOCYTES	PHASMIDS
PESTHOUSES	PETIOLULE	PETTLE	PHALANGAL	PHAT
PESTICIDE	PETIOLULES	PETTLED	PHALANGE	PHATIC
PESTICIDES	PETIT	PETTLES	PHALANGER	PHATTER
PESTILENT	PETITE	PETTLING	PHALANGERS	PHATTEST
PESTLE	PETITION	PETTY	PHALANGES	PHEASANT
PESTLED	PETITIONED	PETULANCE	PHALANGID	PHEASANTS
PESTLES	PETITIONING	PETULANCES	PHALANGIDS	PHEAZAR
PESTLING	PETITIONINGS	PETULANCIES	PHALANX	PHEAZARS
PESTO	PETITIONS	PETULANCY	PHALANXES	PHEER
PESTOLOGIES	PETITORY	PETULANT	PHALAROPE	PHEERE
PESTOLOGY	PETRARIES	PETUNIA	PHALAROPES	PHEERES
PESTOS	PETRARY	PETUNIAS	PHALLI	PHEERS
PESTS	PETRE	PETUNTSE	PHALLIC	PHEESE
PET	PETREL	PETUNTSES	PHALLIN	PHEESED
PETAL	PETRELS	PETUNTZE	PHALLINS	PHEESES
PETALINE	PETRES	PETUNTZES	PHALLISM	PHEESING
PETALISM	PETRIFIC	PEW	PHALLISMS	PHEEZE
PETALISMS	PETRIFIED	PEWIT	PHALLOID	PHEEZED
PETALLED	PETRIFIES	PEWITS	PHALLUS	PHEEZES
PETALODIES	PETRIFY	PEWS	PHALLUSES	PHEEZING
PETALODY	PETRIFYING	PEWTER	PHANG	PHELLEM
PETALOID	PETROGRAM	PEWTERER	PHANGED	PHELLEMS
PETALOUS	PETROGRAMS	PEWTERERS	PHANGING	PHELLOGEN
PETALS	PETROL	PEWTERS	PHANGS	PHELLOGENS
PETANQUE	PETROLAGE	PEYOTE	PHANSIGAR	PHELLOID
PETANQUES	PETROLAGES	PEYOTES	PHANSIGARS	PHELONION
PETAR	PETROLEUM	PEYOTISM	PHANTASIED	PHELONIONS
PETARA	PETROLEUMS	PEYOTISMS	PHANTASIES	PHENACITE
PETARAS	PETROLEUR	PEYOTIST	PHANTASIM	PHENACITES
PETARD	PETROLEURS	PEYOTISTS	PHANTASIMS	PHENAKISM
PETARDS	PETROLIC	PEYSE	PHANTASM	PHENAKISMS
PETARIES	PETROLLED	PEYSED	PHANTASMA	PHENAKITE
PETARS	PETROLLING	PEYSES	PHANTASMATA	PHENAKITES
PETARY	PETROLOGIES	PEYSING	PHANTASMS	PHENATE
PETASUS	PETROLOGY	PEZANT	PHANTASY	PHENATES
PETASUSES	PETROLS	PEZANTS	PHANTASYING	PHENE
PETAURINE	PETRONEL	PEZIZOID	PHANTOM	PHENES
PETAURIST	PETRONELS	PFENNIG	PHANTOMS	PHENETIC
PETAURISTS	PETROSAL	PFENNIGE	PHANTOMY	PHENETICS
PETCHARIES	PETROSALS	PFENNIGS	PHANTOSME	PHENGITE
PETCHARY	PETROUS	PFENNING	PHANTOSMES	PHENGITES

PHENIC	PHILTER	PHONECARDS	PHOSGENES	PHOTOTYPY
PHENOGAM	PHILTERS	PHONED	PHOSPHATE	PHOTS
PHENOGAMS	PHILTRE	PHONEME	PHOSPHATED	PHRASAL
PHENOL	PHILTRES	PHONEMES	PHOSPHATES	PHRASE
PHENOLATE	PHIMOSES	PHONEMIC	PHOSPHATING	PHRASED
PHENOLATES	PHIMOSIS	PHONEMICS	PHOSPHENE	PHRASEMAN
PHENOLIC	PHINNOCK	PHONER	PHOSPHENES	PHRASEMEN
PHENOLOGIES	PHINNOCKS	PHONERS	PHOSPHIDE	PHRASER
PHENOLOGY	PHIS	PHONES	PHOSPHIDES	PHRASERS
PHENOLS	PHISNOMIES	PHONETIC	PHOSPHINE	PHRASES
PHENOM	PHISNOMY	PHONETICS	PHOSPHINES	PHRASIER
PHENOMENA	PHIZ	PHONETISE	PHOSPHITE	PHRASIEST
PHENOMS	PHIZOG	PHONETISED	PHOSPHITES	PHRASING
PHENOTYPE	PHIZOGS	PHONETISES	PHOSPHOR	PHRASINGS
PHENOTYPED	PHIZZES	PHONETISING	PHOSPHORS	PHRASY
PHENOTYPES	PHLEBITIS	PHONETISM	PHOT	PHRATRIES
PHENOTYPING	PHLEBITISES	PHONETISMS	PHOTIC	PHRATRY
PHENYL	PHLEGM	PHONETIST	PHOTICS	PHREAK
PHENYLIC	PHLEGMIER	PHONETISTS	PHOTINIA	PHREAKING
PHENYLS	PHLEGMIEST	PHONETIZE	PHOTINIAS	PHREAKINGS
PHEON	PHLEGMON	PHONETIZED	PHOTISM	PHREAKS
PHEONS	PHLEGMONS	PHONETIZES	PHOTISMS	PHREATIC
PHEROMONE	PHLEGMS	PHONETIZING	PHOTO	PHRENESES
PHEROMONES	PHLEGMY	PHONEY	PHOTOCELL	PHRENESIS
PHESE	PHLOEM	PHONEYED	PHOTOCELLS	PHRENETIC
PHESED	PHLOEMS	PHONEYING	PHOTOCOPIED	PHRENETICS
PHESES	PHLOMIS	PHONEYS	PHOTOCOPIES	PHRENIC
PHESING	PHLOMISES	PHONIC	PHOTOCOPY	PHRENISM
PHEW	PHLOX	PHONICS	PHOTOCOPYING	PHRENISMS
PHI	PHLOXES	PHONIED	PHOTOCOPYINGS	PHRENITIC
PHIAL	PHLYCTENA	PHONIER	PHOTOED	PHRENITIS
PHIALLED	PHLYCTENAE	PHONIES	PHOTOFIT	PHRENITISES
PHIALLING	PHO	PHONIEST	PHOTOFITS	PHRENSIED
PHIALS	PHOBIA	PHONINESS	PHOTOGEN	PHRENSIES
PHILABEG	PHOBIAS	PHONINESSES	PHOTOGENE	PHRENSY
PHILABEGS	PHOBIC	PHONING	PHOTOGENES	PHRENSYING
PHILAMOT	PHOBICS	PHONMETER	PHOTOGENIES	PHRENTICK
PHILAMOTS	PHOBISM	PHONMETERS	PHOTOGENS	PHS
PHILANDER	PHOBISMS	PHONOGRAM	PHOTOGENY	PHTHALATE
PHILANDERED	PHOBIST	PHONOGRAMS	PHOTOGRAM	PHTHALATES
PHILANDERING	PHOBISTS	PHONOLITE	PHOTOGRAMS	PHTHALEIN
PHILANDERS	PHOCA	PHONOLITES	PHOTOING	PHTHALEINS
PHILATELIES	PHOCAE	PHONOLOGIES	PHOTOLYSE	PHTHALIC
PHILATELY	PHOCAS	PHONOLOGY	PHOTOLYSED	PHTHALIN
PHILHORSE	PHOCINE	PHONON	PHOTOLYSES	PHTHALINS
PHILHORSES	PHOEBE	PHONONS	PHOTOLYSING	PHTHISES
PHILIBEG	PHOEBES	PHONOPORE	PHOTON	PHTHISIC
PHILIBEGS	PHOENIX	PHONOPORES	PHOTONICS	PHTHISICS
PHILIPPIC	PHOENIXES	PHONOTYPE	PHOTONS	PHTHISIS
PHILIPPICS	PHOH	PHONOTYPED	PHOTOPHIL	PHUT
PHILLABEG	PHOHS	PHONOTYPES	PHOTOPHILS	PHUTS
PHILLABEGS	PHOLADES	PHONOTYPIES	PHOTOPIA	PHUTTED
PHILLIBEG	PHOLAS	PHONOTYPING	PHOTOPIAS	PHUTTING
PHILLIBEGS	PHON	PHONOTYPY	PHOTOPIC	PHYCOCYAN
PHILOGYNIES	PHONAL	PHONS	PHOTOPSIA	PHYCOCYANS
PHILOGYNY	PHONATE	PHONY	PHOTOPSIAS	PHYCOLOGIES
PHILOLOGIES	PHONATED	PHONYING	PHOTOPSIES	PHYCOLOGY
PHILOLOGY	PHONATES	PHOOEY	PHOTOPSY	PHYLA
PHILOMATH	PHONATING	PHORMINGES	PHOTOS	PHYLAE
PHILOMATHS	PHONATION	PHORMINX	PHOTOTYPE	PHYLARCH
PHILOMOT	PHONATIONS	PHORMIUM	PHOTOTYPED	PHYLARCHIES
PHILOMOTS	PHONATORY	PHORMIUMS	PHOTOTYPES	PHYLARCHS
PHILOPENA	PHONE	PHOS	PHOTOTYPIES	PHYLARCHY
PHILOPENAS	PHONECARD	PHOSGENE	PHOTOTYPING	PHYLE

The Chambers Dictionary is the authority for many longer words; see *OSW* Introduction, page xii

PHYLETIC	PIANETTE	PICKADILL	PICQUETS	PIEING
PHYLLARIES	PIANETTES	PICKADILLS	PICRA	PIEMAN
PHYLLARY	PIANINO	PICKAPACK	PICRAS	PIEMEN
PHYLLITE	PIANINOS	PICKAPACKS	PICRATE	PIEND
PHYLLITES	PIANISM	PICKAXE	PICRATES	PIENDS
PHYLLO	PIANISMS	PICKAXES	PICRIC	PIEPOWDER
PHYLLODE	PIANIST	PICKBACK	PICRITE	PIEPOWDERS
PHYLLODES	PIANISTE	PICKBACKS	PICRITES	PIER
PHYLLODIES	PIANISTES	PICKED	PICS	PIERAGE
PHYLLODY	PIANISTIC	PICKEER	PICTARNIE	PIERAGES
PHYLLOID	PIANISTS	PICKEERED	PICTARNIES	PIERCE
PHYLLOME	PIANO	PICKEERER	PICTOGRAM	PIERCED
PHYLLOMES	PIANOLIST	PICKEERERS	PICTOGRAMS	PIERCER
PHYLLOPOD	PIANOLISTS	PICKEERING	PICTORIAL	PIERCERS
PHYLLOPODS	PIANOS	PICKEERS	PICTORIALS	PIERCES
PHYLLOS	PIARIST	PICKER	PICTURAL	PIERCING
PHYLOGENIES	PIARISTS	PICKEREL	PICTURALS	PIERCINGS
PHYLOGENY	PIAS	PICKERELS	PICTURE	PIERID
PHYLUM	PIASSABA	PICKERIES	PICTURED	PIERIDINE
PHYSALIA	PIASSABAS	PICKERS	PICTURES	PIERIDS
PHYSALIAS	PIASSAVA	PICKERY	PICTURING	PIERRETTE
PHYSALIS	PIASSAVAS	PICKET	PICUL	PIERRETTES
PHYSALISES	PIASTRE	PICKETED	PICULS	PIERROT
PHYSETER	PIASTRES	PICKETER	PIDDLE	PIERROTS
PHYSETERS	PIAZZA	PICKETERS	PIDDLED	PIERS
PHYSIC	PIAZZAS	PICKETING	PIDDLER	PIERST
PHYSICAL	PIAZZIAN	PICKETS	PIDDLERS	PIERT
PHYSICALS	PIBROCH	PICKIER	PIDDLES	PIES
PHYSICIAN	PIBROCHS	PICKIEST	PIDDLING	PIET
PHYSICIANS	PIC	PICKING	PIDDOCK	PIETA
PHYSICISM	PICA	PICKINGS	PIDDOCKS	PIETAS
PHYSICISMS	PICADOR	PICKLE	PIDGEON	PIETIES
PHYSICIST	PICADORS	PICKLED	PIDGEONS	PIETISM
PHYSICISTS	PICAMAR	PICKLER	PIDGIN	PIETISMS
PHYSICKED	PICAMARS	PICKLERS	PIDGINS	PIETIST
PHYSICKING	PICARIAN	PICKLES	PIE	PIETISTIC
PHYSICKY	PICARIANS	PICKLING	PIEBALD	PIETISTS
PHYSICS	PICAROON	PICKLOCK	PIEBALDS	PIETS
PHYSIO	PICAROONS	PICKLOCKS	PIECE	PIETY
PHYSIOS	PICAS	PICKMAW	PIECED	PIEZO
PHYSIQUE	PICAYUNE	PICKMAWS	PIECELESS	PIFFERARI
PHYSIQUES	PICAYUNES	PICKS	PIECEMEAL	PIFFERARO
PHYTOGENIES	PICCADELL	PICKY	PIECEMEALED	PIFFERO
PHYTOGENY	PICCADELLS	PICNIC	PIECEMEALING	PIFFEROS
PHYTOLOGIES	PICCADILL	PICNICKED	PIECEMEALS	PIFFLE
PHYTOLOGY	PICCADILLS	PICNICKER	PIECEN	PIFFLED
PHYTON	PICCANIN	PICNICKERS	PIECENED	PIFFLER
PHYTONS	PICCANINS	PICNICKING	PIECENER	PIFFLERS
PHYTOSES	PICCIES	PICNICKY	PIECENERS	PIFFLES
PHYTOSIS	PICCOLO	PICNICS	PIECENING	PIFFLING
PHYTOTOMIES	PICCOLOS	PICOCURIE	PIECENS	PIG
PHYTOTOMY	PICCY	PICOCURIES	PIECER	PIGBOAT
PHYTOTRON	PICE	PICOT	PIECERS	PIGBOATS
PHYTOTRONS	PICENE	PICOTE	PIECES	PIGEON
PI	PICENES	PICOTED	PIECING	PIGEONED
PIA	PICEOUS	PICOTEE	PIECRUST	PIGEONING
PIACEVOLE	PICHURIM	PICOTEES	PIECRUSTS	PIGEONRIES
PIACULAR	PICHURIMS	PICOTING	PIED	PIGEONRY
PIAFFE	PICINE	PICOTITE	PIEDISH	PIGEONS
PIAFFED	PICK	PICOTITES	PIEDISHES	PIGFEED
PIAFFER	PICKABACK	PICOTS	PIEDMONT	PIGFEEDS
PIAFFERS	PICKABACKS	PICQUET	PIEDMONTS	PIGGED
PIAFFES	PICKADELL	PICQUETED	PIEDNESS	PIGGERIES
PIAFFING	PICKADELLS	PICQUETING	PIEDNESSES	PIGGERY

PIGGIE	PIGWASHES	PILFERY	PILOTAGE	PINCHBECK
PIGGIER	PIGWEED	PILGRIM	PILOTAGES	PINCHBECKS
PIGGIES	PIGWEEDS	PILGRIMER	PILOTED	PINCHCOCK
PIGGIEST	PIKA	PILGRIMERS	PILOTING	PINCHCOCKS
PIGGIN	PIKAS	PILGRIMS	PILOTIS	PINCHED
PIGGING	PIKE	PILHORSE	PILOTLESS	PINCHER
PIGGINGS	PIKED	PILHORSES	PILOTMAN	PINCHERS
PIGGINS	PIKELET	PILI	PILOTMEN	PINCHES
PIGGISH	PIKELETS	PILIFORM	PILOTS	PINCHFIST
PIGGISHLY	PIKEMAN	PILING	PILOUS	PINCHFISTS
PIGGY	PIKEMEN	PILINGS	PILOW	PINCHGUT
PIGGYBACK	PIKER	PILIS	PILOWS	PINCHGUTS
PIGGYBACKS	PIKERS	PILL	PILSENER	PINCHING
PIGHEADED	PIKES	PILLAGE	PILSENERS	PINCHINGS
PIGHT	PIKESTAFF	PILLAGED	PILSNER	PINDAREE
PIGHTED	PIKESTAFFS	PILLAGER	PILSNERS	PINDAREES
PIGHTING	PIKING	PILLAGERS	PILULA	PINDARI
PIGHTLE	PIKUL	PILLAGES	PILULAR	PINDARIS
PIGHTLES	PIKULS	PILLAGING	PILULAS	PINDER
PIGHTS	PILA	PILLAR	PILULE	PINDERS
PIGLET	PILAFF	PILLARIST	PILULES	PINDOWN
PIGLETS	PILAFFS	PILLARISTS	PILUM	PINDOWNS
PIGLING	PILASTER	PILLARS	PILUS	PINE
PIGLINGS	PILASTERS	PILLAU	PIMENT	PINEAL
PIGMAEAN	PILAU	PILLAUS	PIMENTO	PINEAPPLE
PIGMEAN	PILAUS	PILLED	PIMENTOS	PINEAPPLES
PIGMEAT	PILAW	PILLHEAD	PIMENTS	PINED
PIGMEATS	PILAWS	PILLHEADS	PIMIENTO	PINERIES
PIGMENT	PILCH	PILLICOCK	PIMIENTOS	PINERY
PIGMENTAL	PILCHARD	PILLICOCKS	PIMP	PINES
PIGMENTED	PILCHARDS	PILLING	PIMPED	PINETA
PIGMENTS	PILCHER	PILLINGS	PIMPERNEL	PINETUM
PIGMIES	PILCHERS	PILLION	PIMPERNELS	PINEWOOD
PIGMOID	PILCHES	PILLIONED	PIMPING	PINEWOODS
PIGMY	PILCORN	PILLIONING	PIMPLE	PINEY
PIGNERATE	PILCORNS	PILLIONS	PIMPLED	PINFISH
PIGNERATED	PILCROW	PILLOCK	PIMPLES	PINFISHES
PIGNERATES	PILCROWS	PILLOCKS	PIMPLIER	PINFOLD
PIGNERATING	PILE	PILLORIED	PIMPLIEST	PINFOLDED
PIGNORATE	PILEA	PILLORIES	PIMPLY	PINFOLDING
PIGNORATED	PILEATE	PILLORISE	PIMPS	PINFOLDS
PIGNORATES	PILEATED	PILLORISED	PIN	PING
PIGNORATING	PILED	PILLORISES	PINA	PINGED
PIGNUT	PILEI	PILLORISING	PINACOID	PINGER
PIGNUTS	PILEOUS	PILLORIZE	PINACOIDS	PINGERS
PIGPEN	PILER	PILLORIZED	PINAFORE	PINGING
PIGPENS	PILERS	PILLORIZES	PINAFORED	PINGLE
PIGS	PILES	PILLORIZING	PINAFORES	PINGLED
PIGSCONCE	PILEUM	PILLORY	PINAKOID	PINGLER
PIGSCONCES	PILEUS	PILLORYING	PINAKOIDS	PINGLERS
PIGSKIN	PILEWORK	PILLOW	PINAS	PINGLES
PIGSKINS	PILEWORKS	PILLOWED	PINASTER	PINGLING
PIGSNEY	PILEWORT	PILLOWING	PINASTERS	PINGO
PIGSNEYS	PILEWORTS	PILLOWS	PINATA	PINGOES
PIGSNIE	PILFER	PILLOWY	PINATAS	PINGOS
PIGSNIES	PILFERAGE	PILLS	PINBALL	PINGS
PIGSNY	PILFERAGES	PILLWORM	PINBALLS	PINGUEFIED
PIGSTIES	PILFERED	PILLWORMS	PINCASE	PINGUEFIES
PIGSTY	PILFERER	PILLWORT	PINCASES	PINGUEFY
PIGSWILL	PILFERERS	PILLWORTS	PINCER	PINGUEFYING
PIGSWILLS	PILFERIES	PILOSE	PINCERED	PINGUID
PIGTAIL	PILFERING	PILOSITIES	PINCERING	PINGUIN
PIGTAILS	PILFERINGS	PILOSITY	PINCERS	PINGUINS
PIGWASH	PILFERS	PILOT	PINCH	PINHEAD

PINHEADS	PINNOCKS	PIOYS	PIQUANCIES	PISCINAS
PINHOLE	PINNOED	PIP	PIQUANCY	PISCINE
PINHOLES	PINNULA	PIPA	PIQUANT	PISCINES
PINHOOKER	PINNULAS	PIPAGE	PIQUANTLY	PISE
PINHOOKERS	PINNULATE	PIPAGES	PIQUE	PISES
PINIER	PINNULE	PIPAL	PIQUED	PISH
PINIES	PINNULES	PIPALS	PIQUES	PISHED
PINIEST	PINNY	PIPAS	PIQUET	PISHES
PINING	PINOCHLE	PIPE	PIQUETED	PISHING
PINION	PINOCHLES	PIPECLAY	PIQUETING	PISHOGUE
PINIONED	PINOCLE	PIPECLAYED	PIQUETS	PISHOGUES
PINIONING	PINOCLES	PIPECLAYING	PIQUING	PISIFORM
PINIONS	PINOLE	PIPECLAYS	PIR	PISIFORMS
PINITE	PINOLES	PIPED	PIRACIES	PISKIES
PINITES	PINON	PIPEFISH	PIRACY	PISKY
PINK	PINONS	PIPEFISHES	PIRAGUA	PISMIRE
PINKED	PINOT	PIPEFUL	PIRAGUAS	PISMIRES
PINKER	PINOTS	PIPEFULS	PIRAI	PISOLITE
PINKERTON	PINPOINT	PIPELESS	PIRAIS	PISOLITES
PINKERTONS	PINPOINTED	PIPELIKE	PIRANA	PISOLITIC
PINKEST	PINPOINTING	PIPELINE	PIRANAS	PISS
PINKIE	PINPOINTS	PIPELINES	PIRANHA	PISSED
PINKIER	PINS	PIPER	PIRANHAS	PISSES
PINKIES	PINT	PIPERIC	PIRARUCU	PISSHEAD
PINKIEST	PINTA	PIPERINE	PIRARUCUS	PISSHEADS
PINKINESS	PINTABLE	PIPERINES	PIRATE	PISSING
PINKINESSES	PINTABLES	PIPERONAL	PIRATED	PISSOIR
PINKING	PINTADO	PIPERONALS	PIRATES	PISSOIRS
PINKINGS	PINTADOS	PIPERS	PIRATIC	PISTACHIO
PINKISH	PINTAIL	PIPES	PIRATICAL	PISTACHIOS
PINKNESS	PINTAILED	PIPESTONE	PIRATING	PISTAREEN
PINKNESSES	PINTAILS	PIPESTONES	PIRAYA	PISTAREENS
PINKO	PINTAS	PIPETTE	PIRAYAS	PISTE
PINKOES	PINTLE	PIPETTED	PIRL	PISTES
PINKOS	PINTLES	PIPETTES	PIRLICUE	PISTIL
PINKROOT	PINTO	PIPETTING	PIRLICUED	PISTILS
PINKROOTS	PINTOS	PIPEWORK	PIRLICUES	PISTOL
PINKS	PINTS	PIPEWORKS	PIRLICUING	PISTOLE
PINKY	PINXIT	PIPEWORT	PIRLS	PISTOLEER
PINNA	PINY	PIPEWORTS	PIRN	PISTOLEERS
PINNACE	PIOLET	PIPI	PIRNIE	PISTOLES
PINNACES	PIOLETS	PIPIER	PIRNIES	PISTOLET
PINNACLE	PION	PIPIEST	PIRNIT	PISTOLETS
PINNACLED	PIONED	PIPING	PIRNS	PISTOLLED
PINNACLES	PIONEER	PIPINGS	PIROGUE	PISTOLLING
PINNACLING	PIONEERED	PIPIS	PIROGUES	PISTOLS
PINNAE	PIONEERING	PIPIT	PIROSHKI	PISTON
PINNATE	PIONEERS	PIPITS	PIROUETTE	PISTONS
PINNATED	PIONER	PIPKIN	PIROUETTED	PIT
PINNATELY	PIONERS	PIPKINS	PIROUETTES	PITA
PINNED	PIONEY	PIPLESS	PIROUETTING	PITAPAT
PINNER	PIONEYS	PIPPED	PIROZHKI	PITAPATS
PINNERS	PIONIC	PIPPIER	PIRS	PITAPATTED
PINNET	PIONIES	PIPPIEST	PIS	PITAPATTING
PINNETS	PIONING	PIPPIN	PISCARIES	PITARA
PINNIE	PIONINGS	PIPPING	PISCARY	PITARAH
PINNIES	PIONS	PIPPINS	PISCATOR	PITARAHS
PINNING	PIONY	PIPPY	PISCATORS	PITARAS
PINNINGS	PIOTED	PIPS	PISCATORY	PITAS
PINNIPED	PIOUS	PIPSQUEAK	PISCATRIX	PITCH
PINNIPEDE	PIOUSLY	PIPSQUEAKS	PISCATRIXES	PITCHED
PINNIPEDES	PIOY	PIPUL	PISCIFORM	PITCHER
PINNIPEDS	PIOYE	PIPULS	PISCINA	PITCHERS
PINNOCK	PIOYES	PIPY	PISCINAE	PITCHES

PITCHFORK	PITTERS	PLACATIONS	PLAGUY	PLANETIC
PITCHFORKED	PITTING	PLACATORY	PLAICE	PLANETOID
PITCHFORKING	PITTINGS	PLACCAT	PLAICES	PLANETOIDS
PITCHFORKS	PITTITE	PLACCATE	PLAID	PLANETS
PITCHIER	PITTITES	PLACCATES	PLAIDED	PLANGENCIES
PITCHIEST	PITUITA	PLACCATS	PLAIDING	PLANGENCY
PITCHING	PITUITARY	PLACE	PLAIDINGS	PLANGENT
PITCHINGS	PITUITAS	PLACEBO	PLAIDMAN	PLANING
PITCHMAN	PITUITE	PLACEBOES	PLAIDMEN	PLANISH
PITCHMEN	PITUITES	PLACEBOS	PLAIDS	PLANISHED
PITCHPINE	PITUITRIN	PLACED	PLAIN	PLANISHER
PITCHPINES	PITUITRINS	PLACELESS	PLAINANT	PLANISHERS
PITCHPIPE	PITURI	PLACEMAN	PLAINANTS	PLANISHES
PITCHPIPES	PITURIS	PLACEMEN	PLAINED	PLANISHING
PITCHY	PITY	PLACEMENT	PLAINER	PLANK
PITEOUS	PITYING	PLACEMENTS	PLAINEST	PLANKED
PITEOUSLY	PITYINGLY	PLACENTA	PLAINFUL	PLANKING
PITFALL	PITYROID	PLACENTAE	PLAINING	PLANKINGS
PITFALLS	PIU	PLACENTAL	PLAININGS	PLANKS
PITH	PIUM	PLACENTALS	PLAINISH	PLANKTON
PITHBALL	PIUMS	PLACENTAS	PLAINLY	PLANKTONS
PITHBALLS	PIUPIU	PLACER	PLAINNESS	PLANLESS
PITHEAD	PIUPIUS	PLACERS	PLAINNESSES	PLANNED
PITHEADS	PIVOT	PLACES	PLAINS	PLANNER
PITHECOID	PIVOTAL	PLACET	PLAINSMAN	PLANNERS
PITHED	PIVOTALLY	PLACETS	PLAINSMEN	PLANNING
PITHFUL	PIVOTED	PLACID	PLAINSONG	PLANS
PITHIER	PIVOTER	PLACIDER	PLAINSONGS	PLANT
PITHIEST	PIVOTERS	PLACIDEST	PLAINT	PLANTA
PITHILY	PIVOTING	PLACIDITIES	PLAINTFUL	PLANTABLE
PITHINESS	PIVOTINGS	PLACIDITY	PLAINTIFF	PLANTAGE
PITHINESSES	PIVOTS	PLACIDLY	PLAINTIFFS	PLANTAGES
PITHING	PIX	PLACING	PLAINTIVE	PLANTAIN
PITHLESS	PIXEL	PLACINGS	PLAINTS	PLANTAINS
PITHLIKE	PIXELS	PLACIT	PLAINWORK	PLANTAR
PITHOI	PIXES	PLACITA	PLAINWORKS	PLANTAS
PITHOS	PIXIE	PLACITORY	PLAISTER	PLANTED
PITHS	PIXIES	PLACITS	PLAISTERS	PLANTER
PITHY	PIXILATED	PLACITUM	PLAIT	PLANTERS
PITIABLE	PIXY	PLACK	PLAITED	PLANTING
PITIABLY	PIZAZZ	PLACKET	PLAITER	PLANTINGS
PITIED	PIZAZZES	PLACKETS	PLAITERS	PLANTLESS
PITIER	PIZE	PLACKLESS	PLAITING	PLANTLET
PITIERS	PIZES	PLACKS	PLAITINGS	PLANTLETS
PITIES	PIZZA	PLACODERM	PLAITS	PLANTLING
PITIFUL	PIZZAIOLA	PLACODERMS	PLAN	PLANTLINGS
PITIFULLY	PIZZAS	PLACOID	PLANAR	PLANTS
PITILESS	PIZZERIA	PLAFOND	PLANARIAN	PLANTSMAN
PITMAN	PIZZERIAS	PLAFONDS	PLANARIANS	PLANTSMEN
PITMEN	PIZZICATO	PLAGAL	PLANATION	PLANTULE
PITON	PIZZICATOS	PLAGE	PLANATIONS	PLANTULES
PITONS	PIZZLE	PLAGES	PLANCH	PLANULA
PITPROP	PIZZLES	PLAGIARIES	PLANCHED	PLANULAE
PITPROPS	PLACABLE	PLAGIARY	PLANCHES	PLANULAR
PITS	PLACABLY	PLAGIUM	PLANCHET	PLANULOID
PITTA	PLACARD	PLAGIUMS	PLANCHETS	PLANURIA
PITTANCE	PLACARDED	PLAGUE	PLANCHING	PLANURIAS
PITTANCES	PLACARDING	PLAGUED	PLANE	PLANURIES
PITTAS	PLACARDS	PLAGUES	PLANED	PLANURY
PITTED	PLACATE	PLAGUEY	PLANER	PLANXTIES
PITTEN	PLACATED	PLAGUIER	PLANERS	PLANXTY
PITTER	PLACATES	PLAGUIEST	PLANES	PLAP
PITTERED	PLACATING	PLAGUILY	PLANET	PLAPPED
PITTERING	PLACATION	PLAGUING	PLANETARY	PLAPPING

PLAPS	PLATEAUX	PLAY	PLEASANTER	PLENARTY
PLAQUE	PLATED	PLAYA	PLEASANTEST	PLENARY
PLAQUES	PLATEFUL	PLAYABLE	PLEASE	PLENILUNE
PLAQUETTE	PLATEFULS	PLAYAS	PLEASED	PLENILUNES
PLAQUETTES	PLATELET	PLAYBACK	PLEASEMAN	PLENIPO
PLASH	PLATELETS	PLAYBACKS	PLEASEMEN	PLENIPOES
PLASHED	PLATEMAN	PLAYBILL	PLEASER	PLENIPOS
PLASHES	PLATEMARK	PLAYBILLS	PLEASERS	PLENISH
PLASHET	PLATEMARKS	PLAYBOOK	PLEASES	PLENISHED
PLASHETS	PLATEMEN	PLAYBOOKS	PLEASETH	PLENISHES
PLASHIER	PLATEN	PLAYBOY	PLEASING	PLENISHING
PLASHIEST	PLATENS	PLAYBOYS	PLEASINGS	PLENISHINGS
PLASHING	PLATER	PLAYBUS®	PLEASURE	PLENIST
PLASHINGS	PLATERS	PLAYBUSES	PLEASURED	PLENISTS
PLASHY	PLATES	PLAYBUSSES	PLEASURER	PLENITUDE
PLASM	PLATFORM	PLAYED	PLEASURERS	PLENITUDES
PLASMA	PLATFORMED	PLAYER	PLEASURES	PLENTEOUS
PLASMAS	PLATFORMING	PLAYERS	PLEASURING	PLENTIES
PLASMATIC	PLATFORMINGS	PLAYFUL	PLEAT	PLENTIFUL
PLASMIC	PLATFORMS	PLAYFULLY	PLEATED	PLENTY
PLASMID	PLATIER	PLAYGIRL	PLEATER	PLENUM
PLASMIDS	PLATIEST	PLAYGIRLS	PLEATERS	PLENUMS
PLASMIN	PLATINA	PLAYGROUP	PLEATING	PLEON
PLASMINS	PLATINAS	PLAYGROUPS	PLEATS	PLEONASM
PLASMODIA	PLATING	PLAYHOUSE	PLEB	PLEONASMS
PLASMS	PLATINGS	PLAYHOUSES	PLEBBIER	PLEONAST
PLAST	PLATINIC	PLAYING	PLEBBIEST	PLEONASTE
PLASTE	PLATINISE	PLAYLET	PLEBBY	PLEONASTES
PLASTER	PLATINISED	PLAYLETS	PLEBEAN	PLEONASTS
PLASTERED	PLATINISES	PLAYMATE	PLEBEIAN	PLEONEXIA
PLASTERER	PLATINISING	PLAYMATES	PLEBEIANS	PLEONEXIAS
PLASTERERS	PLATINIZE	PLAYPEN	PLEBES	PLEONS
PLASTERING	PLATINIZED	PLAYPENS	PLEBIFIED	PLEOPOD
PLASTERINGS	PLATINIZES	PLAYROOM	PLEBIFIES	PLEOPODS
PLASTERS	PLATINIZING	PLAYROOMS	PLEBIFY	PLEROMA
PLASTERY	PLATINOID	PLAYS	PLEBIFYING	PLEROMAS
PLASTIC	PLATINOIDS	PLAYSOME	PLEBS	PLEROME
PLASTICKY	PLATINOUS	PLAYSUIT	PLECTRA	PLEROMES
PLASTICS	PLATINUM	PLAYSUITS	PLECTRE	PLESH
PLASTID	PLATINUMS	PLAYTHING	PLECTRES	PLESHES
PLASTIDS	PLATITUDE	PLAYTHINGS	PLECTRON	PLESSOR
PLASTIQUE	PLATITUDES	PLAYTIME	PLECTRONS	PLESSORS
PLASTIQUES	PLATONIC	PLAYTIMES	PLECTRUM	PLETHORA
PLASTISOL	PLATONICS	PLAZA	PLECTRUMS	PLETHORAS
PLASTISOLS	PLATOON	PLAZAS	PLED	PLETHORIC
PLASTRAL	PLATOONS	PLEA	PLEDGE	PLEUCH
PLASTRON	PLATS	PLEACH	PLEDGED	PLEUCHS
PLASTRONS	PLATTED	PLEACHED	PLEDGEE	PLEUGH
PLAT	PLATTER	PLEACHES	PLEDGEES	PLEUGHS
PLATAN	PLATTERS	PLEACHING	PLEDGEOR	PLEURA
PLATANE	PLATTING	PLEAD	PLEDGEORS	PLEURAE
PLATANES	PLATTINGS	PLEADABLE	PLEDGER	PLEURAL
PLATANNA	PLATY	PLEADED	PLEDGERS	PLEURISIES
PLATANNAS	PLATYPUS	PLEADER~	PLEDGES	PLEURISY
PLATANS	PLATYPUSES	PLEADERS	PLEDGET	PLEURITIC
PLATBAND	PLATYSMA	PLEADING	PLEDGETS	PLEURITICS
PLATBANDS	PLATYSMAS	PLEADINGS	PLEDGING	PLEURITIS
PLATE	PLAUDIT	PLEADS	PLEDGOR	PLEURITISES
PLATEASM	PLAUDITE	PLEAED	PLEDGORS	PLEURON
PLATEASMS	PLAUDITS	PLEAING	PLEIOMERIES	PLEXIFORM
PLATEAU	PLAUSIBLE	PLEAS	PLEIOMERY	PLEXOR
PLATEAUED	PLAUSIBLY	PLEASANCE	PLENA	PLEXORS
PLATEAUING	PLAUSIVE	PLEASANCES	PLENARILY	PLEXURE
PLATEAUS	PLAUSTRAL	PLEASANT	PLENARTIES	PLEXURES

PLEXUS	PLOIDIES	PLOUTERING	PLUMBS	PLUNGE
PLEXUSES	PLOIDY	PLOUTERS	PLUMBUM	PLUNGED
PLIABLE	PLONG	PLOVER	PLUMBUMS	PLUNGER
PLIABLY	PLONGD	PLOVERS	PLUMCOT	PLUNGERS
PLIANCIES	PLONGE	PLOVERY	PLUMCOTS	PLUNGES
PLIANCY	PLONGED	PLOW	PLUMDAMAS	PLUNGING
PLIANT	PLONGES	PLOWED	PLUMDAMASES	PLUNGINGS
PLIANTLY	PLONGING	PLOWING	PLUME	PLUNK
PLICA	PLONGS	PLOWS	PLUMED	PLUNKED
PLICAE	PLONK	PLOWTER	PLUMELESS	PLUNKER
PLICAL	PLONKED	PLOWTERED	PLUMELET	PLUNKERS
PLICATE	PLONKER	PLOWTERING	PLUMELETS	PLUNKING
PLICATED	PLONKERS	PLOWTERS	PLUMERIES	PLUNKS
PLICATELY	PLONKIER	PLOY	PLUMERY	PLURAL
PLICATES	PLONKIEST	PLOYS	PLUMES	PLURALISE
PLICATING	PLONKING	PLUCK	PLUMIER	PLURALISED
PLICATION	PLONKINGS	PLUCKED	PLUMIEST	PLURALISES
PLICATIONS	PLONKS	PLUCKER	PLUMING	PLURALISING
PLICATURE	PLONKY	PLUCKERS	PLUMIPED	PLURALISM
PLICATURES	PLOOK	PLUCKIER	PLUMIST	PLURALISMS
PLIE	PLOOKIE	PLUCKIEST	PLUMISTS	PLURALIST
PLIED	PLOOKIER	PLUCKILY	PLUMMET	PLURALISTS
PLIER	PLOOKIEST	PLUCKING	PLUMMETED	PLURALITIES
PLIERS	PLOOKS	PLUCKS	PLUMMETING	PLURALITY
PLIES	PLOP	PLUCKY	PLUMMETS	PLURALIZE
PLIGHT	PLOPPED	PLUFF	PLUMMIER	PLURALIZED
PLIGHTED	PLOPPING	PLUFFED	PLUMMIEST	PLURALIZES
PLIGHTER	PLOPS	PLUFFIER	PLUMMY	PLURALIZING
PLIGHTERS	PLOSION	PLUFFIEST	PLUMOSE	PLURALLY
PLIGHTFUL	PLOSIONS	PLUFFING	PLUMOUS	PLURALS
PLIGHTING	PLOSIVE	PLUFFS	PLUMP	PLURIPARA
PLIGHTS	PLOSIVES	PLUFFY	PLUMPED	PLURIPARAE
PLIM	PLOT	PLUG	PLUMPEN	PLURIPARAS
PLIMMED	PLOTFUL	PLUGGED	PLUMPENED	PLURISIE
PLIMMING	PLOTLESS	PLUGGER	PLUMPENING	PLURISIES
PLIMS	PLOTS	PLUGGERS	PLUMPENS	PLUS
PLIMSOLE	PLOTTED	PLUGGING	PLUMPER	PLUSAGE
PLIMSOLES	PLOTTER	PLUGGINGS	PLUMPERS	PLUSAGES
PLIMSOLL	PLOTTERED	PLUGS	PLUMPEST	PLUSED
PLIMSOLLS	PLOTTERING	PLUM	PLUMPIE	PLUSES
PLING	PLOTTERS	PLUMAGE	PLUMPIER	PLUSH
PLINGS	PLOTTIE	PLUMAGED	PLUMPIEST	PLUSHER
PLINK	PLOTTIES	PLUMAGES	PLUMPING	PLUSHES
PLINKED	PLOTTING	PLUMATE	PLUMPISH	PLUSHEST
PLINKING	PLOTTINGS	PLUMB	PLUMPLY	PLUSHIER
PLINKS	PLOTTY	PLUMBAGO	PLUMPNESS	PLUSHIEST
PLINTH	PLOUGH	PLUMBAGOS	PLUMPNESSES	PLUSHY
PLINTHS	PLOUGHBOY	PLUMBATE	PLUMPS	PLUSING
PLIOSAUR	PLOUGHBOYS	PLUMBATES	PLUMPY	PLUSSAGE
PLIOSAURS	PLOUGHED	PLUMBED	PLUMS	PLUSSAGES
PLISKIE	PLOUGHER	PLUMBEOUS	PLUMULA	PLUSSED
PLISKIES	PLOUGHERS	PLUMBER	PLUMULAE	PLUSSES
PLISSE	PLOUGHING	PLUMBERIES	PLUMULAR	PLUSSING
PLOAT	PLOUGHINGS	PLUMBERS	PLUMULATE	PLUTEAL
PLOATED	PLOUGHMAN	PLUMBERY	PLUMULE	PLUTEUS
PLOATING	PLOUGHMEN	PLUMBIC	PLUMULES	PLUTEUSES
PLOATS	PLOUGHS	PLUMBING	PLUMULOSE	PLUTOCRAT
PLOD	PLOUK	PLUMBINGS	PLUMY	PLUTOCRATS
PLODDED	PLOUKIE	PLUMBISM	PLUNDER	PLUTOLOGIES
PLODDER	PLOUKIER	PLUMBISMS	PLUNDERED	PLUTOLOGY
PLODDERS	PLOUKIEST	PLUMBITE	PLUNDERER	PLUTON
PLODDING	PLOUKS	PLUMBITES	PLUNDERERS	PLUTONIC
PLODDINGS	PLOUTER	PLUMBLESS	PLUNDERING	PLUTONIUM
PLODS	PLOUTERED	PLUMBOUS	PLUNDERS	PLUTONIUMS

The Chambers Dictionary is the authority for many longer words; see *OSW* Introduction, page xii

PLUTONOMIES	POCKY	POETIC	POINTEDLY	POLARISES
PLUTONOMY	POCO	POETICAL	POINTEL	POLARISING
PLUTONS	POD	POETICALS	POINTELS	POLARITIES
PLUVIAL	PODAGRA	POETICISE	POINTER	POLARITY
PLUVIALS	PODAGRAL	POETICISED	POINTERS	POLARIZE
PLUVIOSE	PODAGRAS	POETICISES	POINTES	POLARIZED
PLUVIOUS	PODAGRIC	POETICISING	POINTIER	POLARIZER
PLY	PODAGROUS	POETICISM	POINTIEST	POLARIZERS
PLYING	PODAL	POETICISMS	POINTILLE	POLARIZES
PLYWOOD	PODALIC	POETICIZE	POINTING	POLARIZING
PLYWOODS	PODARGUS	POETICIZED	POINTINGS	POLARON
PNEUMA	PODARGUSES	POETICIZES	POINTLESS	POLARONS
PNEUMAS	PODDED	POETICIZING	POINTS	POLARS
PNEUMATIC	PODDIER	POETICS	POINTSMAN	POLDER
PNEUMATICS	PODDIES	POETICULE	POINTSMEN	POLDERED
PNEUMONIA	PODDIEST	POETICULES	POINTY	POLDERING
PNEUMONIAS	PODDING	POETISE	POIS	POLDERS
PNEUMONIC	PODDY	POETISED	POISE	POLE
PNEUMONICS	PODESTA	POETISES	POISED	POLECAT
PO	PODESTAS	POETISING	POISER	POLECATS
POA	PODEX	POETIZE	POISERS	POLED
POACEOUS	PODEXES	POETIZED	POISES	POLEMARCH
POACH	PODGE	POETIZES	POISING	POLEMARCHS
POACHED	PODGES	POETIZING	POISON	POLEMIC
POACHER	PODGIER	POETRESSE	POISONED	POLEMICAL
POACHERS	PODGIEST	POETRESSES	POISONER	POLEMICS
POACHES	PODGINESS	POETRIES	POISONERS	POLEMISE
POACHIER	PODGINESSES	POETRY	POISONING	POLEMISED
POACHIEST	PODGY	POETS	POISONOUS	POLEMISES
POACHING	PODIA	POETSHIP	POISONS	POLEMISING
POACHINGS	PODIAL	POETSHIPS	POISSON	POLEMIST
POACHY	PODIATRIES	POFFLE	POISSONS	POLEMISTS
POAKA	PODIATRY	POFFLES	POITREL	POLEMIZE
POAKAS	PODITE	POGGE	POITRELS	POLEMIZED
POAKE	PODITES	POGGES	POKAL	POLEMIZES
POAKES	PODIUM	POGO	POKALS	POLEMIZING
POAS	PODLEY	POGOED	POKE	POLENTA
POCHARD	PODLEYS	POGOING	POKEBERRIES	POLENTAS
POCHARDS	PODOCARP	POGOS	POKEBERRY	POLER
POCHAY	PODOCARPS	POGROM	POKED	POLERS
POCHAYS	PODOLOGIES	POGROMS	POKEFUL	POLES
POCHETTE	PODOLOGY	POH	POKEFULS	POLEY
POCHETTES	PODS	POI	POKER	POLEYN
POCHOIR	PODSOL	POIGNADO	POKERISH	POLEYNS
POCHOIRS	PODSOLIC	POIGNADOES	POKERS	POLEYS
POCK	PODSOLS	POIGNANCIES	POKES	POLIANITE
POCKARD	PODZOL	POIGNANCY	POKEWEED	POLIANITES
POCKARDS	PODZOLS	POIGNANT	POKEWEEDS	POLICE
POCKED	POEM	POILU	POKEY	POLICED
POCKET	POEMATIC	POILUS	POKEYS	POLICEMAN
POCKETED	POEMS	POINADO	POKIER	POLICEMEN
POCKETFUL	POENOLOGIES	POINADOES	POKIES	POLICES
POCKETFULS	POENOLOGY	POINCIANA	POKIEST	POLICIES
POCKETING	POESIED	POINCIANAS	POKING	POLICING
POCKETS	POESIES	POIND	POKY	POLICY
POCKIER	POESY	POINDED	POLACCA	POLING
POCKIEST	POESYING	POINDER	POLACCAS	POLINGS
POCKMANKIES	POET	POINDERS	POLACRE	POLIO
POCKMANKY	POETASTER	POINDING	POLACRES	POLIOS
POCKMARK	POETASTERS	POINDINGS	POLAR	POLISH
POCKMARKS	POETASTRIES	POINDS	POLARISE	POLISHED
POCKPIT	POETASTRY	POINT	POLARISED	POLISHER
POCKPITS	POETESS	POINTE	POLARISER	POLISHERS
POCKS	POETESSES	POINTED	POLARISERS	POLISHES

POLISHING	POLLIWIGS	POLYACT	POLYOMAS	POLYZOAN
POLISHINGS	POLLIWOG	POLYAMIDE	POLYOMINO	POLYZOANS
POLITE	POLLIWOGS	POLYAMIDES	POLYOMINOS	POLYZOARIES
POLITELY	POLLMAN	POLYANDRIES	POLYONYM	POLYZOARY
POLITER	POLLMEN	POLYANDRY	POLYONYMIES	POLYZOIC
POLITESSE	POLLOCK	POLYARCH	POLYONYMS	POLYZONAL
POLITESSES	POLLOCKS	POLYARCHIES	POLYONYMY	POLYZOOID
POLITEST	POLLS	POLYARCHY	POLYP	POLYZOON
POLITIC	POLLSTER	POLYAXIAL	POLYPARIES	POM
POLITICAL	POLLSTERS	POLYAXIALS	POLYPARY	POMACE
POLITICK	POLLUSION	POLYAXON	POLYPE	POMACEOUS
POLITICKED	POLLUSIONS	POLYAXONS	POLYPES	POMACES
POLITICKING	POLLUTANT	POLYBASIC	POLYPHAGIES	POMADE
POLITICKINGS	POLLUTANTS	POLYCONIC	POLYPHAGY	POMADED
POLITICKS	POLLUTE	POLYESTER	POLYPHASE	POMADES
POLITICLY	POLLUTED	POLYESTERS	POLYPHON	POMADING
POLITICO	POLLUTER	POLYGALA	POLYPHONE	POMANDER
POLITICOES	POLLUTERS	POLYGALAS	POLYPHONES	POMANDERS
POLITICOS	POLLUTES	POLYGAM	POLYPHONIES	POMATO
POLITICS	POLLUTING	POLYGAMIC	POLYPHONS	POMATOES
POLITIES	POLLUTION	POLYGAMIES	POLYPHONY	POMATUM
POLITIQUE	POLLUTIONS	POLYGAMS	POLYPI	POMATUMS
POLITIQUES	POLLUTIVE	POLYGAMY	POLYPIDE	POMBE
POLITY	POLLY	POLYGENE	POLYPIDES	POMBES
POLK	POLLYANNA	POLYGENES	POLYPIDOM	POME
POLKA	POLLYANNAS	POLYGENIC	POLYPIDOMS	POMELO
POLKAS	POLLYWIG	POLYGENIES	POLYPINE	POMELOS
POLKED	POLLYWIGS	POLYGENY	POLYPITE	POMEROY
POLKING	POLLYWOG	POLYGLOT	POLYPITES	POMEROYS
POLKS	POLLYWOGS	POLYGLOTS	POLYPLOID	POMES
POLL	POLO	POLYGLOTT	POLYPOD	POMFRET
POLLACK	POLOIDAL	POLYGLOTTS	POLYPODIES	POMFRETS
POLLACKS	POLOIST	POLYGON	POLYPODS	POMMEL
POLLAN	POLOISTS	POLYGONAL	POLYPODY	POMMELE
POLLANS	POLONAISE	POLYGONIES	POLYPOID	POMMELLED
POLLARD	POLONAISES	POLYGONS	POLYPOSES	POMMELLING
POLLARDED	POLONIE	POLYGONUM	POLYPOSIS	POMMELS
POLLARDING	POLONIES	POLYGONUMS	POLYPOUS	POMMETTY
POLLARDS	POLONISE	POLYGONY	POLYPS	POMMIES
POLLED	POLONISED	POLYGRAPH	POLYPTYCH	POMMY
POLLEN	POLONISES	POLYGRAPHS	POLYPTYCHS	POMOERIUM
POLLENED	POLONISING	POLYGYNIES	POLYPUS	POMOERIUMS
POLLENING	POLONISM	POLYGYNY	POLYS	POMOLOGIES
POLLENS	POLONISMS	POLYHEDRA	POLYSEME	POMOLOGY
POLLENT	POLONIUM	POLYLEMMA	POLYSEMES	POMP
POLLER	POLONIUMS	POLYLEMMAS	POLYSEMIES	POMPADOUR
POLLERS	POLONIZE	POLYMASTIES	POLYSEMY	POMPADOURS
POLLEX	POLONIZED	POLYMASTY	POLYSOME	POMPANO
POLLICAL	POLONIZES	POLYMATH	POLYSOMES	POMPANOS
POLLICES	POLONIZING	POLYMATHIES	POLYSOMIES	POMPELO
POLLICIE	POLONY	POLYMATHS	POLYSOMY	POMPELOS
POLLICIES	POLOS	POLYMATHY	POLYSTYLE	POMPEY
POLLICY	POLT	POLYMER	POLYTENE	POMPEYED
POLLIES	POLTED	POLYMERIC	POLYTHENE	POMPEYING
POLLINATE	POLTFEET	POLYMERIES	POLYTHENES	POMPEYS
POLLINATED	POLTFOOT	POLYMERS	POLYTONAL	POMPHOLYX
POLLINATES	POLTING	POLYMERY	POLYTYPIC	POMPHOLYXES
POLLINATING	POLTROON	POLYMORPH	POLYURIA	POMPIER
POLLING	POLTROONS	POLYMORPHS	POLYURIAS	POMPION
POLLINGS	POLTS	POLYNIA	POLYVINYL	POMPIONS
POLLINIA	POLVERINE	POLYNIAS	POLYVINYLS	POMPOM
POLLINIC	POLVERINES	POLYNYA	POLYWATER	POMPOMS
POLLINIUM	POLY	POLYNYAS	POLYWATERS	POMPON
POLLIWIG	POLYACID	POLYOMA	POLYZOA	POMPONS

POMPOON	PONGING	PONYTAILS	POORNESSES	POPPERS
POMPOONS	PONGO	POO	POORT	POPPET
POMPOSITIES	PONGOES	POOCH	POORTITH	POPPETS
POMPOSITY	PONGOS	POOCHES	POORTITHS	POPPIED
POMPOUS	PONGS	POOD	POORTS	POPPIER
POMPOUSLY	PONGY	POODLE	POORWILL	POPPIES
POMPS	PONIARD	POODLES	POORWILLS	POPPIEST
POMROY	PONIARDED	POODS	POOS	POPPING
POMROYS	PONIARDING	POOED	POOT	POPPISH
POMS	PONIARDS	POOF	POOTED	POPPIT
POMWATER	PONIED	POOFIER	POOTER	POPPITS
POMWATERS	PONIES	POOFIEST	POOTERS	POPPLE
PONCE	PONK	POOFS	POOTING	POPPLED
PONCEAU	PONKED	POOFTAH	POOTS	POPPLES
PONCEAUS	PONKING	POOFTAHS	POOVE	POPPLIER
PONCEAUX	PONKS	POOFTER	POOVERIES	POPPLIEST
PONCED	PONS	POOFTERS	POOVERY	POPPLING
PONCES	PONT	POOFY	POOVES	POPPLY
PONCEY	PONTAGE	POOGYE	POOVIER	POPPY
PONCHO	PONTAGES	POOGYEE	POOVIEST	POPPYCOCK
PONCHOS	PONTAL	POOGYEES	POOVY	POPPYCOCKS
PONCIER	PONTES	POOGYES	POP	POPRIN
PONCIEST	PONTIANAC	POOH	POPADUM	POPRINS
PONCING	PONTIANACS	POOING	POPADUMS	POPS
PONCY	PONTIANAK	POOJA	POPCORN	POPSIES
POND	PONTIANAKS	POOJAH	POPCORNS	POPSY
PONDAGE	PONTIC	POOJAHS	POPE	POPULACE
PONDAGES	PONTIE	POOJAS	POPEDOM	POPULACES
PONDED	PONTIES	POOK	POPEDOMS	POPULAR
PONDER	PONTIFEX	POOKA	POPEHOOD	POPULARLY
PONDERAL	PONTIFF	POOKAS	POPEHOODS	POPULARS
PONDERATE	PONTIFFS	POOKING	POPELING	POPULATE
PONDERATED	PONTIFIC	POOKIT	POPELINGS	POPULATED
PONDERATES	PONTIFICE	POOKS	POPERIES	POPULATES
PONDERATING	PONTIFICES	POOL	POPERIN	POPULATING
PONDERED	PONTIFIED	POOLED	POPERINS	POPULISM
PONDERER	PONTIFIES	POOLING	POPERY	POPULISMS
PONDERERS	PONTIFY	POOLS	POPES	POPULIST
PONDERING	PONTIFYING	POOLSIDE	POPESHIP	POPULISTS
PONDEROUS	PONTIL	POOLSIDES	POPESHIPS	POPULOUS
PONDERS	PONTILE	POON	POPINJAY	PORAL
PONDING	PONTILES	POONAC	POPINJAYS	PORBEAGLE
PONDOK	PONTILS	POONACS	POPISH	PORBEAGLES
PONDOKKIE	PONTLEVIS	POONCE	POPISHLY	PORCELAIN
PONDOKKIES	PONTLEVISES	POONCES	POPJOY	PORCELAINS
PONDOKS	PONTON	POONS	POPJOYED	PORCH
PONDS	PONTONEER	POONTANG	POPJOYING	PORCHES
PONDWEED	PONTONEERS	POONTANGS	POPJOYS	PORCINE
PONDWEEDS	PONTONIER	POOP	POPLAR	PORCPISCE
PONE	PONTONIERS	POOPED	POPLARS	PORCPISCES
PONENT	PONTONS	POOPING	POPLIN	PORCUPINE
PONES	PONTOON	POOPS	POPLINS	PORCUPINES
PONEY	PONTOONED	POOR	POPLITEAL	PORE
PONEYS	PONTOONER	POORER	POPLITIC	PORED
PONG	PONTOONERS	POOREST	POPOVER	PORER
PONGA	PONTOONING	POORHOUSE	POPOVERS	PORERS
PONGAS	PONTOONS	POORHOUSES	POPPA	PORES
PONGED	PONTS	POORI	POPPADUM	PORGE
PONGEE	PONTY	POORIS	POPPADUMS	PORGED
PONGEES	PONY	POORISH	POPPAS	PORGES
PONGID	PONYING	POORLIER	POPPED	PORGIE
PONGIDS	PONYSKIN	POORLIEST	POPPER	PORGIES
PONGIER	PONYSKINS	POORLY	POPPERING	PORGING
PONGIEST	PONYTAIL	POORNESS	POPPERINGS	PORGY

The Chambers Dictionary is the authority for many longer words; see *OSW* Introduction, page xii

PORIER	PORRIDGE	PORTION	POSEY	POSTAGE
PORIEST	PORRIDGES	PORTIONED	POSH	POSTAGES
PORIFER	PORRIGO	PORTIONER	POSHED	POSTAL
PORIFERAL	PORRIGOS	PORTIONERS	POSHER	POSTALLY
PORIFERAN	PORRINGER	PORTIONING	POSHES	POSTALS
PORIFERS	PORRINGERS	PORTIONS	POSHEST	POSTBAG
PORINESS	PORT	PORTLAND	POSHING	POSTBAGS
PORINESSES	PORTA	PORTLANDS	POSHLY	POSTBOX
PORING	PORTABLE	PORTLAST	POSHNESS	POSTBOXES
PORISM	PORTABLES	PORTLASTS	POSHNESSES	POSTBUS
PORISMS	PORTAGE	PORTLIER	POSHTEEN	POSTBUSES
PORISTIC	PORTAGES	PORTLIEST	POSHTEENS	POSTBUSSES
PORK	PORTAGUE	PORTLY	POSIER	POSTCARD
PORKER	PORTAGUES	PORTMAN	POSIES	POSTCARDED
PORKERS	PORTAL	PORTMEN	POSIEST	POSTCARDING
PORKIER	PORTALS	PORTOISE	POSIGRADE	POSTCARDS
PORKIES	PORTANCE	PORTOISES	POSING	POSTCAVA
PORKIEST	PORTANCES	PORTOLAN	POSINGLY	POSTCAVAE
PORKLING	PORTAS	PORTOLANI	POSINGS	POSTCODE
PORKLINGS	PORTASES	PORTOLANO	POSIT	POSTCODED
PORKS	PORTATE	PORTOLANOS	POSITED	POSTCODES
PORKY	PORTATILE	PORTOLANS	POSITING	POSTCODING
PORN	PORTATIVE	PORTOUS	POSITION	POSTDATE
PORNO	PORTATIVES	PORTOUSES	POSITIONED	POSTDATED
PORNOMAG	PORTED	PORTRAIT	POSITIONING	POSTDATES
PORNOMAGS	PORTEND	PORTRAITED	POSITIONS	POSTDATING
PORNOS	PORTENDED	PORTRAITING	POSITIVE	POSTED
PORNS	PORTENDING	PORTRAITS	POSITIVES	POSTEEN
POROGAMIC	PORTENDS	PORTRAY	POSITON	POSTEENS
POROGAMIES	PORTENT	PORTRAYAL	POSITONS	POSTER
POROGAMY	PORTENTS	PORTRAYALS	POSITRON	POSTERED
POROMERIC	PORTEOUS	PORTRAYED	POSITRONS	POSTERING
POROSCOPE	PORTEOUSES	PORTRAYER	POSITS	POSTERIOR
POROSCOPES	PORTER	PORTRAYERS	POSNET	POSTERIORS
POROSCOPIES	PORTERAGE	PORTRAYING	POSNETS	POSTERITIES
POROSCOPY	PORTERAGES	PORTRAYS	POSOLOGIES	POSTERITY
POROSE	PORTERESS	PORTREEVE	POSOLOGY	POSTERN
POROSES	PORTERESSES	PORTREEVES	POSS	POSTERNS
POROSIS	PORTERLY	PORTRESS	POSSE	POSTERS
POROSITIES	PORTERS	PORTRESSES	POSSED	POSTFACE
POROSITY	PORTESS	PORTS	POSSER	POSTFACES
POROUS	PORTESSE	PORTULACA	POSSERS	POSTFIX
PORPESS	PORTESSES	PORTULACAS	POSSES	POSTFIXED
PORPESSE	PORTFOLIO	PORTULAN	POSSESS	POSTFIXES
PORPESSES	PORTFOLIOS	PORTULANS	POSSESSED	POSTFIXING
PORPHYRIA	PORTHOLE	PORTY	POSSESSES	POSTHASTE
PORPHYRIAS	PORTHOLES	PORWIGGLE	POSSESSING	POSTHASTES
PORPHYRIES	PORTHORS	PORWIGGLES	POSSESSOR	POSTHORSE
PORPHYRIN	PORTHORSES	PORY	POSSESSORS	POSTHORSES
PORPHYRINS	PORTHOS	POS	POSSET	POSTHOUSE
PORPHYRIO	PORTHOSES	POSADA	POSSETED	POSTHOUSES
PORPHYRIOS	PORTHOUSE	POSADAS	POSSETING	POSTICHE
PORPHYRY	PORTHOUSES	POSAUNE	POSSETS	POSTICHES
PORPOISE	PORTICO	POSAUNES	POSSIBLE	POSTICOUS
PORPOISED	PORTICOED	POSE	POSSIBLES	POSTIE
PORPOISES	PORTICOES	POSEABLE	POSSIBLY	POSTIES
PORPOISING	PORTICOS	POSED	POSSIE	POSTIL
PORPORATE	PORTIER	POSER	POSSIES	POSTILION
PORRECT	PORTIERE	POSERS	POSSING	POSTILIONS
PORRECTED	PORTIERES	POSES	POSSUM	POSTILLED
PORRECTING	PORTIEST	POSEUR	POSSUMED	POSTILLER
PORRECTS	PORTIGUE	POSEURS	POSSUMING	POSTILLERS
PORRENGER	PORTIGUES	POSEUSE	POSSUMS	POSTILLING
PORRENGERS	PORTING	POSEUSES	POST	POSTILS

The Chambers Dictionary is the authority for many longer words; see *OSW* Introduction, page xii

POSTING	POTATION	POTICHE	POUCHFUL	POUNCING
POSTINGS	POTATIONS	POTICHES	POUCHFULS	POUND
POSTLUDE	POTATO	POTIN	POUCHIER	POUNDAGE
POSTLUDES	POTATOES	POTING	POUCHIEST	POUNDAGES
POSTMAN	POTATORY	POTINS	POUCHING	POUNDAL
POSTMARK	POTBOY	POTION	POUCHY	POUNDALS
POSTMARKS	POTBOYS	POTIONS	POUDER	POUNDED
POSTMEN	POTCH	POTLACH	POUDERS	POUNDER
POSTNASAL	POTCHE	POTLACHES	POUDRE	POUNDERS
POSTNATAL	POTCHED	POTLATCH	POUDRES	POUNDING
POSTNATI	POTCHER	POTLATCHES	POUF	POUNDS
POSTORAL	POTCHERS	POTMAN	POUFED	POUPE
POSTPONE	POTCHES	POTMEN	POUFFE	POUPED
POSTPONED	POTCHING	POTOMETER	POUFFED	POUPES
POSTPONER	POTE	POTOMETERS	POUFFES	POUPING
POSTPONERS	POTED	POTOO	POUFFING	POUPT
POSTPONES	POTEEN	POTOOS	POUFING	POUR
POSTPONING	POTEENS	POTOROO	POUFS	POURABLE
POSTPOSE	POTENCE	POTOROOS	POUFTAH	POURBOIRE
POSTPOSED	POTENCES	POTPOURRI	POUFTAHS	POURBOIRES
POSTPOSES	POTENCIES	POTPOURRIS	POUFTER	POURED
POSTPOSING	POTENCY	POTS	POUFTERS	POURER
POSTRIDER	POTENT	POTSHARD	POUK	POURERS
POSTRIDERS	POTENTATE	POTSHARDS	POUKE	POURIE
POSTS	POTENTATES	POTSHARE	POUKES	POURIES
POSTULANT	POTENTIAL	POTSHARES	POUKING	POURING
POSTULANTS	POTENTIALS	POTSHERD	POUKIT	POURINGS
POSTULATA	POTENTISE	POTSHERDS	POUKS	POURPOINT
POSTULATE	POTENTISED	POTSHOP	POULAINE	POURPOINTS
POSTULATED	POTENTISES	POTSHOPS	POULAINES	POURS
POSTULATES	POTENTISING	POTSTONE	POULARD	POURSEW
POSTULATING	POTENTIZE	POTSTONES	POULARDS	POURSEWED
POSTURAL	POTENTIZED	POTT	POULDER	POURSEWING
POSTURE	POTENTIZES	POTTAGE	POULDERS	POURSEWS
POSTURED	POTENTIZING	POTTAGES	POULDRE	POURSUE
POSTURER	POTENTLY	POTTED	POULDRES	POURSUED
POSTURERS	POTENTS	POTTER	POULDRON	POURSUES
POSTURES	POTES	POTTERED	POULDRONS	POURSUING
POSTURING	POTFUL	POTTERER	POULE	POURSUIT
POSTURIST	POTFULS	POTTERERS	POULES	POURSUITS
POSTURISTS	POTGUN	POTTERIES	POULP	POURSUITT
POSTWAR	POTGUNS	POTTERING	POULPE	POURSUITTS
POSTWOMAN	POTHECARIES	POTTERINGS	POULPES	POURTRAHED
POSTWOMEN	POTHECARY	POTTERS	POULPS	POURTRAY
POSY	POTHEEN	POTTERY	POULT	POURTRAYD
POT	POTHEENS	POTTIER	POULTER	POURTRAYED
POTABLE	POTHER	POTTIES	POULTERER	POURTRAYING
POTABLES	POTHERED	POTTIEST	POULTERERS	POURTRAYS
POTAGE	POTHERING	POTTINESS	POULTERS	POUSOWDIE
POTAGER	POTHERS	POTTINESSES	POULTFEET	POUSOWDIES
POTAGERS	POTHERY	POTTING	POULTFOOT	POUSSE
POTAGES	POTHOLE	POTTINGAR	POULTICE	POUSSES
POTAMIC	POTHOLED	POTTINGARS	POULTICED	POUSSETTE
POTASH	POTHOLER	POTTINGER	POULTICES	POUSSETTED
POTASHED	POTHOLERS	POTTINGERS	POULTICING	POUSSETTES
POTASHES	POTHOLES	POTTLE	POULTRIES	POUSSETTING
POTASHING	POTHOLING	POTTLES	POULTRY	POUSSIN
POTASS	POTHOLINGS	POTTO	POULTS	POUSSINS
POTASSA	POTHOOK	POTTOS	POUNCE	POUT
POTASSAS	POTHOOKS	POTTS	POUNCED	POUTED
POTASSES	POTHOUSE	POTTY	POUNCES	POUTER
POTASSIC	POTHOUSES	POUCH	POUNCET	POUTERS
POTASSIUM	POTICARIES	POUCHED	POUNCETS	POUTHER
POTASSIUMS	POTICARY	POUCHES	POUNCING	POUTHERED

POUTHERING	POWTERS	PRAEAMBLES	PRANKING	PRAYER
POUTHERS	POWWAW	PRAECAVA	PRANKINGS	PRAYERFUL
POUTIER	POWWOW	PRAECAVAE	PRANKISH	PRAYERS
POUTIEST	POWWOWED	PRAECOCES	PRANKLE	PRAYING
POUTING	POWWOWING	PRAEDIAL	PRANKLED	PRAYINGLY
POUTINGLY	POWWOWS	PRAEDIALS	PRANKLES	PRAYINGS
POUTINGS	POX	PRAEFECT	PRANKLING	PRAYS
POUTS	POXED	PRAEFECTS	PRANKS	PRE
POUTY	POXES	PRAELUDIA	PRANKSOME	PREACE
POVERTIES	POXIER	PRAENOMEN	PRANKSTER	PREACED
POVERTY	POXIEST	PRAENOMENS	PRANKSTERS	PREACES
POW	POXING	PRAENOMINA	PRANKY	PREACH
POWAN	POXVIRUS	PRAESES	PRASE	PREACHED
POWANS	POXVIRUSES	PRAESIDIA	PRASES	PREACHER
POWDER	POXY	PRAETOR	PRAT	PREACHERS
POWDERED	POYNANT	PRAETORS	PRATE	PREACHES
POWDERIER	POYNT	PRAGMATIC	PRATED	PREACHIER
POWDERIEST	POYNTED	PRAGMATICS	PRATER	PREACHIEST
POWDERING	POYNTING	PRAHU	PRATERS	PREACHIFIED
POWDERS	POYNTS	PRAHUS	PRATES	PREACHIFIES
POWDERY	POYSE	PRAIRIE	PRATFALL	PREACHIFY
POWELLISE	POYSED	PRAIRIED	PRATFALLEN	PREACHIFYING
POWELLISED	POYSES	PRAIRIES	PRATFALLING	PREACHILY
POWELLISES	POYSING	PRAISE	PRATFALLS	PREACHING
POWELLISING	POYSON	PRAISEACH	PRATFELL	PREACHINGS
POWELLITE	POYSONED	PRAISEACHS	PRATIE	PREACHY
POWELLITES	POYSONING	PRAISED	PRATIES	PREACING
POWELLIZE	POYSONS	PRAISEFUL	PRATING	PREAMBLE
POWELLIZED	POZ	PRAISER	PRATINGLY	PREAMBLED
POWELLIZES	POZZ	PRAISERS	PRATINGS	PREAMBLES
POWELLIZING	POZZIES	PRAISES	PRATIQUE	PREAMBLING
POWER	POZZOLANA	PRAISING	PRATIQUES	PREAMP
POWERBOAT	POZZOLANAS	PRAISINGS	PRATS	PREAMPS
POWERBOATS	POZZY	PRALINE	PRATT	PREASE
POWERED	PRAAM	PRALINES	PRATTED	PREASED
POWERFUL	PRAAMS	PRAM	PRATTING	PREASES
POWERING	PRABBLE	PRAMS	PRATTLE	PREASING
POWERLESS	PRABBLES	PRANA	PRATTLED	PREASSE
POWERPLAY	PRACTIC	PRANAS	PRATTLER	PREASSED
POWERPLAYS	PRACTICAL	PRANAYAMA	PRATTLERS	PREASSES
POWERS	PRACTICALS	PRANAYAMAS	PRATTLES	PREASSING
POWIN	PRACTICE	PRANCE	PRATTLING	PREBEND
POWINS	PRACTICED	PRANCED	PRATTS	PREBENDAL
POWN	PRACTICES	PRANCER	PRATY	PREBENDS
POWND	PRACTICING	PRANCERS	PRAU	PREBIOTIC
POWNDED	PRACTICK	PRANCES	PRAUNCE	PREBORN
POWNDING	PRACTICKS	PRANCING	PRAUNCED	PRECAST
POWNDS	PRACTICS	PRANCINGS	PRAUNCES	PRECATIVE
POWNEY	PRACTICUM	PRANCK	PRAUNCING	PRECATORY
POWNEYS	PRACTICUMS	PRANCKE	PRAUS	PRECAVA
POWNIE	PRACTIQUE	PRANCKED	PRAVITIES	PRECAVAE
POWNIES	PRACTIQUES	PRANCKES	PRAVITY	PRECEDE
POWNS	PRACTISE	PRANCKING	PRAWLE	PRECEDED
POWNY	PRACTISED	PRANCKS	PRAWLES	PRECEDENT
POWRE	PRACTISER	PRANDIAL	PRAWLIN	PRECEDENTS
POWRED	PRACTISERS	PRANG	PRAWLINS	PRECEDES
POWRES	PRACTISES	PRANGED	PRAWN	PRECEDING
POWRING	PRACTISING	PRANGING	PRAWNED	PRECEESE
POWS	PRACTIVE	PRANGS	PRAWNING	PRECENTOR
POWSOWDIES	PRACTOLOL	PRANK	PRAWNS	PRECENTORS
POWSOWDY	PRACTOLOLS	PRANKED	PRAXES	PRECEPIT
POWTER	PRAD	PRANKFUL	PRAXIS	PRECEPITS
POWTERED	PRADS	PRANKIER	PRAY	PRECEPT
POWTERING	PRAEAMBLE	PRANKIEST	PRAYED	PRECEPTOR

The Chambers Dictionary is the authority for many longer words; see *OSW* Introduction, page xii

PRECEPTORS	PREDATES	PREEVES	PREJINK	PREMIERED
PRECEPTS	PREDATING	PREEVING	PREJUDGE	PREMIERES
PRECESS	PREDATION	PREFAB	PREJUDGED	PREMIERING
PRECESSED	PREDATIONS	PREFABS	PREJUDGES	PREMIERS
PRECESSES	PREDATIVE	PREFACE	PREJUDGING	PREMIES
PRECESSING	PREDATOR	PREFACED	PREJUDICE	PREMISE
PRECIEUSE	PREDATORS	PREFACES	PREJUDICED	PREMISED
PRECIEUSES	PREDATORY	PREFACIAL	PREJUDICES	PREMISES
PRECINCT	PREDAWN	PREFACING	PREJUDICING	PREMISING
PRECINCTS	PREDAWNS	PREFADE	PREJUDIZE	PREMISS
PRECIOUS	PREDEFINE	PREFADED	PREJUDIZES	PREMISSES
PRECIOUSES	PREDEFINED	PREFADES	PRELACIES	PREMIUM
PRECIPICE	PREDEFINES	PREFADING	PRELACY	PREMIUMS
PRECIPICES	PREDEFINING	PREFARD	PRELATE	PREMIX
PRECIS	PREDELLA	PREFATORY	PRELATES	PREMIXED
PRECISE	PREDELLAS	PREFECT	PRELATESS	PREMIXES
PRECISED	PREDESIGN	PREFECTS	PRELATESSES	PREMIXING
PRECISELY	PREDESIGNED	PREFER	PRELATIAL	PREMOLAR
PRECISER	PREDESIGNING	PREFERRED	PRELATIC	PREMOLARS
PRECISES	PREDESIGNS	PREFERRER	PRELATIES	PREMONISH
PRECISEST	PREDEVOTE	PREFERRERS	PRELATION	PREMONISHED
PRECISIAN	PREDIAL	PREFERRING	PRELATIONS	PREMONISHES
PRECISIANS	PREDIALS	PREFERS	PRELATISE	PREMONISHING
PRECISING	PREDICANT	PREFIGURE	PRELATISED	PREMORSE
PRECISION	PREDICANTS	PREFIGURED	PRELATISES	PREMOSAIC
PRECISIONS	PREDICATE	PREFIGURES	PRELATISING	PREMOTION
PRECISIVE	PREDICATED	PREFIGURING	PRELATISH	PREMOTIONS
PRECLUDE	PREDICATES	PREFIX	PRELATISM	PREMOVE
PRECLUDED	PREDICATING	PREFIXED	PRELATISMS	PREMOVED
PRECLUDES	PREDICT	PREFIXES	PRELATIST	PREMOVES
PRECLUDING	PREDICTED	PREFIXING	PRELATISTS	PREMOVING
PRECOCIAL	PREDICTER	PREFIXION	PRELATIZE	PREMY
PRECOCITIES	PREDICTERS	PREFIXIONS	PRELATIZED	PRENASAL
PRECOCITY	PREDICTING	PREFLIGHT	PRELATIZES	PRENASALS
PRECOITAL	PREDICTOR	PREFORM	PRELATIZING	PRENATAL
PRECONISE	PREDICTORS	PREFORMED	PRELATURE	PRENOTIFIED
PRECONISED	PREDICTS	PREFORMING	PRELATURES	PRENOTIFIES
PRECONISES	PREDIED	PREFORMS	PRELATY	PRENOTIFY
PRECONISING	PREDIES	PREGGERS	PRELECT	PRENOTIFYING
PRECONIZE	PREDIGEST	PREGNABLE	PRELECTED	PRENOTION
PRECONIZED	PREDIGESTED	PREGNANCE	PRELECTING	PRENOTIONS
PRECONIZES	PREDIGESTING	PREGNANCES	PRELECTOR	PRENT
PRECONIZING	PREDIGESTS	PREGNANCIES	PRELECTORS	PRENTED
PRECOOK	PREDIKANT	PREGNANCY	PRELECTS	PRENTICE
PRECOOKED	PREDIKANTS	PREGNANT	PRELIM	PRENTICED
PRECOOKING	PREDILECT	PREHALLUCES	PRELIMS	PRENTICES
PRECOOKS	PREDOOM	PREHALLUX	PRELUDE	PRENTICING
PRECOOL	PREDOOMED	PREHEAT	PRELUDED	PRENTING
PRECOOLED	PREDOOMING	PREHEATED	PRELUDES	PRENTS
PRECOOLING	PREDOOMS	PREHEATING	PRELUDI	PRENUBILE
PRECOOLS	PREDY	PREHEATS	PRELUDIAL	PRENZIE
PRECURRER	PREDYING	PREHEND	PRELUDING	PREOCCUPIED
PRECURRERS	PREE	PREHENDED	PRELUDIO	PREOCCUPIES
PRECURSE	PREED	PREHENDING	PRELUSIVE	PREOCCUPY
PRECURSES	PREEING	PREHENDS	PRELUSORY	PREOCCUPYING
PRECURSOR	PREEMIE	PREHENSOR	PREMATURE	PREOCULAR
PRECURSORS	PREEMIES	PREHENSORS	PREMED	PREOPTION
PRECUT	PREEN	PREHNITE	PREMEDIC	PREOPTIONS
PRECUTS	PREENED	PREHNITES	PREMEDICS	PREORAL
PRECUTTING	PREENING	PREHUMAN	PREMEDS	PREORDAIN
PREDACITIES	PREENS	PREIF	PREMIA	PREORDAINED
PREDACITY	PREES	PREIFE	PREMIE	PREORDAINING
PREDATE	PREEVE	PREIFES	PREMIER	PREORDAINS
PREDATED	PREEVED	PREIFS	PREMIERE	PREORDER

The Chambers Dictionary is the authority for many longer words; see *OSW* Introduction, page xii

PREORDERED	PRESBYOPIES	PRESSERS	PRETESTS	PREWARN
PREORDERING	PRESBYOPY	PRESSES	PRETEXT	PREWARNED
PREORDERS	PRESBYTE	PRESSFAT	PRETEXTS	PREWARNING
PREP	PRESBYTER	PRESSFATS	PRETOR	PREWARNS
PREPACK	PRESBYTERS	PRESSFUL	PRETORS	PREWYN
PREPACKED	PRESBYTES	PRESSFULS	PRETTIED	PREWYNS
PREPACKING	PRESBYTIC	PRESSIE	PRETTIER	PREX
PREPACKS	PRESCHOOL	PRESSIES	PRETTIES	PREXES
PREPAID	PRESCHOOLS	PRESSING	PRETTIEST	PREXIES
PREPARE	PRESCIENT	PRESSINGS	PRETTIFIED	PREXY
PREPARED	PRESCIND	PRESSION	PRETTIFIES	PREY
PREPARER	PRESCINDED	PRESSIONS	PRETTIFY	PREYED
PREPARERS	PRESCINDING	PRESSMAN	PRETTIFYING	PREYFUL
PREPARES	PRESCINDS	PRESSMARK	PRETTILY	PREYING
PREPARING	PRESCIOUS	PRESSMARKS	PRETTY	PREYS
PREPAY	PRESCRIBE	PRESSMEN	PRETTYING	PREZZIE
PREPAYING	PRESCRIBED	PRESSOR	PRETTYISH	PREZZIES
PREPAYS	PRESCRIBES	PRESSROOM	PRETTYISM	PRIAL
PREPENSE	PRESCRIBING	PRESSROOMS	PRETTYISMS	PRIALS
PREPENSED	PRESCRIPT	PRESSURE	PRETZEL	PRIAPIC
PREPENSES	PRESCRIPTS	PRESSURED	PRETZELS	PRIAPISM
PREPENSING	PRESCUTA	PRESSURES	PREVAIL	PRIAPISMS
PREPOLLEX	PRESCUTUM	PRESSURING	PREVAILED	PRIBBLE
PREPOLLICES	PRESE	PRESSWORK	PREVAILING	PRIBBLES
PREPONE	PRESELECT	PRESSWORKS	PREVAILS	PRICE
PREPONED	PRESELECTED	PREST	PREVALENT	PRICED
PREPONES	PRESELECTING	PRESTED	PREVE	PRICELESS
PREPONING	PRESELECTS	PRESTERNA	PREVED	PRICER
PREPOSE	PRESENCE	PRESTIGE	PREVENE	PRICERS
PREPOSED	PRESENCES	PRESTIGES	PREVENED	PRICES
PREPOSES	PRESENT	PRESTING	PREVENES	PRICEY
PREPOSING	PRESENTED	PRESTO	PREVENING	PRICIER
PREPOSTOR	PRESENTEE	PRESTOS	PREVENT	PRICIEST
PREPOSTORS	PRESENTEES	PRESTS	PREVENTED	PRICINESS
PREPOTENT	PRESENTER	PRESUME	PREVENTER	PRICINESSES
PREPPED	PRESENTERS	PRESUMED	PREVENTERS	PRICING
PREPPIER	PRESENTING	PRESUMER	PREVENTING	PRICK
PREPPIES	PRESENTLY	PRESUMERS	PREVENTS	PRICKED
PREPPIEST	PRESENTS	PRESUMES	PREVERB	PRICKER
PREPPILY	PRESERVE	PRESUMING	PREVERBAL	PRICKERS
PREPPING	PRESERVED	PRETENCE	PREVERBS	PRICKET
PREPPY	PRESERVER	PRETENCES	PREVES	PRICKETS
PREPS	PRESERVERS	PRETEND	PREVIEW	PRICKING
PREPUCE	PRESERVES	PRETENDED	PREVIEWED	PRICKINGS
PREPUCES	PRESERVING	PRETENDER	PREVIEWING	PRICKLE
PREPUTIAL	PRESES	PRETENDERS	PREVIEWS	PRICKLED
PREQUEL	PRESET	PRETENDING	PREVING	PRICKLES
PREQUELS	PRESETS	PRETENDS	PREVIOUS	PRICKLIER
PRERECORD	PRESETTING	PRETENSE	PREVISE	PRICKLIEST
PRERECORDED	PRESIDE	PRETENSES	PREVISED	PRICKLING
PRERECORDING	PRESIDED	PRETERIST	PREVISES	PRICKLINGS
PRERECORDS	PRESIDENT	PRETERISTS	PREVISING	PRICKLY
PREROSION	PRESIDENTS	PRETERIT	PREVISION	PRICKS
PREROSIONS	PRESIDES	PRETERITE	PREVISIONED	PRICKWOOD
PRERUPT	PRESIDIA	PRETERITES	PREVISIONING	PRICKWOODS
PRESA	PRESIDIAL	PRETERITS	PREVISIONS	PRICY
PRESAGE	PRESIDING	PRETERM	PREVUE	PRIDE
PRESAGED	PRESIDIO	PRETERMIT	PREVUED	PRIDED
PRESAGER	PRESIDIOS	PRETERMITS	PREVUES	PRIDEFUL
PRESAGERS	PRESIDIUM	PRETERMITTED	PREVUING	PRIDELESS
PRESAGES	PRESIDIUMS	PRETERMITTING	PREWARM	PRIDES
PRESAGING	PRESS	PRETEST	PREWARMED	PRIDIAN
PRESBYOPE	PRESSED	PRETESTED	PREWARMING	PRIDING
PRESBYOPES	PRESSER	PRETESTING	PREWARMS	PRIED

The Chambers Dictionary is the authority for many longer words; see *OSW* Introduction, page xii

PRIEF	PRIMES	PRINCIPALS	PRISSY	PROBANDS
PRIEFE	PRIMEUR	PRINCIPIA	PRISTANE	PROBANG
PRIEFES	PRIMEURS	PRINCIPLE	PRISTANES	PROBANGS
PRIEFS	PRIMEVAL	PRINCIPLED	PRISTINE	PROBATE
PRIER	PRIMINE	PRINCIPLES	PRITHEE	PROBATED
PRIERS	PRIMINES	PRINCIPLING	PRIVACIES	PROBATES
PRIES	PRIMING	PRINCOCK	PRIVACY	PROBATING
PRIEST	PRIMINGS	PRINCOCKS	PRIVADO	PROBATION
PRIESTED	PRIMIPARA	PRINCOX	PRIVADOES	PROBATIONS
PRIESTESS	PRIMIPARAE	PRINCOXES	PRIVADOS	PROBATIVE
PRIESTESSES	PRIMIPARAS	PRINK	PRIVATE	PROBATORY
PRIESTING	PRIMITIAE	PRINKED	PRIVATEER	PROBE
PRIESTLIER	PRIMITIAL	PRINKING	PRIVATEERED	PROBEABLE
PRIESTLIEST	PRIMITIAS	PRINKS	PRIVATEERING	PROBED
PRIESTLY	PRIMITIVE	PRINT	PRIVATEERINGS	PROBER
PRIESTS	PRIMITIVES	PRINTABLE	PRIVATEERS	PROBERS
PRIEVE	PRIMLY	PRINTED	PRIVATELY	PROBES
PRIEVED	PRIMMED	PRINTER	PRIVATER	PROBING
PRIEVES	PRIMMER	PRINTERS	PRIVATES	PROBIOTIC
PRIEVING	PRIMMERS	PRINTHEAD	PRIVATEST	PROBIOTICS
PRIG	PRIMMEST	PRINTHEADS	PRIVATION	PROBIT
PRIGGED	PRIMMING	PRINTING	PRIVATIONS	PROBITIES
PRIGGER	PRIMNESS	PRINTINGS	PRIVATISE	PROBITS
PRIGGERIES	PRIMNESSES	PRINTLESS	PRIVATISED	PROBITY
PRIGGERS	PRIMO	PRINTOUT	PRIVATISES	PROBLEM
PRIGGERY	PRIMORDIA	PRINTOUTS	PRIVATISING	PROBLEMS
PRIGGING	PRIMOS	PRINTS	PRIVATIVE	PROBOSCIDES
PRIGGINGS	PRIMP	PRION	PRIVATIVES	PROBOSCIS
PRIGGISH	PRIMPED	PRIONS	PRIVATIZE	PROBOSCISES
PRIGGISM	PRIMPING	PRIOR	PRIVATIZED	PROBS
PRIGGISMS	PRIMPS	PRIORATE	PRIVATIZES	PROCACITIES
PRIGS	PRIMROSE	PRIORATES	PRIVATIZING	PROCACITY
PRILL	PRIMROSED	PRIORESS	PRIVET	PROCAINE
PRILLED	PRIMROSES	PRIORESSES	PRIVETS	PROCAINES
PRILLING	PRIMROSING	PRIORIES	PRIVIER	PROCARYON
PRILLS	PRIMROSY	PRIORITIES	PRIVIES	PROCARYONS
PRIM	PRIMS	PRIORITY	PRIVIEST	PROCEDURE
PRIMA	PRIMSIE	PRIORS	PRIVILEGE	PROCEDURES
PRIMACIES	PRIMSIER	PRIORSHIP	PRIVILEGED	PROCEED
PRIMACY	PRIMSIEST	PRIORSHIPS	PRIVILEGES	PROCEEDED
PRIMAEVAL	PRIMULA	PRIORY	PRIVILEGING	PROCEEDER
PRIMAGE	PRIMULAS	PRISAGE	PRIVILY	PROCEEDERS
PRIMAGES	PRIMULINE	PRISAGES	PRIVITIES	PROCEEDING
PRIMAL	PRIMULINES	PRISE	PRIVITY	PROCEEDINGS
PRIMALITIES	PRIMUS	PRISED	PRIVY	PROCEEDS
PRIMALITY	PRIMUSES	PRISER	PRIZABLE	PROCERITIES
PRIMALLY	PRIMY	PRISERS	PRIZE	PROCERITY
PRIMARIES	PRINCE	PRISES	PRIZED	PROCESS
PRIMARILY	PRINCED	PRISING	PRIZEMAN	PROCESSED
PRIMARY	PRINCEDOM	PRISM	PRIZEMEN	PROCESSES
PRIMATAL	PRINCEDOMS	PRISMATIC	PRIZER	PROCESSING
PRIMATE	PRINCEKIN	PRISMOID	PRIZERS	PROCESSOR
PRIMATES	PRINCEKINS	PRISMOIDS	PRIZES	PROCESSORS
PRIMATIAL	PRINCELET	PRISMS	PRIZING	PROCIDENT
PRIMATIC	PRINCELETS	PRISMY	PRO	PROCINCT
PRIME	PRINCELIER	PRISON	PROA	PROCINCTS
PRIMED	PRINCELIEST	PRISONED	PROACTIVE	PROCLAIM
PRIMELY	PRINCELY	PRISONER	PROAS	PROCLAIMED
PRIMENESS	PRINCES	PRISONERS	PROB	PROCLAIMING
PRIMENESSES	PRINCESS	PRISONING	PROBABLE	PROCLAIMS
PRIMER	PRINCESSE	PRISONOUS	PROBABLES	PROCLISES
PRIMERO	PRINCESSES	PRISONS	PROBABLY	PROCLISIS
PRIMEROS	PRINCING	PRISSIER	PROBALL	PROCLITIC
PRIMERS	PRINCIPAL	PRISSIEST	PROBAND	PROCLITICS

PROCLIVE	PROFANE	PROGGING	PROLATE	PROMENADES
PROCONSUL	PROFANED	PROGGINS	PROLATED	PROMENADING
PROCONSULS	PROFANELY	PROGGINSES	PROLATELY	PROMETAL
PROCREANT	PROFANER	PROGNOSES	PROLATES	PROMETALS
PROCREANTS	PROFANERS	PROGNOSIS	PROLATING	PROMINENT
PROCREATE	PROFANES	PROGRADE	PROLATION	PROMISE
PROCREATED	PROFANING	PROGRADED	PROLATIONS	PROMISED
PROCREATES	PROFANITIES	PROGRADES	PROLATIVE	PROMISEE
PROCREATING	PROFANITY	PROGRADING	PROLE	PROMISEES
PROCTAL	PROFESS	PROGRAM	PROLED	PROMISER
PROCTITIS	PROFESSED	PROGRAMME	PROLEG	PROMISERS
PROCTITISES	PROFESSES	PROGRAMMED	PROLEGS	PROMISES
PROCTOR	PROFESSING	PROGRAMMES	PROLEPSES	PROMISING
PROCTORS	PROFESSOR	PROGRAMMING	PROLEPSIS	PROMISOR
PROCURACIES	PROFESSORS	PROGRAMMINGS	PROLEPTIC	PROMISORS
PROCURACY	PROFFER	PROGRAMS	PROLER	PROMISSOR
PROCURE	PROFFERED	PROGRESS	PROLERS	PROMISSORS
PROCURED	PROFFERER	PROGRESSED	PROLES	PROMMER
PROCURER	PROFFERERS	PROGRESSES	PROLETARIES	PROMMERS
PROCURERS	PROFFERING	PROGRESSING	PROLETARY	PROMO
PROCURES	PROFFERS	PROGS	PROLICIDE	PROMOS
PROCURESS	PROFILE	PROHIBIT	PROLICIDES	PROMOTE
PROCURESSES	PROFILED	PROHIBITED	PROLIFIC	PROMOTED
PROCUREUR	PROFILER	PROHIBITING	PROLINE	PROMOTER
PROCUREURS	PROFILERS	PROHIBITS	PROLINES	PROMOTERS
PROCURING	PROFILES	PROIGN	PROLING	PROMOTES
PROD	PROFILING	PROIGNED	PROLIX	PROMOTING
PRODDED	PROFILINGS	PROIGNING	PROLIXITIES	PROMOTION
PRODDING	PROFILIST	PROIGNS	PROLIXITY	PROMOTIONS
PRODIGAL	PROFILISTS	PROIN	PROLIXLY	PROMOTIVE
PRODIGALS	PROFIT	PROINE	PROLL	PROMOTOR
PRODIGIES	PROFITED	PROINED	PROLLED	PROMOTORS
PRODIGY	PROFITEER	PROINES	PROLLER	PROMPT
PRODITOR	PROFITEERED	PROINING	PROLLERS	PROMPTED
PRODITORS	PROFITEERING	PROINS	PROLLING	PROMPTER
PRODITORY	PROFITEERINGS	PROJECT	PROLLS	PROMPTERS
PRODNOSE	PROFITEERS	PROJECTED	PROLOGISE	PROMPTEST
PRODNOSED	PROFITER	PROJECTING	PROLOGISED	PROMPTING
PRODNOSES	PROFITERS	PROJECTINGS	PROLOGISES	PROMPTINGS
PRODNOSING	PROFITING	PROJECTOR	PROLOGISING	PROMPTLY
PRODROMAL	PROFITINGS	PROJECTORS	PROLOGIZE	PROMPTS
PRODROME	PROFITS	PROJECTS	PROLOGIZED	PROMPTURE
PRODROMES	PROFLUENT	PROKARYON	PROLOGIZES	PROMPTURES
PRODROMI	PROFORMA	PROKARYONS	PROLOGIZING	PROMS
PRODROMIC	PROFORMAS	PROKARYOT	PROLOGUE	PROMULGE
PRODROMUS	PROFOUND	PROKARYOTS	PROLOGUED	PROMULGED
PRODS	PROFOUNDER	PROKE	PROLOGUES	PROMULGES
PRODUCE	PROFOUNDEST	PROKED	PROLOGUING	PROMULGING
PRODUCED	PROFOUNDS	PROKER	PROLONG	PROMUSCES
PRODUCER	PROFS	PROKERS	PROLONGE	PROMUSCIDES
PRODUCERS	PROFUSE	PROKES	PROLONGED	PROMUSCIS
PRODUCES	PROFUSELY	PROKING	PROLONGER	PRONAOI
PRODUCING	PROFUSER	PROLACTIN	PROLONGERS	PRONAOS
PRODUCT	PROFUSERS	PROLACTINS	PROLONGES	PRONATE
PRODUCTS	PROFUSION	PROLAMIN	PROLONGING	PRONATED
PROEM	PROFUSIONS	PROLAMINE	PROLONGS	PRONATES
PROEMBRYO	PROG	PROLAMINES	PROLUSION	PRONATING
PROEMBRYOS	PROGENIES	PROLAMINS	PROLUSIONS	PRONATION
PROEMIAL	PROGENY	PROLAPSE	PROLUSORY	PRONATIONS
PROEMS	PROGERIA	PROLAPSED	PROM	PRONATOR
PROENZYME	PROGERIAS	PROLAPSES	PROMACHOS	PRONATORS
PROENZYMES	PROGESTIN	PROLAPSING	PROMACHOSES	PRONE
PROF	PROGESTINS	PROLAPSUS	PROMENADE	PRONELY
PROFACE	PROGGED	PROLAPSUSES	PROMENADED	PRONENESS

PRONENESSES	PROPALING	PROPOSED	PROSECTOR	PROTAMINE
PRONER	PROPANE	PROPOSER	PROSECTORS	PROTAMINES
PRONES	PROPANES	PROPOSERS	PROSECUTE	PROTANDRIES
PRONEST	PROPANOL	PROPOSES	PROSECUTED	PROTANDRY
PRONEUR	PROPANOLS	PROPOSING	PROSECUTES	PROTANOPE
PRONEURS	PROPEL	PROPOUND	PROSECUTING	PROTANOPES
PRONG	PROPELLED	PROPOUNDED	PROSED	PROTASES
PRONGBUCK	PROPELLER	PROPOUNDING	PROSELYTE	PROTASIS
PRONGBUCKS	PROPELLERS	PROPOUNDS	PROSELYTED	PROTATIC
PRONGED	PROPELLING	PROPPANT	PROSELYTES	PROTEA
PRONGHORN	PROPELS	PROPPANTS	PROSELYTING	PROTEAN
PRONGHORNS	PROPEND	PROPPED	PROSEMAN	PROTEAS
PRONGING	PROPENDED	PROPPING	PROSEMEN	PROTEASE
PRONGS	PROPENDING	PROPRIETIES	PROSER	PROTEASES
PRONK	PROPENDS	PROPRIETY	PROSERS	PROTECT
PRONKED	PROPENE	PROPS	PROSES	PROTECTED
PRONKING	PROPENES	PROPTOSES	PROSEUCHA	PROTECTING
PRONKS	PROPENSE	PROPTOSIS	PROSEUCHAE	PROTECTOR
PRONOTA	PROPER	PROPULSOR	PROSEUCHE	PROTECTORS
PRONOTAL	PROPERDIN	PROPULSORS	PROSIER	PROTECTS
PRONOTUM	PROPERDINS	PROPYL	PROSIEST	PROTEGE
PRONOUN	PROPERER	PROPYLA	PROSIFIED	PROTEGEE
PRONOUNCE	PROPEREST	PROPYLAEA	PROSIFIES	PROTEGEES
PRONOUNCED	PROPERLY	PROPYLENE	PROSIFY	PROTEGES
PRONOUNCES	PROPERS	PROPYLENES	PROSIFYING	PROTEID
PRONOUNCING	PROPERTIED	PROPYLIC	PROSILY	PROTEIDS
PRONOUNCINGS	PROPERTIES	PROPYLITE	PROSIMIAN	PROTEIN
PRONOUNS	PROPERTY	PROPYLITES	PROSIMIANS	PROTEINIC
PRONTO	PROPERTYING	PROPYLON	PROSINESS	PROTEINS
PRONUCLEI	PROPHAGE	PROPYLS	PROSINESSES	PROTEND
PRONUNCIO	PROPHAGES	PRORATE	PROSING	PROTENDED
PRONUNCIOS	PROPHASE	PRORATED	PROSINGS	PROTENDING
PROO	PROPHASES	PRORATES	PROSIT	PROTENDS
PROOEMION	PROPHECIES	PRORATING	PROSO	PROTENSE
PROOEMIONS	PROPHECY	PRORATION	PROSODIAL	PROTENSES
PROOEMIUM	PROPHESIED	PRORATIONS	PROSODIAN	PROTEOSE
PROOEMIUMS	PROPHESIES	PRORE	PROSODIANS	PROTEOSES
PROOF	PROPHESY	PRORECTOR	PROSODIC	PROTEST
PROOFED	PROPHESYING	PRORECTORS	PROSODIES	PROTESTED
PROOFING	PROPHESYINGS	PRORES	PROSODIST	PROTESTER
PROOFINGS	PROPHET	PROROGATE	PROSODISTS	PROTESTERS
PROOFLESS	PROPHETIC	PROROGATED	PROSODY	PROTESTING
PROOFREAD	PROPHETS	PROROGATES	PROSOPON	PROTESTOR
PROOFREADING	PROPHYLL	PROROGATING	PROSOPONS	PROTESTORS
PROOFREADINGS	PROPHYLLS	PROROGUE	PROSOS	PROTESTS
PROOFREADS	PROPINE	PROROGUED	PROSPECT	PROTEUS
PROOFS	PROPINED	PROROGUES	PROSPECTED	PROTEUSES
PROOTIC	PROPINES	PROROGUING	PROSPECTING	PROTHALLI
PROOTICS	PROPINING	PROS	PROSPECTINGS	PROTHESES
PROP	PROPODEON	PROSAIC	PROSPECTS	PROTHESIS
PROPAGATE	PROPODEONS	PROSAICAL	PROSPER	PROTHETIC
PROPAGATED	PROPODEUM	PROSAISM	PROSPERED	PROTHORACES
PROPAGATES	PROPODEUMS	PROSAISMS	PROSPERING	PROTHORAX
PROPAGATING	PROPOLIS	PROSAIST	PROSPERS	PROTHORAXES
PROPAGE	PROPOLISES	PROSAISTS	PROSTATE	PROTHYL
PROPAGED	PROPONE	PROSATEUR	PROSTATES	PROTHYLE
PROPAGES	PROPONED	PROSATEURS	PROSTATIC	PROTHYLES
PROPAGING	PROPONENT	PROSCRIBE	PROSTRATE	PROTHYLS
PROPAGULA	PROPONENTS	PROSCRIBED	PROSTRATED	PROTIST
PROPAGULE	PROPONES	PROSCRIBES	PROSTRATES	PROTISTIC
PROPAGULES	PROPONING	PROSCRIBING	PROSTRATING	PROTISTS
PROPALE	PROPOSAL	PROSCRIPT	PROSTYLE	PROTIUM
PROPALED	PROPOSALS	PROSCRIPTS	PROSTYLES	PROTIUMS
PROPALES	PROPOSE	PROSE	PROSY	PROTOAVIS

The Chambers Dictionary is the authority for many longer words; see *OSW* Introduction, page xii

PROTOAVISES
PROTOCOL
PROTOCOLLED
PROTOCOLLING
PROTOCOLS
PROTOGINE
PROTOGINES
PROTOGYNIES
PROTOGYNY
PROTON
PROTONEMA
PROTONEMATA
PROTONIC
PROTONS
PROTORE
PROTORES
PROTOSTAR
PROTOSTARS
PROTOTYPE
PROTOTYPED
PROTOTYPES
PROTOTYPING
PROTOXIDE
PROTOXIDES
PROTOZOA
PROTOZOAL
PROTOZOAN
PROTOZOANS
PROTOZOIC
PROTOZOON
PROTRACT
PROTRACTED
PROTRACTING
PROTRACTS
PROTRUDE
PROTRUDED
PROTRUDES
PROTRUDING
PROTYL
PROTYLE
PROTYLES
PROTYLS
PROUD
PROUDER
PROUDEST
PROUDFUL
PROUDISH
PROUDLY
PROUDNESS
PROUDNESSES
PROUL
PROULED
PROULER
PROULERS
PROULING
PROULS
PROUSTITE
PROUSTITES
PROVABLE
PROVABLY
PROVAND
PROVANDS
PROVANT
PROVE

PROVEABLE
PROVEABLY
PROVED
PROVEDOR
PROVEDORE
PROVEDORES
PROVEDORS
PROVEN
PROVEND
PROVENDER
PROVENDERED
PROVENDERING
PROVENDERS
PROVENDS
PROVER
PROVERB
PROVERBED
PROVERBING
PROVERBS
PROVERS
PROVES
PROVIANT
PROVIANTS
PROVIDE
PROVIDED
PROVIDENT
PROVIDER
PROVIDERS
PROVIDES
PROVIDING
PROVIDOR
PROVIDORS
PROVINCE
PROVINCES
PROVINE
PROVINED
PROVINES
PROVING
PROVINGS
PROVINING
PROVIRAL
PROVIRUS
PROVIRUSES
PROVISION
PROVISIONED
PROVISIONING
PROVISIONS
PROVISO
PROVISOES
PROVISOR
PROVISORS
PROVISORY
PROVISOS
PROVOCANT
PROVOCANTS
PROVOKE
PROVOKED
PROVOKER
PROVOKERS
PROVOKES
PROVOKING
PROVOST
PROVOSTRIES
PROVOSTRY

PROVOSTS
PROW
PROWESS
PROWESSED
PROWESSES
PROWL
PROWLED
PROWLER
PROWLERS
PROWLING
PROWLINGS
PROWLS
PROWS
PROXIES
PROXIMAL
PROXIMATE
PROXIMITIES
PROXIMITY
PROXIMO
PROXY
PROYN
PROYNE
PROYNED
PROYNES
PROYNING
PROYNS
PROZYMITE
PROZYMITES
PRUDE
PRUDENCE
PRUDENCES
PRUDENT
PRUDENTLY
PRUDERIES
PRUDERY
PRUDES
PRUDISH
PRUDISHLY
PRUH
PRUINA
PRUINAS
PRUINE
PRUINES
PRUINOSE
PRUNE
PRUNED
PRUNELLA
PRUNELLAS
PRUNELLE
PRUNELLES
PRUNELLO
PRUNELLOS
PRUNER
PRUNERS
PRUNES
PRUNING
PRUNINGS
PRUNT
PRUNTED
PRUNTS
PRUNUS
PRUNUSES
PRURIENCE
PRURIENCES

PRURIENCIES
PRURIENCY
PRURIENT
PRURIGO
PRURIGOS
PRURITIC
PRURITUS
PRURITUSES
PRUSIK
PRUSIKED
PRUSIKING
PRUSIKS
PRUSSIATE
PRUSSIATES
PRUSSIC
PRY
PRYER
PRYERS
PRYING
PRYINGLY
PRYINGS
PRYS
PRYSE
PRYSED
PRYSES
PRYSING
PRYTANEA
PRYTANEUM
PRYTHEE
PSALM
PSALMIST
PSALMISTS
PSALMODIC
PSALMODIES
PSALMODY
PSALMS
PSALTER
PSALTERIA
PSALTERIES
PSALTERS
PSALTERY
PSALTRESS
PSALTRESSES
PSAMMITE
PSAMMITES
PSAMMITIC
PSCHENT
PSCHENTS
PSELLISM
PSELLISMS
PSEPHISM
PSEPHISMS
PSEPHITE
PSEPHITES
PSEPHITIC
PSEUD
PSEUDAXES
PSEUDAXIS
PSEUDERIES
PSEUDERY
PSEUDISH
PSEUDO
PSEUDONYM
PSEUDONYMS

PSEUDOPOD
PSEUDOPODS
PSEUDS
PSHAW
PSHAWED
PSHAWING
PSHAWS
PSI
PSILOCIN
PSILOCINS
PSILOSES
PSILOSIS
PSILOTIC
PSION
PSIONIC
PSIONICS
PSIONS
PSIS
PSOAS
PSOASES
PSOCID
PSOCIDS
PSORA
PSORALEN
PSORALENS
PSORAS
PSORIASES
PSORIASIS
PSORIATIC
PSORIC
PSST
PST
PSYCH
PSYCHE
PSYCHED
PSYCHES
PSYCHIC
PSYCHICAL
PSYCHICS
PSYCHING
PSYCHISM
PSYCHISMS
PSYCHIST
PSYCHISTS
PSYCHO
PSYCHOGAS
PSYCHOGASES
PSYCHOID
PSYCHOIDS
PSYCHOS
PSYCHOSES
PSYCHOSIS
PSYCHOTIC
PSYCHOTICS
PSYCHS
PSYLLA
PSYLLAS
PSYLLID
PSYLLIDS
PSYOP
PSYOPS
PSYWAR
PSYWARS
PTARMIC

PTARMICS	PUBLICIZED	PUDENDAL	PUGGERIES	PULINGLY
PTARMIGAN	PUBLICIZES	PUDENDOUS	PUGGERY	PULINGS
PTARMIGANS	PUBLICIZING	PUDENDUM	PUGGIE	PULK
PTERIA	PUBLICLY	PUDENT	PUGGIER	PULKA
PTERIN	PUBLICS	PUDGE	PUGGIES	PULKAS
PTERINS	PUBLISH	PUDGES	PUGGIEST	PULKHA
PTERION	PUBLISHED	PUDGIER	PUGGING	PULKHAS
PTEROPOD	PUBLISHER	PUDGIEST	PUGGINGS	PULKS
PTEROPODS	PUBLISHERS	PUDGINESS	PUGGISH	PULL
PTEROSAUR	PUBLISHES	PUDGINESSES	PUGGLE	PULLED
PTEROSAURS	PUBLISHING	PUDGY	PUGGLED	PULLER
PTERYGIA	PUBS	PUDIBUND	PUGGLES	PULLERS
PTERYGIAL	PUCCOON	PUDIC	PUGGLING	PULLET
PTERYGIALS	PUCCOONS	PUDICITIES	PUGGREE	PULLETS
PTERYGIUM	PUCE	PUDICITY	PUGGREES	PULLEY
PTERYGOID	PUCELAGE	PUDOR	PUGGY	PULLEYS
PTERYGOIDS	PUCELAGES	PUDORS	PUGH	PULLING
PTERYLA	PUCELLE	PUDS	PUGIL	PULLOVER
PTERYLAE	PUCELLES	PUDSEY	PUGILISM	PULLOVERS
PTILOSES	PUCER	PUDSIER	PUGILISMS	PULLS
PTILOSIS	PUCES	PUDSIEST	PUGILIST	PULLULATE
PTISAN	PUCEST	PUDSY	PUGILISTS	PULLULATED
PTISANS	PUCK	PUDU	PUGILS	PULLULATES
PTOMAINE	PUCKA	PUDUS	PUGNACITIES	PULLULATING
PTOMAINES	PUCKER	PUEBLO	PUGNACITY	PULMO
PTOSES	PUCKERED	PUEBLOS	PUGS	PULMONARY
PTOSIS	PUCKERING	PUER	PUH	PULMONATE
PTYALIN	PUCKERS	PUERED	PUIR	PULMONATES
PTYALINS	PUCKERY	PUERILE	PUIRER	PULMONES
PTYALISE	PUCKFIST	PUERILISM	PUIREST	PULMONIC
PTYALISED	PUCKFISTS	PUERILISMS	PUISNE	PULMONICS
PTYALISES	PUCKISH	PUERILITIES	PUISNES	PULP
PTYALISING	PUCKLE	PUERILITY	PUISNY	PULPBOARD
PTYALISM	PUCKLES	PUERING	PUISSANCE	PULPBOARDS
PTYALISMS	PUCKS	PUERPERAL	PUISSANCES	PULPED
PTYALIZE	PUD	PUERS	PUISSANT	PULPER
PTYALIZED	PUDDEN	PUFF	PUISSAUNT	PULPERS
PTYALIZES	PUDDENING	PUFFBALL	PUJA	PULPIER
PTYALIZING	PUDDENINGS	PUFFBALLS	PUJAS	PULPIEST
PTYXES	PUDDENS	PUFFBIRD	PUKE	PULPIFIED
PTYXIS	PUDDER	PUFFBIRDS	PUKED	PULPIFIES
PTYXISES	PUDDERED	PUFFED	PUKEKO	PULPIFY
PUB	PUDDERING	PUFFER	PUKEKOS	PULPIFYING
PUBERAL	PUDDERS	PUFFERIES	PUKER	PULPILY
PUBERTAL	PUDDIES	PUFFERS	PUKERS	PULPINESS
PUBERTIES	PUDDING	PUFFERY	PUKES	PULPINESSES
PUBERTY	PUDDINGS	PUFFIER	PUKING	PULPING
PUBES	PUDDINGY	PUFFIEST	PUKKA	PULPIT
PUBESCENT	PUDDLE	PUFFILY	PUKU	PULPITED
PUBIC	PUDDLED	PUFFIN	PUKUS	PULPITEER
PUBIS	PUDDLER	PUFFINESS	PULA	PULPITEERS
PUBISES	PUDDLERS	PUFFINESSES	PULAS	PULPITER
PUBLIC	PUDDLES	PUFFING	PULDRON	PULPITERS
PUBLICAN	PUDDLIER	PUFFINGLY	PULDRONS	PULPITRIES
PUBLICANS	PUDDLIEST	PUFFINGS	PULE	PULPITRY
PUBLICISE	PUDDLING	PUFFINS	PULED	PULPITS
PUBLICISED	PUDDLINGS	PUFFS	PULER	PULPITUM
PUBLICISES	PUDDLY	PUFFY	PULERS	PULPITUMS
PUBLICISING	PUDDOCK	PUFTALOON	PULES	PULPMILL
PUBLICIST	PUDDOCKS	PUFTALOONS	PULICIDE	PULPMILLS
PUBLICISTS	PUDDY	PUG	PULICIDES	PULPOUS
PUBLICITIES	PUDENCIES	PUGGAREE	PULIER	PULPS
PUBLICITY	PUDENCY	PUGGAREES	PULIEST	PULPSTONE
PUBLICIZE	PUDENDA	PUGGED	PULING	PULPSTONES

PULPWOOD	PULVILLI	PUNCHIER	PUNKINESS	PUPPETS
PULPWOODS	PULVILLING	PUNCHIEST	PUNKINESSES	PUPPIED
PULPY	PULVILLIO	PUNCHING	PUNKS	PUPPIES
PULQUE	PULVILLIOS	PUNCHY	PUNNED	PUPPING
PULQUES	PULVILLUS	PUNCING	PUNNER	PUPPODUM
PULSAR	PULVILS	PUNCTA	PUNNERS	PUPPODUMS
PULSARS	PULVINAR	PUNCTATE	PUNNET	PUPPY
PULSATE	PULVINARS	PUNCTATED	PUNNETS	PUPPYDOM
PULSATED	PULVINATE	PUNCTATOR	PUNNING	PUPPYDOMS
PULSATES	PULVINI	PUNCTATORS	PUNNINGLY	PUPPYHOOD
PULSATILE	PULVINULE	PUNCTILIO	PUNNINGS	PUPPYHOODS
PULSATING	PULVINULES	PUNCTILIOS	PUNS	PUPPYING
PULSATION	PULVINUS	PUNCTO	PUNSTER	PUPPYISH
PULSATIONS	PULWAR	PUNCTOS	PUNSTERS	PUPPYISM
PULSATIVE	PULWARS	PUNCTUAL	PUNT	PUPPYISMS
PULSATOR	PULY	PUNCTUATE	PUNTED	PUPS
PULSATORS	PUMA	PUNCTUATED	PUNTEE	PUPUNHA
PULSATORY	PUMAS	PUNCTUATES	PUNTEES	PUPUNHAS
PULSE	PUMELO	PUNCTUATING	PUNTER	PUR
PULSED	PUMELOS	PUNCTULE	PUNTERS	PURBLIND
PULSEJET	PUMICATE	PUNCTULES	PUNTIES	PURCHASE
PULSEJETS	PUMICATED	PUNCTUM	PUNTING	PURCHASED
PULSELESS	PUMICATES	PUNCTURE	PUNTO	PURCHASER
PULSES	PUMICATING	PUNCTURED	PUNTOS	PURCHASERS
PULSIDGE	PUMICE	PUNCTURER	PUNTS	PURCHASES
PULSIDGES	PUMICED	PUNCTURERS	PUNTSMAN	PURCHASING
PULSIFIC	PUMICEOUS	PUNCTURES	PUNTSMEN	PURDAH
PULSING	PUMICES	PUNCTURING	PUNTY	PURDAHED
PULSOJET	PUMICING	PUNDIT	PUNY	PURDAHS
PULSOJETS	PUMIE	PUNDITRIES	PUP	PURDONIUM
PULTAN	PUMIES	PUNDITRY	PUPA	PURDONIUMS
PULTANS	PUMMEL	PUNDITS	PUPAE	PURE
PULTON	PUMMELLED	PUNDONOR	PUPAL	PURED
PULTONS	PUMMELLING	PUNDONORES	PUPARIA	PUREE
PULTOON	PUMMELS	PUNGA	PUPARIAL	PUREED
PULTOONS	PUMP	PUNGAS	PUPARIUM	PUREEING
PULTUN	PUMPED	PUNGENCE	PUPAS	PUREES
PULTUNS	PUMPER	PUNGENCES	PUPATE	PURELY
PULTURE	PUMPERS	PUNGENCIES	PUPATED	PURENESS
PULTURES	PUMPHOOD	PUNGENCY	PUPATES	PURENESSES
PULU	PUMPHOODS	PUNGENT	PUPATING	PURER
PULUS	PUMPING	PUNGENTLY	PUPATION	PURES
PULVER	PUMPION	PUNIER	PUPATIONS	PUREST
PULVERED	PUMPIONS	PUNIEST	PUPFISH	PURFLE
PULVERINE	PUMPKIN	PUNILY	PUPFISHES	PURFLED
PULVERINES	PUMPKINS	PUNINESS	PUPIL	PURFLES
PULVERING	PUMPS	PUNINESSES	PUPILAGE	PURFLING
PULVERISE	PUMY	PUNISH	PUPILAGES	PURFLINGS
PULVERISED	PUN	PUNISHED	PUPILAR	PURFLY
PULVERISES	PUNA	PUNISHER	PUPILARY	PURGATION
PULVERISING	PUNALUA	PUNISHERS	PUPILLAGE	PURGATIONS
PULVERIZE	PUNALUAN	PUNISHES	PUPILLAGES	PURGATIVE
PULVERIZED	PUNALUAS	PUNISHING	PUPILLAR	PURGATIVES
PULVERIZES	PUNAS	PUNITION	PUPILLARY	PURGATORIES
PULVERIZING	PUNCE	PUNITIONS	PUPILLATE	PURGATORY
PULVEROUS	PUNCED	PUNITIVE	PUPILS	PURGE
PULVERS	PUNCES	PUNITORY	PUPILSHIP	PURGED
PULVIL	PUNCH	PUNK	PUPILSHIPS	PURGER
PULVILIO	PUNCHED	PUNKA	PUPPED	PURGERS
PULVILIOS	PUNCHEON	PUNKAH	PUPPET	PURGES
PULVILLAR	PUNCHEONS	PUNKAHS	PUPPETEER	PURGING
PULVILLE	PUNCHER	PUNKAS	PUPPETEERS	PURGINGS
PULVILLED	PUNCHERS	PUNKER	PUPPETRIES	PURI
PULVILLES	PUNCHES	PUNKEST	PUPPETRY	PURIFIED

PURIFIER	PURPOSELY	PURULENCY	PUTCHUK	PUZZLER
PURIFIERS	PURPOSES	PURULENT	PUTCHUKS	PUZZLERS
PURIFIES	PURPOSING	PURVEY	PUTEAL	PUZZLES
PURIFY	PURPOSIVE	PURVEYED	PUTEALS	PUZZLING
PURIFYING	PURPURA	PURVEYING	PUTELI	PUZZOLANA
PURIM	PURPURAS	PURVEYOR	PUTELIS	PUZZOLANAS
PURIMS	PURPURE	PURVEYORS	PUTID	PYAEMIA
PURIN	PURPUREAL	PURVEYS	PUTLOCK	PYAEMIAS
PURINE	PURPURES	PURVIEW	PUTLOCKS	PYAEMIC
PURINES	PURPURIC	PURVIEWS	PUTLOG	PYAT
PURING	PURPURIN	PUS	PUTLOGS	PYATS
PURINS	PURPURINS	PUSES	PUTOIS	PYCNIC
PURIS	PURPY	PUSH	PUTREFIED	PYCNIDIA
PURISM	PURR	PUSHED	PUTREFIES	PYCNIDIUM
PURISMS	PURRED	PUSHER	PUTREFY	PYCNITE
PURIST	PURRING	PUSHERS	PUTREFYING	PYCNITES
PURISTIC	PURRINGLY	PUSHES	PUTRID	PYCNON
PURISTS	PURRINGS	PUSHFUL	PUTRIDER	PYCNONS
PURITAN	PURRS	PUSHFULLY	PUTRIDEST	PYCNOSES
PURITANIC	PURS	PUSHIER	PUTRIDITIES	PYCNOSIS
PURITANS	PURSE	PUSHIEST	PUTRIDITY	PYE
PURITIES	PURSED	PUSHINESS	PUTRIDLY	PYEBALD
PURITY	PURSEFUL	PUSHINESSES	PUTS	PYEBALDS
PURL	PURSEFULS	PUSHING	PUTSCH	PYEING
PURLED	PURSER	PUSHINGLY	PUTSCHES	PYELITIC
PURLER	PURSERS	PUSHROD	PUTSCHIST	PYELITIS
PURLERS	PURSES	PUSHRODS	PUTSCHISTS	PYELITISES
PURLICUE	PURSEW	PUSHY	PUTT	PYELOGRAM
PURLICUED	PURSEWED	PUSLE	PUTTED	PYELOGRAMS
PURLICUES	PURSEWING	PUSLED	PUTTEE	PYEMIA
PURLICUING	PURSEWS	PUSLES	PUTTEES	PYEMIAS
PURLIEU	PURSIER	PUSLING	PUTTEN	PYENGADU
PURLIEUS	PURSIEST	PUSS	PUTTER	PYENGADUS
PURLIN	PURSINESS	PUSSEL	PUTTERED	PYES
PURLINE	PURSINESSES	PUSSELS	PUTTERING	PYET
PURLINES	PURSING	PUSSER	PUTTERS	PYETS
PURLING	PURSLAIN	PUSSERS	PUTTI	PYGAL
PURLINGS	PURSLAINS	PUSSES	PUTTIE	PYGALS
PURLINS	PURSLANE	PUSSIES	PUTTIED	PYGARG
PURLOIN	PURSLANES	PUSSY	PUTTIER	PYGARGS
PURLOINED	PURSUABLE	PUSSYFOOT	PUTTIERS	PYGIDIA
PURLOINER	PURSUAL	PUSSYFOOTED	PUTTIES	PYGIDIAL
PURLOINERS	PURSUALS	PUSSYFOOTING	PUTTING	PYGIDIUM
PURLOINING	PURSUANCE	PUSSYFOOTS	PUTTINGS	PYGIDIUMS
PURLOINS	PURSUANCES	PUSTULANT	PUTTO	PYGMAEAN
PURLS	PURSUANT	PUSTULANTS	PUTTOCK	PYGMEAN
PURPIE	PURSUE	PUSTULAR	PUTTOCKS	PYGMIES
PURPIES	PURSUED	PUSTULATE	PUTTS	PYGMOID
PURPLE	PURSUER	PUSTULATED	PUTTY	PYGMY
PURPLED	PURSUERS	PUSTULATES	PUTTYING	PYGOSTYLE
PURPLER	PURSUES	PUSTULATING	PUTURE	PYGOSTYLES
PURPLES	PURSUING	PUSTULE	PUTURES	PYJAMAED
PURPLEST	PURSUINGS	PUSTULES	PUTZ	PYJAMAS
PURPLIER	PURSUIT	PUSTULOUS	PUTZES	PYKNIC
PURPLIEST	PURSUITS	PUT	PUY	PYKNOSOME
PURPLING	PURSY	PUTAMEN	PUYS	PYKNOSOMES
PURPLISH	PURTIER	PUTAMINA	PUZEL	PYLON
PURPLY	PURTIEST	PUTATIVE	PUZELS	PYLONS
PURPORT	PURTRAID	PUTCHEON	PUZZEL	PYLORIC
PURPORTED	PURTRAYD	PUTCHEONS	PUZZELS	PYLORUS
PURPORTING	PURTY	PUTCHER	PUZZLE	PYLORUSES
PURPORTS	PURULENCE	PUTCHERS	PUZZLED	PYNE
PURPOSE	PURULENCES	PUTCHOCK	PUZZLEDOM	PYNED
PURPOSED	PURULENCIES	PUTCHOCKS	PUZZLEDOMS	PYNES

PYNING	PYRE	PYRITISING	PYROMANIAS	PYRRHICS
PYOGENIC	PYRENE	PYRITIZE	PYROMETER	PYRRHOUS
PYOID	PYRENEITE	PYRITIZED	PYROMETERS	PYRROLE
PYONER	PYRENEITES	PYRITIZES	PYROMETRIES	PYRROLES
PYONERS	PYRENES	PYRITIZING	PYROMETRY	PYRUVATE
PYONINGS	PYRENOID	PYRITOUS	PYROPE	PYRUVATES
PYORRHOEA	PYRENOIDS	PYRO	PYROPES	PYTHIUM
PYORRHOEAS	PYRES	PYROCLAST	PYROPHONE	PYTHIUMS
PYOT	PYRETHRIN	PYROCLASTS	PYROPHONES	PYTHON
PYOTS	PYRETHRINS	PYROGEN	PYROPUS	PYTHONESS
PYRACANTH	PYRETHRUM	PYROGENIC	PYROPUSES	PYTHONESSES
PYRACANTHS	PYRETHRUMS	PYROGENS	PYROS	PYTHONIC
PYRAL	PYRETIC	PYROLATER	PYROSCOPE	PYTHONS
PYRALID	PYREXIA	PYROLATERS	PYROSCOPES	PYURIA
PYRALIDS	PYREXIAL	PYROLATRIES	PYROSES	PYURIAS
PYRALIS	PYREXIAS	PYROLATRY	PYROSIS	PYX
PYRALISES	PYREXIC	PYROLYSE	PYROSOME	PYXED
PYRAMID	PYRIDINE	PYROLYSED	PYROSOMES	PYXES
PYRAMIDAL	PYRIDINES	PYROLYSES	PYROSTAT	PYXIDES
PYRAMIDED	PYRIDOXIN	PYROLYSING	PYROSTATS	PYXIDIA
PYRAMIDES	PYRIDOXINS	PYROLYSIS	PYROXENE	PYXIDIUM
PYRAMIDIA	PYRIFORM	PYROLYTIC	PYROXENES	PYXING
PYRAMIDIC	PYRITE	PYROLYZE	PYROXENIC	PYXIS
PYRAMIDING	PYRITES	PYROLYZED	PYROXYLE	PZAZZ
PYRAMIDON	PYRITIC	PYROLYZES	PYROXYLES	PZAZZES
PYRAMIDONS	PYRITICAL	PYROLYZING	PYROXYLIC	
PYRAMIDS	PYRITISE	PYROMANCIES	PYROXYLIN	
PYRAMIS	PYRITISED	PYROMANCY	PYROXYLINS	
PYRAMISES	PYRITISES	PYROMANIA	PYRRHIC	

Q

QABALAH	QUADRAT	QUAGGY	QUALMIER	QUARREL
QABALAHS	QUADRATE	QUAGMIRE	QUALMIEST	QUARRELLED
QADI	QUADRATED	QUAGMIRED	QUALMING	QUARRELLING
QADIS	QUADRATES	QUAGMIRES	QUALMISH	QUARRELLINGS
QAIMAQAM	QUADRATIC	QUAGMIRIER	QUALMLESS	QUARRELS
QAIMAQAMS	QUADRATICS	QUAGMIRIEST	QUALMS	QUARRIED
QALAMDAN	QUADRATING	QUAGMIRING	QUALMY	QUARRIER
QALAMDANS	QUADRATS	QUAGMIRY	QUAMASH	QUARRIERS
QANAT	QUADRATUS	QUAGS	QUAMASHES	QUARRIES
QANATS	QUADRATUSES	QUAHAUG	QUANDANG	QUARRY
QASIDA	QUADRELLA	QUAHAUGS	QUANDANGS	QUARRYING
QASIDAS	QUADRELLAS	QUAHOG	QUANDARIES	QUARRYMAN
QAT	QUADRIC	QUAHOGS	QUANDARY	QUARRYMEN
QATS	QUADRICS	QUAICH	QUANDONG	QUART
QAWWAL	QUADRIFID	QUAICHS	QUANDONGS	QUARTAN
QAWWALI	QUADRIGA	QUAIGH	QUANGO	QUARTANS
QAWWALIS	QUADRIGAE	QUAIGHS	QUANGOS	QUARTE
QAWWALS	QUADRILLE	QUAIL	QUANNET	QUARTER
QI	QUADRILLED	QUAILED	QUANNETS	QUARTERED
QIBLA	QUADRILLES	QUAILING	QUANT	QUARTERING
QIBLAS	QUADRILLING	QUAILINGS	QUANTA	QUARTERINGS
QIGONG	QUADROON	QUAILS	QUANTAL	QUARTERLIES
QIGONGS	QUADROONS	QUAINT	QUANTED	QUARTERLY
QINDAR	QUADRUMAN	QUAINTER	QUANTIC	QUARTERN
QINDARS	QUADRUMANS	QUAINTEST	QUANTICAL	QUARTERNS
QINGHAOSU	QUADRUPED	QUAINTLY	QUANTICS	QUARTERS
QINGHAOSUS	QUADRUPEDS	QUAIR	QUANTIFIED	QUARTES
QINTAR	QUADRUPLE	QUAIRS	QUANTIFIES	QUARTET
QINTARS	QUADRUPLED	QUAKE	QUANTIFY	QUARTETS
QIS	QUADRUPLES	QUAKED	QUANTIFYING	QUARTETT
QIVIUT	QUADRUPLIES	QUAKER	QUANTING	QUARTETTE
QIVIUTS	QUADRUPLING	QUAKERS	QUANTISE	QUARTETTES
QOPH	QUADRUPLY	QUAKES	QUANTISED	QUARTETTI
QOPHS	QUADS	QUAKIER	QUANTISES	QUARTETTO
QUA	QUAERE	QUAKIEST	QUANTISING	QUARTETTS
QUACK	QUAERED	QUAKINESS	QUANTITIES	QUARTIC
QUACKED	QUAEREING	QUAKINESSES	QUANTITY	QUARTICS
QUACKER	QUAERES	QUAKING	QUANTIZE	QUARTIER
QUACKERIES	QUAERITUR	QUAKINGLY	QUANTIZED	QUARTIERS
QUACKERS	QUAESITUM	QUAKINGS	QUANTIZES	QUARTILE
QUACKERY	QUAESITUMS	QUAKY	QUANTIZING	QUARTILES
QUACKING	QUAESTOR	QUALE	QUANTONG	QUARTO
QUACKLE	QUAESTORS	QUALIA	QUANTONGS	QUARTOS
QUACKLED	QUAFF	QUALIFIED	QUANTS	QUARTS
QUACKLES	QUAFFED	QUALIFIER	QUANTUM	QUARTZ
QUACKLING	QUAFFER	QUALIFIERS	QUARE	QUARTZES
QUACKS	QUAFFERS	QUALIFIES	QUARENDEN	QUARTZIER
QUAD	QUAFFING	QUALIFY	QUARENDENS	QUARTZIEST
QUADDED	QUAFFS	QUALIFYING	QUARENDER	QUARTZITE
QUADDING	QUAG	QUALIFYINGS	QUARENDERS	QUARTZITES
QUADRANS	QUAGGA	QUALITIED	QUARER	QUARTZOSE
QUADRANT	QUAGGAS	QUALITIES	QUAREST	QUARTZY
QUADRANTES	QUAGGIER	QUALITY	QUARK	QUASAR
QUADRANTS	QUAGGIEST	QUALM	QUARKS	QUASARS

The Chambers Dictionary is the authority for many longer words; see *OSW* Introduction, page xii

QUASH	QUEENIER	QUERCETIN	QUIBBLING	QUIETENING
QUASHED	QUEENIES	QUERCETINS	QUIBBLINGS	QUIETENINGS
QUASHEE	QUEENIEST	QUERCETUM	QUIBLIN	QUIETENS
QUASHEES	QUEENING	QUERCETUMS	QUIBLINS	QUIETER
QUASHES	QUEENINGS	QUERIED	QUICH	QUIETERS
QUASHIE	QUEENITE	QUERIES	QUICHE	QUIETEST
QUASHIES	QUEENITES	QUERIMONIES	QUICHED	QUIETING
QUASHING	QUEENLESS	QUERIMONY	QUICHES	QUIETINGS
QUASI	QUEENLET	QUERIST	QUICHING	QUIETISM
QUASSIA	QUEENLETS	QUERISTS	QUICK	QUIETISMS
QUASSIAS	QUEENLIER	QUERN	QUICKBEAM	QUIETIST
QUAT	QUEENLIEST	QUERNS	QUICKBEAMS	QUIETISTS
QUATCH	QUEENLY	QUERULOUS	QUICKEN	QUIETIVE
QUATCHED	QUEENS	QUERY	QUICKENED	QUIETIVES
QUATCHES	QUEENSHIP	QUERYING	QUICKENER	QUIETLY
QUATCHING	QUEENSHIPS	QUERYINGS	QUICKENERS	QUIETNESS
QUATORZE	QUEENY	QUEST	QUICKENING	QUIETNESSES
QUATORZES	QUEER	QUESTANT	QUICKENINGS	QUIETS
QUATRAIN	QUEERCORE	QUESTANTS	QUICKENS	QUIETSOME
QUATRAINS	QUEERCORES	QUESTED	QUICKER	QUIETUDE
QUATS	QUEERDOM	QUESTER	QUICKEST	QUIETUDES
QUAVER	QUEERDOMS	QUESTERS	QUICKIE	QUIETUS
QUAVERED	QUEERED	QUESTING	QUICKIES	QUIETUSES
QUAVERER	QUEERER	QUESTINGS	QUICKLIME	QUIFF
QUAVERERS	QUEEREST	QUESTION	QUICKLIMES	QUIFFS
QUAVERIER	QUEERING	QUESTIONED	QUICKLY	QUIGHT
QUAVERIEST	QUEERISH	QUESTIONING	QUICKNESS	QUIGHTED
QUAVERING	QUEERITIES	QUESTIONINGS	QUICKNESSES	QUIGHTING
QUAVERINGS	QUEERITY	QUESTIONS	QUICKS	QUIGHTS
QUAVERS	QUEERLY	QUESTOR	QUICKSAND	QUILL
QUAVERY	QUEERNESS	QUESTORS	QUICKSANDS	QUILLAI
QUAY	QUEERNESSES	QUESTRIST	QUICKSET	QUILLAIS
QUAYAGE	QUEERS	QUESTRISTS	QUICKSETS	QUILLED
QUAYAGES	QUEEST	QUESTS	QUICKSTEP	QUILLET
QUAYD	QUEESTS	QUETCH	QUICKSTEPPED	QUILLETS
QUAYS	QUEINT	QUETCHED	QUICKSTEPPING	QUILLING
QUAYSIDE	QUELCH	QUETCHES	QUICKSTEPS	QUILLINGS
QUAYSIDES	QUELCHED	QUETCHING	QUID	QUILLMAN
QUEACH	QUELCHES	QUETHE	QUIDAM	QUILLMEN
QUEACHES	QUELCHING	QUETHES	QUIDAMS	QUILLON
QUEACHIER	QUELEA	QUETHING	QUIDDANIES	QUILLONS
QUEACHIEST	QUELEAS	QUETSCH	QUIDDANY	QUILLS
QUEACHY	QUELL	QUETSCHES	QUIDDIT	QUILLWORT
QUEAN	QUELLED	QUETZAL	QUIDDITIES	QUILLWORTS
QUEANS	QUELLER	QUETZALES	QUIDDITS	QUILT
QUEASIER	QUELLERS	QUETZALS	QUIDDITY	QUILTED
QUEASIEST	QUELLING	QUEUE	QUIDDLE	QUILTER
QUEASILY	QUELLS	QUEUED	QUIDDLED	QUILTERS
QUEASY	QUEME	QUEUEING	QUIDDLER	QUILTING
QUEAZIER	QUEMED	QUEUEINGS	QUIDDLERS	QUILTINGS
QUEAZIEST	QUEMES	QUEUES	QUIDDLES	QUILTS
QUEAZY	QUEMING	QUEUING	QUIDDLING	QUIM
QUEBRACHO	QUENA	QUEUINGS	QUIDNUNC	QUIMS
QUEBRACHOS	QUENAS	QUEY	QUIDNUNCS	QUIN
QUEECHIER	QUENCH	QUEYN	QUIDS	QUINA
QUEECHIEST	QUENCHED	QUEYNIE	QUIESCE	QUINARIES
QUEECHY	QUENCHER	QUEYNIES	QUIESCED	QUINARY
QUEEN	QUENCHERS	QUEYNS	QUIESCENT	QUINAS
QUEENDOM	QUENCHES	QUEYS	QUIESCES	QUINATE
QUEENDOMS	QUENCHING	QUIBBLE	QUIESCING	QUINCE
QUEENED	QUENCHINGS	QUIBBLED	QUIET	QUINCES
QUEENHOOD	QUENELLE	QUIBBLER	QUIETED	QUINCHE
QUEENHOODS	QUENELLES	QUIBBLERS	QUIETEN	QUINCHED
QUEENIE	QUEP	QUIBBLES	QUIETENED	QUINCHES

The Chambers Dictionary is the authority for many longer words; see *OSW* Introduction, page xii

QUINCHING
QUINCUNX
QUINCUNXES
QUINE
QUINELLA
QUINELLAS
QUINES
QUINIC
QUINIDINE
QUINIDINES
QUINIE
QUINIES
QUININE
QUININES
QUINNAT
QUINNATS
QUINOA
QUINOAS
QUINOID
QUINOIDAL
QUINOIDS
QUINOL
QUINOLINE
QUINOLINES
QUINOLONE
QUINOLONES
QUINOLS
QUINONE
QUINONES
QUINONOID
QUINQUINA
QUINQUINAS
QUINS
QUINSIED
QUINSIES
QUINSY
QUINT
QUINTA
QUINTAIN
QUINTAINS
QUINTAL
QUINTALS
QUINTAN
QUINTAS
QUINTE
QUINTES

QUINTET
QUINTETS
QUINTETT
QUINTETTE
QUINTETTES
QUINTETTI
QUINTETTO
QUINTETTS
QUINTIC
QUINTILE
QUINTILES
QUINTROON
QUINTROONS
QUINTS
QUINTUPLE
QUINTUPLED
QUINTUPLES
QUINTUPLING
QUINZE
QUINZES
QUIP
QUIPO
QUIPOS
QUIPPED
QUIPPING
QUIPPISH
QUIPS
QUIPSTER
QUIPSTERS
QUIPU
QUIPUS
QUIRE
QUIRED
QUIRES
QUIRING
QUIRISTER
QUIRISTERS
QUIRK
QUIRKED
QUIRKIER
QUIRKIEST
QUIRKILY
QUIRKING
QUIRKISH
QUIRKS
QUIRKY

QUIRT
QUIRTED
QUIRTING
QUIRTS
QUISLING
QUISLINGS
QUIST
QUISTS
QUIT
QUITCH
QUITCHED
QUITCHES
QUITCHING
QUITCLAIM
QUITCLAIMED
QUITCLAIMING
QUITCLAIMS
QUITE
QUITED
QUITES
QUITING
QUITS
QUITTAL
QUITTALS
QUITTANCE
QUITTANCED
QUITTANCES
QUITTANCING
QUITTED
QUITTER
QUITTERS
QUITTING
QUITTOR
QUITTORS
QUIVER
QUIVERED
QUIVERFUL
QUIVERFULS
QUIVERIER
QUIVERIEST
QUIVERING
QUIVERINGS
QUIVERISH
QUIVERS
QUIVERY
QUIXOTIC

QUIXOTISM
QUIXOTISMS
QUIXOTRIES
QUIXOTRY
QUIZ
QUIZZED
QUIZZER
QUIZZERIES
QUIZZERS
QUIZZERY
QUIZZES
QUIZZICAL
QUIZZIFIED
QUIZZIFIES
QUIZZIFY
QUIZZIFYING
QUIZZING
QUIZZINGS
QUOAD
QUOD
QUODDED
QUODDING
QUODLIBET
QUODLIBETS
QUODLIN
QUODLINS
QUODS
QUOIF
QUOIFED
QUOIFING
QUOIFS
QUOIN
QUOINED
QUOINING
QUOINS
QUOIST
QUOISTS
QUOIT
QUOITED
QUOITER
QUOITERS
QUOITING
QUOITS
QUOKKA
QUOKKAS
QUOLL

QUOLLS
QUONDAM
QUONK
QUONKED
QUONKING
QUONKS
QUOOKE
QUOP
QUOPPED
QUOPPING
QUOPS
QUORATE
QUORUM
QUORUMS
QUOTA
QUOTABLE
QUOTABLY
QUOTAS
QUOTATION
QUOTATIONS
QUOTATIVE
QUOTATIVES
QUOTE
QUOTED
QUOTER
QUOTERS
QUOTES
QUOTH
QUOTHA
QUOTIDIAN
QUOTIDIANS
QUOTIENT
QUOTIENTS
QUOTING
QUOTITION
QUOTITIONS
QUOTUM
QUOTUMS
QUYTE
QUYTED
QUYTES
QUYTING
QWERTIES
QWERTY
QWERTYS

R

RABANNA	RABIDEST	RACHIAL	RACKS	RADIANS
RABANNAS	RABIDITIES	RACHIDES	RACKWORK	RADIANT
RABAT	RABIDITY	RACHIDIAL	RACKWORKS	RADIANTLY
RABATINE	RABIDLY	RACHIDIAN	RACLETTE	RADIANTS
RABATINES	RABIDNESS	RACHILLA	RACLETTES	RADIATA
RABATMENT	RABIDNESSES	RACHILLAS	RACLOIR	RADIATAS
RABATMENTS	RABIES	RACHIS	RACLOIRS	RADIATE
RABATO	RABIS	RACHISES	RACON	RADIATED
RABATOES	RACA	RACHITIC	RACONS	RADIATELY
RABATS	RACAHOUT	RACHITIS	RACONTEUR	RADIATES
RABATTE	RACAHOUTS	RACHITISES	RACONTEURS	RADIATING
RABATTED	RACCAHOUT	RACIAL	RACOON	RADIATION
RABATTES	RACCAHOUTS	RACIALISM	RACOONS	RADIATIONS
RABATTING	RACCOON	RACIALISMS	RACQUET	RADIATIVE
RABATTINGS	RACCOONS	RACIALIST	RACQUETS	RADIATOR
RABBET	RACE	RACIALISTS	RACY	RADIATORS
RABBETED	RACECARD	RACIALLY	RAD	RADIATORY
RABBETING	RACECARDS	RACIATION	RADAR	RADICAL
RABBETS	RACED	RACIATIONS	RADARS	RADICALLY
RABBI	RACEGOER	RACIER	RADDER	RADICALS
RABBIN	RACEGOERS	RACIEST	RADDEST	RADICANT
RABBINATE	RACEGOING	RACILY	RADDLE	RADICATE
RABBINATES	RACEGOINGS	RACINESS	RADDLED	RADICATED
RABBINIC	RACEHORSE	RACINESSES	RADDLEMAN	RADICATES
RABBINISM	RACEHORSES	RACING	RADDLEMEN	RADICATING
RABBINISMS	RACEMATE	RACINGS	RADDLES	RADICCHIO
RABBINIST	RACEMATES	RACISM	RADDLING	RADICCHIOS
RABBINISTS	RACEME	RACISMS	RADDOCKE	RADICEL
RABBINITE	RACEMED	RACIST	RADDOCKES	RADICELS
RABBINITES	RACEMES	RACISTS	RADE	RADICES
RABBINS	RACEMIC	RACK	RADGE	RADICLE
RABBIS	RACEMISE	RACKED	RADGER	RADICLES
RABBIT	RACEMISED	RACKER	RADGES	RADICULAR
RABBITED	RACEMISES	RACKERS	RADGEST	RADICULE
RABBITER	RACEMISING	RACKET	RADIAL	RADICULES
RABBITERS	RACEMISM	RACKETED	RADIALE	RADII
RABBITING	RACEMISMS	RACKETEER	RADIALIA	RADIO
RABBITRIES	RACEMIZE	RACKETEERED	RADIALISE	RADIOED
RABBITRY	RACEMIZED	RACKETEERING	RADIALISED	RADIOGRAM
RABBITS	RACEMIZES	RACKETEERINGS	RADIALISES	RADIOGRAMS
RABBITY	RACEMIZING	RACKETEERS	RADIALISING	RADIOING
RABBLE	RACEMOSE	RACKETER	RADIALITIES	RADIOLOGIES
RABBLED	RACEPATH	RACKETERS	RADIALITY	RADIOLOGY
RABBLER	RACEPATHS	RACKETIER	RADIALIZE	RADIONICS
RABBLERS	RACER	RACKETIEST	RADIALIZED	RADIOS
RABBLES	RACERS	RACKETING	RADIALIZES	RADIOTHON
RABBLING	RACES	RACKETRIES	RADIALIZING	RADIOTHONS
RABBLINGS	RACETRACK	RACKETRY	RADIALLY	RADISH
RABBONI	RACETRACKS	RACKETS	RADIALS	RADISHES
RABBONIS	RACEWAY	RACKETT	RADIAN	RADIUM
RABI	RACEWAYS	RACKETTS	RADIANCE	RADIUMS
RABIC	RACH	RACKETY	RADIANCES	RADIUS
RABID	RACHE	RACKING	RADIANCIES	RADIUSES
RABIDER	RACHES	RACKINGS	RADIANCY	RADIX

The Chambers Dictionary is the authority for many longer words; see *OSW* Introduction, page xii

RADOME	RAGGEDLY	RAI	RAINES	RAKER
RADOMES	RAGGEDY	RAID	RAINFALL	RAKERIES
RADON	RAGGEE	RAIDED	RAINFALLS	RAKERS
RADONS	RAGGEES	RAIDER	RAINIER	RAKERY
RADS	RAGGERIES	RAIDERS	RAINIEST	RAKES
RADULA	RAGGERY	RAIDING	RAININESS	RAKESHAME
RADULAE	RAGGIER	RAIDS	RAININESSES	RAKESHAMES
RADULAR	RAGGIES	RAIK	RAINING	RAKI
RADULATE	RAGGIEST	RAIKED	RAINLESS	RAKING
RADWASTE	RAGGING	RAIKING	RAINMAKER	RAKINGS
RADWASTES	RAGGINGS	RAIKS	RAINMAKERS	RAKIS
RAFALE	RAGGLE	RAIL	RAINPROOF	RAKISH
RAFALES	RAGGLED	RAILBED	RAINPROOFED	RAKISHLY
RAFF	RAGGLES	RAILBEDS	RAINPROOFING	RAKSHAS
RAFFIA	RAGGLING	RAILBUS	RAINPROOFS	RAKSHASA
RAFFIAS	RAGGS	RAILBUSES	RAINS	RAKSHASAS
RAFFINATE	RAGGY	RAILBUSSES	RAINSTORM	RAKSHASES
RAFFINATES	RAGHEAD	RAILCARD	RAINSTORMS	RAKU
RAFFINOSE	RAGHEADS	RAILCARDS	RAINTIGHT	RAKUS
RAFFINOSES	RAGI	RAILE	RAINWATER	RALE
RAFFISH	RAGING	RAILED	RAINWATERS	RALES
RAFFISHLY	RAGINGLY	RAILER	RAINWEAR	RALLIED
RAFFLE	RAGINGS	RAILERS	RAINWEARS	RALLIER
RAFFLED	RAGINI	RAILES	RAINY	RALLIERS
RAFFLER	RAGINIS	RAILHEAD	RAIRD	RALLIES
RAFFLERS	RAGIS	RAILHEADS	RAIRDS	RALLINE
RAFFLES	RAGLAN	RAILING	RAIS	RALLY
RAFFLING	RAGLANS	RAILINGLY	RAISABLE	RALLYE
RAFFS	RAGMAN	RAILINGS	RAISE	RALLYES
RAFT	RAGMANS	RAILLERIES	RAISEABLE	RALLYING
RAFTED	RAGMEN	RAILLERY	RAISED	RALLYINGS
RAFTER	RAGMENT	RAILLESS	RAISER	RALLYIST
RAFTERED	RAGMENTS	RAILLIES	RAISERS	RALLYISTS
RAFTERING	RAGOUT	RAILLY	RAISES	RAM
RAFTERINGS	RAGOUTED	RAILMAN	RAISIN	RAMAKIN
RAFTERS	RAGOUTING	RAILMEN	RAISING	RAMAKINS
RAFTING	RAGOUTS	RAILROAD	RAISINGS	RAMAL
RAFTMAN	RAGS	RAILROADED	RAISINS	RAMATE
RAFTMEN	RAGSTONE	RAILROADING	RAISONNE	RAMBLE
RAFTS	RAGSTONES	RAILROADS	RAIT	RAMBLED
RAFTSMAN	RAGTAG	RAILS	RAITA	RAMBLER
RAFTSMEN	RAGTAGS	RAILWAY	RAITAS	RAMBLERS
RAG	RAGTIME	RAILWAYS	RAITED	RAMBLES
RAGA	RAGTIMER	RAILWOMAN	RAITING	RAMBLING
RAGAS	RAGTIMERS	RAILWOMEN	RAITS	RAMBLINGS
RAGBAG	RAGTIMES	RAIMENT	RAIYAT	RAMBUTAN
RAGBAGS	RAGTOP	RAIMENTS	RAIYATS	RAMBUTANS
RAGBOLT	RAGTOPS	RAIN	RAJ	RAMCAT
RAGBOLTS	RAGULED	RAINBAND	RAJA	RAMCATS
RAGDE	RAGULY	RAINBANDS	RAJAH	RAMEAL
RAGE	RAGWEED	RAINBOW	RAJAHS	RAMEE
RAGED	RAGWEEDS	RAINBOWED	RAJAHSHIP	RAMEES
RAGEE	RAGWHEEL	RAINBOWS	RAJAHSHIPS	RAMEKIN
RAGEES	RAGWHEELS	RAINBOWY	RAJAS	RAMEKINS
RAGEFUL	RAGWORK	RAINCHECK	RAJASHIP	RAMEN
RAGER	RAGWORKS	RAINCHECKS	RAJASHIPS	RAMENS
RAGERS	RAGWORM	RAINCOAT	RAJES	RAMENTA
RAGES	RAGWORMS	RAINCOATS	RAKE	RAMENTUM
RAGG	RAGWORT	RAINDATE	RAKED	RAMEOUS
RAGGA	RAGWORTS	RAINDATES	RAKEE	RAMEQUIN
RAGGAS	RAH	RAINDROP	RAKEES	RAMEQUINS
RAGGED	RAHED	RAINDROPS	RAKEHELL	RAMFEEZLE
RAGGEDER	RAHING	RAINE	RAKEHELLS	RAMFEEZLED
RAGGEDEST	RAHS	RAINED	RAKEHELLY	RAMFEEZLES

RAMFEEZLING	RAMSON	RANDOMIZE	RANSOMED	RAPLOCH
RAMI	RAMSONS	RANDOMIZED	RANSOMER	RAPLOCHS
RAMIE	RAMSTAM	RANDOMIZES	RANSOMERS	RAPPAREE
RAMIES	RAMULAR	RANDOMIZING	RANSOMING	RAPPAREES
RAMIFIED	RAMULI	RANDOMLY	RANSOMS	RAPPED
RAMIFIES	RAMULOSE	RANDOMS	RANT	RAPPEE
RAMIFORM	RAMULOUS	RANDON	RANTED	RAPPEES
RAMIFY	RAMULUS	RANDONS	RANTER	RAPPEL
RAMIFYING	RAMUS	RANDS	RANTERISM	RAPPELLED
RAMIN	RAN	RANDY	RANTERISMS	RAPPELLING
RAMINS	RANA	RANEE	RANTERS	RAPPELLINGS
RAMIS	RANARIAN	RANEES	RANTING	RAPPELS
RAMJET	RANARIUM	RANG	RANTINGLY	RAPPER
RAMJETS	RANARIUMS	RANGATIRA	RANTINGS	RAPPERS
RAMMED	RANAS	RANGATIRAS	RANTIPOLE	RAPPING
RAMMER	RANCE	RANGE	RANTIPOLED	RAPPINGS
RAMMERS	RANCED	RANGED	RANTIPOLES	RAPPORT
RAMMIES	RANCEL	RANGELAND	RANTIPOLING	RAPPORTS
RAMMING	RANCELS	RANGELANDS	RANTS	RAPS
RAMMISH	RANCES	RANGER	RANULA	RAPT
RAMMY	RANCH	RANGERS	RANULAS	RAPTLY
RAMOSE	RANCHED	RANGES	RANUNCULI	RAPTOR
RAMOUS	RANCHER	RANGIER	RANZEL	RAPTORIAL
RAMP	RANCHERIA	RANGIEST	RANZELMAN	RAPTORS
RAMPAGE	RANCHERIAS	RANGINESS	RANZELMEN	RAPTURE
RAMPAGED	RANCHERIE	RANGINESSES	RANZELS	RAPTURED
RAMPAGES	RANCHERIES	RANGING	RAOULIA	RAPTURES
RAMPAGING	RANCHERO	RANGOLI	RAOULIAS	RAPTURING
RAMPAGINGS	RANCHEROS	RANGOLIS	RAP	RAPTURISE
RAMPANCIES	RANCHERS	RANGY	RAPACIOUS	RAPTURISED
RAMPANCY	RANCHES	RANI	RAPACITIES	RAPTURISES
RAMPANT	RANCHING	RANIFORM	RAPACITY	RAPTURISING
RAMPANTLY	RANCHINGS	RANINE	RAPE	RAPTURIST
RAMPART	RANCHMAN	RANIS	RAPED	RAPTURISTS
RAMPARTED	RANCHMEN	RANK	RAPER	RAPTURIZE
RAMPARTING	RANCHO	RANKE	RAPERS	RAPTURIZED
RAMPARTS	RANCHOS	RANKED	RAPES	RAPTURIZES
RAMPAUGE	RANCID	RANKER	RAPESEED	RAPTURIZING
RAMPAUGED	RANCIDER	RANKERS	RAPESEEDS	RAPTUROUS
RAMPAUGES	RANCIDEST	RANKES	RAPHANIA	RARE
RAMPAUGING	RANCIDITIES	RANKEST	RAPHANIAS	RAREBIT
RAMPED	RANCIDITY	RANKING	RAPHE	RAREBITS
RAMPER	RANCING	RANKINGS	RAPHES	RAREFIED
RAMPERS	RANCOR	RANKLE	RAPHIA	RAREFIES
RAMPICK	RANCOROUS	RANKLED	RAPHIAS	RAREFY
RAMPICKED	RANCORS	RANKLES	RAPHIDE	RAREFYING
RAMPICKS	RANCOUR	RANKLING	RAPHIDES	RARELY
RAMPIKE	RANCOURS	RANKLY	RAPHIS	RARENESS
RAMPIKES	RAND	RANKNESS	RAPID	RARENESSES
RAMPING	RANDAN	RANKNESSES	RAPIDER	RARER
RAMPINGS	RANDANS	RANKS	RAPIDEST	RAREST
RAMPION	RANDED	RANSACK	RAPIDITIES	RARING
RAMPIONS	RANDEM	RANSACKED	RAPIDITY	RARITIES
RAMPIRE	RANDEMS	RANSACKER	RAPIDLY	RARITY
RAMPIRED	RANDIE	RANSACKERS	RAPIDNESS	RAS
RAMPIRES	RANDIER	RANSACKING	RAPIDNESSES	RASCAILLE
RAMPS	RANDIES	RANSACKS	RAPIDS	RASCAILLES
RAMPSMAN	RANDIEST	RANSEL	RAPIER	RASCAL
RAMPSMEN	RANDING	RANSELS	RAPIERS	RASCALDOM
RAMROD	RANDOM	RANSHAKLE	RAPINE	RASCALDOMS
RAMRODDED	RANDOMISE	RANSHAKLED	RAPINES	RASCALISM
RAMRODDING	RANDOMISED	RANSHAKLES	RAPING	RASCALISMS
RAMRODS	RANDOMISES	RANSHAKLING	RAPIST	RASCALITIES
RAMS	RANDOMISING	RANSOM	RAPISTS	RASCALITY

RASCALLIEST	RATAPLAN	RATOO	RAUNCHES	RAWING
RASCALLY	RATAPLANS	RATOON	RAUNCHIER	RAWINGS
RASCALS	RATAS	RATOONED	RAUNCHIEST	RAWISH
RASCASSE	RATBAG	RATOONER	RAUNCHILY	RAWLY
RASCASSES	RATBAGS	RATOONERS	RAUNCHING	RAWN
RASCHEL	RATCH	RATOONING	RAUNCHY	RAWNESS
RASCHELS	RATCHED	RATOONS	RAUNGE	RAWNESSES
RASE	RATCHES	RATOOS	RAUNGED	RAWNS
RASED	RATCHET	RATPACK	RAUNGES	RAWS
RASES	RATCHETED	RATPACKS	RAUNGING	RAX
RASH	RATCHETING	RATPROOF	RAUNS	RAXED
RASHED	RATCHETS	RATS	RAVAGE	RAXES
RASHER	RATCHING	RATSBANE	RAVAGED	RAXING
RASHERS	RATE	RATSBANES	RAVAGER	RAY
RASHES	RATEABLE	RATTAN	RAVAGERS	RAYAH
RASHEST	RATEABLY	RATTANS	RAVAGES	RAYAHS
RASHING	RATED	RATTED	RAVAGING	RAYED
RASHLY	RATEL	RATTEEN	RAVE	RAYING
RASHNESS	RATELS	RATTEENS	RAVED	RAYLE
RASHNESSES	RATEPAYER	RATTEN	RAVEL	RAYLED
RASING	RATEPAYERS	RATTENED	RAVELIN	RAYLES
RASORIAL	RATER	RATTENING	RAVELINS	RAYLESS
RASP	RATERS	RATTENINGS	RAVELLED	RAYLET
RASPATORIES	RATES	RATTENS	RAVELLING	RAYLETS
RASPATORY	RATFINK	RATTER	RAVELLINGS	RAYLING
RASPBERRIES	RATFINKS	RATTERIES	RAVELMENT	RAYNE
RASPBERRY	RATH	RATTERS	RAVELMENTS	RAYNES
RASPED	RATHE	RATTERY	RAVELS	RAYON
RASPER	RATHER	RATTIER	RAVEN	RAYONS
RASPERS	RATHEREST	RATTIEST	RAVENED	RAYS
RASPIER	RATHERIPE	RATTING	RAVENER	RAZE
RASPIEST	RATHERIPES	RATTINGS	RAVENERS	RAZED
RASPING	RATHERISH	RATTISH	RAVENING	RAZEE
RASPINGLY	RATHEST	RATTLE	RAVENOUS	RAZEED
RASPINGS	RATHRIPE	RATTLEBAG	RAVENS	RAZEEING
RASPS	RATHRIPES	RATTLEBAGS	RAVER	RAZEES
RASPY	RATHS	RATTLED	RAVERS	RAZES
RASSE	RATIFIED	RATTLER	RAVES	RAZING
RASSES	RATIFIER	RATTLERS	RAVIN	RAZMATAZ
RAST	RATIFIERS	RATTLES	RAVINE	RAZMATAZES
RASTA	RATIFIES	RATTLIER	RAVINED	RAZOO
RASTAFARI	RATIFY	RATTLIEST	RAVINES	RAZOOS
RASTER	RATIFYING	RATTLIN	RAVING	RAZOR
RASTERISE	RATINE	RATTLINE	RAVINGLY	RAZORABLE
RASTERISED	RATINES	RATTLINES	RAVINGS	RAZORS
RASTERISES	RATING	RATTLING	RAVINING	RAZURE
RASTERISING	RATINGS	RATTLINGS	RAVINS	RAZURES
RASTERIZE	RATIO	RATTLINS	RAVIOLI	RAZZ
RASTERIZED	RATION	RATTLY	RAVIOLIS	RAZZED
RASTERIZES	RATIONAL	RATTON	RAVISH	RAZZES
RASTERIZING	RATIONALE	RATTONS	RAVISHED	RAZZIA
RASTERS	RATIONALES	RATTY	RAVISHER	RAZZIAS
RASTRUM	RATIONALS	RATU	RAVISHERS	RAZZING
RASTRUMS	RATIONED	RATUS	RAVISHES	RAZZLE
RASURE	RATIONING	RAUCID	RAVISHING	RAZZLES
RASURES	RATIONS	RAUCLE	RAW	RE
RAT	RATIOS	RAUCLER	RAWBONE	REABSORB
RATA	RATITE	RAUCLEST	RAWBONED	REABSORBED
RATABLE	RATLIN	RAUCOUS	RAWER	REABSORBING
RATABLY	RATLINE	RAUCOUSLY	RAWEST	REABSORBS
RATAFIA	RATLINES	RAUGHT	RAWHEAD	REACH
RATAFIAS	RATLING	RAUN	RAWHEADS	REACHABLE
RATAN	RATLINGS	RAUNCH	RAWHIDE	REACHED
RATANS	RATLINS	RAUNCHED	RAWHIDES	REACHER

REACHERS	READVISE	REALMLESS	REAR	REASSUME
REACHES	READVISED	REALMS	REARED	REASSUMED
REACHING	READVISES	REALNESS	REARER	REASSUMES
REACHLESS	READVISING	REALNESSES	REARERS	REASSUMING
REACQUIRE	READY	REALO	REARGUARD	REASSURE
REACQUIRED	READYING	REALOS	REARGUARDS	REASSURED
REACQUIRES	REAEDIFIED	REALS	REARHORSE	REASSURER
REACQUIRING	REAEDIFIES	REALTIE	REARHORSES	REASSURERS
REACT	REAEDIFY	REALTIES	REARING	REASSURES
REACTANCE	REAEDIFYE	REALTIME	REARISE	REASSURING
REACTANCES	REAEDIFYED	REALTOR	REARISEN	REAST
REACTANT	REAEDIFYES	REALTORS	REARISES	REASTED
REACTANTS	REAEDIFYING	REALTY	REARISING	REASTIER
REACTED	REAFFIRM	REAM	REARLY	REASTIEST
REACTING	REAFFIRMED	REAME	REARM	REASTING
REACTION	REAFFIRMING	REAMED	REARMED	REASTS
REACTIONS	REAFFIRMS	REAMEND	REARMICE	REASTY
REACTIVE	REAGENCIES	REAMENDED	REARMING	REATA
REACTOR	REAGENCY	REAMENDING	REARMOST	REATAS
REACTORS	REAGENT	REAMENDS	REARMOUSE	REATE
REACTS	REAGENTS	REAMER	REARMS	REATES
REACTUATE	REAK	REAMERS	REAROSE	REATTACH
REACTUATED	REAKED	REAMES	REAROUSAL	REATTACHED
REACTUATES	REAKING	REAMIER	REAROUSALS	REATTACHES
REACTUATING	REAKS	REAMIEST	REAROUSE	REATTACHING
READ	REAL	REAMING	REAROUSED	REATTAIN
READABLE	REALER	REAMS	REAROUSES	REATTAINED
READABLY	REALEST	REAMY	REAROUSING	REATTAINING
READAPT	REALGAR	REAN	REARRANGE	REATTAINS
READAPTED	REALGARS	REANIMATE	REARRANGED	REATTEMPT
READAPTING	REALIA	REANIMATED	REARRANGES	REATTEMPTED
READAPTS	REALIGN	REANIMATES	REARRANGING	REATTEMPTING
READDRESS	REALIGNED	REANIMATING	REARREST	REATTEMPTS
READDRESSED	REALIGNING	REANNEX	REARRESTED	REAVE
READDRESSES	REALIGNS	REANNEXED	REARRESTING	REAVER
READDRESSING	REALISE	REANNEXES	REARRESTS	REAVERS
READER	REALISED	REANNEXING	REARS	REAVES
READERS	REALISER	REANS	REARWARD	REAVING
READIED	REALISERS	REANSWER	REARWARDS	REAWAKE
READIER	REALISES	REANSWERED	REASCEND	REAWAKED
READIES	REALISING	REANSWERING	REASCENDED	REAWAKEN
READIEST	REALISM	REANSWERS	REASCENDING	REAWAKENED
READILY	REALISMS	REAP	REASCENDS	REAWAKENING
READINESS	REALIST	REAPED	REASCENT	REAWAKENINGS
READINESSES	REALISTIC	REAPER	REASCENTS	REAWAKENS
READING	REALISTS	REAPERS	REASON	REAWAKES
READINGS	REALITIES	REAPING	REASONED	REAWAKING
READJUST	REALITY	REAPPAREL	REASONER	REAWOKE
READJUSTED	REALIZE	REAPPARELLED	REASONERS	REAWOKEN
READJUSTING	REALIZED	REAPPARELLING	REASONING	REBACK
READJUSTS	REALIZER	REAPPARELS	REASONINGS	REBACKED
READMIT	REALIZERS	REAPPEAR	REASONS	REBACKING
READMITS	REALIZES	REAPPEARED	REASSERT	REBACKS
READMITTED	REALIZING	REAPPEARING	REASSERTED	REBADGE
READMITTING	REALLIE	REAPPEARS	REASSERTING	REBADGED
READOPT	REALLIED	REAPPLIED	REASSERTS	REBADGES
READOPTED	REALLIES	REAPPLIES	REASSESS	REBADGING
READOPTING	REALLOT	REAPPLY	REASSESSED	REBAPTISE
READOPTS	REALLOTS	REAPPLYING	REASSESSES	REBAPTISED
READS	REALLOTTED	REAPPOINT	REASSESSING	REBAPTISES
READVANCE	REALLOTTING	REAPPOINTED	REASSIGN	REBAPTISING
READVANCED	REALLY	REAPPOINTING	REASSIGNED	REBAPTISM
READVANCES	REALLYING	REAPPOINTS	REASSIGNING	REBAPTISMS
READVANCING	REALM	REAPS	REASSIGNS	REBAPTIZE

REBAPTIZED
REBAPTIZES
REBAPTIZING
REBATE
REBATED
REBATER
REBATERS
REBATES
REBATING
REBATO
REBATOES
REBBE
REBBES
REBBETZIN
REBBETZINS
REBEC
REBECK
REBECKS
REBECS
REBEL
REBELDOM
REBELDOMS
REBELLED
REBELLER
REBELLERS
REBELLING
REBELLION
REBELLIONS
REBELLOW
REBELLOWED
REBELLOWING
REBELLOWS
REBELS
REBID
REBIDDEN
REBIDDING
REBIDS
REBIND
REBINDING
REBINDS
REBIRTH
REBIRTHS
REBIT
REBITE
REBITES
REBITING
REBITTEN
REBLOOM
REBLOOMED
REBLOOMING
REBLOOMS
REBLOSSOM
REBLOSSOMED
REBLOSSOMING
REBLOSSOMS
REBOANT
REBOATION
REBOATIONS
REBOIL
REBOILED
REBOILING
REBOILS
REBOOT
REBOOTED

REBOOTING
REBOOTS
REBORE
REBORED
REBORES
REBORING
REBORN
REBORROW
REBORROWED
REBORROWING
REBORROWS
REBOUND
REBOUNDED
REBOUNDING
REBOUNDS
REBRACE
REBRACED
REBRACES
REBRACING
REBUFF
REBUFFED
REBUFFING
REBUFFS
REBUILD
REBUILDING
REBUILDS
REBUILT
REBUKABLE
REBUKE
REBUKED
REBUKEFUL
REBUKER
REBUKERS
REBUKES
REBUKING
REBURIAL
REBURIALS
REBURIED
REBURIES
REBURY
REBURYING
REBUS
REBUSES
REBUT
REBUTMENT
REBUTMENTS
REBUTS
REBUTTAL
REBUTTALS
REBUTTED
REBUTTER
REBUTTERS
REBUTTING
REBUTTON
REBUTTONED
REBUTTONING
REBUTTONS
REC
RECAL
RECALESCE
RECALESCED
RECALESCES
RECALESCING
RECALL

RECALLED
RECALLING
RECALLS
RECALMENT
RECALMENTS
RECALS
RECANT
RECANTED
RECANTER
RECANTERS
RECANTING
RECANTS
RECAP
RECAPPED
RECAPPING
RECAPS
RECAPTION
RECAPTIONS
RECAPTOR
RECAPTORS
RECAPTURE
RECAPTURED
RECAPTURES
RECAPTURING
RECAST
RECASTING
RECASTS
RECATCH
RECATCHES
RECATCHING
RECAUGHT
RECCE
RECCED
RECCEED
RECCEING
RECCES
RECCIED
RECCIES
RECCO
RECCOS
RECCY
RECCYING
RECEDE
RECEDED
RECEDES
RECEDING
RECEIPT
RECEIPTED
RECEIPTING
RECEIPTS
RECEIVAL
RECEIVALS
RECEIVE
RECEIVED
RECEIVER
RECEIVERS
RECEIVES
RECEIVING
RECEIVINGS
RECENCIES
RECENCY
RECENSE
RECENSED
RECENSES

RECENSING
RECENSION
RECENSIONS
RECENT
RECENTER
RECENTEST
RECENTLY
RECENTRE
RECENTRED
RECENTRES
RECENTRING
RECEPT
RECEPTION
RECEPTIONS
RECEPTIVE
RECEPTOR
RECEPTORS
RECEPTS
RECESS
RECESSED
RECESSES
RECESSING
RECESSION
RECESSIONS
RECESSIVE
RECESSIVES
RECHARGE
RECHARGED
RECHARGES
RECHARGING
RECHART
RECHARTED
RECHARTER
RECHARTERED
RECHARTERING
RECHARTERS
RECHARTING
RECHARTS
RECHATE
RECHATES
RECHAUFFE
RECHAUFFES
RECHEAT
RECHEATED
RECHEATING
RECHEATS
RECHECK
RECHECKED
RECHECKING
RECHECKS
RECHERCHE
RECHIE
RECHLESSE
RECIPE
RECIPES
RECIPIENT
RECIPIENTS
RECISION
RECISIONS
RECIT
RECITAL
RECITALS
RECITE
RECITED

RECITER
RECITERS
RECITES
RECITING
RECITS
RECK
RECKAN
RECKED
RECKING
RECKLESS
RECKLING
RECKLINGS
RECKON
RECKONED
RECKONER
RECKONERS
RECKONING
RECKONINGS
RECKONS
RECKS
RECLAIM
RECLAIMED
RECLAIMER
RECLAIMERS
RECLAIMING
RECLAIMS
RECLAME
RECLAMES
RECLIMB
RECLIMBED
RECLIMBING
RECLIMBS
RECLINATE
RECLINE
RECLINED
RECLINER
RECLINERS
RECLINES
RECLINING
RECLOSE
RECLOSED
RECLOSES
RECLOSING
RECLOTHE
RECLOTHED
RECLOTHES
RECLOTHING
RECLUSE
RECLUSELY
RECLUSES
RECLUSION
RECLUSIONS
RECLUSIVE
RECLUSORIES
RECLUSORY
RECODE
RECODED
RECODES
RECODING
RECOGNISE
RECOGNISED
RECOGNISES
RECOGNISING
RECOGNIZE

The Chambers Dictionary is the authority for many longer words; see *OSW* Introduction, page xii

RECOGNIZED	RECONVENES	RECREATED	RECULING	REDBUD
RECOGNIZES	RECONVENING	RECREATES	RECUMBENT	REDBUDS
RECOGNIZING	RECONVERT	RECREATING	RECUR	REDCAP
RECOIL	RECONVERTED	RECREMENT	RECURE	REDCAPS
RECOILED	RECONVERTING	RECREMENTS	RECURED	REDCOAT
RECOILER	RECONVERTS	RECROSS	RECURES	REDCOATS
RECOILERS	RECONVEY	RECROSSED	RECURING	REDD
RECOILING	RECONVEYED	RECROSSES	RECURRED	REDDEN
RECOILS	RECONVEYING	RECROSSING	RECURRENT	REDDENDA
RECOIN	RECONVEYS	RECRUIT	RECURRING	REDDENDO
RECOINAGE	RECORD	RECRUITAL	RECURS	REDDENDOS
RECOINAGES	RECORDED	RECRUITALS	RECURSION	REDDENDUM
RECOINED	RECORDER	RECRUITED	RECURSIONS	REDDENED
RECOINING	RECORDERS	RECRUITER	RECURSIVE	REDDENING
RECOINS	RECORDING	RECRUITERS	RECURVE	REDDENS
RECOLLECT	RECORDINGS	RECRUITING	RECURVED	REDDER
RECOLLECTED	RECORDIST	RECRUITS	RECURVES	REDDERS
RECOLLECTING	RECORDISTS	RECS	RECURVING	REDDEST
RECOLLECTS	RECORDS	RECTA	RECUSANCE	REDDIER
RECOLLET	RECOUNT	RECTAL	RECUSANCES	REDDIEST
RECOLLETS	RECOUNTAL	RECTALLY	RECUSANCIES	REDDING
RECOMBINE	RECOUNTALS	RECTANGLE	RECUSANCY	REDDINGS
RECOMBINED	RECOUNTED	RECTANGLES	RECUSANT	REDDISH
RECOMBINES	RECOUNTING	RECTI	RECUSANTS	REDDLE
RECOMBINING	RECOUNTS	RECTIFIED	RECUSE	REDDLED
RECOMFORT	RECOUP	RECTIFIER	RECUSED	REDDLEMAN
RECOMFORTED	RECOUPED	RECTIFIERS	RECUSES	REDDLEMEN
RECOMFORTING	RECOUPING	RECTIFIES	RECUSING	REDDLES
RECOMFORTS	RECOUPS	RECTIFY	RECYCLATE	REDDLING
RECOMMEND	RECOURE	RECTIFYING	RECYCLATES	REDDS
RECOMMENDED	RECOURED	RECTION	RECYCLE	REDDY
RECOMMENDING	RECOURES	RECTIONS	RECYCLED	REDE
RECOMMENDS	RECOURING	RECTITIC	RECYCLES	REDEAL
RECOMMIT	RECOURSE	RECTITIS	RECYCLING	REDEALING
RECOMMITS	RECOURSED	RECTITISES	RECYCLIST	REDEALS
RECOMMITTED	RECOURSES	RECTITUDE	RECYCLISTS	REDEALT
RECOMMITTING	RECOURSING	RECTITUDES	RED	REDECRAFT
RECOMPACT	RECOVER	RECTO	REDACT	REDECRAFTS
RECOMPACTED	RECOVERED	RECTOR	REDACTED	REDEEM
RECOMPACTING	RECOVEREE	RECTORAL	REDACTING	REDEEMED
RECOMPACTS	RECOVEREES	RECTORATE	REDACTION	REDEEMER
RECOMPOSE	RECOVERER	RECTORATES	REDACTIONS	REDEEMERS
RECOMPOSED	RECOVERERS	RECTORESS	REDACTOR	REDEEMING
RECOMPOSES	RECOVERIES	RECTORESSES	REDACTORS	REDEEMS
RECOMPOSING	RECOVERING	RECTORIAL	REDACTS	REDEFINE
RECONCILE	RECOVEROR	RECTORIALS	REDAN	REDEFINED
RECONCILED	RECOVERORS	RECTORIES	REDANS	REDEFINES
RECONCILES	RECOVERS	RECTORS	REDARGUE	REDEFINING
RECONCILING	RECOVERY	RECTORY	REDARGUED	REDELESS
RECONDITE	RECOWER	RECTOS	REDARGUES	REDELIVER
RECONFIRM	RECOWERED	RECTRESS	REDARGUING	REDELIVERED
RECONFIRMED	RECOWERING	RECTRESSES	REDATE	REDELIVERING
RECONFIRMING	RECOWERS	RECTRICES	REDATED	REDELIVERS
RECONFIRMS	RECOYLE	RECTRIX	REDATES	REDEPLOY
RECONNECT	RECOYLED	RECTUM	REDATING	REDEPLOYED
RECONNECTED	RECOYLES	RECTUMS	REDBACK	REDEPLOYING
RECONNECTING	RECOYLING	RECTUS	REDBACKS	REDEPLOYS
RECONNECTS	RECREANCE	RECUILE	REDBELLIES	REDES
RECONQUER	RECREANCES	RECUILED	REDBELLY	REDESCEND
RECONQUERED	RECREANCIES	RECUILES	REDBIRD	REDESCENDED
RECONQUERING	RECREANCY	RECUILING	REDBIRDS	REDESCENDING
RECONQUERS	RECREANT	RECULE	REDBREAST	REDESCENDS
RECONVENE	RECREANTS	RECULED	REDBREASTS	REDESIGN
RECONVENED	RECREATE	RECULES	REDBRICK	REDESIGNED

The Chambers Dictionary is the authority for many longer words; see *OSW* Introduction, page xii

REDESIGNING	REDOUBTS	REDUNDANT	REELINGS	REFIGURING
REDESIGNS	REDOUND	REDUVIID	REELMAN	REFILL
REDEVELOP	REDOUNDED	REDUVIIDS	REELMEN	REFILLED
REDEVELOPED	REDOUNDING	REDWATER	REELS	REFILLING
REDEVELOPING	REDOUNDINGS	REDWATERS	REEN	REFILLS
REDEVELOPS	REDOUNDS	REDWING	REENS	REFINE
REDFISH	REDOWA	REDWINGS	REES	REFINED
REDFISHES	REDOWAS	REDWOOD	REEST	REFINEDLY
REDHANDED	REDOX	REDWOODS	REESTED	REFINER
REDHEAD	REDPOLL	REE	REESTIER	REFINERIES
REDHEADS	REDPOLLS	REEBOK	REESTIEST	REFINERY
REDIA	REDRAFT	REEBOKS	REESTING	REFINES
REDIAE	REDRAFTED	REECH	REESTS	REFINING
REDIAL	REDRAFTING	REECHED	REESTY	REFININGS
REDIALED	REDRAFTS	REECHES	REEVE	REFIT
REDIALING	REDRAW	REECHIE	REEVED	REFITMENT
REDIALLED	REDRAWING	REECHIER	REEVES	REFITMENTS
REDIALLING	REDRAWN	REECHIEST	REEVING	REFITS
REDIALS	REDRAWS	REECHING	REF	REFITTED
REDID	REDRESS	REECHY	REFACE	REFITTING
REDING	REDRESSED	REED	REFACED	REFITTINGS
REDINGOTE	REDRESSER	REEDBED	REFACES	REFLAG
REDINGOTES	REDRESSERS	REEDBEDS	REFACING	REFLAGGED
REDIP	REDRESSES	REEDE	REFASHION	REFLAGGING
REDIPPED	REDRESSING	REEDED	REFASHIONED	REFLAGS
REDIPPING	REDREW	REEDEN	REFASHIONING	REFLATE
REDIPS	REDRIVE	REEDER	REFASHIONS	REFLATED
REDIRECT	REDRIVEN	REEDERS	REFECT	REFLATES
REDIRECTED	REDRIVES	REEDES	REFECTED	REFLATING
REDIRECTING	REDRIVING	REEDIER	REFECTING	REFLATION
REDIRECTS	REDROOT	REEDIEST	REFECTION	REFLATIONS
REDISTIL	REDROOTS	REEDINESS	REFECTIONS	REFLECT
REDISTILLED	REDROVE	REEDINESSES	REFECTORIES	REFLECTED
REDISTILLING	REDS	REEDING	REFECTORY	REFLECTER
REDISTILS	REDSEAR	REEDINGS	REFECTS	REFLECTERS
REDIVIDE	REDSHANK	REEDLING	REFEL	REFLECTING
REDIVIDED	REDSHANKS	REEDLINGS	REFELLED	REFLECTOR
REDIVIDES	REDSHARE	REEDMACE	REFELLING	REFLECTORS
REDIVIDING	REDSHIRE	REEDMACES	REFELS	REFLECTS
REDIVIVUS	REDSHORT	REEDS	REFER	REFLET
REDLEG	REDSKIN	REEDSTOP	REFERABLE	REFLETS
REDLEGS	REDSKINS	REEDSTOPS	REFEREE	REFLEX
REDLY	REDSTART	REEDY	REFEREED	REFLEXED
REDNECK	REDSTARTS	REEF	REFEREEING	REFLEXES
REDNECKS	REDSTREAK	REEFED	REFEREES	REFLEXING
REDNESS	REDSTREAKS	REEFER	REFERENCE	REFLEXION
REDNESSES	REDTOP	REEFERS	REFERENCED	REFLEXIONS
REDO	REDTOPS	REEFING	REFERENCES	REFLEXIVE
REDOES	REDUCE	REEFINGS	REFERENCING	REFLEXLY
REDOING	REDUCED	REEFS	REFERENDA	REFLOAT
REDOLENCE	REDUCER	REEK	REFERENT	REFLOATED
REDOLENCES	REDUCERS	REEKED	REFERENTS	REFLOATING
REDOLENCIES	REDUCES	REEKIE	REFERRAL	REFLOATS
REDOLENCY	REDUCIBLE	REEKIER	REFERRALS	REFLOW
REDOLENT	REDUCING	REEKIEST	REFERRED	REFLOWED
REDONE	REDUCTANT	REEKING	REFERRING	REFLOWER
REDOS	REDUCTANTS	REEKS	REFERS	REFLOWERED
REDOUBLE	REDUCTASE	REEKY	REFFED	REFLOWERING
REDOUBLED	REDUCTASES	REEL	REFFING	REFLOWERINGS
REDOUBLES	REDUCTION	REELED	REFFO	REFLOWERS
REDOUBLING	REDUCTIONS	REELER	REFFOS	REFLOWING
REDOUBT	REDUCTIVE	REELERS	REFIGURE	REFLOWINGS
REDOUBTED	REDUIT	REELING	REFIGURED	REFLOWS
REDOUBTING	REDUITS	REELINGLY	REFIGURES	

REFLUENCE	REFRAMING	REFUTABLE	REGGOS	REGRATES
REFLUENCES	REFREEZE	REFUTABLY	REGICIDAL	REGRATING
REFLUENT	REFREEZES	REFUTAL	REGICIDE	REGRATINGS
REFLUX	REFREEZING	REFUTALS	REGICIDES	REGRATOR
REFLUXED	REFRESH	REFUTE	REGIE	REGRATORS
REFLUXES	REFRESHED	REFUTED	REGIES	REGREDE
REFLUXING	REFRESHEN	REFUTER	REGIME	REGREDED
REFOCUS	REFRESHENED	REFUTERS	REGIMEN	REGREDES
REFOCUSED	REFRESHENING	REFUTES	REGIMENS	REGREDING
REFOCUSES	REFRESHENS	REFUTING	REGIMENT	REGREET
REFOCUSING	REFRESHER	REGAIN	REGIMENTED	REGREETED
REFOCUSSED	REFRESHERS	REGAINED	REGIMENTING	REGREETING
REFOCUSSES	REFRESHES	REGAINER	REGIMENTS	REGREETS
REFOCUSSING	REFRESHING	REGAINERS	REGIMES	REGRESS
REFOOT	REFRINGE	REGAINING	REGIMINAL	REGRESSED
REFOOTED	REFRINGED	REGAINS	REGINA	REGRESSES
REFOOTING	REFRINGES	REGAL	REGINAE	REGRESSING
REFOOTS	REFRINGING	REGALE	REGINAL	REGRET
REFOREST	REFROZE	REGALED	REGINAS	REGRETFUL
REFORESTED	REFROZEN	REGALES	REGION	REGRETS
REFORESTING	REFS	REGALIA	REGIONAL	REGRETTED
REFORESTS	REFT	REGALIAN	REGIONARY	REGRETTING
REFORM	REFUEL	REGALIAS	REGIONS	REGRIND
REFORMADE	REFUELLED	REGALING	REGISSEUR	REGRINDING
REFORMADES	REFUELLING	REGALISM	REGISSEURS	REGRINDS
REFORMADO	REFUELS	REGALISMS	REGISTER	REGROUND
REFORMADOES	REFUGE	REGALIST	REGISTERED	REGROUP
REFORMADOS	REFUGED	REGALISTS	REGISTERING	REGROUPED
REFORMAT	REFUGEE	REGALITIES	REGISTERS	REGROUPING
REFORMATS	REFUGEES	REGALITY	REGISTRAR	REGROUPS
REFORMATTED	REFUGES	REGALLY	REGISTRARS	REGROWTH
REFORMATTING	REFUGIA	REGALS	REGISTRIES	REGROWTHS
REFORMED	REFUGING	REGAR	REGISTRY	REGUERDON
REFORMER	REFUGIUM	REGARD	REGIUS	REGUERDONED
REFORMERS	REFULGENT	REGARDANT	REGIVE	REGUERDONING
REFORMING	REFUND	REGARDED	REGIVEN	REGUERDONS
REFORMISM	REFUNDED	REGARDER	REGIVES	REGULA
REFORMISMS	REFUNDER	REGARDERS	REGIVING	REGULAE
REFORMIST	REFUNDERS	REGARDFUL	REGLET	REGULAR
REFORMISTS	REFUNDING	REGARDING	REGLETS	REGULARLY
REFORMS	REFUNDS	REGARDS	REGMA	REGULARS
REFORTIFIED	REFURBISH	REGARS	REGMATA	REGULATE
REFORTIFIES	REFURBISHED	REGATHER	REGNAL	REGULATED
REFORTIFY	REFURBISHES	REGATHERED	REGNANT	REGULATES
REFORTIFYING	REFURBISHING	REGATHERING	REGO	REGULATING
REFOUND	REFURNISH	REGATHERS	REGOLITH	REGULATOR
REFOUNDED	REFURNISHED	REGATTA	REGOLITHS	REGULATORS
REFOUNDER	REFURNISHES	REGATTAS	REGORGE	REGULINE
REFOUNDERS	REFURNISHING	REGAVE	REGORGED	REGULISE
REFOUNDING	REFUSABLE	REGELATE	REGORGES	REGULISED
REFOUNDS	REFUSAL	REGELATED	REGORGING	REGULISES
REFRACT	REFUSALS	REGELATES	REGOS	REGULISING
REFRACTED	REFUSE	REGELATING	REGRADE	REGULIZE
REFRACTING	REFUSED	REGENCE	REGRADED	REGULIZED
REFRACTOR	REFUSENIK	REGENCES	REGRADES	REGULIZES
REFRACTORS	REFUSENIKS	REGENCIES	REGRADING	REGULIZING
REFRACTS	REFUSER	REGENCY	REGRANT	REGULO®
REFRAIN	REFUSERS	REGENT	REGRANTED	REGULOS
REFRAINED	REFUSES	REGENTS	REGRANTING	REGULUS
REFRAINING	REFUSING	REGEST	REGRANTS	REGULUSES
REFRAINS	REFUSION	REGESTS	REGRATE	REGUR
REFRAME	REFUSIONS	REGGAE	REGRATED	REGURS
REFRAMED	REFUSNIK	REGGAES	REGRATER	REH
REFRAMES	REFUSNIKS	REGGO	REGRATERS	REHANDLE

REHANDLED	REILLUMES	REINSTALLS	REJIGGERING	RELAXANT
REHANDLES	REILLUMING	REINSTATE	REJIGGERS	RELAXANTS
REHANDLING	REIMBURSE	REINSTATED	REJIGGING	RELAXED
REHANDLINGS	REIMBURSED	REINSTATES	REJIGS	RELAXES
REHANG	REIMBURSES	REINSTATING	REJOICE	RELAXIN
REHANGING	REIMBURSING	REINSURE	REJOICED	RELAXING
REHANGS	REIMPLANT	REINSURED	REJOICER	RELAXINS
REHASH	REIMPLANTED	REINSURER	REJOICERS	RELAY
REHASHED	REIMPLANTING	REINSURERS	REJOICES	RELAYED
REHASHES	REIMPLANTS	REINSURES	REJOICING	RELAYING
REHASHING	REIMPORT	REINSURING	REJOICINGS	RELAYS
REHEAR	REIMPORTED	REINTER	REJOIN	RELEASE
REHEARD	REIMPORTING	REINTERRED	REJOINDER	RELEASED
REHEARING	REIMPORTS	REINTERRING	REJOINDERS	RELEASEE
REHEARINGS	REIMPOSE	REINTERS	REJOINED	RELEASEES
REHEARS	REIMPOSED	REINVEST	REJOINING	RELEASER
REHEARSAL	REIMPOSES	REINVESTED	REJOINS	RELEASERS
REHEARSALS	REIMPOSING	REINVESTING	REJON	RELEASES
REHEARSE	REIN	REINVESTS	REJONEO	RELEASING
REHEARSED	REINDEER	REINVOLVE	REJONEOS	RELEASOR
REHEARSER	REINDEERS	REINVOLVED	REJONES	RELEASORS
REHEARSERS	REINED	REINVOLVES	REJOURN	RELEGABLE
REHEARSES	REINETTE	REINVOLVING	REJOURNED	RELEGATE
REHEARSING	REINETTES	REIRD	REJOURNING	RELEGATED
REHEARSINGS	REINFORCE	REIRDS	REJOURNS	RELEGATES
REHEAT	REINFORCED	REIS	REJUDGE	RELEGATING
REHEATED	REINFORCES	REISES	REJUDGED	RELENT
REHEATER	REINFORCING	REISSUE	REJUDGES	RELENTED
REHEATERS	REINFORM	REISSUED	REJUDGING	RELENTING
REHEATING	REINFORMED	REISSUES	REKE	RELENTINGS
REHEATS	REINFORMING	REISSUING	REKED	RELENTS
REHEEL	REINFORMS	REIST	REKES	RELET
REHEELED	REINFUND	REISTAFEL	REKINDLE	RELETS
REHEELING	REINFUNDED	REISTAFELS	REKINDLED	RELETTING
REHEELS	REINFUNDING	REISTED	REKINDLES	RELEVANCE
REHOBOAM	REINFUNDS	REISTING	REKINDLING	RELEVANCES
REHOBOAMS	REINFUSE	REISTS	REKING	RELEVANCIES
REHOUSE	REINFUSED	REITER	RELACHE	RELEVANCY
REHOUSED	REINFUSES	REITERANT	RELACHES	RELEVANT
REHOUSES	REINFUSING	REITERATE	RELAID	RELIABLE
REHOUSING	REINHABIT	REITERATED	RELAPSE	RELIABLY
REHOUSINGS	REINHABITED	REITERATES	RELAPSED	RELIANCE
REHS	REINHABITING	REITERATING	RELAPSER	RELIANCES
REHUNG	REINHABITS	REITERS	RELAPSERS	RELIANT
REHYDRATE	REINING	REIVE	RELAPSES	RELIC
REHYDRATED	REINLESS	REIVER	RELAPSING	RELICS
REHYDRATES	REINS	REIVERS	RELATE	RELICT
REHYDRATING	REINSERT	REIVES	RELATED	RELICTS
REIF	REINSERTED	REIVING	RELATER	RELIDE
REIFIED	REINSERTING	REJECT	RELATERS	RELIE
REIFIES	REINSERTS	REJECTED	RELATES	RELIED
REIFS	REINSMAN	REJECTER	RELATING	RELIEF
REIFY	REINSMEN	REJECTERS	RELATION	RELIEFS
REIFYING	REINSPECT	REJECTING	RELATIONS	RELIER
REIGN	REINSPECTED	REJECTION	RELATIVAL	RELIERS
REIGNED	REINSPECTING	REJECTIONS	RELATIVE	RELIES
REIGNING	REINSPECTS	REJECTIVE	RELATIVES	RELIEVE
REIGNS	REINSPIRE	REJECTOR	RELATOR	RELIEVED
REIK	REINSPIRED	REJECTORS	RELATORS	RELIEVER
REIKI	REINSPIRES	REJECTS	RELAUNCH	RELIEVERS
REIKIS	REINSPIRING	REJIG	RELAUNCHED	RELIEVES
REIKS	REINSTALL	REJIGGED	RELAUNCHES	RELIEVING
REILLUME	REINSTALLED	REJIGGER	RELAUNCHING	RELIEVO
REILLUMED	REINSTALLING	REJIGGERED	RELAX	RELIEVOS

RELIGHT	RELYING	REMEASURE	REMISSION	REMOVE
RELIGHTED	REM	REMEASURED	REMISSIONS	REMOVED
RELIGHTING	REMADE	REMEASURES	REMISSIVE	REMOVER
RELIGHTS	REMADES	REMEASURING	REMISSLY	REMOVERS
RELIGIEUX	REMAIN	REMEDE	REMISSORY	REMOVES
RELIGION	REMAINDER	REMEDED	REMIT	REMOVING
RELIGIONS	REMAINDERED	REMEDES	REMITMENT	REMS
RELIGIOSE	REMAINDERING	REMEDIAL	REMITMENTS	REMUAGE
RELIGIOSO	REMAINDERS	REMEDIAT	REMITS	REMUAGES
RELIGIOUS	REMAINED	REMEDIATE	REMITTAL	REMUDA
RELIGIOUSES	REMAINING	REMEDIED	REMITTALS	REMUDAS
RELINE	REMAINS	REMEDIES	REMITTED	REMUEUR
RELINED	REMAKE	REMEDING	REMITTEE	REMUEURS
RELINES	REMAKES	REMEDY	REMITTEES	REMURMUR
RELINING	REMAKING	REMEDYING	REMITTENT	REMURMURED
RELIQUARIES	REMAN	REMEID	REMITTER	REMURMURING
RELIQUARY	REMAND	REMEIDED	REMITTERS	REMURMURS
RELIQUE	REMANDED	REMEIDING	REMITTING	REN
RELIQUES	REMANDING	REMEIDS	REMITTOR	RENAGUE
RELIQUIAE	REMANDS	REMEMBER	REMITTORS	RENAGUED
RELISH	REMANENCE	REMEMBERED	REMIX	RENAGUES
RELISHED	REMANENCES	REMEMBERING	REMIXED	RENAGUING
RELISHES	REMANENCIES	REMEMBERS	REMIXES	RENAL
RELISHING	REMANENCY	REMEN	REMIXING	RENAME
RELIT	REMANENT	REMENS	REMNANT	RENAMED
RELIVE	REMANENTS	REMERCIED	REMNANTS	RENAMES
RELIVED	REMANET	REMERCIES	REMODEL	RENAMING
RELIVER	REMANETS	REMERCY	REMODELED	RENASCENT
RELIVERED	REMANIE	REMERCYING	REMODELING	RENAY
RELIVERING	REMANIES	REMERGE	REMODELLED	RENAYED
RELIVERS	REMANNED	REMERGED	REMODELLING	RENAYING
RELIVES	REMANNING	REMERGES	REMODELS	RENAYS
RELIVING	REMANS	REMERGING	REMODIFIED	RENCONTRE
RELLISH	REMARK	REMEX	REMODIFIES	RENCONTRES
RELLISHED	REMARKED	REMIGATE	REMODIFY	REND
RELLISHES	REMARKER	REMIGATED	REMODIFYING	RENDER
RELLISHING	REMARKERS	REMIGATES	REMONTANT	RENDERED
RELOAD	REMARKING	REMIGATING	REMONTANTS	RENDERER
RELOADED	REMARKS	REMIGES	REMORA	RENDERERS
RELOADING	REMARQUE	REMIGIAL	REMORAS	RENDERING
RELOADS	REMARQUED	REMIGRATE	REMORSE	RENDERINGS
RELOCATE	REMARQUES	REMIGRATED	REMORSES	RENDERS
RELOCATED	REMARRIED	REMIGRATES	REMOTE	RENDING
RELOCATES	REMARRIES	REMIGRATING	REMOTELY	RENDITION
RELOCATING	REMARRY	REMIND	REMOTER	RENDITIONS
RELUCENT	REMARRYING	REMINDED	REMOTES	RENDS
RELUCT	REMASTER	REMINDER	REMOTEST	RENDZINA
RELUCTANT	REMASTERED	REMINDERS	REMOTION	RENDZINAS
RELUCTATE	REMASTERING	REMINDFUL	REMOTIONS	RENEGADE
RELUCTATED	REMASTERS	REMINDING	REMOUD	RENEGADED
RELUCTATES	REMATCH	REMINDS	REMOULADE	RENEGADES
RELUCTATING	REMATCHED	REMINISCE	REMOULADES	RENEGADING
RELUCTED	REMATCHES	REMINISCED	REMOULD	RENEGADO
RELUCTING	REMATCHING	REMINISCES	REMOULDED	RENEGADOS
RELUCTS	REMBLAI	REMINISCING	REMOULDING	RENEGATE
RELUME	REMBLAIS	REMINT	REMOULDS	RENEGATES
RELUMED	REMBLE	REMINTED	REMOUNT	RENEGE
RELUMES	REMBLED	REMINTING	REMOUNTED	RENEGED
RELUMINE	REMBLES	REMINTS	REMOUNTING	RENEGER
RELUMINED	REMBLING	REMISE	REMOUNTS	RENEGERS
RELUMINES	REMEAD	REMISED	REMOVABLE	RENEGES
RELUMING	REMEADED	REMISES	REMOVABLY	RENEGING
RELUMINING	REMEADING	REMISING	REMOVAL	RENEGUE
RELY	REMEADS	REMISS	REMOVALS	RENEGUED

The Chambers Dictionary is the authority for many longer words; see *OSW* Introduction, page xii

RENEGUER	RENOWNER	REPACKAGED	REPEL	REPLANTING
RENEGUERS	RENOWNERS	REPACKAGES	REPELLANT	REPLANTS
RENEGUES	RENOWNING	REPACKAGING	REPELLANTS	REPLAY
RENEGUING	RENOWNS	REPACKED	REPELLED	REPLAYED
RENEW	RENS	REPACKING	REPELLENT	REPLAYING
RENEWABLE	RENT	REPACKS	REPELLENTS	REPLAYS
RENEWABLES	RENTABLE	REPAID	REPELLER	REPLENISH
RENEWAL	RENTAL	REPAINT	REPELLERS	REPLENISHED
RENEWALS	RENTALLER	REPAINTED	REPELLING	REPLENISHES
RENEWED	RENTALLERS	REPAINTING	REPELS	REPLENISHING
RENEWER	RENTALS	REPAINTINGS	REPENT	REPLETE
RENEWERS	RENTE	REPAINTS	REPENTANT	REPLETED
RENEWING	RENTED	REPAIR	REPENTANTS	REPLETES
RENEWINGS	RENTER	REPAIRED	REPENTED	REPLETING
RENEWS	RENTERS	REPAIRER	REPENTER	REPLETION
RENEY	RENTES	REPAIRERS	REPENTERS	REPLETIONS
RENEYED	RENTIER	REPAIRING	REPENTING	REPLEVIED
RENEYING	RENTIERS	REPAIRMAN	REPENTS	REPLEVIES
RENEYS	RENTING	REPAIRMEN	REPEOPLE	REPLEVIN
RENFIERST	RENTS	REPAIRS	REPEOPLED	REPLEVINED
RENFORCE	RENUMBER	REPAND	REPEOPLES	REPLEVINING
RENFORCED	RENUMBERED	REPAPER	REPEOPLING	REPLEVINS
RENFORCES	RENUMBERING	REPAPERED	REPERCUSS	REPLEVY
RENFORCING	RENUMBERS	REPAPERING	REPERCUSSED	REPLEVYING
RENFORST	RENVERSE	REPAPERS	REPERCUSSES	REPLICA
RENGA	RENVERSED	REPARABLE	REPERCUSSING	REPLICAS
RENGAS	RENVERSES	REPARABLY	REPERTORIES	REPLICATE
RENIED	RENVERSING	REPARTEE	REPERTORY	REPLICATED
RENIES	RENVERST	REPARTEED	REPERUSAL	REPLICATES
RENIFORM	RENVOI	REPARTEEING	REPERUSALS	REPLICATING
RENIG	RENVOIS	REPARTEES	REPERUSE	REPLICON
RENIGGED	RENVOY	REPASS	REPERUSED	REPLICONS
RENIGGING	RENVOYS	REPASSAGE	REPERUSES	REPLIED
RENIGS	RENY	REPASSAGES	REPERUSING	REPLIER
RENIN	RENYING	REPASSED	REPETEND	REPLIERS
RENINS	REOCCUPIED	REPASSES	REPETENDS	REPLIES
RENITENCIES	REOCCUPIES	REPASSING	REPHRASE	REPLUM
RENITENCY	REOCCUPY	REPAST	REPHRASED	REPLY
RENITENT	REOCCUPYING	REPASTED	REPHRASES	REPLYING
RENMINBI	REOFFEND	REPASTING	REPHRASING	REPO
RENMINBIS	REOFFENDED	REPASTS	REPINE	REPOINT
RENNE	REOFFENDING	REPASTURE	REPINED	REPOINTED
RENNED	REOFFENDS	REPASTURES	REPINER	REPOINTING
RENNES	REOPEN	REPAY	REPINERS	REPOINTS
RENNET	REOPENED	REPAYABLE	REPINES	REPOMAN
RENNETS	REOPENER	REPAYING	REPINING	REPOMEN
RENNIN	REOPENERS	REPAYMENT	REPININGS	REPONE
RENNING	REOPENING	REPAYMENTS	REPIQUE	REPONED
RENNINGS	REOPENS	REPAYS	REPIQUED	REPONES
RENNINS	REORDAIN	REPEAL	REPIQUES	REPONING
RENOUNCE	REORDAINED	REPEALED	REPIQUING	REPORT
RENOUNCED	REORDAINING	REPEALER	REPLA	REPORTAGE
RENOUNCER	REORDAINS	REPEALERS	REPLACE	REPORTAGES
RENOUNCERS	REORDER	REPEALING	REPLACED	REPORTED
RENOUNCES	REORDERED	REPEALS	REPLACER	REPORTER
RENOUNCING	REORDERING	REPEAT	REPLACERS	REPORTERS
RENOVATE	REORDERS	REPEATED	REPLACES	REPORTING
RENOVATED	REORIENT	REPEATER	REPLACING	REPORTINGS
RENOVATES	REORIENTED	REPEATERS	REPLAN	REPORTS
RENOVATING	REORIENTING	REPEATING	REPLANNED	REPOS
RENOVATOR	REORIENTS	REPEATINGS	REPLANNING	REPOSAL
RENOVATORS	REP	REPEATS	REPLANS	REPOSALL
RENOWN	REPACK	REPECHAGE	REPLANT	REPOSALLS
RENOWNED	REPACKAGE	REPECHAGES	REPLANTED	REPOSALS

REPOSE
REPOSED
REPOSEDLY
REPOSEFUL
REPOSES
REPOSING
REPOSIT
REPOSITED
REPOSITING
REPOSITOR
REPOSITORS
REPOSITS
REPOSSESS
REPOSSESSED
REPOSSESSES
REPOSSESSING
REPOST
REPOSTED
REPOSTING
REPOSTS
REPOSURE
REPOSURES
REPOT
REPOTS
REPOTTED
REPOTTING
REPOTTINGS
REPOUSSE
REPOUSSES
REPP
REPPED
REPPING
REPPINGS
REPPS
REPREEVE
REPREEVED
REPREEVES
REPREEVING
REPREHEND
REPREHENDED
REPREHENDING
REPREHENDS
REPRESENT
REPRESENTED
REPRESENTING
REPRESENTS
REPRESS
REPRESSED
REPRESSES
REPRESSING
REPRESSOR
REPRESSORS
REPRIEFE
REPRIEFES
REPRIEVAL
REPRIEVALS
REPRIEVE
REPRIEVED
REPRIEVES
REPRIEVING
REPRIMAND
REPRIMANDED
REPRIMANDING
REPRIMANDS

REPRIME
REPRIMED
REPRIMES
REPRIMING
REPRINT
REPRINTED
REPRINTING
REPRINTS
REPRISAL
REPRISALS
REPRISE
REPRISED
REPRISES
REPRISING
REPRIVE
REPRIVED
REPRIVES
REPRIVING
REPRIZE
REPRIZED
REPRIZES
REPRIZING
REPRO
REPROACH
REPROACHED
REPROACHES
REPROACHING
REPROBACIES
REPROBACY
REPROBATE
REPROBATED
REPROBATES
REPROBATING
REPROCESS
REPROCESSED
REPROCESSES
REPROCESSING
REPRODUCE
REPRODUCED
REPRODUCES
REPRODUCING
REPROGRAM
REPROGRAMMED
REPROGRAMMING
REPROGRAMS
REPROOF
REPROOFED
REPROOFING
REPROOFS
REPROS
REPROVAL
REPROVALS
REPROVE
REPROVED
REPROVER
REPROVERS
REPROVES
REPROVING
REPROVINGS
REPRYVE
REPRYVED
REPRYVES
REPRYVING
REPS

REPTANT
REPTATION
REPTATIONS
REPTILE
REPTILES
REPTILIAN
REPTILOID
REPUBLIC
REPUBLICS
REPUBLISH
REPUBLISHED
REPUBLISHES
REPUBLISHING
REPUDIATE
REPUDIATED
REPUDIATES
REPUDIATING
REPUGN
REPUGNANT
REPUGNED
REPUGNING
REPUGNS
REPULP
REPULPED
REPULPING
REPULPS
REPULSE
REPULSED
REPULSES
REPULSING
REPULSION
REPULSIONS
REPULSIVE
REPUNIT
REPUNITS
REPURE
REPURED
REPURES
REPURIFIED
REPURIFIES
REPURIFY
REPURIFYING
REPURING
REPUTABLE
REPUTABLY
REPUTE
REPUTED
REPUTEDLY
REPUTES
REPUTING
REPUTINGS
REQUERE
REQUERED
REQUERES
REQUERING
REQUEST
REQUESTED
REQUESTER
REQUESTERS
REQUESTING
REQUESTS
REQUICKEN
REQUICKENED
REQUICKENING

REQUICKENS
REQUIEM
REQUIEMS
REQUIGHT
REQUIGHTED
REQUIGHTING
REQUIGHTS
REQUIRE
REQUIRED
REQUIRER
REQUIRERS
REQUIRES
REQUIRING
REQUIRINGS
REQUISITE
REQUISITES
REQUIT
REQUITAL
REQUITALS
REQUITE
REQUITED
REQUITER
REQUITERS
REQUITES
REQUITING
REQUITS
REQUITTED
REQUITTING
REQUOTE
REQUOTED
REQUOTES
REQUOTING
REQUOYLE
REQUOYLED
REQUOYLES
REQUOYLING
RERADIATE
RERADIATED
RERADIATES
RERADIATING
RERAIL
RERAILED
RERAILING
RERAILS
RERAN
REREAD
REREADING
REREADS
REREBRACE
REREBRACES
REREDORSE
REREDORSES
REREDOS
REREDOSES
REREDOSSE
REREDOSSES
REREMICE
REREMOUSE
REREVISE
REREVISED
REREVISES
REREVISING
REREWARD
REREWARDS

REROUTE
REROUTED
REROUTEING
REROUTES
REROUTING
RERUN
RERUNNING
RERUNS
RES
RESAID
RESALE
RESALES
RESALGAR
RESALGARS
RESALUTE
RESALUTED
RESALUTES
RESALUTING
RESAT
RESAY
RESAYING
RESAYS
RESCALE
RESCALED
RESCALES
RESCALING
RESCIND
RESCINDED
RESCINDING
RESCINDS
RESCORE
RESCORED
RESCORES
RESCORING
RESCRIPT
RESCRIPTED
RESCRIPTING
RESCRIPTS
RESCUABLE
RESCUE
RESCUED
RESCUER
RESCUERS
RESCUES
RESCUING
RESEAL
RESEALED
RESEALING
RESEALS
RESEARCH
RESEARCHED
RESEARCHES
RESEARCHING
RESEAT
RESEATED
RESEATING
RESEATS
RESEAU
RESEAUS
RESEAUX
RESECT
RESECTED
RESECTING
RESECTION

RESECTIONS	RESIANCE	RESISTANTS	RESOUND	RESTAGES
RESECTS	RESIANCES	RESISTED	RESOUNDED	RESTAGING
RESEDA	RESIANT	RESISTENT	RESOUNDING	RESTART
RESEDAS	RESIANTS	RESISTENTS	RESOUNDS	RESTARTED
RESEIZE	RESIDE	RESISTING	RESOURCE	RESTARTER
RESEIZED	RESIDED	RESISTIVE	RESOURCED	RESTARTERS
RESEIZES	RESIDENCE	RESISTOR	RESOURCES	RESTARTING
RESEIZING	RESIDENCES	RESISTORS	RESOURCING	RESTARTS
RESELECT	RESIDENCIES	RESISTS	RESPEAK	RESTATE
RESELECTED	RESIDENCY	RESIT	RESPEAKING	RESTATED
RESELECTING	RESIDENT	RESITS	RESPEAKS	RESTATES
RESELECTS	RESIDENTS	RESITTING	RESPECT	RESTATING
RESELL	RESIDER	RESKEW	RESPECTED	RESTED
RESELLING	RESIDERS	RESKEWED	RESPECTER	RESTEM
RESELLS	RESIDES	RESKEWING	RESPECTERS	RESTEMMED
RESEMBLE	RESIDING	RESKEWS	RESPECTING	RESTEMMING
RESEMBLED	RESIDUA	RESKILL	RESPECTS	RESTEMS
RESEMBLER	RESIDUAL	RESKILLED	RESPELL	RESTER
RESEMBLERS	RESIDUALS	RESKILLING	RESPELLED	RESTERS
RESEMBLES	RESIDUARY	RESKILLS	RESPELLING	RESTFUL
RESEMBLING	RESIDUE	RESKUE	RESPELLS	RESTFULLER
RESENT	RESIDUES	RESKUED	RESPELT	RESTFULLEST
RESENTED	RESIDUOUS	RESKUES	RESPIRE	RESTFULLY
RESENTER	RESIDUUM	RESKUING	RESPIRED	RESTIER
RESENTERS	RESIGN	RESNATRON	RESPIRES	RESTIEST
RESENTFUL	RESIGNED	RESNATRONS	RESPIRING	RESTIFF
RESENTING	RESIGNER	RESOLD	RESPITE	RESTIFORM
RESENTIVE	RESIGNERS	RESOLE	RESPITED	RESTING
RESENTS	RESIGNING	RESOLED	RESPITES	RESTINGS
RESERPINE	RESIGNS	RESOLES	RESPITING	RESTITUTE
RESERPINES	RESILE	RESOLING	RESPLEND	RESTITUTED
RESERVE	RESILED	RESOLUBLE	RESPLENDED	RESTITUTES
RESERVED	RESILES	RESOLUTE	RESPLENDING	RESTITUTING
RESERVES	RESILIENT	RESOLUTES	RESPLENDS	RESTIVE
RESERVING	RESILING	RESOLVE	RESPOKE	RESTIVELY
RESERVIST	RESIN	RESOLVED	RESPOKEN	RESTLESS
RESERVISTS	RESINATA	RESOLVENT	RESPOND	RESTOCK
RESERVOIR	RESINATAS	RESOLVENTS	RESPONDED	RESTOCKED
RESERVOIRED	RESINATE	RESOLVER	RESPONDER	RESTOCKING
RESERVOIRING	RESINATES	RESOLVERS	RESPONDERS	RESTOCKS
RESERVOIRS	RESINED	RESOLVES	RESPONDING	RESTORE
RESES	RESINER	RESOLVING	RESPONDS	RESTORED
RESET	RESINERS	RESONANCE	RESPONSA	RESTORER
RESETS	RESINIFIED	RESONANCES	RESPONSE	RESTORERS
RESETTED	RESINIFIES	RESONANT	RESPONSER	RESTORES
RESETTER	RESINIFY	RESONATE	RESPONSERS	RESTORING
RESETTERS	RESINIFYING	RESONATED	RESPONSES	RESTRAIN
RESETTING	RESINING	RESONATES	RESPONSOR	RESTRAINED
RESETTLE	RESINISE	RESONATING	RESPONSORS	RESTRAINING
RESETTLED	RESINISED	RESONATOR	RESPONSUM	RESTRAININGS
RESETTLES	RESINISES	RESONATORS	RESPONSUMS	RESTRAINS
RESETTLING	RESINISING	RESORB	RESPRAY	RESTRAINT
RESHAPE	RESINIZE	RESORBED	RESPRAYED	RESTRAINTS
RESHAPED	RESINIZED	RESORBENT	RESPRAYING	RESTRICT
RESHAPES	RESINIZES	RESORBING	RESPRAYS	RESTRICTED
RESHAPING	RESINIZING	RESORBS	RESSALDAR	RESTRICTING
RESHIP	RESINOID	RESORCIN	RESSALDARS	RESTRICTS
RESHIPPED	RESINOIDS	RESORCINS	REST	RESTRING
RESHIPPING	RESINOSES	RESORT	RESTAFF	RESTRINGE
RESHIPS	RESINOSIS	RESORTED	RESTAFFED	RESTRINGED
RESHUFFLE	RESINOUS	RESORTER	RESTAFFING	RESTRINGEING
RESHUFFLED	RESINS	RESORTERS	RESTAFFS	RESTRINGES
RESHUFFLES	RESIST	RESORTING	RESTAGE	RESTRINGING
RESHUFFLING	RESISTANT	RESORTS	RESTAGED	RESTRINGS

The Chambers Dictionary is the authority for many longer words; see *OSW* Introduction, page xii

RESTRUNG	RETALIATED	RETILED	RETOUR	RETRIMMED
RESTS	RETALIATES	RETILES	RETOURED	RETRIMMING
RESTY	RETALIATING	RETILING	RETOURING	RETRIMS
RESTYLE	RETAMA	RETIME	RETOURS	RETRO
RESTYLED	RETAMAS	RETIMED	RETRACE	RETROACT
RESTYLES	RETARD	RETIMES	RETRACED	RETROACTED
RESTYLING	RETARDANT	RETIMING	RETRACES	RETROACTING
RESUBMIT	RETARDANTS	RETINA	RETRACING	RETROACTS
RESUBMITS	RETARDATE	RETINAE	RETRACT	RETROCEDE
RESUBMITTED	RETARDATES	RETINAL	RETRACTED	RETROCEDED
RESUBMITTING	RETARDED	RETINAS	RETRACTING	RETROCEDES
RESULT	RETARDER	RETINITE	RETRACTOR	RETROCEDING
RESULTANT	RETARDERS	RETINITES	RETRACTORS	RETROD
RESULTANTS	RETARDING	RETINITIS	RETRACTS	RETRODDEN
RESULTED	RETARDS	RETINITISES	RETRAICT	RETROFIT
RESULTFUL	RETCH	RETINOID	RETRAICTS	RETROFITS
RESULTING	RETCHED	RETINOIDS	RETRAIN	RETROFITTED
RESULTS	RETCHES	RETINOL	RETRAINED	RETROFITTING
RESUMABLE	RETCHING	RETINOLS	RETRAINING	RETROFITTINGS
RESUME	RETCHLESS	RETINUE	RETRAINS	RETROFLEX
RESUMED	RETE	RETINUES	RETRAIT	RETROJECT
RESUMES	RETELL	RETINULA	RETRAITE	RETROJECTED
RESUMING	RETELLER	RETINULAE	RETRAITES	RETROJECTING
RESUPINE	RETELLERS	RETINULAR	RETRAITS	RETROJECTS
RESURFACE	RETELLING	RETIRACIES	RETRAITT	RETRORSE
RESURFACED	RETELLS	RETIRACY	RETRAITTS	RETROS
RESURFACES	RETENE	RETIRAL	RETRAL	RETROUSSE
RESURFACING	RETENES	RETIRALS	RETRALLY	RETROVERT
RESURGE	RETENTION	RETIRE	RETRATE	RETROVERTED
RESURGED	RETENTIONS	RETIRED	RETRATED	RETROVERTING
RESURGENT	RETENTIVE	RETIREDLY	RETRATES	RETROVERTS
RESURGES	RETES	RETIREE	RETRATING	RETRY
RESURGING	RETEXTURE	RETIREES	RETREAD	RETRYING
RESURRECT	RETEXTURED	RETIRER	RETREADED	RETS
RESURRECTED	RETEXTURES	RETIRERS	RETREADING	RETSINA
RESURRECTING	RETEXTURING	RETIRES	RETREADS	RETSINAS
RESURRECTS	RETHINK	RETIRING	RETREAT	RETTED
RESURVEY	RETHINKING	RETITLE	RETREATED	RETTERIES
RESURVEYED	RETHINKS	RETITLED	RETREATING	RETTERY
RESURVEYING	RETHOUGHT	RETITLES	RETREATS	RETTING
RESURVEYS	RETIAL	RETITLING	RETREE	RETUND
RET	RETIARII	RETOLD	RETREES	RETUNDED
RETABLE	RETIARIUS	RETOOK	RETRENCH	RETUNDING
RETABLES	RETIARIUSES	RETOOL	RETRENCHED	RETUNDS
RETAIL	RETIARY	RETOOLED	RETRENCHES	RETUNE
RETAILED	RETICELLA	RETOOLING	RETRENCHING	RETUNED
RETAILER	RETICELLAS	RETOOLS	RETRIAL	RETUNES
RETAILERS	RETICENCE	RETORSION	RETRIALS	RETUNING
RETAILING	RETICENCES	RETORSIONS	RETRIBUTE	RETURF
RETAILS	RETICENCIES	RETORT	RETRIBUTED	RETURFED
RETAIN	RETICENCY	RETORTED	RETRIBUTES	RETURFING
RETAINED	RETICENT	RETORTER	RETRIBUTING	RETURFS
RETAINER	RETICLE	RETORTERS	RETRIED	RETURN
RETAINERS	RETICLES	RETORTING	RETRIES	RETURNED
RETAINING	RETICULAR	RETORTION	RETRIEVAL	RETURNEE
RETAINS	RETICULE	RETORTIONS	RETRIEVALS	RETURNEES
RETAKE	RETICULES	RETORTIVE	RETRIEVE	RETURNER
RETAKEN	RETICULUM	RETORTS	RETRIEVED	RETURNERS
RETAKER	RETICULUMS	RETOUCH	RETRIEVER	RETURNIK
RETAKERS	RETIE	RETOUCHED	RETRIEVERS	RETURNIKS
RETAKES	RETIED	RETOUCHER	RETRIEVES	RETURNING
RETAKING	RETIES	RETOUCHERS	RETRIEVING	RETURNS
RETAKINGS	RETIFORM	RETOUCHES	RETRIEVINGS	RETUSE
RETALIATE	RETILE	RETOUCHING	RETRIM	RETYING

REUNIFIED	REVENGINGS	REVEURS	REVOKED	REWROTE
REUNIFIES	REVENGIVE	REVEUSE	REVOKES	REWS
REUNIFY	REVENUE	REVEUSES	REVOKING	REWTH
REUNIFYING	REVENUED	REVICTUAL	REVOLT	REWTHS
REUNION	REVENUES	REVICTUALLED	REVOLTED	REX
REUNIONS	REVERABLE	REVICTUALLING	REVOLTER	REYNARD
REUNITE	REVERB	REVICTUALS	REVOLTERS	REYNARDS
REUNITED	REVERBED	REVIE	REVOLTING	REZ
REUNITES	REVERBING	REVIED	REVOLTS	REZONE
REUNITING	REVERBS	REVIES	REVOLUTE	REZONED
REURGE	REVERE	REVIEW	REVOLVE	REZONES
REURGED	REVERED	REVIEWAL	REVOLVED	REZONING
REURGES	REVERENCE	REVIEWALS	REVOLVER	REZZES
REURGING	REVERENCED	REVIEWED	REVOLVERS	RHABDOID
REUSABLE	REVERENCES	REVIEWER	REVOLVES	RHABDOIDS
REUSE	REVERENCING	REVIEWERS	REVOLVING	RHABDOM
REUSED	REVEREND	REVIEWING	REVOLVINGS	RHABDOMS
REUSES	REVERENDS	REVIEWS	REVS	RHABDUS
REUSING	REVERENT	REVILE	REVUE	RHABDUSES
REUTTER	REVERER	REVILED	REVUES	RHACHIDES
REUTTERED	REVERERS	REVILER	REVULSION	RHACHIS
REUTTERING	REVERES	REVILERS	REVULSIONS	RHACHISES
REUTTERS	REVERIE	REVILES	REVULSIVE	RHACHITIS
REV	REVERIES	REVILING	REVVED	RHACHITISES
REVALENTA	REVERING	REVILINGS	REVVING	RHAGADES
REVALENTAS	REVERIST	REVISABLE	REVYING	RHAMPHOID
REVALUE	REVERISTS	REVISAL	REW	RHAPHE
REVALUED	REVERS	REVISALS	REWARD	RHAPHES
REVALUES	REVERSAL	REVISE	REWARDED	RHAPHIDE
REVALUING	REVERSALS	REVISED	REWARDER	RHAPHIDES
REVAMP	REVERSE	REVISER	REWARDERS	RHAPHIS
REVAMPED	REVERSED	REVISERS	REWARDFUL	RHAPONTIC
REVAMPING	REVERSELY	REVISES	REWARDING	RHAPONTICS
REVAMPS	REVERSER	REVISING	REWARDS	RHAPSODE
REVANCHE	REVERSERS	REVISION	REWAREWA	RHAPSODES
REVANCHES	REVERSES	REVISIONS	REWAREWAS	RHAPSODIC
REVEAL	REVERSI	REVISIT	REWEIGH	RHAPSODIES
REVEALED	REVERSING	REVISITED	REWEIGHED	RHAPSODY
REVEALER	REVERSINGS	REVISITING	REWEIGHING	RHATANIES
REVEALERS	REVERSION	REVISITS	REWEIGHS	RHATANY
REVEALING	REVERSIONS	REVISOR	REWIND	RHEA
REVEALINGS	REVERSIS	REVISORS	REWINDING	RHEAS
REVEALS	REVERSISES	REVISORY	REWINDS	RHEMATIC
REVEILLE	REVERSO	REVIVABLE	REWIRE	RHENIUM
REVEILLES	REVERSOS	REVIVABLY	REWIRED	RHENIUMS
REVEL	REVERT	REVIVAL	REWIRES	RHEOCHORD
REVELATOR	REVERTED	REVIVALS	REWIRING	RHEOCHORDS
REVELATORS	REVERTING	REVIVE	REWORD	RHEOCORD
REVELLED	REVERTIVE	REVIVED	REWORDED	RHEOCORDS
REVELLER	REVERTS	REVIVER	REWORDING	RHEOLOGIC
REVELLERS	REVERY	REVIVERS	REWORDS	RHEOLOGIES
REVELLING	REVEST	REVIVES	REWORK	RHEOLOGY
REVELLINGS	REVESTED	REVIVIFIED	REWORKED	RHEOMETER
REVELRIES	REVESTING	REVIVIFIES	REWORKING	RHEOMETERS
REVELRY	REVESTRIES	REVIVIFY	REWORKS	RHEOSTAT
REVELS	REVESTRY	REVIVIFYING	REWOUND	RHEOSTATS
REVENANT	REVESTS	REVIVING	REWRAP	RHEOTAXES
REVENANTS	REVET	REVIVINGS	REWRAPPED	RHEOTAXIS
REVENGE	REVETMENT	REVIVOR	REWRAPPING	RHEOTOME
REVENGED	REVETMENTS	REVIVORS	REWRAPS	RHEOTOMES
REVENGER	REVETS	REVOCABLE	REWRITE	RHEOTROPE
REVENGERS	REVETTED	REVOCABLY	REWRITES	RHEOTROPES
REVENGES	REVETTING	REVOKABLE	REWRITING	RHESUS
REVENGING	REVEUR	REVOKE	REWRITTEN	RHESUSES

RHETOR	RHODAMINE	RHUMB	RIBATTUTA	RICHENING
RHETORIC	RHODAMINES	RHUMBA	RIBATTUTAS	RICHENS
RHETORICS	RHODANATE	RHUMBAED	RIBAUD	RICHER
RHETORISE	RHODANATES	RHUMBAING	RIBAUDRED	RICHES
RHETORISED	RHODANIC	RHUMBAS	RIBAUDRIES	RICHESSE
RHETORISES	RHODANISE	RHUMBS	RIBAUDRY	RICHESSES
RHETORISING	RHODANISED	RHUS	RIBAUDS	RICHEST
RHETORIZE	RHODANISES	RHUSES	RIBBAND	RICHING
RHETORIZED	RHODANISING	RHY	RIBBANDS	RICHLY
RHETORIZES	RHODANIZE	RHYME	RIBBED	RICHNESS
RHETORIZING	RHODANIZED	RHYMED	RIBBIER	RICHNESSES
RHETORS	RHODANIZES	RHYMELESS	RIBBIEST	RICHT
RHEUM	RHODANIZING	RHYMER	RIBBING	RICHTED
RHEUMATIC	RHODIC	RHYMERS	RIBBINGS	RICHTER
RHEUMATICS	RHODIE	RHYMES	RIBBON	RICHTEST
RHEUMATIZ	RHODIES	RHYMESTER	RIBBONED	RICHTING
RHEUMATIZES	RHODIUM	RHYMESTERS	RIBBONING	RICHTS
RHEUMED	RHODIUMS	RHYMING	RIBBONRIES	RICIER
RHEUMIER	RHODOLITE	RHYMIST	RIBBONRY	RICIEST
RHEUMIEST	RHODOLITES	RHYMISTS	RIBBONS	RICIN
RHEUMS	RHODONITE	RHYNE	RIBBONY	RICING
RHEUMY	RHODONITES	RHYNES	RIBBY	RICINS
RHEXES	RHODOPSIN	RHYOLITE	RIBCAGE	RICK
RHEXIS	RHODOPSINS	RHYOLITES	RIBCAGES	RICKED
RHEXISES	RHODORA	RHYOLITIC	RIBIBE	RICKER
RHIES	RHODORAS	RHYTA	RIBIBES	RICKERS
RHIME	RHODOUS	RHYTHM	RIBIBLE	RICKETIER
RHIMES	RHODY	RHYTHMAL	RIBIBLES	RICKETIEST
RHINAL	RHOEADINE	RHYTHMED	RIBLESS	RICKETILY
RHINE	RHOEADINES	RHYTHMI	RIBLET	RICKETS
RHINES	RHOMB	RHYTHMIC	RIBLETS	RICKETTIER
RHINITIS	RHOMBI	RHYTHMICS	RIBLIKE	RICKETTIEST
RHINITISES	RHOMBIC	RHYTHMISE	RIBOSE	RICKETTY
RHINO	RHOMBOI	RHYTHMISED	RIBOSES	RICKETY
RHINOLITH	RHOMBOID	RHYTHMISES	RIBOSOMAL	RICKING
RHINOLITHS	RHOMBOIDS	RHYTHMISING	RIBOSOME	RICKLE
RHINOLOGIES	RHOMBOS	RHYTHMIST	RIBOSOMES	RICKLES
RHINOLOGY	RHOMBS	RHYTHMISTS	RIBOZYME	RICKLY
RHINOS	RHOMBUS	RHYTHMIZE	RIBOZYMES	RICKS
RHIPIDATE	RHOMBUSES	RHYTHMIZED	RIBS	RICKSHA
RHIPIDION	RHONCHAL	RHYTHMIZES	RIBSTON	RICKSHAS
RHIPIDIONS	RHONCHI	RHYTHMIZING	RIBSTONE	RICKSHAW
RHIPIDIUM	RHONCHIAL	RHYTHMS	RIBSTONES	RICKSHAWS
RHIPIDIUMS	RHONCHUS	RHYTHMUS	RIBSTONS	RICKSTAND
RHIZIC	RHONE	RHYTHMUSES	RIBWORK	RICKSTANDS
RHIZINE	RHONES	RHYTINA	RIBWORKS	RICKSTICK
RHIZINES	RHOPALIC	RHYTINAS	RIBWORT	RICKSTICKS
RHIZOBIA	RHOPALISM	RHYTON	RIBWORTS	RICKYARD
RHIZOBIUM	RHOPALISMS	RIA	RICE	RICKYARDS
RHIZOCARP	RHOS	RIAL	RICED	RICOCHET
RHIZOCARPS	RHOTACISE	RIALS	RICER	RICOCHETED
RHIZOCAUL	RHOTACISED	RIANCIES	RICERCAR	RICOCHETING
RHIZOCAULS	RHOTACISES	RIANCY	RICERCARE	RICOCHETS
RHIZOID	RHOTACISING	RIANT	RICERCARES	RICOCHETTED
RHIZOIDAL	RHOTACISM	RIAS	RICERCARS	RICOCHETTING
RHIZOIDS	RHOTACISMS	RIATA	RICERCATA	RICOTTA
RHIZOME	RHOTACIZE	RIATAS	RICERCATAS	RICOTTAS
RHIZOMES	RHOTACIZED	RIB	RICERS	RICTAL
RHIZOPI	RHOTACIZES	RIBALD	RICES	RICTUS
RHIZOPOD	RHOTACIZING	RIBALDRIES	RICEY	RICTUSES
RHIZOPODS	RHOTIC	RIBALDRY	RICH	RICY
RHIZOPUS	RHUBARB	RIBALDS	RICHED	RID
RHIZOPUSES	RHUBARBS	RIBAND	RICHEN	RIDABLE
RHO	RHUBARBY	RIBANDS	RICHENED	RIDDANCE

RIDDANCES	RIFELY	RIGHTLY	RILIER	RINGLESS
RIDDED	RIFENESS	RIGHTNESS	RILIEST	RINGLET
RIDDEN	RIFENESSES	RIGHTNESSES	RILIEVI	RINGLETED
RIDDER	RIFER	RIGHTO	RILIEVO	RINGLETS
RIDDERS	RIFEST	RIGHTOS	RILING	RINGMAN
RIDDING	RIFF	RIGHTS	RILL	RINGMEN
RIDDLE	RIFFLE	RIGHTSIZE	RILLE	RINGS
RIDDLED	RIFFLED	RIGHTSIZED	RILLED	RINGSIDE
RIDDLER	RIFFLER	RIGHTSIZES	RILLES	RINGSIDER
RIDDLERS	RIFFLERS	RIGHTSIZING	RILLET	RINGSIDERS
RIDDLES	RIFFLES	RIGHTWARD	RILLETS	RINGSIDES
RIDDLING	RIFFLING	RIGHTWARDS	RILLETTES	RINGSTAND
RIDDLINGS	RIFFS	RIGID	RILLING	RINGSTANDS
RIDE	RIFLE	RIGIDER	RILLMARK	RINGSTER
RIDEABLE	RIFLED	RIGIDEST	RILLMARKS	RINGSTERS
RIDENT	RIFLEMAN	RIGIDIFIED	RILLS	RINGTAIL
RIDER	RIFLEMEN	RIGIDIFIES	RIM	RINGTAILS
RIDERED	RIFLER	RIGIDIFY	RIMA	RINGWAY
RIDERLESS	RIFLERS	RIGIDIFYING	RIMAE	RINGWAYS
RIDERS	RIFLES	RIGIDISE	RIME	RINGWISE
RIDES	RIFLING	RIGIDISED	RIMED	RINGWORK
RIDGE	RIFLINGS	RIGIDISES	RIMER	RINGWORKS
RIDGEBACK	RIFT	RIGIDISING	RIMERS	RINGWORM
RIDGEBACKS	RIFTE	RIGIDITIES	RIMES	RINGWORMS
RIDGED	RIFTED	RIGIDITY	RIMIER	RINK
RIDGEL	RIFTIER	RIGIDIZE	RIMIEST	RINKED
RIDGELS	RIFTIEST	RIGIDIZED	RIMING	RINKHALS
RIDGER	RIFTING	RIGIDIZES	RIMLESS	RINKHALSES
RIDGERS	RIFTLESS	RIGIDIZING	RIMMED	RINKING
RIDGES	RIFTS	RIGIDLY	RIMMING	RINKS
RIDGEWAY	RIFTY	RIGIDNESS	RIMMINGS	RINNING
RIDGEWAYS	RIG	RIGIDNESSES	RIMOSE	RINS
RIDGIER	RIGADOON	RIGIDS	RIMOUS	RINSABLE
RIDGIEST	RIGADOONS	RIGLIN	RIMS	RINSE
RIDGIL	RIGATONI	RIGLING	RIMU	RINSEABLE
RIDGILS	RIGATONIS	RIGLINGS	RIMUS	RINSED
RIDGING	RIGG	RIGLINS	RIMY	RINSER
RIDGINGS	RIGGALD	RIGMAROLE	RIN	RINSERS
RIDGLING	RIGGALDS	RIGMAROLES	RIND	RINSES
RIDGLINGS	RIGGED	RIGOL	RINDED	RINSIBLE
RIDGY	RIGGER	RIGOLL	RINDIER	RINSING
RIDICULE	RIGGERS	RIGOLLS	RINDIEST	RINSINGS
RIDICULED	RIGGING	RIGOLS	RINDING	RIOT
RIDICULER	RIGGINGS	RIGOR	RINDLESS	RIOTED
RIDICULERS	RIGGISH	RIGORISM	RINDS	RIOTER
RIDICULES	RIGGS	RIGORISMS	RINDY	RIOTERS
RIDICULING	RIGHT	RIGORIST	RINE	RIOTING
RIDING	RIGHTABLE	RIGORISTS	RINES	RIOTINGS
RIDINGS	RIGHTED	RIGOROUS	RING	RIOTISE
RIDOTTO	RIGHTEN	RIGORS	RINGBIT	RIOTISES
RIDOTTOS	RIGHTENED	RIGOUR	RINGBITS	RIOTIZE
RIDS	RIGHTENING	RIGOURS	RINGBONE	RIOTIZES
RIEL	RIGHTENS	RIGS	RINGBONES	RIOTOUS
RIELS	RIGHTEOUS	RIGWIDDIE	RINGED	RIOTOUSLY
RIEM	RIGHTER	RIGWIDDIES	RINGENT	RIOTRIES
RIEMPIE	RIGHTERS	RIGWOODIE	RINGER	RIOTRY
RIEMPIES	RIGHTEST	RIGWOODIES	RINGERS	RIOTS
RIEMS	RIGHTFUL	RIJSTAFEL	RINGGIT	RIP
RIEVE	RIGHTING	RIJSTAFELS	RINGGITS	RIPARIAL
RIEVER	RIGHTINGS	RIKISHI	RINGHALS	RIPARIAN
RIEVERS	RIGHTISH	RILE	RINGHALSES	RIPARIANS
RIEVES	RIGHTIST	RILED	RINGING	RIPE
RIEVING	RIGHTISTS	RILES	RINGINGLY	RIPECK
RIFE	RIGHTLESS	RILEY	RINGINGS	RIPECKS

RIPED	RISKER	RIVAGES	RIVIERES	ROAMERS
RIPELY	RISKERS	RIVAL	RIVING	ROAMING
RIPEN	RISKFUL	RIVALESS	RIVLIN	ROAMINGS
RIPENED	RISKIER	RIVALESSES	RIVLINS	ROAMS
RIPENESS	RISKIEST	RIVALISE	RIVO	ROAN
RIPENESSES	RISKILY	RIVALISED	RIVOS	ROANS
RIPENING	RISKINESS	RIVALISES	RIVULET	ROAR
RIPENS	RISKINESSES	RIVALISING	RIVULETS	ROARED
RIPER	RISKING	RIVALITIES	RIYAL	ROARER
RIPERS	RISKS	RIVALITY	RIYALS	ROARERS
RIPES	RISKY	RIVALIZE	RIZ	ROARIE
RIPEST	RISOLUTO	RIVALIZED	RIZA	ROARIER
RIPIENI	RISOTTO	RIVALIZES	RIZARD	ROARIEST
RIPIENIST	RISOTTOS	RIVALIZING	RIZARDS	ROARING
RIPIENISTS	RISP	RIVALLED	RIZAS	ROARINGLY
RIPIENO	RISPED	RIVALLESS	RIZZAR	ROARINGS
RIPIENOS	RISPETTI	RIVALLING	RIZZARED	ROARS
RIPING	RISPETTO	RIVALRIES	RIZZARING	ROARY
RIPOSTE	RISPING	RIVALRY	RIZZARS	ROAST
RIPOSTED	RISPINGS	RIVALS	RIZZART	ROASTED
RIPOSTES	RISPS	RIVALSHIP	RIZZARTS	ROASTER
RIPOSTING	RISQUE	RIVALSHIPS	RIZZER	ROASTERS
RIPP	RISQUES	RIVAS	RIZZERED	ROASTING
RIPPED	RISSOLE	RIVE	RIZZERING	ROASTINGS
RIPPER	RISSOLES	RIVED	RIZZERS	ROASTS
RIPPERS	RISUS	RIVEL	RIZZOR	ROATE
RIPPIER	RISUSES	RIVELLED	RIZZORED	ROATED
RIPPIERS	RIT	RIVELLING	RIZZORING	ROATES
RIPPING	RITE	RIVELS	RIZZORS	ROATING
RIPPINGLY	RITELESS	RIVEN	ROACH	ROB
RIPPLE	RITENUTO	RIVER	ROACHED	ROBALO
RIPPLED	RITENUTOS	RIVERAIN	ROACHES	ROBALOS
RIPPLER	RITES	RIVERAINS	ROACHING	ROBBED
RIPPLERS	RITORNEL	RIVERBANK	ROAD	ROBBER
RIPPLES	RITORNELL	RIVERBANKS	ROADBLOCK	ROBBERIES
RIPPLET	RITORNELLS	RIVERED	ROADBLOCKS	ROBBERS
RIPPLETS	RITORNELS	RIVERET	ROADCRAFT	ROBBERY
RIPPLIER	RITS	RIVERETS	ROADCRAFTS	ROBBING
RIPPLIEST	RITT	RIVERINE	ROADHOUSE	ROBE
RIPPLING	RITTED	RIVERLESS	ROADHOUSES	ROBED
RIPPLINGS	RITTER	RIVERLIKE	ROADIE	ROBES
RIPPLY	RITTERS	RIVERMAN	ROADIES	ROBIN
RIPPS	RITTING	RIVERMEN	ROADING	ROBING
RIPRAP	RITTS	RIVERS	ROADINGS	ROBINGS
RIPRAPS	RITUAL	RIVERSIDE	ROADLESS	ROBINIA
RIPS	RITUALISE	RIVERSIDES	ROADMAN	ROBINIAS
RIPSTOP	RITUALISED	RIVERWAY	ROADMEN	ROBINS
RIPT	RITUALISES	RIVERWAYS	ROADS	ROBLE
RIPTIDE	RITUALISING	RIVERWEED	ROADSHOW	ROBLES
RIPTIDES	RITUALISM	RIVERWEEDS	ROADSHOWS	ROBORANT
RISALDAR	RITUALISMS	RIVERY	ROADSIDE	ROBORANTS
RISALDARS	RITUALIST	RIVES	ROADSIDES	ROBOT
RISE	RITUALISTS	RIVET	ROADSMAN	ROBOTIC
RISEN	RITUALIZE	RIVETED	ROADSMEN	ROBOTICS
RISER	RITUALIZED	RIVETER	ROADSTEAD	ROBOTISE
RISERS	RITUALIZES	RIVETERS	ROADSTEADS	ROBOTISED
RISES	RITUALIZING	RIVETING	ROADSTER	ROBOTISES
RISHI	RITUALLY	RIVETINGS	ROADSTERS	ROBOTISING
RISHIS	RITUALS	RIVETS	ROADWAY	ROBOTIZE
RISIBLE	RITZIER	RIVETTED	ROADWAYS	ROBOTIZED
RISING	RITZIEST	RIVETTING	ROADWORKS	ROBOTIZES
RISINGS	RITZY	RIVIERA	ROAM	ROBOTIZING
RISK	RIVA	RIVIERAS	ROAMED	ROBOTS
RISKED	RIVAGE	RIVIERE	ROAMER	ROBS

ROBURITE	ROD	ROILY	ROMAIKA	RONYON
ROBURITES	RODDED	ROIN	ROMAIKAS	RONYONS
ROBUST	RODDING	ROINED	ROMAL	ROO
ROBUSTA	RODDINGS	ROINING	ROMALS	ROOD
ROBUSTAS	RODE	ROINISH	ROMAN	ROODS
ROBUSTER	RODED	ROINS	ROMANCE	ROOF
ROBUSTEST	RODENT	ROIST	ROMANCED	ROOFED
ROBUSTLY	RODENTS	ROISTED	ROMANCER	ROOFER
ROC	RODEO	ROISTER	ROMANCERS	ROOFERS
ROCAILLE	RODEOS	ROISTERED	ROMANCES	ROOFIER
ROCAILLES	RODES	ROISTERER	ROMANCING	ROOFIEST
ROCAMBOLE	RODEWAY	ROISTERERS	ROMANCINGS	ROOFING
ROCAMBOLES	RODEWAYS	ROISTERING	ROMANS	ROOFINGS
ROCH	RODFISHER	ROISTERINGS	ROMANTIC	ROOFLESS
ROCHES	RODFISHERS	ROISTERS	ROMANTICS	ROOFLIKE
ROCHET	RODGERSIA	ROISTING	ROMAS	ROOFS
ROCHETS	RODGERSIAS	ROISTS	ROMAUNT	ROOFSCAPE
ROCK	RODING	ROJI	ROMAUNTS	ROOFSCAPES
ROCKAWAY	RODINGS	ROJIS	ROMNEYA	ROOFTOP
ROCKAWAYS	RODLESS	ROK	ROMNEYAS	ROOFTOPS
ROCKCRESS	RODLIKE	ROKE	ROMP	ROOFTREE
ROCKCRESSES	RODMAN	ROKED	ROMPED	ROOFTREES
ROCKED	RODMEN	ROKELAY	ROMPER	ROOFY
ROCKER	RODS	ROKELAYS	ROMPERS	ROOINEK
ROCKERIES	RODSMAN	ROKER	ROMPING	ROOINEKS
ROCKERS	RODSMEN	ROKERS	ROMPINGLY	ROOK
ROCKERY	RODSTER	ROKES	ROMPISH	ROOKED
ROCKET	RODSTERS	ROKIER	ROMPISHLY	ROOKERIES
ROCKETED	ROE	ROKIEST	ROMPS	ROOKERY
ROCKETEER	ROEBUCK	ROKING	RONCADOR	ROOKIE
ROCKETEERS	ROEBUCKS	ROKKAKU	RONCADORS	ROOKIER
ROCKETER	ROED	ROKS	RONDACHE	ROOKIES
ROCKETERS	ROEMER	ROKY	RONDACHES	ROOKIEST
ROCKETING	ROEMERS	ROLAG	RONDAVEL	ROOKING
ROCKETRIES	ROENTGEN	ROLAGS	RONDAVELS	ROOKISH
ROCKETRY	ROENTGENS	ROLE	RONDE	ROOKS
ROCKETS	ROES	ROLES	RONDEAU	ROOKY
ROCKFISH	ROESTONE	ROLFER	RONDEAUX	ROOM
ROCKFISHES	ROESTONES	ROLFERS	RONDEL	ROOMED
ROCKIER	ROGATION	ROLFING	RONDELS	ROOMER
ROCKIERS	ROGATIONS	ROLFINGS	RONDES	ROOMERS
ROCKIEST	ROGATORY	ROLL	RONDINO	ROOMETTE
ROCKILY	ROGER	ROLLABLE	RONDINOS	ROOMETTES
ROCKINESS	ROGERED	ROLLED	RONDO	ROOMFUL
ROCKINESSES	ROGERING	ROLLER	RONDOS	ROOMFULS
ROCKING	ROGERINGS	ROLLERS	RONDURE	ROOMIE
ROCKINGS	ROGERS	ROLLICK	RONDURES	ROOMIER
ROCKLAY	ROGUE	ROLLICKED	RONE	ROOMIES
ROCKLAYS	ROGUED	ROLLICKING	RONEO	ROOMIEST
ROCKLING	ROGUERIES	ROLLICKINGS	RONEOED	ROOMILY
ROCKLINGS	ROGUERY	ROLLICKS	RONEOING	ROOMINESS
ROCKS	ROGUES	ROLLING	RONEOS	ROOMINESSES
ROCKWATER	ROGUESHIP	ROLLINGS	RONES	ROOMING
ROCKWATERS	ROGUESHIPS	ROLLMOP	RONG	ROOMS
ROCKWEED	ROGUING	ROLLMOPS	RONGGENG	ROOMSOME
ROCKWEEDS	ROGUISH	ROLLOCK	RONGGENGS	ROOMY
ROCKWORK	ROGUISHLY	ROLLOCKS	RONNE	ROON
ROCKWORKS	ROGUY	ROLLOUT	RONNING	ROONS
ROCKY	ROIL	ROLLOUTS	RONT	ROOP
ROCOCO	ROILED	ROLLS	RONTE	ROOPED
ROCOCOS	ROILIER	ROM	RONTES	ROOPIER
ROCQUET	ROILIEST	ROMA	RONTGEN	ROOPIEST
ROCQUETS	ROILING	ROMAGE	RONTGENS	ROOPING
ROCS	ROILS	ROMAGES	RONTS	ROOPIT

ROOPS	ROPINGS	ROSELESS	ROSTERINGS	ROTL
ROOPY	ROPY	ROSELIKE	ROSTERS	ROTLS
ROOS	ROQUE	ROSELLA	ROSTING	ROTOGRAPH
ROOSA	ROQUES	ROSELLAS	ROSTRA	ROTOGRAPHED
ROOSAS	ROQUET	ROSELLE	ROSTRAL	ROTOGRAPHING
ROOSE	ROQUETED	ROSELLES	ROSTRATE	ROTOGRAPHS
ROOSED	ROQUETING	ROSEMARIES	ROSTRATED	ROTOLO
ROOSES	ROQUETS	ROSEMARY	ROSTRUM	ROTOLOS
ROOSING	ROQUETTE	ROSEOLA	ROSTRUMS	ROTOR
ROOST	ROQUETTES	ROSEOLAS	ROSTS	ROTORS
ROOSTED	RORAL	ROSERIES	ROSULA	ROTOVATE
ROOSTER	RORE	ROSERY	ROSULAS	ROTOVATED
ROOSTERS	RORES	ROSES	ROSULATE	ROTOVATES
ROOSTING	RORIC	ROSET	ROSY	ROTOVATING
ROOSTS	RORID	ROSETED	ROSYING	ROTOVATOR
ROOT	RORIE	ROSETING	ROT	ROTOVATORS
ROOTAGE	RORIER	ROSETS	ROTA	ROTS
ROOTAGES	RORIEST	ROSETTE	ROTAL	ROTTAN
ROOTED	RORQUAL	ROSETTED	ROTAPLANE	ROTTANS
ROOTEDLY	RORQUALS	ROSETTES	ROTAPLANES	ROTTED
ROOTER	RORT	ROSETTY	ROTARIES	ROTTEN
ROOTERS	RORTED	ROSETY	ROTARY	ROTTENER
ROOTHOLD	RORTER	ROSEWATER	ROTAS	ROTTENEST
ROOTHOLDS	RORTERS	ROSEWATERS	ROTATABLE	ROTTENLY
ROOTIER	RORTIER	ROSEWOOD	ROTATE	ROTTENS
ROOTIES	RORTIEST	ROSEWOODS	ROTATED	ROTTER
ROOTIEST	RORTING	ROSIED	ROTATES	ROTTERS
ROOTING	RORTS	ROSIER	ROTATING	ROTTING
ROOTINGS	RORTY	ROSIERE	ROTATION	ROTULA
ROOTLE	RORY	ROSIERES	ROTATIONS	ROTULAS
ROOTLED	ROSACE	ROSIERS	ROTATIVE	ROTUND
ROOTLES	ROSACEA	ROSIES	ROTATOR	ROTUNDA
ROOTLESS	ROSACEAS	ROSIEST	ROTATORS	ROTUNDAS
ROOTLET	ROSACEOUS	ROSILY	ROTATORY	ROTUNDATE
ROOTLETS	ROSACES	ROSIN	ROTAVATE	ROTUNDED
ROOTLIKE	ROSAKER	ROSINATE	ROTAVATED	ROTUNDER
ROOTLING	ROSAKERS	ROSINATES	ROTAVATES	ROTUNDEST
ROOTS	ROSALIA	ROSINED	ROTAVATING	ROTUNDING
ROOTSIER	ROSALIAS	ROSINESS	ROTAVATOR	ROTUNDITIES
ROOTSIEST	ROSARIAN	ROSINESSES	ROTAVATORS	ROTUNDITY
ROOTSTOCK	ROSARIANS	ROSING	ROTAVIRUS	ROTUNDLY
ROOTSTOCKS	ROSARIES	ROSINING	ROTAVIRUSES	ROTUNDS
ROOTSY	ROSARIUM	ROSINS	ROTCH	ROTURIER
ROOTY	ROSARIUMS	ROSINY	ROTCHE	ROTURIERS
ROPABLE	ROSARY	ROSIT	ROTCHES	ROUBLE
ROPE	ROSCID	ROSITED	ROTCHIE	ROUBLES
ROPEABLE	ROSE	ROSITING	ROTCHIES	ROUCOU
ROPED	ROSEAL	ROSITS	ROTE	ROUCOUS
ROPER	ROSEATE	ROSMARINE	ROTED	ROUE
ROPERIES	ROSEBAY	ROSMARINES	ROTENONE	ROUES
ROPERS	ROSEBAYS	ROSOGLIO	ROTENONES	ROUGE
ROPERY	ROSEBOWL	ROSOGLIOS	ROTES	ROUGED
ROPES	ROSEBOWLS	ROSOLIO	ROTGRASS	ROUGES
ROPEWAY	ROSEBUD	ROSOLIOS	ROTGRASSES	ROUGH
ROPEWAYS	ROSEBUDS	ROSSER	ROTGUT	ROUGHAGE
ROPEWORK	ROSEBUSH	ROSSERS	ROTGUTS	ROUGHAGES
ROPEWORKS	ROSEBUSHES	ROST	ROTHER	ROUGHCAST
ROPEY	ROSED	ROSTED	ROTHERS	ROUGHCASTED
ROPIER	ROSEFINCH	ROSTELLAR	ROTI	ROUGHCASTING
ROPIEST	ROSEFINCHES	ROSTELLUM	ROTIFER	ROUGHCASTS
ROPILY	ROSEFISH	ROSTELLUMS	ROTIFERAL	ROUGHED
ROPINESS	ROSEFISHES	ROSTER	ROTIFERS	ROUGHEN
ROPINESSES	ROSEHIP	ROSTERED	ROTING	ROUGHENED
ROPING	ROSEHIPS	ROSTERING	ROTIS	ROUGHENING

ROUGHENS	ROUNDNESSES	ROUTINIZED	ROYALET	RUBBERISING
ROUGHER	ROUNDS	ROUTINIZES	ROYALETS	RUBBERIZE
ROUGHERS	ROUNDSMAN	ROUTINIZING	ROYALISE	RUBBERIZED
ROUGHEST	ROUNDSMEN	ROUTOUS	ROYALISED	RUBBERIZES
ROUGHIE	ROUNDURE	ROUTOUSLY	ROYALISES	RUBBERIZING
ROUGHIES	ROUNDURES	ROUTS	ROYALISING	RUBBERS
ROUGHING	ROUNDWORM	ROUX	ROYALISM	RUBBERY
ROUGHISH	ROUNDWORMS	ROVE	ROYALISMS	RUBBET
ROUGHLY	ROUP	ROVED	ROYALIST	RUBBING
ROUGHNECK	ROUPED	ROVER	ROYALISTS	RUBBINGS
ROUGHNECKED	ROUPIER	ROVERS	ROYALIZE	RUBBISH
ROUGHNECKING	ROUPIEST	ROVES	ROYALIZED	RUBBISHED
ROUGHNECKS	ROUPING	ROVING	ROYALIZES	RUBBISHES
ROUGHNESS	ROUPIT	ROVINGLY	ROYALIZING	RUBBISHING
ROUGHNESSES	ROUPS	ROVINGS	ROYALLER	RUBBISHLY
ROUGHS	ROUPY	ROW	ROYALLEST	RUBBISHY
ROUGHSHOD	ROUSANT	ROWABLE	ROYALLY	RUBBIT
ROUGHT	ROUSE	ROWAN	ROYALS	RUBBLE
ROUGHY	ROUSED	ROWANS	ROYALTIES	RUBBLES
ROUGING	ROUSEMENT	ROWBOAT	ROYALTY	RUBBLIER
ROUILLE	ROUSEMENTS	ROWBOATS	ROYNE	RUBBLIEST
ROUILLES	ROUSER	ROWDEDOW	ROYNED	RUBBLY
ROUL	ROUSERS	ROWDEDOWS	ROYNES	RUBDOWN
ROULADE	ROUSES	ROWDIER	ROYNING	RUBDOWNS
ROULADES	ROUSING	ROWDIES	ROYNISH	RUBE
ROULE	ROUSINGLY	ROWDIEST	ROYST	RUBEFIED
ROULEAU	ROUSSETTE	ROWDILY	ROYSTED	RUBEFIES
ROULEAUS	ROUSSETTES	ROWDINESS	ROYSTER	RUBEFY
ROULEAUX	ROUST	ROWDINESSES	ROYSTERED	RUBEFYING
ROULES	ROUSTED	ROWDY	ROYSTERER	RUBELLA
ROULETTE	ROUSTER	ROWDYDOW	ROYSTERERS	RUBELLAN
ROULETTES	ROUSTERS	ROWDYDOWS	ROYSTERING	RUBELLANS
ROULS	ROUSTING	ROWDYISH	ROYSTERS	RUBELLAS
ROUM	ROUSTS	ROWDYISM	ROYSTING	RUBELLITE
ROUMING	ROUT	ROWDYISMS	ROYSTS	RUBELLITES
ROUMINGS	ROUTE	ROWED	ROZELLE	RUBEOLA
ROUMS	ROUTED	ROWEL	ROZELLES	RUBEOLAS
ROUNCE	ROUTEING	ROWELLED	ROZET	RUBES
ROUNCES	ROUTEMAN	ROWELLING	ROZETED	RUBESCENT
ROUNCEVAL	ROUTEMEN	ROWELS	ROZETING	RUBICELLE
ROUNCEVALS	ROUTER	ROWEN	ROZETS	RUBICELLES
ROUNCIES	ROUTERS	ROWENS	ROZIT	RUBICON
ROUNCY	ROUTES	ROWER	ROZITED	RUBICONED
ROUND	ROUTH	ROWERS	ROZITING	RUBICONING
ROUNDARCH	ROUTHIE	ROWING	ROZITS	RUBICONS
ROUNDED	ROUTHIER	ROWINGS	ROZZER	RUBICUND
ROUNDEL	ROUTHIEST	ROWLOCK	ROZZERS	RUBIDIUM
ROUNDELAY	ROUTHS	ROWLOCKS	RUANA	RUBIDIUMS
ROUNDELAYS	ROUTINE	ROWME	RUANAS	RUBIED
ROUNDELS	ROUTINEER	ROWMES	RUB	RUBIER
ROUNDER	ROUTINEERS	ROWND	RUBAI	RUBIES
ROUNDERS	ROUTINELY	ROWNDED	RUBAIYAT	RUBIEST
ROUNDEST	ROUTINES	ROWNDELL	RUBATI	RUBIFIED
ROUNDHAND	ROUTING	ROWNDELLS	RUBATO	RUBIFIES
ROUNDHANDS	ROUTINGS	ROWNDING	RUBATOS	RUBIFY
ROUNDING	ROUTINISE	ROWNDS	RUBBED	RUBIFYING
ROUNDINGS	ROUTINISED	ROWS	RUBBER	RUBIN
ROUNDISH	ROUTINISES	ROWT	RUBBERED	RUBINE
ROUNDLE	ROUTINISING	ROWTED	RUBBERIER	RUBINEOUS
ROUNDLES	ROUTINISM	ROWTH	RUBBERIEST	RUBINES
ROUNDLET	ROUTINISMS	ROWTHS	RUBBERING	RUBINS
ROUNDLETS	ROUTINIST	ROWTING	RUBBERISE	RUBIOUS
ROUNDLY	ROUTINISTS	ROWTS	RUBBERISED	RUBLE
ROUNDNESS	ROUTINIZE	ROYAL	RUBBERISES	RUBLES

RUBOUT	RUDDLES	RUGBY	RULINGS	RUMOROUS
RUBOUTS	RUDDLING	RUGELACH	RULLION	RUMORS
RUBRIC	RUDDOCK	RUGGED	RULLIONS	RUMOUR
RUBRICAL	RUDDOCKS	RUGGEDER	RULLOCK	RUMOURED
RUBRICATE	RUDDS	RUGGEDEST	RULLOCKS	RUMOURER
RUBRICATED	RUDDY	RUGGEDISE	RULY	RUMOURERS
RUBRICATES	RUDDYING	RUGGEDISED	RUM	RUMOURING
RUBRICATING	RUDE	RUGGEDISES	RUMAL	RUMOURS
RUBRICIAN	RUDELY	RUGGEDISING	RUMALS	RUMP
RUBRICIANS	RUDENESS	RUGGEDIZE	RUMBA	RUMPED
RUBRICS	RUDENESSES	RUGGEDIZED	RUMBAED	RUMPIES
RUBS	RUDER	RUGGEDIZES	RUMBAING	RUMPING
RUBSTONE	RUDERAL	RUGGEDIZING	RUMBAS	RUMPLE
RUBSTONES	RUDERALS	RUGGEDLY	RUMBELOW	RUMPLED
RUBY	RUDERIES	RUGGELACH	RUMBELOWS	RUMPLES
RUBYING	RUDERY	RUGGER	RUMBLE	RUMPLESS
RUC	RUDES	RUGGERS	RUMBLED	RUMPLING
RUCHE	RUDESBIES	RUGGIER	RUMBLER	RUMPS
RUCHED	RUDESBY	RUGGIEST	RUMBLERS	RUMPUS
RUCHES	RUDEST	RUGGING	RUMBLES	RUMPUSES
RUCHING	RUDIE	RUGGINGS	RUMBLIER	RUMPY
RUCHINGS	RUDIES	RUGGY	RUMBLIEST	RUMS
RUCK	RUDIMENT	RUGOSE	RUMBLING	RUN
RUCKED	RUDIMENTS	RUGOSELY	RUMBLINGS	RUNABOUT
RUCKING	RUDISH	RUGOSITIES	RUMBLY	RUNABOUTS
RUCKLE	RUDS	RUGOSITY	RUMBO	RUNAGATE
RUCKLED	RUE	RUGOUS	RUMBOS	RUNAGATES
RUCKLES	RUED	RUGS	RUME	RUNAROUND
RUCKLING	RUEFUL	RUGULOSE	RUMEN	RUNAROUNDS
RUCKS	RUEFULLY	RUIN	RUMES	RUNAWAY
RUCKSACK	RUEING	RUINABLE	RUMINA	RUNAWAYS
RUCKSACKS	RUEINGS	RUINATE	RUMINANT	RUNBACK
RUCKSEAT	RUELLE	RUINATED	RUMINANTS	RUNBACKS
RUCKSEATS	RUELLES	RUINATES	RUMINATE	RUNCH
RUCKUS	RUELLIA	RUINATING	RUMINATED	RUNCHES
RUCKUSES	RUELLIAS	RUINATION	RUMINATES	RUNCIBLE
RUCOLA	RUES	RUINATIONS	RUMINATING	RUNCINATE
RUCOLAS	RUFESCENT	RUINED	RUMINATOR	RUND
RUCS	RUFF	RUINER	RUMINATORS	RUNDALE
RUCTATION	RUFFE	RUINERS	RUMKIN	RUNDALES
RUCTATIONS	RUFFED	RUING	RUMKINS	RUNDLE
RUCTION	RUFFES	RUINGS	RUMLY	RUNDLED
RUCTIONS	RUFFIAN	RUINING	RUMMAGE	RUNDLES
RUD	RUFFIANED	RUININGS	RUMMAGED	RUNDLET
RUDAS	RUFFIANING	RUINOUS	RUMMAGER	RUNDLETS
RUDASES	RUFFIANLY	RUINOUSLY	RUMMAGERS	RUNDOWN
RUDBECKIA	RUFFIANS	RUINS	RUMMAGES	RUNDOWNS
RUDBECKIAS	RUFFIN	RUKH	RUMMAGING	RUNDS
RUDD	RUFFING	RUKHS	RUMMER	RUNE
RUDDED	RUFFINS	RULABLE	RUMMERS	RUNECRAFT
RUDDER	RUFFLE	RULE	RUMMEST	RUNECRAFTS
RUDDERS	RUFFLED	RULED	RUMMIER	RUNED
RUDDIED	RUFFLER	RULELESS	RUMMIES	RUNES
RUDDIER	RUFFLERS	RULER	RUMMIEST	RUNFLAT
RUDDIES	RUFFLES	RULERED	RUMMILY	RUNG
RUDDIEST	RUFFLING	RULERING	RUMMINESS	RUNGS
RUDDILY	RUFFLINGS	RULERS	RUMMINESSES	RUNIC
RUDDINESS	RUFFS	RULERSHIP	RUMMISH	RUNKLE
RUDDINESSES	RUFIYAA	RULERSHIPS	RUMMY	RUNKLED
RUDDING	RUFIYAAS	RULES	RUMNESS	RUNKLES
RUDDLE	RUFOUS	RULESSE	RUMNESSES	RUNKLING
RUDDLED	RUG	RULIER	RUMOR	RUNLET
RUDDLEMAN	RUGATE	RULIEST	RUMORED	RUNLETS
RUDDLEMEN	RUGBIES	RULING	RUMORING	RUNNABLE

The Chambers Dictionary is the authority for many longer words; see *OSW* Introduction, page xii

RUNNEL
RUNNELS
RUNNER
RUNNERS
RUNNET
RUNNETS
RUNNIER
RUNNIEST
RUNNING
RUNNINGLY
RUNNINGS
RUNNION
RUNNIONS
RUNNY
RUNRIG
RUNRIGS
RUNS
RUNT
RUNTED
RUNTIER
RUNTIEST
RUNTISH
RUNTS
RUNTY
RUNWAY
RUNWAYS
RUPEE
RUPEES
RUPIA
RUPIAH
RUPIAHS
RUPIAS
RUPTURE
RUPTURED
RUPTURES
RUPTURING
RURAL
RURALISE
RURALISED
RURALISES
RURALISING
RURALISM

RURALISMS
RURALIST
RURALISTS
RURALITIES
RURALITY
RURALIZE
RURALIZED
RURALIZES
RURALIZING
RURALLY
RURALNESS
RURALNESSES
RURALS
RURP
RURPS
RURU
RURUS
RUSA
RUSALKA
RUSALKAS
RUSAS
RUSCUS
RUSCUSES
RUSE
RUSES
RUSH
RUSHED
RUSHEE
RUSHEES
RUSHEN
RUSHER
RUSHERS
RUSHES
RUSHIER
RUSHIEST
RUSHINESS
RUSHINESSES
RUSHING
RUSHLIGHT
RUSHLIGHTS
RUSHLIKE
RUSHY

RUSINE
RUSK
RUSKS
RUSMA
RUSMAS
RUSSEL
RUSSELS
RUSSET
RUSSETED
RUSSETING
RUSSETINGS
RUSSETS
RUSSETY
RUSSIA
RUSSIAS
RUST
RUSTED
RUSTIC
RUSTICAL
RUSTICALS
RUSTICATE
RUSTICATED
RUSTICATES
RUSTICATING
RUSTICIAL
RUSTICISE
RUSTICISED
RUSTICISES
RUSTICISING
RUSTICISM
RUSTICISMS
RUSTICITIES
RUSTICITY
RUSTICIZE
RUSTICIZED
RUSTICIZES
RUSTICIZING
RUSTICS
RUSTIER
RUSTIEST
RUSTILY
RUSTINESS

RUSTINESSES
RUSTING
RUSTINGS
RUSTLE
RUSTLED
RUSTLER
RUSTLERS
RUSTLES
RUSTLESS
RUSTLING
RUSTLINGS
RUSTRE
RUSTRED
RUSTRES
RUSTS
RUSTY
RUT
RUTABAGA
RUTABAGAS
RUTACEOUS
RUTH
RUTHENIC
RUTHENIUM
RUTHENIUMS
RUTHFUL
RUTHFULLY
RUTHLESS
RUTHS
RUTILANT
RUTILATED
RUTILE
RUTILES
RUTIN
RUTINS
RUTS
RUTTED
RUTTER
RUTTERS
RUTTIER
RUTTIEST
RUTTING
RUTTINGS

RUTTISH
RUTTY
RYA
RYAL
RYALS
RYAS
RYBAT
RYBATS
RYBAUDRYE
RYBAUDRYES
RYBAULD
RYBAULDS
RYE
RYEBREAD
RYEBREADS
RYEFLOUR
RYEFLOURS
RYEPECK
RYEPECKS
RYES
RYFE
RYKE
RYKED
RYKES
RYKING
RYMME
RYMMED
RYMMES
RYMMING
RYND
RYNDS
RYOKAN
RYOKANS
RYOT
RYOTS
RYOTWARI
RYOTWARIS
RYPE
RYPECK
RYPECKS
RYPER

S

SAB
SABADILLA
SABADILLAS
SABATON
SABATONS
SABBAT
SABBATIC
SABBATICS
SABBATINE
SABBATISE
SABBATISED
SABBATISES
SABBATISING
SABBATISM
SABBATISMS
SABBATIZE
SABBATIZED
SABBATIZES
SABBATIZING
SABBATS
SABELLA
SABELLAS
SABER
SABERED
SABERING
SABERS
SABIN
SABINS
SABKHA
SABKHAH
SABKHAHS
SABKHAS
SABKHAT
SABKHATS
SABLE
SABLED
SABLES
SABLING
SABOT
SABOTAGE
SABOTAGED
SABOTAGES
SABOTAGING
SABOTEUR
SABOTEURS
SABOTIER
SABOTIERS
SABOTS
SABRA
SABRAS
SABRE
SABRED
SABRES
SABREUR

SABREURS
SABRING
SABS
SABULINE
SABULOSE
SABULOUS
SABURRA
SABURRAL
SABURRAS
SAC
SACATON
SACATONS
SACCADE
SACCADES
SACCADIC
SACCATE
SACCHARIC
SACCHARIN
SACCHARINS
SACCHARUM
SACCHARUMS
SACCIFORM
SACCOI
SACCOS
SACCOSES
SACCULAR
SACCULATE
SACCULE
SACCULES
SACCULI
SACCULUS
SACELLA
SACELLUM
SACHEM
SACHEMDOM
SACHEMDOMS
SACHEMIC
SACHEMS
SACHET
SACHETS
SACK
SACKAGE
SACKAGES
SACKBUT
SACKBUTS
SACKCLOTH
SACKCLOTHS
SACKED
SACKER
SACKERS
SACKFUL
SACKFULS
SACKING
SACKINGS

SACKLESS
SACKS
SACLESS
SACLIKE
SACQUE
SACQUES
SACRA
SACRAL
SACRALGIA
SACRALGIAS
SACRALISE
SACRALISED
SACRALISES
SACRALISING
SACRALIZE
SACRALIZED
SACRALIZES
SACRALIZING
SACRAMENT
SACRAMENTED
SACRAMENTING
SACRAMENTS
SACRARIA
SACRARIUM
SACRED
SACREDLY
SACRIFICE
SACRIFICED
SACRIFICES
SACRIFICING
SACRIFIDE
SACRIFIED
SACRIFIES
SACRIFY
SACRIFYING
SACRILEGE
SACRILEGES
SACRING
SACRINGS
SACRIST
SACRISTAN
SACRISTANS
SACRISTIES
SACRISTS
SACRISTY
SACRUM
SACS
SAD
SADDEN
SADDENED
SADDENING
SADDENS
SADDER
SADDEST

SADDHU
SADDHUS
SADDISH
SADDLE
SADDLEBAG
SADDLEBAGS
SADDLEBOW
SADDLEBOWS
SADDLED
SADDLER
SADDLERIES
SADDLERS
SADDLERY
SADDLES
SADDLING
SADDO
SADDOS
SADE
SADES
SADHE
SADHES
SADHU
SADHUS
SADIRON
SADIRONS
SADISM
SADISMS
SADIST
SADISTIC
SADISTS
SADLY
SADNESS
SADNESSES
SADZA
SADZAS
SAE
SAECULUM
SAECULUMS
SAETER
SAETERS
SAFARI
SAFARIED
SAFARIING
SAFARIS
SAFARIST
SAFARISTS
SAFE
SAFED
SAFEGUARD
SAFEGUARDED
SAFEGUARDING
SAFEGUARDS
SAFELY
SAFENESS

SAFENESSES
SAFER
SAFES
SAFEST
SAFETIES
SAFETY
SAFETYMAN
SAFETYMEN
SAFFIAN
SAFFIANS
SAFFLOWER
SAFFLOWERS
SAFFRON
SAFFRONED
SAFFRONS
SAFFRONY
SAFING
SAFRANIN
SAFRANINE
SAFRANINES
SAFRANINS
SAFROLE
SAFROLES
SAFRONAL
SAFRONALS
SAG
SAGA
SAGACIOUS
SAGACITIES
SAGACITY
SAGAMAN
SAGAMEN
SAGAMORE
SAGAMORES
SAGAPENUM
SAGAPENUMS
SAGAS
SAGATHIES
SAGATHY
SAGE
SAGEBRUSH
SAGEBRUSHES
SAGELY
SAGENE
SAGENES
SAGENESS
SAGENESSES
SAGENITE
SAGENITES
SAGENITIC
SAGER
SAGES
SAGEST
SAGGAR

SAGGARD	SAILCLOTH	SAIS	SALEABLE	SALIVATING
SAGGARDS	SAILCLOTHS	SAIST	SALEABLY	SALIX
SAGGARS	SAILED	SAITH	SALEP	SALLAD
SAGGED	SAILER	SAITHE	SALEPS	SALLADS
SAGGER	SAILERS	SAITHES	SALERATUS	SALLAL
SAGGERS	SAILFISH	SAITHS	SALERATUSES	SALLALS
SAGGIER	SAILFISHES	SAJOU	SALERING	SALLE
SAGGIEST	SAILING	SAJOUS	SALERINGS	SALLEE
SAGGING	SAILINGS	SAKE	SALEROOM	SALLEES
SAGGINGS	SAILLESS	SAKER	SALEROOMS	SALLES
SAGGY	SAILOR	SAKERET	SALES	SALLET
SAGIER	SAILORING	SAKERETS	SALESMAN	SALLETS
SAGIEST	SAILORINGS	SAKERS	SALESMEN	SALLIED
SAGINATE	SAILORLY	SAKES	SALESROOM	SALLIES
SAGINATED	SAILORS	SAKI	SALESROOMS	SALLOW
SAGINATES	SAILPLANE	SAKIA	SALET	SALLOWED
SAGINATING	SAILPLANED	SAKIAS	SALETS	SALLOWER
SAGITTA	SAILPLANES	SAKIEH	SALEWD	SALLOWEST
SAGITTAL	SAILPLANING	SAKIEHS	SALEYARD	SALLOWING
SAGITTARIES	SAILROOM	SAKIS	SALEYARDS	SALLOWISH
SAGITTARY	SAILROOMS	SAKIYEH	SALFERN	SALLOWS
SAGITTAS	SAILS	SAKIYEHS	SALFERNS	SALLOWY
SAGITTATE	SAIM	SAKKOI	SALIAUNCE	SALLY
SAGO	SAIMIRI	SAKKOS	SALIAUNCES	SALLYING
SAGOIN	SAIMIRIS	SAKKOSES	SALIC	SALLYPORT
SAGOINS	SAIMS	SAKSAUL	SALICES	SALLYPORTS
SAGOS	SAIN	SAKSAULS	SALICET	SALMI
SAGOUIN	SAINE	SAL	SALICETA	SALMIS
SAGOUINS	SAINED	SALAAM	SALICETS	SALMON
SAGS	SAINFOIN	SALAAMED	SALICETUM	SALMONET
SAGUARO	SAINFOINS	SALAAMING	SALICETUMS	SALMONETS
SAGUAROS	SAINING	SALAAMS	SALICIN	SALMONID
SAGUIN	SAINS	SALABLE	SALICINE	SALMONIDS
SAGUINS	SAINT	SALABLY	SALICINES	SALMONOID
SAGUM	SAINTDOM	SALACIOUS	SALICINS	SALMONOIDS
SAGY	SAINTDOMS	SALACITIES	SALICYLIC	SALMONS
SAHIB	SAINTED	SALACITY	SALIENCE	SALON
SAHIBA	SAINTESS	SALAD	SALIENCES	SALONS
SAHIBAH	SAINTESSES	SALADE	SALIENCIES	SALOON
SAHIBAHS	SAINTFOIN	SALADES	SALIENCY	SALOONS
SAHIBAS	SAINTFOINS	SALADING	SALIENT	SALOOP
SAHIBS	SAINTHOOD	SALADINGS	SALIENTLY	SALOOPS
SAI	SAINTHOODS	SALADS	SALIENTS	SALOP
SAIBLING	SAINTING	SALAL	SALIFIED	SALOPIAN
SAIBLINGS	SAINTISH	SALALS	SALIFIES	SALOPS
SAIC	SAINTISM	SALAMI	SALIFY	SALP
SAICE	SAINTISMS	SALAMIS	SALIFYING	SALPA
SAICES	SAINTLIER	SALAMON	SALIGOT	SALPAE
SAICK	SAINTLIEST	SALAMONS	SALIGOTS	SALPAS
SAICKS	SAINTLIKE	SALANGANE	SALIMETER	SALPIAN
SAICS	SAINTLING	SALANGANES	SALIMETERS	SALPIANS
SAID	SAINTLINGS	SALARIAT	SALINA	SALPICON
SAIDEST	SAINTLY	SALARIATS	SALINAS	SALPICONS
SAIDS	SAINTS	SALARIED	SALINE	SALPIFORM
SAIDST	SAINTSHIP	SALARIES	SALINES	SALPINGES
SAIGA	SAINTSHIPS	SALARY	SALINITIES	SALPINX
SAIGAS	SAIQUE	SALARYING	SALINITY	SALPINXES
SAIKEI	SAIQUES	SALARYMAN	SALIVA	SALPS
SAIKEIS	SAIR	SALARYMEN	SALIVAL	SALS
SAIKLESS	SAIRED	SALBAND	SALIVARY	SALSA
SAIL	SAIRER	SALBANDS	SALIVAS	SALSAED
SAILABLE	SAIREST	SALCHOW	SALIVATE	SALSAING
SAILBOARD	SAIRING	SALCHOWS	SALIVATED	SALSAS
SAILBOARDS	SAIRS	SALE	SALIVATES	SALSE

SALSES	SALUBRITY	SAMBOS	SAMSHU	SANDHILLS
SALSIFIES	SALUE	SAMBUCA	SAMSHUS	SANDHIS
SALSIFY	SALUED	SAMBUCAS	SAMURAI	SANDIER
SALT	SALUES	SAMBUR	SAN	SANDIEST
SALTANDO	SALUING	SAMBURS	SANATIVE	SANDINESS
SALTANT	SALUKI	SAME	SANATORIA	SANDINESSES
SALTANTS	SALUKIS	SAMEKH	SANATORY	SANDING
SALTATE	SALUTARY	SAMEKHS	SANBENITO	SANDINGS
SALTATED	SALUTE	SAMEL	SANBENITOS	SANDIVER
SALTATES	SALUTED	SAMELY	SANCAI	SANDIVERS
SALTATING	SALUTER	SAMEN	SANCAIS	SANDLING
SALTATION	SALUTERS	SAMENESS	SANCHO	SANDLINGS
SALTATIONS	SALUTES	SAMENESSES	SANCHOS	SANDMAN
SALTATO	SALUTING	SAMES	SANCTA	SANDMEN
SALTATORY	SALVABLE	SAMEY	SANCTIFIED	SANDPAPER
SALTBOX	SALVAGE	SAMFOO	SANCTIFIES	SANDPAPERED
SALTBOXES	SALVAGED	SAMFOOS	SANCTIFY	SANDPAPERING
SALTBUSH	SALVAGES	SAMFU	SANCTIFYING	SANDPAPERS
SALTBUSHES	SALVAGING	SAMFUS	SANCTIFYINGS	SANDPIPER
SALTCAT	SALVARSAN	SAMIEL	SANCTION	SANDPIPERS
SALTCATS	SALVARSANS	SAMIELS	SANCTIONED	SANDPIT
SALTCHUCK	SALVATION	SAMIER	SANCTIONING	SANDPITS
SALTCHUCKS	SALVATIONS	SAMIEST	SANCTIONS	SANDPUMP
SALTED	SALVATORIES	SAMISEN	SANCTITIES	SANDPUMPS
SALTER	SALVATORY	SAMISENS	SANCTITY	SANDS
SALTERN	SALVE	SAMITE	SANCTUARIES	SANDSHOE
SALTERNS	SALVED	SAMITES	SANCTUARY	SANDSHOES
SALTERS	SALVER	SAMITI	SANCTUM	SANDSPOUT
SALTEST	SALVERS	SAMITIS	SANCTUMS	SANDSPOUTS
SALTFISH	SALVES	SAMIZDAT	SAND	SANDSTONE
SALTFISHES	SALVETE	SAMIZDATS	SANDAL	SANDSTONES
SALTIER	SALVETES	SAMLET	SANDALLED	SANDSTORM
SALTIERS	SALVIA	SAMLETS	SANDALS	SANDSTORMS
SALTIEST	SALVIAS	SAMLOR	SANDARAC	SANDWICH
SALTILY	SALVIFIC	SAMLORS	SANDARACH	SANDWICHED
SALTINESS	SALVING	SAMNITIS	SANDARACHS	SANDWICHES
SALTINESSES	SALVINGS	SAMNITISES	SANDARACS	SANDWICHING
SALTING	SALVO	SAMOSA	SANDBAG	SANDWORM
SALTINGS	SALVOES	SAMOSAS	SANDBAGGED	SANDWORMS
SALTIRE	SALVOR	SAMOVAR	SANDBAGGING	SANDWORT
SALTIRES	SALVORS	SAMOVARS	SANDBAGS	SANDWORTS
SALTISH	SALVOS	SAMP	SANDBANK	SANDY
SALTISHLY	SAM	SAMPAN	SANDBANKS	SANE
SALTLESS	SAMA	SAMPANS	SANDBLAST	SANELY
SALTLY	SAMAAN	SAMPHIRE	SANDBLASTED	SANENESS
SALTNESS	SAMAANS	SAMPHIRES	SANDBLASTING	SANENESSES
SALTNESSES	SAMADHI	SAMPI	SANDBLASTINGS	SANER
SALTO	SAMADHIS	SAMPIRE	SANDBLASTS	SANEST
SALTOED	SAMAN	SAMPIRES	SANDBOX	SANG
SALTOING	SAMANS	SAMPIS	SANDBOXES	SANGAR
SALTOS	SAMARA	SAMPLE	SANDBOY	SANGAREE
SALTPETER	SAMARAS	SAMPLED	SANDBOYS	SANGAREES
SALTPETERS	SAMARIUM	SAMPLER	SANDED	SANGARS
SALTPETRE	SAMARIUMS	SAMPLERIES	SANDER	SANGFROID
SALTPETRES	SAMAS	SAMPLERS	SANDERS	SANGFROIDS
SALTS	SAMBA	SAMPLERY	SANDERSES	SANGLIER
SALTUS	SAMBAED	SAMPLES	SANDFLIES	SANGLIERS
SALTUSES	SAMBAING	SAMPLING	SANDFLY	SANGOMA
SALTWATER	SAMBAL	SAMPLINGS	SANDGLASS	SANGOMAS
SALTWORKS	SAMBALS	SAMPS	SANDGLASSES	SANGRIA
SALTWORT	SAMBAR	SAMSARA	SANDHEAP	SANGRIAS
SALTWORTS	SAMBARS	SAMSARAS	SANDHEAPS	SANGS
SALTY	SAMBAS	SAMSHOO	SANDHI	SANGUIFIED
SALUBRITIES	SAMBO	SAMSHOOS	SANDHILL	SANGUIFIES

SANGUIFY	SANTONICA	SAPPANS	SARCODIC	SAROD
SANGUIFYING	SANTONICAS	SAPPED	SARCOID	SARODS
SANGUINE	SANTONIN	SAPPER	SARCOIDS	SARONG
SANGUINED	SANTONINS	SAPPERS	SARCOLOGIES	SARONGS
SANGUINES	SANTONS	SAPPHIC	SARCOLOGY	SARONIC
SANGUINING	SANTOUR	SAPPHICS	SARCOMA	SAROS
SANICLE	SANTOURS	SAPPHIRE	SARCOMAS	SAROSES
SANICLES	SANTS	SAPPHIRED	SARCOMATA	SARPANCH
SANIDINE	SANTUR	SAPPHIRES	SARCOMERE	SARPANCHES
SANIDINES	SANTURS	SAPPHISM	SARCOMERES	SARRASIN
SANIES	SAOUARI	SAPPHISMS	SARCONET	SARRASINS
SANIFIED	SAOUARIS	SAPPHIST	SARCONETS	SARRAZIN
SANIFIES	SAP	SAPPHISTS	SARCOPTIC	SARRAZINS
SANIFY	SAPAJOU	SAPPIER	SARCOUS	SARS
SANIFYING	SAPAJOUS	SAPPIEST	SARD	SARSDEN
SANIOUS	SAPAN	SAPPINESS	SARDANA	SARSDENS
SANITARIA	SAPANS	SAPPINESSES	SARDANAS	SARSEN
SANITARY	SAPANWOOD	SAPPING	SARDEL	SARSENET
SANITATE	SAPANWOODS	SAPPLE	SARDELLE	SARSENETS
SANITATED	SAPEGO	SAPPLED	SARDELLES	SARSENS
SANITATES	SAPEGOES	SAPPLES	SARDELS	SARSNET
SANITATING	SAPELE	SAPPLING	SARDINE	SARSNETS
SANITIES	SAPELES	SAPPY	SARDINES	SARTOR
SANITISE	SAPFUL	SAPRAEMIA	SARDIUS	SARTORIAL
SANITISED	SAPHEAD	SAPRAEMIAS	SARDIUSES	SARTORIAN
SANITISES	SAPHEADED	SAPRAEMIC	SARDONIAN	SARTORII
SANITISING	SAPHEADS	SAPROBE	SARDONIC	SARTORIUS
SANITIZE	SAPHENA	SAPROBES	SARDONYX	SARTORIUSES
SANITIZED	SAPHENAS	SAPROLITE	SARDONYXES	SARTORS
SANITIZES	SAPHENOUS	SAPROLITES	SARDS	SARUS
SANITIZING	SAPID	SAPROPEL	SARED	SARUSES
SANITY	SAPIDITIES	SAPROPELS	SAREE	SASARARA
SANJAK	SAPIDITY	SAPROZOIC	SAREES	SASARARAS
SANJAKS	SAPIDLESS	SAPS	SARGASSO	SASH
SANK	SAPIDNESS	SAPSAGO	SARGASSOS	SASHAY
SANKO	SAPIDNESSES	SAPSAGOS	SARGASSUM	SASHAYED
SANKOS	SAPIENCE	SAPSUCKER	SARGASSUMS	SASHAYING
SANNIE	SAPIENCES	SAPSUCKERS	SARGE	SASHAYS
SANNIES	SAPIENT	SAPUCAIA	SARGES	SASHED
SANNUP	SAPIENTLY	SAPUCAIAS	SARGO	SASHES
SANNUPS	SAPLESS	SAPWOOD	SARGOS	SASHIMI
SANNYASI	SAPLING	SAPWOODS	SARGOSES	SASHIMIS
SANNYASIN	SAPLINGS	SAR	SARGUS	SASHING
SANNYASINS	SAPODILLA	SARABAND	SARGUSES	SASIN
SANNYASIS	SAPODILLAS	SARABANDE	SARI	SASINE
SANPAN	SAPOGENIN	SARABANDES	SARIN	SASINES
SANPANS	SAPOGENINS	SARABANDS	SARING	SASINS
SANS	SAPONARIA	SARAFAN	SARINS	SASKATOON
SANSA	SAPONARIAS	SARAFANS	SARIS	SASKATOONS
SANSAS	SAPONIFIED	SARANGI	SARK	SASQUATCH
SANSEI	SAPONIFIES	SARANGIS	SARKIER	SASQUATCHES
SANSEIS	SAPONIFY	SARAPE	SARKIEST	SASS
SANSERIF	SAPONIFYING	SARAPES	SARKING	SASSABIES
SANSERIFS	SAPONIN	SARBACANE	SARKINGS	SASSABY
SANT	SAPONINS	SARBACANES	SARKS	SASSAFRAS
SANTAL	SAPONITE	SARCASM	SARKY	SASSAFRASES
SANTALIN	SAPONITES	SARCASMS	SARMENT	SASSARARA
SANTALINS	SAPOR	SARCASTIC	SARMENTA	SASSARARAS
SANTALS	SAPORIFIC	SARCENET	SARMENTS	SASSE
SANTIR	SAPOROUS	SARCENETS	SARMENTUM	SASSED
SANTIRS	SAPORS	SARCOCARP	SARNEY	SASSES
SANTOLINA	SAPOTA	SARCOCARPS	SARNEYS	SASSIER
SANTOLINAS	SAPOTAS	SARCODE	SARNIE	SASSIEST
SANTON	SAPPAN	SARCODES	SARNIES	SASSING

The Chambers Dictionary is the authority for many longer words; see *OSW* Introduction, page xii

SASSOLIN	SATIRISES	SAUCEBOX	SAUTEED	SAVOUR
SASSOLINS	SATIRISING	SAUCEBOXES	SAUTEEING	SAVOURED
SASSOLITE	SATIRIST	SAUCED	SAUTEES	SAVOURIES
SASSOLITES	SATIRISTS	SAUCEPAN	SAUTEING	SAVOURILY
SASSY	SATIRIZE	SAUCEPANS	SAUTES	SAVOURING
SASTRUGA	SATIRIZED	SAUCER	SAUTING	SAVOURLY
SASTRUGI	SATIRIZES	SAUCERFUL	SAUTOIR	SAVOURS
SAT	SATIRIZING	SAUCERFULS	SAUTOIRS	SAVOURY
SATANG	SATIS	SAUCERS	SAUTS	SAVOY
SATANIC	SATISFICE	SAUCES	SAVABLE	SAVOYARD
SATANICAL	SATISFICED	SAUCH	SAVAGE	SAVOYARDS
SATANISM	SATISFICES	SAUCHS	SAVAGED	SAVOYS
SATANISMS	SATISFICING	SAUCIER	SAVAGEDOM	SAVVEY
SATANITIES	SATISFICINGS	SAUCIEST	SAVAGEDOMS	SAVVEYED
SATANITY	SATISFIED	SAUCILY	SAVAGELY	SAVVEYING
SATARA	SATISFIER	SAUCINESS	SAVAGER	SAVVEYS
SATARAS	SATISFIERS	SAUCINESSES	SAVAGERIES	SAVVIED
SATAY	SATISFIES	SAUCING	SAVAGERY	SAVVIER
SATAYS	SATISFY	SAUCISSE	SAVAGES	SAVVIES
SATCHEL	SATISFYING	SAUCISSES	SAVAGEST	SAVVIEST
SATCHELS	SATIVE	SAUCISSON	SAVAGING	SAVVY
SATE	SATORI	SAUCISSONS	SAVAGISM	SAVVYING
SATED	SATORIS	SAUCY	SAVAGISMS	SAW
SATEDNESS	SATRAP	SAUFGARD	SAVANNA	SAWAH
SATEDNESSES	SATRAPAL	SAUFGARDS	SAVANNAH	SAWAHS
SATEEN	SATRAPIES	SAUGER	SAVANNAHS	SAWBILL
SATEENS	SATRAPS	SAUGERS	SAVANNAS	SAWBILLS
SATELESS	SATRAPY	SAUGH	SAVANT	SAWBLADE
SATELLES	SATSUMA	SAUGHS	SAVANTS	SAWBLADES
SATELLITE	SATSUMAS	SAUL	SAVARIN	SAWBONES
SATELLITED	SATURABLE	SAULGE	SAVARINS	SAWBUCK
SATELLITES	SATURANT	SAULGES	SAVATE	SAWBUCKS
SATELLITING	SATURANTS	SAULIE	SAVATES	SAWDER
SATES	SATURATE	SAULIES	SAVE	SAWDERED
SATI	SATURATED	SAULS	SAVED	SAWDERING
SATIABLE	SATURATES	SAULT	SAVEGARD	SAWDERS
SATIATE	SATURATING	SAULTS	SAVEGARDED	SAWDUST
SATIATED	SATURATOR	SAUNA	SAVEGARDING	SAWDUSTED
SATIATES	SATURATORS	SAUNAS	SAVEGARDS	SAWDUSTING
SATIATING	SATURNIC	SAUNT	SAVELOY	SAWDUSTS
SATIATION	SATURNIID	SAUNTED	SAVELOYS	SAWDUSTY
SATIATIONS	SATURNIIDS	SAUNTER	SAVER	SAWED
SATIETIES	SATURNINE	SAUNTERED	SAVERS	SAWER
SATIETY	SATURNISM	SAUNTERER	SAVES	SAWERS
SATIN	SATURNISMS	SAUNTERERS	SAVEY	SAWFISH
SATINED	SATURNIST	SAUNTERING	SAVEYED	SAWFISHES
SATINET	SATURNISTS	SAUNTERINGS	SAVEYING	SAWHORSE
SATINETS	SATYR	SAUNTERS	SAVEYS	SAWHORSES
SATINETTA	SATYRA	SAUNTING	SAVIN	SAWING
SATINETTAS	SATYRAL	SAUNTS	SAVINE	SAWINGS
SATINETTE	SATYRALS	SAUREL	SAVINES	SAWMILL
SATINETTES	SATYRAS	SAURELS	SAVING	SAWMILLS
SATING	SATYRESS	SAURIAN	SAVINGLY	SAWN
SATINING	SATYRESSES	SAURIANS	SAVINGS	SAWNEY
SATINS	SATYRIC	SAURIES	SAVINS	SAWNEYS
SATINWOOD	SATYRICAL	SAUROID	SAVIOUR	SAWPIT
SATINWOODS	SATYRID	SAUROPOD	SAVIOURS	SAWPITS
SATINY	SATYRIDS	SAUROPODS	SAVOR	SAWS
SATIRE	SATYRISK	SAURY	SAVORED	SAWSHARK
SATIRES	SATYRISKS	SAUSAGE	SAVORIES	SAWSHARKS
SATIRIC	SATYRS	SAUSAGES	SAVORING	SAWTEETH
SATIRICAL	SAUBA	SAUT	SAVOROUS	SAWTOOTH
SATIRISE	SAUBAS	SAUTE	SAVORS	SAWYER
SATIRISED	SAUCE	SAUTED	SAVORY	SAWYERS

The Chambers Dictionary is the authority for many longer words; see *OSW* Introduction, page xii

SAX	SCABROUS	SCALEWORK	SCAN	SCAPPLING
SAXATILE	SCABS	SCALEWORKS	SCAND	SCAPULA
SAXAUL	SCAD	SCALIER	SCANDAL	SCAPULAE
SAXAULS	SCADS	SCALIEST	SCANDALLED	SCAPULAR
SAXES	SCAFF	SCALINESS	SCANDALLING	SCAPULARIES
SAXHORN	SCAFFIE	SCALINESSES	SCANDALS	SCAPULARS
SAXHORNS	SCAFFIES	SCALING	SCANDENT	SCAPULARY
SAXIFRAGE	SCAFFOLD	SCALINGS	SCANDIUM	SCAPULAS
SAXIFRAGES	SCAFFOLDED	SCALL	SCANDIUMS	SCAPUS
SAXITOXIN	SCAFFOLDING	SCALLAWAG	SCANNED	SCAR
SAXITOXINS	SCAFFOLDINGS	SCALLAWAGS	SCANNER	SCARAB
SAXONIES	SCAFFOLDS	SCALLED	SCANNERS	SCARABAEI
SAXONITE	SCAFFS	SCALLIES	SCANNING	SCARABEE
SAXONITES	SCAG	SCALLION	SCANNINGS	SCARABEES
SAXONY	SCAGLIA	SCALLIONS	SCANS	SCARABOID
SAXOPHONE	SCAGLIAS	SCALLOP	SCANSION	SCARABOIDS
SAXOPHONES	SCAGLIOLA	SCALLOPED	SCANSIONS	SCARABS
SAY	SCAGLIOLAS	SCALLOPING	SCANT	SCARCE
SAYABLE	SCAGS	SCALLOPS	SCANTED	SCARCELY
SAYED	SCAIL	SCALLS	SCANTER	SCARCER
SAYER	SCAILED	SCALLY	SCANTEST	SCARCEST
SAYERS	SCAILING	SCALLYWAG	SCANTIER	SCARCITIES
SAYEST	SCAILS	SCALLYWAGS	SCANTIES	SCARCITY
SAYID	SCAITH	SCALP	SCANTIEST	SCARE
SAYIDS	SCAITHED	SCALPED	SCANTILY	SCARECROW
SAYING	SCAITHING	SCALPEL	SCANTING	SCARECROWS
SAYINGS	SCAITHS	SCALPELS	SCANTITIES	SCARED
SAYNE	SCALA	SCALPER	SCANTITY	SCAREDER
SAYON	SCALABLE	SCALPERS	SCANTLE	SCAREDEST
SAYONARA	SCALADE	SCALPING	SCANTLED	SCARER
SAYONARAS	SCALADES	SCALPINGS	SCANTLES	SCARERS
SAYONS	SCALADO	SCALPINS	SCANTLING	SCARES
SAYS	SCALADOS	SCALPLESS	SCANTLINGS	SCAREY
SAYST	SCALAE	SCALPRUM	SCANTLY	SCARF
SAYYID	SCALAR	SCALPRUMS	SCANTNESS	SCARFED
SAYYIDS	SCALARS	SCALPS	SCANTNESSES	SCARFING
SAZ	SCALAWAG	SCALY	SCANTS	SCARFINGS
SAZERAC®	SCALAWAGS	SCAM	SCANTY	SCARFISH
SAZERACS	SCALD	SCAMBLE	SCAPA	SCARFISHES
SAZES	SCALDED	SCAMBLED	SCAPAED	SCARFS
SAZHEN	SCALDER	SCAMBLER	SCAPAING	SCARFSKIN
SAZHENS	SCALDERS	SCAMBLERS	SCAPAS	SCARFSKINS
SAZZES	SCALDFISH	SCAMBLES	SCAPE	SCARFWISE
SBIRRI	SCALDFISHES	SCAMBLING	SCAPED	SCARIER
SBIRRO	SCALDHEAD	SCAMBLINGS	SCAPEGOAT	SCARIEST
SCAB	SCALDHEADS	SCAMEL	SCAPEGOATED	SCARIFIED
SCABBARD	SCALDIC	SCAMELS	SCAPEGOATING	SCARIFIER
SCABBARDED	SCALDING	SCAMMED	SCAPEGOATINGS	SCARIFIERS
SCABBARDING	SCALDINGS	SCAMMING	SCAPEGOATS	SCARIFIES
SCABBARDS	SCALDINI	SCAMMONIES	SCAPELESS	SCARIFY
SCABBED	SCALDINO	SCAMMONY	SCAPEMENT	SCARIFYING
SCABBIER	SCALDS	SCAMP	SCAPEMENTS	SCARING
SCABBIEST	SCALDSHIP	SCAMPED	SCAPES	SCARIOUS
SCABBING	SCALDSHIPS	SCAMPER	SCAPHOID	SCARLESS
SCABBLE	SCALE	SCAMPERED	SCAPHOIDS	SCARLET
SCABBLED	SCALED	SCAMPERING	SCAPHOPOD	SCARLETED
SCABBLES	SCALELESS	SCAMPERS	SCAPHOPODS	SCARLETING
SCABBLING	SCALELIKE	SCAMPI	SCAPI	SCARLETS
SCABBY	SCALENE	SCAMPING	SCAPING	SCARMOGE
SCABIES	SCALENI	SCAMPINGS	SCAPOLITE	SCARMOGES
SCABIOUS	SCALENUS	SCAMPIS	SCAPOLITES	SCARP
SCABIOUSES	SCALER	SCAMPISH	SCAPPLE	SCARPA
SCABLANDS	SCALERS	SCAMPS	SCAPPLED	SCARPAED
SCABRID	SCALES	SCAMS	SCAPPLES	SCARPAING

SCARPAS	SCAUD	SCENARY	SCHELMS	SCHLOCKIEST
SCARPED	SCAUDED	SCEND	SCHEMA	SCHLOCKS
SCARPER	SCAUDING	SCENDED	SCHEMATA	SCHLOCKY
SCARPERED	SCAUDS	SCENDING	SCHEMATIC	SCHLOSS
SCARPERING	SCAUP	SCENDS	SCHEME	SCHLOSSES
SCARPERS	SCAUPED	SCENE	SCHEMED	SCHMALTZ
SCARPETTI	SCAUPER	SCENED	SCHEMER	SCHMALTZES
SCARPETTO	SCAUPERS	SCENEMAN	SCHEMERS	SCHMALTZIER
SCARPH	SCAUPING	SCENEMEN	SCHEMES	SCHMALTZIEST
SCARPHED	SCAUPS	SCENERIES	SCHEMING	SCHMALTZY
SCARPHING	SCAUR	SCENERY	SCHEMINGS	SCHMECK
SCARPHS	SCAURED	SCENES	SCHERZI	SCHMECKS
SCARPINES	SCAURIES	SCENIC	SCHERZO	SCHMELZ
SCARPING	SCAURING	SCENICAL	SCHERZOS	SCHMELZES
SCARPINGS	SCAURS	SCENING	SCHIAVONE	SCHMO
SCARPS	SCAURY	SCENT	SCHIAVONES	SCHMOCK
SCARRE	SCAVAGE	SCENTED	SCHIEDAM	SCHMOCKS
SCARRED	SCAVAGER	SCENTFUL	SCHIEDAMS	SCHMOE
SCARRES	SCAVAGERS	SCENTING	SCHILLER	SCHMOES
SCARRIER	SCAVAGES	SCENTINGS	SCHILLERS	SCHMOOZ
SCARRIEST	SCAVENGE	SCENTLESS	SCHILLING	SCHMOOZE
SCARRING	SCAVENGED	SCENTS	SCHILLINGS	SCHMOOZED
SCARRINGS	SCAVENGER	SCEPSIS	SCHIMMEL	SCHMOOZES
SCARRY	SCAVENGERED	SCEPSISES	SCHIMMELS	SCHMOOZING
SCARS	SCAVENGERING	SCEPTER	SCHISM	SCHMUCK
SCART	SCAVENGERINGS	SCEPTERED	SCHISMA	SCHMUCKS
SCARTED	SCAVENGERS	SCEPTERS	SCHISMAS	SCHMUTTER
SCARTH	SCAVENGES	SCEPTIC	SCHISMS	SCHMUTTERS
SCARTHS	SCAVENGING	SCEPTICAL	SCHIST	SCHNAPPER
SCARTING	SCAVENGINGS	SCEPTICS	SCHISTOSE	SCHNAPPERS
SCARTS	SCAW	SCEPTRAL	SCHISTOUS	SCHNAPPS
SCARVES	SCAWS	SCEPTRE	SCHISTS	SCHNAPPSES
SCARY	SCAWTITE	SCEPTRED	SCHIZO	SCHNAPS
SCAT	SCAWTITES	SCEPTRES	SCHIZOID	SCHNAPSES
SCATCH	SCAZON	SCEPTRY	SCHIZOIDS	SCHNAUZER
SCATCHES	SCAZONS	SCERNE	SCHIZONT	SCHNAUZERS
SCATH	SCAZONTES	SCERNED	SCHIZONTS	SCHNECKE
SCATHE	SCAZONTIC	SCERNES	SCHIZOPOD	SCHNECKEN
SCATHED	SCAZONTICS	SCERNING	SCHIZOPODS	SCHNELL
SCATHEFUL	SCEAT	SCHANSE	SCHIZOS	SCHNITZEL
SCATHES	SCEATT	SCHANSES	SCHLAGER	SCHNITZELS
SCATHING	SCEATTAS	SCHANTZE	SCHLAGERS	SCHNOOK
SCATHS	SCEDULE	SCHANTZES	SCHLEMIEL	SCHNOOKS
SCATOLE	SCEDULED	SCHANZE	SCHLEMIELS	SCHNORKEL
SCATOLES	SCEDULES	SCHANZES	SCHLEMIHL	SCHNORKELS
SCATOLOGIES	SCEDULING	SCHAPPE	SCHLEMIHLS	SCHNORR
SCATOLOGY	SCELERAT	SCHAPPED	SCHLEP	SCHNORRED
SCATS	SCELERATE	SCHAPPEING	SCHLEPP	SCHNORRER
SCATT	SCELERATES	SCHAPPES	SCHLEPPED	SCHNORRERS
SCATTED	SCELERATS	SCHAPSKA	SCHLEPPER	SCHNORRING
SCATTER	SCENA	SCHAPSKAS	SCHLEPPERS	SCHNORRS
SCATTERED	SCENARIES	SCHECHITA	SCHLEPPIER	SCHNOZZLE
SCATTERER	SCENARIO	SCHECHITAS	SCHLEPPIEST	SCHNOZZLES
SCATTERERS	SCENARIOS	SCHEDULE	SCHLEPPING	SCHOLAR
SCATTERING	SCENARISE	SCHEDULED	SCHLEPPS	SCHOLARCH
SCATTERINGS	SCENARISED	SCHEDULER	SCHLEPPY	SCHOLARCHS
SCATTERS	SCENARISES	SCHEDULERS	SCHLEPS	SCHOLARLIER
SCATTERY	SCENARISING	SCHEDULES	SCHLICH	SCHOLARLIEST
SCATTIER	SCENARIST	SCHEDULING	SCHLICHS	SCHOLARLY
SCATTIEST	SCENARISTS	SCHEELITE	SCHLIEREN	SCHOLARS
SCATTING	SCENARIZE	SCHEELITES	SCHLOCK	SCHOLIA
SCATTINGS	SCENARIZED	SCHELLUM	SCHLOCKER	SCHOLIAST
SCATTS	SCENARIZES	SCHELLUMS	SCHLOCKERS	SCHOLIASTS
SCATTY	SCENARIZING	SCHELM	SCHLOCKIER	SCHOLION

SCHOLIUM	SCIENTISING	SCLAVE	SCOLECID	SCOPE
SCHOOL	SCIENTISM	SCLAVES	SCOLECIDS	SCOPED
SCHOOLBAG	SCIENTISMS	SCLERA	SCOLECITE	SCOPELID
SCHOOLBAGS	SCIENTIST	SCLERAL	SCOLECITES	SCOPELIDS
SCHOOLBOY	SCIENTISTS	SCLERAS	SCOLECOID	SCOPELOID
SCHOOLBOYS	SCIENTIZE	SCLERE	SCOLEX	SCOPELOIDS
SCHOOLDAY	SCIENTIZED	SCLEREID	SCOLIA	SCOPES
SCHOOLDAYS	SCIENTIZES	SCLEREIDE	SCOLICES	SCOPING
SCHOOLE	SCIENTIZING	SCLEREIDES	SCOLIOMA	SCOPULA
SCHOOLED	SCILICET	SCLEREIDS	SCOLIOMAS	SCOPULAS
SCHOOLERIES	SCILLA	SCLEREMA	SCOLION	SCOPULATE
SCHOOLERY	SCILLAS	SCLEREMAS	SCOLIOSES	SCORBUTIC
SCHOOLES	SCIMITAR	SCLERES	SCOLIOSIS	SCORCH
SCHOOLING	SCIMITARS	SCLERITE	SCOLIOTIC	SCORCHED
SCHOOLINGS	SCINCOID	SCLERITES	SCOLLOP	SCORCHER
SCHOOLMAN	SCINCOIDS	SCLERITIS	SCOLLOPED	SCORCHERS
SCHOOLMEN	SCINTILLA	SCLERITISES	SCOLLOPING	SCORCHES
SCHOOLS	SCINTILLAS	SCLEROID	SCOLLOPS	SCORCHING
SCHOONER	SCIOLISM	SCLEROMA	SCOLYTID	SCORCHINGS
SCHOONERS	SCIOLISMS	SCLEROMAS	SCOLYTIDS	SCORDATO
SCHORL	SCIOLIST	SCLEROMATA	SCOLYTOID	SCORE
SCHORLS	SCIOLISTS	SCLEROSAL	SCOLYTOIDS	SCORECARD
SCHOUT	SCIOLOUS	SCLEROSE	SCOMBRID	SCORECARDS
SCHOUTS	SCIOLTO	SCLEROSED	SCOMBRIDS	SCORED
SCHTICK	SCION	SCLEROSES	SCOMBROID	SCORELINE
SCHTICKS	SCIONS	SCLEROSING	SCOMBROIDS	SCORELINES
SCHTIK	SCIOSOPHIES	SCLEROSIS	SCOMFISH	SCORER
SCHTIKS	SCIOSOPHY	SCLEROTAL	SCOMFISHED	SCORERS
SCHTOOK	SCIROC	SCLEROTALS	SCOMFISHES	SCORES
SCHTOOKS	SCIROCCO	SCLEROTIA	SCOMFISHING	SCORIA
SCHTOOM	SCIROCCOS	SCLEROTIC	SCONCE	SCORIAC
SCHTUCK	SCIROCS	SCLEROTICS	SCONCED	SCORIAE
SCHTUCKS	SCIRRHOID	SCLEROTIN	SCONCES	SCORIFIED
SCHUIT	SCIRRHOUS	SCLEROTINS	SCONCHEON	SCORIFIER
SCHUITS	SCIRRHUS	SCLEROUS	SCONCHEONS	SCORIFIERS
SCHUSS	SCIRRHUSES	SCLIFF	SCONCING	SCORIFIES
SCHUSSED	SCISSEL	SCLIFFS	SCONE	SCORIFY
SCHUSSES	SCISSELS	SCLIM	SCONES	SCORIFYING
SCHUSSING	SCISSIL	SCLIMMED	SCONTION	SCORING
SCHUYT	SCISSILE	SCLIMMING	SCONTIONS	SCORINGS
SCHUYTS	SCISSILS	SCLIMS	SCOOG	SCORIOUS
SCHWA	SCISSION	SCOFF	SCOOGED	SCORN
SCHWAS	SCISSIONS	SCOFFED	SCOOGING	SCORNED
SCIAENID	SCISSOR	SCOFFER	SCOOGS	SCORNER
SCIAENIDS	SCISSORED	SCOFFERS	SCOOP	SCORNERS
SCIAENOID	SCISSORER	SCOFFING	SCOOPED	SCORNFUL
SCIAENOIDS	SCISSORERS	SCOFFINGS	SCOOPER	SCORNING
SCIAMACHIES	SCISSORING	SCOFFLAW	SCOOPERS	SCORNINGS
SCIAMACHY	SCISSORS	SCOFFLAWS	SCOOPFUL	SCORNS
SCIARID	SCISSURE	SCOFFS	SCOOPFULS	SCORODITE
SCIARIDS	SCISSURES	SCOG	SCOOPING	SCORODITES
SCIATIC	SCIURINE	SCOGGED	SCOOPINGS	SCORPER
SCIATICA	SCIURINES	SCOGGING	SCOOPS	SCORPERS
SCIATICAL	SCIUROID	SCOGS	SCOOT	SCORPIOID
SCIATICAS	SCLAFF	SCOINSON	SCOOTED	SCORPIOIDS
SCIENCE	SCLAFFED	SCOINSONS	SCOOTER	SCORPION
SCIENCED	SCLAFFING	SCOLD	SCOOTERS	SCORPIONS
SCIENCES	SCLAFFS	SCOLDED	SCOOTING	SCORRENDO
SCIENT	SCLATE	SCOLDER	SCOOTS	SCORSE
SCIENTER	SCLATED	SCOLDERS	SCOP	SCORSED
SCIENTIAL	SCLATES	SCOLDING	SCOPA	SCORSER
SCIENTISE	SCLATING	SCOLDINGS	SCOPAE	SCORSERS
SCIENTISED	SCLAUNDER	SCOLDS	SCOPAS	SCORSES
SCIENTISES	SCLAUNDERS	SCOLECES	SCOPATE	SCORSING

The Chambers Dictionary is the authority for many longer words; see *OSW* Introduction, page xii

SCOT	SCOUTHS	SCRAMBLE	SCRATTLE	SCREEDS
SCOTCH	SCOUTING	SCRAMBLED	SCRATTLED	SCREEN
SCOTCHED	SCOUTINGS	SCRAMBLER	SCRATTLES	SCREENED
SCOTCHES	SCOUTS	SCRAMBLERS	SCRATTLING	SCREENER
SCOTCHING	SCOW	SCRAMBLES	SCRAUCH	SCREENERS
SCOTER	SCOWDER	SCRAMBLING	SCRAUCHED	SCREENING
SCOTERS	SCOWDERED	SCRAMBLINGS	SCRAUCHING	SCREENINGS
SCOTIA	SCOWDERING	SCRAMBS	SCRAUCHS	SCREENS
SCOTIAS	SCOWDERINGS	SCRAMJET	SCRAUGH	SCREES
SCOTOMA	SCOWDERS	SCRAMJETS	SCRAUGHED	SCREEVE
SCOTOMAS	SCOWL	SCRAMMED	SCRAUGHING	SCREEVED
SCOTOMATA	SCOWLED	SCRAMMING	SCRAUGHS	SCREEVER
SCOTOMIA	SCOWLING	SCRAMS	SCRAW	SCREEVERS
SCOTOMIAS	SCOWLS	SCRAN	SCRAWL	SCREEVES
SCOTOMIES	SCOWP	SCRANCH	SCRAWLED	SCREEVING
SCOTOMY	SCOWPED	SCRANCHED	SCRAWLER	SCREEVINGS
SCOTOPIA	SCOWPING	SCRANCHES	SCRAWLERS	SCREICH
SCOTOPIAS	SCOWPS	SCRANCHING	SCRAWLIER	SCREICHED
SCOTOPIC	SCOWRER	SCRANNEL	SCRAWLIEST	SCREICHING
SCOTS	SCOWRERS	SCRANNIER	SCRAWLING	SCREICHS
SCOUG	SCOWRIE	SCRANNIEST	SCRAWLINGS	SCREIGH
SCOUGED	SCOWRIES	SCRANNY	SCRAWLS	SCREIGHED
SCOUGING	SCOWS	SCRANS	SCRAWLY	SCREIGHING
SCOUGS	SCOWTH	SCRAP	SCRAWM	SCREIGHS
SCOUNDREL	SCOWTHER	SCRAPBOOK	SCRAWMED	SCREW
SCOUNDRELS	SCOWTHERED	SCRAPBOOKS	SCRAWMING	SCREWBALL
SCOUP	SCOWTHERING	SCRAPE	SCRAWMS	SCREWBALLS
SCOUPED	SCOWTHERS	SCRAPED	SCRAWNIER	SCREWED
SCOUPING	SCOWTHS	SCRAPEGUT	SCRAWNIEST	SCREWER
SCOUPS	SCRAB	SCRAPEGUTS	SCRAWNY	SCREWERS
SCOUR	SCRABBED	SCRAPER	SCRAWS	SCREWIER
SCOURED	SCRABBING	SCRAPERS	SCRAY	SCREWIEST
SCOURER	SCRABBLE	SCRAPES	SCRAYE	SCREWING
SCOURERS	SCRABBLED	SCRAPHEAP	SCRAYES	SCREWINGS
SCOURGE	SCRABBLER	SCRAPHEAPS	SCRAYS	SCREWS
SCOURGED	SCRABBLERS	SCRAPIE	SCREAK	SCREWTOP
SCOURGER	SCRABBLES	SCRAPIES	SCREAKED	SCREWTOPS
SCOURGERS	SCRABBLING	SCRAPING	SCREAKIER	SCREWY
SCOURGES	SCRABS	SCRAPINGS	SCREAKIEST	SCRIBABLE
SCOURGING	SCRAE	SCRAPPED	SCREAKING	SCRIBAL
SCOURIE	SCRAES	SCRAPPIER	SCREAKS	SCRIBBLE
SCOURIES	SCRAG	SCRAPPIEST	SCREAKY	SCRIBBLED
SCOURING	SCRAGGED	SCRAPPILY	SCREAM	SCRIBBLER
SCOURINGS	SCRAGGIER	SCRAPPING	SCREAMED	SCRIBBLERS
SCOURS	SCRAGGIEST	SCRAPPLE	SCREAMER	SCRIBBLES
SCOURSE	SCRAGGILY	SCRAPPLES	SCREAMERS	SCRIBBLIER
SCOURSED	SCRAGGING	SCRAPPY	SCREAMING	SCRIBBLIEST
SCOURSES	SCRAGGLIER	SCRAPS	SCREAMS	SCRIBBLING
SCOURSING	SCRAGGLIEST	SCRAPYARD	SCREE	SCRIBBLINGS
SCOUSE	SCRAGGLY	SCRAPYARDS	SCREECH	SCRIBBLY
SCOUSER	SCRAGS	SCRAT	SCREECHED	SCRIBE
SCOUSERS	SCRAICH	SCRATCH	SCREECHER	SCRIBED
SCOUSES	SCRAICHED	SCRATCHED	SCREECHERS	SCRIBER
SCOUT	SCRAICHING	SCRATCHER	SCREECHES	SCRIBERS
SCOUTED	SCRAICHS	SCRATCHERS	SCREECHIER	SCRIBES
SCOUTER	SCRAIGH	SCRATCHES	SCREECHIEST	SCRIBING
SCOUTERS	SCRAIGHED	SCRATCHIEST	SCREECHING	SCRIBINGS
SCOUTH	SCRAIGHING	SCRATCHING	SCREECHY	SCRIBISM
SCOUTHER	SCRAIGHS	SCRATCHINGS	SCREED	SCRIBISMS
SCOUTHERED	SCRAM	SCRATCHY	SCREEDED	SCRIECH
SCOUTHERING	SCRAMB	SCRATS	SCREEDER	SCRIECHED
SCOUTHERINGS	SCRAMBED	SCRATTED	SCREEDERS	SCRIECHING
SCOUTHERS	SCRAMBING	SCRATTING	SCREEDING	SCRIECHS
SCOUTHERY			SCREEDINGS	SCRIED

The Chambers Dictionary is the authority for many longer words; see *OSW* Introduction, page xii

SCRIENE
SCRIENES
SCRIES
SCRIEVE
SCRIEVED
SCRIEVES
SCRIEVING
SCRIGGLE
SCRIGGLED
SCRIGGLES
SCRIGGLIER
SCRIGGLIEST
SCRIGGLING
SCRIGGLY
SCRIKE
SCRIKED
SCRIKES
SCRIKING
SCRIM
SCRIMMAGE
SCRIMMAGED
SCRIMMAGES
SCRIMMAGING
SCRIMP
SCRIMPED
SCRIMPIER
SCRIMPIEST
SCRIMPILY
SCRIMPING
SCRIMPLY
SCRIMPS
SCRIMPY
SCRIMS
SCRIMSHAW
SCRIMSHAWED
SCRIMSHAWING
SCRIMSHAWS
SCRIMURE
SCRIMURES
SCRINE
SCRINES
SCRIP
SCRIPPAGE
SCRIPPAGES
SCRIPS
SCRIPT
SCRIPTED
SCRIPTING
SCRIPTORY
SCRIPTS
SCRIPTURE
SCRIPTURES
SCRITCH
SCRITCHED
SCRITCHES
SCRITCHING
SCRIVE
SCRIVED
SCRIVENER
SCRIVENERS
SCRIVES
SCRIVING
SCROBE
SCROBES

SCROD
SCRODDLED
SCRODS
SCROFULA
SCROFULAS
SCROG
SCROGGIE
SCROGGIER
SCROGGIEST
SCROGGY
SCROGS
SCROLL
SCROLLED
SCROLLING
SCROLLS
SCROOGE
SCROOGED
SCROOGES
SCROOGING
SCROOP
SCROOPED
SCROOPING
SCROOPS
SCROTA
SCROTAL
SCROTUM
SCROTUMS
SCROUGE
SCROUGED
SCROUGER
SCROUGERS
SCROUGES
SCROUGING
SCROUNGE
SCROUNGED
SCROUNGER
SCROUNGERS
SCROUNGES
SCROUNGING
SCROUNGINGS
SCROW
SCROWDGE
SCROWDGED
SCROWDGES
SCROWDGING
SCROWL
SCROWLE
SCROWLED
SCROWLES
SCROWLING
SCROWLS
SCROWS
SCROYLE
SCROYLES
SCRUB
SCRUBBED
SCRUBBER
SCRUBBERS
SCRUBBIER
SCRUBBIEST
SCRUBBING
SCRUBBINGS
SCRUBBY
SCRUBLAND

SCRUBLANDS
SCRUBS
SCRUFF
SCRUFFIER
SCRUFFIEST
SCRUFFS
SCRUFFY
SCRUM
SCRUMDOWN
SCRUMDOWNS
SCRUMMAGE
SCRUMMAGED
SCRUMMAGES
SCRUMMAGING
SCRUMMED
SCRUMMIER
SCRUMMIEST
SCRUMMING
SCRUMMY
SCRUMP
SCRUMPED
SCRUMPIES
SCRUMPING
SCRUMPOX
SCRUMPOXES
SCRUMPS
SCRUMPY
SCRUMS
SCRUNCH
SCRUNCHED
SCRUNCHES
SCRUNCHIER
SCRUNCHIES
SCRUNCHIEST
SCRUNCHING
SCRUNCHY
SCRUNT
SCRUNTIER
SCRUNTIEST
SCRUNTS
SCRUNTY
SCRUPLE
SCRUPLED
SCRUPLER
SCRUPLERS
SCRUPLES
SCRUPLING
SCRUTABLE
SCRUTATOR
SCRUTATORS
SCRUTINIES
SCRUTINY
SCRUTO
SCRUTOIRE
SCRUTOIRES
SCRUTOS
SCRUZE
SCRUZED
SCRUZES
SCRUZING
SCRY
SCRYDE
SCRYER
SCRYERS

SCRYING
SCRYINGS
SCRYNE
SCRYNES
SCUBA
SCUBAS
SCUCHIN
SCUCHINS
SCUCHION
SCUCHIONS
SCUD
SCUDDALER
SCUDDALERS
SCUDDED
SCUDDER
SCUDDERS
SCUDDING
SCUDDLE
SCUDDLED
SCUDDLES
SCUDDLING
SCUDI
SCUDLER
SCUDLERS
SCUDO
SCUDS
SCUFF
SCUFFED
SCUFFING
SCUFFLE
SCUFFLED
SCUFFLER
SCUFFLERS
SCUFFLES
SCUFFLING
SCUFFS
SCUFT
SCUFTS
SCUG
SCUGGED
SCUGGING
SCUGS
SCUL
SCULK
SCULKED
SCULKING
SCULKS
SCULL
SCULLE
SCULLED
SCULLER
SCULLERIES
SCULLERS
SCULLERY
SCULLES
SCULLING
SCULLINGS
SCULLION
SCULLIONS
SCULLS
SCULP
SCULPED
SCULPIN
SCULPING

SCULPINS
SCULPS
SCULPSIT
SCULPT
SCULPTED
SCULPTING
SCULPTOR
SCULPTORS
SCULPTS
SCULPTURE
SCULPTURED
SCULPTURES
SCULPTURING
SCULPTURINGS
SCULS
SCUM
SCUMBAG
SCUMBAGS
SCUMBER
SCUMBERED
SCUMBERING
SCUMBERS
SCUMBLE
SCUMBLED
SCUMBLES
SCUMBLING
SCUMBLINGS
SCUMFISH
SCUMFISHED
SCUMFISHES
SCUMFISHING
SCUMMED
SCUMMER
SCUMMERS
SCUMMIER
SCUMMIEST
SCUMMING
SCUMMINGS
SCUMMY
SCUMS
SCUNCHEON
SCUNCHEONS
SCUNGE
SCUNGED
SCUNGES
SCUNGIER
SCUNGIEST
SCUNGING
SCUNGY
SCUNNER
SCUNNERED
SCUNNERING
SCUNNERS
SCUP
SCUPPAUG
SCUPPAUGS
SCUPPER
SCUPPERED
SCUPPERING
SCUPPERS
SCUPS
SCUR
SCURF
SCURFIER

SCURFIEST	SCUZZIER	SEAFARING	SEAMING	SEASONAL
SCURFS	SCUZZIEST	SEAFARINGS	SEAMLESS	SEASONED
SCURFY	SCUZZY	SEAFOLK	SEAMOUNT	SEASONER
SCURRED	SCYBALA	SEAFOLKS	SEAMOUNTS	SEASONERS
SCURRIED	SCYBALOUS	SEAFOOD	SEAMS	SEASONING
SCURRIER	SCYBALUM	SEAFOODS	SEAMSET	SEASONINGS
SCURRIERS	SCYE	SEAFOWL	SEAMSETS	SEASONS
SCURRIES	SCYES	SEAFOWLS	SEAMSTER	SEASPEAK
SCURRIL	SCYPHI	SEAFRONT	SEAMSTERS	SEASPEAKS
SCURRILE	SCYPHUS	SEAFRONTS	SEAMY	SEASURE
SCURRING	SCYTALE	SEAGULL	SEAN	SEASURES
SCURRIOUR	SCYTALES	SEAGULLS	SEANCE	SEAT
SCURRIOURS	SCYTHE	SEAHAWK	SEANCES	SEATED
SCURRY	SCYTHED	SEAHAWKS	SEANED	SEATER
SCURRYING	SCYTHEMAN	SEAHOG	SEANING	SEATERS
SCURS	SCYTHEMEN	SEAHOGS	SEANNACHIES	SEATING
SCURVIER	SCYTHER	SEAHORSE	SEANNACHY	SEATINGS
SCURVIES	SCYTHERS	SEAHORSES	SEANS	SEATLESS
SCURVIEST	SCYTHES	SEAHOUND	SEAPLANE	SEATS
SCURVILY	SCYTHING	SEAHOUNDS	SEAPLANES	SEAWARD
SCURVY	SDAINE	SEAKALE	SEAPORT	SEAWARDLY
SCUSE	SDAINED	SEAKALES	SEAPORTS	SEAWARDS
SCUSED	SDAINES	SEAL	SEAQUAKE	SEAWARE
SCUSES	SDAINING	SEALANT	SEAQUAKES	SEAWARES
SCUSING	SDAYN	SEALANTS	SEAQUARIA	SEAWATER
SCUT	SDAYNED	SEALCH	SEAR	SEAWATERS
SCUTA	SDAYNING	SEALCHS	SEARAT	SEAWAY
SCUTAGE	SDAYNS	SEALED	SEARATS	SEAWAYS
SCUTAGES	SDEIGN	SEALER	SEARCE	SEAWEED
SCUTAL	SDEIGNE	SEALERIES	SEARCED	SEAWEEDS
SCUTATE	SDEIGNED	SEALERS	SEARCES	SEAWIFE
SCUTCH	SDEIGNES	SEALERY	SEARCH	SEAWIVES
SCUTCHED	SDEIGNING	SEALGH	SEARCHED	SEAWOMAN
SCUTCHEON	SDEIGNS	SEALGHS	SEARCHER	SEAWOMEN
SCUTCHEONS	SDEIN	SEALINE	SEARCHERS	SEAWORM
SCUTCHER	SDEINED	SEALINES	SEARCHES	SEAWORMS
SCUTCHERS	SDEINING	SEALING	SEARCHING	SEAWORTHY
SCUTCHES	SDEINS	SEALINGS	SEARCING	SEAZE
SCUTCHING	SEA	SEALPOINT	SEARE	SEAZED
SCUTCHINGS	SEABANK	SEALPOINTS	SEARED	SEAZES
SCUTE	SEABANKS	SEALS	SEARER	SEAZING
SCUTELLA	SEABED	SEALSKIN	SEAREST	SEBACEOUS
SCUTELLAR	SEABEDS	SEALSKINS	SEARING	SEBACIC
SCUTELLUM	SEABIRD	SEALWAX	SEARINGS	SEBATE
SCUTES	SEABIRDS	SEALWAXES	SEARNESS	SEBATES
SCUTIFORM	SEABLITE	SEALYHAM	SEARNESSES	SEBESTEN
SCUTIGER	SEABLITES	SEALYHAMS	SEARS	SEBESTENS
SCUTIGERS	SEABOARD	SEAM	SEAS	SEBIFIC
SCUTS	SEABOARDS	SEAMAID	SEASCAPE	SEBUM
SCUTTER	SEABORNE	SEAMAIDS	SEASCAPES	SEBUMS
SCUTTERED	SEABOTTLE	SEAMAN	SEASE	SEBUNDIES
SCUTTERING	SEABOTTLES	SEAMANLY	SEASED	SEBUNDY
SCUTTERS	SEACOAST	SEAMARK	SEASES	SEC
SCUTTLE	SEACOASTS	SEAMARKS	SEASHELL	SECANT
SCUTTLED	SEACOCK	SEAME	SEASHELLS	SECANTLY
SCUTTLER	SEACOCKS	SEAMED	SEASHORE	SECANTS
SCUTTLERS	SEACRAFT	SEAMEN	SEASHORES	SECATEURS
SCUTTLES	SEACRAFTS	SEAMER	SEASICK	SECCO
SCUTTLING	SEACUNNIES	SEAMERS	SEASICKER	SECCOS
SCUTUM	SEACUNNY	SEAMES	SEASICKEST	SECEDE
SCUZZ	SEADROME	SEAMIER	SEASIDE	SECEDED
SCUZZBALL	SEADROMES	SEAMIEST	SEASIDES	SECEDER
SCUZZBALLS	SEAFARER	SEAMINESS	SEASING	SECEDERS
SCUZZES	SEAFARERS	SEAMINESSES	SEASON	SECEDES

SECEDING	SECTARIAL	SEDATING	SEEDINESSES	SEESAWING
SECERN	SECTARIAN	SEDATION	SEEDING	SEESAWS
SECERNED	SECTARIANS	SEDATIONS	SEEDINGS	SEETHE
SECERNENT	SECTARIES	SEDATIVE	SEEDLESS	SEETHED
SECERNENTS	SECTARY	SEDATIVES	SEEDLIKE	SEETHER
SECERNING	SECTATOR	SEDENT	SEEDLING	SEETHERS
SECERNS	SECTATORS	SEDENTARY	SEEDLINGS	SEETHES
SECESH	SECTILE	SEDERUNT	SEEDLIP	SEETHING
SECESHER	SECTILITIES	SEDERUNTS	SEEDLIPS	SEETHINGS
SECESHERS	SECTILITY	SEDES	SEEDNESS	SEEWING
SECESHES	SECTION	SEDGE	SEEDNESSES	SEG
SECESSION	SECTIONAL	SEDGED	SEEDS	SEGAR
SECESSIONS	SECTIONED	SEDGELAND	SEEDSMAN	SEGARS
SECKEL	SECTIONING	SEDGELANDS	SEEDSMEN	SEGGAR
SECKELS	SECTIONS	SEDGES	SEEDY	SEGGARS
SECKLE	SECTOR	SEDGIER	SEEING	SEGHOL
SECKLES	SECTORAL	SEDGIEST	SEEINGS	SEGHOLATE
SECLUDE	SECTORED	SEDGY	SEEK	SEGHOLATES
SECLUDED	SECTORIAL	SEDILE	SEEKER	SEGHOLS
SECLUDES	SECTORIALS	SEDILIA	SEEKERS	SEGMENT
SECLUDING	SECTORING	SEDIMENT	SEEKING	SEGMENTAL
SECLUSION	SECTORISE	SEDIMENTED	SEEKS	SEGMENTED
SECLUSIONS	SECTORISED	SEDIMENTING	SEEL	SEGMENTING
SECLUSIVE	SECTORISES	SEDIMENTS	SEELD	SEGMENTS
SECO	SECTORISING	SEDITION	SEELED	SEGNO
SECODONT	SECTORIZE	SEDITIONS	SEELIER	SEGNOS
SECODONTS	SECTORIZED	SEDITIOUS	SEELIEST	SEGO
SECOND	SECTORIZES	SEDUCE	SEELING	SEGOL
SECONDARIES	SECTORIZING	SEDUCED	SEELINGS	SEGOLATE
SECONDARY	SECTORS	SEDUCER	SEELS	SEGOLATES
SECONDE	SECTS	SEDUCERS	SEELY	SEGOLS
SECONDED	SECULAR	SEDUCES	SEEM	SEGOS
SECONDEE	SECULARLY	SEDUCING	SEEMED	SEGREANT
SECONDEES	SECULARS	SEDUCINGS	SEEMER	SEGREGATE
SECONDER	SECULUM	SEDUCTION	SEEMERS	SEGREGATED
SECONDERS	SECULUMS	SEDUCTIONS	SEEMING	SEGREGATES
SECONDES	SECUND	SEDUCTIVE	SEEMINGLY	SEGREGATING
SECONDI	SECUNDINE	SEDUCTOR	SEEMINGS	SEGS
SECONDING	SECUNDINES	SEDUCTORS	SEEMLESS	SEGUE
SECONDLY	SECUNDUM	SEDULITIES	SEEMLIER	SEGUED
SECONDO	SECURABLE	SEDULITY	SEEMLIEST	SEGUEING
SECONDS	SECURANCE	SEDULOUS	SEEMLIHED	SEGUES
SECRECIES	SECURANCES	SEDUM	SEEMLIHEDS	SEI
SECRECY	SECURE	SEDUMS	SEEMLY	SEICENTO
SECRET	SECURED	SEE	SEEMLYHED	SEICENTOS
SECRETA	SECURELY	SEEABLE	SEEMLYHEDS	SEICHE
SECRETAGE	SECURER	SEECATCH	SEEMS	SEICHES
SECRETAGES	SECURERS	SEECATCHIE	SEEN	SEIF
SECRETARIES	SECURES	SEED	SEEP	SEIFS
SECRETARY	SECUREST	SEEDBED	SEEPAGE	SEIGNEUR
SECRETE	SECURING	SEEDBEDS	SEEPAGES	SEIGNEURS
SECRETED	SECURITAN	SEEDBOX	SEEPED	SEIGNIOR
SECRETES	SECURITANS	SEEDBOXES	SEEPIER	SEIGNIORIES
SECRETIN	SECURITIES	SEEDCAKE	SEEPIEST	SEIGNIORS
SECRETING	SECURITY	SEEDCAKES	SEEPING	SEIGNIORY
SECRETINS	SED	SEEDCASE	SEEPS	SEIGNORAL
SECRETION	SEDAN	SEEDCASES	SEEPY	SEIGNORIES
SECRETIONS	SEDANS	SEEDED	SEER	SEIGNORY
SECRETIVE	SEDATE	SEEDER	SEERESS	SEIK
SECRETLY	SEDATED	SEEDERS	SEERESSES	SEIKER
SECRETORY	SEDATELY	SEEDIER	SEERS	SEIKEST
SECRETS	SEDATER	SEEDIEST	SEES	SEIL
SECS	SEDATES	SEEDILY	SEESAW	SEILED
SECT	SEDATEST	SEEDINESS	SEESAWED	SEILING

SEILS	SELECTION	SELVAGEES	SEMIFLUID	SENATORS
SEINE	SELECTIONS	SELVAGES	SEMIFLUIDS	SEND
SEINED	SELECTIVE	SELVAGING	SEMILUNAR	SENDAL
SEINER	SELECTOR	SELVAS	SEMILUNE	SENDALS
SEINERS	SELECTORS	SELVEDGE	SEMILUNES	SENDED
SEINES	SELECTS	SELVEDGED	SEMINAL	SENDER
SEINING	SELENATE	SELVEDGES	SEMINALLY	SENDERS
SEININGS	SELENATES	SELVEDGING	SEMINAR	SENDING
SEIR	SELENIAN	SELVES	SEMINARIES	SENDINGS
SEIRS	SELENIC	SEMANTEME	SEMINARS	SENDS
SEIS	SELENIDE	SEMANTEMES	SEMINARY	SENECIO
SEISE	SELENIDES	SEMANTIC	SEMINATE	SENECIOS
SEISED	SELENIOUS	SEMANTICS	SEMINATED	SENEGA
SEISES	SELENITE	SEMANTIDE	SEMINATES	SENEGAS
SEISIN	SELENITES	SEMANTIDES	SEMINATING	SENESCENT
SEISING	SELENITIC	SEMANTRA	SEMIOLOGIES	SENESCHAL
SEISINS	SELENIUM	SEMANTRON	SEMIOLOGY	SENESCHALS
SEISM	SELENIUMS	SEMAPHORE	SEMIOTIC	SENGREEN
SEISMAL	SELENOUS	SEMAPHORED	SEMIOTICS	SENGREENS
SEISMIC	SELES	SEMAPHORES	SEMIPED	SENILE
SEISMICAL	SELF	SEMAPHORING	SEMIPEDS	SENILELY
SEISMISM	SELFED	SEMATIC	SEMIPLUME	SENILITIES
SEISMISMS	SELFHEAL	SEMBLABLE	SEMIPLUMES	SENILITY
SEISMS	SELFHEALS	SEMBLABLES	SEMIS	SENIOR
SEITEN	SELFHOOD	SEMBLABLY	SEMISES	SENIORITIES
SEITENS	SELFHOODS	SEMBLANCE	SEMISOLID	SENIORITY
SEITIES	SELFING	SEMBLANCES	SEMISOLIDS	SENIORS
SEITY	SELFINGS	SEMBLANT	SEMITAR	SENNA
SEIZABLE	SELFISH	SEMBLANTS	SEMITARS	SENNACHIE
SEIZE	SELFISHLY	SEMBLE	SEMITAUR	SENNACHIES
SEIZED	SELFISM	SEMBLED	SEMITAURS	SENNAS
SEIZER	SELFISMS	SEMBLES	SEMITONE	SENNET
SEIZERS	SELFIST	SEMBLING	SEMITONES	SENNETS
SEIZES	SELFISTS	SEME	SEMITONIC	SENNIGHT
SEIZIN	SELFLESS	SEMEE	SEMIVOWEL	SENNIGHTS
SEIZING	SELFNESS	SEMEED	SEMIVOWELS	SENNIT
SEIZINGS	SELFNESSES	SEMEIA	SEMMIT	SENNITS
SEIZINS	SELFS	SEMEION	SEMMITS	SENS
SEIZURE	SELICTAR	SEMEIOTIC	SEMOLINA	SENSA
SEIZURES	SELICTARS	SEMEIOTICS	SEMOLINAS	SENSATE
SEJANT	SELKIE	SEMEME	SEMPER	SENSATION
SEJEANT	SELKIES	SEMEMES	SEMPLE	SENSATIONS
SEKOS	SELL	SEMEN	SEMPLER	SENSE
SEKOSES	SELLA	SEMENS	SEMPLEST	SENSED
SEKT	SELLABLE	SEMESTER	SEMPLICE	SENSEFUL
SEKTS	SELLAE	SEMESTERS	SEMPRE	SENSELESS
SEL	SELLAS	SEMESTRAL	SEMPSTER	SENSES
SELACHIAN	SELLE	SEMI	SEMPSTERS	SENSIBLE
SELACHIANS	SELLER	SEMIANGLE	SEMSEM	SENSIBLER
SELADANG	SELLERS	SEMIANGLES	SEMSEMS	SENSIBLES
SELADANGS	SELLES	SEMIBOLD	SEMUNCIA	SENSIBLEST
SELAH	SELLING	SEMIBOLDS	SEMUNCIAE	SENSIBLY
SELAHS	SELLOTAPE	SEMIBREVE	SEMUNCIAL	SENSILE
SELCOUTH	SELLOTAPED	SEMIBREVES	SEMUNCIAS	SENSILLA
SELD	SELLOTAPES	SEMIBULL	SEN	SENSILLUM
SELDOM	SELLOTAPING	SEMIBULLS	SENA	SENSING
SELDSEEN	SELLS	SEMICOLON	SENARIES	SENSINGS
SELDSHOWN	SELS	SEMICOLONS	SENARII	SENSISM
SELE	SELTZER	SEMICOMA	SENARIUS	SENSISMS
SELECT	SELTZERS	SEMICOMAS	SENARY	SENSIST
SELECTED	SELVA	SEMIE	SENAS	SENSISTS
SELECTEE	SELVAGE	SEMIES	SENATE	SENSITISE
SELECTEES	SELVAGED	SEMIFINAL	SENATES	SENSITISED
SELECTING	SELVAGEE	SEMIFINALS	SENATOR	SENSITISES

SENSITISING	SEPARATOR	SEPTUPLING	SERAPHINS	SERIALIZING
SENSITIVE	SEPARATORS	SEPULCHER	SERAPHS	SERIALLY
SENSITIVES	SEPARATUM	SEPULCHERED	SERASKIER	SERIALS
SENSITIZE	SEPARATUMS	SEPULCHERING	SERASKIERS	SERIATE
SENSITIZED	SEPHEN	SEPULCHERS	SERDAB	SERIATED
SENSITIZES	SEPHENS	SEPULCHRE	SERDABS	SERIATELY
SENSITIZING	SEPIA	SEPULCHRED	SERE	SERIATES
SENSOR	SEPIAS	SEPULCHRES	SERED	SERIATIM
SENSORIA	SEPIMENT	SEPULCHRING	SEREIN	SERIATING
SENSORIAL	SEPIMENTS	SEPULTURE	SEREINS	SERIATION
SENSORILY	SEPIOLITE	SEPULTURED	SERENADE	SERIATIONS
SENSORIUM	SEPIOLITES	SEPULTURES	SERENADED	SERIC
SENSORIUMS	SEPIOST	SEPULTURING	SERENADER	SERICEOUS
SENSORS	SEPIOSTS	SEQUACITIES	SERENADERS	SERICIN
SENSORY	SEPIUM	SEQUACITY	SERENADES	SERICINS
SENSUAL	SEPIUMS	SEQUEL	SERENADING	SERICITE
SENSUALLY	SEPMAG	SEQUELA	SERENATA	SERICITES
SENSUM	SEPOY	SEQUELAE	SERENATAS	SERICITIC
SENSUOUS	SEPOYS	SEQUELS	SERENATE	SERICON
SENT	SEPPUKU	SEQUENCE	SERENATES	SERICONS
SENTED	SEPPUKUS	SEQUENCED	SERENE	SERIEMA
SENTENCE	SEPS	SEQUENCER	SERENED	SERIEMAS
SENTENCED	SEPSES	SEQUENCERS	SERENELY	SERIES
SENTENCER	SEPSIS	SEQUENCES	SERENER	SERIF
SENTENCERS	SEPT	SEQUENCING	SERENES	SERIFS
SENTENCES	SEPTA	SEQUENCINGS	SERENEST	SERIGRAPH
SENTENCING	SEPTAL	SEQUENT	SERENING	SERIGRAPHS
SENTIENCE	SEPTARIA	SEQUENTS	SERENITIES	SERIN
SENTIENCES	SEPTARIAN	SEQUESTER	SERENITY	SERINE
SENTIENCIES	SEPTARIUM	SEQUESTERED	SERER	SERINES
SENTIENCY	SEPTATE	SEQUESTERING	SERES	SERINETTE
SENTIENT	SEPTATION	SEQUESTERS	SEREST	SERINETTES
SENTIENTS	SEPTATIONS	SEQUESTRA	SERF	SERING
SENTIMENT	SEPTEMFID	SEQUIN	SERFAGE	SERINGA
SENTIMENTS	SEPTEMVIR	SEQUINED	SERFAGES	SERINGAS
SENTINEL	SEPTEMVIRI	SEQUINNED	SERFDOM	SERINS
SENTINELLED	SEPTEMVIRS	SEQUINS	SERFDOMS	SERIOUS
SENTINELLING	SEPTENARIES	SEQUOIA	SERFHOOD	SERIOUSLY
SENTINELS	SEPTENARY	SEQUOIAS	SERFHOODS	SERIPH
SENTING	SEPTENNIA	SERA	SERFISH	SERIPHS
SENTRIES	SEPTET	SERAC	SERFLIKE	SERJEANCIES
SENTRY	SEPTETS	SERACS	SERFS	SERJEANCY
SENTS	SEPTETTE	SERAFILE	SERFSHIP	SERJEANT
SENVIES	SEPTETTES	SERAFILES	SERFSHIPS	SERJEANTIES
SENVY	SEPTIC	SERAFIN	SERGE	SERJEANTS
SENZA	SEPTICITIES	SERAFINS	SERGEANCIES	SERJEANTY
SEPAD	SEPTICITY	SERAGLIO	SERGEANCY	SERK
SEPADDED	SEPTIFORM	SERAGLIOS	SERGEANT	SERKALI
SEPADDING	SEPTIMAL	SERAI	SERGEANTS	SERKALIS
SEPADS	SEPTIME	SERAIL	SERGES	SERKS
SEPAL	SEPTIMES	SERAILS	SERIAL	SERMON
SEPALINE	SEPTIMOLE	SERAIS	SERIALISE	SERMONED
SEPALODIES	SEPTIMOLES	SERAL	SERIALISED	SERMONEER
SEPALODY	SEPTLEVA	SERANG	SERIALISES	SERMONEERS
SEPALOID	SEPTLEVAS	SERANGS	SERIALISING	SERMONER
SEPALOUS	SEPTS	SERAPE	SERIALISM	SERMONERS
SEPALS	SEPTUM	SERAPES	SERIALISMS	SERMONET
SEPARABLE	SEPTUOR	SERAPH	SERIALIST	SERMONETS
SEPARABLY	SEPTUORS	SERAPHIC	SERIALISTS	SERMONIC
SEPARATA	SEPTUPLE	SERAPHIM	SERIALITIES	SERMONING
SEPARATE	SEPTUPLED	SERAPHIMS	SERIALITY	SERMONINGS
SEPARATED	SEPTUPLES	SERAPHIN	SERIALIZE	SERMONISE
SEPARATES	SEPTUPLET	SERAPHINE	SERIALIZED	SERMONISED
SEPARATING	SEPTUPLETS	SERAPHINES	SERIALIZES	SERMONISES

SERMONISING	SERRE	SESELI	SETTS	SEX
SERMONIZE	SERRED	SESELIS	SETUALE	SEXED
SERMONIZED	SERREFILE	SESEY	SETUALES	SEXENNIAL
SERMONIZES	SERREFILES	SESS	SETULE	SEXER
SERMONIZING	SERRES	SESSA	SETULES	SEXERS
SERMONS	SERRICORN	SESSES	SETULOSE	SEXES
SEROLOGIES	SERRIED	SESSILE	SETULOUS	SEXFID
SEROLOGY	SERRIES	SESSION	SETWALL	SEXFOIL
SERON	SERRING	SESSIONAL	SETWALLS	SEXFOILS
SERONS	SERRS	SESSIONS	SEVEN	SEXIER
SEROON	SERRULATE	SESSPOOL	SEVENFOLD	SEXIEST
SEROONS	SERRY	SESSPOOLS	SEVENS	SEXINESS
SEROPUS	SERRYING	SESTERCE	SEVENTEEN	SEXINESSES
SEROPUSES	SERUEWE	SESTERCES	SEVENTEENS	SEXING
SEROSA	SERUEWED	SESTERTIA	SEVENTH	SEXISM
SEROSAE	SERUEWES	SESTET	SEVENTHLY	SEXISMS
SEROSAS	SERUEWING	SESTETS	SEVENTHS	SEXIST
SEROSITIES	SERUM	SESTETT	SEVENTIES	SEXISTS
SEROSITY	SERUMS	SESTETTE	SEVENTY	SEXLESS
SEROTINAL	SERVAL	SESTETTES	SEVER	SEXOLOGIES
SEROTINE	SERVALS	SESTETTO	SEVERABLE	SEXOLOGY
SEROTINES	SERVANT	SESTETTOS	SEVERAL	SEXPERT
SEROTONIN	SERVANTED	SESTETTS	SEVERALLY	SEXPERTS
SEROTONINS	SERVANTING	SESTINA	SEVERALS	SEXPOT
SEROTYPE	SERVANTRIES	SESTINAS	SEVERALTIES	SEXPOTS
SEROTYPED	SERVANTRY	SESTINE	SEVERALTY	SEXT
SEROTYPES	SERVANTS	SESTINES	SEVERANCE	SEXTAN
SEROTYPING	SERVE	SESTON	SEVERANCES	SEXTANS
SEROTYPINGS	SERVED	SESTONS	SEVERE	SEXTANSES
SEROUS	SERVER	SET	SEVERED	SEXTANT
SEROW	SERVERIES	SETA	SEVERELY	SEXTANTAL
SEROWS	SERVERS	SETACEOUS	SEVERER	SEXTANTS
SERPENT	SERVERY	SETAE	SEVEREST	SEXTET
SERPENTRIES	SERVES	SETBACK	SEVERIES	SEXTETS
SERPENTRY	SERVEWE	SETBACKS	SEVERITIES	SEXTETT
SERPENTS	SERVEWED	SETIFORM	SEVERITY	SEXTETTE
SERPIGINES	SERVEWES	SETLINE	SEVERS	SEXTETTES
SERPIGO	SERVEWING	SETLINES	SEVERY	SEXTETTS
SERPIGOES	SERVICE	SETNESS	SEVRUGA	SEXTILE
SERPULA	SERVICED	SETNESSES	SEVRUGAS	SEXTILES
SERPULAE	SERVICES	SETON	SEW	SEXTOLET
SERPULITE	SERVICING	SETONS	SEWAGE	SEXTOLETS
SERPULITES	SERVIENT	SETOSE	SEWAGES	SEXTON
SERR	SERVIETTE	SETS	SEWED	SEXTONESS
SERRA	SERVIETTES	SETSCREW	SEWEL	SEXTONESSES
SERRAE	SERVILE	SETSCREWS	SEWELLEL	SEXTONS
SERRAN	SERVILELY	SETT	SEWELLELS	SEXTS
SERRANID	SERVILES	SETTEE	SEWELS	SEXTUOR
SERRANIDS	SERVILISM	SETTEES	SEWEN	SEXTUORS
SERRANOID	SERVILISMS	SETTER	SEWENS	SEXTUPLE
SERRANOIDS	SERVILITIES	SETTERED	SEWER	SEXTUPLED
SERRANS	SERVILITY	SETTERING	SEWERAGE	SEXTUPLES
SERRAS	SERVING	SETTERS	SEWERAGES	SEXTUPLET
SERRATE	SERVINGS	SETTING	SEWERED	SEXTUPLETS
SERRATED	SERVITOR	SETTINGS	SEWERING	SEXTUPLING
SERRATES	SERVITORS	SETTLE	SEWERINGS	SEXUAL
SERRATI	SERVITUDE	SETTLED	SEWERS	SEXUALISE
SERRATING	SERVITUDES	SETTLER	SEWIN	SEXUALISED
SERRATION	SERVO	SETTLERS	SEWING	SEXUALISES
SERRATIONS	SESAME	SETTLES	SEWINGS	SEXUALISING
SERRATURE	SESAMES	SETTLING	SEWINS	SEXUALISM
SERRATURES	SESAMOID	SETTLINGS	SEWN	SEXUALISMS
SERRATUS	SESAMOIDS	SETTLOR	SEWS	SEXUALIST
SERRATUSES	SESE	SETTLORS	SEWS	SEXUALISTS

SEXUALITIES	SHADINGS	SHAKOES	SHAME	SHANTEYS
SEXUALITY	SHADOOF	SHAKOS	SHAMEABLE	SHANTIES
SEXUALIZE	SHADOOFS	SHAKT	SHAMED	SHANTUNG
SEXUALIZED	SHADOW	SHAKUDO	SHAMEFAST	SHANTUNGS
SEXUALIZES	SHADOWED	SHAKUDOS	SHAMEFUL	SHANTY
SEXUALIZING	SHADOWER	SHAKY	SHAMELESS	SHANTYMAN
SEXUALLY	SHADOWERS	SHALE	SHAMER	SHANTYMEN
SEXVALENT	SHADOWIER	SHALED	SHAMERS	SHAPABLE
SEXY	SHADOWIEST	SHALES	SHAMES	SHAPE
SEY	SHADOWING	SHALIER	SHAMIANA	SHAPEABLE
SEYEN	SHADOWINGS	SHALIEST	SHAMIANAH	SHAPED
SEYENS	SHADOWS	SHALING	SHAMIANAHS	SHAPELESS
SEYS	SHADOWY	SHALL	SHAMIANAS	SHAPELIER
SEYSURE	SHADS	SHALLI	SHAMING	SHAPELIEST
SEYSURES	SHADUF	SHALLIS	SHAMISEN	SHAPELY
SEZ	SHADUFS	SHALLON	SHAMISENS	SHAPEN
SFERICS	SHADY	SHALLONS	SHAMMASH	SHAPER
SFORZANDI	SHAFT	SHALLOON	SHAMMASHIM	SHAPERS
SFORZANDO	SHAFTED	SHALLOONS	SHAMMED	SHAPES
SFORZANDOS	SHAFTER	SHALLOP	SHAMMER	SHAPING
SFORZATI	SHAFTERS	SHALLOPS	SHAMMERS	SHAPINGS
SFORZATO	SHAFTING	SHALLOT	SHAMMES	SHAPS
SFORZATOS	SHAFTINGS	SHALLOTS	SHAMMIES	SHARD
SFUMATO	SHAFTLESS	SHALLOW	SHAMMING	SHARDED
SFUMATOS	SHAFTS	SHALLOWED	SHAMMOSIM	SHARDS
SGRAFFITI	SHAG	SHALLOWER	SHAMMY	SHARE
SGRAFFITO	SHAGGED	SHALLOWEST	SHAMOY	SHARECROP
SH	SHAGGIER	SHALLOWING	SHAMOYED	SHARECROPPED
SHABBIER	SHAGGIEST	SHALLOWINGS	SHAMOYING	SHARECROPPING
SHABBIEST	SHAGGILY	SHALLOWLY	SHAMOYS	SHARECROPS
SHABBILY	SHAGGING	SHALLOWS	SHAMPOO	SHARED
SHABBLE	SHAGGY	SHALM	SHAMPOOED	SHAREMAN
SHABBLES	SHAGPILE	SHALMS	SHAMPOOER	SHAREMEN
SHABBY	SHAGREEN	SHALOM	SHAMPOOERS	SHARER
SHABRACK	SHAGREENS	SHALOT	SHAMPOOING	SHARERS
SHABRACKS	SHAGROON	SHALOTS	SHAMPOOS	SHARES
SHACK	SHAGROONS	SHALT	SHAMROCK	SHARESMAN
SHACKLE	SHAGS	SHALWAR	SHAMROCKS	SHARESMEN
SHACKLED	SHAH	SHALWARS	SHAMS	SHAREWARE
SHACKLES	SHAHS	SHALY	SHAMUS	SHAREWARES
SHACKLING	SHAIKH	SHAM	SHAMUSES	SHARIA
SHACKO	SHAIKHS	SHAMA	SHAN	SHARIAS
SHACKOES	SHAIRN	SHAMABLE	SHANACHIE	SHARIAT
SHACKOS	SHAIRNS	SHAMAN	SHANACHIES	SHARIATS
SHACKS	SHAITAN	SHAMANIC	SHAND	SHARIF
SHAD	SHAITANS	SHAMANISM	SHANDIES	SHARIFS
SHADBERRIES	SHAKABLE	SHAMANISMS	SHANDRIES	SHARING
SHADBERRY	SHAKE	SHAMANIST	SHANDRY	SHARINGS
SHADBLOW	SHAKEABLE	SHAMANISTS	SHANDS	SHARK
SHADBLOWS	SHAKED	SHAMANS	SHANDY	SHARKED
SHADBUSH	SHAKEDOWN	SHAMAS	SHANGHAI	SHARKER
SHADBUSHES	SHAKEDOWNS	SHAMATEUR	SHANGHAIED	SHARKERS
SHADDOCK	SHAKEN	SHAMATEURS	SHANGHAIING	SHARKING
SHADDOCKS	SHAKER	SHAMBA	SHANGHAIS	SHARKINGS
SHADE	SHAKERS	SHAMBAS	SHANK	SHARKS
SHADED	SHAKES	SHAMBLE	SHANKBONE	SHARKSKIN
SHADELESS	SHAKIER	SHAMBLED	SHANKBONES	SHARKSKINS
SHADES	SHAKIEST	SHAMBLES	SHANKED	SHARN
SHADIER	SHAKILY	SHAMBLIER	SHANKING	SHARNIER
SHADIEST	SHAKINESS	SHAMBLIEST	SHANKS	SHARNIEST
SHADILY	SHAKINESSES	SHAMBLING	SHANNIES	SHARNS
SHADINESS	SHAKING	SHAMBLINGS	SHANNY	SHARNY
SHADINESSES	SHAKINGS	SHAMBLY	SHANS	SHARP
SHADING	SHAKO	SHAMBOLIC	SHANTEY	SHARPED

The Chambers Dictionary is the authority for many longer words; see *OSW* Introduction, page xii

SHARPEN	SHAWLLESS	SHEBEENINGS	SHEIKDOMS	SHELTERINGS
SHARPENED	SHAWLS	SHEBEENS	SHEIKH	SHELTERS
SHARPENER	SHAWM	SHECHITA	SHEIKHA	SHELTERY
SHARPENERS	SHAWMS	SHECHITAH	SHEIKHAS	SHELTIE
SHARPENING	SHAWS	SHECHITAHS	SHEIKHDOM	SHELTIES
SHARPENS	SHAY	SHECHITAS	SHEIKHDOMS	SHELTY
SHARPER	SHAYA	SHED	SHEIKHS	SHELVE
SHARPERS	SHAYAS	SHEDDER	SHEIKS	SHELVED
SHARPEST	SHAYS	SHEDDERS	SHEILA	SHELVES
SHARPIE	SHCHI	SHEDDING	SHEILAS	SHELVIER
SHARPIES	SHCHIS	SHEDDINGS	SHEILING	SHELVIEST
SHARPING	SHE	SHEDS	SHEILINGS	SHELVING
SHARPINGS	SHEA	SHEEL	SHEKEL	SHELVINGS
SHARPISH	SHEADING	SHEELED	SHEKELS	SHELVY
SHARPLY	SHEADINGS	SHEELING	SHELDDUCK	SHEMOZZLE
SHARPNESS	SHEAF	SHEELS	SHELDDUCKS	SHEMOZZLED
SHARPNESSES	SHEAFED	SHEEN	SHELDRAKE	SHEMOZZLES
SHARPS	SHEAFIER	SHEENED	SHELDRAKES	SHEMOZZLING
SHASH	SHEAFIEST	SHEENIER	SHELDUCK	SHEND
SHASHED	SHEAFING	SHEENIES	SHELDUCKS	SHENDING
SHASHES	SHEAFS	SHEENIEST	SHELF	SHENDS
SHASHING	SHEAFY	SHEENING	SHELFED	SHENT
SHASHLICK	SHEAL	SHEENS	SHELFIER	SHEOL
SHASHLICKS	SHEALED	SHEENY	SHELFIEST	SHEOLS
SHASHLIK	SHEALING	SHEEP	SHELFING	SHEPHERD
SHASHLIKS	SHEALINGS	SHEEPCOTE	SHELFLIKE	SHEPHERDED
SHASTER	SHEALS	SHEEPCOTES	SHELFROOM	SHEPHERDING
SHASTERS	SHEAR	SHEEPDOG	SHELFROOMS	SHEPHERDS
SHASTRA	SHEARED	SHEEPDOGS	SHELFS	SHERBET
SHASTRAS	SHEARER	SHEEPFOLD	SHELFY	SHERBETS
SHAT	SHEARERS	SHEEPFOLDS	SHELL	SHERD
SHATTER	SHEARING	SHEEPIER	SHELLAC	SHERDS
SHATTERED	SHEARINGS	SHEEPIEST	SHELLACKED	SHERE
SHATTERING	SHEARLEG	SHEEPISH	SHELLACKING	SHEREEF
SHATTERS	SHEARLEGS	SHEEPO	SHELLACKINGS	SHEREEFS
SHATTERY	SHEARLING	SHEEPOS	SHELLACS	SHERIA
SHAUCHLE	SHEARLINGS	SHEEPSKIN	SHELLBACK	SHERIAS
SHAUCHLED	SHEARMAN	SHEEPSKINS	SHELLBACKS	SHERIAT
SHAUCHLES	SHEARMEN	SHEEPWALK	SHELLBARK	SHERIATS
SHAUCHLIER	SHEARS	SHEEPWALKS	SHELLBARKS	SHERIF
SHAUCHLIEST	SHEAS	SHEEPY	SHELLDUCK	SHERIFF
SHAUCHLING	SHEATFISH	SHEER	SHELLDUCKS	SHERIFFS
SHAUCHLY	SHEATFISHES	SHEERED	SHELLED	SHERIFIAN
SHAVE	SHEATH	SHEERER	SHELLER	SHERIFS
SHAVED	SHEATHE	SHEEREST	SHELLERS	SHERLOCK
SHAVELING	SHEATHED	SHEERING	SHELLFIRE	SHERLOCKS
SHAVELINGS	SHEATHES	SHEERLEG	SHELLFIRES	SHERPA
SHAVEN	SHEATHIER	SHEERLEGS	SHELLFISH	SHERPAS
SHAVER	SHEATHIEST	SHEERLY	SHELLFISHES	SHERRIES
SHAVERS	SHEATHING	SHEERS	SHELLFUL	SHERRIS
SHAVES	SHEATHINGS	SHEET	SHELLFULS	SHERRISES
SHAVIE	SHEATHS	SHEETED	SHELLIER	SHERRY
SHAVIES	SHEATHY	SHEETIER	SHELLIEST	SHERWANI
SHAVING	SHEAVE	SHEETIEST	SHELLING	SHERWANIS
SHAVINGS	SHEAVED	SHEETING	SHELLINGS	SHES
SHAW	SHEAVES	SHEETINGS	SHELLS	SHET
SHAWL	SHEAVING	SHEETS	SHELLWORK	SHETLAND
SHAWLED	SHEBANG	SHEETY	SHELLWORKS	SHETS
SHAWLEY	SHEBANGS	SHEHITA	SHELLY	SHETTING
SHAWLEYS	SHEBEEN	SHEHITAH	SHELTER	SHEUCH
SHAWLIE	SHEBEENED	SHEHITAHS	SHELTERED	SHEUCHED
SHAWLIES	SHEBEENER	SHEHITAS	SHELTERER	SHEUCHING
SHAWLING	SHEBEENERS	SHEIK	SHELTERERS	SHEUCHS
SHAWLINGS	SHEBEENING	SHEIKDOM	SHELTERING	SHEUGH

SHEUGHED	SHIKAREE	SHINGLY	SHIRALEE	SHIVERIEST
SHEUGHING	SHIKAREES	SHINIER	SHIRALEES	SHIVERING
SHEUGHS	SHIKARI	SHINIES	SHIRE	SHIVERINGS
SHEVA	SHIKARIS	SHINIEST	SHIREMAN	SHIVERS
SHEVAS	SHIKARS	SHININESS	SHIREMEN	SHIVERY
SHEW	SHIKSA	SHININESSES	SHIRES	SHIVES
SHEWBREAD	SHIKSAS	SHINING	SHIRK	SHIVOO
SHEWBREADS	SHIKSE	SHININGLY	SHIRKED	SHIVOOS
SHEWED	SHIKSES	SHINNE	SHIRKER	SHIVS
SHEWEL	SHILL	SHINNED	SHIRKERS	SHIVVED
SHEWELS	SHILLABER	SHINNES	SHIRKING	SHIVVING
SHEWING	SHILLABERS	SHINNIED	SHIRKS	SHLEMIEL
SHEWN	SHILLALAH	SHINNIES	SHIRR	SHLEMIELS
SHEWS	SHILLALAHS	SHINNING	SHIRRA	SHLEP
SHIATSU	SHILLED	SHINNY	SHIRRALEE	SHLEPPED
SHIATSUS	SHILLING	SHINNYING	SHIRRALEES	SHLEPPER
SHIATZU	SHILLINGS	SHINS	SHIRRAS	SHLEPPERS
SHIATZUS	SHILLS	SHINTIES	SHIRRED	SHLEPPING
SHIBAH	SHILPIT	SHINTY	SHIRRING	SHLEPS
SHIBAHS	SHILY	SHINY	SHIRRINGS	SHLIMAZEL
SHIBUICHI	SHIM	SHIP	SHIRRS	SHLIMAZELS
SHIBUICHIS	SHIMAAL	SHIPBOARD	SHIRS	SHLOCK
SHICKER	SHIMAALS	SHIPBOARDS	SHIRT	SHLOCKS
SHICKERED	SHIMMED	SHIPFUL	SHIRTBAND	SHMALTZ
SHICKERS	SHIMMER	SHIPFULS	SHIRTBANDS	SHMALTZES
SHICKSA	SHIMMERED	SHIPLAP	SHIRTED	SHMALTZIER
SHICKSAS	SHIMMERING	SHIPLAPPED	SHIRTIER	SHMALTZIEST
SHIDDER	SHIMMERINGS	SHIPLAPPING	SHIRTIEST	SHMALTZY
SHIDDERS	SHIMMERS	SHIPLAPS	SHIRTILY	SHMEK
SHIED	SHIMMERY	SHIPLESS	SHIRTING	SHMEKS
SHIEL	SHIMMEY	SHIPLOAD	SHIRTINGS	SHMO
SHIELD	SHIMMEYS	SHIPLOADS	SHIRTLESS	SHMOCK
SHIELDED	SHIMMIED	SHIPMAN	SHIRTS	SHMOCKS
SHIELDER	SHIMMIES	SHIPMATE	SHIRTY	SHMOES
SHIELDERS	SHIMMING	SHIPMATES	SHIT	SHMOOSE
SHIELDING	SHIMMY	SHIPMEN	SHITE	SHMOOSED
SHIELDINGS	SHIMMYING	SHIPMENT	SHITED	SHMOOSES
SHIELDS	SHIMOZZLE	SHIPMENTS	SHITES	SHMOOSING
SHIELDUCK	SHIMOZZLES	SHIPPED	SHITHEAD	SHMOOZE
SHIELDUCKS	SHIMS	SHIPPEN	SHITHEADS	SHMOOZED
SHIELED	SHIN	SHIPPENS	SHITHOLE	SHMOOZES
SHIELING	SHINBONE	SHIPPER	SHITHOLES	SHMOOZING
SHIELINGS	SHINBONES	SHIPPERS	SHITING	SHMUCK
SHIELS	SHINDIES	SHIPPING	SHITS	SHMUCKS
SHIER	SHINDIG	SHIPPINGS	SHITTAH	SHOAL
SHIERS	SHINDIGS	SHIPPO	SHITTAHS	SHOALED
SHIES	SHINDY	SHIPPON	SHITTED	SHOALER
SHIEST	SHINE	SHIPPONS	SHITTIER	SHOALEST
SHIFT	SHINED	SHIPPOS	SHITTIEST	SHOALIER
SHIFTED	SHINELESS	SHIPPOUND	SHITTIM	SHOALIEST
SHIFTER	SHINER	SHIPPOUNDS	SHITTIMS	SHOALING
SHIFTERS	SHINERS	SHIPS	SHITTING	SHOALINGS
SHIFTIER	SHINES	SHIPSHAPE	SHITTY	SHOALNESS
SHIFTIEST	SHINESS	SHIPWAY	SHIV	SHOALNESSES
SHIFTILY	SHINESSES	SHIPWAYS	SHIVAH	SHOALS
SHIFTING	SHINGLE	SHIPWORM	SHIVAHS	SHOALWISE
SHIFTINGS	SHINGLED	SHIPWORMS	SHIVAREE	SHOALY
SHIFTLESS	SHINGLER	SHIPWRECK	SHIVAREES	SHOAT
SHIFTS	SHINGLERS	SHIPWRECKED	SHIVE	SHOATS
SHIFTY	SHINGLES	SHIPWRECKING	SHIVER	SHOCHET
SHIGELLA	SHINGLIER	SHIPWRECKS	SHIVERED	SHOCHETIM
SHIGELLAS	SHINGLIEST	SHIPYARD	SHIVERER	SHOCK
SHIITAKE	SHINGLING	SHIPYARDS	SHIVERERS	SHOCKABLE
SHIKAR	SHINGLINGS	SHIR	SHIVERIER	SHOCKED

SHOCKER	SHONEENS	SHORE	SHOTHOLE	SHOWBOX
SHOCKERS	SHONKIER	SHOREBIRD	SHOTHOLES	SHOWBOXES
SHOCKING	SHONKIEST	SHOREBIRDS	SHOTMAKER	SHOWBREAD
SHOCKS	SHONKY	SHORED	SHOTMAKERS	SHOWBREADS
SHOD	SHOO	SHORELESS	SHOTPROOF	SHOWCASE
SHODDIER	SHOOED	SHORELINE	SHOTPUT	SHOWCASED
SHODDIES	SHOOFLIES	SHORELINES	SHOTPUTS	SHOWCASES
SHODDIEST	SHOOFLY	SHOREMAN	SHOTS	SHOWCASING
SHODDILY	SHOOGIE	SHOREMEN	SHOTT	SHOWDOWN
SHODDY	SHOOGIED	SHORER	SHOTTE	SHOWDOWNS
SHODER	SHOOGIEING	SHORERS	SHOTTED	SHOWED
SHODERS	SHOOGIES	SHORES	SHOTTEN	SHOWER
SHOE	SHOOGLE	SHORESMAN	SHOTTES	SHOWERED
SHOEBILL	SHOOGLED	SHORESMEN	SHOTTING	SHOWERFUL
SHOEBILLS	SHOOGLES	SHOREWARD	SHOTTLE	SHOWERIER
SHOEBLACK	SHOOGLIER	SHOREWARDS	SHOTTLES	SHOWERIEST
SHOEBLACKS	SHOOGLIEST	SHOREWEED	SHOTTS	SHOWERING
SHOED	SHOOGLING	SHOREWEEDS	SHOUGH	SHOWERINGS
SHOEHORN	SHOOGLY	SHORING	SHOUGHS	SHOWERS
SHOEHORNED	SHOOING	SHORINGS	SHOULD	SHOWERY
SHOEHORNING	SHOOK	SHORN	SHOULDER	SHOWGHE
SHOEHORNS	SHOOKS	SHORT	SHOULDERED	SHOWGHES
SHOEING	SHOOL	SHORTAGE	SHOULDERING	SHOWGIRL
SHOEINGS	SHOOLE	SHORTAGES	SHOULDERINGS	SHOWGIRLS
SHOELACE	SHOOLED	SHORTARM	SHOULDERS	SHOWIER
SHOELACES	SHOOLES	SHORTCAKE	SHOULDEST	SHOWIEST
SHOELESS	SHOOLING	SHORTCAKES	SHOULDST	SHOWILY
SHOEMAKER	SHOOLS	SHORTED	SHOUT	SHOWINESS
SHOEMAKERS	SHOON	SHORTEN	SHOUTED	SHOWINESSES
SHOER	SHOOS	SHORTENED	SHOUTER	SHOWING
SHOERS	SHOOT	SHORTENER	SHOUTERS	SHOWINGS
SHOES	SHOOTABLE	SHORTENERS	SHOUTHER	SHOWMAN
SHOESHINE	SHOOTER	SHORTENING	SHOUTHERED	SHOWMANLY
SHOESHINES	SHOOTERS	SHORTENINGS	SHOUTHERING	SHOWMEN
SHOETREE	SHOOTING	SHORTENS	SHOUTHERS	SHOWN
SHOETREES	SHOOTINGS	SHORTER	SHOUTING	SHOWPIECE
SHOFAR	SHOOTIST	SHORTEST	SHOUTINGS	SHOWPIECES
SHOFARS	SHOOTISTS	SHORTFALL	SHOUTLINE	SHOWPLACE
SHOFROTH	SHOOTS	SHORTFALLS	SHOUTLINES	SHOWPLACES
SHOG	SHOP	SHORTGOWN	SHOUTS	SHOWROOM
SHOGGED	SHOPBOARD	SHORTGOWNS	SHOVE	SHOWROOMS
SHOGGING	SHOPBOARDS	SHORTHAND	SHOVED	SHOWS
SHOGGLE	SHOPE	SHORTHANDS	SHOVEL	SHOWY
SHOGGLED	SHOPFRONT	SHORTHOLD	SHOVELER	SHOWYARD
SHOGGLES	SHOPFRONTS	SHORTHORN	SHOVELERS	SHOWYARDS
SHOGGLIER	SHOPFUL	SHORTHORNS	SHOVELFUL	SHOYU
SHOGGLIEST	SHOPFULS	SHORTIE	SHOVELFULS	SHOYUS
SHOGGLING	SHOPHAR	SHORTIES	SHOVELLED	SHRADDHA
SHOGGLY	SHOPHARS	SHORTING	SHOVELLER	SHRADDHAS
SHOGI	SHOPHROTH	SHORTISH	SHOVELLERS	SHRANK
SHOGIS	SHOPMAN	SHORTLY	SHOVELLING	SHRAPNEL
SHOGS	SHOPMEN	SHORTNESS	SHOVELS	SHRAPNELS
SHOGUN	SHOPPED	SHORTNESSES	SHOVER	SHRED
SHOGUNAL	SHOPPER	SHORTS	SHOVERS	SHREDDED
SHOGUNATE	SHOPPERS	SHORTSTOP	SHOVES	SHREDDER
SHOGUNATES	SHOPPIER	SHORTSTOPS	SHOVING	SHREDDERS
SHOGUNS	SHOPPIEST	SHORTY	SHOW	SHREDDIER
SHOJI	SHOPPING	SHOT	SHOWBIZ	SHREDDIEST
SHOJIS	SHOPPINGS	SHOTE	SHOWBIZZES	SHREDDING
SHOLA	SHOPPY	SHOTES	SHOWBIZZY	SHREDDINGS
SHOLAS	SHOPS	SHOTFIRER	SHOWBOAT	SHREDDY
SHOLOM	SHOPWORN	SHOTFIRERS	SHOWBOATED	SHREDLESS
SHONE	SHORAN	SHOTGUN	SHOWBOATING	SHREDS
SHONEEN	SHORANS	SHOTGUNS	SHOWBOATS	SHREEK

SHREEKED	SHRINE	SHRUGGED	SHUNNERS	SIAMEZES
SHREEKING	SHRINED	SHRUGGING	SHUNNING	SIAMEZING
SHREEKS	SHRINES	SHRUGS	SHUNS	SIB
SHREIK	SHRINING	SHRUNK	SHUNT	SIBB
SHREIKED	SHRINK	SHRUNKEN	SHUNTED	SIBBS
SHREIKING	SHRINKAGE	SHTCHI	SHUNTER	SIBILANCE
SHREIKS	SHRINKAGES	SHTCHIS	SHUNTERS	SIBILANCES
SHREW	SHRINKER	SHTETEL	SHUNTING	SIBILANCIES
SHREWD	SHRINKERS	SHTETELACH	SHUNTINGS	SIBILANCY
SHREWDER	SHRINKING	SHTETELS	SHUNTS	SIBILANT
SHREWDEST	SHRINKS	SHTETL	SHURA	SIBILANTS
SHREWDIE	SHRITCH	SHTETLACH	SHURAS	SIBILATE
SHREWDIES	SHRITCHED	SHTETLS	SHUSH	SIBILATED
SHREWDLY	SHRITCHES	SHTICK	SHUSHED	SIBILATES
SHREWED	SHRITCHING	SHTICKS	SHUSHES	SIBILATING
SHREWING	SHRIVE	SHTOOK	SHUSHING	SIBILATOR
SHREWISH	SHRIVED	SHTOOKS	SHUT	SIBILATORS
SHREWMICE	SHRIVEL	SHTOOM	SHUTDOWN	SIBILOUS
SHREWS	SHRIVELED	SHTUCK	SHUTDOWNS	SIBLING
SHRIECH	SHRIVELING	SHTUCKS	SHUTE	SIBLINGS
SHRIECHED	SHRIVELLED	SHTUM	SHUTES	SIBS
SHRIECHES	SHRIVELLING	SHTUMM	SHUTS	SIBSHIP
SHRIECHING	SHRIVELS	SHTUP	SHUTTER	SIBSHIPS
SHRIEK	SHRIVEN	SHTUPPED	SHUTTERED	SIBYL
SHRIEKED	SHRIVER	SHTUPPING	SHUTTERING	SIBYLIC
SHRIEKER	SHRIVERS	SHTUPS	SHUTTERINGS	SIBYLLIC
SHRIEKERS	SHRIVES	SHUBUNKIN	SHUTTERS	SIBYLLINE
SHRIEKING	SHRIVING	SHUBUNKINS	SHUTTING	SIBYLS
SHRIEKINGS	SHRIVINGS	SHUCK	SHUTTLE	SIC
SHRIEKS	SHROFF	SHUCKED	SHUTTLED	SICCAN
SHRIEVAL	SHROFFAGE	SHUCKER	SHUTTLES	SICCAR
SHRIEVE	SHROFFAGES	SHUCKERS	SHUTTLING	SICCATIVE
SHRIEVED	SHROFFED	SHUCKING	SHWA	SICCATIVES
SHRIEVES	SHROFFING	SHUCKINGS	SHWAS	SICCED
SHRIEVING	SHROFFS	SHUCKS	SHY	SICCING
SHRIFT	SHROUD	SHUDDER	SHYER	SICCITIES
SHRIFTS	SHROUDED	SHUDDERED	SHYERS	SICCITY
SHRIGHT	SHROUDIER	SHUDDERING	SHYEST	SICE
SHRIGHTS	SHROUDIEST	SHUDDERINGS	SHYING	SICES
SHRIKE	SHROUDING	SHUDDERS	SHYISH	SICH
SHRIKED	SHROUDINGS	SHUDDERY	SHYLY	SICILIANA
SHRIKES	SHROUDS	SHUFFLE	SHYNESS	SICILIANE
SHRIKING	SHROUDY	SHUFFLED	SHYNESSES	SICILIANO
SHRILL	SHROVE	SHUFFLER	SHYSTER	SICILIANOS
SHRILLED	SHROVED	SHUFFLERS	SHYSTERS	SICK
SHRILLER	SHROVES	SHUFFLES	SI	SICKBED
SHRILLEST	SHROVING	SHUFFLING	SIAL	SICKBEDS
SHRILLIER	SHROW	SHUFFLINGS	SIALIC	SICKED
SHRILLIEST	SHROWD	SHUFTI	SIALOGRAM	SICKEN
SHRILLING	SHROWED	SHUFTIES	SIALOGRAMS	SICKENED
SHRILLINGS	SHROWING	SHUFTIS	SIALOID	SICKENER
SHRILLS	SHROWS	SHUFTY	SIALOLITH	SICKENERS
SHRILLY	SHRUB	SHUL	SIALOLITHS	SICKENING
SHRIMP	SHRUBBED	SHULE	SIALON	SICKENINGS
SHRIMPED	SHRUBBERIES	SHULED	SIALONS	SICKENS
SHRIMPER	SHRUBBERY	SHULES	SIALS	SICKER
SHRIMPERS	SHRUBBIER	SHULING	SIAMANG	SICKERLY
SHRIMPIER	SHRUBBIEST	SHULN	SIAMANGS	SICKEST
SHRIMPIEST	SHRUBBING	SHULS	SIAMESE	SICKIE
SHRIMPING	SHRUBBY	SHUN	SIAMESED	SICKIES
SHRIMPINGS	SHRUBLESS	SHUNLESS	SIAMESES	SICKING
SHRIMPS	SHRUBLIKE	SHUNNABLE	SIAMESING	SICKISH
SHRIMPY	SHRUBS	SHUNNED	SIAMEZE	SICKISHLY
SHRINAL	SHRUG	SHUNNER	SIAMEZED	SICKLE

The Chambers Dictionary is the authority for many longer words; see *OSW* Introduction, page xii

SICKLED	SIDEPATH	SIEN	SIGHTSEER	SIGNET
SICKLEMAN	SIDEPATHS	SIENNA	SIGHTSEERS	SIGNETED
SICKLEMEN	SIDER	SIENNAS	SIGHTSEES	SIGNETING
SICKLEMIA	SIDERAL	SIENS	SIGHTSMAN	SIGNETS
SICKLEMIAS	SIDERATE	SIENT	SIGHTSMEN	SIGNEUR
SICKLES	SIDERATED	SIENTS	SIGIL	SIGNEURIE
SICKLIED	SIDERATES	SIERRA	SIGILLARY	SIGNEURIES
SICKLIER	SIDERATING	SIERRAN	SIGILLATE	SIGNIEUR
SICKLIES	SIDEREAL	SIERRAS	SIGILS	SIGNIEURS
SICKLIEST	SIDERITE	SIESTA	SIGISBEI	SIGNIFICS
SICKLILY	SIDERITES	SIESTAS	SIGISBEO	SIGNIFIED
SICKLY	SIDERITIC	SIETH	SIGLA	SIGNIFIER
SICKLYING	SIDEROAD	SIETHS	SIGMA	SIGNIFIERS
SICKNESS	SIDEROADS	SIEVE	SIGMAS	SIGNIFIES
SICKNESSES	SIDEROSES	SIEVED	SIGMATE	SIGNIFY
SICKNURSE	SIDEROSIS	SIEVERT	SIGMATED	SIGNIFYING
SICKNURSES	SIDERS	SIEVERTS	SIGMATES	SIGNING
SICKO	SIDES	SIEVES	SIGMATIC	SIGNINGS
SICKOS	SIDESHOOT	SIEVING	SIGMATING	SIGNIOR
SICKROOM	SIDESHOOTS	SIFAKA	SIGMATION	SIGNIORS
SICKROOMS	SIDESHOW	SIFAKAS	SIGMATIONS	SIGNLESS
SICKS	SIDESHOWS	SIFFLE	SIGMATISM	SIGNOR
SICLIKE	SIDESLIP	SIFFLED	SIGMATISMS	SIGNORA
SICS	SIDESLIPPED	SIFFLES	SIGMATRON	SIGNORE
SIDA	SIDESLIPPING	SIFFLEUR	SIGMATRONS	SIGNORES
SIDALCEA	SIDESLIPS	SIFFLEURS	SIGMOID	SIGNORI
SIDALCEAS	SIDESMAN	SIFFLEUSE	SIGMOIDAL	SIGNORIA
SIDAS	SIDESMEN	SIFFLEUSES	SIGN	SIGNORIAL
SIDDHA	SIDESTEP	SIFFLING	SIGNAGE	SIGNORIAS
SIDDHAS	SIDESTEPPED	SIFT	SIGNAGES	SIGNORIES
SIDDHI	SIDESTEPPING	SIFTED	SIGNAL	SIGNORINA
SIDDHIS	SIDESTEPS	SIFTER	SIGNALED	SIGNORINE
SIDDUR	SIDESWIPE	SIFTERS	SIGNALER	SIGNORINI
SIDDURIM	SIDESWIPED	SIFTING	SIGNALERS	SIGNORINO
SIDE	SIDESWIPES	SIFTINGLY	SIGNALING	SIGNORS
SIDEARM	SIDESWIPING	SIFTINGS	SIGNALINGS	SIGNORY
SIDEARMS	SIDETRACK	SIFTS	SIGNALISE	SIGNPOST
SIDEBAND	SIDETRACKED	SIGH	SIGNALISED	SIGNPOSTED
SIDEBANDS	SIDETRACKING	SIGHED	SIGNALISES	SIGNPOSTING
SIDEBAR	SIDETRACKS	SIGHER	SIGNALISING	SIGNPOSTS
SIDEBARS	SIDEWALK	SIGHERS	SIGNALIZE	SIGNS
SIDEBOARD	SIDEWALKS	SIGHFUL	SIGNALIZED	SIJO
SIDEBOARDS	SIDEWALL	SIGHING	SIGNALIZES	SIJOS
SIDEBONES	SIDEWALLS	SIGHINGLY	SIGNALIZING	SIKA
SIDEBURNS	SIDEWARD	SIGHS	SIGNALLED	SIKAS
SIDECAR	SIDEWARDS	SIGHT	SIGNALLER	SIKE
SIDECARS	SIDEWAYS	SIGHTABLE	SIGNALLERS	SIKES
SIDED	SIDEWISE	SIGHTED	SIGNALLING	SIKORSKIES
SIDEKICK	SIDHA	SIGHTER	SIGNALLINGS	SIKORSKY
SIDEKICKS	SIDHAS	SIGHTERS	SIGNALLY	SILAGE
SIDELIGHT	SIDING	SIGHTING	SIGNALMAN	SILAGED
SIDELIGHTS	SIDINGS	SIGHTINGS	SIGNALMEN	SILAGEING
SIDELINE	SIDLE	SIGHTLESS	SIGNALS	SILAGES
SIDELINED	SIDLED	SIGHTLIER	SIGNARIES	SILAGING
SIDELINES	SIDLES	SIGHTLIEST	SIGNARY	SILANE
SIDELING	SIDLING	SIGHTLINE	SIGNATORIES	SILANES
SIDELINING	SIEGE	SIGHTLINES	SIGNATORY	SILASTIC
SIDELOCK	SIEGED	SIGHTLY	SIGNATURE	SILASTICS
SIDELOCKS	SIEGER	SIGHTS	SIGNATURES	SILD
SIDELONG	SIEGERS	SIGHTSAW	SIGNBOARD	SILDS
SIDEMAN	SIEGES	SIGHTSEE	SIGNBOARDS	SILE
SIDEMEN	SIEGING	SIGHTSEEING	SIGNED	SILED
SIDENOTE	SIELD	SIGHTSEEINGS	SIGNER	SILEN
SIDENOTES	SIEMENS	SIGHTSEEN	SIGNERS	SILENCE

SILENCED	SILKENS	SILVERED	SIMONIST	SIMULCASTS
SILENCER	SILKIE	SILVERIER	SIMONISTS	SIMULIUM
SILENCERS	SILKIER	SILVERIEST	SIMONY	SIMULIUMS
SILENCES	SILKIES	SILVERING	SIMOOM	SIMULS
SILENCING	SILKIEST	SILVERINGS	SIMOOMS	SIMURG
SILENE	SILKILY	SILVERISE	SIMOON	SIMURGH
SILENES	SILKINESS	SILVERISED	SIMOONS	SIMURGHS
SILENI	SILKINESSES	SILVERISES	SIMORG	SIMURGS
SILENS	SILKING	SILVERISING	SIMORGS	SIN
SILENT	SILKS	SILVERIZE	SIMP	SINAPISM
SILENTER	SILKTAIL	SILVERIZED	SIMPAI	SINAPISMS
SILENTEST	SILKTAILS	SILVERIZES	SIMPAIS	SINCE
SILENTLY	SILKWEED	SILVERIZING	SIMPATICO	SINCERE
SILENTS	SILKWEEDS	SILVERLY	SIMPER	SINCERELY
SILENUS	SILKWORM	SILVERN	SIMPERED	SINCERER
SILER	SILKWORMS	SILVERS	SIMPERER	SINCEREST
SILERS	SILKY	SILVERY	SIMPERERS	SINCERITIES
SILES	SILL	SIM	SIMPERING	SINCERITY
SILESIA	SILLABUB	SIMA	SIMPERS	SINCIPITA
SILESIAS	SILLABUBS	SIMAR	SIMPKIN	SINCIPUT
SILEX	SILLADAR	SIMAROUBA	SIMPKINS	SINCIPUTS
SILEXES	SILLADARS	SIMAROUBAS	SIMPLE	SIND
SILICA	SILLER	SIMARRE	SIMPLED	SINDED
SILICAS	SILLERS	SIMARRES	SIMPLER	SINDING
SILICATE	SILLIER	SIMARS	SIMPLERS	SINDINGS
SILICATED	SILLIES	SIMARUBA	SIMPLES	SINDON
SILICATES	SILLIEST	SIMARUBAS	SIMPLESSE	SINDONS
SILICATING	SILLILY	SIMAS	SIMPLESSES	SINDS
SILICEOUS	SILLINESS	SIMAZINE	SIMPLEST	SINE
SILICIC	SILLINESSES	SIMAZINES	SIMPLETON	SINECURE
SILICIDE	SILLOCK	SIMI	SIMPLETONS	SINECURES
SILICIDES	SILLOCKS	SIMIAL	SIMPLEX	SINED
SILICIFIED	SILLS	SIMIAN	SIMPLICES	SINES
SILICIFIES	SILLY	SIMIANS	SIMPLIFIED	SINEW
SILICIFY	SILO	SIMILAR	SIMPLIFIES	SINEWED
SILICIFYING	SILOED	SIMILARLY	SIMPLIFY	SINEWIER
SILICIOUS	SILOING	SIMILE	SIMPLIFYING	SINEWIEST
SILICIUM	SILOS	SIMILES	SIMPLING	SINEWING
SILICIUMS	SILPHIA	SIMILISE	SIMPLINGS	SINEWLESS
SILICLE	SILPHIUM	SIMILISED	SIMPLISM	SINEWS
SILICLES	SILPHIUMS	SIMILISES	SIMPLISMS	SINEWY
SILICON	SILT	SIMILISING	SIMPLIST	SINFONIA
SILICONE	SILTATION	SIMILIZE	SIMPLISTE	SINFONIAS
SILICONES	SILTATIONS	SIMILIZED	SIMPLISTS	SINFUL
SILICONS	SILTED	SIMILIZES	SIMPLY	SINFULLY
SILICOSES	SILTIER	SIMILIZING	SIMPS	SING
SILICOSIS	SILTIEST	SIMILOR	SIMS	SINGABLE
SILICOTIC	SILTING	SIMILORS	SIMUL	SINGALONG
SILICOTICS	SILTS	SIMIOUS	SIMULACRA	SINGALONGS
SILICULA	SILTSTONE	SIMIS	SIMULACRE	SINGE
SILICULAS	SILTSTONES	SIMITAR	SIMULACRES	SINGED
SILICULE	SILTY	SIMITARS	SIMULANT	SINGEING
SILICULES	SILURID	SIMKIN	SIMULANTS	SINGER
SILING	SILURIDS	SIMKINS	SIMULAR	SINGERS
SILIQUA	SILURIST	SIMMER	SIMULARS	SINGES
SILIQUAS	SILURISTS	SIMMERED	SIMULATE	SINGING
SILIQUE	SILUROID	SIMMERING	SIMULATED	SINGINGLY
SILIQUES	SILVA	SIMMERS	SIMULATES	SINGINGS
SILIQUOSE	SILVAE	SIMNEL	SIMULATING	SINGLE
SILK	SILVAN	SIMNELS	SIMULATOR	SINGLED
SILKED	SILVANS	SIMONIAC	SIMULATORS	SINGLES
SILKEN	SILVAS	SIMONIACS	SIMULCAST	SINGLET
SILKENED	SILVATIC	SIMONIES	SIMULCASTED	SINGLETON
SILKENING	SILVER	SIMONIOUS	SIMULCASTING	SINGLETONS

SINGLETS	SINTERED	SIRENISES	SISTERED	SIXAINS
SINGLING	SINTERING	SIRENISING	SISTERING	SIXER
SINGLINGS	SINTERS	SIRENIZE	SISTERLY	SIXERS
SINGLY	SINTERY	SIRENIZED	SISTERS	SIXES
SINGS	SINUATE	SIRENIZES	SISTING	SIXFOLD
SINGSONG	SINUATED	SIRENIZING	SISTRA	SIXPENCE
SINGSONGED	SINUATELY	SIRENS	SISTRUM	SIXPENCES
SINGSONGING	SINUATION	SIRES	SISTS	SIXPENNIES
SINGSONGS	SINUATIONS	SIRGANG	SIT	SIXPENNY
SINGSPIEL	SINUITIS	SIRGANGS	SITAR	SIXSCORE
SINGSPIELS	SINUITISES	SIRI	SITARS	SIXSCORES
SINGULAR	SINUOSE	SIRIASES	SITATUNGA	SIXTE
SINGULARS	SINUOSITIES	SIRIASIS	SITATUNGAS	SIXTEEN
SINGULT	SINUOSITY	SIRIH	SITCOM	SIXTEENER
SINGULTS	SINUOUS	SIRIHS	SITCOMS	SIXTEENERS
SINGULTUS	SINUOUSLY	SIRING	SITE	SIXTEENMO
SINGULTUSES	SINUS	SIRIS	SITED	SIXTEENMOS
SINICAL	SINUSES	SIRKAR	SITES	SIXTEENS
SINICISE	SINUSITIS	SIRKARS	SITFAST	SIXTEENTH
SINICISED	SINUSITISES	SIRLOIN	SITFASTS	SIXTEENTHS
SINICISES	SINUSOID	SIRLOINS	SITH	SIXTES
SINICISING	SINUSOIDS	SIRNAME	SITHE	SIXTH
SINICIZE	SIP	SIRNAMED	SITHED	SIXTHLY
SINICIZED	SIPE	SIRNAMES	SITHEN	SIXTHS
SINICIZES	SIPED	SIRNAMING	SITHENCE	SIXTIES
SINICIZING	SIPES	SIROC	SITHENS	SIXTIETH
SINING	SIPHON	SIROCCO	SITHES	SIXTIETHS
SINISTER	SIPHONAGE	SIROCCOS	SITHING	SIXTY
SINISTRAL	SIPHONAGES	SIROCS	SITING	SIZABLE
SINISTRALS	SIPHONAL	SIRRAH	SITIOLOGIES	SIZAR
SINK	SIPHONATE	SIRRAHS	SITIOLOGY	SIZARS
SINKAGE	SIPHONED	SIRRED	SITOLOGIES	SIZARSHIP
SINKAGES	SIPHONET	SIRREE	SITOLOGY	SIZARSHIPS
SINKER	SIPHONETS	SIRREES	SITREP	SIZE
SINKERS	SIPHONIC	SIRRING	SITREPS	SIZEABLE
SINKHOLE	SIPHONING	SIRS	SITS	SIZED
SINKHOLES	SIPHONS	SIRUP	SITTAR	SIZEISM
SINKIER	SIPHUNCLE	SIRUPED	SITTARS	SIZEISMS
SINKIEST	SIPHUNCLES	SIRUPING	SITTER	SIZEIST
SINKING	SIPING	SIRUPS	SITTERS	SIZEISTS
SINKINGS	SIPPED	SIRVENTE	SITTINE	SIZEL
SINKS	SIPPER	SIRVENTES	SITTING	SIZELS
SINKY	SIPPERS	SIS	SITTINGS	SIZER
SINLESS	SIPPET	SISAL	SITUATE	SIZERS
SINLESSLY	SIPPETS	SISALS	SITUATED	SIZES
SINNED	SIPPING	SISERARIES	SITUATES	SIZIER
SINNER	SIPPLE	SISERARY	SITUATING	SIZIEST
SINNERED	SIPPLED	SISES	SITUATION	SIZINESS
SINNERING	SIPPLES	SISKIN	SITUATIONS	SIZINESSES
SINNERS	SIPPLING	SISKINS	SITULA	SIZING
SINNET	SIPS	SISS	SITULAE	SIZINGS
SINNETS	SIR	SISSERARIES	SITUS	SIZISM
SINNING	SIRCAR	SISSERARY	SITUTUNGA	SIZISMS
SINNINGIA	SIRCARS	SISSES	SITUTUNGAS	SIZIST
SINNINGIAS	SIRDAR	SISSIER	SITZKRIEG	SIZISTS
SINOPIA	SIRDARS	SISSIES	SITZKRIEGS	SIZY
SINOPIAS	SIRE	SISSIEST	SIVER	SIZZLE
SINOPIS	SIRED	SISSIFIED	SIVERS	SIZZLED
SINOPISES	SIREN	SISSOO	SIWASH	SIZZLER
SINOPITE	SIRENIAN	SISSOOS	SIWASHES	SIZZLERS
SINOPITES	SIRENIANS	SISSY	SIX	SIZZLES
SINS	SIRENIC	SIST	SIXAIN	SIZZLING
SINSYNE	SIRENISE	SISTED	SIXAINE	SIZZLINGS
SINTER	SIRENISED	SISTER	SIXAINES	SJAMBOK

SJAMBOKKED	SKEER	SKEP	SKIDDERS	SKINFLINT
SJAMBOKKING	SKEERED	SKEPFUL	SKIDDING	SKINFLINTS
SJAMBOKS	SKEERIER	SKEPFULS	SKIDOO	SKINFOOD
SKA	SKEERIEST	SKEPPED	SKIDOOS	SKINFOODS
SKAG	SKEERING	SKEPPING	SKIDPAN	SKINFUL
SKAGS	SKEERS	SKEPS	SKIDPANS	SKINFULS
SKAIL	SKEERY	SKEPSIS	SKIDPROOF	SKINHEAD
SKAILED	SKEESICKS	SKEPSISES	SKIDS	SKINHEADS
SKAILING	SKEET	SKEPTIC	SKIED	SKINK
SKAILS	SKEETER	SKEPTICAL	SKIER	SKINKED
SKAITH	SKEETERS	SKEPTICS	SKIERS	SKINKER
SKAITHED	SKEETS	SKER	SKIES	SKINKERS
SKAITHING	SKEG	SKERRED	SKIEY	SKINKING
SKAITHS	SKEGG	SKERRICK	SKIEYER	SKINKS
SKALD	SKEGGER	SKERRICKS	SKIEYEST	SKINLESS
SKALDIC	SKEGGERS	SKERRIES	SKIFF	SKINNED
SKALDS	SKEGGS	SKERRING	SKIFFED	SKINNER
SKALDSHIP	SKEGS	SKERRY	SKIFFING	SKINNERS
SKALDSHIPS	SKEIGH	SKERS	SKIFFLE	SKINNIER
SKANK	SKEIGHER	SKETCH	SKIFFLES	SKINNIEST
SKANKED	SKEIGHEST	SKETCHED	SKIFFS	SKINNING
SKANKING	SKEIN	SKETCHER	SKIING	SKINNY
SKANKINGS	SKEINS	SKETCHERS	SKIINGS	SKINS
SKANKS	SKELDER	SKETCHES	SKIJORING	SKINT
SKART	SKELDERED	SKETCHIER	SKIJORINGS	SKINTER
SKARTH	SKELDERING	SKETCHIEST	SKILFUL	SKINTEST
SKARTHS	SKELDERS	SKETCHILY	SKILFULLY	SKIO
SKARTS	SKELETAL	SKETCHING	SKILL	SKIOS
SKAS	SKELETON	SKETCHY	SKILLED	SKIP
SKAT	SKELETONS	SKEW	SKILLESS	SKIPJACK
SKATE	SKELF	SKEWBACK	SKILLET	SKIPJACKS
SKATED	SKELFS	SKEWBACKS	SKILLETS	SKIPPED
SKATEPARK	SKELL	SKEWBALD	SKILLFUL	SKIPPER
SKATEPARKS	SKELLIE	SKEWBALDS	SKILLIER	SKIPPERED
SKATER	SKELLIED	SKEWED	SKILLIES	SKIPPERING
SKATERS	SKELLIER	SKEWER	SKILLIEST	SKIPPERINGS
SKATES	SKELLIES	SKEWERED	SKILLING	SKIPPERS
SKATING	SKELLIEST	SKEWERING	SKILLINGS	SKIPPET
SKATINGS	SKELLOCH	SKEWERS	SKILLION	SKIPPETS
SKATOLE	SKELLOCHED	SKEWEST	SKILLIONS	SKIPPIER
SKATOLES	SKELLOCHING	SKEWING	SKILLS	SKIPPIEST
SKATS	SKELLOCHS	SKEWNESS	SKILLY	SKIPPING
SKATT	SKELLS	SKEWNESSES	SKIM	SKIPPINGS
SKATTS	SKELLUM	SKEWS	SKIMMED	SKIPPY
SKAW	SKELLUMS	SKI	SKIMMER	SKIPS
SKAWS	SKELLY	SKIABLE	SKIMMERS	SKIRL
SKEAN	SKELLYING	SKIAGRAM	SKIMMIA	SKIRLED
SKEANS	SKELM	SKIAGRAMS	SKIMMIAS	SKIRLING
SKEAR	SKELMS	SKIAGRAPH	SKIMMING	SKIRLINGS
SKEARED	SKELP	SKIAGRAPHS	SKIMMINGS	SKIRLS
SKEARIER	SKELPED	SKIAMACHIES	SKIMP	SKIRMISH
SKEARIEST	SKELPING	SKIAMACHY	SKIMPED	SKIRMISHED
SKEARING	SKELPINGS	SKIASCOPIES	SKIMPIER	SKIRMISHES
SKEARS	SKELPS	SKIASCOPY	SKIMPIEST	SKIRMISHING
SKEARY	SKELTER	SKIATRON	SKIMPILY	SKIRMISHINGS
SKEDADDLE	SKELTERED	SKIATRONS	SKIMPING	SKIRR
SKEDADDLED	SKELTERING	SKIBOB	SKIMPS	SKIRRED
SKEDADDLES	SKELTERS	SKIBOBBED	SKIMPY	SKIRRET
SKEDADDLING	SKELUM	SKIBOBBING	SKIMS	SKIRRETS
SKEECHAN	SKELUMS	SKIBOBBINGS	SKIN	SKIRRING
SKEECHANS	SKENE	SKIBOBS	SKINCARE	SKIRRS
SKEELIER	SKENES	SKID	SKINCARES	SKIRT
SKEELIEST	SKEO	SKIDDED	SKINFLICK	SKIRTED
SKEELY	SKEOS	SKIDDER	SKINFLICKS	SKIRTER

SKIRTERS	SKOLLY	SKUMMERING	SKYSCAPE	SLAISTERING
SKIRTING	SKOOSH	SKUMMERS	SKYSCAPES	SLAISTERS
SKIRTINGS	SKOOSHED	SKUNK	SKYTE	SLAISTERY
SKIRTLESS	SKOOSHES	SKUNKBIRD	SKYTED	SLAKE
SKIRTS	SKOOSHING	SKUNKBIRDS	SKYTES	SLAKED
SKIS	SKRAN	SKUNKED	SKYTING	SLAKELESS
SKIT	SKRANS	SKUNKING	SKYWARD	SLAKES
SKITE	SKREEN	SKUNKS	SKYWARDS	SLAKING
SKITED	SKREENS	SKURRIED	SKYWAY	SLALOM
SKITES	SKREIGH	SKURRIES	SKYWAYS	SLALOMED
SKITING	SKREIGHED	SKURRY	SLAB	SLALOMING
SKITS	SKREIGHING	SKURRYING	SLABBED	SLALOMS
SKITTER	SKREIGHS	SKUTTLE	SLABBER	SLAM
SKITTERED	SKRIECH	SKUTTLED	SLABBERED	SLAMMAKIN
SKITTERING	SKRIECHED	SKUTTLES	SLABBERER	SLAMMAKINS
SKITTERS	SKRIECHING	SKUTTLING	SLABBERERS	SLAMMED
SKITTISH	SKRIECHS	SKY	SLABBERING	SLAMMER
SKITTLE	SKRIED	SKYBORN	SLABBERS	SLAMMERS
SKITTLED	SKRIEGH	SKYCLAD	SLABBERY	SLAMMING
SKITTLES	SKRIEGHED	SKYDIVER	SLABBIER	SLAMMINGS
SKITTLING	SKRIEGHING	SKYDIVERS	SLABBIEST	SLAMS
SKIVE	SKRIEGHS	SKYER	SLABBING	SLANDER
SKIVED	SKRIES	SKYERS	SLABBY	SLANDERED
SKIVER	SKRIK	SKYEY	SLABS	SLANDERER
SKIVERED	SKRIKS	SKYHOOK	SLABSTONE	SLANDERERS
SKIVERING	SKRIMMAGE	SKYHOOKS	SLABSTONES	SLANDERING
SKIVERS	SKRIMMAGED	SKYIER	SLACK	SLANDERS
SKIVES	SKRIMMAGES	SKYIEST	SLACKED	SLANE
SKIVIE	SKRIMMAGING	SKYING	SLACKEN	SLANES
SKIVIER	SKRIMP	SKYISH	SLACKENED	SLANG
SKIVIEST	SKRIMPED	SKYJACK	SLACKENING	SLANGED
SKIVING	SKRIMPING	SKYJACKED	SLACKENINGS	SLANGER
SKIVINGS	SKRIMPS	SKYJACKER	SLACKENS	SLANGERS
SKIVVIED	SKRUMP	SKYJACKERS	SLACKER	SLANGIER
SKIVVIES	SKRUMPED	SKYJACKING	SLACKERS	SLANGIEST
SKIVVY	SKRUMPING	SKYJACKINGS	SLACKEST	SLANGILY
SKIVVYING	SKRUMPS	SKYJACKS	SLACKING	SLANGING
SKIVY	SKRY	SKYLAB	SLACKLY	SLANGINGS
SKLATE	SKRYER	SKYLABS	SLACKNESS	SLANGISH
SKLATED	SKRYERS	SKYLARK	SLACKNESSES	SLANGS
SKLATES	SKRYING	SKYLARKED	SLACKS	SLANGULAR
SKLATING	SKUA	SKYLARKER	SLADANG	SLANGY
SKLENT	SKUAS	SKYLARKERS	SLADANGS	SLANT
SKLENTED	SKUDLER	SKYLARKING	SLADE	SLANTED
SKLENTING	SKUDLERS	SKYLARKINGS	SLADES	SLANTING
SKLENTS	SKUG	SKYLARKS	SLAE	SLANTLY
SKLIFF	SKUGGED	SKYLIGHT	SLAES	SLANTS
SKLIFFS	SKUGGING	SKYLIGHTS	SLAG	SLANTWAYS
SKLIM	SKUGS	SKYLINE	SLAGGED	SLANTWISE
SKLIMMED	SKULK	SKYLINES	SLAGGER	SLAP
SKLIMMING	SKULKED	SKYMAN	SLAGGIEST	SLAPHEAD
SKLIMS	SKULKER	SKYMEN	SLAGGING	SLAPHEADS
SKOAL	SKULKERS	SKYR	SLAGGY	SLAPJACK
SKOFF	SKULKING	SKYRE	SLAGS	SLAPJACKS
SKOFFED	SKULKINGS	SKYRED	SLAID	SLAPPED
SKOFFING	SKULKS	SKYRES	SLAIN	SLAPPER
SKOFFS	SKULL	SKYRING	SLAINTE	SLAPPERS
SKOKIAAN	SKULLCAP	SKYROCKET	SLAIRG	SLAPPING
SKOKIAANS	SKULLCAPS	SKYROCKETED	SLAIRGED	SLAPS
SKOL	SKULLS	SKYROCKETING	SLAIRGING	SLAPSHOT
SKOLIA	SKULPIN	SKYROCKETS	SLAIRGS	SLAPSHOTS
SKOLION	SKULPINS	SKYRS	SLAISTER	SLAPSTICK
SKOLLIE	SKUMMER	SKYSAIL	SLAISTERED	SLAPSTICKS
SKOLLIES	SKUMMERED	SKYSAILS	SLAISTERIES	SLASH

SLASHED	SLAYS	SLEEPOVERS	SLICKENED	SLIMSIEST
SLASHER	SLEAVE	SLEEPRY	SLICKENING	SLIMSY
SLASHERS	SLEAVED	SLEEPS	SLICKENS	SLIMY
SLASHES	SLEAVES	SLEEPSUIT	SLICKER	SLING
SLASHING	SLEAVING	SLEEPSUITS	SLICKERED	SLINGBACK
SLASHINGS	SLEAZE	SLEEPY	SLICKERS	SLINGBACKS
SLAT	SLEAZEBAG	SLEER	SLICKEST	SLINGER
SLATCH	SLEAZEBAGS	SLEEST	SLICKING	SLINGERS
SLATCHES	SLEAZES	SLEET	SLICKINGS	SLINGING
SLATE	SLEAZIER	SLEETED	SLICKLY	SLINGS
SLATED	SLEAZIEST	SLEETIER	SLICKNESS	SLINGSHOT
SLATER	SLEAZILY	SLEETIEST	SLICKNESSES	SLINGSHOTS
SLATERS	SLEAZY	SLEETING	SLICKS	SLINK
SLATES	SLED	SLEETS	SLID	SLINKER
SLATHER	SLEDDED	SLEETY	SLIDDEN	SLINKERS
SLATHERED	SLEDDING	SLEEVE	SLIDDER	SLINKIER
SLATHERING	SLEDDINGS	SLEEVED	SLIDDERED	SLINKIEST
SLATHERS	SLEDED	SLEEVEEN	SLIDDERING	SLINKING
SLATIER	SLEDGE	SLEEVEENS	SLIDDERS	SLINKS
SLATIEST	SLEDGED	SLEEVER	SLIDDERY	SLINKSKIN
SLATINESS	SLEDGER	SLEEVERS	SLIDE	SLINKSKINS
SLATINESSES	SLEDGERS	SLEEVES	SLIDED	SLINKWEED
SLATING	SLEDGES	SLEEVING	SLIDER	SLINKWEEDS
SLATINGS	SLEDGING	SLEEVINGS	SLIDERS	SLINKY
SLATS	SLEDGINGS	SLEEZIER	SLIDES	SLINTER
SLATTED	SLEDS	SLEEZIEST	SLIDING	SLINTERS
SLATTER	SLEE	SLEEZY	SLIDINGLY	SLIP
SLATTERED	SLEECH	SLEIDED	SLIDINGS	SLIPCASE
SLATTERING	SLEECHES	SLEIGH	SLIER	SLIPCASES
SLATTERN	SLEECHIER	SLEIGHED	SLIEST	SLIPE
SLATTERNS	SLEECHIEST	SLEIGHER	SLIGHT	SLIPES
SLATTERS	SLEECHY	SLEIGHERS	SLIGHTED	SLIPFORM
SLATTERY	SLEEK	SLEIGHING	SLIGHTER	SLIPKNOT
SLATTING	SLEEKED	SLEIGHINGS	SLIGHTEST	SLIPKNOTS
SLATY	SLEEKEN	SLEIGHS	SLIGHTING	SLIPPAGE
SLAUGHTER	SLEEKENED	SLEIGHT	SLIGHTISH	SLIPPAGES
SLAUGHTERED	SLEEKENING	SLEIGHTS	SLIGHTLY	SLIPPED
SLAUGHTERING	SLEEKENS	SLENDER	SLIGHTS	SLIPPER
SLAUGHTERS	SLEEKER	SLENDERER	SLILY	SLIPPERED
SLAVE	SLEEKERS	SLENDEREST	SLIM	SLIPPERIER
SLAVED	SLEEKEST	SLENDERLY	SLIME	SLIPPERIEST
SLAVER	SLEEKIER	SLENTER	SLIMEBALL	SLIPPERING
SLAVERED	SLEEKIEST	SLENTERS	SLIMEBALLS	SLIPPERS
SLAVERER	SLEEKING	SLEPT	SLIMED	SLIPPERY
SLAVERERS	SLEEKINGS	SLEUTH	SLIMES	SLIPPIER
SLAVERIES	SLEEKIT	SLEUTHED	SLIMIER	SLIPPIEST
SLAVERING	SLEEKLY	SLEUTHING	SLIMIEST	SLIPPING
SLAVERS	SLEEKNESS	SLEUTHS	SLIMILY	SLIPPY
SLAVERY	SLEEKNESSES	SLEW	SLIMINESS	SLIPRAIL
SLAVES	SLEEKS	SLEWED	SLIMINESSES	SLIPRAILS
SLAVEY	SLEEKY	SLEWING	SLIMING	SLIPS
SLAVEYS	SLEEP	SLEWS	SLIMLINE	SLIPSHOD
SLAVING	SLEEPER	SLEY	SLIMLY	SLIPSLOP
SLAVISH	SLEEPERS	SLEYS	SLIMMED	SLIPSLOPS
SLAVISHLY	SLEEPERY	SLICE	SLIMMER	SLIPT
SLAVOCRAT	SLEEPIER	SLICED	SLIMMERS	SLIPWARE
SLAVOCRATS	SLEEPIEST	SLICER	SLIMMEST	SLIPWARES
SLAW	SLEEPILY	SLICERS	SLIMMING	SLIPWAY
SLAWS	SLEEPING	SLICES	SLIMMINGS	SLIPWAYS
SLAY	SLEEPINGS	SLICING	SLIMMISH	SLISH
SLAYED	SLEEPLESS	SLICINGS	SLIMNESS	SLISHES
SLAYER	SLEEPOUT	SLICK	SLIMNESSES	SLIT
SLAYERS	SLEEPOUTS	SLICKED	SLIMS	SLITHER
SLAYING	SLEEPOVER	SLICKEN	SLIMSIER	SLITHERED

SLITHERIER
SLITHERIEST
SLITHERING
SLITHERS
SLITHERY
SLITS
SLITTER
SLITTERS
SLITTING
SLIVE
SLIVED
SLIVEN
SLIVER
SLIVERED
SLIVERING
SLIVERS
SLIVES
SLIVING
SLIVOVIC
SLIVOVICA
SLIVOVICAS
SLIVOVICES
SLIVOVITZ
SLIVOVITZES
SLIVOWITZ
SLIVOWITZES
SLOAN
SLOANS
SLOB
SLOBBER
SLOBBERED
SLOBBERIER
SLOBBERIEST
SLOBBERING
SLOBBERS
SLOBBERY
SLOBBIER
SLOBBIEST
SLOBBISH
SLOBBY
SLOBLAND
SLOBLANDS
SLOBS
SLOCKEN
SLOCKENED
SLOCKENING
SLOCKENS
SLOE
SLOEBUSH
SLOEBUSHES
SLOES
SLOETHORN
SLOETHORNS
SLOETREE
SLOETREES
SLOG
SLOGAN
SLOGANEER
SLOGANEERED
SLOGANEERING
SLOGANEERINGS
SLOGANEERS
SLOGANISE
SLOGANISED

SLOGANISES
SLOGANISING
SLOGANISINGS
SLOGANIZE
SLOGANIZED
SLOGANIZES
SLOGANIZING
SLOGANIZINGS
SLOGANS
SLOGGED
SLOGGER
SLOGGERS
SLOGGING
SLOGS
SLOID
SLOIDS
SLOKEN
SLOKENED
SLOKENING
SLOKENS
SLOOM
SLOOMED
SLOOMIER
SLOOMIEST
SLOOMING
SLOOMS
SLOOMY
SLOOP
SLOOPS
SLOOSH
SLOOSHED
SLOOSHES
SLOOSHING
SLOOT
SLOOTS
SLOP
SLOPE
SLOPED
SLOPES
SLOPEWISE
SLOPIER
SLOPIEST
SLOPING
SLOPINGLY
SLOPPED
SLOPPIER
SLOPPIEST
SLOPPILY
SLOPPING
SLOPPY
SLOPS
SLOPWORK
SLOPWORKS
SLOPY
SLOSH
SLOSHED
SLOSHES
SLOSHIER
SLOSHIEST
SLOSHING
SLOSHINGS
SLOSHY
SLOT
SLOTH

SLOTHED
SLOTHFUL
SLOTHING
SLOTHS
SLOTS
SLOTTED
SLOTTER
SLOTTERS
SLOTTING
SLOUCH
SLOUCHED
SLOUCHER
SLOUCHERS
SLOUCHES
SLOUCHIER
SLOUCHIEST
SLOUCHING
SLOUCHY
SLOUGH
SLOUGHED
SLOUGHIER
SLOUGHIEST
SLOUGHING
SLOUGHS
SLOUGHY
SLOVE
SLOVEN
SLOVENLIER
SLOVENLIEST
SLOVENLY
SLOVENRIES
SLOVENRY
SLOVENS
SLOW
SLOWBACK
SLOWBACKS
SLOWCOACH
SLOWCOACHES
SLOWED
SLOWER
SLOWEST
SLOWING
SLOWINGS
SLOWISH
SLOWLY
SLOWNESS
SLOWNESSES
SLOWPOKE
SLOWPOKES
SLOWS
SLOWWORM
SLOWWORMS
SLOYD
SLOYDS
SLUB
SLUBB
SLUBBED
SLUBBER
SLUBBERED
SLUBBERING
SLUBBERINGS
SLUBBERS
SLUBBIER
SLUBBIEST

SLUBBING
SLUBBINGS
SLUBBS
SLUBBY
SLUBS
SLUDGE
SLUDGES
SLUDGIER
SLUDGIEST
SLUDGY
SLUE
SLUED
SLUEING
SLUES
SLUG
SLUGFEST
SLUGFESTS
SLUGGABED
SLUGGABEDS
SLUGGARD
SLUGGARDS
SLUGGED
SLUGGER
SLUGGERS
SLUGGING
SLUGGISH
SLUGHORN
SLUGHORNE
SLUGHORNES
SLUGHORNS
SLUGS
SLUICE
SLUICED
SLUICES
SLUICIER
SLUICIEST
SLUICING
SLUICY
SLUING
SLUIT
SLUITS
SLUM
SLUMBER
SLUMBERED
SLUMBERER
SLUMBERERS
SLUMBERING
SLUMBERINGS
SLUMBERS
SLUMBERY
SLUMBROUS
SLUMBRY
SLUMLORD
SLUMLORDS
SLUMMED
SLUMMER
SLUMMERS
SLUMMIER
SLUMMIEST
SLUMMING
SLUMMINGS
SLUMMOCK
SLUMMOCKED
SLUMMOCKING

SLUMMOCKS
SLUMMY
SLUMP
SLUMPED
SLUMPIER
SLUMPIEST
SLUMPING
SLUMPS
SLUMPY
SLUMS
SLUNG
SLUNK
SLUR
SLURB
SLURBS
SLURP
SLURPED
SLURPER
SLURPERS
SLURPING
SLURPS
SLURRED
SLURRIES
SLURRING
SLURRY
SLURS
SLUSE
SLUSES
SLUSH
SLUSHED
SLUSHES
SLUSHIER
SLUSHIEST
SLUSHING
SLUSHY
SLUT
SLUTS
SLUTTERIES
SLUTTERY
SLUTTISH
SLY
SLYBOOTS
SLYER
SLYEST
SLYISH
SLYLY
SLYNESS
SLYNESSES
SLYPE
SLYPES
SMA
SMACK
SMACKED
SMACKER
SMACKERS
SMACKING
SMACKINGS
SMACKS
SMAIK
SMAIKS
SMALL
SMALLAGE
SMALLAGES
SMALLED

SMALLER	SMASHING	SMEWS	SMITES	SMOOCHES
SMALLEST	SMASHINGS	SMICKER	SMITH	SMOOCHING
SMALLING	SMATCH	SMICKERED	SMITHED	SMOOR
SMALLISH	SMATCHED	SMICKERING	SMITHERIES	SMOORED
SMALLNESS	SMATCHES	SMICKERINGS	SMITHERS	SMOORING
SMALLNESSES	SMATCHING	SMICKERS	SMITHERY	SMOORS
SMALLPOX	SMATTER	SMICKET	SMITHIED	SMOOT
SMALLPOXES	SMATTERED	SMICKETS	SMITHIES	SMOOTED
SMALLS	SMATTERER	SMICKLY	SMITHING	SMOOTH
SMALLSAT	SMATTERERS	SMIDDIED	SMITHS	SMOOTHED
SMALLSATS	SMATTERING	SMIDDIES	SMITHY	SMOOTHEN
SMALM	SMATTERINGS	SMIDDY	SMITHYING	SMOOTHENED
SMALMED	SMATTERS	SMIDDYING	SMITING	SMOOTHENING
SMALMILY	SMEAR	SMIDGEN	SMITS	SMOOTHENS
SMALMING	SMEARED	SMIDGENS	SMITTED	SMOOTHER
SMALMS	SMEARIER	SMIDGEON	SMITTEN	SMOOTHERS
SMALMY	SMEARIEST	SMIDGEONS	SMITTING	SMOOTHEST
SMALT	SMEARILY	SMIDGIN	SMITTLE	SMOOTHIE
SMALTI	SMEARING	SMIDGINS	SMOCK	SMOOTHIES
SMALTITE	SMEARS	SMIGHT	SMOCKED	SMOOTHING
SMALTITES	SMEARY	SMIGHTING	SMOCKING	SMOOTHINGS
SMALTO	SMEATH	SMIGHTS	SMOCKINGS	SMOOTHISH
SMALTOS	SMEATHS	SMILAX	SMOCKS	SMOOTHLY
SMALTS	SMECTIC	SMILAXES	SMOG	SMOOTHS
SMARAGD	SMECTITE	SMILE	SMOGGIER	SMOOTING
SMARAGDS	SMECTITES	SMILED	SMOGGIEST	SMOOTS
SMARM	SMEDDUM	SMILEFUL	SMOGGY	SMORBROD
SMARMED	SMEDDUMS	SMILELESS	SMOGS	SMORBRODS
SMARMIER	SMEE	SMILER	SMOILE	SMORE
SMARMIEST	SMEECH	SMILERS	SMOILED	SMORED
SMARMILY	SMEECHED	SMILES	SMOILES	SMORES
SMARMING	SMEECHES	SMILET	SMOILING	SMORING
SMARMS	SMEECHING	SMILETS	SMOKABLE	SMORZANDO
SMARMY	SMEEK	SMILEY	SMOKE	SMORZATO
SMART	SMEEKED	SMILEYS	SMOKEBUSH	SMOTE
SMARTARSE	SMEEKING	SMILING	SMOKEBUSHES	SMOTHER
SMARTARSES	SMEEKS	SMILINGLY	SMOKED	SMOTHERED
SMARTASS	SMEES	SMILINGS	SMOKEHOOD	SMOTHERER
SMARTASSES	SMEETH	SMILODON	SMOKEHOODS	SMOTHERERS
SMARTED	SMEETHS	SMILODONS	SMOKELESS	SMOTHERING
SMARTEN	SMEGMA	SMIR	SMOKER	SMOTHERINGS
SMARTENED	SMEGMAS	SMIRCH	SMOKERS	SMOTHERS
SMARTENING	SMELL	SMIRCHED	SMOKES	SMOTHERY
SMARTENS	SMELLED	SMIRCHES	SMOKETREE	SMOUCH
SMARTER	SMELLER	SMIRCHING	SMOKETREES	SMOUCHED
SMARTEST	SMELLERS	SMIRK	SMOKIER	SMOUCHES
SMARTIE	SMELLIER	SMIRKED	SMOKIES	SMOUCHING
SMARTIES	SMELLIEST	SMIRKIER	SMOKIEST	SMOULDER
SMARTING	SMELLING	SMIRKIEST	SMOKILY	SMOULDERED
SMARTISH	SMELLINGS	SMIRKING	SMOKINESS	SMOULDERING
SMARTLY	SMELLS	SMIRKS	SMOKINESSES	SMOULDERINGS
SMARTNESS	SMELLY	SMIRKY	SMOKING	SMOULDERS
SMARTNESSES	SMELT	SMIRR	SMOKINGS	SMOULDRY
SMARTS	SMELTED	SMIRRED	SMOKO	SMOUSE
SMARTWEED	SMELTER	SMIRRIER	SMOKOS	SMOUSED
SMARTWEEDS	SMELTERIES	SMIRRIEST	SMOKY	SMOUSER
SMARTY	SMELTERS	SMIRRING	SMOLDER	SMOUSERS
SMASH	SMELTERY	SMIRRS	SMOLDERED	SMOUSES
SMASHED	SMELTING	SMIRRY	SMOLDERING	SMOUSING
SMASHER	SMELTINGS	SMIRS	SMOLDERS	SMOUT
SMASHEROO	SMELTS	SMIT	SMOLT	SMOUTED
SMASHEROOS	SMEUSE	SMITE	SMOLTS	SMOUTING
SMASHERS	SMEUSES	SMITER	SMOOCH	SMOUTS
SMASHES	SMEW	SMITERS	SMOOCHED	SMOWT

SMOWTS
SMOYLE
SMOYLED
SMOYLES
SMOYLING
SMUDGE
SMUDGED
SMUDGER
SMUDGERS
SMUDGES
SMUDGIER
SMUDGIEST
SMUDGILY
SMUDGING
SMUDGY
SMUG
SMUGGED
SMUGGER
SMUGGEST
SMUGGING
SMUGGLE
SMUGGLED
SMUGGLER
SMUGGLERS
SMUGGLES
SMUGGLING
SMUGGLINGS
SMUGLY
SMUGNESS
SMUGNESSES
SMUGS
SMUR
SMURRED
SMURRIER
SMURRIEST
SMURRING
SMURRY
SMURS
SMUT
SMUTCH
SMUTCHED
SMUTCHES
SMUTCHING
SMUTS
SMUTTED
SMUTTIER
SMUTTIEST
SMUTTILY
SMUTTING
SMUTTY
SMYTRIE
SMYTRIES
SNAB
SNABBLE
SNABBLED
SNABBLES
SNABBLING
SNABS
SNACK
SNACKED
SNACKING
SNACKS
SNAFFLE
SNAFFLED

SNAFFLES
SNAFFLING
SNAFU
SNAFUS
SNAG
SNAGGED
SNAGGIER
SNAGGIEST
SNAGGING
SNAGGY
SNAGS
SNAIL
SNAILED
SNAILERIES
SNAILERY
SNAILIER
SNAILIEST
SNAILING
SNAILS
SNAILY
SNAKE
SNAKEBIRD
SNAKEBIRDS
SNAKEBITE
SNAKEBITES
SNAKED
SNAKELIKE
SNAKEROOT
SNAKEROOTS
SNAKES
SNAKESKIN
SNAKESKINS
SNAKEWEED
SNAKEWEEDS
SNAKEWISE
SNAKEWOOD
SNAKEWOODS
SNAKIER
SNAKIEST
SNAKILY
SNAKINESS
SNAKINESSES
SNAKING
SNAKISH
SNAKY
SNAP
SNAPHANCE
SNAPHANCES
SNAPPED
SNAPPER
SNAPPERED
SNAPPERING
SNAPPERS
SNAPPIER
SNAPPIEST
SNAPPILY
SNAPPING
SNAPPINGS
SNAPPISH
SNAPPY
SNAPS
SNAPSHOT
SNAPSHOTS
SNAR

SNARE
SNARED
SNARER
SNARERS
SNARES
SNARIER
SNARIEST
SNARING
SNARINGS
SNARK
SNARKS
SNARL
SNARLED
SNARLER
SNARLERS
SNARLIER
SNARLIEST
SNARLING
SNARLINGS
SNARLS
SNARLY
SNARRED
SNARRING
SNARS
SNARY
SNASH
SNASHED
SNASHES
SNASHING
SNASTE
SNASTES
SNATCH
SNATCHED
SNATCHER
SNATCHERS
SNATCHES
SNATCHIER
SNATCHIEST
SNATCHILY
SNATCHING
SNATCHY
SNATH
SNATHE
SNATHES
SNATHS
SNAZZIER
SNAZZIEST
SNAZZY
SNEAD
SNEADS
SNEAK
SNEAKED
SNEAKER
SNEAKERS
SNEAKEUP
SNEAKEUPS
SNEAKIER
SNEAKIEST
SNEAKILY
SNEAKING
SNEAKISH
SNEAKS
SNEAKSBIES
SNEAKSBY

SNEAKY
SNEAP
SNEAPED
SNEAPING
SNEAPS
SNEATH
SNEATHS
SNEB
SNEBBE
SNEBBED
SNEBBES
SNEBBING
SNEBS
SNECK
SNECKED
SNECKING
SNECKS
SNED
SNEDDED
SNEDDING
SNEDS
SNEE
SNEED
SNEEING
SNEER
SNEERED
SNEERER
SNEERERS
SNEERIER
SNEERIEST
SNEERING
SNEERINGS
SNEERS
SNEERY
SNEES
SNEESH
SNEESHAN
SNEESHANS
SNEESHES
SNEESHIN
SNEESHING
SNEESHINGS
SNEESHINS
SNEEZE
SNEEZED
SNEEZER
SNEEZERS
SNEEZES
SNEEZIER
SNEEZIEST
SNEEZING
SNEEZINGS
SNEEZY
SNELL
SNELLED
SNELLER
SNELLEST
SNELLING
SNELLS
SNELLY
SNIB
SNIBBED
SNIBBING
SNIBS

SNICK
SNICKED
SNICKER
SNICKERED
SNICKERING
SNICKERS
SNICKET
SNICKETS
SNICKING
SNICKS
SNIDE
SNIDELY
SNIDENESS
SNIDENESSES
SNIDER
SNIDES
SNIDEST
SNIES
SNIFF
SNIFFED
SNIFFER
SNIFFERS
SNIFFIER
SNIFFIEST
SNIFFILY
SNIFFING
SNIFFINGS
SNIFFLE
SNIFFLED
SNIFFLER
SNIFFLERS
SNIFFLES
SNIFFLING
SNIFFS
SNIFFY
SNIFT
SNIFTED
SNIFTER
SNIFTERED
SNIFTERING
SNIFTERS
SNIFTIER
SNIFTIEST
SNIFTING
SNIFTS
SNIFTY
SNIG
SNIGGED
SNIGGER
SNIGGERED
SNIGGERER
SNIGGERERS
SNIGGERING
SNIGGERINGS
SNIGGERS
SNIGGING
SNIGGLE
SNIGGLED
SNIGGLER
SNIGGLERS
SNIGGLES
SNIGGLING
SNIGGLINGS
SNIGS

SNIP	SNODS	SNORING	SNOWFALL	SNUFFIEST
SNIPE	SNOEK	SNORINGS	SNOWFALLS	SNUFFING
SNIPED	SNOEKS	SNORKEL	SNOWFIELD	SNUFFINGS
SNIPEFISH	SNOG	SNORKELER	SNOWFIELDS	SNUFFLE
SNIPEFISHES	SNOGGED	SNORKELERS	SNOWFLAKE	SNUFFLED
SNIPER	SNOGGING	SNORKELS	SNOWFLAKES	SNUFFLER
SNIPERS	SNOGS	SNORT	SNOWFLECK	SNUFFLERS
SNIPES	SNOKE	SNORTED	SNOWFLECKS	SNUFFLES
SNIPIER	SNOKED	SNORTER	SNOWFLICK	SNUFFLIER
SNIPIEST	SNOKES	SNORTERS	SNOWFLICKS	SNUFFLIEST
SNIPING	SNOKING	SNORTIER	SNOWIER	SNUFFLING
SNIPINGS	SNOOD	SNORTIEST	SNOWIEST	SNUFFLINGS
SNIPPED	SNOODED	SNORTING	SNOWILY	SNUFFLY
SNIPPER	SNOODING	SNORTINGS	SNOWINESS	SNUFFS
SNIPPERS	SNOODS	SNORTS	SNOWINESSES	SNUFFY
SNIPPET	SNOOK	SNORTY	SNOWING	SNUG
SNIPPETIER	SNOOKED	SNOT	SNOWISH	SNUGGED
SNIPPETIEST	SNOOKER	SNOTS	SNOWK	SNUGGER
SNIPPETS	SNOOKERED	SNOTTED	SNOWKED	SNUGGERIES
SNIPPETY	SNOOKERING	SNOTTER	SNOWKING	SNUGGERY
SNIPPIER	SNOOKERS	SNOTTERED	SNOWKS	SNUGGEST
SNIPPIEST	SNOOKING	SNOTTERIES	SNOWLESS	SNUGGING
SNIPPING	SNOOKS	SNOTTERING	SNOWLIKE	SNUGGLE
SNIPPINGS	SNOOL	SNOTTERS	SNOWLINE	SNUGGLED
SNIPPY	SNOOLED	SNOTTERY	SNOWLINES	SNUGGLES
SNIPS	SNOOLING	SNOTTIE	SNOWMAN	SNUGGLING
SNIPY	SNOOLS	SNOTTIER	SNOWMEN	SNUGLY
SNIRT	SNOOP	SNOTTIES	SNOWS	SNUGNESS
SNIRTLE	SNOOPED	SNOTTIEST	SNOWSCAPE	SNUGNESSES
SNIRTLED	SNOOPER	SNOTTILY	SNOWSCAPES	SNUGS
SNIRTLES	SNOOPERS	SNOTTING	SNOWSHOE	SNUSH
SNIRTLING	SNOOPIER	SNOTTY	SNOWSHOED	SNUSHED
SNIRTS	SNOOPIEST	SNOUT	SNOWSHOEING	SNUSHES
SNITCH	SNOOPING	SNOUTED	SNOWSHOES	SNUSHING
SNITCHED	SNOOPS	SNOUTIER	SNOWSLIP	SNUZZLE
SNITCHER	SNOOPY	SNOUTIEST	SNOWSLIPS	SNUZZLED
SNITCHERS	SNOOT	SNOUTING	SNOWSTORM	SNUZZLES
SNITCHES	SNOOTED	SNOUTS	SNOWSTORMS	SNUZZLING
SNITCHING	SNOOTFUL	SNOUTY	SNOWY	SNY
SNIVEL	SNOOTFULS	SNOW	SNUB	SNYE
SNIVELLED	SNOOTIER	SNOWBALL	SNUBBE	SNYES
SNIVELLER	SNOOTIEST	SNOWBALLED	SNUBBED	SO
SNIVELLERS	SNOOTILY	SNOWBALLING	SNUBBER	SOAK
SNIVELLING	SNOOTING	SNOWBALLS	SNUBBERS	SOAKAGE
SNIVELLY	SNOOTS	SNOWBERRIES	SNUBBES	SOAKAGES
SNIVELS	SNOOTY	SNOWBERRY	SNUBBIER	SOAKAWAY
SNOB	SNOOZE	SNOWBIRD	SNUBBIEST	SOAKAWAYS
SNOBBERIES	SNOOZED	SNOWBIRDS	SNUBBING	SOAKED
SNOBBERY	SNOOZER	SNOWBLINK	SNUBBINGS	SOAKEN
SNOBBIER	SNOOZERS	SNOWBLINKS	SNUBBISH	SOAKER
SNOBBIEST	SNOOZES	SNOWBOARD	SNUBBY	SOAKERS
SNOBBISH	SNOOZIER	SNOWBOARDS	SNUBS	SOAKING
SNOBBISM	SNOOZIEST	SNOWBOOT	SNUCK	SOAKINGLY
SNOBBISMS	SNOOZING	SNOWBOOTS	SNUDGE	SOAKINGS
SNOBBY	SNOOZLE	SNOWBOUND	SNUDGED	SOAKS
SNOBLING	SNOOZLED	SNOWBUSH	SNUDGES	SOAP
SNOBLINGS	SNOOZLES	SNOWBUSHES	SNUDGING	SOAPBARK
SNOBS	SNOOZLING	SNOWCAP	SNUFF	SOAPBARKS
SNOD	SNOOZY	SNOWCAPS	SNUFFBOX	SOAPBERRIES
SNODDED	SNORE	SNOWDRIFT	SNUFFBOXES	SOAPBERRY
SNODDER	SNORED	SNOWDRIFTS	SNUFFED	SOAPBOX
SNODDEST	SNORER	SNOWDROP	SNUFFER	SOAPBOXES
SNODDING	SNORERS	SNOWDROPS	SNUFFERS	SOAPED
SNODDIT	SNORES	SNOWED	SNUFFIER	SOAPER

The Chambers Dictionary is the authority for many longer words; see *OSW* Introduction, page xii

SOAPERS	SOCAGE	SOCS	SOFTENERS	SOJOURNERS
SOAPIE	SOCAGER	SOD	SOFTENING	SOJOURNING
SOAPIER	SOCAGERS	SODA	SOFTENINGS	SOJOURNINGS
SOAPIES	SOCAGES	SODAIC	SOFTENS	SOJOURNS
SOAPIEST	SOCAS	SODAIN	SOFTER	SOKAH
SOAPILY	SOCCAGE	SODAINE	SOFTEST	SOKAHS
SOAPINESS	SOCCAGES	SODALITE	SOFTHEAD	SOKAIYA
SOAPINESSES	SOCCER	SODALITES	SOFTHEADS	SOKE
SOAPING	SOCCERS	SODALITIES	SOFTIE	SOKEMAN
SOAPLAND	SOCIABLE	SODALITY	SOFTIES	SOKEMANRIES
SOAPLANDS	SOCIABLES	SODAMIDE	SOFTING	SOKEMANRY
SOAPLESS	SOCIABLY	SODAMIDES	SOFTISH	SOKEMEN
SOAPROOT	SOCIAL	SODAS	SOFTLING	SOKEN
SOAPROOTS	SOCIALISE	SODBUSTER	SOFTLINGS	SOKENS
SOAPS	SOCIALISED	SODBUSTERS	SOFTLY	SOKES
SOAPSTONE	SOCIALISES	SODDED	SOFTNESS	SOL
SOAPSTONES	SOCIALISING	SODDEN	SOFTNESSES	SOLA
SOAPSUDS	SOCIALISM	SODDENED	SOFTPASTE	SOLACE
SOAPWORT	SOCIALISMS	SODDENING	SOFTS	SOLACED
SOAPWORTS	SOCIALIST	SODDENS	SOFTWARE	SOLACES
SOAPY	SOCIALISTS	SODDIER	SOFTWARES	SOLACING
SOAR	SOCIALITE	SODDIEST	SOFTWOOD	SOLACIOUS
SOARAWAY	SOCIALITES	SODDING	SOFTWOODS	SOLAH
SOARE	SOCIALITIES	SODDY	SOFTY	SOLAHS
SOARED	SOCIALITY	SODGER	SOG	SOLAN
SOARER	SOCIALIZE	SODGERS	SOGER	SOLANDER
SOARERS	SOCIALIZED	SODIC	SOGERS	SOLANDERS
SOARES	SOCIALIZES	SODIUM	SOGGED	SOLANINE
SOARING	SOCIALIZING	SODIUMS	SOGGIER	SOLANINES
SOARINGLY	SOCIALLY	SODOMIES	SOGGIEST	SOLANO
SOARINGS	SOCIALS	SODOMISE	SOGGILY	SOLANOS
SOARS	SOCIATE	SODOMISED	SOGGINESS	SOLANS
SOB	SOCIATES	SODOMISES	SOGGINESSES	SOLANUM
SOBBED	SOCIATION	SODOMISING	SOGGING	SOLANUMS
SOBBING	SOCIATIONS	SODOMITE	SOGGINGS	SOLAR
SOBBINGLY	SOCIATIVE	SODOMITES	SOGGY	SOLARIA
SOBBINGS	SOCIETAL	SODOMITIC	SOGS	SOLARISE
SOBEIT	SOCIETIES	SODOMIZE	SOH	SOLARISED
SOBER	SOCIETY	SODOMIZED	SOHO	SOLARISES
SOBERED	SOCIOGRAM	SODOMIZES	SOHS	SOLARISING
SOBERER	SOCIOGRAMS	SODOMIZING	SOIGNE	SOLARISM
SOBEREST	SOCIOLECT	SODOMY	SOIGNEE	SOLARISMS
SOBERING	SOCIOLECTS	SODS	SOIL	SOLARIST
SOBERISE	SOCIOLOGIES	SOEVER	SOILAGE	SOLARISTS
SOBERISED	SOCIOLOGY	SOFA	SOILAGES	SOLARIUM
SOBERISES	SOCIOPATH	SOFAR	SOILED	SOLARIUMS
SOBERISING	SOCIOPATHS	SOFARS	SOILIER	SOLARIZE
SOBERIZE	SOCK	SOFAS	SOILIEST	SOLARIZED
SOBERIZED	SOCKED	SOFFIONI	SOILINESS	SOLARIZES
SOBERIZES	SOCKET	SOFFIT	SOILINESSES	SOLARIZING
SOBERIZING	SOCKETED	SOFFITS	SOILING	SOLARS
SOBERLY	SOCKETING	SOFT	SOILINGS	SOLAS
SOBERNESS	SOCKETS	SOFTA	SOILLESS	SOLATIA
SOBERNESSES	SOCKETTE	SOFTAS	SOILS	SOLATION
SOBERS	SOCKETTES	SOFTBACK	SOILURE	SOLATIONS
SOBOLE	SOCKEYE	SOFTBACKS	SOILURES	SOLATIUM
SOBOLES	SOCKEYES	SOFTBALL	SOILY	SOLD
SOBRIETIES	SOCKING	SOFTBALLS	SOIREE	SOLDADO
SOBRIETY	SOCKO	SOFTCOVER	SOIREES	SOLDADOS
SOBRIQUET	SOCKS	SOFTCOVERS	SOJA	SOLDAN
SOBRIQUETS	SOCLE	SOFTED	SOJAS	SOLDANS
SOBS	SOCLES	SOFTEN	SOJOURN	SOLDE
SOC	SOCMAN	SOFTENED	SOJOURNED	SOLDER
SOCA	SOCMEN	SOFTENER	SOJOURNER	SOLDERED

SOLDERER	SOLERA	SOLIPSISM	SOLVES	SOMMELIERS
SOLDERERS	SOLERAS	SOLIPSISMS	SOLVING	SOMNIAL
SOLDERING	SOLERS	SOLIPSIST	SOMA	SOMNIATE
SOLDERINGS	SOLES	SOLIPSISTS	SOMAN	SOMNIATED
SOLDERS	SOLEUS	SOLITAIRE	SOMANS	SOMNIATES
SOLDES	SOLEUSES	SOLITAIRES	SOMAS	SOMNIATING
SOLDI	SOLFATARA	SOLITARIES	SOMASCOPE	SOMNIFIC
SOLDIER	SOLFATARAS	SOLITARY	SOMASCOPES	SOMNOLENT
SOLDIERED	SOLFEGE	SOLITO	SOMATA	SON
SOLDIERIES	SOLFEGES	SOLITON	SOMATIC	SONANCE
SOLDIERING	SOLFEGGI	SOLITONS	SOMATISM	SONANCES
SOLDIERINGS	SOLFEGGIO	SOLITUDE	SOMATISMS	SONANCIES
SOLDIERLY	SOLFEGGIOS	SOLITUDES	SOMATIST	SONANCY
SOLDIERS	SOLFERINO	SOLIVE	SOMATISTS	SONANT
SOLDIERY	SOLFERINOS	SOLIVES	SOMBER	SONANTS
SOLDO	SOLGEL	SOLLAR	SOMBERED	SONAR
SOLDS	SOLI	SOLLARS	SOMBERER	SONARS
SOLE	SOLICIT	SOLLER	SOMBEREST	SONATA
SOLECISE	SOLICITED	SOLLERET	SOMBERING	SONATAS
SOLECISED	SOLICITIES	SOLLERETS	SOMBERS	SONATINA
SOLECISES	SOLICITING	SOLLERS	SOMBRE	SONATINAS
SOLECISING	SOLICITINGS	SOLO	SOMBRED	SONCE
SOLECISM	SOLICITOR	SOLOED	SOMBRELY	SONCES
SOLECISMS	SOLICITORS	SOLOING	SOMBRER	SONDAGE
SOLECIST	SOLICITS	SOLOIST	SOMBRERO	SONDAGES
SOLECISTS	SOLICITY	SOLOISTS	SOMBREROS	SONDE
SOLECIZE	SOLID	SOLONCHAK	SOMBRES	SONDELI
SOLECIZED	SOLIDAGO	SOLONCHAKS	SOMBREST	SONDELIS
SOLECIZES	SOLIDAGOS	SOLONETS	SOMBRING	SONDES
SOLECIZING	SOLIDARE	SOLONETSES	SOMBROUS	SONE
SOLED	SOLIDARES	SOLONETZ	SOME	SONERI
SOLEIN	SOLIDARY	SOLONETZES	SOMEBODIES	SONERIS
SOLELY	SOLIDATE	SOLOS	SOMEBODY	SONES
SOLEMN	SOLIDATED	SOLPUGID	SOMEDAY	SONG
SOLEMNER	SOLIDATES	SOLPUGIDS	SOMEDEAL	SONGBIRD
SOLEMNESS	SOLIDATING	SOLS	SOMEDELE	SONGBIRDS
SOLEMNESSES	SOLIDER	SOLSTICE	SOMEGATE	SONGBOOK
SOLEMNEST	SOLIDEST	SOLSTICES	SOMEHOW	SONGBOOKS
SOLEMNIFIED	SOLIDI	SOLUBLE	SOMEONE	SONGCRAFT
SOLEMNIFIES	SOLIDIFIED	SOLUM	SOMEONES	SONGCRAFTS
SOLEMNIFY	SOLIDIFIES	SOLUMS	SOMEPLACE	SONGFEST
SOLEMNIFYING	SOLIDIFY	SOLUS	SOMERSET	SONGFESTS
SOLEMNISE	SOLIDIFYING	SOLUTE	SOMERSETS	SONGFUL
SOLEMNISED	SOLIDISH	SOLUTES	SOMERSETTED	SONGFULLY
SOLEMNISES	SOLIDISM	SOLUTION	SOMERSETTING	SONGLESS
SOLEMNISING	SOLIDISMS	SOLUTIONED	SOMETHING	SONGLIKE
SOLEMNITIES	SOLIDIST	SOLUTIONING	SOMETHINGS	SONGMAN
SOLEMNITY	SOLIDISTS	SOLUTIONS	SOMETIME	SONGMEN
SOLEMNIZE	SOLIDITIES	SOLUTIVE	SOMETIMES	SONGS
SOLEMNIZED	SOLIDITY	SOLVABLE	SOMEWAY	SONGSMITH
SOLEMNIZES	SOLIDLY	SOLVATE	SOMEWAYS	SONGSMITHS
SOLEMNIZING	SOLIDNESS	SOLVATED	SOMEWHAT	SONGSTER
SOLEMNLY	SOLIDNESSES	SOLVATES	SOMEWHATS	SONGSTERS
SOLENESS	SOLIDS	SOLVATING	SOMEWHEN	SONIC
SOLENESSES	SOLIDUM	SOLVATION	SOMEWHERE	SONICS
SOLENETTE	SOLIDUMS	SOLVATIONS	SOMEWHILE	SONLESS
SOLENETTES	SOLIDUS	SOLVE	SOMEWHILES	SONNE
SOLENODON	SOLILOQUIES	SOLVED	SOMEWHY	SONNES
SOLENODONS	SOLILOQUY	SOLVENCIES	SOMEWISE	SONNET
SOLENOID	SOLING	SOLVENCY	SOMITAL	SONNETARY
SOLENOIDS	SOLION	SOLVENT	SOMITE	SONNETED
SOLEPLATE	SOLIONS	SOLVENTS	SOMITES	SONNETEER
SOLEPLATES	SOLIPED	SOLVER	SOMITIC	SONNETEERS
SOLER	SOLIPEDS	SOLVERS	SOMMELIER	SONNETING

SONNETISE	SOOTE	SOPPIER	SORDINO	SORORIZING
SONNETISED	SOOTED	SOPPIEST	SORDO	SOROSES
SONNETISES	SOOTERKIN	SOPPILY	SORDS	SOROSIS
SONNETISING	SOOTERKINS	SOPPINESS	SORE	SOROSISES
SONNETIZE	SOOTES	SOPPINESSES	SORED	SORPTION
SONNETIZED	SOOTFLAKE	SOPPING	SOREDIA	SORPTIONS
SONNETIZES	SOOTFLAKES	SOPPINGS	SOREDIAL	SORRA
SONNETIZING	SOOTH	SOPPY	SOREDIATE	SORRAS
SONNETS	SOOTHE	SOPRA	SOREDIUM	SORREL
SONNIES	SOOTHED	SOPRANI	SOREE	SORRELS
SONNY	SOOTHER	SOPRANINI	SOREES	SORRIER
SONOBUOY	SOOTHERED	SOPRANINO	SOREHEAD	SORRIEST
SONOBUOYS	SOOTHERING	SOPRANINOS	SOREHEADS	SORRILY
SONOGRAM	SOOTHERS	SOPRANIST	SOREHON	SORRINESS
SONOGRAMS	SOOTHES	SOPRANISTS	SOREHONS	SORRINESSES
SONOGRAPH	SOOTHEST	SOPRANO	SOREL	SORROW
SONOGRAPHS	SOOTHFAST	SOPRANOS	SORELL	SORROWED
SONORANT	SOOTHFUL	SOPS	SORELLS	SORROWER
SONORANTS	SOOTHING	SORA	SORELS	SORROWERS
SONORITIES	SOOTHINGS	SORAGE	SORELY	SORROWFUL
SONORITY	SOOTHLICH	SORAGES	SORENESS	SORROWING
SONOROUS	SOOTHLY	SORAL	SORENESSES	SORROWINGS
SONS	SOOTHS	SORAS	SORER	SORROWS
SONSE	SOOTHSAID	SORB	SORES	SORRY
SONSES	SOOTHSAY	SORBARIA	SOREST	SORRYISH
SONSHIP	SOOTHSAYING	SORBARIAS	SOREX	SORT
SONSHIPS	SOOTHSAYINGS	SORBATE	SOREXES	SORTABLE
SONSIE	SOOTHSAYS	SORBATES	SORGHO	SORTANCE
SONSIER	SOOTIER	SORBED	SORGHOS	SORTANCES
SONSIEST	SOOTIEST	SORBENT	SORGHUM	SORTATION
SONSY	SOOTILY	SORBENTS	SORGHUMS	SORTATIONS
SONTAG	SOOTINESS	SORBET	SORGO	SORTED
SONTAGS	SOOTINESSES	SORBETS	SORGOS	SORTER
SONTIES	SOOTING	SORBING	SORI	SORTERS
SOOGEE	SOOTLESS	SORBITE	SORICINE	SORTES
SOOGEED	SOOTS	SORBITES	SORICOID	SORTIE
SOOGEEING	SOOTY	SORBITIC	SORING	SORTIED
SOOGEES	SOP	SORBITISE	SORITES	SORTIEING
SOOGIE	SOPH	SORBITISED	SORITIC	SORTILEGE
SOOGIED	SOPHERIC	SORBITISES	SORITICAL	SORTILEGES
SOOGIEING	SOPHERIM	SORBITISING	SORN	SORTILEGIES
SOOGIES	SOPHISM	SORBITIZE	SORNED	SORTILEGY
SOOJEY	SOPHISMS	SORBITIZED	SORNER	SORTING
SOOJEYS	SOPHIST	SORBITIZES	SORNERS	SORTINGS
SOOK	SOPHISTER	SORBITIZING	SORNING	SORTITION
SOOKS	SOPHISTERS	SORBITOL	SORNINGS	SORTITIONS
SOOLE	SOPHISTIC	SORBITOLS	SORNS	SORTMENT
SOOLED	SOPHISTRIES	SORBS	SOROBAN	SORTMENTS
SOOLES	SOPHISTRY	SORBUS	SOROBANS	SORTS
SOOLING	SOPHISTS	SORBUSES	SOROCHE	SORUS
SOOM	SOPHOMORE	SORCERER	SOROCHES	SOS
SOOMED	SOPHOMORES	SORCERERS	SOROROL	SOSS
SOOMING	SOPHS	SORCERESS	SORORATE	SOSSED
SOOMS	SOPITE	SORCERESSES	SORORATES	SOSSES
SOON	SOPITED	SORCERIES	SORORIAL	SOSSING
SOONER	SOPITES	SORCEROUS	SORORISE	SOSSINGS
SOONEST	SOPITING	SORCERY	SORORISED	SOSTENUTO
SOOP	SOPOR	SORD	SORORISES	SOT
SOOPED	SOPORIFIC	SORDA	SORORISING	SOTERIAL
SOOPING	SOPORIFICS	SORDID	SORORITIES	SOTS
SOOPINGS	SOPOROSE	SORDIDER	SORORITY	SOTTED
SOOPS	SOPOROUS	SORDIDEST	SORORIZE	SOTTING
SOOPSTAKE	SOPORS	SORDIDLY	SORORIZED	SOTTINGS
SOOT	SOPPED	SORDINI	SORORIZES	

SOTTISH	SOUP	SOUTH	SOWBACK	SOZZLED
SOTTISHLY	SOUPCON	SOUTHED	SOWBACKS	SOZZLES
SOTTISIER	SOUPCONS	SOUTHER	SOWBREAD	SOZZLIER
SOTTISIERS	SOUPER	SOUTHERED	SOWBREADS	SOZZLIEST
SOU	SOUPERS	SOUTHERING	SOWCE	SOZZLING
SOUARI	SOUPIER	SOUTHERLY	SOWCED	SOZZLY
SOUARIS	SOUPIEST	SOUTHERN	SOWCES	SPA
SOUBISE	SOUPLE	SOUTHERNS	SOWCING	SPACE
SOUBISES	SOUPLED	SOUTHERS	SOWED	SPACED
SOUBRETTE	SOUPLES	SOUTHING	SOWENS	SPACELESS
SOUBRETTES	SOUPLING	SOUTHINGS	SOWER	SPACEMAN
SOUCE	SOUPS	SOUTHLAND	SOWERS	SPACEMEN
SOUCED	SOUPSPOON	SOUTHLANDS	SOWF	SPACER
SOUCES	SOUPSPOONS	SOUTHMOST	SOWFED	SPACERS
SOUCHONG	SOUPY	SOUTHPAW	SOWFF	SPACES
SOUCHONGS	SOUR	SOUTHPAWS	SOWFFED	SPACESHIP
SOUCING	SOURCE	SOUTHRON	SOWFFING	SPACESHIPS
SOUCT	SOURCED	SOUTHRONS	SOWFFS	SPACESUIT
SOUFFLE	SOURCES	SOUTHS	SOWFING	SPACESUITS
SOUFFLES	SOURCING	SOUTHSAID	SOWFS	SPACEY
SOUGH	SOURCINGS	SOUTHSAY	SOWING	SPACIAL
SOUGHED	SOURDINE	SOUTHSAYING	SOWINGS	SPACIER
SOUGHING	SOURDINES	SOUTHSAYS	SOWL	SPACIEST
SOUGHS	SOURDOUGH	SOUTHWARD	SOWLE	SPACING
SOUGHT	SOURDOUGHS	SOUTHWARDS	SOWLED	SPACINGS
SOUK	SOURED	SOUTS	SOWLES	SPACIOUS
SOUKOUS	SOURER	SOUVENIR	SOWLING	SPACY
SOUKOUSES	SOUREST	SOUVENIRED	SOWLS	SPADASSIN
SOUKS	SOURING	SOUVENIRING	SOWM	SPADASSINS
SOUL	SOURINGS	SOUVENIRS	SOWMED	SPADE
SOULDAN	SOURISH	SOUVLAKI	SOWMING	SPADED
SOULDANS	SOURISHLY	SOUVLAKIA	SOWMS	SPADEFISH
SOULDIER	SOURLY	SOV	SOWN	SPADEFISHES
SOULDIERED	SOURNESS	SOVENANCE	SOWND	SPADEFUL
SOULDIERING	SOURNESSES	SOVENANCES	SOWNDED	SPADEFULS
SOULDIERS	SOUROCK	SOVEREIGN	SOWNDING	SPADELIKE
SOULED	SOUROCKS	SOVEREIGNS	SOWNDS	SPADEMAN
SOULFUL	SOURPUSS	SOVIET	SOWNE	SPADEMEN
SOULFULLY	SOURPUSSES	SOVIETIC	SOWNES	SPADER
SOULLESS	SOURS	SOVIETISE	SOWP	SPADERS
SOULS	SOURSE	SOVIETISED	SOWPS	SPADES
SOUM	SOURSES	SOVIETISES	SOWS	SPADESMAN
SOUMED	SOURSOP	SOVIETISING	SOWSE	SPADESMEN
SOUMING	SOURSOPS	SOVIETISM	SOWSED	SPADEWORK
SOUMINGS	SOUS	SOVIETISMS	SOWSES	SPADEWORKS
SOUMS	SOUSE	SOVIETIZE	SOWSING	SPADGER
SOUND	SOUSED	SOVIETIZED	SOWSSE	SPADGERS
SOUNDBITE	SOUSES	SOVIETIZES	SOWSSED	SPADICES
SOUNDBITES	SOUSING	SOVIETIZING	SOWSSES	SPADILLE
SOUNDCARD	SOUSINGS	SOVIETS	SOWSSING	SPADILLES
SOUNDCARDS	SOUSLIK	SOVRAN	SOWTER	SPADILLIO
SOUNDED	SOUSLIKS	SOVRANLY	SOWTERS	SPADILLIOS
SOUNDER	SOUT	SOVRANS	SOWTH	SPADILLO
SOUNDERS	SOUTACHE	SOVRANTIES	SOWTHED	SPADILLOS
SOUNDEST	SOUTACHES	SOVRANTY	SOWTHING	SPADING
SOUNDING	SOUTANE	SOVS	SOWTHS	SPADIX
SOUNDINGS	SOUTANES	SOW	SOX	SPADO
SOUNDLESS	SOUTAR	SOWANS	SOY	SPADOES
SOUNDLY	SOUTARS	SOWAR	SOYA	SPADONES
SOUNDMAN	SOUTENEUR	SOWARREE	SOYAS	SPADOS
SOUNDMEN	SOUTENEURS	SOWARREES	SOYLE	SPADROON
SOUNDNESS	SOUTER	SOWARRIES	SOYLES	SPADROONS
SOUNDNESSES	SOUTERLY	SOWARRY	SOYS	SPAE
SOUNDS	SOUTERS	SOWARS	SOZZLE	SPAED

The Chambers Dictionary is the authority for many longer words; see *OSW* Introduction, page xii

SPAEING	SPAMMY	SPARD	SPARSE	SPAVIES
SPAEMAN	SPAMS	SPARE	SPARSEDLY	SPAVIN
SPAEMEN	SPAN	SPARED	SPARSELY	SPAVINED
SPAER	SPANAEMIA	SPARELESS	SPARSER	SPAVINS
SPAERS	SPANAEMIAS	SPARELY	SPARSEST	SPAW
SPAES	SPANAEMIC	SPARENESS	SPARSITIES	SPAWL
SPAEWIFE	SPANCEL	SPARENESSES	SPARSITY	SPAWLED
SPAEWIVES	SPANCELLED	SPARER	SPART	SPAWLING
SPAG	SPANCELLING	SPARERS	SPARTAN	SPAWLS
SPAGERIC	SPANCELS	SPARES	SPARTANS	SPAWN
SPAGERICS	SPANDEX	SPAREST	SPARTEINE	SPAWNED
SPAGERIST	SPANDEXES	SPARGE	SPARTEINES	SPAWNER
SPAGERISTS	SPANDREL	SPARGED	SPARTERIE	SPAWNERS
SPAGHETTI	SPANDRELS	SPARGER	SPARTERIES	SPAWNIER
SPAGHETTIS	SPANDRIL	SPARGERS	SPARTH	SPAWNIEST
SPAGIRIC	SPANDRILS	SPARGES	SPARTHE	SPAWNING
SPAGIRICS	SPANE	SPARGING	SPARTHES	SPAWNINGS
SPAGIRIST	SPANED	SPARID	SPARTHS	SPAWNS
SPAGIRISTS	SPANES	SPARIDS	SPARTS	SPAWNY
SPAGS	SPANG	SPARING	SPAS	SPAWS
SPAGYRIC	SPANGED	SPARINGLY	SPASM	SPAY
SPAGYRICS	SPANGHEW	SPARK	SPASMATIC	SPAYAD
SPAGYRIST	SPANGHEWED	SPARKE	SPASMED	SPAYADS
SPAGYRISTS	SPANGHEWING	SPARKED	SPASMIC	SPAYD
SPAHEE	SPANGHEWS	SPARKES	SPASMING	SPAYDS
SPAHEES	SPANGING	SPARKIE	SPASMODIC	SPAYED
SPAHI	SPANGLE	SPARKIER	SPASMS	SPAYING
SPAHIS	SPANGLED	SPARKIES	SPASTIC	SPAYS
SPAIN	SPANGLER	SPARKIEST	SPASTICS	SPAZZ
SPAINED	SPANGLERS	SPARKING	SPAT	SPAZZED
SPAING	SPANGLES	SPARKISH	SPATE	SPAZZES
SPAINGS	SPANGLET	SPARKLE	SPATES	SPAZZING
SPAINING	SPANGLETS	SPARKLED	SPATFALL	SPEAK
SPAINS	SPANGLIER	SPARKLER	SPATFALLS	SPEAKABLE
SPAIRGE	SPANGLIEST	SPARKLERS	SPATHE	SPEAKEASIES
SPAIRGED	SPANGLING	SPARKLES	SPATHED	SPEAKEASY
SPAIRGES	SPANGLINGS	SPARKLESS	SPATHES	SPEAKER
SPAIRGING	SPANGLY	SPARKLET	SPATHIC	SPEAKERS
SPAKE	SPANGS	SPARKLETS	SPATHOSE	SPEAKING
SPALD	SPANIEL	SPARKLIER	SPATIAL	SPEAKINGS
SPALDS	SPANIELLED	SPARKLIES	SPATIALLY	SPEAKOUT
SPALE	SPANIELLING	SPARKLIEST	SPATLESE	SPEAKOUTS
SPALES	SPANIELS	SPARKLING	SPATLESEN	SPEAKS
SPALL	SPANING	SPARKLINGS	SPATLESES	SPEAL
SPALLE	SPANK	SPARKLY	SPATS	SPEALS
SPALLED	SPANKED	SPARKS	SPATTED	SPEAN
SPALLES	SPANKER	SPARKY	SPATTEE	SPEANED
SPALLING	SPANKERS	SPARLING	SPATTEES	SPEANING
SPALLINGS	SPANKING	SPARLINGS	SPATTER	SPEANS
SPALLS	SPANKINGS	SPAROID	SPATTERED	SPEAR
SPALPEEN	SPANKS	SPAROIDS	SPATTERING	SPEARED
SPALPEENS	SPANLESS	SPARRE	SPATTERS	SPEARFISH
SPALT	SPANNED	SPARRED	SPATTING	SPEARFISHES
SPALTED	SPANNER	SPARRER	SPATULA	SPEARHEAD
SPALTING	SPANNERS	SPARRERS	SPATULAR	SPEARHEADED
SPALTS	SPANNING	SPARRES	SPATULAS	SPEARHEADING
SPAM	SPANS	SPARRIER	SPATULATE	SPEARHEADS
SPAMMED	SPANSULE	SPARRIEST	SPATULE	SPEARIER
SPAMMER	SPANSULES	SPARRING	SPATULES	SPEARIEST
SPAMMERS	SPAR	SPARRINGS	SPAUL	SPEARING
SPAMMIER	SPARABLE	SPARROW	SPAULD	SPEARMAN
SPAMMIEST	SPARABLES	SPARROWS	SPAULDS	SPEARMEN
SPAMMING	SPARAXIS	SPARRY	SPAULS	SPEARMINT
SPAMMINGS	SPARAXISES	SPARS	SPAVIE	SPEARMINTS

The Chambers Dictionary is the authority for many longer words; see *OSW* Introduction, page xii

SPEARS	SPED	SPELDIN	SPERMS	SPHERIEST
SPEARWORT	SPEECH	SPELDING	SPERRE	SPHERING
SPEARWORTS	SPEECHED	SPELDINGS	SPERRED	SPHEROID
SPEARY	SPEECHES	SPELDINS	SPERRES	SPHEROIDS
SPEAT	SPEECHFUL	SPELDRIN	SPERRING	SPHERULAR
SPEATS	SPEECHIFIED	SPELDRING	SPERSE	SPHERULE
SPEC	SPEECHIFIES	SPELDRINGS	SPERSED	SPHERULES
SPECCIES	SPEECHIFY	SPELDRINS	SPERSES	SPHERY
SPECCY	SPEECHIFYING	SPELDS	SPERSING	SPHINCTER
SPECIAL	SPEECHING	SPELEAN	SPERST	SPHINCTERS
SPECIALLY	SPEED	SPELK	SPERTHE	SPHINGES
SPECIALS	SPEEDBALL	SPELKS	SPERTHES	SPHINGID
SPECIALTIES	SPEEDBALLS	SPELL	SPET	SPHINGIDS
SPECIALTY	SPEEDBOAT	SPELLABLE	SPETCH	SPHINX
SPECIATE	SPEEDBOATS	SPELLBIND	SPETCHES	SPHINXES
SPECIATED	SPEEDED	SPELLBINDING	SPETS	SPHYGMIC
SPECIATES	SPEEDER	SPELLBINDS	SPETSNAZ	SPHYGMOID
SPECIATING	SPEEDERS	SPELLBOUND	SPETSNAZES	SPHYGMUS
SPECIE	SPEEDFUL	SPELLDOWN	SPETTING	SPHYGMUSES
SPECIES	SPEEDIER	SPELLDOWNS	SPETZNAZ	SPIAL
SPECIFIC	SPEEDIEST	SPELLED	SPETZNAZES	SPIALS
SPECIFICS	SPEEDILY	SPELLER	SPEW	SPIC
SPECIFIED	SPEEDING	SPELLERS	SPEWED	SPICA
SPECIFIES	SPEEDINGS	SPELLFUL	SPEWER	SPICAE
SPECIFY	SPEEDLESS	SPELLICAN	SPEWERS	SPICAS
SPECIFYING	SPEEDO	SPELLICANS	SPEWIER	SPICATE
SPECIMEN	SPEEDOS	SPELLING	SPEWIEST	SPICATED
SPECIMENS	SPEEDS	SPELLINGS	SPEWINESS	SPICCATO
SPECIOUS	SPEEDSTER	SPELLS	SPEWINESSES	SPICCATOS
SPECK	SPEEDSTERS	SPELT	SPEWING	SPICE
SPECKED	SPEEDWAY	SPELTER	SPEWS	SPICEBUSH
SPECKIER	SPEEDWAYS	SPELTERS	SPEWY	SPICEBUSHES
SPECKIEST	SPEEDWELL	SPELTS	SPHACELUS	SPICED
SPECKING	SPEEDWELLS	SPELUNKER	SPHACELUSES	SPICER
SPECKLE	SPEEDY	SPELUNKERS	SPHAER	SPICERIES
SPECKLED	SPEEL	SPENCE	SPHAERE	SPICERS
SPECKLES	SPEELED	SPENCER	SPHAERES	SPICERY
SPECKLESS	SPEELER	SPENCERS	SPHAERITE	SPICES
SPECKLING	SPEELERS	SPENCES	SPHAERITES	SPICIER
SPECKS	SPEELING	SPEND	SPHAERS	SPICIEST
SPECKY	SPEELS	SPENDABLE	SPHAGNOUS	SPICILEGE
SPECS	SPEER	SPENDALL	SPHAGNUM	SPICILEGES
SPECTACLE	SPEERED	SPENDALLS	SPHAGNUMS	SPICILY
SPECTACLES	SPEERING	SPENDER	SPHEAR	SPICINESS
SPECTATE	SPEERINGS	SPENDERS	SPHEARE	SPICINESSES
SPECTATED	SPEERS	SPENDING	SPHEARES	SPICING
SPECTATES	SPEIR	SPENDINGS	SPHEARS	SPICK
SPECTATING	SPEIRED	SPENDS	SPHENDONE	SPICKER
SPECTATOR	SPEIRING	SPENT	SPHENDONES	SPICKEST
SPECTATORS	SPEIRINGS	SPEOS	SPHENE	SPICKNEL
SPECTER	SPEIRS	SPEOSES	SPHENES	SPICKNELS
SPECTERS	SPEISS	SPERLING	SPHENIC	SPICKS
SPECTRA	SPEISSES	SPERLINGS	SPHENODON	SPICS
SPECTRAL	SPEK	SPERM	SPHENODONS	SPICULA
SPECTRE	SPEKBOOM	SPERMARIA	SPHENOID	SPICULAE
SPECTRES	SPEKBOOMS	SPERMARIES	SPHENOIDS	SPICULAR
SPECTRUM	SPEKS	SPERMARY	SPHERAL	SPICULATE
SPECULA	SPELAEAN	SPERMATIA	SPHERE	SPICULE
SPECULAR	SPELD	SPERMATIC	SPHERED	SPICULES
SPECULATE	SPELDED	SPERMATICS	SPHERES	SPICULUM
SPECULATED	SPELDER	SPERMATID	SPHERIC	SPICY
SPECULATES	SPELDERED	SPERMATIDS	SPHERICAL	SPIDE
SPECULATING	SPELDERING	SPERMIC	SPHERICS	SPIDER
SPECULUM	SPELDERS	SPERMOUS	SPHERIER	SPIDERIER

The Chambers Dictionary is the authority for many longer words; see *OSW* Introduction, page xii

SPIDERIEST	SPILLIKINS	SPINNET	SPIRILLA	SPIVVERIES
SPIDERMAN	SPILLING	SPINNETS	SPIRILLAR	SPIVVERY
SPIDERMEN	SPILLINGS	SPINNEY	SPIRILLUM	SPIVVIER
SPIDERS	SPILLOVER	SPINNEYS	SPIRING	SPIVVIEST
SPIDERY	SPILLOVERS	SPINNIES	SPIRIT	SPIVVY
SPIE	SPILLS	SPINNING	SPIRITED	SPLASH
SPIED	SPILLWAY	SPINNINGS	SPIRITFUL	SPLASHED
SPIEL	SPILLWAYS	SPINNY	SPIRITING	SPLASHER
SPIELED	SPILOSITE	SPINODE	SPIRITINGS	SPLASHERS
SPIELER	SPILOSITES	SPINODES	SPIRITISM	SPLASHES
SPIELERS	SPILT	SPINOSE	SPIRITISMS	SPLASHIER
SPIELING	SPILTH	SPINOSITIES	SPIRITIST	SPLASHIEST
SPIELS	SPILTHS	SPINOSITY	SPIRITISTS	SPLASHILY
SPIES	SPIN	SPINOUS	SPIRITOSO	SPLASHING
SPIFF	SPINA	SPINOUT	SPIRITOUS	SPLASHINGS
SPIFFIER	SPINACENE	SPINOUTS	SPIRITS	SPLASHY
SPIFFIEST	SPINACENES	SPINS	SPIRITUAL	SPLAT
SPIFFING	SPINACH	SPINSTER	SPIRITUALS	SPLATCH
SPIFFY	SPINACHES	SPINSTERS	SPIRITUEL	SPLATCHED
SPIGHT	SPINAE	SPINTEXT	SPIRITUS	SPLATCHES
SPIGHTED	SPINAGE	SPINTEXTS	SPIRITUSES	SPLATCHING
SPIGHTING	SPINAGES	SPINTO	SPIRITY	SPLATS
SPIGHTS	SPINAL	SPINULATE	SPIRLING	SPLATTED
SPIGNEL	SPINAR	SPINULE	SPIRLINGS	SPLATTER
SPIGNELS	SPINARS	SPINULES	SPIROGRAM	SPLATTERED
SPIGOT	SPINAS	SPINULOSE	SPIROGRAMS	SPLATTERING
SPIGOTS	SPINATE	SPINULOUS	SPIROGYRA	SPLATTERS
SPIK	SPINDLE	SPINY	SPIROGYRAS	SPLATTING
SPIKE	SPINDLED	SPIRACLE	SPIROID	SPLATTINGS
SPIKED	SPINDLES	SPIRACLES	SPIRT	SPLAY
SPIKEFISH	SPINDLIER	SPIRACULA	SPIRTED	SPLAYED
SPIKEFISHES	SPINDLIEST	SPIRAEA	SPIRTING	SPLAYING
SPIKELET	SPINDLING	SPIRAEAS	SPIRTLE	SPLAYS
SPIKELETS	SPINDLINGS	SPIRAL	SPIRTLES	SPLEEN
SPIKENARD	SPINDLY	SPIRALISM	SPIRTS	SPLEENFUL
SPIKENARDS	SPINDRIFT	SPIRALISMS	SPIRY	SPLEENISH
SPIKERIES	SPINDRIFTS	SPIRALIST	SPIT	SPLEENS
SPIKERY	SPINE	SPIRALISTS	SPITAL	SPLEENY
SPIKES	SPINED	SPIRALITIES	SPITALS	SPLENDENT
SPIKIER	SPINEL	SPIRALITY	SPITCHER	SPLENDID
SPIKIEST	SPINELESS	SPIRALLED	SPITE	SPLENDIDER
SPIKILY	SPINELS	SPIRALLING	SPITED	SPLENDIDEST
SPIKINESS	SPINES	SPIRALLY	SPITEFUL	SPLENDOR
SPIKINESSES	SPINET	SPIRALS	SPITEFULLER	SPLENDORS
SPIKING	SPINETS	SPIRANT	SPITEFULLEST	SPLENDOUR
SPIKS	SPINETTE	SPIRANTS	SPITES	SPLENDOURS
SPIKY	SPINETTES	SPIRASTER	SPITFIRE	SPLENETIC
SPILE	SPINIER	SPIRASTERS	SPITFIRES	SPLENETICS
SPILED	SPINIEST	SPIRATED	SPITING	SPLENIA
SPILES	SPINIFEX	SPIRATION	SPITS	SPLENIAL
SPILIKIN	SPINIFEXES	SPIRATIONS	SPITTED	SPLENIC
SPILIKINS	SPINIFORM	SPIRE	SPITTEN	SPLENII
SPILING	SPININESS	SPIREA	SPITTER	SPLENITIS
SPILINGS	SPININESSES	SPIREAS	SPITTERS	SPLENITISES
SPILITE	SPINK	SPIRED	SPITTING	SPLENIUM
SPILITES	SPINKS	SPIRELESS	SPITTINGS	SPLENIUMS
SPILITIC	SPINNAKER	SPIREME	SPITTLE	SPLENIUS
SPILL	SPINNAKERS	SPIREMES	SPITTLES	SPLENIUSES
SPILLAGE	SPINNER	SPIRES	SPITTOON	SPLENT
SPILLAGES	SPINNERET	SPIREWISE	SPITTOONS	SPLENTS
SPILLED	SPINNERETS	SPIRIC	SPITZ	SPLEUCHAN
SPILLER	SPINNERIES	SPIRICS	SPITZES	SPLEUCHANS
SPILLERS	SPINNERS	SPIRIER	SPIV	SPLICE
SPILLIKIN	SPINNERY	SPIRIEST	SPIVS	SPLICED

SPLICER	SPODIUMS	SPONSIONS	SPOORING	SPOTTER
SPLICERS	SPODOGRAM	SPONSON	SPOORS	SPOTTERS
SPLICES	SPODOGRAMS	SPONSONS	SPOOT	SPOTTIER
SPLICING	SPODUMENE	SPONSOR	SPOOTS	SPOTTIEST
SPLIFF	SPODUMENES	SPONSORED	SPORADIC	SPOTTILY
SPLIFFS	SPOFFISH	SPONSORING	SPORANGIA	SPOTTING
SPLINE	SPOFFY	SPONSORS	SPORE	SPOTTINGS
SPLINED	SPOIL	SPONTOON	SPORES	SPOTTY
SPLINES	SPOILAGE	SPONTOONS	SPORIDESM	SPOUSAGE
SPLINING	SPOILAGES	SPOOF	SPORIDESMS	SPOUSAGES
SPLINT	SPOILED	SPOOFED	SPORIDIA	SPOUSAL
SPLINTED	SPOILER	SPOOFER	SPORIDIAL	SPOUSALS
SPLINTER	SPOILERS	SPOOFERIES	SPORIDIUM	SPOUSE
SPLINTERED	SPOILFIVE	SPOOFERS	SPOROCARP	SPOUSED
SPLINTERIER	SPOILFIVES	SPOOFERY	SPOROCARPS	SPOUSES
SPLINTERIEST	SPOILFUL	SPOOFING	SPOROCYST	SPOUSING
SPLINTERING	SPOILING	SPOOFS	SPOROCYSTS	SPOUT
SPLINTERS	SPOILS	SPOOK	SPOROGENIES	SPOUTED
SPLINTERY	SPOILSMAN	SPOOKED	SPOROGENY	SPOUTER
SPLINTING	SPOILSMEN	SPOOKERIES	SPOROPHYL	SPOUTERS
SPLINTS	SPOILT	SPOOKERY	SPOROPHYLS	SPOUTIER
SPLIT	SPOKE	SPOOKIER	SPOROZOAN	SPOUTIEST
SPLITS	SPOKED	SPOOKIEST	SPOROZOANS	SPOUTING
SPLITTED	SPOKEN	SPOOKILY	SPORRAN	SPOUTINGS
SPLITTER	SPOKES	SPOOKING	SPORRANS	SPOUTLESS
SPLITTERS	SPOKESMAN	SPOOKISH	SPORT	SPOUTS
SPLITTING	SPOKESMEN	SPOOKS	SPORTABLE	SPOUTY
SPLODGE	SPOKEWISE	SPOOKY	SPORTANCE	SPRACK
SPLODGED	SPOLIATE	SPOOL	SPORTANCES	SPRACKLE
SPLODGES	SPOLIATED	SPOOLED	SPORTED	SPRACKLED
SPLODGIER	SPOLIATES	SPOOLER	SPORTER	SPRACKLES
SPLODGIEST	SPOLIATING	SPOOLERS	SPORTERS	SPRACKLING
SPLODGILY	SPOLIATOR	SPOOLING	SPORTFUL	SPRAD
SPLODGING	SPOLIATORS	SPOOLS	SPORTIER	SPRAG
SPLODGY	SPONDAIC	SPOOM	SPORTIEST	SPRAGGED
SPLORE	SPONDEE	SPOOMED	SPORTILY	SPRAGGING
SPLORES	SPONDEES	SPOOMING	SPORTING	SPRAGS
SPLOSH	SPONDULIX	SPOOMS	SPORTIVE	SPRAICKLE
SPLOSHED	SPONDYL	SPOON	SPORTLESS	SPRAICKLED
SPLOSHES	SPONDYLS	SPOONBAIT	SPORTS	SPRAICKLES
SPLOSHING	SPONGE	SPOONBAITS	SPORTSMAN	SPRAICKLING
SPLOTCH	SPONGEBAG	SPOONBILL	SPORTSMEN	SPRAID
SPLOTCHED	SPONGEBAGS	SPOONBILLS	SPORTY	SPRAIN
SPLOTCHES	SPONGED	SPOONED	SPORULAR	SPRAINED
SPLOTCHIER	SPONGEOUS	SPOONEY	SPORULATE	SPRAINING
SPLOTCHIEST	SPONGER	SPOONEYS	SPORULATED	SPRAINS
SPLOTCHING	SPONGERS	SPOONFED	SPORULATES	SPRAINT
SPLOTCHY	SPONGES	SPOONFUL	SPORULATING	SPRAINTS
SPLURGE	SPONGIER	SPOONFULS	SPORULE	SPRANG
SPLURGED	SPONGIEST	SPOONHOOK	SPORULES	SPRANGLE
SPLURGES	SPONGILY	SPOONHOOKS	SPOSH	SPRANGLED
SPLURGIER	SPONGIN	SPOONIER	SPOSHES	SPRANGLES
SPLURGIEST	SPONGING	SPOONIES	SPOSHIER	SPRANGLING
SPLURGING	SPONGINS	SPOONIEST	SPOSHIEST	SPRAT
SPLURGY	SPONGIOSE	SPOONILY	SPOSHY	SPRATS
SPLUTTER	SPONGIOUS	SPOONING	SPOT	SPRATTLE
SPLUTTERED	SPONGOID	SPOONS	SPOTLESS	SPRATTLED
SPLUTTERING	SPONGY	SPOONWAYS	SPOTLIGHT	SPRATTLES
SPLUTTERINGS	SPONSAL	SPOONWISE	SPOTLIGHTED	SPRATTLING
SPLUTTERS	SPONSALIA	SPOONY	SPOTLIGHTING	SPRAUCHLE
SPLUTTERY	SPONSIBLE	SPOOR	SPOTLIGHTS	SPRAUCHLED
SPODE	SPONSING	SPOORED	SPOTLIT	SPRAUCHLES
SPODES	SPONSINGS	SPOORER	SPOTS	SPRAUCHLING
SPODIUM	SPONSION	SPOORERS	SPOTTED	SPRAUNCIER

SPRAUNCIEST
SPRAUNCY
SPRAWL
SPRAWLED
SPRAWLER
SPRAWLERS
SPRAWLIER
SPRAWLIEST
SPRAWLING
SPRAWLS
SPRAWLY
SPRAY
SPRAYED
SPRAYER
SPRAYERS
SPRAYEY
SPRAYIER
SPRAYIEST
SPRAYING
SPRAYS
SPREAD
SPREADER
SPREADERS
SPREADING
SPREADINGS
SPREADS
SPREAGH
SPREAGHS
SPREATHE
SPREATHED
SPREATHES
SPREATHING
SPREAZE
SPREAZED
SPREAZES
SPREAZING
SPRECHERIES
SPRECHERY
SPRECKLED
SPRED
SPREDD
SPREDDE
SPREDDEN
SPREDDES
SPREDDING
SPREDDS
SPREDS
SPREE
SPREED
SPREEING
SPREES
SPREETHE
SPREETHED
SPREETHES
SPREETHING
SPREEZE
SPREEZED
SPREEZES
SPREEZING
SPRENT
SPREW
SPREWS
SPRIG
SPRIGGED

SPRIGGIER
SPRIGGIEST
SPRIGGING
SPRIGGY
SPRIGHT
SPRIGHTED
SPRIGHTING
SPRIGHTLIER
SPRIGHTLIEST
SPRIGHTLY
SPRIGHTS
SPRIGS
SPRING
SPRINGAL
SPRINGALD
SPRINGALDS
SPRINGALS
SPRINGBOK
SPRINGBOKS
SPRINGE
SPRINGED
SPRINGER
SPRINGERS
SPRINGES
SPRINGIER
SPRINGIEST
SPRINGILY
SPRINGING
SPRINGINGS
SPRINGLE
SPRINGLES
SPRINGLET
SPRINGLETS
SPRINGS
SPRINGY
SPRINKLE
SPRINKLED
SPRINKLER
SPRINKLERS
SPRINKLES
SPRINKLING
SPRINKLINGS
SPRINT
SPRINTED
SPRINTER
SPRINTERS
SPRINTING
SPRINTINGS
SPRINTS
SPRIT
SPRITE
SPRITEFUL
SPRITELIER
SPRITELIEST
SPRITELY
SPRITES
SPRITS
SPRITSAIL
SPRITSAILS
SPRITZ
SPRITZED
SPRITZER
SPRITZERS
SPRITZES

SPRITZIG
SPRITZIGS
SPRITZING
SPROCKET
SPROCKETS
SPROD
SPRODS
SPROG
SPROGS
SPRONG
SPROUT
SPROUTED
SPROUTING
SPROUTINGS
SPROUTS
SPRUCE
SPRUCED
SPRUCELY
SPRUCER
SPRUCES
SPRUCEST
SPRUCING
SPRUE
SPRUES
SPRUG
SPRUGS
SPRUIK
SPRUIKED
SPRUIKER
SPRUIKERS
SPRUIKING
SPRUIKS
SPRUIT
SPRUITS
SPRUSH
SPRUSHED
SPRUSHES
SPRUSHING
SPRY
SPRYER
SPRYEST
SPRYLY
SPRYNESS
SPRYNESSES
SPUD
SPUDDED
SPUDDIER
SPUDDIEST
SPUDDING
SPUDDINGS
SPUDDY
SPUDS
SPUE
SPUED
SPUEING
SPUES
SPUILZIE
SPUILZIED
SPUILZIEING
SPUILZIES
SPUING
SPULE

SPULEBANES
SPULEBONE
SPULEBONES
SPULES
SPULYE
SPULYED
SPULYEING
SPULYES
SPULYIE
SPULYIED
SPULYIEING
SPULYIES
SPULZIE
SPULZIED
SPULZIEING
SPULZIES
SPUMANTE
SPUMANTES
SPUME
SPUMED
SPUMES
SPUMIER
SPUMIEST
SPUMING
SPUMOUS
SPUMY
SPUN
SPUNGE
SPUNGES
SPUNK
SPUNKED
SPUNKIE
SPUNKIER
SPUNKIES
SPUNKIEST
SPUNKING
SPUNKS
SPUNKY
SPUNYARN
SPUNYARNS
SPUR
SPURGE
SPURGES
SPURIAE
SPURIOUS
SPURLESS
SPURLING
SPURLINGS
SPURN
SPURNE
SPURNED
SPURNER
SPURNERS
SPURNES
SPURNING
SPURNINGS
SPURNS
SPURRED
SPURRER
SPURRERS
SPURREY
SPURREYS
SPURRIER
SPURRIERS

SPURRIES
SPURRIEST
SPURRING
SPURRINGS
SPURRY
SPURS
SPURT
SPURTED
SPURTING
SPURTLE
SPURTLES
SPURTS
SPURWAY
SPURWAYS
SPUTA
SPUTNIK
SPUTNIKS
SPUTTER
SPUTTERED
SPUTTERER
SPUTTERERS
SPUTTERING
SPUTTERINGS
SPUTTERS
SPUTTERY
SPUTUM
SPY
SPYAL
SPYALS
SPYGLASS
SPYGLASSES
SPYHOLE
SPYHOLES
SPYING
SPYINGS
SPYMASTER
SPYMASTERS
SPYPLANE
SPYPLANES
SPYRE
SPYRES
SQUAB
SQUABASH
SQUABASHED
SQUABASHES
SQUABASHING
SQUABBED
SQUABBER
SQUABBEST
SQUABBIER
SQUABBIEST
SQUABBING
SQUABBISH
SQUABBLE
SQUABBLED
SQUABBLER
SQUABBLERS
SQUABBLES
SQUABBLING
SQUABBY
SQUABS
SQUACCO
SQUACCOS
SQUAD

SQUADDIE	SQUARIALS	SQUEALER	SQUIGGLIER	SQUIRRELY
SQUADDIES	SQUARING	SQUEALERS	SQUIGGLIEST	SQUIRRING
SQUADDY	SQUARINGS	SQUEALING	SQUIGGLING	SQUIRRS
SQUADRON	SQUARISH	SQUEALINGS	SQUIGGLY	SQUIRT
SQUADRONE	SQUARROSE	SQUEALS	SQUILGEE	SQUIRTED
SQUADRONED	SQUARSON	SQUEAMISH	SQUILGEED	SQUIRTER
SQUADRONES	SQUARSONS	SQUEEGEE	SQUILGEEING	SQUIRTERS
SQUADRONING	SQUASH	SQUEEGEED	SQUILGEES	SQUIRTING
SQUADRONS	SQUASHED	SQUEEGEEING	SQUILL	SQUIRTINGS
SQUADS	SQUASHER	SQUEEGEES	SQUILLA	SQUIRTS
SQUAIL	SQUASHERS	SQUEEZE	SQUILLAS	SQUISH
SQUAILED	SQUASHES	SQUEEZED	SQUILLS	SQUISHED
SQUAILER	SQUASHIER	SQUEEZER	SQUINANCIES	SQUISHES
SQUAILERS	SQUASHIEST	SQUEEZERS	SQUINANCY	SQUISHIER
SQUAILING	SQUASHILY	SQUEEZES	SQUINCH	SQUISHIEST
SQUAILINGS	SQUASHING	SQUEEZIER	SQUINCHES	SQUISHING
SQUAILS	SQUASHY	SQUEEZIEST	SQUINIED	SQUISHY
SQUALENE	SQUAT	SQUEEZING	SQUINIES	SQUIT
SQUALENES	SQUATNESS	SQUEEZINGS	SQUINNIED	SQUITCH
SQUALID	SQUATNESSES	SQUEEZY	SQUINNIES	SQUITCHES
SQUALIDER	SQUATS	SQUEG	SQUINNY	SQUITS
SQUALIDEST	SQUATTED	SQUEGGED	SQUINNYING	SQUIZ
SQUALIDLY	SQUATTER	SQUEGGER	SQUINT	SQUIZZES
SQUALL	SQUATTERED	SQUEGGERS	SQUINTED	SRADDHA
SQUALLED	SQUATTERING	SQUEGGING	SQUINTER	SRADDHAS
SQUALLER	SQUATTERS	SQUEGGINGS	SQUINTERS	ST
SQUALLERS	SQUATTEST	SQUEGS	SQUINTEST	STAB
SQUALLIER	SQUATTIER	SQUELCH	SQUINTING	STABBED
SQUALLIEST	SQUATTIEST	SQUELCHED	SQUINTINGS	STABBER
SQUALLING	SQUATTING	SQUELCHER	SQUINTS	STABBERS
SQUALLINGS	SQUATTLE	SQUELCHERS	SQUINY	STABBING
SQUALLS	SQUATTLED	SQUELCHES	SQUINYING	STABBINGS
SQUALLY	SQUATTLES	SQUELCHIER	SQUIRAGE	STABILATE
SQUALOID	SQUATTLING	SQUELCHIEST	SQUIRAGES	STABILATES
SQUALOR	SQUATTY	SQUELCHING	SQUIRALTIES	STABILE
SQUALORS	SQUAW	SQUELCHINGS	SQUIRALTY	STABILES
SQUAMA	SQUAWK	SQUELCHY	SQUIRARCH	STABILISE
SQUAMAE	SQUAWKED	SQUIB	SQUIRARCHS	STABILISED
SQUAMATE	SQUAWKER	SQUIBBED	SQUIRE	STABILISES
SQUAME	SQUAWKERS	SQUIBBING	SQUIREAGE	STABILISING
SQUAMELLA	SQUAWKIER	SQUIBBINGS	SQUIREAGES	STABILITIES
SQUAMELLAS	SQUAWKIEST	SQUIBS	SQUIRED	STABILITY
SQUAMES	SQUAWKING	SQUID	SQUIREDOM	STABILIZE
SQUAMOSAL	SQUAWKINGS	SQUIDDED	SQUIREDOMS	STABILIZED
SQUAMOSALS	SQUAWKS	SQUIDDING	SQUIREEN	STABILIZES
SQUAMOSE	SQUAWKY	SQUIDGE	SQUIREENS	STABILIZING
SQUAMOUS	SQUAWMAN	SQUIDGED	SQUIRELY	STABLE
SQUAMULA	SQUAWMEN	SQUIDGES	SQUIRES	STABLEBOY
SQUAMULAS	SQUAWS	SQUIDGIER	SQUIRESS	STABLEBOYS
SQUAMULE	SQUEAK	SQUIDGIEST	SQUIRESSES	STABLED
SQUAMULES	SQUEAKED	SQUIDGING	SQUIRING	STABLEMAN
SQUANDER	SQUEAKER	SQUIDGY	SQUIRM	STABLEMEN
SQUANDERED	SQUEAKERIES	SQUIDS	SQUIRMED	STABLER
SQUANDERING	SQUEAKERS	SQUIER	SQUIRMIER	STABLERS
SQUANDERINGS	SQUEAKERY	SQUIERS	SQUIRMIEST	STABLES
SQUANDERS	SQUEAKIER	SQUIFF	SQUIRMING	STABLEST
SQUARE	SQUEAKIEST	SQUIFFER	SQUIRMS	STABLING
SQUARED	SQUEAKILY	SQUIFFERS	SQUIRMY	STABLINGS
SQUARELY	SQUEAKING	SQUIFFIER	SQUIRR	STABLISH
SQUARER	SQUEAKINGS	SQUIFFIEST	SQUIRRED	STABLISHED
SQUARERS	SQUEAKS	SQUIFFY	SQUIRREL	STABLISHES
SQUARES	SQUEAKY	SQUIGGLE	SQUIRRELLED	STABLISHING
SQUAREST	SQUEAL	SQUIGGLED	SQUIRRELLING	STABLY
SQUARIAL	SQUEALED	SQUIGGLES	SQUIRRELS	STABS

STACCATO	STAGIEST	STALED	STAMP	STANHOPE
STACCATOS	STAGILY	STALELY	STAMPED	STANHOPES
STACHYS	STAGINESS	STALEMATE	STAMPEDE	STANIEL
STACHYSES	STAGINESSES	STALEMATED	STAMPEDED	STANIELS
STACK	STAGING	STALEMATES	STAMPEDES	STANING
STACKED	STAGINGS	STALEMATING	STAMPEDING	STANK
STACKER	STAGNANCIES	STALENESS	STAMPEDO	STANKS
STACKERS	STAGNANCY	STALENESSES	STAMPEDOED	STANNARIES
STACKET	STAGNANT	STALER	STAMPEDOING	STANNARY
STACKETS	STAGNATE	STALES	STAMPEDOS	STANNATE
STACKING	STAGNATED	STALEST	STAMPER	STANNATES
STACKINGS	STAGNATES	STALING	STAMPERS	STANNATOR
STACKROOM	STAGNATING	STALK	STAMPING	STANNATORS
STACKROOMS	STAGS	STALKED	STAMPINGS	STANNEL
STACKS	STAGY	STALKER	STAMPS	STANNELS
STACKYARD	STAID	STALKERS	STANCE	STANNIC
STACKYARDS	STAIDER	STALKIER	STANCES	STANNITE
STACTE	STAIDEST	STALKIEST	STANCH	STANNITES
STACTES	STAIDLY	STALKING	STANCHED	STANNOUS
STADDA	STAIDNESS	STALKINGS	STANCHEL	STANYEL
STADDAS	STAIDNESSES	STALKLESS	STANCHELLED	STANYELS
STADDLE	STAIG	STALKO	STANCHELLING	STANZA
STADDLES	STAIGS	STALKOES	STANCHELS	STANZAIC
STADE	STAIN	STALKS	STANCHER	STANZAS
STADES	STAINED	STALKY	STANCHERED	STANZE
STADIA	STAINER	STALL	STANCHERING	STANZES
STADIAL	STAINERS	STALLAGE	STANCHERS	STANZO
STADIALS	STAINING	STALLAGES	STANCHES	STANZOES
STADIAS	STAININGS	STALLED	STANCHEST	STANZOS
STADIUM	STAINLESS	STALLING	STANCHING	STAP
STADIUMS	STAINS	STALLINGS	STANCHINGS	STAPEDES
STAFF	STAIR	STALLION	STANCHION	STAPEDIAL
STAFFAGE	STAIRCASE	STALLIONS	STANCHIONED	STAPEDII
STAFFAGES	STAIRCASED	STALLMAN	STANCHIONING	STAPEDIUS
STAFFED	STAIRCASES	STALLMEN	STANCHIONS	STAPEDIUSES
STAFFER	STAIRCASING	STALLS	STANCHLY	STAPELIA
STAFFERS	STAIRCASINGS	STALWART	STANCK	STAPELIAS
STAFFING	STAIRED	STALWARTS	STAND	STAPES
STAFFROOM	STAIRFOOT	STALWORTH	STANDARD	STAPH
STAFFROOMS	STAIRFOOTS	STALWORTHS	STANDARDS	STAPHS
STAFFS	STAIRHEAD	STAMEN	STANDEE	STAPLE
STAG	STAIRHEADS	STAMENED	STANDEES	STAPLED
STAGE	STAIRLIFT	STAMENS	STANDEN	STAPLER
STAGED	STAIRLIFTS	STAMINA	STANDER	STAPLERS
STAGER	STAIRS	STAMINAL	STANDERS	STAPLES
STAGERIES	STAIRWAY	STAMINAS	STANDGALE	STAPLING
STAGERS	STAIRWAYS	STAMINATE	STANDGALES	STAPPED
STAGERY	STAIRWELL	STAMINEAL	STANDING	STAPPING
STAGES	STAIRWELLS	STAMINODE	STANDINGS	STAPPLE
STAGEY	STAIRWISE	STAMINODES	STANDISH	STAPPLES
STAGGARD	STAIRWORK	STAMINODIES	STANDISHES	STAPS
STAGGARDS	STAIRWORKS	STAMINODY	STANDOFF	STAR
STAGGED	STAITH	STAMINOID	STANDOUT	STARAGEN
STAGGER	STAITHE	STAMMEL	STANDOUTS	STARAGENS
STAGGERED	STAITHES	STAMMELS	STANDPIPE	STARBOARD
STAGGERER	STAITHS	STAMMER	STANDPIPES	STARBOARDED
STAGGERERS	STAKE	STAMMERED	STANDS	STARBOARDING
STAGGERING	STAKED	STAMMERER	STANE	STARBOARDS
STAGGERINGS	STAKES	STAMMERERS	STANED	STARCH
STAGGERS	STAKING	STAMMERING	STANES	STARCHED
STAGGING	STALACTIC	STAMMERINGS	STANG	STARCHER
STAGHOUND	STALAG	STAMMERS	STANGED	STARCHERS
STAGHOUNDS	STALAGS	STAMNOI	STANGING	STARCHES
STAGIER	STALE	STAMNOS	STANGS	STARCHIER

STARCHIEST	STARRING	STATEMENTINGS	STAVE	STEAMBOATS
STARCHILY	STARRINGS	STATEMENTS	STAVED	STEAMED
STARCHING	STARRS	STATER	STAVES	STEAMER
STARCHY	STARRY	STATEROOM	STAVING	STEAMERS
STARDOM	STARS	STATEROOMS	STAW	STEAMIE
STARDOMS	STARSHINE	STATERS	STAWED	STEAMIER
STARDRIFT	STARSHINES	STATES	STAWING	STEAMIES
STARDRIFTS	STARSPOT	STATESIDE	STAWS	STEAMIEST
STARDUST	STARSPOTS	STATESMAN	STAY	STEAMILY
STARDUSTS	STARSTONE	STATESMEN	STAYAWAY	STEAMING
STARE	STARSTONES	STATEWIDE	STAYAWAYS	STEAMINGS
STARED	START	STATIC	STAYED	STEAMS
STARER	STARTED	STATICAL	STAYER	STEAMSHIP
STARERS	STARTER	STATICE	STAYERS	STEAMSHIPS
STARES	STARTERS	STATICES	STAYING	STEAMY
STARETS	STARTFUL	STATICS	STAYLESS	STEAN
STARETSES	STARTING	STATIM	STAYMAKER	STEANE
STARETZ	STARTINGS	STATING	STAYMAKERS	STEANED
STARETZES	STARTISH	STATION	STAYNE	STEANES
STARFISH	STARTLE	STATIONAL	STAYNED	STEANING
STARFISHES	STARTLED	STATIONED	STAYNES	STEANINGS
STARGAZER	STARTLER	STATIONER	STAYNING	STEANS
STARGAZERS	STARTLERS	STATIONERS	STAYRE	STEAPSIN
STARING	STARTLES	STATIONING	STAYRES	STEAPSINS
STARINGLY	STARTLING	STATIONS	STAYS	STEAR
STARINGS	STARTLINGS	STATISM	STAYSAIL	STEARAGE
STARK	STARTLISH	STATISMS	STAYSAILS	STEARAGES
STARKED	STARTLY	STATIST	STEAD	STEARATE
STARKEN	STARTS	STATISTIC	STEADED	STEARATES
STARKENED	STARVE	STATISTICS	STEADFAST	STEARD
STARKENING	STARVED	STATISTS	STEADICAM®	STEARE
STARKENS	STARVES	STATIVE	STEADICAMS	STEARED
STARKER	STARVING	STATOCYST	STEADIED	STEARES
STARKERS	STARVINGS	STATOCYSTS	STEADIER	STEARIC
STARKEST	STARWORT	STATOLITH	STEADIES	STEARIN
STARKING	STARWORTS	STATOLITHS	STEADIEST	STEARINE
STARKLY	STASES	STATOR	STEADILY	STEARINES
STARKNESS	STASH	STATORS	STEADING	STEARING
STARKNESSES	STASHED	STATUA	STEADINGS	STEARINS
STARKS	STASHES	STATUARIES	STEADS	STEARS
STARLESS	STASHIE	STATUARY	STEADY	STEARSMAN
STARLET	STASHIES	STATUAS	STEADYING	STEARSMEN
STARLETS	STASHING	STATUE	STEAK	STEATITE
STARLIGHT	STASIDION	STATUED	STEAKS	STEATITES
STARLIGHTS	STASIDIONS	STATUES	STEAL	STEATITIC
STARLIKE	STASIMA	STATUETTE	STEALE	STEATOMA
STARLING	STASIMON	STATUETTES	STEALED	STEATOMAS
STARLINGS	STASIS	STATURE	STEALER	STEATOSES
STARLIT	STATABLE	STATURED	STEALERS	STEATOSIS
STARN	STATAL	STATURES	STEALES	STED
STARNED	STATANT	STATUS	STEALING	STEDD
STARNIE	STATE	STATUSES	STEALINGS	STEDDE
STARNIES	STATED	STATUTE	STEALS	STEDDED
STARNING	STATEDLY	STATUTES	STEALT	STEDDES
STARNS	STATEHOOD	STATUTORY	STEALTH	STEDDIED
STAROSTA	STATEHOODS	STAUNCH	STEALTHED	STEDDIES
STAROSTAS	STATELESS	STAUNCHED	STEALTHIER	STEDDING
STAROSTIES	STATELIER	STAUNCHER	STEALTHIEST	STEDDS
STAROSTY	STATELIEST	STAUNCHERS	STEALTHING	STEDDY
STARR	STATELILY	STAUNCHES	STEALTHINGS	STEDDYING
STARRED	STATELY	STAUNCHEST	STEALTHS	STEDE
STARRIER	STATEMENT	STAUNCHING	STEALTHY	STEDED
STARRIEST	STATEMENTED	STAUNCHINGS	STEAM	STEDES
STARRILY	STATEMENTING	STAUNCHLY	STEAMBOAT	STEDFAST

STEDING
STEDS
STEED
STEEDED
STEEDIED
STEEDIES
STEEDING
STEEDS
STEEDY
STEEDYING
STEEK
STEEKING
STEEKIT
STEEKS
STEEL
STEELBOW
STEELBOWS
STEELD
STEELED
STEELIER
STEELIEST
STEELING
STEELINGS
STEELMAN
STEELMEN
STEELS
STEELWARE
STEELWARES
STEELWORK
STEELWORKS
STEELY
STEELYARD
STEELYARDS
STEEM
STEEMED
STEEMING
STEEMS
STEEN
STEENBOK
STEENBOKS
STEENBRAS
STEENBRASES
STEENED
STEENING
STEENINGS
STEENKIRK
STEENKIRKS
STEENS
STEEP
STEEPED
STEEPEN
STEEPENED
STEEPENING
STEEPENS
STEEPER
STEEPERS
STEEPEST
STEEPEUP
STEEPIER
STEEPIEST
STEEPING
STEEPISH
STEEPLE
STEEPLED

STEEPLES
STEEPLY
STEEPNESS
STEEPNESSES
STEEPS
STEEPUP
STEEPY
STEER
STEERABLE
STEERAGE
STEERAGES
STEERED
STEERER
STEERERS
STEERIES
STEERING
STEERINGS
STEERLING
STEERLINGS
STEERS
STEERSMAN
STEERSMEN
STEERY
STEEVE
STEEVED
STEEVELY
STEEVER
STEEVES
STEEVEST
STEEVING
STEEVINGS
STEGNOSES
STEGNOSIS
STEGNOTIC
STEGODON
STEGODONS
STEGODONT
STEGODONTS
STEGOSAUR
STEGOSAURS
STEIL
STEILS
STEIN
STEINBOCK
STEINBOCKS
STEINED
STEINING
STEININGS
STEINKIRK
STEINKIRKS
STEINS
STELA
STELAE
STELAR
STELE
STELENE
STELES
STELL
STELLAR
STELLATE
STELLATED
STELLED
STELLERID
STELLERIDS

STELLIFIED
STELLIFIES
STELLIFY
STELLIFYING
STELLIFYINGS
STELLING
STELLION
STELLIONS
STELLS
STELLULAR
STEM
STEMBOK
STEMBOKS
STEMBUCK
STEMBUCKS
STEME
STEMED
STEMES
STEMING
STEMLESS
STEMLET
STEMLETS
STEMMA
STEMMATA
STEMME
STEMMED
STEMMER
STEMMERS
STEMMES
STEMMING
STEMMINGS
STEMPEL
STEMPELS
STEMPLE
STEMPLES
STEMS
STEMSON
STEMSONS
STEN
STENCH
STENCHED
STENCHES
STENCHIER
STENCHIEST
STENCHING
STENCHY
STENCIL
STENCILED
STENCILING
STENCILLED
STENCILLING
STENCILLINGS
STENCILS
STEND
STENDED
STENDING
STENDS
STENGAH
STENGAHS
STENLOCK
STENLOCKS
STENNED
STENNING
STENOPAIC

STENOSED
STENOSES
STENOSIS
STENOTIC
STENOTYPIES
STENOTYPY
STENS
STENT
STENTED
STENTING
STENTOR
STENTORS
STENTOUR
STENTOURS
STENTS
STEP
STEPBAIRN
STEPBAIRNS
STEPCHILD
STEPCHILDREN
STEPDAME
STEPDAMES
STEPHANE
STEPHANES
STEPNEY
STEPNEYS
STEPPE
STEPPED
STEPPER
STEPPERS
STEPPES
STEPPING
STEPS
STEPSON
STEPSONS
STEPT
STEPWISE
STERADIAN
STERADIANS
STERCORAL
STERCULIA
STERCULIAS
STERE
STEREO
STEREOME
STEREOMES
STEREOS
STERES
STERIC
STERIGMA
STERIGMATA
STERILANT
STERILANTS
STERILE
STERILISE
STERILISED
STERILISES
STERILISING
STERILITIES
STERILITY
STERILIZE
STERILIZED
STERILIZES
STERILIZING

STERLET
STERLETS
STERLING
STERLINGS
STERN
STERNA
STERNAGE
STERNAGES
STERNAL
STERNEBRA
STERNEBRAE
STERNED
STERNER
STERNEST
STERNFAST
STERNFASTS
STERNING
STERNITE
STERNITES
STERNITIC
STERNLY
STERNMOST
STERNNESS
STERNNESSES
STERNPORT
STERNPORTS
STERNPOST
STERNPOSTS
STERNS
STERNSON
STERNSONS
STERNUM
STERNUMS
STERNWARD
STERNWARDS
STERNWAY
STERNWAYS
STEROID
STEROIDS
STEROL
STEROLS
STERVE
STERVED
STERVES
STERVING
STET
STETS
STETTED
STETTING
STEVEDORE
STEVEDORED
STEVEDORES
STEVEDORING
STEVEN
STEVENS
STEW
STEWARD
STEWARDRIES
STEWARDRY
STEWARDS
STEWARTRIES
STEWARTRY
STEWED
STEWER

The Chambers Dictionary is the authority for many longer words; see *OSW* Introduction, page xii

STEWERS	STICKLERS	STILE	STINGBULL	STIPULATING
STEWIER	STICKLES	STILED	STINGBULLS	STIPULE
STEWIEST	STICKLING	STILES	STINGED	STIPULED
STEWING	STICKS	STILET	STINGER	STIPULES
STEWINGS	STICKWORK	STILETS	STINGERS	STIR
STEWPAN	STICKWORKS	STILETTO	STINGFISH	STIRABOUT
STEWPANS	STICKY	STILETTOED	STINGFISHES	STIRABOUTS
STEWPOND	STICKYING	STILETTOING	STINGIER	STIRE
STEWPONDS	STICTION	STILETTOS	STINGIEST	STIRED
STEWPOT	STICTIONS	STILING	STINGILY	STIRES
STEWPOTS	STIDDIE	STILL	STINGING	STIRING
STEWS	STIDDIED	STILLAGE	STINGINGS	STIRK
STEWY	STIDDIEING	STILLAGES	STINGLESS	STIRKS
STEY	STIDDIES	STILLBORN	STINGO	STIRLESS
STEYER	STIDDYING	STILLED	STINGOS	STIRP
STEYEST	STIE	STILLER	STINGS	STIRPES
STHENIC	STIED	STILLERS	STINGY	STIRPS
STIBBLE	STIES	STILLEST	STINK	STIRRA
STIBBLER	STIEVE	STILLIER	STINKARD	STIRRAH
STIBBLERS	STIEVELY	STILLIEST	STINKARDS	STIRRAHS
STIBBLES	STIEVER	STILLING	STINKER	STIRRAS
STIBIAL	STIEVEST	STILLINGS	STINKERS	STIRRE
STIBINE	STIFF	STILLION	STINKHORN	STIRRED
STIBINES	STIFFED	STILLIONS	STINKHORNS	STIRRER
STIBIUM	STIFFEN	STILLNESS	STINKING	STIRRERS
STIBIUMS	STIFFENED	STILLNESSES	STINKINGS	STIRRES
STIBNITE	STIFFENER	STILLROOM	STINKO	STIRRING
STIBNITES	STIFFENERS	STILLROOMS	STINKS	STIRRINGS
STICCADO	STIFFENING	STILLS	STINKWOOD	STIRRUP
STICCADOES	STIFFENINGS	STILLY	STINKWOODS	STIRRUPS
STICCADOS	STIFFENS	STILT	STINT	STIRS
STICCATO	STIFFER	STILTBIRD	STINTED	STISHIE
STICCATOES	STIFFEST	STILTBIRDS	STINTEDLY	STISHIES
STICCATOS	STIFFIE	STILTED	STINTER	STITCH
STICH	STIFFIES	STILTEDLY	STINTERS	STITCHED
STICHARIA	STIFFING	STILTER	STINTIER	STITCHER
STICHERA	STIFFISH	STILTERS	STINTIEST	STITCHERIES
STICHERON	STIFFLY	STILTIER	STINTING	STITCHERS
STICHIC	STIFFNESS	STILTIEST	STINTINGS	STITCHERY
STICHIDIA	STIFFNESSES	STILTING	STINTLESS	STITCHES
STICHOI	STIFFS	STILTINGS	STINTS	STITCHING
STICHOS	STIFFWARE	STILTISH	STINTY	STITCHINGS
STICHS	STIFFWARES	STILTS	STIPA	STITHIED
STICK	STIFFY	STILTY	STIPAS	STITHIES
STICKED	STIFLE	STIME	STIPE	STITHY
STICKER	STIFLED	STIMED	STIPEL	STITHYING
STICKERED	STIFLER	STIMES	STIPELS	STIVE
STICKERING	STIFLERS	STIMIE	STIPEND	STIVED
STICKERS	STIFLES	STIMIED	STIPENDS	STIVER
STICKFUL	STIFLING	STIMIES	STIPES	STIVERS
STICKFULS	STIFLINGS	STIMING	STIPITATE	STIVES
STICKIED	STIGMA	STIMULANT	STIPITES	STIVIER
STICKIER	STIGMAS	STIMULANTS	STIPPLE	STIVIEST
STICKIES	STIGMATA	STIMULATE	STIPPLED	STIVING
STICKIEST	STIGMATIC	STIMULATED	STIPPLER	STIVY
STICKILY	STIGMATICS	STIMULATES	STIPPLERS	STOA
STICKING	STIGME	STIMULATING	STIPPLES	STOAE
STICKINGS	STIGMES	STIMULI	STIPPLING	STOAI
STICKIT	STILB	STIMULUS	STIPPLINGS	STOAS
STICKJAW	STILBENE	STIMY	STIPULAR	STOAT
STICKJAWS	STILBENES	STIMYING	STIPULARY	STOATS
STICKLE	STILBITE	STING	STIPULATE	STOB
STICKLED	STILBITES	STINGAREE	STIPULATED	STOBS
STICKLER	STILBS	STINGAREES	STIPULATES	STOCCADO

The Chambers Dictionary is the authority for many longer words; see *OSW* Introduction, page xii

STOCCADOS	STOEPS	STOMP	STONN	STOPPERING
STOCCATA	STOGEY	STOMPED	STONNE	STOPPERS
STOCCATAS	STOGEYS	STOMPER	STONNED	STOPPING
STOCIOUS	STOGIE	STOMPERS	STONNES	STOPPINGS
STOCK	STOGIES	STOMPING	STONNING	STOPPLE
STOCKADE	STOGY	STOMPS	STONNS	STOPPLED
STOCKADED	STOIC	STOND	STONY	STOPPLES
STOCKADES	STOICAL	STONDS	STONYING	STOPPLING
STOCKADING	STOICALLY	STONE	STOOD	STOPS
STOCKED	STOICISM	STONEBOAT	STOODEN	STOPWATCH
STOCKER	STOICISMS	STONEBOATS	STOOGE	STOPWATCHES
STOCKERS	STOICS	STONECAST	STOOGED	STORABLE
STOCKFISH	STOIT	STONECASTS	STOOGES	STORAGE
STOCKFISHES	STOITED	STONECHAT	STOOGING	STORAGES
STOCKHORN	STOITER	STONECHATS	STOOK	STORAX
STOCKHORNS	STOITERED	STONECROP	STOOKED	STORAXES
STOCKIER	STOITERING	STONECROPS	STOOKER	STORE
STOCKIEST	STOITERS	STONED	STOOKERS	STORED
STOCKILY	STOITING	STONEFISH	STOOKING	STOREMAN
STOCKINET	STOITS	STONEFISHES	STOOKS	STOREMEN
STOCKINETS	STOKE	STONEFLIES	STOOL	STORER
STOCKING	STOKED	STONEFLY	STOOLBALL	STOREROOM
STOCKINGS	STOKEHOLD	STONEHAND	STOOLBALLS	STOREROOMS
STOCKIST	STOKEHOLDS	STONEHANDS	STOOLED	STORERS
STOCKISTS	STOKEHOLE	STONELESS	STOOLIE	STORES
STOCKLESS	STOKEHOLES	STONEN	STOOLIES	STOREY
STOCKLIST	STOKER	STONER	STOOLING	STOREYED
STOCKLISTS	STOKERS	STONERAG	STOOLS	STOREYS
STOCKLOCK	STOKES	STONERAGS	STOOP	STORGE
STOCKLOCKS	STOKING	STONERAW	STOOPE	STORGES
STOCKMAN	STOLE	STONERAWS	STOOPED	STORIATED
STOCKMEN	STOLED	STONERN	STOOPER	STORIED
STOCKPILE	STOLEN	STONERS	STOOPERS	STORIES
STOCKPILED	STOLES	STONES	STOOPES	STORIETTE
STOCKPILES	STOLID	STONESHOT	STOOPING	STORIETTES
STOCKPILING	STOLIDER	STONESHOTS	STOOPS	STORING
STOCKPILINGS	STOLIDEST	STONEWALL	STOOR	STORK
STOCKPOT	STOLIDITIES	STONEWALLED	STOORS	STORKS
STOCKPOTS	STOLIDITY	STONEWALLING	STOOSHIE	STORM
STOCKROOM	STOLIDLY	STONEWALLINGS	STOOSHIES	STORMBIRD
STOCKROOMS	STOLLEN	STONEWALLS	STOP	STORMBIRDS
STOCKS	STOLLENS	STONEWARE	STOPBANK	STORMED
STOCKTAKE	STOLN	STONEWARES	STOPBANKS	STORMFUL
STOCKTAKEN	STOLON	STONEWORK	STOPCOCK	STORMIER
STOCKTAKES	STOLONS	STONEWORKS	STOPCOCKS	STORMIEST
STOCKTAKING	STOMA	STONEWORT	STOPE	STORMILY
STOCKTAKINGS	STOMACH	STONEWORTS	STOPED	STORMING
STOCKTOOK	STOMACHAL	STONG	STOPES	STORMINGS
STOCKWORK	STOMACHED	STONIED	STOPGAP	STORMLESS
STOCKWORKS	STOMACHER	STONIER	STOPGAPS	STORMS
STOCKY	STOMACHERS	STONIES	STOPING	STORMY
STOCKYARD	STOMACHIC	STONIEST	STOPINGS	STORNELLI
STOCKYARDS	STOMACHICS	STONILY	STOPLESS	STORNELLO
STODGE	STOMACHING	STONINESS	STOPLIGHT	STORY
STODGED	STOMACHS	STONINESSES	STOPLIGHTS	STORYBOOK
STODGER	STOMACHY	STONING	STOPOFF	STORYBOOKS
STODGERS	STOMAL	STONINGS	STOPOFFS	STORYETTE
STODGES	STOMATA	STONK	STOPOVER	STORYETTES
STODGIER	STOMATAL	STONKER	STOPOVERS	STORYING
STODGIEST	STOMATIC	STONKERED	STOPPAGE	STORYINGS
STODGILY	STOMODAEA	STONKERING	STOPPAGES	STORYLINE
STODGING	STOMODEA	STONKERS	STOPPED	STORYLINES
STODGY	STOMODEUM	STONKING	STOPPER	STOSS
STOEP	STOMODEUMS	STONKS	STOPPERED	STOSSES

STOT	STOWERS	STRAINTS	STRAPWORT	STREAKER
STOTINKA	STOWING	STRAIT	STRAPWORTS	STREAKERS
STOTINKI	STOWINGS	STRAITED	STRASS	STREAKIER
STOTIOUS	STOWLINS	STRAITEN	STRASSES	STREAKIEST
STOTS	STOWN	STRAITENED	STRATA	STREAKILY
STOTTED	STOWND	STRAITENING	STRATAGEM	STREAKING
STOTTER	STOWNDED	STRAITENS	STRATAGEMS	STREAKINGS
STOTTERS	STOWNDING	STRAITER	STRATEGIC	STREAKS
STOTTING	STOWNDS	STRAITEST	STRATEGICS	STREAKY
STOUN	STOWNLINS	STRAITING	STRATEGIES	STREAM
STOUND	STOWRE	STRAITLY	STRATEGY	STREAMED
STOUNDED	STOWRES	STRAITS	STRATH	STREAMER
STOUNDING	STOWS	STRAKE	STRATHS	STREAMERS
STOUNDS	STRABISM	STRAKES	STRATI	STREAMIER
STOUNING	STRABISMS	STRAMACON	STRATIFIED	STREAMIEST
STOUNS	STRAD	STRAMACONS	STRATIFIES	STREAMING
STOUP	STRADDLE	STRAMASH	STRATIFY	STREAMINGS
STOUPS	STRADDLED	STRAMASHED	STRATIFYING	STREAMLET
STOUR	STRADDLES	STRAMASHES	STRATONIC	STREAMLETS
STOURIER	STRADDLING	STRAMASHING	STRATOSE	STREAMS
STOURIEST	STRADIOT	STRAMAZON	STRATOUS	STREAMY
STOURS	STRADIOTS	STRAMAZONS	STRATUM	STREEK
STOURY	STRADS	STRAMMEL	STRATUS	STREEKED
STOUSH	STRAE	STRAMMELS	STRAUCHT	STREEKING
STOUSHED	STRAES	STRAMP	STRAUCHTED	STREEKS
STOUSHES	STRAFE	STRAMPED	STRAUCHTER	STREEL
STOUSHING	STRAFED	STRAMPING	STRAUCHTEST	STREELED
STOUT	STRAFES	STRAMPS	STRAUCHTING	STREELING
STOUTEN	STRAFF	STRAND	STRAUCHTS	STREELS
STOUTENED	STRAFFED	STRANDED	STRAUGHT	STREET
STOUTENING	STRAFFING	STRANDING	STRAUGHTED	STREETAGE
STOUTENS	STRAFFS	STRANDS	STRAUGHTER	STREETAGES
STOUTER	STRAFING	STRANGE	STRAUGHTEST	STREETBOY
STOUTEST	STRAG	STRANGELY	STRAUGHTING	STREETBOYS
STOUTH	STRAGGLE	STRANGER	STRAUGHTS	STREETCAR
STOUTHRIE	STRAGGLED	STRANGERED	STRAUNGE	STREETCARS
STOUTHRIES	STRAGGLER	STRANGERING	STRAVAIG	STREETED
STOUTHS	STRAGGLERS	STRANGERS	STRAVAIGED	STREETFUL
STOUTISH	STRAGGLES	STRANGEST	STRAVAIGING	STREETFULS
STOUTLY	STRAGGLIER	STRANGLE	STRAVAIGS	STREETIER
STOUTNESS	STRAGGLIEST	STRANGLED	STRAW	STREETIEST
STOUTNESSES	STRAGGLING	STRANGLER	STRAWED	STREETS
STOUTS	STRAGGLINGS	STRANGLERS	STRAWEN	STREETY
STOVAINE	STRAGGLY	STRANGLES	STRAWIER	STREIGHT
STOVAINES	STRAGS	STRANGLING	STRAWIEST	STREIGHTS
STOVE	STRAICHT	STRANGURIES	STRAWING	STREIGNE
STOVED	STRAICHTER	STRANGURY	STRAWLESS	STREIGNED
STOVEPIPE	STRAICHTEST	STRAP	STRAWLIKE	STREIGNES
STOVEPIPES	STRAIGHT	STRAPLESS	STRAWN	STREIGNING
STOVER	STRAIGHTER	STRAPLINE	STRAWS	STRELITZ
STOVERS	STRAIGHTEST	STRAPLINES	STRAWWORM	STRELITZES
STOVES	STRAIGHTS	STRAPPADO	STRAWWORMS	STRELITZI
STOVIES	STRAIK	STRAPPADOED	STRAWY	STRENE
STOVING	STRAIKED	STRAPPADOING	STRAY	STRENES
STOVINGS	STRAIKING	STRAPPADOS	STRAYED	STRENGTH
STOW	STRAIKS	STRAPPED	STRAYER	STRENGTHS
STOWAGE	STRAIN	STRAPPER	STRAYERS	STRENUITIES
STOWAGES	STRAINED	STRAPPERS	STRAYING	STRENUITY
STOWAWAY	STRAINER	STRAPPIER	STRAYINGS	STRENUOUS
STOWAWAYS	STRAINERS	STRAPPIEST	STRAYLING	STREP
STOWDOWN	STRAINING	STRAPPING	STRAYLINGS	STREPENT
STOWDOWNS	STRAININGS	STRAPPINGS	STRAYS	STREPS
STOWED	STRAINS	STRAPPY	STREAK	STRESS
STOWER	STRAINT	STRAPS	STREAKED	STRESSED

STRESSES	STRIDDLING	STRIPPED	STRONG	STROYS
STRESSFUL	STRIDE	STRIPPER	STRONGARM	STRUCK
STRESSING	STRIDENCE	STRIPPERS	STRONGARMED	STRUCTURE
STRESSOR	STRIDENCES	STRIPPING	STRONGARMING	STRUCTURED
STRESSORS	STRIDENCIES	STRIPPINGS	STRONGARMS	STRUCTURES
STRETCH	STRIDENCY	STRIPS	STRONGBOX	STRUCTURING
STRETCHED	STRIDENT	STRIPY	STRONGBOXES	STRUDEL
STRETCHER	STRIDES	STRIVE	STRONGER	STRUDELS
STRETCHERED	STRIDING	STRIVED	STRONGEST	STRUGGLE
STRETCHERING	STRIDLING	STRIVEN	STRONGISH	STRUGGLED
STRETCHERS	STRIDOR	STRIVER	STRONGLY	STRUGGLER
STRETCHES	STRIDORS	STRIVERS	STRONGMAN	STRUGGLERS
STRETCHIER	STRIFE	STRIVES	STRONGMEN	STRUGGLES
STRETCHIEST	STRIFEFUL	STRIVING	STRONGYL	STRUGGLING
STRETCHING	STRIFES	STRIVINGS	STRONGYLE	STRUGGLINGS
STRETCHY	STRIFT	STROAM	STRONGYLES	STRUM
STRETTA	STRIFTS	STROAMED	STRONGYLS	STRUMA
STRETTE	STRIG	STROAMING	STRONTIA	STRUMAE
STRETTI	STRIGA	STROAMS	STRONTIAN	STRUMATIC
STRETTO	STRIGAE	STROBE	STRONTIANS	STRUMITIS
STREW	STRIGATE	STROBED	STRONTIAS	STRUMITISES
STREWAGE	STRIGGED	STROBES	STRONTIUM	STRUMMED
STREWAGES	STRIGGING	STROBIC	STRONTIUMS	STRUMMEL
STREWED	STRIGIL	STROBILA	STROOK	STRUMMELS
STREWER	STRIGILS	STROBILAE	STROOKE	STRUMMING
STREWERS	STRIGINE	STROBILE	STROOKEN	STRUMOSE
STREWING	STRIGOSE	STROBILES	STROOKES	STRUMOUS
STREWINGS	STRIGS	STROBILI	STROP	STRUMPET
STREWMENT	STRIKE	STROBILUS	STROPHE	STRUMPETED
STREWMENTS	STRIKEOUT	STROBING	STROPHES	STRUMPETING
STREWN	STRIKEOUTS	STROBINGS	STROPHIC	STRUMPETS
STREWS	STRIKER	STRODDLE	STROPPED	STRUMS
STREWTH	STRIKERS	STRODDLED	STROPPIER	STRUNG
STRIA	STRIKES	STRODDLES	STROPPIEST	STRUNT
STRIAE	STRIKING	STRODDLING	STROPPING	STRUNTED
STRIATA	STRIKINGS	STRODE	STROPPY	STRUNTING
STRIATE	STRING	STRODLE	STROPS	STRUNTS
STRIATED	STRINGED	STRODLED	STROSSERS	STRUT
STRIATES	STRINGENT	STRODLES	STROUD	STRUTS
STRIATING	STRINGER	STRODLING	STROUDING	STRUTTED
STRIATION	STRINGERS	STROKE	STROUDINGS	STRUTTER
STRIATIONS	STRINGIER	STROKED	STROUDS	STRUTTERS
STRIATUM	STRINGIEST	STROKEN	STROUP	STRUTTING
STRIATUMS	STRINGILY	STROKER	STROUPACH	STRUTTINGS
STRIATURE	STRINGING	STROKERS	STROUPACHS	STRYCHNIA
STRIATURES	STRINGINGS	STROKES	STROUPAN	STRYCHNIAS
STRICH	STRINGS	STROKING	STROUPANS	STRYCHNIC
STRICHES	STRINGY	STROKINGS	STROUPS	STUB
STRICKEN	STRINKLE	STROLL	STROUT	STUBBED
STRICKLE	STRINKLED	STROLLED	STROUTED	STUBBIER
STRICKLED	STRINKLES	STROLLER	STROUTING	STUBBIES
STRICKLES	STRINKLING	STROLLERS	STROUTS	STUBBIEST
STRICKLING	STRINKLINGS	STROLLING	STROVE	STUBBING
STRICT	STRIP	STROLLINGS	STROW	STUBBLE
STRICTER	STRIPE	STROLLS	STROWED	STUBBLED
STRICTEST	STRIPED	STROMA	STROWER	STUBBLES
STRICTISH	STRIPES	STROMATA	STROWERS	STUBBLIER
STRICTLY	STRIPEY	STROMATIC	STROWING	STUBBLIEST
STRICTURE	STRIPIER	STROMB	STROWINGS	STUBBLY
STRICTURES	STRIPIEST	STROMBS	STROWN	STUBBORN
STRIDDEN	STRIPING	STROMBUS	STROWS	STUBBORNED
STRIDDLE	STRIPINGS	STROMBUSES	STROY	STUBBORNER
STRIDDLED	STRIPLING	STROND	STROYED	STUBBORNEST
STRIDDLES	STRIPLINGS	STRONDS	STROYING	STUBBORNING

The Chambers Dictionary is the authority for many longer words; see *OSW* Introduction, page xii

STUBBORNS	STUMBLER	STUPIDS	STYLISTS	SUBACIDLY
STUBBY	STUMBLERS	STUPING	STYLITE	SUBACRID
STUBS	STUMBLES	STUPOR	STYLITES	SUBACT
STUCCO	STUMBLIER	STUPOROUS	STYLIZE	SUBACTED
STUCCOED	STUMBLIEST	STUPORS	STYLIZED	SUBACTING
STUCCOER	STUMBLING	STUPRATE	STYLIZES	SUBACTION
STUCCOERS	STUMBLY	STUPRATED	STYLIZING	SUBACTIONS
STUCCOING	STUMER	STUPRATES	STYLO	SUBACTS
STUCCOS	STUMERS	STUPRATING	STYLOBATE	SUBACUTE
STUCK	STUMM	STURDIED	STYLOBATES	SUBADAR
STUCKS	STUMMED	STURDIER	STYLOID	SUBADARS
STUD	STUMMEL	STURDIES	STYLOIDS	SUBADULT
STUDBOOK	STUMMELS	STURDIEST	STYLOLITE	SUBADULTS
STUDBOOKS	STUMMING	STURDILY	STYLOLITES	SUBAERIAL
STUDDED	STUMP	STURDY	STYLOS	SUBAGENCIES
STUDDEN	STUMPAGE	STURE	STYLUS	SUBAGENCY
STUDDING	STUMPAGES	STURGEON	STYLUSES	SUBAGENT
STUDDINGS	STUMPED	STURGEONS	STYME	SUBAGENTS
STUDDLE	STUMPER	STURMER	STYMED	SUBAH
STUDDLES	STUMPERS	STURMERS	STYMES	SUBAHDAR
STUDENT	STUMPIER	STURNINE	STYMIE	SUBAHDARIES
STUDENTRIES	STUMPIES	STURNOID	STYMIED	SUBAHDARS
STUDENTRY	STUMPIEST	STURNUS	STYMIEING	SUBAHDARY
STUDENTS	STUMPILY	STURNUSES	STYMIES	SUBAHS
STUDFARM	STUMPING	STURT	STYMING	SUBAHSHIP
STUDFARMS	STUMPS	STURTED	STYPSIS	SUBAHSHIPS
STUDIED	STUMPY	STURTING	STYPSISES	SUBALPINE
STUDIEDLY	STUMS	STURTS	STYPTIC	SUBALTERN
STUDIER	STUN	STUSHIE	STYPTICAL	SUBALTERNS
STUDIERS	STUNG	STUSHIES	STYPTICS	SUBAPICAL
STUDIES	STUNK	STUTTER	STYRAX	SUBAQUA
STUDIO	STUNKARD	STUTTERED	STYRAXES	SUBARCTIC
STUDIOS	STUNNED	STUTTERER	STYRE	SUBAREA
STUDIOUS	STUNNER	STUTTERERS	STYRED	SUBAREAS
STUDS	STUNNERS	STUTTERING	STYRENE	SUBARID
STUDWORK	STUNNING	STUTTERINGS	STYRENES	SUBASTRAL
STUDWORKS	STUNNINGS	STUTTERS	STYRES	SUBATOM
STUDY	STUNS	STY	STYRING	SUBATOMIC
STUDYING	STUNSAIL	STYE	STYROFOAM	SUBATOMICS
STUFF	STUNSAILS	STYED	STYROFOAMS	SUBATOMS
STUFFED	STUNT	STYES	STYTE	SUBAUDIO
STUFFER	STUNTED	STYING	STYTED	SUBAURAL
STUFFERS	STUNTING	STYLAR	STYTES	SUBBASAL
STUFFIER	STUNTMAN	STYLATE	STYTING	SUBBASE
STUFFIEST	STUNTMEN	STYLE	SUABILITIES	SUBBASES
STUFFILY	STUNTS	STYLEBOOK	SUABILITY	SUBBED
STUFFING	STUPA	STYLEBOOKS	SUABLE	SUBBIE
STUFFINGS	STUPAS	STYLED	SUABLY	SUBBIES
STUFFS	STUPE	STYLELESS	SUASIBLE	SUBBING
STUFFY	STUPED	STYLES	SUASION	SUBBINGS
STUGGIER	STUPEFIED	STYLET	SUASIONS	SUBBRANCH
STUGGIEST	STUPEFIER	STYLETS	SUASIVE	SUBBRANCHES
STUGGY	STUPEFIERS	STYLI	SUASIVELY	SUBBREED
STULL	STUPEFIES	STYLIFORM	SUASORY	SUBBREEDS
STULLS	STUPEFY	STYLING	SUAVE	SUBBUREAU
STULM	STUPEFYING	STYLISE	SUAVELY	SUBBUREAUS
STULMS	STUPENT	STYLISED	SUAVER	SUBBUREAUX
STULTIFIED	STUPES	STYLISES	SUAVEST	SUBBY
STULTIFIES	STUPID	STYLISH	SUAVITIES	SUBCANTOR
STULTIFY	STUPIDER	STYLISHLY	SUAVITY	SUBCANTORS
STULTIFYING	STUPIDEST	STYLISING	SUB	SUBCASTE
STUM	STUPIDITIES	STYLIST	SUBABBOT	SUBCASTES
STUMBLE	STUPIDITY	STYLISTIC	SUBABBOTS	SUBCAUDAL
STUMBLED	STUPIDLY	STYLISTICS	SUBACID	SUBCAVITIES

The Chambers Dictionary is the authority for many longer words; see *OSW* Introduction, page xii

SUBCAVITY	SUBEDITING	SUBINCISES	SUBLIMIZED	SUBPLOT
SUBCELLAR	SUBEDITOR	SUBINCISING	SUBLIMIZES	SUBPLOTS
SUBCELLARS	SUBEDITORS	SUBITISE	SUBLIMIZING	SUBPOENA
SUBCHIEF	SUBEDITS	SUBITISED	SUBLINEAR	SUBPOENAED
SUBCHIEFS	SUBENTIRE	SUBITISES	SUBLUNAR	SUBPOENAING
SUBCHORD	SUBEQUAL	SUBITISING	SUBLUNARY	SUBPOENAS
SUBCHORDS	SUBER	SUBITIZE	SUBLUNATE	SUBPOLAR
SUBCLAIM	SUBERATE	SUBITIZED	SUBMAN	SUBPOTENT
SUBCLAIMS	SUBERATES	SUBITIZES	SUBMARINE	SUBPRIOR
SUBCLASS	SUBERECT	SUBITIZING	SUBMARINED	SUBPRIORS
SUBCLASSES	SUBEREOUS	SUBITO	SUBMARINES	SUBREGION
SUBCLAUSE	SUBERIC	SUBJACENT	SUBMARINING	SUBREGIONS
SUBCLAUSES	SUBERIN	SUBJECT	SUBMATRICES	SUBRING
SUBCLIMAX	SUBERINS	SUBJECTED	SUBMATRIX	SUBRINGS
SUBCLIMAXES	SUBERISE	SUBJECTING	SUBMATRIXES	SUBROGATE
SUBCOOL	SUBERISED	SUBJECTS	SUBMEN	SUBROGATED
SUBCORTEX	SUBERISES	SUBJOIN	SUBMENTA	SUBROGATES
SUBCORTEXES	SUBERISING	SUBJOINED	SUBMENTAL	SUBROGATING
SUBCORTICES	SUBERIZE	SUBJOINING	SUBMENTUM	SUBS
SUBCOSTA	SUBERIZED	SUBJOINS	SUBMERGE	SUBSACRAL
SUBCOSTAE	SUBERIZES	SUBJUGATE	SUBMERGED	SUBSAMPLE
SUBCOSTAL	SUBERIZING	SUBJUGATED	SUBMERGES	SUBSAMPLED
SUBCOSTALS	SUBEROSE	SUBJUGATES	SUBMERGING	SUBSAMPLES
SUBCRUST	SUBEROUS	SUBJUGATING	SUBMERSE	SUBSAMPLING
SUBCRUSTS	SUBERS	SUBLATE	SUBMERSED	SUBSCHEMA
SUBDEACON	SUBFAMILIES	SUBLATED	SUBMERSES	SUBSCHEMATA
SUBDEACONS	SUBFAMILY	SUBLATES	SUBMERSING	SUBSCRIBE
SUBDEAN	SUBFEU	SUBLATING	SUBMICRON	SUBSCRIBED
SUBDEANS	SUBFEUED	SUBLATION	SUBMICRONS	SUBSCRIBES
SUBDERMAL	SUBFEUING	SUBLATIONS	SUBMISS	SUBSCRIBING
SUBDEW	SUBFEUS	SUBLEASE	SUBMISSLY	SUBSCRIBINGS
SUBDEWED	SUBFIELD	SUBLEASED	SUBMIT	SUBSCRIPT
SUBDEWING	SUBFIELDS	SUBLEASES	SUBMITS	SUBSCRIPTS
SUBDEWS	SUBFLOOR	SUBLEASING	SUBMITTED	SUBSEA
SUBDIVIDE	SUBFLOORS	SUBLESSEE	SUBMITTER	SUBSECIVE
SUBDIVIDED	SUBFRAME	SUBLESSEES	SUBMITTERS	SUBSELLIA
SUBDIVIDES	SUBFRAMES	SUBLESSOR	SUBMITTING	SUBSERE
SUBDIVIDING	SUBFUSC	SUBLESSORS	SUBMITTINGS	SUBSERES
SUBDOLOUS	SUBFUSCS	SUBLET	SUBMUCOSA	SUBSERIES
SUBDORSAL	SUBFUSK	SUBLETHAL	SUBMUCOSAE	SUBSERVE
SUBDUABLE	SUBFUSKS	SUBLETS	SUBMUCOUS	SUBSERVED
SUBDUAL	SUBGENERA	SUBLETTER	SUBNEURAL	SUBSERVES
SUBDUALS	SUBGENRE	SUBLETTERS	SUBNIVEAL	SUBSERVING
SUBDUCE	SUBGENRES	SUBLETTING	SUBNIVEAN	SUBSET
SUBDUCED	SUBGENUS	SUBLETTINGS	SUBNORMAL	SUBSETS
SUBDUCES	SUBGENUSES	SUBLIMATE	SUBNORMALS	SUBSHRUB
SUBDUCING	SUBGOAL	SUBLIMATED	SUBOCTAVE	SUBSHRUBS
SUBDUCT	SUBGOALS	SUBLIMATES	SUBOCTAVES	SUBSIDE
SUBDUCTED	SUBGRADE	SUBLIMATING	SUBOCULAR	SUBSIDED
SUBDUCTING	SUBGRADES	SUBLIME	SUBOFFICE	SUBSIDES
SUBDUCTS	SUBGROUP	SUBLIMED	SUBOFFICES	SUBSIDIES
SUBDUE	SUBGROUPS	SUBLIMELY	SUBORDER	SUBSIDING
SUBDUED	SUBGUM	SUBLIMER	SUBORDERS	SUBSIDISE
SUBDUEDLY	SUBGUMS	SUBLIMES	SUBORN	SUBSIDISED
SUBDUER	SUBHEAD	SUBLIMEST	SUBORNED	SUBSIDISES
SUBDUERS	SUBHEADS	SUBLIMING	SUBORNER	SUBSIDISING
SUBDUES	SUBHEDRAL	SUBLIMINGS	SUBORNERS	SUBSIDIZE
SUBDUING	SUBHUMAN	SUBLIMISE	SUBORNING	SUBSIDIZED
SUBDUPLE	SUBHUMID	SUBLIMISED	SUBORNS	SUBSIDIZES
SUBDURAL	SUBIMAGINES	SUBLIMISES	SUBOVATE	SUBSIDIZING
SUBEDAR	SUBIMAGO	SUBLIMISING	SUBOXIDE	SUBSIDY
SUBEDARS	SUBIMAGOS	SUBLIMITIES	SUBOXIDES	SUBSIST
SUBEDIT	SUBINCISE	SUBLIMITY	SUBPHYLA	SUBSISTED
SUBEDITED	SUBINCISED	SUBLIMIZE	SUBPHYLUM	SUBSISTING

SUBSISTS	SUBTILISED	SUBVERTED	SUCCOUS	SUD
SUBSIZAR	SUBTILISES	SUBVERTER	SUCCUBA	SUDAMEN
SUBSIZARS	SUBTILISING	SUBVERTERS	SUCCUBAE	SUDAMINA
SUBSOIL	SUBTILIZE	SUBVERTING	SUCCUBAS	SUDAMINAL
SUBSOILED	SUBTILIZED	SUBVERTS	SUCCUBI	SUDARIA
SUBSOILER	SUBTILIZES	SUBVIRAL	SUCCUBINE	SUDARIES
SUBSOILERS	SUBTILIZING	SUBVOCAL	SUCCUBOUS	SUDARIUM
SUBSOILING	SUBTITLE	SUBWARDEN	SUCCUBUS	SUDARY
SUBSOILINGS	SUBTITLED	SUBWARDENS	SUCCUBUSES	SUDATE
SUBSOILS	SUBTITLES	SUBWAY	SUCCULENT	SUDATED
SUBSOLAR	SUBTITLING	SUBWAYS	SUCCULENTS	SUDATES
SUBSONG	SUBTLE	SUBWOOFER	SUCCUMB	SUDATING
SUBSONGS	SUBTLER	SUBWOOFERS	SUCCUMBED	SUDATION
SUBSONIC	SUBTLEST	SUBZERO	SUCCUMBING	SUDATIONS
SUBSTAGE	SUBTLETIES	SUBZONAL	SUCCUMBS	SUDATORIA
SUBSTAGES	SUBTLETY	SUBZONE	SUCCURSAL	SUDATORIES
SUBSTANCE	SUBTLY	SUBZONES	SUCCURSALS	SUDATORY
SUBSTANCES	SUBTONIC	SUCCADE	SUCCUS	SUDD
SUBSTATE	SUBTONICS	SUCCADES	SUCCUSS	SUDDEN
SUBSTATES	SUBTOPIA	SUCCAH	SUCCUSSED	SUDDENLY
SUBSTRACT	SUBTOPIAN	SUCCAHS	SUCCUSSES	SUDDENTIES
SUBSTRACTED	SUBTOPIAS	SUCCEED	SUCCUSSING	SUDDENTY
SUBSTRACTING	SUBTORRID	SUCCEEDED	SUCH	SUDDER
SUBSTRACTS	SUBTOTAL	SUCCEEDER	SUCHLIKE	SUDDERS
SUBSTRATA	SUBTOTALLED	SUCCEEDERS	SUCHNESS	SUDDS
SUBSTRATE	SUBTOTALLING	SUCCEEDING	SUCHNESSES	SUDOR
SUBSTRATES	SUBTOTALS	SUCCEEDS	SUCHWISE	SUDORAL
SUBSTRUCT	SUBTRACT	SUCCENTOR	SUCK	SUDORIFIC
SUBSTRUCTED	SUBTRACTED	SUCCENTORS	SUCKED	SUDORIFICS
SUBSTRUCTING	SUBTRACTING	SUCCES	SUCKEN	SUDOROUS
SUBSTRUCTS	SUBTRACTS	SUCCESS	SUCKENER	SUDORS
SUBSTYLAR	SUBTRIBE	SUCCESSES	SUCKENERS	SUDS
SUBSTYLE	SUBTRIBES	SUCCESSOR	SUCKENS	SUDSED
SUBSTYLES	SUBTRIST	SUCCESSORS	SUCKER	SUDSER
SUBSULTUS	SUBTROPIC	SUCCI	SUCKERED	SUDSERS
SUBSULTUSES	SUBTROPICS	SUCCINATE	SUCKERING	SUDSES
SUBSUME	SUBTRUDE	SUCCINATES	SUCKERS	SUDSIER
SUBSUMED	SUBTRUDED	SUCCINCT	SUCKET	SUDSIEST
SUBSUMES	SUBTRUDES	SUCCINCTER	SUCKETS	SUDSING
SUBSUMING	SUBTRUDING	SUCCINCTEST	SUCKING	SUDSY
SUBSYSTEM	SUBTYPE	SUCCINIC	SUCKINGS	SUE
SUBSYSTEMS	SUBTYPES	SUCCINITE	SUCKLE	SUEABLE
SUBTACK	SUBUCULA	SUCCINITES	SUCKLED	SUED
SUBTACKS	SUBUCULAS	SUCCINYL	SUCKLER	SUEDE
SUBTEEN	SUBULATE	SUCCINYLS	SUCKLERS	SUEDED
SUBTEENS	SUBUNIT	SUCCISE	SUCKLES	SUEDES
SUBTENANT	SUBUNITS	SUCCOR	SUCKLING	SUEDETTE
SUBTENANTS	SUBURB	SUCCORED	SUCKLINGS	SUEDETTES
SUBTEND	SUBURBAN	SUCCORIES	SUCKS	SUEDING
SUBTENDED	SUBURBANS	SUCCORING	SUCRASE	SUER
SUBTENDING	SUBURBIA	SUCCORS	SUCRASES	SUERS
SUBTENDS	SUBURBIAS	SUCCORY	SUCRE	SUES
SUBTENSE	SUBURBS	SUCCOS	SUCRES	SUET
SUBTENSES	SUBURSINE	SUCCOSE	SUCRIER	SUETIER
SUBTENURE	SUBVASSAL	SUCCOT	SUCRIERS	SUETIEST
SUBTENURES	SUBVASSALS	SUCCOTASH	SUCROSE	SUETS
SUBTEXT	SUBVERSAL	SUCCOTASHES	SUCROSES	SUETTIER
SUBTEXTS	SUBVERSALS	SUCCOTH	SUCTION	SUETTIEST
SUBTIDAL	SUBVERSE	SUCCOUR	SUCTIONS	SUETTY
SUBTIL	SUBVERSED	SUCCOURED	SUCTORIAL	SUETY
SUBTILE	SUBVERSES	SUCCOURER	SUCTORIAN	SUFFECT
SUBTILER	SUBVERSING	SUCCOURERS	SUCTORIANS	SUFFER
SUBTILEST	SUBVERST	SUCCOURING	SUCURUJU	SUFFERED
SUBTILISE	SUBVERT	SUCCOURS	SUCURUJUS	SUFFERER

SUFFERERS	SUI	SULFATASES	SULPHITES	SUMMATS
SUFFERING	SUICIDAL	SULFATE	SULPHONE	SUMMED
SUFFERINGS	SUICIDE	SULFATED	SULPHONES	SUMMER
SUFFERS	SUICIDES	SULFATES	SULPHUR	SUMMERED
SUFFETE	SUID	SULFATIC	SULPHURED	SUMMERIER
SUFFETES	SUIDIAN	SULFATING	SULPHURET	SUMMERIEST
SUFFICE	SUIDIANS	SULFATION	SULPHURETED	SUMMERING
SUFFICED	SUIDS	SULFATIONS	SULPHURETING	SUMMERINGS
SUFFICER	SUILLINE	SULFIDE	SULPHURETS	SUMMERLY
SUFFICERS	SUING	SULFIDES	SULPHURETTED	SUMMERS
SUFFICES	SUINGS	SULFINYL	SULPHURETTING	SUMMERSET
SUFFICING	SUINT	SULFINYLS	SULPHURIC	SUMMERSETS
SUFFIX	SUINTS	SULFITE	SULPHURING	SUMMERSETTED
SUFFIXAL	SUIT	SULFITES	SULPHURS	SUMMERSETTING
SUFFIXED	SUITABLE	SULFONATE	SULPHURY	SUMMERY
SUFFIXES	SUITABLY	SULFONATED	SULTAN	SUMMING
SUFFIXING	SUITCASE	SULFONATES	SULTANA	SUMMINGS
SUFFIXION	SUITCASES	SULFONATING	SULTANAS	SUMMIST
SUFFIXIONS	SUITE	SULFONE	SULTANATE	SUMMISTS
SUFFLATE	SUITED	SULFONES	SULTANATES	SUMMIT
SUFFLATED	SUITES	SULFONIUM	SULTANESS	SUMMITAL
SUFFLATES	SUITING	SULFONIUMS	SULTANESSES	SUMMITEER
SUFFLATING	SUITINGS	SULFUR	SULTANIC	SUMMITEERS
SUFFOCATE	SUITOR	SULFURATE	SULTANS	SUMMITRIES
SUFFOCATED	SUITORED	SULFURATED	SULTRIER	SUMMITRY
SUFFOCATES	SUITORING	SULFURATES	SULTRIEST	SUMMITS
SUFFOCATING	SUITORS	SULFURATING	SULTRILY	SUMMON
SUFFOCATINGS	SUITRESS	SULFURED	SULTRY	SUMMONED
SUFFRAGAN	SUITRESSES	SULFURIC	SULU	SUMMONER
SUFFRAGANS	SUITS	SULFURING	SULUS	SUMMONERS
SUFFRAGE	SUIVANTE	SULFURS	SUM	SUMMONING
SUFFRAGES	SUIVANTES	SULK	SUMAC	SUMMONS
SUFFUSE	SUIVEZ	SULKED	SUMACH	SUMMONSED
SUFFUSED	SUJEE	SULKIER	SUMACHS	SUMMONSES
SUFFUSES	SUJEES	SULKIES	SUMACS	SUMMONSING
SUFFUSING	SUK	SULKIEST	SUMATRA	SUMO
SUFFUSION	SUKH	SULKILY	SUMATRAS	SUMOS
SUFFUSIONS	SUKHS	SULKINESS	SUMLESS	SUMOTORI
SUFFUSIVE	SUKIYAKI	SULKINESSES	SUMMA	SUMOTORIS
SUGAR	SUKIYAKIS	SULKING	SUMMAE	SUMP
SUGARALLIES	SUKKAH	SULKS	SUMMAND	SUMPH
SUGARALLY	SUKKAHS	SULKY	SUMMANDS	SUMPHISH
SUGARCANE	SUKKOS	SULLAGE	SUMMAR	SUMPHS
SUGARCANES	SUKKOT	SULLAGES	SUMMARIES	SUMPIT
SUGARED	SUKKOTH	SULLEN	SUMMARILY	SUMPITAN
SUGARIER	SUKS	SULLENER	SUMMARISE	SUMPITANS
SUGARIEST	SULCAL	SULLENEST	SUMMARISED	SUMPITS
SUGARING	SULCALISE	SULLENLY	SUMMARISES	SUMPS
SUGARINGS	SULCALISED	SULLIED	SUMMARISING	SUMPSIMUS
SUGARLESS	SULCALISES	SULLIES	SUMMARIST	SUMPSIMUSES
SUGARLOAF	SULCALISING	SULLY	SUMMARISTS	SUMPTER
SUGARLOAVES	SULCALIZE	SULLYING	SUMMARIZE	SUMPTERS
SUGARPLUM	SULCALIZED	SULPHA	SUMMARIZED	SUMPTUARY
SUGARPLUMS	SULCALIZES	SULPHAS	SUMMARIZES	SUMPTUOUS
SUGARS	SULCALIZING	SULPHATE	SUMMARIZING	SUMS
SUGARY	SULCATE	SULPHATED	SUMMARY	SUN
SUGGEST	SULCATED	SULPHATES	SUMMAT	SUNBAKE
SUGGESTED	SULCATION	SULPHATIC	SUMMATE	SUNBAKED
SUGGESTER	SULCATIONS	SULPHATING	SUMMATED	SUNBAKES
SUGGESTERS	SULCI	SULPHIDE	SUMMATES	SUNBAKING
SUGGESTING	SULCUS	SULPHIDES	SUMMATING	SUNBATH
SUGGESTS	SULFA	SULPHINYL	SUMMATION	SUNBATHE
SUGGING	SULFAS	SULPHINYLS	SUMMATIONS	SUNBATHED
SUGGINGS	SULFATASE	SULPHITE	SUMMATIVE	SUNBATHER

The Chambers Dictionary is the authority for many longer words; see *OSW* Introduction, page xii

SUNBATHERS	SUNDRY	SUNSTRUCK	SUPERGLUING	SUPINATED
SUNBATHES	SUNFAST	SUNSUIT	SUPERGUN	SUPINATES
SUNBATHING	SUNFISH	SUNSUITS	SUPERGUNS	SUPINATING
SUNBATHINGS	SUNFISHES	SUNTAN	SUPERHEAT	SUPINATOR
SUNBATHS	SUNFLOWER	SUNTANNED	SUPERHEATED	SUPINATORS
SUNBEAM	SUNFLOWERS	SUNTANS	SUPERHEATING	SUPINE
SUNBEAMED	SUNG	SUNTRAP	SUPERHEATS	SUPINELY
SUNBEAMS	SUNGAR	SUNTRAPS	SUPERHERO	SUPINES
SUNBEAMY	SUNGARS	SUNUP	SUPERHEROES	SUPPAWN
SUNBEAT	SUNGLASS	SUNUPS	SUPERHIVE	SUPPAWNS
SUNBEATEN	SUNGLASSES	SUNWARD	SUPERHIVES	SUPPEAGO
SUNBED	SUNGLOW	SUNWARDS	SUPERIOR	SUPPEAGOES
SUNBEDS	SUNGLOWS	SUNWISE	SUPERIORS	SUPPED
SUNBELT	SUNHAT	SUP	SUPERJET	SUPPER
SUNBELTS	SUNHATS	SUPAWN	SUPERJETS	SUPPERED
SUNBERRIES	SUNK	SUPAWNS	SUPERLOO	SUPPERING
SUNBERRY	SUNKEN	SUPE	SUPERLOOS	SUPPERS
SUNBIRD	SUNKET	SUPER	SUPERMAN	SUPPING
SUNBIRDS	SUNKETS	SUPERABLE	SUPERMART	SUPPLANT
SUNBLIND	SUNKIE	SUPERABLY	SUPERMARTS	SUPPLANTED
SUNBLINDS	SUNKIES	SUPERADD	SUPERMEN	SUPPLANTING
SUNBLOCK	SUNKS	SUPERADDED	SUPERMINI	SUPPLANTS
SUNBLOCKS	SUNLAMP	SUPERADDING	SUPERMINIS	SUPPLE
SUNBOW	SUNLAMPS	SUPERADDS	SUPERNAL	SUPPLED
SUNBOWS	SUNLESS	SUPERATE	SUPERNOVA	SUPPLELY
SUNBRIGHT	SUNLIGHT	SUPERATED	SUPERNOVAE	SUPPLER
SUNBURN	SUNLIGHTS	SUPERATES	SUPERNOVAS	SUPPLES
SUNBURNED	SUNLIKE	SUPERATING	SUPERPLUS	SUPPLEST
SUNBURNING	SUNLIT	SUPERB	SUPERPLUSES	SUPPLIAL
SUNBURNS	SUNN	SUPERBER	SUPERPOSE	SUPPLIALS
SUNBURNT	SUNNED	SUPERBEST	SUPERPOSED	SUPPLIANT
SUNBURST	SUNNIER	SUPERBITIES	SUPERPOSES	SUPPLIANTS
SUNBURSTS	SUNNIEST	SUPERBITY	SUPERPOSING	SUPPLICAT
SUNDAE	SUNNILY	SUPERBLY	SUPERRICH	SUPPLICATS
SUNDAES	SUNNINESS	SUPERBOLD	SUPERS	SUPPLIED
SUNDARI	SUNNINESSES	SUPERBRAT	SUPERSAFE	SUPPLIER
SUNDARIS	SUNNING	SUPERBRATS	SUPERSALT	SUPPLIERS
SUNDECK	SUNNS	SUPERBUG	SUPERSALTS	SUPPLIES
SUNDECKS	SUNNY	SUPERBUGS	SUPERSEDE	SUPPLING
SUNDER	SUNPROOF	SUPERCOIL	SUPERSEDED	SUPPLY
SUNDERED	SUNRAY	SUPERCOILS	SUPERSEDES	SUPPLYING
SUNDERER	SUNRAYS	SUPERCOLD	SUPERSEDING	SUPPORT
SUNDERERS	SUNRISE	SUPERCOOL	SUPERSELL	SUPPORTED
SUNDERING	SUNRISES	SUPERCOOLED	SUPERSELLS	SUPPORTER
SUNDERINGS	SUNRISING	SUPERCOOLING	SUPERSOFT	SUPPORTERS
SUNDERS	SUNRISINGS	SUPERCOOLS	SUPERSPIES	SUPPORTING
SUNDEW	SUNROOF	SUPEREGO	SUPERSPY	SUPPORTINGS
SUNDEWS	SUNROOFS	SUPEREGOS	SUPERSTAR	SUPPORTS
SUNDIAL	SUNS	SUPERETTE	SUPERSTARS	SUPPOSAL
SUNDIALS	SUNSCREEN	SUPERETTES	SUPERTAX	SUPPOSALS
SUNDOG	SUNSCREENS	SUPERFAST	SUPERTAXES	SUPPOSE
SUNDOGS	SUNSET	SUPERFINE	SUPERTHIN	SUPPOSED
SUNDOWN	SUNSETS	SUPERFIT	SUPERVENE	SUPPOSER
SUNDOWNER	SUNSHADE	SUPERFLUX	SUPERVENED	SUPPOSERS
SUNDOWNERS	SUNSHADES	SUPERFLUXES	SUPERVENES	SUPPOSES
SUNDOWNS	SUNSHINE	SUPERFUSE	SUPERVENING	SUPPOSING
SUNDRA	SUNSHINES	SUPERFUSED	SUPERVISE	SUPPOSINGS
SUNDRAS	SUNSHINY	SUPERFUSES	SUPERVISED	SUPPRESS
SUNDRESS	SUNSPOT	SUPERFUSING	SUPERVISES	SUPPRESSED
SUNDRESSES	SUNSPOTS	SUPERGENE	SUPERVISING	SUPPRESSES
SUNDRI	SUNSTONE	SUPERGENES	SUPERWAIF	SUPPRESSING
SUNDRIES	SUNSTONES	SUPERGLUE	SUPERWAIFS	SUPPURATE
SUNDRIS	SUNSTROKE	SUPERGLUED	SUPES	SUPPURATED
SUNDROPS	SUNSTROKES	SUPERGLUES	SUPINATE	SUPPURATES

The Chambers Dictionary is the authority for many longer words; see *OSW* Introduction, page xii

SUPPURATING	SURED	SURGINGS	SURREINED	SURVIVORS
SUPREMACIES	SURELY	SURGY	SURREJOIN	SUS
SUPREMACY	SURENESS	SURICATE	SURREJOINED	SUSCEPTOR
SUPREME	SURENESSES	SURICATES	SURREJOINING	SUSCEPTORS
SUPREMELY	SURER	SURING	SURREJOINS	SUSCITATE
SUPREMER	SURES	SURLIER	SURRENDER	SUSCITATED
SUPREMES	SUREST	SURLIEST	SURRENDERED	SUSCITATES
SUPREMEST	SURETIED	SURLILY	SURRENDERING	SUSCITATING
SUPREMITIES	SURETIES	SURLINESS	SURRENDERS	SUSES
SUPREMITY	SURETY	SURLINESSES	SURRENDRIES	SUSHI
SUPREMO	SURETYING	SURLOIN	SURRENDRY	SUSHIS
SUPREMOS	SURF	SURLOINS	SURREY	SUSLIK
SUPS	SURFACE	SURLY	SURREYS	SUSLIKS
SUQ	SURFACED	SURMASTER	SURROGACIES	SUSPECT
SUQS	SURFACER	SURMASTERS	SURROGACY	SUSPECTED
SUR	SURFACERS	SURMISAL	SURROGATE	SUSPECTING
SURA	SURFACES	SURMISALS	SURROGATES	SUSPECTS
SURAH	SURFACING	SURMISE	SURROUND	SUSPENCE
SURAHS	SURFACINGS	SURMISED	SURROUNDED	SUSPEND
SURAL	SURFBIRD	SURMISER	SURROUNDING	SUSPENDED
SURAMIN	SURFBIRDS	SURMISERS	SURROUNDINGS	SUSPENDER
SURAMINS	SURFBOARD	SURMISES	SURROUNDS	SUSPENDERS
SURANCE	SURFBOARDS	SURMISING	SURROYAL	SUSPENDING
SURANCES	SURFED	SURMISINGS	SURROYALS	SUSPENDS
SURAS	SURFEIT	SURMOUNT	SURTAX	SUSPENS
SURAT	SURFEITED	SURMOUNTED	SURTAXED	SUSPENSE
SURATS	SURFEITER	SURMOUNTING	SURTAXES	SUSPENSER
SURBAHAR	SURFEITERS	SURMOUNTINGS	SURTAXING	SUSPENSERS
SURBAHARS	SURFEITING	SURMOUNTS	SURTITLE	SUSPENSES
SURBASE	SURFEITINGS	SURMULLET	SURTITLES	SUSPENSOR
SURBASED	SURFEITS	SURMULLETS	SURTOUT	SUSPENSORS
SURBASES	SURFER	SURNAME	SURTOUTS	SUSPICION
SURBATE	SURFERS	SURNAMED	SURUCUCU	SUSPICIONED
SURBATED	SURFFISH	SURNAMES	SURUCUCUS	SUSPICIONING
SURBATES	SURFFISHES	SURNAMING	SURVEILLE	SUSPICIONS
SURBATING	SURFICIAL	SURPASS	SURVEILLED	SUSPIRE
SURBED	SURFIE	SURPASSED	SURVEILLES	SUSPIRED
SURBEDDED	SURFIER	SURPASSES	SURVEILLING	SUSPIRES
SURBEDDING	SURFIES	SURPASSING	SURVEW	SUSPIRING
SURBEDS	SURFIEST	SURPLICE	SURVEWE	SUSS
SURBET	SURFING	SURPLICED	SURVEWED	SUSSARARA
SURCEASE	SURFINGS	SURPLICES	SURVEWES	SUSSARARAS
SURCEASED	SURFMAN	SURPLUS	SURVEWING	SUSSED
SURCEASES	SURFMEN	SURPLUSES	SURVEWS	SUSSES
SURCEASING	SURFPERCH	SURPRISAL	SURVEY	SUSSING
SURCHARGE	SURFPERCHES	SURPRISALS	SURVEYAL	SUSTAIN
SURCHARGED	SURFS	SURPRISE	SURVEYALS	SUSTAINED
SURCHARGES	SURFY	SURPRISED	SURVEYED	SUSTAINER
SURCHARGING	SURGE	SURPRISER	SURVEYING	SUSTAINERS
SURCINGLE	SURGED	SURPRISERS	SURVEYINGS	SUSTAINING
SURCINGLED	SURGEFUL	SURPRISES	SURVEYOR	SUSTAININGS
SURCINGLES	SURGELESS	SURPRISING	SURVEYORS	SUSTAINS
SURCINGLING	SURGENT	SURPRISINGS	SURVEYS	SUSTINENT
SURCOAT	SURGEON	SURQUEDIES	SURVIEW	SUSURRANT
SURCOATS	SURGEONCIES	SURQUEDRIES	SURVIEWED	SUSURRATE
SURCULI	SURGEONCY	SURQUEDRY	SURVIEWING	SUSURRATED
SURCULOSE	SURGEONS	SURQUEDY	SURVIEWS	SUSURRATES
SURCULUS	SURGERIES	SURRA	SURVIVAL	SUSURRATING
SURCULUSES	SURGERY	SURRAS	SURVIVALS	SUSURRUS
SURD	SURGES	SURREAL	SURVIVE	SUSURRUSES
SURDITIES	SURGICAL	SURREBUT	SURVIVED	SUTILE
SURDITY	SURGIER	SURREBUTS	SURVIVES	SUTLER
SURDS	SURGIEST	SURREBUTTED	SURVIVING	SUTLERIES
SURE	SURGING	SURREBUTTING	SURVIVOR	SUTLERS

SUTLERY	SWAGGIES	SWANKY	SWASHED	SWEATER
SUTOR	SWAGGING	SWANLIKE	SWASHER	SWEATERS
SUTORIAL	SWAGING	SWANNED	SWASHERS	SWEATIER
SUTORIAN	SWAGMAN	SWANNERIES	SWASHES	SWEATIEST
SUTORS	SWAGMEN	SWANNERY	SWASHIER	SWEATING
SUTRA	SWAGS	SWANNIER	SWASHIEST	SWEATINGS
SUTRAS	SWAGSHOP	SWANNIEST	SWASHING	SWEATS
SUTTEE	SWAGSHOPS	SWANNING	SWASHINGS	SWEATSUIT
SUTTEEISM	SWAGSMAN	SWANNINGS	SWASHWORK	SWEATSUITS
SUTTEEISMS	SWAGSMEN	SWANNY	SWASHWORKS	SWEATY
SUTTEES	SWAIN	SWANS	SWASHY	SWEDE
SUTTLE	SWAINING	SWANSDOWN	SWASTIKA	SWEDES
SUTTLED	SWAININGS	SWANSDOWNS	SWASTIKAS	SWEE
SUTTLES	SWAINISH	SWANSKIN	SWAT	SWEED
SUTTLETIE	SWAINS	SWANSKINS	SWATCH	SWEEING
SUTTLETIES	SWALE	SWAP	SWATCHES	SWEEL
SUTTLING	SWALED	SWAPPED	SWATH	SWEELED
SUTTLY	SWALES	SWAPPER	SWATHE	SWEELING
SUTURAL	SWALIER	SWAPPERS	SWATHED	SWEELS
SUTURALLY	SWALIEST	SWAPPING	SWATHES	SWEENEY
SUTURE	SWALING	SWAPPINGS	SWATHIER	SWEENEYS
SUTURED	SWALINGS	SWAPS	SWATHIEST	SWEENIES
SUTURES	SWALLET	SWAPT	SWATHING	SWEENY
SUTURING	SWALLETS	SWAPTION	SWATHS	SWEEP
SUVERSED	SWALLOW	SWAPTIONS	SWATHY	SWEEPBACK
SUZERAIN	SWALLOWED	SWARAJ	SWATS	SWEEPBACKS
SUZERAINS	SWALLOWER	SWARAJES	SWATTED	SWEEPER
SVASTIKA	SWALLOWERS	SWARAJISM	SWATTER	SWEEPERS
SVASTIKAS	SWALLOWING	SWARAJISMS	SWATTERED	SWEEPIER
SVELTE	SWALLOWS	SWARAJIST	SWATTERING	SWEEPIEST
SVELTER	SWALY	SWARAJISTS	SWATTERS	SWEEPING
SVELTEST	SWAM	SWARD	SWATTING	SWEEPINGS
SWAB	SWAMI	SWARDED	SWATTINGS	SWEEPS
SWABBED	SWAMIS	SWARDIER	SWAY	SWEEPY
SWABBER	SWAMP	SWARDIEST	SWAYBACK	SWEER
SWABBERS	SWAMPED	SWARDING	SWAYBACKS	SWEERED
SWABBIES	SWAMPER	SWARDS	SWAYED	SWEERT
SWABBING	SWAMPERS	SWARDY	SWAYER	SWEES
SWABBY	SWAMPIER	SWARE	SWAYERS	SWEET
SWABS	SWAMPIEST	SWARF	SWAYING	SWEETCORN
SWACK	SWAMPING	SWARFED	SWAYINGS	SWEETCORNS
SWAD	SWAMPLAND	SWARFING	SWAYL	SWEETED
SWADDIES	SWAMPLANDS	SWARFS	SWAYLED	SWEETEN
SWADDLE	SWAMPS	SWARM	SWAYLING	SWEETENED
SWADDLED	SWAMPY	SWARMED	SWAYLINGS	SWEETENER
SWADDLER	SWAN	SWARMER	SWAYLS	SWEETENERS
SWADDLERS	SWANG	SWARMERS	SWAYS	SWEETENING
SWADDLES	SWANHERD	SWARMING	SWAZZLE	SWEETENINGS
SWADDLING	SWANHERDS	SWARMINGS	SWAZZLES	SWEETENS
SWADDY	SWANK	SWARMS	SWEAL	SWEETER
SWADS	SWANKED	SWART	SWEALED	SWEETEST
SWAG	SWANKER	SWARTH	SWEALING	SWEETFISH
SWAGE	SWANKERS	SWARTHIER	SWEALINGS	SWEETFISHES
SWAGED	SWANKEY	SWARTHIEST	SWEALS	SWEETIE
SWAGES	SWANKEYS	SWARTHS	SWEAR	SWEETIES
SWAGGED	SWANKIE	SWARTHY	SWEARD	SWEETING
SWAGGER	SWANKIER	SWARTNESS	SWEARDS	SWEETINGS
SWAGGERED	SWANKIES	SWARTNESSES	SWEARER	SWEETISH
SWAGGERER	SWANKIEST	SWARTY	SWEARERS	SWEETLY
SWAGGERERS	SWANKING	SWARVE	SWEARING	SWEETMEAL
SWAGGERING	SWANKPOT	SWARVED	SWEARINGS	SWEETMEAT
SWAGGERINGS	SWANKPOTS	SWARVES	SWEARS	SWEETMEATS
SWAGGERS	SWANKS	SWARVING	SWEAT	SWEETNESS
SWAGGIE		SWASH	SWEATED	SWEETNESSES

SWEETPEA	SWIFTEST	SWINGERS	SWITCHINGS	SWORDFISH
SWEETPEAS	SWIFTING	SWINGES	SWITCHMAN	SWORDFISHES
SWEETS	SWIFTLET	SWINGIER	SWITCHMEN	SWORDING
SWEETSOP	SWIFTLETS	SWINGIEST	SWITCHY	SWORDLESS
SWEETSOPS	SWIFTLY	SWINGING	SWITH	SWORDLIKE
SWEETWOOD	SWIFTNESS	SWINGINGS	SWITHER	SWORDMAN
SWEETWOODS	SWIFTNESSES	SWINGISM	SWITHERED	SWORDMEN
SWEETY	SWIFTS	SWINGISMS	SWITHERING	SWORDPLAY
SWEIR	SWIG	SWINGLE	SWITHERS	SWORDPLAYS
SWEIRNESS	SWIGGED	SWINGLED	SWITS	SWORDS
SWEIRNESSES	SWIGGER	SWINGLES	SWITSES	SWORDSMAN
SWEIRT	SWIGGERS	SWINGLING	SWIVE	SWORDSMEN
SWELCHIE	SWIGGING	SWINGLINGS	SWIVED	SWORE
SWELCHIES	SWIGS	SWINGS	SWIVEL	SWORN
SWELL	SWILL	SWINGTREE	SWIVELLED	SWOT
SWELLDOM	SWILLED	SWINGTREES	SWIVELLING	SWOTS
SWELLDOMS	SWILLER	SWINGY	SWIVELS	SWOTTED
SWELLED	SWILLERS	SWINISH	SWIVES	SWOTTER
SWELLER	SWILLING	SWINISHLY	SWIVET	SWOTTERS
SWELLERS	SWILLINGS	SWINK	SWIVETS	SWOTTING
SWELLEST	SWILLS	SWINKED	SWIVING	SWOTTINGS
SWELLING	SWIM	SWINKING	SWIZ	SWOUN
SWELLINGS	SWIMMABLE	SWINKS	SWIZZED	SWOUND
SWELLISH	SWIMMER	SWIPE	SWIZZES	SWOUNDED
SWELLS	SWIMMERET	SWIPED	SWIZZING	SWOUNDING
SWELT	SWIMMERETS	SWIPER	SWIZZLE	SWOUNDS
SWELTED	SWIMMERS	SWIPERS	SWIZZLED	SWOUNE
SWELTER	SWIMMIER	SWIPES	SWIZZLES	SWOUNED
SWELTERED	SWIMMIEST	SWIPEY	SWIZZLING	SWOUNES
SWELTERING	SWIMMING	SWIPIER	SWOB	SWOUNING
SWELTERINGS	SWIMMINGS	SWIPIEST	SWOBBED	SWOUNS
SWELTERS	SWIMMY	SWIPING	SWOBBER	SWOWND
SWELTING	SWIMS	SWIPPLE	SWOBBERS	SWOWNDS
SWELTRIER	SWIMSUIT	SWIPPLES	SWOBBING	SWOWNE
SWELTRIEST	SWIMSUITS	SWIRE	SWOBS	SWOWNES
SWELTRY	SWIMWEAR	SWIRES	SWOLLEN	SWOZZLE
SWELTS	SWIMWEARS	SWIRL	SWOLN	SWOZZLES
SWEPT	SWINDGE	SWIRLED	SWONE	SWUM
SWEPTBACK	SWINDGED	SWIRLIER	SWONES	SWUNG
SWEPTWING	SWINDGES	SWIRLIEST	SWOON	SWY
SWERF	SWINDGING	SWIRLING	SWOONED	SYBARITE
SWERFED	SWINDLE	SWIRLS	SWOONING	SYBARITES
SWERFING	SWINDLED	SWIRLY	SWOONINGS	SYBARITIC
SWERFS	SWINDLER	SWISH	SWOONS	SYBBE
SWERVE	SWINDLERS	SWISHED	SWOOP	SYBBES
SWERVED	SWINDLES	SWISHER	SWOOPED	SYBIL
SWERVER	SWINDLING	SWISHERS	SWOOPING	SYBILS
SWERVERS	SWINDLINGS	SWISHES	SWOOPS	SYBO
SWERVES	SWINE	SWISHEST	SWOOSH	SYBOE
SWERVING	SWINEHERD	SWISHIER	SWOOSHED	SYBOES
SWERVINGS	SWINEHERDS	SWISHIEST	SWOOSHES	SYBOTIC
SWEVEN	SWINEHOOD	SWISHING	SWOOSHING	SYBOTISM
SWEVENS	SWINEHOODS	SWISHINGS	SWOP	SYBOTISMS
SWEY	SWINERIES	SWISHY	SWOPPED	SYBOW
SWEYED	SWINERY	SWISSING	SWOPPER	SYBOWS
SWEYING	SWING	SWISSINGS	SWOPPERS	SYCAMINE
SWEYS	SWINGBEAT	SWITCH	SWOPPING	SYCAMINES
SWIDDEN	SWINGBEATS	SWITCHED	SWOPPINGS	SYCAMORE
SWIDDENS	SWINGBOAT	SWITCHEL	SWOPS	SYCAMORES
SWIES	SWINGBOATS	SWITCHELS	SWOPT	SYCE
SWIFT	SWINGE	SWITCHES	SWORD	SYCEE
SWIFTED	SWINGED	SWITCHIER	SWORDED	SYCEES
SWIFTER	SWINGEING	SWITCHIEST	SWORDER	SYCES
SWIFTERS	SWINGER	SWITCHING	SWORDERS	SYCOMORE

SYCOMORES	SYLPHIER	SYMPATHIES	SYNCED	SYNERGID
SYCONIA	SYLPHIEST	SYMPATHIN	SYNCH	SYNERGIDS
SYCONIUM	SYLPHINE	SYMPATHINS	SYNCHED	SYNERGIES
SYCOPHANT	SYLPHISH	SYMPATHY	SYNCHING	SYNERGISE
SYCOPHANTS	SYLPHS	SYMPATRIC	SYNCHRO	SYNERGISED
SYCOSES	SYLPHY	SYMPHILE	SYNCHRONIES	SYNERGISES
SYCOSIS	SYLVA	SYMPHILES	SYNCHRONY	SYNERGISING
SYE	SYLVAE	SYMPHILIES	SYNCHROS	SYNERGISM
SYED	SYLVAN	SYMPHILY	SYNCHS	SYNERGISMS
SYEING	SYLVANER	SYMPHONIC	SYNCHYSES	SYNERGIST
SYEN	SYLVANERS	SYMPHONIES	SYNCHYSIS	SYNERGISTS
SYENITE	SYLVANITE	SYMPHONY	SYNCING	SYNERGIZE
SYENITES	SYLVANITES	SYMPHYSES	SYNCLINAL	SYNERGIZED
SYENITIC	SYLVANS	SYMPHYSIS	SYNCLINALS	SYNERGIZES
SYENS	SYLVAS	SYMPHYTIC	SYNCLINE	SYNERGIZING
SYES	SYLVATIC	SYMPLAST	SYNCLINES	SYNERGY
SYKE	SYLVIA	SYMPLASTS	SYNCOPAL	SYNES
SYKER	SYLVIAS	SYMPLOCE	SYNCOPATE	SYNESES
SYKES	SYLVIINE	SYMPLOCES	SYNCOPATED	SYNESIS
SYLLABARIES	SYLVINE	SYMPODIA	SYNCOPATES	SYNFUEL
SYLLABARY	SYLVINES	SYMPODIAL	SYNCOPATING	SYNFUELS
SYLLABI	SYLVINITE	SYMPODIUM	SYNCOPE	SYNGAMIC
SYLLABIC	SYLVINITES	SYMPOSIA	SYNCOPES	SYNGAMIES
SYLLABICS	SYLVITE	SYMPOSIAC	SYNCOPIC	SYNGAMOUS
SYLLABIFIED	SYLVITES	SYMPOSIAL	SYNCOPTIC	SYNGAMY
SYLLABIFIES	SYMAR	SYMPOSIUM	SYNCRETIC	SYNGAS
SYLLABIFY	SYMARS	SYMPTOM	SYNCS	SYNGASES
SYLLABIFYING	SYMBION	SYMPTOMS	SYNCYTIA	SYNGENEIC
SYLLABISE	SYMBIONS	SYMPTOSES	SYNCYTIAL	SYNGRAPH
SYLLABISED	SYMBIONT	SYMPTOSIS	SYNCYTIUM	SYNGRAPHS
SYLLABISES	SYMBIONTS	SYMPTOTIC	SYND	SYNING
SYLLABISING	SYMBIOSES	SYNAGOGAL	SYNDACTYL	SYNIZESES
SYLLABISM	SYMBIOSIS	SYNAGOGUE	SYNDED	SYNIZESIS
SYLLABISMS	SYMBIOTIC	SYNAGOGUES	SYNDESES	SYNKARYON
SYLLABIZE	SYMBOL	SYNANDRIA	SYNDESIS	SYNKARYONS
SYLLABIZED	SYMBOLE	SYNANGIA	SYNDET	SYNOD
SYLLABIZES	SYMBOLES	SYNANGIUM	SYNDETIC	SYNODAL
SYLLABIZING	SYMBOLIC	SYNANTHIC	SYNDETS	SYNODALS
SYLLABLE	SYMBOLICS	SYNANTHIES	SYNDIC	SYNODIC
SYLLABLED	SYMBOLISE	SYNANTHY	SYNDICAL	SYNODICAL
SYLLABLES	SYMBOLISED	SYNAPHEA	SYNDICATE	SYNODS
SYLLABLING	SYMBOLISES	SYNAPHEAS	SYNDICATED	SYNODSMAN
SYLLABUB	SYMBOLISING	SYNAPHEIA	SYNDICATES	SYNODSMEN
SYLLABUBS	SYMBOLISM	SYNAPHEIAS	SYNDICATING	SYNOECETE
SYLLABUS	SYMBOLISMS	SYNAPSE	SYNDICS	SYNOECETES
SYLLABUSES	SYMBOLIST	SYNAPSES	SYNDING	SYNOECISE
SYLLEPSES	SYMBOLISTS	SYNAPSIS	SYNDINGS	SYNOECISED
SYLLEPSIS	SYMBOLIZE	SYNAPTASE	SYNDROME	SYNOECISES
SYLLEPTIC	SYMBOLIZED	SYNAPTASES	SYNDROMES	SYNOECISING
SYLLOGISE	SYMBOLIZES	SYNAPTE	SYNDROMIC	SYNOECISM
SYLLOGISED	SYMBOLIZING	SYNAPTES	SYNDS	SYNOECISMS
SYLLOGISES	SYMBOLLED	SYNAPTIC	SYNE	SYNOECIZE
SYLLOGISING	SYMBOLLING	SYNARCHIES	SYNECHIA	SYNOECIZED
SYLLOGISM	SYMBOLOGIES	SYNARCHY	SYNECHIAS	SYNOECIZES
SYLLOGISMS	SYMBOLOGY	SYNASTRIES	SYNECTIC	SYNOECIZING
SYLLOGIZE	SYMBOLS	SYNASTRY	SYNECTICS	SYNOEKETE
SYLLOGIZED	SYMITAR	SYNAXARIA	SYNED	SYNOEKETES
SYLLOGIZES	SYMITARE	SYNAXES	SYNEDRIA	SYNOICOUS
SYLLOGIZING	SYMITARES	SYNAXIS	SYNEDRIAL	SYNONYM
SYLPH	SYMITARS	SYNC	SYNEDRION	SYNONYMIC
SYLPHID	SYMMETRAL	SYNCARP	SYNEDRIUM	SYNONYMIES
SYLPHIDE	SYMMETRIC	SYNCARPIES	SYNERESES	SYNONYMS
SYLPHIDES	SYMMETRIES	SYNCARPS	SYNERESIS	SYNONYMY
SYLPHIDS	SYMMETRY	SYNCARPY	SYNERGIC	SYNOPSES

SYNOPSIS
SYNOPSISE
SYNOPSISED
SYNOPSISES
SYNOPSISING
SYNOPSIZE
SYNOPSIZED
SYNOPSIZES
SYNOPSIZING
SYNOPTIC
SYNOPTIST
SYNOPTISTS
SYNOVIA
SYNOVIAL
SYNOVIAS
SYNOVITIC
SYNOVITIS
SYNOVITISES
SYNROC
SYNROCS
SYNTACTIC
SYNTAGM
SYNTAGMA
SYNTAGMATA
SYNTAGMS
SYNTAN
SYNTANS

SYNTAX
SYNTAXES
SYNTECTIC
SYNTEXIS
SYNTEXISES
SYNTH
SYNTHESES
SYNTHESIS
SYNTHETIC
SYNTHETICS
SYNTHON
SYNTHONS
SYNTHRONI
SYNTHS
SYNTONIC
SYNTONIES
SYNTONIN
SYNTONINS
SYNTONISE
SYNTONISED
SYNTONISES
SYNTONISING
SYNTONIZE
SYNTONIZED
SYNTONIZES
SYNTONIZING
SYNTONOUS

SYNTONY
SYPE
SYPED
SYPES
SYPHER
SYPHERED
SYPHERING
SYPHERS
SYPHILIS
SYPHILISE
SYPHILISED
SYPHILISES
SYPHILISING
SYPHILIZE
SYPHILIZED
SYPHILIZES
SYPHILIZING
SYPHILOID
SYPHILOMA
SYPHILOMAS
SYPHON
SYPHONED
SYPHONING
SYPHONS
SYPING
SYRAH
SYRAHS

SYREN
SYRENS
SYRINGA
SYRINGAS
SYRINGE
SYRINGEAL
SYRINGED
SYRINGES
SYRINGING
SYRINX
SYRINXES
SYRLYE
SYRPHID
SYRPHIDS
SYRTES
SYRTIS
SYRUP
SYRUPED
SYRUPIER
SYRUPIEST
SYRUPING
SYRUPS
SYRUPY
SYSOP
SYSOPS
SYSSITIA
SYSSITIAS

SYSTALTIC
SYSTEM
SYSTEMED
SYSTEMIC
SYSTEMISE
SYSTEMISED
SYSTEMISES
SYSTEMISING
SYSTEMIZE
SYSTEMIZED
SYSTEMIZES
SYSTEMIZING
SYSTEMS
SYSTOLE
SYSTOLES
SYSTOLIC
SYSTYLE
SYSTYLES
SYTHE
SYTHES
SYVER
SYVERS
SYZYGIAL
SYZYGIES
SYZYGY

T

TA	TABLELANDS	TABULAR	TACKET	TADPOLE
TAB	TABLES	TABULARLY	TACKETS	TADPOLES
TABANID	TABLET	TABULATE	TACKETY	TADS
TABANIDS	TABLETED	TABULATED	TACKIER	TADVANCE
TABARD	TABLETING	TABULATES	TACKIES	TAE
TABARDS	TABLETOP	TABULATING	TACKIEST	TAED
TABARET	TABLETOPS	TABULATOR	TACKILY	TAEDIUM
TABARETS	TABLETS	TABULATORS	TACKINESS	TAEDIUMS
TABASHEER	TABLEWARE	TABUN	TACKINESSES	TAEING
TABASHEERS	TABLEWARES	TABUNS	TACKING	TAEL
TABASHIR	TABLEWISE	TABUS	TACKINGS	TAELS
TABASHIRS	TABLIER	TACAHOUT	TACKLE	TAENIA
TABBED	TABLIERS	TACAHOUTS	TACKLED	TAENIAE
TABBIED	TABLING	TACAMAHAC	TACKLER	TAENIAS
TABBIES	TABLINGS	TACAMAHACS	TACKLERS	TAENIASES
TABBINET	TABLOID	TACAN	TACKLES	TAENIASIS
TABBINETS	TABLOIDS	TACANS	TACKLING	TAENIATE
TABBING	TABLOIDY	TACE	TACKLINGS	TAENIOID
TABBOULEH	TABOGGAN	TACES	TACKS	TAES
TABBOULEHS	TABOGGANED	TACET	TACKSMAN	TAFFEREL
TABBY	TABOGGANING	TACH	TACKSMEN	TAFFERELS
TABBYHOOD	TABOGGANS	TACHE	TACKY	TAFFETA
TABBYHOODS	TABOO	TACHES	TACMAHACK	TAFFETAS
TABBYING	TABOOED	TACHINID	TACMAHACKS	TAFFETASES
TABEFIED	TABOOING	TACHINIDS	TACO	TAFFETIES
TABEFIES	TABOOS	TACHISM	TACONITE	TAFFETY
TABEFY	TABOR	TACHISME	TACONITES	TAFFIA
TABEFYING	TABORED	TACHISMES	TACOS	TAFFIAS
TABELLION	TABORER	TACHISMS	TACT	TAFFIES
TABELLIONS	TABORERS	TACHIST	TACTFUL	TAFFRAIL
TABERD	TABORET	TACHISTE	TACTFULLY	TAFFRAILS
TABERDAR	TABORETS	TACHISTES	TACTIC	TAFFY
TABERDARS	TABORIN	TACHISTS	TACTICAL	TAFIA
TABERDS	TABORING	TACHO	TACTICIAN	TAFIAS
TABES	TABORINS	TACHOGRAM	TACTICIANS	TAG
TABESCENT	TABORS	TACHOGRAMS	TACTICITIES	TAGETES
TABETIC	TABOUR	TACHOS	TACTICITY	TAGGED
TABETICS	TABOURED	TACHYLITE	TACTICS	TAGGEE
TABI	TABOURET	TACHYLITES	TACTILE	TAGGEES
TABID	TABOURETS	TACHYLYTE	TACTILIST	TAGGER
TABINET	TABOURIN	TACHYLYTES	TACTILISTS	TAGGERS
TABINETS	TABOURING	TACHYON	TACTILITIES	TAGGIER
TABIS	TABOURINS	TACHYONS	TACTILITY	TAGGIEST
TABLA	TABOURS	TACHYPNEA	TACTION	TAGGING
TABLAS	TABRERE	TACHYPNEAS	TACTIONS	TAGGINGS
TABLATURE	TABRERES	TACIT	TACTISM	TAGGY
TABLATURES	TABRET	TACITLY	TACTISMS	TAGHAIRM
TABLE	TABRETS	TACITNESS	TACTLESS	TAGHAIRMS
TABLEAU	TABS	TACITNESSES	TACTS	TAGLIONI
TABLEAUX	TABU	TACITURN	TACTUAL	TAGLIONIS
TABLED	TABUED	TACK	TACTUALLY	TAGMA
TABLEFUL	TABUING	TACKED	TAD	TAGMATA
TABLEFULS	TABULA	TACKER	TADDIE	TAGMEME
TABLELAND	TABULAE	TACKERS	TADDIES	TAGMEMES

TAGMEMIC	TAILPIPES	TAKERS	TALESMAN	TALLNESS
TAGMEMICS	TAILPIPING	TAKES	TALESMEN	TALLNESSES
TAGRAG	TAILPLANE	TAKHI	TALI	TALLOT
TAGRAGS	TAILPLANES	TAKHIS	TALIGRADE	TALLOTS
TAGS	TAILRACE	TAKI	TALION	TALLOW
TAGUAN	TAILRACES	TAKIER	TALIONIC	TALLOWED
TAGUANS	TAILS	TAKIEST	TALIONS	TALLOWING
TAHA	TAILSKID	TAKIN	TALIPAT	TALLOWISH
TAHAS	TAILSKIDS	TAKING	TALIPATS	TALLOWS
TAHINA	TAILSPIN	TAKINGLY	TALIPED	TALLOWY
TAHINAS	TAILSPINS	TAKINGS	TALIPEDS	TALLY
TAHINI	TAILSTOCK	TAKINS	TALIPES	TALLYING
TAHINIS	TAILSTOCKS	TAKIS	TALIPOT	TALLYMAN
TAHR	TAILWHEEL	TAKS	TALIPOTS	TALLYMEN
TAHRS	TAILWHEELS	TAKY	TALISMAN	TALLYSHOP
TAHSIL	TAILYE	TALA	TALISMANS	TALLYSHOPS
TAHSILDAR	TAILYES	TALAK	TALK	TALMA
TAHSILDARS	TAILZIE	TALAKS	TALKABLE	TALMAS
TAHSILS	TAILZIES	TALANT	TALKATHON	TALMUD
TAI	TAINT	TALANTS	TALKATHONS	TALMUDS
TAIAHA	TAINTED	TALAPOIN	TALKATIVE	TALON
TAIAHAS	TAINTING	TALAPOINS	TALKBACK	TALONED
TAIGA	TAINTLESS	TALAQ	TALKBACKS	TALONS
TAIGAS	TAINTS	TALAQS	TALKED	TALOOKA
TAIGLE	TAINTURE	TALAR	TALKER	TALOOKAS
TAIGLED	TAINTURES	TALARIA	TALKERS	TALPA
TAIGLES	TAIPAN	TALARS	TALKFEST	TALPAE
TAIGLING	TAIPANS	TALAS	TALKFESTS	TALPAS
TAIL	TAIRA	TALAUNT	TALKIE	TALUK
TAILARD	TAIRAS	TALAUNTS	TALKIER	TALUKA
TAILARDS	TAIS	TALAYOT	TALKIES	TALUKAS
TAILBACK	TAISCH	TALAYOTS	TALKIEST	TALUKDAR
TAILBACKS	TAISCHES	TALBOT	TALKING	TALUKDARS
TAILBOARD	TAISH	TALBOTS	TALKINGS	TALUKS
TAILBOARDS	TAISHES	TALBOTYPE	TALKS	TALUS
TAILED	TAIT	TALBOTYPES	TALKY	TALUSES
TAILERON	TAITS	TALC	TALL	TALWEG
TAILERONS	TAIVER	TALCED	TALLAGE	TALWEGS
TAILGATE	TAIVERED	TALCIER	TALLAGED	TAM
TAILGATED	TAIVERING	TALCIEST	TALLAGES	TAMABLE
TAILGATER	TAIVERS	TALCING	TALLAGING	TAMAL
TAILGATERS	TAIVERT	TALCKED	TALLAT	TAMALE
TAILGATES	TAJ	TALCKIER	TALLATS	TAMALES
TAILGATING	TAJES	TALCKIEST	TALLBOY	TAMALS
TAILING	TAJINE	TALCKING	TALLBOYS	TAMANDU
TAILINGS	TAJINES	TALCKY	TALLENT	TAMANDUA
TAILLE	TAK	TALCOSE	TALLENTS	TAMANDUAS
TAILLES	TAKA	TALCOUS	TALLER	TAMANDUS
TAILLESS	TAKABLE	TALCS	TALLEST	TAMANOIR
TAILLEUR	TAKAHE	TALCUM	TALLET	TAMANOIRS
TAILLEURS	TAKAHES	TALCUMS	TALLETS	TAMANU
TAILLIE	TAKAMAKA	TALCY	TALLIABLE	TAMANUS
TAILLIES	TAKAMAKAS	TALE	TALLIATE	TAMARA
TAILOR	TAKAS	TALEA	TALLIATED	TAMARACK
TAILORED	TAKE	TALEAE	TALLIATES	TAMARACKS
TAILORESS	TAKEABLE	TALEFUL	TALLIATING	TAMARAO
TAILORESSES	TAKEAWAY	TALEGALLA	TALLIED	TAMARAOS
TAILORING	TAKEAWAYS	TALEGALLAS	TALLIER	TAMARAS
TAILORINGS	TAKEN	TALENT	TALLIERS	TAMARAU
TAILORS	TAKEOUT	TALENTED	TALLIES	TAMARAUS
TAILPIECE	TAKEOUTS	TALENTS	TALLISH	TAMARI
TAILPIECES	TAKEOVER	TALER	TALLITH	TAMARILLO
TAILPIPE	TAKEOVERS	TALERS	TALLITHIM	TAMARILLOS
TAILPIPED	TAKER	TALES	TALLITHS	TAMARIN

TAMARIND
TAMARINDS
TAMARINS
TAMARIS
TAMARISK
TAMARISKS
TAMASHA
TAMASHAS
TAMBAC
TAMBACS
TAMBER
TAMBERS
TAMBOUR
TAMBOURA
TAMBOURAS
TAMBOURED
TAMBOURIN
TAMBOURING
TAMBOURINS
TAMBOURS
TAMBURA
TAMBURAS
TAMBURIN
TAMBURINS
TAME
TAMEABLE
TAMED
TAMELESS
TAMELY
TAMENESS
TAMENESSES
TAMER
TAMERS
TAMES
TAMEST
TAMIN
TAMINE
TAMINES
TAMING
TAMINGS
TAMINS
TAMIS
TAMISE
TAMISES
TAMMAR
TAMMARS
TAMMIES
TAMMY
TAMOXIFEN
TAMOXIFENS
TAMP
TAMPED
TAMPER
TAMPERED
TAMPERER
TAMPERERS
TAMPERING
TAMPERINGS
TAMPERS
TAMPING
TAMPINGS
TAMPION
TAMPIONS
TAMPON

TAMPONADE
TAMPONADES
TAMPONAGE
TAMPONAGES
TAMPONED
TAMPONING
TAMPONS
TAMPS
TAMS
TAMWORTH
TAMWORTHS
TAN
TANA
TANADAR
TANADARS
TANAGER
TANAGERS
TANAGRA
TANAGRAS
TANAGRINE
TANAISTE
TANAISTES
TANALISED
TANALIZED
TANAS
TANBARK
TANBARKS
TANDEM
TANDEMS
TANDOOR
TANDOORI
TANDOORIS
TANDOORS
TANE
TANG
TANGA
TANGAS
TANGED
TANGELO
TANGELOS
TANGENCIES
TANGENCY
TANGENT
TANGENTS
TANGERINE
TANGERINES
TANGHIN
TANGHININ
TANGHININS
TANGHINS
TANGI
TANGIBLE
TANGIBLES
TANGIBLY
TANGIE
TANGIER
TANGIES
TANGIEST
TANGING
TANGIS
TANGLE
TANGLED
TANGLER
TANGLERS

TANGLES
TANGLIER
TANGLIEST
TANGLING
TANGLINGS
TANGLY
TANGO
TANGOED
TANGOING
TANGOIST
TANGOISTS
TANGOS
TANGRAM
TANGRAMS
TANGS
TANGUN
TANGUNS
TANGY
TANH
TANHS
TANIST
TANISTRIES
TANISTRY
TANISTS
TANIWHA
TANIWHAS
TANK
TANKA
TANKAGE
TANKAGES
TANKARD
TANKARDS
TANKAS
TANKED
TANKER
TANKERS
TANKFUL
TANKFULS
TANKIA
TANKIAS
TANKIES
TANKING
TANKINGS
TANKS
TANKY
TANLING
TANLINGS
TANNA
TANNABLE
TANNAGE
TANNAGES
TANNAH
TANNAHS
TANNAS
TANNATE
TANNATES
TANNED
TANNER
TANNERIES
TANNERS
TANNERY
TANNEST
TANNIC
TANNIN

TANNING
TANNINGS
TANNINS
TANNOY
TANNOYED
TANNOYING
TANNOYS
TANREC
TANRECS
TANS
TANSIES
TANSY
TANTALATE
TANTALATES
TANTALIC
TANTALISE
TANTALISED
TANTALISES
TANTALISING
TANTALISINGS
TANTALISM
TANTALISMS
TANTALITE
TANTALITES
TANTALIZE
TANTALIZED
TANTALIZES
TANTALIZING
TANTALIZINGS
TANTALOUS
TANTALUM
TANTALUMS
TANTALUS
TANTALUSES
TANTARA
TANTARARA
TANTARARAS
TANTARAS
TANTI
TANTIVIES
TANTIVY
TANTO
TANTONIES
TANTONY
TANTRA
TANTRAS
TANTRIC
TANTRUM
TANTRUMS
TANYARD
TANYARDS
TAOISEACH
TAOISEACHS
TAP
TAPA
TAPACOLO
TAPACOLOS
TAPACULO
TAPACULOS
TAPADERA
TAPADERAS
TAPADERO
TAPADEROS
TAPAS

TAPE
TAPEABLE
TAPED
TAPELESS
TAPELIKE
TAPELINE
TAPELINES
TAPEN
TAPENADE
TAPENADES
TAPER
TAPERED
TAPERER
TAPERERS
TAPERING
TAPERINGS
TAPERNESS
TAPERNESSES
TAPERS
TAPERWISE
TAPES
TAPESTRIED
TAPESTRIES
TAPESTRY
TAPESTRYING
TAPET
TAPETA
TAPETAL
TAPETI
TAPETIS
TAPETS
TAPETUM
TAPEWORM
TAPEWORMS
TAPHONOMIES
TAPHONOMY
TAPING
TAPIOCA
TAPIOCAS
TAPIR
TAPIROID
TAPIRS
TAPIS
TAPISES
TAPIST
TAPISTS
TAPLASH
TAPLASHES
TAPPA
TAPPABLE
TAPPAS
TAPPED
TAPPER
TAPPERS
TAPPET
TAPPETS
TAPPICE
TAPPICED
TAPPICES
TAPPICING
TAPPING
TAPPINGS
TAPPIT
TAPROOM

TAPROOMS	TARGED	TARRING	TARTRATE	TASTY
TAPROOT	TARGES	TARRINGS	TARTRATES	TAT
TAPROOTS	TARGET	TARROCK	TARTS	TATAMI
TAPS	TARGETED	TARROCKS	TARTY	TATAMIS
TAPSMAN	TARGETEER	TARROW	TARWEED	TATE
TAPSMEN	TARGETEERS	TARROWED	TARWEEDS	TATER
TAPSTER	TARGETING	TARROWING	TARWHINE	TATERS
TAPSTERS	TARGETS	TARROWS	TARWHINES	TATES
TAPSTRY	TARGING	TARRY	TASAR	TATH
TAPU	TARIFF	TARRYING	TASARS	TATHED
TAPUED	TARIFFED	TARS	TASER	TATHING
TAPUING	TARIFFING	TARSAL	TASERED	TATHS
TAPUS	TARIFFS	TARSALGIA	TASERING	TATIE
TAQUERIA	TARING	TARSALGIAS	TASERS	TATIES
TAQUERIAS	TARINGS	TARSALS	TASH	TATLER
TAR	TARLATAN	TARSEL	TASHED	TATLERS
TARA	TARLATANS	TARSELS	TASHES	TATOU
TARAKIHI	TARMAC	TARSI	TASHING	TATOUAY
TARAKIHIS	TARMACKED	TARSIA	TASIMETER	TATOUAYS
TARAND	TARMACKING	TARSIAS	TASIMETERS	TATOUS
TARANDS	TARMACS	TARSIER	TASK	TATS
TARANTARA	TARN	TARSIERS	TASKED	TATT
TARANTARAED	TARNAL	TARSIOID	TASKER	TATTED
TARANTARAING	TARNALLY	TARSIPED	TASKERS	TATTER
TARANTARAS	TARNATION	TARSIPEDS	TASKING	TATTERED
TARANTAS	TARNISH	TARSUS	TASKINGS	TATTERING
TARANTASES	TARNISHED	TART	TASKS	TATTERS
TARANTASS	TARNISHER	TARTAN	TASLET	TATTERY
TARANTASSES	TARNISHERS	TARTANA	TASLETS	TATTIE
TARANTISM	TARNISHES	TARTANAS	TASS	TATTIER
TARANTISMS	TARNISHING	TARTANE	TASSE	TATTIES
TARANTULA	TARNS	TARTANED	TASSEL	TATTIEST
TARANTULAS	TARO	TARTANES	TASSELED	TATTILY
TARAS	TAROC	TARTANRIES	TASSELING	TATTINESS
TARAXACUM	TAROCS	TARTANRY	TASSELL	TATTINESSES
TARAXACUMS	TAROK	TARTANS	TASSELLED	TATTING
TARBOGGIN	TAROKS	TARTAR	TASSELLING	TATTINGS
TARBOGGINED	TAROS	TARTARE	TASSELLINGS	TATTLE
TARBOGGINING	TAROT	TARTARES	TASSELLS	TATTLED
TARBOGGINS	TAROTS	TARTARIC	TASSELLY	TATTLER
TARBOOSH	TARP	TARTARISE	TASSELS	TATTLERS
TARBOOSHES	TARPAN	TARTARISED	TASSES	TATTLES
TARBOUSH	TARPANS	TARTARISES	TASSET	TATTLING
TARBOUSHES	TARPAULIN	TARTARISING	TASSETS	TATTLINGS
TARBOY	TARPAULINS	TARTARIZE	TASSIE	TATTOO
TARBOYS	TARPON	TARTARIZED	TASSIES	TATTOOED
TARBUSH	TARPONS	TARTARIZES	TASSWAGE	TATTOOER
TARBUSHES	TARPS	TARTARIZING	TASTABLE	TATTOOERS
TARCEL	TARRAGON	TARTARLY	TASTE	TATTOOING
TARCELS	TARRAGONS	TARTARS	TASTED	TATTOOIST
TARDIED	TARRAS	TARTER	TASTEFUL	TATTOOISTS
TARDIER	TARRASES	TARTEST	TASTELESS	TATTOOS
TARDIES	TARRE	TARTIER	TASTER	TATTOW
TARDIEST	TARRED	TARTIEST	TASTERS	TATTOWED
TARDILY	TARRES	TARTINE	TASTES	TATTOWING
TARDINESS	TARRIANCE	TARTINES	TASTEVIN	TATTOWS
TARDINESSES	TARRIANCES	TARTINESS	TASTEVINS	TATTS
TARDIVE	TARRIED	TARTINESSES	TASTIER	TATTY
TARDY	TARRIER	TARTISH	TASTIEST	TATU
TARDYING	TARRIERS	TARTLET	TASTILY	TATUED
TARE	TARRIES	TARTLETS	TASTINESS	TATUING
TARED	TARRIEST	TARTLY	TASTINESSES	TATUS
TARES	TARRINESS	TARTNESS	TASTING	TAU
TARGE	TARRINESSES	TARTNESSES	TASTINGS	TAUBE

TAUBES	TAWDRY	TAXLESS	TEAMED	TEAZELLED
TAUGHT	TAWED	TAXMAN	TEAMER	TEAZELLING
TAULD	TAWER	TAXMEN	TEAMERS	TEAZELS
TAUNT	TAWERIES	TAXOL	TEAMING	TEAZES
TAUNTED	TAWERS	TAXOLS	TEAMINGS	TEAZING
TAUNTER	TAWERY	TAXON	TEAMS	TEAZLE
TAUNTERS	TAWIE	TAXONOMER	TEAMSTER	TEAZLED
TAUNTING	TAWIER	TAXONOMERS	TEAMSTERS	TEAZLES
TAUNTINGS	TAWIEST	TAXONOMIC	TEAMWISE	TEAZLING
TAUNTS	TAWING	TAXONOMIES	TEAMWORK	TEBBAD
TAUPE	TAWINGS	TAXONOMY	TEAMWORKS	TEBBADS
TAUPES	TAWNEY	TAXOR	TEAPOT	TECH
TAUPIE	TAWNEYS	TAXORS	TEAPOTS	TECHIE
TAUPIES	TAWNIER	TAXYING	TEAPOY	TECHIER
TAUREAN	TAWNIES	TAY	TEAPOYS	TECHIES
TAURIC	TAWNIEST	TAYASSUID	TEAR	TECHIEST
TAURIFORM	TAWNINESS	TAYASSUIDS	TEARABLE	TECHILY
TAURINE	TAWNINESSES	TAYBERRIES	TEARAWAY	TECHINESS
TAURINES	TAWNY	TAYBERRY	TEARAWAYS	TECHINESSES
TAUS	TAWPIE	TAYRA	TEARER	TECHNIC
TAUT	TAWPIES	TAYRAS	TEARERS	TECHNICAL
TAUTED	TAWS	TAYS	TEARFUL	TECHNICS
TAUTEN	TAWSE	TAZZA	TEARFULLY	TECHNIQUE
TAUTENED	TAWSES	TAZZAS	TEARIER	TECHNIQUES
TAUTENING	TAWT	TAZZE	TEARIEST	TECHNO
TAUTENS	TAWTED	TCHICK	TEARING	TECHNOPOP
TAUTER	TAWTIE	TCHICKED	TEARLESS	TECHNOPOPS
TAUTEST	TAWTIER	TCHICKING	TEARS	TECHNOS
TAUTING	TAWTIEST	TCHICKS	TEARSHEET	TECHS
TAUTIT	TAWTING	TE	TEARSHEETS	TECHY
TAUTLY	TAWTS	TEA	TEARY	TECKEL
TAUTNESS	TAX	TEABERRIES	TEAS	TECKELS
TAUTNESSES	TAXA	TEABERRY	TEASE	TECTA
TAUTOG	TAXABLE	TEABOARD	TEASED	TECTIFORM
TAUTOGS	TAXABLY	TEABOARDS	TEASEL	TECTONIC
TAUTOLOGIES	TAXACEOUS	TEACH	TEASELED	TECTONICS
TAUTOLOGY	TAXAMETER	TEACHABLE	TEASELER	TECTORIAL
TAUTOMER	TAXAMETERS	TEACHER	TEASELERS	TECTRICES
TAUTOMERS	TAXATION	TEACHERLY	TEASELING	TECTRIX
TAUTONYM	TAXATIONS	TEACHERS	TEASELINGS	TECTUM
TAUTONYMS	TAXATIVE	TEACHES	TEASELLED	TED
TAUTS	TAXED	TEACHIE	TEASELLER	TEDDED
TAVA	TAXER	TEACHING	TEASELLERS	TEDDER
TAVAH	TAXERS	TEACHINGS	TEASELLING	TEDDERS
TAVAHS	TAXES	TEACHLESS	TEASELLINGS	TEDDIE
TAVAS	TAXI	TEACUP	TEASELS	TEDDIES
TAVER	TAXIARCH	TEACUPFUL	TEASER	TEDDING
TAVERED	TAXIARCHS	TEACUPFULS	TEASERS	TEDDY
TAVERING	TAXICAB	TEACUPS	TEASES	TEDESCA
TAVERN	TAXICABS	TEAD	TEASING	TEDESCHE
TAVERNA	TAXIDERMIES	TEADE	TEASINGLY	TEDESCHI
TAVERNAS	TAXIDERMY	TEADES	TEASINGS	TEDESCO
TAVERNER	TAXIED	TEADS	TEASPOON	TEDIER
TAVERNERS	TAXIES	TEAED	TEASPOONS	TEDIEST
TAVERNS	TAXIING	TEAGLE	TEAT	TEDIOSITIES
TAVERS	TAXIMAN	TEAGLED	TEATED	TEDIOSITY
TAVERT	TAXIMEN	TEAGLES	TEATIME	TEDIOUS
TAW	TAXIMETER	TEAGLING	TEATIMES	TEDIOUSLY
TAWA	TAXIMETERS	TEAING	TEATS	TEDISOME
TAWAS	TAXING	TEAK	TEAZE	TEDIUM
TAWDRIER	TAXINGS	TEAKS	TEAZED	TEDIUMS
TAWDRIES	TAXIS	TEAL	TEAZEL	TEDS
TAWDRIEST	TAXIWAY	TEALS	TEAZELED	TEDY
TAWDRILY	TAXIWAYS	TEAM	TEAZELING	TEE

TEED	TEFS	TELEGRAM	TELESM	TELLURATES
TEEING	TEG	TELEGRAMS	TELESMS	TELLURIAN
TEEL	TEGG	TELEGRAPH	TELESTIC	TELLURIANS
TEELS	TEGGS	TELEGRAPHED	TELESTICH	TELLURIC
TEEM	TEGMEN	TELEGRAPHING	TELESTICHS	TELLURIDE
TEEMED	TEGMENTA	TELEGRAPHS	TELETEX	TELLURIDES
TEEMER	TEGMENTAL	TELEMARK	TELETEXES	TELLURION
TEEMERS	TEGMENTUM	TELEMARKED	TELETEXT	TELLURIONS
TEEMFUL	TEGMINA	TELEMARKING	TELETEXTS	TELLURISE
TEEMING	TEGS	TELEMARKS	TELETHON	TELLURISED
TEEMLESS	TEGU	TELEMATIC	TELETHONS	TELLURISES
TEEMS	TEGUEXIN	TELEMATICS	TELETRON	TELLURISING
TEEN	TEGUEXINS	TELEMETER	TELETRONS	TELLURITE
TEENAGE	TEGULA	TELEMETERED	TELEVIEW	TELLURITES
TEENAGED	TEGULAE	TELEMETERING	TELEVIEWED	TELLURIUM
TEENAGER	TEGULAR	TELEMETERS	TELEVIEWING	TELLURIUMS
TEENAGERS	TEGULARLY	TELEMETRIES	TELEVIEWS	TELLURIZE
TEEND	TEGULATED	TELEMETRY	TELEVISE	TELLURIZED
TEENDED	TEGUMENT	TELEOLOGIES	TELEVISED	TELLURIZES
TEENDING	TEGUMENTS	TELEOLOGY	TELEVISER	TELLURIZING
TEENDS	TEGUS	TELEONOMIES	TELEVISERS	TELLUROUS
TEENE	TEHR	TELEONOMY	TELEVISES	TELLUS
TEENED	TEHRS	TELEOSAUR	TELEVISING	TELLUSES
TEENES	TEIL	TELEOSAURS	TELEVISOR	TELLY
TEENIER	TEILS	TELEOST	TELEVISORS	TELNET
TEENIEST	TEIND	TELEOSTS	TELEX	TELNETS
TEENING	TEINDED	TELEPATH	TELEXED	TELOMERE
TEENS	TEINDING	TELEPATHED	TELEXES	TELOMERES
TEENSIER	TEINDS	TELEPATHIES	TELEXING	TELOPHASE
TEENSIEST	TEKNONYMIES	TELEPATHING	TELFER	TELOPHASES
TEENSY	TEKNONYMY	TELEPATHS	TELFERAGE	TELOS
TEENTIER	TEKTITE	TELEPATHY	TELFERAGES	TELOSES
TEENTIEST	TEKTITES	TELEPHEME	TELFERED	TELPHER
TEENTSIER	TEL	TELEPHEMES	TELFERIC	TELPHERED
TEENTSIEST	TELA	TELEPHONE	TELFERING	TELPHERIC
TEENTSY	TELAE	TELEPHONED	TELFERS	TELPHERING
TEENTY	TELAMON	TELEPHONES	TELIA	TELPHERS
TEENY	TELAMONES	TELEPHONIES	TELIAL	TELS
TEEPEE	TELARY	TELEPHONING	TELIC	TELSON
TEEPEES	TELD	TELEPHONY	TELIUM	TELSONS
TEER	TELECAST	TELEPHOTO	TELL	TELT
TEERED	TELECASTED	TELEPLAY	TELLABLE	TEMAZEPAM
TEERING	TELECASTING	TELEPLAYS	TELLAR	TEMAZEPAMS
TEERS	TELECASTS	TELEPOINT	TELLARED	TEMBLOR
TEES	TELECHIR	TELEPOINTS	TELLARING	TEMBLORES
TEETER	TELECHIRS	TELEPORT	TELLARS	TEMBLORS
TEETERED	TELECINE	TELEPORTED	TELLEN	TEME
TEETERING	TELECINES	TELEPORTING	TELLENS	TEMED
TEETERS	TELECOM	TELEPORTS	TELLER	TEMENE
TEETH	TELECOMS	TELERGIC	TELLERED	TEMENOS
TEETHE	TELEDU	TELERGIES	TELLERING	TEMERITIES
TEETHED	TELEDUS	TELERGY	TELLERS	TEMERITY
TEETHES	TELEFAX	TELESALE	TELLIES	TEMEROUS
TEETHING	TELEFAXED	TELESALES	TELLIN	TEMES
TEETHINGS	TELEFAXES	TELESCOPE	TELLING	TEMP
TEETOTAL	TELEFAXING	TELESCOPED	TELLINGLY	TEMPED
TEETOTALS	TELEFILM	TELESCOPES	TELLINGS	TEMPEH
TEETOTUM	TELEFILMS	TELESCOPIES	TELLINOID	TEMPEHS
TEETOTUMS	TELEGA	TELESCOPING	TELLINS	TEMPER
TEF	TELEGAS	TELESCOPY	TELLS	TEMPERA
TEFF	TELEGENIC	TELESEME	TELLTALE	TEMPERAS
TEFFS	TELEGONIC	TELESEMES	TELLTALES	TEMPERATE
TEFILLAH	TELEGONIES	TELESES	TELLURAL	TEMPERATED
TEFILLIN	TELEGONY	TELESIS	TELLURATE	TEMPERATES

TEMPERATING
TEMPERED
TEMPERER
TEMPERERS
TEMPERING
TEMPERINGS
TEMPERS
TEMPEST
TEMPESTED
TEMPESTING
TEMPESTS
TEMPI
TEMPING
TEMPLAR
TEMPLARS
TEMPLATE
TEMPLATES
TEMPLE
TEMPLED
TEMPLES
TEMPLET
TEMPLETS
TEMPO
TEMPORAL
TEMPORALS
TEMPORARIES
TEMPORARY
TEMPORE
TEMPORISE
TEMPORISED
TEMPORISES
TEMPORISING
TEMPORISINGS
TEMPORIZE
TEMPORIZED
TEMPORIZES
TEMPORIZING
TEMPORIZINGS
TEMPOS
TEMPS
TEMPT
TEMPTABLE
TEMPTED
TEMPTER
TEMPTERS
TEMPTING
TEMPTINGS
TEMPTRESS
TEMPTRESSES
TEMPTS
TEMPURA
TEMPURAS
TEMS
TEMSE
TEMSED
TEMSES
TEMSING
TEMULENCE
TEMULENCES
TEMULENCIES
TEMULENCY
TEMULENT
TEN
TENABLE

TENACE
TENACES
TENACIOUS
TENACITIES
TENACITY
TENACULA
TENACULUM
TENAIL
TENAILLE
TENAILLES
TENAILLON
TENAILLONS
TENAILS
TENANCIES
TENANCY
TENANT
TENANTED
TENANTING
TENANTRIES
TENANTRY
TENANTS
TENCH
TENCHES
TEND
TENDANCE
TENDANCES
TENDED
TENDENCE
TENDENCES
TENDENCIES
TENDENCY
TENDENZ
TENDENZEN
TENDER
TENDERED
TENDERER
TENDERERS
TENDEREST
TENDERING
TENDERINGS
TENDERISE
TENDERISED
TENDERISES
TENDERISING
TENDERIZE
TENDERIZED
TENDERIZES
TENDERIZING
TENDERLY
TENDERS
TENDING
TENDINOUS
TENDON
TENDONS
TENDRE
TENDRES
TENDRIL
TENDRILS
TENDRON
TENDRONS
TENDS
TENE
TENEBRAE
TENEBRIO

TENEBRIOS
TENEBRISM
TENEBRISMS
TENEBRIST
TENEBRISTS
TENEBRITIES
TENEBRITY
TENEBROSE
TENEBROUS
TENEMENT
TENEMENTS
TENENDUM
TENENDUMS
TENES
TENESMUS
TENESMUSES
TENET
TENETS
TENFOLD
TENIA
TENIAE
TENIAS
TENIOID
TENNE
TENNER
TENNERS
TENNES
TENNIES
TENNIS
TENNISES
TENNO
TENNOS
TENNY
TENON
TENONED
TENONER
TENONERS
TENONING
TENONS
TENOR
TENORIST
TENORISTS
TENORITE
TENORITES
TENOROON
TENOROONS
TENORS
TENOTOMIES
TENOTOMY
TENOUR
TENOURS
TENPENCE
TENPENCES
TENPENNY
TENPINS
TENREC
TENRECS
TENS
TENSE
TENSED
TENSELESS
TENSELY
TENSENESS
TENSENESSES

TENSER
TENSES
TENSEST
TENSIBLE
TENSILE
TENSILITIES
TENSILITY
TENSING
TENSION
TENSIONAL
TENSIONED
TENSIONING
TENSIONS
TENSITIES
TENSITY
TENSIVE
TENSON
TENSONS
TENSOR
TENSORS
TENT
TENTACLE
TENTACLED
TENTACLES
TENTACULA
TENTAGE
TENTAGES
TENTATION
TENTATIONS
TENTATIVE
TENTATIVES
TENTED
TENTER
TENTERED
TENTERING
TENTERS
TENTFUL
TENTFULS
TENTH
TENTHLY
TENTHS
TENTIE
TENTIER
TENTIEST
TENTIGO
TENTIGOS
TENTING
TENTINGS
TENTLESS
TENTORIA
TENTORIAL
TENTORIUM
TENTORIUMS
TENTS
TENTWISE
TENTY
TENUE
TENUES
TENUIOUS
TENUIS
TENUITIES
TENUITY
TENUOUS
TENUOUSLY

TENURABLE
TENURE
TENURED
TENURES
TENURIAL
TENUTO
TENUTOS
TENZON
TENZONS
TEOCALLI
TEOCALLIS
TEOSINTE
TEOSINTES
TEPAL
TEPALS
TEPEE
TEPEES
TEPEFIED
TEPEFIES
TEPEFY
TEPEFYING
TEPHIGRAM
TEPHIGRAMS
TEPHILLAH
TEPHILLIN
TEPHRA
TEPHRAS
TEPHRITE
TEPHRITES
TEPHRITIC
TEPHROITE
TEPHROITES
TEPID
TEPIDARIA
TEPIDER
TEPIDEST
TEPIDITIES
TEPIDITY
TEPIDLY
TEPIDNESS
TEPIDNESSES
TEQUILA
TEQUILAS
TEQUILLA
TEQUILLAS
TERAFLOP
TERAI
TERAIS
TERAKIHI
TERAKIHIS
TERAPH
TERAPHIM
TERAPHIMS
TERAS
TERATA
TERATISM
TERATISMS
TERATOGEN
TERATOGENS
TERATOID
TERATOMA
TERATOMATA
TERBIC
TERBIUM

TERBIUMS	TERMINISTS	TERRENE	TERZETTI	TESTING
TERCE	TERMINUS	TERRENELY	TERZETTO	TESTINGS
TERCEL	TERMINUSES	TERRENES	TERZETTOS	TESTIS
TERCELET	TERMITARIES	TERRET	TES	TESTON
TERCELETS	TERMITARY	TERRETS	TESLA	TESTONS
TERCELS	TERMITE	TERRIBLE	TESLAS	TESTOON
TERCES	TERMITES	TERRIBLES	TESSELLA	TESTOONS
TERCET	TERMLESS	TERRIBLY	TESSELLAE	TESTRIL
TERCETS	TERMLIES	TERRICOLE	TESSELLAR	TESTRILL
TERCIO	TERMLY	TERRICOLES	TESSERA	TESTRILLS
TERCIOS	TERMOR	TERRIER	TESSERACT	TESTRILS
TEREBENE	TERMORS	TERRIERS	TESSERACTS	TESTS
TEREBENES	TERMS	TERRIES	TESSERAE	TESTUDINES
TEREBINTH	TERN	TERRIFIC	TESSERAL	TESTUDO
TEREBINTHS	TERNAL	TERRIFIED	TESSITURA	TESTUDOS
TEREBRA	TERNARIES	TERRIFIER	TESSITURAS	TESTY
TEREBRAE	TERNARY	TERRIFIERS	TEST	TETANAL
TEREBRANT	TERNATE	TERRIFIES	TESTA	TETANIC
TEREBRANTS	TERNATELY	TERRIFY	TESTABLE	TETANICS
TEREBRAS	TERNE	TERRIFYING	TESTACIES	TETANIES
TEREBRATE	TERNED	TERRINE	TESTACY	TETANISE
TEREBRATED	TERNES	TERRINES	TESTAE	TETANISED
TEREBRATES	TERNING	TERRIT	TESTAMENT	TETANISES
TEREBRATING	TERNION	TERRITORIES	TESTAMENTS	TETANISING
TEREDINES	TERNIONS	TERRITORY	TESTAMUR	TETANIZE
TEREDO	TERNS	TERRITS	TESTAMURS	TETANIZED
TEREDOS	TERPENE	TERROR	TESTATE	TETANIZES
TEREFA	TERPENES	TERRORFUL	TESTATION	TETANIZING
TEREFAH	TERPENOID	TERRORISE	TESTATIONS	TETANOID
TEREK	TERPENOIDS	TERRORISED	TESTATOR	TETANUS
TEREKS	TERPINEOL	TERRORISES	TESTATORS	TETANUSES
TERES	TERPINEOLS	TERRORISING	TESTATRICES	TETANY
TERETE	TERRA	TERRORISM	TESTATRIX	TETCHIER
TERETES	TERRACE	TERRORISMS	TESTATRIXES	TETCHIEST
TERF	TERRACED	TERRORIST	TESTATUM	TETCHILY
TERFE	TERRACES	TERRORISTS	TESTATUMS	TETCHY
TERFES	TERRACING	TERRORIZE	TESTE	TETE
TERFS	TERRACINGS	TERRORIZED	TESTED	TETES
TERGA	TERRAE	TERRORIZES	TESTEE	TETHER
TERGAL	TERRAFORM	TERRORIZING	TESTEES	TETHERED
TERGITE	TERRAFORMED	TERRORS	TESTER	TETHERING
TERGITES	TERRAFORMING	TERRY	TESTERN	TETHERS
TERGUM	TERRAFORMINGS	TERSE	TESTERNED	TETRA
TERIYAKI	TERRAFORMS	TERSELY	TESTERNING	TETRACID
TERIYAKIS	TERRAIN	TERSENESS	TESTERNS	TETRACT
TERM	TERRAINS	TERSENESSES	TESTERS	TETRACTS
TERMAGANT	TERRAMARA	TERSER	TESTES	TETRAD
TERMAGANTS	TERRAMARE	TERSEST	TESTICLE	TETRADIC
TERMED	TERRAMARES	TERSION	TESTICLES	TETRADITE
TERMER	TERRANE	TERSIONS	TESTIER	TETRADITES
TERMERS	TERRANES	TERTIA	TESTIEST	TETRADS
TERMINAL	TERRAPIN	TERTIAL	TESTIFIED	TETRAGON
TERMINALS	TERRAPINS	TERTIALS	TESTIFIER	TETRAGONS
TERMINATE	TERRARIA	TERTIAN	TESTIFIERS	TETRAGRAM
TERMINATED	TERRARIUM	TERTIANS	TESTIFIES	TETRAGRAMS
TERMINATES	TERRARIUMS	TERTIARIES	TESTIFY	TETRALOGIES
TERMINATING	TERRAS	TERTIARY	TESTIFYING	TETRALOGY
TERMINER	TERRASES	TERTIAS	TESTILY	TETRAPLA
TERMINERS	TERRAZZO	TERTIUS	TESTIMONIED	TETRAPLAS
TERMING	TERRAZZOS	TERTIUSES	TESTIMONIES	TETRAPOD
TERMINI	TERREEN	TERTS	TESTIMONY	TETRAPODIES
TERMINISM	TERREENS	TERVALENT	TESTIMONYING	TETRAPODS
TERMINISMS	TERRELLA	TERZETTA	TESTINESS	TETRAPODY
TERMINIST	TERRELLAS	TERZETTAS	TESTINESSES	TETRARCH

TETRARCHIES	TEXTURISE	THANKLESS	THEEKING	THEOMACHIES
TETRARCHS	TEXTURISED	THANKS	THEEKS	THEOMACHY
TETRARCHY	TEXTURISES	THANKYOU	THEES	THEOMANCIES
TETRAS	TEXTURISING	THANKYOUS	THEFT	THEOMANCY
TETRAXON	TEXTURIZE	THANNA	THEFTBOOT	THEOMANIA
TETRAXONS	TEXTURIZED	THANNAH	THEFTBOOTS	THEOMANIAS
TETRODE	TEXTURIZES	THANNAHS	THEFTS	THEONOMIES
TETRODES	TEXTURIZING	THANNAS	THEFTUOUS	THEONOMY
TETRONAL	THACK	THANS	THEGITHER	THEOPATHIES
TETRONALS	THACKS	THAR	THEGN	THEOPATHY
TETROXIDE	THAE	THARS	THEGNS	THEOPHAGIES
TETROXIDES	THAGI	THAT	THEIC	THEOPHAGY
TETRYL	THAGIS	THATAWAY	THEICS	THEOPHANIES
TETRYLS	THAIM	THATCH	THEINE	THEOPHANY
TETTER	THAIRM	THATCHED	THEINES	THEORBIST
TETTERED	THAIRMS	THATCHER	THEIR	THEORBISTS
TETTERING	THALAMI	THATCHERS	THEIRS	THEORBO
TETTEROUS	THALAMIC	THATCHES	THEISM	THEORBOS
TETTERS	THALAMUS	THATCHING	THEISMS	THEOREM
TETTIX	THALASSIC	THATCHINGS	THEIST	THEOREMS
TETTIXES	THALER	THATCHT	THEISTIC	THEORETIC
TEUCH	THALERS	THATNESS	THEISTS	THEORETICS
TEUCHAT	THALIAN	THATNESSES	THELEMENT	THEORIC
TEUCHATS	THALLI	THAUMATIN	THELEMENTS	THEORICS
TEUCHER	THALLIC	THAUMATINS	THELF	THEORIES
TEUCHEST	THALLINE	THAW	THELVES	THEORIQUE
TEUCHTER	THALLIUM	THAWED	THELYTOKIES	THEORIQUES
TEUCHTERS	THALLIUMS	THAWER	THELYTOKY	THEORISE
TEUGH	THALLOID	THAWERS	THEM	THEORISED
TEUGHER	THALLOUS	THAWIER	THEMA	THEORISER
TEUGHEST	THALLUS	THAWIEST	THEMATA	THEORISERS
TEW	THALLUSES	THAWING	THEMATIC	THEORISES
TEWART	THALWEG	THAWINGS	THEME	THEORISING
TEWARTS	THALWEGS	THAWLESS	THEMED	THEORIST
TEWED	THAN	THAWS	THEMELESS	THEORISTS
TEWEL	THANA	THAWY	THEMES	THEORIZE
TEWELS	THANADAR	THE	THEMING	THEORIZED
TEWHIT	THANADARS	THEACEOUS	THEMSELF	THEORIZER
TEWHITS	THANAGE	THEANDRIC	THEMSELVES	THEORIZERS
TEWING	THANAGES	THEARCHIC	THEN	THEORIZES
TEWIT	THANAH	THEARCHIES	THENABOUT	THEORIZING
TEWITS	THANAHS	THEARCHY	THENABOUTS	THEORY
TEWS	THANAS	THEATER	THENAR	THEOSOPH
TEXAS	THANATISM	THEATERS	THENARS	THEOSOPHIES
TEXASES	THANATISMS	THEATRAL	THENCE	THEOSOPHS
TEXT	THANATIST	THEATRE	THENS	THEOSOPHY
TEXTBOOK	THANATISTS	THEATRES	THEOCRACIES	THEOTOKOI
TEXTBOOKS	THANATOID	THEATRIC	THEOCRACY	THEOTOKOS
TEXTILE	THANE	THEATRICS	THEOCRASIES	THEOW
TEXTILES	THANEDOM	THEAVE	THEOCRASY	THEOWS
TEXTLESS	THANEDOMS	THEAVES	THEOCRAT	THERALITE
TEXTORIAL	THANEHOOD	THEBAINE	THEOCRATS	THERALITES
TEXTPHONE	THANEHOODS	THEBAINES	THEODICIES	THERAPIES
TEXTPHONES	THANES	THECA	THEODICY	THERAPIST
TEXTS	THANESHIP	THECAE	THEOGONIC	THERAPISTS
TEXTUAL	THANESHIPS	THECAL	THEOGONIES	THERAPSID
TEXTUALLY	THANK	THECATE	THEOGONY	THERAPSIDS
TEXTUARIES	THANKED	THECODONT	THEOLOGER	THERAPY
TEXTUARY	THANKEE	THECODONTS	THEOLOGERS	THERBLIG
TEXTURAL	THANKER	THEE	THEOLOGIC	THERBLIGS
TEXTURE	THANKERS	THEED	THEOLOGIES	THERE
TEXTURED	THANKFUL	THEEING	THEOLOGUE	THEREAT
TEXTURES	THANKING	THEEK	THEOLOGUES	THEREAWAY
TEXTURING	THANKINGS	THEEKED	THEOLOGY	THEREBY

THEREFOR	THEURGISTS	THIEVISH	THIR	THIRAM	THONGED
THEREFORE	THEURGY	THIG	THIRAM	THIRAMS	THONGS
THEREFROM	THEW	THIGGER	THIRAMS	THIRD	THORACAL
THEREIN	THEWED	THIGGERS	THIRD	THIRDED	THORACES
THEREINTO	THEWES	THIGGING	THIRDED	THIRDING	THORACIC
THERENESS	THEWIER	THIGGINGS	THIRDING	THIRDINGS	THORAX
THERENESSES	THEWIEST	THIGGIT	THIRDINGS	THIRDLY	THORAXES
THEREOF	THEWLESS	THIGH	THIRDLY	THIRDS	THORIA
THEREON	THEWS	THIGHBONE	THIRDS	THIRDSMAN	THORIAS
THEREOUT	THEWY	THIGHBONES	THIRDSMAN	THIRDSMEN	THORITE
THERES	THEY	THIGHS	THIRDSMEN	THIRL	THORITES
THERETO	THIAMIN	THIGS	THIRL	THIRLAGE	THORIUM
THEREUNTO	THIAMINE	THILK	THIRLAGE	THIRLAGES	THORIUMS
THEREUPON	THIAMINES	THILL	THIRLAGES	THIRLED	THORN
THEREWITH	THIAMINS	THILLER	THIRLED	THIRLING	THORNBACK
THERIAC	THIASUS	THILLERS	THIRLING	THIRLS	THORNBACKS
THERIACA	THIASUSES	THILLS	THIRLS	THIRST	THORNBILL
THERIACAL	THIAZIDE	THIMBLE	THIRST	THIRSTED	THORNBILLS
THERIACAS	THIAZIDES	THIMBLED	THIRSTED	THIRSTER	THORNBUSH
THERIACS	THIAZINE	THIMBLES	THIRSTER	THIRSTERS	THORNBUSHES
THERIAN	THIAZINES	THIMBLING	THIRSTERS	THIRSTFUL	THORNED
THERIANS	THIBET	THIN	THIRSTFUL	THIRSTIER	THORNIER
THERM	THIBETS	THINE	THIRSTIER	THIRSTIEST	THORNIEST
THERMAE	THIBLE	THING	THIRSTIEST	THIRSTILY	THORNING
THERMAL	THIBLES	THINGAMIES	THIRSTILY	THIRSTING	THORNLESS
THERMALLY	THICK	THINGAMY	THIRSTING	THIRSTS	THORNS
THERMALS	THICKED	THINGHOOD	THIRSTS	THIRSTY	THORNSET
THERMIC	THICKEN	THINGHOODS	THIRSTY	THIRTEEN	THORNTREE
THERMICAL	THICKENED	THINGIER	THIRTEEN	THIRTEENS	THORNTREES
THERMIDOR	THICKENER	THINGIES	THIRTEENS	THIRTIES	THORNY
THERMION	THICKENERS	THINGIEST	THIRTIES	THIRTIETH	THORON
THERMIONS	THICKENING	THINGNESS	THIRTIETH	THIRTIETHS	THORONS
THERMITE	THICKENINGS	THINGNESSES	THIRTIETHS	THIRTY	THOROUGH
THERMITES	THICKENS	THINGS	THIRTY	THIRTYISH	THOROUGHER
THERMOTIC	THICKER	THINGUMMIES	THIRTYISH	THIS	THOROUGHEST
THERMOTICS	THICKEST	THINGUMMY	THIS	THISNESS	THOROUGHS
THERMS	THICKET	THINGY	THISNESS	THISNESSES	THORP
THEROID	THICKETED	THINK	THISNESSES	THISTLE	THORPE
THEROLOGIES	THICKETS	THINKABLE	THISTLE	THISTLES	THORPES
THEROLOGY	THICKETY	THINKER	THISTLES	THISTLIER	THORPS
THEROPOD	THICKHEAD	THINKERS	THISTLIER	THISTLIEST	THOSE
THEROPODS	THICKHEADS	THINKING	THISTLIEST	THISTLY	THOTHER
THESAURI	THICKING	THINKINGS	THISTLY	THITHER	THOU
THESAURUS	THICKISH	THINKS	THITHER	THIVEL	THOUGH
THESAURUSES	THICKLY	THINLY	THIVEL	THIVELS	THOUGHT
THESE	THICKNESS	THINNED	THIVELS	THLIPSES	THOUGHTED
THESES	THICKNESSES	THINNER	THLIPSES	THLIPSIS	THOUGHTEN
THESIS	THICKO	THINNERS	THLIPSIS	THO	THOUGHTS
THESPIAN	THICKOES	THINNESS	THO	THOFT	THOUING
THESPIANS	THICKOS	THINNESSES	THOFT	THOFTS	THOUS
THETA	THICKS	THINNEST	THOFTS	THOLE	THOUSAND
THETAS	THICKSET	THINNING	THOLE	THOLED	THOUSANDS
THETCH	THICKSETS	THINNINGS	THOLED	THOLES	THOWEL
THETCHED	THICKSKIN	THINNISH	THOLES	THOLI	THOWELS
THETCHES	THICKSKINS	THINS	THOLI	THOLING	THOWL
THETCHING	THICKY	THIOL	THOLING	THOLOBATE	THOWLESS
THETE	THIEF	THIOLS	THOLOBATE	THOLOBATES	THOWLS
THETES	THIEVE	THIOPHEN	THOLOBATES	THOLOI	THRAE
THETHER	THIEVED	THIOPHENE	THOLOI	THOLOS	THRALDOM
THETIC	THIEVERIES	THIOPHENES	THOLOS	THOLUS	THRALDOMS
THETICAL	THIEVERY	THIOPHENS	THOLUS	THON	THRALL
THEURGIC	THIEVES	THIOPHIL	THON	THONDER	THRALLDOM
THEURGIES	THIEVING	THIOUREA	THONDER	THONG	THRALLDOMS
THEURGIST	THIEVINGS	THIOUREAS	THONG	THONGED	THRALLED

THRALLING	THREESOMES	THRIVED	THROWE	THUMBING
THRALLS	THRENE	THRIVEN	THROWER	THUMBKINS
THRANG	THRENES	THRIVER	THROWERS	THUMBLESS
THRANGED	THRENETIC	THRIVERS	THROWES	THUMBLIKE
THRANGING	THRENODE	THRIVES	THROWING	THUMBLING
THRANGS	THRENODES	THRIVING	THROWINGS	THUMBLINGS
THRAPPLE	THRENODIC	THRIVINGS	THROWN	THUMBNAIL
THRAPPLED	THRENODIES	THRO	THROWS	THUMBNAILS
THRAPPLES	THRENODY	THROAT	THROWSTER	THUMBNUT
THRAPPLING	THRENOS	THROATED	THROWSTERS	THUMBNUTS
THRASH	THRENOSES	THROATIER	THRU	THUMBPOT
THRASHED	THREONINE	THROATIEST	THRUM	THUMBPOTS
THRASHER	THREONINES	THROATILY	THRUMMED	THUMBS
THRASHERS	THRESH	THROATS	THRUMMER	THUMBTACK
THRASHES	THRESHED	THROATY	THRUMMERS	THUMBTACKS
THRASHING	THRESHEL	THROB	THRUMMIER	THUMBY
THRASHINGS	THRESHELS	THROBBED	THRUMMIEST	THUMP
THRASONIC	THRESHER	THROBBING	THRUMMING	THUMPED
THRAVE	THRESHERS	THROBBINGS	THRUMMINGS	THUMPER
THRAVES	THRESHES	THROBLESS	THRUMMY	THUMPERS
THRAW	THRESHING	THROBS	THRUMS	THUMPING
THRAWARD	THRESHINGS	THROE	THRUSH	THUMPS
THRAWART	THRESHOLD	THROED	THRUSHES	THUNDER
THRAWING	THRESHOLDS	THROEING	THRUST	THUNDERED
THRAWN	THRETTIES	THROES	THRUSTED	THUNDERER
THRAWS	THRETTY	THROMBI	THRUSTER	THUNDERERS
THREAD	THREW	THROMBIN	THRUSTERS	THUNDERIER
THREADED	THRICE	THROMBINS	THRUSTING	THUNDERIEST
THREADEN	THRID	THROMBOSE	THRUSTINGS	THUNDERING
THREADER	THRIDACE	THROMBOSED	THRUSTS	THUNDERINGS
THREADERS	THRIDACES	THROMBOSES	THRUTCH	THUNDERS
THREADFIN	THRIDDED	THROMBOSING	THRUTCHED	THUNDERY
THREADFINS	THRIDDING	THROMBUS	THRUTCHES	THUNDROUS
THREADIER	THRIDS	THRONE	THRUTCHING	THURIBLE
THREADIEST	THRIFT	THRONED	THRUWAY	THURIBLES
THREADING	THRIFTIER	THRONES	THRUWAYS	THURIFER
THREADS	THRIFTIEST	THRONG	THRYMSA	THURIFERS
THREADY	THRIFTILY	THRONGED	THRYMSAS	THURIFIED
THREAP	THRIFTS	THRONGFUL	THUD	THURIFIES
THREAPING	THRIFTY	THRONGING	THUDDED	THURIFY
THREAPIT	THRILL	THRONGINGS	THUDDING	THURIFYING
THREAPS	THRILLANT	THRONGS	THUDS	THUS
THREAT	THRILLED	THRONING	THUG	THUSES
THREATED	THRILLER	THROPPLE	THUGGEE	THUSNESS
THREATEN	THRILLERS	THROPPLED	THUGGEES	THUSNESSES
THREATENED	THRILLIER	THROPPLES	THUGGERIES	THUSWISE
THREATENING	THRILLIEST	THROPPLING	THUGGERY	THUYA
THREATENINGS	THRILLING	THROSTLE	THUGGISM	THUYAS
THREATENS	THRILLS	THROSTLES	THUGGISMS	THWACK
THREATFUL	THRILLY	THROTTLE	THUGGO	THWACKED
THREATING	THRIMSA	THROTTLED	THUGGOS	THWACKER
THREATS	THRIMSAS	THROTTLER	THUGS	THWACKERS
THREAVE	THRIPS	THROTTLERS	THUJA	THWACKING
THREAVES	THRIPSES	THROTTLES	THUJAS	THWACKINGS
THREE	THRISSEL	THROTTLING	THULIA	THWACKS
THREEFOLD	THRISSELS	THROTTLINGS	THULIAS	THWAITE
THREENESS	THRIST	THROUGH	THULITE	THWAITES
THREENESSES	THRISTED	THROUGHLY	THULITES	THWART
THREEP	THRISTING	THROVE	THULIUM	THWARTED
THREEPING	THRISTLE	THROW	THULIUMS	THWARTER
THREEPIT	THRISTLES	THROWAWAY	THUMB	THWARTERS
THREEPS	THRISTS	THROWAWAYS	THUMBED	THWARTING
THREES	THRISTY	THROWBACK	THUMBIER	THWARTINGS
THREESOME	THRIVE	THROWBACKS	THUMBIEST	THWARTLY

THWARTS	TICING	TIDEWAVE	TIG	TILING
THY	TICK	TIDEWAVES	TIGE	TILINGS
THYINE	TICKED	TIDEWAY	TIGER	TILL
THYLACINE	TICKEN	TIDEWAYS	TIGERISH	TILLABLE
THYLACINES	TICKENS	TIDIED	TIGERISM	TILLAGE
THYLOSE	TICKER	TIDIER	TIGERISMS	TILLAGES
THYLOSES	TICKERS	TIDIES	TIGERLY	TILLED
THYLOSIS	TICKET	TIDIEST	TIGERS	TILLER
THYME	TICKETED	TIDILY	TIGERY	TILLERED
THYMES	TICKETING	TIDINESS	TIGES	TILLERING
THYMI	TICKETS	TIDINESSES	TIGGED	TILLERS
THYMIC	TICKEY	TIDING	TIGGING	TILLIER
THYMIDINE	TICKEYS	TIDINGS	TIGHT	TILLIEST
THYMIDINES	TICKIES	TIDIVATE	TIGHTEN	TILLING
THYMIER	TICKING	TIDIVATED	TIGHTENED	TILLINGS
THYMIEST	TICKINGS	TIDIVATES	TIGHTENER	TILLITE
THYMINE	TICKLE	TIDIVATING	TIGHTENERS	TILLITES
THYMINES	TICKLED	TIDS	TIGHTENING	TILLS
THYMOCYTE	TICKLER	TIDY	TIGHTENS	TILLY
THYMOCYTES	TICKLERS	TIDYING	TIGHTER	TILS
THYMOL	TICKLES	TIE	TIGHTEST	TILT
THYMOLS	TICKLIER	TIEBACK	TIGHTISH	TILTABLE
THYMUS	TICKLIEST	TIEBACKS	TIGHTLY	TILTED
THYMY	TICKLING	TIED	TIGHTNESS	TILTER
THYRATRON	TICKLINGS	TIELESS	TIGHTNESSES	TILTERS
THYRATRONS	TICKLISH	TIEPIN	TIGHTROPE	TILTH
THYREOID	TICKLY	TIEPINS	TIGHTROPES	TILTHS
THYREOIDS	TICKS	TIER	TIGHTS	TILTING
THYRISTOR	TICKY	TIERCE	TIGHTWAD	TILTINGS
THYRISTORS	TICS	TIERCED	TIGHTWADS	TILTS
THYROID	TID	TIERCEL	TIGLON	TIMARAU
THYROIDS	TIDAL	TIERCELET	TIGLONS	TIMARAUS
THYROXIN	TIDBIT	TIERCELETS	TIGON	TIMARIOT
THYROXINE	TIDBITS	TIERCELS	TIGONS	TIMARIOTS
THYROXINES	TIDDIER	TIERCERON	TIGRESS	TIMBAL
THYROXINS	TIDDIES	TIERCERONS	TIGRESSES	TIMBALE
THYRSE	TIDDIEST	TIERCES	TIGRINE	TIMBALES
THYRSES	TIDDLE	TIERCET	TIGRISH	TIMBALS
THYRSI	TIDDLED	TIERCETS	TIGRISHLY	TIMBER
THYRSOID	TIDDLER	TIERED	TIGROID	TIMBERED
THYRSUS	TIDDLERS	TIERING	TIGS	TIMBERING
THYSELF	TIDDLES	TIEROD	TIKA	TIMBERINGS
TI	TIDDLEY	TIERODS	TIKAS	TIMBERS
TIAR	TIDDLEYS	TIERS	TIKE	TIMBO
TIARA	TIDDLIER	TIES	TIKES	TIMBOS
TIARAED	TIDDLIES	TIETAC	TIKI	TIMBRE
TIARAS	TIDDLIEST	TIETACK	TIKIS	TIMBREL
TIARS	TIDDLING	TIETACKS	TIKKA	TIMBRELS
TIBIA	TIDDLY	TIETACS	TIL	TIMBRES
TIBIAE	TIDDY	TIFF	TILAPIA	TIME
TIBIAL	TIDE	TIFFANIES	TILAPIAS	TIMECARD
TIBIAS	TIDED	TIFFANY	TILBURIES	TIMECARDS
TIC	TIDELAND	TIFFED	TILBURY	TIMED
TICAL	TIDELANDS	TIFFIN	TILDE	TIMEFRAME
TICALS	TIDELESS	TIFFING	TILDES	TIMEFRAMES
TICCA	TIDEMARK	TIFFINGS	TILE	TIMELESS
TICE	TIDEMARKS	TIFFINS	TILED	TIMELIER
TICED	TIDEMILL	TIFFS	TILEFISH	TIMELIEST
TICES	TIDEMILLS	TIFOSI	TILEFISHES	TIMELINE
TICH	TIDES	TIFOSO	TILER	TIMELINES
TICHES	TIDESMAN	TIFT	TILERIES	TIMELY
TICHIER	TIDESMEN	TIFTED	TILERS	TIMENOGUY
TICHIEST	TIDEWATER	TIFTING	TILERY	TIMENOGUYS
TICHY	TIDEWATERS	TIFTS	TILES	TIMEOUS

The Chambers Dictionary is the authority for many longer words; see *OSW* Introduction, page xii

TIMEOUSLY	TINDERBOXES	TINKLINGS	TIPIS	TIRLED
TIMEPIECE	TINDERS	TINKLY	TIPPABLE	TIRLING
TIMEPIECES	TINDERY	TINKS	TIPPED	TIRLS
TIMER	TINDING	TINMAN	TIPPER	TIRO
TIMERS	TINDS	TINMEN	TIPPERS	TIROES
TIMES	TINE	TINNED	TIPPET	TIROS
TIMESCALE	TINEA	TINNER	TIPPETS	TIRR
TIMESCALES	TINEAL	TINNERS	TIPPIER	TIRRED
TIMETABLE	TINEAS	TINNIE	TIPPIEST	TIRRING
TIMETABLED	TINED	TINNIER	TIPPING	TIRRIT
TIMETABLES	TINEID	TINNIES	TIPPINGS	TIRRITS
TIMETABLING	TINEIDS	TINNIEST	TIPPLE	TIRRIVEE
TIMID	TINES	TINNING	TIPPLED	TIRRIVEES
TIMIDER	TINFOIL	TINNINGS	TIPPLER	TIRRIVIE
TIMIDEST	TINFOILS	TINNITUS	TIPPLERS	TIRRIVIES
TIMIDITIES	TINFUL	TINNITUSES	TIPPLES	TIRRS
TIMIDITY	TINFULS	TINNY	TIPPLING	TIS
TIMIDLY	TING	TINPLATE	TIPPY	TISANE
TIMIDNESS	TINGE	TINPLATED	TIPS	TISANES
TIMIDNESSES	TINGED	TINPLATES	TIPSIER	TISICK
TIMING	TINGEING	TINPLATING	TIPSIEST	TISICKS
TIMINGS	TINGES	TINPOT	TIPSIFIED	TISSUE
TIMIST	TINGING	TINPOTS	TIPSIFIES	TISSUED
TIMISTS	TINGLE	TINS	TIPSIFY	TISSUES
TIMOCRACIES	TINGLED	TINSEL	TIPSIFYING	TISSUING
TIMOCRACY	TINGLER	TINSELED	TIPSILY	TISWAS
TIMON	TINGLERS	TINSELING	TIPSINESS	TISWASES
TIMONEER	TINGLES	TINSELLED	TIPSINESSES	TIT
TIMONEERS	TINGLIER	TINSELLING	TIPSTAFF	TITAN
TIMONS	TINGLIEST	TINSELLY	TIPSTAFFS	TITANATE
TIMOROUS	TINGLING	TINSELRIES	TIPSTAVES	TITANATES
TIMORSOME	TINGLINGS	TINSELRY	TIPSTER	TITANESS
TIMOTHIES	TINGLISH	TINSELS	TIPSTERS	TITANESSES
TIMOTHY	TINGLY	TINSEY	TIPSY	TITANIC
TIMOUS	TINGS	TINSEYS	TIPT	TITANIS
TIMOUSLY	TINGUAITE	TINSMITH	TIPTOE	TITANISES
TIMPANI	TINGUAITES	TINSMITHS	TIPTOED	TITANISM
TIMPANIST	TINHORN	TINSNIPS	TIPTOEING	TITANISMS
TIMPANISTS	TINHORNS	TINSTONE	TIPTOES	TITANITE
TIMPANO	TINIER	TINSTONES	TIPTOP	TITANITES
TIMPS	TINIES	TINT	TIPTOPS	TITANIUM
TIN	TINIEST	TINTACK	TIPULA	TITANIUMS
TINAJA	TINILY	TINTACKS	TIPULAS	TITANOUS
TINAJAS	TININESS	TINTED	TIRADE	TITANS
TINAMOU	TININESSES	TINTER	TIRADES	TITBIT
TINAMOUS	TINING	TINTERS	TIRAMISU	TITBITS
TINCAL	TINK	TINTIER	TIRAMISUS	TITCH
TINCALS	TINKED	TINTIEST	TIRASSE	TITCHES
TINCHEL	TINKER	TINTINESS	TIRASSES	TITCHIER
TINCHELS	TINKERED	TINTINESSES	TIRE	TITCHIEST
TINCT	TINKERER	TINTING	TIRED	TITCHY
TINCTED	TINKERERS	TINTINGS	TIREDER	TITE
TINCTING	TINKERING	TINTLESS	TIREDEST	TITELY
TINCTS	TINKERINGS	TINTS	TIREDLY	TITER
TINCTURE	TINKERS	TINTY	TIREDNESS	TITERS
TINCTURED	TINKING	TINTYPE	TIREDNESSES	TITFER
TINCTURES	TINKLE	TINTYPES	TIRELESS	TITFERS
TINCTURING	TINKLED	TINWARE	TIRELING	TITHABLE
TIND	TINKLER	TINWARES	TIRELINGS	TITHE
TINDAL	TINKLERS	TINY	TIRES	TITHED
TINDALS	TINKLES	TIP	TIRESOME	TITHER
TINDED	TINKLIER	TIPCAT	TIRING	TITHERS
TINDER	TINKLIEST	TIPCATS	TIRINGS	TITHES
TINDERBOX	TINKLING	TIPI	TIRL	TITHING

The Chambers Dictionary is the authority for many longer words; see *OSW* Introduction, page xii

TITHINGS	TITTUPY	TOASTINGS	TOECLIP	TOILED
TITI	TITTY	TOASTS	TOECLIPS	TOILER
TITIAN	TITUBANCIES	TOASTY	TOED	TOILERS
TITIANS	TITUBANCY	TOAZE	TOEHOLD	TOILES
TITILLATE	TITUBANT	TOAZED	TOEHOLDS	TOILET
TITILLATED	TITUBATE	TOAZES	TOEIER	TOILETED
TITILLATES	TITUBATED	TOAZING	TOEIEST	TOILETING
TITILLATING	TITUBATES	TOBACCO	TOEING	TOILETRIES
TITIS	TITUBATING	TOBACCOES	TOELESS	TOILETRY
TITIVATE	TITULAR	TOBACCOS	TOENAIL	TOILETS
TITIVATED	TITULARIES	TOBIES	TOENAILED	TOILETTE
TITIVATES	TITULARLY	TOBOGGAN	TOENAILING	TOILETTES
TITIVATING	TITULARS	TOBOGGANED	TOENAILS	TOILFUL
TITLARK	TITULARY	TOBOGGANING	TOERAG	TOILINET
TITLARKS	TITULE	TOBOGGANINGS	TOERAGGER	TOILINETS
TITLE	TITULED	TOBOGGANS	TOERAGGERS	TOILING
TITLED	TITULES	TOBOGGIN	TOERAGS	TOILINGS
TITLELESS	TITULING	TOBOGGINED	TOES	TOILLESS
TITLER	TITUP	TOBOGGINING	TOETOE	TOILS
TITLERS	TITUPED	TOBOGGINS	TOETOES	TOILSOME
TITLES	TITUPING	TOBY	TOEY	TOISE
TITLING	TITUPPED	TOC	TOFF	TOISEACH
TITLINGS	TITUPPING	TOCCATA	TOFFEE	TOISEACHS
TITMICE	TITUPS	TOCCATAS	TOFFEES	TOISECH
TITMOSE	TITUPY	TOCCATINA	TOFFIER	TOISECHS
TITMOUSE	TIZWAS	TOCCATINAS	TOFFIES	TOISES
TITOKI	TIZWASES	TOCHER	TOFFIEST	TOISON
TITOKIS	TIZZ	TOCHERED	TOFFISH	TOISONS
TITRATE	TIZZES	TOCHERING	TOFFS	TOITOI
TITRATED	TIZZIES	TOCHERS	TOFFY	TOITOIS
TITRATES	TIZZY	TOCK	TOFORE	TOKAMAK
TITRATING	TJANTING	TOCKED	TOFT	TOKAMAKS
TITRATION	TJANTINGS	TOCKING	TOFTS	TOKAY
TITRATIONS	TMESES	TOCKS	TOFU	TOKAYS
TITRE	TMESIS	TOCO	TOFUS	TOKE
TITRES	TO	TOCOLOGIES	TOG	TOKED
TITS	TOAD	TOCOLOGY	TOGA	TOKEN
TITTED	TOADFISH	TOCOS	TOGAED	TOKENED
TITTER	TOADFISHES	TOCS	TOGAS	TOKENING
TITTERED	TOADFLAX	TOCSIN	TOGATE	TOKENISM
TITTERER	TOADFLAXES	TOCSINS	TOGATED	TOKENISMS
TITTERERS	TOADGRASS	TOD	TOGE	TOKENS
TITTERING	TOADGRASSES	TODAY	TOGED	TOKES
TITTERINGS	TOADIED	TODAYS	TOGES	TOKING
TITTERS	TOADIES	TODDE	TOGETHER	TOKO
TITTIES	TOADRUSH	TODDED	TOGGED	TOKOLOGIES
TITTING	TOADRUSHES	TODDES	TOGGERIES	TOKOLOGY
TITTISH	TOADS	TODDIES	TOGGERY	TOKOLOSHE
TITTIVATE	TOADSTONE	TODDING	TOGGING	TOKOLOSHES
TITTIVATED	TOADSTONES	TODDLE	TOGGLE	TOKOS
TITTIVATES	TOADSTOOL	TODDLED	TOGGLED	TOLA
TITTIVATING	TOADSTOOLS	TODDLER	TOGGLES	TOLAS
TITTLE	TOADY	TODDLERS	TOGGLING	TOLBOOTH
TITTLEBAT	TOADYING	TODDLES	TOGS	TOLBOOTHS
TITTLEBATS	TOADYISH	TODDLING	TOGUE	TOLD
TITTLED	TOADYISM	TODDY	TOGUES	TOLE
TITTLES	TOADYISMS	TODIES	TOHEROA	TOLED
TITTLING	TOAST	TODS	TOHEROAS	TOLERABLE
TITTUP	TOASTED	TODY	TOHO	TOLERABLY
TITTUPED	TOASTER	TOE	TOHOS	TOLERANCE
TITTUPING	TOASTERS	TOEA	TOHUNGA	TOLERANCES
TITTUPPED	TOASTIE	TOEAS	TOHUNGAS	TOLERANT
TITTUPPING	TOASTIES	TOECAP	TOIL	TOLERATE
TITTUPS	TOASTING	TOECAPS	TOILE	TOLERATED

TOLERATES	TOMATOEY	TONDI	TONNEAUX	TOORIES
TOLERATING	TOMB	TONDINI	TONNELL	TOOT
TOLERATOR	TOMBAC	TONDINO	TONNELLS	TOOTED
TOLERATORS	TOMBACS	TONDINOS	TONNES	TOOTER
TOLES	TOMBAK	TONDO	TONNISH	TOOTERS
TOLEWARE	TOMBAKS	TONDOS	TONNISHLY	TOOTH
TOLEWARES	TOMBED	TONE	TONOMETER	TOOTHACHE
TOLING	TOMBIC	TONED	TONOMETERS	TOOTHACHES
TOLINGS	TOMBING	TONELESS	TONOMETRIES	TOOTHCOMB
TOLL	TOMBLESS	TONEME	TONOMETRY	TOOTHCOMBS
TOLLABLE	TOMBOC	TONEMES	TONS	TOOTHED
TOLLAGE	TOMBOCS	TONEMIC	TONSIL	TOOTHFUL
TOLLAGES	TOMBOLA	TONEPAD	TONSILLAR	TOOTHFULS
TOLLBOOTH	TOMBOLAS	TONEPADS	TONSILS	TOOTHIER
TOLLBOOTHS	TOMBOLO	TONER	TONSOR	TOOTHIEST
TOLLDISH	TOMBOLOS	TONERS	TONSORIAL	TOOTHILY
TOLLDISHES	TOMBOY	TONES	TONSORS	TOOTHING
TOLLED	TOMBOYISH	TONETIC	TONSURE	TOOTHLESS
TOLLER	TOMBOYS	TONEY	TONSURED	TOOTHLIKE
TOLLERS	TOMBS	TONG	TONSURES	TOOTHPICK
TOLLHOUSE	TOMBSTONE	TONGA	TONSURING	TOOTHPICKS
TOLLHOUSES	TOMBSTONES	TONGAS	TONTINE	TOOTHS
TOLLING	TOMCAT	TONGED	TONTINER	TOOTHSOME
TOLLINGS	TOMCATS	TONGING	TONTINERS	TOOTHWASH
TOLLMAN	TOME	TONGS	TONTINES	TOOTHWASHES
TOLLMEN	TOMENTA	TONGSTER	TONUS	TOOTHWORT
TOLLS	TOMENTOSE	TONGSTERS	TONUSES	TOOTHWORTS
TOLSEL	TOMENTOUS	TONGUE	TONY	TOOTHY
TOLSELS	TOMENTUM	TONGUED	TOO	TOOTING
TOLSEY	TOMES	TONGUELET	TOOART	TOOTLE
TOLSEYS	TOMFOOL	TONGUELETS	TOOARTS	TOOTLED
TOLT	TOMFOOLED	TONGUES	TOOK	TOOTLES
TOLTER	TOMFOOLING	TONGUING	TOOL	TOOTLING
TOLTERED	TOMFOOLS	TONGUINGS	TOOLBAG	TOOTS
TOLTERING	TOMIA	TONIC	TOOLBAGS	TOOTSED
TOLTERS	TOMIAL	TONICITIES	TOOLBAR	TOOTSES
TOLTS	TOMIUM	TONICITY	TOOLBARS	TOOTSIE
TOLU	TOMMIED	TONICS	TOOLBOX	TOOTSIES
TOLUATE	TOMMIES	TONIER	TOOLBOXES	TOOTSING
TOLUATES	TOMMY	TONIES	TOOLED	TOOTSY
TOLUENE	TOMMYING	TONIEST	TOOLER	TOP
TOLUENES	TOMOGRAM	TONIGHT	TOOLERS	TOPARCH
TOLUIC	TOMOGRAMS	TONIGHTS	TOOLHOUSE	TOPARCHIES
TOLUIDINE	TOMOGRAPH	TONING	TOOLHOUSES	TOPARCHS
TOLUIDINES	TOMOGRAPHS	TONINGS	TOOLING	TOPARCHY
TOLUOL	TOMORROW	TONISH	TOOLINGS	TOPAZ
TOLUOLS	TOMORROWS	TONISHLY	TOOLKIT	TOPAZES
TOLUS	TOMPION	TONITE	TOOLKITS	TOPAZINE
TOLZEY	TOMPIONS	TONITES	TOOLMAKER	TOPCOAT
TOLZEYS	TOMPON	TONK	TOOLMAKERS	TOPCOATS
TOM	TOMPONED	TONKED	TOOLMAN	TOPE
TOMAHAWK	TOMPONING	TONKER	TOOLMEN	TOPECTOMIES
TOMAHAWKED	TOMPONS	TONKERS	TOOLROOM	TOPECTOMY
TOMAHAWKING	TOMS	TONKING	TOOLROOMS	TOPED
TOMAHAWKS	TOMTIT	TONKS	TOOLS	TOPEE
TOMALLEY	TOMTITS	TONLET	TOOM	TOPEES
TOMALLEYS	TON	TONLETS	TOOMED	TOPEK
TOMAN	TONAL	TONNAG	TOOMER	TOPEKS
TOMANS	TONALITE	TONNAGE	TOOMEST	TOPER
TOMATILLO	TONALITES	TONNAGES	TOOMING	TOPERS
TOMATILLOES	TONALITIES	TONNAGS	TOOMS	TOPES
TOMATILLOS	TONALITY	TONNE	TOON	TOPFULL
TOMATO	TONALLY	TONNEAU	TOONS	TOPHI
TOMATOES	TONANT	TONNEAUS	TOORIE	TOPHUS

The Chambers Dictionary is the authority for many longer words; see *OSW* Introduction, page xii

TOPI	TOPSOIL	TORMENTUMS	TORSI	TOSHY
TOPIARIAN	TOPSOILS	TORMINA	TORSION	TOSING
TOPIARIES	TOPSPIN	TORMINAL	TORSIONAL	TOSS
TOPIARIST	TOPSPINS	TORMINOUS	TORSIONS	TOSSED
TOPIARISTS	TOQUE	TORN	TORSIVE	TOSSEN
TOPIARY	TOQUES	TORNADE	TORSK	TOSSER
TOPIC	TOQUILLA	TORNADES	TORSKS	TOSSERS
TOPICAL	TOQUILLAS	TORNADIC	TORSO	TOSSES
TOPICALLY	TOR	TORNADO	TORSOS	TOSSIER
TOPICS	TORAN	TORNADOES	TORT	TOSSIEST
TOPING	TORANA	TORNADOS	TORTE	TOSSILY
TOPIS	TORANAS	TOROID	TORTEN	TOSSING
TOPKNOT	TORANS	TOROIDAL	TORTES	TOSSINGS
TOPKNOTS	TORBANITE	TOROIDS	TORTILE	TOSSPOT
TOPLESS	TORBANITES	TOROSE	TORTILITIES	TOSSPOTS
TOPLINE	TORC	TOROUS	TORTILITY	TOSSY
TOPLINED	TORCH	TORPEDO	TORTILLA	TOST
TOPLINER	TORCHED	TORPEDOED	TORTILLAS	TOSTADA
TOPLINERS	TORCHER	TORPEDOER	TORTIOUS	TOSTADAS
TOPLINES	TORCHERE	TORPEDOERS	TORTIVE	TOT
TOPLINING	TORCHERES	TORPEDOES	TORTOISE	TOTAL
TOPLOFTY	TORCHERS	TORPEDOING	TORTOISES	TOTALISE
TOPMAKER	TORCHES	TORPEDOS	TORTONI	TOTALISED
TOPMAKERS	TORCHIER	TORPEFIED	TORTONIS	TOTALISER
TOPMAKING	TORCHIERE	TORPEFIES	TORTRICES	TOTALISERS
TOPMAKINGS	TORCHIERES	TORPEFY	TORTRICID	TOTALISES
TOPMAN	TORCHIERS	TORPEFYING	TORTRICIDS	TOTALISING
TOPMAST	TORCHING	TORPID	TORTRIX	TOTALITIES
TOPMASTS	TORCHINGS	TORPIDITIES	TORTS	TOTALITY
TOPMEN	TORCHON	TORPIDITY	TORTUOUS	TOTALIZE
TOPMINNOW	TORCHONS	TORPIDLY	TORTURE	TOTALIZED
TOPMINNOWS	TORCHWOOD	TORPIDS	TORTURED	TOTALIZER
TOPMOST	TORCHWOODS	TORPITUDE	TORTURER	TOTALIZERS
TOPOI	TORCS	TORPITUDES	TORTURERS	TOTALIZES
TOPOLOGIC	TORCULAR	TORPOR	TORTURES	TOTALIZING
TOPOLOGIES	TORCULARS	TORPORS	TORTURING	TOTALLED
TOPOLOGY	TORDION	TORQUATE	TORTURINGS	TOTALLING
TOPONYM	TORDIONS	TORQUATED	TORTUROUS	TOTALLY
TOPONYMAL	TORE	TORQUE	TORUFFLED	TOTALS
TOPONYMIC	TOREADOR	TORQUED	TORULA	TOTANUS
TOPONYMICS	TOREADORS	TORQUES	TORULAE	TOTANUSES
TOPONYMIES	TORERO	TORR	TORULI	TOTAQUINE
TOPONYMS	TOREROS	TORREFIED	TORULIN	TOTAQUINES
TOPONYMY	TORES	TORREFIES	TORULINS	TOTARA
TOPOS	TOREUTIC	TORREFY	TORULOSE	TOTARAS
TOPOTYPE	TOREUTICS	TORREFYING	TORULOSES	TOTE
TOPOTYPES	TORGOCH	TORRENT	TORULOSIS	TOTED
TOPPED	TORGOCHS	TORRENTS	TORULUS	TOTEM
TOPPER	TORI	TORRET	TORUS	TOTEMIC
TOPPERS	TORIC	TORRETS	TOSA	TOTEMISM
TOPPING	TORII	TORRID	TOSAS	TOTEMISMS
TOPPINGLY	TORMENT	TORRIDER	TOSE	TOTEMIST
TOPPINGS	TORMENTA	TORRIDEST	TOSED	TOTEMISTS
TOPPLE	TORMENTED	TORRIDITIES	TOSES	TOTEMS
TOPPLED	TORMENTER	TORRIDITY	TOSH	TOTES
TOPPLES	TORMENTERS	TORRIDLY	TOSHACH	TOTHER
TOPPLING	TORMENTIL	TORRS	TOSHACHS	TOTIENT
TOPS	TORMENTILS	TORS	TOSHED	TOTIENTS
TOPSAIL	TORMENTING	TORSADE	TOSHER	TOTING
TOPSAILS	TORMENTINGS	TORSADES	TOSHERS	TOTITIVE
TOPSIDE	TORMENTOR	TORSE	TOSHES	TOTITIVES
TOPSIDES	TORMENTORS	TORSEL	TOSHIER	TOTS
TOPSMAN	TORMENTS	TORSELS	TOSHIEST	TOTTED
TOPSMEN	TORMENTUM	TORSES	TOSHING	TOTTER

The Chambers Dictionary is the authority for many longer words; see *OSW* Introduction, page xii

TOTTERED	TOUN	TOUZLE	TOWNLAND	TOXIN
TOTTERER	TOUNS	TOUZLED	TOWNLANDS	TOXINS
TOTTERERS	TOUPEE	TOUZLES	TOWNLESS	TOXOCARA
TOTTERING	TOUPEES	TOUZLING	TOWNLIER	TOXOCARAS
TOTTERINGS	TOUPET	TOUZY	TOWNLIEST	TOXOID
TOTTERS	TOUPETS	TOVARICH	TOWNLING	TOXOIDS
TOTTERY	TOUR	TOVARICHES	TOWNLINGS	TOXOPHILIES
TOTTIE	TOURACO	TOVARISCH	TOWNLY	TOXOPHILY
TOTTIER	TOURACOS	TOVARISCHES	TOWNS	TOY
TOTTIES	TOURED	TOVARISH	TOWNSCAPE	TOYED
TOTTIEST	TOURER	TOVARISHES	TOWNSCAPED	TOYER
TOTTING	TOURERS	TOW	TOWNSCAPES	TOYERS
TOTTINGS	TOURIE	TOWABLE	TOWNSCAPING	TOYING
TOTTY	TOURIES	TOWAGE	TOWNSCAPINGS	TOYINGS
TOUCAN	TOURING	TOWAGES	TOWNSFOLK	TOYISH
TOUCANET	TOURINGS	TOWARD	TOWNSFOLKS	TOYISHLY
TOUCANETS	TOURISM	TOWARDLY	TOWNSHIP	TOYLESOME
TOUCANS	TOURISMS	TOWARDS	TOWNSHIPS	TOYLESS
TOUCH	TOURIST	TOWBAR	TOWNSKIP	TOYLIKE
TOUCHABLE	TOURISTIC	TOWBARS	TOWNSKIPS	TOYLSOM
TOUCHBACK	TOURISTS	TOWBOAT	TOWNSMAN	TOYMAN
TOUCHBACKS	TOURISTY	TOWBOATS	TOWNSMEN	TOYMEN
TOUCHDOWN	TOURNEDOS	TOWED	TOWNY	TOYS
TOUCHDOWNS	TOURNEY	TOWEL	TOWPATH	TOYSHOP
TOUCHE	TOURNEYED	TOWELED	TOWPATHS	TOYSHOPS
TOUCHED	TOURNEYER	TOWELHEAD	TOWROPE	TOYSOME
TOUCHER	TOURNEYERS	TOWELHEADS	TOWROPES	TOYWOMAN
TOUCHERS	TOURNEYING	TOWELING	TOWS	TOYWOMEN
TOUCHES	TOURNEYS	TOWELLED	TOWSE	TOZE
TOUCHIER	TOURNURE	TOWELLING	TOWSED	TOZED
TOUCHIEST	TOURNURES	TOWELLINGS	TOWSER	TOZES
TOUCHILY	TOURS	TOWELS	TOWSERS	TOZIE
TOUCHING	TOUSE	TOWER	TOWSES	TOZIES
TOUCHINGS	TOUSED	TOWERED	TOWSIER	TOZING
TOUCHLESS	TOUSER	TOWERIER	TOWSIEST	TRABEATE
TOUCHLINE	TOUSERS	TOWERIEST	TOWSING	TRABEATED
TOUCHLINES	TOUSES	TOWERING	TOWSY	TRABECULA
TOUCHMARK	TOUSIER	TOWERLESS	TOWT	TRABECULAE
TOUCHMARKS	TOUSIEST	TOWERS	TOWTED	TRACE
TOUCHTONE	TOUSING	TOWERY	TOWTING	TRACEABLE
TOUCHWOOD	TOUSINGS	TOWHEE	TOWTS	TRACEABLY
TOUCHWOODS	TOUSLE	TOWHEES	TOWY	TRACED
TOUCHY	TOUSLED	TOWIER	TOWZE	TRACELESS
TOUGH	TOUSLES	TOWIEST	TOWZED	TRACER
TOUGHEN	TOUSLING	TOWING	TOWZES	TRACERIED
TOUGHENED	TOUSTIE	TOWINGS	TOWZIER	TRACERIES
TOUGHENER	TOUSTIER	TOWLINE	TOWZIEST	TRACERS
TOUGHENERS	TOUSTIEST	TOWLINES	TOWZING	TRACERY
TOUGHENING	TOUSY	TOWMON	TOWZY	TRACES
TOUGHENINGS	TOUT	TOWMOND	TOXAEMIA	TRACHEA
TOUGHENS	TOUTED	TOWMONDS	TOXAEMIAS	TRACHEAE
TOUGHER	TOUTER	TOWMONS	TOXAEMIC	TRACHEAL
TOUGHEST	TOUTERS	TOWMONT	TOXAPHENE	TRACHEARIES
TOUGHIE	TOUTIE	TOWMONTS	TOXAPHENES	TRACHEARY
TOUGHIES	TOUTIER	TOWN	TOXEMIA	TRACHEATE
TOUGHISH	TOUTIEST	TOWNEE	TOXEMIAS	TRACHEID
TOUGHLY	TOUTING	TOWNEES	TOXEMIC	TRACHEIDE
TOUGHNESS	TOUTS	TOWNHOUSE	TOXIC	TRACHEIDES
TOUGHNESSES	TOUZE	TOWNHOUSES	TOXICAL	TRACHEIDS
TOUGHS	TOUZED	TOWNIE	TOXICALLY	TRACHINUS
TOUK	TOUZES	TOWNIER	TOXICANT	TRACHINUSES
TOUKED	TOUZIER	TOWNIES	TOXICANTS	TRACHITIS
TOUKING	TOUZIEST	TOWNIEST	TOXICITIES	TRACHITISES
TOUKS	TOUZING	TOWNISH	TOXICITY	TRACHOMA

TRACHOMAS	TRADITIONS	TRAIPSES	TRANECTS	TRANSHUMING
TRACHYTE	TRADITIVE	TRAIPSING	TRANGAM	TRANSIENT
TRACHYTES	TRADITOR	TRAIPSINGS	TRANGAMS	TRANSIENTS
TRACHYTIC	TRADITORES	TRAIT	TRANGLE	TRANSIRE
TRACING	TRADITORS	TRAITOR	TRANGLES	TRANSIRES
TRACINGS	TRADS	TRAITORLY	TRANKUM	TRANSIT
TRACK	TRADUCE	TRAITORS	TRANKUMS	TRANSITED
TRACKABLE	TRADUCED	TRAITRESS	TRANNIE	TRANSITING
TRACKAGE	TRADUCER	TRAITRESSES	TRANNIES	TRANSITS
TRACKAGES	TRADUCERS	TRAITS	TRANNY	TRANSLATE
TRACKBALL	TRADUCES	TRAJECT	TRANQUIL	TRANSLATED
TRACKBALLS	TRADUCING	TRAJECTED	TRANQUILLER	TRANSLATES
TRACKED	TRADUCINGS	TRAJECTING	TRANQUILLEST	TRANSLATING
TRACKER	TRAFFIC	TRAJECTS	TRANSACT	TRANSMEW
TRACKERS	TRAFFICKED	TRAM	TRANSACTED	TRANSMEWED
TRACKING	TRAFFICKING	TRAMCAR	TRANSACTING	TRANSMEWING
TRACKINGS	TRAFFICKINGS	TRAMCARS	TRANSACTS	TRANSMEWS
TRACKLESS	TRAFFICS	TRAMLINE	TRANSAXLE	TRANSMIT
TRACKMAN	TRAGEDIAN	TRAMLINED	TRANSAXLES	TRANSMITS
TRACKMEN	TRAGEDIANS	TRAMLINES	TRANSCEND	TRANSMITTED
TRACKROAD	TRAGEDIES	TRAMMED	TRANSCENDED	TRANSMITTING
TRACKROADS	TRAGEDY	TRAMMEL	TRANSCENDING	TRANSMOVE
TRACKS	TRAGELAPH	TRAMMELLED	TRANSCENDS	TRANSMOVED
TRACKWAY	TRAGELAPHS	TRAMMELLING	TRANSE	TRANSMOVES
TRACKWAYS	TRAGI	TRAMMELS	TRANSECT	TRANSMOVING
TRACT	TRAGIC	TRAMMING	TRANSECTED	TRANSMUTE
TRACTABLE	TRAGICAL	TRAMP	TRANSECTING	TRANSMUTED
TRACTABLY	TRAGOPAN	TRAMPED	TRANSECTS	TRANSMUTES
TRACTATE	TRAGOPANS	TRAMPER	TRANSENNA	TRANSMUTING
TRACTATES	TRAGULE	TRAMPERS	TRANSENNAS	TRANSOM
TRACTATOR	TRAGULES	TRAMPET	TRANSEPT	TRANSOMS
TRACTATORS	TRAGULINE	TRAMPETS	TRANSEPTS	TRANSONIC
TRACTED	TRAGUS	TRAMPETTE	TRANSES	TRANSONICS
TRACTILE	TRAHISON	TRAMPETTES	TRANSEUNT	TRANSPIRE
TRACTING	TRAHISONS	TRAMPING	TRANSFARD	TRANSPIRED
TRACTION	TRAIK	TRAMPINGS	TRANSFECT	TRANSPIRES
TRACTIONS	TRAIKED	TRAMPISH	TRANSFECTED	TRANSPIRING
TRACTIVE	TRAIKING	TRAMPLE	TRANSFECTING	TRANSPORT
TRACTOR	TRAIKIT	TRAMPLED	TRANSFECTS	TRANSPORTED
TRACTORS	TRAIKS	TRAMPLER	TRANSFER	TRANSPORTING
TRACTRICES	TRAIL	TRAMPLERS	TRANSFERRED	TRANSPORTINGS
TRACTRIX	TRAILABLE	TRAMPLES	TRANSFERRING	TRANSPORTS
TRACTS	TRAILED	TRAMPLING	TRANSFERS	TRANSPOSE
TRACTUS	TRAILER	TRAMPLINGS	TRANSFIX	TRANSPOSED
TRACTUSES	TRAILERED	TRAMPOLIN	TRANSFIXED	TRANSPOSES
TRAD	TRAILERING	TRAMPOLINED	TRANSFIXES	TRANSPOSING
TRADABLE	TRAILERS	TRAMPOLINING	TRANSFIXING	TRANSPOSINGS
TRADE	TRAILING	TRAMPOLINS	TRANSFORM	TRANSSHIP
TRADEABLE	TRAILS	TRAMPS	TRANSFORMED	TRANSSHIPPED
TRADED	TRAIN	TRAMROAD	TRANSFORMING	TRANSSHIPPING
TRADEFUL	TRAINABLE	TRAMROADS	TRANSFORMINGS	TRANSSHIPPINGS
TRADELESS	TRAINBAND	TRAMS	TRANSFORMS	TRANSSHIPS
TRADEMARK	TRAINBANDS	TRAMWAY	TRANSFUSE	TRANSUDE
TRADEMARKS	TRAINED	TRAMWAYS	TRANSFUSED	TRANSUDED
TRADENAME	TRAINEE	TRANCE	TRANSFUSES	TRANSUDES
TRADENAMES	TRAINEES	TRANCED	TRANSFUSING	TRANSUDING
TRADER	TRAINER	TRANCEDLY	TRANSHIP	TRANSUME
TRADERS	TRAINERS	TRANCES	TRANSHIPPED	TRANSUMED
TRADES	TRAINING	TRANCHE	TRANSHIPPING	TRANSUMES
TRADESMAN	TRAININGS	TRANCHES	TRANSHIPPINGS	TRANSUMING
TRADESMEN	TRAINLESS	TRANCHET	TRANSHIPS	TRANSUMPT
TRADING	TRAINS	TRANCHETS	TRANSHUME	TRANSUMPTS
TRADINGS	TRAIPSE	TRANCING	TRANSHUMED	TRANSVEST
TRADITION	TRAIPSED	TRANECT	TRANSHUMES	TRANSVESTED

TRANSVESTING	TRASHTRIE	TRAWLS	TREATY	TREMATODE
TRANSVESTS	TRASHTRIES	TRAY	TREBLE	TREMATODES
TRANT	TRASHY	TRAYBIT	TREBLED	TREMATOID
TRANTED	TRASS	TRAYBITS	TREBLES	TREMATOIDS
TRANTER	TRASSES	TRAYFUL	TREBLING	TREMBLANT
TRANTERS	TRAT	TRAYFULS	TREBLY	TREMBLE
TRANTING	TRATS	TRAYNE	TREBUCHET	TREMBLED
TRANTS	TRATT	TRAYNED	TREBUCHETS	TREMBLER
TRAP	TRATTORIA	TRAYNES	TRECENTO	TREMBLERS
TRAPAN	TRATTORIAS	TRAYNING	TRECENTOS	TREMBLES
TRAPANNED	TRATTORIE	TRAYS	TRECK	TREMBLIER
TRAPANNING	TRATTS	TREACHER	TRECKED	TREMBLIEST
TRAPANS	TRAUCHLE	TREACHERIES	TRECKING	TREMBLING
TRAPDOOR	TRAUCHLED	TREACHERS	TRECKS	TREMBLINGS
TRAPDOORS	TRAUCHLES	TREACHERY	TREDDLE	TREMBLY
TRAPE	TRAUCHLING	TREACHOUR	TREDDLED	TREMIE
TRAPED	TRAUMA	TREACHOURS	TREDDLES	TREMIES
TRAPES	TRAUMAS	TREACLE	TREDDLING	TREMOLANT
TRAPESED	TRAUMATA	TREACLED	TREDILLE	TREMOLANTS
TRAPESES	TRAUMATIC	TREACLES	TREDILLES	TREMOLITE
TRAPESING	TRAVAIL	TREACLIER	TREDRILLE	TREMOLITES
TRAPESINGS	TRAVAILED	TREACLIEST	TREDRILLES	TREMOLO
TRAPEZE	TRAVAILING	TREACLING	TREE	TREMOLOS
TRAPEZED	TRAVAILS	TREACLY	TREED	TREMOR
TRAPEZES	TRAVE	TREAD	TREEING	TREMORED
TRAPEZIA	TRAVEL	TREADER	TREELESS	TREMORING
TRAPEZIAL	TRAVELED	TREADERS	TREEN	TREMORS
TRAPEZII	TRAVELER	TREADING	TREENAIL	TREMULANT
TRAPEZING	TRAVELERS	TREADINGS	TREENAILS	TREMULANTS
TRAPEZIUM	TRAVELING	TREADLE	TREENS	TREMULATE
TRAPEZIUMS	TRAVELINGS	TREADLED	TREENWARE	TREMULATED
TRAPEZIUS	TRAVELLED	TREADLER	TREENWARES	TREMULATES
TRAPEZIUSES	TRAVELLER	TREADLERS	TREES	TREMULATING
TRAPEZOID	TRAVELLERS	TREADLES	TREESHIP	TREMULOUS
TRAPEZOIDS	TRAVELLING	TREADLING	TREESHIPS	TRENAIL
TRAPING	TRAVELLINGS	TREADLINGS	TREETOP	TRENAILS
TRAPLIKE	TRAVELOG	TREADMILL	TREETOPS	TRENCH
TRAPPEAN	TRAVELOGS	TREADMILLS	TREF	TRENCHAND
TRAPPED	TRAVELS	TREADS	TREFA	TRENCHANT
TRAPPER	TRAVERSAL	TREAGUE	TREFOIL	TRENCHARD
TRAPPERS	TRAVERSALS	TREAGUES	TREFOILED	TRENCHARDS
TRAPPIER	TRAVERSE	TREASON	TREFOILS	TRENCHED
TRAPPIEST	TRAVERSED	TREASONS	TREGETOUR	TRENCHER
TRAPPING	TRAVERSER	TREASURE	TREGETOURS	TRENCHERS
TRAPPINGS	TRAVERSERS	TREASURED	TREHALA	TRENCHES
TRAPPY	TRAVERSES	TREASURER	TREHALAS	TRENCHING
TRAPROCK	TRAVERSING	TREASURERS	TREIF	TREND
TRAPROCKS	TRAVERSINGS	TREASURES	TREILLAGE	TRENDED
TRAPS	TRAVERTIN	TREASURIES	TREILLAGES	TRENDIER
TRAPUNTO	TRAVERTINS	TREASURING	TREILLE	TRENDIES
TRAPUNTOS	TRAVES	TREASURY	TREILLES	TRENDIEST
TRASH	TRAVESTIED	TREAT	TREK	TRENDILY
TRASHCAN	TRAVESTIES	TREATABLE	TREKKED	TRENDING
TRASHCANS	TRAVESTY	TREATED	TREKKER	TRENDS
TRASHED	TRAVESTYING	TREATER	TREKKERS	TRENDY
TRASHERIES	TRAVIS	TREATERS	TREKKING	TRENDYISM
TRASHERY	TRAVISES	TREATIES	TREKS	TRENDYISMS
TRASHES	TRAVOIS	TREATING	TRELLIS	TRENISE
TRASHIER	TRAWL	TREATINGS	TRELLISED	TRENISES
TRASHIEST	TRAWLED	TREATISE	TRELLISES	TRENTAL
TRASHILY	TRAWLER	TREATISES	TRELLISING	TRENTALS
TRASHING	TRAWLERS	TREATMENT	TREMA	TREPAN
TRASHMAN	TRAWLING	TREATMENTS	TREMAS	TREPANG
TRASHMEN	TRAWLINGS	TREATS	TREMATIC	TREPANGS

TREPANNED	TRIADIC	TRIBUNAL	TRICKSTER	TRIFLED
TREPANNER	TRIADIST	TRIBUNALS	TRICKSTERS	TRIFLER
TREPANNERS	TRIADISTS	TRIBUNATE	TRICKSY	TRIFLERS
TREPANNING	TRIADS	TRIBUNATES	TRICKY	TRIFLES
TREPANNINGS	TRIAGE	TRIBUNE	TRICLINIA	TRIFLING
TREPANS	TRIAGES	TRIBUNES	TRICLINIC	TRIFOCAL
TREPHINE	TRIAL	TRIBUTARIES	TRICOLOR	TRIFOCALS
TREPHINED	TRIALISM	TRIBUTARY	TRICOLORS	TRIFOLIES
TREPHINER	TRIALISMS	TRIBUTE	TRICOLOUR	TRIFOLIUM
TREPHINERS	TRIALIST	TRIBUTER	TRICOLOURS	TRIFOLIUMS
TREPHINES	TRIALISTS	TRIBUTERS	TRICORN	TRIFOLY
TREPHINING	TRIALITIES	TRIBUTES	TRICORNE	TRIFORIA
TREPHININGS	TRIALITY	TRICAR	TRICORNES	TRIFORIUM
TREPID	TRIALLED	TRICARS	TRICORNS	TRIFORM
TREPIDANT	TRIALLING	TRICE	TRICOT	TRIFORMED
TREPONEMA	TRIALLIST	TRICED	TRICOTS	TRIG
TREPONEMAS	TRIALLISTS	TRICEPS	TRICROTIC	TRIGAMIES
TREPONEMATA	TRIALOGUE	TRICEPSES	TRICUSPID	TRIGAMIST
TREPONEME	TRIALOGUES	TRICERION	TRICYCLE	TRIGAMISTS
TREPONEMES	TRIALS	TRICERIONS	TRICYCLED	TRIGAMOUS
TRES	TRIANGLE	TRICES	TRICYCLER	TRIGAMY
TRESPASS	TRIANGLED	TRICHINA	TRICYCLERS	TRIGGED
TRESPASSED	TRIANGLES	TRICHINAE	TRICYCLES	TRIGGER
TRESPASSES	TRIAPSAL	TRICHINAS	TRICYCLIC	TRIGGERED
TRESPASSING	TRIARCH	TRICHITE	TRICYCLING	TRIGGERING
TRESS	TRIARCHIES	TRICHITES	TRICYCLINGS	TRIGGERS
TRESSED	TRIARCHS	TRICHITIC	TRIDACNA	TRIGGEST
TRESSEL	TRIARCHY	TRICHOID	TRIDACNAS	TRIGGING
TRESSELS	TRIATHLON	TRICHOME	TRIDACTYL	TRIGLOT
TRESSES	TRIATHLONS	TRICHOMES	TRIDARN	TRIGLOTS
TRESSIER	TRIATIC	TRICHORD	TRIDARNS	TRIGLY
TRESSIEST	TRIATICS	TRICHORDS	TRIDE	TRIGLYPH
TRESSING	TRIATOMIC	TRICHOSES	TRIDENT	TRIGLYPHS
TRESSURE	TRIAXIAL	TRICHOSIS	TRIDENTAL	TRIGNESS
TRESSURED	TRIAXIALS	TRICHROIC	TRIDENTED	TRIGNESSES
TRESSURES	TRIAXON	TRICHROME	TRIDENTS	TRIGON
TRESSY	TRIAXONS	TRICING	TRIDUAN	TRIGONAL
TREST	TRIBADE	TRICK	TRIDUUM	TRIGONIC
TRESTLE	TRIBADES	TRICKED	TRIDUUMS	TRIGONOUS
TRESTLES	TRIBADIC	TRICKER	TRIDYMITE	TRIGONS
TRESTS	TRIBADIES	TRICKERIES	TRIDYMITES	TRIGRAM
TRET	TRIBADISM	TRICKERS	TRIE	TRIGRAMS
TRETS	TRIBADISMS	TRICKERY	TRIECIOUS	TRIGRAPH
TREVALLIES	TRIBADY	TRICKIER	TRIED	TRIGRAPHS
TREVALLY	TRIBAL	TRICKIEST	TRIENNIAL	TRIGS
TREVIS	TRIBALISM	TRICKILY	TRIER	TRIGYNIAN
TREVISES	TRIBALISMS	TRICKING	TRIERARCH	TRIGYNOUS
TREVISS	TRIBALIST	TRICKINGS	TRIERARCHS	TRIHEDRAL
TREVISSES	TRIBALISTS	TRICKISH	TRIERS	TRIHEDRALS
TREW	TRIBALLY	TRICKLE	TRIES	TRIHEDRON
TREWS	TRIBASIC	TRICKLED	TRIETERIC	TRIHEDRONS
TREWSMAN	TRIBBLE	TRICKLES	TRIETHYL	TRIHYBRID
TREWSMEN	TRIBBLES	TRICKLESS	TRIFACIAL	TRIHYBRIDS
TREY	TRIBE	TRICKLET	TRIFECTA	TRIHYDRIC
TREYBIT	TRIBELESS	TRICKLETS	TRIFECTAS	TRIKE
TREYBITS	TRIBES	TRICKLIER	TRIFF	TRIKES
TREYS	TRIBESMAN	TRICKLIEST	TRIFFER	TRILBIES
TREZ	TRIBESMEN	TRICKLING	TRIFFEST	TRILBY
TREZES	TRIBLET	TRICKLINGS	TRIFFIC	TRILBYS
TRIABLE	TRIBLETS	TRICKLY	TRIFFID	TRILD
TRIACID	TRIBOLOGIES	TRICKS	TRIFFIDS	TRILEMMA
TRIACT	TRIBOLOGY	TRICKSIER	TRIFFIDY	TRILEMMAS
TRIACTINE	TRIBRACH	TRICKSIEST	TRIFID	TRILINEAR
TRIAD	TRIBRACHS	TRICKSOME	TRIFLE	TRILITH

TRILITHIC	TRINITY	TRIPODY	TRISOMES	TRIUNES
TRILITHON	TRINKET	TRIPOLI	TRISOMIC	TRIUNITIES
TRILITHONS	TRINKETED	TRIPOLIS	TRISOMIES	TRIUNITY
TRILITHS	TRINKETER	TRIPOS	TRISOMY	TRIVALENT
TRILL	TRINKETERS	TRIPOSES	TRIST	TRIVALVE
TRILLED	TRINKETING	TRIPPANT	TRISTE	TRIVALVED
TRILLING	TRINKETINGS	TRIPPED	TRISTESSE	TRIVALVES
TRILLINGS	TRINKETRIES	TRIPPER	TRISTESSES	TRIVET
TRILLION	TRINKETRY	TRIPPERS	TRISTFUL	TRIVETS
TRILLIONS	TRINKETS	TRIPPERY	TRISTICH	TRIVIA
TRILLIUM	TRINKUM	TRIPPET	TRISTICHS	TRIVIAL
TRILLIUMS	TRINKUMS	TRIPPETS	TRISUL	TRIVIALLY
TRILLO	TRINOMIAL	TRIPPIER	TRISULA	TRIVIUM
TRILLOES	TRINOMIALS	TRIPPIEST	TRISULAS	TRIVIUMS
TRILLS	TRINS	TRIPPING	TRISULS	TRIZONAL
TRILOBATE	TRIO	TRIPPINGS	TRITE	TRIZONE
TRILOBE	TRIODE	TRIPPLE	TRITELY	TRIZONES
TRILOBED	TRIODES	TRIPPLED	TRITENESS	TROAD
TRILOBES	TRIOLET	TRIPPLER	TRITENESSES	TROADE
TRILOBITE	TRIOLETS	TRIPPLERS	TRITER	TROADES
TRILOBITES	TRIONES	TRIPPLES	TRITES	TROADS
TRILOGIES	TRIONYM	TRIPPLING	TRITEST	TROAT
TRILOGY	TRIONYMAL	TRIPPY	TRITHEISM	TROATED
TRIM	TRIONYMS	TRIPS	TRITHEISMS	TROATING
TRIMARAN	TRIOR	TRIPSES	TRITHEIST	TROATS
TRIMARANS	TRIORS	TRIPSIS	TRITHEISTS	TROCAR
TRIMER	TRIOS	TRIPTANE	TRITIATE	TROCARS
TRIMERIC	TRIOXIDE	TRIPTANES	TRITIATED	TROCHAIC
TRIMEROUS	TRIOXIDES	TRIPTOTE	TRITIATES	TROCHAICS
TRIMERS	TRIP	TRIPTOTES	TRITIATING	TROCHAL
TRIMESTER	TRIPE	TRIPTYCH	TRITICAL	TROCHE
TRIMESTERS	TRIPEDAL	TRIPTYCHS	TRITICALE	TROCHEE
TRIMETER	TRIPERIES	TRIPTYQUE	TRITICALES	TROCHEES
TRIMETERS	TRIPERY	TRIPTYQUES	TRITICISM	TROCHES
TRIMETHYL	TRIPES	TRIPUDIA	TRITICISMS	TROCHI
TRIMETRIC	TRIPEY	TRIPUDIUM	TRITIDE	TROCHILIC
TRIMLY	TRIPHONE	TRIPUDIUMS	TRITIDES	TROCHILUS
TRIMMED	TRIPHONES	TRIPWIRE	TRITIUM	TROCHILUSES
TRIMMER	TRIPIER	TRIPWIRES	TRITIUMS	TROCHISK
TRIMMERS	TRIPIEST	TRIPY	TRITON	TROCHISKS
TRIMMEST	TRIPITAKA	TRIQUETRA	TRITONE	TROCHITE
TRIMMING	TRIPITAKAS	TRIQUETRAS	TRITONES	TROCHITES
TRIMMINGS	TRIPLANE	TRIRADIAL	TRITONIA	TROCHLEA
TRIMNESS	TRIPLANES	TRIREME	TRITONIAS	TROCHLEAR
TRIMNESSES	TRIPLE	TRIREMES	TRITONS	TROCHLEAS
TRIMS	TRIPLED	TRISAGION	TRITURATE	TROCHOID
TRIMTAB	TRIPLES	TRISAGIONS	TRITURATED	TROCHOIDS
TRIMTABS	TRIPLET	TRISECT	TRITURATES	TROCHUS
TRIN	TRIPLETS	TRISECTED	TRITURATING	TROCHUSES
TRINAL	TRIPLEX	TRISECTING	TRIUMPH	TROCK
TRINARY	TRIPLEXES	TRISECTOR	TRIUMPHAL	TROCKED
TRINDLE	TRIPLIED	TRISECTORS	TRIUMPHALS	TROCKEN
TRINDLED	TRIPLIES	TRISECTS	TRIUMPHED	TROCKING
TRINDLES	TRIPLING	TRISEME	TRIUMPHER	TROCKS
TRINDLING	TRIPLINGS	TRISEMES	TRIUMPHERS	TROD
TRINE	TRIPLOID	TRISEMIC	TRIUMPHING	TRODDEN
TRINED	TRIPLOIDIES	TRISHAW	TRIUMPHINGS	TRODE
TRINES	TRIPLOIDY	TRISHAWS	TRIUMPHS	TRODES
TRINGLE	TRIPLY	TRISKELE	TRIUMVIR	TRODS
TRINGLES	TRIPLYING	TRISKELES	TRIUMVIRI	TROELIE
TRINING	TRIPOD	TRISKELIA	TRIUMVIRIES	TROELIES
TRINITIES	TRIPODAL	TRISMUS	TRIUMVIRS	TROELY
TRINITRIN	TRIPODIES	TRISMUSES	TRIUMVIRY	TROG
TRINITRINS	TRIPODS	TRISOME	TRIUNE	TROGGED

TROGGING	TROOPER	TROULING	TRUANTING	TRUING
TROGGS	TROOPERS	TROUNCE	TRUANTRIES	TRUISM
TROGON	TROOPIAL	TROUNCED	TRUANTRY	TRUISMS
TROGONS	TROOPIALS	TROUNCER	TRUANTS	TRUISTIC
TROGS	TROOPING	TROUNCERS	TRUCAGE	TRULL
TROIKA	TROOPS	TROUNCES	TRUCAGES	TRULLS
TROIKAS	TROPARIA	TROUNCING	TRUCE	TRULY
TROILISM	TROPARION	TROUNCINGS	TRUCELESS	TRUMEAU
TROILISMS	TROPE	TROUPE	TRUCES	TRUMEAUX
TROILIST	TROPED	TROUPED	TRUCHMAN	TRUMP
TROILISTS	TROPES	TROUPER	TRUCHMANS	TRUMPED
TROILITE	TROPHESIES	TROUPERS	TRUCHMEN	TRUMPERIES
TROILITES	TROPHESY	TROUPES	TRUCIAL	TRUMPERY
TROKE	TROPHI	TROUPIAL	TRUCK	TRUMPET
TROKED	TROPHIC	TROUPIALS	TRUCKAGE	TRUMPETED
TROKES	TROPHIED	TROUPING	TRUCKAGES	TRUMPETER
TROKING	TROPHIES	TROUSE	TRUCKED	TRUMPETERS
TROLL	TROPHY	TROUSER	TRUCKER	TRUMPETING
TROLLED	TROPHYING	TROUSERED	TRUCKERS	TRUMPETINGS
TROLLER	TROPIC	TROUSERING	TRUCKIE	TRUMPETS
TROLLERS	TROPICAL	TROUSERINGS	TRUCKIES	TRUMPING
TROLLEY	TROPICS	TROUSERS	TRUCKING	TRUMPINGS
TROLLEYED	TROPING	TROUSES	TRUCKINGS	TRUMPS
TROLLEYING	TROPISM	TROUSSEAU	TRUCKLE	TRUNCAL
TROLLEYS	TROPISMS	TROUSSEAUS	TRUCKLED	TRUNCATE
TROLLIES	TROPIST	TROUSSEAUX	TRUCKLER	TRUNCATED
TROLLING	TROPISTIC	TROUT	TRUCKLERS	TRUNCATES
TROLLINGS	TROPISTS	TROUTER	TRUCKLES	TRUNCATING
TROLLIUS	TROPOLOGIES	TROUTERS	TRUCKLING	TRUNCHEON
TROLLIUSES	TROPOLOGY	TROUTFUL	TRUCKLINGS	TRUNCHEONED
TROLLOP	TROPPO	TROUTIER	TRUCKMAN	TRUNCHEONING
TROLLOPED	TROSSERS	TROUTIEST	TRUCKMEN	TRUNCHEONS
TROLLOPEE	TROT	TROUTING	TRUCKS	TRUNDLE
TROLLOPEES	TROTH	TROUTINGS	TRUCULENT	TRUNDLED
TROLLOPING	TROTHED	TROUTLESS	TRUDGE	TRUNDLER
TROLLOPS	TROTHFUL	TROUTLET	TRUDGED	TRUNDLERS
TROLLOPY	TROTHING	TROUTLETS	TRUDGEN	TRUNDLES
TROLLS	TROTHLESS	TROUTLING	TRUDGENS	TRUNDLING
TROLLY	TROTHS	TROUTLINGS	TRUDGEON	TRUNK
TROMBONE	TROTLINE	TROUTS	TRUDGEONS	TRUNKED
TROMBONES	TROTLINES	TROUTY	TRUDGER	TRUNKFISH
TROMINO	TROTS	TROUVERE	TRUDGERS	TRUNKFISHES
TROMINOES	TROTTED	TROUVERES	TRUDGES	TRUNKFUL
TROMINOS	TROTTER	TROUVEUR	TRUDGING	TRUNKFULS
TROMMEL	TROTTERS	TROUVEURS	TRUDGINGS	TRUNKING
TROMMELS	TROTTING	TROVER	TRUE	TRUNKINGS
TROMP	TROTTINGS	TROVERS	TRUED	TRUNKS
TROMPE	TROTTOIR	TROW	TRUEING	TRUNNION
TROMPED	TROTTOIRS	TROWED	TRUEMAN	TRUNNIONS
TROMPES	TROTYL	TROWEL	TRUEMEN	TRUQUAGE
TROMPING	TROTYLS	TROWELLED	TRUENESS	TRUQUAGES
TROMPS	TROUBLE	TROWELLER	TRUENESSES	TRUQUEUR
TRON	TROUBLED	TROWELLERS	TRUEPENNIES	TRUQUEURS
TRONA	TROUBLER	TROWELLING	TRUEPENNY	TRUSS
TRONAS	TROUBLERS	TROWELS	TRUER	TRUSSED
TRONC	TROUBLES	TROWING	TRUES	TRUSSER
TRONCS	TROUBLING	TROWS	TRUEST	TRUSSERS
TRONE	TROUBLINGS	TROWSERS	TRUFFLE	TRUSSES
TRONES	TROUBLOUS	TROY	TRUFFLED	TRUSSING
TRONS	TROUGH	TROYS	TRUFFLES	TRUSSINGS
TROOLIE	TROUGHS	TRUANCIES	TRUFFLING	TRUST
TROOLIES	TROULE	TRUANCY	TRUFFLINGS	TRUSTED
TROOP	TROULED	TRUANT	TRUG	TRUSTEE
TROOPED	TROULES	TRUANTED	TRUGS	TRUSTEES

TRUSTER	TSESSEBES	TUBEROUS	TUFTIEST	TUMBLE
TRUSTERS	TSETSE	TUBERS	TUFTING	TUMBLED
TRUSTFUL	TSETSES	TUBES	TUFTINGS	TUMBLER
TRUSTIER	TSIGANE	TUBFAST	TUFTS	TUMBLERS
TRUSTIES	TSIGANES	TUBFASTS	TUFTY	TUMBLES
TRUSTIEST	TSOTSI	TUBFISH	TUG	TUMBLING
TRUSTILY	TSOTSIS	TUBFISHES	TUGBOAT	TUMBLINGS
TRUSTING	TSOURIS	TUBFUL	TUGBOATS	TUMBREL
TRUSTLESS	TSOURISES	TUBFULS	TUGGED	TUMBRELS
TRUSTS	TSUBA	TUBICOLAR	TUGGER	TUMBRIL
TRUSTY	TSUBAS	TUBICOLE	TUGGERS	TUMBRILS
TRUTH	TSUNAMI	TUBICOLES	TUGGING	TUMEFIED
TRUTHFUL	TSUNAMIS	TUBIFEX	TUGGINGLY	TUMEFIES
TRUTHIER	TSURIS	TUBIFEXES	TUGGINGS	TUMEFY
TRUTHIEST	TSURISES	TUBIFORM	TUGHRA	TUMEFYING
TRUTHLESS	TSUTSUMU	TUBING	TUGHRAS	TUMESCE
TRUTHLIKE	TSUTSUMUS	TUBINGS	TUGHRIK	TUMESCED
TRUTHS	TUAN	TUBS	TUGHRIKS	TUMESCENT
TRUTHY	TUANS	TUBULAR	TUGRA	TUMESCES
TRY	TUART	TUBULATE	TUGRAS	TUMESCING
TRYE	TUARTS	TUBULATED	TUGRIK	TUMID
TRYER	TUATARA	TUBULATES	TUGRIKS	TUMIDITIES
TRYERS	TUATARAS	TUBULATING	TUGS	TUMIDITY
TRYING	TUATH	TUBULE	TUI	TUMIDLY
TRYINGLY	TUATHS	TUBULES	TUILLE	TUMIDNESS
TRYINGS	TUB	TUBULIN	TUILLES	TUMIDNESSES
TRYP	TUBA	TUBULINS	TUILLETTE	TUMMIES
TRYPS	TUBAE	TUBULOUS	TUILLETTES	TUMMY
TRYPSIN	TUBAGE	TUCHUN	TUILYIE	TUMOR
TRYPSINS	TUBAGES	TUCHUNS	TUILYIED	TUMOROUS
TRYPTIC	TUBAL	TUCK	TUILYIEING	TUMORS
TRYSAIL	TUBAR	TUCKAHOE	TUILYIES	TUMOUR
TRYSAILS	TUBAS	TUCKAHOES	TUILZIE	TUMOURS
TRYST	TUBATE	TUCKED	TUILZIED	TUMP
TRYSTED	TUBBED	TUCKER	TUILZIEING	TUMPED
TRYSTER	TUBBER	TUCKERBAG	TUILZIES	TUMPHIES
TRYSTERS	TUBBERS	TUCKERBAGS	TUINA	TUMPHY
TRYSTING	TUBBIER	TUCKERBOX	TUINAS	TUMPIER
TRYSTS	TUBBIEST	TUCKERBOXES	TUIS	TUMPIEST
TSADDIK	TUBBINESS	TUCKERED	TUISM	TUMPING
TSADDIKIM	TUBBINESSES	TUCKERING	TUISMS	TUMPS
TSADDIKS	TUBBING	TUCKERS	TUITION	TUMPY
TSADDIQ	TUBBINGS	TUCKET	TUITIONAL	TUMS
TSADDIQIM	TUBBISH	TUCKETS	TUITIONS	TUMSHIE
TSADDIQS	TUBBY	TUCKING	TULAREMIA	TUMSHIES
TSAMBA	TUBE	TUCKS	TULAREMIAS	TUMULAR
TSAMBAS	TUBECTOMIES	TUCOTUCO	TULAREMIC	TUMULARY
TSAR	TUBECTOMY	TUCOTUCOS	TULBAN	TUMULI
TSARDOM	TUBED	TUCUTUCO	TULBANS	TUMULT
TSARDOMS	TUBEFUL	TUCUTUCOS	TULCHAN	TUMULTED
TSAREVICH	TUBEFULS	TUFA	TULCHANS	TUMULTING
TSAREVICHES	TUBELESS	TUFACEOUS	TULE	TUMULTS
TSAREVNA	TUBELIKE	TUFAS	TULES	TUMULUS
TSAREVNAS	TUBENOSE	TUFF	TULIP	TUN
TSARINA	TUBENOSES	TUFFE	TULIPANT	TUNA
TSARINAS	TUBER	TUFFES	TULIPANTS	TUNABLE
TSARISM	TUBERCLE	TUFFET	TULIPS	TUNABLY
TSARISMS	TUBERCLED	TUFFETS	TULIPWOOD	TUNAS
TSARIST	TUBERCLES	TUFFS	TULIPWOODS	TUNBELLIES
TSARISTS	TUBERCULA	TUFT	TULLE	TUNBELLY
TSARITSA	TUBERCULE	TUFTED	TULLES	TUND
TSARITSAS	TUBERCULES	TUFTER	TULWAR	TUNDED
TSARS	TUBEROSE	TUFTERS	TULWARS	TUNDING
TSESSEBE	TUBEROSES	TUFTIER	TUM	TUNDRA

TUNDRAS	TUPPENNY	TURFIER	TURNIPING	TUSKARS
TUNDS	TUPPING	TURFIEST	TURNIPS	TUSKED
TUNDUN	TUPS	TURFINESS	TURNKEY	TUSKER
TUNDUNS	TUPTOWING	TURFINESSES	TURNKEYS	TUSKERS
TUNE	TUQUE	TURFING	TURNOFF	TUSKIER
TUNEABLE	TUQUES	TURFINGS	TURNOFFS	TUSKIEST
TUNED	TURACIN	TURFITE	TURNOUT	TUSKING
TUNEFUL	TURACINS	TURFITES	TURNOUTS	TUSKINGS
TUNEFULLY	TURACO	TURFMAN	TURNOVER	TUSKLESS
TUNELESS	TURACOS	TURFMEN	TURNOVERS	TUSKS
TUNER	TURBAN	TURFS	TURNPIKE	TUSKY
TUNERS	TURBAND	TURFY	TURNPIKES	TUSSAH
TUNES	TURBANDS	TURGENT	TURNROUND	TUSSAHS
TUNESMITH	TURBANED	TURGENTLY	TURNROUNDS	TUSSAL
TUNESMITHS	TURBANS	TURGID	TURNS	TUSSEH
TUNGSTATE	TURBANT	TURGIDER	TURNSKIN	TUSSEHS
TUNGSTATES	TURBANTS	TURGIDEST	TURNSKINS	TUSSER
TUNGSTEN	TURBARIES	TURGIDITIES	TURNSOLE	TUSSERS
TUNGSTENS	TURBARY	TURGIDITY	TURNSOLES	TUSSIS
TUNIC	TURBID	TURGIDLY	TURNSPIT	TUSSISES
TUNICATE	TURBIDITE	TURGOR	TURNSPITS	TUSSIVE
TUNICATED	TURBIDITES	TURGORS	TURNSTILE	TUSSLE
TUNICATES	TURBIDITIES	TURION	TURNSTILES	TUSSLED
TUNICIN	TURBIDITY	TURIONS	TURNSTONE	TUSSLES
TUNICINS	TURBIDLY	TURKEY	TURNSTONES	TUSSLING
TUNICKED	TURBINAL	TURKEYS	TURNTABLE	TUSSOCK
TUNICLE	TURBINALS	TURKIES	TURNTABLES	TUSSOCKS
TUNICLES	TURBINATE	TURKIESES	TURPETH	TUSSOCKY
TUNICS	TURBINATES	TURKIS	TURPETHS	TUSSORE
TUNIER	TURBINE	TURKISES	TURPITUDE	TUSSORES
TUNIEST	TURBINED	TURLOUGH	TURPITUDES	TUT
TUNING	TURBINES	TURLOUGHS	TURPS	TUTANIA
TUNINGS	TURBIT	TURM	TURQUOISE	TUTANIAS
TUNNAGE	TURBITH	TURME	TURQUOISES	TUTEE
TUNNAGES	TURBITHS	TURMERIC	TURRET	TUTEES
TUNNED	TURBITS	TURMERICS	TURRETED	TUTELAGE
TUNNEL	TURBO	TURMES	TURRETS	TUTELAGES
TUNNELED	TURBOCAR	TURMOIL	TURRIBANT	TUTELAR
TUNNELER	TURBOCARS	TURMOILED	TURRIBANTS	TUTELARIES
TUNNELERS	TURBOFAN	TURMOILING	TURTLE	TUTELARS
TUNNELING	TURBOFANS	TURMOILS	TURTLED	TUTELARY
TUNNELLED	TURBOJET	TURMS	TURTLER	TUTENAG
TUNNELLER	TURBOJETS	TURN	TURTLERS	TUTENAGS
TUNNELLERS	TURBOND	TURNABOUT	TURTLES	TUTIORISM
TUNNELLING	TURBONDS	TURNABOUTS	TURTLING	TUTIORISMS
TUNNELLINGS	TURBOPROP	TURNAGAIN	TURTLINGS	TUTIORIST
TUNNELS	TURBOPROPS	TURNAGAINS	TURVES	TUTIORISTS
TUNNIES	TURBOS	TURNBACK	TUSCHE	TUTMAN
TUNNING	TURBOT	TURNBACKS	TUSCHES	TUTMEN
TUNNINGS	TURBOTS	TURNCOAT	TUSH	TUTOR
TUNNY	TURBULENT	TURNCOATS	TUSHED	TUTORAGE
TUNS	TURCOPOLE	TURNCOCK	TUSHERIES	TUTORAGES
TUNY	TURCOPOLES	TURNCOCKS	TUSHERY	TUTORED
TUP	TURD	TURNDUN	TUSHES	TUTORESS
TUPEK	TURDINE	TURNDUNS	TUSHIE	TUTORESSES
TUPEKS	TURDION	TURNED	TUSHIES	TUTORIAL
TUPELO	TURDIONS	TURNER	TUSHING	TUTORIALS
TUPELOS	TURDOID	TURNERIES	TUSHKAR	TUTORING
TUPIK	TURDS	TURNERS	TUSHKARS	TUTORINGS
TUPIKS	TUREEN	TURNERY	TUSHKER	TUTORISE
TUPPED	TUREENS	TURNING	TUSHKERS	TUTORISED
TUPPENCE	TURF	TURNINGS	TUSHY	TUTORISES
TUPPENCES	TURFED	TURNIP	TUSK	TUTORISING
TUPPENNIES	TURFEN	TURNIPED	TUSKAR	TUTORISM

The Chambers Dictionary is the authority for many longer words; see *OSW* Introduction, page xii

TUTORISMS	TWANG	TWEETER	TWILIGHTING	TWIRLY
TUTORIZE	TWANGED	TWEETERS	TWILIGHTS	TWIRP
TUTORIZED	TWANGIER	TWEETING	TWILIT	TWIRPS
TUTORIZES	TWANGIEST	TWEETS	TWILL	TWISCAR
TUTORIZING	TWANGING	TWEEZE	TWILLED	TWISCARS
TUTORS	TWANGINGS	TWEEZED	TWILLIES	TWIST
TUTORSHIP	TWANGLE	TWEEZERS	TWILLING	TWISTABLE
TUTORSHIPS	TWANGLED	TWEEZES	TWILLS	TWISTED
TUTRESS	TWANGLES	TWEEZING	TWILLY	TWISTER
TUTRESSES	TWANGLING	TWELFTH	TWILT	TWISTERS
TUTRICES	TWANGLINGS	TWELFTHLY	TWILTED	TWISTIER
TUTRIX	TWANGS	TWELFTHS	TWILTING	TWISTIEST
TUTRIXES	TWANGY	TWELVE	TWILTS	TWISTING
TUTS	TWANK	TWELVEMO	TWIN	TWISTINGS
TUTSAN	TWANKAY	TWELVEMOS	TWINE	TWISTOR
TUTSANS	TWANKAYS	TWELVES	TWINED	TWISTORS
TUTSED	TWANKS	TWENTIES	TWINER	TWISTS
TUTSES	TWAS	TWENTIETH	TWINERS	TWISTY
TUTSING	TWASOME	TWENTIETHS	TWINES	TWIT
TUTTED	TWASOMES	TWENTY	TWINGE	TWITCH
TUTTI	TWAT	TWENTYISH	TWINGED	TWITCHED
TUTTIES	TWATS	TWERP	TWINGES	TWITCHER
TUTTING	TWATTLE	TWERPS	TWINGING	TWITCHERS
TUTTINGS	TWATTLED	TWIBILL	TWINIER	TWITCHES
TUTTIS	TWATTLER	TWIBILLS	TWINIEST	TWITCHIER
TUTTY	TWATTLERS	TWICE	TWINING	TWITCHIEST
TUTU	TWATTLES	TWICER	TWININGLY	TWITCHING
TUTUS	TWATTLING	TWICERS	TWININGS	TWITCHINGS
TUTWORK	TWATTLINGS	TWICHILD	TWINK	TWITCHY
TUTWORKER	TWAY	TWICHILDREN	TWINKED	TWITE
TUTWORKERS	TWAYS	TWIDDLE	TWINKING	TWITES
TUTWORKS	TWEAK	TWIDDLED	TWINKLE	TWITS
TUX	TWEAKED	TWIDDLER	TWINKLED	TWITTED
TUXEDO	TWEAKING	TWIDDLERS	TWINKLER	TWITTEN
TUXEDOES	TWEAKINGS	TWIDDLES	TWINKLERS	TWITTENS
TUXEDOS	TWEAKS	TWIDDLIER	TWINKLES	TWITTER
TUXES	TWEE	TWIDDLIEST	TWINKLING	TWITTERED
TUYERE	TWEED	TWIDDLING	TWINKLINGS	TWITTERER
TUYERES	TWEEDIER	TWIDDLINGS	TWINKS	TWITTERERS
TUZZ	TWEEDIEST	TWIDDLY	TWINLING	TWITTERING
TUZZES	TWEEDLE	TWIER	TWINLINGS	TWITTERINGS
TWA	TWEEDLED	TWIERS	TWINNED	TWITTERS
TWADDLE	TWEEDLER	TWIFOLD	TWINNING	TWITTERY
TWADDLED	TWEEDLERS	TWIFORKED	TWINNINGS	TWITTING
TWADDLER	TWEEDLES	TWIFORMED	TWINS	TWITTINGS
TWADDLERS	TWEEDLING	TWIG	TWINSET	TWIZZLE
TWADDLES	TWEEDS	TWIGGED	TWINSETS	TWIZZLED
TWADDLIER	TWEEDY	TWIGGEN	TWINSHIP	TWIZZLES
TWADDLIEST	TWEEL	TWIGGER	TWINSHIPS	TWIZZLING
TWADDLING	TWEELED	TWIGGERS	TWINTER	TWO
TWADDLINGS	TWEELING	TWIGGIER	TWINTERS	TWOCCER
TWADDLY	TWEELS	TWIGGIEST	TWINY	TWOCCERS
TWAE	TWEELY	TWIGGING	TWIRE	TWOCCING
TWAES	TWEENESS	TWIGGY	TWIRED	TWOCCINGS
TWAFALD	TWEENESSES	TWIGHT	TWIRES	TWOER
TWAIN	TWEENIES	TWIGHTED	TWIRING	TWOERS
TWAINS	TWEENY	TWIGHTING	TWIRL	TWOFOLD
TWAITE	TWEER	TWIGHTS	TWIRLED	TWONESS
TWAITES	TWEERED	TWIGLOO	TWIRLER	TWONESSES
TWAL	TWEERING	TWIGLOOS	TWIRLERS	TWOPENCE
TWALHOURS	TWEERS	TWIGS	TWIRLIER	TWOPENCES
TWALPENNIES	TWEEST	TWIGSOME	TWIRLIEST	TWOPENNIES
TWALPENNY	TWEET	TWILIGHT	TWIRLING	TWOPENNY
TWALS	TWEETED	TWILIGHTED	TWIRLS	TWOS

TWOSEATER
TWOSEATERS
TWOSOME
TWOSOMES
TWOSTROKE
TWP
TWYER
TWYERE
TWYERES
TWYERS
TWYFOLD
TWYFORKED
TWYFORMED
TYCHISM
TYCHISMS
TYCOON
TYCOONATE
TYCOONATES
TYCOONERIES
TYCOONERY
TYCOONS
TYDE
TYE
TYED
TYEING
TYES
TYG
TYGS
TYING
TYKE
TYKES
TYKISH
TYLECTOMIES
TYLECTOMY
TYLER
TYLERS

TYLOPOD
TYLOPODS
TYLOSES
TYLOSIS
TYLOTE
TYLOTES
TYMBAL
TYMBALS
TYMP
TYMPAN
TYMPANA
TYMPANAL
TYMPANI
TYMPANIC
TYMPANICS
TYMPANIES
TYMPANIST
TYMPANISTS
TYMPANO
TYMPANS
TYMPANUM
TYMPANY
TYMPS
TYND
TYNDE
TYNE
TYNED
TYNES
TYNING
TYPAL
TYPE
TYPECAST
TYPECASTING
TYPECASTS
TYPED
TYPES

TYPESET
TYPEWRITE
TYPEWRITES
TYPEWRITING
TYPEWRITINGS
TYPEWRITTEN
TYPEWROTE
TYPHLITIC
TYPHLITIS
TYPHLITISES
TYPHOID
TYPHOIDAL
TYPHOIDS
TYPHON
TYPHONIAN
TYPHONIC
TYPHONS
TYPHOON
TYPHOONS
TYPHOUS
TYPHUS
TYPHUSES
TYPIC
TYPICAL
TYPICALLY
TYPIFIED
TYPIFIER
TYPIFIERS
TYPIFIES
TYPIFY
TYPIFYING
TYPING
TYPINGS
TYPIST
TYPISTS
TYPO

TYPOLOGIES
TYPOLOGY
TYPOMANIA
TYPOMANIAS
TYPOS
TYPTO
TYPTOED
TYPTOING
TYPTOS
TYRAMINE
TYRAMINES
TYRAN
TYRANED
TYRANING
TYRANNE
TYRANNED
TYRANNES
TYRANNESS
TYRANNESSES
TYRANNIC
TYRANNIES
TYRANNING
TYRANNIS
TYRANNISE
TYRANNISED
TYRANNISES
TYRANNISING
TYRANNIZE
TYRANNIZED
TYRANNIZES
TYRANNIZING
TYRANNOUS
TYRANNY
TYRANS
TYRANT
TYRANTED

TYRANTING
TYRANTS
TYRE
TYRED
TYRELESS
TYRES
TYRO
TYROES
TYRONES
TYROS
TYROSINE
TYROSINES
TYSTIE
TYSTIES
TYTE
TYTHE
TYTHED
TYTHES
TYTHING
TZADDIK
TZADDIKIM
TZADDIKS
TZADDIQ
TZADDIQIM
TZADDIQS
TZAR
TZARS
TZATZIKI
TZATZIKIS
TZETSE
TZETSES
TZIGANIES
TZIGANY
TZIMMES

U

UAKARI	UHLAN	ULNA	UMBERS	UMPIRES
UAKARIS	UHLANS	ULNAE	UMBERY	UMPIRING
UBEROUS	UHURU	ULNAR	UMBILICAL	UMPTEEN
UBERTIES	UHURUS	ULNARE	UMBILICI	UMPTEENTH
UBERTY	UINTAHITE	ULNARIA	UMBILICUS	UMPTIETH
UBIETIES	UINTAHITES	ULOSES	UMBILICUSES	UMPTY
UBIETY	UINTAITE	ULOSIS	UMBLES	UMQUHILE
UBIQUE	UINTAITES	ULOTRICHIES	UMBO	UMWHILE
UBIQUITIES	UITLANDER	ULOTRICHY	UMBONAL	UN
UBIQUITY	UITLANDERS	ULSTER	UMBONATE	UNABASHED
UCKERS	UJAMAA	ULSTERED	UMBONES	UNABATED
UDAL	UJAMAAS	ULSTERS	UMBOS	UNABLE
UDALLER	UKASE	ULTERIOR	UMBRA	UNACCUSED
UDALLERS	UKASES	ULTIMA	UMBRACULA	UNACHING
UDALS	UKE	ULTIMACIES	UMBRAE	UNACTABLE
UDDER	UKELELE	ULTIMACY	UMBRAGE	UNACTED
UDDERED	UKELELES	ULTIMAS	UMBRAGED	UNACTIVE
UDDERFUL	UKES	ULTIMATA	UMBRAGES	UNADAPTED
UDDERLESS	UKULELE	ULTIMATE	UMBRAGING	UNADMIRED
UDDERS	UKULELES	ULTIMATES	UMBRAL	UNADOPTED
UDO	ULCER	ULTIMATUM	UMBRAS	UNADORED
UDOMETER	ULCERATE	ULTIMO	UMBRATED	UNADORNED
UDOMETERS	ULCERATED	ULTION	UMBRATIC	UNADVISED
UDOMETRIC	ULCERATES	ULTIONS	UMBRATILE	UNAFRAID
UDOS	ULCERATING	ULTRA	UMBRE	UNAIDABLE
UDS	ULCERED	ULTRAISM	UMBREL	UNAIDED
UEY	ULCERING	ULTRAISMS	UMBRELLA	UNAIMED
UEYS	ULCEROUS	ULTRAIST	UMBRELLAS	UNAIRED
UFO	ULCERS	ULTRAISTS	UMBRELLO	UNAKING
UFOLOGIES	ULE	ULTRARED	UMBRELLOES	UNALIGNED
UFOLOGIST	ULEMA	ULTRAS	UMBRELLOS	UNALIKE
UFOLOGISTS	ULEMAS	ULULANT	UMBRELS	UNALIST
UFOLOGY	ULES	ULULATE	UMBRERE	UNALISTS
UFOS	ULEX	ULULATED	UMBRERES	UNALIVE
UG	ULEXES	ULULATES	UMBRES	UNALLAYED
UGGED	ULICHON	ULULATING	UMBRETTE	UNALLIED
UGGING	ULICHONS	ULULATION	UMBRETTES	UNALLOYED
UGH	ULICON	ULULATIONS	UMBRIERE	UNALTERED
UGHS	ULICONS	ULVA	UMBRIERES	UNAMAZED
UGLIED	ULIGINOSE	ULVAS	UMBRIL	UNAMENDED
UGLIER	ULIGINOUS	ULYIE	UMBRILS	UNAMERCED
UGLIES	ULIKON	ULYIES	UMBROSE	UNAMIABLE
UGLIEST	ULIKONS	ULZIE	UMBROUS	UNAMUSED
UGLIFIED	ULITIS	ULZIES	UMIAK	UNAMUSING
UGLIFIES	ULITISES	UM	UMIAKS	UNANCHOR
UGLIFY	ULLAGE	UMBEL	UMLAUT	UNANCHORED
UGLIFYING	ULLAGED	UMBELLAR	UMLAUTED	UNANCHORING
UGLILY	ULLAGES	UMBELLATE	UMLAUTING	UNANCHORS
UGLINESS	ULLAGING	UMBELLULE	UMLAUTS	UNANELED
UGLINESSES	ULLING	UMBELLULES	UMPH	UNANIMITIES
UGLY	ULLINGS	UMBELS	UMPIRAGE	UNANIMITY
UGLYING	ULMACEOUS	UMBER	UMPIRAGES	UNANIMOUS
UGS	ULMIN	UMBERED	UMPIRE	UNANXIOUS
UGSOME	ULMINS	UMBERING	UMPIRED	UNAPPAREL

The Chambers Dictionary is the authority for many longer words; see *OSW* Introduction, page xii

UNAPPARELLED	UNBARS	UNBIASSING	UNBOSOMING	UNBURY
UNAPPARELLING	UNBASHFUL	UNBID	UNBOSOMS	UNBURYING
UNAPPARELS	UNBATED	UNBIDDEN	UNBOUGHT	UNBUSY
UNAPPLIED	UNBATHED	UNBIND	UNBOUND	UNBUTTON
UNAPT	UNBE	UNBINDING	UNBOUNDED	UNBUTTONED
UNAPTLY	UNBEAR	UNBINDINGS	UNBOWED	UNBUTTONING
UNAPTNESS	UNBEARDED	UNBINDS	UNBOX	UNBUTTONS
UNAPTNESSES	UNBEARING	UNBISHOP	UNBOXED	UNCAGE
UNARGUED	UNBEARS	UNBISHOPED	UNBOXES	UNCAGED
UNARISEN	UNBEATEN	UNBISHOPING	UNBOXING	UNCAGES
UNARM	UNBED	UNBISHOPS	UNBRACE	UNCAGING
UNARMED	UNBEDDED	UNBITT	UNBRACED	UNCALLED
UNARMING	UNBEDDING	UNBITTED	UNBRACES	UNCANDID
UNARMS	UNBEDS	UNBITTING	UNBRACING	UNCANDOUR
UNARTFUL	UNBEEN	UNBITTS	UNBRAIDED	UNCANDOURS
UNASHAMED	UNBEGET	UNBLAMED	UNBRASTE	UNCANNIER
UNASKED	UNBEGETS	UNBLENDED	UNBRED	UNCANNIEST
UNASSAYED	UNBEGETTING	UNBLENT	UNBREECH	UNCANNILY
UNASSUMED	UNBEGGED	UNBLESS	UNBREECHED	UNCANNY
UNASSURED	UNBEGOT	UNBLESSED	UNBREECHES	UNCANONIC
UNATONED	UNBEGOTTEN	UNBLESSES	UNBREECHING	UNCAP
UNATTIRED	UNBEGUILE	UNBLESSING	UNBRIDGED	UNCAPABLE
UNAU	UNBEGUILED	UNBLEST	UNBRIDLE	UNCAPE
UNAUS	UNBEGUILES	UNBLIND	UNBRIDLED	UNCAPED
UNAVENGED	UNBEGUILING	UNBLINDED	UNBRIDLES	UNCAPES
UNAVOIDED	UNBEGUN	UNBLINDING	UNBRIDLING	UNCAPING
UNAVOWED	UNBEING	UNBLINDS	UNBRIZZED	UNCAPPED
UNAWARE	UNBEINGS	UNBLOCK	UNBROKE	UNCAPPING
UNAWARES	UNBEKNOWN	UNBLOCKED	UNBROKEN	UNCAPS
UNAWED	UNBELIEF	UNBLOCKING	UNBRUISED	UNCAREFUL
UNBACKED	UNBELIEFS	UNBLOCKS	UNBRUSED	UNCARING
UNBAFFLED	UNBELIEVE	UNBLOODED	UNBRUSHED	UNCART
UNBAG	UNBELIEVED	UNBLOODY	UNBUCKLE	UNCARTED
UNBAGGED	UNBELIEVES	UNBLOTTED	UNBUCKLED	UNCARTING
UNBAGGING	UNBELIEVING	UNBLOWED	UNBUCKLES	UNCARTS
UNBAGS	UNBELOVED	UNBLOWN	UNBUCKLING	UNCASE
UNBAITED	UNBELT	UNBLUNTED	UNBUDDED	UNCASED
UNBAKED	UNBELTED	UNBODIED	UNBUILD	UNCASES
UNBALANCE	UNBELTING	UNBODING	UNBUILDING	UNCASHED
UNBALANCED	UNBELTS	UNBOLT	UNBUILDS	UNCASING
UNBALANCES	UNBEND	UNBOLTED	UNBUILT	UNCATE
UNBALANCING	UNBENDED	UNBOLTING	UNBUNDLE	UNCAUGHT
UNBANDED	UNBENDING	UNBOLTS	UNBUNDLED	UNCAUSED
UNBANKED	UNBENDINGS	UNBONE	UNBUNDLER	UNCE
UNBAPTISE	UNBENDS	UNBONED	UNBUNDLERS	UNCEASING
UNBAPTISED	UNBENIGN	UNBONES	UNBUNDLES	UNCERTAIN
UNBAPTISES	UNBENT	UNBONING	UNBUNDLING	UNCES
UNBAPTISING	UNBEREFT	UNBONNET	UNBUNDLINGS	UNCESSANT
UNBAPTIZE	UNBERUFEN	UNBONNETED	UNBURDEN	UNCHAIN
UNBAPTIZED	UNBESEEM	UNBONNETING	UNBURDENED	UNCHAINED
UNBAPTIZES	UNBESEEMED	UNBONNETS	UNBURDENING	UNCHAINING
UNBAPTIZING	UNBESEEMING	UNBOOKED	UNBURDENS	UNCHAINS
UNBAR	UNBESEEMS	UNBOOKISH	UNBURIED	UNCHANCIER
UNBARBED	UNBESPEAK	UNBOOT	UNBURIES	UNCHANCIEST
UNBARE	UNBESPEAKING	UNBOOTED	UNBURNED	UNCHANCY
UNBARED	UNBESPEAKS	UNBOOTING	UNBURNT	UNCHANGED
UNBARES	UNBESPOKE	UNBOOTS	UNBURROW	UNCHARGE
UNBARING	UNBESPOKEN	UNBORE	UNBURROWED	UNCHARGED
UNBARK	UNBIAS	UNBORN	UNBURROWING	UNCHARGES
UNBARKED	UNBIASED	UNBORNE	UNBURROWS	UNCHARGING
UNBARKING	UNBIASES	UNBOSOM	UNBURTHEN	UNCHARITIES
UNBARKS	UNBIASING	UNBOSOMED	UNBURTHENED	UNCHARITY
UNBARRED	UNBIASSED	UNBOSOMER	UNBURTHENING	UNCHARM
UNBARRING	UNBIASSES	UNBOSOMERS	UNBURTHENS	UNCHARMED

UNCHARMING	UNCLES	UNCONFINES	UNCRUMPLED	UNDECKS
UNCHARMS	UNCLESHIP	UNCONFINING	UNCRUMPLES	UNDEE
UNCHARNEL	UNCLESHIPS	UNCONFORM	UNCRUMPLING	UNDEEDED
UNCHARNELLED	UNCLEW	UNCONGEAL	UNCTION	UNDEFACED
UNCHARNELLING	UNCLEWED	UNCONGEALED	UNCTIONS	UNDEFIDE
UNCHARNELS	UNCLEWING	UNCONGEALING	UNCTUOUS	UNDEFIED
UNCHARTED	UNCLEWS	UNCONGEALS	UNCULLED	UNDEFILED
UNCHARY	UNCLING	UNCOOKED	UNCURABLE	UNDEFINED
UNCHASTE	UNCLIPPED	UNCOOL	UNCURBED	UNDEIFIED
UNCHECK	UNCLIPT	UNCOPE	UNCURDLED	UNDEIFIES
UNCHECKED	UNCLOAK	UNCOPED	UNCURED	UNDEIFY
UNCHECKING	UNCLOAKED	UNCOPES	UNCURIOUS	UNDEIFYING
UNCHECKS	UNCLOAKING	UNCOPING	UNCURL	UNDELAYED
UNCHEERED	UNCLOAKS	UNCORD	UNCURLED	UNDELIGHT
UNCHEWED	UNCLOG	UNCORDED	UNCURLING	UNDELIGHTS
UNCHILD	UNCLOGGED	UNCORDING	UNCURLS	UNDELUDED
UNCHILDED	UNCLOGGING	UNCORDS	UNCURRENT	UNDER
UNCHILDING	UNCLOGS	UNCORK	UNCURSE	UNDERACT
UNCHILDS	UNCLOSE	UNCORKED	UNCURSED	UNDERACTED
UNCHOSEN	UNCLOSED	UNCORKING	UNCURSES	UNDERACTING
UNCHRISOM	UNCLOSES	UNCORKS	UNCURSING	UNDERACTS
UNCHURCH	UNCLOSING	UNCORRUPT	UNCURTAIN	UNDERARM
UNCHURCHED	UNCLOTHE	UNCOS	UNCURTAINED	UNDERBEAR
UNCHURCHES	UNCLOTHED	UNCOSTLY	UNCURTAINING	UNDERBEARING
UNCHURCHING	UNCLOTHES	UNCOUNTED	UNCURTAINS	UNDERBEARINGS
UNCI	UNCLOTHING	UNCOUPLE	UNCURVED	UNDERBEARS
UNCIAL	UNCLOUD	UNCOUPLED	UNCUS	UNDERBID
UNCIALS	UNCLOUDED	UNCOUPLES	UNCUT	UNDERBIDDING
UNCIFORM	UNCLOUDING	UNCOUPLING	UNDAM	UNDERBIDS
UNCINATE	UNCLOUDS	UNCOURTLY	UNDAMAGED	UNDERBIT
UNCINATED	UNCLOUDY	UNCOUTH	UNDAMMED	UNDERBITE
UNCINI	UNCLOVEN	UNCOUTHER	UNDAMMING	UNDERBITES
UNCINUS	UNCLUTCH	UNCOUTHEST	UNDAMNED	UNDERBITING
UNCIPHER	UNCLUTCHED	UNCOUTHLY	UNDAMPED	UNDERBITTEN
UNCIPHERED	UNCLUTCHES	UNCOVER	UNDAMS	UNDERBORE
UNCIPHERING	UNCLUTCHING	UNCOVERED	UNDASHED	UNDERBORNE
UNCIPHERS	UNCO	UNCOVERING	UNDATE	UNDERBOUGHT
UNCITED	UNCOATED	UNCOVERS	UNDATED	UNDERBRED
UNCIVIL	UNCOCK	UNCOWL	UNDAUNTED	UNDERBUSH
UNCIVILLY	UNCOCKED	UNCOWLED	UNDAWNING	UNDERBUSHED
UNCLAD	UNCOCKING	UNCOWLING	UNDAZZLE	UNDERBUSHES
UNCLAIMED	UNCOCKS	UNCOWLS	UNDAZZLED	UNDERBUSHING
UNCLASP	UNCOIL	UNCOYNED	UNDAZZLES	UNDERBUY
UNCLASPED	UNCOILED	UNCRATE	UNDAZZLING	UNDERBUYING
UNCLASPING	UNCOILING	UNCRATED	UNDE	UNDERBUYS
UNCLASPS	UNCOILS	UNCRATES	UNDEAD	UNDERCARD
UNCLASSED	UNCOINED	UNCRATING	UNDEAF	UNDERCARDS
UNCLASSY	UNCOLT	UNCREATE	UNDEAFED	UNDERCART
UNCLE	UNCOLTED	UNCREATED	UNDEAFING	UNDERCARTS
UNCLEAN	UNCOLTING	UNCREATES	UNDEAFS	UNDERCAST
UNCLEANED	UNCOLTS	UNCREATING	UNDEALT	UNDERCASTS
UNCLEANER	UNCOMBED	UNCROPPED	UNDEAR	UNDERCLAD
UNCLEANEST	UNCOMBINE	UNCROSS	UNDEBASED	UNDERCLAY
UNCLEANLY	UNCOMBINED	UNCROSSED	UNDECAYED	UNDERCLAYS
UNCLEAR	UNCOMBINES	UNCROSSES	UNDECEIVE	UNDERCLUB
UNCLEARED	UNCOMBINING	UNCROSSING	UNDECEIVED	UNDERCLUBBED
UNCLEARER	UNCOMELY	UNCROWDED	UNDECEIVES	UNDERCLUBBING
UNCLEAREST	UNCOMMON	UNCROWN	UNDECEIVING	UNDERCLUBS
UNCLEARLY	UNCOMMONER	UNCROWNED	UNDECENT	UNDERCOAT
UNCLED	UNCOMMONEST	UNCROWNING	UNDECIDED	UNDERCOATS
UNCLENCH	UNCONCERN	UNCROWNS	UNDECIMAL	UNDERCOOK
UNCLENCHED	UNCONCERNS	UNCRUDDED	UNDECK	UNDERCOOKED
UNCLENCHES	UNCONFINE	UNCRUMPLE	UNDECKED	UNDERCOOKING
UNCLENCHING	UNCONFINED	UNCRUMPLED	UNDECKING	UNDERCOOKS

UNDERCOOL	UNDERGOWN	UNDERPEEPING	UNDERTAKINGS	UNDOER
UNDERCOOLED	UNDERGOWNS	UNDERPEEPS	UNDERTANE	UNDOERS
UNDERCOOLING	UNDERGRAD	UNDERPIN	UNDERTIME	UNDOES
UNDERCOOLS	UNDERGRADS	UNDERPINNED	UNDERTIMES	UNDOING
UNDERCUT	UNDERHAND	UNDERPINNING	UNDERTINT	UNDOINGS
UNDERCUTS	UNDERHANDS	UNDERPINNINGS	UNDERTINTS	UNDONE
UNDERCUTTING	UNDERHUNG	UNDERPINS	UNDERTONE	UNDOOMED
UNDERDECK	UNDERKEEP	UNDERPLAY	UNDERTONES	UNDOUBLE
UNDERDECKS	UNDERKEEPING	UNDERPLAYED	UNDERTOOK	UNDOUBLED
UNDERDID	UNDERKEEPS	UNDERPLAYING	UNDERTOW	UNDOUBLES
UNDERDO	UNDERKEPT	UNDERPLAYS	UNDERTOWS	UNDOUBLING
UNDERDOER	UNDERKING	UNDERPLOT	UNDERUSE	UNDOUBTED
UNDERDOERS	UNDERKINGS	UNDERPLOTS	UNDERUSED	UNDRAINED
UNDERDOES	UNDERLAID	UNDERPROP	UNDERUSES	UNDRAPED
UNDERDOG	UNDERLAIN	UNDERPROPPED	UNDERUSING	UNDRAW
UNDERDOGS	UNDERLAP	UNDERPROPPING	UNDERVEST	UNDRAWING
UNDERDOING	UNDERLAPPED	UNDERPROPS	UNDERVESTS	UNDRAWN
UNDERDONE	UNDERLAPPING	UNDERRAN	UNDERWAY	UNDRAWS
UNDERDRAW	UNDERLAPS	UNDERRATE	UNDERWEAR	UNDREADED
UNDERDRAWING	UNDERLAY	UNDERRATED	UNDERWEARS	UNDREAMED
UNDERDRAWINGS	UNDERLAYING	UNDERRATES	UNDERWENT	UNDREAMT
UNDERDRAWN	UNDERLAYS	UNDERRATING	UNDERWING	UNDRESS
UNDERDRAWS	UNDERLET	UNDERRUN	UNDERWINGS	UNDRESSED
UNDERDREW	UNDERLETS	UNDERRUNNING	UNDERWIT	UNDRESSES
UNDERFED	UNDERLETTING	UNDERRUNNINGS	UNDERWITS	UNDRESSING
UNDERFEED	UNDERLETTINGS	UNDERRUNS	UNDERWOOD	UNDRESSINGS
UNDERFEEDING	UNDERLIE	UNDERSAID	UNDERWOODS	UNDREW
UNDERFEEDS	UNDERLIES	UNDERSAY	UNDERWORK	UNDRIED
UNDERFELT	UNDERLINE	UNDERSAYE	UNDERWORKED	UNDRILLED
UNDERFELTS	UNDERLINED	UNDERSAYES	UNDERWORKING	UNDRIVEN
UNDERFIRE	UNDERLINES	UNDERSAYING	UNDERWORKS	UNDROSSY
UNDERFIRED	UNDERLING	UNDERSAYS	UNDERWROUGHT	UNDROWNED
UNDERFIRES	UNDERLINGS	UNDERSEA	UNDESERT	UNDRUNK
UNDERFIRING	UNDERLINING	UNDERSEAL	UNDESERTS	UNDUBBED
UNDERFISH	UNDERLIP	UNDERSEALED	UNDESERVE	UNDUE
UNDERFISHED	UNDERLIPS	UNDERSEALING	UNDESERVED	UNDUG
UNDERFISHES	UNDERLYING	UNDERSEALINGS	UNDESERVES	UNDULANCIES
UNDERFISHING	UNDERMAN	UNDERSEALS	UNDESERVING	UNDULANCY
UNDERFLOW	UNDERMANNED	UNDERSELF	UNDESIRED	UNDULANT
UNDERFLOWS	UNDERMANNING	UNDERSELL	UNDEVOUT	UNDULATE
UNDERFONG	UNDERMANS	UNDERSELLING	UNDID	UNDULATED
UNDERFONGED	UNDERMEN	UNDERSELLS	UNDIES	UNDULATES
UNDERFONGING	UNDERMINE	UNDERSELVES	UNDIGHT	UNDULATING
UNDERFONGS	UNDERMINED	UNDERSET	UNDIGHTING	UNDULLED
UNDERFOOT	UNDERMINES	UNDERSETS	UNDIGHTS	UNDULOSE
UNDERFOOTED	UNDERMINING	UNDERSETTING	UNDIGNIFIED	UNDULOUS
UNDERFOOTING	UNDERMININGS	UNDERSHOT	UNDIGNIFIES	UNDULY
UNDERFOOTS	UNDERMOST	UNDERSIDE	UNDIGNIFY	UNDUTEOUS
UNDERFUND	UNDERN	UNDERSIDES	UNDIGNIFYING	UNDUTIFUL
UNDERFUNDED	UNDERNOTE	UNDERSIGN	UNDILUTED	UNDYED
UNDERFUNDING	UNDERNOTED	UNDERSIGNED	UNDIMMED	UNDYING
UNDERFUNDINGS	UNDERNOTES	UNDERSIGNING	UNDINE	UNDYINGLY
UNDERFUNDS	UNDERNOTING	UNDERSIGNS	UNDINES	UNEARED
UNDERFUR	UNDERNS	UNDERSKIES	UNDINISM	UNEARNED
UNDERFURS	UNDERPAID	UNDERSKY	UNDINISMS	UNEARTH
UNDERGIRD	UNDERPART	UNDERSOIL	UNDINTED	UNEARTHED
UNDERGIRDED	UNDERPARTS	UNDERSOILS	UNDIPPED	UNEARTHING
UNDERGIRDING	UNDERPASS	UNDERSOLD	UNDIVIDED	UNEARTHLIER
UNDERGIRDS	UNDERPASSES	UNDERSONG	UNDIVINE	UNEARTHLIEST
UNDERGIRT	UNDERPAY	UNDERSONGS	UNDO	UNEARTHLY
UNDERGO	UNDERPAYING	UNDERTAKE	UNDOCK	UNEARTHS
UNDERGOES	UNDERPAYS	UNDERTAKEN	UNDOCKED	UNEASE
UNDERGOING	UNDERPEEP	UNDERTAKES	UNDOCKING	UNEASES
UNDERGONE	UNDERPEEPED	UNDERTAKING	UNDOCKS	UNEASIER

UNEASIEST	UNFAMED	UNFOLDER	UNGAINFUL	UNGOWNED
UNEASILY	UNFANNED	UNFOLDERS	UNGAINLIER	UNGOWNING
UNEASY	UNFASTEN	UNFOLDING	UNGAINLIEST	UNGOWNS
UNEATABLE	UNFASTENED	UNFOLDINGS	UNGAINLY	UNGRACED
UNEATEN	UNFASTENING	UNFOLDS	UNGALLANT	UNGRADED
UNEATH	UNFASTENS	UNFOOL	UNGALLED	UNGRASSED
UNEATHES	UNFAULTY	UNFOOLED	UNGARBLED	UNGRAVELY
UNEDGE	UNFAZED	UNFOOLING	UNGAUGED	UNGRAZED
UNEDGED	UNFEARED	UNFOOLS	UNGEAR	UNGROOMED
UNEDGES	UNFEARFUL	UNFOOTED	UNGEARED	UNGROUND
UNEDGING	UNFEARING	UNFORBID	UNGEARING	UNGROWN
UNEDITED	UNFED	UNFORCED	UNGEARS	UNGRUDGED
UNEFFACED	UNFEEDED	UNFORGED	UNGENIAL	UNGUAL
UNELATED	UNFEELING	UNFORGOT	UNGENTEEL	UNGUARD
UNELECTED	UNFEIGNED	UNFORM	UNGENTLE	UNGUARDED
UNEMPTIED	UNFELLED	UNFORMAL	UNGENTLY	UNGUARDING
UNENDING	UNFELT	UNFORMED	UNGENUINE	UNGUARDS
UNENDOWED	UNFENCED	UNFORMING	UNGERMANE	UNGUENT
UNENGAGED	UNFETTER	UNFORMS	UNGET	UNGUENTS
UNENTERED	UNFETTERED	UNFORTUNE	UNGETS	UNGUES
UNENVIED	UNFETTERING	UNFORTUNES	UNGETTING	UNGUESSED
UNENVIOUS	UNFETTERS	UNFOUGHT	UNGHOSTLY	UNGUIDED
UNENVYING	UNFEUDAL	UNFOUND	UNGIFTED	UNGUIFORM
UNEQUABLE	UNFEUED	UNFOUNDED	UNGILD	UNGUILTY
UNEQUAL	UNFIGURED	UNFRAMED	UNGILDED	UNGUIS
UNEQUALLY	UNFILDE	UNFRANKED	UNGILDING	UNGULA
UNEQUALS	UNFILED	UNFRAUGHT	UNGILDS	UNGULAE
UNERRING	UNFILIAL	UNFRAUGHTED	UNGILT	UNGULATE
UNESPIED	UNFILLED	UNFRAUGHTING	UNGIRD	UNGULATES
UNESSAYED	UNFILMED	UNFRAUGHTS	UNGIRDED	UNGULED
UNESSENCE	UNFINE	UNFREE	UNGIRDING	UNGUM
UNESSENCED	UNFIRED	UNFREED	UNGIRDS	UNGUMMED
UNESSENCES	UNFIRM	UNFREEMAN	UNGIRT	UNGUMMING
UNESSENCING	UNFISHED	UNFREEMEN	UNGIRTH	UNGUMS
UNETH	UNFIT	UNFREEZE	UNGIRTHED	UNGYVE
UNETHICAL	UNFITLY	UNFREEZES	UNGIRTHING	UNGYVED
UNEVEN	UNFITNESS	UNFREEZING	UNGIRTHS	UNGYVES
UNEVENER	UNFITNESSES	UNFRETTED	UNGIVING	UNGYVING
UNEVENEST	UNFITS	UNFRIEND	UNGLAD	UNHABLE
UNEVENLY	UNFITTED	UNFRIENDS	UNGLAZED	UNHACKED
UNEXALTED	UNFITTER	UNFROCK	UNGLOSSED	UNHAILED
UNEXCITED	UNFITTEST	UNFROCKED	UNGLOVE	UNHAIR
UNEXPIRED	UNFITTING	UNFROCKING	UNGLOVED	UNHAIRED
UNEXPOSED	UNFIX	UNFROCKS	UNGLOVES	UNHAIRING
UNEXTINCT	UNFIXED	UNFROZE	UNGLOVING	UNHAIRS
UNEXTREME	UNFIXES	UNFROZEN	UNGLUE	UNHALLOW
UNEYED	UNFIXING	UNFUELLED	UNGLUED	UNHALLOWED
UNFABLED	UNFIXITIES	UNFUMED	UNGLUES	UNHALLOWING
UNFACT	UNFIXITY	UNFUNDED	UNGLUING	UNHALLOWS
UNFACTS	UNFLAWED	UNFUNNY	UNGOD	UNHALSED
UNFADABLE	UNFLEDGED	UNFURL	UNGODDED	UNHAND
UNFADED	UNFLESH	UNFURLED	UNGODDING	UNHANDED
UNFADING	UNFLESHED	UNFURLING	UNGODLIER	UNHANDILY
UNFAILING	UNFLESHES	UNFURLS	UNGODLIEST	UNHANDING
UNFAIR	UNFLESHING	UNFURNISH	UNGODLIKE	UNHANDLED
UNFAIRED	UNFLESHLY	UNFURNISHED	UNGODLILY	UNHANDS
UNFAIRER	UNFLOORED	UNFURNISHES	UNGODLY	UNHANDY
UNFAIREST	UNFLUSH	UNFURNISHING	UNGODS	UNHANG
UNFAIRING	UNFLUSHED	UNFURRED	UNGORD	UNHANGED
UNFAIRLY	UNFLUSHES	UNGAG	UNGORED	UNHANGING
UNFAIRS	UNFLUSHING	UNGAGGED	UNGORGED	UNHANGS
UNFAITH	UNFOCUSED	UNGAGGING	UNGOT	UNHAPPIED
UNFAITHS	UNFOLD	UNGAGS	UNGOTTEN	UNHAPPIER
UNFALLEN	UNFOLDED	UNGAIN	UNGOWN	UNHAPPIES

UNHAPPIEST	UNHELMING	UNHUSKED	UNIPODS	UNJOYFUL
UNHAPPILY	UNHELMS	UNHUSKING	UNIPOLAR	UNJOYOUS
UNHAPPY	UNHELPED	UNHUSKS	UNIQUE	UNJUST
UNHAPPYING	UNHELPFUL	UNI	UNIQUELY	UNJUSTER
UNHARBOUR	UNHEPPEN	UNIAXIAL	UNIQUER	UNJUSTEST
UNHARBOURED	UNHEROIC	UNICITIES	UNIQUES	UNJUSTLY
UNHARBOURING	UNHERST	UNICITY	UNIQUEST	UNKED
UNHARBOURS	UNHEWN	UNICOLOR	UNIRAMOUS	UNKEMPT
UNHARDY	UNHIDDEN	UNICOLOUR	UNIRONED	UNKENNED
UNHARMED	UNHINGE	UNICORN	UNIS	UNKENNEL
UNHARMFUL	UNHINGED	UNICORNS	UNISEX	UNKENNELLED
UNHARMING	UNHINGES	UNICYCLE	UNISEXUAL	UNKENNELLING
UNHARNESS	UNHINGING	UNICYCLES	UNISON	UNKENNELS
UNHARNESSED	UNHIP	UNIDEAL	UNISONAL	UNKENT
UNHARNESSES	UNHIRED	UNIFIABLE	UNISONANT	UNKEPT
UNHARNESSING	UNHITCH	UNIFIC	UNISONOUS	UNKET
UNHASP	UNHITCHED	UNIFIED	UNISONS	UNKID
UNHASPED	UNHITCHES	UNIFIER	UNIT	UNKIND
UNHASPING	UNHITCHING	UNIFIERS	UNITAL	UNKINDER
UNHASPS	UNHIVE	UNIFIES	UNITARD	UNKINDEST
UNHASTING	UNHIVED	UNIFILAR	UNITARDS	UNKINDLED
UNHASTY	UNHIVES	UNIFORM	UNITARIAN	UNKINDLIER
UNHAT	UNHIVING	UNIFORMED	UNITARIANS	UNKINDLIEST
UNHATCHED	UNHOARD	UNIFORMING	UNITARY	UNKINDLY
UNHATS	UNHOARDED	UNIFORMLY	UNITE	UNKING
UNHATTED	UNHOARDING	UNIFORMS	UNITED	UNKINGED
UNHATTING	UNHOARDS	UNIFY	UNITEDLY	UNKINGING
UNHATTINGS	UNHOLIER	UNIFYING	UNITER	UNKINGLIER
UNHAUNTED	UNHOLIEST	UNIFYINGS	UNITERS	UNKINGLIEST
UNHEAD	UNHOLILY	UNILLUMED	UNITES	UNKINGLY
UNHEADED	UNHOLPEN	UNILOBAR	UNITIES	UNKINGS
UNHEADING	UNHOLY	UNILOBED	UNITING	UNKISS
UNHEADS	UNHOMELY	UNIMBUED	UNITINGS	UNKISSED
UNHEAL	UNHONEST	UNIMPEDED	UNITION	UNKISSES
UNHEALED	UNHOOD	UNIMPOSED	UNITIONS	UNKISSING
UNHEALING	UNHOODED	UNINCITED	UNITISE	UNKNELLED
UNHEALS	UNHOODING	UNINDEXED	UNITISED	UNKNIGHT
UNHEALTH	UNHOODS	UNINJURED	UNITISES	UNKNIGHTED
UNHEALTHIER	UNHOOK	UNINSTALL	UNITISING	UNKNIGHTING
UNHEALTHIEST	UNHOOKED	UNINSTALLED	UNITIVE	UNKNIGHTS
UNHEALTHS	UNHOOKING	UNINSTALLING	UNITIVELY	UNKNIT
UNHEALTHY	UNHOOKS	UNINSTALLS	UNITIZE	UNKNITS
UNHEARD	UNHOOP	UNINSURED	UNITIZED	UNKNITTED
UNHEARSE	UNHOOPED	UNINURED	UNITIZES	UNKNITTING
UNHEARSED	UNHOOPING	UNINVITED	UNITIZING	UNKNOT
UNHEARSES	UNHOOPS	UNION	UNITS	UNKNOTS
UNHEARSING	UNHOPED	UNIONISE	UNITY	UNKNOTTED
UNHEART	UNHOPEFUL	UNIONISED	UNIVALENT	UNKNOTTING
UNHEARTED	UNHORSE	UNIONISES	UNIVALENTS	UNKNOWING
UNHEARTING	UNHORSED	UNIONISING	UNIVALVE	UNKNOWN
UNHEARTS	UNHORSES	UNIONISM	UNIVALVES	UNKNOWNS
UNHEATED	UNHORSING	UNIONISMS	UNIVERSAL	UNLACE
UNHEDGED	UNHOUSE	UNIONIST	UNIVERSALS	UNLACED
UNHEEDED	UNHOUSED	UNIONISTS	UNIVERSE	UNLACES
UNHEEDFUL	UNHOUSES	UNIONIZE	UNIVERSES	UNLACING
UNHEEDILY	UNHOUSING	UNIONIZED	UNIVOCAL	UNLADE
UNHEEDING	UNHUMAN	UNIONIZES	UNIVOCALS	UNLADED
UNHEEDY	UNHUMBLED	UNIONIZING	UNJADED	UNLADEN
UNHELE	UNHUNG	UNIONS	UNJEALOUS	UNLADES
UNHELED	UNHUNTED	UNIPAROUS	UNJOINT	UNLADING
UNHELES	UNHURRIED	UNIPED	UNJOINTED	UNLADINGS
UNHELING	UNHURT	UNIPEDS	UNJOINTING	UNLAID
UNHELM	UNHURTFUL	UNIPLANAR	UNJOINTS	UNLASH
UNHELMED	UNHUSK	UNIPOD		UNLASHED

The Chambers Dictionary is the authority for many longer words; see *OSW* Introduction, page xii

UNLASHES	UNLINKS	UNMANAGED	UNMOULDING	UNOWNED
UNLASHING	UNLISTED	UNMANLIER	UNMOULDS	UNPACED
UNLAST	UNLIT	UNMANLIEST	UNMOUNT	UNPACK
UNLASTE	UNLIVABLE	UNMANLIKE	UNMOUNTED	UNPACKED
UNLATCH	UNLIVE	UNMANLY	UNMOUNTING	UNPACKER
UNLATCHED	UNLIVED	UNMANNED	UNMOUNTS	UNPACKERS
UNLATCHES	UNLIVELY	UNMANNING	UNMOURNED	UNPACKING
UNLATCHING	UNLIVES	UNMANS	UNMOVABLE	UNPACKINGS
UNLAW	UNLIVING	UNMANTLE	UNMOVABLY	UNPACKS
UNLAWED	UNLOAD	UNMANTLED	UNMOVED	UNPAGED
UNLAWFUL	UNLOADED	UNMANTLES	UNMOVEDLY	UNPAID
UNLAWING	UNLOADER	UNMANTLING	UNMOVING	UNPAINED
UNLAWS	UNLOADERS	UNMANURED	UNMOWN	UNPAINFUL
UNLAY	UNLOADING	UNMARD	UNMUFFLE	UNPAINT
UNLAYING	UNLOADINGS	UNMARKED	UNMUFFLED	UNPAINTED
UNLAYS	UNLOADS	UNMARRED	UNMUFFLES	UNPAINTING
UNLEAD	UNLOCATED	UNMARRIED	UNMUFFLING	UNPAINTS
UNLEADED	UNLOCK	UNMARRIES	UNMUSICAL	UNPAIRED
UNLEADING	UNLOCKED	UNMARRY	UNMUZZLE	UNPALSIED
UNLEADS	UNLOCKING	UNMARRYING	UNMUZZLED	UNPANEL
UNLEAL	UNLOCKS	UNMASK	UNMUZZLES	UNPANELLED
UNLEARN	UNLOGICAL	UNMASKED	UNMUZZLING	UNPANELLING
UNLEARNED	UNLOOKED	UNMASKER	UNMUZZLINGS	UNPANELS
UNLEARNING	UNLOOSE	UNMASKERS	UNNAIL	UNPANGED
UNLEARNS	UNLOOSED	UNMASKING	UNNAILED	UNPANNEL
UNLEARNT	UNLOOSEN	UNMASKINGS	UNNAILING	UNPANNELLED
UNLEASED	UNLOOSENED	UNMASKS	UNNAILS	UNPANNELLING
UNLEASH	UNLOOSENING	UNMATCHED	UNNAMABLE	UNPANNELS
UNLEASHED	UNLOOSENS	UNMATED	UNNAMED	UNPAPER
UNLEASHES	UNLOOSES	UNMATURED	UNNANELD	UNPAPERED
UNLEASHING	UNLOOSING	UNMEANING	UNNATIVE	UNPAPERING
UNLED	UNLOPPED	UNMEANT	UNNATURAL	UNPAPERS
UNLESS	UNLORD	UNMEEK	UNNEATH	UNPARED
UNLET	UNLORDED	UNMEET	UNNEEDED	UNPARTIAL
UNLICH	UNLORDING	UNMEETLY	UNNEEDFUL	UNPATHED
UNLICKED	UNLORDLY	UNMELTED	UNNERVE	UNPAVED
UNLID	UNLORDS	UNMERITED	UNNERVED	UNPAY
UNLIDDED	UNLOSABLE	UNMET	UNNERVES	UNPAYABLE
UNLIDDING	UNLOST	UNMETED	UNNERVING	UNPAYING
UNLIDS	UNLOVABLE	UNMEW	UNNEST	UNPAYS
UNLIGHTED	UNLOVE	UNMEWED	UNNESTED	UNPEELED
UNLIKABLE	UNLOVED	UNMEWING	UNNESTING	UNPEERED
UNLIKE	UNLOVELIER	UNMEWS	UNNESTS	UNPEG
UNLIKELIER	UNLOVELIEST	UNMILKED	UNNETHES	UNPEGGED
UNLIKELIEST	UNLOVELY	UNMILLED	UNNETTED	UNPEGGING
UNLIKELY	UNLOVES	UNMINDED	UNNOBLE	UNPEGS
UNLIKES	UNLOVING	UNMINDFUL	UNNOBLED	UNPEN
UNLIMBER	UNLUCKIER	UNMINGLED	UNNOBLES	UNPENNED
UNLIMBERED	UNLUCKIEST	UNMIRY	UNNOBLING	UNPENNIED
UNLIMBERING	UNLUCKILY	UNMISSED	UNNOTED	UNPENNING
UNLIMBERS	UNLUCKY	UNMIXED	UNNOTICED	UNPENS
UNLIME	UNMADE	UNMIXEDLY	UNOBEYED	UNPENT
UNLIMED	UNMAILED	UNMOANED	UNOBVIOUS	UNPEOPLE
UNLIMES	UNMAIMED	UNMODISH	UNOFFERED	UNPEOPLED
UNLIMING	UNMAKABLE	UNMONEYED	UNOFTEN	UNPEOPLES
UNLIMITED	UNMAKE	UNMONIED	UNOILED	UNPEOPLING
UNLINE	UNMAKES	UNMOOR	UNOPENED	UNPERCH
UNLINEAL	UNMAKING	UNMOORED	UNOPPOSED	UNPERCHED
UNLINED	UNMAKINGS	UNMOORING	UNORDER	UNPERCHES
UNLINES	UNMAN	UNMOORS	UNORDERED	UNPERCHING
UNLINING	UNMANACLE	UNMORAL	UNORDERING	UNPERFECT
UNLINK	UNMANACLED	UNMOTIVED	UNORDERLY	UNPERPLEX
UNLINKED	UNMANACLES	UNMOULD	UNORDERS	UNPERPLEXED
UNLINKING	UNMANACLING	UNMOULDED	UNOWED	UNPERPLEXES

UNPERPLEXING	UNPOLICED	UNPROVOKES	UNREALLY	UNRINGED
UNPERSON	UNPOLISH	UNPROVOKING	UNREAPED	UNRIP
UNPERSONED	UNPOLISHED	UNPRUNED	UNREASON	UNRIPE
UNPERSONING	UNPOLISHES	UNPULLED	UNREASONS	UNRIPENED
UNPERSONS	UNPOLISHING	UNPURGED	UNREAVE	UNRIPER
UNPERVERT	UNPOLITE	UNPURSE	UNREAVED	UNRIPEST
UNPERVERTED	UNPOLITIC	UNPURSED	UNREAVES	UNRIPPED
UNPERVERTING	UNPOLLED	UNPURSES	UNREAVING	UNRIPPING
UNPERVERTS	UNPOPE	UNPURSING	UNREBATED	UNRIPPINGS
UNPICK	UNPOPED	UNPURSUED	UNREBUKED	UNRIPS
UNPICKED	UNPOPES	UNQUALIFIED	UNRECKED	UNRISEN
UNPICKING	UNPOPING	UNQUALIFIES	UNRED	UNRIVEN
UNPICKS	UNPOPULAR	UNQUALIFY	UNREDREST	UNRIVET
UNPIERCED	UNPOSED	UNQUALIFYING	UNREDUCED	UNRIVETED
UNPILOTED	UNPOSTED	UNQUEEN	UNREDY	UNRIVETING
UNPIN	UNPOTABLE	UNQUEENED	UNREEL	UNRIVETS
UNPINKED	UNPRAISE	UNQUEENING	UNREELED	UNROBE
UNPINKT	UNPRAISED	UNQUEENLIER	UNREELING	UNROBED
UNPINNED	UNPRAISES	UNQUEENLIEST	UNREELS	UNROBES
UNPINNING	UNPRAISING	UNQUEENLY	UNREEVE	UNROBING
UNPINS	UNPRAY	UNQUEENS	UNREEVED	UNROLL
UNPITIED	UNPRAYED	UNQUELLED	UNREEVES	UNROLLED
UNPITIFUL	UNPRAYING	UNQUIET	UNREEVING	UNROLLING
UNPITYING	UNPRAYS	UNQUIETED	UNREFINED	UNROLLS
UNPLACE	UNPREACH	UNQUIETING	UNREFUTED	UNROOF
UNPLACED	UNPREACHED	UNQUIETLY	UNREIN	UNROOFED
UNPLACES	UNPREACHES	UNQUIETS	UNREINED	UNROOFING
UNPLACING	UNPREACHING	UNQUOTE	UNREINING	UNROOFS
UNPLAGUED	UNPRECISE	UNQUOTED	UNREINS	UNROOST
UNPLAINED	UNPREDICT	UNQUOTES	UNRELATED	UNROOSTED
UNPLAIT	UNPREDICTED	UNQUOTING	UNRELAXED	UNROOSTING
UNPLAITED	UNPREDICTING	UNRACED	UNREMOVED	UNROOSTS
UNPLAITING	UNPREDICTS	UNRACKED	UNRENEWED	UNROOT
UNPLAITS	UNPREPARE	UNRAISED	UNRENT	UNROOTED
UNPLANKED	UNPREPARED	UNRAKE	UNREPAID	UNROOTING
UNPLANNED	UNPREPARES	UNRAKED	UNREPAIR	UNROOTS
UNPLANTED	UNPREPARING	UNRAKES	UNREPAIRS	UNROPE
UNPLAYED	UNPRESSED	UNRAKING	UNRESERVE	UNROPED
UNPLEASED	UNPRETTY	UNRATED	UNRESERVES	UNROPES
UNPLEATED	UNPRICED	UNRAVEL	UNREST	UNROPING
UNPLEDGED	UNPRIEST	UNRAVELLED	UNRESTFUL	UNROSINED
UNPLIABLE	UNPRIESTED	UNRAVELLING	UNRESTING	UNROTTED
UNPLIABLY	UNPRIESTING	UNRAVELLINGS	UNRESTS	UNROTTEN
UNPLIANT	UNPRIESTS	UNRAVELS	UNREVISED	UNROUGED
UNPLUCKED	UNPRIMED	UNRAZORED	UNREVOKED	UNROUGH
UNPLUG	UNPRINTED	UNREACHED	UNRHYMED	UNROUND
UNPLUGGED	UNPRISON	UNREAD	UNRIBBED	UNROUNDED
UNPLUGGING	UNPRISONED	UNREADIER	UNRID	UNROUNDING
UNPLUGS	UNPRISONING	UNREADIEST	UNRIDABLE	UNROUNDS
UNPLUMB	UNPRISONS	UNREADILY	UNRIDDEN	UNROUSED
UNPLUMBED	UNPRIZED	UNREADY	UNRIDDLE	UNROVE
UNPLUMBING	UNPROP	UNREAL	UNRIDDLED	UNROYAL
UNPLUMBS	UNPROPER	UNREALISE	UNRIDDLER	UNROYALLY
UNPLUME	UNPROPPED	UNREALISED	UNRIDDLERS	UNRUBBED
UNPLUMED	UNPROPPING	UNREALISES	UNRIDDLES	UNRUDE
UNPLUMES	UNPROPS	UNREALISING	UNRIDDLING	UNRUFFE
UNPLUMING	UNPROVED	UNREALISM	UNRIFLED	UNRUFFLE
UNPOETIC	UNPROVEN	UNREALISMS	UNRIG	UNRUFFLED
UNPOINTED	UNPROVIDE	UNREALITIES	UNRIGGED	UNRUFFLES
UNPOISED	UNPROVIDED	UNREALITY	UNRIGGING	UNRUFFLING
UNPOISON	UNPROVIDES	UNREALIZE	UNRIGHT	UNRULE
UNPOISONED	UNPROVIDING	UNREALIZED	UNRIGHTS	UNRULED
UNPOISONING	UNPROVOKE	UNREALIZES	UNRIGS	UNRULES
UNPOISONS	UNPROVOKED	UNREALIZING	UNRIMED	UNRULIER

UNRULIEST	UNSEASONING	UNSHADOWED	UNSHUTTERED	UNSODDEN
UNRULY	UNSEASONS	UNSHADOWING	UNSHUTTERING	UNSOFT
UNRUMPLED	UNSEAT	UNSHADOWS	UNSHUTTERS	UNSOILED
UNS	UNSEATED	UNSHAKED	UNSHUTTING	UNSOLACED
UNSADDLE	UNSEATING	UNSHAKEN	UNSICKER	UNSOLD
UNSADDLED	UNSEATS	UNSHALE	UNSICKLED	UNSOLDER
UNSADDLES	UNSECRET	UNSHALED	UNSIFTED	UNSOLDERED
UNSADDLING	UNSECULAR	UNSHALES	UNSIGHING	UNSOLDERING
UNSAFE	UNSECURED	UNSHALING	UNSIGHT	UNSOLDERS
UNSAFELY	UNSEDUCED	UNSHAMED	UNSIGHTED	UNSOLEMN
UNSAFER	UNSEEABLE	UNSHAPE	UNSIGHTLIER	UNSOLID
UNSAFEST	UNSEEDED	UNSHAPED	UNSIGHTLIEST	UNSOLIDLY
UNSAFETIES	UNSEEING	UNSHAPELIER	UNSIGHTLY	UNSOLVED
UNSAFETY	UNSEEL	UNSHAPELIEST	UNSIGNED	UNSONSY
UNSAID	UNSEELED	UNSHAPELY	UNSINEW	UNSOOTE
UNSAILED	UNSEELING	UNSHAPEN	UNSINEWED	UNSORTED
UNSAINED	UNSEELS	UNSHAPES	UNSINEWING	UNSOUGHT
UNSAINT	UNSEEMING	UNSHAPING	UNSINEWS	UNSOUL
UNSAINTED	UNSEEMINGS	UNSHARED	UNSISTING	UNSOULED
UNSAINTING	UNSEEMLIER	UNSHAVED	UNSIZABLE	UNSOULING
UNSAINTLIER	UNSEEMLIEST	UNSHAVEN	UNSIZED	UNSOULS
UNSAINTLIEST	UNSEEMLY	UNSHEATHE	UNSKILFUL	UNSOUND
UNSAINTLY	UNSEEN	UNSHEATHED	UNSKILLED	UNSOUNDED
UNSAINTS	UNSEENS	UNSHEATHES	UNSKIMMED	UNSOUNDER
UNSALABLE	UNSEIZED	UNSHEATHING	UNSKINNED	UNSOUNDEST
UNSALTED	UNSELDOM	UNSHED	UNSLAIN	UNSOUNDLY
UNSALUTED	UNSELF	UNSHELL	UNSLAKED	UNSOURCED
UNSAPPED	UNSELFED	UNSHELLED	UNSLICED	UNSOURED
UNSASHED	UNSELFING	UNSHELLING	UNSLING	UNSOWN
UNSATABLE	UNSELFISH	UNSHELLS	UNSLINGING	UNSPAR
UNSATED	UNSELFS	UNSHENT	UNSLINGS	UNSPARED
UNSATIATE	UNSELVES	UNSHEWN	UNSLUICE	UNSPARING
UNSATING	UNSENSE	UNSHIP	UNSLUICED	UNSPARRED
UNSAVED	UNSENSED	UNSHIPPED	UNSLUICES	UNSPARRING
UNSAVOURY	UNSENSES	UNSHIPPING	UNSLUICING	UNSPARS
UNSAY	UNSENSING	UNSHIPS	UNSLUNG	UNSPEAK
UNSAYABLE	UNSENT	UNSHOCKED	UNSMART	UNSPEAKING
UNSAYING	UNSERIOUS	UNSHOD	UNSMILING	UNSPEAKS
UNSAYS	UNSET	UNSHOE	UNSMITTEN	UNSPED
UNSCALE	UNSETS	UNSHOED	UNSMOOTH	UNSPELL
UNSCALED	UNSETTING	UNSHOEING	UNSMOOTHED	UNSPELLED
UNSCALES	UNSETTLE	UNSHOES	UNSMOOTHING	UNSPELLING
UNSCALING	UNSETTLED	UNSHOOT	UNSMOOTHS	UNSPELLS
UNSCANNED	UNSETTLES	UNSHOOTED	UNSMOTE	UNSPENT
UNSCARRED	UNSETTLING	UNSHOOTING	UNSNAP	UNSPHERE
UNSCARY	UNSETTLINGS	UNSHOOTS	UNSNAPPED	UNSPHERED
UNSCATHED	UNSEVERED	UNSHORN	UNSNAPPING	UNSPHERES
UNSCENTED	UNSEW	UNSHOT	UNSNAPS	UNSPHERING
UNSCOURED	UNSEWED	UNSHOUT	UNSNARL	UNSPIDE
UNSCREW	UNSEWING	UNSHOUTED	UNSNARLED	UNSPIED
UNSCREWED	UNSEWN	UNSHOUTING	UNSNARLING	UNSPILLED
UNSCREWING	UNSEWS	UNSHOUTS	UNSNARLS	UNSPILT
UNSCREWS	UNSEX	UNSHOWN	UNSNECK	UNSPOILED
UNSCYTHED	UNSEXED	UNSHRIVED	UNSNECKED	UNSPOILT
UNSEAL	UNSEXES	UNSHRIVEN	UNSNECKING	UNSPOKE
UNSEALED	UNSEXING	UNSHROUD	UNSNECKS	UNSPOKEN
UNSEALING	UNSEXIST	UNSHROUDED	UNSNUFFED	UNSPOTTED
UNSEALS	UNSEXUAL	UNSHROUDING	UNSOAPED	UNSPRUNG
UNSEAM	UNSHACKLE	UNSHRUBD	UNSOCIAL	UNSPUN
UNSEAMED	UNSHACKLED	UNSHRUBD	UNSOCKET	UNSQUARED
UNSEAMING	UNSHACKLES	UNSHUNNED	UNSOCKETED	UNSTABLE
UNSEAMS	UNSHACKLING	UNSHUT	UNSOCKETING	UNSTABLER
UNSEASON	UNSHADED	UNSHUTS	UNSOCKETS	UNSTABLEST
UNSEASONED	UNSHADOW	UNSHUTTER	UNSOD	UNSTACK

UNSTACKED	UNSTRINGING	UNTAMABLY	UNTHRIFT	UNTRIMS
UNSTACKING	UNSTRINGS	UNTAME	UNTHRIFTS	UNTROD
UNSTACKS	UNSTRIP	UNTAMED	UNTHRIFTY	UNTRODDEN
UNSTAID	UNSTRIPED	UNTAMES	UNTHRONE	UNTRUE
UNSTAINED	UNSTRIPPED	UNTAMING	UNTHRONED	UNTRUER
UNSTAMPED	UNSTRIPPING	UNTANGLE	UNTHRONES	UNTRUEST
UNSTARCH	UNSTRIPS	UNTANGLED	UNTHRONING	UNTRUISM
UNSTARCHED	UNSTRUCK	UNTANGLES	UNTIDIED	UNTRUISMS
UNSTARCHES	UNSTRUNG	UNTANGLING	UNTIDIER	UNTRULY
UNSTARCHING	UNSTUCK	UNTANNED	UNTIDIES	UNTRUSS
UNSTATE	UNSTUDIED	UNTAPPED	UNTIDIEST	UNTRUSSED
UNSTATED	UNSTUFFED	UNTARRED	UNTIDILY	UNTRUSSER
UNSTATES	UNSTUFFY	UNTASTED	UNTIDY	UNTRUSSERS
UNSTATING	UNSTUFT	UNTAUGHT	UNTIDYING	UNTRUSSES
UNSTAYED	UNSUBDUED	UNTAX	UNTIE	UNTRUSSING
UNSTAYING	UNSUBJECT	UNTAXED	UNTIED	UNTRUSSINGS
UNSTEADIED	UNSUBTLE	UNTAXES	UNTIES	UNTRUST
UNSTEADIER	UNSUCCESS	UNTAXING	UNTIL	UNTRUSTS
UNSTEADIES	UNSUCCESSES	UNTEACH	UNTILE	UNTRUSTY
UNSTEADIEST	UNSUCKED	UNTEACHES	UNTILED	UNTRUTH
UNSTEADY	UNSUIT	UNTEACHING	UNTILES	UNTRUTHS
UNSTEADYING	UNSUITED	UNTEAM	UNTILING	UNTUCK
UNSTEEL	UNSUITING	UNTEAMED	UNTILLED	UNTUCKED
UNSTEELED	UNSUITS	UNTEAMING	UNTIMELIER	UNTUCKING
UNSTEELING	UNSULLIED	UNTEAMS	UNTIMELIEST	UNTUCKS
UNSTEELS	UNSUMMED	UNTEMPER	UNTIMELY	UNTUMBLED
UNSTEP	UNSUNG	UNTEMPERED	UNTIMEOUS	UNTUNABLE
UNSTEPPED	UNSUNNED	UNTEMPERING	UNTIN	UNTUNABLY
UNSTEPPING	UNSUNNY	UNTEMPERS	UNTINGED	UNTUNE
UNSTEPS	UNSUPPLE	UNTEMPTED	UNTINNED	UNTUNED
UNSTERILE	UNSURE	UNTENABLE	UNTINNING	UNTUNEFUL
UNSTICK	UNSURED	UNTENANT	UNTINS	UNTUNES
UNSTICKING	UNSURER	UNTENANTED	UNTIRABLE	UNTUNING
UNSTICKS	UNSUREST	UNTENANTING	UNTIRED	UNTURBID
UNSTIFLED	UNSUSPECT	UNTENANTS	UNTIRING	UNTURF
UNSTILLED	UNSWADDLE	UNTENDED	UNTITLED	UNTURFED
UNSTINTED	UNSWADDLED	UNTENDER	UNTO	UNTURFING
UNSTIRRED	UNSWADDLES	UNTENT	UNTOILING	UNTURFS
UNSTITCH	UNSWADDLING	UNTENTED	UNTOLD	UNTURN
UNSTITCHED	UNSWATHE	UNTENTING	UNTOMB	UNTURNED
UNSTITCHES	UNSWATHED	UNTENTS	UNTOMBED	UNTURNING
UNSTITCHING	UNSWATHES	UNTENTY	UNTOMBING	UNTURNS
UNSTOCK	UNSWATHING	UNTESTED	UNTOMBS	UNTUTORED
UNSTOCKED	UNSWAYED	UNTETHER	UNTONED	UNTWINE
UNSTOCKING	UNSWEAR	UNTETHERED	UNTORN	UNTWINED
UNSTOCKS	UNSWEARING	UNTETHERING	UNTOUCHED	UNTWINES
UNSTOP	UNSWEARINGS	UNTETHERS	UNTOWARD	UNTWINING
UNSTOPPED	UNSWEARS	UNTHANKED	UNTRACE	UNTWIST
UNSTOPPER	UNSWEET	UNTHATCH	UNTRACED	UNTWISTED
UNSTOPPERED	UNSWEPT	UNTHATCHED	UNTRACES	UNTWISTING
UNSTOPPERING	UNSWORE	UNTHATCHES	UNTRACING	UNTWISTINGS
UNSTOPPERS	UNSWORN	UNTHATCHING	UNTRACKED	UNTWISTS
UNSTOPPING	UNTACK	UNTHAW	UNTRADED	UNTYING
UNSTOPS	UNTACKED	UNTHAWED	UNTRAINED	UNTYINGS
UNSTOW	UNTACKING	UNTHAWING	UNTREAD	UNTYPABLE
UNSTOWED	UNTACKLE	UNTHAWS	UNTREADING	UNTYPICAL
UNSTOWING	UNTACKLED	UNTHINK	UNTREADS	UNURGED
UNSTOWS	UNTACKLES	UNTHINKING	UNTREATED	UNUSABLE
UNSTRAP	UNTACKLING	UNTHINKS	UNTRESSED	UNUSABLY
UNSTRAPPED	UNTACKS	UNTHOUGHT	UNTRIDE	UNUSED
UNSTRAPPING	UNTAILED	UNTHREAD	UNTRIED	UNUSEFUL
UNSTRAPS	UNTAINTED	UNTHREADED	UNTRIM	UNUSHERED
UNSTRING	UNTAKEN	UNTHREADING	UNTRIMMED	UNUSUAL
UNSTRINGED	UNTAMABLE	UNTHREADS	UNTRIMMING	UNUSUALLY

UNUTTERED	UNWATCHED	UNWISHED	UNWRITE	UPBROUGHT
UNVAIL	UNWATER	UNWISHES	UNWRITES	UPBUILD
UNVAILE	UNWATERED	UNWISHFUL	UNWRITING	UPBUILDING
UNVAILED	UNWATERING	UNWISHING	UNWRITTEN	UPBUILDINGS
UNVAILES	UNWATERS	UNWIST	UNWROTE	UPBUILDS
UNVAILING	UNWATERY	UNWIT	UNWROUGHT	UPBUILT
UNVAILS	UNWAYED	UNWITCH	UNWRUNG	UPBURNING
UNVALUED	UNWEAL	UNWITCHED	UNYEANED	UPBURST
UNVARIED	UNWEALS	UNWITCHES	UNYOKE	UPBURSTING
UNVARYING	UNWEANED	UNWITCHING	UNYOKED	UPBURSTS
UNVEIL	UNWEAPON	UNWITS	UNYOKES	UPBY
UNVEILED	UNWEAPONED	UNWITTED	UNYOKING	UPBYE
UNVEILER	UNWEAPONING	UNWITTILY	UNZEALOUS	UPCAST
UNVEILERS	UNWEAPONS	UNWITTING	UNZIP	UPCASTING
UNVEILING	UNWEARIED	UNWITTY	UNZIPPED	UPCASTS
UNVEILINGS	UNWEARY	UNWIVE	UNZIPPING	UPCATCH
UNVEILS	UNWEAVE	UNWIVED	UNZIPS	UPCATCHES
UNVENTED	UNWEAVES	UNWIVES	UNZONED	UPCATCHING
UNVERSED	UNWEAVING	UNWIVING	UP	UPCAUGHT
UNVETTED	UNWEBBED	UNWOMAN	UPADAISY	UPCHEARD
UNVEXED	UNWED	UNWOMANED	UPAITHRIC	UPCHEER
UNVIABLE	UNWEDDED	UNWOMANING	UPAS	UPCHEERED
UNVIEWED	UNWEEDED	UNWOMANLIER	UPASES	UPCHEERING
UNVIRTUE	UNWEENED	UNWOMANLIEST	UPBEAR	UPCHEERS
UNVIRTUES	UNWEETING	UNWOMANLY	UPBEARING	UPCHUCK
UNVISITED	UNWEIGHED	UNWOMANS	UPBEARS	UPCHUCKED
UNVISOR	UNWELCOME	UNWON	UPBEAT	UPCHUCKING
UNVISORED	UNWELDY	UNWONT	UPBIND	UPCHUCKS
UNVISORING	UNWELL	UNWONTED	UPBINDING	UPCLIMB
UNVISORS	UNWEPT	UNWOODED	UPBINDS	UPCLIMBED
UNVITAL	UNWET	UNWOOED	UPBLEW	UPCLIMBING
UNVIZARD	UNWETTED	UNWORDED	UPBLOW	UPCLIMBS
UNVIZARDED	UNWHIPPED	UNWORK	UPBLOWING	UPCLOSE
UNVIZARDING	UNWHIPT	UNWORKED	UPBLOWN	UPCLOSED
UNVIZARDS	UNWIELDIER	UNWORKING	UPBLOWS	UPCLOSES
UNVOCAL	UNWIELDIEST	UNWORKS	UPBOIL	UPCLOSING
UNVOICE	UNWIELDY	UNWORLDLIER	UPBOILED	UPCOAST
UNVOICED	UNWIFELIER	UNWORLDLIEST	UPBOILING	UPCOIL
UNVOICES	UNWIFELIEST	UNWORLDLY	UPBOILS	UPCOILED
UNVOICING	UNWIFELY	UNWORMED	UPBORE	UPCOILING
UNVOICINGS	UNWIGGED	UNWORN	UPBORNE	UPCOILS
UNVULGAR	UNWILFUL	UNWORRIED	UPBOUND	UPCOME
UNWAGED	UNWILL	UNWORTH	UPBOUNDEN	UPCOMES
UNWAKED	UNWILLED	UNWORTHIER	UPBRAID	UPCOMING
UNWAKENED	UNWILLING	UNWORTHIEST	UPBRAIDED	UPCURL
UNWALLED	UNWILLS	UNWORTHS	UPBRAIDER	UPCURLED
UNWANTED	UNWIND	UNWORTHY	UPBRAIDERS	UPCURLING
UNWARDED	UNWINDING	UNWOUND	UPBRAIDING	UPCURLS
UNWARE	UNWINDINGS	UNWOUNDED	UPBRAIDINGS	UPCURVED
UNWARELY	UNWINDS	UNWOVE	UPBRAIDS	UPDATE
UNWARES	UNWINGED	UNWOVEN	UPBRAST	UPDATED
UNWARIE	UNWINKING	UNWRAP	UPBRAY	UPDATES
UNWARIER	UNWIPED	UNWRAPPED	UPBRAYED	UPDATING
UNWARIEST	UNWIRE	UNWRAPPING	UPBRAYING	UPDRAG
UNWARILY	UNWIRED	UNWRAPS	UPBRAYS	UPDRAGGED
UNWARLIKE	UNWIRES	UNWREAKED	UPBREAK	UPDRAGGING
UNWARMED	UNWIRING	UNWREATHE	UPBREAKING	UPDRAGS
UNWARNED	UNWISDOM	UNWREATHED	UPBREAKS	UPDRAW
UNWARPED	UNWISDOMS	UNWREATHES	UPBRING	UPDRAWING
UNWARY	UNWISE	UNWREATHING	UPBRINGING	UPDRAWN
UNWASHED	UNWISELY	UNWRINKLE	UPBRINGINGS	UPDRAWS
UNWASHEN	UNWISER	UNWRINKLED	UPBRINGS	UPDREW
UNWASTED	UNWISEST	UNWRINKLES	UPBROKE	UPEND
UNWASTING	UNWISH	UNWRINKLING	UPBROKEN	UPENDED

UPENDING	UPHEAPINGS	UPLEAN	UPRAN	UPSET
UPENDS	UPHEAPS	UPLEANED	UPRATE	UPSETS
UPFILL	UPHEAVAL	UPLEANING	UPRATED	UPSETTER
UPFILLED	UPHEAVALS	UPLEANS	UPRATES	UPSETTERS
UPFILLING	UPHEAVE	UPLEANT	UPRATING	UPSETTING
UPFILLINGS	UPHEAVED	UPLEAP	UPREAR	UPSETTINGS
UPFILLS	UPHEAVES	UPLEAPED	UPREARED	UPSEY
UPFLOW	UPHEAVING	UPLEAPING	UPREARING	UPSEYS
UPFLOWED	UPHELD	UPLEAPS	UPREARS	UPSHOOT
UPFLOWING	UPHILD	UPLEAPT	UPREST	UPSHOOTING
UPFLOWS	UPHILL	UPLED	UPRESTS	UPSHOOTS
UPFLUNG	UPHILLS	UPLIFT	UPRIGHT	UPSHOT
UPFOLLOW	UPHOARD	UPLIFTED	UPRIGHTED	UPSHOTS
UPFOLLOWED	UPHOARDED	UPLIFTER	UPRIGHTING	UPSIDE
UPFOLLOWING	UPHOARDING	UPLIFTERS	UPRIGHTLY	UPSIDES
UPFOLLOWS	UPHOARDS	UPLIFTING	UPRIGHTS	UPSIES
UPFRONT	UPHOIST	UPLIFTINGS	UPRISAL	UPSILON
UPFURL	UPHOISTED	UPLIFTS	UPRISALS	UPSILONS
UPFURLED	UPHOISTING	UPLIGHTED	UPRISE	UPSITTING
UPFURLING	UPHOISTS	UPLIGHTER	UPRISEN	UPSITTINGS
UPFURLS	UPHOLD	UPLIGHTERS	UPRISES	UPSPAKE
UPGANG	UPHOLDER	UPLINK	UPRISING	UPSPEAK
UPGANGS	UPHOLDERS	UPLINKING	UPRISINGS	UPSPEAKING
UPGATHER	UPHOLDING	UPLINKINGS	UPRIST	UPSPEAKS
UPGATHERED	UPHOLDINGS	UPLINKS	UPRISTS	UPSPEAR
UPGATHERING	UPHOLDS	UPLOAD	UPRIVER	UPSPEARED
UPGATHERS	UPHOLSTER	UPLOADED	UPROAR	UPSPEARING
UPGAZE	UPHOLSTERED	UPLOADING	UPROARED	UPSPEARS
UPGAZED	UPHOLSTERING	UPLOADS	UPROARING	UPSPOKE
UPGAZES	UPHOLSTERS	UPLOCK	UPROARS	UPSPOKEN
UPGAZING	UPHOORD	UPLOCKED	UPROLL	UPSPRANG
UPGO	UPHOORDED	UPLOCKING	UPROLLED	UPSPRING
UPGOES	UPHOORDING	UPLOCKS	UPROLLING	UPSPRINGING
UPGOING	UPHOORDS	UPLOOK	UPROLLS	UPSPRINGS
UPGOINGS	UPHROE	UPLOOKED	UPROOT	UPSPRUNG
UPGONE	UPHROES	UPLOOKING	UPROOTAL	UPSTAGE
UPGRADE	UPHUDDEN	UPLOOKS	UPROOTALS	UPSTAGED
UPGRADED	UPHUNG	UPLYING	UPROOTED	UPSTAGES
UPGRADER	UPHURL	UPMAKE	UPROOTER	UPSTAGING
UPGRADERS	UPHURLED	UPMAKER	UPROOTERS	UPSTAIR
UPGRADES	UPHURLING	UPMAKERS	UPROOTING	UPSTAIRS
UPGRADING	UPHURLS	UPMAKES	UPROOTINGS	UPSTAND
UPGREW	UPJET	UPMAKING	UPROOTS	UPSTANDING
UPGROW	UPJETS	UPMAKINGS	UPROSE	UPSTANDS
UPGROWING	UPJETTED	UPMANSHIP	UPROUSE	UPSTARE
UPGROWINGS	UPJETTING	UPMANSHIPS	UPROUSED	UPSTARED
UPGROWN	UPKEEP	UPMOST	UPROUSES	UPSTARES
UPGROWS	UPKEEPS	UPON	UPROUSING	UPSTARING
UPGROWTH	UPKNIT	UPPED	UPRUN	UPSTART
UPGROWTHS	UPKNITS	UPPER	UPRUNNING	UPSTARTED
UPGUSH	UPKNITTED	UPPERCUT	UPRUNS	UPSTARTING
UPGUSHED	UPKNITTING	UPPERCUTS	UPRUSH	UPSTARTS
UPGUSHES	UPLAID	UPPERMOST	UPRUSHED	UPSTATE
UPGUSHING	UPLAND	UPPERS	UPRUSHES	UPSTAY
UPHAND	UPLANDER	UPPILED	UPRUSHING	UPSTAYED
UPHANG	UPLANDERS	UPPING	UPRYST	UPSTAYING
UPHANGING	UPLANDISH	UPPINGS	UPS	UPSTAYS
UPHANGS	UPLANDS	UPPISH	UPSCALE	UPSTOOD
UPHAUD	UPLAY	UPPISHLY	UPSEE	UPSTREAM
UPHAUDING	UPLAYING	UPPITY	UPSEES	UPSTREAMED
UPHAUDS	UPLAYS	UPRAISE	UPSEND	UPSTREAMING
UPHEAP	UPLEAD	UPRAISED	UPSENDING	UPSTREAMS
UPHEAPED	UPLEADING	UPRAISES	UPSENDS	UPSTROKE
UPHEAPING	UPLEADS	UPRAISING	UPSENT	UPSTROKES

UPSURGE	UPTRAINS	URANIC	UREDINIAL	URINATORS
UPSURGED	UPTREND	URANIDE	UREDINIUM	URINE
UPSURGES	UPTRENDS	URANIDES	UREDINOUS	URINED
UPSURGING	UPTRILLED	URANIN	UREDIUM	URINES
UPSWARM	UPTURN	URANINITE	UREDO	URINING
UPSWARMED	UPTURNED	URANINITES	UREDOSORI	URINOLOGIES
UPSWARMING	UPTURNING	URANINS	UREIC	URINOLOGY
UPSWARMS	UPTURNINGS	URANISCI	UREIDE	URINOSE
UPSWAY	UPTURNS	URANISCUS	UREIDES	URINOUS
UPSWAYED	UPTYING	URANISM	UREMIA	URITE
UPSWAYING	UPVALUE	URANISMS	UREMIAS	URITES
UPSWAYS	UPVALUED	URANITE	UREMIC	URMAN
UPSWEEP	UPVALUES	URANITES	URENA	URMANS
UPSWEEPS	UPVALUING	URANITIC	URENAS	URN
UPSWELL	UPWAFT	URANIUM	URENT	URNAL
UPSWELLED	UPWAFTED	URANIUMS	URES	URNED
UPSWELLING	UPWAFTING	URANOLOGIES	URESES	URNFIELD
UPSWELLS	UPWAFTS	URANOLOGY	URESIS	URNFIELDS
UPSWEPT	UPWARD	URANOUS	URETER	URNFUL
UPSWING	UPWARDLY	URANYL	URETERAL	URNFULS
UPSWINGS	UPWARDS	URANYLIC	URETERIC	URNING
UPSWOLLEN	UPWELL	URANYLS	URETERS	URNINGS
UPSY	UPWELLED	URAO	URETHAN	URNS
UPTAK	UPWELLING	URAOS	URETHANE	UROCHORD
UPTAKE	UPWELLINGS	URARI	URETHANES	UROCHORDS
UPTAKEN	UPWELLS	URARIS	URETHANS	UROCHROME
UPTAKES	UPWENT	URATE	URETHRA	UROCHROMES
UPTAKING	UPWHIRL	URATES	URETHRAE	URODELAN
UPTAKS	UPWHIRLED	URBAN	URETHRAL	URODELANS
UPTEAR	UPWHIRLING	URBANE	URETHRAS	URODELE
UPTEARING	UPWHIRLS	URBANELY	URETIC	URODELES
UPTEARS	UPWIND	URBANER	URGE	URODELOUS
UPTHREW	UPWINDING	URBANEST	URGED	UROGENOUS
UPTHROW	UPWINDS	URBANISE	URGENCE	UROGRAPHIES
UPTHROWING	UPWOUND	URBANISED	URGENCES	UROGRAPHY
UPTHROWN	UPWRAP	URBANISES	URGENCIES	UROKINASE
UPTHROWS	UPWRAPS	URBANISING	URGENCY	UROKINASES
UPTHRUST	UPWROUGHT	URBANITE	URGENT	UROLAGNIA
UPTHRUSTING	UR	URBANITES	URGENTLY	UROLAGNIAS
UPTHRUSTS	URACHI	URBANITIES	URGER	UROLITH
UPTHUNDER	URACHUS	URBANITY	URGERS	UROLITHIC
UPTHUNDERED	URACHUSES	URBANIZE	URGES	UROLITHS
UPTHUNDERING	URACIL	URBANIZED	URGING	UROLOGIC
UPTHUNDERS	URACILS	URBANIZES	URGINGS	UROLOGIES
UPTIE	URAEI	URBANIZING	URIAL	UROLOGIST
UPTIED	URAEMIA	URCEOLATE	URIALS	UROLOGISTS
UPTIES	URAEMIAS	URCEOLI	URIC	UROLOGY
UPTIGHT	URAEMIC	URCEOLUS	URICASE	UROMERE
UPTIGHTER	URAEUS	URCEOLUSES	URICASES	UROMERES
UPTIGHTEST	URAEUSES	URCHIN	URIDINE	UROPOD
UPTILT	URALI	URCHINS	URIDINES	UROPODS
UPTILTED	URALIS	URD	URINAL	UROPYGIA
UPTILTING	URALITE	URDE	URINALS	UROPYGIAL
UPTILTS	URALITES	URDEE	URINANT	UROPYGIUM
UPTOOK	URALITIC	URDS	URINARIES	UROPYGIUMS
UPTORE	URALITISE	URDY	URINARY	UROSCOPIC
UPTORN	URALITISED	URE	URINATE	UROSCOPIES
UPTOWN	URALITISES	UREA	URINATED	UROSCOPY
UPTOWNER	URALITISING	UREAL	URINATES	UROSES
UPTOWNERS	URALITIZE	UREAS	URINATING	UROSIS
UPTOWNS	URALITIZED	UREDIA	URINATION	UROSOME
UPTRAIN	URALITIZES	UREDINE	URINATIONS	UROSOMES
UPTRAINED	URALITIZING	UREDINES	URINATIVE	UROSTEGE
UPTRAINING	URANIAN	UREDINIA	URINATOR	UROSTEGES

The Chambers Dictionary is the authority for many longer words; see *OSW* Introduction, page xii

UROSTOMIES
UROSTOMY
UROSTYLE
UROSTYLES
URSINE
URSON
URSONS
URTEXT
URTEXTS
URTICA
URTICANT
URTICARIA
URTICARIAS
URTICAS
URTICATE
URTICATED
URTICATES
URTICATING
URUBU
URUBUS
URUS
URUSES
URVA
URVAS
US
USABILITIES
USABILITY
USABLE
USABLY
USAGE
USAGER
USAGERS
USAGES
USANCE
USANCES
USE
USED
USEFUL

USEFULLY
USELESS
USELESSLY
USER
USERS
USES
USHER
USHERED
USHERESS
USHERESSES
USHERETTE
USHERETTES
USHERING
USHERINGS
USHERS
USHERSHIP
USHERSHIPS
USING
USNEA
USNEAS
USTION
USTIONS
USUAL
USUALLY
USUALNESS
USUALNESSES
USUALS
USUCAPION
USUCAPIONS
USUCAPT
USUCAPTED
USUCAPTING
USUCAPTS
USUFRUCT
USUFRUCTED
USUFRUCTING
USUFRUCTS
USURE

USURED
USURER
USURERS
USURES
USURESS
USURESSES
USURIES
USURING
USURIOUS
USUROUS
USURP
USURPED
USURPEDLY
USURPER
USURPERS
USURPING
USURPINGS
USURPS
USURY
USWARD
USWARDS
UT
UTAS
UTASES
UTE
UTENSIL
UTENSILS
UTERI
UTERINE
UTERITIS
UTERITISES
UTEROTOMIES
UTEROTOMY
UTERUS
UTES
UTILE
UTILISE
UTILISED

UTILISER
UTILISERS
UTILISES
UTILISING
UTILITIES
UTILITY
UTILIZE
UTILIZED
UTILIZER
UTILIZERS
UTILIZES
UTILIZING
UTIS
UTISES
UTMOST
UTMOSTS
UTOPIA
UTOPIAN
UTOPIANS
UTOPIAS
UTOPIAST
UTOPIASTS
UTOPISM
UTOPISMS
UTOPIST
UTOPISTS
UTRICLE
UTRICLES
UTRICULAR
UTRICULI
UTRICULUS
UTS
UTTER
UTTERABLE
UTTERANCE
UTTERANCES
UTTERED
UTTERER

UTTERERS
UTTEREST
UTTERING
UTTERINGS
UTTERLESS
UTTERLY
UTTERMOST
UTTERMOSTS
UTTERNESS
UTTERNESSES
UTTERS
UTU
UTUS
UVA
UVAE
UVAROVITE
UVAROVITES
UVAS
UVEA
UVEAL
UVEAS
UVEITIC
UVEITIS
UVEITISES
UVEOUS
UVULA
UVULAE
UVULAR
UVULARLY
UVULAS
UVULITIS
UVULITISES
UXORIAL
UXORIALLY
UXORICIDE
UXORICIDES
UXORIOUS

V

VAC
VACANCE
VACANCES
VACANCIES
VACANCY
VACANTLY
VACATE
VACATED
VACATES
VACATING
VACATION
VACATIONED
VACATIONING
VACATIONS
VACATUR
VACATURS
VACCINAL
VACCINATE
VACCINATED
VACCINATES
VACCINATING
VACCINE
VACCINES
VACCINIA
VACCINIAL
VACCINIAS
VACCINIUM
VACCINIUMS
VACHERIN
VACHERINS
VACILLANT
VACILLATE
VACILLATED
VACILLATES
VACILLATING
VACKED
VACKING
VACS
VACUA
VACUATE
VACUATED
VACUATES
VACUATING
VACUATION
VACUATIONS
VACUIST
VACUISTS
VACUITIES
VACUITY
VACUOLAR
VACUOLATE
VACUOLE
VACUOLES

VACUOUS
VACUOUSLY
VACUUM
VACUUMED
VACUUMING
VACUUMS
VADE
VADED
VADES
VADING
VADOSE
VAE
VAES
VAGABOND
VAGABONDED
VAGABONDING
VAGABONDS
VAGAL
VAGARIES
VAGARIOUS
VAGARISH
VAGARY
VAGI
VAGILE
VAGILITIES
VAGILITY
VAGINA
VAGINAE
VAGINAL
VAGINALLY
VAGINANT
VAGINAS
VAGINATE
VAGINATED
VAGINITIS
VAGINITISES
VAGINULA
VAGINULAE
VAGINULE
VAGINULES
VAGITUS
VAGITUSES
VAGRANCIES
VAGRANCY
VAGRANT
VAGRANTS
VAGROM
VAGUE
VAGUED
VAGUELY
VAGUENESS
VAGUENESSES
VAGUER
VAGUES

VAGUEST
VAGUING
VAGUS
VAHINE
VAHINES
VAIL
VAILED
VAILING
VAILS
VAIN
VAINER
VAINESSE
VAINESSES
VAINEST
VAINGLORIED
VAINGLORIES
VAINGLORY
VAINGLORYING
VAINLY
VAINNESS
VAINNESSES
VAIR
VAIRE
VAIRIER
VAIRIEST
VAIRS
VAIRY
VAIVODE
VAIVODES
VAKASS
VAKASSES
VAKEEL
VAKEELS
VAKIL
VAKILS
VALANCE
VALANCED
VALANCES
VALE
VALENCE
VALENCES
VALENCIES
VALENCY
VALENTINE
VALENTINES
VALERIAN
VALERIANS
VALES
VALET
VALETA
VALETAS
VALETE
VALETED
VALETES

VALETING
VALETINGS
VALETS
VALGOUS
VALGUS
VALGUSES
VALI
VALIANCE
VALIANCES
VALIANCIES
VALIANCY
VALIANT
VALIANTLY
VALIANTS
VALID
VALIDATE
VALIDATED
VALIDATES
VALIDATING
VALIDER
VALIDEST
VALIDITIES
VALIDITY
VALIDLY
VALIDNESS
VALIDNESSES
VALINE
VALINES
VALIS
VALISE
VALISES
VALLAR
VALLARY
VALLECULA
VALLECULAE
VALLEY
VALLEYS
VALLONIA
VALLONIAS
VALLUM
VALLUMS
VALONEA
VALONEAS
VALONIA
VALONIAS
VALOR
VALORISE
VALORISED
VALORISES
VALORISING
VALORIZE
VALORIZED
VALORIZES
VALORIZING

VALOROUS
VALORS
VALOUR
VALOURS
VALSE
VALSED
VALSES
VALSING
VALUABLE
VALUABLES
VALUABLY
VALUATE
VALUATED
VALUATES
VALUATING
VALUATION
VALUATIONS
VALUATOR
VALUATORS
VALUE
VALUED
VALUELESS
VALUER
VALUERS
VALUES
VALUING
VALUTA
VALUTAS
VALVAL
VALVAR
VALVASSOR
VALVASSORS
VALVATE
VALVE
VALVED
VALVELESS
VALVELET
VALVELETS
VALVES
VALVING
VALVULA
VALVULAE
VALVULAR
VALVULE
VALVULES
VAMBRACE
VAMBRACED
VAMBRACES
VAMOOSE
VAMOOSED
VAMOOSES
VAMOOSING
VAMOSE
VAMOSED

The Chambers Dictionary is the authority for many longer words; see *OSW* Introduction, page xii

VAMOSES	VANISH	VAPOUR	VARIFOCAL	VARYINGS
VAMOSING	VANISHED	VAPOURED	VARIFOCALS	VAS
VAMP	VANISHER	VAPOURER	VARIFORM	VASA
VAMPED	VANISHERS	VAPOURERS	VARIOLA	VASAL
VAMPER	VANISHES	VAPOURING	VARIOLAR	VASCULA
VAMPERS	VANISHING	VAPOURINGS	VARIOLAS	VASCULAR
VAMPING	VANISHINGS	VAPOURISH	VARIOLATE	VASCULUM
VAMPINGS	VANITAS	VAPOURS	VARIOLATED	VASCULUMS
VAMPIRE	VANITASES	VAPOURY	VARIOLATES	VASE
VAMPIRED	VANITIES	VAPULATE	VARIOLATING	VASECTOMIES
VAMPIRES	VANITORIES	VAPULATED	VARIOLE	VASECTOMY
VAMPIRIC	VANITORY	VAPULATES	VARIOLES	VASES
VAMPIRING	VANITY	VAPULATING	VARIOLITE	VASIFORM
VAMPIRISE	VANNED	VAQUERO	VARIOLITES	VASOMOTOR
VAMPIRISED	VANNER	VAQUEROS	VARIOLOID	VASSAIL
VAMPIRISES	VANNERS	VARA	VARIOLOIDS	VASSAILS
VAMPIRISING	VANNING	VARACTOR	VARIOLOUS	VASSAL
VAMPIRISM	VANNINGS	VARACTORS	VARIORUM	VASSALAGE
VAMPIRISMS	VANQUISH	VARAN	VARIORUMS	VASSALAGES
VAMPIRIZE	VANQUISHED	VARANS	VARIOUS	VASSALESS
VAMPIRIZED	VANQUISHES	VARAS	VARIOUSLY	VASSALESSES
VAMPIRIZES	VANQUISHING	VARDIES	VARISCITE	VASSALLED
VAMPIRIZING	VANS	VARDY	VARISCITES	VASSALLING
VAMPISH	VANT	VARE	VARISTOR	VASSALRIES
VAMPLATE	VANTAGE	VAREC	VARISTORS	VASSALRY
VAMPLATES	VANTAGED	VARECH	VARIX	VASSALS
VAMPS	VANTAGES	VARECHS	VARLET	VAST
VAN	VANTAGING	VARECS	VARLETESS	VASTER
VANADATE	VANTBRACE	VARES	VARLETESSES	VASTEST
VANADATES	VANTBRACES	VAREUSE	VARLETRIES	VASTIDITIES
VANADIC	VANTS	VAREUSES	VARLETRY	VASTIDITY
VANADIUM	VANWARD	VARGUENO	VARLETS	VASTIER
VANADIUMS	VAPID	VARGUENOS	VARLETTO	VASTIEST
VANADOUS	VAPIDER	VARIABLE	VARLETTOS	VASTITIES
VANDAL	VAPIDEST	VARIABLES	VARMENT	VASTITUDE
VANDALISE	VAPIDITIES	VARIABLY	VARMENTS	VASTITUDES
VANDALISED	VAPIDITY	VARIANCE	VARMINT	VASTITY
VANDALISES	VAPIDLY	VARIANCES	VARMINTS	VASTLY
VANDALISING	VAPIDNESS	VARIANT	VARNA	VASTNESS
VANDALISM	VAPIDNESSES	VARIANTS	VARNAS	VASTNESSES
VANDALISMS	VAPOR	VARIATE	VARNISH	VASTS
VANDALIZE	VAPORABLE	VARIATED	VARNISHED	VASTY
VANDALIZED	VAPORED	VARIATES	VARNISHER	VAT
VANDALIZES	VAPORETTI	VARIATING	VARNISHERS	VATABLE
VANDALIZING	VAPORETTO	VARIATION	VARNISHES	VATFUL
VANDALS	VAPORETTOS	VARIATIONS	VARNISHING	VATFULS
VANDYKE	VAPORIFIC	VARIATIVE	VARNISHINGS	VATIC
VANDYKED	VAPORING	VARICELLA	VARROA	VATICIDE
VANDYKES	VAPORISE	VARICELLAS	VARROAS	VATICIDES
VANDYKING	VAPORISED	VARICES	VARSAL	VATICINAL
VANE	VAPORISER	VARICOSE	VARSITIES	VATMAN
VANED	VAPORISERS	VARIED	VARSITY	VATMEN
VANELESS	VAPORISES	VARIEDLY	VARTABED	VATS
VANES	VAPORISING	VARIEGATE	VARTABEDS	VATTED
VANESSA	VAPORIZE	VARIEGATED	VARUS	VATTER
VANESSAS	VAPORIZED	VARIEGATES	VARUSES	VATTERS
VANG	VAPORIZER	VARIEGATING	VARVE	VATTING
VANGS	VAPORIZERS	VARIER	VARVED	VATU
VANGUARD	VAPORIZES	VARIERS	VARVEL	VATUS
VANGUARDS	VAPORIZING	VARIES	VARVELLED	VAU
VANILLA	VAPOROUS	VARIETAL	VARVELS	VAUDOO
VANILLAS	VAPORS	VARIETALS	VARVES	VAUDOOS
VANILLIN	VAPORWARE	VARIETIES	VARY	VAUDOUX
VANILLINS	VAPORWARES	VARIETY	VARYING	VAULT

VAULTAGE	VECTORISING	VEHEMENT	VELIGER	VENDAGES
VAULTAGES	VECTORIZE	VEHICLE	VELIGERS	VENDANGE
VAULTED	VECTORIZED	VEHICLES	VELL	VENDANGES
VAULTER	VECTORIZES	VEHICULAR	VELLEITIES	VENDED
VAULTERS	VECTORIZING	VEHM	VELLEITY	VENDEE
VAULTING	VECTORS	VEHME	VELLENAGE	VENDEES
VAULTINGS	VEDALIA	VEHMIC	VELLENAGES	VENDER
VAULTS	VEDALIAS	VEHMIQUE	VELLET	VENDERS
VAULTY	VEDETTE	VEIL	VELLETS	VENDETTA
VAUNCE	VEDETTES	VEILED	VELLICATE	VENDETTAS
VAUNCED	VEDUTA	VEILIER	VELLICATED	VENDEUSE
VAUNCES	VEDUTE	VEILIEST	VELLICATES	VENDEUSES
VAUNCING	VEDUTISTA	VEILING	VELLICATING	VENDIBLE
VAUNT	VEDUTISTI	VEILINGS	VELLON	VENDIBLES
VAUNTAGE	VEE	VEILLESS	VELLONS	VENDIBLY
VAUNTAGES	VEENA	VEILLEUSE	VELLS	VENDING
VAUNTED	VEENAS	VEILLEUSES	VELLUM	VENDIS
VAUNTER	VEEP	VEILS	VELLUMS	VENDISES
VAUNTERIES	VEEPS	VEILY	VELOCE	VENDISS
VAUNTERS	VEER	VEIN	VELOCITIES	VENDISSES
VAUNTERY	VEERED	VEINED	VELOCITY	VENDITION
VAUNTFUL	VEERIES	VEINIER	VELODROME	VENDITIONS
VAUNTIER	VEERING	VEINIEST	VELODROMES	VENDOR
VAUNTIEST	VEERINGLY	VEINING	VELOUR	VENDORS
VAUNTING	VEERINGS	VEININGS	VELOURS	VENDS
VAUNTINGS	VEERS	VEINLET	VELOUTE	VENDUE
VAUNTS	VEERY	VEINLETS	VELOUTES	VENDUES
VAUNTY	VEES	VEINOUS	VELOUTINE	VENEER
VAURIEN	VEG	VEINS	VELOUTINES	VENEERED
VAURIENS	VEGA	VEINSTONE	VELSKOEN	VENEERER
VAUS	VEGAN	VEINSTONES	VELSKOENS	VENEERERS
VAUT	VEGANIC	VEINSTUFF	VELUM	VENEERING
VAUTE	VEGANISM	VEINSTUFFS	VELURE	VENEERINGS
VAUTED	VEGANISMS	VEINY	VELURED	VENEERS
VAUTES	VEGANS	VELA	VELURES	VENEFIC
VAUTING	VEGAS	VELAMEN	VELURING	VENEFICAL
VAUTS	VEGELATE	VELAMINA	VELVERET	VENERABLE
VAVASORIES	VEGELATES	VELAR	VELVERETS	VENERABLY
VAVASORY	VEGES	VELARIA	VELVET	VENERATE
VAVASOUR	VEGETABLE	VELARIC	VELVETED	VENERATED
VAVASOURS	VEGETABLES	VELARISE	VELVETEEN	VENERATES
VAWARD	VEGETABLY	VELARISED	VELVETEENS	VENERATING
VAWARDS	VEGETAL	VELARISES	VELVETIER	VENERATOR
VAWTE	VEGETALS	VELARISING	VELVETIEST	VENERATORS
VAWTED	VEGETANT	VELARIUM	VELVETING	VENEREAL
VAWTES	VEGETATE	VELARIZE	VELVETINGS	VENEREAN
VAWTING	VEGETATED	VELARIZED	VELVETS	VENEREANS
VEAL	VEGETATES	VELARIZES	VELVETY	VENEREOUS
VEALE	VEGETATING	VELARIZING	VENA	VENERER
VEALER	VEGETATINGS	VELARS	VENAE	VENERERS
VEALERS	VEGETE	VELATE	VENAL	VENERIES
VEALES	VEGETIVE	VELATED	VENALITIES	VENERY
VEALIER	VEGETIVES	VELATURA	VENALITY	VENEWE
VEALIEST	VEGGED	VELATURAS	VENALLY	VENEWES
VEALS	VEGGES	VELD	VENATIC	VENEY
VEALY	VEGGIE	VELDS	VENATICAL	VENEYS
VECTOR	VEGGIES	VELDSKOEN	VENATION	VENGE
VECTORED	VEGGING	VELDSKOENS	VENATIONS	VENGEABLE
VECTORIAL	VEGIE	VELDT	VENATOR	VENGEABLY
VECTORING	VEGIES	VELDTS	VENATORS	VENGEANCE
VECTORINGS	VEHEMENCE	VELE	VEND	VENGEANCES
VECTORISE	VEHEMENCES	VELES	VENDACE	VENGED
VECTORISED	VEHEMENCIES	VELETA	VENDACES	VENGEFUL
VECTORISES	VEHEMENCY	VELETAS	VENDAGE	VENGEMENT

The Chambers Dictionary is the authority for many longer words; see *OSW* Introduction, page xii

VENGEMENTS	VENTRALLY	VERBATIM	VERGER	VERMIN
VENGER	VENTRALS	VERBENA	VERGERS	VERMINATE
VENGERS	VENTRE	VERBENAS	VERGES	VERMINATED
VENGES	VENTRED	VERBERATE	VERGING	VERMINATES
VENGING	VENTRES	VERBERATED	VERGLAS	VERMINATING
VENIAL	VENTRICLE	VERBERATES	VERGLASES	VERMINED
VENIALITIES	VENTRICLES	VERBERATING	VERIDICAL	VERMINOUS
VENIALITY	VENTRING	VERBIAGE	VERIER	VERMINS
VENIALLY	VENTRINGS	VERBIAGES	VERIEST	VERMINY
VENIDIUM	VENTROUS	VERBICIDE	VERIFIED	VERMIS
VENIDIUMS	VENTS	VERBICIDES	VERIFIER	VERMOUTH
VENIN	VENTURE	VERBID	VERIFIERS	VERMOUTHS
VENINS	VENTURED	VERBIDS	VERIFIES	VERNAL
VENIRE	VENTURER	VERBIFIED	VERIFY	VERNALISE
VENIREMAN	VENTURERS	VERBIFIES	VERIFYING	VERNALISED
VENIREMEN	VENTURES	VERBIFY	VERILY	VERNALISES
VENIRES	VENTURI	VERBIFYING	VERISM	VERNALISING
VENISON	VENTURING	VERBLESS	VERISMO	VERNALITIES
VENISONS	VENTURINGS	VERBOSE	VERISMOS	VERNALITY
VENITE	VENTURIS	VERBOSELY	VERISMS	VERNALIZE
VENITES	VENTUROUS	VERBOSER	VERIST	VERNALIZED
VENNEL	VENUE	VERBOSEST	VERISTIC	VERNALIZES
VENNELS	VENUES	VERBOSITIES	VERISTS	VERNALIZING
VENOM	VENULE	VERBOSITY	VERITABLE	VERNALLY
VENOMED	VENULES	VERBOTEN	VERITABLY	VERNANT
VENOMING	VENUS	VERBS	VERITIES	VERNATION
VENOMOUS	VENUSES	VERDANCIES	VERITY	VERNATIONS
VENOMS	VENVILLE	VERDANCY	VERJUICE	VERNICLE
VENOSE	VENVILLES	VERDANT	VERJUICED	VERNICLES
VENOSITIES	VERACIOUS	VERDANTLY	VERJUICES	VERNIER
VENOSITY	VERACITIES	VERDELHO	VERKRAMP	VERNIERS
VENOUS	VERACITY	VERDELHOS	VERLIG	VERONAL
VENT	VERANDA	VERDERER	VERLIGTE	VERONALS
VENTAGE	VERANDAH	VERDERERS	VERLIGTES	VERONICA
VENTAGES	VERANDAHS	VERDEROR	VERMAL	VERONICAS
VENTAIL	VERANDAS	VERDERORS	VERMEIL	VERONIQUE
VENTAILE	VERATRIN	VERDET	VERMEILED	VERQUERE
VENTAILES	VERATRINE	VERDETS	VERMEILING	VERQUERES
VENTAILS	VERATRINES	VERDICT	VERMEILLE	VERQUIRE
VENTANA	VERATRINS	VERDICTS	VERMEILLED	VERQUIRES
VENTANAS	VERATRUM	VERDIGRIS	VERMEILLES	VERREL
VENTAYLE	VERATRUMS	VERDIGRISED	VERMEILLING	VERRELS
VENTAYLES	VERB	VERDIGRISES	VERMEILS	VERREY
VENTED	VERBAL	VERDIGRISING	VERMELL	VERRUCA
VENTER	VERBALISE	VERDIN	VERMELLS	VERRUCAE
VENTERS	VERBALISED	VERDINS	VERMES	VERRUCAS
VENTIDUCT	VERBALISES	VERDIT	VERMIAN	VERRUCOSE
VENTIDUCTS	VERBALISING	VERDITE	VERMICIDE	VERRUCOUS
VENTIFACT	VERBALISM	VERDITER	VERMICIDES	VERRUGA
VENTIFACTS	VERBALISMS	VERDITERS	VERMICULE	VERRUGAS
VENTIGE	VERBALIST	VERDITES	VERMICULES	VERRY
VENTIGES	VERBALISTS	VERDITS	VERMIFORM	VERS
VENTIL	VERBALITIES	VERDOY	VERMIFUGE	VERSAL
VENTILATE	VERBALITY	VERDURE	VERMIFUGES	VERSALS
VENTILATED	VERBALIZE	VERDURED	VERMIL	VERSANT
VENTILATES	VERBALIZED	VERDURES	VERMILIES	VERSANTS
VENTILATING	VERBALIZES	VERDUROUS	VERMILION	VERSATILE
VENTILS	VERBALIZING	VERECUND	VERMILIONED	VERSE
VENTING	VERBALLED	VERGE	VERMILIONING	VERSED
VENTINGS	VERBALLING	VERGED	VERMILIONS	VERSELET
VENTOSE	VERBALLY	VERGENCE	VERMILLED	VERSELETS
VENTOSITIES	VERBALS	VERGENCES	VERMILLING	VERSER
VENTOSITY	VERBARIAN	VERGENCIES	VERMILS	VERSERS
VENTRAL	VERBARIANS	VERGENCY	VERMILY	VERSES

VERSET	VERVET	VESTURED	VIALLED	VICARSHIP
VERSETS	VERVETS	VESTURER	VIALS	VICARSHIPS
VERSICLE	VERY	VESTURERS	VIAMETER	VICARY
VERSICLES	VESICA	VESTURES	VIAMETERS	VICE
VERSIFIED	VESICAE	VESTURING	VIAND	VICED
VERSIFIER	VESICAL	VESUVIAN	VIANDS	VICELESS
VERSIFIERS	VESICANT	VESUVIANS	VIAS	VICENARY
VERSIFIES	VESICANTS	VET	VIATICA	VICENNIAL
VERSIFORM	VESICATE	VETCH	VIATICALS	VICEREINE
VERSIFY	VESICATED	VETCHES	VIATICUM	VICEREINES
VERSIFYING	VESICATES	VETCHIER	VIATICUMS	VICEROY
VERSIN	VESICATING	VETCHIEST	VIATOR	VICEROYS
VERSINE	VESICLE	VETCHLING	VIATORES	VICES
VERSINES	VESICLES	VETCHLINGS	VIATORIAL	VICESIMAL
VERSING	VESICULA	VETCHY	VIATORS	VICHIES
VERSINGS	VESICULAE	VETERAN	VIBE	VICHY
VERSINS	VESICULAR	VETERANS	VIBES	VICIATE
VERSION	VESPA	VETIVER	VIBEX	VICIATED
VERSIONAL	VESPAS	VETIVERS	VIBICES	VICIATES
VERSIONER	VESPER	VETKOEK	VIBIST	VICIATING
VERSIONERS	VESPERAL	VETKOEKS	VIBISTS	VICINAGE
VERSIONS	VESPERS	VETO	VIBRACULA	VICINAGES
VERSO	VESPIARIES	VETOED	VIBRAHARP	VICINAL
VERSOS	VESPIARY	VETOES	VIBRAHARPS	VICING
VERST	VESPINE	VETOING	VIBRANCIES	VICINITIES
VERSTS	VESPOID	VETS	VIBRANCY	VICINITY
VERSUS	VESSAIL	VETTED	VIBRANT	VICIOSITIES
VERSUTE	VESSAILS	VETTING	VIBRANTLY	VICIOSITY
VERT	VESSEL	VETTURA	VIBRATE	VICIOUS
VERTEBRA	VESSELS	VETTURAS	VIBRATED	VICIOUSLY
VERTEBRAE	VEST	VETTURINI	VIBRATES	VICOMTE
VERTEBRAL	VESTA	VETTURINO	VIBRATILE	VICOMTES
VERTED	VESTAL	VEX	VIBRATING	VICTIM
VERTEX	VESTALS	VEXATION	VIBRATION	VICTIMISE
VERTEXES	VESTAS	VEXATIONS	VIBRATIONS	VICTIMISED
VERTICAL	VESTED	VEXATIOUS	VIBRATIVE	VICTIMISES
VERTICALS	VESTIARIES	VEXATORY	VIBRATO	VICTIMISING
VERTICES	VESTIARY	VEXED	VIBRATOR	VICTIMIZE
VERTICIL	VESTIBULA	VEXEDLY	VIBRATORS	VICTIMIZED
VERTICILS	VESTIBULE	VEXEDNESS	VIBRATORY	VICTIMIZES
VERTICITIES	VESTIBULED	VEXEDNESSES	VIBRATOS	VICTIMIZING
VERTICITY	VESTIBULES	VEXER	VIBRIO	VICTIMS
VERTIGINES	VESTIBULING	VEXERS	VIBRIOS	VICTOR
VERTIGO	VESTIGE	VEXES	VIBRIOSES	VICTORESS
VERTIGOES	VESTIGES	VEXILLA	VIBRIOSIS	VICTORESSES
VERTIGOS	VESTIGIA	VEXILLARIES	VIBRISSA	VICTORIA
VERTING	VESTIGIAL	VEXILLARY	VIBRISSAE	VICTORIAS
VERTIPORT	VESTIGIUM	VEXILLUM	VIBRONIC	VICTORIES
VERTIPORTS	VESTIMENT	VEXING	VIBS	VICTORINE
VERTS	VESTIMENTS	VEXINGLY	VIBURNUM	VICTORINES
VERTU	VESTING	VEXINGS	VIBURNUMS	VICTORS
VERTUE	VESTINGS	VEXT	VICAR	VICTORY
VERTUES	VESTITURE	VEZIR	VICARAGE	VICTRESS
VERTUOUS	VESTITURES	VEZIRS	VICARAGES	VICTRESSES
VERTUS	VESTMENT	VIA	VICARATE	VICTRIX
VERVAIN	VESTMENTS	VIABILITIES	VICARATES	VICTRIXES
VERVAINS	VESTRAL	VIABILITY	VICARESS	VICTROLLA
VERVE	VESTRIES	VIABLE	VICARESSES	VICTROLLAS
VERVEL	VESTRY	VIADUCT	VICARIAL	VICTUAL
VERVELLED	VESTRYMAN	VIADUCTS	VICARIATE	VICTUALLED
VERVELS	VESTRYMEN	VIAE	VICARIATES	VICTUALLING
VERVEN	VESTS	VIAL	VICARIES	VICTUALS
VERVENS	VESTURAL	VIALFUL	VICARIOUS	VICUNA
VERVES	VESTURE	VIALFULS	VICARS	VICUNAS

VID	VIFDA	VILIPENDING	VINDALOOS	VIOLATING
VIDAME	VIFDAS	VILIPENDS	VINDEMIAL	VIOLATION
VIDAMES	VIGESIMAL	VILL	VINDICATE	VIOLATIONS
VIDE	VIGIA	VILLA	VINDICATED	VIOLATIVE
VIDELICET	VIGIAS	VILLADOM	VINDICATES	VIOLATOR
VIDENDA	VIGIL	VILLADOMS	VINDICATING	VIOLATORS
VIDENDUM	VIGILANCE	VILLAGE	VINE	VIOLD
VIDEO	VIGILANCES	VILLAGER	VINED	VIOLENCE
VIDEODISC	VIGILANT	VILLAGERIES	VINEGAR	VIOLENCES
VIDEODISCS	VIGILANTE	VILLAGERS	VINEGARED	VIOLENT
VIDEOED	VIGILANTES	VILLAGERY	VINEGARING	VIOLENTED
VIDEOFIT	VIGILS	VILLAGES	VINEGARS	VIOLENTING
VIDEOFITS	VIGNERON	VILLAGIO	VINEGARY	VIOLENTLY
VIDEOGRAM	VIGNERONS	VILLAGIOES	VINER	VIOLENTS
VIDEOGRAMS	VIGNETTE	VILLAGIOS	VINERIES	VIOLER
VIDEOING	VIGNETTED	VILLAGREE	VINERS	VIOLERS
VIDEOS	VIGNETTER	VILLAGREES	VINERY	VIOLET
VIDEOTAPE	VIGNETTERS	VILLAIN	VINES	VIOLETS
VIDEOTAPED	VIGNETTES	VILLAINIES	VINEW	VIOLIN
VIDEOTAPES	VIGNETTING	VILLAINS	VINEWED	VIOLINIST
VIDEOTAPING	VIGOR	VILLAINY	VINEWING	VIOLINISTS
VIDEOTEX	VIGORISH	VILLAN	VINEWS	VIOLINS
VIDEOTEXES	VIGORISHES	VILLANAGE	VINEYARD	VIOLIST
VIDEOTEXT	VIGORO	VILLANAGES	VINEYARDS	VIOLISTS
VIDEOTEXTS	VIGOROS	VILLANIES	VINIER	VIOLONE
VIDETTE	VIGOROUS	VILLANOUS	VINIEST	VIOLONES
VIDETTES	VIGORS	VILLANS	VINING	VIOLS
VIDIMUS	VIGOUR	VILLANY	VINO	VIPER
VIDIMUSES	VIGOURS	VILLAR	VINOLENT	VIPERINE
VIDS	VIHARA	VILLAS	VINOLOGIES	VIPERISH
VIDUAGE	VIHARAS	VILLATIC	VINOLOGY	VIPEROUS
VIDUAGES	VIHUELA	VILLEIN	VINOS	VIPERS
VIDUAL	VIHUELAS	VILLEINS	VINOSITIES	VIRAEMIA
VIDUITIES	VIKING	VILLENAGE	VINOSITY	VIRAEMIAS
VIDUITY	VIKINGISM	VILLENAGES	VINOUS	VIRAEMIC
VIDUOUS	VIKINGISMS	VILLI	VINS	VIRAGO
VIE	VIKINGS	VILLIAGO	VINT	VIRAGOES
VIED	VILAYET	VILLIAGOES	VINTAGE	VIRAGOISH
VIELLE	VILAYETS	VILLIAGOS	VINTAGED	VIRAGOS
VIELLES	VILD	VILLIFORM	VINTAGER	VIRAL
VIER	VILDE	VILLOSE	VINTAGERS	VIRANDA
VIERS	VILDLY	VILLOSITIES	VINTAGES	VIRANDAS
VIES	VILDNESS	VILLOSITY	VINTAGING	VIRANDO
VIEW	VILDNESSES	VILLOUS	VINTAGINGS	VIRANDOS
VIEWABLE	VILE	VILLS	VINTED	VIRE
VIEWDATA	VILELY	VILLUS	VINTING	VIRED
VIEWDATAS	VILENESS	VIM	VINTNER	VIRELAY
VIEWED	VILENESSES	VIMANA	VINTNERS	VIRELAYS
VIEWER	VILER	VIMANAS	VINTRIES	VIREMENT
VIEWERS	VILEST	VIMINEOUS	VINTRY	VIREMENTS
VIEWIER	VILIACO	VIMS	VINTS	VIRENT
VIEWIEST	VILIACOES	VIN	VINY	VIREO
VIEWINESS	VILIACOS	VINA	VINYL	VIREOS
VIEWINESSES	VILIAGO	VINACEOUS	VINYLS	VIRES
VIEWING	VILIAGOES	VINAL	VIOL	VIRESCENT
VIEWINGS	VILIAGOS	VINAS	VIOLA	VIRETOT
VIEWLESS	VILIFIED	VINASSE	VIOLABLE	VIRETOTS
VIEWLY	VILIFIER	VINASSES	VIOLABLY	VIRGA
VIEWPHONE	VILIFIERS	VINCA	VIOLAS	VIRGAS
VIEWPHONES	VILIFIES	VINCAS	VIOLATE	VIRGATE
VIEWPOINT	VILIFY	VINCIBLE	VIOLATED	VIRGATES
VIEWPOINTS	VILIFYING	VINCULA	VIOLATER	VIRGE
VIEWS	VILIPEND	VINCULUM	VIOLATERS	VIRGER
VIEWY	VILIPENDED	VINDALOO	VIOLATES	VIRGERS

VIRGES	VIRUCIDAL	VISION	VISUALIZING	VITRAIL
VIRGIN	VIRUCIDE	VISIONAL	VISUALLY	VITRAIN
VIRGINAL	VIRUCIDES	VISIONARIES	VISUALS	VITRAINS
VIRGINALLED	VIRULENCE	VISIONARY	VITA	VITRAUX
VIRGINALLING	VIRULENCES	VISIONED	VITAE	VITREOUS
VIRGINALS	VIRULENCIES	VISIONER	VITAL	VITREUM
VIRGINED	VIRULENCY	VISIONERS	VITALISE	VITREUMS
VIRGINING	VIRULENT	VISIONING	VITALISED	VITRIC
VIRGINITIES	VIRUS	VISIONINGS	VITALISER	VITRICS
VIRGINITY	VIRUSES	VISIONIST	VITALISERS	VITRIFIED
VIRGINIUM	VIS	VISIONISTS	VITALISES	VITRIFIES
VIRGINIUMS	VISA	VISIONS	VITALISING	VITRIFORM
VIRGINLY	VISAED	VISIT	VITALISM	VITRIFY
VIRGINS	VISAGE	VISITABLE	VITALISMS	VITRIFYING
VIRGULATE	VISAGED	VISITANT	VITALIST	VITRINE
VIRGULE	VISAGES	VISITANTS	VITALISTS	VITRINES
VIRGULES	VISAGIST	VISITATOR	VITALITIES	VITRIOL
VIRICIDAL	VISAGISTE	VISITATORS	VITALITY	VITRIOLIC
VIRICIDE	VISAGISTES	VISITE	VITALIZE	VITRIOLS
VIRICIDES	VISAGISTS	VISITED	VITALIZED	VITTA
VIRID	VISAING	VISITEE	VITALIZER	VITTAE
VIRIDIAN	VISAS	VISITEES	VITALIZERS	VITTATE
VIRIDIANS	VISCACHA	VISITER	VITALIZES	VITTLE
VIRIDITE	VISCACHAS	VISITERS	VITALIZING	VITTLES
VIRIDITES	VISCERA	VISITES	VITALLY	VITULAR
VIRIDITIES	VISCERAL	VISITING	VITALS	VITULINE
VIRIDITY	VISCERATE	VISITINGS	VITAMIN	VIVA
VIRILE	VISCERATED	VISITOR	VITAMINE	VIVACE
VIRILISED	VISCERATES	VISITORS	VITAMINES	VIVACIOUS
VIRILISM	VISCERATING	VISITRESS	VITAMINS	VIVACITIES
VIRILISMS	VISCID	VISITRESSES	VITAS	VIVACITY
VIRILITIES	VISCIDITIES	VISITS	VITASCOPE	VIVAED
VIRILITY	VISCIDITY	VISIVE	VITASCOPES	VIVAING
VIRILIZED	VISCIN	VISNE	VITATIVE	VIVAMENTE
VIRING	VISCINS	VISNES	VITE	VIVANDIER
VIRINO	VISCOSE	VISNOMIE	VITELLARY	VIVANDIERS
VIRINOS	VISCOSES	VISNOMIES	VITELLI	VIVARIA
VIRION	VISCOSITIES	VISNOMY	VITELLIN	VIVARIES
VIRIONS	VISCOSITY	VISON	VITELLINE	VIVARIUM
VIRL	VISCOUNT	VISONS	VITELLINES	VIVARIUMS
VIRLS	VISCOUNTIES	VISOR	VITELLINS	VIVARY
VIROGENE	VISCOUNTS	VISORED	VITELLUS	VIVAS
VIROGENES	VISCOUNTY	VISORING	VITEX	VIVAT
VIROID	VISCOUS	VISORS	VITEXES	VIVATS
VIROIDS	VISCUM	VISTA	VITIABLE	VIVDA
VIROLOGIES	VISCUMS	VISTAED	VITIATE	VIVDAS
VIROLOGY	VISCUS	VISTAING	VITIATED	VIVE
VIROSE	VISE	VISTAL	VITIATES	VIVELY
VIROSES	VISED	VISTALESS	VITIATING	VIVENCIES
VIROSIS	VISEED	VISTAS	VITIATION	VIVENCY
VIROUS	VISEING	VISTO	VITIATIONS	VIVER
VIRTU	VISES	VISTOS	VITIATOR	VIVERRA
VIRTUAL	VISIBLE	VISUAL	VITIATORS	VIVERRAS
VIRTUALLY	VISIBLES	VISUALISE	VITICETA	VIVERRINE
VIRTUE	VISIBLY	VISUALISED	VITICETUM	VIVERS
VIRTUES	VISIE	VISUALISES	VITICETUMS	VIVES
VIRTUOSA	VISIED	VISUALISING	VITICIDE	VIVIANITE
VIRTUOSE	VISIEING	VISUALIST	VITICIDES	VIVIANITES
VIRTUOSI	VISIER	VISUALISTS	VITILIGO	VIVID
VIRTUOSIC	VISIERS	VISUALITIES	VITILIGOS	VIVIDER
VIRTUOSO	VISIES	VISUALITY	VITIOSITIES	VIVIDEST
VIRTUOSOS	VISILE	VISUALIZE	VITIOSITY	VIVIDITIES
VIRTUOUS	VISILES	VISUALIZED	VITRAGE	VIVIDITY
VIRTUS	VISING	VISUALIZES	VITRAGES	VIVIDLY

VIVIDNESS	VOCABS	VOICER	VOLERIES	VOLUMISES
VIVIDNESSES	VOCABULAR	VOICERS	VOLERY	VOLUMISING
VIVIFIC	VOCAL	VOICES	VOLES	VOLUMIST
VIVIFIED	VOCALESE	VOICING	VOLET	VOLUMISTS
VIVIFIER	VOCALESES	VOICINGS	VOLETS	VOLUMIZE
VIVIFIERS	VOCALIC	VOID	VOLING	VOLUMIZED
VIVIFIES	VOCALION	VOIDABLE	VOLITANT	VOLUMIZES
VIVIFY	VOCALIONS	VOIDANCE	VOLITATE	VOLUMIZING
VIVIFYING	VOCALISE	VOIDANCES	VOLITATED	VOLUNTARIES
VIVIPARIES	VOCALISED	VOIDED	VOLITATES	VOLUNTARY
VIVIPARY	VOCALISER	VOIDEE	VOLITATING	VOLUNTEER
VIVISECT	VOCALISERS	VOIDEES	VOLITIENT	VOLUNTEERED
VIVISECTED	VOCALISES	VOIDER	VOLITION	VOLUNTEERING
VIVISECTING	VOCALISING	VOIDERS	VOLITIONS	VOLUNTEERS
VIVISECTS	VOCALISM	VOIDING	VOLITIVE	VOLUSPA
VIVO	VOCALISMS	VOIDINGS	VOLITIVES	VOLUSPAS
VIVRES	VOCALIST	VOIDNESS	VOLK	VOLUTE
VIXEN	VOCALISTS	VOIDNESSES	VOLKS	VOLUTED
VIXENISH	VOCALITIES	VOIDS	VOLKSRAAD	VOLUTES
VIXENLY	VOCALITY	VOILA	VOLKSRAADS	VOLUTIN
VIXENS	VOCALIZE	VOILE	VOLLEY	VOLUTINS
VIZAMENT	VOCALIZED	VOILES	VOLLEYED	VOLUTION
VIZAMENTS	VOCALIZER	VOISINAGE	VOLLEYER	VOLUTIONS
VIZARD	VOCALIZERS	VOISINAGES	VOLLEYERS	VOLUTOID
VIZARDED	VOCALIZES	VOITURE	VOLLEYING	VOLVA
VIZARDING	VOCALIZING	VOITURES	VOLLEYS	VOLVAS
VIZARDS	VOCALLY	VOITURIER	VOLOST	VOLVATE
VIZCACHA	VOCALNESS	VOITURIERS	VOLOSTS	VOLVE
VIZCACHAS	VOCALNESSES	VOIVODE	VOLPINO	VOLVED
VIZIED	VOCALS	VOIVODES	VOLPINOS	VOLVES
VIZIER	VOCATION	VOL	VOLPLANE	VOLVING
VIZIERATE	VOCATIONS	VOLA	VOLPLANED	VOLVOX
VIZIERATES	VOCATIVE	VOLABLE	VOLPLANES	VOLVOXES
VIZIERIAL	VOCATIVES	VOLAE	VOLPLANING	VOLVULI
VIZIERS	VOCES	VOLAGE	VOLS	VOLVULUS
VIZIES	VOCODER	VOLAGEOUS	VOLT	VOLVULUSES
VIZIR	VOCODERS	VOLANT	VOLTA	VOMER
VIZIRATE	VOCULAR	VOLANTE	VOLTAGE	VOMERINE
VIZIRATES	VOCULE	VOLANTES	VOLTAGES	VOMERS
VIZIRIAL	VOCULES	VOLAR	VOLTAIC	VOMICA
VIZIRS	VODKA	VOLARIES	VOLTAISM	VOMICAE
VIZIRSHIP	VODKAS	VOLARY	VOLTAISMS	VOMICAS
VIZIRSHIPS	VOE	VOLATIC	VOLTE	VOMIT
VIZOR	VOES	VOLATILE	VOLTES	VOMITED
VIZORED	VOGIE	VOLATILES	VOLTIGEUR	VOMITING
VIZORING	VOGIER	VOLCANIAN	VOLTIGEURS	VOMITINGS
VIZORS	VOGIEST	VOLCANIC	VOLTINISM	VOMITIVE
VIZSLA	VOGUE	VOLCANISE	VOLTINISMS	VOMITIVES
VIZSLAS	VOGUED	VOLCANISED	VOLTMETER	VOMITO
VIZY	VOGUEING	VOLCANISES	VOLTMETERS	VOMITORIA
VIZYING	VOGUEINGS	VOLCANISING	VOLTS	VOMITORIES
VIZZIE	VOGUER	VOLCANISM	VOLUBIL	VOMITORY
VIZZIED	VOGUERS	VOLCANISMS	VOLUBLE	VOMITOS
VIZZIEING	VOGUES	VOLCANIST	VOLUBLY	VOMITS
VIZZIES	VOGUEY	VOLCANISTS	VOLUCRINE	VOMITUS
VLEI	VOGUIER	VOLCANIZE	VOLUME	VOMITUSES
VLEIS	VOGUIEST	VOLCANIZED	VOLUMED	VOODOO
VLIES	VOGUING	VOLCANIZES	VOLUMES	VOODOOED
VLY	VOGUINGS	VOLCANIZING	VOLUMETER	VOODOOING
VOAR	VOGUISH	VOLCANO	VOLUMETERS	VOODOOISM
VOARS	VOICE	VOLCANOES	VOLUMINAL	VOODOOISMS
VOCAB	VOICED	VOLE	VOLUMING	VOODOOIST
VOCABLE	VOICEFUL	VOLED	VOLUMISE	VOODOOISTS
VOCABLES	VOICELESS	VOLENS	VOLUMISED	VOODOOS

VOR	VOUCHER	VOWESS	VULCANIC	VULNERATE
VORACIOUS	VOUCHERS	VOWESSES	VULCANISE	VULNERATED
VORACITIES	VOUCHES	VOWING	VULCANISED	VULNERATES
VORACITY	VOUCHING	VOWS	VULCANISES	VULNERATING
VORAGO	VOUCHSAFE	VOX	VULCANISING	VULNING
VORAGOES	VOUCHSAFED	VOXEL	VULCANISM	VULNS
VORANT	VOUCHSAFES	VOXELS	VULCANISMS	VULPICIDE
VORPAL	VOUCHSAFING	VOYAGE	VULCANIST	VULPICIDES
VORRED	VOUCHSAFINGS	VOYAGED	VULCANISTS	VULPINE
VORRING	VOUDOU	VOYAGER	VULCANITE	VULPINISM
VORS	VOUDOUED	VOYAGERS	VULCANITES	VULPINISMS
VORTEX	VOUDOUING	VOYAGES	VULCANIZE	VULPINITE
VORTEXES	VOUDOUS	VOYAGEUR	VULCANIZED	VULPINITES
VORTICAL	VOUGE	VOYAGEURS	VULCANIZES	VULSELLA
VORTICES	VOUGES	VOYAGING	VULCANIZING	VULSELLAE
VORTICISM	VOULGE	VOYEUR	VULCANS	VULSELLUM
VORTICISMS	VOULGES	VOYEURISM	VULGAR	VULTURE
VORTICIST	VOULU	VOYEURISMS	VULGARER	VULTURES
VORTICISTS	VOUSSOIR	VOYEURS	VULGAREST	VULTURINE
VORTICITIES	VOUSSOIRED	VOZHD	VULGARIAN	VULTURISH
VORTICITY	VOUSSOIRING	VOZHDS	VULGARIANS	VULTURISM
VORTICOSE	VOUSSOIRS	VRAIC	VULGARISE	VULTURISMS
VOTARESS	VOUTSAFE	VRAICKER	VULGARISED	VULTURN
VOTARESSES	VOUTSAFED	VRAICKERS	VULGARISES	VULTURNS
VOTARIES	VOUTSAFES	VRAICKING	VULGARISING	VULTUROUS
VOTARIST	VOUTSAFING	VRAICKINGS	VULGARISM	VULVA
VOTARISTS	VOW	VRAICS	VULGARISMS	VULVAE
VOTARY	VOWED	VRIL	VULGARITIES	VULVAL
VOTE	VOWEL	VRILS	VULGARITY	VULVAR
VOTED	VOWELISE	VROOM	VULGARIZE	VULVAS
VOTEEN	VOWELISED	VROOMED	VULGARIZED	VULVATE
VOTEENS	VOWELISES	VROOMING	VULGARIZES	VULVIFORM
VOTELESS	VOWELISING	VROOMS	VULGARIZING	VULVITIS
VOTER	VOWELIZE	VROUW	VULGARLY	VULVITISES
VOTERS	VOWELIZED	VROUWS	VULGARS	VUM
VOTES	VOWELIZES	VROW	VULGATE	VUMMED
VOTING	VOWELIZING	VROWS	VULGATES	VUMMING
VOTIVE	VOWELLED	VUG	VULGO	VUMS
VOTRESS	VOWELLESS	VUGGIER	VULGUS	VYING
VOTRESSES	VOWELLING	VUGGIEST	VULGUSES	VYINGLY
VOUCH	VOWELLY	VUGGY	VULN	
VOUCHED	VOWELS	VUGS	VULNED	
VOUCHEE	VOWER	VULCAN	VULNERARIES	
VOUCHEES	VOWERS	VULCANIAN	VULNERARY	

W

WABAIN	WADMAL	WAFTURES	WAGTAILS	WAITER
WABAINS	WADMALS	WAG	WAHINE	WAITERAGE
WABBIT	WADMOL	WAGE	WAHINES	WAITERAGES
WABBLE	WADMOLL	WAGED	WAHOO	WAITERING
WABBLED	WADMOLLS	WAGELESS	WAHOOS	WAITERINGS
WABBLER	WADMOLS	WAGENBOOM	WAID	WAITERS
WABBLERS	WADS	WAGENBOOMS	WAIDE	WAITES
WABBLES	WADSET	WAGER	WAIF	WAITING
WABBLING	WADSETS	WAGERED	WAIFED	WAITINGLY
WABOOM	WADSETT	WAGERER	WAIFING	WAITINGS
WABOOMS	WADSETTED	WAGERERS	WAIFS	WAITRESS
WABSTER	WADSETTER	WAGERING	WAIFT	WAITRESSES
WABSTERS	WADSETTERS	WAGERS	WAIFTS	WAITS
WACK	WADSETTING	WAGES	WAIL	WAIVE
WACKE	WADSETTS	WAGGED	WAILED	WAIVED
WACKER	WADT	WAGGERIES	WAILER	WAIVER
WACKERS	WADTS	WAGGERY	WAILERS	WAIVERS
WACKES	WADY	WAGGING	WAILFUL	WAIVES
WACKIER	WAE	WAGGISH	WAILING	WAIVING
WACKIEST	WAEFUL	WAGGISHLY	WAILINGLY	WAIVODE
WACKINESS	WAENESS	WAGGLE	WAILINGS	WAIVODES
WACKINESSES	WAENESSES	WAGGLED	WAILS	WAIWODE
WACKO	WAES	WAGGLES	WAIN	WAIWODES
WACKS	WAESOME	WAGGLIER	WAINAGE	WAKA
WACKY	WAESUCKS	WAGGLIEST	WAINAGES	WAKANE
WAD	WAFER	WAGGLING	WAINED	WAKANES
WADD	WAFERED	WAGGLY	WAINING	WAKAS
WADDED	WAFERING	WAGGON	WAINS	WAKE
WADDIE	WAFERS	WAGGONED	WAINSCOT	WAKED
WADDIED	WAFERY	WAGGONER	WAINSCOTED	WAKEFUL
WADDIES	WAFF	WAGGONERS	WAINSCOTING	WAKEFULLY
WADDING	WAFFED	WAGGONING	WAINSCOTINGS	WAKELESS
WADDINGS	WAFFING	WAGGONS	WAINSCOTS	WAKEMAN
WADDLE	WAFFLE	WAGHALTER	WAINSCOTTED	WAKEMEN
WADDLED	WAFFLED	WAGHALTERS	WAINSCOTTING	WAKEN
WADDLER	WAFFLER	WAGING	WAINSCOTTINGS	WAKENED
WADDLERS	WAFFLERS	WAGMOIRE	WAIST	WAKENER
WADDLES	WAFFLES	WAGMOIRES	WAISTBAND	WAKENERS
WADDLING	WAFFLIER	WAGON	WAISTBANDS	WAKENING
WADDS	WAFFLIEST	WAGONAGE	WAISTBELT	WAKENINGS
WADDY	WAFFLING	WAGONAGES	WAISTBELTS	WAKENS
WADDYING	WAFFLINGS	WAGONED	WAISTBOAT	WAKER
WADE	WAFFLY	WAGONER	WAISTBOATS	WAKERIFE
WADED	WAFFS	WAGONERS	WAISTCOAT	WAKERS
WADER	WAFT	WAGONETTE	WAISTCOATS	WAKES
WADERS	WAFTAGE	WAGONETTES	WAISTED	WAKF
WADES	WAFTAGES	WAGONFUL	WAISTER	WAKFS
WADI	WAFTED	WAGONFULS	WAISTERS	WAKIKI
WADIES	WAFTER	WAGONING	WAISTLINE	WAKIKIS
WADING	WAFTERS	WAGONLOAD	WAISTLINES	WAKING
WADINGS	WAFTING	WAGONLOADS	WAISTS	WAKINGS
WADIS	WAFTINGS	WAGONS	WAIT	WALD
WADMAAL	WAFTS	WAGS	WAITE	WALDFLUTE
WADMAALS	WAFTURE	WAGTAIL	WAITED	WALDFLUTES

The Chambers Dictionary is the authority for many longer words; see *OSW* Introduction, page xii

WALDGRAVE	WALLOP	WAMPUS	WANNER	WARATAHS
WALDGRAVES	WALLOPED	WAMPUSES	WANNESS	WARBIER
WALDHORN	WALLOPER	WAMUS	WANNESSES	WARBIEST
WALDHORNS	WALLOPERS	WAMUSES	WANNEST	WARBLE
WALDRAPP	WALLOPING	WAN	WANNING	WARBLED
WALDRAPPS	WALLOPINGS	WANCHANCY	WANNISH	WARBLER
WALDS	WALLOPS	WAND	WANS	WARBLERS
WALE	WALLOW	WANDER	WANT	WARBLES
WALED	WALLOWED	WANDERED	WANTAGE	WARBLING
WALER	WALLOWER	WANDERER	WANTAGES	WARBLINGS
WALERS	WALLOWERS	WANDERERS	WANTED	WARBY
WALES	WALLOWING	WANDERING	WANTER	WARD
WALI	WALLOWINGS	WANDERINGS	WANTERS	WARDCORN
WALIER	WALLOWS	WANDEROO	WANTHILL	WARDCORNS
WALIES	WALLPAPER	WANDEROOS	WANTHILLS	WARDED
WALIEST	WALLPAPERS	WANDERS	WANTIES	WARDEN
WALING	WALLS	WANDLE	WANTING	WARDENED
WALIS	WALLSEND	WANDOO	WANTINGS	WARDENING
WALISE	WALLSENDS	WANDOOS	WANTON	WARDENRIES
WALISES	WALLWORT	WANDS	WANTONED	WARDENRY
WALK	WALLWORTS	WANE	WANTONER	WARDENS
WALKABLE	WALLY	WANED	WANTONEST	WARDER
WALKABOUT	WALLYDRAG	WANES	WANTONING	WARDERED
WALKABOUTS	WALLYDRAGS	WANEY	WANTONISE	WARDERING
WALKATHON	WALNUT	WANG	WANTONISED	WARDERS
WALKATHONS	WALNUTS	WANGAN	WANTONISES	WARDING
WALKED	WALRUS	WANGANS	WANTONISING	WARDINGS
WALKER	WALRUSES	WANGLE	WANTONIZE	WARDMOTE
WALKERS	WALTIER	WANGLED	WANTONIZED	WARDMOTES
WALKING	WALTIEST	WANGLER	WANTONIZES	WARDOG
WALKINGS	WALTY	WANGLERS	WANTONIZING	WARDOGS
WALKMILL	WALTZ	WANGLES	WANTONLY	WARDRESS
WALKMILLS	WALTZED	WANGLING	WANTONS	WARDRESSES
WALKS	WALTZER	WANGLINGS	WANTS	WARDROBE
WALKWAY	WALTZERS	WANGS	WANTY	WARDROBER
WALKWAYS	WALTZES	WANGUN	WANWORDY	WARDROBERS
WALL	WALTZING	WANGUNS	WANWORTH	WARDROBES
WALLA	WALTZINGS	WANHOPE	WANWORTHS	WARDROOM
WALLABA	WALY	WANHOPES	WANY	WARDROOMS
WALLABAS	WAMBENGER	WANIER	WANZE	WARDROP
WALLABIES	WAMBENGERS	WANIEST	WANZED	WARDROPS
WALLABY	WAMBLE	WANIGAN	WANZES	WARDS
WALLAH	WAMBLED	WANIGANS	WANZING	WARDSHIP
WALLAHS	WAMBLES	WANING	WAP	WARDSHIPS
WALLAROO	WAMBLIER	WANINGS	WAPENSHAW	WARE
WALLAROOS	WAMBLIEST	WANK	WAPENSHAWS	WARED
WALLAS	WAMBLING	WANKED	WAPENTAKE	WAREHOUSE
WALLBOARD	WAMBLINGS	WANKER	WAPENTAKES	WAREHOUSED
WALLBOARDS	WAMBLY	WANKERS	WAPINSHAW	WAREHOUSES
WALLCHART	WAME	WANKIER	WAPINSHAWS	WAREHOUSING
WALLCHARTS	WAMED	WANKIEST	WAPITI	WAREHOUSINGS
WALLED	WAMEFUL	WANKING	WAPITIS	WARELESS
WALLER	WAMEFULS	WANKLE	WAPPED	WARES
WALLERS	WAMES	WANKS	WAPPEND	WARFARE
WALLET	WAMMUS	WANKY	WAPPER	WARFARED
WALLETS	WAMMUSES	WANLE	WAPPERED	WARFARER
WALLFISH	WAMPEE	WANLY	WAPPERING	WARFARERS
WALLFISHES	WAMPEES	WANNA	WAPPERS	WARFARES
WALLIE	WAMPISH	WANNABE	WAPPING	WARFARIN
WALLIER	WAMPISHED	WANNABEE	WAPS	WARFARING
WALLIES	WAMPISHES	WANNABEES	WAQF	WARFARINGS
WALLIEST	WAMPISHING	WANNABES	WAQFS	WARFARINS
WALLING	WAMPUM	WANNED	WAR	WARHABLE
WALLINGS	WAMPUMS	WANNEL	WARATAH	WARHEAD

WARHEADS	WARPS	WARTIMES	WASHWIPE	WAT
WARHORSE	WARRAGAL	WARTLESS	WASHWIPES	WATAP
WARHORSES	WARRAGALS	WARTLIKE	WASHY	WATAPS
WARIBASHI	WARRAGLE	WARTS	WASM	WATCH
WARIBASHIS	WARRAGLES	WARTWEED	WASMS	WATCHABLE
WARIER	WARRAGUL	WARTWEEDS	WASP	WATCHBOX
WARIEST	WARRAGULS	WARTWORT	WASPIE	WATCHBOXES
WARILY	WARRAN	WARTWORTS	WASPIER	WATCHCASE
WARIMENT	WARRAND	WARTY	WASPIES	WATCHCASES
WARIMENTS	WARRANDED	WARWOLF	WASPIEST	WATCHDOG
WARINESS	WARRANDING	WARWOLVES	WASPISH	WATCHDOGS
WARINESSES	WARRANDS	WARY	WASPISHLY	WATCHED
WARING	WARRANED	WAS	WASPNEST	WATCHER
WARISON	WARRANING	WASE	WASPNESTS	WATCHERS
WARISONS	WARRANS	WASEGOOSE	WASPS	WATCHES
WARK	WARRANT	WASEGOOSES	WASPY	WATCHET
WARKS	WARRANTED	WASES	WASSAIL	WATCHETS
WARLIKE	WARRANTEE	WASH	WASSAILED	WATCHFUL
WARLING	WARRANTEES	WASHABLE	WASSAILER	WATCHING
WARLINGS	WARRANTER	WASHBALL	WASSAILERS	WATCHMAN
WARLOCK	WARRANTERS	WASHBALLS	WASSAILING	WATCHMEN
WARLOCKRIES	WARRANTIES	WASHBASIN	WASSAILINGS	WATCHWORD
WARLOCKRY	WARRANTING	WASHBASINS	WASSAILRIES	WATCHWORDS
WARLOCKS	WARRANTINGS	WASHBOARD	WASSAILRY	WATE
WARLORD	WARRANTOR	WASHBOARDS	WASSAILS	WATER
WARLORDS	WARRANTORS	WASHBOWL	WASSERMAN	WATERAGE
WARM	WARRANTS	WASHBOWLS	WASSERMEN	WATERAGES
WARMAN	WARRANTY	WASHCLOTH	WAST	WATERED
WARMBLOOD	WARRAY	WASHCLOTHS	WASTABLE	WATERER
WARMBLOODS	WARRAYED	WASHDAY	WASTAGE	WATERERS
WARMED	WARRAYING	WASHDAYS	WASTAGES	WATERFALL
WARMEN	WARRAYS	WASHED	WASTE	WATERFALLS
WARMER	WARRE	WASHEN	WASTED	WATERFOWL
WARMERS	WARRED	WASHER	WASTEFUL	WATERFOWLS
WARMEST	WARREN	WASHERED	WASTEL	WATERHEN
WARMING	WARRENER	WASHERIES	WASTELAND	WATERHENS
WARMINGS	WARRENERS	WASHERING	WASTELANDS	WATERIER
WARMISH	WARRENS	WASHERMAN	WASTELOT	WATERIEST
WARMLY	WARREY	WASHERMEN	WASTELOTS	WATERING
WARMNESS	WARREYED	WASHERS	WASTELS	WATERINGS
WARMNESSES	WARREYING	WASHERY	WASTENESS	WATERISH
WARMONGER	WARREYS	WASHES	WASTENESSES	WATERLESS
WARMONGERS	WARRIGAL	WASHHOUSE	WASTER	WATERLILIES
WARMS	WARRIGALS	WASHHOUSES	WASTERED	WATERLILY
WARMTH	WARRING	WASHIER	WASTERFUL	WATERLINE
WARMTHS	WARRIOR	WASHIEST	WASTERIES	WATERLINES
WARN	WARRIORS	WASHINESS	WASTERIFE	WATERLOG
WARNED	WARRISON	WASHINESSES	WASTERIFES	WATERLOGGED
WARNER	WARRISONS	WASHING	WASTERING	WATERLOGGING
WARNERS	WARS	WASHINGS	WASTERS	WATERLOGS
WARNING	WARSHIP	WASHLAND	WASTERY	WATERMAN
WARNINGLY	WARSHIPS	WASHLANDS	WASTES	WATERMARK
WARNINGS	WARSLE	WASHOUT	WASTFULL	WATERMARKED
WARNS	WARSLED	WASHOUTS	WASTING	WATERMARKING
WARP	WARSLES	WASHPOT	WASTINGS	WATERMARKS
WARPATH	WARSLING	WASHPOTS	WASTNESS	WATERMEN
WARPATHS	WARST	WASHRAG	WASTNESSES	WATERPOX
WARPED	WART	WASHRAGS	WASTREL	WATERPOXES
WARPER	WARTED	WASHROOM	WASTRELS	WATERS
WARPERS	WARTHOG	WASHROOMS	WASTRIES	WATERSHED
WARPING	WARTHOGS	WASHSTAND	WASTRIFE	WATERSHEDS
WARPINGS	WARTIER	WASHSTANDS	WASTRIFES	WATERSIDE
WARPLANE	WARTIEST	WASHTUB	WASTRY	WATERSIDES
WARPLANES	WARTIME	WASHTUBS	WASTS	WATERWAY

The Chambers Dictionary is the authority for many longer words; see *OSW* Introduction, page xii

WATERWAYS	WAVEBAND	WAXES	WAYZGOOSES	WEARINESSES
WATERWEED	WAVEBANDS	WAXIER	WAZIR	WEARING
WATERWEEDS	WAVED	WAXIEST	WAZIRS	WEARINGLY
WATERWORK	WAVEFORM	WAXILY	WE	WEARINGS
WATERWORKS	WAVEFORMS	WAXINESS	WEAK	WEARISH
WATERY	WAVEFRONT	WAXINESSES	WEAKEN	WEARISOME
WATS	WAVEFRONTS	WAXING	WEAKENED	WEARS
WATT	WAVEGUIDE	WAXINGS	WEAKENER	WEARY
WATTAGE	WAVEGUIDES	WAXWING	WEAKENERS	WEARYING
WATTAGES	WAVELESS	WAXWINGS	WEAKENING	WEASAND
WATTER	WAVELET	WAXWORK	WEAKENS	WEASANDS
WATTEST	WAVELETS	WAXWORKER	WEAKER	WEASEL
WATTLE	WAVELIKE	WAXWORKERS	WEAKEST	WEASELED
WATTLED	WAVELLITE	WAXWORKS	WEAKFISH	WEASELER
WATTLES	WAVELLITES	WAXY	WEAKFISHES	WEASELERS
WATTLING	WAVEMETER	WAY	WEAKLIER	WEASELING
WATTLINGS	WAVEMETERS	WAYBILL	WEAKLIEST	WEASELLED
WATTMETER	WAVER	WAYBILLS	WEAKLING	WEASELLER
WATTMETERS	WAVERED	WAYBOARD	WEAKLINGS	WEASELLERS
WATTS	WAVERER	WAYBOARDS	WEAKLY	WEASELLING
WAUCHT	WAVERERS	WAYBREAD	WEAKNESS	WEASELLY
WAUCHTED	WAVERIER	WAYBREADS	WEAKNESSES	WEASELS
WAUCHTING	WAVERIEST	WAYED	WEAL	WEATHER
WAUCHTS	WAVERING	WAYFARE	WEALD	WEATHERED
WAUFF	WAVERINGS	WAYFARED	WEALDS	WEATHERING
WAUFFED	WAVEROUS	WAYFARER	WEALS	WEATHERINGS
WAUFFING	WAVERS	WAYFARERS	WEALSMAN	WEATHERLY
WAUFFS	WAVERY	WAYFARES	WEALSMEN	WEATHERS
WAUGH	WAVES	WAYFARING	WEALTH	WEAVE
WAUGHED	WAVESHAPE	WAYFARINGS	WEALTHIER	WEAVED
WAUGHING	WAVESHAPES	WAYGONE	WEALTHIEST	WEAVER
WAUGHS	WAVESON	WAYGOOSE	WEALTHILY	WEAVERS
WAUGHT	WAVESONS	WAYGOOSES	WEALTHS	WEAVES
WAUGHTED	WAVEY	WAYING	WEALTHY	WEAVING
WAUGHTING	WAVEYS	WAYLAID	WEAMB	WEAVINGS
WAUGHTS	WAVIER	WAYLAY	WEAMBS	WEAZAND
WAUK	WAVIES	WAYLAYER	WEAN	WEAZANDS
WAUKED	WAVIEST	WAYLAYERS	WEANED	WEAZEN
WAUKER	WAVILY	WAYLAYING	WEANEL	WEAZENED
WAUKERS	WAVINESS	WAYLAYS	WEANELS	WEAZENING
WAUKING	WAVINESSES	WAYLEAVE	WEANER	WEAZENS
WAUKMILL	WAVING	WAYLEAVES	WEANERS	WEB
WAUKMILLS	WAVINGS	WAYLESS	WEANING	WEBBED
WAUKRIFE	WAVY	WAYMARK	WEANLING	WEBBIER
WAUKS	WAW	WAYMARKED	WEANLINGS	WEBBIEST
WAUL	WAWE	WAYMARKING	WEANS	WEBBING
WAULED	WAWES	WAYMARKS	WEAPON	WEBBINGS
WAULING	WAWL	WAYMENT	WEAPONED	WEBBY
WAULINGS	WAWLED	WAYMENTED	WEAPONRIES	WEBER
WAULK	WAWLING	WAYMENTING	WEAPONRY	WEBERS
WAULKED	WAWLINGS	WAYMENTS	WEAPONS	WEBFEET
WAULKER	WAWLS	WAYPOST	WEAR	WEBFOOT
WAULKERS	WAWS	WAYPOSTS	WEARABLE	WEBFOOTED
WAULKING	WAX	WAYS	WEARED	WEBS
WAULKMILL	WAXBERRIES	WAYSIDE	WEARER	WEBSITE
WAULKMILLS	WAXBERRY	WAYSIDES	WEARERS	WEBSITES
WAULKS	WAXBILL	WAYWARD	WEARIED	WEBSTER
WAULS	WAXBILLS	WAYWARDLY	WEARIER	WEBSTERS
WAUR	WAXCLOTH	WAYWISER	WEARIES	WEBWHEEL
WAURED	WAXCLOTHS	WAYWISERS	WEARIEST	WEBWHEELS
WAURING	WAXED	WAYWODE	WEARIFUL	WEBWORM
WAURS	WAXEN	WAYWODES	WEARILESS	WEBWORMS
WAURST	WAXER	WAYWORN	WEARILY	WECHT
WAVE	WAXERS	WAYZGOOSE	WEARINESS	WECHTS

The Chambers Dictionary is the authority for many longer words; see *OSW* Introduction, page xii

WED	WEEM	WEIGHING	WELDMESH®	WEND
WEDDED	WEEMS	WEIGHINGS	WELDMESHES	WENDED
WEDDER	WEEN	WEIGHS	WELDOR	WENDIGO
WEDDERED	WEENED	WEIGHT	WELDORS	WENDIGOS
WEDDERING	WEENIER	WEIGHTED	WELDS	WENDING
WEDDERS	WEENIES	WEIGHTIER	WELFARE	WENDS
WEDDING	WEENIEST	WEIGHTIEST	WELFARES	WENNIER
WEDDINGS	WEENING	WEIGHTILY	WELFARISM	WENNIEST
WEDELN	WEENS	WEIGHTING	WELFARISMS	WENNISH
WEDELNED	WEENY	WEIGHTINGS	WELFARIST	WENNY
WEDELNING	WEEP	WEIGHTS	WELFARISTS	WENS
WEDELNS	WEEPER	WEIGHTY	WELK	WENT
WEDGE	WEEPERS	WEIL	WELKE	WENTS
WEDGED	WEEPHOLE	WEILS	WELKED	WEPT
WEDGES	WEEPHOLES	WEIR	WELKES	WERE
WEDGEWISE	WEEPIE	WEIRD	WELKIN	WEREGILD
WEDGIE	WEEPIER	WEIRDED	WELKING	WEREGILDS
WEDGIER	WEEPIES	WEIRDER	WELKINS	WEREWOLF
WEDGIES	WEEPIEST	WEIRDEST	WELKS	WEREWOLVES
WEDGIEST	WEEPING	WEIRDIE	WELKT	WERGILD
WEDGING	WEEPINGLY	WEIRDIES	WELL	WERGILDS
WEDGINGS	WEEPINGS	WEIRDING	WELLADAY	WERNERITE
WEDGY	WEEPS	WEIRDLY	WELLANEAR	WERNERITES
WEDLOCK	WEEPY	WEIRDNESS	WELLAWAY	WERSH
WEDLOCKS	WEER	WEIRDNESSES	WELLBEING	WERSHER
WEDS	WEES	WEIRDO	WELLBEINGS	WERSHEST
WEE	WEEST	WEIRDOS	WELLED	WERT
WEED	WEET	WEIRDS	WELLHEAD	WERWOLF
WEEDED	WEETE	WEIRED	WELLHEADS	WERWOLVES
WEEDER	WEETED	WEIRING	WELLHOUSE	WESAND
WEEDERIES	WEETEN	WEIRS	WELLHOUSES	WESANDS
WEEDERS	WEETER	WEISE	WELLIE	WEST
WEEDERY	WEETEST	WEISED	WELLIES	WESTBOUND
WEEDICIDE	WEETING	WEISES	WELLING	WESTED
WEEDICIDES	WEETINGLY	WEISING	WELLINGS	WESTER
WEEDIER	WEETLESS	WEIZE	WELLNESS	WESTERED
WEEDIEST	WEETS	WEIZED	WELLNESSES	WESTERING
WEEDINESS	WEEVER	WEIZES	WELLS	WESTERINGS
WEEDINESSES	WEEVERS	WEIZING	WELLY	WESTERLIES
WEEDING	WEEVIL	WEKA	WELSH	WESTERLY
WEEDINGS	WEEVILED	WEKAS	WELSHED	WESTERN
WEEDLESS	WEEVILED	WELAWAY	WELSHER	WESTERNER
WEEDS	WEEVILLED	WELCH	WELSHERS	WESTERNERS
WEEDY	WEEVILLY	WELCHED	WELSHES	WESTERNS
WEEING	WEEVILS	WELCHER	WELSHING	WESTERS
WEEK	WEEVILY	WELCHERS	WELT	WESTING
WEEKDAY	WEFT	WELCHES	WELTED	WESTINGS
WEEKDAYS	WEFTAGE	WELCHING	WELTER	WESTLIN
WEEKE	WEFTAGES	WELCOME	WELTERED	WESTLINS
WEEKEND	WEFTE	WELCOMED	WELTERING	WESTMOST
WEEKENDED	WEFTED	WELCOMER	WELTERS	WESTS
WEEKENDER	WEFTES	WELCOMERS	WELTING	WESTWARD
WEEKENDERS	WEFTING	WELCOMES	WELTS	WESTWARDS
WEEKENDING	WEFTS	WELCOMING	WEM	WET
WEEKENDINGS	WEID	WELD	WEMB	WETA
WEEKENDS	WEIDS	WELDABLE	WEMBS	WETAS
WEEKES	WEIGELA	WELDED	WEMS	WETBACK
WEEKLIES	WEIGELAS	WELDER	WEN	WETBACKS
WEEKLY	WEIGH	WELDERS	WENCH	WETHER
WEEKNIGHT	WEIGHABLE	WELDING	WENCHED	WETHERS
WEEKNIGHTS	WEIGHAGE	WELDINGS	WENCHER	WETLAND
WEEKS	WEIGHAGES	WELDLESS	WENCHERS	WETLANDS
WEEL	WEIGHED	WELDMENT	WENCHES	WETLY
WEELS	WEIGHER	WELDMENTS	WENCHING	WETNESS

WETNESSES	WHAMMO	WHEE	WHELKED	WHEUGH
WETS	WHAMMOS	WHEECH	WHELKIER	WHEUGHED
WETTED	WHAMMY	WHEECHED	WHELKIEST	WHEUGHING
WETTER	WHAMPLE	WHEECHING	WHELKS	WHEUGHS
WETTEST	WHAMPLES	WHEECHS	WHELKY	WHEW
WETTING	WHAMS	WHEEDLE	WHELM	WHEWED
WETTISH	WHANG	WHEEDLED	WHELMED	WHEWING
WETWARE	WHANGAM	WHEEDLER	WHELMING	WHEWS
WETWARES	WHANGAMS	WHEEDLERS	WHELMS	WHEY
WEX	WHANGED	WHEEDLES	WHELP	WHEYEY
WEXE	WHANGEE	WHEEDLING	WHELPED	WHEYIER
WEXED	WHANGEES	WHEEDLINGS	WHELPING	WHEYIEST
WEXES	WHANGING	WHEEL	WHELPS	WHEYISH
WEXING	WHANGS	WHEELBASE	WHEMMLE	WHEYS
WEY	WHAP	WHEELBASES	WHEMMLED	WHICH
WEYARD	WHAPPED	WHEELED	WHEMMLES	WHICHEVER
WEYS	WHAPPING	WHEELER	WHEMMLING	WHICKER
WEYWARD	WHAPS	WHEELERS	WHEN	WHICKERED
WEZAND	WHARE	WHEELIE	WHENAS	WHICKERING
WEZANDS	WHARES	WHEELIER	WHENCE	WHICKERS
WHA	WHARF	WHEELIES	WHENCES	WHID
WHACK	WHARFAGE	WHEELIEST	WHENCEVER	WHIDAH
WHACKED	WHARFAGES	WHEELING	WHENEVER	WHIDAHS
WHACKER	WHARFED	WHEELINGS	WHENS	WHIDDED
WHACKERS	WHARFING	WHEELMAN	WHERE	WHIDDER
WHACKIER	WHARFINGS	WHEELMEN	WHEREAS	WHIDDERED
WHACKIEST	WHARFS	WHEELS	WHEREAT	WHIDDERING
WHACKING	WHARVE	WHEELWORK	WHEREBY	WHIDDERS
WHACKINGS	WHARVES	WHEELWORKS	WHEREFOR	WHIDDING
WHACKO	WHAT	WHEELY	WHEREFORE	WHIDS
WHACKOES	WHATEN	WHEEN	WHEREFORES	WHIFF
WHACKOS	WHATEVER	WHEENGE	WHEREFROM	WHIFFED
WHACKS	WHATNA	WHEENGED	WHEREIN	WHIFFER
WHACKY	WHATNESS	WHEENGES	WHEREINTO	WHIFFERS
WHAISLE	WHATNESSES	WHEENGING	WHERENESS	WHIFFET
WHAISLED	WHATNOT	WHEENS	WHERENESSES	WHIFFETS
WHAISLES	WHATNOTS	WHEEPLE	WHEREOF	WHIFFIER
WHAISLING	WHATS	WHEEPLED	WHEREON	WHIFFIEST
WHAIZLE	WHATSIS	WHEEPLES	WHEREOUT	WHIFFING
WHAIZLED	WHATSISES	WHEEPLING	WHERES	WHIFFINGS
WHAIZLES	WHATSIT	WHEESH	WHERESO	WHIFFLE
WHAIZLING	WHATSITS	WHEESHED	WHERETO	WHIFFLED
WHALE	WHATSO	WHEESHES	WHEREUNTO	WHIFFLER
WHALEBACK	WHATTEN	WHEESHING	WHEREUPON	WHIFFLERIES
WHALEBACKS	WHAUP	WHEESHT	WHEREVER	WHIFFLERS
WHALEBOAT	WHAUPS	WHEESHTED	WHEREWITH	WHIFFLERY
WHALEBOATS	WHAUR	WHEESHTING	WHEREWITHS	WHIFFLES
WHALEBONE	WHAURS	WHEESHTS	WHERRET	WHIFFLING
WHALEBONES	WHEAL	WHEEZE	WHERRETED	WHIFFLINGS
WHALED	WHEALS	WHEEZED	WHERRETING	WHIFFS
WHALEMAN	WHEAR	WHEEZES	WHERRETS	WHIFFY
WHALEMEN	WHEARE	WHEEZIER	WHERRIES	WHIFT
WHALER	WHEAT	WHEEZIEST	WHERRY	WHIFTS
WHALERIES	WHEATEAR	WHEEZILY	WHERRYMAN	WHIG
WHALERS	WHEATEARS	WHEEZING	WHERRYMEN	WHIGGED
WHALERY	WHEATEN	WHEEZINGS	WHET	WHIGGING
WHALES	WHEATIER	WHEEZLE	WHETHER	WHIGS
WHALING	WHEATIEST	WHEEZLED	WHETS	WHILE
WHALINGS	WHEATMEAL	WHEEZLES	WHETSTONE	WHILED
WHALLY	WHEATMEALS	WHEEZLING	WHETSTONES	WHILERE
WHAM	WHEATS	WHEEZY	WHETTED	WHILES
WHAMMED	WHEATWORM	WHEFT	WHETTER	WHILING
WHAMMIES	WHEATWORMS	WHEFTS	WHETTERS	WHILK
WHAMMING	WHEATY	WHELK	WHETTING	WHILLIED

The Chambers Dictionary is the authority for many longer words; see *OSW* Introduction, page xii

WHILLIES	WHININGS	WHIRLIER	WHISTING	WHITISH
WHILLY	WHINNIED	WHIRLIEST	WHISTLE	WHITLING
WHILLYING	WHINNIER	WHIRLIGIG	WHISTLED	WHITLINGS
WHILLYWHA	WHINNIES	WHIRLIGIGS	WHISTLER	WHITLOW
WHILLYWHAED	WHINNIEST	WHIRLING	WHISTLERS	WHITLOWS
WHILLYWHAING	WHINNY	WHIRLINGS	WHISTLES	WHITRET
WHILLYWHAS	WHINNYING	WHIRLPOOL	WHISTLING	WHITRETS
WHILOM	WHINS	WHIRLPOOLS	WHISTLINGS	WHITS
WHILST	WHINSTONE	WHIRLS	WHISTS	WHITSTER
WHIM	WHINSTONES	WHIRLWIND	WHIT	WHITSTERS
WHIMBERRIES	WHINY	WHIRLWINDS	WHITE	WHITTAW
WHIMBERRY	WHINYARD	WHIRLY	WHITEBAIT	WHITTAWER
WHIMBREL	WHINYARDS	WHIRR	WHITEBAITS	WHITTAWERS
WHIMBRELS	WHIP	WHIRRED	WHITEBASS	WHITTAWS
WHIMMED	WHIPBIRD	WHIRRET	WHITEBASSES	WHITTER
WHIMMIER	WHIPBIRDS	WHIRRETED	WHITEBEAM	WHITTERED
WHIMMIEST	WHIPCAT	WHIRRETING	WHITEBEAMS	WHITTERING
WHIMMING	WHIPCATS	WHIRRETS	WHITECAP	WHITTERS
WHIMMY	WHIPCORD	WHIRRIED	WHITECAPS	WHITTLE
WHIMPER	WHIPCORDS	WHIRRIES	WHITECOAT	WHITTLED
WHIMPERED	WHIPCORDY	WHIRRING	WHITECOATS	WHITTLER
WHIMPERER	WHIPJACK	WHIRRINGS	WHITED	WHITTLERS
WHIMPERERS	WHIPJACKS	WHIRRS	WHITEFLIES	WHITTLES
WHIMPERING	WHIPLASH	WHIRRY	WHITEFLY	WHITTLING
WHIMPERINGS	WHIPLASHED	WHIRRYING	WHITEHEAD	WHITTLINGS
WHIMPERS	WHIPLASHES	WHIRS	WHITEHEADS	WHITTRET
WHIMPLE	WHIPLASHING	WHIRTLE	WHITELY	WHITTRETS
WHIMPLED	WHIPLIKE	WHIRTLES	WHITEN	WHITY
WHIMPLES	WHIPPED	WHISH	WHITENED	WHIZ
WHIMPLING	WHIPPER	WHISHED	WHITENER	WHIZBANG
WHIMS	WHIPPERS	WHISHES	WHITENERS	WHIZBANGS
WHIMSEY	WHIPPET	WHISHING	WHITENESS	WHIZZ
WHIMSEYS	WHIPPETS	WHISHT	WHITENESSES	WHIZZED
WHIMSICAL	WHIPPIER	WHISHTED	WHITENING	WHIZZER
WHIMSIER	WHIPPIEST	WHISHTING	WHITENINGS	WHIZZERS
WHIMSIES	WHIPPING	WHISHTS	WHITENS	WHIZZES
WHIMSIEST	WHIPPINGS	WHISK	WHITEPOT	WHIZZING
WHIMSILY	WHIPPY	WHISKED	WHITEPOTS	WHIZZINGS
WHIMSY	WHIPS	WHISKER	WHITER	WHO
WHIN	WHIPSAW	WHISKERED	WHITES	WHOA
WHINBERRIES	WHIPSAWED	WHISKERS	WHITEST	WHODUNNIT
WHINBERRY	WHIPSAWING	WHISKERY	WHITEWALL	WHODUNNITS
WHINCHAT	WHIPSAWS	WHISKET	WHITEWALLS	WHOEVER
WHINCHATS	WHIPSTAFF	WHISKETS	WHITEWARE	WHOLE
WHINE	WHIPSTAFFS	WHISKEY	WHITEWARES	WHOLEFOOD
WHINED	WHIPSTALL	WHISKEYS	WHITEWASH	WHOLEFOODS
WHINER	WHIPSTALLED	WHISKIES	WHITEWASHED	WHOLEMEAL
WHINERS	WHIPSTALLING	WHISKING	WHITEWASHES	WHOLEMEALS
WHINES	WHIPSTALLS	WHISKS	WHITEWASHING	WHOLENESS
WHINGE	WHIPSTER	WHISKY	WHITEWING	WHOLENESSES
WHINGED	WHIPSTERS	WHISPER	WHITEWINGS	WHOLES
WHINGEING	WHIPSTOCK	WHISPERED	WHITEWOOD	WHOLESALE
WHINGEINGS	WHIPSTOCKS	WHISPERER	WHITEWOODS	WHOLESALES
WHINGER	WHIPT	WHISPERERS	WHITEY	WHOLESOME
WHINGERS	WHIPTAIL	WHISPERING	WHITEYS	WHOLESOMER
WHINGES	WHIPWORM	WHISPERINGS	WHITHER	WHOLESOMEST
WHINIARD	WHIPWORMS	WHISPERS	WHITHERED	WHOLISM
WHINIARDS	WHIR	WHISPERY	WHITHERING	WHOLISMS
WHINIER	WHIRL	WHISS	WHITHERS	WHOLIST
WHINIEST	WHIRLBAT	WHISSED	WHITIER	WHOLISTIC
WHININESS	WHIRLBATS	WHISSES	WHITIES	WHOLISTS
WHININESSES	WHIRLED	WHISSING	WHITIEST	WHOLLY
WHINING	WHIRLER	WHIST	WHITING	WHOM
WHININGLY	WHIRLERS	WHISTED	WHITINGS	WHOMBLE

WHOMBLED	WHUNSTANES	WIDOWHOOD	WIGWAGGING	WILLEYING
WHOMBLES	WHY	WIDOWHOODS	WIGWAGS	WILLEYS
WHOMBLING	WHYDAH	WIDOWING	WIGWAM	WILLFUL
WHOMEVER	WHYDAHS	WIDOWMAN	WIGWAMS	WILLIE
WHOMMLE	WHYEVER	WIDOWMEN	WILD	WILLIED
WHOMMLED	WICCA	WIDOWS	WILDCAT	WILLIES
WHOMMLES	WICCAN	WIDTH	WILDCATS	WILLING
WHOMMLING	WICCANS	WIDTHS	WILDCATTED	WILLINGLY
WHOOBUB	WICCAS	WIDTHWAYS	WILDCATTING	WILLIWAW
WHOOBUBS	WICE	WIDTHWISE	WILDED	WILLIWAWS
WHOOP	WICH	WIEL	WILDER	WILLOW
WHOOPED	WICHES	WIELD	WILDERED	WILLOWED
WHOOPEE	WICK	WIELDABLE	WILDERING	WILLOWIER
WHOOPEES	WICKED	WIELDED	WILDERS	WILLOWIEST
WHOOPER	WICKEDER	WIELDER	WILDEST	WILLOWING
WHOOPERS	WICKEDEST	WIELDERS	WILDFIRE	WILLOWISH
WHOOPING	WICKEDLY	WIELDIER	WILDFIRES	WILLOWS
WHOOPINGS	WICKEDS	WIELDIEST	WILDFOWL	WILLOWY
WHOOPS	WICKEN	WIELDING	WILDFOWLS	WILLPOWER
WHOOPSIE	WICKENS	WIELDLESS	WILDGRAVE	WILLPOWERS
WHOOPSIES	WICKER	WIELDS	WILDGRAVES	WILLS
WHOOSH	WICKERED	WIELDY	WILDING	WILLY
WHOOSHED	WICKERS	WIELS	WILDINGS	WILLYARD
WHOOSHES	WICKET	WIENIE	WILDISH	WILLYART
WHOOSHING	WICKETS	WIENIES	WILDLAND	WILLYING
WHOOT	WICKIES	WIFE	WILDLANDS	WILT
WHOOTED	WICKING	WIFEHOOD	WILDLIFE	WILTED
WHOOTING	WICKIUP	WIFEHOODS	WILDLIFES	WILTING
WHOOTS	WICKIUPS	WIFELESS	WILDLY	WILTJA
WHOP	WICKS	WIFELIER	WILDNESS	WILTJAS
WHOPPED	WICKY	WIFELIEST	WILDNESSES	WILTS
WHOPPER	WIDDIES	WIFELIKE	WILDS	WILY
WHOPPERS	WIDDLE	WIFELY	WILDWOOD	WIMBLE
WHOPPING	WIDDLED	WIFIE	WILDWOODS	WIMBLED
WHOPPINGS	WIDDLES	WIFIES	WILE	WIMBLES
WHOPS	WIDDLING	WIG	WILED	WIMBLING
WHORE	WIDDY	WIGAN	WILEFUL	WIMBREL
WHORED	WIDE	WIGANS	WILES	WIMBRELS
WHOREDOM	WIDEAWAKE	WIGEON	WILFUL	WIMP
WHOREDOMS	WIDEAWAKES	WIGEONS	WILFULLY	WIMPIER
WHORES	WIDEBODY	WIGGED	WILGA	WIMPIEST
WHORESON	WIDELY	WIGGERIES	WILGAS	WIMPISH
WHORESONS	WIDEN	WIGGERY	WILI	WIMPISHLY
WHORING	WIDENED	WIGGING	WILIER	WIMPLE
WHORISH	WIDENER	WIGGINGS	WILIEST	WIMPLED
WHORISHLY	WIDENERS	WIGGLE	WILILY	WIMPLES
WHORL	WIDENESS	WIGGLED	WILINESS	WIMPLING
WHORLBAT	WIDENESSES	WIGGLER	WILINESSES	WIMPS
WHORLBATS	WIDENING	WIGGLERS	WILING	WIMPY
WHORLED	WIDENS	WIGGLES	WILIS	WIN
WHORLS	WIDER	WIGGLIER	WILJA	WINCE
WHORT	WIDES	WIGGLIEST	WILJAS	WINCED
WHORTS	WIDEST	WIGGLING	WILL	WINCER
WHOSE	WIDGEON	WIGGLY	WILLABLE	WINCERS
WHOSEVER	WIDGEONS	WIGHT	WILLED	WINCES
WHOSO	WIDGET	WIGHTED	WILLEMITE	WINCEY
WHOSOEVER	WIDGETS	WIGHTING	WILLEMITES	WINCEYS
WHOT	WIDGIE	WIGHTLY	WILLER	WINCH
WHOW	WIDGIES	WIGHTS	WILLERS	WINCHED
WHUMMLE	WIDISH	WIGLESS	WILLEST	WINCHES
WHUMMLED	WIDOW	WIGLIKE	WILLET	WINCHING
WHUMMLES	WIDOWED	WIGS	WILLETS	WINCHMAN
WHUMMLING	WIDOWER	WIGWAG	WILLEY	WINCHMEN
WHUNSTANE	WIDOWERS	WIGWAGGED	WILLEYED	WINCING

WINCINGS	WINDPROOF	WINGS	WINTERS	WISARD
WINCOPIPE	WINDRING	WINGSPAN	WINTERY	WISARDS
WINCOPIPES	WINDROSE	WINGSPANS	WINTLE	WISDOM
WIND	WINDROSES	WINGY	WINTLED	WISDOMS
WINDAC	WINDROW	WINIER	WINTLES	WISE
WINDACS	WINDROWED	WINIEST	WINTLING	WISEACRE
WINDAGE	WINDROWING	WINING	WINTRIER	WISEACRES
WINDAGES	WINDROWS	WINK	WINTRIEST	WISECRACK
WINDAS	WINDS	WINKED	WINTRY	WISECRACKED
WINDASES	WINDSAIL	WINKER	WINY	WISECRACKING
WINDBAG	WINDSAILS	WINKERS	WINZE	WISECRACKS
WINDBAGS	WINDSES	WINKING	WINZES	WISED
WINDBLOW	WINDSHAKE	WINKINGLY	WIPE	WISELING
WINDBLOWN	WINDSHAKES	WINKINGS	WIPED	WISELINGS
WINDBLOWS	WINDSHIP	WINKLE	WIPEOUT	WISELY
WINDBORNE	WINDSHIPS	WINKLED	WIPEOUTS	WISENESS
WINDBOUND	WINDSOCK	WINKLER	WIPER	WISENESSES
WINDBREAK	WINDSOCKS	WINKLERS	WIPERS	WISENT
WINDBREAKS	WINDSTORM	WINKLES	WIPES	WISENTS
WINDBURN	WINDSTORMS	WINKLING	WIPING	WISER
WINDBURNS	WINDSURF	WINKS	WIPINGS	WISES
WINDED	WINDSURFED	WINN	WIPPEN	WISEST
WINDER	WINDSURFING	WINNA	WIPPENS	WISH
WINDERS	WINDSURFINGS	WINNABLE	WIRE	WISHBONE
WINDFALL	WINDSURFS	WINNER	WIRED	WISHBONES
WINDFALLS	WINDSWEPT	WINNERS	WIREDRAW	WISHED
WINDGALL	WINDTHROW	WINNING	WIREDRAWING	WISHER
WINDGALLS	WINDTHROWS	WINNINGLY	WIREDRAWINGS	WISHERS
WINDGUN	WINDTIGHT	WINNINGS	WIREDRAWN	WISHES
WINDGUNS	WINDWARD	WINNLE	WIREDRAWS	WISHFUL
WINDHOVER	WINDWARDS	WINNLES	WIREDREW	WISHFULLY
WINDHOVERS	WINDY	WINNOCK	WIRELESS	WISHING
WINDIER	WINE	WINNOCKS	WIRELESSED	WISHINGS
WINDIEST	WINEBERRIES	WINNOW	WIRELESSES	WISING
WINDIGO	WINEBERRY	WINNOWED	WIRELESSING	WISKET
WINDIGOS	WINED	WINNOWER	WIREMAN	WISKETS
WINDILY	WINEGLASS	WINNOWERS	WIREMEN	WISP
WINDINESS	WINEGLASSES	WINNOWING	WIREPHOTO	WISPED
WINDINESSES	WINEPRESS	WINNOWINGS	WIREPHOTOS	WISPIER
WINDING	WINEPRESSES	WINNOWS	WIRER	WISPIEST
WINDINGLY	WINERIES	WINNS	WIRERS	WISPING
WINDINGS	WINERY	WINO	WIRES	WISPS
WINDLASS	WINES	WINOS	WIRETAP	WISPY
WINDLASSED	WINESKIN	WINS	WIRETAPPED	WISSED
WINDLASSES	WINESKINS	WINSEY	WIRETAPPING	WISSES
WINDLASSING	WINEY	WINSEYS	WIRETAPS	WISSING
WINDLE	WING	WINSOME	WIREWAY	WIST
WINDLES	WINGBEAT	WINSOMELY	WIREWAYS	WISTARIA
WINDLESS	WINGBEATS	WINSOMER	WIREWORK	WISTARIAS
WINDMILL	WINGDING	WINSOMEST	WIREWORKS	WISTED
WINDMILLED	WINGDINGS	WINTER	WIREWORM	WISTERIA
WINDMILLING	WINGE	WINTERED	WIREWORMS	WISTERIAS
WINDMILLS	WINGED	WINTERIER	WIREWOVE	WISTFUL
WINDOCK	WINGEDLY	WINTERIEST	WIRIER	WISTFULLY
WINDOCKS	WINGEING	WINTERING	WIRIEST	WISTING
WINDORE	WINGER	WINTERISE	WIRILY	WISTITI
WINDORES	WINGERS	WINTERISED	WIRINESS	WISTITIS
WINDOW	WINGES	WINTERISES	WIRINESSES	WISTLY
WINDOWED	WINGIER	WINTERISING	WIRING	WISTS
WINDOWING	WINGIEST	WINTERIZE	WIRINGS	WIT
WINDOWINGS	WINGING	WINTERIZED	WIRRICOW	WITAN
WINDOWS	WINGLESS	WINTERIZES	WIRRICOWS	WITBLITS
WINDPIPE	WINGLET	WINTERIZING	WIRY	WITBLITSES
WINDPIPES	WINGLETS	WINTERLY	WIS	WITCH

The Chambers Dictionary is the authority for many longer words; see *OSW* Introduction, page xii

WITCHED	WITING	WOBBLE	WOLLY	WONDERS
WITCHEN	WITLESS	WOBBLED	WOLVE	WONDRED
WITCHENS	WITLESSLY	WOBBLER	WOLVED	WONDROUS
WITCHERIES	WITLING	WOBBLERS	WOLVER	WONGA
WITCHERY	WITLINGS	WOBBLES	WOLVERENE	WONGAS
WITCHES	WITLOOF	WOBBLIER	WOLVERENES	WONGI
WITCHETTIES	WITLOOFS	WOBBLIES	WOLVERINE	WONGIED
WITCHETTY	WITNESS	WOBBLIEST	WOLVERINES	WONGIING
WITCHIER	WITNESSED	WOBBLING	WOLVERS	WONGIS
WITCHIEST	WITNESSER	WOBBLINGS	WOLVES	WONING
WITCHING	WITNESSERS	WOBBLY	WOLVING	WONINGS
WITCHINGS	WITNESSES	WOBEGONE	WOLVINGS	WONK
WITCHKNOT	WITNESSING	WOCK	WOLVISH	WONKIER
WITCHKNOTS	WITS	WOCKS	WOLVISHLY	WONKIEST
WITCHLIKE	WITTED	WODGE	WOMAN	WONKS
WITCHMEAL	WITTER	WODGES	WOMANED	WONKY
WITCHMEALS	WITTERED	WOE	WOMANHOOD	WONNED
WITCHY	WITTERING	WOEBEGONE	WOMANHOODS	WONNING
WITE	WITTERS	WOEFUL	WOMANING	WONNINGS
WITED	WITTICISM	WOEFULLER	WOMANISE	WONS
WITELESS	WITTICISMS	WOEFULLEST	WOMANISED	WONT
WITES	WITTIER	WOEFULLY	WOMANISER	WONTED
WITGAT	WITTIEST	WOES	WOMANISERS	WONTING
WITGATS	WITTILY	WOESOME	WOMANISES	WONTLESS
WITH	WITTINESS	WOFUL	WOMANISH	WONTS
WITHAL	WITTINESSES	WOFULLY	WOMANISING	WOO
WITHDRAW	WITTING	WOFULNESS	WOMANIZE	WOOBUT
WITHDRAWING	WITTINGLY	WOFULNESSES	WOMANIZED	WOOBUTS
WITHDRAWN	WITTINGS	WOG	WOMANIZER	WOOD
WITHDRAWS	WITTOL	WOGGLE	WOMANIZERS	WOODBIND
WITHDREW	WITTOLLY	WOGGLES	WOMANIZES	WOODBINDS
WITHE	WITTOLS	WOGS	WOMANIZING	WOODBINE
WITHED	WITTY	WOIWODE	WOMANKIND	WOODBINES
WITHER	WITWALL	WOIWODES	WOMANKINDS	WOODBLOCK
WITHERED	WITWALLS	WOK	WOMANLESS	WOODBLOCKS
WITHERING	WITWANTON	WOKE	WOMANLIER	WOODCHAT
WITHERINGS	WITWANTONED	WOKEN	WOMANLIEST	WOODCHATS
WITHERITE	WITWANTONING	WOKS	WOMANLIKE	WOODCHIP
WITHERITES	WITWANTONS	WOLD	WOMANLY	WOODCHIPS
WITHERS	WIVE	WOLDS	WOMANS	WOODCHUCK
WITHES	WIVED	WOLF	WOMB	WOODCHUCKS
WITHHAULT	WIVEHOOD	WOLFBERRIES	WOMBAT	WOODCOCK
WITHHELD	WIVEHOODS	WOLFBERRY	WOMBATS	WOODCOCKS
WITHHOLD	WIVERN	WOLFED	WOMBED	WOODCRAFT
WITHHOLDEN	WIVERNS	WOLFER	WOMBING	WOODCRAFTS
WITHHOLDING	WIVES	WOLFERS	WOMBLIKE	WOODCUT
WITHHOLDS	WIVING	WOLFHOUND	WOMBS	WOODCUTS
WITHIER	WIZARD	WOLFHOUNDS	WOMBY	WOODED
WITHIES	WIZARDLY	WOLFING	WOMEN	WOODEN
WITHIEST	WIZARDRIES	WOLFINGS	WOMENFOLK	WOODENER
WITHIN	WIZARDRY	WOLFISH	WOMENFOLKS	WOODENEST
WITHING	WIZARDS	WOLFISHLY	WOMENKIND	WOODENLY
WITHOUT	WIZEN	WOLFKIN	WOMENKINDS	WOODENTOP
WITHOUTEN	WIZENED	WOLFKINS	WOMERA	WOODENTOPS
WITHS	WIZENING	WOLFLING	WOMERAS	WOODHOLE
WITHSTAND	WIZENS	WOLFLINGS	WON	WOODHOLES
WITHSTANDING	WIZIER	WOLFRAM	WONDER	WOODHORSE
WITHSTANDS	WIZIERS	WOLFRAMS	WONDERED	WOODHORSES
WITHSTOOD	WO	WOLFS	WONDERER	WOODHOUSE
WITHWIND	WOAD	WOLFSBANE	WONDERERS	WOODHOUSES
WITHWINDS	WOADED	WOLFSBANES	WONDERFUL	WOODIE
WITHY	WOADS	WOLFSKIN	WONDERING	WOODIER
WITHYWIND	WOBBEGONG	WOLFSKINS	WONDERINGS	WOODIES
WITHYWINDS	WOBBEGONGS	WOLLIES	WONDEROUS	WOODIEST

WOODINESS	WOODWORKS	WOON	WORKABLE	WORKWEAR
WOODINESSES	WOODWORM	WOONED	WORKADAY	WORKWEARS
WOODING	WOODWORMS	WOONING	WORKADAYS	WORKWEEK
WOODLAND	WOODWOSE	WOONS	WORKBAG	WORKWEEKS
WOODLANDS	WOODWOSES	WOOPIE	WORKBAGS	WORKWOMAN
WOODLARK	WOODY	WOOPIES	WORKBENCH	WORKWOMEN
WOODLARKS	WOODYARD	WOORALI	WORKBENCHES	WORLD
WOODLESS	WOODYARDS	WOORALIS	WORKBOAT	WORLDED
WOODLICE	WOOED	WOORARA	WORKBOATS	WORLDLIER
WOODLOUSE	WOOER	WOORARAS	WORKBOOK	WORLDLIEST
WOODMAN	WOOERS	WOOS	WORKBOOKS	WORLDLING
WOODMEAL	WOOF	WOOSEL	WORKBOX	WORLDLINGS
WOODMEALS	WOOFED	WOOSELL	WORKBOXES	WORLDLY
WOODMEN	WOOFER	WOOSELLS	WORKDAY	WORLDS
WOODMICE	WOOFERS	WOOSELS	WORKDAYS	WORLDWIDE
WOODMOUSE	WOOFIER	WOOSH	WORKED	WORM
WOODNESS	WOOFIEST	WOOSHED	WORKER	WORMCAST
WOODNESSES	WOOFING	WOOSHES	WORKERIST	WORMCASTS
WOODNOTE	WOOFS	WOOSHING	WORKERISTS	WORMED
WOODNOTES	WOOFTER	WOOT	WORKERS	WORMER
WOODPILE	WOOFTERS	WOOTZ	WORKFARE	WORMERIES
WOODPILES	WOOFY	WOOTZES	WORKFARES	WORMERS
WOODREEVE	WOOING	WOOZIER	WORKFOLK	WORMERY
WOODREEVES	WOOINGLY	WOOZIEST	WORKFOLKS	WORMHOLE
WOODROOF	WOOINGS	WOOZILY	WORKFORCE	WORMHOLED
WOODROOFS	WOOL	WOOZINESS	WORKFORCES	WORMHOLES
WOODRUFF	WOOLD	WOOZINESSES	WORKFUL	WORMIER
WOODRUFFS	WOOLDED	WOOZY	WORKGIRL	WORMIEST
WOODRUSH	WOOLDER	WOP	WORKGIRLS	WORMING
WOODRUSHES	WOOLDERS	WOPPED	WORKGROUP	WORMS
WOODS	WOOLDING	WOPPING	WORKGROUPS	WORMSEED
WOODSCREW	WOOLDINGS	WOPS	WORKHORSE	WORMSEEDS
WOODSCREWS	WOOLDS	WORCESTER	WORKHORSES	WORMWOOD
WOODSHED	WOOLEN	WORCESTERS	WORKHOUSE	WORMWOODS
WOODSHEDDED	WOOLENS	WORD	WORKHOUSES	WORMY
WOODSHEDDING	WOOLFAT	WORDAGE	WORKING	WORN
WOODSHEDDINGS	WOOLFATS	WORDAGES	WORKINGS	WORRAL
WOODSHEDS	WOOLFELL	WORDBOOK	WORKLESS	WORRALS
WOODSHOCK	WOOLFELLS	WORDBOOKS	WORKLOAD	WORREL
WOODSHOCKS	WOOLLED	WORDBOUND	WORKLOADS	WORRELS
WOODSIA	WOOLLEN	WORDBREAK	WORKMAN	WORRICOW
WOODSIAS	WOOLLENS	WORDBREAKS	WORKMANLY	WORRICOWS
WOODSIER	WOOLLIER	WORDED	WORKMATE	WORRIED
WOODSIEST	WOOLLIES	WORDGAME	WORKMATES	WORRIEDLY
WOODSKIN	WOOLLIEST	WORDGAMES	WORKMEN	WORRIER
WOODSKINS	WOOLLY	WORDIER	WORKPIECE	WORRIERS
WOODSMAN	WOOLMAN	WORDIEST	WORKPIECES	WORRIES
WOODSMEN	WOOLMEN	WORDILY	WORKPLACE	WORRIMENT
WOODSPITE	WOOLPACK	WORDINESS	WORKPLACES	WORRIMENTS
WOODSPITES	WOOLPACKS	WORDINESSES	WORKROOM	WORRISOME
WOODSTONE	WOOLS	WORDING	WORKROOMS	WORRIT
WOODSTONES	WOOLSACK	WORDINGS	WORKS	WORRITED
WOODSY	WOOLSACKS	WORDISH	WORKSHEET	WORRITING
WOODWALE	WOOLSEY	WORDLESS	WORKSHEETS	WORRITS
WOODWALES	WOOLSEYS	WORDLORE	WORKSHOP	WORRY
WOODWARD	WOOLSHED	WORDLORES	WORKSHOPPED	WORRYCOW
WOODWARDS	WOOLSHEDS	WORDPLAY	WORKSHOPPING	WORRYCOWS
WOODWAX	WOOLWARD	WORDPLAYS	WORKSHOPS	WORRYGUTS
WOODWAXEN	WOOLWORK	WORDS	WORKSHY	WORRYING
WOODWAXENS	WOOLWORKS	WORDSMITH	WORKSOME	WORRYINGS
WOODWAXES	WOOMERA	WORDSMITHS	WORKTABLE	WORRYWART
WOODWIND	WOOMERANG	WORDY	WORKTABLES	WORRYWARTS
WOODWINDS	WOOMERANGS	WORE	WORKTOP	WORSE
WOODWORK	WOOMERAS	WORK	WORKTOPS	WORSED

The Chambers Dictionary is the authority for many longer words; see *OSW* Introduction, page xii

WORSEN	WOURALI	WRAWLED	WRETCHES	WRITHINGS
WORSENED	WOURALIS	WRAWLING	WRETHE	WRITHLED
WORSENESS	WOVE	WRAWLS	WRETHED	WRITING
WORSENESSES	WOVEN	WRAXLE	WRETHES	WRITINGS
WORSENING	WOW	WRAXLED	WRETHING	WRITS
WORSENS	WOWED	WRAXLES	WRICK	WRITTEN
WORSER	WOWEE	WRAXLING	WRICKED	WRIZLED
WORSES	WOWF	WRAXLINGS	WRICKING	WROATH
WORSHIP	WOWFER	WREAK	WRICKS	WROATHS
WORSHIPPED	WOWFEST	WREAKED	WRIED	WROKE
WORSHIPPING	WOWING	WREAKER	WRIER	WROKEN
WORSHIPS	WOWS	WREAKERS	WRIES	WRONG
WORSING	WOWSER	WREAKFUL	WRIEST	WRONGDOER
WORST	WOWSERS	WREAKING	WRIGGLE	WRONGDOERS
WORSTED	WOX	WREAKLESS	WRIGGLED	WRONGED
WORSTEDS	WOXEN	WREAKS	WRIGGLER	WRONGER
WORSTING	WRACK	WREATH	WRIGGLERS	WRONGERS
WORSTS	WRACKED	WREATHE	WRIGGLES	WRONGEST
WORT	WRACKFUL	WREATHED	WRIGGLIER	WRONGFUL
WORTH	WRACKING	WREATHEN	WRIGGLIEST	WRONGING
WORTHED	WRACKS	WREATHER	WRIGGLING	WRONGLY
WORTHFUL	WRAITH	WREATHERS	WRIGGLINGS	WRONGNESS
WORTHIED	WRAITHS	WREATHES	WRIGGLY	WRONGNESSES
WORTHIER	WRANGLE	WREATHIER	WRIGHT	WRONGOUS
WORTHIES	WRANGLED	WREATHIEST	WRIGHTS	WRONGS
WORTHIEST	WRANGLER	WREATHING	WRING	WROOT
WORTHILY	WRANGLERS	WREATHS	WRINGED	WROOTED
WORTHING	WRANGLES	WREATHY	WRINGER	WROOTING
WORTHLESS	WRANGLING	WRECK	WRINGERS	WROOTS
WORTHS	WRANGLINGS	WRECKAGE	WRINGING	WROTE
WORTHY	WRAP	WRECKAGES	WRINGINGS	WROTH
WORTHYING	WRAPOVER	WRECKED	WRINGS	WROUGHT
WORTLE	WRAPOVERS	WRECKER	WRINKLE	WRUNG
WORTLES	WRAPPAGE	WRECKERS	WRINKLED	WRY
WORTS	WRAPPAGES	WRECKFISH	WRINKLES	WRYBILL
WOS	WRAPPED	WRECKFISHES	WRINKLIER	WRYBILLS
WOSBIRD	WRAPPER	WRECKFUL	WRINKLIES	WRYER
WOSBIRDS	WRAPPERED	WRECKING	WRINKLIEST	WRYEST
WOST	WRAPPERING	WRECKINGS	WRINKLING	WRYING
WOT	WRAPPERS	WRECKS	WRINKLY	WRYLY
WOTCHER	WRAPPING	WREN	WRIST	WRYNECK
WOTS	WRAPPINGS	WRENCH	WRISTBAND	WRYNECKS
WOTTED	WRAPROUND	WRENCHED	WRISTBANDS	WRYNESS
WOTTEST	WRAPROUNDS	WRENCHES	WRISTIER	WRYNESSES
WOTTETH	WRAPS	WRENCHING	WRISTIEST	WRYTHEN
WOTTING	WRAPT	WRENCHINGS	WRISTLET	WUD
WOUBIT	WRASSE	WRENS	WRISTLETS	WUDDED
WOUBITS	WRASSES	WREST	WRISTS	WUDDING
WOULD	WRAST	WRESTED	WRISTY	WUDS
WOULDS	WRASTED	WRESTER	WRIT	WULFENITE
WOULDST	WRASTING	WRESTERS	WRITABLE	WULFENITES
WOUND	WRASTS	WRESTING	WRITATIVE	WULL
WOUNDABLE	WRATE	WRESTLE	WRITE	WULLED
WOUNDED	WRATH	WRESTLED	WRITER	WULLING
WOUNDER	WRATHED	WRESTLER	WRITERESS	WULLS
WOUNDERS	WRATHFUL	WRESTLERS	WRITERESSES	WUNNER
WOUNDILY	WRATHIER	WRESTLES	WRITERLY	WUNNERS
WOUNDING	WRATHIEST	WRESTLING	WRITERS	WURLEY
WOUNDINGS	WRATHILY	WRESTLINGS	WRITES	WURLEYS
WOUNDLESS	WRATHING	WRESTS	WRITHE	WURLIES
WOUNDS	WRATHLESS	WRETCH	WRITHED	WURST
WOUNDWORT	WRATHS	WRETCHED	WRITHEN	WURSTS
WOUNDWORTS	WRATHY	WRETCHEDER	WRITHES	WURTZITE
WOUNDY	WRAWL	WRETCHEDEST	WRITHING	WURTZITES

The Chambers Dictionary is the authority for many longer words; see *OSW* Introduction, page xii

WUS	WUTHERED	WYANDOTTE	WYLIECOATS	WYSIWYG
WUSES	WUTHERING	WYANDOTTES	WYN	WYTE
WUSHU	WUTHERS	WYCH	WYND	WYTED
WUSHUS	WUZZLE	WYCHES	WYNDS	WYTES
WUSS	WUZZLED	WYE	WYNN	WYTING
WUSSES	WUZZLES	WYES	WYNNS	WYVERN
WUTHER	WUZZLING	WYLIECOAT	WYNS	WYVERNS

X

XANTHAM
XANTHAMS
XANTHAN
XANTHANS
XANTHATE
XANTHATES
XANTHEIN
XANTHEINS
XANTHENE
XANTHENES
XANTHIC
XANTHIN
XANTHINE
XANTHINES
XANTHINS
XANTHOMA
XANTHOMAS
XANTHOMATA
XANTHOUS
XANTHOXYL
XANTHOXYLS
XEBEC
XEBECS
XENIA
XENIAL
XENIAS
XENIUM
XENOCRYST
XENOCRYSTS

XENOGAMIES
XENOGAMY
XENOGRAFT
XENOGRAFTS
XENOLITH
XENOLITHS
XENOMANIA
XENOMANIAS
XENOMENIA
XENOMENIAS
XENON
XENONS
XENOPHILE
XENOPHILES
XENOPHOBE
XENOPHOBES
XENOPHOBIES
XENOPHOBY
XENOPHYA
XENOTIME
XENOTIMES
XENURINE
XERAFIN
XERAFINS
XERANSES
XERANSIS
XERANTIC
XERAPHIM
XERAPHIMS

XERARCH
XERASIA
XERASIAS
XERIC
XEROCHASIES
XEROCHASY
XERODERMA
XERODERMAS
XEROMA
XEROMAS
XEROMATA
XEROMORPH
XEROMORPHS
XEROPHAGIES
XEROPHAGY
XEROPHILIES
XEROPHILY
XEROPHYTE
XEROPHYTES
XEROSES
XEROSIS
XEROSTOMA
XEROSTOMAS
XEROSTOMATA
XEROTES
XEROTIC
XI
XIPHOID
XIPHOIDAL

XIPHOPAGI
XIS
XOANA
XOANON
XU
XYLEM
XYLEMS
XYLENE
XYLENES
XYLENOL
XYLENOLS
XYLIC
XYLITOL
XYLITOLS
XYLOCARP
XYLOCARPS
XYLOGEN
XYLOGENS
XYLOGRAPH
XYLOGRAPHS
XYLOID
XYLOIDIN
XYLOIDINE
XYLOIDINES
XYLOIDINS
XYLOL
XYLOLOGIES
XYLOLOGY
XYLOLS

XYLOMA
XYLOMAS
XYLOMATA
XYLOMETER
XYLOMETERS
XYLONIC
XYLONITE
XYLONITES
XYLOPHAGE
XYLOPHAGES
XYLOPHONE
XYLOPHONES
XYLORIMBA
XYLORIMBAS
XYLOSE
XYLOSES
XYLYL
XYLYLS
XYST
XYSTER
XYSTERS
XYSTI
XYSTOI
XYSTOS
XYSTS
XYSTUS

Y

YABBER	YAKOWS	YARD	YATTERING	YEADING
YABBERED	YAKS	YARDAGE	YATTERINGS	YEADS
YABBERING	YAKUZA	YARDAGES	YATTERS	YEAH
YABBERS	YALD	YARDANG	YAUD	YEALDON
YABBIE	YALE	YARDANGS	YAUDS	YEALDONS
YABBIES	YALES	YARDBIRD	YAULD	YEALM
YABBY	YAM	YARDBIRDS	YAUP	YEALMED
YACCA	YAMEN	YARDED	YAUPON	YEALMING
YACCAS	YAMENS	YARDING	YAUPONS	YEALMS
YACHT	YAMMER	YARDLAND	YAW	YEAN
YACHTED	YAMMERED	YARDLANDS	YAWED	YEANED
YACHTER	YAMMERING	YARDMAN	YAWEY	YEANING
YACHTERS	YAMMERINGS	YARDMEN	YAWING	YEANLING
YACHTIE	YAMMERS	YARDS	YAWL	YEANLINGS
YACHTIES	YAMS	YARDSTICK	YAWLED	YEANS
YACHTING	YAMULKA	YARDSTICKS	YAWLING	YEAR
YACHTINGS	YAMULKAS	YARDWAND	YAWLS	YEARBOOK
YACHTS	YANG	YARDWANDS	YAWN	YEARBOOKS
YACHTSMAN	YANGS	YARE	YAWNED	YEARD
YACHTSMEN	YANK	YARELY	YAWNER	YEARDED
YACK	YANKED	YARER	YAWNIER	YEARDING
YACKED	YANKER	YAREST	YAWNIEST	YEARDS
YACKER	YANKERS	YARFA	YAWNING	YEARLIES
YACKERS	YANKIE	YARFAS	YAWNINGLY	YEARLING
YACKING	YANKIES	YARMULKA	YAWNINGS	YEARLINGS
YACKS	YANKING	YARMULKAS	YAWNS	YEARLONG
YAFF	YANKS	YARMULKE	YAWNY	YEARLY
YAFFED	YANQUI	YARMULKES	YAWP	YEARN
YAFFING	YANQUIS	YARN	YAWPED	YEARNED
YAFFLE	YAOURT	YARNED	YAWPER	YEARNER
YAFFLES	YAOURTS	YARNING	YAWPERS	YEARNERS
YAFFS	YAP	YARNS	YAWPING	YEARNING
YAGER	YAPOCK	YARPHA	YAWPS	YEARNINGS
YAGERS	YAPOCKS	YARPHAS	YAWS	YEARNS
YAGGER	YAPOK	YARR	YAWY	YEARS
YAGGERS	YAPOKS	YARRAMAN	YBET	YEAS
YAH	YAPON	YARRAMANS	YBLENT	YEAST
YAHOO	YAPONS	YARROW	YBORE	YEASTED
YAHOOS	YAPP	YARROWS	YBOUND	YEASTIER
YAHS	YAPPED	YARRS	YBOUNDEN	YEASTIEST
YAK	YAPPER	YARTA	YBRENT	YEASTING
YAKHDAN	YAPPERS	YARTAS	YCLAD	YEASTLIKE
YAKHDANS	YAPPIE	YARTO	YCLED	YEASTS
YAKIMONO	YAPPIER	YARTOS	YCLEEPE	YEASTY
YAKIMONOS	YAPPIES	YASHMAK	YCLEEPED	YECH
YAKITORI	YAPPIEST	YASHMAKS	YCLEEPES	YEDE
YAKITORIS	YAPPING	YATAGAN	YCLEEPING	YEDES
YAKKA	YAPPS	YATAGANS	YCLEPED	YEDING
YAKKAS	YAPPY	YATAGHAN	YCLEPT	YEED
YAKKED	YAPS	YATAGHANS	YCOND	YEEDING
YAKKER	YAPSTER	YATE	YDRAD	YEEDS
YAKKERS	YAPSTERS	YATES	YDRED	YEGG
YAKKING	YAQONA	YATTER	YE	YEGGMAN
YAKOW	YAQONAS	YATTERED	YEA	YEGGMEN

The Chambers Dictionary is the authority for many longer words; see *OSW* Introduction, page xii

YEGGS	YERSINIAE	YIKKER	YODELS	YOMPED
YELD	YERSINIAS	YIKKERED	YODLE	YOMPING
YELDRING	YES	YIKKERING	YODLED	YOMPS
YELDRINGS	YESES	YIKKERS	YODLER	YON
YELDROCK	YESHIVA	YILL	YODLERS	YOND
YELDROCKS	YESHIVAH	YILLS	YODLES	YONDER
YELK	YESHIVAHS	YIN	YODLING	YONDERLY
YELKS	YESHIVAS	YINCE	YOGA	YONDERS
YELL	YESHIVOT	YINS	YOGAS	YONGTHLY
YELLED	YESHIVOTH	YIP	YOGH	YONI
YELLING	YESK	YIPPED	YOGHOURT	YONIS
YELLINGS	YESKED	YIPPEE	YOGHOURTS	YONKER
YELLOCH	YESKING	YIPPER	YOGHS	YONKERS
YELLOCHED	YESKS	YIPPERS	YOGHURT	YONKS
YELLOCHING	YESSES	YIPPIES	YOGHURTS	YONT
YELLOCHS	YEST	YIPPING	YOGI	YOOF
YELLOW	YESTER	YIPPY	YOGIC	YOOFS
YELLOWED	YESTERDAY	YIPS	YOGIN	YOOP
YELLOWER	YESTERDAYS	YIRD	YOGINI	YOOPS
YELLOWEST	YESTEREVE	YIRDED	YOGINIS	YOPPER
YELLOWIER	YESTEREVES	YIRDING	YOGINS	YOPPERS
YELLOWIEST	YESTERN	YIRDS	YOGIS	YORE
YELLOWING	YESTREEN	YIRK	YOGISM	YORES
YELLOWISH	YESTS	YIRKED	YOGISMS	YORK
YELLOWS	YESTY	YIRKING	YOGURT	YORKED
YELLOWY	YET	YIRKS	YOGURTS	YORKER
YELLS	YETI	YITE	YOHIMBINE	YORKERS
YELM	YETIS	YITES	YOHIMBINES	YORKIE
YELMED	YETT	YLEM	YOICK	YORKIES
YELMING	YETTS	YLEMS	YOICKED	YORKING
YELMS	YEUK	YLIKE	YOICKING	YORKS
YELP	YEUKED	YLKE	YOICKS	YOS
YELPED	YEUKING	YLKES	YOICKSED	YOU
YELPER	YEUKS	YMOLT	YOICKSES	YOUK
YELPERS	YEVE	YMOLTEN	YOICKSING	YOUKED
YELPING	YEVEN	YMPE	YOJAN	YOUKING
YELPINGS	YEVES	YMPES	YOJANA	YOUKS
YELPS	YEVING	YMPING	YOJANAS	YOUNG
YELT	YEW	YMPT	YOJANS	YOUNGER
YELTS	YEWEN	YNAMBU	YOK	YOUNGEST
YEN	YEWS	YNAMBUS	YOKE	YOUNGISH
YENNED	YEX	YO	YOKED	YOUNGLING
YENNING	YEXED	YOB	YOKEL	YOUNGLINGS
YENS	YEXES	YOBBERIES	YOKELISH	YOUNGLY
YENTA	YEXING	YOBBERY	YOKELS	YOUNGNESS
YENTAS	YFERE	YOBBISH	YOKES	YOUNGNESSES
YEOMAN	YGLAUNST	YOBBISHLY	YOKING	YOUNGS
YEOMANLY	YGO	YOBBISM	YOKINGS	YOUNGSTER
YEOMANRIES	YGOE	YOBBISMS	YOKKED	YOUNGSTERS
YEOMANRY	YIBBLES	YOBBO	YOKKING	YOUNGTH
YEOMEN	YICKER	YOBBOES	YOKOZUNA	YOUNGTHLY
YEP	YICKERED	YOBBOS	YOKOZUNAS	YOUNGTHS
YEPS	YICKERING	YOBS	YOKS	YOUNKER
YERBA	YICKERS	YOCK	YOKUL	YOUNKERS
YERBAS	YIELD	YOCKED	YOLD	YOUR
YERD	YIELDABLE	YOCKING	YOLDRING	YOURN
YERDED	YIELDED	YOCKS	YOLDRINGS	YOURS
YERDING	YIELDER	YOD	YOLK	YOURSELF
YERDS	YIELDERS	YODE	YOLKED	YOURSELVES
YERK	YIELDING	YODEL	YOLKIER	YOURT
YERKED	YIELDINGS	YODELLED	YOLKIEST	YOURTS
YERKING	YIELDS	YODELLER	YOLKS	YOUTH
YERKS	YIKE	YODELLERS	YOLKY	YOUTHFUL
YERSINIA	YIKES	YODELLING	YOMP	YOUTHHEAD

YOUTHHEADS	YPSILOID	YTTRIUMS	YUKE	YUMPIES
YOUTHHOOD	YPSILON	YU	YUKED	YUMPING
YOUTHHOODS	YPSILONS	YUAN	YUKES	YUMPS
YOUTHIER	YRAPT	YUCA	YUKIER	YUNX
YOUTHIEST	YRAVISHED	YUCAS	YUKIEST	YUNXES
YOUTHLY	YRENT	YUCCA	YUKING	YUP
YOUTHS	YRIVD	YUCCAS	YUKKIER	YUPON
YOUTHSOME	YRNEH	YUCK	YUKKIEST	YUPONS
YOUTHY	YRNEHS	YUCKED	YUKKY	YUPPIE
YOW	YSAME	YUCKER	YUKO	YUPPIEDOM
YOWE	YSHEND	YUCKERS	YUKOS	YUPPIEDOMS
YOWES	YSHENDING	YUCKIER	YUKS	YUPPIES
YOWIE	YSHENDS	YUCKIEST	YUKY	YUPPIFIED
YOWIES	YSHENT	YUCKING	YULAN	YUPPIFIES
YOWL	YSLAKED	YUCKS	YULANS	YUPPIFY
YOWLED	YTOST	YUCKY	YULE	YUPPIFYING
YOWLEY	YTTERBIA	YUFT	YULES	YUPPY
YOWLEYS	YTTERBIAS	YUFTS	YULETIDE	YUPS
YOWLING	YTTERBIUM	YUG	YULETIDES	YURT
YOWLINGS	YTTERBIUMS	YUGA	YUMMIER	YURTS
YOWLS	YTTRIA	YUGAS	YUMMIEST	YUS
YOWS	YTTRIAS	YUGS	YUMMY	YWIS
YPIGHT	YTTRIC	YUK	YUMP	YWROKE
YPLAST	YTTRIOUS	YUKATA	YUMPED	
YPLIGHT	YTTRIUM	YUKATAS	YUMPIE	

Z

ZABAIONE	ZAMOUSE	ZAREEBA	ZEBUBS	ZEPPELINS
ZABAIONES	ZAMOUSES	ZAREEBAS	ZEBUS	ZERDA
ZABETA	ZAMPOGNA	ZARF	ZECCHINE	ZERDAS
ZABETAS	ZAMPOGNAS	ZARFS	ZECCHINES	ZEREBA
ZABRA	ZAMPONE	ZARIBA	ZECCHINI	ZEREBAS
ZABRAS	ZAMPONI	ZARIBAS	ZECCHINO	ZERIBA
ZABTIEH	ZANDER	ZARNEC	ZECCHINOS	ZERIBAS
ZABTIEHS	ZANDERS	ZARNECS	ZED	ZERO
ZACK	ZANELLA	ZARNICH	ZEDOARIES	ZEROED
ZACKS	ZANELLAS	ZARNICHS	ZEDOARY	ZEROING
ZADDIK	ZANIED	ZARZUELA	ZEDS	ZEROS
ZADDIKIM	ZANIER	ZARZUELAS	ZEE	ZEROTH
ZADDIKS	ZANIES	ZASTRUGA	ZEES	ZERUMBET
ZAFFER	ZANIEST	ZASTRUGI	ZEIN	ZERUMBETS
ZAFFERS	ZANINESS	ZATI	ZEINS	ZEST
ZAFFRE	ZANINESSES	ZATIS	ZEITGEIST	ZESTED
ZAFFRES	ZANJA	ZAX	ZEITGEISTS	ZESTER
ZAG	ZANJAS	ZAXES	ZEK	ZESTERS
ZAGGED	ZANJERO	ZEA	ZEKS	ZESTFUL
ZAGGING	ZANJEROS	ZEAL	ZEL	ZESTFULLY
ZAGS	ZANTE	ZEALANT	ZELANT	ZESTIER
ZAIRE	ZANTES	ZEALANTS	ZELANTS	ZESTIEST
ZAITECH	ZANTHOXYL	ZEALFUL	ZELATOR	ZESTING
ZAITECHS	ZANTHOXYLS	ZEALLESS	ZELATORS	ZESTS
ZAKAT	ZANY	ZEALOT	ZELATRICE	ZESTY
ZAKATS	ZANYING	ZEALOTISM	ZELATRICES	ZETA
ZAKUSKA	ZANYISM	ZEALOTISMS	ZELATRIX	ZETAS
ZAKUSKI	ZANYISMS	ZEALOTRIES	ZELATRIXES	ZETETIC
ZAMAN	ZANZE	ZEALOTRY	ZELOSO	ZETETICS
ZAMANG	ZANZES	ZEALOTS	ZELOTYPIA	ZEUGMA
ZAMANGS	ZAP	ZEALOUS	ZELOTYPIAS	ZEUGMAS
ZAMANS	ZAPATA	ZEALOUSLY	ZELS	ZEUGMATIC
ZAMARRA	ZAPATEADO	ZEALS	ZEMINDAR	ZEUXITE
ZAMARRAS	ZAPATEADOS	ZEAS	ZEMINDARI	ZEUXITES
ZAMARRO	ZAPOTILLA	ZEBEC	ZEMINDARIES	ZEX
ZAMARROS	ZAPOTILLAS	ZEBECK	ZEMINDARIS	ZEXES
ZAMBO	ZAPPED	ZEBECKS	ZEMINDARS	ZEZE
ZAMBOMBA	ZAPPER	ZEBECS	ZEMINDARY	ZEZES
ZAMBOMBAS	ZAPPERS	ZEBRA	ZEMSTVA	ZHO
ZAMBOORAK	ZAPPIER	ZEBRAS	ZEMSTVO	ZHOMO
ZAMBOORAKS	ZAPPIEST	ZEBRASS	ZEMSTVOS	ZHOMOS
ZAMBOS	ZAPPING	ZEBRASSES	ZENANA	ZHOS
ZAMBUCK	ZAPS	ZEBRINA	ZENANAS	ZIBELINE
ZAMBUCKS	ZAPTIAH	ZEBRINAS	ZENDIK	ZIBELINES
ZAMBUK	ZAPTIAHS	ZEBRINE	ZENDIKS	ZIBELLINE
ZAMBUKS	ZAPTIEH	ZEBRINNIES	ZENITH	ZIBELLINES
ZAMIA	ZAPTIEHS	ZEBRINNY	ZENITHAL	ZIBET
ZAMIAS	ZARAPE	ZEBROID	ZENITHS	ZIBETS
ZAMINDAR	ZARAPES	ZEBRULA	ZEOLITE	ZIFF
ZAMINDARI	ZARATITE	ZEBRULAS	ZEOLITES	ZIFFIUS
ZAMINDARIES	ZARATITES	ZEBRULE	ZEOLITIC	ZIFFIUSES
ZAMINDARIS	ZAREBA	ZEBRULES	ZEPHYR	ZIFFS
ZAMINDARS	ZAREBAS	ZEBU	ZEPHYRS	ZIG
ZAMINDARY		ZEBUB	ZEPPELIN	ZIGAN

The Chambers Dictionary is the authority for many longer words; see *OSW* Introduction, page xii

ZIGANKA	ZINES	ZIZANIAS	ZONATED	ZOOIDS
ZIGANKAS	ZINFANDEL	ZIZEL	ZONATION	ZOOKS
ZIGANS	ZINFANDELS	ZIZELS	ZONATIONS	ZOOLATER
ZIGGED	ZING	ZIZYPHUS	ZONDA	ZOOLATERS
ZIGGING	ZINGED	ZIZYPHUSES	ZONDAS	ZOOLATRIA
ZIGGURAT	ZINGEL	ZIZZ	ZONE	ZOOLATRIAS
ZIGGURATS	ZINGELS	ZIZZED	ZONED	ZOOLATRIES
ZIGS	ZINGER	ZIZZES	ZONELESS	ZOOLATRY
ZIGZAG	ZINGERS	ZIZZING	ZONES	ZOOLITE
ZIGZAGGED	ZINGIBER	ZLOTY	ZONING	ZOOLITES
ZIGZAGGING	ZINGIBERS	ZLOTYS	ZONINGS	ZOOLITH
ZIGZAGGY	ZINGIER	ZO	ZONK	ZOOLITHIC
ZIGZAGS	ZINGIEST	ZOA	ZONKED	ZOOLITHS
ZIKKURAT	ZINGING	ZOARIA	ZONKING	ZOOLITIC
ZIKKURATS	ZINGS	ZOARIUM	ZONKS	ZOOLOGIES
ZILA	ZINGY	ZOBO	ZONOID	ZOOLOGIST
ZILAS	ZINKE	ZOBOS	ZONULA	ZOOLOGISTS
ZILCH	ZINKED	ZOBU	ZONULAE	ZOOLOGY
ZILCHES	ZINKENITE	ZOBUS	ZONULAR	ZOOM
ZILLAH	ZINKENITES	ZOCCO	ZONULAS	ZOOMANCIES
ZILLAHS	ZINKES	ZOCCOLO	ZONULE	ZOOMANCY
ZILLION	ZINKIER	ZOCCOLOS	ZONULES	ZOOMANTIC
ZILLIONS	ZINKIEST	ZOCCOS	ZONULET	ZOOMED
ZILLIONTH	ZINKIFIED	ZODIAC	ZONULETS	ZOOMETRIC
ZILLIONTHS	ZINKIFIES	ZODIACAL	ZONURE	ZOOMETRIES
ZIMB	ZINKIFY	ZODIACS	ZONURES	ZOOMETRY
ZIMBI	ZINKIFYING	ZOEA	ZOO	ZOOMING
ZIMBIS	ZINKING	ZOEAE	ZOOBIOTIC	ZOOMORPH
ZIMBS	ZINKY	ZOEAL	ZOOBLAST	ZOOMORPHIES
ZIMMER	ZINNIA	ZOEAS	ZOOBLASTS	ZOOMORPHS
ZIMMERS	ZINNIAS	ZOECHROME	ZOOCHORE	ZOOMORPHY
ZIMOCCA	ZIP	ZOECHROMES	ZOOCHORES	ZOOMS
ZIMOCCAS	ZIPLOCK	ZOEFORM	ZOOCHORIES	ZOON
ZINC	ZIPPED	ZOETIC	ZOOCHORY	ZOONAL
ZINCED	ZIPPER	ZOETROPE	ZOOCYTIA	ZOONIC
ZINCIER	ZIPPERED	ZOETROPES	ZOOCYTIUM	ZOONITE
ZINCIEST	ZIPPERS	ZOETROPIC	ZOOEA	ZOONITES
ZINCIFIED	ZIPPIER	ZOIATRIA	ZOOEAE	ZOONITIC
ZINCIFIES	ZIPPIEST	ZOIATRIAS	ZOOEAL	ZOONOMIA
ZINCIFY	ZIPPING	ZOIATRICS	ZOOEAS	ZOONOMIAS
ZINCIFYING	ZIPPO	ZOIC	ZOOECIA	ZOONOMIC
ZINCING	ZIPPOS	ZOISITE	ZOOECIUM	ZOONOMIES
ZINCITE	ZIPPY	ZOISITES	ZOOGAMETE	ZOONOMIST
ZINCITES	ZIPS	ZOISM	ZOOGAMETES	ZOONOMISTS
ZINCKED	ZIPTOP	ZOISMS	ZOOGAMIES	ZOONOMY
ZINCKIER	ZIRCALOY	ZOIST	ZOOGAMOUS	ZOONOSES
ZINCKIEST	ZIRCALOYS	ZOISTS	ZOOGAMY	ZOONOSIS
ZINCKIFIED	ZIRCON	ZOMBI	ZOOGENIC	ZOONOTIC
ZINCKIFIES	ZIRCONIA	ZOMBIE	ZOOGENIES	ZOONS
ZINCKIFY	ZIRCONIAS	ZOMBIES	ZOOGENOUS	ZOOPATHIES
ZINCKIFYING	ZIRCONIC	ZOMBIFIED	ZOOGENY	ZOOPATHY
ZINCKING	ZIRCONIUM	ZOMBIFIES	ZOOGLOEA	ZOOPERAL
ZINCKY	ZIRCONIUMS	ZOMBIFY	ZOOGLOEAE	ZOOPERIES
ZINCO	ZIRCONS	ZOMBIFYING	ZOOGLOEAS	ZOOPERIST
ZINCODE	ZIT	ZOMBIISM	ZOOGLOEIC	ZOOPERISTS
ZINCODES	ZITE	ZOMBIISMS	ZOOGONIES	ZOOPERY
ZINCOID	ZITHER	ZOMBIS	ZOOGONOUS	ZOOPHAGAN
ZINCOS	ZITHERN	ZOMBORUK	ZOOGONY	ZOOPHAGANS
ZINCOUS	ZITHERNS	ZOMBORUKS	ZOOGRAFT	ZOOPHAGIES
ZINCS	ZITHERS	ZONA	ZOOGRAFTS	ZOOPHAGY
ZINCY	ZITI	ZONAE	ZOOGRAPHIES	ZOOPHILE
ZINE	ZITS	ZONAL	ZOOGRAPHY	ZOOPHILES
ZINEB	ZIZ	ZONARY	ZOOID	ZOOPHILIA
ZINEBS	ZIZANIA	ZONATE	ZOOIDAL	ZOOPHILIAS

ZOOPHILIES
ZOOPHILY
ZOOPHOBIA
ZOOPHOBIAS
ZOOPHORI
ZOOPHORIC
ZOOPHORUS
ZOOPHYTE
ZOOPHYTES
ZOOPHYTIC
ZOOPLASTIES
ZOOPLASTY
ZOOS
ZOOSCOPIC
ZOOSCOPIES
ZOOSCOPY
ZOOSPERM
ZOOSPERMS
ZOOSPORE
ZOOSPORES
ZOOSPORIC
ZOOTAXIES
ZOOTAXY
ZOOTECHNIES
ZOOTECHNY
ZOOTHECIA
ZOOTHEISM
ZOOTHEISMS
ZOOTHOME
ZOOTHOMES
ZOOTOMIC
ZOOTOMIES

ZOOTOMIST
ZOOTOMISTS
ZOOTOMY
ZOOTOXIN
ZOOTOXINS
ZOOTROPE
ZOOTROPES
ZOOTROPHIES
ZOOTROPHY
ZOOTYPE
ZOOTYPES
ZOOTYPIC
ZOOZOO
ZOOZOOS
ZOPILOTE
ZOPILOTES
ZOPPA
ZOPPO
ZORGITE
ZORGITES
ZORI
ZORIL
ZORILLE
ZORILLES
ZORILLO
ZORILLOS
ZORILS
ZORINO
ZORINOS
ZORIS
ZORRO
ZORROS

ZOS
ZOSTER
ZOSTERS
ZOUK
ZOUKS
ZOUNDS
ZOWIE
ZUCCHETTO
ZUCCHETTOS
ZUCCHINI
ZUCCHINIS
ZUCHETTA
ZUCHETTAS
ZUCHETTO
ZUCHETTOS
ZUFFOLI
ZUFFOLO
ZUFOLI
ZUFOLO
ZUGZWANG
ZUGZWANGS
ZULU
ZULUS
ZUMBOORUK
ZUMBOORUKS
ZUPA
ZUPAN
ZUPANS
ZUPAS
ZURF
ZURFS
ZUZ

ZUZIM
ZYDECO
ZYDECOS
ZYGA
ZYGAENID
ZYGAENINE
ZYGAENOID
ZYGAL
ZYGANTRA
ZYGANTRUM
ZYGANTRUMS
ZYGOCACTI
ZYGODONT
ZYGOMA
ZYGOMAS
ZYGOMATA
ZYGOMATIC
ZYGON
ZYGOPHYTE
ZYGOPHYTES
ZYGOSE
ZYGOSES
ZYGOSIS
ZYGOSPERM
ZYGOSPERMS
ZYGOSPORE
ZYGOSPORES
ZYGOTE
ZYGOTES
ZYGOTIC
ZYLONITE
ZYLONITES

ZYMASE
ZYMASES
ZYME
ZYMES
ZYMIC
ZYMITE
ZYMITES
ZYMOGEN
ZYMOGENIC
ZYMOGENS
ZYMOID
ZYMOLOGIC
ZYMOLOGIES
ZYMOLOGY
ZYMOLYSES
ZYMOLYSIS
ZYMOLYTIC
ZYMOME
ZYMOMES
ZYMOMETER
ZYMOMETERS
ZYMOSES
ZYMOSIS
ZYMOTIC
ZYMOTICS
ZYMURGIES
ZYMURGY
ZYTHUM
ZYTHUMS

Dictionary of 2- and 3-letter words allowable for Scrabble®

Note that, although these are complete lists of all the 2- and 3-letter words allowable for Scrabble, the meanings are not necessarily comprehensive; the full range can be found in *The Chambers Dictionary*.

The definitions have been selected to help players to remember the words, and at the same time to act as guides to possible derivatives. For example, CUE is defined both as 'a signal to begin a speech, etc' (the plural CUES being implied) and as 'to give such a signal' (implying the forms CUES (again), CUEING, and CUED). Remember however that this dictionary is intended only as an aide-mémoire. *Official Scrabble® Words*, in conjunction with *The Chambers Dictionary*, is the final authority.

Different parts of speech are separated by '❑', and different meanings of the same word by ';'.

Bold type is used when reference is being made to other words. Often these words are defined in the lists; when, however, the reference is to longer words, definitions have been given for those that are felt to be less familiar.

2-LETTER WORDS

AA	a type of lava
AD	colloquial for **advertisement**
AE	Scots word for **one** (adjective)
AH	interjection expressing surprise, joy, etc ◻ to make such an interjection
AI	the three-toed sloth; same as **ayu**
AM	present tense of **be**
AN	the indefinite article used before a vowel
AR	the letter 'R'
AS	in whatever way ◻ so ◻ a mythological Norse god; a Roman unit of weight; a Roman coin
ÅS	a **kame**, a gravel ridge
AT	preposition denoting position in space or time
AW	interjection expressing disappointment, sympathy, etc
AX	US form of **axe**
AY	always ◻ yes ◻ an affirmative vote or voter
BA	in ancient Egyptian religion, the soul
BE	to exist or live
BI	colloquial short form of **bisexual**, (a person who is) attracted sexually to both sexes
BO	interjection intended to startle ◻ in US slang, a term of address to a man
BY	beside; near; through ◻ same as **bye**
CH	obsolete dialect pronoun meaning **I**
DA	a Burmese knife; a dialect form of **dad**, a father
DI	a plural of **deus**, Latin word for **god**
DO	to perform ◻ a celebration; same as **doh**
EA	dialect word meaning **river**
EE	Scots word for **eye** (noun)
EF	the letter 'F'
EH	interjection expressing inquiry ◻ to say 'eh'
EL	the letter 'L', or anything of that shape; an elevated railway
EM	the letter 'M'; a unit of measurement in printing
EN	the letter 'N'; in printing, half of an **em**
ER	interjection expressing hesitation
ES	the letter 'S', or anything of that shape
EX	the letter 'X'; someone no longer in a previous relationship
FA	a musical note (in sol-fa)
FY	same as **fie**
GI	same as **gie**, a judo or karate costume
GO	to pass from one place to another ◻ energy or activity; a Japanese board game
GU	same as **gue**
HA	interjection expressing a wide range of emotions or responses
HE	pronoun used in referring to a male person or thing ◻ a male
HI	interjection calling attention
HO	interjection calling attention, expressing surprise, etc ◻ stopping, cessation ◻ obsolete word meaning to stop
ID	a fish of the carp family; part of the human personality
IF	on condition that; whether ◻ a condition
IN	not out ◻ someone or something that is in ◻ to take in
IO	interjection expressing joy, triumph or grief ◻ a cry of 'io'
IS	present tense of **be**
IT	pronoun referring to an inanimate thing ◻ an indefinable quality; Italian vermouth
JO	Scots word for a loved one
KA	the spirit or soul; a god; same as **kae**, a jackdaw
KO	a Maori digging-stick
KY	same as **kye**
LA	a musical note (in sol-fa) ◻ interjection with various meanings
LI	a Chinese unit of distance
LO	interjection meaning see, look or behold
MA	childish or familiar word for **mother** (noun)
ME	pronoun representing oneself
MI	a musical note (in sol-fa)
MO	old word for **more**

MU a letter in the Greek alphabet
MY of or belonging to me

NA Scots word for **no**, not at all
NE obsolete word meaning not
NÉ (of a man) born
NO a word of negation; not at all □ a
negative vote or voter
NU a letter in the Greek alphabet
NY obsolete spelling of **nigh** (adjective
and verb)

OB an objection
OD a hypothetical force; old word for
god, often used as a mild oath
OE same as **oy**
OF belonging to
OH interjection expressing surprise,
interest, pain, etc
OI interjection used to attract attention
OM an intoned Hindu sacred symbol
ON not off; available □ in cricket, the on-
side □ to go on
OO Scots form of **wool** □ Scots form of
we
OP short form of **operation**
OR in heraldry, the tincture gold or yellow
□ a word expressing alternatives
OS a bone
OU Scots interjection expressing
concession
OW interjection expressing pain; same as
ou
OX a general name for a bovine animal
OY Scots word for **grandchild**

PA childish or familiar word for **father**; a
Maori fort
PH a number used to express degree of
acidity or alkalinity
PI a letter in the Greek alphabet □ pious
or sanctimonious

PO short form of **chamberpot**

QI an individual's life force

RE a musical note (in sol-fa) □ about

SH interjection requesting silence
SI an earlier form of **ti**, a musical note
SO in such a way □ same as **sol**, a musical
note
ST interjection requesting silence

TA interjection expressing thanks
TE same as **ti**, a musical note
TI a musical note (in sol-fa); a small
Pacific tree
TO in the direction of, towards

UG to loathe
UM interjection expressing doubt or
hesitation
UN dialect word for **one** (noun)
UP in a higher place □ a rise; a spell of
prosperity □ to move up
UR interjection expressing hesitation
US pronoun used in referring to oneself
and others
UT a syllable representing **doh**

WE pronoun used in referring to oneself
and others
WO variant of **woe**

XI a letter in the Greek alphabet
XU a Vietnamese coin

YE old word for **you**; old spelling of **the**
YO interjection calling for effort or
attention
YU precious jade

ZO same as **zho**

3-LETTER WORDS

AAS plural of **aa**

ABA an outer garment worn by some Arab women

ABB a textile yarn

ABY to pay (as) a penalty

ACE a winning serve in tennis □ outstanding □ to play an ace

ACH same as **och**

ACT to do in a specified way □ something done

ADD to make an addition

ADO bustle or fuss

ADS plural of **ad**

ADZ US form of **adze**, a cutting tool

AFT behind; near the stern of a vessel, etc

AGA a Turkish commander or chief officer

AGE the time during which a person has existed □ to grow old

AGO past; since

AHA interjection expressing exultation, pleasure, surprise, etc

AHS present tense of **ah**

AIA an Indian or South African nursemaid

AID to help or assist □ help; something that helps

AIL to be indisposed □ a trouble

AIM to point or direct □ a purpose

AIN Scots word for **own** (adjective)

AIR the mixture of gases breathed by people and animals; an appearance or manner □ to make known publicly

AIS plural of **ai**

AIT a small island

AKE old spelling of **ache** (verb)

ALA an outgrowth on a fruit

ALB a priest's long white vestment

ALE a kind of beer

ALL comprising the whole amount, extent, etc of □ the whole; everybody or everything

ALP a high mountain; a mountain pasture

ALS obsolete form of **also**, or **as** (adverb)

ALT a high tone; a halt or rest

AMI French word for **friend**

AMP short form of **ampere** and **amplifier**

ANA in equal quantities (in recipes and prescriptions)

AND also; indicating addition □ something added

ANE Scots word for **one**

ANI a tropical American bird

ANN old Scots word for a payment to a parish minister's widow

ANT a small industrious insect

ANY some; whichever, no matter which

APE a monkey □ to imitate

APT suitable □ obsolete word meaning to adapt

ARB short form of **arbitrageur**, a person who profits by judicious dealing in stocks and shares

ARC a part of the circumference of a circle □ to form an arc

ARD a primitive type of plough

ARE present tense of **be** □ a unit of metric land measure

ARK a floating vessel □ obsolete word meaning to put in an ark

ARM a limb; a weapon □ to provide with weapons

ARS plural of **ar**

ART the creation of works of beauty; a human skill

ARY dialect word for **any**

ASH a kind of tree; the remains of anything burnt

ASK to request, inquire, or invite □ dialect word for **newt**

ASP a venomous snake

ASS a long-eared animal like a small horse; a stupid person

ATE past tense of **eat**

AUF obsolete word for an elf's child

AUK a heavy black-and-white seabird

AVA Scots word meaning **at all**

AVE a recitation of the address or prayer to the Virgin Mary

AWA Scots word for **away**

AWE fear or dread □ to strike with or influence by awe

AWL a pointed instrument for boring

AWN the beard of barley, etc □ to shelter with an awning

AXE a tool for chopping □ to chop or cut down

AYE ever; yes □ an affirmative vote or voter

AYS plural of **ay**

AYU a small edible Japanese fruit

BAA the cry of a sheep □ to bleat

BAC colloquial short form of **baccalaureate**, a degree or diploma

BAD evil; wicked; faulty □ something evil, wicked, etc

BAG a receptacle for containing something ❑ to put into a bag

BAH interjection expressing disgust or contempt

BAM a hoax ❑ to hoax or cheat

BAN a prohibition ❑ to forbid or prohibit

BAP a large, flat breakfast roll

BAR a block of a solid substance; an obstruction ❑ to obstruct or prevent

BAS plural of **ba**

BAT a flying mammal; an implement for striking a ball ❑ to strike with a bat

BAY an inlet of the sea; the barking (of hounds) ❑ to bark or howl

BED a place to sleep on ❑ to put to bed

BEE an insect that makes honey; the letter 'B'

BEG to ask for ❑ another word for **bey**

BEL a measure of noise

BEN Scots or Irish word for **mountain**

BET a sum of money, etc, gambled ❑ to gamble (money, etc)

BEY a Turkish governor

BEZ the second tine of a deer's horn

BIB a protective piece of material fastened under a child's chin ❑ to tipple

BID an offer ❑ to make an offer

BIG large; very important ❑ Scots word for **build** (verb)

BIN a container for rubbish; a case for wine ❑ to put into a bin

BIO short form of **biography**

BIS twice

BIT a small piece; a curb or restraint ❑ to curb or restrain

BIZ slang word for **business**

BOA a large constricting snake

BOB to move quickly up and down ❑ a curtsy

BOD a person

BOG a marsh ❑ to sink

BOH same as **bo** (interjection)

BOK South African word for a goat or an antelope

BON French word for **good**

BOO a sound expressing disapproval or contempt ❑ to make such a sound

BOP short for **bebop**, a variety of jazz music ❑ to dance to pop music

BOR East Anglian form of address meaning **neighbour**

BOS plural of **bo**

BOT the maggot of a botfly ❑ Australian word meaning to cadge

BOW a bending of the neck or body in greeting ❑ to bend or incline downwards

BOX a case or receptacle for holding anything; a blow with the hand or fists ❑ to put into a box; to strike with the hand or fists

BOY a male child ❑ Shakespearean word meaning to play (a female part) as a boy

BRA short for **brassière**, an undergarment worn to support a woman's breasts

BRO a place for which one feels a strong affinity

BUB old word for a strong drink

BUD a flower not yet opened ❑ to produce buds

BUG a kind of insect ❑ to pester or irritate

BUM a tramp or sponger ❑ to sponge or live dissolutely

BUN a kind of sweet roll or cake

BUR a prickly seed-case; a throaty sound of 'r' ❑ to whisper hoarsely

BUS a road vehicle for passengers ❑ to transport by bus

BUT except; nevertheless ❑ an objection ❑ to put forward as an objection

BUY to purchase ❑ something purchased

BYE a pass to the next round (of a competition, etc)

BYS plural of **by**

CAB a taxi-cab

CAD a dishonourable man

CAM a projection on a revolving shaft; a whitening stone ❑ to whiten with a cam

CAN a container of tin-plate ❑ to store in such a container

CAP a covering for the head, a chimney, etc ❑ to put a cap on or cover the top of

CAR a self-propelled wheeled vehicle

CAT a small, furry domestic animal ❑ to vomit

CAW to cry as a crow ❑ the cry of a crow

CAY a low islet

CEE the letter 'C', or anything of that shape

CEL short form of **celluloid**, a strong, often transparent, plastic material

CEP a kind of edible mushroom

CHA tea

CHE dialect form of **I**, used by Shakespeare

CHI feminine of **chal**, a fellow or person

CID a chief, captain or hero

CIG colloquial short form of **cigarette**

CIT contemptuous term for someone who is not a gentleman

CLY old word meaning to seize or steal

COB a male swan; a wicker basket ❑ to strike

COD a kind of fish; a hoax ❑ to hoax or make fun of

COG a projection on a toothed wheel ❑ to furnish with cogs

COL a pass in a mountain range

CON a trick or swindle ❑ to trick; to persuade by dishonest means

COO to make a sound like a dove ❑ the sound made by a dove

COP to capture ❑ a policeman; a capture or arrest

COR interjection expressing surprise ❑ a Hebrew measure

COS a crisp, long-leaved lettuce

COT a small bed for a young child

COW the female of bovine and some other animals ❑ to subdue

COX short for **coxswain**, (to act as) a person who steers a boat

COY bashful or modest ❑ Shakespearean word meaning to caress or to disdain

COZ short for **cousin**

CRU French word meaning **vineyard** or **vintage**

CRY to utter a sound of pain or grief, or loudly ❑ such a sound

CUB the young of some animals, eg a fox ❑ to produce cubs

CUD food chewed again by a ruminating animal

CUE a signal to begin a speech, etc ❑ to give such a signal

CUM combined with; with the addition of

CUP a small round drinking-vessel ❑ to form into a cup shape

CUR a worthless mongrel dog

CUT to make an incision in; to reduce ❑ an incision or reduction

CUZ obsolete form of **coz**

CWM Welsh word for **valley**

DAB to touch or press gently ❑ a gentle touch or wipe; an expert ❑ expert

DAD a father; a thump ❑ to thump

DAE Scots form of **do** (verb)

DAG a dirty tuft of wool on a sheep ❑ to cut off dags

DAH same as **da**, a Burmese knife

DAK in India, the mail or post; a letter

DAL a kind of Indian edible pea

DAM an embankment to restrain water ❑ to restrain (water) with an embankment or bank

DAN a level of efficiency (in Japanese combative sports)

DAP to dip bait gently into the water (in fishing) ❑ bait so dipped

DAS plural of **da**

DAW a jackdaw ❑ to dawn

DAY the time when it is light; 24 hours

DEB colloquial form of **débutante**, a young woman making her first formal appearance in society

DEE the letter 'D', or anything of that shape ❑ euphemism for **damn**

DEF excellent, brilliant

DEI a plural of **deus**, Latin word for **god**

DEL another word for **nabla**, a mathematical symbol

DEN the lair of a wild animal; a private place ❑ to retire to a den

DEW moisture deposited from the air on cooling ❑ to moisten (as) with dew

DEY formerly, the pasha of Algiers

DIB to fish by dapping ❑ a small bone in a sheep's leg

DID past tense of **do**

DIE to lose life ❑ a small cube, a dice

DIG to use a spade; to excavate ❑ an act of digging

DIM not bright ❑ to make dim

DIN a loud jarring noise ❑ to annoy with such a noise

DIP to immerse briefly; to lower ❑ an act or period of dipping

DIT named or reputed (French) ❑ Scots word meaning to block

DIV an evil spirit of Persian mythology

DOB to inform on or betray

DOC contraction of **doctor** (noun)

DOD dialect word meaning to cut the hair of ❑ Scots word for a rounded hill

DOE the female of a deer, rabbit, and some other animals

DOG one of a family of four-legged animals, often the domestic variety ❑ to follow like a dog

DOH a musical note (in sol-fa)

DON a university lecturer, etc ❑ to put on (clothes, etc)

DOO Scots word for **dove**, a pigeon

DOP a kind of brandy ❑ obsolete word meaning to dip

DOR a dung-beetle ❑ obsolete word meaning to mock

DOS plural of **do**, a musical note

DOT   a very small spot ❑ to make such a spot

DOW   same as **dhow**, an Arab sailing vessel ❑ obsolete and Scots word meaning to be able

DRY   without liquid ❑ to make or become dry

DSO   same as **zho**

DUB   to add sound effects, etc, to ❑ Scots word for **puddle**

DUD   something or someone ineffectual ❑ ineffective; useless

DUE   something owed ❑ Shakespearean word meaning to endue

DUG   past tense of **dig** ❑ a nipple of an animal

DUN   greyish brown ❑ a greyish-brown horse ❑ to press for payment

DUO   two people considered a pair for a specific reason

DUP   Shakespearean word meaning to undo

DUX   a leader

DYE   to stain ❑ a colour produced by dyeing

DZO   same as **zho**

EAN   Shakespearean word meaning to give birth to

EAR   the organ of hearing; the part of corn, etc, containing the seeds ❑ to produce (corn) ears; obsolete word meaning to plough

EAS   plural of **ea**

EAT   to take in food ❑ an archaic word for **food**

EAU   French word for **water**; same as **ea**

EBB   to move back from the land (of the tide) ❑ such a movement of the tide

ECH   Shakespearean word meaning to eke out

ECU   a European unit of currency

EDH   same as **eth**

EEK   interjection expressing fright

EEL   a long, smooth cylindrical fish

EEN   plural of **ee**

EFF   euphemism for **fuck**

EFS   plural of **ef**

EFT   a newt

EGG   an oval or round body from which young are hatched ❑ to add eggs to (in cooking, etc)

EGO   the 'I' or self

EHS   present tense of **eh**

EIK   Scots form of **eke**

EKE   to add ❑ an addition

ELD   old word for age or old age

ELF   a diminutive, mischievous supernatural being ❑ Shakespearean word meaning to entangle (hair)

ELK   a kind of large deer

ELL   a measure of length

ELM   a tree with serrated leaves

ELS   plural of **el**

ELT   dialect word for a young sow

EME   obsolete word for **uncle**

EMS   plural of **em**

EMU   a flightless, fast-running bird

END   the last point; termination or close ❑ to finish or close

ENE   obsolete, dialect or poetic word for **even**

ENG   a phonetic symbol

ENS   plural of **en**; being or existence

EON   same as **aeon**, an eternity

ERA   a series of years; an age

ERE   before ❑ same as **ear**, to plough

ERF   South African word for a garden plot

ERG   a unit of work

ERK   slang word for **aircraftsman**

ERN   old spelling of **earn**

ERR   to make a mistake

ERS   the bitter vetch

ESS   same as **es**

EST   a programme designed to develop human potential

ETA   a letter in the Greek alphabet

ETH   a letter used in Old English

EUK   dialect word meaning to itch ❑ an itching

EVE   poetic word for **evening**

EWE   a female sheep

EWK   same as **euk**

EWT   old form of **newt**, a tailed amphibious animal

EYE   the organ of sight ❑ to look at carefully

FAB   marvellous

FAD   an interest intensely but briefly pursued; a craze

FAG   a cigarette; drudgery ❑ to work, or be worked, hard

FAH   same as **fa**

FAN   an instrument used for cooling ❑ to cool, (as) with a fan

FAP   Shakespearean word meaning fuddled or drunk

FAR   remote or distant ❑ dialect word meaning to remove to a distance

FAS   plural of **fa**

FAT   plump; obese ❑ solid vegetable or animal oil ❑ to make or grow fat

FAW   a gypsy

FAX	a machine that scans electronically ❑ to send messages by such a machine
FAY	poetic word for a fairy ❑ dialect word meaning to clean out (eg a ditch) ❑ same as **fey** (adjective)
FED	past tense of **feed** ❑ US slang for a Federal agent
FEE	the price paid for services ❑ to pay a fee to
FEN	low marshy land
FET	obsolete form of **fetch** (verb)
FEU	a Scottish form of land tenure ❑ to grant or hold land in feu
FEW	not many
FEY	whimsical; fairylike; foreseeing the future ❑ same as **fay** (verb)
FEZ	a red brimless cap of wool or felt
FIB	a little lie ❑ to tell such a lie
FID	a conical pin of hard wood
FIE	old interjection expressing disapproval ❑ same as **fey** (adjective)
FIG	a kind of tropical fruit packed with seeds ❑ Shakespearean word meaning to make an insulting gesture at
FIL	Shakespearean word for the shaft of a vehicle
FIN	a steering, swimming, or balancing organ on an aquatic animal
FIR	a kind of conifer
FIT	healthy; suitable ❑ something that fits ❑ to make suitable
FIX	to make firm; to arrange ❑ a difficulty; something fraudulently arranged
FIZ	to make a hissing or sputtering sound ❑ such a sound; a fizzy drink
FLU	short form of **influenza**
FLY	to move through the air ❑ a kind of flying insect ❑ surreptitious or sly
FOB	a small watch pocket ❑ obsolete word meaning to pocket
FOE	an enemy
FOG	a thick mist ❑ to be affected by fog
FOH	an expression of disgust or contempt
FON	obsolete word for a fool ❑ to play the fool
FOP	an affected dandy
FOR	in the place of; in favour of; towards
FOU	Scots word for **drunk** (adjective)
FOX	a wild animal related to the dog ❑ to act cunningly, to cheat
FOY	Spenserian word meaning **allegiance**, loyalty
FRA	Italian word meaning **brother** or **friar**
FRO	obsolete word for **from**

FRY	to cook in oil or fat ❑ a dish so cooked; a number of young fish
FUB	old word meaning to put off
FUD	Scots word for a rabbit's or hare's tail
FUG	a very hot, close atmosphere ❑ to cause a fug in
FUM	same word as **fung**, a fabulous Chinese bird
FUN	pleasure, enjoyment, merriment ❑ to play
FUR	the thick, soft, fine hair of some animals; a crust formed by hard water ❑ to cover or coat with fur
GAB	to chatter ❑ idle talk
GAD	to wander about idly ❑ a miner's chisel
GAE	Scots word for **go** (verb)
GAG	to silence ❑ something that gags the mouth
GAL	dialect word for **girl**
GAM	a school of whales ❑ to join up in a gam
GAN	past tense of the old verb **gin**, to begin
GAP	an opening ❑ to make a gap in
GAR	Scots word meaning to compel ❑ a garfish
GAS	a substance which is neither solid nor liquid ❑ to poison with gas
GAT	slang word for a gun
GAU	under the Nazi regime, a German political district
GAY	lively ❑ a homosexual
GED	dialect word for **pike** (fish)
GEE	the letter 'G' ❑ of horses, to move on
GEL	a jelly-like solution ❑ to form a gel
GEM	a precious stone ❑ old word meaning to adorn with gems
GEN	general information
GEO	a gully or creek
GET	to obtain ❑ a stupid person
GEY	Scots word meaning **fairly** ❑ Scots word meaning **considerable**
GHI	clarified butter
GIB	a wedge-shaped piece of metal ❑ to fasten with a gib
GID	a sheep disease
GIE	Scots word for **give** (verb) ❑ a judo costume
GIF	old word meaning **if**
GIG	a band or pop group's engagement ❑ to play a gig
GIN	an alcoholic spirit ❑ to snare in a gin trap
GIO	same as **geo**
GIP	same as **gyp** (noun)
GIS	plural of **gis**

GIT	a stupid person
GJU	same as **gue**
GNU	an African antelope
GOA	a Tibetan gazelle
GOB	slang word for the mouth □ to spit
GOD	an object of worship □ to deify
GOE	older form of **geo** □ old form of **go** (verb)
GON	a geometrical grade
GOO	a sticky substance
GOS	plural of **go**
GOT	past tense of **get**
GOV	short form of **governor**
GOY	a Gentile
GUB	Australian word for a white man
GUE	a kind of violin formerly used in Shetland
GUM	a sticky substance □ to smear, coat, etc with gum
GUN	a weapon for discharging explosive projectiles, etc □ to discharge such projectiles, etc
GUP	slang word for gossip or prattle
GUR	an unrefined cane sugar
GUS	plural of **gu**
GUT	the intestine □ to take the guts out of (fish, etc)
GUV	same as **gov**
GUY	colloquial term for a person generally □ to make fun of
GYM	short form of **gymnasium, gymnastics**, etc
GYP	slang word for a cheat □ to swindle
HAD	past tense of **have**
HAE	Scots form of **have**
HAG	an ugly old woman □ Scots word meaning to hack or hew
HAH	an interjection expressing various emotions, such as surprise, exultation, dismay
HAJ	a Muslim pilgrimage to Mecca
HAM	salted and smoked flesh from the leg of a pig; a bad actor □ to overact, exaggerate
HAN	Spenserian plural form of **have** (verb)
HAP	chance, fortune □ to happen by chance
HAS	present tense of **have**
HAT	a covering for the head □ to provide or cover with a hat
HAW	the fruit of the hawthorn □ to make indecisive noises
HAY	cut grass, used for fodder □ to make hay
HEM	an edge or border □ to form a hem on

HEN	a female domestic fowl □ to challenge to a daring act
HEP	slang word meaning knowing, abreast of knowledge and taste □ a rosehip
HER	pronoun representing a female person or thing □ of or belonging to such a person or thing
HES	plural of **he**
HET	slang word for **heterosexual**
HEW	to cut with blows □ Spenserian form of **hue**
HEX	something that brings misfortune □ to bring misfortune
HEY	interjection calling attention, etc □ a winding country-dance □ to dance this dance
HIC	interjection representing a hiccup
HID	past tense of **hide**
HIE	to turn (a horse) to the left □ a cry requesting such a turn
HIM	pronoun representing a male person or thing
HIN	a Hebrew liquid measure
HIP	part of the thigh □ to carry on the hip
HIS	of or belonging to a male person or thing
HIT	to strike □ an act of striking
HOA	interjection expressing exultation, surprise, etc □ cessation □ obsolete word meaning to stop
HOB	a flat surface on a cooker
HOC	Latin word for **this**
HOD	a trough for carrying bricks □ Scots word meaning to bob or jog
HOE	a tool for loosening the earth □ to use a hoe
HOG	a kind of pig □ to use selfishly
HOH	same as **ho**
HOI	interjection used to attract attention
HON	short for **honey**, as a term of endearment
HOO	Shakespearean interjection expressing boisterous emotion
HOP	to leap on one leg □ a leap on one leg
HOS	plural of **ho**
HOT	very warm □ to heat
HOW	in what way □ a manner or means
HOX	Shakespearean word meaning to hock or hamstring
HOY	a large one-decked boat □ interjection requesting someone or something to stop □ to incite
HUB	the centre of a wheel
HUE	a colour or tint
HUG	to embrace □ an embrace
HUH	interjection expressing disgust

HUI   a Maori gathering; a social gathering

HUM   to make a sound like bees □ the noise of bees

HUP   to turn (a horse) to the right □ a cry requesting such a turn

HUT   a small house or shelter □ to settle in a hut

HYE   obsolete form of **hie** or **high**

HYP   old word for **hypochondria**, excessive worry about one's health □ to offend

ICE   frozen water □ to cool with ice

ICH   Shakespearean word meaning to eke or augment □ dialect word for **I**

ICY   covered with ice; frosty

IDE   same as **id**, a fish

IDS   plural of **id**

IFF   conjunction used in logic to express 'if and only if'

IFS   plural of **if**

ILK   a type or kind

ILL   unwell □ harm; misfortune

IMP   a mischievous child; a wicked spirit □ to engraft (a hawk) with new feathers

INK   a coloured liquid used in writing □ to colour with ink

INN   a small hotel □ old word meaning to lodge

INS   plural of **in**

ION   an electrically-charged particle

IOS   plural of **io**

IRE   anger

IRK   to annoy or weary

ISH   Scottish legal word meaning issue or expiry

ISM   any distinctive theory or fad

ISO   short for **isolated replay**, a TV and film facility

ITA   the miriti palm

ITS   of or belonging to something

IVY   a climbing evergreen plant

JAB   to poke or stab □ a poke or stab, an injection

JAG   a sharp projection □ to pierce

JAK   same as **jack**, an East Indian tree

JAM   a conserve made with fruit and sugar; a blockage □ to block up (eg a street) by crowding

JAP   same as **jaup**, a Scots word meaning to splash or a splash

JAR   a wide-mouthed container □ to put in jars

JAW   part of the skull holding the teeth □ to chatter at length

JAY   a bird of the crow family

JEE   same as **gee**

JET   a stream of liquid; a jetplane □ to spout; to travel by jet

JEU   French word for **game**

JEW   offensive word meaning to cheat or get the better of

JIB   a triangular sail □ to show objection

JIG   a lively dance □ to dance a jig; to jump up and down

JIZ   same as **gizz**, Scots word for a wig

JOB   a piece of work □ to work at jobs

JOE   same as **jo**

JOG   to run at a slow, steady pace □ a spell of jogging

JOR   the second movement of a raga

JOT   a little bit, an iota □ to note down

JOW   Scots word meaning to toll □ a stroke of a bell

JOY   gladness, delight □ an obsolete word meaning to rejoice

JUD   a mass of coal

JUG   a container for liquids □ to stew (eg hare) in a closed pottery jar

JUS   Latin word for a law or a legal right

JUT   to project □ a projection

KAE   Scots word for **jackdaw** □ to serve

KAI   in New Zealand, etc, food, a meal

KAM   Shakespearean word meaning **awry**, twisted or distorted

KAS   plural of **ka**

KAT   same as **khat**, an E African shrub; an ancient Egyptian unit of weight

KAW   same as **caw**

KAY   the letter 'K'

KEA   a large New Zealand parrot

KEB   Scots word meaning to give birth to a premature or stillborn lamb □ a ewe giving birth to such a lamb

KED   a wingless fly that infests sheep

KEF   a drug that produces a dreamy repose; such repose

KEG   a small cask

KEN   to know □ a range of knowledge

KEP   dialect word meaning to catch □ a catch

KET   Scots word for **carrion**, rotting flesh of an animal

KEX   a dry stalk

KEY   an instrument for locking, tuning, etc □ to enter (data) into a computer

KID   a young goat; a child □ to hoax or deceive

KIF same as **kef**
KIN one's relations
KIP a nap ▢ to have a nap or sleep
KIR a wine and blackcurrant drink
KIT equipment ▢ to provide with equipment
KOA a Hawaiian acacia
KOB an African waterbuck
KOI a Japanese carp, an edible fish (plural also **koi**)
KON Spenserian word meaning to know
KOP South African word for **hill**
KOS same as **coss**, an Indian measure of distance
KOW same as **cow**, Scots word for a bunch of twigs
KYE Scots word for **cows**, cattle
KYU in judo, one of the novice grades

LAB contraction of **laboratory**
LAC a dark-red resin
LAD a boy or youth
LAG a delay; insulating material ▢ to fall behind; to cover (eg pipes) with insulating material
LAH same as **la**, a musical note
LAM to beat ▢ a hurried flight from the police (US slang)
LAP a circuit of a race-track ▢ to scoop up with the tongue
LAR the god relating to a house
LAS plural of **la**
LAT short form of **latrine**, a lavatory
LAV short form of **lavatory**
LAW a rule or statute ▢ obsolete word meaning to take to court
LAX slack, careless, or negligent ▢ a kind of salmon
LAY to place or set down; to produce eggs ▢ a lyric or song
LEA meadow or pasture ▢ fallow
LED past tense of **lead**
LEE shelter; the sheltered side ▢ Scots word meaning to tell a lie
LEG a limb for walking and standing ▢ to walk briskly
LEI a garland or wreath; plural of **leu**
LEK the unit of Albanian currency ▢ of blackcocks, etc, to gather and display
LEP dialect word meaning to leap
LES same as **lez**
LET to allow; to grant use of in return for payment ▢ a hindrance; an instance of letting for payment
LEU the unit of Romanian currency
LEV the unit of Bulgarian currency

LEW same as **lev** ▢ tepid
LEX Latin word for **law**
LEY a straight line between landscape features; same as **lea**
LEZ short form of **lesbian**, a female homosexual
LIB short form of **liberation**, setting free, from discrimination, prejudice, etc ▢ dialect word meaning to geld
LID a cover or covering
LIE a false statement ▢ to tell a lie; to be in a horizontal position
LIG a dialect form of **lie**
LIN Spenserian word meaning to cease ▢ same as **linn**, a waterfall
LIP one of the folds of flesh round the mouth ▢ to use or touch with the lips
LIS a fleur-de-lis
LIT past tense of **light**
LOB a ball hit (in tennis) or thrown (in cricket) in a specific way ▢ to hit or throw a ball in this way
LOD in statistics, the logarithm of the odds
LOG a fallen or cut tree-trunk ▢ to enter in a record
LOO colloquial form of **lavatory**; a card game ▢ to subject to a forfeit at loo
LOP to cut off unnecessary parts ▢ an act of lopping
LOR colloquial form of **lord**, interjection expressing surprise
LOS praise, reputation
LOT a great deal; a set of things offered together for sale ▢ to allot
LOW not tall or high ▢ an area where things (eg spirits, health, finances, etc) are low ▢ to make the noise of cattle
LOX liquid oxygen; a kind of smoked salmon
LOY in Ireland, a long, narrow spade
LUD a form of **lord**, a judge
LUG to pull or drag with difficulty ▢ dialect word for **ear**
LUM Scots word for **chimney**
LUR same as **lure**, a Bronze Age trumpet
LUV love, a term of endearment
LUX a unit of illumination
LUZ a supposedly indestructible bone, possibly the sacrum
LYE a short branch of a railway; an alkaline solution
LYM Shakespearean for **lyam**, a leash

MAA of a goat, to bleat
MAC contraction of **mackintosh**

MAD insane; angry ▢Shakespearean word meaning to drive mad

MAE Scots word for **mo**

MAG short form of **magazine**; an old word for a halfpenny ▢dialect word for to tease or to chatter

MAK Scots word meaning to make

MAL French word for **pain, sickness**

MAM dialect word for **mother**

MAN an adult human male ▢to provide with a (human) operator

MAP a diagram of the surface of the earth, etc ▢to make a map of

MAR to spoil or damage

MAS a house or farm in the south of France; plural of **ma**

MAT a floor covering ▢to tangle

MAW the stomach of an animal

MAX obsolete word for **gin**, the drink

MAY may blossom ▢to gather may blossom

MEG variant form of **mag**, a halfpenny

MEL honey

MEN plural of **man**

MES plural of **me**

MET past tense of **meet** ▢short form of **meteorology**, the study of weather

MEU the plant spignel

MEW (of a cat) to make a thin, high-pitched cry ▢this cry; a gull

MHO a former unit of electrical inductance

MID middle ▢the middle; short for **midshipman**

MIL a unit of wire measurement; a Cyprian coin

MIM Scots and dialect word meaning **prim**

MIR a Russian peasant farming commune; a Muslim ruler

MIS Spenserian word meaning to fail ▢plural of **mi**

MIX to mingle ▢a mixture

MIZ short form of **misery** or **miserable**

MNA same as **mina**, a Greek unit of weight or money

MOA a gigantic extinct bird like an ostrich

MOB a disorderly crowd ▢to form into a mob

MOD a Highland Gaelic festival

MOE obsolete form of **mo**, more ▢obsolete form of **mow**, a wry face

MOG same as **moggy**, a cat

MOI French word meaning **me**, facetiously used in English

MOM US colloquial word for **mother**

MON a Japanese family badge or crest

MOO (of cattle) to low ▢a cow's low

MOP a sponge, etc, on a stick ▢to clean with a mop

MOR a layer of humus

MOT French word meaning **word**

MOU Scots word for a mouth

MOW to cut the grass on ▢a pile of hay; obsolete word for a wry face

MOY Shakespearean word for a coin or a measure

MOZ Australian word meaning a type of curse

MUD wet soft earth ▢to bury or hide in mud

MUG a cup with vertical sides ▢to attack from behind

MUM child's word for **mother** (noun) ▢silent ▢to act in a mime

MUN dialect word for **must** (verb) ▢dialect word for **man** (noun)

MUS plural of **mu**

MUX US and dialect word meaning to spoil, botch ▢a mess

NAB to seize ▢a hilltop

NAE Scots form of **no**, not any, certainly not

NAG a small horse ▢to worry or annoy constantly

NAM same as **naam**, distraint ▢past tense of **nim**

NAN same as **naan**, slightly leavened bread

NAP to take a short sleep ▢a short sleep

NAS form of obsolete **ne has**, has not, and **ne was**, was not

NAT colloquial form of **nationalist**, a person who strives for the unity or independence of a nation

NAY old form of **no** ▢a denial

NEB a beak or bill ▢to put a bill on

NED a young hooligan

NÉE (of a woman) born

NEF obsolete word for a church nave

NEK South African word for **col**

NEP dialect word for **catmint**, a plant attractive to cats

NET an open material, formed into meshes ▢to catch (fish) in a net

NEW recently made, bought, produced, etc ▢something new ▢old word meaning to renew

NIB the writing point of a pen ▢to provide with a nib

NID a pheasant's nest or brood

NIE obsolete spelling of **nigh** (adjective and verb)

NIL nothing; zero

NIM obsolete word meaning to take or steal □ an old game involving taking objects (usually matches) alternately from heaps

NIP a small quantity of spirits □ to pinch

NIS in Scandinavian folklore, a brownie or goblin

NIT a young louse; a fool; a unit of information

NIX nothing; □ to veto or cancel

NOB a person of high social rank

NOD to move the head forward in assent or greeting □ such a movement of the head

NOG an egg and alcohol drink; a wooden peg or cog □ to fix with a nog

NOH same as **no**, a traditional style of Japanese drama

NOM French word for **name**

NON Latin word for **not**

NOR and not; neither

NOS plural of **no**

NOT word expressing denial, negation, or refusal

NOW at the present time; immediately □ the present time

NOX nitrogen oxide

NOY Spenserian word meaning to hurt or annoy □ vexation, hurt or trouble

NTH adjective implying a large number

NUB the point or gist; same as **knub**, a knob □ to hang

NUN a female member of a religious order

NUR same as **knur**, a knot on a tree

NUS plural of **nu**

NUT an edible seed in a hard shell □ to look for and gather nuts

NYE obsolete spelling of **nigh** (adjective and verb) □ another word for **nid**

NYS Spenserian word meaning **is not**

OAF a lout; an idiot

OAK a kind of tree; its wood

OAR a pole with a blade for rowing a boat □ to row a boat

OAT a kind of grass, the seeds of which are used as food

OBA in West Africa, a chief or ruler

OBI West Indian, etc witchcraft; a fetish or charm □ to bewitch

OBO a vessel for carrying oil and bulk ore

OBS plural of **ob**

OCA a South American wood-sorrel

OCH Scots or Irish interjection expressing impatience or regret

ODA a room in a harem

ODD strange; unpaired, left over □ in golf, an additional or allowed stroke

ODE an elaborate lyric addressed to someone or something

ODS plural of **od**

OES plural of **oe**

OFF not on; away; not available □ in cricket, the off-side □ to go off

OFT often

OHM a unit of electrical resistance

OHO an expression of triumph and surprise or gratification

OIK an inferior person; a lout

OIL a greasy, flammable liquid □ to smear or lubricate with oil

OKE a Turkish weight

OLD advanced in years; worn out □ times past, olden times

OLE Spanish interjection expressing approval or support

OLM a blind salamander

OMS plural of **om**

ONE single; undivided; only □ an individual thing or person; the number or figure 1; a symbol representing it

ONS plural of **on**

OOF slang word for money

OOH an expression of pleasure, surprise, etc □ to make such an expression

OOM South African word for **uncle**

OON Scots word for **oven**

OOP same as **oup**

OOR Scots word for **our**

OOS plural of **oo**, Scots word for **wool**

OPE poetic word meaning to open

OPS plural of **op**

OPT to decide or choose

ORB a circle or sphere □ to form into an orb

ORC an orca, a killer whale

ORD obsolete word meaning a point, eg of a weapon

ORE a solid mineral aggregate

ORF a viral infection of sheep

ORS plural of **or**

ORT dialect word for a leftover from a meal

OUD an Arab stringed instrument

OUK Scots word for **week**

OUP Scots word meaning to bind with thread or to join

OUR of or belonging to us

OUT not in; excluded □ someone or something that is out □ to put or throw out; to make public

OVA plural of **ovum**, an egg

OWE to be in debt for

OWL a nocturnal predacious bird; a wiseacre ❏ to behave like an owl

OWN to possess ❏ belonging to oneself

OWT dialect word for **anything**

OYE same as **oy**

OYS plural of **oy**

PAD a wad of soft material used to cushion, protect, fill out, etc ❏ to cover or fill with soft material

PAH same as **pa**, a Maori fort or settlement

PAL colloquial word for **friend** ❏ to associate as a pal

PAM the knave of clubs

PAN a broad, shallow container ❏ to wash earth for gold

PAP soft food for infants ❏ to feed with such food

PAR a state of equality; same as **parr**, a young fish, especially a young salmon

PAS French word for **step**; plural of **pa**

PAT a gentle stroke with the palm of the hand ❏ to stroke gently

PAW a clawed foot ❏ to scrape with a paw

PAX the kiss of peace; Latin word for **peace**

PAY to hand over money; to be profitable ❏ salary or wages

PEA a vegetable, the rounded seed of a climbing plant

PEC colloquial short form for a pectoral muscle

PED short for **pedestrian**, a person who travels on foot

PEE the letter 'P' ❏ to urinate

PEG a pin or fixture ❏ to fasten with a peg

PEN an implement for writing ❏ to write down on paper

PEP vigour or spirit ❏ to put pep into

PER for each; by

PET a tame animal; a favourite ❏ to treat as a pet

PEW a bench in a church

PHI a letter in the Greek alphabet

PHO same as **foh**

PHS plural of **ph**

PIA a tropical plant

PIC colloquial word for **picture** (noun)

PIE meat, fruit, etc baked in a pastry; confusion ❏ to reduce to confusion

PIG a farm animal bred for food ❏ slang word meaning to eat greedily

PIN a piece of wood or metal used for fastening ❏ to fasten with a pin

PIP a small hard seed in a fruit; offence or disgust ❏ to offend or disgust

PIR a Muslim title of honour, given to a holy man

PIS plural of **pi**

PIT a hole in the earth ❏ to put in a pit

PIU Italian word for **more**

PIX same as **pyx**

PLY a fold ❏ to bend or fold

POA a meadow-grass plant

POD the shell of leguminous plants ❏ to shell (eg peas)

POH interjection expressing impatient contempt

POI a Hawaiian dish, fermented taro

POM colloquial word for a Pomeranian dog

POO slang word for **faeces**, excrement ❏ to defecate

POP a mild explosive sound ❏ to make a pop

POS plural of **po**

POT a utensil for cooking or storing ❏ to cook or put in a pot

POW Scots word for **head** (noun)

POX any of several viral diseases with pustules ❏ obsolete word meaning to infect with pox

POZ old short form of **positive** (adjective)

PRE colloquial word meaning **before**

PRO in favour ❏ someone who is in favour; colloquial short form of **professional** and **prostitute** (nouns)

PRY to examine things with curiosity ❏ an act of prying

PSI a letter in the Greek alphabet

PST interjection used to attract attention

PUB a public house

PUD colloquial word for **pudding**

PUG a small dog with a wrinkled face; clay, ground with water ❏ to grind with water

PUH Shakespearean spelling of **pooh**, interjection expressing disgust, etc

PUN to play on words ❏ a play on words

PUP a young dog ❏ to give birth to pups

PUR obsolete spelling of **purr**, (of a cat) to make a contented sound ❏ the sound made

PUS thick yellowish fluid formed by suppuration

PUT to place; to throw ❏ a push; a throw

PUY a small volcanic cone

PYE same as **pie**, confusion ❏ to reduce to confusion

PYX a box in which coins are kept for testing ❏ to test

QAT same as **kat**, an E African shrub
QIS plural of **qi**
QUA in the capacity of

RAD a unit of radiation dosage
RAG a worn scrap of cloth ❑ to tease or ridicule
RAH an expression of approbation or joy ❑ to make such an expression
RAI a modern, North African form of popular music
RAJ rule, government, or sovereignty
RAM a male sheep ❑ to push or cram down hard
RAN past tense of **run**
RAP a sharp blow ❑ to strike sharply
RAS a headland; an Ethiopian prince
RAT a rodent like a large mouse ❑ to hunt rats
RAW uncooked
RAX dialect word meaning to stretch ❑ a stretch
RAY a beam of light ❑ to radiate
REC a recreation ground
RED of a colour like blood ❑ the colour of blood; something that is red ❑ Scots word meaning to tidy
REE Scots word for an enclosure (for sheep, etc)
REF short form of **referee**, (to act as) an umpire or judge
REH an efflorescence of salts on soil in India, etc
REM a unit of radiation dosage
REN old spelling of **run**
REP a commercial representative ❑ to work or act as a rep
RES short form of (North American Indian) **reservation**
RET to expose to moisture; to soak
REV a revolution in an internal-combustion engine ❑ to increase the speed of revolution
REW Spenserian spelling of **row** (noun)
REX obsolete plural word meaning tricks or pranks
REZ same as **res**
RHO a letter in the Greek alphabet
RHY Spenserian spelling of **rye**, the grass
RIA a drowned valley
RIB a bone curving forward from the backbone ❑ to tease
RID to free or clear
RIG to fit with sails; to equip or clothe ❑ an arrangement of sails and masts; an outfit

RIM an edge or border ❑ to provide with a rim
RIN Scots form of **run**
RIP to tear open or apart ❑ a rent or tear
RIT Scots word meaning to slit ❑ a slit
RIZ US past tense of **rise**
ROB to steal ❑ a fruit syrup
ROC an enormous bird in Arabian legend
ROD a slender stick or bar ❑ to push a rod through
ROE a mass of fish eggs; a small species of deer
ROK same as **roc**
ROM a gypsy man
ROO short form of **kangaroo**
ROT to decay ❑ decay or corruption
ROW a line or rank; a noisy squabble ❑ to quarrel ❑ to propel through water with oars
RUB to apply friction ❑ an impediment or difficulty
RUC same as **roc**
RUD archaic or dialect word meaning redness or complexion ❑ Spenserian word meaning to redden
RUE a strong smelling plant; regret ❑ to regret
RUG a heavy floor-mat ❑ Scots word meaning to pull roughly
RUM a spirit distilled from sugar cane ❑ odd, droll
RUN to move quickly ❑ an act or instance of running
RUT a furrow made by wheels ❑ to make such a furrow
RYA a type of Scandinavian rug
RYE a cereal grass; its grain

SAB a saboteur
SAC in biology, a baglike structure
SAD unhappy, sorrowful
SAE Scots form of **so**, in this way, accordingly, etc
SAG to bend or hang down ❑ an act or instance of sagging
SAI the capuchin monkey
SAL a large North Indian tree; a salt
SAM Spenserian word meaning **together**
SAN old short form of **sanatorium**, a kind of hospital; a Japanese form of address
SAP a liquid circulating through plants ❑ to drain
SAR Scots form of **savour**, (to) taste; a sea bream
SAT past tense of **sit**

SAW a cutting tool with a toothed blade □ to use a saw; past tense of **see**

SAX short form of **saxophone**, a musical instrument; a chopper for trimming slates

SAY to utter in words, speak □ something said or stated

SAZ a stringed instrument of Turkey, North Africa, etc

SEA a great expanse of water

SEC a secant □ of wines, dry

SED Miltonic spelling of **said** (verb)

SEE to perceive by the eye □ an area under the authority of a bishop

SEG a stud in the sole of a shoe

SEI a whale, a kind of rorqual

SEL Scots form of **self**

SEN a monetary unit (in Japan, etc) of various values ; a coin of these values

SET to put or place in position □ a group; a complete series

SEW to work on with a needle and thread

SEX the quality of being male or female □ to identify the sex of

SEY Scots word for a part of a carcase of beef

SEZ slang spelling of **says** (verb)

SHE pronoun used in referring to a female person or thing □ a female

SHY embarrassed; bashful □ to jump aside; to recoil

SIB a blood relation, a kinsman

SIC thus □ Scots word for **such** □ to incite (a dog to attack)

SIM short for **Simeonite**, an evangelical

SIN moral offence □ to commit sin

SIP to drink in small mouthfuls □ a quantity sipped

SIR a word used in addressing a man □ to address as 'sir'

SIS contracted form of **sister**

SIT to rest on the buttocks □ a spell of sitting

SIX the number after five

SKA Jamaican music similar to reggae

SKI a narrow strip attached to a boot for gliding over snow □ to move on skis

SKY the space visible above the earth □ to hit high into the air

SLY cunning, wily; surreptitious

SMA Scots word for **small**

SNY same as **snye**, a side channel of a river

SOB to cry uncontrollably, taking intermittent breaths □ the sound of a breath so taken

SOC historically, the right of holding a local court

SOD an obnoxious person; a piece of cut turf □ to cover with sods

SOG dialect word for a soft, wet place □ to soak

SOH same as **sol**, a musical note

SOL a musical note (in sol-fa); a colloidal suspension in a liquid

SON a male offspring

SOP bread, etc soaked in liquid □ to soak

SOS plural of **so**, a musical note

SOT a habitual drunkard □ to act as a sot

SOU an old small French coin

SOV short form of **sovereign**, a gold coin

SOW a female pig □ to scatter seed on the ground

SOX slang spelling of **socks** (plural noun)

SOY dark, salty sauce made from fermented beans

SPA a resort with a mineral spring □ to stay at a spa

SPY a secret agent employed to watch □ to watch secretly

STY a pen for pigs □ to keep in a sty

SUB colloquial shortening of **subscription**, **subeditor**, and many other words □ to subscribe, subedit, etc

SUD rare singular form of **suds**, froth of soapy water

SUE to prosecute at law

SUI Latin word meaning of himself, herself, itself

SUK same as **souk**, a market-place

SUM the total, whole amount □ to add, make up the total of

SUN the star that is the source of light □ to expose to the sun's rays

SUP to take (liquid) into the mouth □ a small mouthful

SUQ same as **souk**, a market-place

SUR French word for **on**, **above**

SUS a suspect □ to arrest for suspicious behaviour

SWY an Australian game, two-up

SYE dialect word meaning to strain □ a sieve

TAB a small tag, flap, or other attachment □ to fix a tab to

TAD a small amount

TAE Scots form of **toe**, **too**, and **to**

TAG a tab or label □ to put a tag on

TAI a Japanese sea bream

TAJ a crown; a dervish's conical cap

TAK Scots form of **take**

TAM a cap with a broad circular flat top

TAN brown colour of the skin after exposure to the sun's rays ▢ to become brown in the sun

TAP a gentle knock or its sound ▢ to knock gently

TAR a black bituminous substance ▢ to coat with tar

TAT shabby articles ▢ to touch up

TAU a letter in the Greek alphabet

TAW to prepare skins for white leather ▢ a thong

TAX a contribution levied towards a country's revenue ▢ to impose a tax on

TAY dialect, especially Irish, word for **tea**

TEA a drink made from the dried leaves of a shrub ▢ to take tea

TED a Teddy boy or girl ▢ to spread out (cut grass) for drying

TEE a support for a golf ball ▢ to place on a tee

TEF an Ethiopian cereal grass

TEG a sheep in its second year

TEL in Arab countries, a hill or mound

TEN the number after nine

TES plural of **te**

TEW to hustle ▢ excitement

THE the definite article

THO Spenserian word for **those** or **then**

THY of thee

TIC an involuntary twitching of muscles

TID Scots word meaning mood, a temporary state of mind

TIE to bind, fasten or knot ▢ something for tying

TIG a touch; a game involving touching ▢ to touch

TIL sesame

TIN a silvery-white metal ▢ to coat with tin

TIP a gratuity; a helpful piece of advice ▢ to give a tip

TIS plural of **ti**

TIT a nipple; a small bird; a tug ▢ to tug

TOC telecommunications code for signalling the letter 'T'

TOD an old wool weight ▢ to yield a tod

TOE a digit at the end of a foot ▢ to kick or touch with the toes

TOG a unit of measurement of thermal insulation ▢ to dress

TOM a male cat

TON a unit of weight

TOO also

TOP the highest point, part or level ▢ to cover the top; to surpass

TOR a hill

TOT a small child or drink ▢ to add or total

TOW to pull along (behind) ▢ an act of towing; prepared fibres of flax or hemp

TOY an object for playing with ▢ to play idly with

TRY to attempt; to make an effort ▢ an effort

TUB a small carton; a bath ▢ to bath in a tub

TUG to pull forcibly ▢ a forcible pull, a jerk

TUI a New Zealand bird, a honey-guide

TUM colloquial word for **stomach**

TUN a large cask ▢ to put in a tun

TUP a ram ▢ of a ram, to copulate

TUT interjection expressing rebuke or disapproval ▢ to say 'tut'

TUX short for **tuxedo**, a dinner-jacket

TWA Scots form of **two**

TWO the number after one

TWP dim-witted, stupid (Welsh)

TYE a trough for washing ore ▢ to wash in a tye

TYG an old drinking-cup with two or more handles

UDO a Japanese ivy

UDS old interjection meaning **God's** or **God save**

UEY a U-turn

UFO an unidentified flying object

UGH interjection expressing repugnance ▢ an old representation of a cough or grunt

UGS present tense of ug

UKE a ukulele

ULE a Central American rubber tree

UNI colloquial for **university**

UNS plural of **un**

UPS plural and present tense of **up**

URD an Indian bean

URE an extinct wild ox

URN a type of vase ▢ to put in an urn

USE to put to some purpose ▢ the purpose for which something is used

UTE Australian short form of **utility**, a small truck

UTS plural of **ut**

UTU settlement of a debt (Maori)

UVA a grape or grape-like berry

VAC vacation; a vacuum-cleaner ▢ to clean with a vac

VAE same as **voe**

VAN a light transport vehicle ▢ to go or send in a van

VAS a duct carrying liquid

VAT a large vessel or tank ❑ to put or treat in a vat

VAU an obsolete letter in the Greek alphabet

VEE the letter 'V', or anything of that shape or angle

VEG short for **vegetable(s)** ❑ to laze about

VET a veterinary surgeon ❑ to treat an animal medically; to examine

VEX to distress or annoy ❑ Scots word meaning **grief**

VIA Latin word for **way** or **road** ❑ by way of, through

VID short form of **video**

VIE to contend in rivalry ❑ obsolete word meaning a bid

VIM energy, vigour

VIN French word for **wine**

VIS Latin word for **force**

VLY low-lying wet ground, a swamp

VOE in Orkney and Shetland, a bay or creek

VOL in heraldry, two wings displayed and conjoined

VOR Shakespearean word meaning to warn

VOW a solemn promise ❑ to make a vow or vows

VOX voice

VUG Cornish word for a cavity in a rock

VUM US word meaning to vow

WAD a pad or mass of loose material ❑ to form into a wad

WAE Scots word for **woe**

WAG to move from side to side ❑ an act of wagging; a habitual joker

WAN lacking colour, pale ❑ to make or become wan

WAP to throw or pull quickly ❑ a sharp blow

WAR a state of conflict ❑ to make war

WAS past tense of **be**

WAT a Thai Buddhist temple or monastery

WAW Spenserian or Scott word meaning a wave

WAX a fatty substance ❑ to treat with wax; to grow larger

WAY a route or passage ❑ Spenserian word meaning to journey

WEB a fine structure spun by a spider ❑ to envelop with a web

WED to marry ❑ a pledge, security

WEE small ❑ a short distance ❑ to urinate

WEM old word for **wame**, the womb or belly

WEN a sebaceous cyst; former name for **wyn**

WET containing, or soaked or covered with, liquid ❑ to make wet

WEX obsolete form of **wax**

WEY a measure for dry goods

WHA Scots form of **who**

WHO pronoun used in referring to a person or people

WHY for what reason; because of which

WIG an artificial covering of hair ❑ to scold

WIN to gain; to be successful ❑ a gain or victory

WIS sham archaic word meaning to know

WIT humour; intelligence ❑ archaic word meaning to know

WOE misery

WOG offensive word for a non-white foreigner

WOK a pan used in Chinese cookery

WON past tense of **win** ❑ the monetary unit of Korea

WOO to court; to seek the support of

WOP offensive word for someone of a Mediterranean or Latin race; ❑ variant of **whop**, to whip or thrash

WOS plural of **wo**, woe

WOT facetious spelling of **what** ❑ variant of **wit**, to know

WOW interjection expressing wonder ❑ to impress ❑ anything thrillingly impressive

WOX obsolete past tense of **wax**

WRY twisted to one side; sardonic ❑ to give a twist to

WUD Scots form of **wood**

WUS a term used in addressing a companion (Welsh)

WYE the letter 'Y', or anything shaped like it

WYN a rune, having the value of modern English 'w'

XIS plural of **xi**

YAH variant of **yea** ❑ interjection expressing derision, etc

YAK a species of ox; persistent talk ❑ to talk persistently

YAM a sweet potato

YAP to bark sharply or constantly ❑ a yelp

YAW to deviate from course ❑ such a deviation

YEA yes ❑ an affirmative vote or voter

YEN a Japanese coin; an intense desire ❑ to desire or yearn

YEP	variant of **yes**
YES	a word of affirmation ▫ an affirmative vote or voter
YET	in addition, besides; nevertheless
YEW	a type of evergreen tree
YEX	Scots word for **hiccup**
YGO	Spenserian past participle of **go**
YIN	one of the two opposing principles of Chinese philosophy
YIP	to give a short, sudden cry ▫ such a cry
YOB	a lout
YOD	past tense of Spenserian **yead**, to go
YOK	a laugh ▫ to laugh
YON	that, the thing known ▫ yonder
YOS	plural of **yo**
YOU	pronoun referring to the person being spoken or written to
YOW	variant of **ewe**
YUG	same as **yuga**, one of the four Hindu ages of the world
YUK	something unpleasantly messy, disgusting or sickly
YUP	same as **yep**
YUS	plural of **yu**
ZAG	a change of direction on a zigzag course ▫ to change direction on such a course
ZAP	to destroy ▫ vitality or force
ZAX	variant of **sax**, a chopper for trimming slates
ZEA	part of a cereal plant, once used as a diuretic
ZED	the letter 'Z'; a bar of metal of this shape
ZEE	US form of **zed**
ZEK	in the former USSR, an inmate of a prison or labour camp
ZEL	an Oriental cymbal
ZEX	variant of **zax**
ZHO	in the Himalayas, an animal that is a cross between a yak and a cow
ZIG	same as **zag**
ZIP	energy, vitality ▫ to be full of or act with energy
ZIT	a pimple
ZIZ	a nap or sleep ▫ to take a nap
ZOA	plural of **zoon**, a unified individual creature
ZOO	a garden or park where animals are kept
ZOS	plural of **zo**
ZUZ	an ancient Palestinian coin